# CONSTITUTIONAL LAW AND HUMAN RIGHTS

### Consultant Editors

LORD LESTER OF HERNE HILL
one of Her Majesty's Counsel; Bencher of Lincoln's Inn;
Honorary Visiting Professor of Public Law, University College London

DAWN OLIVER M.A., Ph.D.
of the Middle Temple, Barrister;
Professor of Constitutional Law, University College London

### Contributors

## CONSTITUTIONAL LAW

LORD LESTER OF HERNE HILL, one of Her Majesty's Counsel; Bencher of
Lincoln's Inn; Honorary Visiting Professor of Public Law, University College London
DAWN OLIVER, M.A., Ph.D., of the Middle Temple, Barrister; Professor of
Constitutional Law, University College London
KATYA LESTER, M.A., LL.B., LL.M., of Lincoln's Inn, Barrister

*with assistance from*
CHARLES BARTON, SUSAN COCHRANE and JANE KRON, of Her Majesty's
Treasury Legal Department
SIR FRANKLIN BERMAN, K.C.M.G., one of Her Majesty's Counsel, the Legal
Adviser to the Foreign and Commonwealth Office, and his staff
ADAM ROBB, B.A., B.C.L., of the Inner Temple, Barrister

### NORTHERN IRELAND

LORD LOWRY, Lord of Appeal in Ordinary (retired)
and former Lord Chief Justice of Northern Ireland

### SCOTLAND

ANTHONY W. BRADLEY, M.A., LL.M., of the Inner Temple, Barrister;
Emeritus Professor of Constitutional Law, University of Edinburgh

## HUMAN RIGHTS

MONICA CARSS-FRISK, LL.B., B.C.L., of Gray's Inn, Barrister
DINAH ROSE, B.A., of Gray's Inn, Barrister
PUSHPINDER SAINI, B.A., B.C.L., of Gray's Inn, Barrister

The contributors gratefully acknowledge the co-operation and assistance
of members of Her Majesty's Civil Service and
the staff of the House of Lords Library in the reissue of the title.

The law stated in this work is in general that in force on 31 May 1996,
although subsequent changes have been included wherever possible.

**Editor**

SIMON HETHERINGTON, LL.B.


**Managing Editor (Commissioning)**

DEBORAH SAUNDERS, B.A.,

OF GRAY'S INN, BARRISTER

Constitutional Law
and
Human Rights

# Constitutional Law
## and
# Human Rights

Consultant Editors

## Lord Lester of Herne Hill QC
## Professor Dawn Oliver

with a foreword by

The Rt Hon Lord Woolf
Master of the Rolls

BUTTERWORTHS

LONDON          1997

| UNITED KINGDOM | Butterworths, a Division of Reed Elsevier (UK) Ltd Halsbury House, 35 Chancery Lane, **London** WC2A 1EL and 4 Hill Street, **Edinburgh** EH2 3JZ |
| AUSTRALIA | Butterworths, **Sydney, Melbourne, Brisbane, Adelaide, Perth, Canberra** and **Hobart** |
| CANADA | Butterworths Canada Ltd, **Toronto** and **Vancouver** |
| HONG KONG | Butterworths Asia, **Hong Kong** |
| IRELAND | Butterworth (Ireland) Ltd, **Dublin** |
| MALAYSIA | Malayan Law Journal Sdn Bhd, **Kuala Lumpur** |
| NEW ZEALAND | Butterworths of New Zealand Ltd, **Wellington** and **Auckland** |
| SINGAPORE | Butterworths Asia, **Singapore** |
| SOUTH AFRICA | Butterworth Publishers (Pty) Ltd, **Durban** |
| USA | Michie, **Charlottesville**, Virginia |

First published in 1996 as Volume 8(2) of *Halsbury's Laws of England*

Editor in Chief

The Right Honourable
LORD HAILSHAM OF ST. MARYLEBONE
Lord High Chancellor of Great Britain
1970–74 and 1979–87

Printed and bound in Great Britain by Redwood Books, Trowbridge, Wilts.

# FOREWORD BY THE RT HON LORD WOOLF
## MASTER OF THE ROLLS

Lawyers in the United Kingdom can no longer afford to neglect Constitutional Law and Human Rights. These rights can no longer be left as part of the back cloth to our domestic law, something of which we are dimly conscious but upon which it is not necessary to focus accurately. Our attention can no longer remain riveted only on our common and statute law which admittedly still dominate centre stage. We are about to embark on a period of dramatic constitutional change, change which will fundamentally affect our legal institutions and culture. We could even become a federal state within a united states of Europe.

Devolution, reform of the House of Lords and legislation incorporating the European Convention of Human Rights are now manifesto commitments of a government with a dominating majority of the House of Commons as a result of the election of 1st May 1997.

For lawyers, the removal of the legislative role of the hereditary peers will not be significant, although it could have a dramatic impact on the role of the Lords. Devolution, however, will give rise to a whole additional range of legal issues which will have to be resolved by the court designated to determine demarcation disputes between Westminster and the legislative bodies of Scotland and Wales. When the Convention becomes part of our domestic law, which now appears inevitable, human rights will have a central role to play in our legal affairs. Our public law will be transformed.

These changes will not happen overnight. In the meantime, in order to understand what the proposals involve it is necessary to have an authoritative account of our existing constitutional framework. In addition it is already necessary to be aware of the provisions of the various conventions, and in particular the European Convention, in order to advise on or litigate about, or determine, public law issues. To perform any of these functions effectively lawyers need access to the considerable learning on this subject which has now accumulated in this jurisdiction and abroad.

No doubt like other members of the judiciary, since its publication I have turned to volume 8(2) of *Halsbury's Laws of England* for the assistance that I have needed on this subject. When I have done so I have not been disappointed. Having the conventional "Halsbury's Laws" format, the helpful paragraph headings enable you to "zoom in" rapidly on the correct portion of the text. You there find the clear statement of legal principles which is of such assistance. If this is not sufficient you have the copious and usually exhaustive notes to guide you to the relevant authorities.

That this should be the position is no surprise if you know who are the two consulting editors of this volume. They are undoubtedly an extraordinarily well qualified combination to perform this task. Anthony Lester QC has probably done more than any other advocate to educate the judiciary in this country on this subject, and Dawn Oliver is a most distinguished professor of law in this field. They are supported by a galaxy of contributors of the very highest repute in their respective fields. It is not necessary to say more than that the volume is of the standard you would expect from such editors and contributors.

The one disadvantage of volume 8(2) is that in order to have access to the volume you normally need to have access to a set of Halsbury's Laws, and this for many lawyers is not always practical for reasons of both expense and space. It is therefore good news indeed that the volume is to be republished as a text book in its own right. There is no difficulty in doing this because, unlike some sections of Halsbury, volume 8(2) is a self-contained work which is not dependent for its usefulness upon the ability to consult other parts of the parent work.

Having gained its independence, I wish it the very great success it deserves. I am sure it is destined to become generally recognised as a leading text book on these subjects. I am confident that in one of its incarnations it is going to be on the great majority of bookshelves of those involved in public law. All lawyers in the field will benefit from this praiseworthy initiative. Constitutional lawyers are about to confront an exciting but also extremely challenging period in the law. We will need the help this book can give.

Woolf MR
Royal Courts of Justice
8th May 1997

# TABLE OF CONTENTS

# TABLE OF STATUTES

# TABLE OF STATUTORY
# INSTRUMENTS

Reference should be made to the Supreme Court Practice for the
Rules of the Supreme Court.

# TABLE OF EUROPEAN
# COMMUNITY LEGISLATION

# TABLE OF TREATIES AND CONVENTIONS

# TABLE OF PARLIAMENTARY PAPERS

# TABLE OF SCHEMES AND CODES OF CONDUCT

# TABLE OF CASES

## A

## B

## E

# H

I

## N

PARA

## V

## W

# X

Decisions of the European Court of Justice are listed below numerically.
These decisions are also included in the preceding alphabetical list.

# CONSTITUTIONAL LAW AND HUMAN RIGHTS

## 9. NON-DEPARTMENTAL PUBLIC BODIES AND INFORMATION-GATHERING INSTITUTIONS

For further coverage of the subject areas listed in the first column of the table below, reference may be had to the titles in *Halsbury's Laws of England* (4th Edn) listed in the second column.

# 1. INTRODUCTION: BASIC PRINCIPLES OF THE CONSTITUTION OF THE UNITED KINGDOM

## (1) DEFINITION OF CONSTITUTIONAL LAW

**1. Definition of constitutional law.** Constitutional law is that part of English law which (together with the law of Scotland[1] and Northern Ireland[2]) governs the system of public administration of the United Kingdom, and relationships between the individual and the state[3]. The task of defining English constitutional law is peculiarly difficult because of the absence of a written constitution for the United Kingdom as the sole or supreme source of legal authority for all public action, whether executive, legislative or judicial.

The task is made even more difficult because of the United Kingdom's membership of the European Community which has its own constitutional framework[4]. European Community law forms part of the law of England, and within its sphere it is paramount[5]. Community law has a profound effect on traditional English constitutional principles and rules, including the doctrine of parliamentary sovereignty[6], the royal prerogative[7], the functions of the judiciary[8], and concepts of citizenship[9]. Membership of the European Community also means that European institutions exercise governmental functions in relation to the United Kingdom[10]. In addition, a modern restatement of English constitutional law has to take account of the increasing influence of the Convention for the Protection of Human Rights and Fundamental Freedoms (1950)[11] upon rights, duties, and remedies which in other European states are protected by written constitutions and enforceable Bills of Rights.

The United Kingdom is unusual in that it lacks a comprehensive constitutional charter[12] which establishes and gives limited powers to the institutions of government; confers and protects the civil and political rights of citizens; may be repealed or amended only in accordance with special procedural requirements; and enjoys particular sanctity[13]. There is a framework of rules[14] defining the functions, composition and interrelationship of the institutions of government in the United Kingdom, their relationships with institutions of the European Community[15], and the rights and duties of the governed[16]. These rules describe the location, conferment, distribution, exercise and limitation of political power among the instruments of the state and may be said to embody the elements of a constitution in the sense of a regulated and legally established system of government.

However, United Kingdom constitutional law is an incomplete system, consisting of piecemeal legislation, ancient common law doctrines, and constitutional conventions which are binding in a political rather than in a legal sense. The United Kingdom constitution lacks the coherence of comprehensive written constitutions[17].

The boundaries of English constitutional law have never been satisfactorily defined, partly because there is no constitutional document possessing an extraordinary sanctity or legally protected status, partly because the constitutional rules are susceptible to change by more or less formal means[18], partly because many of the rules are not justiciable[19], and partly because the differences between public law and private law are not clear[20].

Nor is there any clear distinction between state bodies and others in the United Kingdom[21]. It has been said that even public bodies may have private lives[22]; and generally public bodies may be sued in the ordinary courts for breaches of private law obligations[23].

There have, especially over the past two decades, been criticisms of many aspects of British government[24]; and many proposals for constitutional reform[25].

1 See 5 *Stair Memorial Encyclopaedia* CONSTITUTIONAL LAW; Mitchell *Constitutional Law* (2nd Edn, 1968). See also paras 51–66 post.

2 See paras 67–86 post.

3 It is impossible in this work to concentrate the whole treatment of constitutional law in one place. Certain portions of the subject have attained such large proportions as to demand titles to themselves. See eg ADMINISTRATIVE LAW; BRITISH NATIONALITY, IMMIGRATION AND RACE RELATIONS; CROWN LANDS AND PRIVILEGES; CROWN PROCEEDINGS; EUROPEAN COMMUNITIES; FOREIGN RELATIONS LAW; LOCAL GOVERNMENT; PARLIAMENT; PEERAGES AND DIGNITIES; POLICE; PRISONS; PUBLIC HEALTH.

4 See para 23 post.

5 See the European Communities Act 1972 s 2(1); *H P Bulmer Ltd v J Bollinger SA* [1974] Ch 401, [1974] 2 All ER 1226, CA; para 24 post; and EUROPEAN COMMUNITIES.

6 As to the doctrine of parliamentary sovereignty see paras 232–237 post.

7 As to the royal prerogative see paras 367–372 post.

8 As to the judiciary generally see paras 301–311 post.

9 See further paras 23, 25 post.

10 See further EUROPEAN COMMUNITIES vol 51 para 1.70 et seq.

11 Ie the Convention for the Protection of Human Rights and Fundamental Freedoms (Rome, 4 November 1950; TS 71 (1953); Cmd 8969) (commonly referred to as the European Convention on Human Rights): see paras 25, 122–181 post.

12 Eg within the Commonwealth every country has a written constitution except New Zealand, which has an enforceable Bill of Rights (Bill of Rights Act 1990). Within the Council of Europe, all of the other 33 member states have written constitutions. As to the Council of Europe see FOREIGN RELATIONS LAW.

13 For this reason, it is sometimes said that the United Kingdom has an unwritten constitution. But many of the constitutional rules by which the country is governed are individually to be found in written documents such as statutes, law reports and parliamentary standing orders.

   Although the Magna Carta of Edward I (25 Edw 1) (1297) and other constitutional documents of the same kind, such as the Petition of Right (1627) and the Bill of Rights, are sometimes regarded as forming a written constitution they are not complete, and are not immune from change by the ordinary process of legislation. 'Magna Carta has not remained untouched; and, like every other law of England, it is not condemned to that immunity from development or improvement which was attributed to the laws of the Medes and Persians'; see *Chester v Bateson* [1920] 1 KB 829 at 832, DC, per Darling J. Thus the Magna Carta of Edward I has, with the exception of cc 1, 9, 29 and 37, been repealed by a long series of Acts of which the most recent is the Statute Law (Repeals) Act 1969; the Petition of Right (1627), except for ss ss 1, 2, 6–8 was repealed by the Justices of the Peace Act 1968 s 8(2), Sch 5 Pt II; and parts of the Bill of Rights (especially that relating to the declaration against transubstantiation) by the Juries Act 1825 s 62, the Accession Declaration Act 1910, and the Statute Law Revision Acts of 1888, 1948, 1950. In their susceptibility of ordinary change, even the most important of English constitutional documents are different from the Constitution of the United States of America for example, which can only be changed by a complicated process of constitutional amendment. Thus the constitution of the United Kingdom is not a 'controlled' but an 'uncontrolled' constitution: see the distinction drawn by Lord Birkenhead in *McCawley v R* [1920] AC 691 at 704, PC. As to Parliament's power to repeal statutes see further para 234 post. As to the history and citation of the Bill of Rights see para 35 note 3 post.

14 As to the varying nature of these rules see para 7 post.

15 See para 23 post.

16 See paras 25, 101 et seq post.

17 Eg unlike other Commonwealth and European states, the United Kingdom has no enforceable constitutional guarantee of equality without discrimination applicable to everyone within and throughout its jurisdiction. Instead, there is specific legislation forbidding religious and political discrimination in employment, and in the exercise of public powers in Northern Ireland (but not in Great Britain) (see para 80 post); forbidding racial discrimination in employment (and elsewhere) in Great Britain (but not in Northern Ireland) (see BRITISH NATIONALITY, IMMIGRATION AND RACE RELATIONS vol 4(2) (Reissue) para 151 et seq); and forbidding sex discrimination in employment (and elsewhere) throughout the United Kingdom as a whole (see generally the Sex Discrimination Act 1975).

18 While all constitutional rules are susceptible to change the possibility of change in practical terms varies with the nature and standing of the rule: see eg the statutes cited in note 13 supra; and cf the Statute of Westminster 1931 s 4 (Parliament not to legislate for Dominion except by consent); '... the Imperial Parliament could, as a matter of abstract law, repeal or disregard s 4 of the Statute. But that is theory and has no relation to realities': *British Coal Corpn v R* [1935] AC 500 at 520, PC, obiter. Some constitutional conventions, especially those of a political nature, are less rigid than others and are liable to be reinterpreted in the light of new situations (eg the conventions regarding the choice of a Prime Minister) while some, it seems, are deliberately vague and ill-defined (eg the conventions regarding ministerial

responsibility and the working of the Cabinet system). As to the Prime Minister see paras 394–398 post; as to the Cabinet see paras 402–413 post.

19　See para 7 post.

20　See eg *O'Reilly v Mackman* [1983] 2 AC 237, [1982] 3 All ER, HL; and ADMINISTRATIVE LAW vol 1(1) (Reissue) paras 63–65.

21　While it is accepted that minister of the Crown, local authorities, National Health Service authorities and police officers are state or 'public' bodies, it is not clear to what extent other bodies are to be regarded as subject to public law and in that sense performing public functions or acting as state or public bodies. See eg *R v Panel on Take-overs and Mergers, ex p Datafin plc* [1987] QB 815, [1987] 1 All ER 564, CA; *R v Disciplinary Committee of the Jockey Club, ex p Aga Khan* [1993] 2 All ER 853, [1993] 1 WLR 909, CA. See para 5 post; and ADMINISTRATIVE LAW.

22　See Lord Woolf 'Public law, private law: Why the divide?' [1986] Public Law 220 at 223.

23　Proceedings against the Crown which, although brought in the same courts as actions against private persons, were formerly by way of petition of right, are now by way of action and are for the most part assimilated to private actions (see CROWN PROCEEDINGS); actions in private law (eg in tort or for breach of contract) against local authorities have always been brought in the same courts and according to the same rules of substantive law and procedure as actions against private persons; and in England and Wales the same writ of habeas corpus may be used to obtain the release of a person subject to any form of illegal custody or restraint whether public or private: see eg *Sommersett's Case* (1772) 20 State Tr 1 (slave released from private custody); *Barnardo v Ford* [1892] AC 326, HL (custody of child); *Armah v Government of Ghana* [1968] AC 192, [1966] 3 All ER 177, HL (extradition); *Secretary of State for Home Affairs v O'Brien* [1923] AC 603, HL (deportation); *R v Governor of Brixton Prison, ex p Ahsan* [1969] 2 QB 222, [1969] 2 All ER 347, DC (removal on grounds of illegal entry); *R v Secretary of State for the Home Department, ex p Mubojayi* [1992] QB 244, [1991] 4 All ER 72, DC (discussion of the differences in the use of habeas corpus and judicial review as a way of questioning an administrative decision to remove an asylum seeker from this country).

　　There are, however, certain courts such as courts-martial which have no concern with private law and the same might be said of many statutory tribunals.

24　See eg *Report of the Royal Commission on the Constitution 1969–73* (Cmnd 5460) (1973) (the Kilbrandon Report); Scarman *English Law: The New Dimension* (1974); Hailsham *Elective Dictatorship* (1976); Bogdanor *The People and the Party System* (1981); Holme and Elliott (eds) *1688–1988: Time for a New Constitution* (1988); Wright *Citizens and Subjects* (1994); Jowell and Oliver (eds) *The Changing Constitution* (3rd Edn, 1994).

25　See eg *Report of the Royal Commission on the Constitution 1969–73* (Cmnd 5460) (1973) (the Kilbrandon Report); *House of Lords Select Committee on a Bill of Rights* (HL Paper (1977–78) No 176); *Standing Advisory Committee on a Bill of Rights in Northern Ireland, The Protection of Human Rights by Law in Northern Ireland* (Cmnd 7009) (1977); *Report of the Committee of Inquiry into the Conduct of Local Authority Business* (Cmnd 9797) (1986) (the Widdecombe Report); Charter 88 *Charter* (1988); Lester et al *A British Bill of Rights* (1990); Institute for Public Policy Research *The Constitution of the United Kingdom, Constitution Paper No 4* (1991); McDonald *The Future of Whitehall* (1991); Oliver *Government in the United Kingdom: The Search for Accountability, Effectiveness and Citizenship* (1991); Woodhouse *Ministers and Parliament* (1994); publications of the Scottish Constitutional Convention, namely; *The Scottish Claim of Right* (1988), *Towards a Scottish Parliament* (1989), *Key Elements of Proposals for a Scottish Parliament* (1990), *Towards Scotland's Parliament* (1990), *Further Steps Towards a Scheme for Scotland's Parliament* (1994); publications of the Constitution Unit, namely: *Delivering Constitutional Reform* (1996), *Reform of the House of Lords* (1996), *Scotland's Parliament: Fundamentals for a New Scotland Act* (1996), *An Assembly for Wales* (1996), *Regional Government in England* (1996).

## (2) CHARACTERISTICS OF THE BRITISH CONSTITUTION

**2. Characteristics of the constitution.** The principal characteristics of the constitution of the United Kingdom, in the sense of its system of government, are as follows:

(1)　the constitution is based on the premise that no body or political party is infallible[1] or has a monopoly of wisdom, that state bodies should be democratically and legally accountable[2], and that they should promote good government in the general interest, rather than in their personal interests or the interests of limited sections of society[3];

(2)　the United Kingdom is bound by membership of the European Community[4], and the obligations imposed by ratification of the European Convention on

Human Rights[5], and the other international human rights codes to which the United Kingdom is party[6];

(3)    the constitution is unwritten[7] and flexible[8];

(4)    the United Kingdom has a constitutional monarchy[9];

(5)    the United Kingdom has a parliamentary executive[10];

(6)    Parliament is sovereign[11];

(7)    Parliament consists in law of the House of Commons, the House of Lords and the monarch, but for practical purposes the legislature is divided into two parts, the House of Commons and the House of Lords[12];

(8)    the House of Commons, the first and dominant chamber of Parliament, is elected and so the system is one of representative democracy[13];

(9)    the judiciary is separate from the other organs of government and independent from them[14], but in other respects there is not a separation of powers;

(10)   there is a permanent, politically neutral, professional Civil Service[15];

(11)   the system is unitary[16];

(12)   below the level of central government there is a local government tier which has only local legislative power, and is limited by law and government policy as to how it spends the money it is granted by central government and how much it may raise from the council tax[17];

(13)   the liberties of the individual derive from a person's status as a subject of the Crown, and are residual in nature[18], and there is no developed concept of citizenship conferring positive civil rights and liberties in relation to the state[19].

These characteristics result from a combination of legal rules and constitutional conventions[20]. For example, the fact that there is a parliamentary executive is a matter of convention only. It follows that a treatment of the law of the constitution must take into account constitutional conventions.

1    Contrast the position as set out by Blackstone: 'Besides the attribute of sovereignty, the law also ascribes to the king, in his political capacity, absolute perfection. The King can do no wrong.' 1 Bl Com 245. Although the monarch remains personally immune from action in the courts, the position now is that the Crown may be sued for wrongful acts: see para 15 post; and CROWN PROCEEDINGS. Ministers of the Crown are accountable to the courts and to Parliament for all actions of government, thus confining the application of the doctrine of perfection to the person of the monarch: see paras 14, 16 note 4 post.

2    As to accountability and responsibility see paras 16 note 4, 21 post; Marshall *Constitutional Conventions: the rules and forms of political accountability* (1987); Oliver *Government in the United Kingdom: The Search for Accountability, Effectiveness and Citizenship* (1991) chs 1, 2. See also *Eighth Report of the Treasury and Civil Service Committee: Civil Service Management Reform: The Next Steps* (HC Paper (1987–88) no 494); *Fifth Report of the Treasury and Civil Service Committee: The Role of the Civil Service* (HC Paper (1993–94) no 27); the government White Paper *The Civil Service: Taking Forward Continuity and Change* (Cm 2748) (1995); *Report of the Inquiry into the Export of Defence Equipment and Dual-Use Goods to Iraq and related Prosecutions* (HC Paper (1995–96) no 115) (the 'Scott Report').

3    See Burke (1774) 'Parliament is not a congress of ambassadors from different and hostile interests; which interests each must maintain, as an agent and advocate, against other agents and advocates; but Parliament is a deliberative assembly of one nation, with one interest, that of the whole; where, not local purposes, not local prejudices ought to guide, but the general good, resulting from the general reason of the whole. You choose a member indeed; but when you have chosen him, he is not member of Bristol, but he is a member of Parliament (Speech to the Electors of Bristol, 3 November 1774); and see also 1 Bl Com ch 7.
     The Committee on Standards in Public Life identified seven principles of public life which emphasise the importance of serving the public interest, and which apply to all aspects of public life. Those principles are: selflessness; integrity; objectivity; accountability; openness; honesty; and leadership: see the *First Report of the Committee on Standards in Public Life* (Cm 2850) (1995) p 14; and para 12 post. Those principles have been adopted by the House of Commons: see para 211 post.

4    See para 23 post; and EUROPEAN COMMUNITIES.

5    Ie the Convention for the Protection of Human Rights and Fundamental Freedoms: see para 122–181 post.

6    See paras 1 ante; 103 post.

7    See para 1 ante.

8    For the distinction between flexible and rigid constitutions see Bryce 'Flexible and Rigid Constitutions', in *Studies in History and Jurisprudence* (1901) ch III; Wheare *Modern Constitution* (2nd Edn, 1966) ch 1. It follows from the absence of a written constitutional charter containing the fundamental and supreme law of the United Kingdom that European and international legal principles and rules readily infiltrate English law, by means of primary and subordinate legislation and judicial development of the common law. In this respect the United Kingdom system is more porous as well as more flexible than those of most other states. For full parliamentary debate to tke note of the United Kingdom's existing constitutional settlement and of the implications of proposals for change see 573 HC Official Report (6th series), 3 July 1996, cols 1449–1570; and 573 HC Official Report (6th series), 4 July 1996, cols 1581–1690.

9    The monarch is Head of State and possesses important legal powers: see further paras 14 et seq, 34–40, 367–372 post. By convention the powers of the monarch in relation to the United Kingdom are exercised on advice of relevant ministers: see for examples paras 19–22 post. By convention ministers are required to be members of one or other of the two Houses of Parliament, of which the House of Commons, the elected chamber, is dominant. As to the House of Commons generally see PARLIAMENT. As to the House of Lords generally see para 204 post; and PARLIAMENT. The exercise of statutory powers exercised in the name of the Crown and of many prerogative powers is also subject to judicial review: *Council of Civil Service Unions v Minister for the Civil Service* [1985] AC 374, [1984] 3 All ER 935, HL; and see paras 367–380 post; and ADMINISTRATIVE LAW. It is because the powers of the monarch are subject to parliamentary and judicial control that the monarchy is said to be constitutional. See also Bogdanor *The Monarchy and the Constitution* (1995) chs 1, 3.

10   By convention the monarch, who appoints ministers under prerogative powers (see paras 394, 399 post) must appoint from members of one or other of the Houses of Parliament. Convention requires that the Prime Minister and the Chancellor of the Exchequer be members of the House of Commons. See para 21 post.

11   See paras 232–237 post.

12   See Loveland *Constitutional Law: A Critical Introduction* (1996) p 191. See further para 201 et seq post; and PARLIAMENT.

13   As to parliamentary elections see paras 206–209 post; and ELECTIONS. The primacy of the House of Commons flows both from the provisions of the Parliament Acts 1911 and 1949 (which provide that Bills may in certain circumstances receive the royal assent after having been approved only by the House of Commons) (see PARLIAMENT), and from the fact that its legitimacy is greater than that of the House of Lords because its members are elected while those of the House of Lords are hereditary or appointed: see PARLIAMENT; it is because of these two considerations that convention requires that the Prime Minister and the Chancellor of the Exchequer are members of the House of Commons, so that the focus of party political activity is in that chamber, which further reinforces its dominance: see further paras 394, 477 post.

14   See paras 8, 10, 18 post; and COURTS; ADMINISTRATIVE LAW.

15   As to the Civil Service see paras 549–564 post.

16   See para 4 post. Note that the structure of government provided for Northern Ireland under the Northern Ireland Constitution Act 1973, which, however, is not in place, would be federal in nature: see para 67 et seq post.

17   See para 4 post; and LOCAL GOVERNMENT.

18   See eg *Malone v Metropolitan Police Comr* [1979] Ch 344, sub nom *Malone v Metropolitan Police Comr (No 2)* [1979] 2 All ER 620. See also para 26 post.

19   See paras 25, 101 et seq post.

20   As to constitutional conventions see paras 19–22 post.

### 3.  The United Kingdom.

In every Act and public document passed and issued after 12 April 1927, 'the United Kingdom' means Great Britain and Northern Ireland, unless the context otherwise requires[1], exclusive of the Channel Islands and the Isle of Man[2]. 'Great Britain' means England and Scotland[3], and any reference in any Act passed before 1 April 1974 to 'England' includes Berwick upon Tweed and Monmouthshire and, in the case of an Act passed before the Welsh Language Act 1967[4], Wales[5], although the practice has been to use the form 'England and Wales'[6].

It is declared by the Northern Ireland Constitution Act 1973 that Northern Ireland is a part of Her Majesty's dominions and of the United Kingdom and will not cease to be either without the consent of the majority of the people of Northern Ireland voting in a poll[7].

1    Royal and Parliamentary Titles Act 1927 s 2(2) (amended by the Interpretation Act 1978 s 25(1), Sch 3); Interpretation Act 1978 ss 5, 22, Sch 1, Sch 2 para 4(1)(a). For an example of an Act incorporating annexed territory into a part of the United Kingdom see the Island of Rockall Act 1972 making the island

a part of the Scotland (see s 1 (amended by the Local Government (Scotland) Act 1973 s 214(2), Sch 27 Pt II para 202)), following the formal taking possession of the island in pursuance of a royal warrant.

A gift for the defence of the United Kingdom has been held to be for the defence of the United Kingdom as constituted from time to time: *Re Driffill, Harvey v Chamberlain* [1950] Ch 92, [1949] 2 All ER 933. A British ship on the high seas has been held not to be part of the United Kingdom for the purposes of what is now the Army Act 1955 s 70(4) (as amended) (civil offences committed by persons subject to military law): *R v Gordon-Finlayson, ex p An Officer* [1941] 1 KB 171, DC; see ROYAL FORCES vol 41 para 433.

2 See *Navigators and General Insurance Co Ltd v Ringrose* [1962] 1 All ER 97, [1962] 1 WLR 173, CA (doubting *Stoneham v Ocean Rly and General Accident Insurance Co* (1887) 19 QBD 237 at 239 per Mathew J); *R v Prowes* (1832) 1 Mood CC 349. Various provisions of the Immigration Act 1971, the Criminal Justice Act 1982, the Immigration (Carriers' Liability) Act 1987 and the Immigration Act 1988 have been extended by Orders in Council to the Isle of Man, Guernsey and Jersey: Immigration (Isle of Man) Order 1991, SI 1991/2630; Immigration (Guernsey) Order 1993, SI 1993/1796; and the Immigration (Jersey) Order 1993, SI 1993/1797. A power exists to extend the provisions of the Asylum and Immigration Appeals Act 1993 to the Channel Islands and the Isle of Man (see s 15). At the date at which this volume states the law, no Order in Council had been made in exercise of this power.

References to the United Kingdom in the Army Act 1955 (except in ss 119 (as amended), 126, 127 (as amended), 143 and Pt IV (ss 154–176) (as amended)), the Air Force Act 1955 (except in ss 119 (as amended), 126, 127 (as amended), 143 and Pt IV (ss 154–176) (as amended)), and the Naval Discipline Act 1957 (except in ss 80 (as amended), 82A (as added), 88(3), (4) (as amended) are to be construed as including references to the Channel Islands and the Isle of Man: Army Act 1955 s 216 (amended by the Armed Forces Act 1991 s 24(1)); Air Force Act 1955 s 214 (amended by the Armed Forces Act 1991 s 24(1)); Naval Discipline Act 1957 s 125 (amended by the Armed Forces Act 1971 s 52(2); and the Armed Forces Act 1991 s 24(2)). See also the Army Act 1955 (Isle of Man) Order 1996, SI 1996/723. For the constitutional position of the Isle of Man and the Channel Islands generally see COMMONWEALTH vol 6 (Reissue) paras 838–850. As to the extension of English law to the Isle of Man and the Channel Islands see COMMONWEALTH vol 6 (Reissue) paras 1107–1108. For the position of the Isle of Man and the Channel Islands in relation to the European Communities see the Act of Accession (1972) arts 25–27, Protocol 3; and EUROPEAN COMMUNITIES.

3 Union with Scotland Act 1706 art I (embodying art I of the Treaty of Union). See further para 51–66 post.

4 Ie before 27 July 1967.

5 Interpretation Act 1978 Sch 2 para 5(a). The Welsh Language Act 1967 s 4, which provided that references to England in future Acts of Parliament were no longer to include Wales, was repealed by the Interpretation Act 1978 s 25, Sch 3, but the effect is preserved by the Interpretation Act 1978 Sch 2 para 5(a). The remainder of the Welsh Language Act 1967 was repealed by the Welsh Language Act 1993 s 35, Sch 2.

6 'Wales' in any enactment made or passed on or after 1 April 1974 is the area consisting of the counties established by the Local Government Act 1972 s 20 as originally enacted (ie those created out of Wales and the former county of Monmouth and county borough of Newport, and subject to any subsequent alteration of boundaries made under s 73 (as amended) (consequential alteration of boundary following the alteration of a watercourse)): Interpretation Act 1978 Sch 1 (definition substituted by the Local Government (Wales) Act 1994 s 1(3), Sch 2 para 9). Those counties are referred to as the 'preserved counties': Local Government Act 1972 s 270(1) (definition added by the Local Government (Wales) Act 1994 s 1(4), (7)). In the Local Government Act 1972, 'Wales' means the combined area of the preserved counties and 'England' does not include any area included in any of the preserved counties: s 269 (substituted by the Local Government (Wales) Act 1994 Sch 2 para 8). The preserved counties are Clwyd, Dyfed, Gwent, Gwynedd, Mid Glamorgan, Powys, South Glamorgan and West Glamorgan: Local Government Act 1972 s 20, Sch 4 Pt I (both as originally enacted). As to the reorganisation of local government in Wales, including the creation of new counties, see s 20, Sch 4 (as substituted by the Local Government (Wales) Act 1994 ss 1, 66, Schs 1, 15, 17, 18). See also paras 41–50 post; and LOCAL GOVERNMENT.

7 Northern Ireland Constitution Act 1973 s 1. As to the constitutional position of Northern Ireland see paras 67–86 post.

**4. Unitary government.** The government of the United Kingdom is unitary in character, for although most local authorities are elected and able to pursue, within limits, an independent policy[1], and although Scotland and Northern Ireland have their own legal systems and the administration of Northern Ireland[2], Scotland[3], and, to some extent, of Wales[4], differs from that of England, the whole country is, subject to the powers of the European Community[5], under the direct operation of one central government and the

United Kingdom Parliament[6]. Where bodies other than the United Kingdom Parliament possess legislative powers[7], these either derive from the royal prerogative[8] or have been granted by the United Kingdom Parliament and may be amended or repealed by the Parliament[9].

1   See generally the Local Government Act 1972; and LOCAL GOVERNMENT.
2   See paras 67–86 post.
3   See paras 51–66 post.
4   As to the Welsh Office see para 46 post.
5   See paras 23–24 post; and EUROPEAN COMMUNITIES.
6   However, as to the particular provisions relating to the government of Northern Ireland see para 68 et seq post.
7   Eg powers of delegated legislation by statutory instrument (see STATUTES); or powers to make Orders in Council (see para 907 post).
8   See paras 367, 907, 916–918 post.
9   See para 232 post.

**5. The legal basis of government.** From the legal point of view, government may be described as the exercise of certain powers and the performance of certain duties by public authorities or officers, together with certain private persons or corporations[1] exercising public or governmental[2] functions. The principal elements of the structure of the machinery of government, and the regulation of the powers and duties which belong to the different parts of this structure, are defined by the law[3], which also prescribes, to some extent, the mode in which these powers are to be exercised and these duties are to be performed[4].

1   *R v Panel on Take-overs and Mergers, ex p Datafin plc* [1987] QB 815, [1987] 1 All ER 564, CA
2   *R v Disciplinary Committee of the Jockey Club, ex p Aga Khan* [1993] 2 All ER 853, [1993] 1 WLR 909, CA (jockey club not exercising governmental functions).
3   However, the organisation of the Civil Service is not fully regulated by law and so it was possible in the period from 1988 for the government to reorganise the Civil Service into executive agencies without changing the law: see the Report of the Efficiency Unit to the Prime Minister *Improving Management in Government: The Next Steps* (Efficiency Unit of the Cabinet Office, 1988); and para 549–564 post. It is unclear whether the exercise of statutory discretions by chief executives and other civil servants working in executive agencies falls within the Carltona principle (as to which see para 365 post); see further Freedland 'The rule against delegation and the *Carltona* doctrine in an agency context' [1996] Public Law 19; and para 551 post.
4   As to the modifications introduced by conventions see para 21 post. As to the elaboration of the exercise of powers and duties in the form of administrative rules see para 7 post.

**6. The principle of legality.** The legal basis of government gives rise to the principle of legality, sometimes referred to as the rule of law[1]. This may be expressed as a number of propositions, as described below.

(1) The existence or non-existence of a power or duty is a matter of law and not of fact, and so must be determined by reference either to the nature of the legal personality of the body in question and the capacities that go with it, or to some enactment or reported case. As far as the capacities that go with legal personality are concerned, many public bodies are incorporated by statute and so statutory provisions will define and limit their legal capacities[2]. Individuals who are public office-holders have the capacities that go with the legal personality that they have as natural persons[3]. The Crown is a corporation sole or aggregate[4] and so has general legal capacity, including (subject to some statutory limitations and limitations imposed by European law) the capacity to enter into contracts and to own and dispose of property[5]. The fact of a continued undisputed exercise of a power by a public body is immaterial, unless it points to a customary power

exercised from time immemorial[6]. In particular, the existence of a power cannot be proved by the practice of a private office[7].

(2) The argument of state necessity is not sufficient to establish the existence of a power or duty which would entitle a public body to act in a way that interferes with the rights or liberties of individuals[8]. However, the common law does recognise that in case of extreme urgency, when the ordinary machinery of the state cannot function, there is a justification for the doing of acts needed to restore the regular functioning of the machinery of government[9].

(3) If effect is to be given to the doctrine that the existence or non-existence of a power or duty is a matter of law, it should be possible for the courts to determine whether or not a particular power or duty exists, to define its ambit[10] and provide an effective remedy for unlawful action[11]. The independence of the judiciary is essential to the principle of legality[12]. The right of access to the courts can be excluded by statute, but this is not often done in express terms[13]. A person whose civil or political rights and freedoms as guaranteed by the Convention for the Protection of Human Rights and Fundamental Freedoms (the European Convention on Human Rights) have been infringed is entitled under the Convention to an effective right of access to the courts and an effective national remedy[14]. On the other hand, powers are often given to bodies other than the ordinary courts, to decide questions of law without appeal to the ordinary courts, and sometimes in such terms that their freedom from appellate jurisdiction extends to their findings of fact or law on which the existence of their powers depends[15].

(4) Since the principal elements of the structure of the machinery of government, and the powers and duties which belong to its several parts, are defined by law, its form and course can be altered only by a change of law[16]. Conversely, since the legislative power of Parliament is unrestricted, save where European Community law has primacy[17], its form and course can at any time be altered by Parliament[18]. Consequently there are no powers or duties inseparably annexed to the executive government[19].

1    The rule of law is a political principle the classic exposition of which is in Dicey *Law of the Constitution* (10th Edn, 1959) p 187 et seq. Dicey identified three principles which together establish the rule of law: (1) the absolute supremacy or predominance of regular law as opposed to the influence of arbitrary power; (2) equality before the law or the equal subjection of all classes to the ordinary law of the land administered by the ordinary courts; and (3) the law of the constitution is a consequence of the rights of individuals as defined and enforced by the courts. This exposition was not entirely accurate at the time of its publication, but the spirit of this doctrine has since been very influential in constitutional law. Dicey was criticised for his dislike of discretion, as this made provision under the welfare state unacceptable in terms of the rule of law: Jennings *The Law and the Constitution* (1933). Experience in European countries indicates that special administrative courts, such as the Conseil d'Etat in France, can provide strong control of government and protections for the individual, contrary to Dicey's assertion that only the ordinary courts could do so. The 'rule of law' nowadays has a range of meanings, including the idea that it embodies institutional morality, ie that there should be feasible limits on official power so as to constrain abuses which occur: see Jowell 'The Rule of Law Today' in Jowell and Oliver (eds) *The Changing Constitution* (3rd Edn, 1994). See Wade and Bradley *Constitutional and Administrative Law* (11th Edn, 1993) ch 6.

2    Eg local authorities are incorporated by the Local Government Act 1972 ss 2(3), 13(3), 14(2), 21 (as substituted), 33 (as substituted), and have power to do such acts as are provided for by statute, supplemented by local legislation. As a consequence of their corporate status, they are limited in their actions by the doctrine of ultra vires. See *R v Somerset County Council, ex p Fewings* [1995] 3 All ER 20, [1995] 1 WLR 1037, CA; and LOCAL GOVERNMENT vol 28 para 1315.

3    Eg the Metropolitan Police Commissioner. See per Sir Robert Megarry V-C in *Malone v Metropolitan Police Comr* [1979] Ch 344 at 357, sub nom *Malone v Metropolitan Police Comr (No 2)* [1979] 2 All ER 620 at 630: 'England...is not a country where everything is forbidden except what is expressly permitted: it is a country where everything is permitted except what is expressly forbidden'. See also at 366, 638: 'The notion that some express authorisation of law is required for acts which meet with 'general disfavour', and 'offend against proper standards of behaviour,' and so on, would make the state of the law dependent on subjective views on indefinite concepts, and would be likely to produce some remarkable and

contentious results'. Cf Laws J in *R v Somerset County Council, ex p Fewings* [1995] 1 All ER 513; affd on other grounds [1995] 3 All ER 20, [1995] 1 WLR 1037, CA. However, some acts that are not prohibited in English law may be contrary to the Convention for the Protection of Human Rights and Fundamental Freedoms (the European Convention on Human Rights): see paras 122–181 post.

4    See *Re M* [1994] 1 AC 377 at 424, sub nom *M v Home Office* [1993] 3 All ER 537 at 566, HL, per Lord Woolf; and *Town Investments Ltd v Department of the Environment* [1978] AC 359, [1977] 1 All ER 813, HL, in which Lord Diplock held that the Crown is a corporation sole, and Lord Simon of Glaisdale held that it is a corporation aggregate. As to corporations sole and aggregate see CORPORATIONS.

5    In exercising its common law contractual power the Crown is not subject to judicial review: *R v Lord Chancellor, ex p Hibbit and Saunders (a firm)* (1993) Times, 12 March, DC; Oliver 'Judicial review and the shorthand writers' [1993] Public Law 214. The position as to the exercise of contracting power by local authorities is different and they are subject to judicial review: see for instance *R v Lewisham London Borough Council, ex p Shell UK Ltd* [1988] 1 All ER 938, DC.

6    *Entick v Carrington* (1765) 19 State Tr 1029 at 1068. Lord Camden CJ there pointed out that the acquiescence of the victims of general warrants could not render them legal; the defendants could not prove that the practice started before the Revolution of 1688.

7    *Entick v Carrington* (1765) 19 State Tr 1029 at 1068. The executive is not limited to exercising executive powers (see para 9 post), but all the powers exercised by the executive are subject to the principle that the exercise of governmental authority directly affecting individual interests must rest on legitimate foundations. For a case where a ministerial announcement (of an extra-statutory tax concession) which appeared to 'outweigh the law of the land' was seriously questioned see *R v Customs and Excise Comrs, ex p Cooke and Stevenson* [1970] 1 All ER 1068 at 1071–1072, [1970] 1 WLR 450 at 454–455, DC, per Lord Parker CJ. See also *R v LCC, ex p Entertainments Protection Association Ltd* [1931] 2 KB 215 at 228, CA, per Scrutton LJ (local authority has no power to dispense with the provisions of the Sunday Observance Act 1780); *Vestey v IRC* [1980] AC 1148 at 1172–1173, sub nom *Vestey v IRC (Nos 1 and 2)* [1979] 3 All ER 976 at 985, HL, per Lord Wilberforce (Inland Revenue has no power to dispense with the duty to pay tax).

8    *Entick v Carrington* (1765) 19 State Tr 1029 at 1073, per Lord Camden CJ: 'With respect to the argument of state necessity or a distinction which has been aimed at between state offences and others, the common law does not understand that kind of reasoning, nor do our books take notice of any such distinction'. Lord Camden CJ was probably concerned to prevent the intrusion into English law of 'reason of state' (raison d'état) which was characteristic of continental despotisms. If this is correct, he was certainly successful; 'reason of state' has not effected an entry into English law. Within a few years, in *R v Stratton* (1779) 21 State Tr 1045, Lord Mansfield CJ had to try a case arising out of a coup d'état in Madras, where the Governor had been imprisoned by his own Council. Members of the Council were subsequently put on trial in England and argued that they had acted under the stress of necessity. In charging the jury, Lord Mansfield said at 1230: 'To amount to a justification, there must appear imminent danger to the government and individuals; the mischief must be extreme, and such as would not admit a possibility of waiting for a legal remedy; that the safety of the government must well warrant the experiment'. The defendants were in fact convicted. Necessity has been held to justify abnormal action in other countries outside the United Kingdom. Lord Mansfield later admitted that cases where it might become necessary to act without regard to law in the special circumstances of a distant territory (but could not exist in England) had presented themselves to his imagination, but that he had not dared to state them to the jury. In *Sabally and N'Jie v A-G* [1965] 1 QB 273 at 293, [1964] 3 All ER 377 at 380–381, CA, Lord Denning MR stated that the Crown, having granted a representative legislature to a colony and having thus renounced its prerogative to legislate, could nevertheless intervene to break a deadlock and fill a gap caused by a failure to elect a legislature; see de Smith and Brazier *Constitutional and Administrative Law* (7th Edn, 1994) p 74.

    In the United Kingdom the only occasions on which the interests of the state have been successfully pleaded as a defence to what would otherwise be tortious conduct or an unlawful invasion of an individual's rights, eg in the confidentiality of information, have been in connection with the seizure of documents by the police on the occasion of an arrest, or the use of confidential documents which have come lawfully into the possession of the prosecution: see infra. *Entick v Carrington* supra itself arose out of the seizure of documents under a general warrant to search premises for papers thought to be seditious, and Lord Camden CJ held that neither the seizure nor the warrant itself could be supported in the absence of a statute. Police powers of search and seizure are now regulated by statute: Police and Criminal Evidence Act 1984 Pt II (ss 8–23) (as amended); see CRIMINAL LAW vol 11(1) (Reissue) para 668 et seq.

    The use of confidential documents by the police has involved invasions of the property rights of the owner of the documents. In *Elias v Pasmore* [1934] 2 KB 164, the police, while executing a valid warrant for the arrest of one person, lawfully seized his papers, but also seized papers of another person whom they later successfully charged with the same offence. In rejecting an action of trespass brought against the police by that other person, Horridge J said at 173: 'the interests of the state must excuse the seizure of documents, which seizure would otherwise be unlawful, if it appears in fact that such documents were evidence of a crime committed by anyone'.

In *Ghani v Jones* [1970] 1 QB 693 at 706, [1969] 3 All ER 1700 at 1703, CA, where the police were held to have acted illegally in impounding the passports of persons whom they suspected of having committed a murder, Lord Denning MR criticised, obiter, Horridge J's statement, as being not only too wide, as including any crime committed by anyone, but also unnecessary for the purpose of excusing the particular seizure; he was also of the opinion (at 708–709, and at 1705) that the police might excusably search for and seize papers in the course of investigating crime, although only under very strict conditions. In *Butler v Board of Trade* [1971] Ch 680, [1970] 3 All ER 593 a confidential document had lawfully come into the possession of the liquidator of a company. Goff J refused to restrain its use to support a prosecution of a director of the company, following in this Horridge J's statement in *Elias v Pasmore* supra, as criticised by Lord Denning MR in *Ghani v Jones* supra, and also the wider opinion he had expressed in that case. The decisions and obiter dicta in these cases disclose a willingness on the part of the courts to extend, subject to safeguards, the powers of the police in their attempts to deal with crime. Only in *Elias v Pasmore* supra was there a general reference to the interests of the state, and even there it need not have been mentioned. In *Ghani v Jones* supra the state was not mentioned. In all the cases the court was concerned to balance the needs of investigating and repressing crime against the property rights of the subject. In *Butler v Board of Trade* supra Goff J spoke (at 691 and at 600) of the interest of the state to apprehend and prosecute criminals and said that 'the interest and duty of the defendants as a department of the state to prosecute offenders under the Companies Act must prevail over the offender's limited proprietary right in equity to restrain a breach of confidence'. None of these cases provides any foundation for a generalised doctrine of state necessity. For a critical appraisal see de Smith and Brazier *Constitutional and Administrative Law* (7th Edn, 1994) p 570 et seq. As to the confidentiality of information and breach of confidence generally see CONFIDENCE AND DATA PROTECTION.

9   *R v Hampden, Ship Money Case* (1637) 3 State Tr 826 at 1012–1013, per Holborne, in argument. See further paras 168, 820–822 post. The state's power to deal with riots and rebellions, to which the term 'martial law' is sometimes applied, rests on this principle. As to martial law see further para 821 post. In such cases necessary acts not in accordance with law may subsequently be the subject of indemnifying legislation: see eg the Indemnity Act 1920 (repealed), and the War Damage Act 1965, which retrospectively negatived the decision in *Burmah Oil Co (Burma Trading) Ltd v Lord Advocate* [1965] AC 75, [1964] 2 All ER 348, HL; see para 820 post. Alternatively, the illegality of those rights of redress may be removed; see eg the Enemy Property Act 1953 ss 6, 7 (repealed). If the exercise of these powers interferes with civil and political rights that are protected by the Convention for the Protection of Human Rights and Fundamental Freedoms (as to which see paras 122–181 post) then under the terms of the Convention they will be regarded as unlawful unless justified on grounds set out in the Convention. These may include, in respect of certain rights, necessity in a democratic society in the interests of national security or public safety, the prevention of disorder or crime, and the protection of the rights and freedoms of others. Article 15 provides that in time of war or other public emergency threatening the life of the nation measures may be taken derogating from the obligations under the Convention to the extent strictly required by the exigencies of the situation: see para 168 post.

10   This doctrine is inherent in all the seventeenth century cases on prerogative: see *Prohibitions del Roy* (1607) 12 Co Rep 63 (the monarch may not sit as a judge in the royal courts); *Brownlow v Cox and Michil* (1615) 3 Bulst 32 (the monarch may not withdraw matters of state from the cognisance of the courts); and see in particular *Proclamations' Case* (1611) 12 Co Rep 74 at 76: 'Also it was resolved that the King hath no prerogative, but that which the law of the land allows him'. In *Stockdale v Hansard* (1839) 9 Ad & El 1 the Court of Queen's Bench refused to acknowledge the right of the House of Commons to determine the limits of its privileges, and held that they were a matter of common law to be determined, like any other matter of common law, by the common law courts.

11   A minister or other public official or body that is in breach of a court order may be found to be in contempt of court: *Re M* [1994] 1 AC 377, sub nom *M v Home Office* [1993] 3 All ER 537, HL. Injunctions and interim injunctions may be granted against officers of the Crown: *Re M* supra. As to remedies against public bodies or in respect of exercises of public or governmental functions see generally ADMINISTRATIVE LAW.

12   See para 10 post. As to the judiciary see further paras 301–311 post.

13   Examples may be found in the Parliament Act 1911 s 3 (which provides that any certificate of the Speaker under that Act may not be questioned in any court of law). See also the Immigration Act 1971 s 14(3) (which provides that a discretionary decision by the Secretary of State on 'public good' grounds concerning variation of limited leave to enter and remain in the United Kingdom may not be the subject of appeal). The courts have consistently attempted to hold that a provision in an enactment making the decision of an administrative authority final does not oust their supervisory jurisdictions: see *R v Medical Appeal Tribunal, ex p Gilmore* [1957] 1 QB 574, sub nom *Re Gilmore's Application* [1957] 1 All ER 796, CA; *Anisminic Ltd v Foreign Compensation Commission* [1969] 2 AC 147, [1969] 1 All ER 208,

HL. This has now received statutory recognition; any provision in any Act passed before 1 August 1958 to the effect that any order or determination is not to be called into question in any court, or any provision which by similar words excludes any of the powers of the High Court, does not prevent the High Court from making orders of certiorari and mandamus: Tribunals and Inquiries Act 1992 s 12(1). See further ADMINISTRATIVE LAW vol 1(1) (Reissue) paras 21, 59, 73.

For an example of an unsuccessful attempt in one of the Defence of the Realm Regulations to prevent access to the courts see *Chester v Bateson* [1920] 1 KB 829. For the special restrictions created by the doctrine of act of state see FOREIGN RELATIONS.

14  See the Convention for the Protection of Human Rights and Fundamental Freedoms Arts 6(1), 13; and paras 134, 163 post.

15  There are various forms. Thus it may be provided that the certificate of an administrative authority is conclusive evidence that the requirements of an Act have been complied with, or an administrative authority or tribunal may have power to determine the ambit of its own authority or jurisdiction, or the power to act may be conferred in subjective terms, or it may be provided that an order under an Act is to have effect as if enacted in the enabling Act: see generally ADMINISTRATIVE LAW vol 1(1) (Reissue) paras 21, 68.

16  But see para 5 note 3 ante, where an exception is noted regarding the organisation of the Civil Service. As to the Civil Service see para 549–564 post.

17  See paras 1 ante; 23–24 post.

18  See paras 1 ante; 232 post.

19  The contrary doctrine, that certain prerogatives were inseparable, was upheld by the majority of the judges in *R v Hampden, Ship Money Case* (1637) 3 State Tr 826 at 1085, 1190, 1194–1195, 1235. The same doctrine appears in *Godden v Hales* (1686) 11 State Tr 1166. The decision in *R v Hampden, Ship Money Case* supra was, however, overruled by the Ship Money Act 1640 (repealed), and the Bill of Rights declared that the pretended prerogatives of taxing without recourse to Parliament, of suspending the laws, and of dispensing with the obligation to observe the law in individual cases, were illegal. As to the history and citation of the Bill of Rights see para 35 note 3 post.

**7. Sources of powers and duties.** Much of what government and Parliament do is regulated by rules which are not law in the sense that they are not justiciable. These rules include statements of policy, practice and procedure and govern matters such as the relationships between ministers and civil servants, the appearance of civil servants before select committees and the financial interests of ministers[1]. The development of these rules, if they are published, facilitates the holding of government to account for its actions, and amounts to a process of establishing non-legal norms. Some but not all of these rules are properly regarded as constitutional conventions[2].

The specific legal sources of governmental powers and duties are the specific sources of law, that is to say:

(1) the common law, equity, admiralty law and ecclesiastical law, all of which are largely embodied in judicial decisions[3];

(2) the common law powers enjoyed by the Crown by virtue of its legal personality as a corporation[4] and under the royal prerogative[5];

(3) prerogative rules and orders made and issued by the Crown, acting in exercise of the power entrusted to it by virtue of the common law, and embodied in Orders in Council[6], treaties[7], charters, proclamations relating to the colonies or dependencies[8] and other executive documents[9];

(4) Acts of Parliament[10];

(5) subordinate legislation made by the Crown, government departments, local authorities or other bodies on whom legislative powers have been conferred by statute; such subordinate legislation includes proclamations, declarations, Orders in Council, rules, regulations, warrants, schemes, directions, orders and byelaws[11];

(6) the *lex et consuetudo Parliamenti*, or, in other words, the privileges of each House of Parliament and the rules relating to contempt of Parliament[12];

(7) custom[13];

(8) where the exercise of powers or the performance of duties admits of some discretion, judgment or choice it may be useful to refer to ministerial announcements as to future action[14], or to extra-statutory concessions[15];

(9) in a field such as constitutional law, where case law is often scanty, the views of writers of repute enjoy considerable persuasive authority[16];

(10) directly applicable and directly effective European Community law[17];

(11) undertakings given to government by organisations which regulate in some part the conduct of the organisations or confer rights on others[18];

(12) authorisations to conduct services and pursue programmes implied in grants and appropriations of money by Parliament for such purposes[19]: there may in consequence exist a broad and undefined power whereby a government department, as representative of the Crown, may act in a benevolent manner much as an individual might do provided the payments it makes are covered by an appropriation[20]; and in so acting it may impose conditions upon the receipt of its benevolence. An example of this benevolence might be the making of an extra-statutory payment subject to a specified form of application[21]; and

(13) the provisions of the Convention for the Protection of Human Rights and Fundamental Freedoms[22] and the other international human rights treaties to which the United Kingdom is party[23].

1   See eg *Questions of Procedure for Ministers* (Cabinet Office, May 1992) (as now revised: see para 416 note 1 post); *Departmental Evidence and Response to Select Committees* (Cabinet Office, December 1994); and the Civil Service Management Code (1996) (including the Civil Service Code): see para 554 note 1 head (2) post.

2   As to constitutional conventions as sources of law see paras 19–21 post. For examples of important written non-legal rules see *Questions of Procedure for Ministers* (Cabinet Office, May 1992) (as now revised: see para 416 note 1 post); and para 21 note 26 post; *Departmental Evidence and Response to Select Committees* (Cabinet Office, December 1994) (formerly the Osmotherly Rules); *Duties and Responsibilities of Civil Servants in relation to Ministers: A Note by the Head of the Home Civil Service* 123 HC Official Report (6th series), 2 December 1987, written answers cols 572–575 (the 'Armstrong memorandum'); (reproduced as revised in *The Role of the Civil Service* (minutes of evidence) (HC Paper (1993–94) no 27-II)).

3   Some of the most important principles of constitutional law have been enunciated by judges. The principle of legality is largely a judicial creation: see para 6 ante; and the cases cited in notes thereto. In the *Prohibitions Del Roy* (1607) 12 Co Rep 63, Sir Edward Coke CJ declared that 'the King in his own person cannot adjudge any case…but this ought to be determined and adjudged in some Court of Justice' thus establishing the principle of the separation of powers between the judiciary and other branches of government which is an important pillar of the principle of legality (see paras 8, 10 post; and COURTS). In the *Proclamations' Case* (1611) 12 Co Rep 74 Sir Edward Coke CJ, declaring that 'the King hath no prerogative, but that which the law of the land allows him' held that the King could not by proclamation create a new criminal offence, although he may use proclamations to exhort his subjects. By implication this could only be done with the consent of Parliament (paras 917–918 post). Thus the importance of procedure in constitutional law has a firm basis in judicial decisions. In *Entick v Carrington* (1765) 19 State Tr 1029 (see para 6 notes 6–8 ante) Lord Camden CJ held that the exercise of governmental authority directly affecting individual interests must rest on legal foundations. *R v Pinney* (1832) 3 B & Ad 947 enunciated the powers and duties of the mayor of a borough in putting down riots. *Malone v Metropolitan Police Comr* [1979] Ch 344, sub nom *Malone v Metropolitan Police Comr (No 2)* [1979] 2 All ER 620 establishes that an aspect of the principle of legality is that England is a country where everything is permitted except what is expressly forbidden (see para 6 ante). *O'Reilly v Mackman* [1983] 2 AC 237, [1982] 3 All ER 1124, HL, establishes that there is a separate system of public law and that in principle public law issues should be adjudicated through the procedure laid down in the Supreme Court Act 1981 s 31 and RSC Ord 53 (see ADMINISTRATIVE LAW). *Council of Civil Service Unions v Minister for the Civil Service* [1985] AC 374, [1984] 3 All ER 935, HL, decided that the test for determining whether a decision is susceptible to judicial review is the nature and not the source of the power, and thus that exercises of the royal prerogative (see para 367 et seq post) will be susceptible to judicial review unless they are not justiciable (see and ADMINISTRATIVE LAW). The judiciary also promulgates practice directions and notes which do not exactly fit into any categorisation of the sources of law but which might be regarded as an inherent part of the judicial function: see further para 10 note 1 post.

4   See para 10 text and note 4 ante.

5   See para 367 et seq post.

6    See para 907 post.

7    Agreements or treaties embodied in statutes, such as the Union with Scotland Act 1706 and the Union with Ireland Act 1800 (now for the most part repealed), or incorporated referentially such as by the European Communities Act 1972, the European Communities (Amendment) Act 1986, the European Economic Area Act 1993 and the European Communities (Amendment) Act 1994, are sometimes designated 'quasi-treaties'. As to the Community Treaties see para 24 note 2 post.

8    As to the legal use of proclamations see note 3 supra; and para 917 post. As to colonies and dependencies see COMMONWEALTH vol 6 (Reissue) paras 802, 805.

9    As to executive documents generally see paras 906–922 post. Included under the head of prerogative rules and orders are some administrative regulations such as the Civil Service Management Code (1996) and a separate guide for the use of establishment officers: 897 HC Official Report (5th series), 15 October 1975, written answers col 711; see para 559 post.

10   The powers of the Queen in Parliament to enact laws are discussed in para 232 post. The Magna Carta of Edward I (1297), the Petition of Right (1627), the Bill of Rights, and the Act of Settlement, being in the nature of solemn compacts between the monarch and people, are usually designated quasi-statutes. As to the history and citation of the Bill of Rights see para 35 note 3 post. For repeals which affect Magna Carta (1297), the Petition of Right (1627), and the Bill of Rights see para 1 note 13 ante. In relation to the power to enact statutes, the practice of linking an announcement of a proposed change in the law and retrospective legislation should be noted. See eg the announcement (804 HC Official Report (5th series), 22 July 1970, col 548) that betterment levy would no longer be chargeable; this was followed by the Land Commission (Dissolution) Act 1971 which received the royal assent on 8 April 1971 and which operated retrospectively: see s 1(1). See also Department of the Environment Circular 140/1973 and the Valuation (Statutory Deductions) Order 1973, SI 1973/2139. The attitude of the courts to such announcements has not been tested but regard might be had to the remarks of Lord Parker CJ in *R v Customs and Excise Comrs, ex p Cooke and Stevenson* [1970] 1 All ER 1068 at 1072, [1970] 1 WLR 450 at 454–455, DC; see also *R v Secretary of State for the Home Department, ex p Fire Brigades Union* [1995] 1 All ER 888 at 896–897, CA, per Sir Thomas Bingham MR, and at 911 per Morritt LJ.

11   See para 9 post. Many items of subordinate legislation are termed 'statutory instruments'; see the Statutory Instruments Act 1946 s 1(1); and STATUTES vol 44(1) (Reissue) para 1503. See also ADMINISTRATIVE LAW vol 1(1) (Reissue) paras 4, 35. Their validity may be questioned in judicial proceedings on the ground that they are ultra vires or that the correct procedure for making them has not been followed: see eg *Customs and Excise Comrs v Cure and Deeley Ltd* [1962] 1 QB 340, [1961] 3 All ER 641; *Agricultural, Horticultural and Forestry Industry Training Board v Aylesbury Mushrooms Ltd* [1972] 1 All ER 280, [1972] 1 WLR 190 (lack of proper consultation); *Daymond v South West Water Authority* [1976] AC 609, [1976] 1 All ER 39, HL (ultra vires); *Raymond v Honey* [1983] 1 AC 1, [1982] 1 All ER 756, HL (ultra vires); *R v Secretary of State for Social Services, ex p Association of Metropolitan Authorities* [1986] 1 All ER 164, [1986] 1 WLR 1 (ultra vires); *Woolwich Equitable Building Society v IRC* [1991] 4 All ER 92, sub nom *R v IRC, ex p Woolwich Equitable Building Society* [1990] 1 WLR 1400, HL (ultra vires). Properly included under the head subordinate legislation are orders of an administrative nature, often not published as statutory instruments. See eg Statements of Changes in Immigration Rules (see the Immigration Act 1971 s 3(2); and BRITISH NATIONALITY, IMMIGRATION AND RACE RELATIONS vol 4(2) (Reissue) para 72 note 10); see also the Codes of Practice issued by the Secretary of State under the Police and Criminal Evidence Act 1984 (see CRIMINAL LAW vol 11(1) (Reissue) para 657), issued to provide 'clear and workable guidelines for the police, balanced by strengthened safeguards for the public': Foreword to the original Codes); guidance issued by the Secretary of State under what is now the Social Security Contributions and Benefits Act 1992 s 140(2), (4), concerning the award of Social Fund payments (see *R v Secretary of State for Social Services, ex p Stitt* [1991] COD 68, CA). On this see Feldman 'The Constitution and the Social Fund: A Novel Form of Legislation' (1991) 107 LQR 39, highly critical of the fact that such guidance avoids the parliamentary scrutiny undergone by subordinate legislation under social security legislation; Departmental Circulars and Planning Policy Guidance Notes under town and country planning legislation which are intended to provide precise and practical guidance on planning policies (Department of the Environment Circular 1/88 para 2). An act of subordinate legislation 'is a law, and is obligatory to all persons bound by it ... as any Act of Parliament, only with this difference that it is liable to have its validity brought into question': see *City of London v Wood* (1701) 12 Mod Rep 669 at 678 per Holt CJ, speaking of byelaws.

12   See generally PARLIAMENT.

13   See generally CUSTOM AND USAGE. Most of the law relating to custom, in the strict sense of the term, can have little relevance to constitutional law since, in a paraphrase of the words of Lord Camden CJ in *Entick v Carrington* (1765) 19 State Tr 1029, it is incredible that any custom of a public character should have existed from the time whereof the memory of man runneth not to the contrary and never yet have found a place in any book of law. Yet the so-called conventions have a customary character, and it was

doubtless for that reason that Anson entitled his book on the constitution *The Law and Custom of the Constitution*. For the constitutional conventions see paras 19–22 post.

14 A minister is entitled to adopt from time to time general policies according to which he proposes to exercise his discretion, and there is nothing to preclude him from announcing such policies; it may indeed be of great convenience to the public that he should do so. But a minister charged with the duty of making administrative decisions in a fair and impartial manner must not allow such a policy to preclude him from fairly judging all the issues which are relevant to each individual case (*British Oxygen Co Ltd v Board of Trade* [1971] AC 610, HL). These principles apply also to local and, indeed, all public bodies endowed with a statutory discretion: see ADMINISTRATIVE LAW vol 1(1) (Reissue) paras 29–32. The courts have been prepared to recognise and, where necessary, give effect to administrative practices adopted by public authorities, even where they are not expressly allowed or prescribed by law. For central government departments see *Carltona Ltd v Works Comrs* [1943] 2 All ER 560, CA (civil servant may take decisions in the name of the minister or the department), and for local authorities see *Lever Finance Ltd v Westminster (City) London Borough Council* [1971] 1 QB 222, [1970] 3 All ER 496, CA: for a full discussion of this case see Bradley (Case and Comment) [1971] CLJ 3; and for the extent to which a public authority may be estopped from denying the validity of acts done according to a non-statutory practice see ADMINISTRATIVE LAW vol 1(1) (Reissue) para 23; and Wade and Bradley *Constitutional and Administrative Law* (11th Edn, 1993) pp 700–703. There are a number statements of practice issued by government which, though not legally binding, effectively regulate the operation of Cabinet government: *Questions of Procedure for Ministers* (Cabinet Office, May 1992) (as now revised: see para 416 note 1 post); and of relations between ministers and civil servants: *Departmental Evidence and Response to Select Committees* (Cabinet Office, December 1994) (formerly the Osmotherly Rules); *Duties and Responsibilities of Civil Servants in relation to Ministers: A Note by the Head of the Home Civil Service* 123 HC Official Report (6th series), 2 December 1987, written answers cols 572–575 (the 'Armstrong memorandum'); (reproduced as revised in *The Role of the Civil Service* (minutes of evidence) (HC Paper (1993–94) no 27-II)); *Civil Servants and Ministers: Duties and Responsibilities* (Cmnd 9841) (1986); and the Civil Service Code (incorporated in the Civil Service Management Code (1996): see para 554 note 1 head (2) post.

15 These have been termed 'administrative quasi-legislation'; see Megarry 60 LQR 125, 218; and Ganz *Quasi-Legislation* (1987). They are not legally enforceable, and may have doubtful validity in law: see para 6 note 7 ante. For a case where a statute was enforced despite a concession see *R v Berry* [1969] 2 QB 73, [1969] 1 All ER 689, CA, where the concession had been abused. An extra-statutory concession may give rise to a legitimate expectation that executive discretion or power will be exercised in accordance with the concession, but not if an attempt has been made to abuse the concession (eg for tax avoidance): *R v IRC, ex p Fulford-Dobson* [1987] STC 344. A legitimate expectation may also be raised by a statement of practice, a notice or a ruling, for instance issued by the Inland Revenue, but only if the applicant has been frank with the government body concerned: *Re Preston* [1985] AC 835, sub nom *Preston v IRC* [1985] 2 All ER 327, HL; *R v IRC, ex p MFK Underwriting Agencies Ltd* [1989] STC 873. Extra-statutory concessions are often published (eg the tax concessions are set out in a booklet IR 1 (1994), and are revised periodically; explanatory notes are issued by the Board of Inland Revenue).

16 'It is fair to say that in the diffuse field of constitutional law the opinions of authorities are resorted to more often than in other branches of English law. In administrative law cases the opinions of modern writers ... have come to be quoted in argument and are occasionally cited in judgments': de Smith and Brazier *Constitutional and Administrative Law* (7th Edn, 1994) p 27. Hence they are frequently cited in this title.

17 See paras 23–24 post; and EUROPEAN COMMUNITIES.

18 Eg the Motor Insurers' Bureau (Compensation of Victims of Uninsured Drivers) Agreement (1988); and the Motor Insurers' Bureau (Compensation of Victims of Untraced Drivers) Agreement (1972) (see further INSURANCE vol 25 (Reissue) paras 759–760). It is believed that the essential validity of such undertakings does not appear to have been tested in the courts but the courts have recognised that an individual who, as a third party, has no rights against the Motor Insurers' Bureau can rely on receiving the benefits of the agreement: see *Albert v Motor Insurers' Bureau* [1972] AC 301, [1971] 2 All ER 1345, HL. It is thought that the courts would uphold the essential validity of the Motor Insurers' Bureau agreements as a binding contractual obligation, but the sanction behind such undertakings is probably the implied threat of legislation which might be enacted to effect the purpose of the undertakings: see further INSURANCE vol 25 (Reissue) para 758.

19 Clear statutory authority is needed for public expenditure, and there is a constitutional convention which jealously safeguards the exclusive control exercised by Parliament over both the levying and the expenditure of public revenue: *Steele Ford & Newton v Crown Prosecution Service (No 2)* [1994] 1 AC 22, [1993] 2 All ER 769, HL. Conformity to appropriations and the estimates on which they are based is assured by the Comptroller and Auditor-General: see generally para 715 et seq post. As to the Comptroller and Auditor General see paras 724–726 post.

20 The amount that can be paid may be further limited by any express statutory provision to pay grants, subsidies, etc of the same nature.

21 Eg the payments made by the Criminal Injuries Compensation Board. The board was established by virtue of the royal prerogative and it prescribes conditions subject to which it may make gratuitous payments to the victims of criminal acts. The Criminal Injuries Compensation Scheme was placed on a statutory basis by virtue of the Criminal Justice Act 1988 ss 108–117 (now repealed: see infra). However, at the date at which this volume states the law, those provisions had not been brought into force and the scheme still operates under the prerogative. The government introduced a White Paper *Compensating Victims of Violent Crime: Changes to the Criminal Injuries Compensation Scheme* (Cm 2434) (1993), which introduces changes to the system of compensation awards, and which was heavily criticised in the House of Lords (552 HL Official Report (5th series), 2 March 1994 col 1071) for its failure to put the scheme on the intended statutory footing. The new proposals were declared unlawful in *R v Secretary of State for the Home Department, ex p Fire Brigades Union* [1995] 1 All ER 888, CA, on the ground that the Home Secretary could not use prerogative powers to introduce a new scheme that was different from that provided for by the Act, even though the Act was not in force, without first repealing the Act. As from 1 April 1996 there is a Criminal Injuries Compensation Scheme in place under the Criminal Injuries Compensation Act 1995, introduced to replace the withdrawn scheme. The Criminal Justice Act 1988 ss 108–117 are repealed: Criminal Injuries Compensation Act 1995 s 12(7), Schedule.

Ministerial circulars are not regarded as a 'source' of law except in such rare instances. More usually they are issued for purposes of information, eg stating ministerial policy, explaining legislation, providing administrative machinery; and in practice they are particularly important in certain areas of law, eg education and town and country planning. Only on the rare occasions when they exceed their 'information' function or give rise to legitimate expectations might they properly be seen as a 'source' of law. For a case where a ministerial circular gave rise to legitimate expectations as to how ministerial discretion would be exercised see *R v Secretary of State for the Home Department, ex p Khan* [1985] 1 All ER 40, [1984] 1 WLR 1337, CA, where it was held that where a member of the public affected by a decision of a public authority had a legitimate expectation based on a statement or undertaking by the authority that it would apply certain criteria or follow certain procedures in making its decision, the authority was under a duty to follow those criteria or procedures in reaching its decision, provided that the statement or undertaking in question did not conflict with the authority's statutory duty. See also Lester 'Government compliance with international human rights law: a new year's legitimate expectation' [1996] Public Law 187.

22 See paras 122–181 post.

23 See para 103 post.

## 8. Absence of a strict separation of powers.
It is clear that the powers of government are distributed among a number of institutions, so that the original concentration of power in the monarch no longer exists; in the eighteenth century this division of the powers of government seemed to be such an essential characteristic of the English constitution that it was made the basis for the doctrine of separation of powers[1].

This doctrine, which is to the effect that in a nation which has political liberty as the direct object of its constitution no one person or body of persons ought to be allowed to control the legislative, executive and judicial powers, or any two of them[2], has never in its strict form corresponded with the facts of English government[3] mainly because, although the functions and powers of government are largely separated[4], the membership of the separate instruments of state overlap[5]. Only in one aspect of the constitution can it be said that the doctrine is strictly adhered to, namely that by tradition, convention and law the judiciary is insulated from political matters[6].

1 The doctrine in its developed form derives from the writings of Montesquieu (Esprit des Lois, Book XI, Chs V, VI), who attributed that object and those principles to England. His theory was not so obviously inconsistent with the English constitution of his time as it has since become, for the concentration of legislative and executive power in the hands of the Cabinet is due to conventional rules, which had not been fully developed in his time: see para 403 note 3 post. The doctrine has had a very great influence everywhere, and was applied extensively in the framing of the constitution of the United States of America. See Vile *Constitutionalism and the Separation of Powers* (1967); and Barendt 'Separation of Powers and Constitutional Government' [1995] Public Law 599.

2 This is an abbreviated form of Montesquieu's theory. For other interpretations of the doctrine see ADMINISTRATIVE LAW vol 1(1) (Reissue) para 5.

3 A concern, most strongly expressed by Lord Hewart of Bury in *The New Despotism*, that the distinctions between legislative, executive and judicial functions were being unduly disregarded, formed the background for the inquiry conducted by the Committee on Ministers' Powers (the Donoughmore-Scott

Committee): see the *Report of the Committee on Ministers' Powers* (Cmd 4060) (1932). The committee was led to lay emphasis on some rather dubious distinctions, eg between judicial and quasi-judicial functions. These were carefully avoided by the Committee on Administrative Tribunals and Inquiries (the Franks Committee), which reported in 1957 (*Report of the Committee on Administrative Tribunals and Inquiries* (Cmnd 218) (1957). See Jennings *The Law and the Constitution* ch 1 and Appendix I. For an examination of the tests to be applied to discover whether a court or tribunal has genuine judicial characteristics in a constitutional system which reserves certain functions to the judiciary see *Liyanage v R* [1967] 1 AC 259, [1966] 1 All ER 650, PC; *United Engineering Workers' Union v Devanayagam* [1968] AC 356, [1967] 2 All ER 367, PC; and see further ADMINISTRATIVE LAW vol 1(1) (Reissue) para 5.

4    There is, however, some overlapping of functions: see eg para 9 note 2 post.

5    See para 9 note 2 post.

6    See para 303 post.

**9. Executive functions.** Although the legislative, executive and judicial functions of the state are formally distinct, it is not the case that executive functions are exclusively performed by the executive[1], or that the executive does not engage in functions which would normally be described as legislative or judicial in character[2].

Executive functions are incapable of comprehensive definition, for they are merely the residue of functions of government after legislative and judicial functions have been taken away. They may, however, be said to entail the formulation or application of general policy in relation to particular situations or cases, or the making or execution of individual discretionary decisions. More specifically, they include the execution of law and policy, the maintenance of public order, the management of Crown property and nationalised industries and services, the direction of foreign policy, the conduct of military operations, and the provision, regulation, financing or supervision of such services as education, public health, transport and national insurance[3].

In the performance of these functions, executive bodies may be empowered by statute to exercise functions which are strictly legislative in character[4]; in addition certain discretionary actions of the executive are not far removed from legislation[5] and certain decisions affecting personal and proprietary rights, whilst not strictly judicial, have been held to give rise to a duty to act judicially[6].

1    For the various meanings which may be attributed to the term 'executive' see ADMINISTRATIVE LAW vol 1(1) (Reissue) para 16.

2    For a thorough discussion of this topic see Jennings *The Law and the Constitution* 280–304; *Report of the Committee on Ministers' Powers* (Cmd 4060) (1932) 8–15. The overlapping of functions and the interrelationship of membership of the various branches of government may be seen in the fact that ministers are by convention members of both the executive and the legislature; and legislative powers are conferred by Parliament on the executive (see further note 4 infra).

3    For a general characterisation, to be supplemented to take account of later developments, see Maitland *Constitutional History of England* (1908) p 196.

4    These are instanced by rules, regulations, orders, and other forms of subordinate legislation. A measure of parliamentary control over such legislation is exercised under the Statutory Instruments Act 1946 ss 4–7; see further STATUTES vol 44(1) (Reissue) para 1515 et seq. For other forms of parliamentary control over the actions of the executive see ADMINISTRATIVE LAW vol 1(1) (Reissue) para 35.

5    Eg police notices for the regulation of traffic, and extra-statutory tax concessions (see para 7 ante; and ADMINISTRATIVE LAW vol 1(1) (Reissue) para 2 note 11). Prerogative powers may also be exercise in lieu of legislation, as in the case of the royal warrant under which various army pensions are paid (see ROYAL FORCES); and the establishment of the Criminal Injuries Compensation Board by administrative action under the prerogative: see 694 HC Official Report (5th series), 5 May 1964, col 1138; and *Compensation for Victims of Crimes of Violence* (Cmnd 2323) (1964). Departmental circulars have on occasion been described as 'sub-delegated legislation'; see the cases cited in ADMINISTRATIVE LAW vol 1(1) (Reissue) para 2 note 7.

6    For the distinction between a judicial function, and a function in the exercise of which there is a duty to act judicially (ie to observe the rules of fairness and natural justice) see ADMINISTRATIVE LAW vol 1(1) (Reissue) para 85.

**10. Non-judicial functions of the judiciary.** Some of the judges exercise legislative functions in the making of rules of procedure[1]; and the rules of common law, of equity, of admiralty and of ecclesiastical law have all been enunciated by the judges[2]. They also perform executive functions such as the appointment of guardians and trustees, the administration of estates, and the protection of the interests of persons suffering from mental disorder and other disabilities[3]. Justices of the peace, who are primarily subordinate criminal and family law judges, at one time carried on or supervised almost the whole of county government[4], and although they have lost most of their executive powers they are still intimately associated with the police[5], and control the granting of certain types of licences[6].

1　Eg along with other members of the legal profession, in the Rules Committee which frames the Rules of the Supreme Court: see the Supreme Court Act 1981 ss 84, 85 (as amended); and COURTS. Certain practice notes made by the judges under their inherent jurisdiction might be said to be legislation: see eg *Practice Note* [1966] 3 All ER 77, sub nom *Practice Statement (Judicial Precedent)* [1966] 1 WLR 1234 (where the House of Lords modified its strict adherence to the doctrine of binding precedent). For a rare extra-judicial pronouncement which has been regarded as a statement of law see the M'Naghten Rules, which were answers given by the judges to the House of Lords in *M'Naghten's Case* (1843) 10 Cl & Fin 200: see CRIMINAL LAW vol 11(1) (Reissue) para 31.

2　The orthodox view derived from Blackstone was that judges do not make law, but only declare what has always been the law: 1 Bl Com (14th Edn) 88. Judges have often declared that defects in legislation can only be cured by Parliament: see eg *Magor and St Mellons RDC v Newport Corpn* [1952] AC 189 at 191, [1951] 2 All ER 839 at 841, HL, per Viscount Simonds; *Hill v East and West India Dock Co* (1884) 9 App Cas 448 at 465 per Lord Bramwell; *Kaye v Robertson* [1991] FSR 62, CA; *Malone v Metropolitan Police Comr* [1979] Ch 344, sub nom *Malone v Metropolitan Police Comr (No 2)* [1979] 2 All ER 620; cf however *Haley v London Electricity Board* [1965] AC 778 at 800–801, [1964] 3 All ER 185 at 194, HL, per Lord Evershed; *Myers v DPP* [1965] AC 1001 at 1021, [1964] 2 All ER 881 at 885, HL, per Lord Reid; *Pettitt v Pettitt* [1970] AC 777 at 794–795, [1969] 2 All ER 385 at 390, HL, per Lord Reid; *Woolwich Equitable Building Society v IRC* [1993] AC 70 at 173–174, sub nom *Woolwich Building Society v IRC (No 2)* [1992] 3 All ER 737 at 760–761, HL, per Lord Goff of Chieveley; *R v R* [1992] 1 AC 599, [1991] 4 All ER 481, HL; *Pepper v Hart* [1993] AC 593, [1993] 1 All ER 42, HL. See also Lord Reid 'The Judge as Law Maker' XII Journal of Society of Public Teachers of Law (NS) 22; Lester 'English Judges as Law Makers' [1993] Public Law 269; Lord Mackay of Clashfern 'Can Judges change the Law?' [1987] Proceedings of the British Academy 285.

3　See *Scott v Scott* [1913] AC 417 at 437, HL, where Viscount Haldane explained that proceedings in such matters may be held in camera, on the ground that they are not really judicial but administrative in character; and see also at 482–483 per Lord Shaw. See also Jennings *The Law and the Constitution*.

4　See Maitland *Constitutional History of England* (1908) pp 206–209, 232, 233.

5　Eg in the issuing of warrants: see MAGISTRATES vol 29 para 321.

6　See eg BETTING vol 4(1) (Reissue) para 61.

**11. Non-legislative functions of the legislature.** Both Houses of Parliament exercise judicial functions, the House of Lords as the final court of appeal in most matters arising within the United Kingdom[1], and both Houses in questions concerning their own privileges. Not only do officers of the Houses execute the decisions of the Houses in matters of privilege, but the Houses themselves, in proceedings in respect of private bills, follow a procedure which is in substance judicial[2].

1　See generally COURTS vol 10 para 733 et seq.

2　See generally PARLIAMENT.

**12. Standards in public life.** Standards of conduct in public life are nowhere comprehensively set out, but they may be inferred from the general law and conventions of the constitution. They are set out in non-legal form in guidelines used in parliament, government and the Civil Service, and in the Civil Service Code[1].

The Committee on Standards in Public Life has identified seven principles of public life which emphasise the importance of serving the public interest, and which apply to all who serve the public[2]. The seven principles are as follows:

(1) Selflessness: holders of public office should take decisions solely in terms of the public interest; they should not do so in order to gain financial or other material benefits for themselves, their family, or their friends.

(2) Integrity: holders of public office should not place themselves under any financial or other obligation to outside individuals or organisations that might influence them in the performance of their official duties.

(3) Objectivity: in carrying out public business, including making public appointments, awarding contracts, or recommending individuals for rewards and benefits, holders of public office should make choices on merit.

(4) Accountability: holders of public office are accountable for their decisions and actions to the public and must subject themselves to whatever scrutiny is appropriate to their office.

(5) Openness: holders of public office should be as open as possible about all the decisions and actions that they take; they should give reasons for their decisions and restrict information only when the wider public interest clearly demands.

(6) Honesty: holders of public office have a duty to declare any private interests relating to their public duties and to take steps to resolve any conflicts arising in a way that protects the public interest.

(7) Leadership: holders of public office should promote and support these principles by leadership and example.

Misbehaviour in a public office is a common law offence[3]. Corruption of or by members or servants of public bodies is a statutory offence[4] and in some circumstances is punishable at common law[5]. Misfeasance in a public office is a tort[6].

1   See further paras 211, 401, 560 post. See also *Questions of Procedure for Ministers* (Cabinet Office, May 1992) (as now revised: see para 416 note 1 post); *Departmental Evidence and Response to Select Committees* (Cabinet Office, December 1994); and the Civil Service Code, set out in the Civil Service Management Code (1996) para 4.1 Annex A, 566 HL Official Report (5th series), 30 October 1995, written answers, cols *146–148*. As to the Civil Service see paras 549–564 post.
    *Questions of Procedure for Ministers* (Cabinet Office, May 1992) (as revised) para 1 summarises the ethical standards expected of ministers (see para 416 post). Membership of Lloyd's is covered by the amendment set out in 247 HC Official Report (6th series), 21 July 1994, written answers cols *551–553*. See also paras 416, 420 post; the *Third Report of the Committee on Standards and Privileges: The Code of Conduct and the Guide to the Rules relating to the Conduct of Members* (HC Paper (1995–96) no 604).
2   *First Report of the Committee on Standards in Public Life* (Cm 2850-I) (1995) p 14. As to the adoption by the House of Commons of a code setting out those principles see para 211 note 3 post.
3   *R v Bembridge* (1783) 3 Doug KB 327; *R v Hall* [1891] 1 QB 747; *R v Whitaker* [1914] 3 KB 1283, CCA; *R v Llewellyn-Jones* [1968] 1 QB 429, [1967] 3 All ER 225, CA; *R v Dytham* [1979] QB 722, [1979] 3 All ER 641, CA; *R v Bowden* [1995] 4 All ER 505, CA. See generally CRIMINAL LAW vol 11(1) para 290 et seq. See also *Lyme Regis Corpn v Henley* (1834) 2 Cl & Fin 331, HL.
4   Public Bodies Corrupt Practices Act 1889 ss 1, 2 (as amended), 3(2), 4 (as amended), 7: see CRIMINAL LAW vol 11(1) (Reissue) para 283.
5   It is an offence at common law to bribe a privy councillor (*R v Vaughan* (1769) 4 Burr 2494) or a juryman (*R v Young* (1801) 2 East 14); it is a crime for a judicial or ministerial officer to take a bribe (*R v Vaughan* supra), or to offer a bribe to the holder of a public office (*R v Lancaster and Worrall* (1890) 16 Cox CC 737).
    The acceptance of a bribe by a member of either House of Parliament is a breach of privilege: Erskine May's *Treatise on the Law, Privileges, Proceedings and Usage of Parliament* (21st Edn, 1989) pp 119, 128 (that work is referred to subsequently in this title as 'Erskine May *Parliamentary Practice* (21st Edn, 1989)). It is not clear whether it is a criminal offence to bribe or to offer a bribe to a member of Parliament or for a member of Parliament to accept a bribe: see *Report of the Royal Commission on Standards of Conduct in Public Life* (Cmnd 6524) (1976) (the Salmon Commission); 917 HC Official Report (5th series), 20 October 1976, col 1446; Zellick 'Bribery of Members of Parliament and the Criminal Law' [1979] Public Law 31; Zellick 'MPs and the Law of Bribery' [1981] Public Law 287; Williams *Conflict of Interest* (1985) pp 85–

86; *R v Currie, Jurasek, Brooks, Greenway and Plasser Railway Machinery (GB) Ltd* (1992, unreported) per Buckley J: 'That a member of Parliament against whom there is a prima facie case of corruption should be immune from prosecution in the Courts of Law is to my mind an unacceptable proposition at the present time. I do not believe it to be the law. The Committee of Privileges is not well equipped to conduct an enquiry into such a case (see Lord Salmon, 378 HL Official Report (5th series), 8 December 1976, col 632), nor is it an appropriate or experienced body to pass sentence. Unless it is to be assumed that it would be prejudiced in his favour I cannot see that it would be in the member's own interest for the matter to be dealt with by the Committee. The courts and the legislature have over the years built up a formidable body of law and codes of practice to achieve fair treatment of suspects and persons ultimately charged and brought to trial. Again, unless it is to be assumed that his peers would lean in his favour why should a member be deprived of a jury and an experienced judge to consider his guilt or innocence and, if appropriate, sentence? Why should the public be similarly deprived?' (quoted in the Note on 'Payments to Members of Parliament for Parliamentary Services' prepared for the Committee on Standards in Public Life by Sir Clifford Boulton, GCB, August 1994. That committee ('the Nolan Committee') recommended that this question be clarified (*First Report of the Committee on Standards in Public Life* (Cm 2850-I, p 43) (1995)), and the government agreed to consider whether this matter should be referred to the Law Commission: *The Government's Response to the First Report of the Committee on Standards in Public Life* (Cm 2931) (1995) p 2.

6    *Dunlop v Woollahra Municipal Council* [1982] AC 158, [1981] 1 All ER 1202, PC; *Jones v Swansea City Council* [1990] 3 All ER 737, [1990] 1 WLR 1453, HL; *Three Rivers District Council v Bank of England* [1996] 3 All ER 558; and see ADMINISTRATIVE LAW vol 1(1) Reissue para 203. See also De Smith, Woolf and Jowell *Judicial Review of Administrative Action* (5th Edn, 1995) pp 783–785; and Clerk and Lindsell *Torts* (17th Edn, 1995) p 134.

# (3) STATE INSTITUTIONS

**13.  Bodies exercising public or governmental functions.** Nowadays,      though many functions are exercised by or in the name of the Crown, many other bodies also exercise public or governmental functions and are thus subject to public law controls, including judicial review[1]. The authorities exercising public or governmental functions include the following: (1) the Queen[2]; (2) the two Houses of Parliament[3]; (3) the courts[4] and other tribunals[5]; (4) the servants of the Crown[6]; (5) officers of the Houses of Parliament[7]; (6) local authorities or members or servants of local authorities[8]; (7) the police[9]; (8) the armed forces[10]; (9) non-departmental public bodies, including tribunals and advisory bodies and miscellaneous other bodies[11]. In addition some private persons or corporations exercise functions of a public or governmental nature[12].

1    As to judicial review generally see ADMINISTRATIVE LAW.
2    See paras 14, 15, 17 post. The exercise of these powers by the monarch is generally required by convention to be on the advice of an appropriate minister. Commonly the exercise of these powers is entrusted to some servant of the Crown.
3    See paras 17, 201 et seq post; and generally PARLIAMENT.
4    See generally COURTS; COUNTY COURTS.
5    These are of many kinds: see generally de Smith and Brazier *Constitutional and Administrative Law* (7th Edn, 1994) pp 658–661; Wade and Bradley *Constitutional and Administrative Law* (11th Edn, 1993) pp 643–653.
6    Many powers are now conferred directly on servants of the Crown, eg the Secretaries of State, so that it is no longer correct to say that all executive powers of the central government are powers of the Crown (cf Maitland *Constitutional History of England* (1908) pp 415–416); but these officers are all appointed, mediately or immediately, by the monarch, so the point is somewhat academic.
7    See further PARLIAMENT.
8    See eg EDUCATION; HIGHWAYS; LOCAL GOVERNMENT; NATIONAL HEALTH SERVICE; PUBLIC HEALTH; TOWN AND COUNTRY PLANNING.
9    See generally POLICE.
10   See paras 883–890 post; and generally ROYAL FORCES.
11   See para 951 et seq post.
12   Eg the universities, many of which are established by royal charter and are in the main independent of government control, and are not public authorities, yet they receive large parts of their income from

public funds. The Inns of Court, the Law Society, and the General Medical Council perform some public or governmental functions and are subject to judicial review in respect of those, yet they are not public authorities: see further ADMINISTRATIVE LAW vol 1(1) para 6 et seq.

**14. The Head of State.** The monarch is Head of State, and the supreme executive officer in the state; she is the titular head of the Church of England, the Law, the Navy, the Army and the Air Force, and the source of justice and all titles of honour, distinctions and dignities; foreign affairs are conducted, declarations of war and peace made, and the law executed and administered, solely in her name, although the monarch acts in such matters only on the advice of her ministers.

At first the whole of the central government of the realm was the King's government in fact as well as in name and no very clear distinction was drawn between the executive, legislative, judicial and other powers of the Crown[1]. From the time of the Norman Conquest to the middle of the thirteenth century the power of the Crown was limited only by its obligation to rule according to law[2]. Until the rise of Parliament in the latter years of the thirteenth century this was a vague and unsubstantial limitation. The rise of Parliament, and the development of its powers and privileges, substituted a limitation which has become, in the course of centuries, more and more strict, and has introduced a distinction between the monarch's powers when acting in association with Parliament and when not acting in association with Parliament[3].

The power of doing justice in the courts has been irrevocably delegated to the judges and magistrates, so that the monarch may take no part in the proceedings of a court of justice[4]. Since, in addition, the monarch can no longer without the consent of both Houses of Parliament remove any of the judges of the superior courts[5], and all decisions of inferior courts are subject to review by the superior courts, the monarch has lost all power of influencing judicial decisions.

Where the monarch acts with the co-operation of other persons, those persons are responsible for her acts. For since it is a maxim of the common law that the monarch can do no wrong[6], and is therefore incapable of authorising wrong to be done[7], they cannot defend themselves by pleading her orders[8]. However, since the monarch cannot now in general act save in accordance with the advice and on the initiative of her ministers, there could be no question of their pleading her orders for what they do. Accordingly, although the monarch may legally choose such ministers as she wishes, she cannot use them to circumvent the law. But she still has the right to be consulted, the right to encourage, and the right to warn[9]. However, she also has the right to offer, on her own initiative, suggestions and advice to her ministers even when she is obliged in the last resort to accept the formal advice tendered to her[10].

1   YB 24 Edw 3, Mich pl 70 ('Tout fuit in luy et vient de lui al commencement').

2   Bracton, fo 5b 'But the King himself ought not to be subject to man, but subject to God and to the law, for the law makes the King. Let the King, then, attribute to the law what the law attributes to him, namely dominion and power, for there is no king where the will and not the law has dominion'. The first sentence was quoted by Coke CJ to James I in the *Prohibitions del Roy* (1607) 12 Co Rep 63. See also YB 19 Hen 6, Pasch pl 1: 'La ley est le plus haute inheritance, que le roy ad; car par la ley il même et toutes ses sujets sont rulés, et si la ley ne fuit, nul roy, et nul inheritance sera'.

3   Hearn *Government of England* 18: 'The mode by which the English monarchy obtains in practice its limited character is very remarkable. The law places no restriction upon the extent of the royal power, but rigorously defines the manner in which the several branches of that power may be exercised. In every part of public affairs the expression of the royal will is conclusive; but in each case the royal will must be intimated through the appropriate channel'. See also Dicey *Law of the Constitution* (10th Edn, 1959) p 490 note 2. Thus, in theory, even in the making of a statute, 'the King is pars agens, the rest (ie the Lords and Commons) are but consentientes': *R v Hampden, Ship Money Case* (1637) 3 State Tr 826 at 863 per St John in argument.

4   *Prohibitions del Roy* (1607) 12 Co Rep 63 at 64; see para 6 ante.

5   See the Act of Settlement s 3 (repealed in this regard); and see now the Supreme Court Act 1981 s 11(3); the Appellate Jurisdiction Act 1876 s 6 (as amended); see also paras 8 ante; 21, 303 post; and COURTS; PARLIAMENT.

6   *Re M* [1994] 1 AC 377 at 395, sub nom *M v Home Office* [1993] 3 All ER 537 at 540, HL, per Lord Templeman; and see paras 15, 367 post.

7   *Feather v R* (1865) 6 B & s 257 at 295–296.

8   *R v Earl of Danby* (1685) 11 State Tr 600, HL; and see para 388 text and note 10 post; and *Entick v Carrington* (1765) 19 State Tr 1029. However, the Crown Proceedings Act 1947 s 2 (as amended) makes the Crown liable, as well as the servant, for torts committed in the course of employment: see generally CROWN PROCEEDINGS.

9   Bagehot *The English Constitution* (1963 Edn) p 111; Brazier *Constitutional Practice* (2nd Edn, 1994) ch 9.

10   de Smith and Brazier *Constitutional and Administrative Law* (7th Edn, 1994) p 124; Brazier *Constitutional Practice* (2nd Edn, 1994) ch 9; and see generally Bogdanor *The Monarchy and the Constitution* (1995).

**15. The Crown.** The expression 'the Crown' may be used to refer either to the monarch or to the executive[1]. Nowadays it is used primarily to refer to the latter and to the executive powers of the monarch in whose name many of the activities of government are carried on. In effect the limitations on the powers of the monarch are now limitations on the powers of the Crown or executive. In this sense the Crown has legal status as a corporation sole or aggregate[2].

Historically the principal source of legislative, executive and judicial power was the monarch and it is still the case today that the exercise of many of these powers is carried out in the name of, or with the concurrence of, the monarch. The greater part of the machinery of central government is still regarded, historically and substantially, as an emanation from the Crown. The judges of the Supreme Court are regarded as 'Her Majesty's judges'. Acts of Parliament require the royal assent. But as a result of legislation[3] and decisions of the courts[4] many of the former powers of the monarch have been abolished or transferred to the Queen in Parliament, the courts or minister of the Crown.

In general the present position is that the Crown may not exercise primary legislative powers except with the consent of Parliament[5], and the exercise of secondary legislative powers depends on statutory authority or on the extent of residual royal prerogative powers to legislate by Order in Council[6].

The machinery for securing that the Crown governed according to law was defective until the separation between the King and the courts and the independence of the judiciary[7] were achieved and the common law immunity of the Crown from proceedings in court was restricted[8]. At one time it was thought that neither the Crown nor minister of the Crown could be subject to injunctive orders or found to be in contempt of court, but it is now clear that injunctions may be granted against minister of the Crown acting in their official capacity, and that they may be found to be in contempt of court[9].

1   *Re M* [1994] 1 AC 377 at 395, sub nom *M v Home Office* [1993] 3 All ER 537 at 540, HL, per Lord Templeman. See Mitchell *Constitutional Law* (2nd Edn, 1968) 167.

2   See para 6 text and note 4 ante.

3   See especially the Bill of Rights, by which a number of powers thitherto claimed by the monarch without parliamentary authority were declared illegal. Of these the principal ones were: the powers to suspend laws and to dispense with laws; the levying of taxation without the consent of Parliament; the raising or keeping of a standing army within the kingdom in time of peace: see paras 376, 378, 883 post. In addition the Bill of Rights maintained the right of subjects to petition the King (see para 419 post), that election of members of Parliament should be free (see para 207 post), and that the freedom of speech and debates or proceedings in Parliament ought not to be impeached or questioned in any court or place out of Parliament (see para 210 post), thus seeking to put an end to attempts by the King to interfere in these matters. As to the history and citation of the Bill of Rights see para 35 note 3 post.

4   See para 6 note 7 ante for decisions which have removed or limited the powers of the monarch.

5   See *Proclamations' Case* (1611) 12 Co Rep 74; paras 8, 10, 21 post. See also COURTS; ADMINISTRATIVE LAW.

6   See *Proclamations' Case* (1611) 12 Co Rep 74; see also note 3 supra; and para 907 post.

7   See para 18, 21, 303 post. See also COURTS; ADMINISTRATIVE LAW.

8    See the Crown Proceedings Act 1947; paras 382–383 post; and CROWN PROCEEDINGS.
9    *Re M* [1994] 1 AC 377, sub nom *M v Home Office* [1993] 3 All ER 537, HL.

**16. The executive** As indicated previously most of the functions of government are carried out in the name of the Crown by ministers appointed by the Crown[1]. The executive consists of (1) ministers who are members of the Cabinet[2]; (2)ministers who are not of Cabinet rank; and (3) the Civil Service[3]. The phrase 'the government' or 'Her Majesty's government' normally refers to ministerial members of the executive, although strictly civil servants have no constitutional personality or responsibility separate from that of the government[4].

1    See paras 15 ante; 21 post.
2    As to the Cabinet see paras 402–413 post.
3    As to the Civil Service see paras 549–564 post.
4    See the *Duties and Responsibilities of Civil Servants in relation to Ministers: A Note by the Head of the Home Civil Service*, 123 HC Official Report (6th series), 2 December 1987, written answers cols 572–575: '...in general the executive powers of the Crown are exercised by and on the advice of Her Majesty's Ministers, who in turn are answerable to Parliament. The Civil Service as such, has no constitutional personality or responsibility separate from the duly constituted Government of the day'. See also generally the and the Civil Service Code, set out in the Civil Service Management Code (1996) para 4.1 Annex A (see para 554 note 1 post); and *Questions of Procedure for Ministers* (Cabinet Office, May 1992) (as now revised: see para 416 note 1 post).

**17. The legislature.** Subject to the powers of institutions of the European Community and the provision of the Treaties of the Community[1], the body having supreme legislative power in the United Kingdom is the Queen in Parliament[2], known as the Parliament[3] of the United Kingdom of Great Britain and Northern Ireland[4]. It consists of the monarch[5] and the three estates of the realm, namely the lords spiritual and temporal (sitting together in the House of Lords[6]) and the persons elected for the people (sitting in the House of Commons)[7]. The House of Commons consists of members elected by ballot for single-member constituencies, by an electorate based on the principle of universal adult suffrage[8]. The House of Lords and the House of Commons, whether sitting separately or jointly, do not have corporate status or legal personality[9].

In practice the monarch now plays a purely formal part in the making of statutes for, by convention, she has lost the power of refusing her assent to a bill passed by both Houses[10], or, in terms of the Parliament Acts 1911 and 1949, by the House of Commons alone[11]. Where a bill affects royal interests or the royal prerogative, by convention the monarch's consent is required.

1    Case C-213/89 *R v Secretary of State for Transport, ex p Factortame Ltd (No 2)* [1991] 1 AC 603, sub nom *Factortame Ltd v Secretary of State for Transport (No 2)* [1991] 1 All ER 70, ECJ and HL. See also *R v Secretary of State for Employment, ex p Equal Opportunities Commission* [1995] 1 AC 1, sub nom *Equal Opportunities Commission v Secretary of State for Employment* [1994] 1 All ER 910, HL; paras 23–24 post; and EUROPEAN COMMUNITIES.
2    The words of enactment for public general acts illustrate the technical position of the monarch in the legislative process: 'Be it enacted by the Queen's most Excellent Majesty, by and with the advice and consent of the Lords Spiritual and Temporal, and Commons, in this present Parliament assembled, and by the authority of the same'. See further STATUTES.
3    Parliament is not a corporate institution, but an assembly or assemblies of those entitled to attend: see 204 HC Official Report (6th series), 24 February 1992, cols 778–785; 536 HL Official Report (5th series), 6 March 1992, cols 1109–1111. For a further discussion of the use of the term 'Parliament' see para 201 post.
4    See the Royal and Parliamentary Titles Act 1927 s 2; and para 201 post.
5    See para 14 ante.
6    The House of Lords comprises the Lords Spiritual, consisting of the two archbishops and 24 bishops of the Church of England, and the Lords Temporal, consisting of hereditary peers and peeresses and holders of life peerages, some of which are held by Lords of Appeal in Ordinary: see para 204 post; and PARLIAMENT.

7   1 Bl Com (4th edn) 122. The House of Commons refuses to permit the monarch to attend its meetings in person: Erskine May *Parliamentary Practice* (21st Edn, 1989) p 80.

8   See generally PARLIAMENT. See also para 206 post; and ELECTIONS.

9   See note 3 supra. For arrangements relating to the administration of the two Houses which reflect the non-corporate legal status of the Houses see the House of Commons (Administration) Act 1978; the Parliamentary Corporate Bodies Act 1992; and para 201 post. See also Erskine May *Parliamentary Practice* (21st Edn, 1989) pp 192–193; and the Report to the House of Commons Commission by a team led by Sir Robin Ibbs *House of Commons Services* (HC Paper (1990–91) no 38).

10  See PARLIAMENT. For a discussion of the role of the Queen in Parliament today see McGrath 'The Monarchy and Parliament' (1996) Parliamentary Monitor no 6 (6 May 1996) p 30.

11  See the Parliament Act 1911 s 4(1) (amended by the Parliament Act 1949 s 2(2)). See further para 21 note 6 post; and STATUTES vol 44(1) (Reissue) para 1273.

**18. The judiciary.** The judiciary is the third of the three principal branches of government. It is essential to the principle of legality or the rule of law[1] that those having the power to adjudicate in disputes between individuals and state institutions should be independent from the other branches of government. Judges of the Supreme Court in England and Wales, and the superior courts in Scotland[2] and in Northern Ireland[3] enjoy very substantial security of tenure and independence[4] but other judicial officers, including magistrates[5], coroners[6] and tribunal members[7] enjoy less security. Their independence is protected by convention rather than by law[8].

1   See paras 6 ante, 303–304 post.

2   See para 61 post.

3   See para 84 post.

4   See COURTS vol 10 para 867. Note, however, the different position of circuit judges acting in the Crown Court (notwithstanding that it is part of the Supreme Court).

5   See MAGISTRATES vol 29 para 218 et seq.

6   See CORONERS vol 9 paras 1019–1029.

7   See ADMINISTRATIVE LAW vol 1(1) (Reissue) para 14.

8   See further para 21 post.

# (4) CONSTITUTIONAL CONVENTIONS

**19. The importance of constitutional conventions in the British constitution.** In any system of government it is likely that there will be rules and practices that are not to be found in the formal sources of law but which are nevertheless habitually obeyed and generally regarded as binding. These rules, commonly referred to in the United Kingdom as conventions, were first identified[1] as being limited to the regulation of the residual legal powers of the Crown[2], but in practice conventions regulate the conduct of holders of many public offices[3].

1   See Dicey *Law of the Constitution* (10th Edn, 1959) Chs XIV, XV, pp 417–473. There is also a large conventional element in the Constitution of the United States of America: see Dicey *Law of the Constitution* (10th Edn, 1959) pp 28–30; Horwill *Usages of the American Constitution*.

2   Dicey *Law of the Constitution* (10th Edn, 1959) p 426.

3   See Marshall *Constitutional Conventions: the rules and forms of political accountability* (1987); Wade and Bradley *Constitutional and Administrative Law* (11th Edn, 1993) p 24; de Smith and Brazier *Constitutional and Administrative Law* (7th Edn, 1994) pp 27–48; and para 21 post.

**20. The nature of conventions.** In general it may be said that conventions differ from rules of law in that they are not enforceable by judicial process, but are sanctioned by settled practice and political convenience[1]. The existence of some conventions is certain and they can be defined accurately[2]. The nature and even the existence of others are subject to varying degrees of doubt[3]. Although the existence and contents of some, such as the standing orders of the Houses of Parliament, are quite certain, whether they are mere conventions or genuine rules of law is entirely a matter of definition[4]. Conventions may or may not be more flexible than rules of law[5].

To be a genuine convention, a rule or principle must be regarded as binding; but here again there may be doubt, not only whether it is not a mere convenient practice, but also when a rule of practice turns into a binding convention[6].

There can therefore be no authoritative source to which reference can be made to ascertain whether a convention exists or what it is. One can only refer to works on constitutional law[7] or on constitutional or political history[8] or the biographies of public figures[9], more especially where they deal with crises of one kind or another.

1　Dicey (see *Law of the Constitution* (10th Edn) pp 24–27, 417, 422) insisted on this distinction. See also Hood Phillips 'Constitutional Conventions: a Conventional Reply' (VIII Journal of the Society of Public Teachers of Law (NS) 60). It cannot be maintained in its entirety, partly because many undoubted rules of law cannot be judicially enforced. Moreover, certain rules of law depend on the existence of conventions: see de Smith and Brazier *Constitutional and Administrative Law* (7th Edn) pp 39–40. Dicey also insisted that conventions were indirectly sanctioned by law, because a breach of a convention would eventually lead to a breach of law or a breakdown of government. Thus if Parliament were not summoned to meet in a particular year, income tax could not be collected and the army could not be kept in existence without a breach of law. Although there can be no doubt that these considerations were present to the minds of politicians in the early years of the eighteenth century, when the leading conventions regulating ministerial responsibility were developed, they no longer operate psychologically. See also Marshall *Constitutional Conventions: the rules and forms of political accountability* (1987); de Smith and Brazier *Constitutional and Administrative Law* (7th Edn, 1994) pp 27–34; Wade and Bradley *Constitutional and Administrative Law* (11th Edn, 1993) pp 19–28.

2　Eg that the monarch should not refuse assent to a bill passed by both Houses of Parliament.

3　Eg those regulating the part to be played by the monarch in choosing a Prime Minister, when there is no clear majority in the House of Commons: see para 21 post.

4　They have all the characteristics of law, except that they cannot be enforced judicially.

5　Eg the convention that Parliament must meet at least once a year could not be said to be at all flexible.

6　Eg it is not certain whether a binding convention that the Prime Minister must be a member of the House of Commons arose when George V called upon Mr Baldwin rather than Lord Curzon to form a government in 1923. It may surely be taken to have become a convention by the time that Lord Home renounced his peerage in 1963 immediately after becoming Prime Minister.

7　Eg Jennings *Cabinet Government* (3rd Edn, 1959); de Smith and Brazier *Constitutional and Administrative Law* (7th Edn, 1994); Wade and Bradley *Constitutional and Administrative Law* (11th Edn, 1993); Marshall *Constitutional Conventions: the rules and forms of political accountability* (1987).

8　Eg Mackintosh *The British Cabinet* (3rd Edn, 1977).

9　Eg Nicolson *King George V*.

**21. Principal conventions.** The paramount convention is that the monarch must act on the advice tendered to her by her ministers, in particular the Prime Minister[1]. She must appoint as Prime Minister that member of the House of Commons[2] who can acquire the confidence of the House[3], and must appoint such persons, being members of one or other of the Houses of Parliament, to be members of the government and Cabinet as the Prime Minister recommends[4]. She must, in ordinary circumstances, accept any recommendation the Prime Minister may submit that Parliament be dissolved[5]. The monarch must assent to any bill that has passed both Houses of Parliament (or the House of Commons alone under the Parliament Acts 1911 and 1949)[6]. If the government does not have, or loses, the confidence of the House of Commons the Prime Minister must either recommend a dissolution of Parliament or tender the resignation of himself and the government[7].

Since the monarch must always act upon ministerial advice, ministers are always politically responsible to the House of Commons for their acts, even if done in her name[8]. Their responsibility is both personal and collective[9]. Civil servants are not responsible to the House, since they must carry out the policy for which the departmental minister is responsible and must obey any instructions he may give[10]. They must be politically neutral, in the sense that they must co-operate loyally with whatever government is for the time being in power. Accordingly, they are not to be dismissed upon a change of government but are removable only for misconduct or inefficiency[11].

The independence of the superior judges is fortified by the conventional rule that the conduct of a judge cannot be called in question in the House of Commons except on a motion specifically criticising him or supporting an address for his removal[12]; and in general a matter cannot be raised in Parliament if it is sub judice[13]. The separation of the judicial from the legislative functions of the House of Lords is protected by the convention that lay peers may not take part in the hearing of an appeal[14]. For the purpose of maintaining the impartiality of the administration of criminal justice, the Attorney General is required to act upon his own independent judgment in such matters as deciding whether to institute or approve a prosecution or to take or defend or intervene in civil proceedings on behalf of the Crown[15].

Certain conventions govern the conduct of the Houses of Parliament. Thus it is a convention that all money bills must originate in the House of Commons[16]. The Speaker of the House of Commons must control debate impartially and must do his best to see that all parties have fair opportunities to take part[17]. Although the Speaker has normally been elected from among members of the party in power at the time for electing a new Speaker[18], he can expect to retain office even though that party ceases to hold office[19]. The membership of committees is conventionally arranged so as to afford a proper party representation[20]. Moreover, although each House can change its standing orders at will, there is a convention that some of them must not be abolished or substantially altered. Such are the standing orders that require that every amendment or motion to authorise central government expenditure, or to increase or impose a tax, must have the monarch's recommendation[21], and those that lay down an elaborate quasi-judicial procedure for legislation by private bill[22].

Certain conventions regulate the relations between members of the Commonwealth[23].

Some practices of fairly long standing may or may not have become conventions. Such are the rule that the Public Accounts Committee of the House of Commons[24] is not to consider policy questions, and that its chairman is a member of the Opposition[25]; and that members of a government should relinquish company directorships the holding of which might affect their conduct in office[26]. Many understandings operative in local administration have the same ambiguous character.

1   See paras 351, 412 post; and Bogdanor *The Monarchy and the Constitution* (1995).
2   See para 20 note 6 ante.
3   See para 394 post.
4   See para 404 post.
5   No Prime Minister in the United Kingdom has been refused a dissolution for over a century, although in 1924 Asquith expressed the opinion that a Prime Minister leading a minority government was not entitled to a dissolution, and George V regarded himself as exercising an unfettered discretion in granting a dissolution to MacDonald: see Nicholson *King George V* (1952) p 400. It would seem therefore that the monarch is not in all circumstances obliged to grant a Prime Minister's request for a dissolution. The exercise of the royal prerogative in this respect is unlikely to be determined solely by past usages and precedents. The minimum criteria which are likely to be met before the monarch would consider refusing such a request from the Prince Minister are: (1) belief that the existing Parliament was still vital, viable and capable of doing its job; (2) belief that a general election would be detrimental to the national economy; and (3) an alternative Prime Minister could be found who would be capable of commanding a working majority in the House of Commons and thus able to form a government for a reasonable period. A clear distinction must be drawn between the existence of the prerogative to refuse a request for a dissolution and the question whether in any particular set of circumstances the monarch would regard it as in the best interests of the nation to refuse a dissolution. See further the letter attributed to the Private Secretary to George VI quoted by Douglas-Home in 'Who decides when Parliament should be dissolved?', The Times, 6 May 1974; and also the letter from the Leader of the House of Commons to

backbench members of Parliament, The Times, 11 May 1974. The matter is fully discussed in de Smith and Brazier *Constitutional and Administrative Law* (7th Edn, 1994) pp 128–130; Wade and Bradley *Constitutional and Administrative Law* (11th Edn, 1993) pp 255–258; Markesinis *The Theory and Practice of Dissolution of Parliament* (1972); Marshall *Constitutional Conventions: the rules and forms of political accountability* (1987); and Bogdanor *The Monarchy and the Constitution* (1995) pp 157–163.

6 The last exercise of a veto was in 1708. The rule follows automatically from the obligation on the monarch to act on ministerial advice, for the government has ample opportunities to prevent a bill obnoxious to it from passing the House of Commons. If per incuriam one should pass, the proper course would be to procure the passing of an Act repealing it. See Bogdanor *The Monarchy and the Constitution* (1995) pp 129–132.

7 See paras 397, 418 post.

8 See para 416 post.

9 See para 416 post.

10 See paras 365, 560 post. As to the Civil Service see para 549–564 post.

11 In strict law they hold office at the pleasure of the Crown: see para 557 post.

12 Members of Parliament have a greater degree of freedom to criticise judges than ministers. Ministers may and do criticise judgments and sentences and make general statements about the judiciary (Mr Baldwin 'It was obviously undesirable that His Majesty's judges should write for publication on matters of political controversy': 303 HC Official Report (5th series), 24 June 1935, col 799) but they must not criticise a judge and they should show due restraint when commenting in Parliament on judicial words and deeds: see generally Erskine May *Parliamentary Practice* (21st Edn, 1989) pp 377–380. As to the position in relation to members of Parliament see 865 HC Official Report (5th series), 4 December 1973 col 1092: Mr Speaker 'It can be argued that a judge has made a mistake, that he was wrong, and the reasons for those contentions can be given, within certain limits ... Reflections on the judge's character or motives cannot be made except on a motion. Any suggestion that a judge should be dismissed can be made only on a motion.' See also 120 HC Official Report (6th series), 23 July 1987, col 492: Mr Speaker: 'Judges are not to be criticised unless there is a substantive issue motion before the House'. On parliamentary criticism of judges generally see also Erskine May *Parliamentary Practice* (21st Edn, 1989) pp 377–380; and Brazier *Constitutional Practice* (1994) pp 274–279.

13 Subject to the discretion of the chair, reference may be made in the House of Commons to matters awaiting or under adjudication in all civil courts in so far as such matters relate to a ministerial decision which cannot be challenged in court except on the grounds of misdirection or bad faith, or concern matters of national importance such as the national economy, public order or the essentials of life: see 839 HC Official Report (5th series), 28 June 1972, col 1627; and see further Brazier *Constitutional Practice* (1994) pp 274–279; and PARLIAMENT.

14 See COURTS vol 10 para 746. Note, however, that the Lords of Appeal in Ordinary (the Law Lords), while generally abstaining from participation in political controversial debate, are not precluded from taking part in debate: see de Smith and Brazier *Constitutional and Administrative Law* (7th Edn, 1994) pp 20, 322.

15 See para 537 note 1 post.

16 See further PARLIAMENT.

17 See generally PARLIAMENT.

18 But note that the Speaker at the date at which this volume states the law, Madame Speaker Boothroyd, was elected in 1992 from the Opposition (Labour) benches: 207 HC Official Report (6th series), 27 April 1992, cols 2–27.

19 See further PARLIAMENT.

20 See further PARLIAMENT.

21 See para 706 post.

22 See PARLIAMENT.

23 See COMMONWEALTH vol 6 (Reissue) para 811.

24 As to the Committee of Public Accounts of the House of Commons see para 719 post.

25 See para 716 post.

26 This convention has been put into the form of published rules: 496 HC Official Report (5th series), 25 February 1952, cols 701–703; see also *Questions of Procedure for Ministers* (Cabinet Office, May 1992) (as now revised: see para 416 note 1 post) paras 103–127.

## 22. Cabinet control of legislative and executive functions.

As the result of these conventions a marked feature of the modern British system of government is the concentration of the control of both legislative and executive functions in a small body of people, presided over by the Prime Minister[1], who are agreed on fundamentals and decide the most important questions of policy secretly in the Cabinet[2]. Legal controls, whether directed to procedure or organisation, over the relationship between the legislature and the executive are almost non-existent, and the operation of the Cabinet is also carried on outside any system of legal control. Within the framework of a Parliament that is sovereign, save where European law applies, and an unwritten constitution lacking a comprehensive Bill of Rights or public rights of access to official information, the principal constitutional checks on the power of the Cabinet are the existence of a powerful and organised parliamentary opposition, and the possibility that measures proposed or carried by the government may subject them to popular disapproval and enable the Opposition to defeat them at the next general election and supplant them in their control of the executive. At times when opposition parties are weak, whether because of lack of popular support or because their numbers are small in the House of Commons[3], the ability of Parliament to hold the government to account, to promote efficiency and effectiveness in government and to protect the interests of individuals and minorities is limited.

1    The relation of the Prime Minister to the Cabinet is necessarily ill-defined and obscure, and depends to
     a great extent on personal characteristics and the current political environment and atmosphere. See para
     398 post. As to the Prime Minister see paras 394–398 post.
2    As to the Cabinet see paras 402–413 post.
3    See para 206 post; and ELECTIONS.

## (5) THE EUROPEAN DIMENSION TO THE CONSTITUTION

**23. United Kingdom membership of the European Community.** The United Kingdom joined the European Economic Community with effect from 1 January 1973, and the United Kingdom's membership of the Community was given legal effect in the domestic law of England by the European Communities Act 1972[1]. The Community has been renamed the European Community under the Treaty on European Union[2], which came into force on 1 November 1993, having been ratified by all 12 member states[3].

Under Community law certain measures are to be given direct effect[4] or to have direct applicability[5] in member states. The European Court of Justice[6] has developed the doctrine of primacy or supremacy of European Community law, according to which member states have restricted their own legislative powers, and the courts of member states are bound to give effect to directly effective Community law even if it is incompatible with the national law of a state[7], including its constitutional law[8]. English courts have accepted this requirement. The result may be that a United Kingdom Act of Parliament or other law that is incompatible with Community law will not be given effect by English courts, which will give effect instead to the Community law[9].

In legal proceedings the English courts must decide in accordance with principles laid down by the European Court of Justice questions as to the meaning or effect of any of the Treaties[10] or as to the validity, meaning or effect of any Community instrument[11]. Judicial notice must be taken of the Treaties, the Official Journal[12] of the Community and of decisions or expressions of opinion by the European Court of Justice (or any court attached to it) on questions as to the meaning or effect of any of the Treaties or the validity, meaning or effect of Community instruments[13].

The United Kingdom is party to the European Economic Area Agreement[14], which is largely given the force of law in the United Kingdom[15]. In consequence there is statutory provision extending to member states of the European Free Trade Association and nationals of those states, the same rights as to European Community states and nationals, in respect of matters which are covered by the European Economic Area Agreement[16].

1    See the Treaty of Accession (1972) (TS 16 (1979); Cmnd 7461); the Act of Accession (1972); the
     European Communities Act 1972; and EUROPEAN COMMUNITIES vol 51 para 1.16. As to the

referendum held on 5 June 1975 on whether the United Kingdom should remain a member of the European Communities see the Referendum Act 1975 (repealed); and EUROPEAN COMMUNITIES vol 51 para 1.24. As to the incorporation of Community Treaties into United Kingdom law see para 24 post.

2    Ie the Treaty on European Union signed at Maastricht on 7 February 1992 (the 'Maastricht Treaty') (Cm 1934); and taking effect on 1 November 1993 (OJ L293, 27.11.1993, p 61); see EUROPEAN COMMUNITIES. By virtue of Title II art G para (1), the phrase 'European Economic Community' is replaced by the term 'Economic Community', and as a result all future references to the Treaty of Rome should be to the EC Treaty as opposed to the EEC Treaty. As to the establishment of the European Union see the Treaty on European Union Articles A–F.

3    The Treaty on European Union is given effect in the United Kingdom by the European Communities (Amendment) Act 1993.

4    Case 26/62 *NV Algemene Transport-en Expeditie Onderneming van Gend & Loos v Nederlandse administratie der belastingen* [1963] ECR 1, [1963] CMLR 105, ECJ. See also Winter 'Direct applicability and direct effect: two distinct and different concepts in Community law' (1972) 9 CMLRev 425; and EUROPEAN COMMUNITIES.

5    See EC Treaty art 189; and Winter 'Direct applicability and direct effect: two distinct and different concepts in Community law' (1972) 9 CMLRev 425; and EUROPEAN COMMUNITIES.

6    In English statutes, the Court of Justice of the European Communities is known as the 'European Court': see the European Communities Act 1972 s 1, Sch 1 Pt II, applied by the Interpretation Act 1978 s 5, Sch 1. However, in this title, the longer form 'European Court of Justice' is preferred to avoid confusion with the European Court of Human Rights.

7    Case 6/64 *Costa v ENEL* [1964] ECR585, [1964] CMLR 425, ECJ; see also Case 35/76 *Simmenthal SpA v Ministero delle Finanze* [1976] ECR 1871, [1977] 2 CMLR 1, ECJ; Case 70/77 *Simmenthal SpA v Amministrazione delle Finanze dello Stato* [1978] ECR 1453, [1978] 2 CMLR 733, ECJ; Case 106/77 *Amministrazione delle Finanze dello Stato v Simmenthal SpA* [1978] ECR 629, [1978] 3 CMLR 263, ECJ. See also para 24 post.

8    Case 11/70 *Internationale Handelsgesellschaft mbH v Einfuhr und Vorratsstelle für Getreide und Futtermittel* [1970] ECR 1125, [1972] CMLR 255, ECJ.

9    *Factortame Ltd v Secretary of State for Transport* [1990] 2 AC 85, [1989] 2 All ER 692, HL, per Lord Bridge of Harwich (there is a presumption that Acts of Parliament are compatible with Community law unless and until declared to be incompatible); Case C-213/89 *R v Secretary of State for Transport, ex p Factortame Ltd* [1990] ECR I-2433, ECJ; *R v Secretary of State for Transport, ex p Factortame Ltd (No 2)* [1991] 1 AC 603, sub nom *Factortame Ltd v Secretary of State for Transport (No 2)* [1991] 1 All ER 70, ECJ and HL. Additionally the High Court has jurisdiction under RSC Ord 53 to grant a declaration that a statutory provision is incompatible with Community law: see *R v Secretary of State for Employment, ex p Equal Opportunities Commission* [1995] 1 AC 1, sub nom *Equal Opportunities Commission v Secretary of State for Employment* [1994] 1 All ER 910, HL; and EUROPEAN COMMUNITIES.

10   As to Community treaties see para 24 note 2 post.

11   European Communities Act 1972 s 3(1) (amended by the European Communities (Amendment) Act 1986 s 2); and see EUROPEAN COMMUNITIES.

12   The Official Journal is admissible as evidence of any instrument or other act thereby communicated: European Communities Act 1972 s 3(2). Alternatively, evidence of any instrument may be by the production of a certified true copy by an official of a Community instrument, or of a copy purporting to be printed by the Queen's printer, or by production of a copy certified by an officer of a government department: s 3(3) (amended by the European Communities (Amendment) Act 1986 s 2). This also has effect in relation to the EFTA court and the EFTA Surveillance Authority: see the European Economic Area Act 1993 s 4.

13   European Communities Act 1972 s 3(2) (amended by the European Communities (Amendment) Act 1986 s 2); and see EUROPEAN COMMUNITIES.

14   Ie the Agreement on the European Economic Area signed at Oporto on 2 May 1992 (Cm 2073).

15   That Agreement is made one of the Treaties listed in the European Communities Act 1972 s 2 (as amended): European Economic Area Act 1993 s 1.

16   Where legislation is limited in its operation by reference to the Community or some connection with it, those references are now to operates as references to European Free Trade Association (EFTA): s 2. This generally equates the treatment of EFTA nationals to that of EC nationals, but in so far as it fails to do so, and in relation to instruments which are not statutory, s 3 operates to confer equality of treatment.

## 24.   The primacy of European Community law.

The legal powers and functions of United Kingdom state institutions are, since the accession of the United Kingdom to the European Communities in 1973[1], now to be exercised subject to or in accordance with European Community law[2].

The primacy of Community law over inconsistent national law is illustrated by the principles and decisions of the European Court of Justice described below.

(1) Member states are obliged to take all appropriate measures, whether general or particular, to ensure fulfilment of the obligations arising out of the EC Treaty or resulting from action taken by the institutions of the Community. Member states must facilitate the achievement of the Community's tasks. They must abstain from any measure which could jeopardise the attainment of the objectives of the Treaty[3].

(2) Within its sphere, Community law is supreme law. Independently of national legislation, Community law imposes obligations on individuals and confers rights upon them which become part of their legal heritage[4]. Appropriately worded Treaty provisions, regulations, and directives are capable of giving rise to rights in individuals which national courts are bound to safeguard without the need for national implementing legislation (the principle of 'direct effect')[5].

(3) Community law takes precedence over inconsistent national legislation; and member states must not maintain in force measures which are liable to impair the useful effects of the EC Treaty[6].

(4) Community law takes precedence even over inconsistent national constitutional provisions[7]. In applying national law, whether the relevant provisions were made before or after a directive, the national court must interpret the national provision so as to comply with the directive[8].

(5) Even where Community rules lack direct effect, (for example, because they are contained in a directive which binds only public authorities) they may influence the interpretation of national implementing rules[9].

(6) National courts must ensure the full protection which persons derive from the direct effect of Community law, without waiting for national implementing legislation[10]. Time limits do not apply while a state has failed to implement a directive correctly[11]. Individuals wronged by the State's failure properly to implement a directive may obtain compensation from the state for the loss and damage they have suffered[12].

(7) In the absence of any relevant Community rules, it is for the national legal order of each member state to designate the competent courts and to lay down the procedural rules for proceedings designated to ensure the protection of the rights which individuals acquire through the direct effect of Community law, provided that such rules are not less favourable than those governing the same right of action on an internal matter[13].

1   See para 23 text and note 1 ante.
2   All such rights, powers, liabilities, obligations and restrictions from time to time created or arising by or under the Treaties, and all such remedies and procedures from time to time provided for by or under the Treaties, as in accordance with the Treaties are without further enactment to be given legal effect or used in the United Kingdom must be recognised and available in law, and be enforced, allowed and followed accordingly; and the expression 'enforceable Community right' and similar expressions must be read as referring to one to which this provision applies: European Communities Act 1972 s 2(1). Any enactment passed or to be passed is to be construed and to have effect subject to s 2(1)–(3): see EUROPEAN COMMUNITIES vol 51 paras 3.04–3.06. 'When we come to matters with a European element, the Treaty is like an incoming tide. It flows into the estuaries and up the rivers. It cannot be held back. Parliament has decreed that the treaty is henceforward to be part of our law': *H P Bulmer Ltd v J Bollinger SA* [1974] Ch 401 at 418, [1974] 2 All ER 1226 at 1231, CA, per Lord Denning MR. See also Case 9/70 *Grad v Finanzamt Traunstein* [1970] ECR 825, [1971] CMLR 1, ECJ.
    Community Treaties, ie those which are incorporated into United Kingdom law by the European Communities Act 1972 s 1 (as amended), are listed in s 1(2) (as amended), or are regarded as Community Treaties by virtue of declaration by Order in Council under s 1(3) (as amended): see EUROPEAN COMMUNITIES vol 51 para 1.22. Treaties entered into after 22 January 1972 (the date of the accession of the United Kingdom to the European Community) must in addition be approved by resolution of each House of Parliament: s 1(3). The European Economic Area Agreement is a Community Treaty: see para 23 text and notes 14–16 ante.
3   See the EC Treaty art 5; and EUROPEAN COMMUNITIES vol 51 paras 1.39–1.40

4  Case 26/62 *NV Algemene Transport-en Expeditie Ondememing van Gend & Loos v Nederlandse administratie der belastingen* [1963] ECR 1, [1963] CMLR 105, ECJ.

5  Case 148/78 *Pubblico Ministero v Ratti* [1979] ECR 1629, [1980] 1 CMLR 96, ECJ; Case 6/64 *Costa v ENEL* [1964] ECR 585, [1964] CMLR 425, ECJ; *Factortame Ltd v Secretary of State for Transport* [1990] 2 AC 85, [1989] 2 All ER 692, HL; Case C-213/89 *R v Secretary of State for Transport, ex p Factortame Ltd* [1990] ECR I-2433, ECJ; *R v Secretary of State for Transport, ex p Factortame Ltd (No 2)* [1991] 1 AC 603, sub nom *Factortame Ltd v Secretary of State for Transport (No 2)* [1991] 1 All ER 70, ECJ and HL; Case 41/74 *Van Duyn v Home Office* [1974] ECR 1337, [1975] 1 CMLR 1, ECJ (this includes provisions of directives which are absolute, unconditional and precise); Case 152/84 *Marshall v Southampton and South West Area Health Authority (Teaching)* [1986] QB 401, [1986] 2 All ER 584, [1986] ECR 723, ECJ.

6  'Any national court must, in a case within its jurisdiction, apply Community law in its entirety and protect rights which the latter confers on individuals and must accordingly set aside any provision of national law which may conflict with it, whether prior to or subsequent to the Community rule.' Case 106/77 *Amministrazione delle Finanze dello Stato v Simmenthal SpA* [1978] ECR 629, [1978] 3 CMLR 263, ECJ; see also *Marshall v Southampton and South-West Hampshire Area Health Authority (No 2)* [1990] 3 CMLR 426, [1990] IRLR 481, CA.

7  Case 11/70 *Internationale Handelsgesellschaft mbH v Einfuhr und Vorratsstelle für Getreide und Futtermittel* [1970] ECR 1125, [1972] CMLR 255, ECJ; *Factortame Ltd v Secretary of State for Transport* [1990] 2 AC 85, [1989] 2 All ER 692, HL; Case C-213/89 *R v Secretary of State for Transport, ex p Factortame Ltd* [1990] ECR I-2433, ECJ; *R v Secretary of State for Transport, ex p Factortame Ltd (No 2)* [1991] 1 AC 603, sub nom *Factortame Ltd v Secretary of State for Transport (No 2)* [1991] 1 All ER 70, ECJ and HL; Joined Cases C-46/93 and C-48/93 *Brasserie du Pêcheur SA v Germany, R v Secretary of State for Transport, ex p Factortame Ltd* [1996] All ER (EC) 301, ECJ.

8  Case C-106/89 *Marleasing SA v La Comercial Internacional de Alimentacion SA* [1990] ECR I-4135, [1992] 1 CMLR 305, ECJ (effectively overruling *Duke v GEC Reliance Ltd* [1988] AC 618, [1988] 1 All ER 626, HL; and *Finnegan v Clowney Youth Training Programme Ltd* [1990] 2 AC 407, [1990] 2 All ER 546, HL.

9  Case 14/83 *Von Colson and Kamann v Land Nordrhein-Westfalen* [1984] ECR 1891, [1986] 2 CMLR 430, ECJ (directive had no direct effect on the parties to the case; European Court of Justice stated that in dealing with national legislation designed to give effect to a directive 'It is for the national court to interpret and apply the legislation adopted for the implementation of the directive in conformity with the requirements of Community law, in so far as it is given discretion to do so under national law').

10  Case C-184/89 *Nimz v Freie und Hansestadt Hamburg* [1991] ECR 297, [1992] 3 CMLR 699, ECJ.

11  Case C-208/90 *Emmott v Minister for Social Welfare and A-G* [1991] ECR I-4269, [1991] 3 CMLR 894, ECJ.

12  Joined Cases C-6/90 and C-9/90 *Francovich and Bonifaci v Italy* [1991] ECR I-5357, [1992] IRLR 84, ECJ. Remedies must be sufficiently effective to deter employers from discriminating on the basis of sex: *Marshall v Southampton and South West Hampshire Health Authority (No 2)* [1990] 3 CMLR 425, [1990] IRLR 481, CA.

13  Case 45/76 *Comet BV v Produktschap voor Siergewassen* [1976] ECR 2043, [1977] 1 CMLR 533, ECJ.

## (6)  THE INDIVIDUAL AND THE STATE

**25.  Citizenship rights in English law.** In other democratic countries, the status of citizenship (as distinct from nationality[1]) embodies the basic constitutional concept that, by virtue of that status: (1) the individual has legally enforceable rights which are fundamental in the sense that they have a specially protected status in domestic law in relation to the public authorities of the state; (2) the individual has legal duties towards the state and the community; and (3) the state has legally enforceable duties towards the individual. However, in the absence of an enforceable, constitutionally protected Bill of Rights, citizens of the United Kingdom[2] do not have procedurally entrenched fundamental rights in relation to the state[3]. In the absence of a written constitution, nor do any English laws define the principles governing either the duties of the individual to the state, or the duties of the state to the individual.

Nevertheless, a range of statutory provisions and common law rules together give the individual (a) the principal civil[4] and political[5] rights or liberties usually associated with citizenship; and (b) certain social[6] and economic[7] entitlements[8]. Statutory provisions also impose duties on the state to secure the protection of civil, political, social and economic rights[9], normally regardless of the nationality of the individual[10]. English laws also impose duties on the citizen[11].

Under European Community law, nationals of the member states are entitled to certain rights of the kind associated with the status of citizenship. These rights include the four freedoms of movement, namely, of persons, services, capital[12], and goods[13], and the right to equal pay and equal treatment in employment and social security, without discrimination on grounds of sex[14]. The Treaty on European Union has introduced the status of 'Citizenship of the Union'[15] which confers on its holders (i) the right to move and reside freely within the territory of member states[16]; (ii) the right to vote and stand as a candidate at municipal elections in the member state in which they reside[17]; (iii) the right to protection by the diplomatic or consular authorities of any member state if the individual's own state is not so represented[18]; (iv) the right to petition the European Parliament[19]; and (v) the right to apply to the European Community Ombudsman[20].

A number of international human rights codes to which the United Kingdom is a party guarantee fundamental human rights and freedoms, and provide for international supervisory and enforcement mechanisms[21]. Although these codes have not been directly incorporated into English law, and are binding only in international law, their provisions are influential in the way in which legislation is drafted, and in the way in which English law is interpreted and applied in English courts[22]. Ministers are acknowledged to have a duty to comply with international law and treaty obligations and citizens may reasonably expect ministers and civil servants to do so[23].

1    See BRITISH NATIONALITY, IMMIGRATION AND RACE RELATIONS.

2    The British Nationality Act 1981 Pt I (ss 1–14) (as amended) refers to British citizens, but defines these by reference to the United Kingdom; see s 1; and BRITISH NATIONALITY, IMMIGRATION AND RACE RELATIONS vol 4(2) (Reissue) para 14. See also Dummett and Nicol *Subjects, Citizens, Aliens and Others* (1990).

3    The notion of 'natural' and 'unalienable' or 'imprescriptible' rights, enshrined in the American Declaration of Independence and in the French Declaration of the Rights of Man, with antecedents in John Locke's writings (Two Treatises of Government, 1690) was described by Bentham as 'nonsense upon stilts': Hart *Essays on Bentham* (1982) 63 and 79. For Dicey the 'one fundamental dogma of English constitutional law' was 'the absolute legislative sovereignty or despotism of the King in Parliament': Dicey *Law of the Constitution* (10th Edn, 1959) p 145. This means that although 'we have laws which may be called fundamental or constitutional because they deal with important principles (as for example, the descent of the Crown (see paras 34–40 post) or the terms of the Union with Scotland (see paras 51, 53 post)) lying at the basis of our institutions, but with us there is no such thing as a supreme law, or law which tests the validity of other laws': Dicey *Law of the Constitution* (10th Edn, 1959) p 145. Dicey also observed that 'with us the law of the constitution, the rules which in foreign countries naturally form part of a constitutional code, are not the source but the consequence of the rights of individuals as defined and enforced by the courts': Dicey *Law of the Constitution* (10th Edn, 1959) p 203. However, the written constitutions of most other Commonwealth countries guarantee fundamental human rights and freedoms (see generally COMMONWEALTH), as do the international human rights codes to which the United Kingdom is party (see para 103 post), and as does European Community law (see para 104 post). The doctrine of parliamentary sovereignty, together with the absence of an enforceable Bill of Fundamental Human Rights, made it possible for Parliament to enact provisions in the Commonwealth Immigrants Act 1968 which discriminated in effect against British Asians from East Africa on the basis of their colour or ethnic origins, and thereby subjected them to degrading treatment in breach of Article 3 of the Convention for the Protection of Human Rights and Fundamental Freedoms (the European Convention on Human Rights): see *East African Asians Cases* (1973) 3 EHRR 76, EComHR, para 220,; and para 124 post.

4    Civil rights are often regarded as 'first generation' rights of citizenship, having been won largely in the courts in the seventeenth and eighteenth centuries: see *Proclamations' Case* (1611) 12 Co Rep 74; *Prohibitions Del Roy* (1607) 12 Co Rep 63; *Entick v Carrington* (1765) 19 State Tr 1029. See Marshall *Citizenship and Social Class* (1950). Examples of traditional civil rights include the right to personal liberty, including freedom from arbitrary arrest or detention; the right not to be subjected to torture or to inhuman or degrading treatment or punishment; the right not to be held in slavery or servitude, or subjected to forced labour; the right to equality before the law and to the equal protection of the law; the

right to, and of access to, a fair hearing by independent and impartial courts and tribunals established by law; the right not to be held guilty retrospectively for a criminal offence; the right to freedom of expression, thought, conscience and religion; the right to peaceful assembly and to freedom of association with others; the right to freedom of movement; the right to respect for private and family life, home, and correspondence; the right to marry and to found a family; and the right to own property, including the peaceful enjoyment of one's possessions: see paras 105–121 post.

5    Political rights are often regarded as 'second generation' rights of citizenship, having been won in the nineteenth century, notably through the Representation of the People Act 1832 (repealed) and the Representation of the People Act 1867; see para 118 post. Political rights entitle individuals to participate in the political process. See Marshall *Citizenship and Social Class* (1950). Some civil rights, notably the right to freedom of expression and association, are also political rights because they enable individuals, organised interests and parties to participate in the political process. Political rights include the right to take part in the conduct of public affairs, directly or through freely chosen representatives; the right to vote and to be elected at genuine periodic elections, by universal and equal suffrage, held by secret ballot, guaranteeing the free expression of the will of the electors: see paras 117–118 post.

6    Social rights are commonly regarded as 'third generation' rights, having been won for the most part after the Second World War. Their importance to citizenship is that they give individuals security and enable them to 'share to the full in the social heritage and to live the life of a civilised being according to the standards prevailing in society': Marshall *Citizenship and Social Class* (1950) p 11. They make a reality of participation in society and in the political process. Commonly no distinction is made between social rights and economic rights; see note 7 infra.

7    'Economic rights' is an ambiguous phrase. It may be used to refer to freedom to operate in the marketplace, generally associated with freedom of contract. But in the context of citizenship it is generally used to refer to the entitlement of the individual to the receipt of cash benefits from public authorities of the state, eg rights to state pensions, child benefit, income support and other benefits payable in the case of sickness, disability and unemployment: see generally NATIONAL HEALTH AND SOCIAL SECURITY.

8    See Marshall *Citizenship and Social Class* (1950).

9    Eg duties (1) to provide or secure the provision of social and economic entitlements: see NATIONAL HEALTH AND SOCIAL SECURITY; (2) to secure or provide remedies for interferences with rights or unlawful interferences with liberties (see generally para 105 et seq post); (3) to make real, if necessary through the provision of legal aid or legal services, rights of access to the courts for the enforcement of these rights and entitlements or the performance of duties by state organs, and for the resolution of private disputes: see para 119 post.

10   Enjoyment of civil liberties does not generally depend on nationality, save that enemy aliens' liberties may be interfered with in time of war (see para 168 post), and some non-nationals residing in the United Kingdom do not have the right of abode: see BRITISH NATIONALITY, IMMIGRATION AND RACE RELATIONS vol 4(2) (Reissue) paras 11, 64. Of political rights, the rights to vote and stand for election are not limited to British citizens: citizens of the Republic of Ireland and Commonwealth citizens resident in the United Kingdom have the right to vote and stand for election in British parliamentary and local elections; citizens of member states of the European Community resident in the United Kingdom are entitled to vote and stand for election in European Parliamentary elections and in local government elections: EC Treaty art 8B (added by the Treaty on European Union (Cm 1934) art G(9)). As to those treaties see further para 23 ante. As to the right to vote see generally ELECTIONS. Entitlement to social and economic rights does not generally depend on nationality but on residence: see NATIONAL HEALTH AND SOCIAL SECURITY. International human rights instruments generally prohibit discrimination on grounds of nationality in the enjoyment of protected rights. See eg the Universal Declaration of Human Rights 1948; the International Covenant on Civil and Political Rights 1966; and the International Covenant on Economic, Social and Cultural Rights 1966.

11   Eg duties to obey the law, to pay taxes, to do jury service, to do military service in time of war: see CRIMINAL LAW; INCOME TAXATION; COURTS; WAR.

12   See the EC Treaty Title III (amended by the Treaty on European Union art G(10)–(15)).

13   See the EC Treaty Title I (amended by the Treaty on European Union art G(2)–(9)).

14   See EUROPEAN COMMUNITIES vol 52 para 21.12–21.14.

15   See the EC Treaty Pt 2 (arts 8–8E) (art 8 substituted, and arts 8A–8E added, by the Treaty on European Union art G(9)). The status of citizen of the Union is established, and conferred on every national of a member state, by the EC Treaty art 8 (as so substituted). As to the conferring of rights on nationals of EFTA states see para 23 ante.

16   Ibid art 8A (as added: see note 15 supra).

17   Ibid art 8B (as added: see note 15 supra).

18   Ibid art 8C (as added: see note 15 supra).

19   Ibid art 8D (as added: see note 15 supra).

20   Ibid art 8D (as added: see note 15 supra).

21   See para 103 post.
22   See para 104 post.
23   See 567 HL Official Report (5th series), 29 November 1995, written answers, cols *44–45*; 567 HL
      Official Report (5th series), 30 November 1995, written answers, col 57; and *Questions of Procedure for
      Ministers* (Cabinet Office, May 1992) (as now revised: see para 416 note 1 post), para 8.

**26. The relationship between subject and monarch.** English law is still informed by the ancient conception of the relationship between the individual and the state as being one between the subject[1] and the monarch. The relationship of subject and monarch was conceived of as a personal one[2], involving a bargain under which the monarch gave the subject protection and undertook to govern according to the laws of the land[3], and the subject owed the monarch legally enforceable allegiance[4]. It did not involve the subject having any legally enforceable rights against the Crown, and the duties of protection owed by the Crown were not justiciable. With the development of the principle of legality[5] the individual has become progressively emancipated from the control of the monarch or Crown and now has a high degree of autonomy and personal liberty[6].

1   The term 'subject' is commonly used instead of 'citizen' or 'individual' in case law and legal texts. As to the origin of the term in this context see para 29 post.
2   See para 29 post.
3   The Crown's duty towards the subject rested originally upon a semi-feudal bond, whereby the King, as liege lord, was bound to maintain and defend his people in return for service and obedience: see *Calvin's Case* (1608) 7 Co Rep 1a at 5a. There is, however, no legal duty on the Crown to afford by its military forces protection to British ships trading in foreign waters, and, if it does so, it is entitled to demand payment for so doing: *China Navigation Co Ltd v A-G* [1932] 2 KB 197, CA. See also para 28 post.
4   See para 29 post.
5   See para 6 ante.
6   See para 105 et seq post. See also Oliver 'What is happening to relations between the individual and the State' in Jowell and Oliver (eds) *The Changing Constitution* (3rd Edn, 1994) ch 15.

**27. The duties of the individual to the state.** The individual is under certain common law duties to serve the public[1]. In practice he or she will now be called upon only in exceptional circumstances. Thus, although the maintenance of order is the function of professional police forces, every citizen is under a duty to assist in the quelling of disturbances and the maintenance of the Queen's peace[2]; and if a person refuses to accede to the request of a magistrate, a sheriff or a constable to assist in preserving the peace, he commits an offence at common law[3].

Many duties of service to the public are laid on individuals by statute. In general these duties, with the exception of those arising from service in the armed forces or in a civil capacity, are incumbent upon resident aliens no less than upon subjects[4]. Qualified persons may be compelled to serve on juries[5] and to give evidence in a criminal trial[6] or civil proceedings[7]. There are duties relating to the registration of births and deaths[8], the notification of infectious disease[9], and making returns for the purpose of registering electors[10], for the compilation of the decennial census[11], and for purposes of direct[12] and indirect[13] taxation. The parent or guardian of every child is under a duty to cause that child to attend school[14].

Many active duties are imposed on persons who voluntarily engage in certain occupations. Thus employers of labour have to make returns, for example under the legislation relating to public passenger vehicles[15], and under social security legislation[16], and also to collect and pay over sums by way of taxation under the PAYE scheme[17]; and all who serve the public in the armed forces[18] or in a civil capacity[19] bring themselves under active duties.

1   The first writer to draw special attention to the active duties of the subject was Maitland: see Maitland *Constitutional History of England* (1908) pp 501–506. Very few of the duties of the subject to serve the

public if called upon to do so remain. The prerogative right to impress seamen to serve in the Royal Navy has never been abolished, but is no longer exercised. Statutes requiring service in the militia and national service in times of war continued in force for some years after the termination of the Second World War, but are no longer in force. Duties to serve, if called upon, as a sheriff (see SHERIFFS vol 42 paras 1101–1107) or parish constable (see POLICE vol 36 para 201), are now theoretical. However, in so far as they remain, the Crown has power also to grant exemptions from them: see *R v Larwood* (1694) 1 Ld Raym 29; *R v Clarke* (1787) 1 Term Rep 679; *Morris v Burdett* (1813) 2 M & s 212.

2 See de Smith and Brazier *Constitutional and Administrative Law* (7th Edn) p 416; Wade and Bradley *Constitutional and Administrative Law* (11th Edn, 1993) p 549. The duty of the police to maintain the peace is initially based on the duty of the constable as an ordinary individual, but their powers and duties have been greatly extended by statute: see generally POLICE.

3 *R v Brown* (1841) Car & M 314. There is Irish authority to the effect that the police, in their capacity as ordinary subjects, must, if called upon, assist in the execution of civil judgments: see *Miller v Knox* (1838) 4 Bing NC 574, HL.

4 See BRITISH NATIONALITY, IMMIGRATION AND RACE RELATIONS vol 4(2) (Reissue) para 66.

5 See the Juries Act 1974 s 1 (as amended); and JURIES vol 26 para 604.

6 See CRIMINAL LAW vol 11(2) para 1167.

7 See EVIDENCE vol 17 para 234.

8 See the Births and Deaths Registration Act 1953 ss 1 (as amended), 15; and REGISTRATION CONCERNING THE INDIVIDUAL vol 39 paras 1025 et seq, 1045 et seq.

9 See the Public Health (Control of Disease) Act 1984 ss 10–20 (as amended); and PUBLIC HEALTH vol 38 para 74 et seq.

10 See the Representation of the People Regulations 1986, SI 1986/1081, reg 29 (as amended); and ELECTIONS vol 15 (Reissue) para 348.

11 See the Census Act 1920 ss 3, 8 (both as amended); regulations from time to time made thereunder; and REGISTRATION CONCERNING THE INDIVIDUAL vol 39 paras 1093, 1098.

12 See eg the Inheritance Tax Act 1984 s 218; and the Taxes Management Act 1970 s 8(1) (as substituted and amended); and generally INCOME TAXATION vol 23 (Reissue) para 1606; INHERITANCE TAXATION vol 24 (Reissue) para 663.

13 See eg the Value Added Tax Act 1994 s 58, Sch 11 para 2, and regulations made thereunder: see VALUE ADDED TAX.

14 See the Education Act 1944 s 36 (as amended); and EDUCATION vol 15 (Reissue) para 59.

15 See the Public Passenger Vehicles Act 1981 ss 19, 20 (both as amended).

16 See eg the Social Security Administration Act 1992 s 8; and NATIONAL HEALTH AND SOCIAL SECURITY.

17 See the Income and Corporation Taxes Act 1988 s 203 (as amended), and regulations made thereunder; and INCOME TAXATION vol 23 (Reissue) para 778.

18 See eg the Army Act 1955 s 32; and ROYAL FORCES vol 41 para 412.

19 See paras 901 et seq, 560 et seq post; and generally LOCAL GOVERNMENT.

**28. The Crown's duty towards the subject.** The essential duties of the Crown towards the subject[1] are now to be found expressed in the terms of the oaths which every monarch is required to take before or at the coronation. The duties imposed by the coronation oath[2] are:

(1) to govern the peoples of the United Kingdom of Great Britain and Northern Ireland, and the dominions etc belonging or pertaining to them according to their respective laws and customs[3];

(2) to cause law and justice in mercy to be executed in all judgments, to the monarch's power;

(3) to maintain the laws of God, the true profession of the Gospel, and the protestant reformed religion established by law, to the utmost of the Sovereign's power;

(4) to maintain and preserve inviolable the settlement of the Church of England, and its doctrine, worship, discipline and government as by law established in England; and

(5) to preserve unto the bishops and clergy of England, and to the Churches there committed to their charge, all such rights and privileges as by law do or shall appertain to them or any of them[4].

The monarch is also bound by oath to preserve the Presbyterian Church in Scotland[5].

1    See para 26 ante.

2    The coronation oath must be taken at the coronation under the Act of Settlement s 2. As to the statutory
     form of the oath and the alteration in the oath as at present administered see para 39 note 3 post. As to
     the citation of the Act of Settlement see para 35 note 3 post.

3    By the Act of Settlement s 4, it is declared that 'whereas the laws of England are the birthright of the
     people thereof and all the kings and queens who shall ascend the throne of this realm ought to administer
     the government of the same according to the said laws and all their officers and ministers ought to serve
     them respectively according to the same…the same are…ratified and confirmed accordingly'. As to the
     Crown's duty to exercise the prerogative in conformity to law see para 368 post.

4    The duties as set out above are based on the coronation oath in the Form and Order of the Service In
     the Coronation of Queen Elizabeth II, 1953. These duties incorporate the duties set out in the coronation
     oath as enacted in the Coronation Oath Act 1688 s 3.

5    Union with Scotland Act 1706 art XXV (embodying art XXV of the Treaty of Union), ss 2–5; and see
     paras 51–66 post. This oath is taken before the coronation: see para 39 note 4 post. As to the accession
     declaration see para 39 post.

**29. The natural allegiance of the subject.** As, in feudal phraseology, the King was
styled 'liege lord', so his subjects were termed 'liege subjects', and were bound as such to
serve and obey him[1]. Hence the duty of the subject towards the monarch is known legally
as allegiance.

Allegiance is by statute due to the monarch, whether the rightful heir to the Crown or
not, and the subjects are bound to serve in war against every rebellion, power and might
reared against the monarch, and are protected in so doing from attainder of high treason and
from all forfeitures and penalties[2]. The duty of allegiance is applicable to the monarch in
both capacities, that is to say, in the natural as well as in the regal or political capacity[3].

Allegiance has been distinguished as being of three kinds, according to the persons
from whom it is due, namely natural, local and acquired[4]. The practical effect of owing
allegiance is to be liable for the offence of treason[5].

1    *Calvin's Case* (1608) 7 Co Rep 1a at 5a.

2    11 Hen 7, c 1 (Treason) (1495). This statute is not authority for the proposition that a usurping
     government in control must be regarded as a lawful government: *Madzimbamuto v Lardner-Burke* [1969]
     1 AC 645 at 726, [1968] 3 All ER 561 at 575, PC. It was said by Lord Hale (1 Hale PC 134) that if
     the right heir once had possession and then a usurper obtained possession but the right heir continued
     his claim and ultimately regained possession, a compassing of his death during the interval was treason,
     but this may be doubted in view of the provisions of 11 Hen 7, c 1. After the Battle of Bosworth in
     1485 Henry VII, who assumed the Crown after the death of Richard III in the battle, antedated the
     commencement of his reign to the eve of the battle, and passed through his first Parliament a bill of
     attainder for high treason against Richard III and 28 of his supporters. The bill was, however, frowned
     upon on constitutional grounds: see Kendall *Richard the Third* p 377. As to treason see generally
     CRIMINAL LAW.

3    For withholding their allegiance to the King in his natural capacity, and treating him with asperity and
     harshness, the Despencers were banished in the reign of Edward II: see *Despencers' Case* (1320) 1 State
     Tr 23; *Calvin's Case* (1608) 7 Co Rep 1a; 1 Bl Com (14th Edn) 370; *Axtell's Case* (1660) 5 State Tr 1146
     at 1175. For the differences between the natural and politic capacities of the monarch see CROWN LANDS
     AND PRIVILEGES.

4    *Calvin's Case* (1608) 7 Co Rep 1a at 5b; and Co Litt 129a.

5    *Joyce v DPP* [1946] AC 347: see BRITISH NATIONALITY, IMMIGRATION AND RACE RELATIONS vol 4(2)
     (Reissue) para 66; see also CRIMINAL LAW for a full discussion of the offence of treason.

**30. Who owes allegiance.** Allegiance is due from all British subjects and British
nationals[1], wherever they may be[2]. A British subject or national cannot divest himself of
his duty of allegiance in time of war[3], nor can he by so doing commit acts of treason with
impunity[4]; and the very fact of naturalisation in an enemy's country with a view to
escaping liability for treasonable acts may, it seems, constitute an act of treason[5]. Similarly
there is a discretion to withhold registration of a renunciation of citizenship during any

war in which Her Majesty may be engaged in right of Her Majesty's government in the United Kingdom[6].

1    For the meanings of these terms see BRITISH NATIONALITY, IMMIGRATION AND RACE RELATIONS vol 4(2) (Reissue) para 3.

2    *Cundell's Case* (1812) 4 Newgate Calendar 62; *R v Casement* [1917] 1 KB 98 at 137, CCA; and see *Macdonald's Case* (1747) 18 State Tr 857; *Re Stepney Election Petition, Isaacson v Durant* (1886) 17 QBD 54 at 63, DC. The effects of allegiance depend on citizenship in a Commonwealth country (if such citizenship exists), and on the laws of the Commonwealth country: see BRITISH NATIONALITY, IMMIGRATION AND RACE RELATIONS vol 4(2) (Reissue) para 52; and COMMONWEALTH vol 6 (Reissue) para 812.

3    *R v Lynch* [1903] 1 KB 444 at 458 per Lord Alverstone CJ: 'Whatever a declaration of war may or may not do, it at any rate prevents British subjects from making arrangements with the King's enemies when such arrangements would constitute crimes against the law of the country to which they owe allegiance'.

4    *R v Lynch* [1903] 1 KB 444.

5    *R v Lynch* [1903] 1 KB 444 at 459 per Wills J ('Naturalisation under the circumstances was itself an act of treason').

6    British Nationality Act 1981 s 12(4). See BRITISH NATIONALITY, IMMIGRATION AND RACE RELATIONS vol 4(2) (Reissue) paras 28, 57. This provision (and its predecessor provisions) extend the effect of *R v Commanding Officer, 30th Battalion Middlesex Regiment, ex p Freyberger* [1917] 2 KB 129, CA (no declaration of alienage (or more latterly, renunciation of citizenship) in time of war for the purpose of evading military service).

**31. Local allegiance.** Local allegiance is due from all persons[1] resident within the realm, and, so long as they or their families or effects remain within the monarch's protection, they are punishable as traitors for acts of treason, whether their country is at amity with this country or not[2]; but allegiance is not due from an alien enemy coming to invade the realm[3]. If a resident alien goes abroad with a British passport (whether or not obtained by misrepresentation) the Crown assumes the burden of protection and the alien correspondingly extends his duty of allegiance[4].

1    At common law persons were either subjects, denizens ('A denizen is an alien born, but who has obtained *ex donatione regis* letters patent to make him an English subject': 1 Bl Com (14th Edn) 373) or aliens, and aliens owed local allegiance. Under the Ireland Act 1949 s 2(1) citizens of the Republic of Ireland are neither British subjects nor aliens, but it is assumed that they owe local allegiance if resident within the realm. See further COMMONWEALTH vol 6 (Reissue) para 853.

2    *R v De la Motte* (1781) 21 State Tr 687; *Calvin's Case* (1608) 7 Co Rep 1a at 6a; 3 Co Inst 4; 1 Bl Com (14th Edn) 370 note 2; *De Jager v A-G of Natal* [1907] AC 326, PC; *Markwald v A-G* [1920] 1 Ch 348 at 363–364, CA. The duty of allegiance ceases only when the alien withdraws himself and his family and effects, and he remains liable for acts or purposes of hostility, even in the case of aiding his own countrymen. This rule was laid down by all the judges in 1707: see 1 East PC 52–53; 1 Bl Com (14th Edn) 370 note 2; *Joyce v DPP* [1946] AC 347 at 367, 374–375, [1946] 1 All ER 186 at 190, 194, HL. In return, so long as they owe allegiance, the defence of act of state cannot be set up against them in an action brought by them against a servant of the Crown: see *Johnstone v Pedlar* [1921] 2 AC 262, HL.

3    *Calvin's Case* (1608) 7 Co Rep 1a at 4b; 3 Co Inst 4. For a curious attempt to renounce allegiance without acquiring a different nationality and without leaving the country see *Tejendrasingh v Lord Adrian* (1971) Times, 12 January, CA.

4    *Joyce v DPP* [1946] AC 347, [1946] 1 All ER 186, HL.

**32. The oath of allegiance.** Persons entering on certain offices[1] are required by law to take the oath of allegiance, or an affirmation or declaration in lieu of the oath, in the manner provided by statute, and aliens becoming naturalised are also required to take the oath[2].

The taking of the statutory oath does not add to the natural duty of a British subject, who is in all cases bound as though he had taken the oath[3]. Refusal to take the oath in certain cases, however, entails disqualification from holding office, or vacation of the office if the person has already entered upon it[4], whilst in the case of clerical orders and preferments the taking of the oath is a condition precedent to ordination, or to institution or collation or to the granting of a licence in the case of benefices[5]. As regards peers and members of Parliament, sitting or voting in either House without having first taken and subscribed the oath entails a fine in certain cases[6].

1    As to the persons required to take the oath see para 923 et seq post.
2    See BRITISH NATIONALITY, IMMIGRATION AND RACE RELATIONS vol 4(2) (Reissue) para 68.
3    2 Co Inst 121; 1 Bl Com (14th Edn) 369; *Marryat v Wilson* (1799) 1 Bos & P 430, Ex Ch.
4    See the Promissory Oaths Act 1868 s 7 (amended by the Statute Law (Repeals) Act 1981). As to the officers required to take the oath under that Act see para 923 post.
5    Clerical Subscription Act 1865 ss 4, 5 (both as amended): see ECCLESIASTICAL LAW vol 14 para 660.
6    Parliamentary Oaths Act 1866 s 5; and see *A-G v Bradlaugh* (1885) 14 QBD 667, CA; and PARLIAMENT.

**33. Affirmation in lieu of oath.** In all cases and for all purposes where the oath of allegiance is required to be taken, a solemn affirmation may be made in lieu of taking the oath by any person who objects to being sworn[1]. The affirmation is of the same force and effect as the taking of the oath itself[2]. Where an oath of allegiance has been duly administered and taken, the fact that the person to whom it was administered had at the time of taking the oath no religious belief does not affect the validity of the oath[3].

1    Oaths Act 1978 s 5(1). See further para 923 post; and EVIDENCE vol 17 para 265.
2    Ibid s 5(4).
3    Ibid s 4(2).

# (7)  THE DESCENT OF THE CROWN AND PROVISIONS SECURING THE SUCCESSION

## (i)  Descent of the Crown

**34. Descent of the Crown at common law.** At common law the title to the Crown of England was governed by the feudal rules of hereditary descent formerly applicable to land[1], subject to the distinctions that in the case of females the title devolved upon the eldest daughter alone and her issue[2]; and that the ancient doctrines relating to the exclusion of the half-blood from the inheritance had no application[3]. In the absence of statutory limitations, therefore, the Crown would descend lineally to the issue of the reigning monarch[4], males being preferred to females, and subject to the right of primogeniture amongst both males and females of equal degree, whilst children would represent their deceased ancestors *per stirpes in infinitum*[5]. Upon failure of lineal descendants, the Crown would pass under the rule to the nearest collateral relation descended from the blood royal[6].

1    This is the substance of the rule as deduced by Blackstone (see 1 Bl Com (14th Edn) 192–193); but the principal authority for the existence of the rule is to be found in the course of descent in the past, and in the fact that where the rule has been broken, or where any doubt as to the validity of the title has existed, it has usually been found necessary to fortify the title by statute. See 7 Hen 4 c 2 (Succession to the Crown) (1405–6); 1 Mar sess 2 c 1 (Legitimacy of the Queen) (1553); 1 Eliz 1 c 3 (Recognition of the Queen's Title to the Crown) (1558–9); 1 Jac 1 c 1 (Recognition of the King's Title to the Crown) (1603–4) (all repealed); and the Succession to the Crown Act 1707. See further CROWN LANDS AND PRIVILEGES; PARLIAMENT. As to the present title, which depends primarily upon statute, see para 36 post. For the laws of descent of land see EXECUTORS; REAL PROPERTY.
2    Co Litt 135a; 1 Bl Com (14th Edn) 194. In the case of land, the title devolved upon all the daughters equally as coparceners: see REAL PROPERTY. The point is fully discussed by Farran 'The Law of the Accession (1953) 16 Mod LR 140. Queen Elizabeth II succeeded in accordance with Blackstone's rule.
3    See note 6 infra.
4    It is expressly declared that the law of the Crown of England is and always hath been such, that the children of the Kings of England, in whatsoever parts they be born, in England or elsewhere, be able and

ought to bear the inheritance after the death of their ancestors: 25 Edw 3 stat 1 (Status of Children Born Abroad) (1350–1) (amended by the British Nationality and Status of Aliens Act 1914 s 28, Sch 3; and the Statute Law Revision Act 1948).

5    Ie the children take the place which would have been occupied by theose ancestors: 1 Bl Com (14th Edn) 194.

6    There can be no doubt that the ancient doctrines with regard to land, relating to the exclusion of the half-blood from the inheritance, never had any application to the descent of the Crown, and that collaterals were always admitted provided they could trace descent from the first monarch purchaser: 1 Bl Com (14th Edn) 202; Bac Abr, Prerogative, A; *Willion v Berkley* (1561) 1 Plowd 223 at 245; Co Litt 15b. Thus the Crown descended from Edward VI to Mary, and from Mary to Elizabeth I, although this instance is not conclusive, because the descent was regulated by 35 Hen 8 c 1 (Succession to the Crown) (1543) (repealed). It is also said that the maxim *possessio fratris haeredem facit sororem* (possession of an estate by a brother such as would entitle his sister [of the whole blood] to succeed him as heir [to the exclusion of a half-brother]) does not apply to the descent of the Crown, and that, therefore, in the absence of lineal issue, the brother of the half-blood may succeed in preference to the sister of the whole blood: see Co Litt 15b.

## 35. Parliament's power to limit descent of the Crown. The common law right of inheritance is liable to be defeated by parliamentary grant[1].

Moreover, although the right of the two Houses of Parliament to vary and limit the descent of the Crown, in cases of misgovernment amounting to a breach of the original contract between the Crown and people, cannot be said to be admitted as a definite constitutional principle[2], due weight must be attributed to the fact that the tenure of the Crown since 1688 has depended primarily upon the action taken by the Lords and Commons convened in an irregular manner[3].

Therefore the Crown descends now according to the statutory limitations, but retaining its hereditary and descendible qualities as at common law, subject to the statutory provisions[4].

1    See para 36 note 2 post.

2    The title to the Crown was originally elective, and the notion of hereditary right grew gradually. What survives of the elective principle is still to be seen in the terms of the coronation ceremony (see CROWN LANDS AND PRIVILEGES). It has been said that 'we have never cast wholly aside either the hereditary or the elective principle: our Sovereign is still crowned and announced with the same rites as Edward, Harold and William': Freeman *Comparative Politics* 178.

3    On the flight of James II in 1688, all those who had served as members of the Parliaments of Charles II, together with the Court of Aldermen and members of the Common Council of the City of London, assembled on 26 December 1688, at the desire of the Prince of Orange, and requested the Prince to take over the civil and military administration and the disposal of the public revenue, and likewise to summon a Convention Parliament: see the Commons Journals dated 26 December 1688. A Convention Parliament (see para 208 note 1 post) was accordingly summoned by the Prince of Orange by letters directed to the Lords Spiritual and Temporal, being Protestants, and to the coroners, clerks of the peace, and others. This Convention Parliament met on 22 January 1688 (or 1689: as to change of date, see infra): see the Commons Journals dated 26 December 1688 and 22 January 1688 (or 1689). On 28 January the Commons so convened resolved that 'King James II having endeavoured to subvert the constitution of the kingdom by breaking the original contract between the King and people and by the advice of Jesuits and other wicked persons having violated the fundamental laws; and having withdrawn himself out of this kingdom; has abdicated the government; and that the throne is thereby vacant': see the Commons Journals dated 28 January 1688 (or 1689). On 12 February a declaration was drawn up and agreed by the Lords and Commons affirming the rights and liberties of the People, and settling the Crown and regal government of England, France and Ireland upon William and Mary of Orange, during their joint lives and the life of the survivor; the further limitations being: (1) to the heirs of the body of Mary; (2) to the Princess Anne of Denmark and the heirs of her body; (3) to the heirs of the body of William, Prince of Orange. This declaration was offered on the following day to William and Mary, who accepted its terms, and the declaration was then published to the nation in the form of a proclamation: (see the Commons Journals dated 12 February 1688 (or 1689) and 13 February 1688 (or 1689)). The declaration was subsequently enacted with certain additions in the form of the Bill of Rights, and the Acts of the Convention Parliament were subsequently ratified and confirmed by the Crown and Parliament Recognition Act 1689 (see infra), which also acknowledged the King and Queen. The Bill of Rights, being thus confirmed by a Parliament summoned in the constitutional manner, was formally credited

with the force of a legal statute, and appears upon the statute books as such (see infra). For a full discussion of the logical difficulties involved in the irregular procedure employed see Maitland *Constitutional History of England* (1908) pp 283–285.

The dates of the declaration as given above must be read subject to the change from the old style (Julian calendar) to the new style made by the Calendar (New Style) Act 1750 s 1, by which, as from and after the last day of December 1751, the legal commencement of the year was changed from 25 March to 1 January. Modern practice frequently refers to the Bill of Rights as made in 1689, though by its own terms it was made in February 1688 and is often referred to as the Bill of Rights (1688). The Crown and Parliament Recognition Act 1689 refers to the proceedings of 'the Parliament assembled at Westminster the thirteenth day of February one thousand six hundred eighty-eight' and declares 'that all and singular the Acts made and enacted in the said Parliament were and are laws and statutes of this kingdom and as such ought to be reputed taken and obeyed by all the people of this Kingdom.'

The Short Titles Act 1896 conferred the short title 'Bill of Rights' without a date. Similarly, the Act of Settlement (1700 or 1701) was given a short title without a date.

4    These are contained in the Act of Settlement; and His Majesty's Declaration of Abdication Act 1936. Nothing in the Legitimacy Act 1976 (see CHILDREN vol 5(2) (Reissue) paras 723–728) affects the succession to the throne: s 11, Sch 1 para 5.

**36. The present succession.** As from the dates of the Unions of England with Scotland and Ireland, the succession of the imperial crown of the United Kingdom of Great Britain, and of Great Britain and Northern Ireland respectively, is to be as it then stood limited and settled under the Act of Settlement[1]. This succession is vested in the heirs of the body of the Princess Sophia who are protestants[2].

1    Union with Scotland Act 1706 art II; Union with Ireland Act 1800 art 2; Ireland Act 1949 s 1(1). As to the Union with Scotland Act see para 53 post; as to union with Ireland see para 67 post. As to the citation of the Act of Settlement see para 35 note 3 ante.

2    The Princess Sophia having predeceased Anne, the Crown descended, under this provision, to George I, son of Sophia. It then descended lineally to George IV, from George IV to his brother William IV, from whom it descended to Queen Victoria, niece of William IV, then lineally to Edward VIII, who, on 10 December 1936, executed an Instrument of Abdication, and, on 11 December 1936, gave his assent to His Majesty's Declaration of Abdication Act 1936. Thereupon His Majesty ceased to be King and the Crown passed to George VI (see s 1(1)) from whom it descended lineally to Her present Majesty Queen Elizabeth II. The Duke of Windsor (the former Edward VIII) and any issue he might have had were excluded from the succession: s 1(2).

**37. Assent of Parliaments to alterations.** Any alteration by Parliament in the law touching the succession to the throne would, except perhaps in the case of Canada and Australia, be ineffective to alter the succession to the throne in respect of, and in accordance with the law of, any other independent member of the Commonwealth which was within Her Majesty's dominions at the time of such alteration, unless the alteration were effected by legislation expressly reciting the request and consent of the member concerned[1]. Constitutional convention therefore requires that the assent of the Parliament of each member of the Commonwealth within Her Majesty's dominions be obtained in respect of any such alteration in the law[2].

1    See COMMONWEALTH vol 6 (Reissue) paras 813–816.
2    See the Statute of Westminster 1931 preamble; and His Majesty's Declaration of Abdication Act 1936 preamble.

### (ii) Provisions securing the Succession

**38. The succession under the Act of Settlement.** The descent of the Crown in the present protestant line is secured by the Act which regulates the succession[1], in which it is enacted that to the form of government so established the lords spiritual and temporal and commons shall and will, in the name of all the people of the realm, most humbly and faithfully submit themselves, their heirs and posterities, and faithfully promise[2] to stand to, maintain and defend the heirs of the body of the Princess Sophia, being protestants, according to the limitation and succession of the Crown in the Act specified and contained, to the utmost of their powers, with their lives and estates, against all persons whatsoever that shall attempt anything to the contrary[3].

1    Ie the Act of Settlement s 1. As to the citation of the Act of Settlement see para 35 note 3 ante.
2    The words of the Act which follow here are 'after the deceases of His Majesty [ie William III] and Her Royal Highness [ie Princess Anne of Denmark, subsequently Queen Anne] and the failure of the heirs of their respective bodies.'
3    Act of Settlement s 1; as to the effect of that Act and of the subsequent statute, 4 & 5 Anne c 14 (Princess Sophia, naturalization) (1705) (otherwise 4 & 5 Anne c 16) (repealed) on the lineal descendants of Princess Sophia, see *A-G v Prince Ernest Augustus of Hanover* [1957] AC 436, [1957] 1 All ER 49, HL (lineal descendants are British subjects).

**39. Statutory conditions of tenure.** The descent of the Crown in the present line of succession is subject to certain statutory conditions as follows:

(1)    a person who is a Roman Catholic or marries a Roman Catholic[1], is excluded from inheriting, possessing or enjoying the Crown, and in such case the people are absolved of their allegiance, and the Crown is to descend to such person or persons, being protestants, as would have inherited it in case the person so reconciled etc were dead[2];

(2)    every person inheriting the Crown must take the coronation oath in the form provided by statute[3];

(3)    every king or queen must make, subscribe and repeat, sitting on the throne in the House of Lords, either on the first day of the meeting of the first Parliament after the accession, or at the coronation, whichever shall first happen, a declaration that he or she is a faithful protestant, and will, according to the true intent of the enactments which secure the protestant succession to the throne, uphold and maintain those enactments to the best of his or her powers according to law[4];

(4)    any person coming into possession of the Crown must join in communion with the Church of England[5]; and

(5)    it is also provided as a fundamental term of the union of England with Scotland that every person who succeeds to the Crown must take and subscribe the oaths for the preservation of the Established Church in England and the Presbyterian Church in Scotland[6].

1    The terms of the Act of Settlement are 'any person who shall be reconciled to, or hold communion with, the see or Church of Rome, or profess the popish religion, or marry a papist': s 2. As to the citation of the Act of Settlement see para 35 note 3 ante.
2    This is the joint effect of the Act of Settlement s 2, and the Bill of Rights s 1. As to the history and citation of the Bill of Rights see para 35 note 3 ante.
3    Act of Settlement s 2. The form of the oath is provided by the Coronation Oath Act 1688 s 3, and must be administered by the Archbishop of Canterbury or York, or any other bishop of the realm appointed by the monarch for that purpose, in the presence of all persons attending, assisting or otherwise present at the coronation: s 4. The form of the oath as at present administered differs from that provided by the Act owing to the disestablishment of the Irish Church (by the Irish Church Act 1869), and to the provisions of the Union with Scotland Act 1706 art XXV. As to the oath for the preservation of the Established Church of England see the text and note 6 infra. For the form of oath as administered to Her present Majesty see para 28 ante.
4    Bill of Rights s 1; Act of Settlement s 2; Accession Declaration Act 1910. The declaration was made by King George V at the opening of Parliament, and therefore the necessity for making it at the coronation did not arise: 7 HL Official Report (5th series) col 4. The same was true in the case of Queen Elizabeth II. King George VI made the declaration during the coronation service: see Supplement to the London Gazette, 10 November 1937, p 7054. For the purposes of any enactment requiring an oath or declaration to be taken, made or subscribed by the monarch on or after the accession, the date on which the monarch attains the age of 18 years is deemed to be the date of the accession: Regency Act 1937 s 1(2). However, it should be

noted that the monarch has no minority, and his exercise of the prerogative is valid even if he has not attained 18 (see Co Litt 43a, b; 2 Co Inst, proem, 3; 1 Bl Com (14th Edn) 248), although the Regency Acts (see para 40 post) mean that the prerogative is exercised in the monarch's name while the monarch is under 18. By 28 Hen 8 c 27 (Succession to the Crown) (1536), power was given to future monarchs to revoke all enactments made by Parliament whilst they should be under the age of 24. This enactment was repealed temporarily by 1 Edw 6 c 11 (Repeal of 28 Hen 8 c 17) (1547), and both these statutes were determined and annulled by 24 Geo 2 c 24 (Minority of Successor to Crown) (1750), s 23 (repealed).

5    Act of Settlement s 3.

6    See paras 51, 53 post. The oath for the preservation of the Established Church of England is now administered as part of the coronation oath: see text and note 4 supra. The oath for the preservation of the Presbyterian Church was taken by Queen Elizabeth II at a meeting of the Privy Council held immediately after her accession, the instrument being subscribed in duplicate, and one part sent to the Court of Session to be recorded in the Books of Sederunt, and afterwards to be lodged in the Public Register of Scotland, the other part remaining among the records of the Council to be entered in the Council Book: see the London Gazette Extraordinary, 8 February 1952, p 839; London Gazette, 12 February 1952, p 861.

**40. Accession and regency.** On the death of the reigning monarch[1] the Crown vests immediately in the person who is entitled to succeed, it being a maxim of the common law that the King never dies[2]. The new monarch is therefore entitled to exercise full prerogative rights without further ceremony[3].

The fact of the accession of the new monarch is published to the nation by a proclamation which is issued as soon as conveniently may be after the death of the former monarch by the lords spiritual and temporal, members of the late monarch's Privy Council and the principal gentlemen of quality, with the Lord Mayor, aldermen and citizens of London[4].

Where at the accession the monarch is under 18 years of age, provision is made for the exercise of the royal functions[5] by a regent in the name and on behalf of the monarch[6], and for the guardianship of the monarch until that age is reached[7].

1    The death of the monarch is termed legally 'demise', meaning the transfer of the kingdom (ie demissio) to the successor: *Hill v Grange* (1555) 1 Plowd 164 at 177; *Willion v Berkley* (1561) 1 Plowd 223 at 243; *Wroth's Case* (1572) 2 Plowd 452 at 457. As to the effect of the demise of the Crown generally see CROWN LANDS AND PRIVILEGES.

2    1 Bl Com (14th Edn) 249; *Calvin's Case* (1608) 7 Co Rep 1a at 10b; and 3 Co Inst 7; 4 Co Inst 156, 201, 352; Bac Abr, Prerogative, A. The acceptance of this doctrine appears to have been gradual, the importance of the ceremonies of the oath of recognition and coronation being originally far greater than it is now. As to the early doctrine of election see para 35 note 2 ante. Edward I commenced to reign in 1272, although his coronation did not take place until 1274. Edward II dated his reign from the day after his father's death. See 2 Stubbs' Constitutional History of England, its Origin and Development 102. See further CROWN LANDS AND PRIVILEGES.

3    See Bl Com (14th Edn) 249. According to Coke, the Crown descends to the rightful heir before coronation, for by the law of England there is no interregnum, and coronation is but an ornament or solemnity of honour; and so it was resolved by all the judges: *Calvin's Case* (1608) 7 Co Rep 1a. Coronation is a solemn recognition on the part of the nation that the regal authority is vested in the person of the monarch, and on the part of the monarch a solemn recognition of the fundamental rights of the people (see Bac Abr, Prerogative, A, 390, note (a)); and it may be said to be a necessary ceremony, since otherwise the obligation of the monarch to take the oath in the form prescribed by statute (see the Act of Settlement) would be imperfect. Whether entitled by hereditary descent or not, the person crowned becomes the de facto King, and as such is entitled to allegiance and protected by the law of treason: see para 29 ante. As to the citation of the Act of Settlement see para 35 note 3 ante.

4    This is the established practice, for which there appears to be no direct legal authority other than usage. For the form of proclamation used on the accession of Her Majesty Queen Elizabeth II see the London Gazette, 8 February 1952, p 787.

5    These include all powers and authorities belonging to the Crown, whether prerogative or statutory, together with the receiving of any homage to be done to Her Majesty: Regency Act 1937 s 8(2).

6    Ibid s 1. This Act is unaffected by the Family Law Reform Act 1969: see s 2(4), Sch 2 para 1. The regent is the person next in line, if he is of full age: see s 3. There is also provision for regency in the case of incapacity of the monarch: see s 2 (as amended). As to regency generally see CROWN LANDS AND PRIVILEGES.

7 See ibid s 5; and see further CROWN LANDS AND PRIVILEGES.

The regent will normally be the person next in the line of succession to the Crown, unless he is not qualified to succeed to the Crown or is not a British subject of full age domiciled in some part of the United Kingdom, or is incapable of inheriting, possessing and enjoying the Crown under terms of the Act of Settlement: see the Regency Act 1937 s 3(1), (2). If any person who would at the commencement of a regency have become regent, but for the fact that he was not of full age becomes of full age during the regency, he becomes regent instead: s 3(3). If the regent dies or becomes disqualified, the person becomes regent who would have become regent if the events necessitating the regency had occurred immediately after the death or disqualification: Regency Act 1937 s 3(4). The heir apparent or the heir presumptive to the throne is deemed to be of full age if he has attained 18: Regency Act 1953 s 2. If the regent is declared to be incapable of Carrying out the royal functions, his functions are performed by the person who would have become regent if the regent had died: Regency Act 1937 s 3(5).

If a regency becomes necessary during the reign of Queen Elizabeth II, the Duke of Edinburgh, if living, is to be regent, unless or until there is a child or grandchild of the Queen and the Duke who can be regent: Regency Act 1953 s 1(2).

As to the oaths to be taken by the regent, and the limitations on the regent's powers, see the Regency Act 1937 s 4.

## (8) WALES

**41. England and Wales.** Any reference in any Act passed before 1 April 1974 to 'England' includes, inter alia, Monmouthshire[1], and, in any Act passed before 27 July 1967, includes a reference to 'Wales'[2]. 'Wales' means the combined area of the counties which were created by the Local Government Act 1972[3] but subject to any alterations made following the alteration of a watercourse[4].

1 A new county of Monmouthshire was created and made one of the counties of England by the Laws in Wales Act 1535 (repealed). Monmouthshire was redesignated part of Wales by the Local Government Act 1972 s 20(1), (2), Sch 4 (all as originally enacted), as part of the counties of Gwent, Mid Glamorgan and South Glamorgan. As to the administration of local government in Wales as from 1 April 1996 see s 20, Sch 4 (both substituted by the Local Government (Wales) Act 1994 s 1, Sch 1); para 49 post; and LOCAL GOVERNMENT. For certain purposes (including the definition of 'Wales') references to the counties created by the 1972 Act as originally enacted (the 'preserved counties') are retained: see s 270(1) (definition of 'preserved county' added in s 270(1), by the Local Government (Wales) Act 1994 s 1(7)). In the Local Government Act 1972, 'Wales' now means the combined area of the preserved counties, and 'England' does not include any area which is included in any of the preserved counties: s 269 (substituted by the Local Government (Wales) Act 1994 s 1(3), Sch 2 para 8).

2 Interpretation Act 1978 ss 22, 23, Sch 2 para 5(a); Welsh Language Act 1967 s 4. The Welsh Language Act 1967 received the Royal Assent on 27 July 1967.

3 Ie by the Local Government Act 1972 s 20, Sch 4 as originally enacted: see note 1 supra.

4 Interpretation Act 1978 Sch 1 (definition substituted by the Local Government (Wales) Act 1994 Sch 2 para 9).

**42. The law in Wales.** The Laws in Wales Act 1535[1] provided that England and Wales were united and Welshmen and Englishmen were to be subject to the same laws and have the same privileges[2]. Since that time, there has been one legal system for England and Wales.

In 1973 a minority opinion of the Royal Commission on the Constitution[3] recommended the creation of a Welsh Assembly with limited legislative powers[4]. A scheme was contained in the Wales Act 1978[5], providing for an elected assembly for Wales[6]. However, in a referendum on 1 March 1979, the proposed assembly was rejected by the Welsh electorate, and after the general election in 1979, the Wales Act 1978 was repealed by Order in Council[7].

Wales is represented in the United Kingdom Parliament by at least 35 members[8].

1    This short title was conferred by the Statute Law Revision Act 1948.

2    See the Laws in Wales Act 1535 s 1 (repealed); and the Laws in Wales Act 1542 (repealed, except for s 47 (sale in market in Wales not to transfer property in stolen goods), by the Welsh Language Act 1993 s 35, Sch 2). See 7 Co Rep 191–236; Holdsworth vol IV, pp 80–81. Before the Laws in Wales Act 1535 the law in Wales was of Welsh custom and English law, known as the Custom of the Marches, administered under the jurisdiction of the Lords Marchers: Holdsworth vol 1, 121 et seq. From soon after the Conquest, Norman kings permitted their nobles to conquer and hold such parts of Wales as they could. Each noble was given *jura regalia* (sovereign rights), within the area held by him, until the conquest of Wales in 1282. Each noble was known as a lord marcher. The territory held by them included the Welsh administrative counties of Brecknock, Denbigh, Glamorgan, Montgomery, Pembroke and Radnor, the English county of Monmouth and parts of Shropshire, Herefordshire and Gloucestershire. The statute 28 Edw 3, c 11 (1354) declared their territories perpetually annexed to the English Crown. Their quasi-sovereign position was abolished by the Laws in Wales Act 1535.

    The Marches were the boundary between England and Wales (and between England and Scotland). Under the Laws in Wales Acts 1535 and 1542 five new counties were formed: Monmouth as an English county, and Brecknock (or Brecon), Radnor, Montgomery and Denbigh as Welsh counties. The position of the counties of Pembroke and Glamorgan was regularised. Courts were to be kept in English: Laws in Wales Acts 1535 s 20 (repealed). Wales was to be represented in Parliament (s 29) (repealed). Commissioners were appointed to divide Wales into shires.

    The Laws in Wales Act 1542 was passed to provide for local government and judicial organisation in Wales. Wales was divided into 12 counties. Monmouth was an English county: Holdsworth vol 1, 123–124. Four Courts of Great Session were established, to be held twice a year, with power to exercise within their territory the jurisdiction exercised by the courts of Kings Bench. English law, but not the authority of English courts, was to prevail in Wales and so the jurisdiction of the Lords Marchers was practically abolished. By the mid seventeenth century these courts had taken on an equitable jurisdiction too: *Pulfath v Griffith* (1669) 2 Keble 259; Holdsworth vol 1, 125. From the late seventeenth century disputes arose about the jurisdiction of the courts at Westminster over Wales. English courts had jurisdiction by statute over certain cases, and the main controversy was over the claim of the Court of Kings Bench to execute its process in Wales. It was settled in 1779 that the Court of Kings Bench could issue process to compel appearance into Wales: *Penry v Jones* (1779) 1 Dougl 213, Holdsworth vol 1, 130–131. In 1798 Wales was divided into four circuits and there were eight judges. The Law Terms Act 1830 abolished the Palatine Courts of Chester and the Courts of Great Sessions in Wales, added a judge to the three courts of common law and extended the English circuit system to Chester and Wales; the equitable jurisdiction of the Welsh courts was transferred to the Court of Chancery and the courts of Exchequer: Holdsworth vol 1, 131–132.

3    See the *Report of the Royal Commission on the Constitution 1969–73* (Cmnd 5460 and 5460-I) (1973) (the 'Kilbrandon Report'), ch 24.

4    *Report of the Royal Commission on the Constitution 1969–73* (Cmnd 5460 and 5460-I) (1973) ch 24.

5    In the 1976–77 session of Parliament, the government's Scotland and Wales Bill (proposing legislative devolution for Scotland and executive devolution for Wales) had failed to make progress. In the 1977–78 session, separate bills dealing with Scotland and Wales were introduced and both were enacted (see the Scotland Act 1978 (repealed) and the Wales Act 1978 (repealed)), although neither scheme of devolution came into force apart from the holding of separate devolution referendums in March 1979.

6    For consideration of the arguments for and against devolution of executive or legislative power to Wales see: Welsh Grand Committee *The Structure of Government in Wales* (1993); Thomas 'The Welsh Assembly debate: 1979 revisited?' (1995) 15 Public Money and Management (no 2) 6–8; Osmond (ed) *A Parliament for Wales* (1994); Balsom 'The Scottish and Welsh devolution referenda of 1979: constitutional change and popular choice' (1979) Parliamentary Affairs 394–409; Osmond *The Democratic Challenge* (1992); Bogdanor *Devolution* (1979); Constitution Unit *An Assembly for Wales* (1996).

7    Wales Act 1978 (Repeal) Order 1979, SI 1979/933.

8    Parliamentary Constituencies Act 1986 s 3, Sch 2 para 1.

**43. The Church in Wales.** The Church of England, in so far as it existed in Wales (including Monmouthshire) was, as from 31 March 1920, disestablished[1].

1    Welsh Church (Temporalities) Act 1919 s 2. The disestablishment was provided for in the Welsh Church Act 1914 s 1 (amended by the Statute Law Revision Act 1927). The operation of the Welsh Church Act 1914 had been suspended during the Great War by the Suspensory Act 1914 (repealed). Every ecclesiastical corporation in Wales was dissolved and ecclesiastical law and the ecclesiastical courts ceased to operate in Wales: Welsh Church Act 1914 ss 2, 3). The Church in Wales lost its emoluments, but provision was made for the transfer to a representative body of churches, parsonages, certain of the endowments and a sum of £1 million in respect of the commutation of existing interests of individuals. See generally ECCLESIASTICAL LAW vol 14 para 322 et seq.

**44. The Welsh language.** The Welsh Language Act 1993 creates the Welsh Language Board (Bwrdd yr Iaith Gymraeg) whose function is to promote and facilitate the use of the Welsh language[1]. Every public body[2] which provides services to the public in Wales or exercises statutory functions in relation to the provision by other public bodies of such services must prepare and implement schemes as to the use of the Welsh language in connection with provision of these services[3]. The purpose of the schemes is to give effect, so far as is both appropriate in the circumstances and reasonably practicable, to the principle that in the conduct of public business and the administration of justice in Wales, the English and Welsh languages should be treated on a basis of equality[4]. The Welsh Language Board exercises supervision over the preparation, revision and operation of such schemes[5].

The Welsh language may be spoken in any legal proceedings in Wales by any person who desires to use it[6]. Ministers may prescribe the use of Welsh versions of any statutorily prescribed document or form of words[7].

1 Welsh Language Act 1993 ss 1, 3(1). As to the constitution of the Welsh Language Board see s 2, Sch 1; and as to its functions see ss 3, 4.
2 As to the meaning of 'public body' see ibid s 6 (amended by the Local Government (Wales) Act 1994 s 66(6), Sch 16 para 106(1); the Environment Act 1995 s 78, Sch 10 para 37; and the Health Authorities Act 1995 ss 2(1), 5(1), Sch 1 Pt III para 125, Sch 3). It does not generally include a person acting as the servant or agent of the Crown: see the Welsh Language Act 1993 s 21.
3 See ibid ss 5(1), (3), 6 (as amended), 21.
4 See ibid s 5(2).
5 Ibid ss 7–19.
6 Ibid s 22. As to the translation of oaths and affirmations see s 23; and as to the provision of interpreters see s 24.
7 See ibid ss 25–27.

**45. The Secretary of State for Wales.** The Secretary of State for Wales is a member of the Cabinet and presides over the Welsh Office[1]. He is assisted by two Parliamentary Under-Secretaries of State, by a Permanent Secretary and two Deputy Secretaries. The Secretary of State has substantial administrative and subordinate legislative autonomy with full responsibility in Wales for ministerial functions relating to major areas of administration[2]. He is also accountable for the activities of many non-departmental public bodies in Wales[3].

The Secretary of State for Wales is a corporation sole for all purposes relating to the acquisition, holding, management or disposal of property[4]. His corporate seal is to be authenticated by the signature of a Secretary of State or of an Under-Secretary of State in the Welsh Office or of any person authorised by a Secretary of State to act in that behalf[5]. The seal is to be officially and judicially noticed[6]. A document purporting to be an instrument made or issued by the Secretary of State for Wales and to be sealed with his duly authenticated seal or to be signed by an Under-Secretary of State in the Welsh Office or any duly authorised person is to be received in evidence and to be deemed to be so made or issued without further proof unless the contrary is shown[7].

1 The office of Minister for Welsh Affairs was created in 1951 and was held by the Secretary of State for the Home Department until January 1957, and then by the Minister of Housing and Local Government. A Minister of State for Welsh Affairs was appointed in December 1957. A Secretary of State for Wales was for the first time appointed in the administration formed in October 1964. See *Commission on the Constitution, Written Evidence I, The Welsh Office* (1969) para 14. The functions of the Secretary of State for Wales were initially defined in a reply to a parliamentary question given by the Prime Minister: see 702 HC Official Report (5th series), 19 November 1964, cols 623–632. As to the Welsh Office see para 46 post.
2 The Secretary of State for Wales exercises functions transferred to him by the following orders in Council: the Secretary of State for Wales and Minister of Land and Natural Resources Order 1965, SI 1965/319 (as amended); the Transfer of Functions (Cultural Institutions) Order 1965, SI 1965/603; the Transfer of

Functions (Building Control and Historic Buildings) Order 1966, SI 1966/692; the Ministry of Land and Natural Resources (Dissolution) Order 1967, SI 1967/156; the Transfer of Functions (Wales) Order 1969, SI 1969/388; the Transfer of Functions (Wales) Order 1970, SI 1970/1536; the Transfer of Functions (Wales) (No 1) Order 1978, SI 1978/272; the Transfer of Functions (Wales) (No 2) Order 1978, SI 1978/274; the Transfer of Functions (Radioactive Substances) (Wales) Order 1990, SI 1990/2598. See also the Transfer of Functions (Education and Employment) Order 1995, SI 1995/2986, art 5; and para 47 note 10 post. As to the nature of those functions see para 47 post.

3   See para 48 note 2 post. As to non-departmental public bodies see para 951 et seq post.
4   Secretary of State for Wales and Minister of Land and Natural Resources Order 1965, SI 1965/319, art 8(1) (amended by the Ministers of the Crown Act 1974 s 4(3), Sch 3). As to acts done for him by another Secretary of State see the Ministers of the Crown Act 1975 s 3(2); and para 363 ante. As to corporations sole see CORPORATIONS.
5   Secretary of State for Wales and Minister of Land and Natural Resources Order 1965 art 8(2).
6   Ibid art 8(2)(a).
7   Ibid art 8(2)(b).

**46. The Welsh Office.** The Welsh Office was established in 1965, following the creation of the Office of Secretary of State for Wales[1]. The Welsh Office is an authorised government department for the purpose of suing and being sued[2], and is subject to investigation by the Parliamentary Commissioner for Administration[3]. Its expenses are provided by Parliament[4]. It has offices in both London and Cardiff[5].

1   See the Secretary of State for Wales and Minister of Land and Natural Resources Order 1965, SI 1965/319 (as amended).
2   See the list published under the Crown Proceedings Act 1947 s 17(1); and CROWN PROCEEDINGS.
3   Parliamentary Commissioner Act 1967 s 4(1), Sch 2 (substituted by the Parliamentary and Health Services Commissioners Act 1987 s 1(1), and s 1(2), Sch 1 respectively). See further PARLIAMENT.
4   See *Supply Estimates 1995–96 for the year ending 31 March 1996* (HC Paper (1994–95) no 271–XV).
5   See the Civil Service Year Book 1996 col 907.

**47. Functions.** The Welsh Office is concerned with policy development. Its executive functions[1] include overseeing and sometimes directing the execution of government policies by local authorities, the health service, non-departmental public bodies[2] and training and enterprise councils[3].

The Welsh Office has responsibility in Wales for local government[4]; for agriculture, fisheries and food, together with planning, forestry, arterial drainage, flood defence and coastal protection[5]; industry and business, including the Welsh Development Agency[6] and the Development Board for Rural Wales[7]; employment and training[8]; the Welsh language[9] and culture, schools, further and higher education[10], arts, museums and libraries[11]; local public transport as well as motorways and trunk roads and transport policy[12]; housing[13], public health, social services, environmental services[14], including responsibility for two executive agencies, namely Welsh Historic Monuments[15] and the Planning Inspectorate[16]; health including responsibility for health policy and management of the National Health Service in Wales, hospitals and community health services[17].

1   The general principles underlying the transfer of functions orders and also underlying certain legislation which has been passed since the date of the relevant order and under which the Secretary of State for Wales has functions (eg the Town and Country Planning Act 1990) may be described as set out infra.
    (1)  Though certain provisions may apply only to Wales, legislation itself usually applies alike to England and Wales. As a member of the Cabinet, the Secretary of State participates in the formulation of new policies and the preparation of new legislation applying alike to England and Wales.
    (2)  In general, responsibility for making major regulations and other instruments affecting England and Wales alike rests with the appropriate minister in England who makes them together with the Secretary of State for Wales. Indeed, much legislation permits the Secretary of State for Wales to make his own subordinate legislation for Wales.
    (3)  Application of the legislation in Wales is the responsibility of the Secretary of State.

(4)   There are special arrangements for joint or several responsibility in relation to areas (eg of some water authorities) which lie partly in Wales and partly in England, and responsibility in relation to certain other matters affecting England and Wales together is also shared by the Secretary of State for Wales and the appropriate minister; eg there are two joint England and Wales executive agencies (established in 1992) namely: (a) the Agricultural Development Advisory Service (ADAS) (see para 437 post), operated jointly with the Minister of Agriculture, Fisheries and Food; and (b) the Planning Inspectorate, operated jointly with the Secretary of State for the Environment (see para 452 post).

2   See para 48 note 2 post. As to non-departmental public bodies see para 951 et seq post.

3   See the Welsh Office Annual Report: *The Government's Expenditure Plans 1995–96 to 1997–98* (Cm 2815) (1995) para 1.13.

4   See generally the Local Government Act 1972 and the Local Government (Wales) Act 1994; para 49 post; and LOCAL GOVERNMENT.

5   Welsh Office Annual Report: *The Government's Expenditure Plans 1995–96 to 1997–98* (Cm 2815) (1995), ch 2. See generally AGRICULTURE; FISHERIES; FOOD; FORESTRY; WATER.

6   Welsh Office Annual Report: *The Government's Expenditure Plans 1995–96 to 1997–98* (Cm 2815) (1995) para 3.17. See TOWN AND COUNTRY PLANNING vol 46 (Reissue) paras 1185–1257.

7   Welsh Office Annual Report: *The Government's Expenditure Plans 1995–96 to 1997–98* (Cm 2815) (1995) para 3.27. See TRADE, INDUSTRY AND INDUSTRIAL RELATIONS vol 47 (Reissue) para 856 et seq.

8   Welsh Office Annual Report: *The Government's Expenditure Plans 1995–96 to 1997–98* (Cm 2815) (1995) ch 4. See generally EMPLOYMENT; TRADE, INDUSTRY AND INDUSTRIAL RELATIONS.

9   As to the Welsh language see para 44 ante.

10  Note the effect of the Transfer of Functions (Education and Employment) Order 1995, SI 1995/2986, art 5, which transfers the functions of the Secretary of State for Wales relating to education to the Secretary of State, but which does not prevent the continued exercise of those functions by the Secretary of State for Wales.

11  Welsh Office Annual Report: *The Government's Expenditure Plans 1995–96 to 1997–98* (Cm 2815) (1995) ch 5. The Office of Her Majesty's Chief Inspector of Schools in Wales was established in 1992, under the Education (Schools) Act 1992. As to the Curriculum Council for Wales established under the Education Act 1993 s 252 see EDUCATION vol 15 (Reissue) para 107. See generally EDUCATION; LIBRARIES AND CULTURAL AND SCIENTIFIC INSTITUTIONS.

12  Welsh Office Annual Report: *The Government's Expenditure Plans 1995–96 to 1997–98* (Cm 2815) (1995) ch 6. See generally HIGHWAYS.

13  Welsh Office Annual Report: *The Government's Expenditure Plans 1995–96 to 1997–98* (Cm 2815) (1995) ch 7; see also Housing for Wales established under the Housing Act 1988; the Leasehold Reform, Housing and Urban Development Act 1993; and generally HOUSING.

14  Welsh Office Annual Report: *The Government's Expenditure Plans 1995–96 to 1997–98* (Cm 2815) (1995) ch 8. See generally PUBLIC HEALTH; NATIONAL HEALTH AND SOCIAL SECURITY.

15  See the *Next Steps Review 1995* (Cm 3164) (1995) p 4.

16  See the *Next Steps Review 1995* (Cm 3164) (1995) p 132.

17  Welsh Office Annual Report: *The Government's Expenditure Plans 1995–96 to 1997–98* (Cm 2815) (1995) ch 10. See generally NATIONAL HEALTH AND SOCIAL SECURITY.

**48.  Organisation.** The functions of the Welsh Office are reflected in the division of the Office into 11 groups as follows:

(1)   the Economic Development Group has responsibility for urban and rural development policy in Wales, economic policy and the administration of the European Union's structural and regional development funds in Wales[1].

(2)   the Industry and Training Department administers the government's schemes of regional financial assistance, provides advice to businesses, develops training and vocational education and works with seven Training and Enterprise Councils in Wales[2];

(3)   the Agriculture Department participates in the formulation of United Kingdom and European agriculture policy, advises on fisheries, animal health and welfare and administers agricultural grants[3];

(4)   the Health Professionals Group (including the Nursing Division) provides professional advice on health matters[4];

(5)   the Welsh Office Health Department discharges the Secretary of State's responsibilities in the management of the National Health Service in Wales[5];

(6)   the Local Government Group is responsible for policy on all aspects of social services in Wales, policy relating to the provision of standards of housing in Wales' the administration of local government finance and local government, including its reorganisation in Wales[6];

(7)   the Transport, Planning and Environment Group is responsible for transport policy issues, the execution of the trunk road and motorway programme, planning legislation and policy and water legislation, control of pollution and environmental protection matters[7];

(8)   the Education Department is responsible for the National Curriculum in schools in Wales, the administration of nursery, primary and secondary schools, higher and further education including the training of teachers, universities and museums, libraries, broadcasting, the arts and the Welsh language[8].

(9)   the Finance Group, comprising the Finance Programmes Division, the Finance Services Division and the Economic Advice Division[9];

(10) the Legal Group[10]; and

(11) the Establishment Group, dealing with personnel management, management services, planning and review, and statistics[11].

The Deputy Secretary for Economic Affairs is responsible for the Economic Development Group, the Industry and Training Department and the Agriculture Department. The Legal, Establishment and Finance Groups, and the Welsh Office Health Department work directly to the Permanent Secretary. The Deputy Secretary for Social Affairs is responsible for the Health Professionals Group (under the Chief Medical Officer), the Nursing Division (under the Chief Nursing Officer) the Local Government Group, the Transport, Planning and Environment Group and the Education Department[12].

In addition, there are 64 non-departmental public bodies in Wales, 29 of which advise and assist the department, 11 of which are tribunals and 24 of which have executive functions[13].

Some governmental functions, such as those of the Board of Inland Revenue, employment-related functions of the Department of Education and Employment and the social services functions of the Department of Social Security are exercised in Wales not by the Welsh Office but by other government departments[14].

1   See the Civil Service Year Book 1996 cols 919–920.
2   See the Civil Service Year Book 1996 cols 915–918.
3   See the Civil Service Year Book 1996 cols 914–915.
4   See the Civil Service Year Book 1996 cols 921–923.
5   See the Civil Service Year Book 1996 cols 911–913.
6   See the Civil Service Year Book 1996 cols 923–926.
7   See the Civil Service Year Book 1996 cols 926–929.
8   See the Civil Service Year Book 1996 cols 920–921.
9   See the Civil Service Year Book 1996 cols 910–911.
10 See the Civil Service Year Book 1996 col 908.
11 See the Civil Service Year Book 1996 cols 908–910.
12 See the Civil Service Year Book 1996 col 907 et seq.
13 As to non-departmental public bodies generally see para 951 et seq post. The executive bodies in Wales include charter bodies such as the Arts Council for Wales, the National Library of Wales, the National Museum of Wales and the Sports Council of Wales; and statutory bodies such as the Land Authority for Wales; the Development Board for Rural Wales, the Welsh Development Agency, the Higher and Further Education Funding Councils for Wales, the Wales Tourist Board and the Welsh Language Board, the Cardiff Bay Development Corporation, the Countryside Council for Wales. See the Welsh Office Annual Report: *The Government's Expenditure Plans 1995–96 to 1997–98* (Cm 2815) (1995) p 108: 'the Secretary of State is accountable to Parliament for the actions of Welsh non-departmental public bodies and approves individual expenditure proposals that are above delegated limits...the Permanent Secretary of the Welsh Office, as Departmental Accounting Officer, is personally responsible to Parliament through the Public Accounts Committee for the proper payment of money to the non-departmental public

bodies, and for ensuring that the Departmental financial control and management systems are adequate to protect public funds...the sponsoring divisions of the Welsh Office are responsible for providing a suitable framework of rules and guidance and for monitoring non-departmental public bodies' compliance with them'.

14 See the Welsh Office Annual Report: *The Government's Expenditure Plans 1995–96 to 1997–98* (Cm 2815) (1995) chs 6, 8.

**49. Local government in Wales.** A new structure of local government in Wales is established as from 1 April 1996[1]. The eight county councils and 37 district councils established by the Local Government Act 1972 are replaced by 22 new principal councils. They comprise 11 counties and 11 county boroughs. These 22 councils are unitary authorities, replacing the two tiers of district and county councils[2]. The members of the new principal councils were elected in May 1995[3] and assumed responsibility for local government services in Wales on 1 April 1996, when the two tier system of district and county councils ceased[4]. There continue to be community councils and community meetings exercising certain local government functions[5].

1 See the Local Government Act 1972 ss 20, 21 (substituted by the Local Government (Wales) Act 1994 ss 1(1), 2 respectively).

2 See the Local Government Act 1972 ss 20, 21 (as substituted: see note 1 supra), Sch 4 (substituted by the Local Government (Wales) Act 1994 s 1(2)).

3 See the Local Government Act 1972 Sch 5 (substituted by the Local Government (Wales) Act 1994 s 3, Sch 3).

4 For certain purposes, mainly relating to parliamentary boundaries, lord lieutenants and sheriffs, the eight counties established by the Local Government Act 1972 remain as preserved counties: see para 41 note 1 ante.

5 See the Local Government Act 1972 ss 27–35 (as amended); and generally LOCAL GOVERNMENT.

**50. The Prince of Wales.** The eldest son of the reigning monarch is the heir apparent and is usually created Prince of Wales and Earl of Chester by the monarch by letters patent[1].

1 4 Co Inst 243; 1 Bl Com (14th Edn) 194. The title of Prince of Wales was originated by Edward I, who conferred it upon his second son, Edward, on the conquest of Wales in 1284: see 2 Hume's History of England 243. The present Prince of Wales was created Prince of Wales and Earl of Chester on 26 July 1958 and invested with the insignia of those titles on 1 July 1969 at Caernarvon Castle at the age of 20.

As to the titles assumed by the monarch's eldest son in regard to Scotland see para 54 post. As to the other titles held by the heir apparent and other members of the royal family see CROWN LANDS AND PRIVILEGES.

# (9)  SCOTLAND

**51. Historical introduction.** The constitutional position of Scotland in the United Kingdom[1] cannot be understood without reference to the formerly separate kingdoms of Scotland and England. Before 1603, Scotland and England each had their own parliament, legal system, church and monarchy. In 1603, when Elizabeth I died with no direct heir, title to the English throne passed to King James VI of Scotland, who moved his court from Scotland to London. The resulting situation was a personal union rather than a union of the Crowns, since the two Crowns remained distinct in law until 1707. Although James desired to bring about measures for integrating the laws of England and Scotland, the aspiration made little progress and effectively lapsed in 1608[2]. Persons born in Scotland after the accession of James to the throne of England were held to be citizens of both countries as they owed allegiance to the same king[3]. During the seventeenth century, both countries experienced many constitutional problems in relation to the

Stuart kings. In the time of the Commonwealth, they were governed under the same written constitution (Cromwell's Instrument of Government of 1653) until the monarchy was restored in 1660.

In 1688–89 the vesting of the two Crowns in William and Mary occurred through separate measures in each country. In April 1689, the Scottish Estates (ie Parliament) adopted the Claim of Right[4], which set out the conditions on which the Scottish Crown was offered to William and Mary, who by then were already King and Queen of England[5].

Although William III, soon after acceding to the two Crowns, suggested a union of the two kingdoms, the period 1689–1706 was marked by the independence of the Scottish Parliament, which defended the economic and religious interests of the Scottish people, even if this threatened England's security[6]. In 1700, the English Parliament in the Act of Settlement assigned the succession to the English Crown after Queen Anne's death to Electress Sophia of Hanover[7]. However, in 1704 the Scottish Parliament provided that if Anne died without heirs, that Parliament must choose as her successor in Scotland someone other than the English monarch, unless in the meantime 'conditions of government' had been enacted which secured the honour, sovereignty and other interests of Scotland[8]. In 1704, both Parliaments empowered the Queen to appoint commissioners to consult concerning a 'nearer and more complete union' of the two kingdoms[9]. Negotiation between the commissioners brought about the Treaty of Union 1706. This came into effect on 1 May 1707 after its enactment by each Parliament, together with associated legislation, notably the Act for Securing the Protestant Religion and Presbyterian Church Government in Scotland[10].

1    For a fuller discussion see 5 *Stair Memorial Encyclopaedia* CONSTITUTIONAL LAW; Mitchell *Constitutional Law* (2nd Edn, 1968); and Fraser *Constitutional Law* (2nd Edn, 1948).
2    See 22 *Stair Memorial Encyclopedia* SOURCES OF LAW (GENERAL AND HISTORICAL) para 628, summarising the proposals for integration made during the 17th century.
3    *Calvin's Case* (1608) 7 Co Rep 1a.
4    Claim of Right 1689, c 28, APS IX 38. The Claim of Right declared that James VII of Scotland (who was also James II of England) had 'by the advice of evil and wicked Counsellors, invaded the fundamental Constitution of the Kingdom, and altered it from a legal limited Monarchy, to an arbitrary despotic Power' and that the throne had become vacant.
5    See Address to Prince of Orange (1689) c 6, APS IX 9.
6    See Riley *The Union of England and Scotland* (1978) ch 1.
7    See the Act of Settlement. As to the citation of the Act of Settlement see para 35 note 3 ante.
8    Act of Security (1704) c 3, APS XI 136.
9    Ie Union of England and Scotland (1704), 3 & 4 Anne c 6 (England) (repealed); Act for a Treaty with England (1704) c 50, APS XI 295 (Scotland) (repealed).
10   See the Union with Scotland Act 1706 (6 Anne c 11); the Scottish Act of Union (1706) c 7, APS XI 406; and the Act for Securing the Protestant Religion and Presbyterian Church (1706) c 6, APS XI 402.

**52. The Scottish and English legal systems.** The Treaty and Acts of Union created a single monarchy and Parliament for Great Britain[1]. The Union legislation sought by various means to ensure the continued existence of the Scottish legal system, with its own courts and legal profession. In the United Kingdom's legislature since 1707, the majority of members in each House has always been from England. Nonetheless, the formal sources of law are not identical in the two jurisdictions, and the substantive rules of law differ in many ways[2]. The historical origins of Scots law are not found in the English common law, but owe much to the continental systems of civil law. The more recent development of Scots law has been much influenced by the common law, but Scotland continues to have its own criminal law and procedure; and areas of private law (property, succession, family law and obligations) as well as civil procedure display many differences from English law. In areas of government and public administration, the legislation is often the same throughout the United Kingdom, but on matters such as education, local government, social services and housing, separate schemes of legislation exist in the two countries. There is no uniformity even in areas of public law such as judicial review[3] and the legal liability of the Crown to interim measures of relief[4]. In civil matters, the House of Lords sits as the final court of appeal from both jurisdictions, and the view has been expressed in that House that important rules of public law should be the same in both jurisdictions[5]. But in criminal law, where the House of Lords has no appellate function in respect of Scotland, the two separate systems of criminal justice may produce different outcomes on such issues as jurisdiction and abuse of process[6]. Moreover, the approach of the Scottish judiciary to the status in domestic law of the European Convention on Human Rights in domestic law has not always been the same as that of the English courts[7].

While Acts of the United Kingdom Parliament enacted since 1 May 1707 bind the Scottish courts if they extend to Scotland, Acts of the English Parliament enacted before that date do not apply in Scotland unless they have been extended to Scotland by an Act passed since 1707[8]. Scottish courts remain bound by Acts of the former Scottish Parliament which have continued in force since 1707 and have not been repealed by the United Kingdom Parliament. However, by the Scottish doctrine of desuetude, an Act of the Scottish Parliament may be held by the Scottish courts to be no longer in force if it has long been in disuse and the circumstances with which the Act was intended to deal have changed materially since it was enacted[9].

1   See paras 51 ante; 53 post.
2   See 22 *Stair Memorial Encyclopaedia* SOURCES OF LAW (FORMAL); SOURCES OF LAW (GENERAL AND HISTORICAL). See *Orr Ewing's Trustees* (1884) 11 R 600 at 629, Ct of Sess, per Lord President Inglis: 'The judicatories of Scotland and England are as independent of each other within their respective territories, as if they were the judicatories of two foreign states'.
3   Contrast *O'Reilly v Mackman* [1983] 2 AC 237, [1982] 3 All ER 1124, HL, with *West v Secretary of State for Scotland* 1992 SLT 636, where the Court of Session rejected the distinction between public law and private law as the basis for determining the limits of judicial review in Scots law. There are significant differences in the procedure of judicial review between RSC Ord 53 and Court of Session procedure: see Himsworth 'Judicial Review in Scotland' in Hadfield (ed) *Judicial Review, A Thematic Approach* (1995), ch 10. The availability of judicial review in both English and Scots law does not mean that an applicant for judicial review is always entitled to choose whether to seek review in London or Edinburgh: *Bank of Scotland v Investment Management Regulatory Organisation Ltd* 1989 SLT 432, Ct of Sess (no jurisdiction to review regulatory decision taken in London).
4   See *McDonald v Secretary of State for Scotland* 1994 SLT 692, Ct of Sess, not following *Re M* [1994] 1 AC 377, sub nom *M v Home Office* [1993] 3 All ER 537, HL.
5   See *Conway v Rimmer* [1968] AC 910 at 938, [1968] 1 All ER 874 at 879, HL, per Lord Reid: 'There are many chapters of the law where for historical and other reasons it is quite proper that the law should be different in the two countries; but here we are dealing purely with public policy - with the proper relation between the powers of the executive and the powers of the courts - and I can see no rational justification for the law on this matter being different in the two countries'. See also per Lord Morris of Borth-y-Gest at 961, 894, and Lord Pearce at 983, 908; and *Lord Advocate v Dumbarton District Council* [1990] 2 AC 580 at 591, [1990] 1 All ER 1 at 6–7, HL, per Lord Keith of Kinkel.
6   See eg *Bennett v HM Advocate* 1995 SLT 510, Ct of Sess, not following *R v Horseferry Road Magistrates' Court, ex p Bennett* [1994] AC 42, sub nom *Bennett v Horseferry Road Magistrates' Court* [1993] 3 All ER 138, HL.
7   See in particular *Kaur v Lord Advocate* 1981 SLT 322, Ct of Sess; and *Moore v Secretary of State for Scotland* 1985 SLT 38, Ct of Sess; but see also *Re Budh Singh* (13 July 1988, unreported). See 12 *Stair Memorial Encyclopedia* HUMAN RIGHTS IN EUROPE para 8; and Murdoch 'The European Convention on Human Rights in Scots Law' [1991] Public Law 40. As to the Convention for the Protection of Human Rights and Fundamental Freedoms (1950) (commonly known as the European Convention on Human Rights) see generally paras 122–181.
8   See eg the extension to Scotland of the Statute of Treasons 1351 by the Treason Act 1708.
9   See eg *M'Ara v Magistrates of Edinburgh* 1913 SC 1059. For the view that the doctrine of desuetude is redundant today see 22 *Stair Memorial Encyclopaedia* SOURCES OF LAW (FORMAL) paras 129–133; and on the doctrine of precedent as it applies in the law of Scotland, see paras 265–354 thereof. As to the structure of the Scottish courts see paras 59–62 post.

**53. The Treaty of Union between England and Scotland.** With effect from 1 May 1707, the Treaty declared that the two Kingdoms of England and Scotland should be united into one Kingdom by the name of Great Britain[1]; that the Crown in the United Kingdom should after Queen Anne's death descend to members of the Hanoverian line, being protestant[2]; and that the United Kingdom should be represented by one Parliament[3]. As regards the composition of that Parliament, the Treaty provided for 16 Scottish peers to sit in the House of Lords and 45 elected Scottish members in the House of Commons[4]. Freedom of trade within Great Britain was established for all subjects of the United Kingdom[5], and many other economic and financial provisions were made[6].

Apart from the regulation of trade, customs and excise matters, on which the English laws replaced the Scottish laws, and except for laws which were inconsistent with the Treaty, all other laws within Scotland were to remain in force after the Union 'but alterable by the Parliament of Great Britain'. However, laws concerning public right could be made the same in England and Scotland, but laws concerning private right could be altered only if this was in the interests of the Scottish people[7]. The future existence of the Court of Session was guaranteed, and Scottish cases were not to be decided by the English courts[8]. Other guarantees were given for the continuance of Scottish institutions, the most important being to maintain the Presbyterian Church in Scotland which was incorporated in the Treaty and provided also for maintaining the Scottish universities[9].

While the Treaty of Union would appear to have been a treaty according to international law (ius gentium)[10], the legislation which gave effect to it within the two countries dealt with matters vital to the constitutional structure of the new state, the United Kingdom of Great Britain. The effect was to create what was described at the time as an 'incorporating union', not a federal union. The intention must have been to create a union that was permanent: the Treaty and the Acts made no general provision for their own amendment, nor for the recall of the separate English and Scottish Parliaments should amendment of the Treaty be desirable. The articles of the Treaty comprise three categories of provision, namely (1) provisions which expressly confer on the Parliament of Great Britain power of subsequent amendment; (2) those which contain no such power; and (3) those which expressly exclude any subsequent alteration whatsoever (such as those relating to the Court of Session and the Presbyterian Church in Scotland) which were declared fundamental and unalterable[11].

Important questions have arisen as to the effect of these provisions, particularly those declared to be fundamental and unalterable[12]. On one view, which many English jurists have supported, the Treaty of Union is fully subject to the legislative sovereignty of the Westminster Parliament; thus, whatever the intention of its framers may have been, the Treaty has been said to illustrate the futility of a sovereign Parliament seeking to bind itself[13]. An opposing view is that, at least so far as the essential guarantees of Scottish institutions are concerned, the Treaty of Union is a constituent document which created the Parliament of Great Britain in 1707 to take the place of both the former English and Scottish Parliaments[14]. Scope for such widely diverse arguments is left open by the inconclusive nature of the case-law[15]. Certainly, the English and Scottish Acts of Union still have effect within the English and Scottish jurisdictions respectively[16], and many provisions of the Acts of Union have been amended since 1707[17]. It is uncertain: (a) whether any provisions in the Treaty of Union are incapable of being amended by the Westminster Parliament and, in that event, whether the validity of any attempt to amend them is a matter that could be decided by the English or Scottish courts; and (b) whether in the case of legislation seeking to change the law affecting private right in Scotland, the test of 'evident utility'[18] contained in Article 18 is a justiciable question[19].

---

1   See the Union with Scotland Act 1706 art I. That Act embodies the Treaty of Union between England and Scotland. The treaty was given effect in Scotland by the Scottish Act of Union (1706) c 7, APS XI 406.

2   Union with Scotland Act 1706 art II. As to the descent of the Crown see paras 34–40 ante.

3   Ibid s 1 art 3.

4   Ibid s 1 arts 22, (repealed), 23 (as amended). As to the House of Commons see generally PARLIAMENT.

5   Ibid s 1 art 4. For an unsuccessful attempt to use art 4 as a ground for holding unlawful the introduction of the community charge (poll tax) in local government in Scotland one year before it commenced in England see *Pringle, Petitioner* 1991 SLT 330, Ct of Sess. See also *R v Lord Chancellor, ex p Law Society* (1993) Times, 25 June (unsuccessful attempt to challenge legal aid regulations in England for, inter alia, inconsistency with the Union with Scotland Act 1706 art IV).

6   See ibid arts V–XVII (now mostly repealed), dealing inter alia with equality of customs and excise duties, common coinage and weights and measures.

7   See ibid art XVIII; and note 15 infra. Article XVIII requires that any alteration be for the 'evident utility of the Subjects within Scotland'.

8   See ibid art XIX. Article XIX further provided for the future continuance of the Court of Justiciary and its criminal jurisdiction, and certain other courts. See also *R v Metropolitan Police Comr, ex p Bennett* [1995] QB 313, [1995] 3 All ER 248 (English court without power to intervene in execution in England of warrant for arrest issued by a Scottish court).

9   The Act for Securing the Protestant Religion and Presbyterian Church Government, set out in the Union with Scotland Act 1706 s 2, provided inter alia: 'That this Act of Parliament, with the Establishment therein contained, shall be held and observed in all time coming as a fundamental and essential condition of any Treaty or Union to be concluded between the two Kingdoms, without any alteration thereof'.

10  See McNair *Law of Treaties* (1961) p 40; and Smith 'The Union of 1707 as Fundamental Law' [1957] Public Law 99.

11  See *MacCormick v Lord Advocate* 1953 SC 396 at 412, where Lord President Cooper observed that he found in the Union legislation no 'provision that the Parliament of Great Britain should be "absolutely sovereign" in the sense that that Parliament should be free to alter the Treaty at will'.

12  The principal such questions are: 'are the Acts of Union between England and Scotland to be regarded as a form of fundamental (constitutional) law, binding on the United Kingdom Parliament? If so, have the courts power to review the validity of legislation by Parliament which seeks (for instance) to amend 'unalterable' provisions of the Union? Or are the Acts of Union capable of being amended in any or every respect by the Westminster Parliament? See the text and notes infra.

13  See eg Maitland *Constitutional History of England* (1908) p 332; Dicey *Law of the Constitution* (10th Edn, 1959) pp 65–66, 68–70, 145. See also Dicey and Rait *Thoughts on the Scottish Union* (1920); and Munro *Studies in Constitutional Law* (1987) ch 4.

14  One argument is that the Parliament of Great Britain was 'born unfree': Mitchell *Constitutional Law* (2nd edn, 1968) ch 5 and pp 92–98. On this basis, it has been suggested that the 'ultimate rule of recognition' which underlies the United Kingdom's constitutional law is the following: 'Whatever the Queen in Parliament enacts, unless in derogation from the justiciable limits set by the Articles of Union, is law': MacCormick 'Does the United Kingdom have a Constitution? Reflections on MacCormick v Lord Advocate' (1978) 29 NILQ 1, 11. See generally 5 *Stair Memorial Encyclopaedia* CONSTITUTIONAL LAW paras 338–360. See also King Murray 'Devolution in the United Kingdom - a Scottish Perspective' (1980) 96 LQR 35; Upton 'Marriage Vows of the Elephant: the Constitution of 1707' (1989) 105 LQR 79; Himsworth and Walker 'The Poll Tax and Fundamental Law' [1991] Juridical Review 45.

15  See in particular *Laughland v Wansborough Paper Co* 1921 SLT 341, Ct of Sess; *MacCormick v Lord Advocate* 1953 SC 396, Ct of Sess; and *Gibson v Lord Advocate* 1975 SLT 134, Ct of Sess. Decisions arising from the community charge (poll tax) include *Murray v Rogers* 1992 SLT 221, Ct of Sess and *Fraser v MacCorquodale* 1992 SLT 229 and *Pringle, Petitioner* 1991 SLT 330. Arguments founded upon the Treaty of Union were rejected by an English court in *R v Lord Chancellor, ex p Law Society* (1993) Times, 25 June.

16  See eg *R v Metropolitan Police Comr, ex p Bennett* [1995] QB 313, [1995] 3 All ER 248.

17  See eg the list of statutes amending provisions of the Treaty of Union set out by Upton in 'Marriage Vows of the Elephant: the Constitution of 1707' (1989) 105 LQR 79 at 93.

18  See note 7 supra.

19  There are as yet no reported decisions in which the validity of legislation has been successfully impugned for the reason that it does not conform to the Articles of Union. Notwithstanding the emphatic requirement that the Act to maintain the established church in Scotland should be maintained 'as a fundamental and essential condition' of the Union, important aspects of that Act were amended when the requirement that professors in the Scottish universities adhere to the Westminster Confession was revoked by the Universities (Scotland) Act 1853.

**54. The monarch and the succession.** The legislation which implemented the Treaty of Union between England and Scotland created a single kingdom of Great Britain, enlarged in 1800 to become the Kingdom of Great Britain and Ireland. Today the expression 'the United Kingdom' used in legislation means the United Kingdom of Great Britain and Northern Ireland[1]. The succession to the monarchy since 1707 has been governed by the Act of Settlement as applied to the United Kingdom by the Treaty of Union[2] and the Union with Ireland Act 1800[3]. The style and titles of the monarch are the same throughout the United Kingdom[4]. The Queen has responsibilities in relation to the Church of Scotland, but these are of less significance than her role as Supreme Governor of the Church of England[5].

The eldest son of the monarch succeeds at his birth to the titles pertaining to the Principality of Scotland, namely Duke of Rothesay, Earl of Carrick, Baron of Renfrew, Lord of the Isles and Prince and Great Steward of Scotland[6]. For the purposes of administering law and government in Scotland, the Treaty of Union required that separate royal seals should be maintained in Scotland[7].

1  See para 3 ante.
2  Union with Scotland Act 1706 art II, applying the Act of Settlement s 1. As to the citation of the Act of Settlement see para 35 note 3 ante.
3  The monarchy descends according to the rules of succession applicable to real property in English law before 1926, except that Roman Catholics and persons married to Roman Catholics are excluded and, in the absence of a male heir, the older of two sisters succeeds alone, as Elizabeth did in 1952. In 1937 the government was satisfied as to the right of Princess Elizabeth to succeed to the throne as sole heiress presumptive: 319 HC Official Report (5th series), 28 January 1937, col 1055. This position conforms with the rule of Scots feudal law: see 7 *Stair Memorial Encyclopaedia* THE CROWN para 783; and cf Walker (ed) *Stair's Institutions of the Law of Scotland* (1981) p 690 ('rights indivisible fall to the eldest [of female heirs] alone, without anything in lieu thereof to the rest'). The sole departure from the Act of Settlement line of succession since 1707 was authorised by His Majesty's Declaration of Abdication Act 1936: see generally paras 34–40 ante.
4  They are determined by royal proclamation issued from time to time under the authority of the Royal Titles Act 1953: see CROWN LANDS AND PRIVILEGES. The proclamation of the Queen as Elizabeth II in 1952 was challenged unsuccessfully in the Court of Session on the ground that there had never been an Elizabeth I of Scotland; the Court held that the royal numeral derived from the proclamation of the Queen in 1952 and that no citizen had title or interest to challenge its legality: *MacCormick v Lord Advocate* 1953 SC 396. It was subsequently stated by the Prime Minister that on a future succession to the throne, the royal style should refer to the highest appropriate numeral, taking into account the designation of all previous monarchs both in England and Scotland: 514 HC Official Report (5th series), 15 April 1953, cols 199–201.
5  As to the Church of England see ECCLESIASTICAL LAW vol 14 paras 352–360. As to the Church of Scotland see 5 *Stair Memorial Encyclopaedia* CONSTITUTIONAL LAW paras 679–691; and Lyall *Of Presbyters and Kings* (1980). When the Queen (or more commonly her representative, the Lord High Commissioner) attends the General Assembly of the Church of Scotland, she is not a member of the Assembly and plays no direct part in its proceedings. The Lord High Commissioner may not be a Roman Catholic, nor may a Roman Catholic advise the Queen on appointments that she may make in the Church of Scotland: Roman Catholic Relief Act 1829 ss 12, 18 (both amended by the Statute Law Revision (No 2) Act 1888; s 12 also amended by the Statute Law Revision Act 1950).
6  5 *Stair Memorial Encyclopaedia* CONSTITUTIONAL LAW paras 706–711. When there is no heir apparent, the monarch himself is Prince of Scotland. See also 7 *Stair Memorial Encyclopedia* THE CROWN paras 786–787.
7  Union with Scotland Act 1706 art XXIV. For the royal seals in Scotland see 7 *Stair Memorial Encyclopedia* THE CROWN paras 873–1000. The Keeper of the Great Seal of Scotland is now the Secretary of State for Scotland (Secretary for Scotland Act 1885 s 8: see para 64 post) who also is furnished with his own seal: s 4.

**55. The Crown and the Royal Prerogative.** As regards the legal concept of the Crown[1], the law of Scotland is today broadly similar to English law. However, in many detailed respects, particularly as regards proceedings brought by and against the Crown, Scots law differs from English law. The earlier tradition in Scots law was less inclined than English law to grant the Crown special privileges or immunity from the ordinary law[2]. Long before the Crown Proceedings Act 1947, the Crown could be sued in Scotland by means of an action directed against the Officers of State or, after 1857, against the Lord Advocate[3]. It was established only in 1921 that the Crown was not vicariously liable for the delictual acts of Crown servants arising out of and in the course of their employment[4]. The differences between the position of the Crown in English and Scots law explain why the Crown Proceedings Act 1947 does not make the same provision for the two jurisdictions[5].

The concept of the prerogative powers of the Crown, that is to say, powers, privileges, rights and other interests which are recognised in law as pertaining to the Crown even though they have not been vested in the Crown by Act of Parliament, is in broad terms the same in both English and Scots law[6]. However, the detailed powers and other interests of the Crown are not identical in the two jurisdictions[7]. Although the extent of the royal prerogative may differ in detail, the role of the courts in relation to the exercise of the prerogative is the same in both jurisdictions: prerogative decisions are in general subject to judicial review[8] and the exercise of prerogative powers may in some circumstances give rise to a duty to compensate[9].

The Crown is not bound by regulatory statutes unless there is either an express statement in the legislation or a necessary implication to this effect[10]. So far as public interest immunity (formerly Crown privilege) in the law of evidence is concerned, English law is more closely in line with Scots law than had previously been the case[11], but it cannot be assumed that the law of public interest immunity is identical in the two jurisdictions[12].

1   In *British Medical Association v Greater Glasgow Health Board* [1989] AC 1211, [1989] 1 All ER 984, HL, an action against a health board constituted under the National Health Service (Scotland) Act 1978 was held not to be a proceeding against the Crown for the purposes of the Crown Proceedings Act 1947 s 21 (nature of relief in Crown proceedings). See further CROWN PROCEEDINGS.

2   See *British Medical Association v Greater Glasgow London Health Board* [1989] AC 1211 at 1225, [1989] 1 All ER 984 at 990, HL, per Lord Jauncey of Tullichettle, observing that 'Scots law took a more robust view of the individual's rights against the Crown than did the law of England'. See generally 7 *Stair Memorial Encyclopedia* THE CROWN. See also Mitchell 'The Royal Prerogative in Modern Scots Law' [1957] Public Law 304; and Wolffe 'Crown and Prerogative in Scots Law' in Finnie, Himsworth and Walker (eds) *Edinburgh Essays in Public Law* (1991) pp 351–369.

3   See the Crown Suits (Scotland) Act 1857 s 1. Thus the Lord Advocate could be sued as the Crown's representative in respect of claims based on contractual or proprietary rights. For the position before 1857 see *King's Advocate v Lord Dunglass* (1836) 15 Sh 314, Ct of Sess.

4   *MacGregor v Lord Advocate* 1921 SC 847.

5   See the Crown Proceedings Act 1947 Pt V (ss 41–51) (as amended) (application to Scotland). In *McDonald v Secretary of State for Scotland* 1994 SLT 692, Ct of Sess, it was held (not following *Re M* [1994] 1 AC 377, sub nom *M v Home Office* [1993] 3 All ER 537, HL), that because of the Crown Proceedings Act 1947 s 21 the remedy of interdict is not available against the Crown, although it was available before that Act: *Somerville v Lord Advocate* (1893) 20 R 1050, Ct of Sess; *Russell v Magistrates of Hamilton* (1897) 25 R 350, Ct of Sess; *Bell v Secretary of State for Scotland* 1933 SLT 519,Ct of Sess. See also Fraser *Constitutional Law* (2nd Edn, 1948) ch XI; and Mitchell *Constitutional Law* (2nd Edn, 1968) pp 302–314.

6   See eg as to the effects of a royal proclamation *Grieve v Edinburgh and District Water Trustees* 1918 SC 700. A litigant may not rely on the unity of the Crown as a reason for suing a United Kingdom minister in Scotland when the Scottish court is 'forum non conveniens': *Sokha v Secretary of State for the Home Department* 1992 SLT 1049, Ct of Sess (litigant having no connection with Scotland except for having instructed Scottish solicitors could not sue in Scotland in respect of proceedings under the Immigration Act 1971).

7   As to the prerogative in English law see para 367 et seq post; and in Scots law 7 *Stair Memorial Encyclopedia* THE CROWN. See also CROWN LANDS AND PRIVILEGES.

8   See eg *Council of Civil Service Unions v Minister for the Civil Service* [1985] AC 374, [1984] 3 All ER 935, HL.

9   See eg *Burmah Oil Co (Burma Trading) Ltd v Lord Advocate* [1965] AC 75, [1964] 2 All ER 348, HL (Crown under a duty to compensate the owner of property which had been destroyed intentionally by British forces during military operations). This duty to compensate was retrospectively set aside by the War Damage Act 1965.

10   *Lord Advocate v Dumbarton District Council* [1990] 2 AC 580, [1990] 1 All ER 1, HL, reversing a decision by the Court of Session, which had held (at 1988 SLT 546) that the doctrine of Crown immunity from legislation was narrower in Scots law than in English law. See per Lord Keith of Kinkel at 591, 7–8: 'It is not conceivable that Parliament could have a different intention as regards the application of [an Act in force throughout the United Kingdom] to the Crown in the various parts of the Kingdom'. See also Wolffe 'Crown Immunity from Regulatory Statutes' [1988] Public Law 339; and 'Crown Immunity from Legislative Obligations' [1990] Public Law 14.

11   See *Conway v Rimmer* [1968] AC 910, [1968] 1 All ER 874, HL; and cf in particular *Glasgow Corpn v Central Land Board* 1956 SC (HL) 1, with *Duncan v Cammell Laird & Co Ltd* [1942] AC 624, [1942] 1 All ER 587, HL.
12   See McShane 'Crown Privilege in Scotland: The Demerits of Disharmony' (Part I) [1992] Juridical Review 256, and (Part II) [1993] Juridical Review 41.

**56. Scotland's representation in Parliament.** The effect of the implementation of the Treaty of Union in 1707 was to replace the separate English and Scottish Parliaments with the Parliament of Great Britain[1]. However, the two English Houses continued to sit at Westminster with the addition to the House of Lords of 16 Scottish representative peers[2] and to the Commons of (in 1707) 45 members representing Scottish counties and burghs[3]. In 1707 the Union legislation left unchanged the law governing the franchise in Scotland[4], but the successive reforms of the electoral system since 1832 have assimilated the law on the franchise in both England and Scotland, and the Representation of the People Acts apply throughout the United Kingdom. The Registration Appeal Court, which consists of three Court of Session judges, hears appeals concerning the electoral register[5]. Scotland is entitled to be represented in the House of Commons by not less than 71 members[6]. Election petitions arising in Scotland are heard by two judges of the Court of Session, sitting as the Election Petition Court[7]. The law governing disqualification from sitting and voting in the House of Commons applies fully to members from Scottish constituencies[8].

    The changes in the territorial jurisdiction of the Westminster Parliament in 1707 and subsequently had no direct effect on the law, custom and procedures of Parliament[9]. In principle the same process applies whenever Parliament is legislating for any part of the United Kingdom. However, legislation that relates solely to Scotland is subject to special procedure, and the separate organisation of government in Scotland is recognised in Parliament[10].

1   Union with Scotland Act 1706 art III. As to the Treaty of Union, as embodied in the Union with Scotland Act 1706, see paras 51, 53 ante.
2   The Peerage Act 1963 s 4 admitted all surviving Scottish peers to the House of Lords: see PEERAGES AND DIGNITIES vol 35 (Reissue) para 904. Since the Union in 1707, the Crown has had no power to create new Scottish peers. See also 5 *Stair Memorial Encyclopaedia* CONSTITUTIONAL LAW para 367. Significant differences exist in peerage law as between England and Scotland, and claims to Scottish peerages must be decided in accordance with Scots law: see eg *Annandale and Hartfell Earldom* [1986] AC 319, [1985] 3 All ER 577, HL. The Church of Scotland, unlike the Church of England, is not represented directly in the House of Lords.
3   There are now 72 Scottish constituencies. See the Parliamentary Constituencies Act 1986 s 3, Sch 2 para 1(2), providing that the minimum number of constituencies in Scotland is 71.
4   See 5 *Stair Memorial Encyclopaedia* CONSTITUTIONAL LAW paras 467–470.
5   See the Representation of the People Act 1983 s 57. For decisions by the court see eg *Ferris v Wallace* 1936 SC 561 (which was not cited in *Fox v Stirk* [1970] 2 QB 463, [1970] 3 All ER 7, CA); and *Scott v Phillips* 1974 SLT 33.
6   See note 3 supra. There is a separate Boundary Commission for Scotland, of which the Speaker is ex officio chairman and a Court of Session judge is deputy chairman: Parliamentary Constituencies Act 1986 s 2, Sch 1.
7   See the Representation of the People Act 1983 s 125(1).
8   See the House of Commons Disqualification Act 1975; and PARLIAMENT.
9   See para 201 et seq post; and PARLIAMENT.
10   See generally PARLIAMENT.

**57. Scottish committees of the House of Commons.** The     Scottish     Grand Committee consists of all members of the House of Commons who are elected for Scottish constituencies[1]. Thus, unlike most House of Commons committees, its composition bears no necessary relationship to the total strengths of the political parties in the Commons[2]. Among its main items of business are:

(1)    questions tabled for oral answer by Scottish Office ministers or Scottish law officers[3];

(2)    short debates on topics notified by individual members of the Committee[4];

(3)    ministerial statements on matters relating to the discharge of ministerial responsibilities in Scotland or government policy towards Scotland[5];

(4)    the consideration of Bills referred to it for consideration in relation to their principle, being Bills which have been certified by the Speaker as relating exclusively to Scotland[6];

(5)    motions relating to statutory instruments and other items of delegated legislation[7]; and

(6)    motions for the adjournment of the Committee[8].

The debate of the principle of a Bill in the Scottish Grand Committee may obviate the need for a second reading debate of the Bill in the whole House[9]. A Bill which has been considered by the Committee in relation to principle may, after it has been examined in detail at the committee stage, go for consideration on report to the Scottish Grand Committee[10]. The Scottish Grand Committee may hold certain of its meetings in Scotland[11].

The practice of the House in constituting Standing Committees to hear the committee stages of public general Bills[12] includes provision for two Scottish Standing Committees to include not fewer than 16 members representing Scottish constituencies[13], to which Bills certified by the Speaker as relating exclusively to Scotland may be committed, with precedence in one Committee being given to government bills[14]. Occasionally a Scottish Bill is committed for consideration to a Special Standing Committee[15].

The Select Committee on Scottish Affairs is appointed by the House of Commons as one of the select committees which examine the expenditure, administration and policy of the major government departments and their associated public bodies[16].

---

1    HC Standing Orders (1995) (Public Business) no 94A(1).

2    Until 1981, the Committee of Selection of the House of Commons had power to add between 10 and 15 other members to the Scottish Grand Committee.

3    See HC Standing Orders (1995) (Public Business) nos 94A(2)(a), 94B.

4    See HC Standing Orders (1995) (Public Business) nos 94A(2)(b), 94C.

5    See HC Standing Orders (1995) (Public Business) nos 94A(2)(c), 94D.

6    See HC Standing Orders (1995) (Public Business) nos 94A(2)(d), 94E. See also 5 *Stair Memorial Encyclopaedia* CONSTITUTIONAL LAW paras 414–418.

7    See HC Standing Orders (1995) (Public Business) nos 94A(2)(e), 94F.

8    See HC Standing Orders (1995) (Public Business) nos 94A(2)(f), (g), 94G. The subject debated on the motion for the adjournment must relate to Scotland: see HC Standing Orders (1995) (Public Business) no 94G(2). Twelve days are allotted each session for such motions, six at the disposal of the government, four at the disposal of the Leader of the Opposition, and one each at the disposal of the leaders of the two opposition parties which have the next largest number of seats in Scotland: see HC Standing Orders (1995) (Public Business) no 94G(3).

9    See HC Standing Orders (1995) (Public Business) no 94E(5), (6).

10   See HC Standing Orders (1995) (Public Business) no 92. Such a reference may be blocked by at least 20 members of the House rising in their places: see HC Standing Orders (1995) (Public Business) no 92(1). The quorum of the Scottish Grand Committee is 10: HC Standing Orders (1995) (Public Business) no 94A(1)).

11   See HC Standing Orders (1995) (Public Business) no 94H(1). In 1995, the government proposed changes to Standing Orders inter alia to permit regular sittings of the Committee in Scotland and to enable ministers who were not members for Scottish constituencies to take part in proceedings of the Committee in Scotland: see 267 HC Official Report (6th series), 29 November 1995, cols 1228–1242.

12   See HC Standing Orders (1995) (Public Business) nos 84 (constitution of standing committees), 95 (Scottish Standing Committees). See also PARLIAMENT.

13   HC Standing Orders (1995) (Public Business) nos 86(2)(i), 95(1).

14   HC Standing Orders (1995) (Public Business) no 95(2). Private members' bills may be considered by the second Scottish Standing Committee.

15   See HC Standing Orders (1995) (Public Business) no 91. An instance was the Children (Scotland) Bill 1994–95. The Special Standing Committee may on such a bill hold its hearings in Scotland: see HC Standing Orders (1995) (Public Business) no 91(1) proviso.

16   HC Standing Orders (1995) (Public Business) no 130; and see paras 227, 718 post. The Committee's remit includes, (in addition to the activities of the Scottish Office), administration and expenditure of the Lord Advocate's Departments, together with policy functions discharged by the Lord Advocate through the Scottish Courts Administration, but excluding consideration of individual cases and appointments, advice given within government by Scottish Law Officers, and the drafting of bills: HC Standing Orders (1995) (Public Business) no 130(2). The Committee's remit does not extend to inquiring into the activities of all government departments in Scotland. The maximum number of members of the Committee is 11: HC Standing Orders (1995) (Public Business) no 130(2). For the early years of the Committee on Scottish Affairs see Drucker and Kellas, in Drewry (ed) *The New Select Committees* (2nd Edn, 1989), ch 12.

**58.  Private legislation applying to Scotland.** The legislative process of Parliament in respect of private legislation[1] is subject to special machinery which must be followed when public or private bodies seek to obtain parliamentary powers affecting public or private interests in Scotland for which before 1899 the promoter would have been entitled to petition Parliament for leave to bring in a private Bill[2]. Instead of petitioning for a private Bill, such bodies present a petition to the Secretary of State for Scotland, requesting him to issue a provisional order in accordance with the terms of a draft order submitted to him. This procedure makes it possible for an inquiry to be held in Scotland into the proposals by commissioners selected from two parliamentary panels and if necessary from an extra-parliamentary panel of experienced persons, but final control over the proposals is retained by the two Houses at Westminster[3].

1   See PARLIAMENT.

2   See the Private Legislation Procedure (Scotland) Act 1936; Erskine May *Parliamentary Practice* (21st Edn, 1989) ch 39; and 19 *Stair Memorial Encyclopaedia* PROVISIONAL ORDERS AND PRIVATE LEGISLATION. If a proposal primarily affects an undertaking or institution carried on in Scotland and also elsewhere, the Private Legislation Procedure (Scotland) Act s 1(4) enables such a proposal to be carried out by a single private bill, thus making unnecessary a private bill for England and a draft order for Scotland. If proposed legislation raises novel and important questions of public policy, the promoters may be required to proceed by private bill procedure: see s 1(2)–(4).

3   See Erskine May *Parliamentary Practice* (21st Edn, 1989) p 965. If an inquiry is held into the proposed order in Scotland, the proceedings resemble those which take place before a private Bill committee in either House. In certain circumstances, a joint committee of both Houses may at a later stage in the procedure be appointed to consider the contents of any order made to give effect to the proposals: see the Private Legislation Procedure (Scotland) Act 1936 s 9; and Erskine May *Parliamentary Practice* (21st Edn, 1989) pp 973–975.

**59.  Civil and criminal courts in Scotland.** Justice in Scotland is administered mainly through the Scottish courts, although certain specialised courts and tribunals exercise jurisdiction throughout the United Kingdom or Great Britain[1]. Superior civil jurisdiction is exercised by the Court of Session, which derives directly from the creation of the College of Justice in 1532[2]. The Court of Session consists of 24 judges, of whom eight sit in the Inner House with a mainly appellate jurisdiction[3], and 15 sit in the Outer House singly at first instance, as Lords Ordinary[4]. These judges, sitting as the Lord Commissioners of Justiciary[5], constitute the High Court of Justiciary, the superior criminal court in Scotland, whose origin dates back to 1672[6]. For the trial of the more serious criminal offences, individual High Court judges sit with a jury, whether in Edinburgh or on circuit in Scotland. The High Court of Justiciary also sits as a Court of Criminal Appeal[7].

The sheriff court has a broad civil and criminal jurisdiction, but is subordinate to the Court of Session and the High Court. The judges who sit in the sheriff court are the sheriffs principal and the sheriffs, who are for the most part full-time judges. As well as its general civil jurisdiction, the sheriff court exercises an extensive jurisdiction relating to public administration and local government, including functions in respect of licensing, social work, mental health, compulsory acquisition, public health and education[8]. However, the sheriff court has no general power of judicial review in respect of local authorities and other public bodies, this jurisdiction being exclusive to the Court of Session[9]. In civil matters, an appeal lies from the sheriff to the sheriff principal and thence to the Inner House of the Court of Session. In criminal matters, trial in the sheriff court may take the form of either solemn procedure, that is to say with a jury, or summary procedure, that is to say by the sheriff or sheriff principal sitting alone[10].

Criminal jurisdiction is also exercised by the district courts, where summary trial takes place before either lay magistrates or a stipendiary magistrate[11].

1   For the history and present jurisdiction of the courts and tribunals in Scotland see 6 *Stair Memorial Encyclopaedia* COURTS AND COMPETENCY. See also Walker *The Scottish Legal System* (6th Edn, 1992).

2   In 1532 the Scottish Parliament caused the King to appoint a college of 15 members with a president 'for the doing and administration of justice in all civil actions': College of Justice Act 1532, c 2, APS II 335. The Court of Session is now governed by the Court of Session Act 1988 (as variously amended, in particular by the Law Reform (Miscellaneous Provisions) (Scotland) Act 1990).

3   Namely, the Lord President with three of the most senior judges, and the Lord Justice Clerk also with three senior judges: Court of Session Act 1988 s 2(2). Progression to the Inner House was formerly by seniority, but vacancies are now filled by a joint appointment made from the Outer House by the Lord President and the Lord Justice Clerk, with the consent of the Secretary of State and after such consultation with other judges as may appear appropriate in particular circumstances: s 2(3) (amended by the Law Reform (Miscellaneous Provisions) (Scotland) Act 1990 s 35(2), Sch 4 para 4). An extra Division in the Inner House may be formed when necessary: Court of Session Act 1988 s 2(3) (as so amended).

4   One judge regularly acts as chairman of the Scottish Law Commission: see the Law Commissions Act 1965 s 2 (amended by the Law Reform (Miscellaneous Provisions) (Scotland) Act 1985 s 59, Sch 4). Temporary judges may be appointed to the Court of Session: see the Law Reform (Miscellaneous Provisions) (Scotland) Act 1990 s 35(3), Sch 4 paras 5–11.

5   See the Criminal Procedure (Scotland) Act 1995 s 1(2).

6   See the Courts Act 1672, c 40, APS VIII 80, 87 (as amended). The existence and jurisdiction of the High Court of Justiciary are now governed by the Criminal Procedure (Scotland) Act 1995. In the High Court of Justiciary, the Lord President of the Court of Session occupies the office of Lord Justice General: see s 1(2); and 6 *Stair Memorial Encyclopaedia* COURTS AND COMPETENCY para 930.

7   Criminal Procedure (Scotland) Act 1995 s 106. In general, for appellate purposes the High Court comprises either the Lord Justice General or the Lord Justice Clerk sitting with two other judges, but if necessary five or more judges may sit to resolve particularly difficult issues. The quorum of the Court is three judges: see ss 103(2), 173(1).

8   For a full list of these functions see 6 *Stair Memorial Encyclopaedia* COURTS AND COMPETENCY paras 1063–1138.

9   *Brown v Hamilton District Council* 1983 SC (HL) 1.

10  See generally 6 *Stair Memorial Encyclopaedia* COURTS AND COMPETENCY. As to solemn and summary procedures see respectively the Criminal Procedure (Scotland) Act 1995 Pts VII, VIII (solemn), and Pts IX, X (summary); and see also 17 *Stair Memorial Encyclopaedia* PROCEDURE paras 641 et seq, 696 et seq respectively.

11  See generally the District Courts (Scotland) Act 1975; and the Criminal Procedure (Scotland) Act 1995 ss 6, 7; and 6 *Stair Memorial Encyclopaedia* COURTS AND COMPETENCY paras 1155–1168.

**60. Appeals to the House of Lords from Scotland.** As a result of the Union of Scotland and England in 1707[1] the House of Lords acquired an appellate jurisdiction from the Court of Session. In the Claim of Right of 1689, a continuing controversy in Scotland had been resolved by a declaration confirming that subjects could protest to the King and Parliament against decisions of the Court of Session[2]. In the absence of express provision in the Treaty of Union for a forum of appeal to replace the Scottish Parliament, the possibility of appealing to the House of Lords from the Court of Session was confirmed in 1709[3]. On criminal matters, however, the House of Lords exercises no appellate jurisdiction in cases coming from Scotland[4].

One qualification for appointment as a Lord of Appeal in Ordinary is for two years to have been a judge of the Court of Session or for 15 years to have been a practising advocate in Scotland or a solicitor entitled to appear in the Court of Session and the High Court of Justiciary[5]. Since the early years of the twentieth century, there has been a strong convention that two Lords of Appeal in Ordinary should be qualified in the law of Scotland[6].

In general, appeals to the House of Lords from the Court of Session are not subject to a requirement of leave[7], but appeals against interlocutory judgments in the Inner House, Court of Session, require leave to be given, either by the Court or the House of Lords, except where the judges in the division are divided on the issue in question[8]. The statement of the House of Lords in 1966 as to the binding effect of the House's decisions[9] applies to appeals from Scotland as it does to appeals from English courts. As the final court of appeal from England and Wales, Scotland and Northern Ireland, the House of Lords has judicial knowledge of all the legal systems in the United Kingdom[10].

1    See paras 51, 53 ante.
2    See the Claim of Right 1689, c 28, APS IX 38, declaring that it was 'the right and privilege of the subjects to protest for remeed of law to the King and Parliament against sentences pronounced by the Lords of Session, providing the same do not stop execution of these sentences'.
3    *Greenshields v Edinburgh Magistrates* (1710) Colles 427, 1 ER 356, HL. The Union with Scotland Act 1706 art XIX (embodying the Treaty of Union art 19) prohibited the courts that sat in Westminster Hall 'or any court of the like nature' from having power to review decisions of the Scottish courts, but this prohibition did not extend to the House of Lords, which did not sit in Westminster Hall and did not resemble the English courts that did. See also Maclean 'The 1707 Union: Scots Law and the House of Lords' in Kiralfy and MacQueen (eds) *New Perspectives in Scottish Legal History* (1984) pp 50–75.
4    *Mackintosh v Lord Advocate* (1876) 2 App Cas 41, HL. See also the Criminal Procedure (Scotland) Act 1995 s 142.
5    See the Appellate Jurisdiction Act 1876 s 6 (as amended); and COURTS vol 10 para 749.
6    See COURTS vol 10 para 749.
7    See the Appellate Jurisdiction Act 1876 s 3(2); and COURTS vol 10 para 741.
8    6 *Stair Memorial Encyclopaedia* COURTS AND COMPETENCY para 829.
9    *Practice Note (Judgment: judicial decision as authority: House of Lords)* [1966] 3 All ER 77, sub nom *Practice Statement (Judicial Precedent)* [1966] 1 WLR 1234, HL.
10   *Cooper v Cooper* (1888) 15 R 21, HL; *Elliot v Joicey* 1935 SC (HL) 57.

**61. The appointment and tenure of judges.** In the sixteenth century, appointment to the College of Justice[1] appears to have been *ad vitam aut culpam* (for life or until misconduct)[2], but between 1660 and 1689 many judges were stated to hold their office at the king's pleasure. The Claim of Right in 1689 declared that 'changing the nature of the judges' gifts *ad vitam aut culpam* into Commissions *durante bene placito*' was contrary to law[3]. This declaration remains the legal basis for the tenure of Court of Session judges today, subject only to the introduction of a retiring age in 1959[4]. Where a sheriff or a sheriff principal is unfit for office by reason of inability, neglect of duty or misbehaviour, his or her appointment may be terminated by the Secretary of State for Scotland, but only upon a report to this effect having been made by the Lord President of the Court of Session and the Lord Justice-Clerk after a joint investigation made by them into the sheriff's fitness or unfitness for office[5].

Appointments to the offices of Lord President and Lord Justice-Clerk are made by the Crown on the recommendation of the Prime Minister, following consultation with the Lord Chancellor, the Secretary of State for Scotland, the Lord Advocate and the current holders of the two offices if available[6]. Other appointments to the Court of Session are made by the Crown on the recommendation of the Secretary of State, following consultation with the Lord Advocate and, in practice, with the Lord President[7]. Sheriffs and sheriffs principal are appointed by the Crown on the recommendation of the Secretary of State, who is advised by the Lord Advocate[8].

1    As to the College of Justice see para 59 text and note 2 ante.
2    6 *Stair Memorial Encyclopaedia* COURTS AND COMPETENCY para 906.
3    Claim of Right 1689, c 28, APS IX 38, art 13.
4    See now the Judicial Pensions Act 1981 (as amended). The retirement age was introduced by the Judicial Pensions Act 1959 s 2, and reduced to 70 by an amendment made by the Judicial Pensions Act 1993 s 26(10), Sch 6 para 3. The statutory provisions (derived from the Act of Settlement) by which the higher judiciary in the English courts hold office during good behaviour subject to a power of removal by the monarch on an address from both Houses of Parliament) have not been extended to the Scottish judiciary. See however *M'Creadie v Thomson* 1907 SC 1176 at 1182. There is no recent instance of a Court of Session judge having been removed from office. As to the citation of the Act of Settlement see para 35 note 3 ante.
5    See the Sheriff Courts (Scotland) Act 1971 s 12. The Secretary of State's order must be made by statutory instrument, subject to annulment in pursuance of a resolution of either House of Parliament: s 12(3)(a). For use of the procedure in 1977 see 939 HC Official Report (5th series), 25 November 1977, written answers col *922*; 940 HC Official Report (5th series), 6 December 1977, written answers col *1288*.
       The issue of a sheriff's inability to perform judicial duties is not confined to physical or mental ability, but includes the assessment of character defects, even though these fall short of misconduct: *Stewart v Secretary of State for Scotland* 1995 SLT 895, Ct of Sess. As to the procedural fairness to be observed by the investigating judges see *Stewart v Secretary of State for Scotland* supra.
6    6 *Stair Memorial Encyclopaedia* COURTS AND COMPETENCY para 929. The former practice by which the Lord Advocate would be appointed Lord President when that office falls vacant has ceased: Edwards *The Attorney General, Politics and the Public Interest* (1984) p 284; and see 5 *Stair Memorial Encyclopedia* CONSTITUTIONAL LAW para 538 note 10.
7    6 *Stair Memorial Encyclopaedia* COURTS AND COMPETENCY para 929. This reference to consultation with the Lord Advocate needs to be compared with other statements of the practice, indicating that it is for the Lord Advocate to make a nomination to the Secretary of State for approval before it is forwarded to the Crown: see para 63 note 11 post.
       The Union with Scotland Act 1706 art XIX (embodying the Treaty of Union art 19) provided as the qualification required of a person appointed to the Court of Session that he should have been a practising Advocate or a Principal Clerk of Session for five years, or a Writer to the Signet for ten years (subject in this case to an examination of his knowledge of Civil Law by the Faculty of Advocates). In practice, considerably longer than five years practice as an advocate has been required and no Writers to the Signet have ever been appointed. Eligibility for appointment to the Court of Session has been extended to sheriffs principal and sheriffs, thus establishing a route by which Scottish solicitors can be appointed to the Court of Session: see the Law Reform (Miscellaneous Provisions) (Scotland) Act 1990 s 35(1), Sch 4 paras 1–3.
8    Sheriff Courts (Scotland) Act 1907 s 11; 6 *Stair Memorial Encyclopaedia* COURTS AND COMPETENCY para 1038.

**62. Specialised courts and tribunals.** There are many specialised courts and tribunals in Scotland with jurisdictions created by social and economic legislation, some of it directly relating to Scotland's distinctive needs. These bodies may be composed exclusively of judges from the Court of Session[1]. On some tribunals with jurisdiction extending beyond Scotland, one or more Court of Session judges are nominated to sit together with judges from the English High Court and lay persons[2]. The Scottish Land Court was created in 1911, with jurisdiction in respect of certain disputes affecting agricultural holdings and crofting land[3], and its legally qualified chairman has the same rank and tenure of office as if he were a judge of the Court of Session[4]. The Court of Lord Lyon King of Arms is a court of law with both administrative and judicial functions in respect of claims to armorial bearings and various heraldic and genealogical matters; the Court's decisions are subject to review in the Court of Session[5].

There are also in Scotland many tribunals, which operate under the same legislation as equivalent tribunals in England and Wales, the sole difference being that the right of appeal on questions of law lies to the Court of Session[6]. Those that are peculiar to Scotland or exist under Scottish legislation include the Lands Tribunal for Scotland[7], the Crofters Commission[8], and children's hearings[9]. The Council on Tribunals, whose chairman and members are appointed jointly by the Lord Chancellor and the Lord Advocate[10], must appoint a Scottish Committee, consisting of two or three members of the Council designated by the Lord Advocate, three or four other persons appointed to the Committee by the Lord Advocate, and also the Parliamentary Commissioner for Administration ex officio[11]. Powers of appointing and removing tribunal chairmen and members which in England and Wales are vested in the Lord Chancellor are in respect of tribunals which sit only in Scotland exercised by the Lord President of the Court of Session[12].

In 1990, the position of Legal Services Ombudsman for Scotland was created; appointment to the office is made by the Secretary of State for Scotland after consultation with the Lord President of the Court of Session[13].

1 Eg (1) the Lands Valuation Appeal Court (constituted by one or three nominated judges), which has jurisdiction over the valuation of land for rating purposes: see 6 *Stair Memorial Encyclopaedia* COURTS AND COMPETENCY paras 938–951; (2) the Registration Appeal Court (two Inner House judges and one Outer House judge): see para 56 text and note 5 ante; and (3) the Election Petition Court (two Court of Session judges): see para 56 text and note 7 ante. On the selection of judges for the Election Petition Court see the Court of Session Act 1988 s 44.

2 Eg the Employment Appeal Tribunal: see EMPLOYMENT vol 16 (Reissue) para 493.

3 See 6 *Stair Memorial Encyclopaedia* COURTS AND COMPETENCY paras 952–980.

4 See the Scottish Land Court Act 1993.

5 6 *Stair Memorial Encyclopaedia* COURTS AND COMPETENCY paras 1010–1021.

6 See the Tribunals and Inquiries Act 1992 s 11(1) (as amended), (7).

7 See 6 *Stair Memorial Encyclopaedia* COURTS AND COMPETENCY paras 1139–1154. The Tribunal was created in 1971 under powers contained in the Lands Tribunal Act 1949 s 10(2), and inter alia has power under the Conveyancing and Feudal Reform (Scotland) Act 1970 to discharge or vary obligations contained in titles to land.

8 Ie the Commission established under the Crofters (Scotland) Act 1993 s 1: see 6 *Stair Memorial Encyclopaedia* COURTS AND COMPETENCY paras 965–968.

9 Created under the Social Work (Scotland) Act 1968: see 6 *Stair Memorial Encyclopaedia* COURTS AND COMPETENCY para 1074.

10 See the Tribunals and Inquiries Act 1992 s 2(1).

11 See ibid s 2(2), (3).

12 See ibid ss 6(1),(8), 7(1)(e).

13 See the Law Reform (Miscellaneous Provisions) (Scotland) Act 1990 s 34, Sch 3.

**63. The Law Officers of the Crown in Scotland.** The Lord Advocate and the Solicitor-General for Scotland hold posts which are comparable with the offices of Attorney-General and Solicitor-General[1], but which are nonetheless distinctive from their English counterparts[2]. Both offices are political appointments made by the Crown on the advice of the Prime Minister, and only members of the Scottish bar are eligible for appointment[3]. When a new Lord Advocate is not already a member of the House of Commons or the House of Lords, it is now customary for him to receive a life peerage[4]. The Lord Advocate is not a member of the Cabinet, but he is admitted to the Privy Council; he attends Cabinet meetings whenever advice on matters of Scots law may be needed[5].

Until the formation of the Scottish Office in 1885[6], the Lord Advocate was the only minister of the Crown with special responsibility for Scottish affairs. The present functions of the office of Lord Advocate include the following: (1) advising and representing the Crown in respect of civil proceedings by and against the Crown in Scottish courts and in maintaining and protecting the Crown's rights and interests in Scotland[7]; (2) responsibility for the prosecution of crimes in the public interest and on behalf of the Crown, exercising this responsibility through advocates depute appointed by him, the Crown Office in Edinburgh and the system of public prosecutors (procurators fiscal) which operates throughout Scotland[8]; (3) responsibility for important aspects of the Scottish legal system, including (a) law reform[9]; (b) legislative drafting[10]; (c) advice on judicial appointments[11]; (d) appointment, jointly with the Lord Chancellor, of the Council on Tribunals and the Council's Scottish Committee[12]. The head of the Scottish bar is the elected Dean of the Faculty of Advocates, not the Lord Advocate, but when the latter appears in court he has seniority over the Dean of Faculty[13].

1 See paras 529–530 post.

2 See Edwards *The Attorney-General, Politics and the Public Interest* (1984) ch 10; 5 *Stair Memorial Encyclopedia* CONSTITUTIONAL LAW paras 509, 535–543; Milne *The Scottish Office* (1957) ch 23.

3 Edwards *The Attorney-General, Politics and the Public Interest* (1984) pp 282–283. As to the Prime Minister see paras 394–398 post.
    When the office of Lord Advocate is vacant or the Lord Advocate is unable to act through absence or illness or he authorises the Solicitor General for Scotland to act in a particular case, any functions authorised or required by an enactment to be discharged by the Lord Advocate may in general be discharged by the Solicitor General for Scotland: Law Officers' Act 1944 s 2(1). This applies as in the case of s 1(1) (as to which see para 529 note 8 post). When the office of Lord Advocate is vacant notices, proceedings etc required to be served on or taken against him may be served on or taken against the Solicitor General for Scotland except in so far as any enactment passed since 13 July 1944 provides to the contrary: s 2(2).
    As to the salaries of the Scottish law officers see the Ministerial and other Salaries Act 1975 s 1(1)(a), Sch 1 Pt III (amended by the Ministerial and other Salaries Order 1996, SI 1996/1913, art 2, Sch 1 Pt III).

4 5 *Stair Memorial Encyclopedia* CONSTITUTIONAL LAW para 371.

5 As to the Cabinet see paras 402–413 post. As to the Privy Council see paras 521–526 post.

6 See para 64 post. The Secretary for Scotland Act 1885 s 9 provided that the creation of the Scottish Office was not to prejudice or interfere with the rights, privileges etc of the Lord Advocate. The Lord Advocate and his department have a very close relationship with the Secretary of State for Scotland and the Scottish Office departments, but neither the Lord Advocate nor his department is part of the Scottish Office.

7 By the Crown Suits (Scotland) Act 1857 s 1, actions raised on behalf of a department of the Crown in Scotland, or directed against a department in Scotland, may be raised at the instance of, or be directed against, the Lord Advocate. Before that Act, it was customary to name in such actions Her Majesty's Officers of State as representing the Crown. However, actions raised against departments of the Scottish Office may be directed directly against the Secretary of State for Scotland: Reorganisation of Offices (Scotland) Act 1939 s 1(8) (amended by the Requirements of Writing (Scotland) Act 1995 s 14(2), Sch 5). As to the Officers of State see 7 *Stair Memorial Encyclopedia* THE CROWN paras 789–851.

8 The Lord Advocate is expected to carry out this responsibility without regard to party political considerations: see the statement by the Prime Minister (Macmillan) 600 HC Official Report (5th series), 16 February 1959, col 31; 5 *Stair Memorial Encyclopaedia* CONSTITUTIONAL LAW para 535. The scope for prosecutions brought at the initiative of the private individuals affected by criminal conduct is very much narrower in Scotland than in English law: see Edwards *The Attorney General, Politics and the Public Interest* (1984) pp 300–309 and in particular *J & P Coats Ltd v Brown* 1909 SC (J) 39; *M'Bain v Crichton* 1961 JC 25; and *H v Sweeney* 1983 SLT 48.

9 In 1972, before which the division of responsibility for law reform in Scotland between the Scottish Office and the Lord Advocate was uncertain, the Lord Advocate acquired important ministerial functions relating to law reform: see 848 HC Official Report (5th series), 21 December 1972, written answers col 456–457. The Lord Advocate acquired responsibility for appointing the Scottish Law Commission (under the Law Commissions Act 1965) as well as law reform responsibilities in relation to such subjects as civil jurisdiction and proceedings, the enforcement of civil judgments, the law of evidence, arbitration and fatal accident inquiries.

10 The drafting of bills applying solely to Scotland and of the Scottish clauses of British and United Kingdom bills is undertaken by Scottish parliamentary draftsmen who are members of the Lord Advocate's Department in London. If the Lord Advocate or Solicitor-General for Scotland is a member of the House of Commons, he may take part in the deliberations of any standing committee of the Commons, but without having voting rights or being counted in the quorum: HC Standing Orders (1995) (Public Business) no 87.

11 Appointments to the Court of Session and to the offices of sheriff principal and sheriff are made by the Crown on the advice of the Secretary of State for Scotland, but by convention the Lord Advocate's nomination is made to the Secretary of State: Edwards *The Attorney General, Politics and the Public Interest*

(1984) p 292 (citing 623 HC Official Report (5th series), 10 May 1960, col 173. Cf para 61 ante; and 6 *Stair Memorial Encyclopedia* COURTS AND COMPETENCY para 929.

12  See para 62 ante.

13  See 13 *Stair Memorial Encyclopaedia* LEGAL PROFESSION para 1302.

**64.  Executive government in Scotland: the Secretary of State and administrative devolution.** The effect of the Union of England and Scotland in 1707[1], taken with the abolition of the Scottish Privy Council in 1708, was that the seat of Scotland's government moved to London. For many years the Lord Advocate occupied the leading role in the management of Scotland. In 1885 the post of Secretary for Scotland was created, with oversight of numerous Scottish boards and local authorities[2]. The Secretary for Scotland joined the Cabinet in 1892, and was elevated to the position of one of His Majesty's Principal Secretaries of State in 1926[3]. In 1939, he acquired direct responsibility for all the Scottish departments of central government[4], apart from the Lord Advocate's Department and the Crown Office[5]. After 1945 additional functions were vested in the Scottish Office[6]. Whereas in England governmental tasks are dispersed between many Whitehall departments on a functional basis, in Scotland they are brought together with some four or five departments being grouped under a single Cabinet minister[7]. In addition to his specific functions, the Secretary of State is responsible for representing the interests of Scotland in the Cabinet and in Whitehall, and has an indirect interest in all matters affecting Scotland. This system of 'administrative devolution[8]' is not accompanied by the devolution of any legislative or political authority to the electorate in Scotland voting as such[9].

1  See paras 51, 53 ante.

2  The Secretary for Scotland Act 1885 and The Secretary for Scotland Act 1887 vested in the Secretary for Scotland many functions including responsibility for public health, local government, poor law and transport. See Milne *The Scottish Office* (1957); Hanham 'The Creation of the Scottish Office 1881–87' 1965 JR 205; and Hanham 'The Development of the Scottish Office' in Wolfe (ed) *Government and Nationalism in Scotland* ch 5; 5 *Stair Memorial Encyclopaedia* CONSTITUTIONAL LAW paras 512, 516–534.

3  Secretaries of State Act 1926 s 1. See also *Agee v Lord Advocate* 1977 SLT (Notes) 54. As to the office of Secretary of State see para 355 et seq post.

4  Reorganisation of Offices (Scotland) Act 1939; and see the *Report of the Committee on Scottish Administration* (Cmd 5563) (1937). This reorganisation affected only departments which were already organised on a Scottish territorial basis. It did not affect ministerial responsibility for departments which operated throughout the United Kingdom or Great Britain, and necessarily had offices in Scotland. Today these departments include the Ministry of Defence, the Commissioners of Inland Revenue, the Commissioners of Customs and Excise, the Department of Social Security and the Home Office (Immigration and Nationality Division).

5  See para 53 ante.

6  See the *Report of the Royal Commission on Scottish Affairs* (Cmd 9212) (1954).

7  In 1978, a change in the public expenditure control system enabled total Scottish Office expenditure (and also Welsh Office expenditure) to be shown in separate territorial programmes, the effect being to allow the Secretary of State greater freedom to allocate funds within the total expenditure and thus to set priorities for public expenditure which might differ from those in England: see McCrone (ed) *Scottish Government Yearbook 1983* ch 8 (R Parry).

8  See the *Report of the Royal Commission on the Constitution 1969–73* (Cmnd 5460) (1973) (the 'Kilbrandon Report') chs 4, 21.

9  Voters in Scotland vote in elections for the United Kingdom Parliament, the European Parliament and Scottish local authorities (as to which see the Local Government (Scotland) Act 1973 (as variously amended) and the Local Government etc (Scotland) Act 1994), but the only occasion on which they have voted as the Scottish electorate was in the devolution referendum in 1979. See para 66 post.

**65.  The Scottish Office.** The Scottish Office has a ministerial team consisting of the Secretary of State for Scotland, a Minister of State, and three Parliamentary Under-Secretaries of State. The Office comprises five departments (together with central services) namely: (1) the Scottish Office Agriculture, Environment and Fisheries

Department; (2) the Scottish Office Development Department; (3) the Scottish Office Education and Industry Department; (4) the Scottish Office Department of Health; and (5) the Scottish Office Home Department[1].

The Scottish Office Agriculture, Environment and Fisheries Department is responsible for agriculture and the fishing industry in Scotland, food hygiene, participation in negotiations on agricultural matters, participation in international agreements for conservation and other aspects of fishing; the department's environmental responsibilities include pollution control, water, forestry[2], rural affairs and the natural heritage. The department is responsible for certain executive agencies, namely, the Scottish Agricultural Science Agency, the Scottish Environment Protection Agency and the Scottish Fisheries Protection Agency[3].

The Scottish Office Development Department's functions include housing and urban regeneration, new towns, local government organisation and finance, town planning and public inquiries, heritage policy and economic infrastructure, including roads, transport and European funds. The department is responsible for one executive agency, Historic Scotland[4].

The Scottish Office Education and Industry Department's functions include the system of public education (including school education, further and higher education), science and technology, youth and community services, the arts, libraries, museums and galleries and, on the industrial side, industrial assistance and business support, industrial policy and investment. The department maintains two executive agencies, the Student Awards Agency for Scotland and the Scottish Office Pensions Agency[5].

The Scottish Office Department of Health is responsible for managing the National Health Service and for public health policy[6].

The Scottish Office Home Department's responsibilities include civil law and legal aid (which is administered by the Scottish Legal Aid Board), fire services, criminal justice, police services, prisons, social work policy and exercise of the Secretary of State's social work functions[7]. The department maintains one executive agency, the Scottish Prison Service.

Associated with the Scottish Office are several minor departments. These include the General Register Office for Scotland (headed by the Registrar General for Scotland), the Registers of Scotland (headed by the Keeper of the Records of Scotland) and the Scottish Courts Administration (headed by the Director of the Scottish Courts Administration). The Scottish Courts Administration is responsible for advising the Secretary of State for Scotland on the performance of the Scottish Courts Service, and is responsible for the central administration pertaiing to the judiciary in the Supreme Court and the Sheriff Court. It is responsible to the Lord Advocate[8] for certain functions in the field of law, the jurisdiction and procedure of civil courts, enforcement of judgments, procedure in statutory inquiries and certian tribunals, the Council on Tribunals and Scottish Committee of that council, and proposals for the reform of law including the programme of the Scottish Law Commission[9].

These departments, together with central services such as the Solicitor's Office, the Information Directorate, and Liaison, Personnel, and Finance divisions are collectively known as the Scottish Office. Associated with the Scottish Office and its departments are numerous non-departmental public bodies, some of which are advisory to the Secretary of State and others of which have executive functions[10].

The Scottish Office is subject to investigation by the Parliamentary Commissioner for Administration[11]. The office's expenses are provided by Parliament[12]. Civil actions by and against the Crown in Scotland are generally undertaken by or against the Lord Advocate, but it is customary in legal proceedings which relate to functions of the Scottish Office for the Secretary of State for Scotland to be named as a party[13].

1    Certain departments which before 1939 had their own existence and powers as corporate entities were abolished by the Reorganisation of Offices (Scotland) Act 1939 s 1(1); their functions were transferred to the Secretary of State, who thereby became free to reorganise the allocation of business within the Scottish Office from time to time. One such reorganisation took place in 1995, when the distribution of functions between the five departments and the names of the departments were revised. The details of departmental functions in this paragraph are derived from the Civil Service Year Book 1996; the Scottish Office Annual Report: *The Government's Expenditure Plans 1995–96 to 1997–98: Serving Scotland's Needs* (Cm 2814) (1995); the *Next Steps Review 1995* (Cm 3164) (1995); and information supplied by the Solicitor to the Secretary of State for Scotland.

2    The Forestry Commission, whose headquarters is located in Edinburgh, is a government department with responsibility for forestry throughout Great Britain. It reports to the Secretary of State for Scotland (who takes the leading ministerial role), the Minister for Agriculture, Fisheries and Food, and the Secretary of State for Wales: Scottish Office Annual Report: *The Government's Expenditure Plans 1995–96 to 1997–98: Serving Scotland's Needs* (Cm 2814) (1995) p 163.

3    See the Civil Service Year Book 1996 col 849.

4    See the Civil Service Year Book 1996 cols 861, 866.

5    See the Civil Service Year Book 1996 col 868.

6    See the Civil Service Year Book 1996 col 856.

7    See the Civil Service Year Book 1996 col 874.

8    See the Civil Service Year Book 1996 col 900.

9    See para 63 ante.

10   For a full list see the official publication *Public Bodies*. As to non-departmental public bodies see para 951 et seq post.

11   Parliamentary Commissioner Act 1967 s 4(1), Sch 2 (as substituted and amended): see PARLIAMENT.

12   *Supply Estimates 1995–96 for the year ending 31 March 1996* (HC Paper (1994–95) no 271–XIV) (includes the Forestry Commision).

13   Reorganisation of Offices (Scotland) Act 1939 s 1(8) (amended by the Requirements of Writing (Scotland) Act 1995 s 14(2), Sch 5); and see paras 55, 63 ante. See also Fraser *Constitutional Law* (2nd Edn, 1948) p 162; and Mitchell *Constitutional Law* (2nd Edn, 1968) p 311.

**66. Legislative and executive devolution.** Political demands within Scotland for greater autonomy through the devolution of legislative and executive functions than is possible under administrative devolution caused the subject of devolution within the United Kingdom to be considered by the Royal Commission on the Constitution between 1969 and 1973[1]. The Commission's majority report recommended the creation of a Scottish Assembly with legislative powers[2]. A scheme on these lines was contained in the Scotland Act 1978[3], which provided for an elected Scottish Assembly with legislative powers and a ministerial executive responsible to the Assembly[4]. However, in a referendum on 1 March 1979, the proposed Assembly received insufficient support from the Scottish electorate to satisfy the requirement in the 1978 Act[5] that 40 per cent of all electors should vote for the Assembly[6]. After the general election in 1979, the Scotland Act was repealed by Order in Council[7].

In November 1995, the Scottish Constitutional Convention, a self-constituted gathering representing certain political parties in Scotland, as well as churches, trade unions, local authorities and other bodies, adopted proposals for a Scottish parliament that would enjoy significantly broader powers than those proposed by the Scotland Act 1978 for the Scottish Assembly[8]. These proposals coincided with a government statement about the government of Scotland which rejected the notion of a Scottish parliament and sought to expand the role of the Scottish Grand Committee[9].

1    *Report of the Royal Commission on the Constitution 1969–73* (Cmnd 5460 and 5460-I) (1973) (the Kilbrandon Report) chs 4, 21.

2    *Report of the Royal Commission on the Constitution 1969–73* (Cmnd 5460 and 5460-I) (1973) ch 24.

3    In the 1976–77 session of Parliament, the Government's Scotland and Wales Bill (proposing legislative devolution for Scotland and executive devolution for Wales) had failed to make progress. In the 1977–78 session, separate bills dealing with Scotland and Wales were introduced and both were enacted (see the Scotland Act 1978 (repealed) and the Wales Act 1978 (repealed)), although neither scheme of devolution came into force apart from the holding of separate devolution referendums in March 1979.

4   For a detailed commentary on the Scotland Act 1978 (repealed) see the annotations contained in *Current Law Statutes 1978*. See also Bogdanor *Devolution* (1979).

5   Scotland Act 1978 s 85(2) (repealed).

6   In the referendum, 32.9% of the electorate voted in favour of devolution, 30.8% voted against, and the remainder did not vote.

7   See 968 HC Official Report (5th series), 20 June 1979, cols 1327–1462.

8   *Scotland's Parliament; Scotland's Right* (November 1995). See also the Scottish Constitutional Convention's *A Claim of Right for Scotland* (March 1989).

9   267 HC Official Report (6th series), 29 November 1995, cols 1228–1242. These proposals were subsequently adopted: 268 HC Official Report (6th Series), 19 December 1995, cols 1408–1433; and see para 57 ante; and Constitution Unit *Scotland's Parliament: Fundamentals for a New Scotland Act* (1996).

## (10) NORTHERN IRELAND

**67. Historical introduction.** The constitutional status of Northern Ireland may be traced back to the Union with Ireland Act 1800[1], which provided that the kingdoms of Great Britain and Ireland should, on 1 January 1801 and for ever after be united as the United Kingdom of Great Britain and Ireland with a single Parliament at Westminster[2]. The Act also provided for Irish representation in the United Kingdom Parliament[3] and united the Church of England and the Church of Ireland into one Protestant Episcopal Church[4]. The Government of Ireland Act 1920 sought a new solution for Ireland by providing that separate parts of the country, to be known as Northern Ireland and Southern Ireland, would have separate parliaments and executives within the United Kingdom[5]. However, that Act never took effect with respect to Southern Ireland (which, as the Irish Free State, was granted dominion status within the British Commonwealth of Nations[6]), but became the constitutional framework within which Northern Ireland was governed from 1921 to 1972, when its Parliament was prorogued by the Northern Ireland (Temporary Provisions) Act 1972, which placed Northern Ireland under a temporary government[7]. All functions belonging to the former Governor, Governor in Council, the government or any minister of Northern Ireland or head of a department of that government were to be exercised by the Secretary of State for Northern Ireland as chief executive officer[8], and the legislative functions of the former Parliament could be exercised by Order in Council[9]. The Parliament was abolished with effect from 18 July 1973[10].

1   Ie the Union with Ireland Act 1800 (adapted to Northern Ireland by the Irish Free State (Consequential Adaptation of Enactments) Order 1923, SR & O 1923/405, made under the Irish Free State (Consequential Provisions) Act 1922 s 6).

    For an outline of Ireland's constitutional history before and after 1800 see 31 Halsbury's Statutes (4th Edn, 1994 Reissue) NORTHERN IRELAND pp 268–271; and Wade and Bradley *Constitutional and Administrative Law* (11th Edn, 1993) pp 41–42, where it is observed that the Union with Ireland Act 1800 did not contain the same constitutional guarantees as those which had been enacted in a different situation with regard to the Union with Scotland in 1707 (see paras 51, 53 ante). For an account of the progress and results of the Home Rule debate, starting with the Home Rule Bill of 1886 see Hadfield *The Constitution of Northern Ireland* (1989) pp 5–43; and McCrudden 'Northern Ireland and the British Constitution' in Jowell and Oliver (eds) *The Changing Constitution* (3rd Edn, 1994) pp 326–330.

2   Union with Ireland Act 1800 Arts 1–3.

3   See the Union with Ireland Act 1800 Art 4. Spiritual representation ceased on the passing of the Irish Church Act 1869 (see note 4 infra). Temporal peers continued to be elected until 1920 and thereafter peers already elected sat during their lives; the last survivor (until 1961) was the Earl of Kilmorey.

    In 1965 12 Irish peers petitioned the House of Lords for a declaration that the peerage of Ireland was entitled to representation, but it was held that the provisions of the Acts of Union relating to the election of Irish representative peers ceased to be effective on the passing of the Irish Free State (Agreement) Act 1922 and that the right to elect Irish representative peers no longer existed: Report by the Committee of Privileges on the Petition of the Irish Peers (1966) HL Sess P(53)67, adopted by the House: 278 HL Official Report (5th series), 24 November 1966, cols 363–364. See also Calvert *Constitutional Law in Northern Ireland* (1968) pp 23, 80–84.

4    Union with Ireland Act 1800 Article 5 (as amended). The Church of Ireland was disestablished by the Irish Church Act 1869 s 2 (repealed). For an unsuccessful attempt to challenge the validity of that Act see *Ex p Canon Selwyn* (1872) 36 JP Jo 54; and Calvert *Constitutional Law in Northern Ireland* (1968) pp 20–21.

5    See generally Hadfield *The Constitution of Northern Ireland* (1989) pp 45–93.

6    See the Irish Free State (Agreement) Act 1922 (repealed) and the Irish Free State (Consequential Provisions) Act 1922, which amended the Government of Ireland Act 1920 in certain necessary respects, as it continued to apply to Northern Ireland. The Irish Free State became Eire in 1938 pursuant to the new Constitution of 1937 and was named the Republic of Ireland on leaving the Commonwealth in 1949: see the Ireland Act 1949 s 1(2) (repealed: now replaced by the Northern Ireland Constitution Act 1973 s 1), which declared that Northern Ireland would in no event cease to be part of Her Majesty's dominions and the United Kingdom without the consent of the Parliament of Northern Ireland.

7    See the Northern Ireland (Temporary Provisions) Act 1972 s 1 (expired on 1 January 1974 on the coming into force of the Northern Ireland Constitution Act 1973 Pt II (ss 4–16): see s 2(4); and the Northern Ireland Constitution (Devolution) Order 1973, SI 1973/2162).

8    Northern Ireland (Temporary Provisions) Act 1972 s 1(1) (expired: see note 7 supra).

9    Ibid s 1(3) (expired: see note 7 supra). The Secretary of State's Department is the Northern Ireland Office; as to the organisation of that office see para 83 post.

10   Northern Ireland Constitution Act 1973 ss 31(1), 43(5).


**68. Status of Northern Ireland since direct rule.** The Parliament of Northern Ireland having been prorogued and then abolished[1], a statutory declaration has been maintained[2] that Northern Ireland[3] remains part of Her Majesty's dominions and of the United Kingdom, and it is affirmed that in no event will Northern Ireland or any part of it cease to be part of Her Majesty's dominions and of the United Kingdom without the consent of the majority of the people of Northern Ireland voting in a poll[4] held for that purpose[5].

The sovereignty of the Parliament of the United Kingdom over Northern Ireland is maintained[6].

Nothing in the Northern Ireland (Temporary Provisions) Act 1972 derogates or authorises anything to be done in derogation from the status of Northern Ireland as part of the United Kingdom[7].

1    See para 67 ante.

2    The declaration was previously contained in the Ireland Act 1949 s 1(2) (repealed).

3    Northern Ireland consists of the parliamentary counties of Antrim, Armagh, Down, Fermanagh, Londonderry and Tyrone and the parliamentary boroughs of Belfast and Londonderry: Government of Ireland Act 1920 s 1(2); Northern Ireland Constitution Act 1973 s 43(2).

4    In a poll held on 8 March 1973 under the Northern Ireland (Border Poll) Act 1972 (repealed), and the Northern Ireland (Border Poll) Order 1973, SI 1973/97 (NI 3) (lapsed), 591,820 voted in favour of Northern Ireland remaining part of the United Kingdom, 6,463 voted in favour of Northern Ireland being joined with the Republic of Ireland outside the United Kingdom; and some 425,800 people (approximately 41.3% of the electorate), abstained: see Hadfield *The Constitution of Northern Ireland* (1989) p 104.

5    Northern Ireland Constitution Act 1973 s 1, Sch 1. A poll may not be held earlier than ten years after the previous such poll: Sch 1 para 1. The Secretary of State may by order direct the holding of such a poll; any such order must make provision as to the persons entitled to vote, the conduct of the poll, the question or questions to be asked, and other provision as appears expedient, including the application of other enactments with respect to parliamentary or Assembly elections: Sch 1 paras 1, 2. An order is made by statutory instrument, but may not be made until a draft has been approved by resolution of each House of Parliament: Sch 1 para 3.

6    Government of Ireland Act 1920 s 75 (amended by the Northern Ireland Constitution Act 1973 s 41(1), Sch 6 Pt I); and see the Northern Ireland Constitution Act 1973 s 4(4).

     The following operative provisions of subsequent legislation of the United Kingdom Parliament may also be noted: Northern Ireland (Miscellaneous Provisions) Act 1932 s 9 (as amended) (sea, shore and tidal waters); Northern Ireland Act 1947 ss 8, 9 (both as amended) (cesser of reservation of registration of deeds and registration of title); Administration of Justice Act 1956 s 55, Sch 1 (as amended) (Admiralty jurisdiction etc, and registration of judgments of courts outside Northern Ireland); Northern Ireland

Act 1962 s 22 (as amended) (land purchase matters), s 24 (backing of warrants); Administration of Justice Act 1969 s 20 (as amended) (orders for interim payment), s 21 (as amended) (powers of court exercisable before commencement of proceedings).

7    Northern Ireland (Temporary Provisions) Act 1972 s 2.

**69. The present constitutional position.** Following a short period of devolved government in 1974[1], Northern Ireland has reverted to direct rule from Westminster under the Northern Ireland Act 1974[2], with provision for devolved government in accordance with the Northern Ireland Constitution Act 1973 and the Northern Ireland Act 1982[3]. The 1982 Act, as well as providing for staged devolution[4], amended earlier legislation, particularly with regard to the executive[5], and abolished statutory consultative committees[6], and altered the machinery for the dissolution and prorogation of the Northern Ireland Assembly ('the Assembly')[7]. Orders in Council can now be made in respect of any reserved matter[8] and they can, if the matter is urgent, be made before they are laid before Parliament[9]. The number of seats in the Assembly has been increased to 85[10]. Disqualification from office of members of, or candidates for election to, the Northern Ireland Assembly is regulated by the Northern Ireland Assembly Disqualification Act 1975[11]. Members of the Assembly are entitled to certain salaries and allowances[12].

Devolved government in accordance with the Northern Ireland Constitution Act 1973 and the Northern Ireland Act 1982 remains as one of the statutory alternatives. The position in the event of devolution is accordingly described in subsequent paragraphs[13].

1    See para 70 post.
2    See para 71 post. See also para 72 post, which describes the government's further proposals for devolution under the Northern Ireland Acts 1974 and 1982.
3    See para 70 et seq post.
4    See para 72 post.
5    See the Northern Ireland Constitution Act 1973 s 8 (as substituted); and para 74 post.
6    See ibid s 26 (as amended); and para 70 note 6 post.
7    See ibid s 27(2)–(4), (6) (as amended); and para 73 post.
8    See ibid s 38(1)(b) (as amended); and para 78 post.
9    See ibid s 38(5) (as amended).
10   See para 70 note 7 post.
11   Ie the Northern Ireland Assembly Disqualification Act 1975 (variously amended by the Northern Ireland Act 1982 s 7(3), Sch 3).
12   See the Northern Ireland Assembly (Pay and Allowances) Order 1984, SI 1984/823 (amended by SI 1986/222).
13   Ie in paras 73–79 post. The relationship with the Republic of Ireland in the event of devolution, as contemplated by the Northern Ireland Constitution Act 1973, is described in para 85 post.

**70. Initial devolution: transferred matters.** If it appeared to the Secretary of State that the Northern Ireland Assembly ('the Assembly') had made satisfactory provision by its standing orders for legislative procedure and the establishment of consultative committees, and that a Northern Ireland Executive could be formed which, having regard to the support it commanded in the Assembly and to the electorate on which that support was based, was likely to be widely accepted throughout the community, so that there was a reasonable basis for the establishment in Northern Ireland of government by consent, he was under a duty to lay before Parliament the draft of an Order in Council declaring what matters should be transferred matters[1], and, if approved by resolution of each House of Parliament, to submit it to Her Majesty in Council, so that an order might be made in terms of the draft[2]. The Northern Ireland Constitution (Devolution) Order 1973[3] appointed 1 January 1974 for the commencement of Part II of the Northern Ireland Constitution Act 1973 (which deals with legislative powers, executive authorities, relations with the Republic of Ireland and financial provisions), and on that day the temporary government came to an end[4].

The 'transferred matters' do not include 'excepted matters[5]' or 'reserved matters[6]'.

A new unicameral legislature had been established with the name 'Northern Ireland Assembly' (the Assembly), to which 78 members had been elected in June 1973[7], and the Secretary of State had nominated the members of an Executive[8]. The Executive and the Assembly proceeded from 1 January 1974 to discharge their functions, but the Assembly was prorogued on 29 May 1974[9] and dissolved on 25 March 1975[10]. The office of Governor of Northern Ireland and the Parliament of Northern Ireland had already ceased to exist[11].

1   Northern Ireland Constitution Act 1973 s 2(1). The Secretary of State may lay a draft Order in Council before Parliament to provide that a matter become, or cease to be, a transferred matter: see s 3(1). In the case of a matter which is a transferred matter, he may not lay a draft before Parliament unless the Assembly has passed a resolution praying that it cease to be a transferred matter: see s 3(2). If the draft laid before Parliament is approved by resolution by each House, the Secretary of State must submit it to Her Majesty in Council for an Order in Council to be made: ss 2(3), 3(3). This will enable new matters to be added to the list of transferred matters as the new regime establishes itself, and without the need for a statute.

2   Ibid s 2(3).

3   Ie the Northern Ireland Constitution (Devolution) Order 1973, SI 1973/2162.

4   Northern Ireland Constitution Act 1973 s 2(4).

5   The 'excepted matters' under ibid s 2(2), Sch 2 (amended by the Northern Ireland Act 1982 s 6, Sch 2 para 9; and the Child Support Act 1991 s 58(13), Sch 5 para 2) are: (1) the Crown, including the succession to the Crown and a regency, but not (a) functions of Northern Ireland executive authorities or functions in relation to Northern Ireland of any minister of the Crown; (b) property belonging to Her Majesty in right of the Crown or belonging to a government department or held in trust for Her Majesty for the purposes of a government department; (c) foreshore or the sea bed or subsoil or their natural resources as far as vested in Her Majesty in right of the Crown; (2) the Parliament of the United Kingdom; parliamentary elections, including the franchise; disqualifications for membership of that Parliament; (3) international relations, including treaties, the making of peace or war and neutrality, and matters connected therewith, but not (a) the surrender of fugitive offenders between Northern Ireland and the Republic of Ireland; (b) the exercise of legislative powers so far as required for giving effect to any agreement or arrangement made under the Northern Ireland Constitution Act 1973 s 12; (c) the exercise of legislative powers for any of the purposes mentioned in the European Communities Act 1972 s 2(2)(a) or (b), or for purposes similar to those of any of ss 5–12 (as amended), or any paragraph of Sch 4); (4) the armed forces of the Crown but not any matter within the Northern Ireland Constitution Act 1973 ss 2(2)(b), 3(2), Sch 3 para 3 (see note 6 infra); (5) dignities and titles of honour; (6) treason and treason felony, but not powers of arrest or criminal procedure in respect of it; (7) nationality; immigration; aliens as such; (8) taxes for the time being levied under any law applying to the United Kingdom as a whole, existing Northern Ireland taxes (ie any of the following taxes levied in Northern Ireland before 1 January 1974, namely estate duty, stamp duty, general betting duty, pool betting duty, duty on gaming machine licences and duty on licences in respect of mechanically-propelled vehicles), and taxes substantially of the same character as any of those taxes; (9) the appointment and removal of Northern Ireland Supreme Court judges, county court judges, recorders, resident magistrates, justices of the peace, members of juvenile court panels, coroners, the chief and other national insurance commissioners for Northern Ireland, the chief and other child support commissioners for Northern Ireland and the president and other members of the Lands Tribunal for Northern Ireland; (10) the appointment and office of the Director and deputy Director of Public Prosecutions for Northern Ireland; (11) elections, including the franchise, in respect of the Northern Ireland Assembly and local authorities; (12) coinage, legal tender and bank notes; (13) the National Savings Bank; (14) special powers and other provisions for dealing with terrorism or subversion; (15) without prejudice to heads (10) and (11) supra, any matter for which provision is made by the Northern Ireland Assembly Act 1973, or the Northern Ireland Constitution Act 1973, the Northern Ireland Act 1974 or the Northern Ireland Act 1982, but not (a) matters in respect of which it is stated by the Northern Ireland Constitution Act 1973 that provision may be made by Measure; or (b) matters specified in Sch 3 (see note 6 infra). Head (15) is not to be taken to apply to any matters by reason only that provision is made in respect of it by an Order in Council under s 6(4) or (5), s 38 or s 39, or under the Northern Ireland Act 1974 Sch 1 para 1: Northern Ireland Constitution Act 1973 Sch 2 para 15 (as amended).

6   Ibid s 3(4), Sch 3. Cf para 74 post.
    The minimum 'reserved matters' under the Northern Ireland Constitution Act 1973 Sch 3 (amended by the Judicature (Northern Ireland) Act 1978 s 122(2), Sch 7 Pt I; the British Telecommunications Act 1981 ss 87, 89, Sch 3 Pt II para 57(2), Sch 6 Pt II; the Broadcasting Act 1990 s 203(1), Sch 20 para 19;

and the Trustee Savings Banks Act 1985 ss 4(3), 7(3), Sch 4), are: (1) any such property as is mentioned in the Northern Ireland Constitution Act 1973 Sch 2 para 1(b) (see head (1)(b) in note 5 supra), but not as respects any aerodrome or harbour; (2) all matters, other than those specified in Sch 2 para 9 (see head (9) in note 5 supra), relating to the Supreme Court of Judicature of Northern Ireland, county courts, courts of summary jurisdiction (including magistrates' courts and juvenile courts) and coroners, including procedure, evidence, appeals, juries, costs, legal aid and the registration, execution and enforcement of judgments and orders, but not (a) bankruptcy, insolvency, the winding up of corporate and unincorporated bodies or the making of arrangements or compositions with creditors; (b) the regulation of the profession of solicitors; (3) without prejudice to heads (4), (5) and (6) infra, the maintenance of public order including the conferring of powers, authorities, privileges or immunities for that purpose on constables, members of the armed forces of the Crown and other persons, but not any matter within Sch 2 para 14 (see head (14) in note 5 supra); (4)(a) the criminal law, including the creation of offences and penalties; (b) the prevention and detection of crime and powers of arrest and detention in connection with crime or criminal proceedings; (c) prosecutions; (d) the treatment of offenders (including children and young persons, and mental health patients, involved in crime) (this head includes, in particular, prisons and other institutions for treatment or detention); (e) the surrender of fugitive offenders between Northern Ireland and the Republic of Ireland; (f) compensation out of public funds for victims of crime; (5) the establishment, organisation and control of the Royal Ulster Constabulary and of any other police force; the Police Authority for Northern Ireland; traffic wardens; (6) firearms and explosives; (7) disqualification for membership of the Northern Ireland Assembly; privileges, powers and immunities of the Assembly, its members and committees greater than those conferred by s 26(1) (as amended); (8) the exercise of legislative powers so far as required for giving effect to any agreement etc made under s 12; (9) trade with any place outside the United Kingdom, but not (a) the furtherance of the trade of Northern Ireland or the protection of traders in Northern Ireland against fraud; (b) services in connection with, or the regulation of the quality, insurance, transport, marketing or identification of agricultural or food products, including livestock; (c) the prevention of disease or the control of weeds and pests; (d) aerodromes and harbours; (10) navigation, including merchant shipping, but not harbours or inland waters; (11) the foreshore and the sea bed and subsoil and their natural resources (except so far as affecting harbours); submarine pipe-lines, submarine cables, including any land line used solely for the purpose of connecting one submarine cable with another; (12) civil aviation, but not aerodromes; (13) postal services, including the issue, transmission and payment of money and postal orders issued by the Post Office; designs for postage stamps; (14) telecommunications; (15) wireless telegraphy and the provision of programme services within the meaning of the Broadcasting Act 1990; (16) domicile; (17) nuclear installations; (18) trade marks, designs, copyright and patent rights; (19) units of measurement and United Kingdom primary standards; (20) oaths, undertakings in lieu of oaths and declarations other than those excepted from the Northern Ireland Constitution Act 1973 s 21(1) by s 21(3); (21) civil defence; (22) the Emergency Powers Act (Northern Ireland) 1926 or any enactment for similar purposes.

7　See the Northern Ireland Assembly Act 1973. The Assembly was prorogued and dissolved (see the text and notes infra); and a subsequent Assembly was elected and also dissolved in 1986: see para 72 post.

　　It is now provided that the Assembly is to consist of 85 members: s 1(1) (amended by the Parliamentary Constituencies (Northern Ireland) Order 1982, SI 1982/1838, art 3(1)), but no election to the Assembly has been held since that change took effect. The constituencies for which members are to be returned to the Assembly are specified in the Northern Ireland Assembly Act 1973 s 1(2), Schedule (substituted by the Parliamentary Constituencies (Northern Ireland) Order 1982 art 3(2)). Proceedings of the Assembly are not invalidated by a vacancy in their membership: Northern Ireland Assembly Act 1973 s 1(4).

　　As to the procedure on an election to the Assembly see ss 2, 4 (both as amended). As to disqualification for membership of the Assembly see s 3 (as amended); and the Northern Ireland Assembly Disqualification Act 1975.

8　As to the power of the Secretary of State to appoint members of the Northern Ireland Executive under the Northern Ireland Constitution Act 1973 see para 74 post.

9　Northern Ireland Assembly (Prorogation) Order 1974, SI 1974/926, made under the Northern Ireland Constitution Act 1973 s 27(6) as originally enacted. Prorogation was precipitated by the Ulster Workers' Council strike in protest against the Sunningdale Agreement (see para 85 post), and by the resignation on 28 May 1974, of the Unionist members of the Executive.

10　Northern Ireland Assembly (Dissolution) Order 1975, SI 1975/422, made under the Northern Ireland Act 1974 s 1(1).

11　Northern Ireland Constitution Act 1973 ss 31, 32 (as originally enacted), which came into force on 1 September 1973: Northern Ireland Constitution Act 1973 (Commencement No 1) Order 1973, SI 1973/1418. The Northern Ireland Constitution Act 1973 s 32(3) provided that there were to be no further appointments to the Privy Council of Northern Ireland which had been created by the Irish Free State (Consequential Provisions) Act 1922 Sch 1. As to the Secretary of State for Northern Ireland see para 83 post.

**71. Direct rule in Northern Ireland since 1974.** On the dissolution of the Northern Ireland Assembly ('the Assembly') on 25 March 1975[1], direct rule was reintroduced by bringing into force temporary provisions for the government of Northern Ireland[2]. These provisions are expressed to have effect during the interim period[3], which was originally one year from the passing of the Act[4], but may be continued by order[5] for periods of up to one year from the end of the previous such period[6].

Under these temporary provisions Her Majesty may by Order in Council make laws for Northern Ireland and, in particular, provision for any matter for which the Northern Ireland Constitution Act 1973 authorises or requires provision to be made by Measure of the Northern Ireland Assembly[7]. During the interim period no person is to hold office under the Northern Ireland Constitution Act 1973[8], and any functions of the Head of a Northern Ireland department[9] may be discharged by that department subject to the discretion and control of the Secretary of State[10].

The functions of local government are performed by district councils[11] and Northern Ireland continues, as before direct rule, to be represented in the Parliament of the United Kingdom[12].

1 See para 70 text and note 10 ante.
2 Ie the Northern Ireland Act 1974 s 1(3), Sch 1.
3 Ibid s 1(3).
4 Ie one year from 17 July 1974: ibid s 1(4).
5 The power to make such an order is exercisable by statutory instrument, but no order may be made unless a draft has been approved by a resolution of each House of Parliament: ibid s 1(6).
6 Ibid s 1(4), (5). The interim period has been renewed annually by order. At the date of publication, the most recent such order is the Northern Ireland Act 1974 (Interim Period Extension) Order 1996, SI 1996/1748, made on 2 July 1996, extending the interim period until 16 July 1997.
7 Northern Ireland Act 1974 Sch 1 para 1. Such an Order in Council is Northern Ireland legislation for the purpose of the Interpretation Act 1978: see ss 5, 23(4), 24(5)(e), Sch 1. No Measure may be passed by the Assembly during the interim period: Northern Ireland Act 1974 Sch 1 para 1(1)(a). The power to make an Order in Council includes power to vary or revoke a previous Order in Council: Sch 1 para 1(3).

    No recommendation may be made to Her Majesty to make an Order in Council containing a provision in relation to which the Secretary of State would be precluded by the Northern Ireland Constitution Act 1973 s 5(1) (see para 76 post) from giving his consent if it were contained in a proposed measure: Northern Ireland Act 1974 Sch 1 para 1(2). No recommendations to Her Majesty to make an Order in Council may be made unless either a draft has been approved by resolution of each House of Parliament, or the order declares that it was made without a draft by reason of urgency: see Sch 1 para 1(4). An Order in Council made without being approved must subsequently be laid before each House of Parliament, and ceases to have effect if not approved by resolution within 45 days (but without prejudice to anything done during that period: see Sch 1 para 1(5), (6).
8 Ie under the Northern Ireland Constitution Act 1973 s 8 (as substituted: see para 74 post): Northern Ireland Act 1974 Sch 1 para 2(1)(a).
9 The Ministries of Northern Ireland Act (Northern Ireland) 1921 s 1, Sch 1 (both as amended) established (with other ministries now abolished) the Ministry of Finance for Northern Ireland, the Ministry of Agriculture for Northern Ireland and the Ministry of Education for Northern Ireland. By the Ministries Act (Northern Ireland) 1944 s 1 the Ministry of Health and Local Government was established. By the Ministries Act (Northern Ireland) 1946 s 2(1) the name of the Ministry of Labour was changed to the Ministry of Labour and National Insurance. By the Ministries (Transfer of Functions and Adaptation of Enactments) Order (Northern Ireland) 1964, SR & O (NI) 1964/67, certain functions of the Ministry of Health and Local Government were transferred to the Ministry of Education and by the Ministries (Transfer of Functions) (No 2) Order (Northern Ireland) 1964, SR & O (NI) 1964/205, the names of the Ministry of Health and Local Government and the Ministry of Labour and National Insurance were changed to the Ministry of Development and the Ministry of Health and Social Services respectively; and certain functions of the Ministry of Finance, the Ministry of Health and Local Government, the Ministry of Home Affairs and the Ministry of Labour and National Insurance were transferred to the Ministry of Agriculture, the Ministry of Health and Social Services, the Ministry of Development and the Ministry of Education respectively. By the Ministries (Northern Ireland) Order 1973, SI 1973/2161 (NI 24), the Ministry of Home Affairs was abolished and there were established the Ministry of the Environment for Northern Ireland and the Ministry of Manpower Services for Northern Ireland (the name of which was

changed to the Department of Economic Development by the Departments (No 2) (Northern Ireland) Order 1982, SI 1982/846) (NI 11).

The Northern Ireland Constitution Act 1973 s 7(5) provided that the Northern Ireland Ministries existing on the appointed day (1 January 1974: see ss 2, 43(2); Northern Ireland Constitution (Devolution) Order 1973, SI 1973/2162) were to become known as departments instead of ministries. See the Northern Ireland Constitution Act 1973 Sch 5 para 8. By the Departments (Northern Ireland) Order 1982, SI 1982/338, (NI 6), the Department of Finance was renamed the Department of Finance and Personnel.

10  Northern Ireland Act 1974 Sch 1 para 2(1)(b), (2). The functions of any other person appointed under the Northern Ireland Constitution Act 1973 s 8 (as substituted) may be discharged by the Secretary of State: Northern Ireland Act 1974 Sch 1 para 2(1)(b). Similarly, anything required to be done to or in relation to the head of a Northern Ireland department or other appointed person during the interim period may be done to or in relation to the substituted authority: see Sch 1 para 2(3). Instruments and enactments are accordingly amended: see Sch 1 para 2(4).

If action by or in relation to the Assembly is required by any enactment as a condition of taking any step or of the coming of anything into operation, during the interim period the step may be taken or the thing may come into operation without the action specified: see Sch 1 para 3(1)–(3). Provisions requiring the laying of documents before the Assembly, or the passing of a resolution or motion or the presentation of an address by the Assembly, do not have effect during the interim period: see Sch 1 para 3(4), (5). No instrument made during the interim period may be annulled or revoked by any action of the Assembly, which may take no proceedings on such an instrument: see Sch 1 para 3(6), (7). During the interim period, alternative provision is made for the making of reports or complaints in relation to the Parliamentary Commissioner and the Commissioner for Complaints, and specified accounts and reports which would otherwise be required to be laid before the Assembly must instead be laid before the House of Commons: see Sch 1 paras 4, 5.

See further para 83 post; and McCrudden 'Northern Ireland and the British Constitution' in Jowell and Oliver (eds) *The Changing Constitution* (3rd Edn, 1994) p 342.

11  Local government powers are limited since the reorganisation, shortly before the reintroduction of direct rule, of local government, which implemented *Local Government in Northern Ireland* (Cmnd 546) (1970) (the Macrory Report); and involved the abolition of county councils. Many former local government functions are discharged by statutory boards, such as Education and Library Boards, Health and Social Services Boards and the Northern Ireland Housing Executive.

12  Northern Ireland is represented by 17 members of Parliament: Parliamentary Constituencies Act 1986 s 3, Sch 2 para 1(4).

**72.  Devolutionary proposals: the Constitutional Convention and the Northern Ireland Act 1982.** The Northern Ireland Act 1974, as well as legislating for the government of Northern Ireland during the interim period, provided for the election and holding in Northern Ireland of a Convention (a 'Constitutional Convention'[1]) for the purpose of considering what provision for the government of Northern Ireland was likely to command the most widespread acceptance throughout the community there[2]. It was provided that 78 members were to be elected in the same manner as the Northern Ireland Assembly, with a non-voting chairman appointed by Her Majesty and the Convention was to report to the Secretary of State, who would lay the report before Parliament[3].

A new Northern Ireland Assembly ('the Assembly') was elected on 20 October 1982[4], and 60 members took their seats[5].

The Northern Ireland Act 1982[6] provided for the Assembly to make proposals for the general or partial suspension of direct rule, if those proposals had the support of 70 per cent of the members of the Assembly or if they had the support of a majority and the Secretary of State notified the Assembly that he was satisfied that the substance of the proposals was likely to command widespread acceptance throughout the community[7]. Direct rule could then be suspended either generally or partially[8]. Pending general suspension of direct rule, the Assembly was to consider and report on any matter affecting Northern Ireland which was not an excepted matter[9], including proposals referred to it by the Secretary of State, and report on any matter considered by it[10]. The Assembly was also to set up committees in relation to the Northern Ireland departments under the control of the Secretary of State[11]. The Assembly was dissolved on 23 June 1986[12].

1    Northern Ireland Act 1974 long title.
2    Ibid s 2, Sch 2 (repealed).
3    Ibid Sch 2. An election was held on 1 May 1975 and the Convention met on 8 May 1975 under the chairmanship of the Lord Chief Justice of Northern Ireland. It produced a majority report which the Secretary of State laid before Parliament on 20 November 1975 but which he stated to Parliament on 12 January 1976 to be unacceptable because it did not 'command sufficiently widespread acceptance throughout the community to provide stable and effective government'. In the hope of further progress, the Secretary of State reconvened the Convention on 3 February 1976, but agreement was not attained and, following a statement to Parliament by the Secretary of State on 5 March 1976 the Convention was dissolved on 6 March 1976 by the Northern Ireland Constitutional Convention (Dissolution) Order 1976, SI 1976/349. See also Hadfield *The Constitution of Northern Ireland* (1989) pp 126–130.
4    See the Northern Ireland Constitution Act 1973 s 27(7) (as amended); the Northern Ireland Act 1974 s 1(1); and the Northern Ireland Assembly (Day of Election) Order 1982, SI 1982/1078.
5    These members performed functions under the Northern Ireland Act 1982 ss 3, 4 (see text and notes 10–11 infra): see Hadfield *The Constitution of Northern Ireland* (1989) pp 155–172.
6    See generally Hadfield *The Constitution of Northern Ireland* (1989) pp 151–177; Hadfield 'The Northern Ireland Act 1982 - Do-It-Yourself Devolution?' (1982) 33 NILQ pp 301–325; Maguire *The Northern Ireland Act 1982*; Gearty *The Northern Ireland Act 1982*.
7    See the Northern Ireland Act 1982 s 1. As to direct rule see para 71 ante.
8    See ibid s 2.
9    As to excepted matters see para 70 note 5 ante; applied by ibid s 7(2).
10   See ibid s 3.
11   See ibid s 4.
12   Northern Ireland Act 1982 s 5(1); Northern Ireland Assembly (Dissolution) Order 1986, SI 1986/1036.

**73. Legislative powers.** In the event of devolution, legislative powers of the Northern Ireland Assembly ('the Assembly') are to be exercised by Measures passed by the Assembly and approved by Her Majesty in Council[1].

The Northern Ireland Assembly is to consist of 85 members[2] elected on the principle of proportional representation, each vote in the poll being a single transferable vote[3]. The Assembly must make standing orders for regulating its procedure[4]. Each Assembly lasts for four years[5]. It may otherwise be dissolved by Order in Council if its composition appears such that it is not possible to make acceptable Executive appointments from among members of the Assembly[6] and it is in the public interest to dissolve the Assembly[7]. Additionally, the Assembly may be prorogued or further prorogued by Order in Council[8].

A Measure is to have the same force and effect as an Act of the Parliament of the United Kingdom[9], and may amend or repeal any provision made by or under any Act of Parliament in so far as it is part of the law of Northern Ireland[10]. A Measure is not invalid by reason of any failure to comply with certain provisions governing the submission of it for approval by Her Majesty in Council; and no act or omission under any of those provisions is to be called in question in any legal proceedings[11].

1    Northern Ireland Constitution Act 1973 s 4(1), (2); Northern Ireland Constitution (Devolution) Order 1973, SI 1973/2162. For restrictions on legislative powers see para 70 notes 5–6 ante.
2    See para 70 text and note 7 ante. Provision with respect to the first election to the Assembly was made by the Northern Ireland Assembly Elections Order 1973, SI 1973/890.
3    See the Northern Ireland Assembly Act 1973 s 2(3). As to the procedure and conduct of elections under that Act see s 2(4)–(6) (amended by the Northern Ireland Act 1982 s 7(3), Sch 3); the Northern Ireland Assembly (Bye-Elections) Order 1974, SI 1974/545; and the Northern Ireland Assembly (Election) Order 1982, SI 1982/1135 (as amended).
4    Northern Ireland Constitution Act 1973 s 25(1). Those standing orders must include provision for (1) general debate of a proposed Measure with an opportunity to vote on its general principles; (2) the consideration of, and an opportunity to vote on, the details of a proposed Measure; and (3) a final stage at which a proposed Measure can be passed or rejected, but not amended; (4) the procedure to be adopted when the Secretary of State withholds consent to a proposed Measure or refers the Measure back for further consideration; (5) the examination by a committee of the Assembly of the manner in which moneys charged on or appropriated out of the Consolidated Fund of Northern Ireland have been applied: s 25(2), (3), (8). The Secretary of State may give directions pending the making of standing orders: s 25(9).

5    See ibid s 27(2)–(4) (substituted by the Northern Ireland Act 1982 s 6, Sch 2 para 5).

6    Ie appointments under the Northern Ireland Constitution Act 1973 s 8 (as amended), which comply with the requirements of s 8(4) (as so amended) (see para 74 post).

7    See ibid s 27(5). In this event a day may be appointed by Order in Council for the election of a new Assembly: see s 27(7) (amended by the Northern Ireland Act 1982 Sch 3). As to the making of Orders in Council under these provisions see s 27(8), (9).

8    Ibid s 27(6) (substituted by the Northern Ireland Act 1982 Sch 2 para 5). As to the making of Orders in Council under this provision see s 27(8), (10).

9    Northern Ireland Constitution Act 1973 s 4(3), which is expressed to be subject to s 17 (discriminatory provisions void: see para 80 post).

10    Ibid s 4(4), which is expressed to be subject to s 17 (see para 80 post). This does not affect the power of the Parliament of the United Kingdom to make laws for Northern Ireland: s 4(4).

11    Ibid s 4(5).

**74. Executive authorities.** The executive power in Northern Ireland is to continue to be vested in Her Majesty[1]. As respects transferred matters[2], the Secretary of State, as Her Majesty's principal officer in Northern Ireland, is to exercise on Her Majesty's behalf such prerogative or other executive powers of Her Majesty in relation to Northern Ireland as she may delegate to him[3]. The powers so delegated are to be exercised through the members of the Northern Ireland Executive and the Northern Ireland departments[4].

The Secretary of State may appoint[5] persons to be heads of the Northern Ireland departments and persons to discharge such other functions as he may determine[6] and may appoint all or any of such persons to be members of the Northern Ireland Executive and, if he thinks fit, one of these persons to preside over the Executive as Chief Executive member[7]. The total number holding appointments is not to exceed 13 but the Secretary of State may by order increase that number[8]. The appointments are to be made from among the members of the Assembly[9] and are to be such as will in the opinion of the Secretary of State command widespread acceptance throughout the community[10].

The Attorney General for England and Wales continues to be by virtue of that office also Attorney General for Northern Ireland[11].

Arrangements may be made between any department of the government of the United Kingdom and any Northern Ireland department for any functions of one of them to be discharged by, or by officers of, the other[12].

1    Northern Ireland Constitution Act 1973 s 7(1).

2    For the purposes of the Northern Ireland Constitution Act 1973 'transferred matters' are all matters other than those specified in Schs 2, 3 (as amended): see ss 2(2), 3(4), 43(2), Schs 2, 3 (as amended); and the Northern Ireland Constitution (Devolution) Order 1973, SI 1973/2162. See para 70 notes 5, 6 ante.

3    Northern Ireland Constitution Act 1973 s 7(2).

4    Ibid s 7(3) (amended by the Northern Ireland Constitution (Amendment) Act 1973 s 1(2)). As to the members of the Northern Ireland Executive see text and notes 5–7 infra. As to the Northern Ireland departments see para 71 note 9 ante. The Secretary of State, as Her Majesty's principal officer in Northern Ireland, the members of the Northern Ireland Executive, any other persons appointed under s 8 (as amended) and the Northern Ireland departments are known as Northern Ireland executive authorities: s 7(6).

5    Before making any appointment (other than as described in note 9 infra) the Secretary of State must, so far as practicable, consult with the parties represented in the Assembly and take into account proposals submitted under the Northern Ireland Act 1982 s 1 (suspension of direct rule): Northern Ireland Constitution Act 1973 s 8(7) (s 8(1)–(7) substituted by the Northern Ireland Act 1982 s 6, Sch 2 para 1). Persons appointed hold office during Her Majesty's pleasure: Northern Ireland Constitution Act 1973 s 8(8). Every person appointed must take the oath (or affirm) as prescribed by Sch 4: s 8(10).

6    Ibid s 8(1) (as substituted: see note 5 supra).

7    Ibid s 8(2) (as substituted: see note 5 supra).

As to the payment of salary, allowances and pension contributions see s 9; the Executive and Other Salaries (Northern Ireland) Order 1973, SI 1973/2159; and the Assembly Pensions (Northern Ireland) Order 1976, SI 1976/1779 (amended by SI 1984/358).

8    Northern Ireland Constitution Act 1973 s 8(3) (as substituted: see note 5 supra).

9    Two of the persons holding appointments may be persons not appointed from members of the Assembly, but only one such person may be head of a department: s 8(5) (as substituted: see note 5 supra). A person appointed who is not a member of the Assembly may sit and speak at the assembly, but not vote: s 8(8). A person appointed from among the members of the Assembly may not hold office for more than six months after ceasing to be a member of the Assembly: s 8(8).

10   Ibid s 8(4) (as substituted: see note 5 supra). If it is not possible to make an appointment complying with this requirement the Secretary of State may make an appointment which does not so comply, but the person appointed must not hold office for more than six months: s 8(6).

11   See ibid s 10(1); and para 530 post. The Solicitor General for England and Wales may act as deputy for the Attorney General, or where the office of Attorney General is vacant: see s 10(2), (3).

12   Ibid s 11(1). No such arrangements affect the responsibility of the department on whose behalf the functions are discharged: s 11(2).

**75. Other law officers.** In addition to the Attorney General for Northern Ireland[1], there are a Director of Public Prosecutions for Northern Ireland[2], and a Crown Solicitor for Northern Ireland[3].

1    See para 74 ante.
2    See the Prosecution of Offences (Northern Ireland) Order 1972, SI 1972/538 (NI 1); and the Northern Ireland Constitution Act 1973 s 34.
3    See ibid s 35. The Crown Solicitor for Northern Ireland is appointed by the Attorney General for Northern Ireland: s 35(1).

**76. Proposed measures dealing with excepted or reserved matters.** The consent of the Secretary of State is required in relation to a proposed Measure which contains any provision dealing with an excepted matter[1] or reserved matter[2]; and he may not give his consent where a provision deals with an excepted matter unless he considers it to be ancillary to other provisions dealing with reserved or transferred matters[3]. If he withholds consent he must refer the Measure back to the Assembly for further consideration[4].

A proposed Measure to which the Secretary of State has consented is not to be submitted by him to Her Majesty in Council until he has first laid it before Parliament, and, either (1) no notice of a motion[5] praying that it shall not be submitted for approval has been given within 20 sitting days; or (2) such a motion has been rejected or withdrawn[6].

1    As to excepted matters see para 70 note 5 ante.
2    As to reserved matters see para 70 note 6 ante.
3    See the Northern Ireland Constitution Act 1973 s 5(1), (7). As to transferred matters see para 70 ante. As to the procedure on dealing with proposed Measures introduced in the Northern Ireland Assembly ('the Assembly') see s 5(2)–(4). The Secretary of State is not to submit to Her Majesty in Council any Measure dealing with an excepted or reserved matter which has not been referred to him unless he consents to the Measure: s 5(5).
4    Ibid s 5(6). If the Measure is modified by the Assembly and transmitted again to the Secretary of State, s 5(5) (see note 3 supra) applies as if it were a new Measure: s 5(6).
5    The notice of motion must be signed by not less than 20 members of the House in which it is given: ibid s 6(6).
6    Ibid s 6(1), (7). This provision is not to apply if the Secretary of State considers that (1) the proposed Measure does not contain provisions (other than ancillary provisions) dealing with excepted or reserved matters; or (2) by reason of urgency the measure should be submitted to Her Majesty in Council without first being laid before Parliament, but in that case an analogous procedure is provided for moving its repeal subsequently: see s 6(2)–(5).

**77. Financial provisions.** Provisions similar to those in force in the United Kingdom govern the operation and audit of the Consolidated Fund of Northern Ireland[1], and require a recommendation from the head of the Department of Finance for Measures dealing with the raising and spending of public money[2].

A sum equal to the Northern Ireland share of United Kingdom taxes, to be determined in respect of each year by the Treasury, is to be charged on and paid out of the Consolidated Fund of the United Kingdom into the Consolidated Fund of Northern Ireland[3], and the Secretary of State may from time to time pay out of money provided by Parliament into the Consolidated Fund of Northern Ireland such sums by way of grant as he may with the consent of the Treasury determine and may, in connection with any such payment, impose such conditions as he may with the like consent determine[4].

1    See the Northern Ireland Constitution Act 1973 s 13(1)–(3). Section 13(1) abolished the Exchequer of Northern Ireland. Subject to that, these financial provisions are to be read with the Exchequer and Audit Act (Northern Ireland) 1921 and the Exchequer and Financial Provisions Act (Northern Ireland) 1950. As to the operation of the Consolidated Fund in the United Kingdom see para 711 et seq post.

2    See the Northern Ireland Constitution Act 1973 s 14. As to loans to the Consolidated Fund of Northern Ireland see the Northern Ireland (Loans) Act 1975.

3    See ibid s 15(1), (5). The Northern Ireland share of United Kingdom taxes is determined by the Treasury under s 15(2)–(4), (6) and regulations made thereunder: see the Northern Ireland (Share of United Kingdom Taxes) Regulations 1975, SI 1975/1313 (amended by SI 1983/1599; and SI 1988/1667); and the Northern Ireland (Share of United Kingdom Taxes) (National Insurance Surcharge) Regulations 1977, SI 1977/1879.

4    Northern Ireland Constitution Act 1973 s 16(1). As to the Treasury see paras 512–517 post.

**78. Power to legislate by Order in Council.** Her Majesty may by Order in Council, approved by resolution of each House of Parliament, make provision with respect to elections (but not the franchise) and boundaries in respect of local authorities in Northern Ireland, and any reserved matters[1], and generally make such provision, including provision amending the law of any part of the United Kingdom, as appears to Her Majesty to be necessary or expedient in consequence of, or for giving full effect to, the Northern Ireland Constitution Act 1973, or any order under that Act[2] relating to devolved responsibilities[3].

Provision may be made for the payment of sums into or out of the Consolidated Fund or the Consolidated Fund of Northern Ireland, or for sums to be paid out of money provided by Parliament or money appropriated by Measure[4].

1    See the Northern Ireland Constitution Act 1973 s 38 (amended by the Northern Ireland Act 1982 ss 6, 7(3), Sch 2 para 6, Sch 3).

2    Ie under the Northern Ireland Constitution Act 1973 s 3: see para 70 note 1 ante.

3    See ibid s 39(1). As to provisions for transferring functions relating to reserved or excepted matters (see para 70 notes 5–6 ante) see s 39(2), (4), (5), (8); and the Northern Ireland (Modification of Enactments - No 1) Order 1973, SI 1973/2163. This provision extends to the Northern Ireland Act 1982 and any order made thereunder: Sch 2 para 8. Provision may also be made for the transfer of property, rights and liabilities, and the substitution of any authority for any other authority in a document, and transitional or consequential matters: Northern Ireland Constitution Act 1973 s 39(7).

4    Ibid s 39(6). See also para 77 ante. As to the Consolidated Fund of the United Kingdom see para 711 et seq post.

**79. Maintenance of supreme authority of United Kingdom Parliament.** The supreme authority of the Parliament of the United Kingdom remains unaffected[1].

1    Government of Ireland Act 1920 s 75 (amended by the Northern Ireland Constitution Act 1973 s 41(1), Sch 6 Pt I); Northern Ireland Constitution Act 1973 s 4(4).

**80. Prevention of religious and political discrimination and protection of human and civil rights.** To the extent that it discriminates[1] against any person or class of persons on the ground of religious belief or political opinion, any Measure, any Act of the Parliament of Northern Ireland and any relevant subordinate instrument[2] is to be void[3].

If it appears to the Secretary of State to be expedient in the public interest that steps should be taken for the speedy decision of any question whether a provision of a Measure,

Act of the Parliament of Northern Ireland or relevant subordinate instrument is void by virtue of this provision, he may recommend to Her Majesty that the question be referred for decision to the Judicial Committee of the Privy Council[4]. If it appears to him that some provision of a proposed Measure of the Northern Ireland Assembly ('the Assembly') might be void, he must refer it back to the Assembly for further consideration, but if, when it is transmitted to him again, it still appears to contain such a provision, he must recommend the referral of the question to the Judicial Committee[5]. The Judicial Committee may hear any person who appears to it interested in the determination of the question[6]. A decision of the Judicial Committee of the Privy Council is to be stated in open court and is to be binding in all subsequent legal proceedings[7].

There are also provisions rendering discrimination by public authorities unlawful, and affording a remedy by way of injunction, with or without an award of damages to any person who may be adversely affected[8]. A Standing Advisory Commission on Human Rights is constituted to advise the Secretary of State on the adequacy and effectiveness of the law for the time being in force in preventing discrimination and providing redress[9].

Certain authorities and bodies are precluded from requiring any person to take an oath or make a declaration, as a condition of his being appointed to or acting as a member of that authority or body, or of serving with or being employed under that authority or body[10].

A number of other forms of discrimination are the subjects of particular legislation[11].

Having regard to the United Kingdom's international obligations under the Convention for the Protection of Human Rights and Fundamental Freedoms (1950)[12], statutes affecting human rights are interpreted in the same way as in the rest of the United Kingdom[13].

The Parliamentary Commissioner and the Commissioner for Complaints[14] are empowered (as is the commissioner appointed under the Parliamentary Commissioner Act 1967) to investigate a complaint alleging maladministration involving discrimination on the ground of religious belief or political opinion notwithstanding that the person aggrieved has a remedy by way of proceedings in a court of law[15].

The liberty of the individual is protected also by the Habeas Corpus (Ireland) Act 1781[16].

1    An Act, Measure or other instrument so discriminates if it treats that person or class less favourably in any circumstances than other persons are treated in those circumstances by the law for the time being in force in Northern Ireland: Northern Ireland Constitution Act 1973 s 23(1). No such Act, Measure or instrument is treated as discriminating if it has the effect of safeguarding national security or protecting public safety or public order: s 23(3).

     Nothing in the Northern Ireland Constitution Act 1973 Pt III (ss 17–23) (as amended) renders unlawful; anything required or authorised to be done by an Act of the Parliament of the United Kingdom: s 23(6).

2    'Relevant subordinate instrument' means an instrument of a legislative character (including a byelaw) made under any Act of Parliament of the United Kingdom or the Parliament of Northern Ireland or under any Measure and extending only to Northern Ireland or a part of Northern Ireland: ibid s 17(2).

3    Ibid s 17(1).

     The prevention of religious and political discrimination and the protection of human and civil rights are important aspects of constitutional law in Northern Ireland. Issues of equality are closely connected with the individual's conception of his relationship to the state and of the legitimacy of the state itself: see McCrudden 'Northern Ireland and the British Constitution' in Jowell and Oliver (eds) *The Changing Constitution* (3rd Edn, 1994) pp 344–350.

4    Northern Ireland Constitution Act 1973 s 18(1). Nothing in s 18 prejudices any power of her majesty to refer questions to the Judicial Committee otherwise than under s 18: s 18(7). As to the judicial committee of the Privy Council see para 311 post; and generally COURTS.

5    Ibid s 18(2).

6    Ibid s 18(3).

7    Ibid s 18(4). If the Judicial Committee determines that a provision would be void, the Secretary of State may not submit the proposed Measure to Her Majesty in Council: s 18(5). He must again refer the

Measure back to the Assembly: see s 5(6) (applied by s 18(6)). If the Committee determines that the provision would not be void, that decision applies to the provision if contained in the Measure when enacted: s 18(5).

8    See ibid s 19 (amended by the Fair Employment (Northern Ireland) Act 1976 s 58(1), Sch 6 para 1). A person discriminates against another person or a class of persons if he treats that person or class less favourably in any circumstances than he treats or would treat other persons in those circumstances: Northern Ireland Constitution Act 1973 s 23(2). No act done by any person is to be treated as discriminating if it was done for the purpose of safeguarding national security or protecting public safety or public order: s 23(3). A certificate signed by or on behalf of the Secretary of State is conclusive evidence that an act was done for the purpose of safeguarding national security: s 23(4). See also s 23(6); and note 1 supra.

9    See ibid s 20(1) (amended by the Fair Employment (Northern Ireland) Act 1976 s 58(3)). The Commission must report annually to the Secretary of State: see the Northern Ireland Constitution Act 1973 s 20(7). As to the composition of the Commission, its staff and facilities see s 20(2)–(6) (as amended).

10   See ibid s 21(1). Exceptions are mentioned in s 21(2), (3).

11   See eg the Sex Discrimination (Northern Ireland) Order 1976, SI 1976/1042 (NI 15) (amended by SI 1985/1641 (NI 18)); the Police (Northern Ireland) Order 1977, SI 1977/53 (NI 2); the Fair Employment (Northern Ireland) Act 1989 (as amended); see also the Industrial Relations (Northern Ireland) Order 1993, SI 1993/2668 (NI 11).

12   See paras 122–181 post.

13   *R v Deery* [1977] NI 164, CCA.

14   See the Parliamentary Commissioner Act (Northern Ireland) 1969; and the Commissioner for Complaints Act (Northern Ireland) 1969.

15   See the Northern Ireland Constitution Act 1973 s 22.

16   Habeas Corpus (Ireland) Act 1781.


**81.   Emergency provisions.** The Northern Ireland (Emergency Provisions) Act 1996 makes provision for combating terrorism[1]. The Act is subject to annual renewal[2].

In the case of scheduled offences[3], provision is made for preliminary enquiries[4] and limitations are imposed on the power to grant bail[5]. The maximum period of remand in custody in the case of scheduled offences is 28 days[6]. Power is conferred on the Secretary of State to set time limits, with respect to any preliminary stage of proceedings for a scheduled offence, to the completion of that stage by the prosecution and to custody of the accused during that stage[7].

A trial on indictment of a scheduled offence is generally to be conducted at Belfast[8] in the Crown Court without a jury[9]. Special provision is made in relation to the treatment of admissions by the accused[10].

There is also special provision as to the onus of proof in relation to possession of proscribed articles[11] and in relation to the possession of articles in circumstances giving rise to a reasonable suspicion that they are to be used for a purpose connected with an act of terrorism[12]. Wide powers of arrest, search and seizure, and powers to stop and question are conferred on constables and members of the armed forces[13], and explosives inspectors[14] have powers of search and seizure in relation to unlawfully kept explosives or explosive substances[15]. The Secretary of State has the power to direct the closure or diversion of roads[16]. Membership of, and recruitment for, proscribed organisations[17] is an offence[18], as are various forms of support for such organisations[19]. It is also an offence to direct, at any level, the activities of an organisation which is concerned in the commission of acts of terrorism[20].

Particular provision is made for the treatment of young offenders convicted of scheduled offences[21]. There are restricted remission arrangements for persons convicted of scheduled offences[22], and the method is prescribed for dealing with a person who commits a scheduled offence during a period of remission of sentence for a previous conviction[23].

The following are also offences: unlawful collection of certain information[24], giving or receiving instruction or training in the making of use of firearms, explosives or explosive substances[25], and wearing in public without lawful authority or reasonable excuse a hood, mask or other article concealing identity[26].

Persons detained in police custody under the terrorism provisions[27] have a right to have someone informed of the detention[28], and a right of access to legal advice[29]. Fingerprinting is also controlled[30].

An Independent Assessor of Military Complaints Procedures in Northern Ireland has been appointed by the Secretary of State to keep under review procedures adopted by the General Officer Commanding Northern Ireland[31].

The provision of private security services is regulated. It is an offence to provide such services without a certificate[32], or to pay a person for such services who does not hold such a certificate[33]. The Secretary of State must be notified of change of personnel of a provider of such services[34], and records must be kept of employees[35].

Finally, detailed provision is made in relation to compensation for loss resulting from action taken under the emergency provisions[36].

The Prevention of Terrorism (Temporary Provisions) Act 1989 applies throughout the United Kingdom and is renewed annually[37].

1    The Northern Ireland (Emergency Provisions) Act 1996 repeals and replaces the Northern Ireland (Emergency Provisions) Act 1991 as from 25 August 1996: see ss 59, 62(1), 63(7), Sch 7 Pt I. For an account of the history of the legislation prior to the Northern Ireland (Emergency Provisions) Act 1991 see McCrudden 'Northern Ireland and the British Constitution' in Jowell and Oliver (eds) *The Changing Constitution* (3rd Edn, 1994) pp 350–361. See also the Northern Ireland (Emergency Provisions) Regulations 1991, SI 1991/1759. See also Wade and Bradley *Constitutional and Administrative Law* (11th Edn, 1993) pp 591, 595–600.

2    See the Northern Ireland (Emergency Provisions) Act 1996 s 62. As to the power to supplement the Act by regulations for preserving the peace see s 49.

3    See ibid s 1, Sch 1 Pts I, III.

4    See ibid s 2.

5    See ibid s 3. Special provision is made for legal aid to be available to applicants for bail in the case of scheduled offences (s 4), and in relation to the holding in custody of young persons charged with scheduled offences, enabling such young persons to be held in custody in a prison (ss 6, 7). The power to grant bail is generally limited to the High Court, the Court of Appeal and the court of trial: see s 3(2). As to bail for members of the security forces see s 3(6), (7).

6    See ibid s 5.

7    See ibid ss 8, 9. As to the power to prosecute for offences under the Act see s 57.

8    See ibid s 10.

9    See ibid s 11. When convicting for a scheduled offence, the trial judge must deliver a reasoned judgment and an appeal against both conviction and sentence lies to the Court of Appeal without leave (s 11(5), (6)) and thence, with the leave of that court or the House of Lords, to the House of Lords. In practice a reasoned judgment is delivered also in the case of an acquittal.

10   See ibid s 12. A statement by the accused may be given in evidence if the prosecution satisfies the court that it was not obtained by torture, inhuman or degrading treatment or any violence or threat of violence in order to induce him to make the statement. The original words, 'torture or inhuman or degrading treatment', have been expanded to incorporate in the statute rulings given and the practice prevailing in relation to trials without jury, and the common law discretion to exclude admissible evidence which is more prejudicial than probative has been endorsed: see s 12(2), (3); and see also *R v O'Halloran* [1979] NI 45, CA; *R v Corey* (1973) [1979] NI 49n. When a statement is excluded, the trial may in certain circumstances be restarted before a different court, in which the statement will remain excluded: Northern Ireland (Emergency Provisions) Act 1996 s 12(2)(iii), (3).

11   Ibid s 13. A 'proscribed article' is an explosive, firearm, ammunition, substance or other thing possession of which is an offence under any enactment specified in s 13(4): s 13(3). The presence of a person and a proscribed article in the same premises, vessel, aircraft or vehicle is evidence of possession which can be refuted by evidence of that person's knowledge or control: s 13(1), (2). As to the ultimate burden of proof see, however, *R v Killen* [1974] NI 220, CA; and *Measures to deal with Terrorism in Northern Ireland* (Cmnd 5847) (1975) (the 'Gardiner Report') at para 52.

12   See the Northern Ireland (Emergency Provisions) Act 1996 s 32.

13   See ibid ss 17–21, 23–26, 28. As to codes of practice made by the Secretary of State in connection with the exercise by the police or members of the armed forces of their powers under these and other provisions see ss 52–54. These provisions replace the Northern Ireland (Emergency Provisions)

Act 1991 ss 61, 62 (repealed), under which were made the Northern Ireland (Emergency Provisions) Act 1991 (Codes of Practice) (No 1) Order 1993, SI 1993/2761; the Northern Ireland (Emergency Provisions) Act 1991 (Codes of Practice) (No 2) Order 1993, SI 1993/2788 (revoked); and the Northern Ireland (Emergency Provisions) Act 1991 (Codes of Practice) (No 3) Order 1996, SI 1996/1698. Detailed provision is made by the Northern Ireland (Emergency Provisions) Act 1996 s 36, Sch 3 with respect to the detention of terrorists and suspected terrorists, but those provisions are suspended on the coming into force of the Act: see s 62(3)(b), (5). The provisions replaced by s 36, Sch 3, namely the Northern Ireland (Emergency Provisions) Act 1991 s 34, Sch 3 (repealed), were not among those provisions of the Act periodically renewed. Detention without trial has not been resorted to since 1975. As to lawfulness of army procedure for house arrests see *Murray v Ministry of Defence* [1988] 2 All ER 521, [1988] 1 WLR 692, HL.

14  Ie inspectors under the Explosives Act 1875 s 53 (repealed in relation to England and Wales).

15  See the Northern Ireland (Emergency Provisions) Act 1996 s 22. As to the power to reject an application to operate an explosives factory, magazine or store see s 50.

16  See ibid s 27.

17  Ie any organisation listed in ibid Sch 2: s 30.

18  See ibid s 30.

19  See ibid ss 30(1)(d), 31.

20  See ibid s 29, which also sets the maximum penalty for the offence at life imprisonment.

21  See ibid s 14.

22  See ibid s 15.

23  See ibid s 16.

24  Ibid s 33.

25  Ibid s 34.

26  Ibid s 35.

27  Ie the Prevention of Terrorism (Temporary Provisions) Act 1989 s 14, and any provision contained in an order under Sch 2 or Sch 5 and conferring a power of arrest or detention: Northern Ireland (Emergency Provisions) Act 1996 s 45(1). See further CRIMINAL LAW vol 11(1) (Reissue) para 118.

28  See ibid ss 45(2), 46.

29  See ibid s 47.

30  See ibid s 48.

31  See ibid s 51.

32  See ibid s 37. As to applications for such certificates see s 38; as to the duration and revocation of certificates see s 39. As to the liability of directors, etc, for offences committed by a body corporate see s 43.

33  See ibid s 42.

34  See ibid s 40. As to notifications see also s 44.

35  See ibid s 41.

36  See ibid ss 55, 56.

37  See the Northern Ireland (Emergency and Prevention of Terrorism Provisions) (Continuance) Order 1996; and the Prevention of Terrorism (Additional Powers) Act 1996. See also Wade and Bradley *Constitutional and Administrative Law* (11th Edn, 1993) pp 591–595; and CRIMINAL LAW vol 11(1) (Reissue) paras 102–141.

**82. Scrutiny of legislation.** There is a Northern Ireland Grand Committee[1], which considers such specified matters relating exclusively to Northern Ireland as may be referred to it[2]. There is in addition a Northern Ireland Affairs Committee, established in 1994, which is a select committee of the House of Commons[3]. Its role is to look at the administration and expenditure of the Northern Ireland Office and the Northern Ireland departments[4]. Legislation in the form of a bill can be considered and amended in Parliament, but much legislation for Northern Ireland, which may in fact, though not in form, be primary legislation, is effected by Order in Council, and thus can be accepted or rejected but not amended[5].

1  HC Standing Orders (1995) (Public Business) no 99(1). This is to be distinguished from the Northern Ireland Affairs Committee, as to which see text and note 3 infra. The Grand Committee consists of the Northern Ireland members of Parliament and up to 25 other members of Parliament nominated by the Committee of Selection from time to time. The Chairman is nominated by the Speaker.

2  The committee's powers are limited by HC Standing Orders (1995) (Public Business) no 99(1), (2). Matters are referred to it only on the motion of a minister. The committee must then consider the matter

or matters referred to it and report only that it has considered the said matter or matters: HC Standing Orders (1995) (Public Business) no 99(3).

3    As to select committees generally see para 227 post; and PARLIAMENT.

4    The committee reported on 27 April 1995 on employment creation in Northern Ireland and on 22 November 1995 on electricity prices in Northern Ireland.

5    For this reason proposals for a draft Order in Council (in the form of a draft Order) are often circulated to interested parties, including Northern Ireland's political parties, for comment. This informal procedure is described in Hadfield *The Constitution of Northern Ireland* (1989) pp 134–135.

**83. The Secretary of State for Northern Ireland and the Northern Ireland Office.** There is a Secretary of State for Northern Ireland, whose department is the Northern Ireland Office[1]. He is assisted by two Ministers of State, and two Parliamentary Under Secretaries[2]. The department's expenses are provided by Parliament[3] and the department is subject to investigation by the Parliamentary Commissioner for Administration[4].

The Secretary of State has extensive powers in connection with the Northern Ireland Assembly and the Northern Ireland Executive[5] and responsibilities in connection with the administration of justice, public order, security and elections, as well as financial, economic, commercial and social matters. He has overall responsibility for the work of the Northern Ireland Office and the Northern Ireland departments.

The Northern Ireland Office operates both in London and in Belfast, and the Northern Ireland departments are based in Belfast[6]. The office comprises five directorates, each headed by a director[7]. Collectively, and together with a number of other senior officials, the directors form the Departmental Board which, under the chairmanship of the Permanent Under-Secretary of State, provides strategic direction to the department. The Head of the Northern Ireland Civil Service, who also holds the position of Second Permanent Secretary in the Northern Ireland Office, has a seat on the Departmental Board.

A number of the functions of the department are discharged through executive agencies; the chief executives of these agencies are accountable to ministers through the Permanent Under-Secretary of State[8].

1    As to the office of Secretary of State see para 355 et seq post.

2    See the Northern Ireland Office Annual Report: *Expenditure Plans and Priorities: the Government's Expenditure Plans 1995–96 to 1997–98* (Cm 2816) (1995) p iii.

3    See the *Supply Estimates 1995–96 for the year ending 31 March 1996* (HC Paper (1994–95) no 271–XVI).

4    See the Parliamentary Commissioner Act 1967 s 4(1), Sch 2 (both as substituted and amended); and generally PARLIAMENT.

5    See paras 69–76 ante.

6    The structure of the Northern Ireland Office has been overhauled following a review conducted in 1994–95; the changes were put in place after the publication of the Civil Service Year Book 1996.

7    See note 6 supra. The directorates are as follows:

   (1)   the Political Directorate, which deals with a wide range of issues including political and constitutional matters, political development, human rights, electoral policy, the peace process and international aspects on Northern Ireland policy;

   (2)   the Policing Directorate, which deals with policy and funding in relation to the police;

   (3)   the Criminal Justice Directorate is involved in the development of criminal justice policy and the oversight of Training Schools and the Probation Board;

   (4)   the Security Directorate provides advice on security policy and operational matters to ministers; and

   (5)   the Central Services Directorate, headed by the Principal Finance and Establishment Officer, which exercises the personnel, office sevices and financial functions of the department and leads on developing good management practice.

   The head of the Policing Directorate, who is also the Senior Director, Belfast, acts as the equivalent of a Northern Ireland Permanent Secretary and represents the department on the Northern Ireland Civil Service Policy Co-ordinating Committee.

   The Political Directorate is based mainly in London, but has a presence in Belfast through the Political Affairs Division and has responsibility for the Government Information Service based in Stormont Castle. The other four directorates are located in Belfast.

8    At the date at which this volume states the law, there are three such agencies, namely: the Northern
     Ireland Prison Service, the Compensation Agency and the Forensic Science Agency for Northern Ireland:
     see the Civil Service Year Book (1996) cols 801–803.

**84.   The legal system.** Two statutes of the Parliament of Ireland, Poynings' Law 1495[1]
and Yelverton's Act (Ireland) 1781[2] made applicable to Ireland certain statutes of the
Parliaments of England (before 1707) and Great Britain. By the early seventeenth century
English law had spread to all parts of Ireland and applied to all irrespective of their race
or origin[3]. Since then the Irish courts generally have followed and adopted the
developments of English common law and equity. The statute law of Northern Ireland[4]
is in most respects identical with or very similar to that of England and Wales. The legal
systems are, however, separate and distinct, although again, very similar, particularly as
regards the superior courts.

The Supreme Court of Judicature of Northern Ireland is established under the
Judicature (Northern Ireland) Act 1978[5]. It comprises the High Court of Justice in
Northern Ireland, the Court of Appeal and the Crown Court[6]. The High Court consists of
the Lord Chief Justice of Northern Ireland and seven puisne judges[7] and is divided into the
Chancery Division, Queen's Bench Division and Family Division[8]. The Court of Appeal
consists of the Lord Chief Justice and three Lords Justices of Appeal[9] and, as well as its civil
jurisdiction, exercises the jurisdiction formerly exercised by the Court of Criminal Appeal
for Northern Ireland[10]. Every judge of the High Court is a judge of the Court of Appeal
for the purposes of its jurisdiction in a criminal cause or matter[11]. The Crown Court[12] has
jurisdiction in all proceedings on indictment and its jurisdiction is exercisable by the Lord
Chief Justice, any judge of the High Court or the Court of Appeal or any county court
judge. An appeal lies to the House of Lords in both civil and criminal matters[13]. The law
regarding qualifications of judges of the High Court and Court of Appeal, their
appointment and tenure and vacation of office is similar to that of England and Wales[14]. The
Act contains specific provisions relating to the supervisory and declaratory jurisdiction[15] of
the High Court which are the statutory basis of judicial review[16].

The Northern Ireland Court Service is a unified and distinct civil service of the
Crown with the functions, inter alia, of facilitating the conduct of the business of the
Supreme Court, county courts, magistrates' courts and coroners' courts and provides the
staff for those courts as well as for its own office. The officers and staff of the Court Service
are appointed by the Lord Chancellor[17]. The Lord Chancellor also makes appointments
of statutory officers, that is to say, the officers in charge of the different offices of the
Supreme Court, the Official Solicitor and District Judges[18]. The judges of the High Court
and the Court of Appeal must select two of their number on or before 1 October in each
year for the trial of parliamentary election petitions[19].

The county court system which had existed in Ireland continued in Northern Ireland
after partition in accordance with the County Officers and Courts (Ireland) Act 1877
under which full time county court judges were introduced. These judges both exercised
civil jurisdiction and acted as chairmen of quarter sessions to try offences on indictment
and to hear appeals from the magistrates' courts. There are now 13 county court judges
in Northern Ireland (of whom two are styled the Recorder of Belfast and the Recorder
of Londonderry) exercising this civil and criminal jurisdiction under the County Courts
(Northern Ireland) Order 1980[20].

Justices of the Peace were appointed in Ireland from medieval times and their
subsequent history was similar to that in England until the Summary Jurisdiction and
Criminal Justice Act (Northern Ireland) 1935 deprived lay justices of most of their
jurisdiction in petty sessions, which is now exercised by a resident magistrate, who
must be a barrister or solicitor who has practised for not less than seven years. The

statutory basis of the jurisdiction of magistrates courts is now the Magistrates' (Northern Ireland) Order 1981[21].

There are also in Northern Ireland a social security legal system presided over by Social Security Commissioners[22], a system of industrial tribunals[23], the Lands Tribunal[24], the Value Added Tax and Duties Tribunal[25], and Coroners' Courts[26], with jurisdictions similar to those exercised in England and Wales. There is a Boundary Commission for the United Kingdom[27].

The doctrine of judicial precedent is similar to that which holds sway in England and Wales. Decisions of the Court of Appeal in England and Wales and of the Inner House of the Court of Session are of strong persuasive authority, as are decisions before 1921 of the former Irish courts, but they are not binding on the courts in Northern Ireland. Particular attention is also paid to decisions of courts of the Commonwealth countries and of the Republic of Ireland and, where applicable, the United States.

The Incorporated Law Society of Northern Ireland was established by Royal Charter granted on 10 July 1922. The solicitors' profession is governed by the Council of the Society and is also subject to the jurisdiction of the Lord Chief Justice by virtue of a transfer to him of functions formerly exercised by the Lord Chancellor of Ireland[28]. The statutory functions of the Society are provided for by the Solicitors (Northern Ireland) Order 1976[29].

Call to the Bar of Northern Ireland is made by the Lord Chief Justice on the authority of the Executive Council of the Inn of Court of Northern Ireland, which is exercised on behalf of Her Majesty's Judges and with their consent, and call within the Bar is made by the Lord Chief Justice on his own authority, the warrant having been signed by the Secretary of State for Northern Ireland, as successor to the Governor of Northern Ireland. The Executive Council of the Inn of Court of Northern Ireland has since 1983 been the ruling authority of the Bar of Northern Ireland and particular functions are discharged by the Benchers of the Inn and by the General Council of the Bar of Northern Ireland, which deals with the maintenance of the standards, honour and independence of the Bar and investigates complaints against members of the Bar in their professional capacity.

There is in Northern Ireland an Office of Law Reform, set up in 1965 and now within the Department of Finance and Personnel, with functions relating to the civil law of Northern Ireland which are similar to those of the Law Commission.

A member of the Judiciary or the Bar of Northern Ireland may be appointed to be a Lord of Appeal in Ordinary in accordance with the Appellate Jurisdiction Act 1876[30].

1   Ie Poynings' Law 1495 10 Hen 7 c 22, another provision of which prevented the Irish Parliament from being called without permission of the King or from passing legislation which he had not approved, but this was repealed in 1782.

2   Ie Yelverton's Act (Ireland) 1781 21 & 22 Geo 3 c 48. In 1719 a statute of the Parliament of Great Britain, 6 Geo 1 c 5, declared the undoubted right and authority of the Parliament of Great Britain to legislate to bind the Kingdom and people of Ireland; that Act was repealed in 1782 by 22 Geo 3 c 53.

3   See *Tanistry Case* (1608) Dav Ir 28; *Resolution concerning Gavelkind* (1606) Dav Ir 49.

4   As to the sources of Northern Ireland statute law see 31 Halsbury's Statutes (4th Edn, 1994 Reissue) NORTHERN IRELAND pp 271–272.

5   Replacing the Supreme Court of Judicature Act (Ireland) 1877 (repealed) as applied by the Government of Ireland Act 1920 ss 38, 40 (repealed).

6   Judicature (Northern Ireland) Act 1978 s 1.

7   See ibid s 2(1) (amended by the Maximum Number of Judges (Northern Ireland) Order 1993, SI 1993/606). The number may be varied by Order in Council: Judicature (Northern Ireland) Act 1978 s 2(3).

8   See ibid s 5.

9   See ibid s 3. The number may be varied by Order in Council: s 3(4).

10   See ibid s 34(2). See also the Criminal Appeal (Northern Ireland) Act 1980, which governs the making of appeals from the Crown Court in Northern Ireland to the Court of Appeal in Northern Ireland, and from the Court of Appeal in Northern Ireland to the House of Lords.

11  Ibid s 3(2). This includes eg a case stated in a criminal proceeding, and not merely appeals from the Crown Court.
12  See ibid ss 46–53 (as amended). Solicitors have a right of audience: see s 50(1).
13  See ibid ss 41–44; and note 10 supra.
14  See ibid ss 9, 12–14; and see further COURTS.
15  See ibid ss 18–25 (as amended).
16  RSC (NI) (ie the Rules of the Supreme Court (Northern Ireland) (Revision) 1980, SR 1980/346) Ord 53.
17  See the Judicature (Northern Ireland) Act 1978 s 69 (as amended).
18  See ibid s 70, Sch 3 (both as amended).
19  See ibid s 108 (as amended). As to election petitions see the Representation of the People Act 1983 s 123; and the Electoral Law Act (Northern Ireland) 1962 s 72(2); and ELECTIONS vol 15 (Reissue) para 747 et seq.
20  Ie the County Courts (Northern Ireland) Order 1980, SI 1980/397 (NI 3). This Order consolidated with amendments the County Courts Act (Northern Ireland) 1959 and the County Court Appeals Act (Northern Ireland) 1964. Since appeals from the magistrates' courts still go to the county court, it has not been necessary, as in England and Wales, to make the Crown Court an inferior court for the purpose of such appeals.
21  Ie the Magistrates' (Northern Ireland) Order 1981, SI 1981/1675 (NI 26).
22  See the Social Security Administration (Northern Ireland) Act 1992 s 50, Sch 2; and NATIONAL HEALTH AND SOCIAL SECURITY.
23  See the Industrial Training (Northern Ireland) Order 1984, SI 1984/1159 (NI 9) (as amended); and EMPLOYMENT; TRADE, INDUSTRY AND INDUSTRIAL RELATIONS.
24  See the Lands Tribunal and Compensation Act (Northern Ireland) 1964 ss 1–4; and COMPULSORY ACQUISITION.
25  See the Value Added Tax Act 1994 s 82, Sch 12 (as amended); and VALUE ADDED TAX.
26  See the Coroners Act (Northern Ireland) 1959; and CORONERS.
27  See the Parliamentary Constituencies Act 1986 s 2, Sch 1; and ELECTIONS vol 15 (Reissue) para 304.
28  See the Solicitors (Ireland) Act 1898; and the Supreme Court of Judicature (Northern Ireland) Order 1921, SR & O 1921/1802.
29  Ie the Solicitors (Northern Ireland) Order 1976, SI 1976/582 (NI 12) (as amended).
30  There have been two such appointments since 1921.

**85. Relations with the Republic of Ireland.** In the event of devolved government under the Northern Ireland Constitution Act 1973[1], a Northern Ireland executive authority[2] may (1) consult on any matter with any authority of the Republic of Ireland[3]; and (2) enter into agreements or arrangements with any authority of the Republic of Ireland in respect of any transferred matter[4]. Provision may be made by Measure[5] for giving effect to any such agreement or arrangement, including provision for transferring, to any authority designated by or constituted under the agreement or arrangement, any function which would otherwise be exercisable by any authority in Northern Ireland, or for transferring to an authority in Northern Ireland any functions which would otherwise be exercisable by any authority elsewhere[6]. However, any such Measure would need the consent of the Secretary of State[7].

Proposals were made in 1973 to set up a Council of Ireland representing the two parts of Ireland with safeguards for the interests of the United Kingdom government (the 'Sunningdale Agreement')[8], but this did not happen[9].

Following the Sunningdale Agreement, a Joint Law Enforcement Commission appointed by the governments of the United Kingdom and the Republic of Ireland met to consider the possibility of extradition in relation to terrorist offences and the trial of persons in one jurisdiction in Ireland for offences committed in the other[10]. The Criminal Jurisdiction Act 1975 subsequently dealt with the second of these points and ancillary matters and provided for the trial in Northern Ireland of offences committed in the Republic[11].

At talks held on 6 November 1981 between the Prime Minister of the United Kingdom and the Taoiseach[12] the establishment of an Anglo-Irish Inter-Governmental Council was announced, as a means 'through which institutional expression can be given to the unique relationship between the two governments'[13].

In 1985 a further agreement, known as the Anglo-Irish Agreement, was reached between the two governments[14]. The two governments affirmed that any change in the status of Northern Ireland would be effected only with the consent of the majority of the people in Northern Ireland, that the present wish of such majority was for no change in status; but the governments declared that, in the event that in the future a majority of the people clearly wished for and formally consented to the establishment of a United Ireland, they would introduce and support legislation to give effect to that wish. The agreement also recognises the Anglo-Irish Inter-Governmental Council set up in 1981 and provides for the establishment of an Inter-governmental Conference concerned with Northern Ireland; this conference will be concerned with (a) political matters; (b) security and related matters; (c) legal matters, including the administration of justice; and (d) the promotion of cross-border co-operation[15]. It is stated that it is the policy of the United Kingdom government that certain responsibilities of the Secretary of State for Northern Ireland should be devolved on a basis which would secure widespread acceptance within the community; the Irish government affirmed its support for that policy[16]. The Irish government is empowered to advance views and proposals on the role and composition of certain Northern Ireland bodies, including the Standing Advisory Commission on Human Rights, the Fair Employment Agency, the Equal Opportunities Commission, the Policy Authority for Northern Ireland and the Police Complaints Board[17]. The conference is empowered to consider whether there are areas of the criminal law applying in Northern Ireland and the Republic of Ireland which might be harmonised and whether mixed courts should be established in both jurisdictions for the trial of certain offences; the conference will also be concerned with policy aspects of extradition and extra-territorial jurisdiction as between Northern Ireland and the Republic of Ireland[18].

The terms of this agreement remain applicable in Northern Ireland[19].

On 15 December 1993 the Prime Minister of the United Kingdom and the Taoiseach issued a Joint Declaration[20] the object of which was to secure by peaceful negotiation a final political settlement in and concerning Northern Ireland[21].

1    As to devolution under the Northern Ireland Constitution Act 1973 see para 70 et seq ante.

2    As to executive authorities see para 74 ante.

3    Northern Ireland Constitution Act 1973 s 12(1)(a).

4    Ibid s 12(1)(b). As to transferred matters see para 70 ante.

5    Ie by Measure of the Northern Ireland Assembly. As to the Northern Ireland Assembly see para 70 ante

6    Northern Ireland Constitution Act 1973 s 12(2).

7    See ibid s 12(3), read with Sch 3 para 8: the exercise of legislative powers for such a purpose is a reserved matter. See further para 76 ante.

8    See the Sunningdale Agreement (866 HC Official Report (5th series), 10 December 1973, cols 37–41).

9    See para 70 note 9 ante.

10   The Commission's first meeting was on 15 January 1974. It reported in May 1974: *Report of the Law Enforcement Commission to the Secretary of State for Northern Ireland and the Minister for Justice of Ireland* (Cmnd 5627) (1974).

11   The Criminal Jurisdiction Act 1975 was completely in force by 1 June 1976: see the Criminal Jurisdiction Act 1975 (Commencement No 1) Order 1975, SI 1975/1347; and the Criminal Jurisdiction Act 1975 (Commencement No 2) Order 1976, SI 1976/813. Corresponding legislation was passed in the Republic of Ireland.

12   Ie the Prime Minister of the Republic of Ireland.

13   See Hadfield *The Constitution of Northern Ireland* (1989) pp 180, 210 note 9, and, for a description of the discussions which preceded this announcement and of the results achieved, ch VII particularly at pp 179–183. The New Ireland Forum which met in Dublin in May 1983 listed three constitutional options for the government of Northern Ireland, namely a unitary state of Ireland, a federal state of Ireland, with two provinces (the present Northern Ireland and the present Republic of Ireland) and a Northern Ireland ruled by the joint authority of the British and Irish Governments, with or without the devolution of limited powers to a Northern Ireland Assembly. All these options were rejected by the United Kingdom government.

14  *Agreement between the Government of the United Kingdom of Great Britain and Northern Ireland and the Government of the Republic of Ireland* (Cmnd 9657) (1985), signed by the United Kingdom Prime Minister and the Taoiseach at Hillsborough, Co Down on 15 November 1985. See further The Times, 18 November 1985.

15  See the Anglo-Irish Agreement art 2.

16  See ibid art 4.

17  See ibid art 6.

18  See ibid art 8.

19  The Anglo-Irish Agreement has been held by the High Court not to be unlawful since there was no derogation from sovereignty, Northern Ireland citizens were not deprived of any privileges enjoyed by other United Kingdom citizens, and the agreement resulted from the exercise of the prerogative and was not open to review by the courts: *Ex p Molyneaux* [1986] 1 WLR 331. For a description of the practical operation of the Anglo-Irish Agreement see Hadfield *The Constitution of Northern Ireland* (1989) pp 190–209.

20  Ie the *Joint Declaration issued by the Prime Minister, the Rt Hon John Major MP and the Taoiseach, Mr Albert Reynolds TD* (Cm 2442) (1994) signed on 15 December 1993. This is known as the 'Downing Street Declaration'.

21  The Declaration acknowledges the need to remove the causes of conflict and to heal divisions and expresses the belief that the development of an agreed framework for peace, which had been discussed for nearly two years between the two Governments and which was based on a number of key principles articulated by them over the previous 20 years, provides the starting point of a peace process designed to culminate in a political settlement. Both governments made a commitment to promote co-operation at all levels on the basis of the fundamental principles, undertakings and obligations under international agreements, to which they had jointly committed themselves and the guarantees which each government had given and now reaffirmed, including Northern Ireland's statutory guarantee (see para 68 text and note 5 ante). The Declaration envisaged a process of political dialogue to create institutions and structures which, while respecting the diversity of the people of Ireland, would enable them to work together in all areas of common interest. The governments reiterated that the achievement of peace must involve a permanent end to the use of, or support for, paramilitary violence and confirmed that, in those circumstances, democratically mandated parties which established a commitment to exclusively peaceful methods, and which had shown that they abide by the democratic process, were free to participate fully in democratic politics and to join in dialogue and in due course between the governments and the political parties on the way ahead. The Declaration was accompanied by a document entitled 'Frameworks for the Future' ('the framework document'), which was intended as a basis for negotiation.

## 86–100.  Northern Ireland (Entry to Negotiations, etc) Act 1996  The Northern Ireland (Entry to Negotiations, etc) Act 1996 provides for the holding of elections in Northern Ireland for the purpose of providing delegates from among whom participants in negotiations[1] may be drawn[2]. As soon as practicable thereafter, the Secretary of State must invite the nominating representative[3] of each party for which delegates have been returned, to nominate from among those delegates a team to participate in the negotiations[4]. He must, however, refrain from inviting nominations from, and must exclude persons nominated by, any party for so long as certain requirements are not met[5].

The delegates returned are to constitute a forum for the discussion of issues relevant to promoting dialogue and understanding within Northern Ireland[6]. The functions of the forum are deliberative only[7], and it accordingly has no legislative, executive or administrative functions, or any power to determine the conduct, course or outcome of the negotiations[8], but the participants in the negotiations may refer any matter to the forum, which may then consider that matter[9].

The Secretary of State may from time to time by order direct the holding of a referendum for the purpose of obtaining the views of the people of Northern Ireland on any matter relating to Northern Ireland[10].

Allowances may be paid to delegates whether by reference to days on which they attend the forum or participate in negotiations or otherwise[11]. The expenses of the Secretary of State are met out of money provided by Parliament[12].

1   Ie the negotiations referred to in *Northern Ireland: Ground Rules for Substantive All-Party Negotiations* (Cm 3232) (1996): Northern Ireland (Entry to Negotiations, etc) Act 1996 s 2(1).

     The Act received the Royal Assent on 29 April 1996, and came into force on that date.

2   Ibid s 1(1). The elections were held on 30 May 1996: see s 1(2), Sch 1 para 3; and the Elections (Northern Ireland) Order 1996, SI 1996/1220. As to the conduct of the poll see the Northern Ireland (Entry to Negotiations, etc) Act 1996 Sch 1, Pt I; and the Elections (Northern Ireland) Order 1996. As to the potential participants see the Northern Ireland (Entry to Negotiations, etc) Act 1996 Sch 1 Pt II.

3   The nominating representative in relation to a party is the person who at any time appears to the Secretary of State to be the leader of the party or otherwise the most appropriate person to act on behalf of the party for these purposes: s 5(1). An initial list of all the nominating representatives must be published in the Belfast Gazette, as must notice of any change in the nominating representative of any of those parties: s 5(2).

4   Ibid s 2(2). The nominating representative may from time to time substitute for any nominated delegate any other person returned as a delegate in the election: s 2(4).

5   Ibid s 2(3). The requirements are those referred to in *Northern Ireland: Ground Rules for Substantive All-Party Negotiations* (Cm 3232) (1996) paras 8, 9.

6   Ibid s 3(1). As to the chairmanship, meetings, procedure and privileges of the forum see s 3(5), Sch 2.

     Section 3 ceases to have effect at the end of May 1997: s 7(1); but this period may be extended (or shortened) by order by the Secretary of State: see s 7(2)–(4), (5).

7   Ibid s 3(2).

8   Ibid s 3(3).

9   Ibid s 3(4).

10  Ibid s 4(1), (4). A draft of such an order must be laid before Parliament and approved by resolution of each House of Parliament: s 4(2). The order may provide for the conduct of a referendum, including the wording of the question to be put: see s 4(3).

11  See ibid s 6(1).

12  See ibid s 6(2).

# 2. HUMAN RIGHTS AND FREEDOMS

## (1) INTRODUCTORY

**101. Fundamental rights and freedoms of the individual.** The origins of the fundamental rights and liberties of the citizens of this country, like the origins of constitutional government, are matters of continuing historical controversy, reflecting different strands of English political philosophy and Whig and Tory interpretations of the Revolution of 1688[1]. They may be said to derive both from the concept of popular rights and popular sovereignty, reflected in the reference in the Act of Settlement to the laws of England as being the 'birthright of the people'[2], as well as from the concept of parliamentary sovereignty[3] and of a compact between monarch and Parliament, whereby the rights and liberties of the subject were declared in the Bill of Rights, and further secured in the Act of Settlement.

In traditional English legal terms, the concept of popular rights and popular sovereignty has been eclipsed by the concept of parliamentary sovereignty, according to which, since Parliament is sovereign (in place of the monarch), the subject cannot possess fundamental rights such as are guaranteed to the citizen by many foreign and Commonwealth constitutions, as well as by international and European law[4]. According to this traditional view of the doctrine of parliamentary sovereignty, the liberties of the subject are merely implications drawn from two principles, namely: (1) that individuals may say or do what they please, provided they do not transgress the substantive law, or infringe the legal rights of others[5]; and (2) that public authorities (including the Crown) may do nothing but what they are authorised to do by some rule of common law[6] (including the royal prerogative) or statute[7], and in particular may not interfere with the liberties of individuals without statutory authority[8]. Where public authorities are not authorised to interfere with the individual, the individual has liberties[9]. It is in this sense that such liberties are residual, rather than fundamental and positive, in their nature.

Apart from the general provisions ensuring the peaceful enjoyment of rights of property, and the freedom of the individual from illegal detention, duress, punishment or taxation, contained in the four great charters or statutes which regulate the relations between the Crown and people[10], and apart from specific legislation conferring particular rights[11], the fundamental rights and liberties of the individual are not expressly defined in any United Kingdom law or code. However, the provisions of the Convention for the Protection of Human Rights and Fundamental Freedoms[12] are commonly taken into account by English courts when cases involving human rights issues arise[13]. Furthermore, an alleged victim of a violation of that Convention may have recourse to the European Commission and Court of Human Rights for redress, after exhausting any effective domestic remedies[14].

1   See eg Kenyon *Revolution Principles: The Politics of Party 1689–1720* (1977).
2   Act of Settlement s 4. As to the citation of the Act of Settlement see para 35 note 3 ante.
3   As to parliamentary sovereignty see generally para 232–237 post.
4   However, English courts, increasingly influenced by international human rights law, comparative constitutional law, and European law, are becoming more sympathetic to the concept of popular sovereignty and fundamental rights and liberties. See eg *Derbyshire County Council v Times Newspapers Ltd* [1992] 1 QB 770, [1992] 3 All ER 65, CA; affd [1993] AC 534, [1993] 1 All ER 1011, HL; both the Court of Appeal and the House of Lords treated American constitutional case law on federal and state guarantees of free speech (notably in *New York Times Co v Sullivan* 376 US 254 (1964), US SC; and *City of Chicago v Tribune Co* 139 NE 86 (1923) Supreme Court of Illinois as persuasive in the context of English constitutional law: the American constitutional principles, rooted in a republican rather than a monarchical tradition, were regarded as relevant in preventing an English public authority from invoking libel law to protect its so-called governing reputation. See also *Harman v Secretary of state for the Home Department* [1983] 1 AC 280 at 316–318, sub nom *Home Office v Harman* [1982] 1 All ER 532 at 547–548, HL, per Lord Scarman (dissenting).
5   'The law of England is a law of liberty': *R v Cobbett* (1804) 29 State Tr 1 at 49 per Lord Ellenborough CJ; *A-G v Observer Ltd, A-G v Times Newspapers Ltd* [1990] 1 AC 109 at 178, sub nom *A-G v Guardian Newspapers Ltd (No 2)* [1988] 3 All ER 545 at 596, CA, per Sir John Donaldson MR, and at 283, 660, HL, per Lord Goff of Chieveley.
6   At common law the Crown, as a corporation possessing legal personality, has the capacities of a natural person and thus the same liberties as the individual: see para 6 ante.
7   The authorisation may take the form of a simple parliamentary appropriation of money for a particular purpose: see para 7 head (12) ante.
8   *Proclamations' Case* (1611) 12 Co Rep 74; and see para 6 ante.
9   See 2 Hatschek's Englisches Staatsrecht 547–548.
10  Namely: Magna Carta of Edward 1 (1297), c 29; the Petition of Right (1627); the Bill of Rights; and the Act of Settlement. As to the provisions of these, and the extent to which they have been amended or repealed see generally paras 203, 207, 310, 372–378, 883 post. As to the history and citation of the Bill of Rights and the Act of Settlement see para 35 note 3 ante.
11  See para 103 post.
12  Ie the European Convention for the Protection of Human Rights and Fundamental Freedoms (Rome, 4 November 1953; TS 71; Cmd 8969) (frequently referred to as the European Convention on Human Rights): see para 122 post.
13  See para 104 post.
14  For the effect of the United Kingdom's ratification of the Convention for the Protection of Human Rights and Fundamental Freedoms as a guarantee of civil and political rights see generally paras 122–181 post.

**102. Protection of fundamental rights and freedoms.** In the absence of an entrenched Bill of Rights for the United Kingdom, the fundamental rights and liberties of the individual owe their main legal protection to:

(1)   the provisions of the Convention for the Protection of Human Rights and Fundamental Freedoms[1] as applied both in English courts and through the

machinery for their enforcement in the European Commission and Court of Human Rights at Strasbourg[2];

(2)   those provisions of European Community law which protect the rights of individuals[3];

(3)   the development of the action of trespass in its various forms[4];

(4)   the prerogative orders[5], including the writ of habeas corpus, as reinforced by the Habeas Corpus Acts[6];

(5)   the fact that the individual can insist upon having common law actions affecting some of his most treasured rights, as well as all accusations of serious crime, tried by a random collection of ordinary persons, that is by a jury[7];

(6)   the fact that, except in the case of the monarch, who can do no wrong in the eyes of the law[8], and whose person is inviolable[9], and, excepting too the protection afforded to the judiciary whilst acting in their official capacity[10], and the limited protection afforded to magistrates and justices of the peace[11], all persons are subject to the jurisdiction of the courts, and may be made liable for any infringement of the rights and liberties of others unless some statutory authorisation for the infringement is found[12]; and

(7)   the rule of construction that statutes and other legislative acts are so far as possible to be interpreted so as not to cause any interference with the vested rights of the individual[13].

1   Ie the Convention for the Protection of Human Rights and Fundamental Freedoms (Rome, 4 November 1950; TS 71; Cmd 8969) (commonly referred to as the European Convention on Human Rights): see para 122 post. The International Covenant on Civil and Political Rights (1966) (as to which see para 103 note 3 post) is equally significant, but less well known in the United Kingdom. See generally Harris and Joseph (eds) *The International Covenant on Civil and Political Rights and United Kingdom Law* (1995).

2   See paras 122–181 post.

3   See para 104 post; and EUROPEAN COMMUNITIES.

4   In common law systems actions for trespass have been developed to permit an action for trespass to be brought for a mere interference with a personal or property right, unaccompanied by actual damage. There is also a rule that an award of damages by a jury will not lightly be disturbed, however high, if some important constitutional principle is at stake: *Huckle v Money* (1763) 2 Wils 205. As to trespass generally see TORT; and as to damages see DAMAGES.

5   See ADMINISTRATIVE LAW vol 1(1) (Reissue) para 102 et seq; and CROWN PROCEEDINGS.

6   See the Habeas Corpus Acts 1679, 1803 and 1816; and ADMINISTRATIVE LAW vol 1(1) (Reissue) paras 222–265. According to Dicey *Law of the Constitution* (10th Edn, 1959) p 199, although the Habeas Corpus Acts 'declare no principle and define no rights...they are for practical purposes worth a hundred constitutional articles guaranteeing individual liberty'. For similarly exaggerated statements in praise of the English writ of habeas corpus see eg *Secretary of State for Home Affairs v O'Brien* [1923] AC 603 at 609, HL, per Lord Birkenhead; and *Greene v Secretary of State for Home Affairs* [1942] AC 284 at 304, [1941] 3 All ER 388 at 399–400, HL, per Lord Wright. In practice habeas corpus has been attenuated by Parliament and the courts, enabling the Executive to enjoy sweepingly broad powers of detention. The decision in *Liversidge v Anderson* [1942] AC 206, [1941] 3 All ER 338, HL, allowing detention without proof of reasons under the Defence (General) Regulations 1939, SR & O 1939/927 reg 18B (revoked), can no longer be extended beyond the context of the regulation itself: see *Ali v Jayaratne* [1951] AC 66, PC; *IRC v Rossminster Ltd* [1980] AC 952, [1980] 1 All ER 80, HL. See, however, Le Sueur 'Should We Abolish the Writ of Habeas Corpus?' [1992] Public Law 13. Article 5 of the Convention for the Protection of Human Rights and Fundamental Freedoms gives more effective protection: see para 127 post.

7   See CRIMINAL LAW; PRACTICE AND PROCEDURE. A jury is immune from all proceedings in respect of its verdict: *Bushell's Case* (1670) 6 State Tr 999. This is a real safeguard in criminal trials for breach of official secrecy legislation, or for criminal, seditious or blasphemous libel, but it does not apply to other interferences with free speech, eg for breach of confidence, or for contempt of court.

8   See para 367 note 2 post; and see also *Re M* [1994] 1 AC 377 at 395, sub nom *M v Home Office* [1993] 3 All ER 537 at 540, HL, per Lord Templeman.

9   See para 367 note 2 post.

10   See para 388 post.

11   See further para 304 text and note 3 post.

12  *Entick v Carrington* (1765) 19 State Tr 1029; and see Dicey *Law of the Constitution* (10th Edn, 1959) p
    193–195.

13  'It is clear that the burden is on those who seek to establish that the legislature intended to take away
    the private rights of individuals to show that by express words or by necessary implication such an
    intention appears': *Metropolitan Asylum District Managers v Hill* (1881) 6 App Cas 193 at 208, HL, per
    Lord Blackburn. 'Their Lordships consider that, where "fundamental rights and freedoms of the
    individual" are being considered, a court should be cautious before accepting the view that some
    particular disregard of them is of minimal amount': *Olivier v Buttigieg* [1967] 1 AC 115 at 136, [1966]
    2 All ER 459 at 466, PC. See further Lord Browne-Wilkinson 'The Infiltration of a Bill of Rights'
    [1992] Public Law 397. Presumptions in favour of the liberty or property of the individual become
    relatively weak in time of war when the safety of the realm is in danger. The counter-maxim *salus populi
    suprema lex* ('the welfare of the people is the paramount law') is applied as a corrective. See eg *R v
    Halliday* [1917] AC 260 at 270, HL; *Ronnfeldt v Phillips* (1918) 35 TLR 46, CA; *Hudson's Bay Co v
    Maclay* (1920) 36 TLR 469 at 475; *Liversidge v Anderson* [1942] AC 206, [1941] 3 All ER 338, HL; and
    see WAR.

**103.  The International Human Rights Codes.** The United Kingdom is party to
many international human rights codes[1], of which the most notable are the Convention
for the Protection of Human Rights and Fundamental Freedoms (1950)[2] and the
International Covenant on Civil and Political Rights (1966)[3].

There have been many legislative attempts to codify fundamental human rights and
freedoms in the United Kingdom as an enforceable constitutional Bill of Rights, notably
by incorporating the provisions of the Convention into domestic law[4]; however, at the
date at which this volume states the law, incorporation has not been achieved[5]. In the
absence of incorporation, there may nonetheless be some principles, common in
European Community law or the law of other jurisdictions, which are of limited
application in English law[6]; but English law does not provide a protection of civil rights
exactly corresponding to that provided by the Convention for the Protection of Human
Rights and Fundamental Freedoms or other jurisdictions[7].

1   Ie the International Covenant on Economic, Social and Cultural Rights, 16 December 1966 (UN TS
    vol 993, p 3); International Covenant on Civil and Political Rights, 16 December 1966 (UN TS vol 999,
    p 171); Convention for the Protection of Human Rights and Fundamental Freedoms, 4 November 1950
    (Council of Europe, ETS no 5), and Protocols (see note 2 infra; para 122 post); European Agreement
    Relating to Persons Participating in the Proceedings of the European Commission and Court of Human
    Rights, 6 May 1969 (Council of Europe, ETS no 67); European Social Charter, 18 October 1961
    (Council of Europe, ETS no 35); Convention on the Prevention and Punishment of the Crime of
    Genocide, 9 December 1948 (UN TS vol 78 p 277); Slavery Convention signed at Geneva on
    25 September 1926, as amended by Protocol of 7 December 1953 (UN TS vol 212 p 17 and vol 182
    p 51); Supplementary Convention on the Abolition of Slavery, the Slave Trade and Institutions and
    Practices Similar to Slavery, 7 September 1956 (UN TS vol 266 p 3); International Labour Organisation
    Convention no 29 Concerning Forced Labour, 28 June 1930 (UN TS vol 39 p 55); International Labour
    Organisation Convention no 105 Concerning the Abolition of Forced Labour, 25 June 1957 (UN TS
    vol 320 p 291); Convention Against Torture and Other Cruel, Inhuman or Degrading Treatment or
    Punishment, 10 December 1984 (UN General Assembly Resolution 39/46, Doc A/39/51); European
    Convention for the Prevention of Torture and Inhuman or Degrading Treatment or Punishment,
    26 November 1987 (Council of Europe, ETS no 126); Convention for the Protection of Individuals
    With Regard to Automatic Processing of Personal Data, 28 January 1981 (Council of Europe, ETS no
    108); International Labour Organisation Convention no 102 Concerning Minimum Standards of Social
    Security, 28 June 1952 (UN TS vol 210 p 131); European Code of Social Security, 16 April 1964
    (Council of Europe, ETS no 48); Convention Relating to the Status of Refugees, 28 July 1951 (UN TS
    vol 189 p 137); Protocol Relating to the Status of Refugees, 31 January 1967 (UN TS vol 606 p 267);
    European Agreement on the Abolition of Visas for Refugees, 20 April 1959 (Council of Europe, ETS
    no 31); European Agreement on Transfer of Responsibility for Refugees, 16 October 1980 (Council of
    Europe, ETS no 107); Convention Relating to the Status of Stateless Persons, 28 September 1954 (UN
    TS vol 360 p 131); Convention on the Reduction of Statelessness, 30 August 1961 (UN TS vol 989
    p 175); International Labour Organisation Convention no 97 Concerning Migrant Workers, 1 July 1949
    (UN TS vol 120 p 71); International Labour Organisation Convention no 87 Concerning Freedom of
    Association and Protection of the Right to Organise, 9 July 1948 (UN TS vol 68 p 17); International

Labour Organisation Convention no 98 Concerning the Application of the Principles of the Right to Organise and Bargain Collectively, 1 July 1949 (UN TS vol 96 p 257); International Labour Organisation Convention no 122 Concerning Employment Policy, 9 July 1964 (UN TS vol 569 p 65); International Labour Organisation Convention no 135 Concerning Protections and Facilities to be Afforded to Workers' Representatives in the Undertaking, 23 June 1971 (UN TS vol 883 p 111); International Labour Organisation Convention no 141 Concerning Organisations of Rural Workers and their Role in Economic and Social Development, 4 June 1975 (International Labour Organisation Official Bulletin vol LVIII, 1975, Ser A, no 1, pp 28–32); International Labour Organisation Convention no 151 Concerning Protection of the Right to Organise and Procedures for Determining Conditions of Employment in the Public Service, 27 June 1978 (International Labour Organisation Official Bulletin vol LXI, 1978, Ser A, no 2, p 106); Convention on the Political Rights of Women, 20 December 1952 (UN TS vol 193 p 135); Convention on Consent to Marriage, Minimum Age for Marriage and Registration of Marriages, 10 December 1962 (UN TS vol 521 p 231); Convention on the Rights of the Child, 20 November 1989 (UN General Assembly Resolution 44/25; Cm 1976); European Convention on the Legal Status of Children Born Out of Wedlock, 15 October 1975 (Council of Europe, ETS no 85); Geneva Convention Relative to the Protection of Civilian Persons in Time of War, 12 August 1949 (UN TS vol 75 p 287); International Convention on the Elimination of All Forms of Racial Discrimination, 21 December 1965 (UN TS vol 660 p 195); Convention on the Elimination of All Forms of Discrimination Against Women, 18 December 1979 (GA Res 34/180, UN Doc A/34/46); International Labour Organisation Convention no 100 Concerning Equal Remuneration for Men and Women Workers for Work of Equal Value, 29 June 1951 (UN TS vol 165 p 303); Unesco Convention Against Discrimination in Education, 14 December 1960 (UN TS vol 429 p 93).

2    Ie the Convention for the Protection of Human Rights and Fundamental Freedoms (Rome, 4 November 1950; TS 71; Cmd 8969) (frequently referred to as the European Convention on Human Rights): see para 122 post.

3    Ie the International Covenant on Civil and Political Rights (New York, 16 December 1966; ratified by the United Kingdom 20 May 1976; TS 6 (1977): Cmnd 6702;). See generally McGoldrick *The Human Rights Committee* (1990); Harris and Joseph (eds) *The International Covenant on Civil and Political Rights and United Kingdom Law* (1995). Because the United Kingdom has not accepted the Optional Protocol to the International Covenant on Civil and Political Rights, the Human Rights Committee established by Art 28 of that Covenant cannot receive and consider communications from individuals claiming to be victims of violations of the Covenant by the United Kingdom. This, together with the lack of incorporation of the Covenant, explains the relative neglect of the Covenant and of its case law by advocates and courts in this country. However, the United Kingdom is accountable on the international plane to the Human Rights Committee through the reporting procedures under Art 40 of the Covenant. Reports have to be submitted periodically on the measures adopted to give effect to the rights recognised in the Covenant, and on the progress made in the enjoyment of those rights. The United Kingdom has faced pressure from the Human Rights Committee to incorporate the relevant provisions of the Covenant into domestic law. This has been done in the case of Hong Kong by means of the (1991) Hong Kong (Bill of Rights) Ordinance 1991 (Cap 383) Pt II (s 8) arts 1–23. The Human Rights Committee has noted that the legal system of the United Kingdom does not fully ensure that an effective remedy is provided for breaches of the Covenant. The Committee is concerned by the combined effects of the non-incorporation of the Covenant into domestic law, the failure to accede to the Optional Protocol, and the absence of a constitutional Bill of Rights: CCPR/C/79 Add 55, 27 July 1995.

4    For the view that incorporation of the Convention for the Protection of Human Rights and Fundamental Freedoms into English law could be effected by the House of Lords, in its judicial capacity, deciding that it is binding on the English courts, see Loveland *Constitutional Law: A Critical Introduction* (1996) p 600 et seq.

5    For an account of the attempts made to enact a formal constitutional document for the United Kingdom see Zander *A Bill of Rights?* (3rd Edn, 1985) ch 1; and Bailey, Harris and Jones *Civil Liberties: Cases and Materials* (4th Edn, 1995) pp 16–24. See also, subsequent to those texts, the Human Rights Bill of 1994: presented and 1st Reading 559 HL Official Report (5th series), 22 November 1994, col 150; 2nd Reading 560 HL Official Report (5th series), 25 January 1995, col 1136; Committee 561 HL Official Report (5th series), 15 February 1995, col 762; Report 562 HL Official Report (5th series), 29 March 1995, col 1692; 3rd Reading 563 HL Official Report (5th series), 1 May 1995, col 1271.

The absence of incorporation may be seen as a substantial cause of the number of instances in which the European Court of Human Rights and the European Commission of Human Rights have found human rights violations in British cases: see Bailey, Harris and Jones *Civil Liberties: Cases and Materials* (4th Edn, 1995) 20; Loveland *Constitutional Law: A Critical Introduction* (1996) p 589. This has meant that the Convention has been invoked in many significant British cases before the European Commission and Court of Human Rights where, in the other contracting states, constitutional and administrative courts are able to provide effective remedies. The Convention, like European Community law, has therefore come to underpin the British constitution in protecting human rights and freedoms; and both the European Court of Human Rights and the European Court of Justice have served in place of a British constitutional court, able to review the compatibility of legislation with principles which may be seen as constitutional. See eg David Kinley *The European Convention on Human Rights: Compliance without Incorporation* (1993) Appendix 1.

For the view that references to the European Court of Human Rights from states which have not incorporated it into their own law are not disproportionately large see Harris, O'Boyle and Warbrick *Law of the European Convention on Human Rights* (1995) pp 23–24.

For the arguments for and against incorporation of a Bill of Rights see the Green Paper 'Legislation on Human Rights, with particular reference to the European Convention' (Home Office, June 1976). See also *Standing Advisory Commission on a Bill of Rights: The Protection of Human Rights by Law in Northern Ireland* (Cmnd 7009) (1977).

6    The principle of proportionality is a general principle of European Community law and the European Convention on Human Rights: see eg EUROPEAN COMMUNITIES vol 51 para 2.296. It is also well recognised as a legal principle in interpreting alleged infringements of national written constitutions, whether in common law or civil law systems, and it is recognised in some areas of English law, but not yet as an independent ground of judicial review: see generally Jowell and Lester 'Proportionality: Neither Novel nor Dangerous' Current Legal Problems, Special Issue on 'New Directions in Judicial Review' (1990); *R v Secretary of State for the Home Department, ex p Brind* [1991] 1 AC 696 at 747–748, sub nom *Brind v Secretary of State for the Home Department* [1991] 1 All ER 720 at 722–723, HL; *National and Local Government Officers' Association v Secretary of State for the Environment* (1992) Times, 2 December, CA, where the principle of proportionality and Convention jurisprudence were not to be applied when interpreting the Local Government Officers (Political Restrictions) Regulations 1990, SI 1990/851. In *R v Independent Television Commission, ex p TSW Broadcasting Ltd* [1996] EMLR 291, HL, it would seem to have been assumed that it would be appropriate to apply the proportionality principle in cases involving interference with human rights and freedoms. In *R v Secretary of State for the Home Department, ex p Leech* [1994] QB 198, [1993] 4 All ER 539, a proportionality test was adopted in construing a statutory power to censor prisoners' correspondence. In *Rantzen v Mirror Group Newspapers (1986) Ltd* [1994] QB 670 at 690, [1993] 4 All ER 975 at 992, CA, a proportionality test was adopted in construing a statutory power to set aside excessive damages awards in libel cases. In *R v Ministry of Defence, ex p Smith* [1996] 1 All ER 257, CA, in the context of the traditional test of irrationality in English administrative law, it was held that the more substantial the interference with human rights, the more the court would require by way of justification before being satisfied that the decision is reasonable. See also *Cunliffe v Commonwealth* [1995] 1 LRC 54, Aust HC, for differing judicial views on the proportionality test.

7    Eg in the absence of civil wrongdoing amounting to a breach of contract or tort, English administrative law does not provide a remedy in damages for the misuse of public powers in the licensing field, even where there has been an illegal, arbitrary, and unfair misuse of those powers in breach of legitimate expectations: *R v Knowsley Metropolitan Borough Council, ex p Maguire* [1992] NLJR 1375. By contrast, the European Court of Human Rights is empowered, by Art 50 of the European Convention on Human Rights, to afford 'just satisfaction' (which may include damages) to the injured party, if the court finds that a decision or a measure is in conflict with the Convention (see para 180 post), and if internal law allows only partial reparation to be made for the consequences of the decision or measure. Damages may also be awarded for breaches of constitutionally guaranteed rights: see *Maharaj v A-G of Trinidad and Tobago (No 2)* [1979] AC 385, [1978] 2 All ER 670, PC. Member states of the European Community are obliged to make good the damage caused to individuals by a breach of Community law for which they are responsible: Joined Cases C-6/90 and C-9/90 *Francovich and Bonifaci v Italy* [1991] ECR I-5357, [1992] IRLR 84, ECJ.

## 104. International human rights law and English law.

The rights and freedoms contained in the international human rights codes are guaranteed, as a matter of international law, against the misuse of legislative, executive, or judicial powers within the United Kingdom. Their primary purpose is similar to the purpose of much constitutional and administrative law; that is, to protect the individual's rights and interests against the misuse of public powers by public authorities. Both the Convention for the Protection of Human Rights and Fundamental Freedoms[1] and the International Covenant on Civil and Political Rights (1966)[2] oblige the United Kingdom to secure the rights and freedoms in domestic law, and to provide effective remedies before national authorities for breaches of their provisions.

Unless and until the rights contained in the Convention, or the other international human rights instruments to which the United Kingdom is party, are incorporated by statute into domestic law[3], they do not as such form part of English law, and the courts have no power to enforce those rights directly[4]. However, provisions of these instruments are relevant in determining the scope of civil rights and liberties under English law even though these provisions are not a part of English law[5]. This applies in principle to any of the international human rights codes to which the United Kingdom is party. In practice, however, the Convention for the Protection of Human Rights and Fundamental Freedoms is especially influential as a source of protection of civil rights and liberties, because of the right of alleged victims of breaches of the Convention, whether by Parliament, the executive, the judiciary, or any other public authority of the United Kingdom, to complain to the European Commission and Court of Human Rights[6].

This right of recourse to the Convention institutions has led some English courts (especially the House of Lords and the Court of Appeal) to have regard to the Convention and its case law[7]. For example, they may have regard to the provisions of the Convention and to Convention case law to resolve an ambiguity in English primary or subordinate legislation[8]. Where there is an ambiguity, the courts presume that Parliament intended to legislate in conformity with the Convention, and not in conflict with it[9]. They may also have regard to the Convention when contemplating how a judicial discretion is to be exercised, for example, whether or not to grant an interlocutory injunction restricting freedom of expression[10]; or when the common law is developing[11] or uncertain[12], or where it is certain but incomplete[13]. The Convention, and especially the guarantee of freedom of expression[14], may be seen as the articulation of some of the principles underlying the common law[15].

In the absence of statutory incorporation of the international human rights codes into domestic law, it would be a usurpation of the functions of Parliament if the courts were to interpret the statutory powers conferred upon ministers of the Crown as being limited by or subject to those codes[16]. However, stricter judicial scrutiny is called for where fundamental human rights are adversely affected by the administrative decisions of public authorities[17]. The Convention for the Protection of Human Rights and Fundamental Freedoms and the other international human rights codes are also relevant as sources of public policy[18].

Although the European Community has not acceded to the Convention for the Protection of Human Rights and Fundamental Freedoms[19], the European Court of Justice[20] has often had regard to the Convention and to the case law of the European Court of Human Rights as a source of general Community principles of law and interpretation of Community law[21]. In this way, the Convention indirectly influences the laws and practices of the member states of the European Community. Furthermore, where Community legislation is specifically made subject to the Convention[22], the Convention's provisions are indirectly incorporated into domestic law as part of the incorporation of Community law, and domestic courts must then interpret and apply the Convention as part of Community law.

Where Community legislation guarantees fundamental human rights[23], it is a source of rights and remedies which national courts must protect.

1   Ie the Convention for the Protection of Human Rights and Fundamental Freedoms (Rome, 4 November 1950; TS 71; Cmd 8969) Arts 1, 13: see paras 122, 163 post. That Convention is commonly referred to as the European Convention on Human Rights.

2   Ie the International Covenant on Civil and Political Rights (1966) Art 2. As to that Covenant see para 103 note 3 ante.

3   The first international human rights treaty to which the United Kingdom became party after the Second World War was the Convention on the Prevention and Punishment of the Crime of Genocide,

which was approved by the UN General Assembly on 9 December 1948 (Cmnd 4421), came into force in January 1961, and was incorporated into domestic law by the Genocide Act 1969: see s 1, Schedule; and CRIMINAL LAW vol 11(1) (Reissue) para 424. See also the Criminal Justice Act 1988 s 134, which created a crime of torture, defined in accordance with the UN Convention against Torture and Other Cruel, Inhuman or Degrading Treatment or Punishment 1984 (see para 103 note 1 ante); and CRIMINAL LAW vol 11(1) (Reissue) para 504.

4　See eg *Rantzen v Mirror Group Newspapers (1986) Ltd* [1994] QB 670 at 690, [1993] 4 All ER 975 at 992, CA, per Neill LJ.

5　See STATUTES vol 44(1) (Reissue) paras 1455–1468. 'The international human rights instruments and their developing jurisprudence enshrine values and principles long recognised by the common law. These international instruments have inspired many of the constitutional guarantees of fundamental human rights and freedoms within and beyond the Commonwealth. They should be interpreted with the generosity appropriate to charters of freedom. They reflect international law and principle and are of particular importance as aids to interpretation and in helping courts to make choices between competing interests. Whilst not all rights are justiciable in themselves, both civil and political rights and economic and social rights are integral and complementary parts of one coherent system of global human rights. They serve as vital points of reference for judges as they develop the common law and make the choices which it is their responsibility to make in a free and democratic society.' This is part of the so-called 'Balliol Statement' of 1992: (made by the international judicial conference on the domestic application of international human rights norms, held at Balliol College, Oxford 1992): see 'Developing Human Rights Jurisprudence', Commonwealth Secretariat and Interights (1992) p 27 paragraph 5.

6　See the Convention for the Protection of Human Rights and Fundamental Freedoms Art 25; and para 172 post. Successive governments have accepted the right of individual petition, without interruption, since 14 January 1966. For a useful handbook see Clements *European Human Rights: Taking a Case under the Convention* (1994). When the Eleventh Protocol to the Convention comes into force, the right of individual access to the European Court of Human Rights will become direct and permanent: see para 122 post.

7　The decisions in *Sunday Times v United Kingdom* (1979) 2 EHRR 245, ECtHR; and in *Sunday Times v United Kingdom (No 2)* (1992) 14 EHRR 229, ECtHR, were potent influences upon British judicial attitudes, because the European Court of Human Rights there decided that the House of Lords had violated the right to free expression, guaranteed by the Convention for the Protection of Human Rights and Fundamental Freedoms Art 10 (see para 158–159 post), by granting injunctions restraining contempt (in *A-G v Times Newspapers Ltd* [1974] AC 273, [1973] 3 All ER 54, HL), and breach of confidence (in *A-G v Guardian Newspapers Ltd* [1987] 3 All ER 316, [1987] 1 WLR 1248, HL). Similarly, the decision in *Rantzen v Mirror Group Newspapers (1986) Ltd* [1994] QB 670 at 690, [1993] 4 All ER 975 at 992, CA, influenced the European Court of Human Rights in *Tolstoy v United Kingdom* (1995) 20 EHRR 442, in deciding that a jury's award of damages was so excessive as to amount to a breach of Art 10 of the Convention.

8　*R v Secretary of State for the Home Department, ex p Brind* [1991] 1 AC 696 at 747–748, sub nom *Brind v Secretary of State for the Home Department* [1991] 1 All ER 720 at 722–723, HL, 760–761, 734 per Lord Ackner.

9　*R v Secretary of State for the Home Department, ex p Brind* [1991] 1 AC 696 at 747, sub nom *Brind v Secretary of State for the Home Department* [1991] 1 All ER 720 at 723, HL, per Lord Bridge of Harwich.

10　*A-G v Guardian Newspapers Ltd* [1987] 3 All ER 316 at 355, [1987] 1 WLR 1248 at 1296, HL, per Lord Templeman, and at 364, 1307 per Lord Ackner. See also *R v Khan* [1996] 3 All ER 289, HL.

11　In *Mabo v Queensland (No 2)* (1992) 175 CLR 1 at 42, Aust HC, per Brennan J (with whom Mason CJ and McHugh J concurred on this point) observed that 'the common law does not necessarily conform with international law, but international law is a legitimate and important influence on the development of the common law, especially when international law declares the existence of universal human rights.' See also *Dietrich v R* (1992) 177 CLR 292, Aust HC.

12　*A-G v Observer Ltd, A-G v Times Newspapers Ltd* [1990] 1 AC 109, sub nom *A-G v Guardian Newspapers Ltd (No 2)* [1988] 3 All ER 545, HL; *Derbyshire County Council v Times Newspapers Ltd* [1992] QB 770 at 812, [1992] 3 All ER 65 at 77–79, CA, per Balcombe LJ, and at 830, 93 per Butler-Sloss LJ; affd on other grounds [1993] AC 534, [1993] 1 All ER 1011, HL.

13　*Derbyshire County Council v Times Newspapers Ltd* [1992] 1 QB 770 at 812, [1992] 3 All ER 65 at 78–79, CA, per Balcombe LJ, and at 830, 93 per Butler-Sloss LJ; affd on other grounds [1993] AC 534, [1993] 1 All ER 1011, HL; *R v Chief Metropolitan Stipendiary Magistrate, ex p Choudhury* [1991] 1 QB 429 at 449, [1991] 1 All ER 306 at 320, DC, per Watkins LJ. In the absence of legislation incorporating the Convention into English law, it seems unlikely that the courts will use the Convention to create entirely new common law rights and obligations. However, the extent to which a right is entirely new, and so incapable of such judicial development, is controversial. Eg in *Kaye v Robertson* [1991] FSR 62, CA, and in *Malone v Metropolitan Police Comr* [1979] Ch 344, sub nom

*Malone v Metropolitan Police Comr (No 2)* [1979] 2 All ER 620, the courts felt unable to use the guarantee of respect for personal privacy in Art 8 of the Convention (see paras 149–155 post) to develop a right of privacy in English law. For the contrary view (ie that the Convention should inform the common law) see *R v Secretary of State for the Home Department, ex p McQuillan*, [1995] 4 All ER 400 at 422 per Sedley J; and Lester 'English Judges as Law Makers' [1993] Public Law 269 at 284–286. In *R v Khan* [1996] 3 All ER 289, HL, the question whether a right of personal privacy could be developed by reference to Art 8 of the Convention was specifically left open.

14   See the Convention for the Protection of Human Rights and Fundamental Freedoms Art 10; and paras 158–159 post.

15   *Rantzen v Mirror Group Newspapers (1986) Ltd* [1994] QB 670 at 691, [1993] 4 All ER 975 at 993, CA, per Neill LJ. See also *A-G v Observer Ltd, A-G v Times Newspapers Ltd* [1990] 1 AC 109 at 283–284, sub nom *A-G v Guardian Newspapers Ltd (No 2)* [1988] 3 All ER 545 at 660, HL; *Derbyshire County Council v Times Newspapers Ltd* [1993] AC 534 at 551, [1993] 1 All ER 1011 at 1021, HL, per Lord Keith of Kinkel; *R v Secretary of State for the Home Department, ex p Norney* (1995) 7 Administrative Law Reports 861 at 871 per Dyson J.

16   *R v Secretary of State for the Home Department, ex p Brind* [1991] 1 AC 696, sub nom *Brind v Secretary of State for the Home Department* [1991] 1 All ER 720, HL; *National and Local Government Officers' Association v Secretary of State for the Environment* (1992) Times, 2 December, CA. See, however, Sir John Laws 'Is the High Court the Guardian of Fundamental Constitutional Rights?' [1993] Public Law 59 (referred to in *R v Secretary of State for the Home Department, ex p McQuillan* [1995] 4 All ER 400 at 422 per Sedley J); Lester 'Government compliance with international human rights law: a new year's legitimate expectation' [1996] Public Law 187.

17   *Bugdaycay v Secretary of State for the Home Department* [1987] AC 514 at 531, [1987] 1 All ER 940 at 952, HL, per Lord Bridge of Harwich; and at 537, 956 per Lord Templeman (in relation to life and liberty); *R v Secretary of State for the Home Department, ex p Brind* [1991] 1 AC 696, sub nom *Brind v Secretary of State for the Home Department* [1991] 1 All ER 720, HL, (in relation to freedom of expression); *R v Independent Television Commission, ex p TSW Broadcasting Limited* [1996] EMLR 291, HL (obiter in relation to fundamental human rights and freedoms generally). See also *R v Ministry of Defence, ex p Smith* [1996] 1 All ER 257, CA.

18   See eg *Blathwayt v Baron Cawley* [1976] AC 397 at 425–426, [1975] 3 All ER 625 at 636, HL, per Lord Wilberforce (dissenting, but this point agreed by all their Lordships).

19   But see the Treaty on European Union (Cm 1934) Title I Art F para 2, by which the Community, without acceding to the Convention for the Protection of Human Rights and Fundamental Freedoms (1950), agrees to respect the fundamental rights contained in it.

20   As to the European Court of Justice see para 23 note 6 ante. In its opinion 2/94 of 28 March 1996, the European Court of Justice decided that as Community law now stands, the European Community has no competence to accede the Convention.

21   See eg Case 222/84 *Johnston v Chief Constable of the Royal Ulster Constabulary* [1986] ECR 1651, [1987] QB 129, [1986] 3 All ER 135, ECJ; Case 249/86 *Housing of Migrant Workers: EC Commission v Germany* [1989] ECR 1263, [1990] 3 CMLR 540, ECJ; Joined Cases 46/87, 227/88 *Hoechst AG v EC Commission* [1989] ECR 2859, [1991] 4 CMLR 410, ECJ; Case C-260/89 *ERT* [1991] ECR I-2925, [1994] 4 CMLR 540, ECJ; Case C-2/92 *Bostock* [1994] ECR I-955, [1994] 4 CMLR 547, ECJ; *Wachauf*; Case C-168/91 *Konstantinidis* [1993] ECR I-1191, [1993] 3 CMLR 401, ECJ. See further EUROPEAN COMMUNITIES vol 51 para 2.293.

22   Eg the broadcasting and misleading advertising directives which are subject to the guarantee of free expression in the Convention for the Protection of Human Rights and Fundamental Freedoms (1950) Art 10 (see paras 158–159 post): EC Council Directive 84/450 (OJ L250, 19.9.84, p 1) relating to the approximation of the laws of the member states concerning misleading advertising; and EC Council Directive 89/552 (OJ L298, 17.10.89, p 23) on the co-ordination of certain provisions laid down by law, regulation or administrative action in member states concerning the pursuit of television broadcasting facilities.

23   Such as the right to equal pay for men and women (guaranteed by the EC Treaty Art 119 and EC Council Directive 75/117 (OJ L45, 19.2.75, p 19)) on the approximation of the laws of the member states relating to the application of the principle of equal pay for men and women); equal treatment without sex discrimination in employment (guaranteed by EC Council Directive 76/207 (OJ L39, 14.2.76, p 40)) on the implementation of the principle of equal treatment for men and women as regards access to employment, vocational training and promotion and working conditions); social security (guaranteed by EC Council Directive 79/7 (OJ L6, 10.1.79, p 24)) on the progressive implementation of the principle of equal treatment for men and women in matters of social security); occupational social security schemes (guaranteed by EC Council Directive 86/378 (OJ L225, 12.8.86, p 40)) on the implementation of the principle of equal treatment for men and women in occupational social security schemes). See generally EUROPEAN COMMUNITIES vol 52 para 21.01 et seq.

The European Court of Justice has held that EC Council Directive 76/207 (cited supra) prohibits the dismissal of a transsexual for reasons relating to gender reassignment: Case C-13/94 *P v S* [1996] All ER (EC) 397, ECJ.

## (2) HUMAN RIGHTS AND FREEDOMS UNDER ENGLISH LAW

**105. Civil liberties.** The term 'civil liberties' is here used to denote the civil and political rights recognised by the English[1] common law and statutes. The role of civil and political rights[2] in traditional liberal theory is to protect the individual from oppressive actions by the state. In the United Kingdom there is no Bill of Rights against which Acts of Parliament can be tested and as such all the rights enjoyed under English law are residual[3]. Traditionally the English courts have been averse to expressing their reasoning in terms of rights, but recently rights-based reasoning has been adopted[4].

1　Although this paragraph and paras 106–121 post focus on the protection of human rights and civil liberties afforded by English law, frequent reference is made to relevant decisions in other jurisdictions, often those of the Commonwealth, because rights-based reasoning in English law is young, and in the absence of a Bill of Rights, limited (see text and note 4 infra), whereas other Commonwealth jurisdictions have more experience in determining the scope and effect of human rights and competing public interests. Comparison with other jurisdictions is in line with the increasingly international and comparative approach to this branch of the law: see eg *Retrofit (Pte) Ltd v Posts and Telecommunications Corpn (A-G intervening)* 1995 (9) BCLR (Z), Zimb SC; *State v Williams* [1995] 2 LRC 103, SA Const Ct; *Martin v Tauranga District Court* [1995] 2 LRC 788, NZ CA; *Ballina Shire Council v Ringland* (1994) 33 NSWLR 680, Aust CA; *Holomisa v Argus Newspapers Ltd* 1996 (2) SA 588, Witwatersrand Local Div; *A Juvenile v The State* [1989] LRC (Const) 774, Zimb SC; *Catholic Commission for Justice and Peace in Zimbabwe v A-G* [1993] 2 LRC 279, Zimb SC; *Republic v Mbushuu* [1994] 2 LRC 335, Tanz HC; *Rajagopal v State of Tamil Nadu* (1994) 6 SCC 632, Ind SC; *Sata v Post Newspapers Ltd (No 2)* [1995] 2 LRC 61, Zamb HC; *Pointu v Minister of Education and Science* (27 October 1995, unreported), Mauritius SC, where use was made of the principles of the international law of human rights and reference was made to the Convention for the Protection of Human Rights and Fundamental Freedoms (as to which see paras 122–181 post).

2　Rights can be sub-divided into positive rights and negative rights. Positive rights require some action by the state to ensure their fulfilment whilst negative rights merely require that the state refrain from certain forms of action. The common law has traditionally protected only negative rights.

3　By 'residual' is meant that civil liberties under English law are what is left behind after the legal limits have been defined. Civil liberties exist in the interstices of the law. See *A-G v Observer Ltd, A-G v Times Newspapers Ltd* [1990] 1 AC 109 at 178, sub nom *A-G v Guardian Newspapers Ltd (No 2)* [1988] 3 All ER 545 at 596, CA, per Sir John Donaldson MR: 'The starting point of our domestic law is that every citizen has a right to do what he likes, unless restrained by the common law or by statute.' See also at 283, 660, HL, per Lord Goff of Chieveley. For Commonwealth examples of a structure for rights reasoning and the limitations placed upon rights see *R v Big M Drug Mart* (1985) 18 DLR (4th) 321 at 359 et seq, Can SC; *R v Oakes* (1986) 26 DLR (4th) 200.

4　See eg *Derbyshire County Council v Times Newspapers Ltd* [1993] AC 534, [1993] 1 All ER 1011, HL (right to free speech); *Khawaja v Secretary of State for the Home Department* [1984] AC 74, [1983] 1 All ER 765, HL; *Bugdaycay v Secretary of State for the Home Department* [1987] AC 514, [1987] 1 All ER 940, HL (right to life).

**106. Right to life.** The right to life[1] is protected primarily by the criminal law[2], but also by the civil law[3]. Capital punishment has been abolished for all but a few crimes[4]. Abortion is permitted in certain circumstances[5]. Euthanasia, such as by administering a drug, is unlawful[6]. Attempted suicide is no longer unlawful[7], but inciting, aiding, abetting, counselling or procuring suicide are still criminal offences[8].

The right to life is of paramount concern in cases where it is sought to withhold medical treatment from those who cannot give their consent to such withholding[9]. However the courts have declined to interfere with decisions of health authorities not to carry out a treatment on the ground that the patient's right to life has been violated[10]. An adult of sound mind can refuse medical treatment even if in doing so he or she is endangering his own life[11].

A threat to life, such as the perceived risk to a person deported or refused asylum, may have to be balanced against questions of national security[12]. It has been held that, for the purpose of quantifying certain state benefits, those benefits should be sufficient to enable the recipient to carry out a reasonable level of social activity, rather than merely provide attention necessary to maintain life[13]. Under English law, the state and the representatives of the state have no general immunity from the duty to respect the right to life and are subject to the ordinary law of the land save where statute expressly confers special powers[14].

1   For a full judicial discussion of the right to life in English law see *Airedale NHS Trust v Bland* [1993] AC 789 at 826–828, [1993] 1 All ER 821 at 851–852, CA, per Hoffmann LJ, and at 863–864, 865–866, HL, per Lord Goff of Chieveley, where it was observed that the principle of sanctity of human life, although fundamental, was not absolute and must in certain circumstances give way to the principle of self-determination. On the facts of the case it was held to be lawful for doctors to discontinue the patient's treatment even though it was certain that he would die as a result. In *R v Bingley Magistrates, ex p Morrow* (1994) Times, 28 April it was held that the magistrates were correct not to issue a summons for murder against the doctors in the *Airedale NHS Trust v Bland* supra and that the magistrates were bound by the decision in that case. See also *Bugdaycay v Secretary of State for the Home Department* [1987] AC 514 at 531, [1987] 1 All ER 940 at 952, HL, per Lord Bridge of Harwich: 'The most fundamental of all human rights is the individual's right to life and when an administrative decision under challenge is said to be one which may put the applicant's life at risk, the basis of the decision must surely call for the most anxious scrutiny.' For a discussion of the right to life in European Community law and the role of fundamental rights in Community law more generally see Case C-159/90 *Society for the Protection of Unborn Children Ireland Ltd v Grogan* [1991] ECR I-4685, ECJ. As to the right to life under the Convention for the Protection of Human Rights and Fundamental Freedoms see para 123 post.

2   In particular, the criminal offences of murder and manslaughter. It is no defence to a charge of murder or attempted murder that one was acting under the threat of being killed oneself or that others were being so threatened: see *R v Howe* [1987] AC 417, [1987] 1 All ER 771, HL; *R v Gotts* [1992] 2 AC 412, [1992] 1 All ER 832, HL; and CRIMINAL LAW vol 11(1) (Reissue) para 24. Judicial review of a decision not to prosecute is available: *R v DPP, ex p C* (1994) Times, 7 March, DC (although this was not a case involving homicide).

3   The estate of a deceased person has the right to sue for damages by way of compensation where death is caused intentionally or negligently: see NEGLIGENCE vol 34 para 13 et seq.

4   See the Murder (Abolition of the Death Penalty) Act 1965 s 1(1). Capital punishment is still available for treason (Treason Act 1814 s 1) and piracy with violence (Piracy Act 1837 s 2): see CRIMINAL LAW vol 11(2) (Reissue) para 1199. The exercise of the royal prerogative of the pardon may be subject to judicial review: *R v Secretary of State for the Home Department, ex p Bentley* [1994] QB 349, [1993] 4 All ER 442; and see para 823 et seq post. In *The State v Makwanyane* [1995] 1 LRC 269, the Constitutional Court of South Africa unanimously held that capital punishment was contrary to the constitution. See also *S v Ntesang* [1995] 2 LRC 338, Bots CA; *Jabar v Public Prosecutor* [1995] 2 LRC 349, Sing CA; *Pratt v A-G for Jamaica* [1994] 2 AC 1, [1993] 4 All ER 769, PC; *Bradshaw v A-G of Barbados* [1995] 2 WLR 936, PC; *Republic v Mbushuu* [1994] 2 LRC 335, Tanz HC. In *Kindler v Canada* [1993] 4 LRC 85, Can SC, the majority held that there was no violation of the Canadian Charter of Rights and Freedoms in the surrender of a convicted offender to face capital punishment in the United States. See also *Guerra v Baptiste* [1996] 1 AC 397, [1995] 4 All ER 583, PC (appeal from Trinidad and Tobago: notice of execution warrant unconstitutional).

5   See the Abortion Act 1967 s 1 (amended by the Human Fertilisation and Embryology Act 1990 s 37); and MEDICINE vol 30 (Reissue) para 46. There appears to be no right to be aborted (see the Congenital Disabilities (Civil Liability) Act 1976 s 1; and *Report on Injuries to Unborn Children* (Law Com no 60) (1974); *McKay v Essex Area Health Authority* [1982] QB 1166, [1982] 2 All ER 771, CA; and TORT vol 45 para 1277). But also see Fortin 'Is the 'Wrongful Life' Action Really Dead?' [1987] JSWL 306. Although English law protects the foetus in certain circumstances (see eg the Offences Against the Person Act 1861 s 58; and CRIMINAL LAW vol 11(1) (Reissue) para 462 et seq) it does not regard the foetus as having any rights or as being a legal person, so that eg the foetus cannot be made a ward of court (*Re F (in utero)* [1988] Fam 122, [1988] 2 All ER 193, CA; see CHILDREN vol 5(2) (Reissue) para 760) and although the Congenital Disabilities (Civil Liability Act) 1976 does give certain rights to claim damages to children born disabled as a result of an injury to one or both of the parents before birth such rights do not vest until birth (*Paton v British Pregnancy Advisory Service Trustees* [1979] QB 276, [1978] 2 All ER 987). For the position under the Convention for the Protection of Human Rights and Fundamental Freedoms (1950) see para 122 text and note 1 post.

6   In *Airedale NHS Trust v Bland* [1993] AC 789, [1993] 1 All ER 821, HL, it was emphasised that taking active steps, such as administering a drug, to end another's life, no matter how humanitarian the motive, remains murder. See also *R v Cox* (18 September 1992, unreported).

7   See the Suicide Act 1961 s 1; and CRIMINAL LAW vol 11(1) (Reissue) para 442.

8   See the Suicide Act 1961 s 2 (as amended); and CRIMINAL LAW vol 11(1) (Reissue) paras 58, 443.

9   See *Airedale NHS Trust v Bland* [1993] AC 789, [1993] 1 All ER 821, HL. See also *Re B (a minor) (wardship: medical treatment)* (1981) [1990] 3 All ER 927, [1981] 1 WLR 1421, CA (parents' wish to withhold medical treatment from seriously ill and handicapped child who was a ward of court were not conclusive; it is not for a court to say that the life of a seriously handicapped person ought not to be saved); *Re C (a minor) (wardship: medical treatment)* [1990] Fam 26, [1989] 2 All ER 782, CA (doctors allowed to withhold life-prolonging medical treatment but directed to treat to relieve the child's suffering, but it was emphasised that the doctors could not be permitted to take any active steps to end the child's life (see text and note 6 supra); *Re J (a minor) (wardship: medical treatment)* [1991] Fam 33, [1990] 3 All ER 930, CA (the duty to keep alive is qualified: it may not always be in the patient's best interests to be kept alive, and the quality of life if treatment was continued was relevant; the Court of Appeal balanced the interests as they would be seen by a person in the ward's position). In *Re F (mental patient: sterilisation)* [1990] 2 AC 1, sub nom *F v West Berkshire Health Authority (Mental Health Commission intervening)* [1989] 2 All ER 545, HL, the test was whether the proposed treatment was in the best interests of the person, as determined by whether it would be approved by a responsible body of professional medical opinion (*Bolam v Friern Hospital Management Committee* [1957] 2 All ER 118, [1957] 1 WLR 582), observing that an operation would only be in the best interests of a patient if it was carried out in order to save life, or to ensure improvement or prevent deterioration in the patient's condition. For the treatment of the issue by the Irish Supreme Court see *Re a Ward of Court* (27 July 1995, unreported) Record Nos 167/171/175/177–195).

10  See *R v Cambridge Health Authority, ex p B* [1995] 2 All ER 129, CA (in the Divisional Court Laws J said that there was a positive duty on the health authority to sustain life wherever there was a chance, however slim, of survival; but the Court of Appeal disagreed, stating that the health authority had had full regard to all the relevant considerations). See also *Re J (a minor) (child in care: medical treatment)* [1993] Fam 15 at 28, [1992] 4 All ER 614 at 623, CA, per Lord Donaldson MR (the court should not make orders of medical treatment with consequences for the use of health authority's resources since it is in no position to express a view as to how such resources should be deployed).

11  See *Re T (adult: refusal of medical treatment)* [1993] Fam 95, [1992] 4 All ER 649, CA (where, however, the patient's decision was held invalid for want of capacity). In *Rodriguez v A-G of Canada* [1994] 2 LRC 136, Can SC, the court refused an application by an individual suffering from a terminal disease to have a statute which made it an offence to aid or abet a suicide declared unconstitutional on the grounds that it violated her right to life, liberty and security of person as guaranteed by the Canadian Charter of Rights and Freedoms ss 1, 7.

12  *R v Secretary of State for the Home Department, ex p Chahal* [1995] 1 All ER 658, [1995] 1 WLR 526, CA (risk to the applicant had to be balanced against the interests of national security, but because the court could not examine the evidence of danger to national security, it could not say that the decision was wrong, and had to find for the Secretary of State). See also *R v Secretary of State for Home Department, ex p McQuillan* [1995] 4 All ER 400.

13  *Secretary of State for Social Security v Fairey* (1995) 26 BMLR 63, CA.

14  The representatives of the state may take advantage of the ordinary defences of self-defence, the defence of others and duress, but there is no general defence open to members of the armed forces or the police of obedience to superior orders: *R v Clegg* [1995] 1 AC 482, [1995] 1 All ER 334, HL, where the House declined to change the law so that a verdict of manslaughter could be returned where the degree of force used by a member of the armed forces in self-defence was deemed to be excessive, saying that this was a matter for Parliament). As to the application of self-defence in relation to the use of force by agents of the state see *A-G for Northern Ireland's Reference (No 1 of 1975)* [1977] AC 105, [1976] 2 All ER 937, HL; *Farrell v Secretary of State for Defence* [1980] 1 All ER 166, [1980] 1 WLR 172, HL.

**107. Freedom of expression.** The right to freedom of expression¹, particularly the freedom to criticise public bodies, is regarded by the courts as one of the most important freedoms². It is protected by various provisions that positively encourage or require free speech³. The public interest in free speech may, however, be subservient to a competing public interest in (for example):

(1)   national security⁴, under either the civil law⁵ or the criminal law⁶;

(2) the fair administration of justice under the rules relating to contempt of court[7], for contempt in the face of the court[8], scandalizing the court[9], prejudicing legal proceedings[10] and disobeying an order of the court[11];

(3) the restriction of obscene and corrupting or otherwise offensive material[12];

(4) the protection of religious beliefs[13];

(5) the maintenance of public order[14];

(6) the protection of vulnerable groups[15];

(7) the protection of confidence in institutions[16];

(8) certain limitations on the extent to which public authorities can disseminate information[17];

(9) the protection of reputations[18];

(10) the right to personal privacy[19].

The content of information distributed via television[20], radio[21] and video recordings[22] is regulated.

Additionally, the right to freedom of expression has been considered in the context of distribution of leaflets urging the public not to buy certain goods[23], and guidance on advertising issued by the General Medical Council[24].

1 For the role of freedom of expression in European Community law see Case C-159/90 *Society for the Protection of Unborn Children Ireland Ltd v Grogan* [1991] ECR I-4685, ECJ. For judicial discussion of the importance of the right to freedom of expression see *Re X (a minor) (wardship: jurisdiction)* [1975] Fam 47, sub nom *Re X (a minor) (wardship: restriction on publication)* [1975] 1 All ER 697, CA; *Harman v Secretary of State for the Home Department* [1983] 1 AC 280, sub nom *Home Office v Harman* [1982] 1 All ER 532, HL (particularly contrast the speeches of Lord Diplock and Lord Scarman); *Wheeler v Leicester City Council* [1985] AC 1054, [1985] 2 All ER 1106, HL; *R v Secretary of State for the Home Department, ex p Brind* [1991] 1 AC 696, sub nom *Brind v Secretary of State for the Home Department* [1991] 1 All ER 720, HL; *Derbyshire County Council v Times Newspapers Ltd* [1993] AC 534, [1993] 1 All ER 1011, HL; *R v Advertising Standards Authority Ltd, ex p Vernons Organisation Ltd* [1993] 2 All ER 202, [1992] 1 WLR 1289 (general principle that the courts will not restrain the expression of opinion and conveyance of information whether by a private individual or a public body, save on pressing grounds); *R v Central Independent Television plc* [1994] Fam 192, [1994] 3 All ER 641, CA. For a discussion of the role of freedom of expression in Australian law see *Australian Capital Television Pty Ltd v Commonwealth of Australia* (1992) 177 CLR 106, Aust HC; and *Nationwide News Pty Ltd v Wills* (1992) 177 CLR 1, Aust HC, where the majority found an implied freedom of communication within the Constitution, at least in relation to political discussion, and declared invalid a Commonwealth Act of Parliament on the ground that it infringed the freedom. In *Retrofit (Pte) Ltd v Posts and Telecommunications Corpn (A-G intervening)* 1995 (9) BCLR (Z) Zimb SC, it was held that prima facie a state monopoly on telecommunications could offend the constitutional protection of free expression. See also *Government of the Republic of South Africa v Sunday Times Newspaper* [1995] 1 LRC 168, SA SC (Transvaal Division); *Holomisa v Argus Newspapers Ltd* 1996 (2) SA 588, Witwatersrand Local Div. As to the right to freedom of expression under the Convention for the Protection of Human Rights and Fundamental Freedoms see paras 158–159 post.

2 See in particular *Derbyshire County Council v Times Newspapers Ltd* [1993] AC 534 at 551, [1993] 1 All ER 1011 at 1021, HL, per Lord Keith of Kinkel; and *A-G v Observer Ltd, A-G v Times Newspapers Ltd* [1990] 1 AC 109 at 283–284, sub nom *A-G v Guardian Newspapers Ltd (No 2)* [1988] 3 All ER 545 at 660, HL, per Lord Goff of Chieveley, expressing the view that there was no difference between the common law protection of freedom of expression and the protection afforded by the Convention for the Protection of Human Rights and Fundamental Freedoms Art 10: 'It is established in the jurisprudence of the European Court of Human Rights that the word "necessary" in this context implies the existence of a pressing social need, and that interference with freedom of expression should be no more than is proportionate to the legitimate aim pursued. I have no reason to believe that English law, as applied in the courts, leads to any different conclusion.' See also *Rantzen v Mirror Group Newspapers (1986) Ltd* [1994] QB 670, [1993] 4 All ER 975, CA. For Commonwealth examples see *Woods v Minister of Justice, Legal and Parliamentary Affairs* 1995 (1) BCLR 56, Zimb SC (on the right of prisoners to write letters); and *Kauesa v Minister of Home Affairs, Namibia* 1995 (11) BCLR 1540, Namibia SC (police regulation prohibiting serving members of the force from criticising the administration of the force or other government departments declared unconstitutional).

3 Members of the Houses of Parliament when speaking in Parliament are absolutely privileged; what is said in Parliament cannot be made the subject matter of court proceedings: see para 210 post. See also, on the

publication of papers printed by order of Parliament, the Parliamentary Papers Act 1840; and PARLIAMENT. On the relationship between defamation proceedings and Parliamentary proceedings see *Rost v Edwards* [1990] 2 QB 460, [1990] 2 All ER 654; *Prebble v Television New Zealand Ltd* [1995] 1 AC 321, [1994] 3 All ER 407, PC; and *Blackshaw v Lord* [1984] QB 1, [1983] 2 All ER 311, CA. See also the Defamation Act 1996 ss 13, 19(2) which, as from 4 September 1996, permit an individual member of Parliament to waive parliamentary privilege for the purpose of defamation proceedings in which his conduct relating to parliamentary activities is in issue. As to state assistance to freedom of expression see the Representation of the People Act 1983 ss 95, 96, 97 (ss 95, 96 as amended); and ELECTIONS vol 15 (Reissue) paras 676–680. Educational institutions providing further education funded by the state are required to ensure that freedom of speech is available to those speaking on their premises: Education (No 2) Act 1986 s 43; *R v University of Liverpool, ex p Caesar-Gordon* [1991] 1 QB 124, [1990] 3 All ER 821, DC. As to charitable status and political organisations see *McGovern v A-G* [1982] Ch 321, [1981] 3 All ER 493; and CHARITIES vol 5(2) (Reissue) para 60. The Fair Trading Act 1973 s 59(3) requires the Monopolies and Mergers Commission to take account of 'the need for accurate presentation of news and free expression of opinion,' in deciding whether a newspaper merger will operate against the public interest: see TRADE, INDUSTRY AND INDUSTRIAL RELATIONS vol 47 (Reissue) para 126.

4　　In *R v Ponting* [1985] Crim LR 318, Crown Court, McCowan J accepted, in the context of the Official Secrets Act 1911 s 2 (repealed), that the interests of the state were to be defined by the government of the day, and for the purposes of the trial were identical with the interests of the government of the day. But see also *Chandler v DPP* [1964] AC 763, [1962] 3 All ER 142, HL, on the Official Secrets Act 1911 s 1 (as amended).

5　　The doctrine of confidentiality is a private law doctrine that can be used by the state: *A-G v Jonathan Cape Ltd, A-G v Times Newspapers Ltd* [1976] QB 752, [1975] 3 All ER 484, HL. However, there are special rules to be applied when considering whether the government can succeed in a claim for breach of confidence, namely: (1) the government must show a clear public interest in maintaining secrecy; (2) there will be no restraint if the public interest in disclosure outweighs the interest in secrecy; and (3) prior restraint is unlikely if the information is already in the public domain: see *A-G v Observer Ltd, A-G v Times Newspapers Ltd* [1990] 1 AC 109, sub nom *A-G v Guardian Newspapers Ltd (No 2)* [1988] 3 All ER 345, HL. See also *A-G v Blake* (19 April 1996, unreported). In certain circumstances an injunction against one newspaper restraining a breach of confidence will bind any other newspaper that has notice of the injunction: *A-G v Newspaper Publishing plc* [1988] Ch 333, [1987] 3 All ER 276, CA; *A-G v Times Newspapers Ltd* [1992] 1 AC 191, [1991] 2 All ER 398, HL. See generally CONFIDENCE AND DATA PROTECTION vol 8(1) (Reissue) para 434.

6　　Eg offences under the Official Secrets Acts 1911 and 1989; treason; sedition; incitement to mutiny or disaffection: see CRIMINAL LAW vol 11(1) (Reissue) paras 76 et seq, 89–91, 92 et seq, 245 et seq.

7　　See generally CONTEMPT. But note the decision in *R v Solicitor General, ex p Taylor* (1995) Times, 14 August, sub nom *R v A-G, ex p Taylor* (1995) Independent, 3 August, DC, that there is no jurisdiction to review the decisions of the Solicitor General or the Attorney General.

8　　The offence of contempt in the face of the court is designed to protect the conduct of court proceedings from untoward conduct within the court itself: *Morris v Crown Office* [1970] 2 QB 114, [1970] 1 All ER 1079, CA (dealing with a demonstration in court); *Balogh v Crown Court at St Albans* [1975] QB 73, [1974] 3 All ER 283, CA (principles to be applied when dealing with contempt in the face of the court); and see CONTEMPT vol 9 paras 5, 6, 89.

9　　The offence of scandalising the court is designed to protect the judicial process from certain types of comment designed to lower confidence in the judicial process: see *Ambard v A-G for Trinidad and Tobago* [1936] AC 322, [1936] 1 All ER 704, PC; *R v Metropolitan Police Comr, ex p Blackburn (No 2)* [1968] 2 QB 150, [1968] 2 All ER 319, CA; *Badry v DPP of Mauritius* [1983] 2 AC 297, [1982] 3 All ER 973, PC.

10　　Preventing the prejudice of legal proceedings is usually concerned with preventing prejudicial publicity about a case, but it can take the form of interfering with an individual's conduct of a case: see *Raymond v Honey* [1983] 1 AC 1, [1982] 1 All ER 756, HL. As to the former see the Contempt of Court Act 1981; the common law offence of contempt of court (see *A-G v News Group Newspapers plc* [1989] QB 110, [1988] 2 All ER 906, DC; *A-G v Sport Newspapers Ltd* [1992] 1 All ER 503, [1991] 1 WLR 1194, DC); and CONTEMPT. On the question of prejudice see *A-G v English* [1983] 1 AC 116, [1982] 2 All ER 903, HL; *A-G v News Group Newspapers Ltd* [1987] QB 1, [1986] 2 All ER 833, CA). On protecting a journalist's sources see the Contempt of Court Act 1981 s 10; and *Secretary of State for Defence v Guardian Newspapers Ltd* [1985] AC 339, [1984] 3 All ER 601, HL (test under the Contempt of Court Act 1981 s 10 is one of necessity not one of convenience or expedience); *Re an Inquiry under the Companies Securities (Insider Dealing) Act 1985* [1988] AC 660 at 704, [1988] 1 All ER 203 at 208–209, HL, per Lord Griffiths (necessity lies somewhere between 'indispensable' and 'useful' or 'expedient'); *X Ltd v Morgan-Grampian (Publishers) Ltd* [1991] 1 AC 1 at 43, [1990] 2 All ER 1 at 8, HL, per Lord Bridge of Harwich (where national security or crime prevention is concerned an order for disclosure will follow almost automatically). As to the definition of a court for the purposes of contempt of court see *A-G v BBC* [1981] AC 303, [1980] 3 All ER 161, HL; and *Pickering v Associated Newspapers Holdings plc* [1991] 2 AC 370, sub nom *Pickering v Liverpool Daily Post and Echo Newspapers plc* [1991] 1 All ER 622, HL. In *Solicitor General v Radio New Zealand Ltd* [1994] 2 LRC 116, NZ HC, the court decided that the law of contempt was compatible with the right to freedom of expression in s 14 of the New Zealand Bill of Rights Act 1990. See further para 119 note 8 post. In *Television New Zealand Ltd v Police* [1995] 2 LRC 808, NZ HC, search warrants against television companies were upheld.

11  See generally CONTEMPT. If a party does not comply with an order of the court restricting publication then that party will be in contempt of court. In certain circumstances an injunction against one newspaper restraining a breach of confidence will bind any other newspaper that has notice of the injunction: see note 5 supra.

12  See the Post Office Act 1953 s 11 (as amended); the Children and Young Persons (Harmful Publications) Act 1955; the Obscene Publications Act 1959; the Theatres Act 1968; the Protection of Children Act 1978; the Indecent Displays (Control) Act 1981; the Public Order Act 1986 s 20 (as amended); *Shaw v DPP* [1962] AC 220, [1961] 2 All ER 446, HL; *R v Knuller (Publishing, Printing and Promotions) Ltd* [1973] AC 435, [1972] 2 All ER 898, HL; and *R v Gibson* [1990] 2 QB 619, [1991] 1 All ER 439, CA (the common law offence of outraging public decency has survived the Obscene Publications Act 1959 and the prosecution need not show that the defendant intended to cause outrage); *R v Bow Street Metropolitan Stipendary Magistrate, ex p Noncyp Ltd* [1990] 1 QB 123, [1989] 3 WLR 467, CA.

13  As to the right to freedom of conscience contrasted with the right to freedom of expression see para 108 post.

14  See the Public Order Act 1986 ss 4, 4A (as added) 5, and Pt III (ss 17–29) (as amended) (offences relating to racial hatred); and *R v Horseferry Road Metropolitan Stipendiary Magistrate, ex p Siadatan* [1991] 1 QB 260, [1991] 1 All ER 324, DC (the publishing of the novel *The Satanic Verses* did not constitute an offence under Public Order Act 1986 s 4(1)); *DPP v Clarke* (1991) 94 Cr App Rep 359, DC. See also the Public Order Act 1936 s 1 (as amended); and *O'Moran v DPP* [1975], QB 864, [1975] 1 All ER 473, DC. In *Re Criminal Code (Manitoba)* [1993] 1 LRC 367, Can SC, it was held that a provision in the Criminal Code outlawing the stopping of, or communication with, any other person in a public place for the purpose of engaging in prostitution did not infringe the guarantee of free expression, or the right to liberty, notwithstanding that prostitution was not of itself unlawful. In *R v Keegstra* [1991] LRC (Const) 333, Can SC, the court upheld the constitutionality of criminal sanctions against promoting racial hatred (see also *Taylor v Human Rights Commission* [1991] LRC (Const) 445, Can SC; *Andrews v R* [1991] LRC (Const) 431, Can SC).

15  Local education authorities, governing bodies and headteachers of maintained schools are forbidden from promoting any partisan political views when teaching: see EDUCATION vol 15 (Reissue) para 113. Local education authorities are generally forbidden to promote homosexuality by publishing or teaching: see EDUCATION vol 15 (Reissue) para 115. For the use of the wardship jurisdiction to prevent publication of private information see para 110 note 19 post. In *A-G v Able* [1984] 1 QB 795, [1984] 1 All ER 277 the Attorney-General unsuccessfully attempted to obtain an injunction to prevent the distribution of a guide to suicide on the grounds that its publication would amount to the crime of counselling or procuring suicides.

16  For the restrictions on national civil servants see note 4 supra; and paras 560–561 post. For the restrictions on the freedom of expression of local authority employees see the Local Government and Housing Act 1989 ss 1, 2 (as amended); *National and Local Government Officers' Association v Secretary of State for the Environment* (1992) Times, 2 December, CA; and LOCAL GOVERNMENT. In *Osborne v Canada (Treasury Board)* [1993] 2 LRC 1, Can SC, the court held that the prohibition of civil servants from engaging in work for or against a political party infringed the constitutional right to free expression. In *Hector v A-G of Antigua and Barbuda* [1990] 2 AC 312, [1990] 2 All ER 103, PC, an offence of publishing a false statement which was 'likely to undermine public confidence in the conduct of public affairs' offended against the constitutional guarantee of free expression.

17  In relation to central government see *R v Secretary of State for the Environment, ex p Greenwich London Borough Council* (1989) Times, 17 May, DC. In relation to local government see eg the Local Government Act 1986 s 2A (added by the Local Government Act 1988 s 28 ('clause 28', information regarding homosexuality)); and *R v Inner London Education Authority, ex p Westminster City Council* [1986] 1 All ER 19, [1986] 1 WLR 28; *R v Derbyshire County Council, ex p Times Supplements Ltd* [1990] NLJR 1421, DC.

18  In *Derbyshire County Council v Times Newspapers Ltd* [1993] AC 534, [1993] 1 All ER 1011, HL, it was held that at common law a local authority did not have the right to maintain an action for damages for defamation as it would tend to inhibit free criticism of public authorities, and that there was no public interest in allowing either local or central government to maintain such an action. In *Rantzen v Mirror Group Newspapers (1986) Ltd* [1994] QB 670, [1993] 4 All ER 975, CA, it was held that the court's power under the Courts and Legal Services Act 1990 s 8 to order a new trial or substitute another award

in any case where the damages awarded by a jury were excessive should be construed in a manner that was not inconsistent with the Convention for the Protection of Human Rights and Fundamental Freedoms Art 10 (see paras 158–159 post). See also *John v Mirror Group Newspapers Ltd* [1996] 2 All ER 35, CA (damage to reputation compared to personal injury to ensure a proprotionate award in accordance with Art 10 of the Convention); *Bonnard v Perryman* [1891] 2 Ch 269, CA (interim injunction will not generally be ordered to prevent publication of allegedly libellous material especially if the defendants intend to justify the allegations). On the relationship between defamation proceedings and parliamentary proceedings see note 3 supra.

'The defence of fair comment is now recognised to be one of the most valuable parts of the law of libel and slander. It is an essential part of the greater right of free speech. It is the right of every man to comment freely, fairly and honestly on any matter of public interest': *Kemsley v Foot* [1951] 2 KB 34 at 46–47, [1951] 1 All ER 331 at 338, CA, per Birkett LJ; affd [1952] AC 345, [1952] 1 All ER 501, HL. For the effect on defamation law in Australia of the constitutional principle protecting freedom of expression in relation to political matters see *Theophanous v Herald & Weekly Times Ltd* [1994] 3 LRC 369; *Stephens v West Australian Newspapers Ltd* [1994] 3 LRC 446; and *Ballina Shire Council v Ringland* (1994) 33 NSWLR 680. *Holomisa v Argus Newspapers Ltd* 1996 (2) SA 588, Witwatersrand Local Div; *Sata v Post Newspapers Ltd (No 2)* [1995] 2 LRC 61, Zamb HC; *Hill v Church of Scientology of Toronto* (1995) 126 DLR (4th) 129, Can SC; *Rashid v Nizami* (19 February 1996, unreported), Lahore HC. For an analysis of the 'horizontal' versus 'vertical' arguments of the application of fundamental human rights in this context see *Gardener v Whitaker* 1994 (5) BCLR 19, *Jurgen v Editor, Sunday Times Newspaper* 1995 (1) BCLR 97. Cf *Du Plessis v De Klerk* 1996 (5) BCLR 658, SA Const Ct. In *Public Prosecutor v Pung Chen Choon* [1994] 2 LRC 236, Malaysia SC, it was held that the offence of malicious publication of false news was not contrary to the Constitution. See Barendt 'Libel and Freedom of Speech in English Law' [1993] Public Law 449. See generally TORT.

19   See para 110 post.

20   Both the British Broadcasting Corporation and the independent television companies are subject to the Broadcasting Complaints Commission and the Broadcasting Standards Council (see the Broadcasting Act 1990; and TELECOMMUNICATIONS AND BROADCASTING). See *R v Broadcasting Complaints Commission, ex p BBC* (1984) 128 Sol Jo 384, CA; *R v Broadcasting Complaints Commission, ex p BBC* (1992) Times, 16 October; *R v Broadcasting Complaints Commission, ex p Granada Television* [1993] EMLR 426, Times, 31 May; *R v Broadcasting Complaints Commission, ex p Owen* [1985] QB 1153, [1985] 2 All ER 522, DC. The independent television services are also regulated by the Independent Television Commission (see the Broadcasting Act 1990; and *R v Independent Broadcasting Authority, ex p Whitehouse* (1985) Times, 4 April, CA). The Secretary of State may by notice in writing require the BBC to refrain from broadcasting certain matters: see *R v Secretary of State for the Home Department, ex p Brind* [1991] 1 AC 696, sub nom *Brind v Secretary of State for the Home Department* [1991] 1 All ER 720, HL). The Secretary of State may also direct the independent television services not to broadcast certain matters (Broadcasting Act 1990 s 10). As to injunctions against broadcasting organisations see *Cambridge Nutrition Ltd v BBC* [1990] 3 All ER 523, CA (approved in *Secretary of State for Home Department v Central Broadcasting Ltd* [1993] EMLR 253, CA, where Hirst LJ considered *Cambridge Nutrition Ltd v BBC* supra to be fully in line with the Convention for the Protection of Human Rights and Fundamental Freedoms Art 10); and *R v Advertising Standards Authority Ltd, ex p Vernons Organisation Ltd* [1993] 2 All ER 202, [1992] 1 WLR 1289.

21   See the Broadcasting Act s 90 as to the duties of the Radio Authority; and TELECOMMUNICATIONS AND BROADCASTING.

22   See generally the Video Recordings Act 1984; and TELECOMMUNICATIONS AND BROADCASTING.

23   See *Middlebrook Mushrooms Ltd v Transport and General Workers' Union* [1993] ICR 612, CA (Convention for the Protection of Human Rights and Fundamental Freedoms Art 10 should be borne in mind when considering whether to grant an injunction).

24   In *R v General Medical Council, ex p Colman* [1989] COD 313 (the case was subsequently settled in the course of proceedings before the European Court of Human Rights after the relevant restraint on free expression had been abolished: *Colman v United Kingdom* A 258-D (1993), 18 EHRR 119, ECtHR.

## 108. Freedom of conscience. Freedom of conscience[1] is closely related to freedom of expression[2] and includes freedom of religion[3].

1   See *Wheeler v Leicester City Council* [1985] 1 AC 1054 at 1080, [1985] 2 All ER 1106 at 1112–1113, HL, per Lord Templeman: 'The laws of this country are not like the laws of Nazi Germany. A private individual or a private organisation cannot be obliged to display zeal in pursuit of an object sought by a public authority and cannot be obliged to publish views dictated by a public authority,' and in the Court of Appeal [1985] 1 AC 1054 at 1061, [1985] 2 All ER 151 at 156 per Browne-Wilkinson LJ (dissenting):

'The case raises a conflict between two basic principles of a democratic society; viz, on the one hand, the right of a democratically elected body to conduct its affairs in accordance with its own views and, on the other, the right to freedom of speech and conscience enjoyed by each individual in a democratic society.' See also the Human Fertilisation and Embryology Act 1990 s 38, by which no duty may be imposed under the Act on a person who has a conscientious objection to participating in activities governed by the Act; see MEDICINE vol 30 (Reissue) para 69. Parents may insist on their children being excused from attendance at religious worship and instruction: see EDUCATION vol 15 (Reissue) para 60.

2    See para 107 ante.

3    The offence of blasphemous libel is an uncertain offence but appears to involve the denial of the Christian faith in terms of wanton or unnecessary profanity which are likely to shock and outrage the sensibilities of ordinary Christians: see *Whitehouse v Gay News Ltd, Whitehouse v Lemon* [1979] AC 617, sub nom *R v Gay News Ltd* [1979] 1 All ER 898, HL. See further CRIMINAL LAW vol 11(1) (Reissue) para 348. The offence protects only the Christian religion: *R v Chief Metropolitan Stipendiary Magistrate, ex p Choudhury* [1991] 1 QB 429, [1991] 1 All ER 306, DC. Religious organisations can obtain charitable status; for the definition of what is a religion see *Dunne v Byrne* [1912] AC 407, HL; *Bowman v Secular Society* [1917] AC 406, HL; *Re South Place Ethical Society, Barralet v A-G* [1980] 1 WLR 1565. As to recognition of different religions under the law see eg the Local Government Finance Act 1988 s 51, Sch 5 para 11 (amended by the Local Government Finance Act 1992 s 104, Sch 10 para 3) (non-domestic rating: exempt hereditaments). Note the Education Reform Act 1988 s 8, which provides that the agreed syllabus for religious education must reflect the fact that the religious traditions in England are in the main Christian whilst taking account of the teaching and practices of the other principal religions represented in Great Britain. But see also s 9, which provides that religious observance must not be a condition of admission to any maintained school. On the special status of the Church of England see ECCLESIASTICAL LAW vol 14 paras 345–360. For a Commonwealth example of the right to freedom of religion see *Re Chikweche* [1995] 2 LRC 93, Zimb SC (Rastafarian unlawfully barred from legal practice for wearing hair in dreadlocks). For the position under the Convention for the Protection of Human Rights and Fundamental Freedoms see para 156 post.

**109. Right to free assembly.** The right to free assembly is regarded as being an aspect of the right to freedom of expression[1]. However, it is subject to regulation by both common law and statute. Everyone has the prima facie right to pass along the highway[2]. The common law rules relating to breach of the peace[3] remove certain rights from a person who commits or who threatens to commit a breach of the peace[4]. There are several statutory offences that limit the right to free assembly[5]. The police also have powers to regulate demonstrations[6]. There is a statutory right to picket[7].

1    See *Hubbard v Pitt* [1976] QB 142 at 178, [1975] 3 All ER 1 at 10, CA, per Lord Denning MR (dissenting) (application for interlocutory injunction to restrain defendants from demonstrating): 'Here we have to consider the right to demonstrate and the right to protest on matters of public concern. These are rights which it is in the public interest that individuals should possess; and, indeed, that they should exercise without impediment so long as no wrongful act is done. It is often the only means by which grievances can be brought to the knowledge of those in authority...[the courts] should not interfere by interlocutory injunction with the right to demonstrate and to protest any more than they should interfere with the right of free speech.' See also *Verrall v Great Yarmouth Borough Council* [1981] 1 QB 202 at 217–218, [1980] 1 All ER 839 at 845, CA, per Lord Denning MR ('Freedom of assembly is another of our precious freedoms. Everyone is entitled to meet and assemble with his fellows to discuss their affairs and to promote their views'; court ordered specific performance by local authority of contract to allow the National Front to use council building for annual conference). For a Commonwealth example see *Re Munhumeso* 1995 (2) BCLR 125, Zimb SC. As to the position under the Convention for the Protection of Human Rights and Fundamental Freedoms Art 11 see para 160 post.

2    But see the Highways Act 1980 s 137 (as amended) (wilful obstruction of the highway); and *Arrowsmith v Jenkins* [1963] 2 QB 561, [1963] 2 All ER 210, DC. See further HIGHWAYS vol 21 (Reissue) para 466. The court will consider the reasonableness of the activity that causes the obstruction: see *Nagy v Weston* [1965] 1 All ER 78, [1965] 1 WLR 280, DC; and *Hirst v Chief Constable of West Yorkshire* (1986) 85 Cr App Rep 143, DC; and obstructing the highway constitutes a public nuisance if unreasonable. As to what is unreasonable see *R v Clark (No 2)* [1964] 2 QB 315, sub nom *R v Clark* [1963] 3 All ER 884, CCA.

3    Breach of the peace was defined in *R v Howell* [1982] QB 416 at 427, [1981] 3 All ER 383 at 389, CA, as: 'whenever harm is actually done or is likely to be done to a person or in his presence to his property or a person is in fear of being so harmed through an assault, an affray, a riot, unlawful assembly or other disturbance. It is for this breach of the peace when done in his presence or the reasonable apprehension

of it taking place that a constable, or anyone else, may arrest an offender without warrant.' See also *Wise v Dunning* [1902] 1 KB 167 (breach of the peace can be committed by person who, in addressing meeting in public places, although not directly inciting breaches of the peace, uses language the natural consequence of which is that breaches of the peace will be committed by others, and who intends to holds similar meetings, and use similar language in the future); *R v Chief Constable of Devon and Cornwall, ex p Central Electricity Generating Board* [1982] QB 458 at 472, [1981] 3 All ER 826 at 832, CA, per Lord Denning MR ('There is a breach of the peace whenever a person who is lawfully carrying out his work is unlawfully prevented by another from doing it'); *Parkin v Norman* [1983] 1 QB 92, [1982] 2 All ER 583, DC; *Moss v McLachlan* [1984] IRLR 76, DC (arrest for apprehended breach of the peace need not take place in the location where it is apprehended that the breach of the peace will occur); *McConnell v Chief Constable of Greater Manchester Police* [1990] 1 All ER 423, [1990] 1 WLR 364, CA (breach of the peace can occur on private property even if confined to the persons immediately involved in the fracas if a member of the public was likely to be disturbed). For the role of the right to free assembly in breach of the peace see *R v Londonderry Justices* (1891) 28 LR Ir 440, *Beatty v Gillbanks* (1882) 9 QBD 308; and *Hubbard v Pitt* [1976] QB 142, [1975] 3 All ER 1, CA.

4  Ie a police constable or anyone else has the power to take steps to prevent or end the breach of the peace, to arrest and detain the person who has or who threatens the breach of the peace, and may enter upon private premises, and consequently certain acts which would otherwise be tortious or criminal are justified: see *Humphries v Connor* (1864) 17 I CLR 1; *O'Kelly v Harvey* (1883) 15 Cox CC 435; and *Albert v Lavin* [1982] AC 546, [1981] 3 All ER 879, HL.

5  See the Public Order Act 1986 Pt I (ss 1–10) (as amended) (offences of riot, violent disorder, affray, causing fear of or provoking violence, causing intentional harassment, alarm or distress, and causing harassment, alarm or distress), and s 18 (as amended) (offences in connection with stirring up racial hatred) (see CRIMINAL LAW vol 11(1) (Reissue) paras 149–154); the Public Meeting Act 1908 s 1 (as amended) (offence to act at a lawful public meeting in a disorderly manner for the purpose of preventing the transaction of the business for which the meeting was called) (see CRIMINAL LAW vol 11(1) (Reissue) para 147); the Public Order Act 1936 s 1 (as amended) (offence to wear a uniform in any public place or at any public meeting, signifying association with any political object) (see CRIMINAL LAW vol 11(1) (Reissue) para 100); the Highways Act 1980 s 137 (as amended) (see text and note 2 supra); the Trade Union and Labour Relations (Consolidation) Act 1992 s 241 (offences relating to intimidation, violence, harassment, etc with a view to compelling a person not to do or to do something which he has a right to do or not to do (and see *DPP v Fidler* [1992] 1 WLR 91, DC)) (see TRADE, INDUSTRY AND INDUSTRIAL RELATIONS vol 47 (Reissue) para 1441). Under the Prevention of Terrorism (Temporary Provisions) Act 1989 s 1, Sch 1, certain organisations are proscribed, namely, the Irish Republican Army and the Irish National Liberation Army. The Secretary of State may by order add to the list of proscribed organisations any organisation which appears to him to be concerned in, or in promoting or encouraging terrorism in the United Kingdom and connected with the affairs of Northern Ireland, or may remove an organisation from that list: s 1(2)(a). It is an offence to belong to a proscribed oprganisation or to organise a meeting in support of such an organistaion: s 2). See further para 81 ante; and CRIMINAL LAW vol 11(1) (Reissue) para 111.

6  See the Public Order Act 1986 s 14A (as added) (prohibition of trespassory assemblies), s 14C (as added) (power to stop a person on his way to a trespassory assembly); the Criminal Justice and Public Order Act 1994 s 61 (power to remove trespassers from land), s 63 (regulation of 'raves'). The Public Order Act 1986 s 11 (advance notice of public procession, senior police officer may impose conditions and may apply to the local authority to prohibit the procession), s 14 (conditions on public assemblies).

7  Trade Union and Labour Relations (Consolidation) Act 1992 s 220; the Employment Code of Practice (Picketing) Order 1992, SI 1992/476; and see *Hubbard v Pitt* [1976] QB 142 at 177, [1975] 3 All ER 1 at 9, CA, per Lord Denning MR; *Thomas v National Union of Mineworkers (South Wales Area)* [1986] Ch 20, [1985] 2 All ER 1; *News Group Newspapers Ltd v Society of Graphical and Allied Trades 1982 (No 2)* [1987] ICR 181, [1986] IRLR 337. See also TRADE, INDUSTRY AND INDUSTRIAL RELATIONS vol 47 (Reissue) paras 1443–1444.

**110. Right to personal privacy.** The scope of a right to personal privacy is difficult to define, and may be more correctly seen as a bundle of rights which have a variety of justifications[1]. It is uncertain whether there is no general right to privacy[2] recognised by English common law[3]. However, the right to privacy is a broad notion which encompasses a variety of more specific rights. These include: the right to be left alone[4]; the right to communicate privately[5]; the right not to have personal information published[6]; the right to a private life[7]; and the right to have access to personal information[8]. Although primarily protected by the civil law, aspects of the right to privacy are also protected by the criminal law[9]. As there is no general right to privacy, these rights are only protected by English law when the facts of a particular case constitute a recognised cause of action. Trespass to the person[10], trespass to property[11], nuisance[12], harassment[13], defamation[14], malicious falsehood[15], wilful infliction of harm[16], breach of confidence[17], copyright[18] and the court's wardship jurisdiction[19] have all been used as devices to protect different aspects of respect for private life.

1    In addition to the rights mentioned in this paragraph which could be considered within a right to privacy, see also paras 111–115 post (right to be free from arbitrary entries, searches and seizures; right to a private life; right to a family life; right to bodily integrity; and right to personal liberty). For the more formal rights under the Convention for the Protection of Human Rights and Fundamental Freedoms see paras 149–155 post.

2    The right to privacy has been the subject of much public debate: see the Royal Commissions of 1949, 1962 and 1977, chaired by Sir William Ross, Lord Shawcross, and Lord McGregor of Durris respectively; *Report of the Committee on Privacy* (Cmnd 5012) (1972) ('the Younger Committee Report'); the Consultation Paper *Infringement of Privacy* (Lord Chancellor's Department, July 1993); *Report of the Committee on Privacy and Related Matters* (Cm 1102) (1990) ('the Calcutt Committee Report'); *Review of Press Self-Regulation* (Cm 2135) (1993); *Fourth Report of the National Heritage Select Committee: Privacy and Media Intrusion* (HC Paper (1993–94) no 291-I); *Privacy and Media Intrusion - The Government's Response* (Cm 2918) (1995). For an analysis of the right to privacy see Feldman 'Secrecy, Dignity or Autonomy? Views of Privacy as a Civil Liberty' [1995] CLP 41.

3    *Kaye v Robertson* [1991] FSR 62, CA; see particularly at 71 per Leggatt LJ (right to privacy so long disregarded by the common law that only Parliament could provide a remedy). However, see *Morris v Beardmore* [1981] AC 446, [1980] 2 All ER 753, HL (in particular Lord Edmund-Davies at 461, 761–762, Lord Keith of Kinkel at 462, 762, and Lord Scarman at 463–464, 762–764); *A-G v Observer Ltd, A-G v Times Newspapers Ltd* [1990] 1 AC 109 at 255–256, sub nom *A-G v Guardian Newspapers Ltd (No 2)* [1988] 3 All ER 545 at 639–640, HL, per Lord Keith of Kinkel; and Lester [1993] Public Law 269, 284–286 for suggestions that the development of a tort of privacy is within the interpretative reach of the courts. In *R v Khan* [1996] 3 All ER 289, HL, the question whether English law requires a right of privacy was left open. Also note cases such as *Abernethy v Hutchinson* (1825) 3 LJCh 209 (protection of hospital lectures); *Prince Albert v Strange* (1849) 2 De G & Sm 652, on appeal (1849) 1 Mac & G 25; and *Duchess of Argyll v Duke of Argyll* [1967] Ch 302, [1965] 1 All ER 611; and the American cases of *Barber v Time Inc* 159 SW 2d 291 (1942) where the publication of a photograph of the plaintiff in her hospital bed taken without her consent was held to be an invasion of a private right; *Union Pacific Rly Co v Botsford* 141 US 250 (1891) (in which the US judges developed a 'right to be let alone' from old English common law cases); and *Cruzan v Director, Missouri Department of Health* 110 S Ct 2841 (1990). See also *Case v Minister of Safety and Security* 1996 (5) BCLR 609, SA Const Ct (statute making it an offence to possess 'any indecent or obscene pornographic matter' contrary to constitutional right to privacy). See also CONFIDENCE AND DATA PROTECTION vol 8(1) (Reissue) paras 429–433.

4    This is protected by the torts of trespass to the person, trespass to property and possibly by the developing tort of harassment (see text and notes 10–13 infra). In particular see *Morris v Beardmore* [1981] AC 446, [1980] 2 All ER 753, HL. It is protected by the criminal law by the Administration of Justice Act 1970 s 40 (as amended); the Criminal Law Act 1977 s 6 (as amended); the Protection from Eviction Act 1977; the Public Order Act 1986 s 4A, 5 (s 4A added by the Criminal Justice and Public Order Act 1994 s 154); the Trade Union and Labour Relations (Consolidation) Act 1992 s 220; and the Criminal Justice and Public Order Act 1994 Pt V (ss 61–80) (particularly s 68 (aggravated trespass)).

5    See the Interception of Communications Act 1985 s 1 (offence to intercept communication in the course of its transmission by post or by public telecommunication system, except where one of the parties to the communication has consented to the interception or where it has been authorised under a warrant by the Secretary of State); the Contempt of Court Act 1981 s 10; and generally CONFIDENCE AND DATA PROTECTION; CRIMINAL LAW vol 11(1) (Reissue) para 270, vol 11(2) (Reissue) para 1163; DISCOVERY; EVIDENCE; PRESS AND PRINTING.

6    See text and notes 17, 19 infra.

7    See para 112 post.

8    See the Data Protection Act 1984; the Access to Personal Files Act 1987; the Access to Medical Reports Act 1988; the Access to Health Records Act 1990; and CONFIDENCE AND DATA PROTECTION vol 8(1) (Reissue) paras 501–545. See also *Gaskin v Liverpool City Council* [1980] 1 WLR 1549, CA; *Gaskin v United Kingdom* A 160 (1989), 12 EHRR 36, ECtHR; and *W v Egdell* [1990] Ch 359, [1990] 1 All ER 835, CA; *R v Secretary of State for the Home Department, ex p Doody* [1994] 1 AC 531, sub nom *Doody v Secretary of State for the Home Department* [1993] 3 All ER 92, HL, per Lord Mustill (prisoner serving mandatory life sentence seeking to know the reasons why particular penal element had been selected

for his sentence; Lord Mustill recognised three rationales for ordering disclosure: (1) natural human desire to understand and have knowledge of that which will shape one's life; (2) the subject of the information may be able to correct any mistakes in the information; (3) aids the process of appeal and review). See also the White Paper on *Open Government* (Cm 2290) (1993).

9   See the provisions cited in notes 4–5 supra).

10   Note that in *Kaye v Robertson* [1991] FSR 62, CA, it was held that the use of a flash bulb could constitute a battery where the subject was suffering from head injuries.

11   *Morris v Beardmore* [1981] AC 446, [1980] 2 All ER 753, HL; *IRC v Rossminster Ltd* [1980] AC 952, [1980] 1 All ER 80, HL, especially per Lord Scarman at 1021–1022, 101–102; *Kaye v Robertson* [1991] FSR 62, CA, where it was suggested that even if a trespass to the person was established by, for example, a flashlight being used in someone's face the remedies available for such a tort would not be suitable for preventing disclosure of the photographs obtained thereby. See also *Entick v Carrington* (1765) 19 State Tr 1029.

12   See *Baron Bernstein of Leigh v Skyviews and General Ltd* [1978] 1 QB 479, [1977] 2 All ER 902 at 909 per Griffiths J. In *Khorasandjian v Bush* [1993] QB 727, [1993] 3 All ER 669, CA, the court extended the protection of the tort of nuisance to those who had no property interest but were mere licensees and decided that the making of unwanted telephone calls could constitute a nuisance; an injunction could be ordered to prevent the defendant from 'harassing' the plaintiff.

13   See eg the Domestic Violence and Matrimonial Proceedings Act 1976 (power to grant non-molestation orders). For the view that there is no general tort of harassment see *Patel v Patel* [1988] 2 FLR 179. However, *Khorasandjian v Bush* [1993] QB 727, [1993] 3 All ER 669, CA, appears to suggest that there is such a tort. In relation to harassment and industrial disputes see *Thomas v National Union of Mineworkers (South Wales Area)* [1986] Ch 20, [1985] 2 All ER 1 (miners wishing to return to work during strike were entitled to use public highway to enter colliery without unreasonable harassment, which would be tortious); and *News Group Newspapers Ltd v Society of Graphical and Allied Trades 1982 (No 2)* [1987] ICR 181, suggesting that interference with right to use highway could not be actionable per se. See also *Vaughan v Vaughan* (1971) 115 Sol Jo 405.

14   See *Tolley v J S Fry & Sons Ltd* [1931] AC 333, HL; *Kaye v Robertson* [1991] FSR 62, CA.

15   See *Joyce v Sengupta* [1993] 1 All ER 897, [1993] 1 WLR 337, CA. See also *Kaye v Robertson* [1991] FSR 62, CA.

16   See *Wilkinson v Downton* [1897] 2 QB 57; *Janvier v Sweeney* [1919] 2 KB 316; *Kaye v Robertson* [1991] FSR 62, CA.

17   See *Hellewell v Chief Constable of Derbyshire* [1995] 4 All ER 473, [1995] 1 WLR 804 (plaintiff claiming breach of confidence for distribution of photograph of him taken by the police for distribution to help in the prevention of crime, claim struck out. But per Laws J (obiter) at 476, 807 if someone with a telephoto lens were to take from a distance and with no authority a picture of another engaged in some private act, his subsequent disclosure of the photograph would amount to a breach of confidence; *Marcel v Metropolitan Police Comr* [1992] Ch 225, [1992] 1 All ER 72, CA (police should not disclose documents that they had seized to anyone other than the true owner unless the police had been served with a subpoena reflecting a general principle that information gathered for one purpose must not be used for another, see eg the Taxes Management Act 1970 s 6, Sch 1); *A-G v Guardian Newspapers (No 2)* [1990] 1 AC 109, HL (in particular the judgment of Sir John Donaldson MR at 176–178); see further generally CONFIDENCE AND DATA PROTECTION.

18   See generally COPYRIGHT.

19   See *R v Central Independent Television plc* [1994] Fam 192, [1994] 3 All ER 641, CA (mother attempted to invoke the court's inherent wardship jurisdiction to restrain broadcast of information that would harm daughter by disclosing that former husband was a paedophile; court would not engage in balancing exercise between interests of child and those of free speech because threatened publication did not touch matters of direct concern to the court in its supervisory role over the care and upbringing of the child); *Re W (a minor)(wardship: freedom of publication)* [1992] 1 All ER 794, [1992] 1 WLR 100, CA (see in particular the guidelines set out by Neill LJ); *Re M and N (minors) (wardship: publication of information)* [1990] Fam 211, [1990] 1 All ER 205, CA; *X County Council v A* [1985] 1 All ER 53, sub nom *Re X (a minor) (wardship: injunction)* [1984] 1 WLR 1422; *Re X (a minor) (wardship: jurisdiction)* [1975] Fam 47, sub nom *Re X (a minor) (wardship: restriction of publication)* [1975] 1 All ER 697, CA.

**111. Right to be free from arbitrary entries, searches, and seizures.** The right to be free from arbitrary entries, searches and seizures[1] is an aspect of the general rights to liberty[2], privacy[3] and natural justice[4]. The general powers of entry, search and seizure now have a statutory basis[5] and there are several specific statutory powers[6]. However, if an individual consents to entry on to his premises then no other legal basis is required to justify the entry[7]. The civil law also provides for search and seizure[8].

1 See generally CRIMINAL LAW. See also paras 110 ante, 114–115 post. In *British Columbia Securities Commission v Branch* [1995] 2 SCR 3, Can SC, it was held that a statutory provision giving the Securities Commission power to compel subjects of an investigation to produce documents and to answer questions did not offend either s 7 (privilege against self-incrimination and right to silence) or s 8 (protection against unreasonable searches and seizures) Canadian Charter of Rights and Freedoms. See also *Simpson v A-G (Baigent's Case)* [1994] 3 LRC 202, NZ CA (scope of the right to be free from unreasonable search discussed in the context of a search that was known by the police to have no legal justification, and the appropriate remedies considered); and *Auckland Unemployed Workers' Rights Centre Inc v A-G* [1994] 3 LRC 264; *Park-Ross v Director of OSEC* [1995] 1 LRC 178, SA SC (Cape of Good Hope Provincial Division). For the position under the Convention for the Protection of Human Rights and Fundamental Freedoms Art 8 see paras 149–155 post. See also, under European Community law, Case 136/79 *National Panasonic* [1980] ECR 2033 at 2057, ECJ; Case 85/87 *Dow Benelux* [1989] ECR 3137 at 3157, ECJ. In both cases the powers of search and seizure were tested against the Convention for the Protection of Human Rights and Fundamental Freedoms Art 8: see paras 149–155 post. See also *Television New Zealand Ltd v Police* [1995] 2 LRC 808, NZ HC.

2 See *Entick v Carrington* (1765) 19 State Tr 1029 per Lord Camden CJ: 'By the laws of England, every invasion of private property, be it ever so minute, is a trespass...Papers are the owner's goods and chattels: they are his dearest property; and though the eye cannot by the laws of England be guilty of trespass, yet where private papers are removed and carried away, the secret nature of those goods will be an aggravation of the trespass, and demand more considerable damages in that respect.'

3 See *Morris v Beardmore* [1981] AC 446 at 463, [1980] 2 All ER 753 at 763, HL, per Lord Scarman: 'It is not the task of judges, exercising their ingenuity in the field of implication, to go further in the invasion of fundamental private rights and liberties than Parliament has expressly authorised'; and *Marcel v Metropolitan Police Comr* [1992] Ch 225 at 234–235, [1991] 1 All ER 845 at 851 per Browne-Wilkinson V-C: 'Search and seizure under statutory powers constitute fundamental infringements of the individual's immunity from interference by the state with his property and privacy - fundamental human rights'; revsd on the question of use of seized documents [1992] Ch 225, [1992] 1 All ER 72, CA, but this point approved: see per Dillon LJ at 255, 80. See also *R v Khan* [1996] 3 All ER 289, HL.

4 As to the two principal rules of natural justice see further para 119 note 1 post.

5 See the Police and Criminal Evidence Act 1984 s 1 (as amended) (power of a constable to stop and search persons, vehicles etc), s 3 (duty to make records concerning searches), s 4 (as amended) (road checks), s 8 (powers of a justice of the peace to authorise entry and search of premises), s 17 (as amended) (power of a constable to enter premises to effect an arrest), s 18 (powers of a constable to carry out entry and search after an arrest), s 19 (general power of seizure) and s 22 (retention of items seized); the Criminal Justice and Public Order Act 1994 s 60 (a senior police officer may authorise all uniformed police officers in a particular locality to stop any pedestrian and search him or her for offensive weapons or dangerous instruments, and to stop any vehicle and search that vehicle, its driver and passengers for offensive weapons and dangerous instruments whether or not the officer has any grounds for suspecting that the person or vehicle is carrying such items). See, as to the Police and Criminal Evidence Act 1984 s 3, *Chapman v DPP* (1988) 89 Cr App Rep 190, DC). On the exercise of the powers of police officers to stop and search see the Codes of Practice made under the Police and Criminal Evidence Act 1984 CRIMINAL LAW vol 11(1) (Reissue) para 657 et seq. As to judicial review of a defective warrant see *IRC v Rossminster Ltd* [1980] AC 952, [1980] 1 All ER 80, HL; *R v Billericay Justices and Dobbyn, ex p Frank Harris (Coaches) Ltd* [1991] Crim LR 472 (in both cases review was refused) but cf *R v Reading Justices, ex p South West Meats Ltd* [1992] Crim LR 672; and *Darbo v DPP* [1992] Crim LR 56 (review granted). It is also probable that the common law power of search and seizure in cases of grave crime, as set out in *Ghani v Jones* [1970] 1 QB 693, [1969] 3 All ER 1700, CA, has survived the Police and Criminal Evidence Act 1984: see s 19(5).

6 Eg the Prevention of Terrorism (Temporary Provisions) Act 1989 ss 13A, 13B (s 13A added by the Criminal Justice and Public Order Act 1994 s 81(1); s 13B added by the Prevention of Terrorism (Additional Powers) Act 1996 s 1) (special powers of stop and search to counter terrorism). The Intelligence Services Act 1994 ss 5, 6 enables the Secretary of State to issue general warrants for entry on and interference with property if he believes it is necessary for the discharge of the functions of the Service, being the protection of national security from espionage, terrorism and sabotage, and where arrangements are made to ensure that no unnecessary information is obtained. Complaints against the Service may be investigated by the Commissioner or the Tribunal appointed under that Act (see ss 8, 9), decisions of which are not themselves liable to be questioned in any court. As from a day to be appointed, the Secretary of State may enlist the assistance of the security service in the prevention and detection of serious crime: see the Security Service Act 1989 s 2(2) (as prospectively amended) see para 471 note 11 post.

7 See *Faulkner v Willetts* [1982] RTR 159, DC.

8   See *Anton Piller KG v Manufacturing Processes Ltd* [1976] Ch 55, [1976] 1 All ER 779, CA. As to the
    circumstances in which Anton Piller orders may be made, and the scope of such orders, see generally
    INJUNCTIONS vol 24 (Reissue) para 872 et seq.

## 112. Right to respect for private life.

The right of an individual to respect for his private life[1] is affected by the extent to which the state limits consensual activity[2], the extent to which an individual's choices concerning his private life are protected by the state[3], and the extent to which the state will penalise an individual's private thoughts[4].

1   See also paras 110–111 ante, 114–115 post. As to the corresponding position under the Convention for
    the Protection of Human Rights and Fundamental Freedoms Art 8 see paras 149–155 post.
2   See *A-G's Reference (No 6 of 1980)* [1981] QB 715, [1981] 2 All ER 1057, CA (consent not a valid defence
    to a charge including any degree of actual bodily harm unless the activity involved serves some element
    of public interest, and the following were accepted (obiter) as being capable of serving the public interest,
    properly conducted sport, lawful chastisement, reasonable surgical interference and dangerous
    exhibitions; the Court of Appeal held that it was irrelevant whether the assault took place in public or in
    private); *R v Brown* [1994] 1 AC 212, [1993] 2 All ER 75, HL (no defence to charges under the Offences
    Against the Person 1861 ss 20, 47 (both as amended) (see CRIMINAL LAW vol 11(1) (Reissue) paras 471,
    490) that the victim of the assault consented to the assault and the injury caused thereby and in particular
    there was no public interest in sado-masochism between consenting adults). Subsequent proceedings
    before the European Commission of Human Rights have endorsed this decision: see Application 21627/
    93 *Laskey v United Kingdom* (18 January 1995, unreported), EComHR.
3   Ie whether those choices have a bearing on an individual's status and rights. See *R v Ministry of Defence,
    ex p Smith* [1996] 1 All ER 257, CA (question whether homosexuals should be allowed to join or
    remain in the armed forces involved fundamental human rights, but the court would not hold the
    policy of the Ministry of Defence irrational). As to discrimination on the grounds of sexual orientation
    see *R v Director of GCHQ, ex p Hodges* [1988] COD 123; *Bell v Devon and Cornwall Police Authority*
    [1978] IRLR 283; and *Boychuk v H J Symons Holdings Ltd* [1977] IRLR 395, EAT; *Smith v Gardner
    Merchant Ltd* [1996] IRLR 342, EAT. As to homosexual couples adopting children see *C v C* [1991
    FCR 254, [1991] 1 FLR 223, CA (mother being in lesbian relationship not necessarily a bar to
    adoption but is still a factor to be considered); and *Re E* [1995] 1 FCR 65, [1995] 1 FLR 382, CA (not
    reasonable for parents to refuse to consent to adoption on the ground that the proposed adopter is a
    lesbian: refusal of consent should be based on reason not on emotion or prejudice). The age of consent
    for homosexual men is 18: Sexual Offences Act 1967 (amended by the Criminal Justice and Public
    Order Act 1994 s 145(1)). Local authorities may not promote homosexuality by publishing or teaching:
    Local Government Act 1986 s 2A (added by the Local Government Act 1988 s 28). See *R v Brown*
    [1994] 1 AC 212, [1993] 2 All ER 75, HL, cited in note 2 supra. As far as transsexuals are concerned
    the law only looks to the biological sex of the individual at birth (see *Corbett v Corbett (otherwise Ashley)*
    [1971] P 83, [1970] 2 All ER 33; and *White v British Sugar Corpn* [1977] IRLR 121. See also paras 106
    ante, 114 post. In Case C-13/94 *P v S* [1996] All ER (EC) 397, ECJ, discrimnation on the grounds of
    gender reassignment was held to contravene EC Council Directive 76/207 (OJ L39, 14.2.76, p 40)
    (equal treatment).
4   See *R v Court* [1989] AC 28, [1988] 2 All ER 221, HL (test for indecency in relation to the offence of
    indecent assault is whether the assault is unquestionably indecent; if so then the offender's motive is
    irrelevant but if the assault is equivocal as to indecency then the offender's motive is relevant).

## 113. Right to respect for family life.

The right to respect for family life[1] in English law is affected by the following broad principles. In general parental rights are subservient to the welfare of the child[2]. The wardship jurisdiction of the High Court cannot be used to test the correctness of local authority child-care decisions[3] but the courts have implied certain procedural rights for parents when their children are the subject of state attention[4] and children must also be involved in decisions affecting them[5]. There is no common law action based on interference with parental rights[6]. There is no general right to marry[7]. European Community law offers some protection to family life based on the freedom of movement of persons[8].

1   See also paras 110–112 ante. For a Commonwealth example of the application of the right to a family life
    see *Re Wood and Hansard* 1995 (1) BCLR 43, Zimb SC. As to the position under the Convention for the
    Protection of Human Rights and Fundamental Freedoms see para 151 post.

2    See the Children Act 1989 s 1 (welfare of the child is paramount); and CHILDREN vol 5(2) (Reissue) para 809 et seq); *Gillick v West Norfolk Area Health Authority* [1986] AC 112, [1985] 3 All ER 402, HL (parental rights to control a child exist for the benefit not of the parent but of the child, and are justified only in so far as they enable the parent to perform his duties towards the child; such rights yield to the child's right to make his own decisions when he reaches a sufficient understanding and intelligence to be capable of making up his own mind); *Re K D (A minor) (ward: termination of access)* [1988] AC 806, [1988] 1 All ER 577, HL (when determining in wardship proceedings whether a natural parent's access to the ward should be terminated so as to permit the local authority to place the ward for adoption, the first and paramount consideration is the welfare of the child and the parent's claim to access is subservient to the child's welfare); for a thorough discussion of the nature of parental rights see per Lord Oliver of Aylmerton, in particular at 587 et seq, 585 et seq); *Re K (a minor) (ward: care and control)* [1990] 3 All ER 795, [1990] 1 WLR 431, CA (in determining whether care and control of a ward of court who is the child of unmarried parents, one of whom has died, should vest in foster care or the surviving natural parent the correct test is whether the welfare of the child positively demands that the natural parent's role in the care and upbringing of the child should be displaced by the foster parents rather than who would provide a better home); *Re L (a minor)* (1989) Independent, 6 October, CA (parents must act reasonably in opposing adoption; following *Re W* [1971] AC 682, [1971] 2 All ER 49, HL); *R v Gwynedd County Council, ex p B* [1992] 3 All ER 317, CA (rights and duties of local authority in respect of child in its care pursuant to Child Care Act 1980 cease upon child's death; parental right and duty to bury child reverts to natural parents). In *B v Children's Aid Society of Metropolitan Toronto* [1995] 1 SCR 315, Can SC (whether parents could refuse life-saving treatment for their child on religious grounds).

3    *A v Liverpool City Council* [1982] AC 363, [1981] 2 All ER 385, HL; *Re W (a minor: wardship: jurisdiction)* [1985] AC 791, sub nom *W v Hertfordshire County Council* [1985] 2 All ER 301, HL; and after the decision in *O v United Kingdom* A 120 (1987), 10 EHRR 82, ECtHR; *Re M and H (minors) (local authority: parental rights)* [1990] 1 AC 686, sub nom *M v H* [1988] 3 All ER 5, HL.

4    *R v Norfolk County Council Social Services Department, ex p M* [1989] QB 619, [1989] 2 All ER 359; *R v Harrow London Borough Council, ex p D* [1990] Fam 133, [1990] 3 All ER 12, HL.

5    See eg the Children Act 1989 s 1(3) (child's wishes and feelings are the first of the factors listed in the statutory checklist), s 10(2)(b), (8) (child may, with the leave of the court seek an order about his future).

6    See *F v Wirral Metropolitan Borough Council* [1991] Fam 69, [1991] 2 All ER 648, CA (no common law right available to parent against stranger who interfered with parent's rights in respect of his or her relationship with the children; the statutory code for the welfare of children under which local authorities, exercising an administrative function, could interfere with parental rights, was based on the welfare of the child; accordingly breaches by local authority of the statutory code did not give rise to a private right in the parent to claim damages against the local authority but only to public law remedies and to an action for misfeasance in a public office).

7    See *R v Secretary of State for the Home Department, ex p Bhajan Singh* [1976] QB 198, [1975] 2 All ER 1081, CA (illegal immigrant being detained pending deportation had no right to be released in order to be married). In English law two people who were born the same sex cannot be married: *Corbett v Corbett (otherwise Ashley)* [1971] P 83, [1970] 2 All ER 33. As to the right to marry under the Convention for the Protection of Human Rights and Fundamental Freedoms see para 162 post.

8    See the EC Treaty Art 8A (added by the Treaty on European Union (Cm 1934) Title II Art G para (9)); EC Council Regulation 1612/68 (OJ L254, 18.10.68, p 2); and eg Case 76/72 *Michel S v Fonds National de Reclassement Social des Handicapes* [1973] ECR 457, ECJ; Case 9/74 *Casagrande v Landeshauptstadt Munchen* Case [1974] ECR 773, ECJ; Case 389/87 *Echternach* [1989] ECR 723, ECJ. For a Commonwealth example of the application of the right to a family life and the rights of a citizen see *Rattigan v Chief Immigration Officer* 1995 (1) BCLR 1, Zimb SC.

## 114. Right to bodily integrity.

The right to bodily integrity[1] is protected by both the criminal law[2] and the civil law[3]. Consent is a defence to charges of assault in certain circumstances[4]. In some situations, individuals can be required to submit to an assault without any legal redress[5]. The police have powers to take samples from suspects in certain circumstances[6].

1    See further paras 110–111 ante, 115 post. Torture is a specific offence under the Criminal Justice Act 1988 s 134: see CRIMINAL LAW vol 11(1) (Reissue) para 504. In *Pratt v A-G for Jamaica* [1994] 2 AC 1, [1993] 4 All ER 769, PC, it was held that prisoners held on death row for over five years would have strong grounds for arguing that their treatment amounted to 'inhuman or degrading punishment'. See also *Catholic Commission for Justice and Peace in Zimbabwe v A-G* [1993] 2 LRC 279, Zimb SC; *Ex p A-G of Namibia: re Corporal Punishment by Organs of State* [1992] LRC (Const) 515,

Nam SC. As to the position under the Convention for the Protection of Human Rights and Fundamental Freedoms Art 3 see para 124 post.

2   See particularly the Offences Against the Person Act 1861; and generally CRIMINAL LAW. Parents are permitted to use reasonable force when disciplining their children, and if the force used and the manner of its application is reasonable the parents will have a defence to charges of assault and battery (see *R v Hopley* (1860) 2 F & F 202; *R v Mackie* (1973) 57 Cr App Rep 453, CA; and CHILDREN vol 5(2) (Reissue) para 730 note 5). Teachers in schools funded by the state may not use corporal punishment which is inhuman or degrading on the children in their care: see the Education (No 2) Act 1986 s 47 (as amended); and EDUCATION vol 15 (Reissue) para 125; the Children's Homes Regulations 1991, SI 1991/1506, reg 8(2) (made under the Children Act 1989 s 63(11), Sch 6). In *Costello-Roberts v United Kingdom* A 247-C (1993), 19 EHRR 112, ECtHR, the court made clear that it did not wish to be taken as approving in any way the retention of corporal punishment in schools. The Human Rights Committee, which oversees the International Covenant on Civil and Political Rights (1966) (see para 103 note 3 ante) has recommended that corporal punishment administered to privately-funded pupils in independent schools be abolished: CCPR/C/79/Add 55, 27 July 1995.

3   An action for battery will lie if there is physical touching and an action for assault may lie if the victim is put in fear of violence: see generally TORT vol 45 para 1310 et seq. In the absence of specific statutory authority, agents of the state are subject to the general law (see eg *Entick v Carrington* (1765) 19 State Tr 1029).

4   See CRIMINAL LAW vol 11(1) (Reissue) para 494; TORT vol 45 para 1312. As to the effectiveness of consent in non-medical cases see para 112 note 2 ante. In medical cases the test for whether the consent given was real and effective is whether the patient was capable of understanding what he was told and the implications of the consent given, and whether the doctor gave the patient enough information to satisfy a body of responsible medical opinion (see *Sidaway v Board of Governors of the Bethlem Royal Hospital and the Maudsley Hospital* [1985] AC 871, [1985] 1 All ER 643, HL). In *R v Brown* [1994] 1 AC 212, [1993] 2 All ER 75, HL, it was held that consent to sado-masochistic activity was no defence to charges of unlawful wounding and casuing actual bodily harm. Subsequent proceedings before the European Commission of Human Rights have endorsed this decision: see Application 21627/93 *Laskey v United Kingdom* (18 January 1995, unreported), EComHR.

5   If an adult patient is temporarily unable to give consent a doctor may give treatment under the doctrine of implied consent or the doctrine of necessity. If the reason for not being able to give consent is lack of mental capacity and the patient has been detained compulsorily under the Mental Health Act 1983, then s 62 permits a doctor to give urgent treatment (which is not irreversible or hazardous) without the patient's consent for the condition for which the patient was detained, where consent would otherwise be required: see *Re C (adult: refusal of medical treatment)* [1994] 1 All ER 819, [1994] 1 WLR 290; and *B v Croydon Health Authority* [1995] Fam 133, [1995] 1 All ER 683); and MENTAL HEALTH vol 30 (Reissue) para 1349. As to the cirumstances in which under the Mental Health Act 1983 consent would not be required see s 63; and MENTAL HEALTH vol 30 (Reissue) para 1345. Other treatments must have the patient's consent, unless the treatment is declared lawful by the court (see *Re F (mental patient: sterilisation)* [1990] 2 AC 1, sub nom *F v West Berkshire Health Authority (Mental Health Commission intervening)* [1989] 2 All ER 545, HL). If the patient has not been compulsorily detained then there is no statutory provision for treatment without consent, and only the common law doctrines and the principles established by *Re F (mental patient: sterilisation)* supra apply. Although the general rule is that competent adults may refuse treatment, see *Re T (adult: refusal of treatment)* [1993] Fam 95, [1992] 4 All ER 649, CA; and *Re S (adult: refusal of treatment)* [1993] Fam 123, [1992] 4 All ER 671, for an attenuation of the rule in certain circumstances. Parents and persons with parental responsibility may give consent on behalf of their children under 16: see the Children Act 1989 s 3(1); and CHILDREN vol 5(2) (Reissue) paras 604, 730; see also s 3(5) (right of other persons with care but not parental responsibility to act to promote or safeguard welfare of child); and see CHILDREN vol 5(2) (Reissue) para 733. The court may make the relevant decision as part of its wardship jurisdiction (either inherent or under s 8: see CHILDREN vol 5(2) (Reissue) para 746). For a discussion of the principles to be applied by a court in exercising its wardship jurisdiction see *Re R (a minor) (wardship: consent to treatment)* [1992] Fam 11, [1991] 4 All ER 177, CA. As to the consent of prisoners to medical treatment see *Freeman v Home Office (No 2)* [1984] QB 524, [1984] 1 All ER 1036, CA. A prisoner of sound mind cannot be forcibly fed; the right to self-determination prevails: *Secretary of State for the Home Department v Robb* [1995] Fam 127, [1995] 1 All ER 677).

6   See the Police and Criminal Evidence Act 1984 ss 61–65 (as amended); and CRIMINAL LAW.

**115. Right to personal liberty.** The right to liberty[1] is protected as against state interference by two principles: (1) an individual may do anything that is not prohibited by law[2]; and (2) the state may not interfere with the individual save where the law permits[3]. It is further protected as against persons by the offence of kidnapping[4], the writ of habeas corpus[5] and the tort of false imprisonment[6]. A person may be arrested[7] by a warrant issued by a justice of the peace[8] or without a warrant if certain conditions are satisfied[9]. An individual can be detained only for a period of time set out in statute[10] and is afforded certain protections whilst in detention[11].

1   The courts attach great weight to the right to personal liberty, and any infringement of the right will attract intense scrutiny: see eg *Bugdaycay v Secretary of State for the Home Department* [1987] AC 514, [1987] 1 All ER 940, HL; *Khawaja v Secretary of State for the Home Department* [1984] AC 74, [1983] 1 All ER 765, HL. See further paras 110, 112, 114 ante, 116 post. For the position under the Convention for the Protection of Human Rights and Fundamental Freedoms Art 5 see paras 127–133 post.

2   See para 6 note 3 ante.

3   In particular see *Entick v Carrington* (1765) 19 State Tr 1029; *Liversidge v Anderson* [1942] AC 206, [1941] 3 All ER 338, HL; *Ali v Jayaratne* [1951] AC 66, PC; *IRC v Rossminster Ltd* [1980] AC 952, [1980] 1 All ER 80, HL; and also note the prerogative writ of habeas corpus (the Habeas Corpus Acts of 1679, 1816 and 1862). For the police powers of stop and search see further para 111 text and note 5 ante. See also the Road Traffic Act 1988 s 163 (as amended) (no requirement for reasonable cause); and the Sporting Events (Control of Alcohol etc) Act 1985 s 7 (as amended); and see CRIMINAL LAW vol 11(1) (Reissue) para 177. See also para 109 note 6 ante.

4   As to kidnapping see CRIMINAL LAW vol 11(1) (Reissue) para 493.

5   As to habeas corpus see ADMINISTRATIVE LAW vol 1(1) (Reissue) paras 222–265.

6   As to false imprisonment generally see TORT vol 45 paras 1325–1338. An otherwise lawful imprisonment cannot be rendered unlawful by the conditions of the confinement: see *R v Deputy Governor of Parkhurst Prison, ex p Hague* [1992] 1 AC 58, sub nom *Hague v Deputy Governor of Parkhurst Prison* [1991] 3 All ER 733, HL. A soldier required to serve in the armed forces when not lawfully committed to do so could maintain an action for false imprisonment: see *Pritchard v Ministry of Defence* (1995) Times, 27 January.

7   If the arrest does not conform with the conditions set down by law, then actions for false imprisonment and battery will lie, and no proof of special damage is required: see *Murray v Ministry of Defence* [1988] 2 All ER 521, [1988] 1 WLR 692, HL, particularly at 528, 703 per Lord Griffiths. In particular if unreasonable force is used when making the arrest an action for battery will lie: see *Allen v Metropolitan Police Comr of Metropolitan Police* [1980] Crim LR 441; and as to the principles to apply when considering aggravated damages in relation to assaults by police constables on detainees see *O'Connor v Hewitson* [1979] Crim LR 46, CA.

8   As to the prerequisites for the grant of a warrant, and the classes of offence for which a warrant may be granted, see CRIMINAL LAW vol 11(1) (Reissue) para 695.

9   See the Police and Criminal Evidence Act 1984 Pt III (ss 24–33) (as amended), and Sch 2 (as amended) (which preserves pre-existing statutory powers of arrest); and CRIMINAL LAW vol 11(1) (Reissue) paras 693–713. Note that obstructing a police officer in the course of his duty is not per se an arrestable offence: see *Gelberg v Miller* [1961] 1 All ER 291 at 295, DC, per Lord Parker CJ; although several cases have assumed the contrary to be true: see eg *Ledger v DPP* [1991] Crim LR 439 and the note at 441. An arrest would be unlawful if the officer knew that there was no possibility of a charge: *Plange v Chief Constable of South Humberside Police* (1992) Times, 23 March, CA. If the arrest does not conform with the legal requirements then an action for unlawful arrest and assault will lie: see *Wershof v Metropolitan Police Comr* [1978] 3 All ER 580, [1978] Crim LR 424. However, a police officer need only reasonably believe that an arrestable offence has been committed, it is not necessary that an arrestable offence has actually been committed; the test is whether the police officer had reasonable suspicion: see the Police and Criminal Evidence Act 1984 s 24 (as amended); and CRIMINAL LAW vol 11(1) (Reissue) para 705. The arrested person must be told of the reason for the arrest, even if it is obvious: s 28(3), (4). If the reason given renders the arrest unlawful it is irrelevant that there was a valid reason for the arrest if it was not communicated to the arrested person at the time of the arrest: (*Christie v Leachinsky* [1947] AC 573, HL; *Abbassy v Metropolitan Police Comr* [1990] 1 All ER 193, [1990] 1 WLR 385, CA). Private citizens may arrest anyone who is or who they reasonably believe to be in the process of committing an arrestable offence. Where the offence is not taking place at the time of the arrest, private citizens are only permitted to make an arrest where an arrestable offence has in fact taken place, and they are not protected by their reasonable suspicions: see *Walters v W H Smith & Son Ltd* [1914] 1 KB 595, CA; and Bailey, Harris and Jones *Civil Liberties: Cases and Materials* (4th Edn, 1995) pp 108–113. Private citizens have no power to make an arrest in anticipation of a future offence except where they reasonably apprehend a breach of the peace: see CRIMINAL LAW vol 11(1) (Reissue) para 709.

10  See *R v Brown* [1994] 3 SCR 749, Can SC, where the question whether statutory minimum sentences amount to cruel and unusual punishment was considered.

11    See the Police and Criminal Evidence Act 1984 Pt IV (ss 34–45) (as amended); and generally CRIMINAL
      LAW vol 11(1) (Reissue) paras 715–720. See also, as to the admissibility of confessions, ss 76–78; and
      as to the right of silence see Criminal Justice and Public Order Act 1994 ss 34–39; and EVIDENCE. In
      *DPP v Pete* [1991] LRC (Const) 553, Tanz CA, it was held that the denial of bail violated the
      constitutional right to personal liberty. In *Kihoro v A-G of Kenya* [1993] 3 LRC 390, Kenya CA, the
      appellant's detention for 74 days in police custody before being brought before a court infringed his
      right to personal liberty and to freedom from torture and awarded compensatory damages. In *R v
      Narayan* [1992] NZLR 145, [1993] 1 LRC 603, NZ CA, the right of the accused upon arrest to consult
      a lawyer without delay, and to be informed of that right had been denied, in breach of the New
      Zealand Bill of Rights Act 1990. In *Violet v Vidanapathirana* [1995] 2 LRC 53, Sri Lanka CA, it was
      held that, when confronted with a case of obvious disappearance of an individual held in custody and
      a false denial of such custody by a person in authority, the court had to take affirmative action to
      prevent nullification of the rule of law, freedom and the safety of the subject. As regards detention
      under emergency powers and the right to liberty see *State of Punjab v Talwandi* [1985] LRC (Const)
      600; *Minister of Home Affairs v Austin* [1987] LRC (Const) 567, Zimb SC; *Chng Suan Tze v Minister of
      Home Affairs* [1989] LRC (Const) 683, Sing CA; *Karpal Singh v Minister for Home Affairs* [1989] LRC
      (Const) 648, Malaysia SC; *Teo Soh Lung v Minister for Home Affairs* [1990] LRC (Const) 490, Sing HC;
      *Lee Gee Lam v Timbalan Menteri Datam Negeri* [1994] 1 LRC 203, Malaysia HC. In *State of Punjab v
      Sukhpal Singh* [1991] LRC (Const) 213, Ind SC, strong procedural safeguards were required in the
      context of preventive detention.

## 116. Right to freedom of movement.

**116. Right to freedom of movement.** The right to freedom of movement has been
recognised as a valid consideration in assessing the lawfulness of administrative action[1].
However, the right to freedom of movement is circumscribed by the law[2]. European
Community law provides for the free movement of persons[3], and for certain rights
contingent upon citizenship of the European Union[4].

1    Under the Prevention of Terrorism (Temporary Provsions) Act 1989 Pt II (ss 4–8), the Secretary of State
     has the power to make exclusion orders where it appears to him expedient to prevent acts of terrorism
     connected with the affairs of Northern Ireland: see s 4. Exclusion orders may be made against a person
     whom the Secretary of State is satisfied has been concerned in the commission, preparation or instigation
     of such act: see ss 5–7); see *R v Secretary of State for the Home Department, ex p McQuillan* [1995] 4 All ER
     400 at 421 per Sedley J (application for judicial review of an exclusion order made under the Prevention
     of Terrorism (Temporary Provisions) Act 1989): 'Freedom of movement, subject only to the general law,
     is a fundamental value of the common law'. See also *R v Secretary of State for the Home Department, ex p
     Adams* [1995] All ER (EC) 177, DC; *R v Secretary of State for Foreign and Commonwealth Affairs, ex p Everett*
     [1989] QB 811, [1989] 1 All ER 655, CA (freedom to travel in relation to the judicial review of the
     refusal to issue a passport). In *Nyirongo v A-G of Zambia* [1993] 3 LRC 256, Zambia SC, it was held that
     the constitutional guarantee of a citizen's freedom of movement entailed the right to the issue of a
     passport. In *Rattigan v Chief Immigration Officer* [1994] 1 LRC 343, Zimb SC, the refusal to permit alien
     husbands to reside with female citizens of Zimbabwe in that country violated the constitutional guarantee
     of a citizen's freedom of movement. See also *Ruwodo NO v Minister of Home Affairs* 1995 (7) BCLR 903,
     Zimb SC. There is no right of movement free from border controls into and out of the United Kingdom:
     see *R v Secretary of State for the Home Department, ex p Flynn* [1995] 3 CMLR 397.
2    See eg the law of trespass (see para 109 text and notes 4, 6 ante); restrictions imposed by the criminal
     law, such as the Criminal Justice and Public Order Act 1994 ss 61–71; and the Police and Criminal
     Evidence Act 1984 s 4 (as amended) (road checks). The writ of *ne exeat regno* is now obsolete as a
     weapon of the Crown but can be used by private individuals as a remedy to prevent a debtor from
     leaving the jurisdiction: see *Al Nahkel for Contracting and Trading Ltd v Lowe* [1986] QB 235, [1986]
     1 All ER 729; *Felton v Callis* [1969] 1 QB 200, [1968] 3 All ER 673; and also *R v Home Secretary, ex p
     Muboyayi* [1992] 1 QB 244 at 258, [1991] 4 All ER 72 at 82, CA, per Sir John Donaldson MR.
3    Fundamental human rights have been formally integrated into Community law by the Treaty on
     European Union (Cm 1934) Title I Art F para 2. As to that Treaty generally see para 23 ante. On the
     relationship between citizenship of the European Union and fundamental rights see Case C-168/91
     *Christos Konstantinidis v Stadt Altensteig-Standesamt* [1993] 3 CMLR 401 at 420, ECJ, opinion of the
     Advocate-General. The free movement provisions and the implementing directives have been held to
     create directly effective rights in national courts: see the EC Treaty Art 8A (added by the Treaty on
     European Union Title II Art G para (9)); however, this right to move freely between the member
     states is subject to a member state's right to exclude an individual on grounds of public policy (see
     Case 41/74 *Van Duyn v Home Office (No 2)* [1974] ECR 1337, ECJ; and Case 30/77 *R v Pierre
     Bouchereau* [1977] ECR 1999, ECJ: reliance by a national authority upon the concept of public policy

presupposes the existence of a genuine and sufficiently serious threat affecting one of the fundamental interests of society). See *R v Secretary of State for the Home Department, ex p McQuillan* [1995] 4 All ER 400 at 415 et seq per Sedley J. See generally Vincenzi 'European Citizenship and Free Movement Rights in the United Kingdom' [1995] Public Law 259; and EUROPEAN COMMUNITIES. See also the Convention for the Protection of Human Rights and Fundamental Freedoms, Fourth Protocol, Art 2 (which Protocol the United Kingdom has not ratified: see further para 122 post); and Harris, O'Boyle and Warbrick *Law of the European Convention on Human Rights* (1995), pp 559–562. The *East African Asians Cases* (1973) 3 EHHR 76, EComHR, covered by the Fourth Protocol, Art 3 were dealt with under Arts 3, 14 of the Convention itself (see paras 124, 164 post).

4    These rights include the right to move freely within the territory of the member states, subject to the limitations and conditions set out in the Treaty on European Union and by the implementing legislation: see Art 8A (as added: see note 3 supra). In particular the right to free movement applies to those who are working or seeking work: see generally EUROPEAN COMMUNITIES vol 52 para 15.01 et seq.

**117. Freedom of association.** The right to freedom of association[1] is reflected in the doctrine of freedom of contract[2], the ease with which trusts can be constituted[3] and companies formed[4]. It is limited to protect public order[5] and national security[6], and reflected by the absence of regulation of political parties.

The right to freedom of association is most particularly regulated in the field of labour relations. Thus in certain circumstances there is protection of the right to belong to a trade union[7]: (1) a prospective employee is protected from discrimination based on his union status[8]; (2) an employee can claim unfair dismissal if he is dismissed because of his union activity[9]; and (3) an employee has grounds of complaint for unlawful victimisation short of dismissal if the victimisation takes place because of his union activity[10].

1    See *Cheall v Association of Professional Executive Clerical and Computer Staff* [1983] 2 AC 180 at 191, [1983] 1 All ER 1130 at 1136, HL, per Lord Diplock: 'Freedom of association can only be mutual; there can be no right of an individual to associate with other individuals who are not willing to associate with him.'

2    See *Chertsey UDC v Mixnam's Properties Ltd* [1965] AC 735 at 764, [1964] 2 All ER 627 at 638, HL, per Lord Upjohn: 'Freedom to contract between the subjects of this country is a fundamental right even today, and if Parliament intends to empower a third party to make conditions which regulate the terms of contracts to be made between others then it must do so in quite clear terms'. An important aspect of this freedom is the right to form unincorporated associations. See generally CONTRACT.

3    See generally CHARITIES; TRUSTS.

4    See generally COMPANIES.

5    See the Public Order Act 1936 s 1 (as amended); *O'Moran v DPP* [1975] QB 864, [1975] 1 All ER 473, DC; and CRIMINAL LAW vol 11(1) (Reissue) para 100.

6    See the Public Order Act 1936 s 2; the Prevention of Terrorism (Temporary Provisions) Act 1989 s 2; *McEldowney v Forde* [1971] AC 632, [1969] 2 All ER 1039, HL; and CRIMINAL LAW vol 11(1) (Reissue) para 101.

7    But see *Council of Civil Service Unions v Minister for the Civil Service* [1985] AC 374, [1984] 3 All ER 935, HL. For the position under the Convention for the Protection of Human Rights and Fundamental Freedoms Art 11 see para 161 post.

8    See the Trade Union and Labour Relations (Consolidation) Act 1992 s 137; and TRADE, INDUSTRY AND INDUSTRIAL RELATIONS vol 47 (Reissue) para 1141.

9    See ibid s 152; and TRADE, INDUSTRY AND INDUSTRIAL RELATIONS vol 47 (Reissue) para 1150.

10   See ibid s 146; and TRADE, INDUSTRY AND INDUSTRIAL RELATIONS vol 47 (Reissue) para 1147.

**118. Right to participate in government.** The right to participate in government implies universal adult suffrage[1] including the right to a secret ballot[2] and the right to stand for election[3.]

1    See the Representation of the People Act 1983 s 1; and ELECTIONS vol 15 (Reissue) para 309 et seq. Generally any British citizen and those Commonwealth and Republic of Ireland citizens resident in the United Kingdom are entitled to vote. European Union citizens resident in the United Kingdom are entitled to vote in municipal elections and elections to the European Parliament: see para 25 notes 10, 17 ante. The following classes of people are not entitled to vote: (1) peers; (2) minors (ie those under the age of 18); (3) aliens; (4) persons suffering from a mental illness; (5) persons convicted and in prison; (6) persons reported guilty or convicted of corrupt practice: see ELECTIONS vol 15 (Reissue)

paras 309, 314–316. For the position under the Convention for the Protection of Human Rights and Fundamental Freedoms, First Protocol, Art 3 see para 166 post.

2   See ELECTIONS vol 15 (Reissue) paras 598–602.

3   Any person who is a British subject, of full age and not otherwise disqualified, may be a candidate for Parliament. As to the disqualifications for membership of the House of Commons (including clergy, peers, election offenders, persons under 21, aliens (except citizens of the Republic of Ireland), persons under a mental incapacity, certain criminal offenders, bankrupts, specified office holders) see generally PARLIAMENT. Additionally, citizens of member states of the European Community are entitled to stand in the United Kingdom in municipal elections and for election to the European Parliament: see para 25 notes 10, 17 ante. As to disqualifications for membership of a local authority (including holders of politically restricted posts, bankrupts, certain criminal offenders and election offenders) see LOCAL GOVERNMENT vol 28 para 1091. As to disqualification for the office of representative to the European Parliament see ELECTIONS vol 15 (Reissue) para 606.

## 119. Right to protection of the law.

**119. Right to protection of the law.** The right to protection of the law[1] includes the right not to have conduct criminalised retrospectively[2]; the presumption that a person is innocent of a crime of which he is accused until it is proved otherwise, and that the burden of proof is generally on the accuser[3]; the right to confidential legal advice[4]; and the right to a fair[5] and speedy[6] trial. Although the police and the Director of Public Prosecutions have a discretion not to proceed against certain persons, such discretion is subject to review by the courts[7].

For the enforcement of his civil rights an individual is entitled to unimpeded access to the courts[8].

1   For use of the right to protection of the law in a civil matter see *Woolwich Equitable Building Society v IRC* [1993] AC 70, sub nom *Woolwich Building Society v IRC (No 2)* [1992] 3 All ER 737, HL. The presumption of innocence and the human rights implications of statutes which reverse the burden of proof have been widely considered in Commonwealth jurisdictions: see *R v Oakes* [1987] LRC (Const) 477, Can SC; *A-G of Hong Kong v Lee Kwong-kut* [1993] AC 951, [1993] 3 All ER 939, PC; *Seaboyer v R* [1993] 1 LRC 465, Can SC; *Vasquez v R* [1994] 3 All ER 674, [1994] 2 LRC 377, PC; *R v Laba* [1994] 3 SCR 343; *R v Daviault* [1994] 3 SCR 63; *Freiremar SA v Prosecutor-General of Namibia* 1994 (6) BCLR 73, Namibia HC. For a review of the human rights implications of reversing the burden of proof see *State v Zuma* [1995] 1 LRC 145, SA Const Ct, in which it was held a statutory provision that placed the onus on an accused to prove that a confession was made under duress breached the accused's right to a fair trial. See also *State v Mhlungu* [1995] 2 LRC 503, SA Const Ct; *State v Van den Berg* [1995] 2 LRC 619, Nam HC. In *Ridgeway v R* (19 April 1995, unreported), Aust HC, there was considered to be no substantive defence of entrapment in Australian law, but where there was a significant element of government inducement or persuasion in the commission of an offence there was a discretion to exclude the evidence and stay the proceedings. The courts have recognised the importance of equality in the application of laws: see *R v Hertfordshire County Council, ex p Cheung* (1986) Times, 4 April; *Westminster City Council v Great Portland Estates plc* [1985] AC 661, sub nom *Great Portland Estates v Westminster City Council plc* [1984] 3 All ER 744, HL; and *R v Immigration Appeal Tribunal, ex p Manshoora Begum* [1986] Imm AR 385. As to the existence of a general constitutional principle of equality see Jowell (1994) 47(2) CLP 1. Note the decision in *Nyamakazi v President of Bophuthatswana* 1994 (1) BCLR 92, SA SC (Bophuthatswana General Division) which refers to the place of equality in western, liberal and democratic thought. As to the application of the principle of equality with respect to different religions see the dissenting judgment of Kwach JA in *Kaitany v Wamaitha* (1995) Civil Appeal No 108, Kenya CA. As regards affirmative action see *Motala v University of Natal* [1995] 2 LRC 429, SA SC (Durban and Coast Local Division).

As to the two principal rules of natural justice, namely *nemo judex in causa sua* (no one may be judge in his own cause), and *audi alteram partem* under which a decision cannot stand unless the person directly affected by it was given a fair opportunity both to state his case and to know and answer the other side's case, see ADMINISTRATIVE LAW vol 1(1) (Reissue) para 84 et seq. Note the general principle of evidence that evidence illegally obtained is admissible (see *R v Fox* [1986] AC 281, sub nom *Fox v Chief Constable of Gwent* [1985] 3 All ER 392, HL); *R v Khan* [1996] 3 All ER 289, HL.

2   See *Knuller (Publishing, Printing and Promotions) Ltd v DPP* [1973] AC 435, [1972] 2 All ER 498, HL, where it was held that their decision in *Shaw v DPP* [1962] AC 220, [1961] 2 All ER 446, HL, did not support the doctrine that the courts have some general or residual power to create new offences so as to widen existing offences as to punish conduct not previously punishable in law. See, however, the War Crimes Act 1991 s 1, permitting charges of murder or manslaughter to be brought in respect of acts committed during the Second World War; and *Huntley v A-G for Jamaica* [1995] 2 AC 1, [1995] 1

All ER 308, PC. See also *Chan Chi-Hung v R* [1996] 1 AC 442, [1995] 3 WLR 742, PC (lower sentence to be imposed where offence reformulated by statute after commission but before sentence).

3    See eg *State v Zuma* [1995] 1 LRC 145, SA Const Ct; and generally CRIMINAL LAW vol 11(2) (Reissue) paras 1062–1066.

4    See *R v Balkan* (1973) 13 CCC (2d) 482, Alta App Div; and EVIDENCE.

5    As to the conduct of criminal trials see CRIMINAL LAW. Several Commonwealth jurisdictions have considered the human rights implications of trial procedure: *Kunnath v The State* [1993] 4 All ER 30, PC (on the need for interpreters); *R v L* [1994] 2 LRC 204 (on the admissibility of videotape evidence); *R v Cruz* [1994] 2 LRC 390 (right of peremptory challenge of jurors); *R v B* (1995) 1 HRNZ 1 (order for complainant to undergo intimate examination); *Phato v A-G, Eastern Cape* 1994 (5) BCLR 99 (right of an accused to information held by the police); *R v Chaplin* [1995] 1 SCR 727 (relationship between the prosecution's duty of disclosure and the right to silence, and the freedom from self-incrimination). See also *British Columbia Securities Commission v Branch* [1995] 2 SCR 3, Can SC, cited in para 111 note 1 ante; *R v Crawford* [1995] 1 SCR 858, Can SC, (question whether the cross-examination of accused about pre-trial silence offended against right to silence). As to the position under the Convention for the Protection of Human Rights and Fundamental Freedoms Art 6 see paras 134–147 post.

6    The constitutional right to be tried within a reasonable time was breached where the appellant was awaiting retrial more than three years after the Court of Appeal of Jamaica had ordered his retrial: *Bell v DPP* [1985] AC 937, sub nom *Bell v DPP of Jamaica* [1985] 2 All ER 585, PC. Guidelines concerning delays were set out in the Canadian case of *R v Morin* (1992) 71 CCC (3d) 1; and these were considered in *Martin v Tauranga District Court* [1995] 2 LRC 788, NZ CA. As regards the right to a fair hearing of a criminal charge within a reasonable time see generally *Re Mlambo* [1993] 2 LRC 28, Zimb SC; and *Triveniben v State of Gujarat* [1992] LRC (Const) 425; *Daya Singh v Union of India* [1992] LRC (Const) 452; *Catholic Commission for Justice and Peace in Zimbabwe v A-G* [1993] 2 LRC 279, Zimb SC; *Nkomo v A-G* [1993] 2 LRC 375; and *Pratt v A-G for Jamaica* [1994] 2 AC 1, [1993] 4 All ER 769, PC.

7    See *R v DPP, ex p C* [1995] 1 Cr App Rep 136; *R v Chief Constable of Kent, ex p L (a minor)* [1993] 1 All ER 756, DC; *R v Tower Bridge Metropolitan Stipendiary Magistrate, ex p Chaudhry* [1994] QB 340, [1994] 1 All ER 44, DC.

8    Generally see *Pyx Granite Co Ltd v Ministry of Housing and Local Government* [1960] AC 260, [1959] 3 All ER 1, HL; *Khawaja v Secretary of State for the Home Department* [1984] AC 74 at 111, [1983] 1 All ER 765 at 782, HL, per Lord Scarman: 'every person within the jurisdiction enjoys the equal protection of our laws. There is no distinction between English nationals and others'); and *A-G v Times Newspapers* [1974] AC 273 at 310, 313, [1973] 3 All ER 54 at 73, 75, HL, per Lord Diplock: '[Contempt of court] extends also to conduct that is calculated to inhibit suitors generally from availing themselves of their constitutional right to have their legal rights and obligations ascertained and enforced in courts of law, by holding up any suitor to public obloquy for doing so or by exposing him to public and prejudicial discussion of the merits or the facts of his case before they have been determined by the court or the action has been otherwise disposed of in due course of law...[however] discussion, however strongly expressed, on matters of general public interest of this kind is not to be stifled merely because there is litigation pending out of particular facts to which general principles discussed would be applicable. If the arousing of public opinion by this kind of discussion has the indirect effect of bringing pressure to bear on a particular litigant to abandon or settle a pending action, this must be borne because of the greater public interest in upholding freedom of discussion on matters of general public concern.' In *Brandy v HREOC* [1995] 2 LRC 9, Aust HC, statutory provisions were declared invalid to the extent that they provided for the Human Rights and Equal Opportunity Commission to make binding determinations involving judicial power. Prisoners have the right of access to the courts: *Leech v Deputy Governor of Parkhurst Prison* [1988] AC 533, [1988] 1 All ER 485, HL; *Raymond v Honey* [1983] 1 AC 1, [1982] 1 All ER 756, HL (governor could not prevent prisoner sending documents to High Court to pursue claim for contempt); *R v Secretary of State for the Home Department, ex p Anderson* [1984] QB 778, [1984] 1 All ER 920 (prison governor had prevented prisoner from having an interview with his lawyer to discuss potential civil claim concerning his treatment in prison because the prisoner had not simultaneously submitted his claim to the internal disciplinary procedure; the prison rules could not confer power to impede access to the courts); *R v Secretary of State for the Home Department, ex p Leech* [1994] QB 198, [1993] 4 All ER 539, CA (prisoner obtained judicial review of prison rule enabling governor to read letters from his solicitor relating to possible legal proceedings). See also *Maharaj v A-G of Trinidad and Tobago (No 2)* [1979] AC 385, [1978] 2 All ER 670, PC; *Harrikissoon v A-G of Trinidad and Tobago* [1980] AC 265, [1979] 3 WLR 62, PC; and *Chokolingo v A-G of Trinidad and Tobago* [1981] 1 All ER 244, [1981] 1 WLR 106, PC. See further para 107 text and notes 7–11 ante.

**120. Right to property.** The right to property[1] is protected by the law of tort[2], theft[3] and related offences, by the law relating to intellectual property[4], by the principle that there can be no taxation save as required by Parliament[5], and indirectly by the principles of natural justice[6]. The state can compel the sale of land[7].

1   For a discussion of the right to property in European Community law see Case 44/79 *Hauer* [1979] ECR 3727, ECJ; Case 4/73 *Nold* [1974] ECR 491, ECJ; Case 154/78 *Valsabbia* [1980] ECR 907, ECJ. See *Local Government Board v Arlidge* [1915] AC 10, HL, on the standing of the right to property (in particular Viscount Haldane at 130–131); *R v Secretary of State for Transport, ex p de Rothschild* [1989] 1 All ER 933, CA; *Prest v Secretary of State for Wales* (1982) 81 LGR 193 at 198, CA, per Lord Denning MR: 'No citizen is to be deprived of his land by any public authority against his will, unless it is expressly authorised by Parliament and the public interest decisively so demands; and then on condition that proper compensation is paid'; citing *A-G v De Keyser's Royal Hotel Ltd* [1920] AC 508, HL; and *Minister of Housing and Local Government v Hartnell* [1965] AC 1134, [1965] 1 All ER 490, HL. For a Commonwealth example see *Davies v Minister of Land, Agriculture and Water Development* 1995 (1) BCLR 83, Zimb HC. As to the recognition of native title in Australia see *Mabo v Queensland* (1988) 166 CLR 186; and *Mabo v Queensland (No 2)* (1992) 175 CLR 1. In *Tawanda Nyambirai v National Social Security* (Judgment No SC 110/95), Zimb SC, it was held that a compulsory national insurance was not contrary to the constitutional protection of the right to property. For the position under the Convention for the Protection of Human Rights and Fundamental Freedoms, First Protocol, Art 1, see para 165 post.
2   See generally TORT.
3   See generally CRIMINAL LAW.
4   See generally COPYRIGHT; PATENTS AND REGISTERED DESIGNS.
5   See *A-G v De Keyser's Royal Hotel Ltd* [1920] AC 508, HL; *A-G v Wilts United Dairies* (1922) 127 LT 822; *Woolwich Equitable Building Society v IRC* [1991] 4 All ER 92, sub nom *R v IRC, ex p Woolwich Equitable Building Society* [1990] 1 WLR 1400, HL; *Woolwich Equitable Building Society v IRC* [1993] AC 70, sub nom *Woolwich Building Society v IRC (No 2)* [1992] 3 All ER 737, HL; Case 199/82 *Amministrazione delle Finanze dello Stato v San Giorgio SpA* [1983] ECR 3595, [1985] 2 CMLR 658, ECJ; and *Customs and Excise Comrs v Cure & Deeley Ltd* [1962] 1 QB 340, [1961] 3 All ER 641. See further para 228 post.
6   See *Cooper v Wandsworth Board of Works* (1863) 14 CBNS 180, in particular at 190 per Willes J: 'I apprehend that a tribunal which is by law invested with power to affect the property of one of Her Majesty's subjects, is bound to give such subject an opportunity of being heard before it proceeds: and that that rule is of universal application, and founded upon the plainest principles of justice').
7   See generally COMPULSORY ACQUISITION; HIGHWAYS; TOWN AND COUNTRY PLANNING.

**121. Economic and social rights.** The right to work at a trade or profession without being unjustly excluded from it has been recognised by the common law[1]. The right to education is recognised by statute[2], as is the right to be housed[3]. The state provides a minimum income[4]. The courts have not accepted a positive right to health care[5]. There is statutory recognition of the right to strike[6].

1   See *Nagle v Feilden* [1966] 2 QB 633 at 644–645, [1966] 1 All ER 689 at 693, CA, per Lord Denning MR. See also *McInnes v Onslow Fane* [1978] 3 All ER 211, [1978] 1 WLR 1520; *R v Barnsley Metropolitan Borough Council, ex p Hook* [1976] 3 All ER 452, [1976] 1 WLR 1052, CA; *Walker v Leeds City Council* [1978] AC 403, [1976] 3 All ER 709, HL; *Breen v Amalgamated Engineering Union* [1971] 2 QB 175, [1971] 1 All ER 1148, CA; *Edwards v Society of Graphical and Allied Trades* [1971] Ch 354.
2   See the Education Act 1944 s 8 (as amended) (obligation imposed on local education authorities to provide primary and secondary schools in their areas) s 36 (as amended) (duty on parents to ensure that their children receive suitable full time education); *R v Inner London Education Authority, ex p Ali* [1990] COD 317; *Meade v Haringey London Borough Council* [1979] 2 All ER 1016, [1979] 1 WLR 637, CA; *R v Birmingham City Council, ex p Equal Opportunities Commission* [1989] AC 1155, sub nom *Equal Opportunities Commission v Birmingham City Council* [1989] 1 All ER 769, HL). Parents have a choice within the public education system as to which school to send their children: Education Act 1980 s 6 (as amended); and see *R v Cleveland County Council, ex p Commission for Racial Equality* (1991) 91 LGR 139, CA; *R v Governors of Bishop Challoner Roman Catholic Comprehensive Girls' School, ex p Choudhury* [1992] 2 AC 182, sub nom *Choudhury v Governors of Bishop Challoner Roman Catholic Comprehensive Girls' School* [1992] 3 All ER 277, HL; *Cumings v Birkenhead Corpn* [1972] 1 Ch 12, [1971] 2 All ER 881, CA. In certain circumstances a child can be excluded from school: see eg *R v Headmaster of Fernhill Manor School, ex p Brown* (1992) Times, 5 June (private school); *R v Board of Governors of Stoke Newington School, ex p M* [1994] ELR 131; as to publicly funded schools see the Education (No 2) Act 1986 ss 23–26 (as amended). See further EDUCATION vol 15 (Reissue) paras 22 et seq, 59, 99, 118, 120–123.

For the position under the Convention for the Protection of Human Rights and Fundamental Freedoms, First Protocol, Art 2, see para 166 post.

3   See the Housing Act 1985 s 65 (duty to house homeless persons); and generally HOUSING paras 509–523.

4   Ie income support: see the Social Security Contributions and Benefits Act 1992 s 124 (as amended). See NATIONAL HEALTH AND SOCIAL SECURITY.

5   The National Health Service Act 1977 ss 1, 3 place duties on the Secretary of State to provide adequate health care but these duties are probably legally unenforceable (see *R v Secretary of State for Social Services, ex p Hincks* (1979) 123 Sol Jo 436); but the possibility of judicial review on the ground of irrationality has been left open (*R v Cambridge Health Authority, ex p B* [1995] 2 All ER 129, [1995] 1 WLR 898, CA; *Re J (a minor) (child in care: medical treatment)* [1993] Fam 15, [1992] 4 All ER 614, CA; *Re Walker's Application* (1987) Times, 26 November, CA; and *R v Ethical Committee of St Mary's Hospital (Manchester), ex p Harriot* [1988] 1 FLR 512, but note at 518–519 per Schiemann J: 'If the committee had advised, for instance, that the IVF unit should in principle refuse all such treatment to anyone who was a Jew or coloured then I think the courts might well grant a declaration that such a policy was illegal.' See also para 106 note 10 ante.

6   Ie at common law a strike will incur various contractual and tortious liabilities and statute provides an immunity from suit in certain circumstances: see TRADE, INDUSTRY AND INDUSTRIAL RELATIONS vol 47 (Reissue) paras 1401–1440.

## (3)  HUMAN RIGHTS AND FREEDOMS UNDER THE EUROPEAN CONVENTION

### (i)  Introduction

**122. The European Convention on Human Rights and Fundamental Freedoms.** The Convention for the Protection of Human Rights and Fundamental Freedoms[1] (commonly known as the European Convention on Human Rights was signed in 1950 and entered into force in 1953[2]. It was the first comprehensive international human rights treaty, establishing the first international complaints procedure[3], and the first international court dealing exclusively with human rights[4]. The Convention provides for the establishment of a European Commission of Human Rights and a European Court of Human Rights[5].

The Convention is concerned primarily with violations of its rights and freedoms by public authorities. However, the Convention expressly requires contracting states to secure the rights and freedoms contained in the Convention to everyone within their jurisdiction[6]. This, and the nature and wording of some of the substantive guarantees, imposes positive obligations upon states to take action to secure some of those rights and freedoms against infringements by private persons as well as by public authorities[7].

In outline, the Convention provides for the reference to the Commission of a complaint that a state has breached the provisions of the Convention[8]. The Commission may only deal with a complaint after all domestic remedies have been exhausted, according to the general rules of international law, and within a period of six months from the date on which the final decision was taken[9]. If an application is declared admissible[10], then the Commission must attempt to secure a 'friendly settlement' between the applicant and the respondent government[11]. If such a settlement cannot be achieved, the Commission draws up a report, including a legal opinion as to whether there has been a violation of the Convention, and transmits it to the Committee of Ministers[12]. If the state concerned has accepted the jurisdiction of the European Court of Human Rights, then the case may be referred to that court[13].

On receipt of a request from the Secretary General of the Council of Europe, a contracting state must furnish an explanation of the manner in which its internal law ensures the effective implementation of any of the provisions of the Convention[14].

1   Ie the Convention for the Protection of Human Rights and Fundamental Freedoms (1950) (Rome, 4 November 1950; TS 71 (1953); Cmd 8969; ETS no 5). See generally Harris, O'Boyle & Warbrick *Law of the European Convention on Human Rights* (1995). For the relationship between the Convention and the International Covenant on Civil and Political Rights (1966) (see para 103 note 3 ante) see Schmidt 'The Complementarity of the Covenant and the European Convention – Recent Developments' in Harris and Joseph (eds) *The International Covenant on Civil and Political Rights and United Kingdom Law* (1995).

The Convention is based to a large extent on the Universal Declaration of Human Rights (Paris, 10 December 1948; UN 2 (1949); Cmd 7662). The United Kingdom has ratified not only the Convention but also its Protocols, other than the Fourth (which it has signed), Sixth, Seventh and Ninth. The First Protocol contains additional rights and freedoms (20 March 1952; Cmnd 9221; Council of Europe, ETS no 9); the Second Protocol confers on the European Court of Human Rights the competence to give advisory opinions (6 May 1963; Cmnd 4551; Council of Europe, ETS no 44); the Third Protocol amends certain procedural provisions of the Convention (6 May 1963; Cmnd 4552; Council of Europe, ETS no 45); the Fourth Protocol contains further additional rights and freedoms (16 September 1963; Cmnd 2309; Council of Europe, ETS no 46); the Fifth Protocol further amends the procedural provisions of the Convention (20 January 1966; TS 48 (1972); Cmnd 4963; Council of Europe, ETS no 55); the Sixth Protocol concerns the abolition of the death penalty (28 April 1983, Council of Europe, ETS no 114); the Seventh Protocol contains further additional rights and freedoms (22 November 1984, Council of Europe, ETS no 117); the Eighth Protocol amends the procedural provisions relating to the European Court of Human Rights (19 March 1985, Council of Europe, ETS no 118); the projected Ninth Protocol amends the Convention to give complainants the right to refer a case to court (6 November 1990, Council of Europe, ETS no 140). The projected Tenth Protocol (1992, Council of Europe, ETS 146) relates to the Committee of Ministers' decision as to whether or not there has been a violation of the Convention. Once the Protocol is in force only a simple majority of the Committee will be required rather than the present two-thirds majority requirement (25 March 1992, Council of Europe, ETS no 146).

The Eleventh Protocol (11 May 1994; Cm 2634; Council of Europe, ETS no 155) has been ratified by the United Kingdom, but at the date at which this volume states the law is not yet in force. The effect of the Protocol will be to: (1) replace the existing part-time Commission and court with a single permanent court; (2) reform the enforcement procedures; and (3) create a right of access to the court after the exhaustion of effective domestic remedies. For the history of British involvement in the drafting and ratification of the Convention and acceptance of the individual petition see Lester 'Fundamental Rights: the United Kingdom Isolated?' (1984) PL 46 at pp 49–55; see also the fuller account by Geoffrey Marston, 'The United Kingdom's Part in the Preparation of the European Convention on Human Rights 1950' (1993) 42 ICLQ 796; Lester, 'Taking Human Rights Seriously' (1994–95) 5 King's College Law Journal.

2   For an account of the background to the Convention see Harris, O'Boyle and Warbrick *Law of the European Convention on Human Rights* (1995) ch 1. At the date at which this volume states the law, the following states have ratified the Convention: Andorra; Austria; Belgium; Bulgaria; Cyprus; Czech Republic; Denmark; Estonia; Finland; France; Germany; Greece; Hungary; Iceland; Ireland; Italy; Liechtenstein; Lithuania; Luxembourg; Malta; Netherlands; Norway; Poland; Portugal; Romania; San Marino; Slovakia; Slovenia; Spain; Sweden; Switzerland; Turkey; United Kingdom.

At the date at which this volume states the law, the First Protocol (see note 1 supra) had been adopted by all those states except Andorra and Switzerland.

At the date at which this volume states the law, the Fourth Protocol (see note 1 supra) had been adopted by: Austria; Belgium; Cyprus; Czech Republic; Denmark; Estonia; Finland; France; Germany; Hungary; Iceland; Ireland; Italy; Lithuania; Luxembourg; Netherlands; Norway; Poland; Portugal; Romania; San Marino; Slovakia; Slovenia; Sweden.

At the date at which this volume states the law, the Sixth Protocol (see note 1 supra) had been adopted by: Andorra; Austria; Czech Republic; Denmark; Finland; France; Germany; Hungary; Iceland; Ireland; Italy; Liechtenstein; Luxembourg; Malta; Netherlands; Norway; Portugal; Romania; San Marino; Slovakia; Slovenia; Spain; Sweden; Switzerland.

At the date at which this volume states the law, the Seventh Protocol (see note 1 supra) had been adopted by: Austria; Czech Republic; Denmark; Estonia; Finland; France; Greece; Hungary; Iceland; Italy; Lithuania; Luxembourg; Norway; Romania; San Marino; Slovakia; Slovenia; Sweden; Switzerland.

At the date at which this volume states the law, the Second, Third, Fifth and Eighth Protocols (see note 1 supra) had been adopted by all the parties to the Convention.

At the date at which this volume states the law, the Ninth Protocol (see note 1 supra) had been adopted by: Austria; Belgium; Cyprus; Czech Republic; Denmark; Estonia; Finland; Germany; Hungary; Ireland; Italy; Liechtenstein; Luxembourg; Netherlands; Norway; Poland; Portugal; Romania; San Marino; Slovakia; Slovenia; Sweden; Switzerland.

The Tenth and Eleventh Protocols (see note 1 supra) require ratification by all parties to the Convention to enter into force; at the date at which this volume states the law, the necessary ratifications had not been obtained.

A contracting state may by declaration extend the application of the Convention to the territories for whose international relations it is reponsible: see Convention for the Protection of Human Rights and Fundamental Freedoms (1950) Art 63; and *Tyrer v United Kingdom* A 26 (1978), 2 EHRR 1, ECtHR; *Gillow v United Kingdom* A 109 (1986), 11 EHRR 335, ECtHR.

A contracting state may denounce the Convention (in respect of itself or a territory to which it extended the Convention by declaration: see supra) after at least five years' adherence to it, and by sixth months' notice to the Secretary General of the Council of Europe: Art 65(1), (4). This does not release the state from its obligations under the Convention in respect of any alleged violation before the denunciation becomes effective: Art 65(2). A contacting state which ceases to be a member of the Council of Europe ceases also to be a party to the Convention: Art 65(3).

3　As to the making of complaints see para 172 post. The contracting states generally agree not to apply alternative treaties, declarations or conventions in force between them for the purposeof submitting, by way of petition, a dispute arising out of the interpretation or application of the Convention for the Protection of Human Rights and Fundamental Freedoms (1950) to a means of settlement other than those provided by that Convention: Art 62.

4　As to the composition and jurisdiction of the European Court of Human Rights see paras 179–181 post.

5　Convention for the Protection of Human Rights and Fundamental Freedoms Art 19. As to the membership, proceedings and operation of the Commission and the court see paras 172–178 post.

6　Ibid Art 1. As to the extent of the states' responsibilities see eg *Costello-Roberts v United Kingdom* A 247-C (1993), 19 EHRR 112, ECtHR; Applications 6780/74, 6950/75 *Cyprus v Turkey* 2 DR 125 (1976), 4 EHRR 282, EComHR (rapes carried out by Turkish soldiers were imputable to Turkey because it was not shown that adequate measures were taken to prevent them from occurring, and because disciplinary measures were not taken against the perpetrators).

7　See Harris, O'Boyle and Warbrick *Law of the European Convention on Human Rights* (1995) pp 19–22; Clapham *Human Rights in the Private Sphere* (1993). Nothing in the Convention for the Protection of Human Rights and Fundamental Freedoms (1950) may be contrued as limiting or derogating from any of the human rights or fundamental freedoms ensured by the laws of any contracting state or any other agreement to which a state is a party: Art 60.

8　As to references to the Commission see para 172 post

9　See Convention for the Protection of Human Rights and Fundamental Freedoms Art 26; and para 173 post.

10　See ibid Art 27; and paras 174–175 post.

11　See ibid arts 28–30; and para 176 post.

12　See ibid arts 31, 32; and para 177 post.

13　See ibid Art 48; and para 179 post.

14　Ibid Art 57. This power has not in practice been extensively used.

As to the effect on the European Court of Human Rights of the prospective coming into force of the Eleventh Protocol to the Convention see note 1 supra.

### (ii)　The Rights Guaranteed by the Convention

#### A.　RIGHTS RELATING TO LIFE AND LIBERTY

**123. Right to life.** Under the Convention for the Protection of Human Rights and Fundamental Freedoms, everyone's right to life[1] must be protected by law[2], and no one may be deprived of his life intentionally save in the execution of a sentence of a court[3] following his conviction of a crime for which this penalty is provided by law[4].

However, deprivation of life is not regarded as inflicted in contravention of this requirement[5] when it results from the use of force which is no more than absolutely necessary[6] (1) in defence of any person from unlawful violence[7]; (2) in order to effect a lawful[8] arrest or to prevent the escape of a person lawfully detained[9]; or (3) in action lawfully taken for the purpose of quelling a riot or insurrection[10]. No derogation from the application of this requirement may be made except in respect of deaths resulting from lawful acts of war[11].

The requirement of the protection of human life is one of the most fundamental provisions in the Convention, from which no derogation is possible, even in times of national emergency; it enshrines one of the basic values of the democratic societies making up the Council of Europe. As such, its provisions must be strictly construed[12]. The requirement of the protection of human life may prevail over concern for the protection of other rights[13].

The Convention permits the use of force for the purposes enumerated in heads (1) to (3) above, subject to the requirement that the force used is strictly proportionate to the achievement of the permitted purpose. In assessing whether the use of force is strictly proportionate, regard must be had to the nature of the aim pursued, the dangers to life and limb inherent in the situation, and the degree of risk that the force employed might result in loss of life. Deprivations of life must be subjected to careful scrutiny, particularly where deliberate lethal force is used, taking into consideration not only the actions of the agents of the state who actually administer the force, but also all the surrounding circumstances including such matters as the planning and control of the actions under examination[14].

1    As to whether abortion violates the right to life of the foetus see Application 8416/78 *Paton v United Kingdom* (1980) 3 EHRR 408, EComHR; it appears from the Commission's consideration in that case that: (1) by general usage, the term 'everyone' does not include the unborn; (2) the possible construction of the Convention for the Protection of Human Rights and Fundamental Freedoms Art 2 as recognising an absolute right to life of the foetus could be incompatible with the object and purpose of the Convention, as placing a higher value on the foetus' life than on that of the pregnant woman. However, the question whether, and if so how far, Art 2 covered the foetus was left open in the circumstances of the case.

2    The protection of the right to life by law imposes a broader obligation on the state than merely requiring it to refrain from the intentional taking of life. The state is further enjoined to take appropriate steps to safeguard life: Application 7154/75 *X v United Kingdom* 14 DR 31 at 32 (1978).

3    A claim that the execution of a sentence of imprisonment on an applicant's husband violated her right to life where there was medical evidence that she might commit suicide as a result was in the circumstances ill-founded, because the risk of suicide could be addressed by other means: Application 11604/85 *Naddaf v Federal Republic of Germany* (1986) 9 EHRR 561, EComHR. A conviction for a capital offence must be in accordance with the Convention for the Protection of Human Rights and Fundamental Freedoms Arts 3, 6, 7, 14 (see paras 124, 134–148, 164 post). In certain circumstances, the treatment or punishment of condemned persons may constitute inhuman or degrading treatment contrary to Art 3 (see para 124 post). As to the death penalty in English law see CRIMINAL LAW vol 11(2) (Reissue) para 1199. The death penalty is prohibited altogether by the Sixth Protocol to the Convention, which, however, has not been ratified by the United Kingdom: see Harris, O'Boyle and Warbrick *Law of the European Convention on Human Rights* (1995) pp 46, 564. See also note 5 infra.

4    Convention for the Protection of Human Rights and Fundamental Freedoms (1950) Art 2(1). Cf the Universal Declaration of Human Rights (Paris, 10 December 1948) Art 3; and see the International Covenant on Civil and Political Rights (1966) (see para 103 note 3 ante) Art 6. For the position under English law see para 106 ante. As to the Convention for the Protection of Human Rights and Fundamental Freedoms (1950) generally see para 122 ante. As to the Universal Declaration of Human Rights see para 122 note 1 ante. See further Joseph 'The Right to Life' in Harris and Joseph (eds) *The International Covenant on Civil and Political Rights and United Kingdom Law* (1995).

5    The situations defined in the Convention for the Protection of Human Rights and Fundamental Freedoms Art 2(1), (2), where deprivation of life may be justified, are exhaustive and must be narrowly interpreted, being exceptions to, or indicating the limits of, a fundamental Convention right: Application 10044/82 *Stewart v United Kingdom* 39 DR 162 (1984), 7 EHRR 453, EComHR.

6    Convention for the Protection of Human Rights and Fundamental Freedoms Art 2(2). 'Absolutely necessary' indicates that a stricter and more compelling test applies in relation to Art 2 than in relation to other provisions of the Convention. The provision gives protection against more than intentional killings; it also defines situations where it is permitted to use force that may result in the loss of life as an unintentional outcome: *McCann v United Kingdom* A 324 (1995) paras 148–149, ECtHR; Application 10044/82 *Stewart v United Kingdom* 39 DR 162 (1984), 7 EHRR 453, EComHR (13 year old boy killed by plastic baton round during riot in Northern Ireland; on the facts, the force used was absolutely necessary for the purpose of quelling the riot).

7    Convention for the Protection of Human Rights and Fundamental Freedoms (1950) Art 2(2)(a).

8   'Lawful' means lawful under domestic law: See eg Application 9013/80 *Farrell v United Kingdom* 30 DR 96 (1982), 5 EHRR 466, EComHR; Application 2756/66 *X v Belgium* 12 YB 174 (1969), EComHR.
9   Convention for the Protection of Human Rights and Fundamental Freedoms (1950) Art 2(2)(b).
10  Ibid Art 2(2)(c). The action taken to quell·a riot must be lawful under domestic law: Application 2756/66 *X v Belgium* 12 YB 174 (1969), EComHR.
11  Convention for the Protection of Human Rights and Fundamental Freedoms (1950) Art 15 para (2); see para 168 post.
12  *McCann v United Kingdom* A 324 (1995) para 147, ECtHR; see also Application 10044/82 *Stewart v United Kingdom* 39 DR 162 (1984), 7 EHRR 453, EComHR. The requirement does not impose an obligation upon a state to provide a police bodyguard: Application 6040/73 *X v Ireland* 44 CD 121 (1973), EComHR.
13  Application 5207/71 *X v Federal Republic of Germany* 39 CD 99 (1971), EComHR (allegation that repeated court orders for the eviction of an old woman from a house were shown medically to be a threat to her life: admissible; application later rejected for other reasons).
14  *McCann v United Kingdom* A 324 (1995), ECtHR, paras 149–150. See also Application 10444/82 *Stewart v United Kingdom* DR 39 (1984), 7 EHRR 453, EComHR; Application 17579/90 *Kelly v United Kingdom* (1993) 16 EHRR CD 20, EComHR.

**124.  Prohibition of torture; inhuman and degrading treatment or punishment.**
No one may be subjected to torture[1] or to inhuman[2] or degrading[3] treatment or punishment[4]. There may be no derogation from the application of this requirement[5]. Ill-treatment must attain a minimum level of severity if it is to fall within the scope of this provision[6]. Treatment causing mental suffering is sufficient to fall within the provision, provided a sufficient degree of intensity is reached[7]. Provided it is sufficiently real and immediate, a mere threat of conduct prohibited by this provision may itself be in conflict with it[8].

Treatment in connection with arrest[9], the conditions of detention, and treatment during detention[10] in prison[11] or mental hospital[12] may amount to inhuman or degrading treatment. Although this provision does not generally prohibit the death penalty, the treatment or punishment of condemned persons may in some circumstances be considered to be inhuman or degrading[13]. Racial discrimination may in some circumstances be considered degrading treatment[14], but in particular circumstances legislation discriminating against women[15], or against illegitimate children[16], has not been held to be degrading[17].

Although there is no right under the Convention for the Protection of Human Rights and Fundamental Freedoms (1950) to political asylum as such, nor any right not to be expelled or extradited from a state, the expulsion or extradition of a person to another state where there are substantial grounds[18] for believing that he would be in danger[19] of being subjected to torture, or to inhuman or degrading treatment or punishment, constitutes a breach of the Convention by the state which takes the decision to deport or extradite[20].

Corporal punishment as a criminal penalty or as a disciplinary sanction in schools may violate this provision[21].

1   Torture has been defined as deliberate inhuman treatment causing very serious and cruel suffering, referring to Resolution 3452 of the General Assembly of the United Nations, of 9 December 1975, which declared that 'torture constitutes an aggravated and deliberate form of cruel, inhuman or degrading treatment or punishment': see *Ireland v United Kingdom* A 25 (1978), 2 EHRR 25, ECtHR, para 167 (treatment of republican detainees in Northern Ireland), where interrogation techniques constituted inhuman and degrading treatment, but not torture, because they did not occasion suffering of the intensity or cruelty implied by the word torture (see note 2 infra). 'Torture' has been used to describe inhuman treatment which has a purpose, such as the obtaining of information or confessions, or the infliction of punishment, and it is generally an aggravated form of inhuman treatment: *Greek Case* 12 YB 1 at 186 (1969), EComHR (practices including *falanga* (beating the soles of the feet) and severe beating of political detainees in order to obtain confessions or information held

by the Commission to constitute torture; Committee of Ministers confirmed the decision: CM Res DH (70) 1).

2    The notion of inhuman treatment covers at least such treatment as deliberately causes severe suffering, physical or mental: *Greek Case* 12 YB 1 at 186 (1969), EComHR. In *Ireland v United Kingdom* A 25 (1978), 2 EHRR 25, ECtHR, para 167, the treatment of persons arrested and detained in Northern Ireland, including beatings and the use of certain techniques for 'interrogation in depth' (namely: forcing the detainee to stand spread-eagled against a wall for lengthy periods, with the majority of his weight on his fingertips; covering a detainee's head with a hood; subjection of the detainee to a loud hissing noise; deprivation of sleep; and deprivation of food and drink), constituted inhuman treatment as they caused intense physical and mental suffering and acute psychiatric disturbance. Rape, the severe physical ill-treatment of prisoners, and the withholding of food and medicine from detainees have been held to amount to inhuman treatment: See Applications 6780/74, 6950/75 *Cyprus v Turkey* (1976) 4 EHRR 282, EComHR.

3    Treatment is 'degrading' if it arouses in the victim feelings of fear, anguish and inferiority capable of humiliating and debasing him and possibly breaking his physical or moral resistance: *Ireland v United Kingdom* A 25 (1978), 2 EHRR 25, ECtHR, para 167 (the interrogation techniques mentioned in note 2 supra amounted to degrading as well as inhuman treatment). An action which lowers a person in rank, position, reputation or character may be degrading, provided the treatment reaches a certain level of severity, as may be an action which grossly humiliates a victim before others, or drives him to act against his will or conscience: *East African Asians Cases* (1973) 3 EHRR 76 at 80, EComHR. A punishment will be degrading if it entails a degree of humiliation and debasement which attains a particular level, and which is other than that usual element of humilation almost inevitably involved in judicial punishment. The assessment is relative, and depends on all the circumstances of the case and in particular on the nature and context of the punishment itself and the manner and method of its execution: *Tyrer v United Kingdom* A 26 (1978), 2 EHRR 1, ECtHR, para 30. Publicity may be relevant but its absence does not prevent a punishment from being degrading; it may suffice if the victim is humiliated in his own eyes: *Tyrer v United Kingdom* supra. Striking a doctor off a medical register did not constitute a degrading punishment: see *Albert and Le Compte v Belgium* A 58 (1983), 5 EHRR 533, ECtHR. A disciplinary penalty pronounced on a prisoner by a court, consisting of seven days sleeping without a bed, with a diet restricted to bread and water, was not inhuman or degrading, although it did not correspond to modern standards: Application 7408/76 *X v Federal Republic of Germany* 10 DR 221, EComHR.

4    Convention for the Protection of Human Rights and Fundamental Freedoms (1950) Art 3. Cf the Universal Declaration of Human Rights (Paris, 10 December 1948), Art 5; International Covenant on Civil and Political Rights (1966) Art 7; European Convention for the Prevention of Torture and Inhuman and Degrading Treatment or Punishment 1987 (TS 5 (1991), Cmd 1634; ETS 126). As to the Convention for the Protection of Human Rights and Fundamental Freedoms (1950) generally see para 122 ante. As to the Universal Declaration of Human Rights see para 122 note 1 ante.

5    Convention for the Protection of Human Rights and Fundamental Freedoms (1950) Art 15(2). Article 3 enshrines one of the fundamental values of the democratic societies making up the Council of Europe: *Soering v United Kingdom* A 161 (1989), 11 EHRR 439, ECtHR. Thus a degrading punishment may not be justified by its deterrent effect, the fact that it has the support of public opinion, or even if law and order could not be maintained without it: *Tyrer v United Kingdom* A 26 (1978), 2 EHRR 1, ECtHR. The Convention prohibits torture and inhuman and degrading treatment of punishment in absolute terms, irrespective of the victim's conduct: *Ireland v United Kingdom* A 25 (1978), 2 EHRR 25, ECtHR, para 163. The court will be particularly vigilant in scrutinising the facts of a case dealing with rights under Art 3 of the Convention: see *Ribitsch v Austria* A 336 (1995), ECtHR, para 32. See also *Tomasi v France* A 241-A (1992), 15 EHRR 1, ECtHR, para 115 (applicant arrested on suspicion of terrorism and seriously assaulted in police custody; held that Art 3 had been violated, and that the requirements of a criminal investigation and the undeniable difficulties inherent in fighting crime, and particularly terrorism, could not result in limits being placed on the protection to be afforded in respect of the physical integrity of individuals).

6    The assessment of this minimum is, in the nature of things, relative; it depends on all the circumstances of the case, such as the duration of the treatment, its physical or mental effects, and, in some cases the sex, age and state of health of the victim: *Ireland v United Kingdom* A 25 (1978), 2 EHRR 25, ECtHR, para 162. The interference with human dignity resulting from the surveillance of an applicant's home did not reach the minimum level of severity required to constitute degrading treatment (Application 8930/80 *D'Haese and Le Compte v Belgium* (1983) 6 EHRR 114, EComHR); nor did the embarrassment caused to transsexuals under the French legal system arising from the fact that identity documents, including passports, could not be altered to show their new sex (*B v France* A 232-C (1992), 16 EHRR 1). See also *Guzzardi v Italy* A 39 (1980), 3 EHRR 333, ECtHR; and text and note 10 infra.

7 See *X and Y v Netherlands* A 91 (1985), 8 EHRR 235, Com Rep para 93; *Ireland v United Kingdom* A 25 (1978), 2 EHRR 25, ECtHR, para 162.

8 To threaten an individual with torture might, in some circumstances, constitute at least inhuman treatment: *Campbell and Cosans v United Kingdom* A 48 (1982), 4 EHRR 293, ECtHR, para 26 (mere threat of corporal punishment in Scottish schools caused insufficient suffering or humiliation to conflict with Convention for the Protection of Human Rights and Fundamental Freedoms (1950) Art 3).

9 See *Klaas v Germany* A 269 (1993), 18 EHRR 305, ECtHR. See also *Diaz Ruano v Spain* A 285-B (1994), 19 EHRR 555, ECtHR (no violation in circumstances in which it was impossible to determine beyond reasonable doubt whether marks found on a body were the result of ill-treatment). However, where injuries are sustained in police custody, the court will require the government to produce evidence establishing facts which cast doubt on the victim's account of events, particularly if that account is supported by medical evidence: see *Tomasi v France* A 241-A (1992), 15 EHRR 1, ECtHR (violation of Convention inferred where applicant sustained unexplained injuries while in police custody); and *Ribitsch v Austria* A 336 (1995), ECtHR, paras 31–36 (government had failed to establish that applicant's injuries were not caused by his treatment in police custody, even though the national court had acquitted the police officer concerned of misconduct). See also *Hurtado v Switzerland* A 280-A (1994) Com Rep, FSett (being compelled to wear soiled clothing until the day after arrest was degrading, and not being provided with adequate medical treatment until eight days after arrest was inhuman).

10 See *Guzzardi v Italy* A 39 (1980), 3 EHRR 333, ECtHR (conditions of confinement of suspected member of the mafia undoubtedly unpleasant, but did not attain the requisite minimum level of severity).

11 See *Ireland v United Kingdom* A 25 (1978), 2 EHRR 25; *Greek Case* 12 YB 1 at 186 (1969), EComHR; Applications 6780/74, 6950/75 *Cyprus v Turkey* (1976) 4 EHRR 282, EComHR.

The state was not responsible where inhuman and degrading conditions of detention were self-imposed; but the state did have an obligation to exercise custodial authority to safeguard the health and well-being of the prisoners who had imposed such conditions upon themselves, and was required to keep its reaction to the prisoners under constant review: Application 8317/78 *McFeeley v United Kingdom* 20 DR 44 (1980), EComHR.

Solitary confinement may, in some circumstances, constitute a breach of the Convention; regard must be had to its stringency, duration, the objective pursued and the effect on the prisoner. Complete sensory isolation coupled with complete social isolation can ultimately destroy the personality and constitute a form of inhuman treatment which cannot be justified by the requirements of security: Applications 7572/76, 7586/76 and 7587/76 *Ensslin, Baader and Raspe v Federal Republic of Germany* (on the facts the conditions of detention not inhuman, and justified by security requirements). See also Application 8463/78 *Kröcher and Möller v Switzerland* 34 DR 25 (1982), EComHR.

The continued detention of a prisoner whose state of health has deteriorated is not inhuman provided that the necessary medical care is provided: Application 7994/77 *Kotälla v Netherlands* 14 DR 238 (1978), EComHR. Inadequate provision of medical care for detainees may constitute inhuman treatment: *Hurtado v Switzerland* A 280-A (1994), FSett; *Greek Case* supra; Applications 6780/74, 6950/75 *Cyprus v Turkey* supra.

12 See Application 6840/74 *A v United Kingdom* (1980) 3 EHRR 131, FSett (inhuman and degrading treatment arising out of the conditions in secure segregated cell in mental institution); Application 6870/75 *B v United Kingdom* 32 DR 5 (1981), EComHR (overcrowded and insanitary conditions were unsatisfactory, but did not amount to inhuman or degrading treatment); *Herczegfalvy v Austria* A 244 (1992), 15 EHRR 437, ECtHR, para 82 (forcible medical treatment and feeding were therapeutically necessary, and could not, in the circumstances, be regarded as inhuman or degrading).

13 Circumstances to be taken into account include the manner in which the death penalty is imposed or executed, the personal circumstances of the condemned person, the disproportionality of the penalty to the offence, and conditions of detention while awaiting execution: *Soering v United Kingdom* A 161 (1989), 11 EHRR 439, ECtHR, para 104 (applicant faced real risk of treatment contrary to Art 3 of the Convention if he was extradited to Virginia on a charge of capital murder, because of the risk of exposure to the suffering experienced by condemned prisoners who spent on average six to eight years on death row; it was immaterial that delay was likely to be due in part to appeals pursued by the applicant). Cf para 107 note 4 ante.

14 *East African Asians Cases* (1973) 3 EHRR 76, EComHR. The Commission stressed the special importance to be attached to discrimination based on race as an affront to human dignity, and indicated that racial discrimination might therefore be capable of constituting degrading treatment when differential treatment on some other ground would raise no such question. The collective expulsion of aliens is forbidden under the Fourth Protocol, Art 4, which, however, has not been ratified by the United Kingdom; see para 122 note 1 ante.

15 *Abdulaziz, Cabales and Balkandali v United Kingdom* A 94 (1985), 7 EHRR 471, ECtHR, para 91.

16  *Marckx v Belgium* A 31 (1979), 2 EHRR 330, ECtHR.

17  As to the prohibition of discrimination under the Convention for the Protection of Human Rights and Fundamental Freedoms (1950) see para 164 post.

18  In determining whether substantial grounds are shown for believing in the existence of a real risk of treatment contrary to the Convention, the court will assess the issue in the light of all the material before it, including, if necessary, material obtained *proprio motu*. Since the nature of a contracting state's responsibility in such a case lay in exposing the applicant to the risk of ill-treatment, the existence of the risk was primarily to be assessed with reference to the facts which were known or ought to have been known to the state at the time of the expulsion. However, the court could have regard to information coming to light later, which might be of value in confirming or refuting the appreciation made by the state, and the well-foundedness of the applicant's fears: see *Cruz Varas v Sweden* A 201 (1991), 14 EHRR 1, ECtHR.

19  Account may be taken of the risk of ill-treatment by private groups or individuals, as well as the state: Application 10308/83 *Altun v Federal Republic of Germany* 36 DR 209, EComHR; Application 10479/83 *Kirkwood v United Kingdom* (1984) 37 DR 158, EComHR. But see Application 7216/75 *X v Federal Republic of Germany* (1976) 5 DR 137, EComHR; Application 8581/79 *X v United Kingdom* (1980) 29 DR 48, EComHR; and Application 12461/86 *YH v Federal Republic of Germany* (1986) 51 DR 258, EComHR; and Application 24573/94 *HLR v France* (7 December 1995, unreported), EComHR; and *Sharif Hussein Ahmed v Austria* (5 July 1995, unreported), Com Rep.

20  *Soering v United Kingdom* A 161 (1989), 11 EHRR 439, ECtHR, para 88; see note 13 supra. See also *Cruz Varas v Sweden* A 201 (1991), 14 EHRR 1, ECtHR (return of Chilean asylum-seeker did not violate the Convention, because the the the credibility of the applicant's claim that he faced a real risk of torture was doubtful). See also *Vilvarajah v United Kingdom* A 215 (1991), 14 EHRR 248, ECtHR, (return of Tamil asylum seekers to Sri Lanka did not, on the facts, violate the Convention); Application 24573/94 *HLR v France* (7 December 1995, unreported), EComHR; and Application 5961/72 *Amekrane v United Kingdom* 44 CD 101, EComHR (Moroccan officer involved in attempt on the life of the King of Morocco; after escaping to Gibraltar and asking for asylum, was returned to Morocco the next day and there sentenced to death; widow's application admissible). Expulsion to a country where a person will be liable to perform military service is not a breach of Art 3 of the Convention: Application 4314/69 *X v Federal Republic of Germany* 13 YB 900 (1970), EComHR.

As to expulsion orders which, if carried out, might lead to the break up of the family see para 152 post.

21  See *Tyrer v United Kingdom* A 26 (1978), 2 EHRR 1, ECtHR (birching on the Isle of Man constituted degrading punishment). See also *Costello-Roberts v United Kingdom* A 247-C (1993), 19 EHRR 112, ECtHR (punishment of a seven year old boy at a preparatory school, who was beaten with a gym shoe, did not attain the minimum level of severity to constitute a violation of Art 3 of the Convention, though the court expressed its disapproval of corporal punishment in schools: see para 114 note 2 ante); *Y v United Kingdom* A 247-A (1992), 17 EHRR 238, FSett (Commission found breach of Art 3 where a boy at a private school was caned for defacing another student's book, and a civil action for damages for assault had failed); Application 9471/81 *Warwick v United Kingdom* (1986) 60 DR 5, EComHR (the caning of a 16 year old girl on the hand by a male headteacher constituted degrading punishment).

A contracting state may be held responsible for degrading corporal punishment in private schools, because the state has an obligation under the First Protocol, Art 2, to secure to children their right to education (see para 166 post), of which a school's disciplinary system forms a part. The state cannot absolve itself of responsibility by delegating that obligation to private bodies or individuals: *Costello-Roberts v United Kingdom* supra. See also *Y v United Kingdom* supra, in which the European Commission of Human Rights reasoned that the state was responsible because it had a positive obligation to ensure a legal system which provided adequate protection to children's physical and emotional well-being, and must ensure that children were not exposed to inhuman or degrading treatment within its jurisdiction.

The threat of corporal punishment resulting from its availability in Scottish state schools was not sufficiently severe to constitute a violation of Art 3: *Campbell and Cosans v United Kingdom* A 48 (1982), 4 EHRR 293, ECtHR.

## 125. Prohibition of slavery and servitude. No one may be held in slavery or servitude[1]. No derogation may be made in respect of this requirement[2].

1  Convention for the Protection of Human Rights and Fundamental Freedoms (1950) Art 4(1). Cf the Universal Declaration of Human Rights (Paris, 10 December 1948), Art 4. As to the Convention for the Protection of Human Rights and Fundamental Freedoms (1950) generally see para 122 ante. As to the Universal Declaration of Human Rights see para 122 note 1 ante.

An applicant who was placed at the 'disposal of the state' for ten years following the completion of a prison sentence was not held in servitude contrary to this provision; his situation did not violate Art 5(1) of the Convention (see para 127–133 post), and accordingly could have been regarded as servitude only if it involved a particularly serious form of denial of freedom: *Van Droogenbroeck v Belgium* A 50 (1982), 4 EHRR 443, ECtHR. See also Applications 3435–3438/67 *W, X, Y and Z v United Kingdom* 28 CD 109, 11 YB 562 (1968), EComHR.

2    Convention for the Protection of Human Rights and Fundamental Freedoms (1950) Art 15(2).

## 126.  Prohibition of forced or compulsory labour. No one may be required to perform forced[1] or compulsory[2] labour[3]. An obligation to perform labour will not violate this provision provided it is not excessive or disproportionate in the circumstances[4].

Forced or compulsory labour does not include[5] (1) any work required to be done in the ordinary course of detention or during conditional release from detention[6]; (2) any service of a military character[7] or, in case of conscientious objection in countries where it is recognised[8], service exacted instead of compulsory military service[9]; (3) any service exacted in case of an emergency or calamity threatening the life or well-being of the community[10]; or (4) any work or service which forms part of normal civic obligations[11].

1    'Forced' labour suggests physical or mental constraint: *Van der Mussele v Belgium* A 70 (1983), 6 EHRR 163, ECtHR.

2    'Compulsory' labour is to be interpreted, taking into account International Labour Organisation Convention no 29 concerning Forced or Compulsory Labour (see para 103 ante), as any work exacted under the menace of any penalty and performed against the will of the person concerned, that is, work for which the person concerned has not offered himself voluntarily: *Van der Mussele v Belgium* A 70 (1983), 6 EHRR 163, ECtHR.

3    Convention for the Protection of Human Rights and Fundamental Freedoms (1950) Art 4(2). See also the International Covenant on Civil and Political Rights (1966) Art 8; and the International Labour Organisation Convention no 29 concerning Forced or Compulsory Labour; and para 103 ante. As to the Convention for the Protection of Human Rights and Fundamental Freedoms (1950) generally see para 122 ante.

4    See Application 1468/62 *Iversen v Norway* 6 YB 278 (1963), EComHR (Norwegian dentist compelled to work in northern Norway for two years, later reduced to one; the assignment was for a short period, was well remunerated, and fell within the applicant's profession; the fact that work is compulsory and is enforced under threat of punishment is not conclusive as to whether it is a violation of the Convention). See also the Convention for the Protection of Human Rights and Fundamental Freedoms Art 4(3)(c); and text and note 10 infra. See also *Van der Mussele v Belgium* A 70 (1983), 6 EHRR 163, ECtHR (Belgian pupil lawyer obliged to represent a client without remuneration or reimbursement of his expenses under national legal aid arrangements; not disproportionate or excessive in the circumstances; factors considered included: normal activities of a lawyer; professional benefit to him; and his services secured to the client the benefit of Art 6 of the Convention (see paras 134–147 post)).

5    The Convention for the Protection of Human Rights and Fundamental Freedoms (1950) Art 4(3) is not intended to limit the exercise of the right guaranteed by Art 4(2); rather, delimits the content of that right, in that it indicates what the term 'forced or compulsory labour' does not include, and so aids the interpretation of Art 4(2): see *Schmidt v Germany* A 291-B (1994), 18 EHRR 513, ECtHR, para 22; *Van der Mussele v Belgium* A 70 (1983), 6 EHRR 163, ECtHR.

6    Convention for the Protection of Human Rights and Fundamental Freedoms (1950) Art 4(3)(a).
    'Detention' means detention imposed according to the provisions of Art 5 (see paras 127–133 post): Art 4(3)(a). Provided that detention is imposed in accordance with Art 5(1)(e), labour required of the detainee will not constitute forced or compulsory labour for the purpose of Art 4, even if the terms of the detention violate Art 5(4): *De Wilde, Ooms and Versyp v Belgium (Vagrancy Cases)* A 12 (1971), 1 EHRR 373, ECtHR.
    It is immaterial that the conviction of the detained person is later quashed: Application 3245/67 *X v Austria* 12 YB 206 (1969), EComHR; Application 3485/68 *X v United Kingdom* 12 YB 288 (1969), EComHR (imposition of an obligation to work during detention of eight months for incitement to racial hatred was not a breach of the Convention). Nor is it a breach if there is an obligation to work in prison in return for allegedly insufficient pay and without social security benefits: Application 833/ 60 *X v Austria* 3 YB 428, EComHR; Application 2413/65 *X v Germany* 23 CD 1, EComHR. Compulsory work demanded of convicts in a forced labour institution is not forced or compulsory labour within the meaning of the Convention (Application 770/60 *X v Germany* 6 CD 1, EComHR; Application 2742/66 *X v Austria* 9 YB 550 (1966), EComHR), nor is the practice of hiring out prisoners for work to private enterprise, although this is contrary to the International Labour Organisation Convention no 29, and to the International Covenant on Civil and Political Rights

(1966). However, the prohibition contained in the International Labour Organisation Convention was deliberately omitted from the Convention for the Protection of Human Rights and Fundamental Freedoms Art 4: Applications 3134/67, 3172/67, 3188–3206/67 *Twenty-one Detained Persons v Germany* 11 YB 528 (1968), EComHR.

7 'Military service' includes not only compulsory military service, but also military service of a voluntary and contractual nature: Applications 3435–3438/67 *W, X, Y and Z v United Kingdom* 11 YB 562 (1968), EComHR (complaints rejected from applicants who had, with parental consent, committed themselves at the ages of 15 or 16 to service in the armed forces of the Crown until they were 18, and for a further nine years thereafter).

8 States have the freedom to recognise or not to recognise conscientious objections as exempting persons from military service: Application 5591/72 *X v Austria* 43 CD 161 (1973), EComHR.

9 Convention for the Protection of Human Rights and Fundamental Freedoms (1950) Art 4(3)(b); Application 2299/64 *Grandrath v Germany* 8 YB 324, 10 YB 626 (1965), EComHR (refusal by Jehovah's Witness to undertake military or civilian service).

10 Convention for the Protection of Human Rights and Fundamental Freedoms (1950) Art 4(3)(c); Application 1468/62 *Iversen v Norway* 6 YB 278 (1963), EComHR; and see note 1 supra.

11 Convention for the Protection of Human Rights and Fundamental Freedoms (1950) Art 4(3)(d). Normal civic obligations have been held to include: a lessor's obligation to maintain his building (Application 5593/72 *X v Austria* 45 CD 113 (1973), EComHR); the obligation on a holder of a shooting licence to participate in gassing fox holes (Application 9686/82 *X v Federal Republic of Germany* 39 DR 90 (1984), EComHR); and an employer's obligation to deduct tax from his employees' income (Application 7427/76 *Four Companies v Austria* 7 DR 148 (1976), EComHR). The European Court of Human Rights has held that both compulsory fire service, and a financial contribution payable in lieu of such service, are normal civic obligations: *Schmidt v Germany* A 291-B (1994), 18 EHRR 513, ECtHR, para 22.

**127. Right to liberty and security of the person.** Everyone has the right to liberty[1] and security[2] of the person[3]. No one may be deprived of his liberty save in the following cases[4] and in accordance with a procedure prescribed by law[5]: (1) the lawful detention of a person after conviction by a competent court[6]; (2) the lawful arrest or detention of a person for non-compliance with the lawful order of a court or in order to secure the fulfilment of any obligation prescribed by law[7]; (3) the lawful arrest or detention of a person effected for the purpose of bringing him before the competent legal authority on reasonable suspicion of having committed an offence or when it is reasonably considered necessary to prevent his committing an offence or fleeing after having done so[8]; (4) the detention of a minor by lawful order for the purpose of educational supervision or his lawful detention for the purpose of bringing him before the competent legal authority[9]; (5) the lawful detention of persons for the prevention of the spreading of infectious diseases, of persons of unsound mind, alcoholics or drug addicts or vagrants[10]; (6) the lawful arrest or detention of a person to prevent his effecting an unauthorised entry into the country or of a person against whom action is being taken with a view to deportation or extradition[11].

Everyone who is arrested must be informed promptly[12], in a language which he understands[13], of the reasons for his arrest and of any charge against him[14]. Everyone who is deprived of his liberty by arrest or detention is entitled to take proceedings by which the lawfulness of his detention will be decided speedily[15] by a court[16] and his release ordered if the detention is not lawful[17]. Everyone who has been the victim of arrest or detention in contravention of the above principles must have an enforceable right to compensation[18].

1 'Liberty' means the physical liberty of the person: see *Engel v Netherlands* A 22 (1976), 1 EHRR 647, ECtHR, para 58. The purpose of this provision is to ensure than no one should be dispossessed of his liberty in an arbitrary fashion: see eg *Engel v Netherlands* supra; *Bozano v France* A 111 (1986), 9 EHRR 297, ECtHR, para 54. As to the importance of the right see *Winterwerp v Netherlands* A 33 (1979), 2 EHRR 387, ECtHR, para 39.

2 'Security of the person' must be understood in the context of physical liberty: see *East African Asians v United Kingdom* (1973) 3 EHRR 76, EComHR, at para 220. The phrase does not impose any positive

obligation on the state to provide protection from attack by others (Application 6040/73 *X v Ireland* 16 YB 388 (1973), EComHR); nor can it be construed as referring to social security (Application 5287/71 *X v Federal Republic of Germany* 1 Digest 288 (1972), EComHR).

3    Convention for the Protection of Human Rights and Fundamental Freedoms (1950) Art 5(1). As to the Convention for the Protection of Human Rights and Fundamental Freedoms (1950) generally see para 122 ante.

4    The list of permissible exceptions to the right to liberty is exhaustive and, since it consists of restrictions, must be given a narrow interpretation: see *Winterwerp v Netherlands* A 33 (1979), 2 EHRR 387, ECtHR, para 37; and *Quinn v France* A 311 (1995), ECtHR, para 42. It is, however, possible for this provision to be derogated from in times of emergency: see para 168 post.

5    Convention for the Protection of Human Rights and Fundamental Freedoms (1950) Art 5(1). The procedure followed must be in conformity with the applicable municipal law and the Convention, including the general principles contained in the Convention, and not be arbitrary: *Winterwerp v Netherlands* A 33 (1979), 2 EHRR 387, ECtHR, para 37. The same principles apply in relation to the requirement of lawfulness in Art 5(1)(a)–(f) (see text and notes 6–11 infra): *Winterwerp v Netherlands* supra. It is in the first place for the national authorities, notably the courts, to interpret and apply national law (*Winterwerp v Netherlands* supra para 46; *Bozano v France* A 111 (1986), 9 EHRR 297, ECtHR, para 58), although the Convention authorities will intervene if the national authorities can clearly be seen to have infringed national law (*Van der Leer v Netherlands* A 170-A (1990), 12 EHRR 567, ECtHR). The 'general principles' contained in the Convention include the rule of law: see *Engel v Netherlands* A 22 (1976), 1 EHRR 647, ECtHR, para 69. As for the prohibition on arbitrariness, a detention has been held to be arbitrary if not in conformity with the purpose of the particular subparagraph of Art 5 of the Convention or with Art 5 generally: see *Winterwerp v Netherlands* supra para 39; *Bouamar v Belgium* A 129 (1988), 11 EHRR 1, ECtHR, para 50. Thus detention ostensibly for the purpose of deportation which is in reality aimed at illegal extradition would be arbitrary (*Bozano v France* supra at para 60). Even if properly motivated, a detention may also be arbitrary if it is disproportionate to the attainment of its purpose: see eg *Winterwerp v Netherlands* supra at para 39 (requirement of lawfulness in Art 5(1)(e)); Application 6871/75 *Caprino v United Kingdom* 22 DR 5 (1980), EComHR (about the requirement of 'lawfulness' in Art 5(1)(f)); and *Van Droogenbroeck v Belgium* A 50 (1982), 4 EHRR 443, ECtHR (requirement of lawfulness in Art 5(1)(a)).

State authorities are, however, permitted a certain 'margin of appreciation', or discretion, in relation to the measures they take: see *Winterwerp v Netherlands* supra at para 40; *Weeks v United Kingdom* A 114 (1987), 10 EHRR 293, ECtHR, para 50. The requirement of lawfulness may also incorporate the requirement that the municipal law upon which the detention is based is accessible and foreseeable in its application: see Application 9174/80 *Zamir v United Kingdom* 40 DR 42 (1983), EComHR. As to the doctrine of the margin of appreciation see Harris, O'Boyle and Warbrick *Law of the European Convention on Human Rights* (1995) pp 12–15.

6    Convention for the Protection of Human Rights and Fundamental Freedoms (1950) Art 5(1)(a): see para 128 post.

7    Ibid Art 5(1)(b): see para 129 post.

8    Ibid Art 5(1)(c): see para 130 post.

9    Ibid Art 5(1)(d): see para 131 post.

10   Ibid Art 5(1)(e): see para 132 post.

11   Ibid Art 5(1)(f): see para 133 post.

12   This does not mean that the information must be given in its entirety by the arresting officer at the very moment of the arrest: *Fox, Campbell and Hartley v United Kingdom* A 182 (1990), 13 EHRR 157, ECtHR, para 40; the requirement is complied with if the arrested person is informed of the legal and factual grounds for his arrest, whether at one time or in stages, within a sufficient period following his arrest. Cf *Van der Leer v Netherlands* A 170-A (1990), 12 EHRR 567, ECtHR, where a delay of ten days was held to involve a violation of this requirement.

13   This requirement was held to be complied with in Application 2689/65 *Delcourt v Belgium* 10 YB 238 at 270–272 (1967), EComHR, where the arrest warrant for a French speaking person was in Dutch, but the subsequent questioning, in the course of which the reasons became apparent, was in French.

14   Convention for the Protection of Human Rights and Fundamental Freedoms (1950) Art 5(2). This applies to an arrest on any ground, not just in connection with criminal proceedings: see *Van der Leer v Netherlands* A 170-A (1990), 12 EHRR 567, ECtHR, para 27. An arrested person must be told in simple, non-technical language that he can understand, the essential legal and factual grounds for his arrest, so as to be able, if he sees fit, to apply to a court to challenge its lawfulness in accordance with Art 5(4) of the Convention': *Fox, Campbell and Hartley v United Kingdom* A 182 (1990), 13 EHRR 157, ECtHR, para 40. A further purpose of Art 5(2) is to enable the arrested person to deny the offence and obtain his release see Application 8010/77 *X v United Kingdom* 16 DR 101 at 114 (1979), EComHR. Whether an arrested person has been sufficiently informed of the reasons for his arrest must be

determined on the facts of each case: *Fox, Campbell and Hartley v United Kingdom* supra. There may be no need to indicate all the charges that might later be brought against an arrested person who is being detained in circumstances falling within Art 5(1)(c) of the Convention; it is sufficient that the detainee is provided with enough information to justify the arrest: Application 4220/69 *X v United Kingdom* 14 YB 250 at 278 (1971), EComHR. If a person (eg a mentally disordered person) cannot understand the information that is being provided to him, the information must be communicated to a lawyer: see *X v United Kingdom* B 41 (1980), Com Rep para 111. The reasons for an arrest need not be given in any particular way: see Application 2621/65 *X v Netherlands* 9 YB 474 at 480 (1966), EComHR.

15  Time begins to run for this purpose when proceedings are instituted: *Van der Leer v Netherlands* A 170-A (1990), 12 EHRR 567, ECtHR; if an administrative remedy has to be exhausted before there can be recourse to a court, the relevant period begins when the relevant administrative authority is seised of the case: *Sanchez-Reisse v Switzerland* A 107 (1986), 9 EHRR 71, ECtHR, para 54. Article 5(4) of the Convention will be violated if a person has to wait for an unreasonably long period before being able to make an application to challenge the legality of his detention: see eg *X v United Kingdom* B 41 (1980) para 138, Com Rep (possibility of making an application to a Mental Health Review Tribunal after a mental patient had been recalled for six months was not speedy). For the purposes of determining whether there has been a speedy remedy, the relevant period ends with the final decision as to the applicant's detention, not the date of his release; if there is a possibility of appeal under municipal law, the period before the decision on appeal must be taken into account: see *Luberti v Italy* A 75 (1984), 6 EHRR 440, ECtHR. There is no fixed time limit as to what is a speedy remedy. The court noted in *Sanchez-Reisse v Switzerland* supra that each case must be determined in the light of its own circumstances, and that it is relevant to take into account the diligence of the national authorities and any delays caused by the conduct of the detained person, and any other factors causing delay that do not engage the state's responsibility. if the length of time taken before a decision is prima facie incompatible with the notion of speediness, the court will look to the state to explain the reason for the delay. According to *Koendjbiharie v Netherlands* A 185-B (1990), 13 EHRR 820, ECtHR, if the length of time taken is prima facie incompatible with the notion of speediness, the court will look to the state to explain the delay. The judge's workload does not excuse delay, because a state has a general obligation to organise its court system efficiently: see *Bezicheri v Italy* A 164 (1989), 12 EHRR 210, ECtHR, para 25. A period of five days before a decision about detention has been held to be permissible (Application 11256/84 *Egue v France* 57 DR 47 at 71 (1988), EComHR); but a delay of five and a half months was held not acceptable in *Bezicheri v Italy* supra; 16 days before a decision on the continued long-term detention of a recidivist offender satisfied the requirement of speediness: Application 7648/76 *Christinet v Switzerland* 17 DR 35 at 57 (1979), EComHR. It should be noted that for persons arrested under Art 5(1)(c) of the Convention (see para 130 post), Art 5(4) applies concurrently with Art 5(3).

16  The court must be a body which 'provides the guarantees appropriate to the kind of deprivation of liberty in question': *De Wilde, Ooms and Versyp v Belgium* A 12 (1971), 1 EHRR 373, ECtHR, para 76. It does not, however, need to be a 'court of law of the classic kind integrated within the standard judicial machinery of the country' (*Weeks v United Kingdom* A 114 (1987), 10 EHRR 293, ECtHR, para 61); but it must be independent both of the executive and of the parties (*De Wilde, Ooms and Versyp v Belgium* supra at para 77). The medical officer of a person of unsound mind and a government minister (see *X v United Kingdom* A 46 (1981), 4 EHRR 188, ECtHR, para 61) and a public prosecutor (*Winterwerp v Netherlands* A 33 (1979), 2 EHRR 387, ECtHR, para 64) have been held not to satisfy this criterion; the English Parole Board has been held to do so (*Weeks v United Kingdom* supra). A court must be competent to take a legally binding decision about a person's release: see *X v United Kingdom* supra (Mental Health Review Tribunal not competent in this regard); and *Weeks v United Kingdom* supra (Parole Board competent in as much as it had power to make recommendations that were binding on the Home Secretary).

17  Convention for the Protection of Human Rights and Fundamental Freedoms (1950) Art 5(4). Cf the right to apply for habeas corpus under English law (see para 115 ante; and ADMINISTRATIVE LAW vol 1(1) (Reissue) paras 222–265). It applies whatever the ground of detention, and whether the detention is justified under Art 5(1) or not: see *De Wilde, Ooms and Versyp v Belgium* A 12 (1971), 1 EHRR 373, ECtHR, para 73. The purpose of Art 5(4) of the Convention is to enable a person's release from detention, and it does not, therefore, apply once a person is lawfully free (Application 10230/82 *X v Sweden* 32 DR 303 at 304 (1983), EComHR), although such a person may still be able to challenge the speediness of the remedy granted to him (Application 9403/81 *X v United Kingdom* 28 DR 235 at 239 (1982), EComHR). A person who absconds remains entitled to a remedy under Art 5(4) of the Convention because he is still being deprived of his liberty as a matter of law: see *Van der Leer v Netherlands* A 170-A (1990), 12 EHRR 567, ECtHR. Where a person has been lawfully released he may still have a remedy under Art 13 of the Convention (see para 163 post): see Application 10801/84 *L v Sweden* 61 DR 62 at 73 (1988), EComHR. If, however, a person has been speedily

released, the court will not consider whether the remedy he sought complies with Art 5(4): see *Fox, Campbell and Hartley v United Kingdom* A 182 (1990), 13 EHRR 157, ECtHR.

If a state provides a right of appeal against a first instance rejection of a claim to be released, the appeal body must 'in principle' comply with Art 5(4) of the Convention: *Toth v Austria* A 224 (1991), 14 EHRR 551, ECtHR, para 84.

A court must provide guarantees of judicial procedure, although regard must be had to the particular nature of the circumstances in which the proceedings take place: *De Wilde, Ooms and Versyp v Belgium* supra at para 78. Where a person is detained for a short period of time in an emergency, less strict procedural standards may suffice: *Wassink v Netherlands* A 185-A (1990), ECtHR. An oral hearing is required in cases involving detention of persons of unsound mind (*Winterwerp v Netherlands* A 33 (1979), 2 EHRR 387, ECtHR, para 60), or a minor (*Bouamar v Belgium* A 129 (1988), 11 EHRR 1, ECtHR, para 60). Written proceedings were sufficient in a case under Art 5(1)(f) (see para 133 post): *Sanchez-Reisse v Switzerland* A 107 (1986), 9 EHRR 71, ECtHR, para 51. Cf *Farmakopoulos v Belgium* A 235-A (1992), 16 EHRR 187, ECtHR, Com Rep, (Art 5(4) generally requires that the detained person or his representative be permitted to participate in an oral hearing).

Article 5(4) has been held to require the provision of legal assistance (*Bouamar v Belgium* supra (minor); *Megyeri v Germany* A 237-A (1992), 15 EHRR 584, ECtHR (person of unsound mind). The person concerned should not be required to take the initiative to obtain legal representation: *Megyeri v Germany* supra. Legal assistance is required wherever necessary to render the application for release effective: *Woukam Moudefo v France* A 141-B (1988), 13 EHRR 549, ECtHR, Com Rep paras 86–91; in cases of indigency, the right to legal assistance extends to the provision of legal aid where this is necessary for an effective remedy: Application 9174/80 *Zamir v United Kingdom* 40 DR 42 at 60 (1983), EComHR.

It appears that the principle of adversarial proceedings ('equality of arms') applies: eg *Lamy v Belgium* A 151 (1989), 11 EHRR 529, ECtHR (when accused detained under Art 5(1)(c) (see para 130 post) not allowed access to official file when applying for bail; file was available to the Crown: breach of Art 5(4)); *Weeks v United Kingdom* A 114 (1987), 10 EHRR 293, ECtHR, para 66 (prisoner seeking release not allowed full access to adverse material in Parole Board's possession: breach of Art 5(4)); and *Toth v Austria* A 224 (1991), 14 EHRR 551, ECtHR; and see *K v Austria* A 255-B (1993), ECtHR, Com Rep. See the report of the European Commission of Human Rights in *Farmakopoulos v Belgium* supra, where a 24-hour limit was found to be too short on the facts. A person in detention must also be told the reasons for his detention, as part of his right to time and facilities to prepare an application, as this is essential in order to challenge the legality of detention: see *X v United Kingdom* A 46 (1981), 4 EHRR 188, ECtHR, para 66.

A public hearing is not required by this provision: see *Bezicheri v Italy* A 164 (1989), 12 EHRR 210, ECtHR, para 20. Article 5(4) of the Convention does not apply where the initial decision to detain is taken by a court and the required supervision is thus incorporated in the decision of that court: *De Wilde, Ooms and Versyp v Belgium* supra at para 76; *Winterwerp v Netherlands* supra; and *Perez v France* A 325-C (1995), ECtHR, para 30.

In some cases a review of lawfulness at reasonable intervals is required: *Winterwerp v Netherlands* supra at para 55. Thus where the circumstances which provide the legal basis for the decision to detain may cease to exist, there must be a remedy at reasonable intervals: see *X v United Kingdom* supra (possibility that mentally disordered person's condition might improve meant that he had to be provided with an opportunity of review of the lawfulness of his detention at reasonable intervals). This principle was applied to discretionary life sentences in *Thynne, Wilson and Gunnell v United Kingdom* A 190-A (1990), 13 EHRR 666, ECtHR. Cf *Wynne v United Kingdom* A 294 (1994), 19 EHRR 333, ECtHR, para 35 (no requirement of a continuing remedy in the case of a mandatory life sentence). What is a reasonable interval depends on the case: see eg *Bezicheri v Italy* supra (one month was reasonable in the context of detention on remand).

'Lawful' in Art 5(4) of the Convention has the same meaning as in Art 5(1), so that the detained person must be able to challenge his detention not only on the basis of municipal law, but also on the basis of the general principles of the Convention, and on grounds of arbitrariness: see *Van Droogenbroeck v Belgium* A 50 (1982), 4 EHRR 443, ECtHR, para 48. The latter ground has been held to include questions of proportionality: see eg *Winterwerp v Netherlands* supra. This requirement was found not to have been satisfied by the English remedy of habeas corpus in *X v United Kingdom* supra, because this remedy may not be used to challenge the medical grounds for the detention of a mentally disordered person. Cf *Brogan v United Kingdom* A 145-B (1988), 11 EHRR 117, ECtHR, para 65 (habeas corpus was a sufficient remedy to challenge the detention of an accused within Art 5(1)(c) of the Convention). Judicial review in English law does not provide a remedy as required by Art 5(4) in the case of a person detained under a discretionary life sentence, because of the limited grounds of challenge: see *Weeks v United Kingdom* supra. See also *Hussain v United Kingdom* (1996) 22 EHRR 1, ECtHR. Article 5(4) does not require a remedy to challenge the conditions under which a person is detained: *Ashingdane v United Kingdom* A 93 (1985), 7 EHRR 528, ECtHR, para 52.

18   Convention for the Protection of Human Rights and Fundamental Freedoms (1950) Art 5(5). The remedy required is one before a court, which leads to a legally binding award of compensation: *Brogan v United Kingdom* A 145-B (1988), 11 EHRR 117, ECtHR, para 67. See also *Fox, Campbell and Hartley v United Kingdom* A 182 (1990), 13 EHRR 157, ECtHR. Compensation may be broader than mere financial compensation, but it does not include release, which is provided for in Art 5(4): Application 9990/82 *Bozano v France* 39 DR 119 at 144 (1984), EComHR. There is no question of compensation without proof of pecuniary or non-pecuniary damage: *Wassink v Netherlands* A 185-A (1990), ECtHR, para 38. When an applicant alleges a violation of some other part of Art 5 at the same time as alleging a breach of Art 5(5), it will first be considered whether a breach of the former has been established and, if so, whether the requirements of Art 5(5) have been satisfied: *Ciulla v Italy* A 148 (1989), 13 EHRR 346, ECtHR, paras 43–45. Where Art 5(5) alone is alleged to have been breached, the Commission will declare the application inadmissible unless there is a previous final decision that there has been a violation of some part of Art 5(1)–(4), or the national courts have decided, directly or indirectly, that there has been such a breach: see Application 10313/83 *Eggs v Switzerland* 39 DR 225 at 235 (1984), EComHR; Application 7950/77 *X v Austria* 19 DR 213 (1980), EComHR. If there has been a violation of Art 5(5), the applicant may be awarded 'just satisfaction' under Art 50 of the Convention: see *Brogan v United Kingdom* supra. As to Art 50 of the Convention see para 180 post.

## 128. Lawful deprivation of liberty: detention after conviction. The first exception to the rule that no one may be deprived of his liberty[1] is the lawful detention[2] of a person after conviction[3] by a competent[4] court[5].

1   Ie the Convention for the Protection of Human Rights and Fundamental Freedoms (1950) Art 5(1): see para 127 ante. As to the Convention generally see para 122 ante. Note also that the deprivation of liberty authorised by the provision described in the text and notes infra must be in accordance with a procedure prescribed by law: see para 127 note 5 ante.

2   As to the distinction between arrest and detention in relation to ibid Art 5 see para 129 note 2 post.

3   'Conviction' means a 'finding of guilt' in respect of an offence; this exception does not permit detention as a preventive or security measure: see *Guzzardi v Italy* A 39 (1980), 3 EHRR 333, ECtHR, para 100. It includes cases where a person is convicted of an offence and is ordered to be detained in a mental institution for treatment: *X v United Kingdom* A 46 (1981), 4 EHRR 188, ECtHR, para 39. See also Art 5(1)(e) of the Convention: para 132 post. Conviction may be for a disciplinary as well as a criminal offence, if the conviction results in detention of the convicted person: *Engel v Netherlands* A 22 (1976), 1 EHRR 647, ECtHR, para 68. A conviction is a conviction by a trial court, and any detention pending appeal must be justified by reference to Art 5(1)(a) of the Convention, rather than 5(1)(c) (see para 130 post): *Wemhoff v Federal Republic of Germany* A 7 (1968), 1 EHRR 55, ECtHR. The conviction may be that of a foreign court, even if the state of that court is not a party to the Convention: see *Drozd and Janousek v France and Spain* A 240 (1992), 14 EHRR 745, ECtHR.

4   'Competent' means having jurisdiction to hear the case: Application 2645/65 *X v Austria* 11 YB 322 at 348 (1968), EComHR.

5   Convention for the Protection of Human Rights and Fundamental Freedoms (1950) Art 5(1)(a). For the meaning of 'court' in Art 5 see para 127 note 16 ante.

    The judicial guarantees required by Art 5(1)(a) are not necessarily those required by Art 6 (right to fair and public hearing): *Engel v Netherlands* A 22 (1976), 1 EHRR 647, ECtHR, para 68.

    Where a person is detained in one state following conviction in another, non-Convention, state, the detention will be justified under Art 5(1)(a) unless the conviction in the other state was the result of a flagrant denial of justice: *Drozd and Janousek v France and Spain* A 240 (1992), 14 EHRR 745, ECtHR, para 110. Article 5(1)(a) governs only the fact of detention, not the place or conditions of detention: Application 7977/77 *X v United Kingdom* 1 Digest 305 (1981), EComHR (transfer from prison to Broadmoor, as permitted by sentence, did not fall to be considered under Art 5(1)(a)). For detention to be justified it must be lawful (see para 127 note 5 ante); but Art 5(1)(a) does not require a lawful conviction, only lawful detention. Thus the European Court of Human Rights and the European Commission of Human Rights may not review the legality of a conviction (Application 7629/76 *Krzycki v Federal Republic of Germany* 13 DR 57 at 61 (1978), EComHR), or a sentence (*Weeks v United Kingdom* A 114 (1987), 10 EHRR 293, ECtHR, para 50). Nor will detention be rendered retroactively unlawful for the purposes of Art 5(1)(a) if the conviction or sentence upon which it is based is subsequently overturned (Application 7629/76 *Krzycki v Federal Republic of Germany* supra at 61). The requirement of lawfulness also means that the detention must not be arbitrary (see para 127 notes 1, 5 ante), ie its purpose must be the execution of the sentence of imprisonment imposed by the court. Article 5(1)(a) will apply to detention as a result of an administrative decision if the detention follows and depends upon, or occurs by virtue of, an initial conviction and court sentence: *Van Droogenbroeck v Belgium* A 50 (1982),

4 EHRR 443, ECtHR, para 35; and see also *Weeks v United Kingdom* supra. See also *Monnell and Morris v United Kingdom* A 115 (1987), 10 EHRR 205, ECtHR (applicants in person refused leave to appeal to the Court of Appeal, and the Court of Appeal directed that specified periods of the applicants' detention pending appeal would not count towards their sentences, because they had wasted the court's time; the European Court of Human Rights held that this was justified under Art 5(1)(a)).

## 129. Compliance with orders and fulfilment of obligations.

The second exception to the rule that no one may be deprived of his liberty[1] is the lawful arrest or detention[2] of a person for non-compliance with the lawful order of a court[3] or in order to secure the fulfilment of any obligation prescribed by law[4].

1     Ie the Convention for the Protection of Human Rights and Fundamental Freedoms (1950) Art 5(1): see para 127 ante. As to the Convention generally see para 122 ante. Note also that the deprivation of liberty authorised by the provision described in the text and notes infra must be in accordance with a procedure prescribed by law: see para 127 note 5 ante.

2     The distinction between arrest and detention is not important; the question is whether the measure or conduct complained of amounts to a restriction on freedom of movement (guaranteed by the Fourth Protocol, Art 2) sufficiently serious to amount to a deprivation of liberty within the scope of Art 5. The secure detention of a person in a closed prison will obviously fall within Art 5; less extreme interferences with freedom of movement may also be covered: see eg *Guzzardi v Italy* A 39 (1980), 3 EHRR 333, ECtHR, para 100 (applicant required by judicial compulsory residence order to live on restricted part of remote island: violation of Art 5(1)). The distinction between a restriction upon freedom of movement falling only within the Fourth Protocol, Art 2, and one serious enough to fall within Art 5(1), is one of degree or intensity, not of nature or substance: *Guzzardi v Italy* supra at para 93. Regard must be had to a whole range of criteria such as the type, duration, effects and manner of implementation of the measure in question: *Guzzardi v Italy* supra at para 92. In Applications 6780/74 and 6950/75 *Cyprus v Turkey (First and Second Applications)* (1976) 4 EHRR 482 para 285, EComHR, the confinement of Greek Cypriots to detention centres, or to private houses where they were held under guard, or to a hotel which they could not leave without permission or an escort, amounted to detention within Art 5, but a restriction whereby they could not leave a village fell to be considered only under the Fourth Protocol, Art 2. (Note that the United Kingdom has signed but not ratified the Fourth Protocol to the Convention: see para 122 ante). See, similarly, Application 14102/88 *Aygun v Sweden* 63 DR 195 (1989), EComHR (no breach of Art 5 by restriction of the applicant to Stockholm). By contrast, in *Ashingdane v United Kingdom* A 93 (1985), 7 EHRR 528, ECtHR, para 42, Art 5 of the Convention applied where the applicant was compulsorily detained in a mental hospital under a detention order even though he was kept in an unlocked ward and was allowed to leave the hospital unaccompanied during the day and over weekends. The 'strict arrest' of soldiers (locking in cell in army barracks) fell within Art 5, but 'aggravated arrest' (confinement during off-duty hours to designated building) did not: *Engel v Netherlands* A 22 (1976), 1 EHRR 647, ECtHR. The question whether Art 5 applies where a person is taken to a police station for questioning depends on the intention of the police: Application 8819/79 *X v Federal Republic of Germany* 24 DR 158 (1981), EComHR (no deprivation of liberty where 10 year old schoolgirl was taken to a police station for questioning for two hours in connection with a school theft, and was kept in an unlocked cell, because the object of the police had been to question, not to arrest her). Article 5 may apply where the period of detention is very short: see eg in Application 8278/78 *X v Austria* 18 DR 154 (1979), EComHR (period of restraint for the purpose of performing a blood test). It protects children as well as adults, but will not apply in cases involving an exercise of parental rights, rather than a restriction upon the child's freedom of movement imposed by the state: see *Nielsen v Denmark* A 144 (1988), 11 EHRR 175, ECtHR, where a 12 year old boy was placed in a closed psychiatric ward at the request of his mother for treatment for his neurotic condition, the court (by a majority) held that the case did not involve a deprivation of liberty within Art 5, but involved an exercise of parental rights, which was a fundamental element of family life, respect for which is recognised as a right in Art 8 of the Convention. Such an exercise of parental rights did not fall within Art 5, provided that it was for a 'proper purpose' (and was lawful under the relevant domestic law). Article 5 may apply to the arrest or detention of a person by a state's agents outside the state's own territory see Application 14009/88 *Reinette v France*, 63 DR 189 (1989). It may also apply where a person has surrendered himself to custody: *De Wilde, Ooms and Versyp v Belgium* A 12 (1971), 1 EHRR 373, ECtHR, (vagrant who gave himself up to the police for detention was entitled to the protection of Art 5). Article 5 is concerned only with the fact of deprivation of liberty, not with the conditions in which a person is detained (see Art 3; and para 124 ante): *Ashingdane v United Kingdom* supra. It follows that Art 5 does not apply where greater restrictions are placed on the freedom of movement of a person already detained (Application 7754/77 *X v Switzerland*

11 DR 216 (1977), EComHR; Application 11703/85 *D v Federal Republic of Germany* 54 DR 116 (1987), EComHR), although it would apply to an extension of the period of detention by virtue of prison disciplinary proceedings (*Campbell and Fell v United Kingdom* A 80 (1984), 7 EHRR 165, ECtHR).

3    Convention for the Protection of Human Rights and Fundamental Freedoms (1950) Art 5(1)(b). This applies eg in cases of failure to pay a fine (Application 6289/73 *Airey v Ireland* 8 DR 42 (1977), EComHR); refusal to undergo a medical examination ordered by a court (Application 6659/74 *X v Federal Republic of Germany* 3 DR 92 (1975), EComHR); and failure to observe a residence restriction (Application 8916/80 *Freda v Italy* 21 DR 250 (1980), EComHR. Detention must be lawful under municipal law and the Convention and not arbitrary: see *K v Austria* A 255-B (1993), Com Rep (applicant imprisoned for failure to comply with court order to give evidence; order infringed applicant's freedom of expression which was protected by Art 10 (see paras 158–159 post): breach of Art 5(1)) See also the cases cited in note 2 supra.

4    Ibid Art 5(1)(b). This refers to the situation where a person is detained 'to compel him to fulfil a specific and concrete obligation which he has until then failed to satisfy': *Engel v Netherlands* A 22 (1976), 1 EHRR 647, ECtHR, para 69. See eg Application 10179/82 *B v France* 52 DR 111 (1987), EComHR (obligation to carry an identity card and to submit to an identity check); Application 10600/83 *Johansen v Norway* 44 DR 155 (1985), EComHR (obligation to do military service); *Ciulla v Italy* A 148 (1989), 13 EHRR 346, ECtHR (obligation to live in a designated locality); Applications 8022/77, 8025/77 and 8027/77 *McVeigh, O'Neill and Evans v United Kingdom* 25 DR 15 (1981), EComHR (obligation to make a customs or tax return). In *Ciulla v Italy* supra an obligation imposed upon a Mafia suspect to 'change your behaviour' was not sufficiently specific or concrete to fall within Art 5(1)(b). The requirement of a specific and concrete obligation means that Art 5(1)(b) cannot be relied on to compel compliance with the law generally, and cannot justify preventive detention of the kind that a state might introduce in an emergency situation: see *Lawless v Ireland* A 3 (1961), 1 EHRR 15, ECtHR, paras 9, 12; *Guzzardi v Italy* A 39 (1980), 3 EHRR 333, ECtHR, para 101. Provided, however, that it is sufficiently specific and concrete, an obligation imposed in connection with the enforcement of the criminal law may fall within Art 5(1)(b): see Applications 8022/77, 8025/77 and 8027/77 *McVeigh, O'Neill and Evans v United Kingdom* supra (persons entering Great Britain required to submit to 'further examination' at the point of entry pursuant to anti-terrorist legislation; applicants detained for that purpose and released after 45 hours, having been questioned, searched, photographed and fingerprinted, but were not charged with any offence: no breach of Art 5, as the obligation was sufficiently specific and concrete in that it applied only on entering and leaving Great Britain to check the particular matters referred to in the legislation). Cf *Ireland v United Kingdom* A 25 (1978), 2 EHRR 25, ECtHR. For a statement by the European Commission on Human Rights as to the circumstances in which Art 5(1)(b) extends to cases in which a deprivation of liberty is considered necessary to make the execution of an obligation effective at the time that it arises, even though there has been no prior failure to comply with an obligation, see Applications 8022/77, 8025/77 and 8027/77 *McVeigh, O'Neill and Evans v United Kingdom* supra at para 191.

## 130. Suspicion and prevention of offences; and prevention of fleeing. The

third exception to the rule that no one may be deprived of his liberty[1] is the lawful[2] arrest or detention of a person effected for the purpose of bringing him before the competent legal authority[3] on reasonable suspicion[4] of having committed an offence[5] or when it is reasonably considered necessary to prevent his committing an offence[6] or fleeing after having done so[7].

Everyone arrested or detained in accordance with the provisions described above must be brought promptly[8] before a judge or other officer authorised by law[9] to exercise judicial power[10] and is entitled to trial within a reasonable time[11] or to release pending trial[12]. Release may be conditioned by guarantees to appear for trial[13].

1    Ie the Convention for the Protection of Human Rights and Fundamental Freedoms (1950) Art 5(1): see para 127 ante. As to the Convention generally see para 122 ante. As to the International Covenant on Civil and Political Rights (1966) (see para 103 note 3 ante) Art 9 see Bailey 'Rights in the Administration of Justice' in Harris and Joseph (eds) *The International Covenant on Civil and Political Rights and United Kingdom Law* (1995) ch 6.

2    'Lawful' means (as elsewhere in Art 5(1) of the Convention: see para 127 note 5 ante), that the arrest or detention must be lawful under the applicable municipal law and that the applicable law, or the conduct complained of, must not be arbitrary: see *De Jong, Baljet and Van Den Brink v Netherlands* A 77 (1984), 8 EHRR 20, ECtHR, para 44; and *Kemmache v France (No 3)* A 296–C (1994), 19 EHRR 349, ECtHR, para 42.

3   'Competent legal authority' means the same as 'judge or other officer authorised by law to exercise judicial power' in Art 5(3) of the Convention: *Schiesser v Switzerland* A 34 (1979), 2 EHRR 417, ECtHR, para 29; and note 9 infra. An arrest will fall within Art 5(1)(c) even though the person detained is not eventually charged or taken before a competent legal authority, provided that reasonable suspicion existed at the time of arrest: *Brogan v United Kingdom* A 145-B (1988), 11 EHRR 117, ECtHR. The phrase 'for the purpose of bringing him before the competent legal authority' applies to each of the three limbs of Art 5(1)(c); thus the detention of a suspected terrorist could not be justified under Art 5(1)(c) solely as being necessary to prevent his committing an offence, as the detention was not effected with the purpose of initiating a criminal prosecution: *Lawless v Ireland* A 3 (1961), 1 EHRR 15, ECtHR, para 14.

4   It is not necessary to establish that an offence has been committed or that the arrested person has committed it: Application 10803/84 *X v Austria* 11 EHRR 112 (1989), EComHR. See *Fox, Campbell and Hartley v United Kingdom* A 182 (1990), 13 EHRR 157, ECtHR, para 32: 'reasonable suspicion' supposes the existence of facts and information which would satisfy an objective observer that the person concerned may have committed the offence...what may be regarded as reasonable will depend upon all the circumstances'. Even in relation to terrorist offences, the state must furnish at least some facts or information capable of satisfying the court that the arrested person was reasonably suspected of having committed the alleged offence: *Fox, Campbell and Hartley v United Kingdom* supra at para 34 (evidence of previous conviction of terrorist offences and previous questioning about specific terrorist attacks was insufficient to establish reasonable suspicion). See also *Murray v United Kingdom* A 300 (1994), 19 EHRR 193, ECtHR.

5   Convention for the Protection of Human Rights and Fundamental Freedoms (1950) Art 5(1)(c). 'Offence' for this purpose means a criminal offence: *Ciulla v Italy* A 148 (1989), 13 EHRR 346, ECtHR, para 38. It will also include a military offence: *De Jong, Baljet and Van Den Brink v Netherlands* A 77 (1984), 8 EHRR 20, ECtHR. A power to arrest any person concerned in the commission, preparation or instigation of acts of terrorism was justified under Art 5(1)(c) of the Convention although involvement with terrorism was not itself a criminal offence: *Brogan v United Kingdom* A 145-B (1988), 11 EHRR 117, ECtHR. The court observed at para 51 that the definition of 'acts of terrorism' in the relevant national law (ie the use of violence for political ends) was 'well in keeping with the idea of an offence', and in any event following their arrest the applicants had immediately been questioned about specific offences of which they were suspected. Article 5(1)(c) of the Convention is limited to the arrest or detention of persons for the purpose of enforcing the criminal law: *Ciulla v Italy* supra (detention to bring applicant before competent legal authority in connection with compulsory residence order did not fall within Art 5(1)(c)).

6   Ibid Art 5(1)(c). This does not permit a general power of preventive detention, as such an interpretation would lead to 'conclusions repugnant to the fundamental principles of the Convention': *Lawless v Ireland* A 3 (1961), 1 EHRR 15, ECtHR, para 14; and see note 3 supra. In the light of this decision, the meaning of the second limb of Art 5(1)(c) is questionable, although it might cover eg the common law power of arrest to prevent a breach of the peace. See also *Letellier v France* A 207 (1991), 14 EHRR 83, ECtHR (in exceptional circumstances an accused might be detained so as to avoid a disturbance to public order).

7   Convention for the Protection of Human Rights and Fundamental Freedoms (1950) Art 5(1)(c).

8   'The degree of flexibility attaching to the notion of "promptness" is limited...Whereas promptness is to be assessed in each case according to its special features, the significance to be attached to those features can never be taken to the point of impairing the very essence of the right guaranteed by Art 5(3)': *Brogan v United Kingdom* A 145-B (1988), 11 EHRR 117, ECtHR, para 59 (four days and six hours: violation of Art 5(3)). Cf *Brannigan & McBride v United Kingdom* A 258-B (1993), 17 EHRR 539, ECtHR (United Kingdom conceded that detention of suspected terrorists was in breach of Art 5(3), but the court found no violation of the Convention because the United Kingdom had made an emergency derogation under Art 15 (see para 168 post)); *Koster v Netherlands* A 221 (1991), 14 EHRR 396, ECtHR (five days in the context of military criminal law: violation of Art 5(3)); *McGoff v Sweden* A 83 (1984), 8 EHRR 246, ECtHR (15 days: violation of Art 5(3)); Application 2894/66 *X v Netherlands* 9 YB 564 at 568 (1966), EComHR (four days: consistent with Art 5(3)).

9   'Judge or other judicial officer authorised by law' in ibid Art 5(3) has the same meaning as 'competent legal authority' in Art 5(1)(c) (see note 3 supra): *Schiesser v Switzerland* A 34 (1979), 2 EHRR 417, ECtHR, para 29. This means that the 'officer' must be impartial, and impartiality involves an objective as well as subjective element: *Huber v Switzerland* A 188 (1990) para 43. Cf the court's interpretation of the 'impartiality' requirement in the Art 6(1) (see paras 134–147 post) It follows that the functions of investigation and prosecution must be kept separate, and that a prosecutor cannot act as a 'judicial officer' within Art 5(3).

10   The state is obliged to take the initiative for a detained person to be brought before a judge or other judicial officer: Application 9017/80 *McGoff v Sweden* 31 DR 72 (1982), EComHR. The role of the

judge or other judicial officer is to review the circumstances militating for and against detention, of deciding, by reference to legal criteria, whether there are reasons to justify detention, and of ordering release if there are no such reasons: *Schiesser v Switzerland* A 34 (1979), 2 EHRR 417, ECtHR, para 31. A judicial officer must be able to take legally binding decisions: *Ireland v United Kingdom* A 25 (1978), 2 EHRR 25, ECtHR, para 199. Article 5(3) of the Convention for the Protection of Human Rights and Fundamental Freedoms (1950) requires that such an officer himself hears the individual brought before him, but it does not require him to permit the accused's lawyer to be present at the hearing: *Schiesser v Switzerland* supra at paras 31, 36.

11 Detention on remand may continue during the whole of the period between arrest and trial, provided there are relevant and sufficient grounds, but the Convention for the Protection of Human Rights and Fundamental Freedoms (1950) Art 5(3) will be violated if the detention continues beyond a reasonable time because the proceedings have not been conducted with reasonable expedition: see eg *Herczegfalvy v Austria* A 242-B (1992), 15 EHRR 437, ECtHR, para 71 (where a person is in pre-trial detention there must be special diligence in the conduct of the proceedings); *Wemhoff v Federal Republic of Germany* A 7 (1968), 1 EHRR 55, ECtHR, para 17 (an accused person in detention is entitled to have his case given priority and conducted with particular expedition). The standard of diligence required is the same as under Art 6(1) (see paras 134–147 post): *Abdoella v Netherlands* A 248-A (1992), 20 EHRR 585, ECtHR, para 24. There is no absolute limit to the permissible period of pre-trial detention; the reasonableness of the length of proceedings depends on the facts of the case: see eg *W v Switzerland* A 254-A (1993), 17 EHRR 60, ECtHR (four years: no breach of Art 5(3) of the Convention in the circumstances). Cf eg *Toth v Austria* A 224 (1991), 14 EHRR 551, ECtHR, (two years and one month: violation of Art 5(3)); *Tomasi v France* A 241-A (1992), 15 EHRR 1, ECtHR (five years and seven months: violation of Art 5(3)).

12 Ibid Art 5(3). This is intended to minimise the risk of arbitrariness, by providing judicial control of interferences by the executive with the individual's right to liberty in the criminal process: *Brogan v United Kingdom* A 145-B (1988), 11 EHRR 117, ECtHR, para 58. Once Art 5(3) applies, reasonable suspicion that a person has committed an offence is not sufficient; there must also be relevant and sufficient public interest reasons to justify further interference with the right to liberty of a person who is presumed innocent: *Letellier v France* A 207 (1991), 14 EHRR 83, ECtHR, para 35. Article 5(3) applies throughout the period from the arrest of an accused to his acquittal or conviction by the trial court, but not to detention pending an appeal: *Wemhoff v Federal Republic of Germany* A 7 (1968), 1 EHRR 55, ECtHR, paras 7–9 (and see para 128 note 3 ante). On the criteria to be considered in determining whether to refuse bail see eg *Stogmuller v Austria* A 9 (1969), 1 EHRR 155, ECtHR, para 15; *Yagci and Sargin v Turkey* A 319 (1995), 20 EHRR 505, ECtHR, para 52. Such circumstances may include: the danger of flight (*Stogmuller v Austria* supra); the severity of the sentence which the accused may expect if convicted (*Neumeister v Austria* A 8 (1968), 1 EHRR 91, ECtHR, para 10); factors relating to 'the character of the person involved, his morals, his home, his occupation, his assets, his family ties and all kinds of links with the country in which he is being prosecuted' (*Neumeister v Austria* supra at para 10). If the danger of the accused absconding is the only justification for detention, the release of the accused pending trial should be ordered if it is possible to obtain guarantees that will ensure his appearance at trial: *Wemhoff v Federal Republic of Germany* supra at para 15. A justifiable fear that the accused will interfere with the course of justice by suppressing evidence is another permissible reason for refusing bail: *Wemhoff v Federal Republic of Germany* supra at para 14. In special circumstances the detention of an accused in order to prevent the repetition of offences of which he was suspected may be compatible with Art 5(3) of the Convention: *Matznetter v Austria* A 10 (1969), 1 EHRR 198, ECtHR, at paras 9, 11.

13 Convention for the Protection of Human Rights and Fundamental Freedoms (1950) Art 5(3). It is clear that this permits the imposition of conditions of bail. The amount of a guarantee must be calculated by reference to the accused rather than by reference to some other person: *Neumeister v Austria* A 8 (1968), 1 EHRR 91, ECtHR, para 14.

## 131. Detention of minor.

The fourth exception to the rule that no one may be deprived of his liberty[1] is the detention of a minor[2] by lawful[3] order for the purpose of educational supervision[4] or his lawful detention for the purpose of bringing him before the competent legal authority[5].

1 Ie the Convention for the Protection of Human Rights and Fundamental Freedoms (1950) Art 5(1): see para 127 ante. As to the Convention generally see para 122 ante.

2 'Minor' has an autonomous meaning within the Convention: see Application 8500/79 *X v Switzerland* 18 DR 238 (1979), EComHR, where it was noted that in no contracting state is the age of majority less than 18. A person younger than 18 may therefore be taken to be a 'minor'.

3    'Lawful' means (as elsewhere in Art 5(1): see para 127 note 5 ante), that the arrest or detention must comply with municipal law and be in keeping with the purpose of Art 5, ie to protect the individual from arbitrariness: *Bouamar v Belgium* A 129 (1988), 11 EHRR 1, ECtHR, para 47.

4    Thus the detention of a minor in a reformatory for the purpose of educational supervision is authorised by the Convention for the Protection of Human Rights and Fundamental Freedoms (1950) Art 5(1)(d); detention in a remand prison as a preliminary to a transfer speedily to such an institution would also be permitted: *Bouamar v Belgium* A 129 (1988), 11 EHRR 1, ECtHR (16 year old boy detained in remand prison with no educational facilities pursuant to court order for 119 days in one year: violation of Art 5(1)(d)).

5    Ibid Art 5(1)(d). See eg Application 8500/79 *X v Switzerland* 18 DR 238 (1979), EComHR (eight month detention of minor accused of criminal offence pending preparation of psychiatric report needed for the taking of a decision in his case: no violation).

## 132.   Further justifications for deprivation of liberty.

The fifth exception to the rule that no one may be deprived of his liberty[1] is the lawful[2] detention of persons for the prevention of the spreading of infectious diseases, of persons of unsound mind[3], alcoholics or drug addicts or vagrants[4].

1    Ie the Convention for the Protection of Human Rights and Fundamental Freedoms (1950) Art 5(1): see para 127 ante. As to the Convention generally see para 122 ante.

2    The requirement of lawfulness requires that the detention complies with municipal law both as to procedure and substance, and that it is not arbitrary: *Van Der Leer v Netherlands* A 170–A (1990), 12 EHRR 567, ECtHR, para 22; see generally para 127 note 5 ante. Thus the detention must conform with the purpose of the restrictions permitted by Art 5(1)(e) of the Convention: *Winterwerp v Netherlands* A 33 (1979), 2 EHRR 387, ECtHR, para 39. In the context of persons of unsound mind the individual concerned must be reliably shown by objective medical expertise to be of unsound mind; that the individual's mental disorder is of a kind or degree which warrants compulsory confinement; and that the disorder persists throughout the period of detention: *Winterwerp v Netherlands* supra at para 39. The state has a certain discretion in making its own initial assessment of the situation *Winterwerp v Netherlands* supra at para 40. The first of these conditions does not, however, apply in emergencies: *Winterwerp v Netherlands* supra at para 42; *X v United Kingdom* A 46 (1981), 4 EHRR 188, ECtHR. Article 5(1)(e) of the Convention does not govern conditions of detention or guarantee the provision of suitable treatment, which are matters for Art 3 (see para 124 ante). However, in *Ashingdane v United Kingdom* A 93 (1985), 7 EHRR 528, ECtHR, para 44, it was indicated that the detention of a person of unsound mind is required to be in a hospital, clinic or other appropriate institution authorised for the detention of such persons.

3    'Unsound mind' cannot be definitively interpreted, but the deprivation of a person's liberty cannot be justified 'simply because his views or behaviour deviate from the norms prevailing in a particular society': *Winterwerp v Netherlands* A 33 (1979), 2 EHRR 387, ECtHR, para 37. See also note 2 supra.

4    Convention for the Protection of Human Rights and Fundamental Freedoms (1950) Art 5(1)(e). The definition of 'vagrants' in the Belgian Criminal Code, namely, 'persons who have no fixed abode, no means of subsistence and no regular trade or profession' has been held to be within the meaning of 'vagrants' for the purposes of the Convention for the Protection of Human Rights and Fundamental Freedoms (1950) Art 5(1)(e): see *De Wilde, Ooms and Versyp v Belgium* A 12 (1971), 1 EHRR 373, ECtHR. See also *Guzzardi v Italy* A 39 (1980), 3 EHRR 333, ECtHR (suspected Mafia members who lacked identifiable sources of income were not vagrants).

Persons falling into the categories provided by the Convention for the Protection of Human Rights and Fundamental Freedoms (1950) Art 5(1)(e) may be detained not only for public safety but also because their own interests may necessitate their detention: *Guzzardi v Italy* supra at para 98.

## 133.   Deprivation of liberty in relation to immigration, deportation or extradition.

The sixth exception to the rule that no one may be deprived of his liberty[1] is the lawful[2] arrest or detention of a person to prevent his effecting an unauthorised entry into the country or of a person against whom action is being taken with a view to deportation or extradition[3].

1    Ie the Convention for the Protection of Human Rights and Fundamental Freedoms (1950) Art 5(1): see para 127 ante. As to the Convention generally see para 122 ante.

2    'Lawful' means (as elsewhere in Art 5(1) of the Convention: see para 127 note 5 ante), that the arrest
or detention must be lawful under the applicable municipal law and that the applicable law, or the
conduct complained of, must not be arbitrary: see *De Jong, Baljet and Van Den Brink v Netherlands* A 77
(1984), 8 EHRR 20, ECtHR, para 44; and *Kemmache v France* A 296–C (1994), 19 EHRR 349,
ECtHR, para 42.

It is not clear when a ruling by a national court that a measure was invalid under the relevant municipal
law will be held to have retrospective effect. In *Bozano v France* A 111 (1986), 9 EHRR 297, ECtHR,
the court appeared to draw a distinction between the agents of the state acting in good faith but
subsequently found to have acted illegally, and the abuse of power ab initio. In the latter case it would be
much more likely for a finding of retrospective effect to be made by the national court or by the
Strasbourg organs (see paras 179–181 post). Cf Application 6871/75 *Caprino v United Kingdom* 22 DR 5
(1980), EComHR (invalidity of deportation order did not affect the lawfulness of detention based upon
it, because it was still action being taken 'with a view to' deportation); Application 9174/80 *Zamir v
United Kingdom* 40 DR 42 (1983), EComHR (requirement of non-arbitrariness in Art 5(1)(f) of the
Convention does not permit the European Commission of Human Rights to question on its facts a
decision to deport a person). The Commission has, however, been prepared to read into Art 5(1)(f) a
requirement that deportation or extradition proceedings be conducted with 'requisite diligence'. See
Application 7317/75 *Lynas v Switzerland* 6 DR 141 (1976), EComHR, where a requirement that
deportation or extradition proceedings be conducted with 'requisite diligence' was regarded as an aspect
of the requirement that detention be lawful. The national law authorising the detention must be accessible
and foreseeable: Application 9174/80 *Zamir v United Kingdom* supra.

3    Convention for the Protection of Human Rights and Fundamental Freedoms (1950) Art 5(1)(f). In
*Bozano v France* A 111 (1986), 9 EHRR 297, ECtHR. Where an Italian national who had been
convicted in absentia of murder by an Italian court, was forcibly taken by French police officers by car
to the Swiss border and handed to Swiss police custody, pursuant to what subsequently turned out to
be an invalid deportation order, his detention was not lawful within the meaning of Art 5(1)(f) of the
Convention. The European Court of Human Rights took into account (1) that French law might have
been infringed when the applicant was handed into Swiss police custody; and (2) on the question of
'arbitrariness', the circumstances in which the applicant was forcibly conveyed to the Swiss border. The
applicant's detention was not lawful but was designed to achieve 'a disguised form of extradition' which
could not be justified by Art 5(1)(f) of the Convention: *Bozano v France* supra at para 60.

## B.    RIGHT TO A FAIR TRIAL

**134. Right to a fair trial.** In the determination[1] of his civil rights and obligations[2] or
of any criminal charge[3] against him, everyone is entitled to a fair[4] and public[5] hearing
within a reasonable time[6] by an independent and impartial tribunal established by law[7].
Judgment[8] must be pronounced publicly[9] but the press and public may be excluded from
all or part of the trial in the interest of morals, public order or national security in a
democratic society, where the interests of juveniles or the protection of the private life of
the parties so require, or to the extent strictly necessary in the opinion of the court in
special circumstances where publicity would prejudice the interests of justice[10].

Everyone charged with a criminal[11] offence must be presumed innocent until proved
guilty according to law[12]. Everyone charged with a criminal offence has the following
minimum rights: (1) to be informed promptly, in a language which he understands and
in detail, of the nature and cause of the accusation against him[13]; (2) to have adequate time
and facilities for the preparation of his defence[14]; (3) to defend himself in person or
through legal assistance of his own choosing or, if he has not sufficient means to pay for
legal assistance, to be given it free when the interests of justice so require[15]; (4) to examine
or have examined witnesses against him and to obtain the attendance and examination of
witnesses on his behalf under the same conditions as witnesses against him[16]; and (5) to
have the free assistance of an interpreter if he cannot understand or speak the language
used in court[17].

1    For the Convention for the Protection of Human Rights and Fundamental Freedoms (1950) Art 6 to
apply in the context of civil rights and obligations there must be a dispute or 'contestation' concerning
such rights or obligations: *H v Belgium* A 127 (1987), 10 EHRR 339, ECtHR, para 40. 'Dispute' has an

autonomous meaning under the Convention. In conformity with the spirit of the Convention 'dispute' should not be construed technically, but given a substantive rather than formal meaning; it may relate not only to the actual existence of a right, but also to its scope or the manner in which it may be exercised, and may concern questions both of fact and of law; the dispute must be genuine and of a serious nature; Art 6 covers all proceedings the result of which is decisive for civil rights and obligations: see *Benthem v Netherlands* A 97 (1985), 8 EHRR 1, ECtHR. However, a tenuous connection or remote consequences do not suffice: the civil rights and obligations must be the object - or one of the objects - of the dispute; the result of the proceedings must be directly decisive for such a right (*Benthem v Netherlands* supra at para 32). Article 6 does not control the content of national law, but provides a procedural guarantee of a fair hearing in the determination of whatever substantive rights exist as a matter of national law; see eg Application 10475/83 *Dyer v United Kingdom* 39 DR 246 at 251 (1984), EComHR (application inadmissible where there was a statutory immunity from suit by applicant soldier); *Powell and Rayner v United Kingdom* A 172 (1990), 12 EHRR 355, ECtHR, para 36 (statutory exclusion of liability). Contrast however *Fayeds v United Kingdom* A 294-B (1994), 18 EHRR 393, ECtHR, para 65.

As to the Convention for the Protection of Human Rights and Fundamental Freedoms (1950) generally see para 122 ante.

2   As to civil rights and obligations for this purpose see para 135 post.

3   As to criminal charges see para 136 post.

4   As to what constitutes a fair hearing see para 137 post.

5   As to the right to a public hearing see para 138 post.

6   See para 139 post.

7   See para 140 post.

8   It is a requirement of the fair trial guarantee that a court should give reasons for its judgment. The European Court of Human Rights has held that national courts must 'indicate with sufficient clarity the grounds on which they base their decision' so that the 'accused may usefully exercise the right of appeal available to him' see *Hadjianastassiou v Greece* A 252-A (1992), 16 EHRR 219, ECtHR, para 33. It is not necessary for a court to deal with every point raised in argument (*Van der Hurk v Netherlands* A 288 (1994), 18 EHRR 481, ECtHR, para 61), but if a submission would, if accepted, be decisive for the outcome of the case, it must be dealt with in the court's judgment (*Hiro Balani v Spain* A 303-B (1994), 19 EHRR 566, ECtHR, para 28).

9   There are no express restrictions on this right in the Convention for the Protection of Human Rights and Fundamental Freedoms (1950) Art 6. The list of restrictions in text and note 10 infra applies only to the right to a public hearing: *Campbell and Fell v United Kingdom* A 80 (1984), 7 EHRR 165, ECtHR. However, public pronouncement does not necessarily mean pronouncement orally in open court: see *Pretto v Italy* A 71 (1983), 6 EHRR 182, ECtHR, para 26 ('the form of publicity to be given to the "judgment"...must be assessed in the light of the special features of the proceedings in question and by reference to the object and purpose of Article 6(1)') (Art 6(1) satisfied where the judgment was made available to the public in the court registry). See also, concerning a criminal case, *Axen v Germany* A 72 (1983), 6 EHRR 195, ECtHR.

10  Convention for the Protection of Human Rights and Fundamental Freedoms (1950) Art 6(1). The object and purpose of Art 6 is 'to enshrine the fundamental principle of the rule of law': *Salabiaku v France* A 141-A (1988), 13 EHRR 379, ECtHR, para 28; *Golder v United Kingdom* A 18 (1975), 1 EHRR 524, ECtHR, para 35; *Klass v Federal Republic of Germany* A 28 (1978), 2 EHRR 214, ECtHR, para 55. A restrictive interpretation of Art 6(1) would not correspond to the aim and the purpose of the Convention: *Delcourt v Belgium* A 11 (1970), 1 EHRR 355, ECtHR, para 25; *Moreira de Azevedo v Portugal* A 189 (1990), 13 EHRR 721, ECtHR, para 66. This principle applies to Art 6 as a whole, not merely to Art 6(1).

Where Art 6 applies, it guarantees the right of access to a court: *Golder v United Kingdom* supra; and see para 141 post.

Article 6(1) of the Convention does not guarantee a right of appeal from a decision by a court, whether in a criminal or non-criminal case, which complies with the requirements of Art 6(1). (A right of appeal is provided for criminal cases by the Seventh Protocol, Art 2.) If a contracting state provides a right of appeal, Art 6 applies to those proceedings: *Delcourt v Belgium* A 11 (1970), 1 EHRR 355, ECtHR, para 25.

Where the initial determination of a party's civil rights and obligations is carried out by an administrative or professional authority which does not comply with all the requirements of a fair trial, Art 6 is complied with if there is an appeal to a body with full jurisdiction which does comply with those requirements: see *Le Compte, Van Leuven and De Meyere v Belgium* A 43 (1981), 4 EHRR 1, ECtHR, para 51 (violation of Art 6(1) where there was an appeal from a professional association to a court which could only consider points of law); *W v United Kingdom* A 121 (1987), 10 EHRR 29, ECtHR (availability of judicial review did not satisfy the requirements of Art 6(1) where parents wished to challenge local authority decision concerning access to child in care). See also *Obermeier v Austria* A 179 (1990),

13 EHRR 290, ECtHR (right of appeal to the Austrian Administrative Court against a dismissal did not comply with Art 6(1), because review limited to whether government body had exercised its discretion in a manner incompatible with the object and purpose of the law); *Zumtobel v Austria* A 268-A (1993), 17 EHRR 116, ECtHR, para 32 (Art 6(1) complied with where applicant enjoyed right of appeal to the Austrian Administrative Court against an order for the expropriation of his land in order to build a road, because the Administrative Court was able to consider all the submissions the applicant had made to the relevant government office on their merits; *Fischer v Austria* A 312 (1995), 20 EHRR 349, ECtHR (no violation of Art 6(1) where applicant had right of appeal against revocation of tipping licence to Austrian Administrative Court, and that court did not regard itself as being restricted in its review of the facts). See also *Bryan v United Kingdom* A 335-A (1995), 21 EHRR 342, ECtHR, paras 43–47 (proceedings to challenge enforcement notice served under town and country planning legislation). Where a determination is made by 'courts of the classic kind', Art 6 must be fully complied with at the trial stage: *De Cubber v Belgium* A 86 (1984), 7 EHRR 236, ECtHR, para 32. It is possible, however, for the appeal proceedings to make reparation for any breaches of Art 6 by the court at first instance: see eg *Edwards v United Kingdom* A 247-B (1992), 15 EHRR 417, ECtHR.

11 The term 'criminal' in the Convention for the Protection of Human Rights and Fundamental Freedoms (1950) Art 6(2), (3) has the same meaning as is discussed in para 136 post: see *Adolf v Austria* A 49 (1982), 4 EHRR 313, ECtHR.

12 Convention for the Protection of Human Rights and Fundamental Freedoms (1950) Art 6(2): see para 142 post.

13 Ibid Art 6(3)(a): see para 143 post.

14 Ibid Art 6(3)(b): see para 144 post.

15 Ibid Art 6(3)(c): see para 145 post.

16 Ibid Art 6(3)(d): see para 146 post.

17 Ibid Art 6(3)(e): see para 147 post.

**135. Civil proceedings.** In order to determine[1] whether a civil right or obligation is at issue[2], it must first be determined whether a right or obligation is at issue and what is its nature under the relevant domestic law[3]. The phrase 'civil rights and obligations' refers, by use of the word 'civil', to the distinction between private and public law, with civil rights and obligations being rights and obligations in private law[4]. The test is whether according to general objective principles (in which context the legal systems of other contracting states must also be taken into consideration) the character of a 'civil right' or 'civil obligation' can be assigned to the right or obligation at issue, taking into account in particular the capacity of the person claiming the right and the conditions in which he exercises or wishes to exercise it[5]. The protection of the Convention applies irrespective of the parties' status, public or private, and of the nature of the legislation which governs the manner in which the dispute is to be determined, so long as the outcome is decisive of private law rights and obligations[6].

The rights and obligations of private persons in their relations inter se are always civil rights and obligations. Cases where civil rights or obligations have been found involve: commercial law[7]; the law of tort[8]; family law[9]; the law of succession[10]; employment law[11]; and the law of real property[12].

Civil rights may also arise in cases concerning relations between an individual and the state, including cases concerning: the right to property[13]; the right to engage in a commercial activity[14]; and the right to compensation for financial loss resulting from illegal state acts[15].

Rights provided by statute for social security and social assistance are civil rights[16].

Certain rights involving an individual and the state have been classified as public law rights and therefore not 'civil' rights within the meaning of the Convention. These include rights concerning employment in the public sector[17]; an individual's liability to pay tax[18]; immigration and nationality[19]; state education[20]; prison discipline[21]; legal aid[22]; the right to medical treatment[23]; and the validity of elections[24].

The right to an effective remedy guaranteed by the Convention is also a civil right[25].

1 Ie for the purposes of the Convention for the Protection of Human Rights and Fundamental Freedoms (1950) Art 6: see para 134 ante. As to the Convention generally see para 122 ante.

2   The fact that a deciding authority has a discretion does not mean that there is no right at issue, since it follows from generally recognised legal and administrative principles that the discretion is not unfettered: *Pudas v Sweden* A 125 (1987), 10 EHRR 380, ECtHR, para 34.

3   *Konig v Federal Republic of Germany* A 27 (1978), 2 EHRR 170, ECtHR, para 89; *Feldbrugge v Netherlands* A 99 (1986), 8 EHRR 425, ECtHR, paras 26–40; and *Powell and Rayner v United Kingdom* A 172 (1990), 12 EHRR 355, ECtHR, para 36.

4   *Ringeisen v Austria* A 13 (1971), 1 EHRR 455, ECtHR, para 94; *Konig v Federal Republic of Germany* A 27 (1978), 2 EHRR 170, ECtHR, para 95. However, 'civil right' has an autonomous meaning under the Convention: *Konig v Federal Republic of Germany* supra at para 88; *Benthem v Netherlands* A 97 (1985), 8 EHRR 1, ECtHR, paras 32–34. Only the character of the right at issue is relevant: *Ringeisen v Austria (No 1)* supra at para 94; *Konig v Federal Republic of Germany* supra at para 90; *Benthem v Netherlands* supra at para 34.

5   *H v Belgium* A 127 (1987), 10 EHRR 339, ECtHR, paras 44–47.

6   *H v France* A 162-A (1989), 12 EHRR 74, ECtHR, para 47.

7   Application 8734/79 *Barthold v Federal Republic of Germany* 26 DR 145 (1981), EComHR.

8   *Axen v Federal Republic of Germany* A 72 (1983), 6 EHRR 195, ECtHR.

9   *Airey v Ireland* A 32 (1979), 2 EHRR 305, ECtHR.

10  Application 7211/75 *X v Switzerland* 7 DR 104 (1976), EComHR.

11  *Buchholz v Federal Republic of Germany* A 42 (1981), 3 EHRR 597, ECtHR.

12  *Langborger v Sweden* A 155 (1989), 12 EHRR 416, ECtHR.

13  See eg *Ringeisen v Austria* A 13 (1971), 1 EHRR 455, ECtHR (granting of permission to purchase land); *Sporrong and Lönnroth v Sweden* A 52 (1982), 5 EHRR 35, ECtHR (expropriation of land); *Skarby v Sweden* A 180–B (1990), 13 EHRR 90, ECtHR (planning laws); Application 10259/83 *Anca v Belgium* 40 DR 170 (1984), EComHR (bankruptcy); Application 7830/77 *X v Austria* 14 DR 200 (1978), EComHR (patent rights).

14  See eg *Konig v Federal Republic of Germany* A 27 (1978), 2 EHRR 170, ECtHR (licence to run medical clinic); *Tre Traktorer Aktiebolag v Sweden* A 159 (1989), 13 EHRR 309, ECtHR (alcohol licence for a restaurant); *Pudas v Sweden* A 125 (1987), 10 EHRR 380, ECtHR (public service transport licence); *H v Belgium* A 127 (1987), 10 EHRR 339, ECtHR (right to practise law).

15  See eg *X v France* A 234–C (1992), 14 EHRR 483, ECtHR (claim for damages for negligence for contracting AIDS from blood transfusion); *Editions Periscope v France* A 234-B (1992), 14 EHRR 597, ECtHR (claim for compensation by company caused pecuniary loss by illegal refusal of tax concession); *Stran Greek Refineries and Stratis Andreadis v Greece* A 301-B (1994), 19 EHRR 293, ECtHR (financial claim arising out of contract between private company and the state).

16  See eg *Feldbrugge v Netherlands* A 99 (1986), 8 EHRR 425, ECtHR; *Deumeland v Germany* A 120 (1986), 8 EHRR 448, ECtHR; *Schuler-Zgraggen v Switzerland* A 263 (1993), 16 EHRR 405, ECtHR; *Kerojarvi v Finland* A 326 (1995), ECtHR.

17  Application 9248/81 *Leander v Sweden* 34 DR 78 (1983), EComHR (civil servants); Application 9208/80 *Saraiva de Carvalho v Portugal* 26 DR 262 (1981), EComHR (members of the armed forces); Application 9877/82 *X v Portugal* 32 DR 258 (1983), EComHR (judges); although cf *Lombardo v Italy* A 249-B (1992), 21 EHRR 188, ECtHR (dispute concerning judge's pension to which he was entitled by statute concerned a civil right).

18  Application 9908/82 *X v France* 32 DR 266, EComHR; *Schouten and Meldrum v Netherlands* A 304 (1994), 19 EHRR 432, ECtHR, para 50 (some financial obligations belong 'exclusively to the realm of public law and are accordingly not covered by the notion of "civil rights and obligations"' (paragraph 50). The court there indicated that criminal law fines and obligations deriving from tax legislation would fall outside the scope of Art 6(1) of the Convention.

19  Application 7729/76 *Agee v United Kingdom* 7 DR 164 (1976), EComHR; Application 13325/87 *S v Switzerland* 59 DR 256 (1988), EComHR.

20  Application 14688/89 *Simpson v United Kingdom* 64 DR 188 (1989), EComHR.

21  Application 8317/78 *McFeeley v United Kingdom* 20 DR 44 (1980), EComHR.

22  Application 3925/69 *X v Federal Republic of Germany* 32 CD 56 (1970), EComHR.

23  Application 10801/84 *L v Sweden* 61 DR 62 (1988), EComHR.

24  Application 18997/91 *IZ v Greece* 76A DR 65 (1994), EComHR.

25  *De La Pradelle v France* A 253-B (1992), ECtHR: see para 141 text and note 19 post.

**136. Criminal charges.** In order to determine[1] whether an offence with which an individual is charged is criminal[2], three criteria must be applied, namely: (1) the classification of the offence under national law; (2) the nature of the offence; and (3) the degree of severity of the possible punishment[3]. Thus as well as applying to offences which are criminal under national law, offences under prison disciplinary proceedings have been held to be criminal[4], as have offences classified as regulatory under national law[5], and offences relating to parliamentary privilege and the administration of justice[6].

The right to a fair trial applies when a person has been charged with an offence[7]. A charge is the official notification given to an individual by the competent authority of an allegation that he has committed a criminal offence or some other act which carries the implication of such an allegation and which likewise substantially affects the situation of the suspect[8]. A person has been found to have been the subject of a criminal charge for this purpose when arrested for a criminal offence[9]; when as part of a customs investigation he has been required to produce evidence and has had his bank account frozen[10]; and when charged by the police[11]. There is no criminal charge for this purpose against a person, however, where his property is affected by a criminal charge against a third party[12]. Extradition proceedings are not covered by the phrase 'criminal charge'[13].

1   Ie for the purposes of the Convention for the Protection of Human Rights and Fundamental Freedoms (1950) Art 6: see para 134 ante. As to the Convention generally see para 122 ante.

2   The meaning of 'criminal' for the purposes of the Convention is autonomous: *Engel v Netherlands* A 22 (1976), 1 EHRR 647, ECtHR.

3   *Engel v Netherlands* A 22 (1976), 1 EHRR 647, ECtHR, para 82. It follows that an offence which is criminal under national law is automatically so under the Convention, but if an act is not criminal under national law it may yet be so under the Convention. For an example of this see *Benham v United Kingdom* (1996) Times, 24 June, ECtHR (non-payment of community charge incurring possible consequence of committal to prison was a criminal matter for the purposes of the Convention).

4   See eg *Campbell and Fell v United Kingdom* A 80 (1984), 7 EHRR 165, ECtHR, paras 67–73 (mutiny, incitement to mutiny and gross personal violence to a prison officer fell within the concept of 'criminal charge' in the Convention for the Protection of Human Rights and Fundamental Freedoms (1950) Art 6(1)).

5   See eg *Ozturk v Germany* A 73 (1984), 6 EHRR 409, ECtHR, paras 45–56 (careless driving, regulatory under German law: emphasised that the offence was of general application and carried with it a sanction (ie a fine) of a punitive and deterrent kind; it was also relevant that most contracting states continued to treat minor road traffic offences as criminal); *Bendenoun v France* A 284 (1994), 18 EHRR 54, ECtHR (offences imposing large financial penalties for tax evasion); *Belilos v Switzerland* A 132 (1988), 10 EHRR 466, ECtHR (breaches of police regulations prohibiting public demonstrations); *Deweer v Belgium* A 35 (1980), 2 EHRR 439, ECtHR (offences under price-fixing regulations); *Salabiaku v France* A 141-A (1988), 13 EHRR 379, ECtHR (offences contained in customs code).

6   See eg *Ravnsborg v Sweden* A 283-B (1994), 18 EHRR 38, ECtHR; *Demicoli v Malta* A 210 (1991), 14 EHRR 47, ECtHR.

7   Convention for the Protection of Human Rights and Fundamental Freedoms (1950) Art 6(1).

8   *Corigliano v Italy* A 57 (1982), 5 EHRR 334, ECtHR, para 34. 'Charge' has an autonomous Convention meaning, and it is necessary to consider the realities of the procedure in question. The test is whether a person is substantially affected by the steps taken against him: *Deweer v Belgium* A 35 (1980), 2 EHRR 439, ECtHR, paras 42, 44, 46.

9   *Wemhoff v Federal Republic of Germany* A 7 (1968), 1 EHRR 55, ECtHR; Application 8233/78 *X v United Kingdom* 17 DR 122 (1979), EComHR.

10   *Funke v France* A 256-A (1993), 16 EHRR 297, ECtHR.

11   Application 11224/84 *Ewing v United Kingdom* (1986) 10 EHRR 141, EComHR.

12   *Allgemeine Gold-und Silverscheideanstalt v United Kingdom* A 108 (1986), 9 EHRR 1, ECtHR.

13   Application 11683/85 *Farmakopoulos v Belgium* 64 DR 52 (1990), EComHR.

**137.  What constitutes a fair hearing.** The right to a fair hearing guaranteed by the Convention for the Protection of Human Rights and Fundamental Freedoms (1950)[1] applies both to civil and criminal cases, although the contracting states have a greater latitude when dealing with civil cases concerning civil rights and obligations than they have when dealing with criminal cases[2]. A right to a hearing in one's presence is implicit in the concept of a fair hearing in a criminal case[3], but in civil cases, although there is a general right to an oral hearing, the right of a party to be present at the hearing has been held to extend only to certain kinds of cases, such as cases which involve an assessment of a party's conduct[4] or where the 'personal character and manner of life' of a party is in issue[5].

A party may waive his right to be present at an oral hearing[6]. Trial in absentia is also permitted where the state has sought diligently, but failed, to give an accused effective notice of the hearing[7]. A trial may also proceed without the presence of the accused in the interests of the administration of justice, where the accused is unfit through illness to attend[8]. The right of a party to be present at an appeal may not be guaranteed if there was an oral hearing at first instance at which he was entitled to be present. Beyond this, the right to be present at an appeal depends on the role of the appellate court and the particular facts of the case[9].

Everyone who is a party to proceedings must have a reasonable opportunity of presenting his case to the court under conditions which do not place him at a substantial disadvantage[10]. It has been held to be a requirement of the guarantee of a fair trial that the proceedings be adversarial, in that all the evidence must in principle be produced in the presence of the accused with a view to adversarial argument[11]. The fair trial guarantee includes the right to freedom from self-incrimination[12]. The right to a fair trial has been infringed where the accused in a criminal jury trial was subjected to prejudicial publicity[13], or where an accused was not able to participate effectively in the trial because the court room did not have sufficiently good acoustics[14].

The rules of evidence are in principle a matter for each contracting state, although in certain circumstances the use of a particular rule of evidence may cause the trial to be unfair on the facts[15]. A rule permitting the use of illegally obtained evidence in a criminal prosecution does not automatically render the trial unfair, although the application of such a rule in a particular case may do so[16].

The Convention does not guarantee a trial by jury in a criminal prosecution[17]. It has been held not to be a breach of the Convention for an accused to be placed in a glass cage for security reasons[18], or to be handcuffed in court[19].

1   Ie the Convention for the Protection of Human Rights and Fundamental Freedoms (1950) Art 6(1): see para 134 ante. As to the Convention generally see para 122 ante.
2   *Dombo Beheer v Netherlands* A 274-A (1993), 18 EHRR 213, ECtHR, para 32.
3   *Ekbarani v Sweden* A 134 (1988), 13 EHRR 504, ECtHR, para 25 (criminal cases).
4   *Muyldermans v Belgium* A 214-B (1991), 15 EHRR 204, ECtHR, para 64.
5   Application 434/58 *X v Sweden* 2 YB 354, at 372 (1959), EComHR.
6   *Poitrimol v France* A 277-A (1993), 18 EHRR 130, ECtHR, para 31.
7   *Colozza v Italy* A 89 (1985), 7 EHRR 516, ECtHR; *Brozicek v Italy* A 167 (1989), 12 EHRR 371, ECtHR. Where a trial has been permitted to be conducted without the presence of the accused, should the accused later learn of the proceedings he must be able to obtain a fresh determination of the merits of the charge: *Colozza v Italy* supra at para 29.
8   Applications 7572/76, 7586/76 and 7587/76 *Ensslin, Baader and Raspe v Federal Republic of Germany* 14 DR 64 (1978), EComHR.
9   *Ekbarani v Sweden* A 134 (1988), 13 EHRR 504, ECtHR, para 27.
10  This is the concept of 'equality of arms': see Application 10938/84 *Kaufman v Belgium* 50 DR 98 (1986), EComHR; *Dombo Beheer v Netherlands* A 274-A (1993), 18 EHRR 213, ECtHR, para 33. The principle of 'equality of arms' involves a fair balance between the parties: *Dombo Beheer v Netherlands* supra at para 33; *Borgers v Belgium* A 214 (1991), 15 EHRR 92, ECtHR (lack of equal standing between the Procureur General and the applicant before the Court of Cassation involved a breach of Art 6(1) of the Convention for the Protection of Human Rights and Fundamental Freedoms (1950), because the Procureur General was entitled to state his opinion in open court and then retire with the court and take part (though without a vote) in its discussion of the case); *Stran Greek Refineries and Stratis Andreadis v Greece* A 301-B (1994), 19 EHRR 293, ECtHR, at paras 46, 49 (legislation made decision against applicant in claim against Greek government 'inevitable'): 'the principle of the rule of law and the notion of a fair trial enshrined in Article 6 preclude any interference by the legislature with the administration of justice designed to influence the judicial determination of the dispute'; *Ruiz-Mateos v Spain* A 262 (1993), 16 EHRR 505, ECtHR (applicants were not allowed right of reply to written submissions by counsel for the state). The principle of equality of arms requires that an expert witness

appointed by an accused be accorded equal treatment with one appointed by the court who has links with the prosecution (*Bonisch v Austria* A 92 (1985), 9 EHRR 191, ECtHR); that parties to civil proceedings be allowed to cross-examine witnesses (Application 5362/72 *X v Austria* 42 CD 145 (1972), EComHR); and that parties to civil proceedings be informed of the reasons for an administrative decision so as to be able to challenge it (*Hentrich v France* A 296-A (1994), 18 EHRR 440, ECtHR, para 56). See further, as to the right to call and examine witnesses, para 146 post.

11 *Barbera, Messegue and Jabardo v Spain* A 146 (1988), 11 EHRR 360, ECtHR, para 78. See also *Kamasinski v Austria* A 168 (1989), 13 EHRR 36, ECtHR (breach of Art 6 of the Convention where appeal judge had obtained information from trial judge over the telephone without the appellant being informed or being given a chance to comment on the information).

12 See para 142 text and note 13 post.

13 See eg Application 3444/67 *X v Norway* 35 CD 37 at 48 (1970), EComHR; Application 13251/87 *Berns and Ewert v Luxembourg* 68 DR 137 (1991), EComHR.

14 *Stanford v United Kingdom* A 282-A (1994), ECtHR, para 26.

15 Eg where hearsay evidence has been introduced and the accused has had no opportunity of confronting the witnesses: *Unterpertinger v Austria* A 110 (1986), 13 EHRR 175, ECtHR; *Kostovski v Netherlands* A 166 (1989), 12 EHRR 434, ECtHR; *Asch v Austria* A 203 (1991), 15 EHRR 597, ECtHR; *Artner v Austria* A 242-A (1992), ECtHR; *Ludi v Switzerland* A 238 (1992), 15 EHRR 173, ECtHR. It is not clear whether it is only where the hearsay evidence is the only evidence against the accused that there will be a breach of Art 6(1) of the Convention (see eg *Asch v Austria* supra), or whether it is sufficient that it has played a significant part (see eg *Ludi v Switzerland* supra).

16 See eg *Schenk v Switzerland* A 140 (1988), 13 EHRR 242, ECtHR, para 46 (illegally obtained tape recording admitted in criminal trial: no breach of Art 6(1) of the Convention, because defence had been able to challenge use and authenticity of the tape, and there was other evidence against the accused). It has been held not to be a breach of Art 6 of the Convention to admit evidence obtained by an undercover agent (Application 12127/86 *X v Federal Republic of Germany* (1989) 11 EHRR 84, EComHR); to admit evidence of an accomplice who has been promised immunity, provided the jury has been made fully aware of the situation (Application 7306/75 *X v United Kingdom* 7 DR 115 (1976), EComHR); for the court to be informed of the accused's criminal record during the trial (Application 2676/65 *X v Austria* 23 CD 31 at 34 (1967), EComHR); for a conviction to be founded solely on circumstantial evidence (Application 12013/86 *Alberti v Italy* 59 DR 100 (1989), EComHR); or for a confession to be admitted even though it was obtained in the absence of the accused's lawyer (Application 9370/81 *G v United Kingdom* 35 DR 75 (1983), EComHR). However, there will be a breach of Art 6(1) if the prosecution does not disclose to the defence all material evidence for or against the accused, although a failure to do so will be cured where the effect of the non-disclosure on the outcome of the trial is properly considered by an appellate court: see *Edwards v United Kingdom* A 247-B (1992), 15 EHRR 417, ECtHR, para 39.

17 Application 8299/78 *X and Y v Ireland* 22 DR 51 (1980), EComHR.

18 Application 11837/85 *Auguste v France* 69 DR 104 (1990), EComHR.

19 Application 12323/86 *Campbell v United Kingdom* 57 DR 148 (1988), EComHR.

**138. Public hearing.** The Convention for the Protection of Human Rights and Fundamental Freedoms (1950) guarantees the right to a public hearing[1]. The presence of the press is particularly important in this regard[2]. The right to a public hearing implies a right to an oral hearing at the level of the trial court[3].

The right to a public hearing is subject to the restrictions expressly provided for in the Convention, namely that the press and public may be excluded from all or part of the trial in the interests of morals, public order or national security in a democratic society, where the interests of juveniles or the private life of the parties so require, or to the extent strictly necessary in the opinion of the court in special circumstances where publicity would prejudice the interests of justice[4]. It is not expressly provided that a restriction must be a proportionate response to a social need, but the court may apply a proportionality test in deciding whether a restriction on the right to a public hearing is justified[5].

It may be justifiable for witnesses to give evidence in camera in order to ensure their safety[6].

A public hearing is not in all circumstances required for appeal proceedings; provided that there has been a public hearing before the trial court, the absence of a public hearing at the appeal stage may not violate the Convention[7].

The Convention does not require a public hearing if an accused or a party has waived his right to such a hearing, provided that the waiver is unequivocal and there is no important public interest consideration that calls for the public to be present[8].

1   Convention for the Protection of Human Rights and Fundamental Freedoms (1950) Art 6(1); and see para 134 ante. This guarantee protects litigants from the administration of justice in secret with no public scrutiny: *Preto v Italy* A 71 (1983), 6 EHRR 182, ECtHR, para 21. As to the Convention generally see para 122 ante.
2   Application 8273/78 *X v Federal Republic of Germany* 2 Digest 454 (1981), EComHR.
3   *Fredin v Sweden (No 2)* A 283-A (1994), ECtHR, para 21.
4   Convention for the Protection of Human Rights and Fundamental Freedoms (1950) Art 6(1).
5   See *Campbell and Fell v United Kingdom* A 80 (1984), 7 EHRR 165, ECtHR, para 87 (prison disciplinary proceedings conducted in camera for reasons of public order and security: no violation of Art 6 of the Convention because requirement that disciplinary proceedings be in public would impose disproportionate burden on the state).
    For other examples of cases where the holding of a hearing in camera was held to be justified see Application 1913/63 *X v Austria* 2 Digest 438 (1965), EComHR (trial of accused for sexual offences against children); Application 7366/76 *X v United Kingdom* 2 Digest 452 (1977), EComHR (divorce proceedings); and Application 13562/88 *Guenoun v France* 66 DR 181 (1990), EComHR (medical disciplinary proceedings).
6   Application 8016/77 *X v United Kingdom* 2 Digest 456 (1980), EComHR.
7   *Ekbatani v Sweden* A 134 (1988), 13 EHRR 504, ECtHR, para 31.
8   *Hakansson and Sturesson v Sweden* A 171 (1990), 13 EHRR 1, ECtHR, para 66.

**139. Reasonable time.** The Convention for the Protection of Human Rights and Fundamental Freedoms (1950) guarantees the right to a hearing within a reasonable time[1].

In civil cases, time usually begins to run from the initiation of court proceedings[2], and in criminal cases from the time of charge[3]. The guarantee continues to apply until the case is finally determined (which may include appeal proceedings)[4].

There is no absolute time limit; the reasonableness of the length of proceedings will depend on the particular circumstances of the case. In assessing reasonableness, relevant factors are the complexity of the case, the conduct of the applicant and the conduct of the competent administrative and judicial authorities[5].

The state is not responsible for delay that is caused by the conduct of the applicant[6], but it is responsible for delays that result from the conduct of its administrative or judicial authorities[7].

Certain types of cases may require greater urgency than others. This is generally the case in relation to criminal, rather than civil, cases[8]. Particular urgency has been held to be required where the applicant is in detention pending the outcome of his case[9], or in civil cases concerning the applicant's employment[10], title to land[11], mental health[12] or civil status[13], or where delay might render the proceedings pointless[14].

The requirement of trial within a reasonable time may lead to a breach of the Convention not only where there has been a delay in the manner in which a particular case has been dealt with, but also where the delay is caused by the state's failure to provide an efficient system of justice[15].

1   Convention for the Protection of Human Rights and Fundamental Freedoms (1950) Art 6(1): see para 134 ante. This guarantee 'underlines the importance of rendering justice without delays which might jeopardise its effectiveness and credibility': *H v France* A 162-A (1989), 12 EHRR 74, ECtHR, para 58. In a criminal case it is 'designed to avoid that a person charged should remain too long in a state of uncertainty about his fate': *Stogmuller v Austria* A 9 (1969) at 40, 1 EHRR 155, ECtHR. As to the Convention generally see para 122 ante.
2   See eg *Guincho v Portugal* A 81 (1984), 7 EHRR 223, ECtHR, para 29.
3   See para 136 text and notes 7–8 ante.
4   *Eckle v Federal Republic of Germany* A 51 (1982), 5 EHRR 1, ECtHR, para 76.
5   *Konig v Federal Republic of Germany* A 27 (1978), 2 EHRR 170, ECtHR, para 99.

6   *Konig v Federal Republic of Germany* A 27 (1978), 2 EHRR 170, ECtHR, para 103.

7   As regards criminal cases see eg Application 8435/78 *Orchin v United Kingdom* 34 DR 5 (1982), EComHR (delay in entering a nolle prosequi); *Foti v Italy* A 56 (1982), 5 EHRR 313, ECtHR, para 61 (delay in transferring cases between courts); *Eckle v Federal Republic of Germany* A 51 (1982), 5 EHRR 1, ECtHR (delay in conduct of preliminary investigation in civil law system). For the application of the principle to civil cases see eg *Wiesinger v Austria* A 213 (1991), 16 EHRR 258, ECtHR (delays caused by lack of co-ordination between administrative authorities); *Guincho v Portugal* A 81 (1984), 7 EHRR 223, ECtHR (delays by court in performing registry tasks); and *H v United Kingdom* A 120 (1987), 10 EHRR 95, ECtHR (delays in presentation of evidence by the state).

8   See *Baggetta v Italy* A 119 (1987), 10 EHRR 325, ECtHR, para 24.

9   *Abdoella v Netherlands* A 248-A (1992), 20 EHRR 585, ECtHR, para 24.

10  *Buchholz v Federal Republic of Germany* A 42 (1981), 3 EHRR 597, ECtHR, para 52.

11  *Hentrich v France* A 296-A (1994), 18 EHRR 440, ECtHR, para 61.

12  *Bock v Federal Republic of Germany* A 150 (1989), 12 EHRR 247, ECtHR, para 48.

13  *Bock v Federal Republic of Germany* A 150 (1989), 12 EHRR 247, ECtHR, para 48.

14  *X v France* A 234-C (1991), 14 EHRR 483, ECtHR.

15  See eg *Zimmermann and Steiner v Switzerland* A 66 (1983), 6 EHRR 17, ECtHR, para 29, where it was observed that contracting states have a duty to organise their legal systems so as to allow the courts to comply with the requirements of Art 6(1) of the Convention; a breach of Art 6(1) was found where the national court's case load had built up over many years and adequate steps to increase the number of judges and administrative staff or otherwise to reorganise the court system to cope with the situation had not been taken. See also *Guincho v Portugal* A 81 (1984), 7 EHRR 223, ECtHR. Cf *Buchholz v Federal Republic of Germany* A 42 (1981), 3 EHRR 597, ECtHR, where it was held that if a state takes reasonably prompt remedial action it will not be liable for delays that result from a backlog of cases that was not reasonably foreseeable.

**140. Independent and impartial tribunal.** The Convention for the Protection of Human Rights and Fundamental Freedoms (1950) guarantees the right to a hearing before an independent and impartial tribunal established by law[1].

For the purposes of the Convention a tribunal is characterised by its judicial function[2], but it must also satisfy requirements as to independence (in particular of the executive); impartiality; duration of its members' terms of office; and guarantees afforded by its procedure[3]. A tribunal may be composed of persons who are not necessarily professional judges[4]. A body may be a tribunal for the purposes of the Convention although it exercises other than judicial functions[5], but it must be competent to take legally binding decisions[6].

In determining whether a body can be considered independent, regard may be had to the manner of appointment of its members[7] and the duration of their terms of office[8], the existence of guarantees against outside pressures and the question whether the body presents an appearance of independence[9].

'Impartiality' has been held to mean lack of prejudice or bias[10]. The test for impartiality is both subjective, that is to say on the basis of the personal conviction of a particular judge in a given case, and objective, that is to say ascertaining whether the judge offered guarantees sufficient to exclude legitimate doubt[11]. In a criminal case, the existence of some connection between a juror and an important witness does not necessarily prevent the jury from being impartial[12].

1   Convention for the Protection of Human Rights and Fundamental Freedoms (1950) Art 6(1): see para 134 ante. As to the Convention generally see para 122 ante.

    The judicial organisation in a democratic society must not depend on the discretion of the executive, but should be regulated by law emanating from Parliament. This means that the basic rules concerning the organisation and jurisdiction of the court system must be set out in legislation: see Application 7360/76 *Zand v Austria* 15 DR 70 at 80 (1978), EComHR. Article 6(1) of the Convention does not, however, prevent the establishment of special courts, if they are provided for in law see Application 8299/78 *X and Y v Ireland* 22 DR 51 (1980), EComHR.

2 Ie 'determining matters within its competence on the basis of the rules of law and after proceedings conducted in the prescribed manner': *Belilos v Switzerland* A 132 (1988), 10 EHRR 466, ECtHR, para 64.

3 *Belilos v Switzerland* A 132 (1988), 10 EHRR 466, ECtHR, para 64.

4 Eg members of the armed forces may be members of disciplinary tribunals (*Engel v Netherlands* A 22 (1976), 1 EHRR 647, ECtHR, para 89); and civil servants may be members of administrative tribunals (*Ettl v Austria* A 117 (1987), 10 EHRR 255, ECtHR, para 38).

5 *H v Belgium* A 127-B (1987), 10 EHRR 339, ECtHR, para 50.

6 *Benthem v Netherlands* A 97 (1985), 8 EHRR 1, ECtHR.

7 Appointment by the executive is permissible: see eg *Belilos v Switzerland* A 132 (1988), 10 EHRR 466, ECtHR.

8 A very short term is sufficient for members of administrative or disciplinary tribunals: see *Campbell and Fell v United Kingdom* A 80 (1984), 7 EHRR 165, ECtHR. Tribunal members must be protected from removal during their term of office, although this need not be recognised in law provided it is recognised as a matter of practice: see *Sramek v Austria* A 84 (1984), 7 EHRR 351, ECtHR, para 38.

9 See *Campbell and Fell v United Kingdom* A 80 (1984), 7 EHRR 165, ECtHR, para 78. Applying this test, a court did not qualify as an independent court when it sought and accepted as binding Foreign Office advice on the meaning of a treaty that it had to apply: see *Beaumartin v France* A 296-B (1994), 19 EHRR 485, ECtHR, para 38. Tribunal members must not be subject to instructions from the executive: *Sramek v Austria* A 84 (1984), 7 EHRR 351, ECtHR (a member of a tribunal was a civil servant whose immediate superior was representing the government as party to the case).

10 *Piersack v Belgium* A 53 (1982), 5 EHRR 169, ECtHR, para 30.

11 *Hauschildt v Denmark* A 154 (1989), 12 EHRR 266, ECtHR, para 46. See *Fey v Austria* A 255 (1993), 16 EHRR 387, ECtHR, para 30: 'What is at stake is the confidence which the courts in a democratic society must inspire in the public and, above all, as far as criminal proceedings are concerned, in the accused'. If a party believes that the court or tribunal is not impartial, the question is whether that doubt as to impartiality can be objectively justified. If there is a legitimate doubt as to impartiality, the judge must withdraw from the case: *Hauschildt v Denmark* supra at para 48. Legitimate doubt as to impartiality has been found in a number of cases, eg: *De Cubber v Belgium* A 86 (1984), 7 EHRR 236, ECtHR (trial judge had previously acted as an investigating judge); *Piersack v Belgium* A 53 (1982), 5 EHRR 169, ECtHR (trial judge had previously been the head of the section of the public prosecutor's department that had investigated the applicant's case and commenced proceedings against him); *Langborger v Sweden* A 155 (1989), 12 EHRR 416, ECtHR (breach of both the independence and impartiality requirements found when lay members of tribunal whose function was to adjudicate on a clause in a tenancy agreement had close links with and had been nominated by organisations which had an interest in the removal of the clause); and *Procola v Luxembourg* A 326 (1995), ECtHR (four members of the Conseil d'Etat had carried out both advisory and judicial functions).
 It is not clear whether the requirement of impartiality may be waived by an accused or a party: see *Pfeifer and Plankl v Austria* A 227 (1992), 14 EHRR 692, ECtHR, para 37 (waiver in so far as it is permissible must be unequivocally established).

12 See *Pullar v United Kingdom* (1996) Times, 24 June, ECtHR (juror was junior employee in firm of which witness was a partner, but in the circumstances, notably that the employee had been given notice of redundancy, doubts about impartiality could not be objectively justified).

**141. Right of access to a court.** The Convention for the Protection of Human Rights and Fundamental Freedoms (1950) guarantees the right to a fair trial, which involves the right of access to a court[1]. The right of access to a court applies to criminal as well as civil proceedings (ie an accused is entitled to be tried on the charge against him in court)[2].

The right is a right of effective access to a court[3]. It requires that a person be given personal and reasonable notice of an administrative decision which interferes with his civil rights and obligations, so that he has adequate time to challenge it in court[4].

The right of access to a court is not absolute: restrictions may be imposed since the right of access by its nature requires regulation, which may vary according to the needs and resources of the community and of individuals[5]. Any such restriction must not be such that the essence of the right is impaired; it must also have a legitimate aim and comply with the principle of proportionality[6]. Restrictions on the right of access to a court have been allowed in relation to: vexatious litigants[7]; minors[8]; bankrupts[9]; prisoners[10]; a requirement for the payment of fines[11]; reasonable time limits in respect of proceedings[12]; a requirement for payment of security for costs[13]; in a criminal case, a practice whereby there is no hearing as to guilt or innocence (only as to sentence) where an accused pleads guilty at the beginning of his trial[14]; and privilege available in defamation proceedings concerning allegations of fraud in a government inspector's report[15]. Restrictions have been held to be in breach of the Convention where, for example, certain bodies were prevented by statute from bringing proceedings in respect of their property, but were required to bring them before Church authorities[16]; and a professional person was compelled to bring a claim for fees for work done through a professional organisation[17].

The right of access to a court in both criminal and non-criminal cases may be waived, for example by means of an arbitration agreement[18]. The right of access to a court overlaps with the right to an effective national remedy in respect of a breach of a Convention right, in so far as the Convention right is also a civil right[19].

1   Convention for the Protection of Human Rights and Fundamental Freedoms (1950) Art 6(1); *Golder v United Kingdom* A 18 (1975), 1 EHRR 524, ECtHR (refusal to permit convicted prisoner to write to solicitor with a view to instituting civil proceedings for libel against a prison officer involved a breach of applicant's right of access to a court, ie his right to institute proceedings). As to the Convention generally see para 122 ante.
2   *Deweer v Belgium* A 35 (1980), 2 EHRR 439, ECtHR.
3   See eg *Airey v Ireland* A 32 (1979), 2 EHRR 305, ECtHR (indigent wife who wished to bring proceedings for judicial separation and who had been denied legal aid to do so had been denied right of effective access to a court).
4   *De La Pradelle v France* A 253-B (1992), ECtHR.
5   See *Golder v United Kingdom* A 18 (1975), 1 EHRR 524, ECtHR, para 38.
6   *Ashingdane v United Kingdom* A 93 (1985), 7 EHRR 528, ECtHR, para 57 (proceedings by mental patient challenging Secretary of State's decision under statute to continue to detain him; no liability for acts done under the statute unless there was lack of reasonable care or bad faith: no violation of the applicant's right of effective access to a court, because the limitation of liability under the statute served a legitimate aim (ie preventing those who care for mental patients from being unfairly harassed by litigation), the essence of the right was not impaired and the restrictions were consistent with the principle of proportionality in that it was possible for the applicant to claim bad faith or absence of reasonable care). See also *Fayeds v United Kingdom* A 294-B (1994), 18 EHRR 393, ECtHR.
7   Application 11559/85 *H v United Kingdom* 45 DR 281 (1985), EComHR.
8   *Golder v United Kingdom* A 18 (1975), 1 EHRR 524, ECtHR.
9   Application 12040/86 *M v United Kingdom* 52 DR 269 (1987), EComHR.
10  *Campbell and Fell v United Kingdom* A 80 (1984), 7 EHRR 165, ECtHR.
11  Application 10412/83 *P v France* 52 DR 128 (1987), EComHR.
12  Application 9707/82 *X v Sweden* 31 DR 223 (1982), EComHR.
13  Application 17070/90 *Grepne v United Kingdom* 66 DR 268 (1990), EComHR.
14  Application 5076/71 *X v United Kingdom* 40 CD 64 (1972), EComHR.
15  *Fayeds v United Kingdom* A 294-B (1994), 18 EHRR 393, ECtHR (permissible restriction, as it had a legitimate aim, ie to further the public interest in the proper conduct of the affairs of public companies, and was not disproportionate).
16  *Holy Monasteries v Greece* A 301-A (1994), 20 EHRR 1, ECtHR.
17  *Philis v Greece* A 209 (1991), 13 EHRR 741, ECtHR.
18  *Deweer v Belgium* A 35 (1980), 2 EHRR 439, ECtHR, para 49.
19  See *De La Pradelle v France* A 253-B (1992), ECtHR, para 37. The right to an effective remedy is guaranteed by Art 13 of the Convention (see para 163 post). As to civil rights see para 135 ante.

**142. The presumption of innocence.** Everyone charged with a criminal[1] offence must be presumed innocent until proved guilty according to law[2]. The presumption applies until the end of any appeal proceedings against conviction[3]. The guarantee operates in the main at the stage of court proceedings; it does not apply, for example, to practices in the course of a criminal investigation, such as medical examinations[4] or an order to produce documents[5].

The burden of proof must fall upon the prosecution[6], but it may be transferred to the accused when he is seeking to establish a defence[7].

This provision does not prohibit presumptions of fact or law against the accused, although such presumptions must be confined within reasonable limits which take into account the importance of what is at stake and maintain the rights of the defence[8]. Nor does it prohibit offences of strict liability[9]. It does, however, impose certain evidential requirements: a confession obtained as a result of 'maltreatment' must not be admitted in evidence[10], although a confession may be admitted despite the fact that the accused has made it without having been informed of his right to silence[11].

It is a requirement of this provision that the accused be given an opportunity to rebut the evidence presented against him[12].

Although not specifically mentioned as an element of fairness, the right to remain silent under police questioning and the privilege against self-incrimination are international standards which lie at the heart of the notion of fair procedure[13].

1   The term 'criminal' in this context has the same meaning as is discussed in para 136 ante: see *Adolf v Austria* A 49 (1982), 4 EHRR 313, ECtHR.
2   Convention for the Protection of Human Rights and Fundamental Freedoms (1950) Art 6(2). This requires, inter alia, that when carrying out their duties, the members of a court should not start with the preconceived idea that the accused has committed the offence charged...it is for the prosecution to inform the accused of the case that will be made against him, so that he may prepare and present his defence accordingly, and to adduce evidence sufficient to convict him': *Barbera, Messegue and Jabardo v Spain* A 146 (1988), 11 EHRR 360, ECtHR, para 77. As to the Convention for the Protection of Human Rights and Fundamental Freedoms (1950) generally see para 122 ante.
3   *Nolkenbockhoff v Federal Republic of Germany* A 123 (1987), 13 EHRR 360, ECtHR). It does not apply, however, to cases referred to the English Court of Appeal under the Criminal Appeal Act 1968 s 17(1)(a) (as amended) (see CRIMINAL LAW vol 11(2) (Reissue) para 1436): Application 14739/89 *Callaghan v United Kingdom* 60 DR 296 (1989), EComHR.
4   Application 986/61 *X v Federal Republic of Germany* 5 YB 192 (1962), EComHR.
5   *Funke v France* A 256-A (1993), 16 EHRR 297, ECtHR.
6   *Barbera, Messegue and Jabardo v Spain* A 146 (1988), 11 EHRR 360, ECtHR, para 77. See further text and note 13 infra.
7   Application 8803/79 *Lingens v Austria* 26 DR 171 (1981), EComHR (burden of showing truth of statement as defence to criminal defamation proceedings on the defendant).
8   See *Salabiaku v France* A 141-A (1988), 13 EHRR 379, ECtHR, para 28 (no breach of Art 6(2) of the Convention where the actus reus of smuggling prohibited goods presumed from fact of possession of such goods since it was open to the accused under French law to establish force majeure, which he had failed to do); Application 5124/71 *X v United Kingdom* 42 CD 135 (1972), EComHR (rebuttable presumption that accused was living off earnings of prostitute proved to be living with him and under his control).
9   See *Salabiaku v France* A 141-A (1988), 13 EHRR 379, ECtHR, paras 28, 29.
10   *Austria v Italy*, 6 YB 740 at 784 (1963), EComHR.
11   Application 4483/70 *X v Federal Republic of Germany* 38 CD 77 (1971), EComHR.
12   *Austria v Italy*, 6 YB 740 at 784 (1963), EComHR.
13   *Murray v United Kingdom* (1996) 22 EHRR 29, ECtHR, para 45. However, the right to silence is not absolute, and whether the drawing of adverse inferences from the exercise of a right to silence infringes the European Convention on Human Rights Art 6 must be determined in the circumstances of the particular case, having regard to the situations where inferences may be drawn, the weight attached to them by the national courts in their assessment of evidence, and the degree of compulsion inherent in the situation: *Murray v United Kingdom* supra at para 47.
      See also *Funke v France* A 256-A (1993), 16 EHRR 297, ECtHR, at para 44 (applicant's right to silence infringed when he had been convicted of an offence of failing to produce bank statements relevant to investigations into customs offences that might have been committed by him). See also Application 19187/91 *Saunders v United Kingdom* (1994) Com Rep paras 69–75, 18 EHRR CD 23, EComHR (applicant required by law to answer questions, the answers to which were adduced in evidence against him). The freedom from self-incrimination is an important element in safeguarding an accused from oppression and coercion during criminal proceedings, linked to the presumption of innocence guaranteed by Art 6(2) of the Convention: Application 19187/91 *Saunders v United Kingdom* supra at para 72.

**143. Right to be informed of criminal charges.** Everyone charged with a criminal offence[1] has the right to be informed promptly, in a language which he understands[2] and in detail, of the nature and cause of the accusation against him[3].

The accused must be informed of the offence with which he is charged and the material facts upon which the allegation is based[4]. The information should contain the material enabling him to prepare his defence but does not have to mention the evidence on which the charge is based[5]. It should normally be in writing, but this is not necessary if he has been given sufficient information orally or has waived his right to a written communication[6].

1 The term 'criminal' in this context has the same meaning as is discussed in para 136 ante: see *Adolf v Austria* A 49 (1982), 4 EHRR 313, ECtHR.
2 Unless the authorities are able to prove, or have reasonable grounds to believe, that the accused has a sufficient command of the language in which the relevant information is being provided to him, they are obliged to provide him with an appropriate translation: *Brozicek v Italy* A 167 (1989), 12 EHRR 371, ECtHR. It is sufficient if the information is given to the accused's lawyer in a language which the lawyer understands: Application 6185/73 *X v Austria* 2 DR 68 at 71 (1975), EComHR.
3 Convention for the Protection of Human Rights and Fundamental Freedoms (1950) Art 6(3)(a). The purpose of this provision is to give the accused the information he needs to prepare his defence: Application 524/59 *Ofner v Austria* 3 YB 322 at 344 (1960), EComHR. Cf Art 5(2) (see para 127 ante) which provides a similar guarantee for persons detained pending trial, but note that the information required under Art 6(3)(a) is more specific and more detailed: Application 343/57 *Nielsen v Denmark* 2 YB 412 at 462 (1959), EComHR. It is not clear when Art 6(3)(a) begins to apply: in a civil law system it is at the latest when the accused is indicted: *Kamasinski v Austria* A 168 (1989), 13 EHRR 36, ECtHR, paras 78–81. As to the Convention for the Protection of Human Rights and Fundamental Freedoms (1950) generally see para 122 ante.
4 Application 524/59 *Ofner v Austria* 3 YB 322 at 344 (1960), EComHR.
5 Application 7628/76 *X v Belgium* 9 DR 169 at 173 (1977), EComHR. Cf *Brozicek v Italy* A 167 (1989), 12 EHRR 371, ECtHR, para 42 (sufficient that the information listed the offences, stated the place and date thereof, referred to the relevant Article of the Criminal Code and mentioned the name of the victim).
6 *Kamasinski v Austria* A 168 (1989), 13 EHRR 36, ECtHR, paras 79–81.

**144. Right to adequate time and facilities.** Everyone charged with a criminal offence[1] has the right to have adequate time and facilities for the preparation of his defence[2]. The right applies from the time when a person is charged with a criminal offence[3].

The adequacy of the time allowed depends on the facts, taking into account factors such as: the stage of proceedings[4]; the complexity of the case[5]; and the workload of the defence lawyer[6]. The accused must be allowed to appoint his own lawyer in good time before the hearing[7], and if a lawyer is replaced for good reason, additional time must be allowed[8].

The right to adequate facilities entails, in particular, a right for the accused to communicate with his lawyer to the extent necessary to prepare his defence or appeal[9]. A prisoner must be permitted a visit from his lawyer out of the hearing of prison officers and other officials in order to communicate with his lawyer in relation to the preparation of his defence[10]. Restrictions on visits by lawyers may be imposed only if they can be justified in the public interest, for example to prevent the obstruction of justice[11]. An accused must have a right to acquaint himself, for the purposes of preparing his defence, with the results of investigations carried out throughout the proceedings[12].

To establish a breach of this provision it is necessary to show actual prejudice to the accused[13]. Time restrictions placed on the submissions of a defence lawyer might constitute a breach[14].

If there is a right of appeal against the trial decision, the Convention for the Protection of Human Rights and Fundamental Freedoms (1950) applies to guarantee adequate time and facilities to prepare the appeal[15].

1 The term 'criminal' in this context has the same meaning as is discussed in para 136 ante: see *Adolf v Austria* A 49 (1982), 4 EHRR 313, ECtHR.

2 Convention for the Protection of Human Rights and Fundamental Freedoms (1950) Art 6(3)(b). The purpose of this provision is to protect the accused against a hasty trial (Application 8463/78 *Krocher and Moller v Switzerland* 26 DR 24 at 53 (1981), EComHR); and to ensure that the accused has 'the opportunity to organise his defence in an appropriate way and without restrictions as to the possibility to put all relevant defence arguments before the trial court' (*Can v Austria* A 96 (1985), Com Rep paras 53–58). The protection afforded by Art 6(3)(b) extends also to other facilities, such as being granted an adjournment: see Application 6404/73 *X v United Kingdom* 2 Digest 895 (1975), EComHR). As to the Convention for the Protection of Human Rights and Fundamental Freedoms (1950) generally see para 122 ante.

3 Application 7909/74 *X and Y v Austria* 15 DR 160 (1978), EComHR.

4 Application 5523/72 *Huber v Austria* 46 CD 99 (1974), EComHR.

5 *Albert and Le Compte v Belgium* A 58 (1983), 5 EHRR 533, ECtHR.

6 Application 7909, *X Y Z v Austria* 15 DR 160 (1978), EComHR.

7 Application 11022/84 *Perez Mahia v Spain* 9 EHRR 145 (1986), EComHR.

8 *Goddi v Italy* A 76 (1984), 6 EHRR 457, ECtHR.

9 See eg *Goddi v Italy* A 76 (1984), 6 EHRR 457, ECtHR; *Can v Austria* A 96 (1985), Com Rep.

10 *Can v Austria* A 96 (1985), Com Rep.

11 *Can v Austria* A 96 (1985), Com Rep. A refusal to permit a prisoner to take his notes and annotated documents to a meeting with his lawyer was found to have involved no breach of Art 6(3)(b): Application 1850/63 *Koplinger v Austria* 12 YB 438 at 494 (1969), EComHR.

12 Application 8403/78 *Jespers v Belgium* 27 DR 61 at 87 (1984), EComHR. Cf *Edwards v United Kingdom* A 247-B (1992), 15 EHRR 417, ECtHR.

13 Application 4042/69 *X v United Kingdom* 13 YB 690 at 696 (1970), EComHR (no breach of Art 6(3)(b) where legally-aided applicant had met his barrister only ten minutes before a trial that led to a sentence of seven years' imprisonment). Seventeen days' notice of the hearing was held to be sufficient in a 'fairly complex' case of theft: Application 7909/74 *X and Y v Austria* 15 DR 160 at 162 (1978), EComHR.

14 Application 7085/75 *X v Federal Republic of Germany* 2 Digest 809 (1976), EComHR.

15 See eg *Hadjianastassiou v Greece* A 252 (1992), 16 EHRR 219, ECtHR.

**145. Right to defend or to have legal assistance.** Everyone charged with a criminal offence[1] has the right to defend himself in person or through legal assistance[2] of his own choosing or, if he has not sufficient means to pay for legal assistance, to be given it free when the interests of justice so require[3]. This right extends to the pre-trial stage[4], and generally to appeal proceedings[5], but not to remand proceedings[6].

The right is to effective legal assistance, not merely to the nomination of a lawyer[7]. The competent national authorities are only required to intervene, however, if a failure to provide effective representation is manifest or sufficiently brought to their attention[8].

The right of an accused to defend himself in person does not mean that the accused has a completely free choice in this regard: the state may require that an accused be assisted by a lawyer at trial in the interests of justice[9], and that an accused be assisted on appeal[10]. An accused who lawfully elects to defend himself in person, having thereby waived his right to legal representation, is under a duty to show diligence, and there is accordingly no breach of the Convention for the Protection of Human Rights and Fundamental Freedoms (1950) by the state where there is a deficiency in the proceedings resulting from some lack of diligence on the part of the accused[11].

Where the accused is represented by a lawyer, the state may appoint a second lawyer contrary to the wishes of the accused, provided that there is relevant and sufficient justification for doing so[12]. Where an accused is legally represented, he also has a right to be present at the trial[13]. If the accused is not present at the hearing, he is nevertheless entitled to be legally represented[14].

Where the accused chooses to be legally represented by a lawyer for whom he will pay, his choice of lawyer is not absolute: regulation of the qualifications and conduct of lawyers is permissible. Thus a lawyer may, for example, be excluded for refusing to wear robes[15], or for failing to comply with professional ethics[16]. As a general rule, however, the accused's choice of lawyer should be respected[17], although it is permissible to restrict the number of lawyers representing an accused, provided that the defence is able to present its case on an equal footing with the prosecution[18].

The right to effective legal assistance includes a right of private access to a lawyer, both prior to and at the trial[19]. There will be a breach of the right if the state fails to notify an accused's lawyer of a hearing, with the result that the accused is not represented at it[20].

The onus is on the accused who seeks to establish a breach of the right to free legal assistance to show that he lacks the means to pay for his own representation[21]. Where legal aid is granted, it may still be permissible for the state to require the accused upon conviction to pay the costs of the free assistance he has had if he then has the necessary means to do so[22]. The question when the interests of justice require that legal aid should be available should be judged by reference to the facts of the case as a whole, including facts that may materialise after the competent national authority has taken its decision[23].

An accused has no right to be involved in the appointment[24] or functioning[25] of a lawyer representing him on legal aid.

1    The term 'criminal' in this context has the same meaning as is discussed in para 136 ante: see *Adolf v Austria* A 49 (1982), 4 EHRR 313, ECtHR.
2    The state does not have to take the initiative to ensure that an accused's lawyer is present during pre-trial questioning, although if the accused (or his lawyer) requests that the lawyer be present, the provision described in the text probably requires that this is allowed, if there is a risk that the information obtained during questioning will prejudice the defence: *S v Switzerland* A 220 (1991), 14 EHRR 670, ECtHR.
     There is a need to 'ensure the most cost-effective use of the funds available for legal aid', and it may be permissible, therefore, to limit the cost of legally-aided representation: Application 9728/82 *M v United Kingdom* 36 DR 155 at 158 (1983), EComHR. Cf the position in civil cases, where it has been held that legal aid must be provided pursuant to the Convention for the Protection of Human Rights and Fundamental Freedoms (1950) Art 6(1) regardless of economic cost: *Airey v Ireland* A 32 (1979), 2 EHRR 305, ECtHR. As to the Convention for the Protection of Human Rights and Fundamental Freedoms (1950) generally see para 122 ante.
3    Ibid Art 6(3)(c). The purpose of this provision is to ensure that proceedings do not take place without adequate representation of the defence case (*Pakelli v Federal Republic of Germany* A 64 (1983), 6 EHRR 1, ECtHR); and that the accused is placed 'in a position to put his case in such a way that he is not at a disadvantage vis-a-vis the prosecution' Application 10098/82 *X v Federal Republic of Germany* (1984) 8 EHRR 225, EComHR. It follows that the state is not able to require an accused to defend himself in person; Art 6(3)(c) guarantees a right to legal assistance through the accused's own lawyer or, subject to certain conditions, through legal aid: see *Pakelli v Federal Republic of Germany* supra; *Poitrimol v France* A 277-A (1993), 18 EHRR 130, ECtHR, para 34. See also *Benham v United Kingdom* (1996) Times, 24 June, ECtHR.
     Article 6(3)(c) prohibits an interference with the rights set out in it: see *Brandstetter v Austria* A 211 (1991), 15 EHRR 378, ECtHR, para 51 (accused alleged to have made false statements at his trial for an offence, subsequently prosecuted for defamation on the basis of those statements: no violation on the facts, but 'the position might be different if it were established that, as a consequence of national law or practice in this respect being unduly severe, the risk of subsequent prosecution is such that the defendant is genuinely inhibited from freely exercising his right to defend himself (para 53)).
4    *Quaranta v Switzerland* A 205 (1991), ECtHR (accused entitled to the assistance of legal aid lawyer in relation to his appearances before investigating judge, as well as at trial); *S v Switzerland* A 220 (1991), 14 EHRR 670, ECtHR (right of private access to lawyer at pre-trial stage).
5    The requirements may vary depending on the special features of the appeal proceedings in question and their role in the case as a whole: see eg *Monnell and Morris v United Kingdom* A 115 (1987), 10 EHRR 205, ECtHR (Art 6(3)(c) does not guarantee oral hearing for leave to appeal before the Court of Appeal: it is sufficient that the applicant canto present written submissions).
6    Application 10868/84 *Woukam Moudefo v France* 51 DR 62 (1987), EComHR.
7    *Artico v Italy* A 37 (1980), 3 EHRR 1, ECtHR (legal aid lawyer appointed to act, but never in fact acted, claiming other professional commitments and ill health, and the Court of Cassation refused to appoint another lawyer).
8    *Kamasinksi v Austria* A 168 (1989), 13 EHRR 36, ECtHR, para 65.
9    *Croissant v Germany* A 237-B (1992), 16 EHRR 135, ECtHR.

10  Application 16598/90 *Philis v Greece* 66 DR 260 (1990), EComHR.
11  See *Melin v France* A 261-A (1993), 17 EHRR 1, ECtHR, para 25.
12  *Croissant v Germany* A 237-B (1992), 16 EHRR 135, ECtHR, para 27.
13  *FCB v Italy* A 208-B (1991), 14 EHRR 909, ECtHR. Cf the guarantee of an oral hearing in one's presence in Art 6(1) of the Convention (see para 137 ante).
14  *Campbell and Fell v United Kingdom* A 80 (1984), 7 EHRR 165, ECtHR; *Lala v Netherlands* A 297-A (1994), 18 EHRR 586, ECtHR, para 33 (although accused should be present at his trial, the fact that he does not appear, even in the absence of an excuse, cannot justify depriving him of his right to be legally represented).
15  Applications 5217/71 and 5367/72 *X and Y v Federal Republic of Germany* 42 CD 139 (1972), EComHR.
16  Applications 7572/76, 7586/76 and 7587/76 *Ensslin, Baader and Raspe v Federal Republic of Germany* 14 DR 64 (1978), EComHR.
17  *Goddi v Italy* A 76 (1984), 6 EHRR 457, ECtHR.
18  Applications 7572/76, 7586/76 and 7587/76 *Ensslin, Baader and Raspe v Federal Republic of Germany* 14 DR 64 (1978), EComHR, at 114.
19  See *S v Switzerland* A 220 (1991), 14 EHRR 670, ECtHR. This right may be subject to restrictions in the public interest. Cf the right of the accused to adequate facilities to prepare his defence (see para 144 ante).
20  See *Goddi v Italy* A 76 (1984), 6 EHRR 457, ECtHR.
21  See eg *Pakelli v Federal Republic of Germany* A 64 (1983), 6 EHRR 1, ECtHR, para 34. There are no decisions indicating what are sufficient means for this purpose.
22  *Croissant v Germany* A 237-B (1992), 16 EHRR 135, Com Rep para 33.
23  See eg *Granger v United Kingdom* A 174 (1990), 12 EHRR 469, ECtHR. Factors to be taken into account are: the complexity of the case (*Granger v United Kingdom* supra; *Quaranta v Switzerland* A 205 (1991), ECtHR); the accused's ability to make a contribution to his defence (*Granger v United Kingdom* supra; *Quaranta v Switzerland* supra); and the seriousness of the offence with which the accused is charged and the severity of the possible sentence that might result (*Boner v United Kingdom* A 300-B (1994), 19 EHRR 246, ECtHR, para 41; *Quaranta v Switzerland* supra).
    The interests of justice will require legal aid to be granted on appeal where the accused has a right of appeal under national law, even if his chances of succeeding on the appeal are slim see *Boner v United Kingdom* supra.
    The test for the 'interests of justice' requirement is not whether in the absence of legal aid there has been 'actual prejudice' to the presentation of the accused's defence, but rather whether 'it appears plausible in the particular circumstances' that a lawyer would be of assistance: *Artico v Italy* A 37 (1980), 3 EHRR 1, ECtHR, para 35.
24  Eg Application 646/59 *X v Federal Republic of Germany* 3 YB 273 (1960), EComHR.
25  Eg Application 8386/78 *X v United Kingdom* 21 DR 126 (1980), EComHR.

**146. Right to examine witnesses.** Everyone charged with a criminal offence[1] has the right to examine or have examined witnesses[2] against him and to obtain the attendance and examination of witnesses on his behalf under the same conditions as witnesses against him[3]. This right does not apply at the pre-trial stage. It does not, for example, provide a right to cross-examine witnesses prior to trial[4], or a witness being questioned by the police[5]; nor does it oblige an investigating judge to hear a defence witness, provided the witness may be called at trial[6]. The right to cross-examine and call witnesses is not absolute, but any limits on the right must be consistent with the principle of equality of arms[7].

It is not necessarily inconsistent the Convention for the Protection of Human Rights and Fundamental Freedoms (1950) for certain witnesses to be excused from giving oral evidence. It has been held, for example, that a police informer need not be called as a witness[8], and that a member of the accused's family may be excused from giving evidence in recognition of a conflict of interest[9]. There will, however, be a breach of the Convention if a statement by a person not called as a witness at trial is admitted in evidence without the accused having had an opportunity to confront him during the preceding investigation, at least where the statement is the only or main evidence against him[10].

It is generally for the national courts to assess whether it is appropriate to call witnesses, although the court must give reasons for any decision not to hear a witness which the accused has requested should be heard[11]. Where witnesses are properly called by the defence, the court must take appropriate steps to ensure their attendance at trial[12]. There is no breach of the Convention, however, where the accused's counsel fails to call a particular witness[13].

Although in principle an accused should be present when witnesses are being heard in a case against him, the interests of justice may permit an exception to this principle to ensure that the witness is not intimidated and gives an unreserved statement, provided that the accused's lawyer is permitted to remain and to cross-examine the witness[14].

1   The term 'criminal' in this context has the same meaning as is discussed in para 136 ante: see *Adolf v Austria* A 49 (1982), 4 EHRR 313, ECtHR.
2   'Witness' has an autonomous meaning under the Convention for the Protection of Human Rights and Fundamental Freedoms (1950), and includes expert witnesses, whether called by the prosecution or the defence or appointed by the court: see eg *Brandsetter v Austria* A 211 (1991), 15 EHRR 378, ECtHR. A person who does not give oral evidence but provides a statement before the court is a witness for these purposes: *Kostovski v Netherlands* A 166 (1989), 12 EHRR 434, ECtHR, para 40. As to the Convention generally see para 122 ante.
3   Convention for the Protection of Human Rights and Fundamental Freedoms (1950) Art 6(3)(d).
4   Application 9627/81 *Ferrari-Bravo v Italy* 37 DR 15 (1984), EComHR.
5   Application 8414/78 *X v Federal Republic of Germany* 17 DR 231 (1979), EComHR.
6   Application 8339/78 *Schertenleib v Switzerland* 17 DR 180 at 255 (1979), EComHR.
7   *Engel v Netherlands* A 22 (1976), 1 EHRR 647, ECtHR, para 91. As to the principle of 'equality of arms' see para 137 note 10 ante.
8   *Kostovski v Netherlands* A 166 (1989), 12 EHRR 434, ECtHR.
9   *Unterpertinger v Austria* A 110 (1986), 13 EHRR 175, ECtHR.
10  See para 137 note 15 ante.
11  *Vidal v Belgium* A 235-B (1992), ECtHR paras 33–34.
12  Application 3566/68 *X v Federal Republic of Germany* 31 CD 31 (1969), EComHR.
13  Application 18123/91 *F v United Kingdom* (1992) 15 EHRR CD32, EComHR.
14  Application 11219/84 *Kurup v Denmark* 42 DR 287 at 292 (1985), EComHR.

**147. Right to an interpreter.** Everyone charged with a criminal offence[1] has the right to have the free assistance of an interpreter if he cannot understand or speak the language used in court[2].

The obligation to provide the free assistance of an interpreter cannot be restricted. It does not depend on the accused's means, and the accused cannot be made to pay the cost of the interpreter if he is convicted[3]. 'Assistance' may include translations of documents, but need not include all items of written evidence or official documents, only those which are necessary to ensure a fair trial[4]. It is not essential for the accused to be provided with a written translation of the indictment, or of the judgment[5].

It may be that the Convention for the Protection of Human Rights and Fundamental Freedoms (1950) requires an interpreter to be provided where the accused's lawyer can speak the language used in court, and for communications between the accused and his lawyer[6]. There may in certain circumstances be an obligation to exercise a degree of control over the adequacy of the interpretation provided[7].

The right to an interpreter may be waived[8].

The Convention does not guarantee an accused the right to an interpreter to conduct his defence in a language of his choice, including the language of an ethnic minority of which he is a member, if he understands the language used in court[9].

1   The term 'criminal' in this context has the same meaning as is discussed in para 136 ante: see *Adolf v Austria* A 49 (1982), 4 EHRR 313, ECtHR.
2   Convention for the Protection of Human Rights and Fundamental Freedoms (1950) Art 6(3)(e). This right applies as soon as a person is charged with a criminal offence, and continues to apply during any appeal proceedings. See eg *Kamasinski v Austria* A 168 (1989), 13 EHRR 36, ECtHR, para 74 (Convention required an interpreter to be present during police questioning and in the course of the

preliminary investigation into the case). As to the Convention for the Protection of Human Rights and Fundamental Freedoms (1950) generally see para 122 ante.

3   See *Luedicke Belkacem and Koc v Federal Republic of Germany* A 29 (1978), 2 EHRR 149, ECtHR, para 46.
4   *Kamasinski v Austria* A 168 (1989), 13 EHRR 36, ECtHR, para 74.
5   *Kamasinski v Austria* A 168 (1989), 13 EHRR 36, ECtHR, para 74.
6   See *Kamasinski v Austria* A 168 (1989), 13 EHRR 36, ECtHR, para 74 (Art 6(3)(e) extends to all 'statements...which it is necessary for [the accused] to understand in order to have a fair trial'.
7   See *Kamasinski v Austria* A 168 (1989), 13 EHRR 36, ECtHR, para 74.
8   See *Kamasinski v Austria* A 168 (1989), 13 EHRR 36, ECtHR, para 80.
9   Application 10210/82 *K v France* 35 DR 203 at 207 (1983), EComHR.

## C. PROHIBITION OF RETROSPECTIVE LAWS

**148. Prohibition of retrospective laws.** No one may be held guilty of any criminal offence on account of any act or omission which did not constitute a criminal offence under national or international law at the time when it was committed[1]; nor may a heavier penalty[2] be imposed than the one which was applicable at the time the criminal offence was committed[3]. This does not, however, prejudice the trial and punishment of a person for an act or omission which, when it was committed, was criminal according to the general principles of laws recognised by civilised nations[4].

The provision does not apply to the determination of civil rights[5], regulations and conditions governing release from prison on probation[6], deportation orders[7], decisions to extradite[8], preventive measures of detention[9], the entry of past convictions on a person's record[10], or disciplinary offences[11]. It is unclear whether it applies to the detention in a mental institution of a person convicted of a criminal offence[12].

The provision is not confined to prohibiting the restrospective application of the criminal law to the disadvantage of the accused. It also embodies the principle *nullum crimen, nulla poena sine lege*[13], and the principle that the criminal law must not be extensively construed to the detriment of the accused, for instance by analogy. An offence must be clearly defined in law so that an individual may foresee the legal consequences of his actions[14].

1   Convention for the Protection of Human Rights and Fundamental Freedoms (1950) Art 7(1). This does not distinguish between acts or omissions which no longer constitute a criminal offence, and acts or omissions which do not yet constitute a criminal offence. A person cannot be held guilty under an obsolete law if the acts of which he is accused were performed after the abrogation of the law. The European Commission of Human Rights may investigate in order to satisfy itself that domestic courts are not continuing to apply an abrogated law: Application 1169/61 *D v Federal Republic of Germany* 6 YB 520 (1963), EComHR. Cf the Universal Declaration of Human Rights (Paris, 10 December 1948), Art 11 para 1. As to the Convention for the Protection of Human Rights and Fundamental Freedoms (1950) generally see para 122 ante. As to the Universal Declaration of Human Rights see para 122 note 1 ante.
      Under Art 7 of the Convention the supervisory jurisdiction of the European Commission of Human Rights consists in making sure that, at the moment when the accused performed the act which led to prosecution, there was in force a legal provision whch made that act punishable, that the punishment imposed does not exceed the limits fixed by that provision, and that the national court did not act unreasonably in interpreting municipal law and applying it to the applicant: Application 4681/70 *Murphy v United Kingdom* 43 CD 1 (1972), EComHR. This supervisory function is undertaken by the Commission with caution: Application 1852/63 *v Austria* 8 YB 190 (1965), EComHR; Application 1169/61 *D v Federal Republic of Germany* supra.
2   The European Court of Human Rights is free to assess for itself whether a particular measure amounts to a penalty: *Welch v United Kingdom* A 307 (1995), ECtHR, para 27; *Jamil v France* A 320 (1995) ECtHR, para 30. The starting point in any assessment of the existence of a 'penalty' is whether the measure in question is imposed following conviction for a criminal offence. Other factors that may be taken into account are the nature and purpose of the measure in question; its characterisation under national law; the procedures involved in the making and implementation of the measure; and its severity: *Welch v United Kingdom* supra at paras 28–29 (confiscation order under the Drug

Trafficking Offences Act 1986 was a penalty, and its retrospective imposition on the applicant was accordingly a violation of Art 7(1) of the Convention); *Jamil v France* supra at para 31 (imprisonment in default of payment of customs fine was a penalty; retrospective increase in maximum period of imprisonment in default violated Art 7(1), since the penalty was ordered by a criminal court, was intended to be a deterrent and could have led to a punitive deprivation of liberty). See also *Engel v Netherlands* A 22 (1976), 1 EHRR 647, ECtHR, para 82; *Ozturk v Germany* A 73 (1984), 6 EHRR 409, ECtHR, para 53.

More lenient criminal legislation may be applied retroactively, but an offender has no right to be sentenced in accordance with a law passed after the offence was committed, being a law which is more lenient than the law then in force: Application 3777/68 *X v United Kingdom* 31 CD 120 (1969), EComHR; Application 7900/77 *X v Federal Republic of Germany* 13 DR 70 (1978), EComHR.

3    Convention for the Protection of Human Rights and Fundamental Freedoms (1950) Art 7(1).

See *Waddington v Miah* [1974] 2 All ER 377, [1974] 1 WLR 683, HL (offences under the Immigration Act 1971 were not retrospective), particularly at 379, 694 per Lord Reid: 'it is hardly credible that any government department would promote or that Parliament would pass retrospective criminal legislation'. When the Republic of Ireland alleged that the Northern Ireland Act 1972 violated Art 7 of the Convention in that it permitted retrospective prosecutions, the Attorney General undertook to the Commission that no one would be held guilty of any criminal offence under the Act which was not an offence at the date it was committed. The application was accordingly withdrawn: Applications 5310/71 and 5451/72 *Ireland v United Kingdom* 15 YB 76 (1972), EComHR.

4    Convention for the Protection of Human Rights and Fundamental Freedoms (1950) Art 7(2). This provision makes it clear that Art 7 does not affect laws passed at the end of the Second World War to punish war crimes, treason, and collaboration with the enemy: see Application 268/57 *X v Belgium* 1 YB 239 (1957), EComHR; Application 214/56 *De Becker v Belgium* 2 YB 214 (1958), EComHR; Application 1063/61 *X v Federal Republic of Germany* 4 YB 324 (1961), EComHR.

5    Application 8988/80 *X v Belgium* 24 DR 198 (1981), EComHR (adjudication of bankruptcy in commercial court was not 'criminal' for this purpose). Quaere whether civil contempt of court is 'criminal' for the purposes of Art 7 of the Convention: Application 10038/82 *Harman v United Kingdom* 38 DR 53 (1984), FSett.

6    Application 1760/63 *X v Austria* 9 YB 166 at 175 (1966), EComHR; Application 11653/85 *Hogben v United Kingdom* 45 DR 231 (1986), EComHR (stricter parole policy raised no issue under Art 7 of the Convention, because it concerned the execution of a sentence and not the imposition of a penalty).

7    *Moustaquim v Belgium* A 193 (1991), 13 EHRR 802, ECtHR.

8    Application 7512/76 *X v Netherlands* 6 DR 184 (1976), EComHR.

9    *Lawless v Ireland (Merits)* A 3 (1961), ECtHR (preventive detention of suspected terrorist raised no issue under Art 7 of the Convention, because he was not detained as a result of conviction on a criminal charge, and his detention was not a penalty); *De Wilde, Ooms and Versyp v Belgium* A 12 (1971), 1 EHRR 373, ECtHR (detention for vagrancy raised no issue under Art 7 of the Convention because vagrancy is not an offence under Belgian law, and the magistrates did not find applicants guilty or impose a penalty upon them); Application 9167/80 *X v Austria* 26 DR 248 (1981), EComHR (detention of applicant in institution for recidivists did not constitute a penalty within Art 7 of the Convention, because its purpose was preventive and not punitive).

10   Application 448/59 *X v Federal Republic of Germany* 3 YB 254 (1960), EComHR.

11   *Application 4519/70, X v Luxembourg* 14 YB 616 (1971), EComHR; Application 4274/69 *X v Federal Republic of Germany* 13 YB 888 (1970), EComHR. But see *Engel v Netherlands* A 22 (1976), 1 EHRR 647, ECtHR, for the distinction between disciplinary and criminal proceedings.

12   Application 10448/83 *Dhoest v Belgium* 55 DR 5 (1987), EComHR.

13   Ie there can be no crime or punishment without the law.

14   *Kokkinakis v Greece* A 260-A (1993), 17 EHRR 397, ECtHR, para 52 (offence is clearly defined where an individual can to a reasonable degree foresee from the wording of the relevant provision and, if need be, with the assistance of the courts' interpretation of it and with the benefit of legal advice, what acts and omissions will make him liable). See also Application 5493/72 *Handyside v United Kingdom* 17 YB 228 (1974), EComHR (ambit of 'obscenity' under the Obscene Publications Acts 1959 and 1964); Application 8710/79 *X Ltd and Y v United Kingdom* 28 DR 77 (1982), EComHR (prosecution for blasphemous libel); *Sunday Times v United Kingdom* A 30 (1979), 2 EHRR 245, ECtHR (in the context of Art 10 of the Convention (see paras 158–159 post)); *S W v United Kingdom* [1996] 1 FLR 434, ECtHR; and *C R v United Kingdom* [1996] 1 FLR 434, ECtHR; and Application 17862/91 *MC v France* (12 April 1995, unreported), EComHR.

Courts may not find that acts previously unpunishable should entail criminal libility, or that existing offences should be extended to cover facts which previously clearly did not constitute an offence. The constituent elements of an offence may not be essentially changed to the detriment of the accused. On the other hand, the existing elements of an offence may be clarified and adapted to new circumstances that can reasonably be brought under the original concept of the offence: *X Ltd and Y v United Kingdom* supra at 78–82. See also Application 1852/63 *X v Austria* 8 YB 190 (1965), EComHR; Application 10505/83 *Enkelmann v Switzerland* 41 DR 178 (1985), EComHR; Application 11130/84 *Gerlach v Federal Republic of Germany* 43 DR 210 (1985), EComHR; and Application 21627/93 *Laskey v United Kingdom* (18 January 1995, unreported), EComHR.

Art 7 of the Convention is not to be read as outlawing the gradual clarification of the rules of criminal liability through judicial interpretation from case to case, provided that the resultant development is consistent with the essence of the offence and could reasonably be foreseen: see *S W v United Kingdom* supra, and *C R v United Kingdom* supra, in which the court held that the basic ingredients of the offence of rape were not altered by the decision in *R v R* [1992] 1 AC 599, [1991] 2 All ER 257, CA; affd [1992] 1 AC 599, [1991] 4 All ER 481, HL, holding that a man could be guilty of raping his wife. The law had evolved progressively, and judicial recognition of the absence of a husband's immunity from prosecution for rape of his wife was reasonably foreseeable, with appropriate legal advice. The applicants' respective convictions for the rape and attempted rape of their wives prior to the date of the Court of Appeal judgment accordingly did not violate Art 7(1) of the Convention; the character of rape was so manifest that the decisions in *R v R* supra could not be said to be at variance with the object and purpose of Art 7 of the Convention, namely, to ensure that no one should be subject to arbitrary prosecution, conviction or punishment. The abandonment of the husband's immunity from prosecution for the rape of his wife was itself in conformity with the fundamental objectives of the Convention.

### D. RIGHTS RELATING TO PRIVACY

## 149. Respect for private and family life, home and correspondence.

Everyone has the right to respect[1] for his private[2] and family[3] life, his home[4] and his correspondence[5]. There may be no interference[6] by a public authority with the exercise of this right except such as is in accordance with the law[7] and is necessary in a democratic society[8] in the interests of national security[9], public safety or the economic well-being of the country[10], or for the prevention of disorder or crime[11], for the protection of health or morals[12] or for the protection of the rights[13] and freedoms of others[14].

1 As to what constitutes 'respect' see para 154 post.
2 See para 150 post.
3 See para 151 post.
4 See para 152 post.
5 Convention for the Protection of Human Rights and Fundamental Freedoms (1950) Art 8(1). As to the Convention generally see para 122 ante. As to respect for correspondence see para 153 post.
6 As to what constitutes interference see para 155 post.
7 See *Klass v Federal Republic of Germany* A 28 (1978), 2 EHRR 214, ECtHR (German statute governing surveillance was sufficiently precise, and the procedures for ensuring compliance strict enough to meet the legality requirement of Art 8(2) of the Convention); see also Application No 10628/83 *M S v Switzerland* 44 DR 175 (1985), EComHR. See however, in *Malone v United Kingdom* A 82 (1984), 7 EHRR 14, ECtHR (unpublished administrative practice regulating wiretapping (in the absence of legislative regime) too vague to be 'in accordance with law'). The practice of 'metering' (ie maintaining a register of telephone calls from a particular number), which was also in issue in *Malone v United Kingdom* supra, is not based on any legal rules regulating the scope and manner of the exercise of the discretion enjoyed by public authorities to carry out the practice. A challenge to the United Kingdom statutory regime implemented by the Interception of Communications Act 1985, was declared inadmissible in Application 21482/93 *Christie v United Kingdom* 78-A DR 119 (1994), EComHR. European Community law regulating telephone tapping satisfied the legality requirement: see Application 10439/83 *Mersch v Luxembourg* 43 DR 34 (1985), EComHR. See also *Huvig v France* A 176-B (1990), 12 EHRR 528, ECtHR; and *Kruslin v France* A 176-A (1990), 12 EHRR 547, ECtHR (French statutory provisions and case-law on telephone surveillance failed to meet legality requirement); *Eriksson v Sweden* A 156 (1989), 12 EHRR 183, ECtHR; *Olsson v Sweden (No 2)* A 250 (1992), 17 EHRR 134, ECtHR (conditions imposed by social workers restricting access of parents to children in care had no legal basis and were therefore not in accordance with law); *Silver v United Kingdom* A 61 (1983), 5 EHRR 347, ECtHR (stopping prisoner's correspondence on the

basis of standing orders and circular instructions issued to governors but not accessible to the prisoners was not in accordance with law). See also *Campbell v United Kingdom* A 233 (1992), 15 EHRR 137, ECtHR; and *Hercezegfalvy v Austria* A 244 (1992), 15 EHRR 437, ECtHR.

8    See *Dudgeon v United Kingdom* A 45 (1981), 4 EHRR 149, ECtHR; and *Norris v Ireland* A 142 (1988), 13 EHRR 186, ECtHR; in both cases, the European Court of Human Rights was not satisfied that the criminalisation of homosexual acts in private was necessary in a democratic society; the court required particularly serious reasons to justify interference with private enjoyment of sexual relations. However, in Application 21627/93 *Laskey v United Kingdom* (18 January 1995, unreported), EComHR, convictions for consensual sado-masochistic assaults were considered necessary in a democratic society to protect the health of the participants. As to the national proceedings see *R v Brown* [1994] 1 AC 212, [1993] 2 All ER 75, HL.

The European Court of Human Rights has accorded high importance to privilege between lawyer and client, and the right to communicate with legal advisors in rejecting state arguments seeking to justify interference: see *Golder v United Kingdom* A 18 (1975), 1 EHRR 524, ECtHR (not necessary to refuse to transmit letter from prisoner to his solicitor about the possibility of bringing civil proceedings against a police officer); *Campbell v United Kingdom* A 233 (1992), 15 EHRR 137 (reasonable cause must be shown for suspecting that letter from prisoner contains illicit material before intercepting and opening it); *Niemietz v Germany* A 251-B (1992), 16 EHRR 97, ECtHR (search of premises of lawyer in quest for documents to be used in criminal proceedings was disproportionate to purpose of preventing crime and protecting the 'rights of others').

Execution of an Anton Piller Order in civil proceedings can be justified as being necessary for the protection of rights of others: *Chappell v United Kingdom* A 152 (1989), 12 EHRR 1, ECtHR. See also *Klass v Federal Republic of Germany* A 28 (1978), 2 EHRR 214, ECtHR (government's claim that secret surveillance was justified in the interests of national security and public safety was accepted, with the independent judicial supervision of exercise of powers of surveillance as a check against abuse); see also *Leander v Sweden* A 116 (1987), 9 EHRR 433, ECtHR (need to collect and maintain information in secret dossiers on applicants for public employment in security sensitive areas is not an interference provided that there are adequate and effective safeguards against abuse).

In Application 21780/93 *T V v Finland* 76-A DR 140 (1994), EComHR, disclosure that a prisoner was HIV-positive to the prison staff involved in his custody, and who were themselves the subject of a duty of confidentiality, was justified as being necessary for the 'protection of the rights of others'. The state will be required to provide procedural safeguards against arbitrary treatment as a condition of justifying interference: *W v United Kingdom* A 121 (1987), 10 EHRR 29, ECtHR (exclusion of parents from decisions as to placing children in foster care or for adoption not necessary for the protection of the rights of the child); *Olsson v Sweden (No 1)* A 130 (1988), 11 EHRR 259, ECtHR (positive duty on social workers to involve parents in decisions as to care of children). States do, however, enjoy a wide margin of appreciation in deciding what steps are necessary in ensuring re-union of parents and children and protection of children, and the court has emphasised that national courts are better placed to assess the evidence upon which such decisions are made: *Olsson v Sweden (No 2)* A 250 (1992), 17 EHRR 134, ECtHR; *Andersson (M and R) v Sweden* A 226 (1992), 14 EHRR 615, ECtHR; *Hokkanen v Finland* A 299-A (1994), 19 EHRR 139, ECtHR. See also *Funke v France* A 256-A (1993), 16 EHRR 297, ECtHR (absence of prior judicial authorisation required for search and seizure).

9    See eg *Leander v Sweden* A 116 (1987), 9 EHRR 433, ECtHR.

10   See *Funke v France* A 256-A (1993), 16 EHRR 297, ECtHR (search by customs officials of individual's home pursued legitimate aim under the Convention for the Protection of Human Rights and Fundamental Freedoms (1950) Art 8(2) as being in the interest of the economic well-being of the country, but the scope of the powers of search and seizure was too wide to be proportionate to the legitimate aim pursued); *Berrehab v Netherlands* A 138 (1988), 11 EHRR 322, ECtHR (expulsion of Moroccan citizen following divorce from Dutch wife pursued legitimate aim of protecting the Dutch labour market, but was a disproportionate interference with his family relationship with the child of the marriage). See also Application 14501/89 *A and A v Netherlands* 72 DR 118 (1992), 89 LS Gaz, EComHR; and *Gül v Switzerland* (19 February 1996, unreported), ECtHR.

11   *Campbell and Fell v United Kingdom* A 80 (1984), 7 EHRR 165, ECtHR; *Moustaquim v Belgium* A 193 (1991), 13 EHRR 802, ECtHR; and *Nasri v France* A 322-B (1995), ECtHR; *Beldjoudi v France* A 234-A (1992), 14 EHRR 801, ECtHR. In Application 11278/84 *Family K and W v Netherlands* 43 DR 216 (1985), EComHR, the interference with the family life of a convicted drug trafficker resulting from his expulsion from the Netherlands to Hong Kong was justified on grounds of prevention of crime or disorder; see also Application 16009/90 *X v United Kingdom* [1992] 89 LS Gaz R 35, EComHR. The European Court and Commission of Human Rights have on several occasions rejected as justifiable on grounds of prevention of crime or preservation of public order the deportation of aliens with strong

family ties in the host country: *Moustaquim v Belgium* supra; *Beldjoudi v France* supra; Application 23078/
93 *Bouchelkia v France* EComHR; and *Nasri v France* supra.

12  Taking a child into public care may be justified as being necessary to protect the health and morals of
the child, but failing to allow contact between mother and child for a substantial period was
disproportionate to such legitimate aims and not necessary in a democratic society: *Andersson v Sweden*
A 226 (1992), 14 EHRR 615, ECtHR. See also Application 11526/86 *W v Federal Republic of Germany*
50 DR 219 (1986), EComHR; Application 12523/86 *Gribler v United Kingdom* (1987) 10 EHRR 546,
EComHR; *U and G F v Federal Republic of Germany*, Application 11588/85, 47 DR 259 (1986),
EComHR; *Eriksson v Sweden* A 156 (1989), 12 EHRR 183, ECtHR.

13  *Olsson v Sweden* A 130 (1988), 11 EHRR 259, ECtHR. The compulsory psychiatric examination
of a bankrupt is a justifiable interference with the right to respect for private life when ordered for
the protection of the rights of creditors: Application 10996/84 *Meeder v Netherlands* (1986) 9 EHRR
546, EComHR.

14  Convention for the Protection of Human Rights and Fundamental Freedoms Art 8(2).

**150.  Respect for private life.** The Convention for the Protection of Human Rights
and Fundamental Freedoms (1950) guarantees the right to respect for private life[1]. The
concept of a private life within the Convention is wider than the idea of personal privacy
in common law[2], and is not limited to an 'inner circle' within which an individual may
live his personal life as he chooses, but to include to a certain degree the right to establish
and develop relationships (including sexual relationships) with other human beings,
especially in the emotional field, for the development and fulfilment of one's own
personality[3]. Sexual relations fall within this provision as a most intimate aspect of private
life[4], although some aspects of the right to maintain relationships with others fall under
other articles of the Convention[5]. Private life also covers the physical and moral integrity
of the person[6], encompassing protection against compulsory physical interventions and
treatments[7], against serious pollution[8] or substantial noise nuisance[9], but not against the
compulsory wearing of seat belts[10].

The right to determine one's identity is a fundamental part of private life[11].

The right to respect for private life will be infringed if authorities keep an individual
under surveillance, maintain a record of his financial affairs, tap his telephone, or check
his mail[12]. The collection of information about an individual such as by way of a census[13],
fingerprinting by the police[14], or maintaining medical records[15], amount to an interference
with private life. A complaint of infringement was declared admissible where it was
disclosed that a person was HIV-positive[16]. However, there is no invariable and absolute
right for a person to know that information about him has been collected and retained[17].

It is not an interference with private life to prevent someone from keeping a dog[18], or
to institute a voluntary vaccination system without proper information as to the risks
involved with vaccinations[19].

1   Convention for the Protection of Human Rights and Fundamental Freedoms (1950) Art 8(1) (see para
149 ante). As to the Convention generally see para 122 ante. As to what constitutes respect for the rights
guaranteed by the Convention see para 154 post; as to what amounts to interference with those rights see
para 155 post.

2   As to the right of privacy under English law see para 110 ante.

3   See *Niemietz v Germany* A 251 (1992), 16 EHRR 97, ECtHR, para 29; Application 6825/74 *X v
Iceland* 5 DR 86 (1976), EComHR; Application 8317/78 *McFeeley v United Kingdom* 20 DR 44
(1980), EComHR (respect for private life requiring prisoners to be permitted a degree of association
with others).

4   See *Dudgeon v United Kingdom* A 45 (1981), 4 EHRR 149, ECtHR; *Norris v Ireland* A 142 (1988),
13 EHRR 186, ECtHR; and *Modinos v Cyprus* A 259 (1993), 16 EHRR 485, ECtHR. All these cases
concerned legislation criminalising the activities of homosexual adult men in private and which was
held to violate Art 8 of the Convention. See also, however, Application 21627/93 *Laskey v United
Kingdom* (18 January 1995, unreported), EComHR.

5   Eg the right of freedom of association provided by the Convention for the Protection of Human Rights
and Fundamental Freedoms (1950) Art 11 (see para 161 post), or the right to marry and found a family
provided by Art 12 (see para 162 post).

6    See *X and Y v Netherlands* A 91 (1985), 8 EHRR 235, ECtHR, para 22 (failure of Dutch law to provide for the prosecution by mentally handicapped person of a man for sexual assault amounted to a failure to secure respect for her private life).

7    See Application 8278/78 *X v Austria* 18 DR 154 (1979), EComHR (compulsory blood tests in paternity proceedings); and Application 21132/93 *Peters v Netherlands* 77-A DR 75 (1994), EComHR (compulsory urine tests). However, in *Costello-Roberts v United Kingdom* A 247-C (1993), 19 EHRR 112, ECtHR, the relatively slight nature of the corporal punishment complained of by the applicant, and the fact that it was inflicted in the non-personal context of school discipline, did not entail adverse effects for his physical or moral integrity sufficient to amount to a violation of Art 8 of the Convention.

8    *Lopes-Ostra v Spain* A 303-C (1994), ECtHR.

9    Application 9310/81 *Rayner v United Kingdom* 47 DR 5 (1986), EComHR.

10    Application 8707/79 *X v Belgium* 18 DR 255 (1979), EComHR.

11    *Burghartz and Burghartz v Switzerland* A 280-B (1994), 18 EHRR 101, ECtHR; *Stjerna v Finland* A 299-B (1994), ECtHR; Application 22500/93 *Lassaulet v France*, EComHR. These cases concerned the right to use a name. See also *Gaskin v United Kingdom* A 160 (1989), 12 EHRR 36, ECtHR (applicant was entitled to records relating to his upbringing in foster care as an essential part of his identity); and *Rasmussen v Denmark* A 87 (1984), 7 EHRR 371, ECtHR (determination of parentage).

12    *Klass v Federal Republic of Germany* A 28 (1978), 2 EHRR 214, ECtHR; Application 10439/83 *Mersch v Luxembourg* 43 DR 34 (1985), EComHR; *Malone v United Kingdom* A 82 (1984), 7 EHRR 14, ECtHR; and Application 12175/86 *Hewitt and Harman v United Kingdom* 67 DR 88 (1989), Com Rep. See, however, *Friedl v Austria* A 305-B (1995), 21 EHRR 83, ECtHR (applicant's rights not infringed by reason of being photographed during political demonstration).

13    Application 9702/82 *X v United Kingdom* 30 DR 239 (1982), EComHR.

14    *Murray v United Kingdom* A 300 (1994), 19 EHRR 193, ECtHR.

15    Application 14461/88 *Chare née Jullien v France* 71 DR 141 (1991), EComHR.

16    See Application 22009/93 *Z v Finland*, EcomHR. But cf Application 21780/93 *T V v Finland* 76-A DR 140 (1994), EComHR. As to complaints to the European Commission of Human Rights see para 172 et seq post.

17    See *Leander v Sweden* A 116 (1987), 9 EHRR 433, ECtHR; Application 19404/92 *Williams v United Kingdom* (1992, unreported), EComHR; Application 20317/92 *Hewitt and Harman v United Kingdom* (1993, unreported), EComHR.

18    Application 6825/74 *X v Iceland* 5 DR 86 (1976), EComHR.

19    Application 7154/75 *X v United Kingdom* 14 DR 31 (1978), EComHR.

**151. Respect for family life.** The Convention for the Protection of Human Rights and Fundamental Freedoms (1950) guarantees the right to respect for family life[1].

'Family' has been given a wide interpretation, extending beyond formal relationships created by marriage[2] or between parent and child[3] to include de facto relationships where there is a sufficient personal tie; and also taking into account developments in social and cultural practices[4]. Thus the Convention has been held to cover relationships between siblings[5]; uncle and nephew[6]; grandparents and grandchildren[7]; a couple in a current relationship but not living together[8]; an engaged couple[9]; children and foster parents[10]; a child and his adoptive family[11]; a child and his father after the parents' divorce[12]. Family life will exist between father and child even if the parents have ended their union by the time of the birth, as long as the child was the product of a settled union[13], but a man who donates sperm for the purposes of artificial insemination does not as a result of that fact alone have a right to respect for family life with the child, including access rights[14]. In order for family life to continue as a child grows older, a continuing relationship between parent and child is necessary[15].

Homosexual unions are not recognised as entitled to protection under the guarantee of respect for family life, but may be protected as part of private life[16].

Respect for family life includes taking measures for uniting a family[17], but a refusal to grant citizenship to an applicant's children when there is no actual separation of the parent and the children is not a violation of the right to family life[18]. It requires states to implement fair procedures for the determination of matters affecting the integrity of the family unit, including the right of parents to take part in the decision-making process[19].

The exercise of parental rights over children is a fundamental part of family life[20]. Undue delay in determining access proceedings potentially violates the Convention[21].

The right to a respect for family life does not guarantee to a father the right to be consulted as to whether a mother should have an abortion[22]. Nor does it confer a right to establish a family in any particular jurisdiction[23], or a positive right to formal termination of family life or divorce[24]. It does not require a state to make national laws enabling each family to have a home[25].

1   Convention for the Protection of Human Rights and Fundamental Freedoms (1950) Art 8(1) (see para 149 ante). As to the Convention generally see para 122 ante. As to what constitutes respect for the rights guaranteed by the Convention see para 154 post; as to what amounts to interference with those rights see para 155 post.
2   As to polygamous marriages see Application 2991/66 *Alam and Khan v United Kingdom* 10 YB 478 (1967), EComHR; Application 14501/89 *A and A v Netherlands* 72 DR 118 (1992), 89 LS Gaz, EComHR.
3   It is not necessary that a child be legitimate for family life to exist: see *Marckx v Belgium* A 31 (1979), 2 EHRR 330, ECtHR; *Johnston v Ireland* A 112 (1986), 9 EHRR 203, ECtHR.
4   See *Marckx v Belgium* A 31 (1979), 2 EHRR 330, ECtHR; and *Johnston v Ireland* A 112 (1986), 9 EHRR 203, ECtHR.
5   *Moustaquim v Belgium* A 193 (1991), 13 EHRR 802, ECtHR.
6   *Boyle v United Kingdom* A 282-B (1994), Com Rep.
7   *Marckx v Belgium* A 31 (1979), 2 EHRR 330, ECtHR.
8   *Kroon v Netherlands* A 297-C (1994), 19 EHRR 263, ECtHR.
9   Application 15817/89 *Wakefield v United Kingdom* 66 DR 251 (1990), EComHR.
10  *Gaskin v United Kingdom* A 160 (1989), 12 EHRR 36, ECtHR; the court noted, however (at para 49) that the content of family life may depend on the nature of the fostering arrangements.
11  Application 9993/82 *X v France* 31 DR 241 (1982), EComHR.
12  *Berrehab v Netherlands* A 138 (1988), 11 EHRR 322, ECtHR: the absence between father and mother of a relationship which could be called family life for the purposes of the Convention did not mean that family life could not continue between the absent parent and the child.
13  *Keegan v Ireland* A 290 (1994), 18 EHRR 342, ECtHR; *Gül v Switzerland* (19 February 1996, unreported), ECtHR.
14  Application 16944/90 *G v Netherlands* (1993) 16 EHRR CD 38, EComHR.
15  *Berrehab v Netherlands* A 138 (1988), 11 EHRR 322, ECtHR; Application 2992/66 *Singh v United Kingdom* 10 YB 478 (1967), EComHR.
16  Application 11716/85 *S v United Kingdom* 47 DR 272 (1986), EComHR; Application 16106/90 *B v United Kingdom* 64 DR 278 (1990), EComHR.
17  *Andersson v Sweden* A 226 (1992), 14 EHRR 615, ECtHR.
18  Application 5302/71 *X and Y v United Kingdom* 44 CD 29 (1974), EComHR.
19  *W, B and R v United Kingdom* A 121-C (1987), 10 EHRR 29, 87, 74, ECtHR; *Olsson v Sweden* A 130 (1988), 11 EHRR 259, ECtHR.
20  *Nielsen v Denmark* A 144 (1988), 11 EHRR 175, ECtHR. Note that under English law, the concept of 'parental responsibility' has replaced that of 'parental rights': see generally the Children Act 1989; and CHILDREN vol 5(2) (Reissue) para 729 et seq.
21  *H v United Kingdom* A 120 (1987), 10 EHRR 95, ECtHR; and see *O v United Kingdom* A 120 (1987), 10 EHRR 82, ECtHR.
22  Application 8416/78 *X v United Kingdom* 19 DR 244 (1980), EComHR.
23  *Abdulaziz, Cabales and Balkandali v United Kingdom* A 94 (1985), 7 EHRR 471, ECtHR; Application 14112/88 *X v United Kingdom* [1989] 86 LS Gaz R 45, EComHR; *Cruz Varas v Sweden* A 201 (1991), 14 EHRR 1, ECtHR; *Gül v Switzerland* (19 February 1996, unreported), ECtHR.
24  *Johnston v Ireland* A 112 (1986), 9 EHRR 203, ECtHR; see, however, *Airey v Ireland* A 32 (1979), 2 EHRR 305, ECtHR.
25  *Barreto v Portugal* A 334 (1992), ECtHR.

**152. Respect for home.** The Convention for the Protection of Human Rights and Fundamental Freedoms (1950) guarantees the right to respect for the home[1].

The home may extend in certain cicumstances to professional business premises[2]. It need not in every case be the place where a person is actually living[3]. The right to respect for one's home does not involve a positive right to a home[4]. It is a right to occupy and not to be expelled or evicted[5], and a compulsory purchase order may interfere with this right[6]. It includes the right to peaceful enjoyment of the home[7].

1 Convention for the Protection of Human Rights and Fundamental Freedoms (1950) Art 8(1) (see para 149 ante). Cf the Universal Declaration of Human Rights (Paris, 10 December 1948), Art 12; and the International Covenant on Civil and Political Rights (1966) Art 17. As to the Convention for the Protection of Human Rights and Fundamental Freedoms (1950) generally see para 122 ante. As to the Universal Declaration of Human Rights see para 122 note 1 ante. As to the International Covenant on Civil and Political Rights (1966) see para 103 note 3 ante; and see also Michael 'Privacy' in Harris and Joseph (eds) *The International Covenant on Civil and Political Rights and United Kingdom Law* (1995) ch 10.

   As to what constitutes respect for the rights guaranteed by the Convention see para 154 post; as to what amounts to interference with those rights see para 155 post.

2 *Niemietz v Germany* A 251-B (1992), 16 EHRR 97, ECtHR; *Chappell v United Kingdom* A 152-A (1989), Com Rep.

3 See *Gillow v United Kingdom* A 109 (1986), 11 EHRR 335, ECtHR (refusal to give applicant residence permit to return to a home which he had built for himself on Guernsey amounted to failure to respect the applicant's right to respect for his home).

4 Application 159/56 *X v Federal Republic of Germany* 1 YB 202 (1956), EComHR. The right to live in a mobile home has been considered in a number of cases: see eg Application 18401/91 *Smith v United Kingdom* (1994) 18 EHRR CD65, EComHR; Application 20348/92 *Buckley v United Kingdom* (1994) 18 EHRR CD 123, EComHR. See also Harris, O'Boyle and Warbrick *Law of the European Convention on Human Rights* (1995) p 319.

5 Application 7456/76 *Wiggins v United Kingdom* 13 DR 40 (1978), EComHR; Applications 6780/74, 6950/75 *Cyprus v Turkey* (1976) 4 EHRR 282, EComHR.

6 Application 10825/84 *Howard v United Kingdom* 52 DR 198 (1987), EComHR.

7 Application 7889/77 *Arrondelle v United Kingdom* 26 DR 5 (1982), FSett; *Lopes-Ostra v Spain* A 303-C (1994), ECtHR.

## 153. Respect for correspondence. The Convention for the Protection of Human Rights and Fundamental Freedoms (1950) guarantees the right to respect for correspondence[1].

Correspondence includes both written communications and telephone communications[2]. A person sending a letter retains no right to respect for correspondence once it is in the hands of the addressee[3].

1 Convention for the Protection of Human Rights and Fundamental Freedoms (1950) Art 8(1) (see para 149 ante). Cf the Universal Declaration of Human Rights (Paris, 10 December 1948), Art 12; and the International Covenant on Civil and Political Rights (1966) Art 17. As to the Convention for the Protection of Human Rights and Fundamental Freedoms (1950) generally see para 122 ante. As to the Universal Declaration of Human Rights see para 122 note 1 ante. As to the International Covenant on Civil and Political Rights (1966) see para 103 note 3 ante.

   The question of the violation of the right to respect for correspondence has been raised most frequently in respect of restrictions on prisoners' correspondence: see *Golder v United Kingdom* A 18 (1975), 1 EHRR 524, ECtHR (preventing applicant from writing to solicitor interfered with correspondence); *Boyle and Rice v United Kingdom* A 131 (1988), 10 EHRR 425, ECtHR; *Campbell v United Kingdom* A 233 (1992), 15 EHRR 137, ECtHR; *Herczegfalvy v Austria* A 242-B (1992) 15 EHRR 437, ECtHR; and Application 15943/90 *Domenichini v Italy*, EComHR. There was no failure by the United Kingdom to secure respect for correspondence when mail was intercepted by another state: Application 7597 *Bertrand Russell Peace Foundation Ltd v United Kingdom* 14 DR 117 (1978), EComHR.

   As to what constitutes respect for the rights guaranteed by the Convention see para 154 post; as to what amounts to interference with those rights see para 155 post.

2 *Klass v Federal Republic of Germany* A 28 (1978), 2 EHRR 214, ECtHR; *Malone v United Kingdom* A 82 (1984), 7 EHRR 14, ECtHR. There are no reported decisions on the question whether 'correspondence' can be extended to protect other forms of communication. For the view that it should see Harris, O'Boyle and Warbrick *Law of the European Convention on Human Rights* (1995) p 320.

3 Application 21962/93 *A D v Netherlands* 76A DR 157 (1994), EComHR.

**154. What constitutes respect.** The obligation on states to respect the interests specified in the Convention for the Protection of Human Rights and Fundamental Freedoms (1950)[1] is primarily a negative obligation not to interfere with those interests[2], but there are positive obligations inherent in respect for those interests which require the state not merely to refrain from interfering with them, but to adopt measures to secure respect for them[3].

Thus failure by a state: to make legal aid provision for a woman seeking judicial separation from violent husband[4]; to make legal provision for pursuance by a mentally handicapped person of criminal complaints of sexual attack[5]; to provide for full legal status of the child of an unmarried couple[6]; to provide a system of domestic law safeguarding an illegitimate child's integration into its family[7]; to allow a second generation immigrant to remain in the country where his family lived[8]; to enforce court orders granting a father right to access to his child against the maternal grandparents[9]; to provide for independent adjudication on the question of confidentiality of documents relating to foster care[10]; to consult the natural father of a child before placing the child for adoption[11]; and to protect a person from pollution[12], have all been held to violate the right to respect for the rights guaranteed by the Convention. It appears that the failure of the state to provide for the amendment of the birth certificate after a person has changed sex is a failure to respect private life[13]. The development of the common law to remove the marital exemption from criminal liability for rape was held in conformity with the fundamental principles of the Convention[14].

On the other hand, a state has been held under no obligation: to provide a remedy for invasion of privacy by means of untrue statements[15]; to provide financial support so that one parent could stay at home to look after children[16]; to assist prisoners in maintaining contact with their families[17]; to admit the alien spouses of the applicants to join them[18]; to ensure efficient functioning of the postal service as part of the right to respect for correspondence[19].

1    Ie the Convention for the Protection of Human Rights and Fundamental Freedoms (1950) Art 8(1): see paras 149–153 ante. As to the Convention generally see para 122 ante.
2    See *Belgian Linguistics Case (No 2)* A 6 (1968), 1 EHRR 252, ECtHR; *Lingens v Austria* A 103 (1986), 8 EHRR 407, ECtHR.
3    *X and Y v Netherlands* A 91 (1985), 8 EHRR 235, ECtHR, para 23.
4    *Airey v Ireland* A 32 (1979), 2 EHRR 305, ECtHR.
5    *X and Y v Netherlands* A 91 (1985), 8 EHRR 235, ECtHR.
6    *Johnston v Ireland* A 112 (1986), 9 EHRR 203, ECtHR.
7    *Marckx v Belgium* A 31 (1979), 2 EHRR 330, ECtHR.
8    *Moustaquim v Belgium* A 193 (1991), 13 EHRR 802, ECtHR; see also *Beljoudi v France* A 234-A (1992), 14 EHRR 801, ECtHR; *Nasri v France* A 322-B (1995), ECtHR.
9    *Hokkanen v Finland* A 299-A (1994), 19 EHRR 139, ECtHR.
10   *Gaskin v United Kingdom* A 160 (1989), 12 EHRR 36, ECtHR.
11   *Keegan v Ireland* A 290 (1994), 18 EHRR 342, ECtHR.
12   Application 7889/77 *Arrondelle v United Kingdom* 26 DR 5 (1982), FSett; *Lopes-Ostra v Spain* A 303-C (1994), ECtHR; Application 9310/81 *Rayner v United Kingdom* 47 DR 5 (1986), EComHR.
13   Application 7654/76 *Von Oosterwijk v Belgium* B 36 (1979), Com Rep para 52; *B v France* A 232-C (1992), 16 EHRR 1, ECtHR. See contra *Rees v United Kingdom* A 106 (1986), 9 EHRR 56, ECtHR; *Cossey v United Kingdom* A 184 (1990), 13 EHRR 622, ECtHR.
14   See *S W v United Kingdom* [1996] 1 FLR 434, ECtHR; and *C R v United Kingdom* [1996] 1 FLR 434, ECtHR; and para 148 note 14 ante.
15   Application 10871/84 *Winer v United Kingdom* p 48 DR 154 (1986), EComHR (limited range of civil remedies available to the applicant to protect his reputation from both true and false statements about his sexual relations with his wife did not amount to a failure to respect his private life)
16   Application 11776/85 *Andersson and Kullman v Sweden* 46 DR 251 (1986), EComHR.
17   Application 9054/80 *X v United Kingdom* 30 DR 113 (1982), EComHR.
18   *Abdulaziz, Cabalas and Balkandali v United Kingdom* A 94 (1985), 7 EHRR 471, ECtHR (states have wide margin of appreciation as to what steps are necessary to achieve respect for private life); see also

Application 7729/76 *Agee v United Kingdom* 7 DR 164 (1976), EComHR; and *Berrehab v Netherlands* A 138 (1988), 11 EHRR 322, ECtHR.

19  Application 8383/78 *X v Federal Republic of Germany* 17 DR 227 (1979), EComHR. However, where letters are despatched through a prison postal service, the state is under an obligation to ensure that they are posted and delivered: Application 11523/85 *Grace v United Kingdom* 62 DR 22. The state may also in circumstances where a prisoner has limited financial resources be under an obligation to pay for his letters: Application 9659/82 *Boyle v United Kingdom* 41 DR 90 (1985), EComHR.

**155.  What constitutes interference.** The Convention for the Protection of Human Rights and Fundamental Freedoms (1950) prohibits interference, save in specified circumstances, with the right to respect for private and family life, home and correspondence[1]. The burden is upon the applicant to establish a sufficient degree of likelihood that an interference has occured[2]. It is not necessary, however, for an applicant to show, for example, that legislation which affects his private life has actually been applied to him by way of a prosecution since the very existence of such legislation may amount to a sufficient interference[3].

Medical treatment administered to an individual without their consent does not amount to an interference if that individual cannot give informed consent[4]. Nor did the appointment of a guardian ad litem, on application of legal advisers of a person of full age, amount to a breach of the Convention[5]. The denial of an opportunity for a person detained under prevention of terrorism legislation to contact his spouse was a violation of the Convention[6].

1  Convention for the Protection of Human Rights and Fundamental Freedoms (1950) Art 8(2): see paras 149–153 ante. As to the Convention generally see para 122 ante. As to the circumstances in which interference is permissible see para 149 text and notes 7–14 ante.
2  *Campbell v United Kingdom* A 233 (1992), 15 EHRR 137, ECtHR.
3  *Dudgeon v United Kingdom* A 45 (1981), 4 EHRR 149, ECtHR; *Norris v Ireland* A 142 (1988), 13 EHRR 186, ECtHR; and *Modinos v Cyprus* A 259 (1993), 16 EHRR 485, ECtHR. All those cases concerned legislation prohibiting homosexual activities in private, the existence of which was held to interfere with the applicants' rights under Art 8 of the Convention; but contra see Application 21627/93 *Laskey v United Kingdom* (18 January 1995, unreported), EComHR. See also *Klass v Federal Republic of Germany* A 28 (1978), 2 EHRR 214, ECtHR; and *Leander v Sweden* A 116 (1987), 9 EHRR 433, ECtHR; both of which concerned the existence of legislation authorising the state to tap telephones.
4  *Herczegfalvy v Austria* A 242-B (1992), 15 EHRR 437, ECtHR.
5  Application 7940/77 *X v United Kingdom* 14 DR 224 (1978), EComHR.
6  Applications 8022/77, 8025/77, 8027/77 *McVeigh, O'Neill and Evans v United Kingdom* 25 DR 15 (1981), 5 EHRR 71, EComHR.

E.  FREEDOM OF CONSCIENCE

**156.  Freedom of thought, conscience and religion.** Everyone has the right to freedom of thought, conscience and religion, including the right to change his religion or belief[1]. This is a guarantee of protection against indoctrination of religion by the state[2]. It is an absolute right and not subject to the limited permissible interferences by public authorities with the right to manifest one's belief[3]. The burden is on a complainant to show that he is in fact an adherent to a particular religion and that the practice or belief he relies upon is an essential element of that religion[4]. The existence of an established state church does not, of itself, violate the Convention for the Protection of Human Rights and Fundamental Freedoms (1950) if membership is voluntary[5].

1  Convention for the Protection of Human Rights and Fundamental Freedoms (1950) Art 9(1). Cf the Universal Declaration of Human Rights (Paris, 10 December 1948). As to the Convention for the Protection of Human Rights and Fundamental Freedoms (1950) generally see para 122 ante. As to the Universal Declaration of Human Rights see para 122 note 1 ante. As to the International Covenant on Civil and Political Rights (1966) see para 103 note 3 ante; and see Cumper 'Freedom of Thought,

Conscience and Religion' in Harris and Joseph (eds) *The International Covenant on Civil and Political Rights and United Kingdom Law* (1995) ch 11.

    A corporation cannot enjoy this right: Application 3798/68 *Church of X v United Kingdom* 12 YB 306 (1969), EComHR; Application 7865/77 *Company X v Switzerland* 16 DR 85 (1981), EComHR. Conviction of a conscientious objector for failure to perform substitute service imposed in place of military service is not a violation of the right: Application 2299/64 *Grandrath v Federal Republic of Germany* 10 YB 626 at 688 (1966), Com Rep. See also Art 4(3)(b) of the Convention; and para 126 ante.

2    See Application 10491/83 *Angelini v Sweden* 51 DR 41 (1986), EComHR.

3    Ie the Convention for the Protection of Human Rights and Fundamental Freedoms (1950) Art 9(2) applies only to the freedom to manifest religion or belief, not the freedom to hold them: see para 157 post. An interference by public authorities with a publication relates substantially to the freedom of expression and only remotely, if at all, to the freedom of thought and belief: *Application 5493/72 Handyside v United Kingdom* 45 CD 23 (1976), EComHR.

4    Application 8160/78 *X v United Kingdom* 22 DR 27 (1981), EComHR; Application 10180/82 *D v France* 35 DR 199 (1983), EComHR.

5    *Darby v Sweden* A 187 (1990), 13 EHRR 774, ECtHR.

**157. Freedom to manifest religion and belief.** Freedom of thought, conscience and religion[1] includes freedom, alone or in community with others[2], and in public or private, to manifest[3] religion[4] or belief in worship, teaching, practice[5] and observance[6]. This freedom may be subject only to such limitations as are prescribed by law and are necessary in a democratic society in the interests of public safety[7], for the protection of public order, health[8] or morals, for the protection of the rights[9] and freedom of others[10].

1    See para 156 ante. The application of a general law to persons who have reasons of conscience not to comply with it does not violate the Convention for the Protection of Human Rights and Fundamental Freedoms (1950) Art 9(1): Application 88111/79 *Seven Individuals v Sweden* 29 DR 104, EComHR; and Application 10358/83 *C v United Kingdom* 37 DR 142 (1983), EComHR. For the position under English law see para 108 ante. As to the Convention for the Protection of Human Rights and Fundamental Freedoms (1950) generally see para 122 ante.

2    A church or organisation may be a victim of an interference with these rights, as well as an individual: Application 7805/77 *X and Church of Scientology v Sweden* 16 DR 68 (1979), EComHR; Application 12587/86 *Chappell v United Kingdom* 53 DR 241 (1987), EComHR.

3    Advertisements directed at the commercial sale of devices produced by a particular religious group are not protected manifestations of religion: Application 7805/77 *X and Church of Scientology v Sweden* 16 DR 68 (1979), EComHR. Distribution of leaflets to soldiers encouraging them not to serve in Northern Ireland is not a manifestation of pacifist belief: Application 7050/75 *Arrowsmith v United Kingdom* 19 DR 5 (1978), EComHR (although in that case pacifism itself, as a belief, was held to fall within the ambit of of the Convention for the Protection of Human Rights and Fundamental Freedoms (1950) Art 9(1)).

4    The issue of granting custody to a parent who is not a Jehovah's Witness rather than to one who is, should be decided under ibid Art 8 (see paras 149–155 ante): *Hoffman v Austria* A 255-C (1993), 17 EHRR 293, ECtHR. The state has a responsibility to ensure that the holders of religious beliefs can effectively enjoy their rights under the Convention: *Otto Preminger Institut v Austria* A 295-A (1994), 19 EHRR 34, ECtHR, paras 47–49.

5    A law which criminalised the practice of parental chastisement of children is not an interference with Art 9(1) of the Convention even where the applicants maintained that their religion required such measures: Application 8811/79 *Seven Individuals v Sweden* 29 DR 104, EComHR. See also Application 8160/78 *X v United Kingdom* 22 DR 29 (1981), EComHR (refusal of school to allow Moslem teacher to attend prayers at mosque during school hours).

6    Convention for the Protection of Human Rights and Fundamental Freedoms (1950) Art 9(1); cf the Universal Declaration of Human Rights (Paris, 10 December 1948), Art 18; and the International Covenant on Civil and Political Rights (1966) Art 18. As to the Universal Declaration of Human Rights see para 122 note 1 ante. As to the International Covenant on Civil and Political Rights (1966) see para 103 note 3 ante. Article 9 of the Convention does not provide the basis for right to divorce: *Johnstone v Ireland* A 112 (1986), 9 EHRR 203, ECtHR. The absence of criminal sanctions in English law against publications which offended against the religious beliefs of non-Christians was not a violation of Art 9 of the Convention: Application 17439/90 *Choudhury v United Kingdom* (1991) 12 HRLJ 172, EComHR; *R v Chief Metropolitan Stipendiary Magistrate, ex p Choudhury* [1991] 1 QB 429, [1991] 1 All ER 306, DC.

7    Because of the terms of the Convention for the Protection of Human Rights and Fundamental Freedoms (1950) Art 4(3)(b) (see para 126 ante), which excludes from its prohibition of forced or compulsory

labour, military service or, where conscientious objectors are recognised, alternative national service, it has been held that the state may, but need not, recognise conscientious objectors, and only then may it have to consider providing an alternative to military service: Application 2299/64 *Grandrath v Federal Republic of Germany* 10 YB 626 (1966), Com Rep. If a state provides alternative forms of national service, it does not violate Art 9(1) of the Convention if such service is for a longer period than military service, or if it takes measures to enforce such alternative service: Application 17086/90 *Autio v Finland* 72 DR 245 (1991), EComHR; Application 10600/83 *Johansen v Norway* 44 DR 155 (1985), EComHR. There was no violation of Art 9 and Art 14 of the Convention where a conscientious objector complained that Swedish law permitted only Jehovah's Witnesses to enjoy exemption from both military and alternative national service: Application 10410/83 *N v Sweden* 40 DR 203 (1984).

8    See Application 7992/77 *X v United Kingdom* 14 DR 234 (1978), EComHR (requirement that all motorcyclists wear crash helmets justified).

9    Thus the conviction of a farmer who, on religious grounds, refused to take part in a compulsory health scheme designed to prevent illness amongst farm animals was necessary for the protection of health: Application 1068/61 *X v Netherlands* 5 YB 278 (1962).

10   Convention for the Protection of Human Rights and Fundamental Freedoms (1950) Art 9(2). See *Kokkinakis v Greece* A 260-A (1993), 17 EHRR 397, ECtHR (application of Greek law which criminalised the proselytising activities of a Jehovah's Witness interfered with Art 9(1) of the Convention, and was not proportionate to the aim of protecting the rights of others); Application 18748/91 *Manoussokis v Greece*, EComHR (conviction of Jehovah's Witness for renting room for private worship without obtaining prior authorisation from ecclesiastical authority and the state violated the right to freedom of religion). See also Application.6886/75 *X v United Kingdom* 5 DR 100 (1976), EComHR (refusal to grant prisoner access to religious book containing chapter on martial arts). Limitations imposed by which a state insists upon the observance of a particular law may be justifiable: Application 1497/62 *Reformed Church of X v Netherlands* 5 YB 286 at 298 (1962), EComHR; Application 2065/63 *X v Netherlands* 8 YB 266 at 270 (1965), EComHR (compulsory old age pension scheme; domestic law had made provision for conscientious objectors).So may positive limitations placed upon the conduct of religious or kindred activities: Application 1753/63 *X v Austria* 8 YB 174 (1965), EComHR (restriction upon religious practices of Buddhist convert in prison).

## F.  FREEDOM OF EXPRESSION

**158.  Right to freedom of expression.** Everyone[1] has the right to freedom of expression[2], including freedom to hold opinions and to receive[3] and impart information and ideas[4] without interference[5] by public authority[6] and regardless of frontiers[7]. This does not prevent states from requiring the licensing[8] of broadcasting, television or cinema enterprises[9]. The exercise of these freedoms, since it carries with it duties and responsibilities[10], may be subject to such formalities, conditions, restrictions or penalties as are prescribed by law[11] and are necessary in a democratic society, in the interests of national security[12], territorial integrity[13] or public safety, for the prevention of disorder[14] or crime, for the protection of health or morals[15], for the protection of the reputation or rights[16] of others, for preventing the disclosure of information received in confidence[17], or for maintaining the authority and impartiality of the judiciary[18].

1    This provision applies to all legal entities, irrespective of their corporate status or the fact that they pursue commercial objectives: *Autronic AG v Switzerland* A 178 (1990), 12 EHRR 485, ECtHR.

2    See para 159 post.

3    The right to receive information prohibits a government from restricting a person from receiving information that others may wish or may be willing to impart to him, but it does not impose on governments an obligation to supply him with it: *Leander v Sweden* A 116 (1987), 9 EHRR 433, ECtHR (applicant had no right of access to government register containing information on his personal life). See also *Gaskin v United Kingdom* A 160 (1989), 12 EHRR 36, ECtHR (access to records concerning applicant's upbringing in local authority care). If a person is, however, prevented from obtaining information from other sources, the Convention for the Protection of Human Rights and Fundamental Freedoms (1950) Art 10 will be relevant: see *Autronic AG v Switzerland* A 178 (1990), 12 EHRR 485, ECtHR; and *Sunday Times v United Kingdom* A 30 (1979), 2 EHRR 245, ECtHR. The state is prohibited from standing between a speaker and his audience since each has a right of access to the other: *Groppera Radio AG v Switzerland* A 173 (1990), 12 EHRR 321, ECtHR; *Casado Coca v Spain* A 285 (1994),

18 EHRR 1, ECtHR.As to the Convention for the Protection of Human Rights and Fundamental Freedoms (1950) generally see para 122 ante.

4 The meaning of the terms 'ideas' and 'information' was considered in *Groppera Radio AG v Switzerland* A 173 (1990), 12 EHRR 321, ECtHR, where the court declined to give a precise definition, but observed that both broadcasting of programmes over the air and cable re-transmission of such programmes were covered by the Convention for the Protection of Human Rights and Fundamental Freedoms (1950) Art 10(1) without any need to make distinctions according to the content of the programmes. See also *Markt Intern and Beerman v Federal Republic of Germany* A 164 (1989), 12 EHRR 161, ECtHR (information of a commercial nature in trade magazine fell within Art 10(1) of the Convention. Article 10(1) includes opinions, criticism, and speculation: *Thorgierson v Iceland* A 239 (1992), 14 EHRR 843, ECtHR; *Castells v Spain* A 236 (1992), 14 EHRR 445, ECtHR.

5 Where the impact upon speech or expression is collateral to the exercise by the state of authority for other purposes, both the European Court of Human Rights and the European Commission of Human Rights have been reluctant to consider that the interference falls within Art 10 of the Convention for the Protection of Human Rights and Fundamental Freedoms (1950). See eg *Glasenapp v Federal Republic of Germany* A 104 (1986), 9 EHRR 25, ECtHR; *Kosiek v Federal Republic of Germany* A 105 (1986), 9 EHRR 328, ECtHR (claims by teachers that conditions attaching to their employment by German *lander* interfered with their rights under Art 10 of the Convention were, in reality, claims of rights of access to public employment which had been deliberately excluded from the Convention). See, however, Application 10293/83 *B v United Kingdom* 45 DR 41 (1985), EComHR; Application 11389/85 *Morissens v Belgium* 56 DR 127 (1988), EComHR; Application 17851/91 *Vogt v Germany* (1993) Com Rep (interference with civil servant's right to freedom of expression was not justifiable); the European Court of Human Rights agreed: *Vogt v Germany* A 323 (1995), ECtHR. See Application 7729/76 *Agee v United Kingdom* 7 DR 164 (1976), EComHR (interference necessary but unintended corollary of exercise of state's authority in deporting illegal immigrants); Applications 14773/89 and 15774/89 *Piermont v France* (1994) Com Rep para 94. There will be no interference where an individual has agreed or contracted to limit his freedom of expression: Application 11308/84 *Vereiging Rechtswinkels Utrecht v Netherlands* 46 DR 200 (1986), EComHR.

6 This protection goes beyond prior censorship of expression and includes the prohibition of post-expression civil or criminal sanctions: *Barford v Denmark* A 149 (1989), 13 EHRR 493, ECtHR (criminal sanctions); *Lingens v Austria* A 103 (1986), 8 EHRR 407, ECtHR (civil penalty); *Müller v Switzerland* A 133 (1988), 13 EHRR 212, ECtHR (forfeiture); *Autronic AG v Switzerland* A 178 (1990), 12 EHRR 485, ECtHR (denial of licence); *Tolstoy v United Kingdom* A 323 (1995), 20 EHRR 442 (libel damages and injunction). In *Observer and Guardian v United Kingdom* A 216 (1991), 14 EHRR 153, ECtHR, the court would not commit itself to the position that prior censorship was inevitably in breach of the Convention, but stated that prior restraints required the most careful scrutiny.

The state is under a positive obligation to take action where a threat to an individual's freedom of expression comes from a private source: *Plattform Artze für das Leben v Austria* A 139 (1988), 13 EHRR 204, ECtHR (obligation to prevent disruption of demonstration by hostile mob). Penalties imposed by the Spanish Bar Council, a public law corporation, upon a lawyer for engaging in advertising was interference by a public authority: *Casado Coca v Spain* A 285 (1994), 18 EHRR 1, ECtHR. See also Application 12242/86 *Rommelfanger v Federal Republic of Germany* 62 DR 151 (1989), EComHR.

As to the possible obligations upon the state to prevent excessive press concentrations see Application 5178/71 *De Geillerstreede Pers v Netherlands* 8 DR 5 (1976) Com Rep para 88; Application 24744/94 *Huggett v United Kingdom* 82-A DR 98 (1995) (BBC policy of allocating broadcasting time only to political parties presenting candidates in at least 12.5% of seats in an election, being intended to facilitate the public expression of political opinions which are likely to be of general interest, did not disclose any arbitrariness or discrimination violative of Art 14 of the Convention in conjunction with Art 10).

7 Ibid Art 10(1); cf The Universal Declaration of Human Rights (Paris, 10 December 1948), Art 19; and the International Covenant on Civil and Political Rights (1966) Art 19. As to the Universal Declaration of Human Rights see para 122 note 1 ante. As to the International Covenant on Civil and Political Rights (1966) see para 103 note 3 ante; and see also Feldman 'Freedom of Expression' in Harris and Joseph (eds) *The International Covenant on Civil and Political Rights and United Kingdom Law* (1995) ch 12.

8 Early cases suggested that the maintenance of public service monopolies in broadcasting was compatible with the Convention for the Protection of Human Rights and Fundamental Freedoms (1950): see Application 3071/67 *X v Sweden* 26 CD 71 (1968), EComHR ('licensing' did not exclude a public television monopoly); and see Application 8266/78 *X v United Kingdom* 16 DR 190 (1978); Application 10799/84 *Radio X, S, W and A v Switzerland* 37 DR 236 (1984), EComHR. When France ratified the Convention in 1974 it was with an interpretative declaration relating to Art 10 designed to protect its state radio and television monopolies: YB VII (1964) p 454. More recently, however, the compatibility of a broadcasting monopoly with Art 10 of the Convention has been considered under Art 10(2) (see text and notes 12–14 infra) rather than Art 10(1), and requires in each case the justification of being necessary

in a democratic society: Application 17505/90 *Nydahl v Sweden* (1993) 16 EHRR CD 15, EComHR; *Informationsverein Lentia v Austria* A 276 (1993), 17 EHRR 93, ECtHR.

9    Convention for the Protection of Human Rights and Fundamental Freedoms (1950) Art 10(1). Private individuals or organisations do not enjoy a general right to be afforded broadcasting time or a licence to advertise on television: Application 4515/70 *X and Association Z v United Kingdom* 38 CD 86 (1971), EComHR. Nor do they have a right to the grant of a licence for a commercial radio station: Application 4750/71 *X v United Kingdom* 40 CD 29 (1972), EComHR. A refusal by the authorities to grant subsidies for theatre performances is not a violation of the convention: Application 2834/66 *X v Germany* 13 YB 260 (1970), EComHR. See also Application 2690/65 *NV Televizier v Netherlands* 9 YB 521 (1966), 11 YB 782 (1968), FSett (restrictions on publishing magazine caused by literary copyright).

10   See *Engel v Netherlands* A 22 (1976), 1 EHRR 647, ECtHR; Application 10293/83 *B v United Kingdom* 45 DR 41 (1985), EComHR; Application 11389/85 *Morissens v Belgium* 56 DR 127 (1988), EComHR; Application 8010/77 *X v United Kingdom* 16 DR 101 (1979), EComHR. See also *Handyside v United Kingdom* A 24 (1976), 1 EHRR 737, ECtHR (responsibilities of publishers); *Lingens v Austria* A 103 (1986), 8 EHRR 407, ECtHR (duty of press to impart information and ideas on political issues); *Otto Preminger Institut v Austria* A 295-A (1994), 19 EHRR 34, ECtHR (duty of those who exercise freedom of expression to avoid expression which does not contribute to public debate and is gratuitously offensive to others).

11   Foreseeability is inherent in the phrase 'prescribed by law': *Sunday Times v United Kingdom* A 30 (1979), 2 EHRR 245, ECtHR (foreseeability to a degree that was reasonable in the circumstances); *Müller v Switzerland* A 133 (1988), 13 EHRR 212, ECtHR. See also Application 10038/82 *Harman v United Kingdom* 38 DR 53 (1984), EComHR; and *Goodwin v United Kingdom* (27 March 1996, unreported), ECtHR (Contempt of Court Act 1981 s 10 was sufficiently precise). In *Groppera Radio AG v Switzerland* A 173 (1990), 12 EHRR 321, ECtHR, and *Autronic v Switzerland* A 178 (1990), 12 EHRR 485, ECtHR, the state was allowed to rely upon norms of public international law which were applied in municipal law). 'Honest practices', required by German unfair competition legislation, were prescribed by law since in areas such as competition, in which the situation was constantly changing absolute precision could not be achieved, and developed case law contributed to foreseeablility: *Markt Intern and Beerman v Federal Republic of Germany* A 164 (1989), 12 EHRR 161, ECtHR; and *Barthold v Federal Republic of Germany* A 90 (1985), 7 EHRR 383, ECtHR. See also *Tolstoy v United Kingdom* A 323 (1995), 20 EHRR 442, ECtHR (legal rules concerning libel damages were formulated with sufficient precision; Art 10 of the Convention did not require an individual to be able to anticipate the quantum of a jury award: libel awards therefore not too uncertain to be 'prescribed by law').

12   See *Observer and Guardian Newspapers v United Kingdom* A 216 (1991), 14 EHRR 153, ECtHR (interlocutory injunctions restraining publication by newspapers of information obtained from book written by former member of security services: maintaining the authority of the judiciary and safeguarding the operation of the security service were legitimate aims for the purposes of Art 10(2) of the Convention but the continuance of the injunction, in the face of widespread importation of copies of the book published overseas, was disproportionate). See also *Vereinigung Demokratischer Soldaten Osterreichs and Berthold Gubi v Austria* A 302 (1994), 20 EHRR 56, ECtHR (right to distribute journal within military barracks); *Vereniging Weekblad 'Bluf' v Netherlands* A 306-A (1995), ECtHR (seizure of publication which included information obtained from Dutch Internal Security Service record). State restrictions upon broadcasting news items relating to organisations connected with or supporting terrorism were justified as being within the margin of appreciation permitted to states within the area of national security: Application 15404/89 Application 15404/89 *Purcell v Ireland* 70 DR 262 (1991), EComHR; Applications 18714/91, 18759/91 *Brind and McLaughlin v United Kingdom* 77-A DR 42 (1994), EComHR.

13   See *Piermont v France* A 314 (1995), ECtHR.

14   A ban on cable retransmission in Switzerland of programmes broadcast from Italy did not infringe the applicants' right to impart information and ideas regardless of frontiers because it was designed to maintain orderly international telecommunications: *Groppera Radio AG v Switzerland* A 173 (1990), 12 EHRR 321, ECtHR. Restricting expression in order to prevent disorder within the armed forces is a legitimate aim for the purposes of Art 10(2) of the Convention: *Engel v Netherlands* A 22 (1976), 1 EHRR 647, ECtHR; *Vereniging Democratischer Soldaten Osterreichs and Gubi v Austria* A 302 (1994), 20 EHRR 56, ECtHR. See also *Piermont v France* A 314 (1995), ECtHR (adminstrative orders expelling member of the European Parliament from French territories pursued the legitimate aims of preventing disorder and territorial integrity, but was not necessary in a democratic society; a fair balance had not been struck between these aims and freedom of expression).

15   See *Handyside v United Kingdom* A 24 (1976), 1 EHRR 737, ECtHR (banning of publication for children which included substantial chapter on sex: interference was justified (within the state's margin of appreciation) as being necessary for the protection of public morals); *Müller v Switzerland* A 133 (1988), 13 EHRR 212, ECtHR (punishment of artist for exhibiting obscene paintings was within state's margin of appreciation); *Open Door Counselling and Dublin Well Woman v Ireland* A 246 (1992), 15 EHRR 244,

ECtHR (primarily for state to assess the content of morals, but European Court of Human Rights would scrutinise the claim that the action taken by the state to protect its own conception of morals was necessary in a democratic society).

16  See eg *Lingens v Austria* A 103 (1986), 8 EHRR 407, ECtHR (punishment of journalist following private prosecution for defamation brought by leading politician not justified under Art 10(2) of the Convention). See also, as to the limits of acceptable criticism of persons in the public eye: *Oberschlick v Austria* A 204 (1991), 19 EHRR 389, ECtHR; and *Fayed v United Kingdom* A 294-B (1994), 18 EHRR 393, ECtHR. As to the protection of the religious rights of others see *Otto Preminger Institut v Austria* A 295-A (1994), 19 EHRR 34, ECtHR (public showings of satirical film with religious theme; seizure justified as pursuing the legitimate aim of protecting the religious rights of others); and as to the religious rights guaranteed by the Convention see paras 156–157 ante. In Application 25096/94 *Otto E F A Remer v Germany* 82-A DR 117 (1995), EComHR, a conviction for incitement to racial hatred by publishing materials denying mass gassing of Jews in Nazi Germany was held to be an interference with the applicant's rights under Art 10 of the Convention, but was necessary in a democratic society for the protection of the rights and reputations of others). See also Application 17419/90 *Wingrove v United Kingdom* (1995), Com Rep (refusal of British Board of Film Classification to grant a classification to a film on the grounds that it was blasphemous).

17  See eg *Goodwin v United Kingdom* (27 March 1996, unreported), ECtHR (an order requiring a journalist to disclose his sources was not necessary in a democratic society when the disclosure was sought to enable a company to identify a disloyal employee).

18  Convention for the Protection of Human Rights and Fundamental Freedoms (1950) Art 10(2).

Because of the requirements of Art 6(1) (see para 134–147 ante), the state may have a duty to interfere with freedom of expression if the right of an individual to a fair trial would be prejudiced by publication of information about the proceedings: *Observer and Guardian v United Kingdom* A 216 (1991), 14 EHRR 153, ECtHR, para 61. For cases where it was necessary to interfere with freedom of expression on the grounds that it was necessary for maintaining the authority and impartiality of the judiciary, see: *Barfod v Denmark* A 149 (1989), 13 EHRR 493, ECtHR, paras 61–64 (conviction of amateur journalist for criminal defamation in article containing unfounded implication of bias was within the margin of appreciation allowed to states); Application 15974/90 *Prager and Oberschlick v Austria* A 313 (1995), Com Rep (conviction for defamation did not, on the facts, exceed the state's margin of appreciation). For a decision where interference on this ground was rejected see: *Sunday Times v United Kingdom* A 30 (1979), 2 EHRR 245, ECtHR, para 59. On the issue protecting the authority and impartiality of the judiciary see also the recent admissibility decision of the Commission in Application 21861/93 *Zihlmann v Switzerland* (1995) 82-A DR 12.

## 159. What constitutes freedom of expression.

The Convention for the Protection of Human Rights and Fundamental Freedoms (1950) guarantees the right to freedom of expression[1]. Freedom of expression is defined widely and has been given an appropriately broad interpretation when the scope of the concept has had to be considered[2]. Freedom of expression constitutes one of the essential foundations of a democratic society and, subject to the restrictions permitted by the Convention[3], it is applicable not only to information or ideas that are favourably received or regarded as inoffensive but also to those that offend, shock or disturb the state or any sector of the population[4].

Freedom of expression is not limited to the written or spoken word[5]. Similarly, the means of protected expression extend beyond speech to print[6]; radio[7]; television broadcasting[8]; and film[9].

Some types of expression have been regarded as deserving of lesser protection against restriction by the state. Thus racist literature[10] and expressions of political support[11] for terrorism have been denied protection under the Convention.

It is taken for granted that political expression is protected by the Convention[12]. Artistic expression is also covered[13]. The expression of information of a commercial nature is also protected[14].

Freedom of expression includes the negative freedom not to speak[15].

Complaints regarding the seizure by the authorities of a publication are related to the right to freedom of expression rather than the right to freedom of thought or belief[16].

1    Convention for the Protection of Human Rights and Fundamental Freedoms (1950) Art 10(1): see para
     158 ante. As to the Convention generally see para 122 ante.
2    Article 10 of the Convention is based quite closely on the International Covenant on Civil and Political
     Rights (1966), but it is in several respects cast in much weaker language. In particular, Art 10 of the
     Convention does not, in its terms, create an independent right to hold opinions without interference (cf
     Art 19(1) of the Covenant), nor does it expressly refer to the right to seek information (cf Art 19(2) of
     the Covenant). The limitations and restrictions of the right permitted by Art 10(2) of the Convention
     also go beyond those permitted by Art 19(3) of the Covenant. As to the International Covenant on Civil
     and Political Rights (1966) see para 103 note 3 ante.
3    Ie subject to the Convention for the Protection of Human Rights and Fundamental Freedoms (1950)
     Art 10(2): see para 158 ante.
4    *Sunday Times v United Kingdom* A 30 (1979), 2 EHRR 245, ECtHR.
5    See eg *Müller v Switzerland* A 133 (1988), 13 EHRR 212, ECtHR (painting of dubious merit); *Barford v
     Denmark* A 149 (1989), 13 EHRR 493, ECtHR (defamatory criticism of judges); *Chorherr v Austria* A
     266-B (1993), 17 EHRR 358, ECtHR (images); Application 11674/85 *Stevens v United Kingdom*
     46 DR 245 (1986), EComHR (dress); Application 7215/75 *Case of X* 19 DR 66 (1977), EComHR
     (inability to engage in sexual relationship due to incarceration not an interference with expression since
     physical expression of feelings is not within Art 10(1)).
6    *Handyside v United Kingdom* A 24 (1976), 1 EHRR 737, ECtHR.
7    *Groppera Radio AG v Switzerland* A 173 (1990), 12 EHRR 321, ECtHR.
8    *Autronic v Switzerland* A 178 (1990), 12 EHRR 485, ECtHR.
9    *Otto Preminger Institut v Austria* A 295-A (1994), 19 EHRR 34, ECtHR.
10   Applications 8384/78, 8406/78 *Glimmerveen and Hagenbeck v Netherlands* 18 DR 187 (1979), EComHR
     (racist literature); Application 9325/81 *X v Federal Republic of Germany* 29 DR 194 (1982), EComHR
     (Nazi leaflets).
         See, however, *Jersild v Denmark* A 298 (1994), 19 EHRR 1, ECtHR, where a television journalist was
     convicted under criminal legislation prohibiting dissemination of racist insults: even though he had
     solicited such contributions and had edited them to give prominence to the most offensive, the European
     Court of Human Rights found that his conviction was not proportionate to the interest of protecting the
     rights of others, in the context of a factual programme about the holding of racist opinions; see also *Otto
     Preminger Institut v Austria* A 295-A (1994), 19 EHRR 34, ECtHR.
11   Application 15404/89 *Purcell v Ireland* 70 DR 262 (1991), EComHR (political support for terrorism).
12   *Lingens v Austria* A 103 (1986), 8 EHRR 407, ECtHR.
13   *Müller v Switzerland* A 133 27 (1988), 13 EHRR 212, ECtHR.
14   See *Casado Coca v Spain* A 285 (1994), 18 EHRR 1, ECtHR; and *Markt Intern and Beerman v Federal
     Republic of Germany* A 164 (1989), 12 EHRR 161, ECtHR.
15   *K v Austria* A 255-B (1993), Com Rep. Compelling an individual to reveal the souces of information
     may constitute a violation of this negative right: *Goodwin v United Kingdom* (27 March 1996,
     unreported), ECtHR.
16   *Handyside v United Kingdom* A 24 (1976), 1 EHRR 737, ECtHR.

## G.  FREEDOM OF ASSOCIATION AND ASSEMBLY

**160. Freedom of assembly.** Everyone has the right to freedom of peaceful[1] assembly[2].
The exercise of the right may be subject to such restrictions as are prescribed by law[3] and
are necessary in a democratic society in the interests of national security or public safety,
for the prevention of disorder[4] or crime, for the protection of public health or morals and
lawful restrictions on the exercise of this right by members of the armed forces, or of the
police, or of the administration of the state[5] are permitted[6].

1    The term 'peaceful assembly' is not to be interpreted restrictively: Application 13079/87 *G v Federal
     Republic of Germany* 60 DR 256 (1989), EComHR (sit-in blocking entrance to barracks).
2    Convention for the Protection of Human Rights and Fundamental Freedoms (1950) Art 11(1); cf the
     Universal Declaration of Human Rights (Paris, 10 December 1948), Art 20 para 1; and the International
     Covenant on Civil and Political Rights (1966) Art 21. As to the Convention for the Protection of Human
     Rights and Fundamental Freedoms (1950) generally see para 122 ante. As to the Universal Declaration
     of Human Rights see para 122 note 1 ante. As to the International Covenant on Civil and Political Rights
     (1966) see para 103 note 3 ante; and see further Murphy 'Freedom of Assembly' in Harris and Joseph
     (eds) *The International Covenant on Civil and Political Rights and United Kingdom Law* (1995) ch 13.

This freedom is a fundamental right in a democratic society, and covers both the right to private meetings and meetings in public: Application 8191/78 *Rassemblement Jurassien Unité v Switzerland* 17 DR 93 (1979), EComHR. It is an essential part of the activities of any political organisation: *Greek Case* 12 YB 1 at 170–171 (1969), EComHR. States are under a positive obligation to take steps, even in the sphere of relations between individuals, to enable lawful demonstrations to proceed peacefully: *Plattform 'Ärzte für das Leben' v Austria* A 139 (1988), 13 EHRR 204, ECtHR (on the facts the authorities had not failed to take reasonable measures); *Ezelin v France* A 202 (1991), 14 EHRR 362, ECtHR (sanction imposed upon lawyer for not disassociating himself from demonstration at which offences were committed violated Art 11 of the Convention, and although aimed at the prevention of disorder, was disproportionate to that aim). The imposition of a sanction after a demonstration may still be an interference with freedom of assembly: *Ezelin v France* supra.

3    As to the meaning of the phrase 'prescribed by law' see para 158 note 11 ante.

4    Subjecting peaceful demonstrations to an authorisation procedure did not encroach upon the essence of the right: Application 8191/78 *Rassemblement Jurassien Unité v Switzerland* 17 DR 93 (1979), EComHR (temporary ban on all public demonstrations was acceptable under Art 11(2), as there existed a serious danger that public safety and order would be threatened should a particular public demonstration take place); Application 8440/78 *Christians against Racism and Fascism v United Kingdom* 21 D 148 (1980), EComHR (argument that proposed demonstration would fall outside the scope of Art 11 of the Convention if it might evoke violent opposition was rejected).

5    *Vogt v Germany* A 323 (1995), ECtHR; and see the report of the European Commission of Human Rights in that case: Application 17851/91 (1993), Com Rep para 88.

6    Convention for the Protection of Human Rights and Fundamental Freedoms (1950) Art 11(2).

## 161. Freedom of association.

**161.  Freedom of association.** Everyone has the right to freedom of association[1] with others, including the right to form and join[2] trade unions[3] for the protection of his interests[4]. No restrictions[5] may be placed on the exercise of this right other than such as are prescribed by law[6] and are necessary in a democratic society[7] in the interests of national security or public safety, for the prevention of disorder[8] or crime, for the protection of health or morals or for the protection of the rights and freedom of others[9]. The imposition of lawful restrictions on the exercise of this right by members of the armed forces[10], of the police[11], or of the administration of the state[12] is permitted[13].

1    For the purposes of the Convention for the Protection of Human Rights and Fundamental Freedoms (1950) Art 11(2), an association is more formal and organised than an assembly (as to which see para 160 ante). 'Assocation' presupposes a voluntary grouping for a common goal: *Young, James and Webster v United Kingdom* A 44 (1981), ECtHR (relationship between workers employed by same employer could not be understood as 'association' since it depended only upon a contractual relationship between employer and employee). The right to share the company of others does not qualify as 'association' for this purpose: Application 8317/78 *McFeeley v United Kingdom* 20 DR 44 (1980), EComHR (contact between prisoners). The existence of separate legal status for a body does not necessarily render it an association under the Convention: *Le Compte, Van Leaven and De Meyere v Belgium* A 43 (1981), 4 EHRR 1, ECtHR (doctors' professional body); Application 6094/73 *Association X v Sweden* 9 DR 5 (1977), EComHR (university student organisation). Associations may have a wide variety of purposes, and include political parties (Application 250/57 *KPD v Federal Republic of Germany* 1 YB 222 (1957), EComHR), but the activities they pursue may be limited under Art 17 of the Convention (see para 170 post). Associations enjoy rights under Art 11(1) directly against the state: Application 10126/82 *Platform 'Ärzte fur das Leben' v Austria* 44 DR 65 (1985), EComHR. As to the Convention for the Protection of Human Rights and Fundamental Freedoms (1950) generally see para 122 ante.

2    Freedom of association implies also the freedom not to associate or not to be affiliated to a trade union: Application 4072/69 *X v Belgium* 13 YB 708 at 718 (1970), EComHR; and cf the Universal Declaration of Human Rights (Paris, 10 December 1948), Art 20 para 2. See also *Sigurour A Sigurjonsson v Iceland* A 264 (1993), 16 EHRR 462, ECtHR. The threat of dismissal for refusing to join union following the conclusion of closed shop agreement between employers and recognised union is an interference which strikes at the very substance of the right to freedom of association: *Young, James and Webster v United Kingdom* A 44 (1981), 4 EHRR 38, ECtHR, para 55. The obligation to join the *Ordre des Medecins* in order to practise as a doctor in Belgium did not violate Art 11(1) of the Convention since doctors, though compelled to join the Ordre which was a public law institution, were able to form their own professional associations: *Le Compte, Van Leuven and De Meyere v Belgium* A 43 (1981), 4 EHRR 1, ECtHR. As to the Universal Declaration of Human Rights see para 122 note 1 ante.

3   The freedom to join a trade union does not guarantee any particular treatment of trade unions, or their members, by the state, such as the right to be consulted: *National Union of Belgian Police v Belgium* A 9 (1975), 1 EHRR 578, ECtHR. Article 11(1) of the Convention protects the right of a union to be heard during the course of collective bargaining, but does not protect any right to have a collective agreement concluded: *Swedish Engine Drivers' Union v Sweden* A 20 (1976), 1 EHRR 617, ECtHR. The right to strike, and other means that a union may deploy to protect its members' interests, may be the subject of regulation under national law: *Schmidt and Dahlstrom v Sweden* A 21 (1976), 1 EHRR 632, ECtHR, where the argument that if the state is the employer, its activities in this role are not subject to scrutiny under Art 11(1) of the Convention, was rejected. Obligations upon private employers will arise through the state's positive obligations to ensure that domestic law safeguards Art 11(1) rights by preventing abusive and arbitrary behaviour by private bodies, including trade unions: *Young, James and Webster v United Kingdom* A 44 (1981), 4 EHRR 38, ECtHR; see also Application 10550/83 *Cheall v United Kingdom* 42 DR 178 (1985), EComHR; and *Sibson v United Kingdom* A 258-A (1993), 17 EHRR 193, ECtHR.

4   Convention for the Protection of Human Rights and Fundamental Freedoms (1950) Art 11(1); cf the Universal Declaration of Human Rights (Paris, 10 December 1948), Art 20 para 1, Art 23 para 4; see also the International Labour Organisation Convention no 87 Concerning Freedom of Association and Protection of the Right to Organise, 9 July 1948 (UN TS vol 68 p 17); the European Social Charter (Turin, 18 October 1961; TS 38 (1965); Cmd 2643), Arts 5, 6; and the International Covenant on Civil and Political Rights (1966) Art 11. See further Ewing 'Freedom of Association and Trade Union Rights' in Harris and Joseph (eds) *The International Covenant on Civil and Political Rights and United Kingdom Law* (1995) ch 14.

    This right does not include the right to manage or organise associations: Application 1038/61 *X v Belgium* 4 YB 324 (1961), EComHR. As to the International Covenant on Civil and Political Rights (1966) see para 103 note 3 ante.

5   A general state policy of restricting the number of organisations with which collective agreements are to be concluded is not in itself incompatible with trade union freedom under the Convention for the Protection of Human Rights and Fundamental Freedoms (1950) Art 11(1): *National Union of Belgian Police v Belgium* A 9 (1975), 1 EHRR 578, ECtHR; *Swedish Engine Drivers' Union v Sweden* A 20 (1976), 1 EHRR 617, ECtHR.

6   As to the meaning of the phrase 'prescribed by law' see para 158 note 11 ante.

7   In order to demonstrate that a restriction is justified, the state must demonstrate a pressing social need, rather than mere expediency: *Sigurour A Sigurjonnson v Iceland* A 264 (1993), 16 EHRR 462, ECtHR (requirement that taxi drivers be members of association not justified as facilitating adminstration of taxi service in public interest).

8   See *Vogt v Germany* A 323 (1995), ECtHR (dismissal of state-employed teacher because of active membership of left-wing political party not proportionate to aim of protecting national security and prevention of disorder).

9   Convention for the Protection of Human Rights and Fundamental Freedoms (1950) Art 11(2). A contracting state is not precluded by Art 11 from imposing restrictions on the political activity of aliens: see Art 16; and para 169 post.

10  See eg *Engel v Netherlands* A 22 (1976), 1 EHRR 647, ECtHR.

11  See eg Application 2977/66 (1969, unreported), EComHR; *National Union of Belgian Police v Belgium* A 9 (1975), 1 EHRR 578, ECtHR.

12  See Application 11603/85 *Council of Civil Service Unions v United Kingdom* 50 DR 228 (1987), EComHR (abolition of right to form and join trade unions representing employees at the United Kingdom Government Communications Headquarters: applicants were involved within the adminstration of the state, and complete ban on union activity was in accordance with law since it was lawful under domestic law, and further that it was within the state's powers of restriction under Art 11(1) of the Convention); Application 17851/91 *Vogt v Germany* (1993), Com Rep para 88 (teachers not members of the administration of the state); this point was not taken before the European Court of Human Rights (see *Vogt v Germany* A 323 (1995)).

13  Convention for the Protection of Human Rights and Fundamental Freedoms (1950) Art 11(2).

## H.  RIGHT TO MARRY AND FOUND A FAMILY

**162. Right to marry and found a family.** Men and women of marriageable age[1] have the right to marry[2] and found a family according to the national laws[3] governing the exercise of this right[4].

The right to marry refers only to marriage between persons of the opposite biological sex; the Convention for the Protection of Human Rights and Fundamental Freedoms (1950) does not give a right to marry to a transsexual under his or her new sex[5], or to homosexuals to marry one another[6].

The Convention does not expressly or by implication guarantee a right to divorce[7].

The right to found a family is absolute in the sense that the state has no right to interfere with it[8]. The state is not however required to facilitate opportunities for a couple to found a family by allowing for consummation of the marriage[9].

Conditions imposed upon adoptions can be the subject of scrutiny under the Convention[10]. States are not, however, under an obligation to provide a system for adoption[11]. Unmarried persons cannot assert a right to adopt[12].

The state may treat a legitimate family more favourably than an illegitimate family as long as such discrimination does not violate the right to a private and family life[13].

The right to marry has been frequently invoked in the context of persons detained by the state[14].

1　The formalities of marriage and questions of capacity and minimum age to marry are for national law: *F v Switzerland* A 128 (1987), 10 EHRR 411, ECtHR; and Application 11579/85 *Khan v United Kingdom* 48 DR 253 (1986).

2　There is no duty to allow any particular form of marriage or to recognise polygamous marriages: Application 6167/73 *X v Federal Republic of Germany* 1 DR 64 (1974), EComHR.

3　National laws must satisfy the principles of legal certainty, and must not so interfere with the substance of the right to deprive it of all content: *Von Oosterwijk v Belgium* A 40 (1980), 3 EHRR 577, ECtHR; Application 7114/75 *Hamer v United Kingdom* 24 DR 5 (1979), Com Rep; *Rees v United Kingdom* A 106 (1986), 9 EHRR 56, ECtHR. It is for the state to decide upon appropriate rules of conflict of laws (as to which see generally CONFLICT OF LAWS): Application 3898/68 *X v United Kingdom* 35 CD 102 (1970), EComHR; Application 9057/80 *X v Switzerland* 26 DR 207 (1981), EComHR.

4　Convention for the Protection of Human Rights and Fundamental Freedoms (1950) Art 12. Cf the Universal Declaration of Human Rights (Paris, 10 December 1948), Art 16; and the International Covenant on Civil and Political Rights (1966), Art 23. As to the Convention for the Protection of Human Rights and Fundamental Freedoms (1950) generally see para 122 ante. As to the Universal Declaration of Human Rights see para 122 note 1 ante. As to the International Covenant on Civil and Political Rights (1966) see para 103 note 3 ante; and see further Ghandi 'Family and Child Rights' in Harris and Joseph (eds) *The International Covenant on Civil and Political Rights and United Kingdom Law* (1995) ch 15.

　　The right to marry is protected in the absence of an intention to found a family, but it has not been accepted that the right to found a family may exist under the Convention in the absence of a marriage: Application 7114/75 *Hamer v United Kingdom* 24 DR 5 (1979), Com Rep; *Rees v United Kingdom* A 106 (1986), 9 EHRR 56, ECtHR. The right of unmarried persons to found a family may fall under Art 8 of the Convention: see para 151 ante.

5　*Rees v United Kingdom* A 106 (1986), 9 EHRR 56, ECtHR, para 49; *Cossey v United Kingdom* A 184 (1990), 13 EHRR 622, ECtHR.

6　Application 11716/85 *S v United Kingdom* 47 DR 274 (1986), EComHR.

7　*Johnston v Ireland* A 122 (1986), 9 EHRR 203, ECtHR; the court also held that there was no obligation to permit divorce under Art 8 of the Convention (right to respect for family life): see para 151 ante. See also *F v Switzerland* A 128 (1987), 10 EHRR 411, ECtHR, where a condition imposed by a domestic court that a man could not marry until three years after the date of his divorce infringed Art 12 of the Convention because of the delay it imposed on the exercise of the right.

8　Application 6564/74 *X v United Kingdom* 2 DR 105 (1975), EComHR.

9　Application 6564/74 *X v United Kingdom* 2 DR 105 (1975), EComHR; Application 8166/78 *X and Y v Switzerland* 13 DR 241 (1978), EComHR. Separation between married couples as a result of deportation decisions falls to be considered under Art 8 of the Convention: see *Beldjoudi v France* A 234-A (1992), 14 EHRR 801, ECtHR; and para 151 ante.

10　Application 7229/75 *X and Y v United Kingdom* 12 DR 32 (1977), EComHR.

11　Application 7229/75 *X and Y v United Kingdom* 12 DR 32 (1977), EComHR.

12　Application 6482/14 *X v Belgium and Netherlands* 7 DR 75 (1975), EComHR.

13　Application 9639/82 *B, R and J v Federal Republic of Germany* 36 DR 130 (1984), EComHR (failure of German law to give custody right to father of child born out of wedlock).

14  See eg Application 862/90 *X v Germany* 4 YB 240 (1961) (refusal to permit prisoner to marry was justified where his sentence was too long for him to found a home for many years to come and the marriage might prejudice the maintenance of good order in prison); Application 3898/68 *X v United Kingdom* 13 YB 674 (refusal to permit polygamous marriage). However, the mere fact of detention is not enough to deny a prisoner the right; it was a violation of Art 12 of the Convention to delay a prisoner's opportunity to marry until he was released on parole, because the effect of the delay would be to infringe in substance the right to marry: Application 7114/75 *Hamer v United Kingdom* 24 DR 5 (1979), Com Rep; and Application 8186/78 *Draper v United Kingdom* 24 DR 72 (1980), Com Rep. As to refusal to permit conjugal visits see Application 3603/68 *X v Germany* 13 YB 336 (1970); and para 1689 post. The English courts have held that a refusal to allow an illegal immigrant, imprisoned while awaiting deportation, to be married at a register office is not contrary to Art 12 of the Convention: *R v Secretary of State for the Home Department, ex p Bhajan Singh* [1976] QB 198 at 203, [1975] 2 All ER 1081, CA.

## I.  EFFECTIVE REMEDIES

**163.  Right to an effective remedy.** Everyone is guaranteed an effective[1] remedy[2] before a national authority[3] for a violation[4] of a right contained in the Convention for the Protection of Human Rights and Fundamental Freedoms (1950), notwithstanding that the violation has been committed by persons acting in an official capacity[5]. This does not, however, guarantee a remedy by which primary legislation can be challenged as violating the Convention[6].

1   This does not require that contracting states give direct effect to the Convention for the Protection of Human Rights and Fundamental Freedoms (1950) in domestic law: *Ireland v United Kingdom* A 25 (1978), 2 EHRR 25, ECtHR. As to the Convention generally see para 122 ante.
    The applicant's substantive arguments concerning his rights under the Convention must have been properly considered by the national body: *Soering v United Kingdom* A 161 (1989), 11 EHRR 439, ECtHR; but see *Costello-Roberts v United Kingdom* A 247-C (1993), 19 EHRR 112, ECtHR, where reference was made only to the technical availability of a remedy before a national authority and no mention was made of whether the applicant would have been able to put forward arguments concerning his Convention rights. It is not necessary that the applicant would have succeeded before the national body: *Costello-Roberts v United Kingdom* supra at para 40. As to the effectiveness of judicial review see *Soering v United Kingdom* supra; *Vilvarajah v United Kingdom* A 215 (1991), 14 EHRR 248, ECtHR. As to the effectiveness of civil actions see *Costello-Roberts v United Kingdom* supra; but see Application 9471/81 *Warwick v United Kingdom* 60 DR 5 (1989), EComHR.

2   A cumulation of remedies in the national legal system is sufficient: *Silver v United Kingdom* A 61 (1983), 5 EHRR 347, ECtHR; *Leander v Sweden* A 61 (1987), 9 EHRR 433, ECtHR. The remedy need not be judicial (see *Leander v Sweden* supra at para 77), and exceptionally a judicial remedy will not be sufficient (*Greek Case* 12 YB 1 at 174 (1969), EComHR). But if the remedy involves the exercise of a political discretion (*Silver v United Kingdom* supra) or does not involve an element of enforceability (eg the Prison Boards of Visitors in *Silver v United Kingdom* supra) the remedy will not be effective. But note that a consistent national practice, even if not legally enforceable, can be considered sufficient: see *Leander v Sweden* supra; and *Soering v United Kingdom* A 161 (1989), 11 EHRR 439, ECtHR, where the absence of interim relief against the Crown was not considered to be in breach of Art 13 of the Convention.

3   The national authority must be sufficiently independent of the body whose actions are alleged to be in violation of the Convention: *Silver v United Kingdom* A 61 (1983), 5 EHRR 347, ECtHR, para 116; Application 12573/86 *M and E F v Switzerland* 51 DR 283 (1987), EComHR.

4   It is not necessary for an applicant to demonstrate that a right guaranteed by the Convention has actually been violated; it is sufficient to show that it is arguable that a right has been violated: *Klass v Federal Republic of Germany* A 28 (1978), 2 EHRR 214, ECtHR, para 64. As to whether a claim is 'arguable' or 'manifestly ill-founded' (see Art 27 of the Convention; and paras 174–175 post) see: *Silver v United Kingdom* A 61 (1983), 5 EHRR 347, ECtHR, para 113; *Leander v Sweden* A 61 (1987), 9 EHRR 433, ECtHR, para 79; Application 10126/82 *Platform 'Arzte fur das Leben' v Austria* 44 DR 65 (1985), EComHR; *Boyle and Rice v United Kingdom* A 131 (1988), 10 EHRR 425, ECtHR (no breach of Art 13 of the Convention despite the fact that there were several breaches of other Articles of the Convention); *Powell and Rayner v United Kingdom* A 172 (1990), 12 EHRR 355, ECtHR (tests of 'manifestly ill-founded' and 'arguable' were the same); *Friedl v Austria* A 305-B (1994), FSett.

5   Convention for the Protection of Human Rights and Fundamental Freedoms (1950) Art 13.

6    See *Leander v Sweden* A 61 (1987), 9 EHRR 433, ECtHR, para 77; *Abdulaziz, Cabales and Balkandali v United Kingdom* A 94 (1985), 7 EHRR 471, ECtHR; *Murray v United Kingdom* A 300-A (1994), 19 EHRR 193, ECtHR. Article 13 does not require a state to provide a remedy against a decision of the final court in a domestic legal system: Applications 8603/79, 8722/79, 8723/79, 8729/79 *Crocianietal v Italy* 22 DR 147 (1981), EComHR, at 223–224).

## J. PROHIBITION OF DISCRIMINATION

**164. Prohibition of discrimination.** The enjoyment of the rights and freedoms as set out in the Convention for the Protection of Human Rights and Fundamental Freedoms (1950)[1] must be secured without discrimination on any ground such as[2] sex[3], race[4], colour, language[5], religion[6], political or other opinion, national or social origin, association with a national minority, property[7], birth[8] or other status[9].

This provision refers only to discrimination in respect of the enjoyment of the guaranteed rights and freedoms. However, its application does not presuppose a breach of any of the other provisions of the Convention[10]. It is sufficient if the facts of a case fall within the ambit of one or more of the substantive articles[11].

The provision may only be violated by a difference in treatment between persons who are in comparable situations[12] which has no objective and reasonable justification[13]. Contracting states enjoy a margin of appreciation in relation to the question of justification, which depends upon the circumstances, subject matter and background of the case[14].

1    For the rights and freedoms set out in the Convention for the Protection of Human Rights and Fundamental Freedoms (1950) see paras 123 et seq ante; 168 et seq post. This also applies to the substantive rights set out in the Protocols, which are to be regarded as additional articles to the Convention: First Protocol, Art 5; Fourth Protocol, Art 6(1); Sixth Protocol, Art 6; Seventh Protocol, Art 7. As to the Convention generally, and as to the Protocols to which the United Kingdom is a signatory, see para 122 ante.

     The Convention contains no express guarantee of equality before the law, or general prohibition of discrimination: contrast the stronger provisions in the International Covenant on Civil and Political Rights (1966) Art 26. As to the International Covenant on Civil and Political Rights (1966) see para 103 note 3 ante; and see further Lester and Joseph 'Obligations of Non-Discrimination' in Harris and Joseph (eds) *The International Covenant on Civil and Political Rights and United Kingdom Law* (1995) ch 17.

2    The words 'such as' show that the list of prohibited grounds is illustrative, and not exhaustive: *Engel v Netherlands* A 22 (1976), 1 EHRR 647, ECtHR, para 72; *James v United Kingdom* A 98 (1986), 8 EHRR 123, ECtHR, para 74. Any difference of treatment between persons who are similarly situated, in an area within the ambit of Convention rights and freedoms, is capable of constituting discrimination: *Sunday Times v United Kingdom (No 2)* A 217 (1991), 14 EHRR 229, ECtHR, para 58. Article 14 of the Convention does not require an applicant to establish that he or she is a member of a particular group, provided that comparable individuals can be identified who are enjoying more favourable treatment without justification. See eg *Pine Valley Developments Ltd v Ireland* A 222 (1991), 14 EHRR 319, ECtHR (legislation to validate planning permission nullified by judgment of Irish Supreme Court benefited all holders of planning permission in the relevant category apart from applicants: violation of Art 14 of the Convention in the absence of any justification for the discrimination). See also *Fredin v Sweden* A 192 (1991), 13 EHRR 784, ECtHR.

3    See eg *Abdulaziz, Cabales and Balkandali v United Kingdom* A 94 (1985), 7 EHRR 471, ECtHR, para 82; *Schuler-Zgraggen v Switzerland* A 263 (1993), 16 EHRR 405, ECtHR, para 67; *Schmidt v Germany* A 291-B (1994), 18 EHRR 513, ECtHR. As to sex discrimination see further EMPLOYMENT.

4    See eg *Abdulaziz, Cabales and Balkandali v United Kingdom* A 94 (1985), 7 EHRR 471, ECtHR, para 85; *East African Asians Cases* (1973) 3 EHRR 76, EComHR. For racial discrimination generally see BRITISH NATIONALITY, IMMIGRATION AND RACE RELATIONS.

5    See eg *Belgian Linguistics Case (No 2)* A 6 (1968), 1 EHRR 252, ECtHR; *Mathieu-Mohin and Clerfayt v Belgium* A 113 (1987), 10 EHRR 1, ECtHR.

6    See eg *Hoffmann v Austria* A 255-C (1993), 17 EHRR 293, ECtHR (refusal of parental rights after divorce because of membership of Jehovah's Witnesses was disproportionate discrimination on grounds of religion).

7    See eg *James v United Kingdom* A 98 (1986), 8 EHRR 123, ECtHR; *Lithgow v United Kingdom* A 102 (1986), 8 EHRR 329, ECtHR.

8   See eg *Abdulaziz, Cabales and Balkandali v United Kingdom* A 94 (1985), 7 EHRR 471, ECtHR.

9   Convention for the Protection of Human Rights and Fundamental Freedoms (1950) Art 14. Cf the Universal Declaration of Human Rights (Paris, 10 December 1948), Art 8. As to the Universal Declaration of Human Rights see para 122 note 1 ante.

The term 'other status' has not been defined, but see eg: *Marckx v Belgium* A 31 (1979), 2 EHRR 330, ECtHR (illegitimacy); *Inze v Austria* A 126 (1987), 10 EHRR 394, ECtHR (illegitimacy); *Vermiere v Belgium* A 214-C (1991), 15 EHRR 488, ECtHR (illegitimacy); *Airey v Ireland* A 32 (1979), 2 EHRR 305, ECtHR (poverty); *Johnston v Ireland* A 112 (1986), 9 EHRR 203, ECtHR (poverty)); *Van der Mussele v Belgium* A 70 (1983), 6 EHRR 163, ECtHR (professional status); *Darby v Sweden* A 187 (1990), 13 EHRR 774, ECtHR (residence); *Dudgeon v United Kingdom* A 45 (1981), 4 EHRR 149, ECtHR (sexual orientation); *Engel v Netherlands* A 22 (1976), 1 EHRR 647, ECtHR (military rank). A contracting state is not precluded by Art 16 of the Convention from imposing restriction on the political activities of aliens: see Art 16; and para 169 post.

10  A measure which in itself conforms with the article of the Convention enshrining the right in question may violate Art 14 because it is discriminatory in nature; Art 14 thus constitutes an integral part of each of the rights safeguarded by the Convention: *Belgian Linguistics Case (No 2)* A 6 (1968), 1 EHRR 252, ECtHR, para 9; *Airey v Ireland* A 32 (1979), 2 EHRR 305, ECtHR, para 30; *Marckx v Belgium* A 31 (1979), 2 EHRR 330, ECtHR, para 32.

Discrimination within Art 14 of the Convention includes, in general, cases where a person or group is treated, without proper justification, less favourably than another, even though the more favourable treatment is not called for by the Convention; accordingly a state cannot argue that it has acted more generously than the Convention requires: *Abdulaziz, Cabales and Balkandali v United Kingdom* A 94 (1985), 7 EHRR 471, ECtHR, para 82.

If the European Court of Human Rights does not find a separate breach of another substantive article of the Convention, that has been invoked by the applicant both on its own and in conjunction with Art 14, it must also examine the case under Art 14; on the other hand, such an examination is rarely required when the court finds a violation of the other article taken alone. The court will only examine the case under Art 14 in such circumstances if a clear inequality of treatment in the enjoyment of the right in question is a fundamental aspect of the case: *Airey v United Kingdom* supra at para 30.

11  *Van der Mussele v Belgium* A 70 (1983), 6 EHRR 163, ECtHR (requirement that student advocate undertake defence work without remuneration within ambit of Art 4); *Rasmussen v Denmark* A 87 (1984), 7 EHRR 371, ECtHR (discrimination beween a husband and wife in relation to paternity proceedings within ambit of Arts 6, 8); *Inze v Austria* A 126 (1987), 10 EHRR 394, ECtHR (discrimination against illegitimate child in relation to inheritance on intestacy within ambit of the First Protocol, Art 1).

12  Where the European Court of Human Rights considers that the persons with whom the applicant seeks to compare himself are not in a similar or analogous situation to the applicant, there will be no discrimination contrary to Art 14 of the Convention: *Van der Mussele v Belgium* A 70 (1983), 6 EHRR 163, ECtHR (fundamental differences between the legal and other professions); see also *Rasmussen v Denmark* A 87 (1984), 7 EHRR 371, ECtHR; *Johnston v Ireland* A 112 (1986), 9 EHRR 203, ECtHR (Irish law recognising divorces obtained abroad by those domiciled abroad was not discriminatory on the grounds of financial means); *Lithgow v United Kingdom* A 102 (1986), 8 EHRR 329, ECtHR.

In the absence of positive evidence, it may be difficult for applicants to establish that those who have been more favourably treated are in a similar situation to their own: see eg *Fredin v Sweden* A 192 (1991), 13 EHRR 784, ECtHR, para 60 (applicants were the only business engaged in extracting gravel to have their permit revoked; the argument that it was for the state to explain the respects in which their business differed from others was rejected).

13  *Belgian Linguistics Case (No 2)* A 6 (1968), 1 EHRR 252, ECtHR, para 10. A difference in treatment will be justified if it pursues a legitimate aim, and if there is a reasonable relationship of proportionality between the means employed and the aim sought to be realised: *Belgian Linguistics Case (No 2)* supra; *Marckx v Belgium* A 31 (1979), 2 EHRR 330, ECtHR, para 32; *Rasmussen v Denmark* A 87 (1984), 7 EHRR 371, ECtHR; *Abdulaziz, Cabales and Balkandali v United Kingdom* A 94 (1985), 7 EHRR 471, ECtHR; *Inze v Austria* A 126 (1987), 10 EHRR 394, ECtHR, para 41. Compare the test for the objective justification of indirect sex discrimination enunciated by the European Court of Justice: Case 170/84 *Bilka-Kaufhaus GmbH v Weber von Hartz* [1986] ECR 1607, ECJ.

14  *Rasmussen v Denmark* A 87 (1984), 7 EHRR 371, ECtHR, para 40. See also *Belgian Linguistics Case (No 2)* A 6 (1968), 1 EHRR 252, ECtHR; *National Union of Belgian Police v Belgium* A 19 (1975), 1 EHRR 578, ECtHR; *Swedish Engine Drivers' Union v Sweden* A 20 (1976), 1 EHRR 617, ECtHR; *Engel v Netherlands* A 22 (1976), 1 EHRR 647, ECtHR.

The width of the margin of appreciation afforded to contracting states will vary according to the grounds upon which persons are differently treated. Thus very weighty reasons would have to be advanced by a state in order to justify discrimination on the grounds of sex: *Abdulaziz, Cabales and*

*Balkandali v United Kingdom* A 94 (1985), 7 EHRR 471, ECtHR, para 72 (sex discrimination in immigration rules which permitted wives but not husbands to join spouses settled in the United Kingdom was not justified by the aim to protect the domestic labour market); *Schuler-Zgraggen v Switzerland* A 263 (1993), 16 EHRR 405, ECtHR (assumption made by court, when determining claim for invalidity pension, that women gave up work when they gave birth to a child constituted unjustified sex discrimination in relation to the right to a fair trial); *Burghartz v Switzerland* A 280-B (1994), 18 EHRR 101, ECtHR. Similar considerations apply to discrimination against illegitimate children: *Inze v Austria* A 126 (1987), 10 EHRR 394, ECtHR, para 41; and see *Marckx v Belgium* A 31 (1979), 2 EHRR 330, ECtHR. It is probable that racial discrimination would attract the same reasoning: see *Abdulaziz, Cabales and Balkandali v United Kingdom* supra; and the *East African Asians Case* (1973) 3 EHRR 76, EComHR.

## K. RIGHT TO PROPERTY

**165. Right to property.** Every natural or legal person is entitled to the peaceful enjoyment of his possessions[1]. No one may be deprived of his possessions[2] except in the public interest[3] and subject to the conditions provided for by law[4] and by the general principles of international law[5]. The preceding principles do not, however, in any way impair the right of a state to enforce such laws as it deems necessary to control the use[6] of property in accordance with the general interest or to secure the payment[7] of taxes or other contributions or penalties[8].

This in substance guarantees the right of property[9].

The rights of corporate bodies are also protected, provided that the applicant is the real victim of a violation[10].

A wide variety of property rights have been held to be protected by this provision, being either movable or immovable property, or tangible or intangible interests, including: shares[11]; patents[12]; the entitlement to use property[13]; the benefit of a restrictive covenant and entitlement to annual rent[14]; a landlord's entitlement to rent[15]; an arbitral award[16]; a licence to carry on an economic activity where the licencee has a reasonable and legitimate expectation as to the lasting nature of the licence and to the continuation of benefit from it[17]; the economic interests connected with the running of a business[18]; the right to exercise a profession[19]; a legitimate expectation that a certain state of affairs will apply[20]; and a legal claim, provided it is a concrete, adequately specified claim[21]. The entitlement to a pension under a contributory pension scheme will be protected provided that the applicant has a legal right to benefits if he satisfies certain conditions[22].

However, the protection does not obtain unless and until it is possible to lay claim to the property concerned[23]. Similarly, claims which a person has as an heir during the testator's lifetime do not fall under the protection of this provision, which protects existing property and not the right to acquire property[24].

An applicant must establish the nature of his property right and his entitlement to enjoy it as a matter of domestic law[25].

1    Convention for the Protection of Human Rights and Fundamental Freedoms (1950), First Protocol (1952), Art 1. As to the relationship between this limb of the First Protocol, Art 1 and the other limbs see *Sporrong and Lönnroth v Sweden* A 52 (1982), 5 EHRR 35, ECtHR, para 61; and note 8 infra. As to the Convention and its Protocols generally see para 122 ante.

2    In determining whether there has been a deprivation of possessions it is necessary to look behind appearances and investigate the realities of the situation complained of, in order to ascertain whether that situation amounted to a de facto expropriation: *Sporrong and Lönnroth v Sweden* A 52 (1982), 5 EHRR 35, ECtHR, para 63 (on the facts, the existence of expropriation permits did not automatically attract the protection of First Protocol, Art 1); see, however, *James v United Kingdom* A 98 (1986), 8 EHRR 123, ECtHR, para 38 (legislation giving tenants right to purchase the rented properties); *Papamichalopoulos v Greece* A 260-B (1993), 16 EHRR 440, ECtHR, para 45 (transfer of land to Greek navy); *Hentrich v France* A 296-A (1994), 18 EHRR 440, ECtHR, paras 34–35 (exercise of a right of pre-emption by the revenue authorities).

3    The review of the object or purpose of a legislative measure or other interference with property is
     limited. Whether an expropriation or other deprivation of possessions is in the public interest will be
     subjected to very marginal review, as the margin of appreciation available to the national legislature in
     implementing social and economic policies is a wide one; the legislature's judgment as to what is in
     the public interest will be respected unless that judgment is manifestly without reasonable foundation:
     see *Handyside v United Kingdom* A 24 (1976), 1 EHRR 737, ECtHR, para 62; *James v United Kingdom*
     A 98 (1986), 8 EHRR 123, ECtHR, para 46. The same applies in relation to measures concerned with
     the use of property within the meaning of the Protocol: see eg *Spadea and Scalabrino v Italy* A 315-B
     (1995), 21 EHRR 482, ECtHR, para 29; *Pressos Compania Naviera SA v Belgium* A 332 (1995), 21
     EHRR 301, ECtHR, para 37. However, whichever of the three limbs of Art 1 of the First Protocol
     applies, the requirements will not be satisfied unless there is a reasonable relationship of proportionality
     between the means employed and the aim sought to be realised. A fair balance must be struck between
     the demands of the general interest of the community and the requirements of the protection of the
     individual's fundamental rights, the search for such a fair balance being inherent in the whole of the
     Convention: *Sporrong and Lönnroth v Sweden* supra at paras 69, 73; *James v United Kingdom* supra at para
     50; *Lithgow v United Kingdom* A 102 (1986), 8 EHRR 329, ECtHR, para 120; *Allgemeine Gold-und
     Silverscheideanstalt v United Kingdom* A 108 (1986), 9 EHRR 1, ECtHR, para 52; *Tre Traktörer
     Aktiebolag v Sweden* A 159 (1989), 13 EHRR 309, ECtHR, para 59; *Mellacher v Austria* A 169 (1989),
     12 EHRR 391, ECtHR, para 48; and *Hentrich v France* A 296-A (1994), 18 EHRR 440, ECtHR, paras
     45–49). See also *Holy Monasteries v Greece* A 301-A (1994), 20 EHRR 1, ECtHR, para 70; *Stran Greek
     Refineries v Greece* A 301-B (1994), 19 EHRR 293, ECtHR, para 74; *Air Canada v United Kingdom*
     A 316 (1995), 20 EHRR 150, ECtHR (availability of judicial review proceedings to challenge
     Customs and Excise Commissioners' decision was taken into account in holding no breach of
     Convention); *Pressos Compania Naviera SA v Belgium* supra at para 38. The powers of the state to secure
     the payment of taxes or other contributions or penalties are particularly wide, but a taxing measure
     may involve a breach of Art 1 of the First Protocol if it fails to strike a fair balance between the demands
     of the general interest of the community and the requirements of the protection of the individual's
     fundamental rights: see *Gasus Dosier-und Fordertechnik v Netherlands* A 306-B (1995), 20 EHRR 403,
     ECtHR, para 62. See also Application 13013/87 *Wasa Liv Omsesidigt v Sweden* 58 DR 163 at 185–187
     (1988), EComHR.

4    This requires the existence of and compliance with adequately accessible and sufficiently precise domestic
     legal provisions: *Lithgow v United Kingdom* A 102 (1986), 8 EHRR 329, ECtHR, para 110. State action
     does not necessarily comply with the requirement that it be prescribed by law merely by reason of the
     fact that it is in conformity with domestic law; it must satisfy the principle of legal certainty and not be
     arbitrary: see *Winterwerp v Netherlands* A 33 (1979), 2 EHRR 387, ECtHR, para 45 (cited in para 127
     ante). See also *Hentrich v France* A 296-A (1994), 18 EHRR 440, ECtHR, paras 45–49.

5    Convention for the Protection of Human Rights and Fundamental Freedoms (1950), First Protocol,
     Art 1. As to the relationship between this limb of the First Protocol, Art 1 and the other limbs see *Sporrong
     and Lönnroth v Sweden* A 52 (1982), 5 EHRR 35, ECtHR, para 61; and note 8 infra.
         Although Art 1 of the First Protocol does not expressly refer to the payment of compensation in respect
     of a taking or other interference with property, the extent to which compensation is payable is material
     to the assessment of whether the requirement of proportionality is satisfied: see *James v United Kingdom*
     A 98 (1986), 8 EHRR 123, ECtHR, para 54; *Lithgow v United Kingdom* A 102 (1986), 8 EHRR 329,
     ECtHR, para 120; *Sporrong and Lönnroth v Sweden* supra at para 73. See also *Holy Monasteries v Greece*
     A 301-A (1994), 20 EHRR 1, ECtHR, paras 70–75; *Hentrich v France* A 296-A (1994), 18 EHRR 440,
     ECtHR, para 48; and *Pressos Compania Naviera SA v Belgium* A 332 (1995), 21 EHRR 301, ECtHR,
     para 38. The taking of property without the payment of an amount reasonably related to its value would
     normally constitute a disproportionate interference which could not be considered justifiable under Art 1
     of the First Protocol, but this does not guarantee a right to full compensation in all circumstances;
     legitimate objectives of public interest, such as pursued in measures of economic reform or measures
     designed to achieve greater social justice, may call for less than reimbursement of the full market value:
     *James v United Kingdom* supra at para 54; *Lithgow v United Kingdom* supra at para 121; *Holy Monasteries v
     Greece* supra at para 71.
         A taking must also be subject to the conditions provided for by the general principles of international
     law: First Protocol Art 1. This does not, however, mean that Art 1 incorporates the standards of general
     international law for the benefit of nationals: the reference to general international law applies only to
     alien property holders: *James v United Kingdom* supra at paras 58–66; *Lithgow v United Kingdom* supra at
     paras 111–119.

6    See *Sporrong and Lönnroth v Sweden* A 52 (1982), 5 EHRR 35, ECtHR, para 65 (expropriation permits
     granted in respect of properties were not intended to limit or control the use of those properties: this limb
     of Art 1 of the First Protocol did not apply). See contra *Mellacher v Austria* A 169 (1989), 12 EHRR 391,
     ECtHR (legislation compelling reduction of rents chargeable by certain landlords: Art 1 applied); *Gillow v*

*United Kingdom* (1986) 7 EHRR 292, EComHR (this point not taken in A 109 (1986), 11 EHRR 335, ECtHR. For other cases falling within the ambit of the 'control of use' limb of Art 1 of the First Protocol see Application 12570/86 *Denev v Sweden* 59 DR 127 (1989), EComHR (obligation on landowner to plant trees in interests of environmental protection); *Pine Valley Developments Ltd v Ireland* A 222 (1991), 14 EHRR 319, ECtHR (planning controls); *Fredin v Sweden* A 192 (1991), 13 EHRR 784, ECtHR (revocation of permit to exploit gravel pit); *Mellacher v Austria* supra (rent control); *Allgemeine Gold-und Silverscheideanstalt v United Kingdom* A 108 (1986), 9 EHRR 1, ECtHR (prohibition on importation); Application 11540/85 *Karni v Sweden* 55 DR 157 (1988), EComHR (economic regulation of professions); Application 9614/81 *G, S and M v Austria* 34 DR 119 (1983), EComHR (seizure of property for legal proceedings); *Inze v Austria* A 126 (1987), 10 EHRR 394, ECtHR (inheritance laws); and *Vendittelli v Italy* A 293-A (1994), 19 EHRR 464, ECtHR (sequestration of flat in connection with alleged infringement of planning regulations).

7   For cases concerning the state's power to tax or to impose other contributions or penalties, falling within the third rule of the First Protocol, Art 1 (see note 8 infra) see Application 11036/84 *Svenska Management Gruppen v Sweden* 45 DR 211 (1985), EComHR; Application 13013/87 *Wasa Liv Omsesidigt v Sweden* 58 DR 163 at 185–187 (1988), EComHR; *Gasus Dosier-und Fordertechnik v Netherlands* A 306-B (1995), 20 EHRR 403, ECtHR, para 59.

8   Convention for the Protection of Human Rights and Fundamental Freedoms (1950), First Protocol, Art 1. This limb of Art 1 of the Protocol applies where there is an interference with the opportunity to use property, as well as in relation to measures to secure the payment of taxes or other contributions or penalties: see *Sporrong and Lönnroth v Sweden* A 52 (1982), 5 EHRR 35, ECtHR, para 65.

The First Protocol, Art 1 comprises three distinct rules: (1) it states the principle of peaceful enjoyment of property (see text and note 1 supra); (2) it regulates the deprivation of possessions and subjects it to certain conditions (see text and notes 2–5 supra); and (3) it recognises that states are entitled to control the use of property in accordance with the general interest (see infra; and text and note 6 supra): *Sporrong and Lönnroth v Sweden* A 52 (1982), 5 EHRR 35, ECtHR, para 61; *James v United Kingdom* A 98 (1986), 8 EHRR 123, ECtHR, para 37; *Lithgow v United Kingdom* A 102 (1986), 8 EHRR 329, ECtHR, para 106; *AGOSI v United Kingdom* A 108 (1986), 9 EHRR 1, ECtHR, para 48; *Erkner and Hofauer v Austria* A 117 (1987), 9 EHRR 464, ECtHR, para 73; *Poiss v Austria* A 117 (1987), 10 EHRR 231, ECtHR, para 63; *Tre Traktörer Aktiebolag v Sweden* A 159 (1989), 13 EHRR 309, ECtHR, para 54; *Mellacher v Austria* A 169 (1989), 12 EHRR 391, ECtHR, para 42; and *Holy Monasteries v Greece* A 301-A (1994), 20 EHRR 1, ECtHR, para 56. In considering whether there has been a violation of the First Protocol, Art 1, it is necessary first to consider which of these three rules applies. The first rule applies where the interference in question is not intended to control the use of property, but nevertheless has the effect of interfering with the use or enjoyment of property: see *Sporrong and Lönnroth v Sweden* supra at para 65. See also *Erkner and Hofauer v Austria* supra at para 74 (provisional transfer of applicants' land to other landowners was neither a formal nor a de facto expropriation, and was not essentially designed to restrict or control the use of land, so the second and third rules did not apply; consequently the first rule applied. The first rule of Art 1 of the First Protocol was also held to apply in Application 7456/76 *Wiggins v United Kingdom* 13 DR 40 at 46–47 (1978), EComHR (refusal of housing licence to applicant to live in his own house); Application 7889/77 *Arrondelle v United Kingdom* 19 DR 186 (1980), EComHR (nuisance caused to houseowner by neighbouring airfield); see further at 26 DR 5 (1982), FSett; *Stran Greek Refineries v Greece* A 301-B (1994), 19 EHRR 293, ECtHR, para 68 (making arbitral award in applicants' favour void and unenforceable by legislation fell within the first rule of Art 1 of the First Protocol, as it did not involve de facto or de iure deprivation within the second rule, nor a measure to control the use of property).

9   *Marckx v Belgium* A 31 (1979), 2 EHRR 330, ECtHR, para 63.

10  Application 9266/81 *Yarrow v United Kingdom* 30 DR 155 at 185 (1983), EComHR (shareholders not victims when the value of their shares affected by reason of damage to the company); but see Application 1706/62 *X v Austria* 21 CD 34 at 44 (1966), EComHR (substantial majority shareholder was victim when the company suffered damage). Piercing the corporate veil will be justified only in exceptional circumstances, in particular when it is clearly established that the company cannot apply to the Convention institutions through the organs set up under its articles of incorporation or through its liquidators: see *Agrotexim v Greece* A 330 (1995), 21 EHRR 250, ECtHR.

11  Applications 8588/79, 8589/79 *Bramelid and Malmström v Sweden* 29 DR 64 (1982), EComHR.

12  Application 12633/87 *Smith Kline and French Laboratories v Netherlands* 66 DR 70 (1990), EComHR.

13  Application 11185/84 *Herrick v United Kingdom* (1985) 8 EHRR 66, EComHR.

14  Application 10741/84 *S v United Kingdom* 41 DR 226 (1984), EComHR.

15  *Mellacher v Austria* A 169 (1989), 12 EHRR 391, ECtHR, paras 43–44.

16  *Stran Greek Refineries v Greece* A 301-B (1994), 19 EHRR 293, ECtHR, paras 61–62.

17  Application 10426/83 *Pudas v Sweden* 40 DR 234 (1984), EComHR.

18  *Tre Traktörer Aktiebolag v Sweden* A 159 (1989), 13 EHRR 309, ECtHR, para 53.

19   *Van Marle v Netherlands* A 101 (1986), 8 EHRR 483, ECtHR, paras 41–42, where the court observed
      that the applicants' professional clientele constituted an asset protected by the First Protocol, Art 1).
20   *Pine Valley Developments Ltd v Ireland* A 222 (1991), 14 EHRR 319, ECtHR, para 51.
21   Application 7742/76 *A, B and Company AS v Federal Republic of Germany* 14 DR 146 (1978), EComHR;
      *Pressos Compania Naviera SA v Belgium* A 332 (1995), 21 EHRR 301, ECtHR (legal claim and legitimate
      expectation that the claims would be determined in accordance with the general law of tort).
22   Application 5849/72 *Müller v Austria* 3 DR 25 (1975), Com Rep.
23   See eg Application 8410/78 *X v Federal Republic of Germany* 18 DR 216 (1979), EComHR (expectation
      that notaries' fees would not be reduced by law is not protected under Art 1 of the Convention unless
      and until it is an actual claim for services rendered).
24   *Marckx v Belgium* A 31 (1979), 2 EHRR 330, ECtHR, para 50; *Inze v Austria* A 126 (1987), 10
      EHRR 394, ECtHR, paras 37–38.
25   Application 11716/85 *S v United Kingdom* 47 DR 274 (1986), EComHR (occupation of property
      without a legal right was not protected under Art 1 of the Convention). However, the fact that domestic
      law does not recognise a particular interest as a property right is not conclusive, as the concept of
      possession is autonomous, and an established economic interest may be sufficient to attract the protection:
      see *Tre Traktörer Aktiebolag v Sweden* A 159 (1989), 13 EHRR 309, ECtHR, para 53.

## L.   RIGHT TO EDUCATION

**166.   The right to education.** No one is to be denied the right to education[1]. This
necessarily implies the right to be educated in the national language or one of the national
languages, and guarantees a right of access to educational institutions[2] existing at a given
time, as well as the right to official recognition of studies successfully completed[3].

This provision is concerned primarily with elementary education and may not apply
to advanced studies[4]. It applies to the education given in public nurseries even though
such education is not compulsory[5].

The right to education does not prevent states from imposing entry requirements for
access to educational establishments, in particular in relation to higher education[6], nor
does it confer a right on students to pursue their education in a particular country[7].

In the exercise of any functions[8] which it assumes in relation to education and
teaching[9], the state must respect[10] the right of parents[11] to ensure such education and
teaching in conformity with their own religious and philosophical convictions[12]. The
United Kingdom has made a reservation to this provision[13].

The state may require children to be educated, whether at school or at home[14].

1   Convention for the Protection of Human Rights and Fundamental Freedoms (1950), First Protocol
     (1952), Art 2. As to the Convention and its Protocols generally see para 122 ante. Although this provision
     involves a positive right to education, its negative formulation indicates that the contracting states did not
     recognise such a right to education as would have required them to establish at their own expense or to
     subsidise education of any particular type or at any particular level: *Belgian Linguistics Case (No 2)* A 6
     (1968), 1 EHRR 252, ECtHR; Application 7782/77 *X v United Kingdom* 14 DR 179 (1978), EComHR.
        The right to education by its very nature calls for regulation by the state, but such regulation must
     never injure the substance of the right nor conflict with other guaranteed rights: *Belgian Linguistics Case
     (No 2)* supra at para 5; *Campbell and Cosans v United Kingdom* A 48 (1982), 4 EHRR 293, ECtHR, para 41
     (suspension of boy from school for almost full school year, which would have ended only if his parents
     agreed to subject him to the risk of corporal punishment, contrary to their philosophical convictions,
     violated the First Protocol, Art 2, because his access to education was conditional upon a requirement
     which conflicted with parents' right to ensure his education in conformity with their own philosophical
     convictions (see text and note 12 infra)); and see Application 11433/85 *Ingrid Jordebo Foundation of
     Christian Schools and Ingrid Jordebo v Sweden* 51 DR 125 (1987), EComHR. As to the prohibition of
     degrading corporal punishment see para 124 ante.
2   This provision does not oblige governments to recognise or continue to recognise any particular
     institution as an educational establishment: Application 3798/68 *Church of X v United Kingdom* 12 YB 306
     (1968), EComHR.
3   *Belgian Linguistics Case (No 2)* A 6 (1968), 1 EHRR 252, ECtHR.
4   Application 5962/72 *X v United Kingdom* 2 DR 50 (1975), EComHR; Application 7671/76 *15 Foreign
     Students v United Kingdom* 9 DR 185 (1977), EComHR.

5   Application 6853/74 9 DR 27 (1977), EComHR.

6   Application 8840/80 *X v United Kingdom* 23 DR 228 (1980), EComHR; Application 6598/74 5 Digest 783.

7   Application 7671/76 *15 Foreign Students v United Kingdom* 9 DR 185 (1977), EComHR (applicants refused leave to remain in United Kingdom as students).

8   This provision is binding upon the contracting states in relation to each and every function that they undertake in the sphere of education and teaching, including ancillary functions: *Campbell and Cosans v United Kingdom* A 48 (1982), 4 EHRR 293, ECtHR, para 33.

9   'The education of children is the whole process whereby adults endeavour to transmit their beliefs, culture and other values to the young, whereas teaching or instruction refers in particular to the transmission of knowledge and to intellectual development'; a school's disciplinary system is an integral part of the educational process: *Campbell and Cosans v United Kingdom* A 48 (1982), 4 EHRR 293, ECtHR, para 33.

10  'Respect' means more than 'take account of' or 'acknowledge'; it implies some positive obligation on the part of the state: *Campbell and Cosans v United Kingdom* A 48 (1982), 4 EHRR 293, ECtHR (policy of gradually eliminating corporal punishment in state schools did not amount to respect for the applicants' convictions against use of corporal punishment).

11  This does not prevent states from imparting information or knowledge of a directly or indirectly religious or philosophical kind through education, but the state must take care that such information or knowledge included in the curriculum must be conveyed in an objective, critical and pluralist manner; the state is forbidden to pursue an aim of indoctrination: *Kjeldsen, Busk Madsen and Pedersen v Denmark* A 23 (1976), 1 EHRR 711, ECtHR (compulsory sex education in state schools did not violate the First Protocol, Art 2, since it was intended to impart knowledge objectively and in the public interest, and heavily state-subsidised private schools, in which sex education was not compulsory, were also available).

    Parents do not lose all their rights under this provision if their children are taken into care: *Olsson v Sweden* A 130 (1988), 11 EHRR 259, ECtHR (no violation of the First Protocol, Art 2, on the facts). An adoption order confers the same rights on the adoptive parents as were previously enjoyed by the natural parents; natural parents whose children are adopted no longer have rights under this provision: Application 7626/76 *X v United Kingdom* 11 DR 160 (1977), EComHR. If one parent has custody of a child, the other parent's rights under this provision cease: Application 7911/77 *X v Sweden* 12 DR 192 (1977), EComHR.

12  Convention for the Protection of Human Rights and Fundamental Freedoms (1950), First Protocol, Art 2; cf the International Covenant on Economic, Social and Cultural Rights, 16 December 1966 (UN TS vol 993, p 3), Art 13; Convention on the Rights of the Child, 20 November 1989 (UN General Assembly Resolution 44/25; Cmd 1976), Art 28(1); Universal Declaration of Human Rights (Paris, 10 December 1948), Art 26(2). See further para 103 ante.

    'Philosophical convictions' denotes such convictions as are worthy of respect in a democratic society and are not incompatible with human dignity. Such convictions must not conflict with the fundamental right of the child to education: *Campbell and Cosans v United Kingdom* A 48 (1982), 4 EHRR 293, ECtHR, para 36 (opposition to corporal punishment was philosophical conviction). Parents' linguistic preferences are not a philosophical conviction for the purposes of Art 2 of the First Protocol: *Belgian Linguistics Case (No 2)* A 6 (1968), 1 EHRR 252, ECtHR.

13  The United Kingdom's reservation states that in view of certain provisions of the Education Acts in force in the United Kingdom, the principle affirmed in the second sentence of Art 2 of the First Protocol is accepted by the United Kingdom only so far as it is compatible with the provision of efficient instruction and training, and the avoidance of unreasonable public expenditure.

14  Application 10233/83 *Family H v United Kingdom* 37 DR 105 (1984), EComHR.

## M. RIGHT TO FREE ELECTIONS

**167. Right to free elections.** The contracting states[1] undertake to hold free elections at reasonable intervals by secret ballot, under conditions which will ensure the free expression of the opinion of the people in the choice of the legislature[2].

The right of free elections to the legislature is regarded as being of fundamental importance in the scheme of the Convention for the Protection of Human Rights and Fundamental Freedoms (1950)[3]. It includes both the right to vote[4] and the right to stand for elections[5], although both these rights may be subjected to conditions by the state[6]. The state has a wide margin of appreciation[7] in the application of these rights and is not required to adopt a specific electoral system[8]. The right to free elections may be invoked by individuals[9].

1　Ie the contracting states to the Convention for the Protection of Human Rights and Fundamental Freedoms (1950), First Protocol (1952). As to the Convention and its Protocols generally see para 122 ante.

2　Convention for the Protection of Human Rights and Fundamental Freedoms (1950), First Protocol, Art 3. With regard to the right to free elections in other international law instruments see the International Covenant on Civil and Political Rights (1966) Art 25; and the Universal Declaration of Human Rights (Paris, 10 December 1948), Art 21; and Joseph 'Rights of Political Participation' in Harris and Joseph (eds) *The International Covenant on Civil and Political Rights and United Kingdom Law* (1995) ch 16. As to the International Covenant on Civil and Political Rights (1966) see para 103 note 3 ante. As to the Universal Declaration of Human Rights see para 122 note 1 ante.

　　　Whether a particular body is a 'legislature' is to be determined by reference to the constitution of the contracting state: *Mathieu-Mohin and Clerfayt v Belgium* A 113 (1987), 10 EHRR 1, ECtHR, para 53. Municipal county councils in the United Kingdom are not legislatures as they do not have autonomous powers: Application 11391/85 *Booth-Clibborn v United Kingdom* 43 DR 236 (1985), EComHR; but this decision now needs to be viewed in the light of *Mathieu-Mohin and Clerfayt v Belgium* supra. The First Protocol, Art 3 does not apply to the appointment of the Head of State: Application 15344/89 *Habsburg-Lothringen v Austria* 64 DR 210 (1989), EComHR.

3　See *Mathieu-Mohin and Clerfayt v Belgium* A 113 (1987), 10 EHRR 1, ECtHR, para 47: 'According to the Preamble to the Convention, fundamental human rights and freedoms are best maintained by "an effective political democracy". Since it enshrines a characteristic principle of democracy, Article 3 of the First Protocol is accordingly of prime importance in the Convention system'.

4　*Mathieu-Mohin and Clerfayt v Belgium* A 113 (1987), 10 EHRR 1, ECtHR, para 51. However, a state has the right to disenfranchise individuals: see eg Application 530/59 *X v Federal Republic of Germany* 3 YB 184 (1960), EComHR (convicted prisoners); Application 9914/82 *H v Netherlands* 33 DR 242 (1979), EComHR; Application 1065/61, *X v Belgium* 4 YB 260 (1961), EComHR (nationals resident overseas).

5　*Mathieu-Mohin and Clerfayt v Belgium* A 113 (1987), 10 EHRR 1, ECtHR, para 51.

6　Eg the requirement of a given number of signatures before a group can stand for election: Application 6850/74 *Association X, Y, Z v Federal Republic of Germany* 5 DR 90 (1986), EComHR.

7　*Mathieu-Mohin and Clerfayt v Belgium* A 113 (1987), 10 EHRR 1, ECtHR, para 52 (but see also at para 54); Application 6850/74 *Association X, Y, Z v Federal Republic of Germany* 5 DR 90 (1986), EComHR.

8　*Mathieu-Mohin and Clerfayt v Belgium* A 113 (1987), 10 EHRR 1, ECtHR, para 54; Application 7140/75 *X v United Kingdom* 7 DR 95 at 96–97 (1977), EComHR; Application 8364/78 *Lindsay v United Kingdom* 15 DR 247 at 251 (1979), EComHR; Application 8765/79 *Liberal Party, R & P v United Kingdom* (1980) 21 DR 211 at 223 (1980), EComHR.

9　*Mathieu-Mohin and Clerfayt v Belgium* A 113 (1987), 10 EHRR 1, ECtHR.

## N. DEROGATIONS

**168. Measures derogating from state obligations.** In time of war or other emergency threatening the life of the nation[1] any state may take measures derogating from its obligations under the Convention for the Protection of Human Rights and Fundamental Freedoms (1950) to the extent strictly required[2] by the exigencies of the situation[3], provided such measures are not inconsistent with its other obligations under international law[4]. However, no derogation from the right to life[5] (except in respect of deaths resulting from lawful acts of war) or from the prohibitions of torture or inhuman or degrading treatment[6] or of slavery, servitude[7] or retrospective criminal laws[8] may be made[9]. Notice of measures taken must be communicated to the Secretary General of the Council of Europe, who must also be informed when such measures have ceased to operate and the general provisions of the Convention are again being fully executed[10].

1　See eg *Lawless v Ireland (No 2)* A 3 (1961), 1 EHRR 13, ECtHR (derogation justified); *Greek Case* 12 YB 1 (1969), EComHR (state cannot invoke a crisis for which it was itself responsible). The government is allowed to exercise a certain margin of appreciation in assessing the extent of derogation strictly required by the exigencies of the situation: Application 176/56 *Greece v United Kingdom (First Cyprus Case)* 2 YB 182 (1958), EComHR. This provision may include situations which do not involve an external threat, such as low intensity, irregular, but organised violence: see *Brannigan and McBride v United Kingdom* A 258-B (1993), 17 EHRR 539, ECtHR.

2　In assessing whether a particular measure is strictly required, the first question is whether it is necessary by examining why the ordinary law is not sufficient to meet the emergency and why the emergency measure may be sufficient: *Lawless v Ireland (No 2)* A 3 (1961), 1 EHRR 13, ECtHR; *Ireland v United Kingdom* A 25 (1978), 2 EHRR 25, ECtHR; *Brannigan and McBride v United Kingdom* A 258-B (1993), 17 EHRR 529, ECtHR. Once the necessity is established it may be examined whether some other, less draconian, emergency measure would suffice: see *Ireland v United Kingdom* supra (alternative of sealing the border between the Republic of Ireland and Northern Ireland was more draconian than the measure proposed); *Brannigan and McBride v United Kingdom* supra (non-judicial safeguards proposed by the British government in respect of administrative detention).

3   See *Ireland v United Kingdom* A 25 (1978), 2 EHRR 25, ECtHR, where the conditions prevailing in Northern Ireland fulfilled this condition and there was no independent assessment by the European Court of Human Rights. But see *Brannigan and McBride v United Kingdom* A 258-B (1993), 17 EHRR 539, ECtHR, where the European Commission of Human Rights stated that it had to make an independent finding. See also *Greek case* 12 YB 1 (1969), EComHR, where the Commission found, contrary to the Greek government's contention (no public emergency); *Ireland v United Kingdom* supra (national authorities are in principle in the best position to decide both on the presence of such an emergency and on the nature of and scope of derogations necessary to avert it; but there is a wide margin of appreciation').

4   Convention for the Protection of Human Rights and Fundamental Freedoms (1950) Art 15(1). As to the Convention see generally para 122 ante.

5   See ibid Art 2; and para 123 ante.

6   See ibid Art 3; and para 124 ante.

7   See ibid Art 4(1); and para 125 ante.

8   See ibid Art 7; and para 148 ante.

9   Ibid Art 15(2).

10  Ibid Art 15(3). The state is not required to give prior notice of derogation: *Lawless v Ireland (No 2)* A 3 (1961), 1 EHRR 13, ECtHR (notice promulgated 12 days after measures were taken); cf *Greek Case* 12 YB 1 (1969), EComHR. A continuing derogation cannot be justified after the emergency has ceased: *De Becker v Belgium* B 2 (1962), EComHR. Accordingly, the measures taken by a state must be kept under review: *Brannigan and McBride v United Kingdom* A 258-B (1993), 17 EHRR 539, ECtHR, para 54.

## 169. Restrictions on the political rights of aliens.

Nothing in the provisions of the Convention for the Protection of Human Rights and Fundamental Freedoms (1950) guaranteeing the right to freedom of expression[1], or the right to freedom of assembly[2], association, and freedom to join of a trade union[3], or in the provision prohibiting discrimination[4], can be regarded as preventing states from imposing restrictions on the political activity of aliens[5].

1   Ie the Convention for the Protection of Human Rights and Fundamental Freedoms (1950) Art 10: see paras 158–159 ante. As to the Convention generally see para 122 ante.

2   Ie ibid Art 11: see para 160 ante.

3   Ie ibid Art 11: see para 161 ante.

4   Ie ibid Art 14: see para 164 ante.

5   Ibid Art 16. This includes restrictions on the right to vote: see *Mathieu-Mohin and Clerfayt v Belgium* A 113 (1987), 10 EHRR 1, ECtHR, para 54. As to the meaning of 'aliens' in this context see *Piermont v France* A 314 (1995), 20 EHRR 301, ECtHR (member of the European Parliament, representing a German constituency, was not an alien with respect to French overseas territories in the South Pacific).

## 170. Activities aimed at the destruction of human rights.

Nothing in the Convention for the Protection of Human Rights and Fundamental Freedoms (1950) may be interpreted as implying for any state[1], group or person[2] any right to engage in any activity or perform any act aimed at the destruction of any of the rights and freedoms set out in the Convention, or at limiting them to a greater extent than is provided for in the Convention[3].

1   When relied upon by individuals this provision essentially constitutes part of an allegation of bad faith by the state: see *Engel v Netherlands* A 22 (1976), 1 EHRR 647, ECtHR; and *Lithgow v United Kingdom* A 102 (1986), Com Rep para 448 (this point not taken at A 102 (1986), 8 EHRR 329, ECtHR). See also *Greek Case* 12 YB 1 at 111–112 (1969), EComHR; *Sporrong and Lönnroth v Sweden* A 52 (1982), 5 EHRR 35, ECtHR.

2   See Applications 8384/78, 8406/78 *Glimmerveen and Hagenbeck v Netherlands* 18 DR 187 (1979), EComHR, where this provision justified interference with rights under the Convention for the Protection of Human Rights and Fundamental Freedoms (1950) Art 10, and the First Protocol, Art 3 (see paras 158–159, 167 ante) where the applicants had been excluded from participating in an election on a racist platform. See also *Jersild v Denmark* A 298 (1994), 19 EHRR 1, ECtHR; Application 250/57 *KPD v Federal Republic of Germany* 1 YB 222 at 223 (1957), EComHR (Art 17 of the Convention successfully relied upon by a government in the case of an application brought by the dissolved German Communist Party which invoked Arts 9–11); Application 12194/86 *Kühnen v Federal Republic of Germany* 56 DR 205 (1988), EComHR. This does not mean, however, that a person whose political activities are aimed at the overthrow of a democratic system of government in a state may be subjected to torture or denied a fair hearing of his case or subjected to unlawful detention: see *Lawless v Ireland* A 3 (1960) 1 EHRR 1, ECtHR, para 7; Application 17851/91 *Vogt v Germany* (1993) Com Rep; Application 15404/89 *Purcell v Ireland* 70 DR 262 at 278 (1991), EComHR.

3   Convention for the Protection of Human Rights and Fundamental Freedoms (1950) Art 17; and see Application 250/57 *KPD v Federal Republic of Germany* 1 YB 222 at 223 (1957), EComHR (Art 17 of the Convention protects 'the rights enshrined in the Convention by safeguarding the free functioning of democratic institutions').

**171. Prohibition of the use of restrictions for an improper purpose.** The restrictions of the rights and freedoms guaranteed in the Convention for the Protection of Human Rights and Fundamental Freedoms (1950) (and its Protocols) may not be applied for any purpose other than those for which they have been prescribed[1].

This prohibition may only be invoked by an applicant who claims that a restriction permitted by the Convention on his protected rights has been used for some purpose other than the one for which it is authorised[2].

1   Convention for the Protection of Human Rights and Fundamental Freedoms (1950) Art 18. As to the restrictions and derogations permitted by the Convention see Arts 8–11, 15; and paras 149–161 ante. As to the Convention and its Protocols see para 122 ante.

2   See *Engel v Netherlands* A 22 (1976), 1 EHRR 647, ECtHR, paras 104–108. Article 18 of the Convention is an integral part of all the limitation provisions of the Convention (Application 753/60 *X v Austria* 3 YB 310 (1960), EComHR), so can have no application where the Convention right is not subject to any restrictons (Application 4771/71 *Kamma v Netherlands* 1 DR 4 (1974), Com Rep). It prevents a state from relying on Art 15 (see para 168 ante) when the emergency has passed: *De Becker v Belgium* B 2 (1962), EComHR.

The European Commission of Human Rights may examine ex officio whether restrictions have been applied for an improper purpose even if this question has not been expressly invoked by the applicant: *De Wilde, Ooms and Versyp v Belgium (Vagrancy Cases)* A 12 (1971), 1 EHRR 373, ECtHR.

### (iii)   Enforcement of the Convention

A.  EUROPEAN COMMISSION OF HUMAN RIGHTS

**172. Complaints to the Commission.** Any contracting state to the Convention for the Protection of Human Rights and Fundamental Freedoms (1950) may refer to the European Commission of Human Rights[1] any alleged breach of the Convention by another contracting state[2].

The Commission may receive petitions[3] from any person, non-governmental organisation or group of individuals claiming to be a victim of a violation by a state of the Convention for the Protection of Human Rights and Fundamental Freedoms (1950)[4].

1   Reference is made through the Secretary General of the Council of Europe: Convention for the Protection of Human Rights and Fundamental Freedoms (1950) Art 24. As to the Convention generally see para 122 ante. As to the states party to the Convention and its Protocols see para 122 note 2 ante.

2   Ibid Art 24.

3   Complaints are made to the Secretary General of the Council of Europe: ibid Art 25(1).

4    Such a complaint may be made only if the state in question has declared that it recognises the Commission's competence to hear it: ibid Art 25(1). Such a declaration may be made for a specific period: Art 25(2); declarations may be deposited with the Secretary General: see Art 25(3). The states which have made such a declaration undertake not to hinder in any way the exercise of this right: Art 25(1): see eg Application 1593/62 *X v Austria* 7 YB 162 at 166, 168 (1964), EComHR.

See further Harris, O'Boyle and Warbrick *Law of the European Convention on Human Rights* (1995) p 580 et seq.

On the coming into force of the Eleventh Protocol to the Convention, the Commission will be abolished, and there will be a permanent right of access to a new, full-time, permanent European Court of Human Rights: see para 122 note 1 ante.

**173. Exhaustion of domestic remedies.** The European Commission of Human Rights may deal with a matter on a complaint or reference to it[1] only after all domestic remedies have been exhausted[2], according to the generally recognised rules of international law[3], and within six months from the date on which the final decision[4] was taken[5].

The respondent state may raise the objection of non-exhaustion of domestic remedies at any stage of the proceedings[6], and may also waive the application of the rule[7].

An application may be allowed notwithstanding non-exhaustion of domestic remedies where a remedy was not available within a reasonable time[8].

1    See para 172 ante. This requirement applies both to individual petitions and to inter-state applications: Application 788/60 *Austria v Italy* 4 YB 116 (1961), EComHR. But it does not apply to an inter-state reference concerning legislative measures or where substantial evidence is provided of an administrative practice in breach of the Convention for the Protection of Human Rights and Fundamental Freedoms (1950): Application 299/57 *Greece v United Kingdom* 2 YB 186 at 192 (1957), EComHR; Applications 5310/71, 5451/72 *Ireland v United Kingdom* 41 CD 3 (1972), EComHR; Applications 6780/74, 6950/75 *Cyprus v Turkey* 2 DR 125 (1975), EComHR. As to the Convention for the Protection of Human Rights and Fundamental Freedoms (1950) generally see para 122 ante.

2    Failure to take steps to accelerate proceedings does not constitute a failure to exhaust domestic remedies: Application 8961/80 *X v Federal Republic of Germany* 26 DR 200 (1981), EComHR; see also Application 8435/78 *X v United Kingdom* 26 DR 18 (1982), EComHR. It is sufficient compliance with Art 26 of the Convention that the domestic remedies are exhausted before the Commission arrives at a decision upon the application, even though they were not exhausted at the time of its presentation: *Ringeisen v Austria* A 13 (1971), ECtHR, paras 90–93.

3    As to the exhaustion of domestic remedies in relation to international agreements see FOREIGN RELATIONS LAW vol 18 para 1751.

4    The refusal of entry clearance and leave to remain in the United Kingdom constituted a final decisions for this purpose: Applications 9214/80, 9473/81, 9474/81 *X, Cabales and Balkandali v United Kingdom* (1982) 5 EHRR 132, EComHR.

5    Convention for the Protection of Human Rights and Fundamental Freedoms (1950) Art 26. The rule is one of admissibility, although, exceptionally, the Commission may join the issue of non-exhaustion of domestic remedies to the merits of the application. This is especially so where the application involves the provisions of Art 6(1) (right to fair trial: see paras 134–147 ante): Application 788/60 *Austria v Italy* 4 YB 116 (1961), EComHR; Application 332/57 *Lawless v Ireland* 2 YB 308 (1958), EComHR; Application 2991/66 Application 2991/66 *Alam and Khan v United Kingdom* 10 YB 478 (1967), EComHR.

As to the abolition of the Commission on the prospective coming into force of the Eleventh Protocol to the Convention see para 122 note 1 ante.

6    Thus the state may raise the objection during oral proceedings, even though it did not do so at the stage of written proceedings: Application 712/60 *Retimag v Federal Republic of Germany* 4 YB 384 (1961), EComHR. However, the objection should be raised at the initial examination for admissibility by the Commission; failure to do so may estop the government concerned from raising it before the court: Applications 8805/79, 8806/79, 9242/81 *De Jong, Baljet, Van Den Brink v Netherlands* A 77 (1984), 8 EHRR 20, ECtHR.

7    Application 1994/63 *57 Inhabitants of Louvain v Belgium* 7 YB 252 (1964), EComHR; Application 8919/80 *Van der Mussele v Belgium* 23 DR 244 (1981), EComHR.

8    Application 7630/76 *Reed v United Kingdom* 19 DR 113, (1979) 3 EHRR 136, EComHR.

**174. Petitions which must be rejected by the Commission.** The European Commission of Human Rights may not deal with any petition[1] which is anonymous[2] or substantially the same as a matter which has already been examined by it or which has been submitted to another procedure of investigation or settlement if it contains no relevant new information[3]. It must consider inadmissible any such petition which it considers incompatible with the provisions of the Convention for the Protection of Human Rights and Fundamental Freedoms (1950)[4], manifestly ill-founded[5] or an abuse of the right of petition[6]. The Commission must reject any such petition which it considers inadmissible because not all domestic remedies have been exhausted or because the petition was not submitted within six months of the final decision being taken[7].

1   Ie a petition under the Convention for the Protection of Human Rights and Fundamental Freedoms (1950) Art 25: see para 172 text and notes 3–4 ante. As to the Convention generally see para 122 ante.
    As to the abolition of the Commission on the prospective coming into force of the Eleventh Protocol to the Convention see para 122 note 1 ante.
2   Ibid Art 27(1)(a). An application will be rejected on this ground if the file does not contain any element enabling the Commission to identify the applicant: Application 361/58 *X v Ireland* 5 Digest 334, EComHR (petition signed by 'lover of tranquillity'); see also Application 3798/68 *Church of X v United Kingdom* 12 YB 306 (1968), EComHR (application on behalf of a church and its members, where members not named).
3   Convention for the Protection of Human Rights and Fundamental Freedoms (1950) Art 27(1)(b).
    A new submission on an application on which a decision on admissibility has already been made is a new application: Application 3806/68 *X & Co (England) Ltd v Germany* 11 YB 609 (1968), EComHR. A new application will be rejected if it merely reiterates previous complaints (Application 2795/66 *X v Germany* 30 CD 23 (1969), EComHR), or if it only contains new legal arguments regarding the national law (Application 261/57 *X v Germany* 1 YB 255 (1957), EComHR) or new factual information which does not affect the substance of previous allegations (Application 2606/65 *X v Germany* 26 CD 22 (1967), EComHR; Application 8206/78 *X v United Kingdom* 25 DR 147 (1981), EComHR (reference to 'travaux préparatoires' of Convention not 'new factual information')). However, a new application containing a new fact which would have required a different decision had it previously been known to the Commission is not substantially the same as the previous petition: Application 3780/68 *X v Belgium* 37 CD 6 (1970), EComHR; Application 4256/69 *X v Federal Republic of Germany* 37 CD 67 (1970), EComHR. An application by a petitioner, other than a petitioner whose application has been rejected previously, is not inadmissible under this provision: Application 493/59 *X v Ireland* 4 YB 302 (1961), EComHR (the earlier case was Application 332/57 *Lawless v Ireland* 2 YB 308 (1958), EComHR). Cf Application 499/59 *X v Federal Republic of Germany* 2 YB 397 (1959), EComHR; Application 3798/68 *Church of X v United Kingdom* 12 YB 306 (1968), EComHR; Application 9028/80 *X v Federal Republic of Germany* 22 DR 236 (1980), EComHR. An application from a petitioner whose earlier petition was rejected for non-exhausted local remedies, but who has now exhausted them, will not be rejected under this provision: Application 3448/67 *Wemhoff v Germany* 30 CD 56 (1967), EComHR.
4   See para 175 post.
5   This basis of inadmissibility is concerned with the merits of the application. An application is regarded as manifestly ill-founded when it does not reveal a violation of any of the rights and freedoms guaranteed in the Convention, or where the application is based upon an interpretation of the Convention which is obviously incorrect in law. The distinction between this and an application incompatible with the Convention is not always observed by the Commission: see eg Application 2992/66 *Singh v United Kingdom* 10 YB 478 (1967), EComHR; Application 86/55 *X v Germany* 1 YB 198 (1958), EComHR. It has been said that an application raising complex issues of law cannot be manifestly ill-founded: Application 5029/71 *Klass v Federal Republic of Germany* 1 DR 20 (1974), EComHR. Nor can a complaint which is 'arguable' be manifestly ill-founded: *Boyle and Rice v United Kingdom* A 131 (1988), ECtHR, paras 53–54.
6   Convention for the Protection of Human Rights and Fundamental Freedoms (1950) Art 27(2).
    Petitions are an abuse of the right of petition where they are submitted in persistent and negligent disregard of the rules laid down to enable the secretariat to prepare applications for presentation (Application 26/55 *X v Germany* 1 YB 194 (1958), EComHR; Application 244/57 *X v Germany* 1 YB 196 (1958), EComHR; Application 13284/87 *M v United Kingdom* 54 DR 214 (1987), EComHR), or where the facts obviously do not indicate any violation of the Convention (Application 1270/61 *Koch v Germany* 5 YB 126 (1962), EComHR), or where the petition makes defamatory or abusive remarks about the respondent government or its agent (Application 2424/65 *Rafael v Austria* 9 YB 426 (1966), EComHR; Application 5267/71 *X v Federal Republic of Germany* 43 CD 154 (1973),

EComHR; Application 6029/73 *X v Austria* 44 CD 134 (1973), EComHR), or where the petition is a repetition of a baseless application (Application 1307/61 *X v Federal Republic of Germany* 5 YB 230 at 236 (1962), EComHR), or where false statements are made deliberately in an attempt to mislead the Commission (Application 2625/65 *X and X v Federal Republic of Germany* 28 CD 26 (1965), EComHR; Application 3934/69 *X v Sweden* 34 CD 27 (1970), EComHR), or where proceedings before the Commission are being used to evade obligations under domestic law (Application 5207/71 *Raupp v Federal Republic of Germany* 14 YB 698 (1971), EComHR; but cf Application 6066/73 *Levy v Federal Republic of Germany* 45 CD 99 (1973), EComHR). However, the fact that the petition is introduced for motives of publicity and propaganda does not necessarily render it an abuse of the right of petition: Application 332/57 *Lawless v Ireland* 2 YB 308 at 338 (1958), EComHR; Application 1468/62 *Iversen v Norway* 6 YB 278 (1963), EComHR.

An inter-state application cannot be rejected as abusive: Applications 6780/74, 6950/75 *Cyprus v Turkey* 2 DR 125 (1976), 4 EHRR 282, EComHR.

7　Ie any petition inadmissible under the Convention for the Protection of Human Rights and Fundamental Freedoms (1950) Art 26 (see para 173 ante): Art 27(3).

**175. Rejection of petition for incompatibility with the Convention.** The European Commission of Human Rights must consider inadmissible any petition submitted by an individual which it considers incompatible with the provisions of the Convention for the Protection of Human Rights and Fundamental Freedoms (1950)[1]. An application cannot be admitted (1) when it is based upon an alleged violation of a right not guaranteed by the Convention[2]; (2) if the applicant or respondent is incompetent to appear before the Commission[3]; (3) when it is within a reservation made by a contracting state[4]; (4) where it deals with a matter which is the subject matter of a derogation[5]; (5) if it claims the right to engage in activities which could nullify the enjoyment of other rights granted by the convention[6]; or (6) if it is an attempt to use the Commission as a court of 'fourth instance'[7].

The following have, inter alia, been held to be rights not guaranteed by the Convention: the right to work[8]; the right to a pension[9]; the right to occupy a public position[10]; the right to exercise a particular profession[11]; the right to paid leave[12]; the right to adequate living accommodation[13]; the right to reputation or character[14]; the right to political asylum[15]; the right to settle in a foreign state[16]; the right to leave a country and to obtain documents for the purpose[17]; the right not to be extradited or expelled[18]; the right to free legal aid in civil matters[19]; the right to an appeal[20]; the right to revision or reopening of a conviction or to habeas corpus for that purpose[21]; the right to a stay of execution of a sentence[22] or its reduction[23] or suspension[24]; the right to conditional freedom[25]; the right to serve a sentence in a particular prison[26]; the right to cause criminal proceedings to be commenced against a third person[27]; the right to registration of a patent[28]; the right to take property out of a country without restrictions[29]; the right to be detained in a particular prison[30]; the right to diplomatic protection[31]; or the right to financial assistance to maintain a particular standard of living[32].

1　Convention for the Protection of Human Rights and Fundamental Freedoms (1950) Art 27(2): see para 174 ante. As to the Convention generally see para 122 ante.

　　As to the abolition of the Commission on the prospective coming into force of the Eleventh Protocol to the Convention see para 122 note 1 ante.

2　As to rights not guaranteed see text and notes 8–32 infra.

3　A state not party to the Convention is not a competent respondent: Application 4517/70 *Huber v Austria* 38 CD 90 at 99 (1971), EComHR; nor is one which, though a party, has not accepted the right of individual petition. There is no jurisdiction to examine a complaint made against the European Community arising from a decision of the EC Council (until, presumably, the European Community accedes to the Convention): Application 8030/77 *Confédération Française Démocratique du Travail v European Communities* 13 DR 231 (1978), [1979] 2 CMLR 229, EComHR. An association cannot be given authority to make a complaint retrospectively by the execution of powers of attorney by individual victims in favour of the association: Applications 9959, 10357/82 *S Association v Sweden* 37 DR 87 (1984), EComHR.

　　In addition, an application is incompatible if the alleged violation took place in a territory to which it does not apply, or at a time before the law entered into force with respect to the respondent state. A 'petition which cites an individual as respondent is incompatible with the convention: see eg Application 2942/66 *X v Germany* 23 CD 51 (1967), EComHR; Application 9022/80 *W v Switzerland* 33 DR 21 (1983), EComHR.

See generally Harris, O'Boyle and Warbrick *Law of the European Convention on Human Rights* (1995) pp 629–647.

4   States were given the right to make reservations to any particular provision of the Convention for the Protection of Human Rights and Fundamental Freedoms (1950) in relation to a particular law in force at the time of ratification, if such a law was not in conformity with the Convention, but reservations of a general nature were permitted: see Art 64.

5   See ibid Art 15; and para 168 ante.

6   See ibid Art 17; and para 170 ante.

7   The Commission (and the court) are established to ensure the observance of the engagements undertaken by the contracting states under the Convention: Art 19. The Commission is not a court of appeal from decisions of the domestic courts, who alone can decide whether a conviction or judgment is correct in terms of that law, or whether a sentence is or is not too severe: see eg Application 254/57 *X v Germany* 1 YB HR 150 at 152 (1957), EComHR; Application 788/60 *Austria v Italy* 4 YB 116 (1961), EComHR; Application 899/60 *R v Federal Republic of Germany* 5 YB 136 (1962), EComHR; Application 1103/61 *X v Belgium* 5 YB 168 at 190 (1962), EComHR; Application 3075/67 *X v United Kingdom* 28 CD 94 (1965), EComHR.

8   Application 852/60 *X v Germany* 4 YB 346 (1961), EComHR; Application 1038/61 *X v Belgium* 4 YB 324 (1961), EComHR; Application 5415/72 *X v United Kingdom* 43 CD 158 (1973), EComHR; Application 6907/75 *X v Denmark* 3 DR 153 (1975), EComHR.

9   Application 2116/64 *X v Federal Republic of Germany* 23 CD 10 (1967), EComHR; Application 4130/69 *X v the Netherlands* 38 CD 9 (1971), EComHR; Application 5713/72 *X and Y v Federal Republic of Germany* 44 CD 76 (1974), EComHR. As to social security benefits see Application 4933/71 *X v United Kingdom* 43 CD 24 (1973), EComHR.

10  Application 1103/61 *X v Belgium* 5 YB 168 (1962), EComHR. As to service in the armed forces see Application 787/60 *X v the Netherlands* 7 CD 75 (1961), EComHR.

11  Application 1197/61 *X v Federal Republic of Germany* 5 YB 88 (1962), EComHR. As to acting as advocate in a particular case see Application 1013/61 *K and Y v Germany* 5 YB 158 (1962), EComHR; and as to participating in the administration of direction of a professional body or in a company see Application 1038/61 *X v Belgium* 4 YB 324 (1961), EComHR.

12  Application 436/58 *X v Federal Republic of Germany* 2 YB 386 (1959), EComHR.

13  Application 2942/66 *X v Federal Republic of Germany* 23 CD 51 (1967), EComHR.

14  Application 2413/65 *X v Federal Republic of Germany* 23 CD 1 (1965), EComHR.

15  Application 1802/62 *X v Federal Republic of Germany* 6 YB 462 (1963), EComHR; Application 3040/67 *X v Germany* 10 YB 518 (1967), EComHR; Application 11278/84 *K and W v Netherlands* 43 DR 216 (1985), EComHR. An alien has no right to reside in a contracting state: Application 858/60 *X v Belgium* 4 YB 224 (1961), EComHR; Application 1465/62 *X v Germany* 5 YB 256 (1962), EComHR; Application 5269/71 *X and Y v United Kingdom* 39 CD 104 (1971), EComHR (exclusion from country where spouse is living); but see the Convention for the Protection of Human Rights and Fundamental Freedoms (1950) Art 3; and para 124 ante; cf Application 2143/64 *X v Austria and Yugoslavia* 7 YB 314 (1964), EComHR. There is no general right to enter or to reside in a certain country or part of it as such, even in the case of a national: Application 3325/66 *X, Y, Z, V and W v United Kingdom* 10 YB 528 (1967), EComHR; Application 3798/68 *Church of X v United Kingdom* 12 YB 306 (1969), EComHR. Cf the Fourth Protocol, Arts 2(4), 3 (which has been signed but not ratified by the United Kingdom); see para 122 ante.

16  Application 10427/83 *C v United Kingdom* 47 DR 85 (1986), EComHR.

17  Application 3110/67 *X v Germany* 11 YB 494 (1968), EComHR. The right to leave a country is guaranteed by the Fourth Protocol, Art 2(2), which has been signed but not, however, ratified by the United Kingdom: see para 122 note 1 ante.

18  Application 1983/63 *X v the Netherlands* 8 YB 228 (1965), EComHR; Application 2143/64 *X v Austria and Yugoslavia* 7 YB 314 (1964), EComHR; Application 3110/67 *X v Federal Republic of Germany* 11 YB 494 (1968), EComHR. In certain circumstances this might amount to a violation of Art 3 of the Convention: see para 124 ante. There is no right to a particular nationality: Application 2699/65 *X v Federal Republic of Germany* 11 YB 366 (1968), EComHR; Application 11278/84 *K and W v Netherlands* 43 DR 216 (1985), EComHR.

19  Application 2942/66 *X v Germany* 23 CD 51 (1967), EComHR; Application 4471/70 *X v United Kingdom* 39 CD 44 at 47 (1971), EComHR; see also Application 2804/66 *Struppat v Germany* 11 YB 380 (1968), EComHR; Application 3925/69 *X v Federal Republic of Germany* 32 CD 56 (1970), EComHR. But see the Convention for the Protection of Human Rights and Fundamental Freedoms Art 6(1); and para 134 et seq ante.

20  Application 2749/66 *De Courcy v United Kingdom* 10 YB 388 (1967), EComHR; see also Application 2366/64 *X v Germany* 10 YB 208 (1967), EComHR; and Application 7761/77 *X v Austria* 14 DR 171 (1978), EComHR.

21  See eg Application 2749/66 *De Courcy v United Kingdom* 10 YB 388 (1967), EComHR; Application 3034/67 *Fletcher v United Kingdom* 25 CD 76 (1967), EComHR; Application 3505/68 *X v United Kingdom* 12 YB 298 (1969), EComHR; Application 4311/69 *X v Denmark* 37 CD 82 (1970), EComHR; Application 5335/72 *X v United Kingdom* 42 CD 144 (1972), EComHR.

22  Application 1140/61 *X v Austria* 8 CD 57 (1961), EComHR; Application 2306/64 *X v Austria* 21 CD 23, EComHR.

23  Application 1789/63 *X v Austria* 11 CD 25 (1963), EComHR.

24  Application 2428/65 *X v Federal Republic of Germany* 25 CD 1 (1967), EComHR.

25  Application 369/58 *X v Belgium* 2 YB 376 (1959), EComHR; Application 1599/62 *X v Austria* 6 YB 348 (1963), EComHR; Application 1760/63 *X v Austria* 9 YB 166 (1966), EComHR.

26  Application 2516/65 *X v Federal Republic of Germany* 9 YB 436 (1966), EComHR.

27  Application 2749/66 *De Courcy v United Kingdom* 10 YB 388 (1967), EComHR, where it was also held that there is no guaranteed right to clemency, or to ensure that an action is brought against a judge; Application 2646/65 *X v Federal Republic of Germany* 9 YB 484 (1966), EComHR; Application 3110/67 *X v Federal Republic of Germany* 11 YB 494 (1968), EComHR.

28  Application 7830/77 *X v Austria* 14 DR 200 (1978), EComHR.

29  Application 10653/83 *S v Sweden* 42 DR 224 (1985), 8 EHRR 310, EComHR.

30  Application 11208/84 *McQuiston v United Kingdom* 46 DR 182 (1986), EComHR.

31  Application 7597 *Bertrand Russell Peace Foundation Ltd v United Kingdom* 14 DR 117 (1978), EComHR; Application 12822/87 *Kaplan v United Kingdom* 54 DR 201 (1987), EComHR.

32  Application 11776/85 *Andersson and Kullman v Sweden* 46 DR 251 (1986), EComHR.

**176. Friendly settlements.** In the event of the European Commission of Human Rights accepting a petition it must undertake, together with the representatives of the parties, with a view to ascertaining the facts, an examination of the petition and, if need be, an investigation, for the effective conduct of which the states concerned must furnish all necessary facilities after an exchange of views with the Commission[1]. The Commission must place itself at the disposal of the parties with a view to securing a friendly settlement of the matter on the basis of respect for human rights[2]. If the Commission succeeds in effecting a friendly settlement it must draw up a report[3] which is sent to the states concerned, to the Committee of Ministers[4] and to the Secretary General of the Council of Europe for publication[5].

1   Convention for the Protection of Human Rights and Fundamental Freedoms (1950) Art 28(a). As to the Convention generally see para 122 ante. The functions of the Commission under Art 28 must be performed by a sub-commission consisting of seven members of the Commission: Art 29(1). Each of the parties concerned may appoint a person of its choice as a member of the sub-commission (Art 29(2)), and the remaining members are chosen by lot (Art 29(3)).
    As to the abolition of the Commission on the prospective coming into force of the Eleventh Protocol to the Convention see para 122 note 1 ante.

2   Ibid Art 28(b).

3   The report must be confined to a brief statement of the facts and of the solution reached: ibid Art 30.

4   Ie the Committee of Ministers of the Council of Europe established by the Statute of the Council of Europe (London, 5 May 1949; TS 51 (1949); Cmd 7778), Art 14. The Committee consists of the ministers of foreign affairs or their deputies of the member states of the Council of Europe. The committee has the authority to suspend a member state from its right to be represented in the Council of Europe, to request it to withdraw, or to determine that it has ceased to be a member of the Council of Europe: see Arts 3, 7, 8. Nothing in the Convention for the Protection of Human Rights and Fundamental Freedoms (1950) prejudices the powers conferred on the committee by the Statute of the Council of Europe: Convention for the Protection of Human Rights and Fundamental Freedoms (1950) Art 61.

5   Ibid Art 30 (amended by the Third Protocol, Art 2 (see para 122 note 2 ante)).

**177. Decisions and reports.** If the European Commission of Human Rights does not succeed in effecting a friendly settlement[1] it must draw up a report on the facts and state its opinion as to whether the facts found disclose a breach by the state concerned of its obligations under the Convention for the Protection of Human Rights and Fundamental Freedoms (1950)[2]. The report must be transmitted to the Committee of Ministers[3] and to the states concerned, which are not at liberty to publish it[4]. In transmitting the report to the committee, the Commission may make such proposals as it thinks fit[5].

If the question is not referred to the European Court of Human Rights[6] within three months from the date of the transmission of the report to the Committee of Ministers, the committee must decide by a majority of two-thirds of the members entitled to sit on the committee whether there has been a violation of the Convention[7]. If the decision is affirmative the committee prescribes a period during which the state concerned must take the measures required by the committee's decision[8]. If the state concerned has not taken satisfactory measures within the prescribed period, the committee must decide by a majority of two-thirds of the members entitled to sit on the committee what effect must be given to its original decision, and must publish the report[9]. Any such decision is binding[10].

1    See para 176 ante.
2    Convention for the Protection of Human Rights and Fundamental Freedoms (1950) Art 31(1). The opinions of all the members of the Commission on this point may be contained in the report: Art 31(1). As to the Convention generally see para 122 ante.
        As to the abolition of the Commission on the prospective coming into force of the Eleventh Protocol to the Convention see para 122 note 1 ante.
3    As to the Committee of Ministers see para 176 note 4 ante.
4    Convention for the Protection of Human Rights and Fundamental Freedoms (1950) Art 31(2).
5    Ibid Art 31(3). For an account of the procedure see Harris, O'Boyle and Warbrick *Law of the European Convention on Human Rights* (1995) p 594 et seq.
6    Ie under the Convention for the Protection of Human Rights and Fundamental Freedoms (1950) Art 48: see para 179 text and note 4 post.
7    Ibid Art 32(1).
8    Ibid Art 32(2).
9    Ibid Art 32(3).
10   Ibid Art 32(4).

**178. Proceedings of the Commission.** The European Commission of Human Rights consists of a number of members equal to the number of states party to the Convention for the Protection of Human Rights and Fundamental Freedoms; no two members may be nationals of the same state[1]. The members are elected by the Committee of Ministers[2] by an absolute majority from a list of names drawn up by the Bureau of the Consultative Assembly[3]. The members are elected for a period of six years and may be re-elected[4]. They sit in their individual capacities[5], and the Commission meets in camera[6]. It meets as the circumstances require, convened by the Secretary General of the Council of Europe[7]. It takes its decisions by a majority of members present and voting[8]. The Commission draws up its own rules of procedure[9]. Its secretariat is provided by the Secretary General of the Council of Europe[10]. The expenses of the Commission are borne by the Council of Europe[11].

The members of the Commission are entitled during the discharge of their functions to the privileges and immunities provided in the Statute of the Council of Europe[12].

1    Convention for the Protection of Human Rights and Fundamental Freedoms (1950) Art 20. As to the Convention generally see para 122 ante.
        As to the abolition of the Commission on the prospective coming into force of the Eleventh Protocol to the Convention see para 122 note 1 ante.
2    As to the Committee of Ministers see para 176 note 4 ante.
3    Convention for the Protection of Human Rights and Fundamental Freedoms (1950) Art 21(1). For the provisions relating to nomination of candidates and filling of casual vacancies, particularly n the event of more states becoming parties to the Convention, see Art 21(2).

4    Ibid Art 22(1). For further provisions relating to terms of office see Art 22(2)–(6) (amended by the Fifth
     Protocol, Arts 1, 2 (see para 122 note 2 ante)).
5    Convention for the Protection of Human Rights and Fundamental Freedoms (1950) Art 23.
6    Ibid Art 33.
7    Ibid Art 35.
8    Ibid Art 34. A sub-commission takes decisions by a majority of its members: Art 34.
9    Ibid Art 36.
10   Ibid Art 37.
11   Ibid Art 58.
12   Ibid Art 59. As to the privileges and immuities referred to see the Statute of the Council of Europe
     (London, 5 May 1949; TS 51; Cmd 7778), Art 40; and the General Agreement on Privileges and
     Immunities of the Council of Europe (Paris, 2 September 1949; TS 34; Cmd 8852); and *Zoernsch v
     Waldock* [1964] 2 All ER 256, [1964] 1 WLR 675, CA.

## B.   EUROPEAN COURT OF HUMAN RIGHTS

**179. Jurisdiction of the court.** The jurisdiction of the European Court of Human
Rights extends to all cases concerning the interpretation or application of the Convention
for the Protection of Human Rights and Fundamental Freedoms (1950), which the
contracting states or the European Commission of Human Rights may refer to it[1]. Only
a contracting state or the Commission[2] has the right to bring a case before the court[3]. The
states which may bring a case before the court are: (1) a state whose national is alleged to
be a victim of a violation of the Convention; (2) a state which referred the case to the
Commission; and (3) a state against which the complaint has been lodged, provided in
each case that the state or states concerned are subject to the compulsory jurisdiction of
the court or have consented to the case being heard by the court[4]. Contracting states may
at any time declare that they recognise as compulsory ipso facto and without special
agreement the jurisdiction of the court in all matters concerning the interpretation or
application of the Convention[5].

1    Convention for the Protection of Human Rights and Fundamental Freedoms (1950) Art 45. References
     are made under Art 48 (see text and note 4 infra). The court also has power to give advisory opinions,
     conferred by the Third Protocol to the Convention (see para 122 note 1 ante). In the event of any dispute
     as to whether the court has jurisdiction, the matter is settled by the decision of the court: Convention for
     the Protection of Human Rights and Fundamental Freedoms (1950) Art 49. As to the Convention
     generally see para 122 ante.
         As to the abolition of the Commission, and the effect on the court, on the prospective coming into
     force of the Eleventh Protocol to the Convention see para 122 note 1 ante.
2    The court may only deal with a case after the Commission has acknowledged the failure of efforts for a
     friendly settlement and within a period of three months from the date of transmission of the report of the
     Commission to the Council of Ministers under the Convention for the Protection of Human Rights and
     Fundamental Freedoms (1950) Art 32 (see para 177 ante): Art 47. When the Commission appears in a
     case which it has referred to the court it is not a party to the case; its function is to clarify the facts of the
     case and attempt an evaluation of them: see Application 332/57 *Lawless v Ireland* 3 YB 492 (1960),
     EComHR; Application 556/59 *X v Austria* 3 Yearbook HR 288 at 294 (1960), EComHR.
3    Convention for the Protection of Human Rights and Fundamental Freedoms (1950) Art 44. An
     individual applicant may not bring a case before the court, but the court may authorise the Commission
     to present the applicant's comments.
4    Ibid Art 48.
5    Ibid Art 46.

**180. Judgments of the court.** The judgment of the European Court of Human
Rights is final[1], and the contracting states undertake to abide by its decision in any case
to which they are party[2]. Reasons must be given for a judgment[3], and if the judgment
does not in whole or in part represent the unanimous opinion of the judges, any judge
may deliver a separate opinion[4].

The decision is transmitted to the Committee of Ministers[5] for the supervision of its execution[6].

If the court finds that a decision or measure taken by a legal or other authority of a contracting state is completely or partially in conflict with the obligations arising from the Convention for the Protection of Human Rights and Fundamental Freedoms (1950), and if the internal law of the state allows for only partial reparation to be made for the consequences of the decision or measure, the decision of the court must, if necessary, afford just satisfaction to the injured party[7].

1   Convention for the Protection of Human Rights and Fundamental Freedoms (1950) Art 52. As to the Convention generally see para 122 ante.
   As to the effect on the European Court of Human Rights of the prospective coming into force of the Eleventh Protocol to the Convention see para 122 note 1 ante.
2   Convention for the Protection of Human Rights and Fundamental Freedoms (1950) Art 53.
3   Ibid Art 51(1).
4   Ibid Art 51(2).
5   As to the Committee of Ministers see para 176 note 4 ante.
6   Convention for the Protection of Human Rights and Fundamental Freedoms (1950) Art 54.
7   Ibid Art 50. See generally Harris, O'Boyle and Warbrick *Law of the European Convention on Human Rights* (1995) pp 682–688.

**181–200.  Composition and procedure of the court.** The  European  Court  of Human Rights consists of a number of judges equal to that of the members of the Council of Europe[1]. No two judges may be nationals of the same state[2]. The members of the court are elected by a majority by the Consultative Assembly from a list of persons[3] nominated by the members of the Council of Europe[4]. Members of the court are elected for a period of nine years, and may be re-elected[5]. The president and vice-president of the court are elected for three years, and may be re-elected[6]. For each day of duty the members of the court receive a compensation determined by the Committee of Ministers[7].

For the consideration of each case referred to it, the court consists of a chamber of seven judges[8]. It draws up its own rules and determines its own procedure[9].

The expenses of the court are borne by the Council of Europe[10].

The members of the Commission are entitled during the discharge of their functions to the privileges and immunities provided in the Statute of the Council of Europe[11].

1   Convention for the Protection of Human Rights and Fundamental Freedoms (1950) Art 38. As to the Convention generally see para 122 ante.
   As to the effect on the European Court of Human Rights of the prospective coming into force of the Eleventh Protocol to the Convention see para 122 note 1 ante.
2   Convention for the Protection of Human Rights and Fundamental Freedoms (1950) Art 38.
3   The persons must be of high moral character and must either possess the qualifications required for appointment to high judicial office or be jurisconsults of recognised competence: ibid Art 39(3).
4   Ibid Art 39(1). Each member nominates three candidates, of which at least two must be its own nationals: Art 39(1). For the provisions relating to the filling of casual vacancies, and in the event of more states becoming parties to the Convention, see Art 39(2).
5   Ibid Art 40(1). For further provisions relating to terms of office see Art 40(2)–(7) (amended by the Fifth Protocol, Arts 3, 4 (see para 122 note 2 ante)).
6   Convention for the Protection of Human Rights and Fundamental Freedoms (1950) Art 41.
7   Ibid Art 42. As to the Committee of Ministers see para 176 note 4 ante.
8   Ibid Art 43. The judge who is a national of any state concerned or, if there is none, a person of its choice, sits in the capacity of a judge as an ex officio member of the chamber: Art 43. The names of the other judges are chosen by lot by the President: Art 43.
9   Ibid Art 55.
10   Ibid Art 58.
11   Ibid Art 59. As to the privileges and immunities referred to see the Statute of the Council of Europe (London, 5 May 1949; TS 51; Cmd 7778), Art 40; and the General Agreement on Privileges and Immunities of the Council of Europe (Paris, 2 September 1949; TS 34; Cmd 8852).

# 3. PARLIAMENT

## (1) BASIC PRINCIPLES

**201. The United Kingdom Parliament.** The United Kingdom Parliament[1] is known as and styled 'the Parliament of the United Kingdom of Great Britain and Northern Ireland'[2]. It owes its origins to the Acts and Treaty of Union between Scotland and England of 1707 and associated legislation, all of whose constituent parts may be summarised as 'the Union Agreement', which came into effect on 1 May 1707[3].

Parliament consists, in law, of the monarch[4], the House of Commons[5] and the House of Lords[6], but for practical purposes the legislature is divided into two chambers, the House of Commons (which is the dominant chamber) and the House of Lords (which is the senior chamber)[7]. The two chambers are independent of one another and communicate by message[8]. The House of Commons is not itself a corporate body in law: it lacks capacity to give or take land or other things, to contract or to sue[9]. Like the House of Commons, the House of Lords is not itself a corporate body in law[10].

The word 'Parliament' may be used to refer to joint assemblies of the members of the two Houses[11]. It may also refer to sittings of either or both of the Houses of Parliament without the participation of the Queen, as in the conventions of individual and collective ministerial responsibility to Parliament[12] or parliamentary scrutiny of government policy in which the Queen has no role.

The Queen in Parliament functions as the supreme domestic legislature[13]. Other bodies within the United Kingdom with legislative power include: (1) the Queen in Council[14]; (2) ministers possessing delegated legislative powers[15]; and (3) local authorities with power to make byelaws[16]. Of these bodies, the Queen in Parliament is supreme[17] but in matters of European Community law the laws of the Community have primacy[18]. In practice, the principal functions of the Queen in Parliament in respect of primary legislation (Acts of Parliament) and of the two Houses of Parliament in respect of secondary or delegated legislation (principally statutory instruments[19]) are those of ratifying or scrutinising proposals brought forward by the administration[20].

The other functions of the two Houses of Parliament include (a) the provision of the political arm of the executive[21]; (b) the extraction of information from the government and the scrutiny of government policy and acts[22]; (c) the granting of supply[23]; (d) in the House of Commons, the scrutiny of public expenditure and taxation[24]; (e) the redress of individual grievances[25]; and (f) the provision of a debating forum and generally acting as 'the grand inquest of the nation'[26]. Both Houses of Parliament must also preserve and enforce the privileges of Parliament, which are necessary for the uninhibited exercise of all their functions[27].

1   As to the law relating to Parliament generally see PARLIAMENT. This part of the title is concerned with the aspects of the United Kingdom Parliament that are of greatest importance in constitutional law, in particular the roles of the Queen in Parliament and the two Houses of Parliament in relation to legislation, taxation and public expenditure, and the legal sovereignty of Parliament.

   The term 'Parliament' was first applied to general assemblies of the State under Louis VII in France about the middle of the twelfth century. The earliest mention of it in the statutes is in the preamble of the Statute of Westminster 1275. Until the reign of Henry IV both Houses sat together (4 Co Inst 5). The term derives from the middle English 'parlement': talk, conference, deliberative assembly. This was its meaning in the thirteenth century. By the fourteenth century the term was used to refer to the Great Council of the Realm: Oxford Dictionary of English Etymology (1966). The usage of the term to refer to meetings survives, for instance at the Honourable Society of the Middle Temple, where meetings of Benchers are called Parliaments.

Those entitled to be summoned to Parliament have changed as new peerages have been created (see for instance *St John's Peerage Claim* [1915] AC 282, PC), life peerages have been introduced (Life Peerages Act 1958) and hereditary peers have been entitled to disclaim their peerages for their life (Peerage Act 1963), and as the franchise has been extended. See generally PARLIAMENT; ELECTIONS; PEERAGES AND DIGNITIES.

2   Royal and Parliamentary Titles Act 1927 s 2(1) (amended by the Statute Law (Repeals) Act 1977).

3   As to the Treaty of Union see paras 51, 53 ante. See also 5 *Stair Memorial Encyclopaedia* CONSTITUTIONAL LAW para 361; Erskine May *Parliamentary Practice* (21st Edn, 1989).

4   As to the monarch as Head of State see para 14 ante.

5   As to the House of Commons see PARLIAMENT.

6   As to the House of Lords see para 204 post; and PARLIAMENT.

7   See Loveland *Constitutional Law: A Critical Introduction* (1996) p 191; and PARLIAMENT. The United Kingdom Parliament is sometimes described as bicameral. This is true in the sense that it has two chambers, the House of Lords and the House of Commons, but in law it also has a third part, the monarch, with whom lies the power of enactment, by and with the advice and consent of the three estates of the realm in Parliament assembled: see further para 17 ante.

8   As to the relations between the two houses see PARLIAMENT.

9   See the Report to the House of Commons Commission by a team led by Sir Robin Ibbs, *House of Commons Services* (HC Paper (1990–91) no 38); 204 HC Official Report (6th series), 24 February 1992, cols 778–785. The administration of the House of Commons is carried out on its behalf by the House of Commons Commission, which appoints all staff in the House Departments except the Clerk of the House of Commons, and Clerk Assistant, the Serjeant at Arms and the Speaker's personal staff: see the House of Commons (Administration) Act 1978 s 2; and PARLIAMENT. See also Erskine May *Parliamentary Practice* (21st Edn, 1989) pp 192–193. The Clerk of the House of Commons (formally the Under Clerk of the Parliaments) is the Corporate Officer of the Commons and has power to deal with property and enter into contracts, and do anything reasonably necessary or expedient for or incidental to those matters for any purpose of the House of Commons, and power to do any other thing which the Under Clerk of Parliaments can do by virtue of his office: see the Parliamentary Corporate Bodies Act 1992 s 2; and PARLIAMENT.

10  See note 9 supra. '...the fact of the matter is that neither House constitutes a legal persona, able to do the sort of things one inevitably has to do as the owner of property. It is not an entirely new problem and I have to concede that up to now we have somehow managed to muddle through. Clerks of Parliament have for instance entered into contracts making themselves personally liable, which has been very brave of them': 536 HL Official Report (5th series), 6 March 1992, col 1110 (The Lord Privy Seal). The Clerk of the Parliaments is the House of Lords' Corporate Officer, and has similar powers to those of the House of Commons' Corporate Officer: see the Parliamentary Corporate Bodies Act 1992 s 1; and PARLIAMENT.

11  As where the Queen meets Parliament in person at the opening of Parliament in the Chamber of the House of Lords: see Erskine May *Parliamentary Practice* (21st Edn, 1989) p 232.

12  As to individual and collective ministerial responsibility see paras 416–417 post.

13  As to the Queen in Parliament see para 17 ante.

14  As to the Queen in Council see para 525 post.

15  See ADMINISTRATIVE LAW vol 1(1) (Reissue) para 55; STATUTES vol 44(1) (Reissue) paras 1499–1526.

16  See ADMINISTRATIVE LAW vol 1(1) (Reissue) para 55; CORPORATIONS vol 9 para 1280; LOCAL GOVERNMENT vol 28 para 1323 et seq.

17  See further paras 17 ante, 202 post.

18  As to the primacy of European Community law see para 24 ante.

19  Some delegated legislation is not confirmed in statutory instruments: see Erskine May *Parliamentary Practice* (21st Edn, 1989) pp 539–540. As to subordinate legislation generally see STATUTES vol 44(1) (Reissue) paras 1499–1526.

20  See the *Report of the House of Commons Select Committee on Procedure* (HC Paper (1977–78) no 588–1 p viii); Norton *The Commons in Perspective* (1981) ch 4; Walkland *The Legislative Process in Great Britain* (1968); Griffith *Parliamentary Scrutiny of Government Bills* (1974); Miers and Page *Legislation* (2nd Edn, 1990); and paras 225–227 post.

21  Ministers are drawn from the membership of the two Houses of Parliament: see para 399 post.

22  As to parliamentary supervision of the executive see paras 225–227 post.

23  As to supply procedures see para 712 post; and PARLIAMENT.

24  As to parliamentary control of taxation and expenditure see paras 228–230 post. The House of Commons claims exclusive privilege in respect of legislation affecting public expenditure and taxation: see PARLIAMENT.

25  As to the redress of grievances see para 226 post; and ADMINISTRATIVE LAW vol 1(1) (Reissue) paras 41–43.

26  As to the examination of the conduct of government see para 225 post.

27  See further PARLIAMENT.

**202. The Queen in Parliament and the legislative functions of Parliament.** The Queen is a necessary party to the enactment of statutes[1] and this is reflected in the wording of the enacting formula[2]. A bill does not become law until it has received the Royal Assent[3]. However, there is provision for bills to receive the Royal Assent without the consent of the House of Lords[4]. An Act may include provisions for bringing it into force at a later date or for the Secretary of State or another member of the administration to bring it into operation by order laid before Parliament[5].

The Crown is therefore a necessary party to primary United Kingdom legislation[6], and neither House of Parliament, whether acting alone or in conjunction with the other House, has any power of making primary legislation without the Crown. Delegated legislation in the form of statutory instruments will have been authorised by Act of Parliament to which the monarch has given Royal Assent[7]. Orders in Council also receive the nominal consent of the Queen in Council[8]. Moreover, the Crown cannot by proclamation or otherwise make or unmake any law on its own authority apart from Parliament[9], except in conquered or ceded colonies to which representative institutions have not been granted[10].

1   As to statutes generally see STATUTES.
2   As to the wording of the enacting formula see para 17 ante; and STATUTES vol 44(1) (Reissue) para 1273. Measures passed by the General Synod of the Church of England are governed by special enactment: see the Church of England Assembly (Powers) Act 1919. As to the General Synod of the Church of England see ECCLESIASTICAL LAW. As to the Crown in relation to the Church of England see CROWN LANDS AND PRIVILEGES.
3   As to the Royal Assent see PARLIAMENT; STATUTES vol 44(1) (Reissue) paras 1245, 1278–1279. See also Bogdanor *The Monarchy and the Constitution* (1995) pp 129–132.
4   See the Parliament Acts 1911 and 1949. Only four Acts have received the Royal Assent without the consent of the House of Lords, namely: (1) the Welsh Church Act 1914; (2) the Government of Ireland Act 1914 (which was never brought into operation); (3) the Parliament Act 1949; and (4) the War Crimes Act 1991. See further PARLIAMENT.
5   Even where this has not happened, the courts will take account of the will of Parliament as expressed in the Act where this is relevant in an application for judicial review: *R v Secretary of State for the Home Department, ex p Fire Brigades Union* [1995] 2 AC 513, [1995] 1 All ER 888, CA. As to the office of Secretary of State see para 355 et seq post.
6   European legislation will often have direct effect in the United Kingdom and other member states without the requirement for an Act of Parliament: see paras 23–24 ante; and EUROPEAN COMMUNITIES.
7   As to delegated or subordinate legislation generally see STATUTES vol 44(1) (Reissue) paras 1499–1526.
8   As to Orders in Council see para 907 post; and the statute 15 Edw 2 (Revocatio Novarum Ordinationum) (1322). In *Stockdale v Hansard* (1839) 9 Ad & El 1 the authority of the House of Commons was pleaded in justification of the publication of a parliamentary report containing a libel upon Stockdale, but it was held that the House could not, by its resolution, alter the law so as to make defamatory matter non-libellous. See also *Bowles v Bank of England* [1913] 1 Ch 57, 82 LJCh 124. Special statutory provision is made for the validity of financial resolutions of the House of Commons by the Provisional Collection of Taxes Act 1968: see paras 228, 705 post; and PARLIAMENT.
9   See *Re Grazebrook, ex p Chavasse* (1865) 4 De GJ & Sm 655 at 662; Bill of Rights s 1. As to proclamations by the Crown see Case of Proclamations 12 Co Rep 74; and see paras 916–918 post. As to the history and citation of the Bill of Rights see para 35 note 3 ante.
10  See COMMONWEALTH vol 6 (Reissue) para 1029. As to the Crown's legislative competence in settled colonies see COMMONWEALTH vol 6 (Reissue) para 990.

**203. The Crown or government in relation to Parliament.** The Crown or its ministers are restrained from ruling without a Parliament, since it is enacted that for redress of all grievances[1] and for the amending, strengthening and preserving of laws Parliaments ought to be held frequently[2].

1   As to the redress of grievances see para 226 post.
2   Bill of Rights s 1. As to the history and citation of the Bill of Rights see para 35 note 3 ante.

**204. Limitation of the role of the House of Lords.** The powers and functions of the House of Lords[1] have been diminished over the years. The Lords no longer have the right to amend, reject or delay money bills[2], and other legislation may receive the Royal Assent without the consent of the House of Lords under the Parliament Acts 1911 and 1949[3]. However, an Act to prolong the duration of a Parliament does require the consent of the Lords[4]

Their powers in relation to legislation are limited by a number of conventions. By the 'Salisbury' doctrine it is unconstitutional for the Lords to refuse their consent to legislation that seeks to give effect to a manifesto commitment of the governing party[5]. On the other hand the Lords are constitutionally entitled to amend or refuse consent to measures which appear to them to be contrary to constitutional principles[6].

1  As to the House of Lords generally see PARLIAMENT.
2  See PARLIAMENT.
3  As to the legislature see paras 17, 202 ante; and PARLIAMENT.
4  See the Parliament Act 1911 s 2(1) (amended by the Parliament Act 1949 s 1); and PARLIAMENT.
5  See 261 HL Official Report (5th series), 4 November 1964, col 66; 545 HL Official Report (5th series) 19 May 1993, cols 1780–1813; Griffith and Ryle *Parliament: Functions, Practice and Procedures* (1989) pp 504–506.
6  See eg the War Crimes Bill 1990, which was opposed in the House of Lords because it retrospectively criminalised conduct. It later received the Royal Assent under the Parliament Acts 1911 and 1949: see 513 HL Official Report (5th series), 4 December 1989, cols 604–679.

**205. No separation of powers between Parliament and the executive.** In the United Kingdom, unlike other countries such as the United States, there is no separation of personnel between Parliament and the political arm of the executive, but a fusion of the two[1]. It is in this sense that Parliament may be said to provide the executive[2], and it is through the fact that ministers are members of one or other of the two Houses of Parliament that the conventions of ministerial responsibility to Parliament are given effect[3].

1  'A Cabinet is a combining committee - a *hyphen* which joins, a *buckle* which fastens, the legislative part of the State to the executive part of the State. In its origin it belongs to the one, in its functions it belongs to the other.' Bagehot *The English Constitution* (1963 Edn) p 68.
   Convention requires that the Queen appoint as Prime Minister the person who commands the support of a majority in the House of Commons (see para 394 post); that the Chancellor of the Exchequer be a member of the House of Commons (see para 399 post); that the Lord Chancellor, a member of the House of Lords, be a member of the administration (see para 482 post); and that other members of the administration normally be members of one or other of the Houses of Parliament (see para 399 post).
2  See Norton *The Commons in Perspective* (1981).
3  There have been exceptions to the convention that members of the administration must be members of one or other House of Parliament. Scottish Solicitors General are frequently not in either House.

## (2) ELECTIONS, SUMMONING, ADJOURNMENT, PROROGATION AND DISSOLUTION OF PARLIAMENT.

**206. Elections.** Members of the House of Commons[1] are elected, following a proclamation by the Queen for the summoning of a new Parliament, under a system known as the 'relative majority' or 'first past the post' system[2].

1  As to the House of Commons see PARLIAMENT.
2  See ELECTIONS vol 15 (Reissue) para 565. As to elections generally *Report of the Hansard Society Commission on Electoral Reform* (1976); Bogdanor *The People and the Party System* (1981); Finer *Adversary Politics and Electoral Reform* (1975); Rogaly *Parliament for the People* (1976); Maude and Sczemerey *Why Electoral Change? The Case for Electoral Reform Examined* (1982); Finer 'Adversarial Politics and the Eighties' (1982) 1 Electoral Studies 221; 1 Anson's Law and Custom of the Constitution (5th Edn, 1922) pp 146–152; and ELECTIONS.

**207. Integrity of elections.** The Crown may not interfere with the election of members of Parliament, which ought to be free[1].

1    Bill of Rights s 1. See also 3 Edw 1 (Statute of Westminster the First) (1275), c 5, which prohibits the subject from interfering with elections by force of arms, malice or menacing; and see ELECTIONS. As to the history and citation of the Bill of Rights see para 35 note 3 ante.

**208. Summons and meeting of Parliament.** A new Parliament cannot legally assemble without the royal writ[1]. On the assembling of a new Parliament in pursuance of the royal writ, or at the commencement of a new session of an already existing Parliament after prorogation, the monarch must meet the two Houses either in person or by representatives[2]; otherwise there can be no legal beginning of a new Parliament, or session of an existing Parliament[3], except in the case of the demise of the Crown[4].

1    1 Bl Com (14th Edn) 149. As to the issue of such writs generally see PARLIAMENT. Although on certain occasions, through the necessity occasioned by the monarch's absence or abdication, the two Houses have met and transacted business in an irregular manner without the royal writ, such meetings are termed Convention Parliaments, to distinguish them from Parliaments proper, and their proceedings are not recognised legally unless subsequently ratified by statute. This was why there had to be a Bill of Rights in 1688 (or 1689): see 13 Car 2, stat 1, cc 7, 14 (Confirmation of Acts) (1661) (repealed). As to the history and citation of the Bill of Rights see para 35 note 3 ante.
2    See PARLIAMENT.
3    4 Co Inst 6; 1 Bl Com (14th Edn) 153.
4    See generally PARLIAMENT.

**209. Dissolution, prorogation and adjournment.** Except in the case of effluxion of time, an existing Parliament can be ended only by an exercise of the royal prerogative[1]. Parliament may be so dissolved at any time, but by the customary or conventional usage of the constitution in the exercise of this prerogative the monarch acts upon the advice of the Prime Minister[2] unless prepared to dismiss him[3].

A session of an existing Parliament can only be terminated by the Crown by prorogation[4]; but an adjournment or postponement of business, either in the House of Lords or the House of Commons, for a definite time, can be effected by resolution of either House, without the intervention of the Crown[5], although in earlier days a desire expressed by the Crown for the adjournment of both or either of the two Houses was usually complied with[6].

1    In practice Parliament is always dissolved before its term has expired: see Erskine May *Parliamentary Practice* (21st Edn, 1989) pp 221–223. As to the manner of dissolving Parliament see PARLIAMENT. The length of a Parliament has been extended beyond five years in time of war: see eg the Parliament and Registration Act 1916, the Prolongation of Parliament Acts 1940, 1941, 1942, 1943 and 1944; and Erskine May *Parliamentary Practice* (21st Edn, 1989) p 62.
2    It was held until recently that the monarch should act on the advice of her ministers; in practice she acts on the advice of the Prime Minister: see the statement of Lord Palmerston in 1859 in 153 Official Report (3rd series) col 1415; Marshall *Constitutional Conventions: the rules and forms of political accountability* (1987) ch III; and paras 21 ante, 351 post. It is impossible to lay down any rule as to when the Prime Minister (or the Cabinet) should advise a dissolution. Generally speaking, the Prime Minister will choose the moment he considers most favourable to the prospects of his party. He is not bound to advise a dissolution merely because he has been defeated by a vote of the House of Commons save on a vote of confidence or if the vote manifestly makes it impossible for him to continue to govern. The conventions as to what amounts to a vote of confidence or no confidence are evolving. In 1994 the administration was defeated on the second reading of measure to introduce Value Added Tax on domestic fuel and did not resign. It seems therefore that a defeat on the second reading of a programme bill or on a taxation measure will not be regarded as requiring resignation or a request for dissolution (see 251 HC Official Report (6th series), 6 December 1994, col 281.
     Three categories of business on which a government defeat will be expected to result in dissolution or resignation are (1) a motion which, in terms, expresses confidence or no confidence in the government

as a whole; (2) a motion or question which the Prime Minister has announced in advance will be treated as a vote of confidence; and (3) the motion for an address in response to the Queen's speech at the start of a session (because the Queen's speech comprises the administration's programme for the session and failure to win approval for it would be tantamount to a vote of no confidence). See Griffith and Ryle *Parliament: Functions, Practice and Procedures* (1989) pp 40–43; Marshall *Constitutional Conventions: the rules and forms of political accountability* (1987) ch III. As to the collective responsibility and dismissal of ministers see paras 417–418 post.

3   The last dismissal of a Prime Minister was in 1783. A dismissal today would be most unlikely, although the power doubtless exists: see para 418 post.

4   1 Bl Com (14th Edn) 187. Parliament is adjourned through the midsummer break and other recesses, for the practical reason that it is much easier to recall an adjourned house in the case of emergency and to enable outstanding business to be completed after the recess. A prorogued Parliament could only be recalled by proclamation. As to the adjournment and prorogation of Parliament see HC Standing Orders (1995) (Public Business) no 22; and PARLIAMENT.

5   1 Bl Com (14th Edn) 186. As to adjournment generally see PARLIAMENT.

6   See Commons Journals, 11 June 1572; 5 April 1604; 4 June, 14 November, 18 December 1621; 11 July 1625; 13 September 1660; 25 July 1667; 4 August 1685; 24 February 1691; 21 June 1712; 16 April 1717; 3 February 1741; 10 December 1745; 21 May 1768.

## (3) MEMBERS OF PARLIAMENT

**210. The constitutional status of members of Parliament.** The        status        of members of Parliament is protected by the law relating to parliamentary privilege and contempt of Parliament[1]. Members of the House of Commons[2] are constitutionally regarded as the representatives of their constituents and not their delegates or delegates of the party organisations to which they belong[3]. The freedom of speech, and debates and proceedings in Parliament, may not be impeached or questioned in any court or place outside Parliament[4]. It would be a breach of parliamentary privilege and a contempt of Parliament for any person outside the House of Commons to seek to mandate a member or even to claim the right to do so[5].

Members of the House of Lords[6], although they have no constituents, are also constitutionally expected to act in accordance with their judgment of the public interest and not to promote their own pecuniary interests[7]. They are also required to declare and register relevant pecuniary interests[8]. In order to protect the principle of representative democracy, members of the House of Commons are obliged to declare any relevant personal pecuniary interests they may have before speaking in a parliamentary debate or in transactions or communications with ministers or other members of Parliament[9], and to register their interests[10].

Ministers who are members of the House of Commons are subject to the rules for the registration and declaration of interests in the same way as other members. In addition they are subject to guidelines and requirements laid down by successive Prime Ministers in order to ensure that no conflict arises or appears to arise between their private interests and public duties[11].

Members of Parliament receive salaries and may claim allowances for subsistence, office expenses, secretarial and research assistance and travel[12].

1   As to the privileges of Parliament see PARLIAMENT.

2   As to the House of Commons see PARLIAMENT.

3   This theory of representation was given its classical expression by Edmund Burke in the speech to the electors of Bristol, 3 November 1774 (see para 2 note 3 ante). See also the *Report of the Royal Commission on the Constitution 1969–73* (Cmnd 5460) (1973) (the 'Kilbrandon Report') para 1236; and *Amalgamated Society of Railway Servants v Osborne* [1910] AC 87, HL; *Bromley London Borough Council v GLC* [1983] 1 AC 768, [1982] 2 WLR 62, HL; *Conservative and Unionist Central Office v Burrell (Inspector of Taxes)* [1983] 1 AC 768, [1982] 1 All ER 129, CA; *R v Waltham Forest London Borough Council, ex p Baxter* [1988] QB 419, [1987] 3 All ER 761, CA. See also *Resolution of the Committee of Privileges and House of*

*Commons* (HC Paper (1946–47) no 118) paras 11–15; 440 HC Official Report (5th series), 15 July 1947, cols 284–365 (the case of W J Brown); *Second Report from the Committee of Privileges: Complaint concerning a Resolution of the Yorkshire Area Council of the National Union of Mineworkers* (HC Paper (1974–75) no 634). See also Oliver 'The Parties and Parliament: Representative or Intra-Party Democracy?' in Jowell and Oliver (eds) *The Changing Constitution* (2nd Edn, 1989) p 115; Birch *Representative and Responsible Government* (1964). This theory of representation was endorsed in the *First Report of the Committee on Standards in Public Life* (Cm 2850–I) (1995) and approved by the House of Commons: see 263 HC Official Report (6th series), 19 July 1995, col 1739; 265 HC Official Report (6th series) 6 November 1995, cols 661, 681.

4　Bill of Rights s 1. As to the history and citation of the Bill of Rights see para 35 note 3 ante.

　　As from 4 September 1996 where the conduct of a person in or in relation to proceedings is in issue in defamation proceedings, he may waive for the purposes of the proceedings, so far as concerns him, the protection of any enactment or rule of law which prevents proceedings in Parliament being impeached or questioned in any court or place out of Parliament, so that evidence may be given, questions asked or statements, submissions, comments or findings made about his conduct, without infringing parliamentary privilege: Defamation Act 1996 ss 13(1), (2), 19(2). This does not affect the operation of any such enactment or rule in relation to another person who has not waived it (s 13(3)), or affect any rule protecting a person from liability for words spoken or things done in relation to parliamentary proceedings: see s 13(4), (5).

　　See also 1 Anson's Law and Custom of the Constitution (5th Edn, 1922) pp 166–177; and PARLIAMENT.

5　See PARLIAMENT.

6　As to the House of Lords see para 204 ante; and PARLIAMENT.

7　See *House of Lords Companion to the Standing Orders* (1989) pp 69–70; *Third Report of the Select Committee on Procedure of the House* (HL Paper (1994–95) no 90); *Fifth Report of the Select Committee on Procedure of the House* (HL Paper (1994–95) no 98; 566 HL Official Report (5th series), 1 November 1995, cols 1428–1488; and Erskine May *Parliamentary Practice* (21st Edn, 1989) pp 432–433.

8　For the institution of a register of interests in the House of Lords see *Third Report of the Select Committee on Procedure of the House* (HL Paper (1994–95) no 90); *Fifth Report of the Select Committee on Procedure of the House* (HL Paper (1994–95) no 98; 566 HL Official Report (5th series), 1 November 1995, cols 1428–1488; and 566 HL Official Report (5th series), 7 November 1995, cols 1630–1640.

9　See Erskine May *Parliamentary Practice* (21st Edn, 1989) pp 120–121, 354–359; Griffith and Ryle *Parliament: Functions, Practice and Procedures* (1989) pp 55–60; Wade and Bradley *Constitutional and Administrative Law* (11th Edn, 1993) pp 238–242.

10　See the *Select Committee on Members' Interests (Declaration)* (HC Paper (1974–75) no 102); the *First Report of the Select Committee on Members' Interests: Registration and Declaration of Members' Financial Interests* (HC Paper (1991–92) no 326); and Erskine May *Parliamentary Practice* (21st Edn, 1989) pp 384–390. See further *First Report of the Committee on Standards in Public Life* (Cm 2850) (1995); *First Report of the Select Committee on Standards in Public Life* (HC Paper (1994–95) no 637); *First Report of the Committee of Privileges: Complaint Concerning an Article in the Sunday Times 10 July 1994 Relating to the Conduct of Members* (HC Paper 1994–95) no 351); *Register of Members' Interests as at 31 March 1996* (HC Paper 1995–96) no 345; *Third Report from the Committee on Standards and Privileges: The Code of Conduct and the Guide to the Rules Relating to the Conduct of Members* (HC Paper (1995–96) no 604) pp 14–20; 282 HC Official Report (6th series) 24 July 1996 cols 392–407.

11　As to the conduct of ministers see para 420 post.

12　See Erskine May *Parliamentary Practice* (21st Edn, 1989) pp 16–17. As from 1 July 1996 the salary was set at £43,000 per annum, but as from 1 April 1997 it is to be linked to senior civil service pay: see 281 HC Official Report (6th series), 10 July 1996, col 533; and see also the Senior Salaries Review Body *Report on Parliamentary Pay and Allowances* (Cm 3330) (1996). As to Civil Service remuneration see para 558 post.

**211. Regulation of conduct of members of Parliament.** The House of Commons[1] has the right to regulate its own proceedings[2], and by virtue of that right can discipline members for breaches of its rules or for conduct which is inconsistent with the standards which the House is entitled to expect of its members[3]. However, members of Parliament are not in principle exempt from the operation of the criminal law[4].

Allegations of serious misconduct, contempt of the House or breach of its rules may be examined by the appropriate Select Committee of the House[5] and subsequently considered by the House in the light of the Select Committee's findings. Disciplinary measures available to the House in such circumstances include committal, formal reprimand, temporary suspension from the House (with or without loss of pay) and expulsion[6].

The rules relating to the conduct of members[7] assist members in the discharge of their obligations to the House, their constituents and the public at large. By virtue of the oath or affirmation of allegiance, members have a duty to be faithful and bear true allegiance to the Queen, her heirs and successors, according to law. They have a duty to uphold the law and to act on all occasions in accordance with the public trust placed in them, a general duty to act in the interests of the nation as a whole, and a special duty to their constituents. Members must base their conduct on a consideration of the public interest, and avoid any conflict between personal and public interest, or immediately resolve such conflict in favour of the latter. They must at all times conduct themselves in a manner which will tend to maintain and strengthen the public's trust and confidence in the integrity of Parliament and never undertake any action which would bring the House or its members into disrepute. Acceptance of a bribe to influence a member's conduct, including any fee, compensation or reward in connection with the promotion of or opposition to any bill, motion or other matter submitted or intended to be submitted to the House or a committee is contrary to the law of Parliament. Members must fulfil conscientiously the requirements relating to the registration of interests, and must draw attention to relevant interests in any proceedings or in communications with ministers, departments or executive agencies. In any activities with or on behalf of an organisation with which a member has a financial relationship (including matters which may not be of public record, such as informal meetings and functions), he must bear in mind the need to be open and frank with ministers, members and officials. No member may act as a paid advocate in proceedings in the House. No improper use may be made of payments or allowances made to members for public purposes, and the administrative rules applying to such payments and allowances must be strictly observed. Information received in confidence in the course of parliamentary duties must be used only in connection with those duties, and never for the purpose of financial gain[8].

1    As to the House of Commons see PARLIAMENT.

2    See Erskine May *Parliamentary Practice* (21st Edn, 1989) p 69. As to the conduct of business generally see PARLIAMENT.

3    The House of Commons has adopted (at 282 HC Official Report (6th series) 24 July 1996 cols 392–407) the *Third Report from the Committee on Standards and Privileges: The Code of Conduct and the Guide to the Rules Relating to the Conduct of Members* (HC Paper (1995–96) no 604). See text and notes 7–8 infra.
      See also *The Report from the Select Committee on Conduct of Members* (HC Paper (1976–77) no 490). A Parliamentary Commissioner for Standards was appointed by the House of Commons in November 1995 whose remit included advising on the interpretation of a code of conduct for members of the House of Commons: HC Official Report (6th series), 6 November 1995, cols 681–682, 699; and *The House of Commons Commission Parliamentary Commissioner for Standards: Nomination of Candidate* (HC Paper (1994–95) no 789; House of Commons Standing Orders (1995) (Public Business) no 121B. See also the *First Report of the Committee on Standards in Public Life* (Cm 2850-I) (1995). As to the standards of conduct in public life see para 12 ante; and text and notes 7–8 infra.

4    There is uncertainty about the law of bribery in relation to members of Parliament: see the *Report of the Royal Commission on Standards of Conduct in Public Life* (the Salmon Commission) (Cmnd 6524) (1976) para 307; *First Report of the Committee on Standards in Public Life* (Cm 2850-I) (1995) (the 'Nolan Committee') paras 103–104; *First Report of the Select Committee on Standards in Public Life* (HC Paper (1994–95) no 637) paras 51–52; *First Report of the Committee of Privileges* (HC Paper (1994–95) no 351-II) pp 154–157, 160–162.

5    In November 1995 the House established a new Select Committee for Standards and Privileges: HC Official Report (6th series), 6 November 1995, cols 610–612, 681; and *House of Commons Commission Parliamentary Commissioner for Standards: Nomination of Candidate* (HC Paper (1994–95) no 789; House of Commons Standing Orders (1995) (Public Business) no 121A.

6    For examples see Commons Journals (1954–55) 25; (1967–68) 362; (1976–77) 448–450; (1989–90) 226–228. See also Erskine May *Parliamentary Practice* (21st Edn, 1989) pp 103–114; and PARLIAMENT.

7    Ie the rules contained in the *Third Report from the Committee on Standards and Privileges: The Code of Conduct and the Guide to the Rules Relating to the Conduct of Members* (HC Paper (1995–96) no 604).

8    *Third Report from the Committee on Standards and Privileges: The Code of Conduct and the Guide to the Rules Relating to the Conduct of Members* (HC Paper (1995–96) no 604) pp 10–11, 14.

# (4) PEERS

**212. Creation of peers.** It seems that the monarch cannot create another sovereign in any part of her dominions[1]; nor can she create a peerage with a right of precedence contrary to the statute[2] by which the precedence of all the nobility and great officers of state is regulated[3]. But she may, it appears, grant rank and precedence before the officers of state and peers of the realm to a foreign prince intermarrying with the royal family[4]; and she may create baronets with precedence before knights baronets (or bannerets), knights of the Bath, and knights bachelor[5].

The right to create new Irish peers has lapsed[6], whilst the right to create new Scottish peers appears to be doubtful[7].

Whether the Crown can limit the descent of a peerage in a manner unknown to the common law is doubtful[8].

Life peerages can be created by the Crown so as to confer a right on a peer, whether man or woman, to sit and vote in the House of Lords[9]. Formerly confined to the lords spiritual and the Lords of Appeal in Ordinary, life peerages are now the general rule, and it is considered inappropriate today to recommend the creation of a new hereditary peerage save perhaps in special cases[10].

1   4 Co Inst 287. Nor, it seems, can she grant palatine rights (as to which see CROWN LANDS AND PRIVILEGES).

2   Ie the House of Lords Precedence Act 1539. As to the provisions of this Act see PEERAGES AND DIGNITIES.

3   *R v Knollys* (1694) 1 Ld Raym 10 at 16. The same principle would, it seems, apply to grants of precedence simply. As to the precedence of the husband of the Queen regnant see CROWN LANDS AND PRIVILEGES.

4   This was done by the Prince Regent (subsequently George IV) on the marriage of the Princess Charlotte of Wales with Prince Leopold: see London Gazette 14 May 1816.

5   *Anon* (1611) 12 Co Rep 81.

6   Writs were formerly sent to the Lord Chancellor of Ireland under the Great Seal of the United Kingdom on a vacancy occurring in the number of Irish representative peers, directing him to cause the election of a new representative peer, but since the abolition of the office of Lord Chancellor of Ireland (see para 477 note 1 post) the issue of writs has been impossible so no new election can be held: see 66 HL Official Report (5th series), 23 March 1927, cols 724–732; and COURTS vol 10 para 740.

7   There is no provision authorising fresh creations in the Union with Scotland Act 1706. As this Act does not expressly bar the creation of Scottish peerages, but only limits the number of representative peers (see s 1, art 22; and para 53 text and note 4 ante), it seems doubtful whether the Crown is restrained (see *Duke of Queensberry's Case* (1719) 1 P Wms 582 at 585, HL). The point is now academic, since s 1, art 22 of the Act of 1706 is repealed and every Scottish peer is now entitled to a summons to Parliament: see the Peerage Act 1963 s 4.

8   *Devon Peerage Case* (1831) 2 State Tr NS 659, HL (earldom granted to a man and his heirs male held good); *Wiltes' Peerage Claim* (1869) LR 4 HL 126 (a similar grant held bad). See also para 870 post; and PEERAGES AND DIGNITIES.

9   See the Life Peerages Act 1958 s 1: and PEERAGES AND DIGNITIES. A hereditary peeress in her own right can sit and vote in the House of Lords: see the Peerage Act 1963 s 6; and PARLIAMENT; PEERAGES AND DIGNITIES vol 35 (Reissue) paras 905, 935–936.

10  See 850 HC Official Report (5th series), 13 February 1973, col 1141. However, in 1983 the Rt Hon William Whitelaw was created Viscount Whitelaw, of Penrith in the County of Cumbria (see London Gazette, 21 June 1983), and the former Speaker of the House of Commons, the Rt Hon George Thomas, was created Viscount Tonypandy, of Rhondda in the County of Mid Glamorgan (see London Gazette, 15 July 1983). See further Brazier *Constitutional Practice* (2nd Edn, 1994) p 238.

**213. Peerage claims.** Uncertain or disputed peerage claims[1] are adjudicated upon by the Committee for Privileges of the House of Lords[2], which, however, has no jurisdiction except upon a reference by the Crown[3]; so the proper procedure in such cases is to petition the Crown[4].

1  As to peerage claims generally see PEERAGES AND DIGNITIES vol 35 (Reissue) para 951 et seq.
2  As to the Committee for Privileges of the House of Lords see PARLIAMENT. As to the House of Lords see para 204 ante; and PARLIAMENT.
3  See *Lord De la Warre's Case* (1597) 11 Co Rep 1a; *Earl of Waterford's Case* (1832) 6 Cl & Fin 133, HL.
4  *R v Knollys* (1694) 1 Ld Raym 10 at 17. For the jurisdiction in peerage cases see COURTS vol 10 para 740. As to the procedure see PEERAGES AND DIGNITIES vol 35 (Reissue) para 953.

**214. Refusal and disclaimer of peerage.** It seems that the subject cannot legally refuse to accept a dignity or honour conferred by the Crown[1], and it is said that a peer may be fined by the Crown for not taking his seat in the House of Lords[2] in compliance with a writ of summons[3]. A hereditary peer, other than one of the first creation, may, however, disclaim his peerage for life[4].

1  4 Co Inst 43, 44: see also *Duke of Queensberry's Case* (1719) 1 P Wms 582 at 592, HL. The Attorney General and Solicitor General in the Labour government elected in February 1974 preferred not to accept the customary knighthoods.
2  As to the House of Lords see para 204 ante; and PARLIAMENT.
3  See note 1 supra.
4  See the Peerage Act 1963 ss 1–3; para 215 note 2 post; and PEERAGES AND DIGNITIES.

**215. Perpetuity of titles.** A peerage cannot be extinguished except by failure of heirs indicated in the creation[1] or by Act of Parliament[2].

Where a title or dignity descends to co-heirs, it is not extinguished, but falls into abeyance and becomes vested in the monarch[3], who can terminate the abeyance by nomination of one of the co-heirs[4].

1  See *R v Knollys* (1694) 1 Ld Raym 10.
2  See 4 Co Inst 355; *Earl of Shrewsbury's Case* (1612) 12 Co Rep 106, PC. A peerage was formerly also extinguished by attainder: see *Nevil's Case* (1604) 7 Co Rep 33a. Attainder for treason or felony was, however, abolished by the Forfeiture Act 1870 s 1 (as amended and repealed). As to attainder see PEERAGES AND DIGNITIES vol 35 (Reissue) para 948 note 1; COURTS vol 10 para 735; PARLIAMENT. Disclaimer under the Peerage Act 1963 does not affect the devolution of a peerage on the death of the person disclaiming: see s 3(1); and PEERAGES AND DIGNITIES vol 35 (Reissue) para 947.
3  See 3 Lords Journals 535 (8 March 1625); Cruise, Dignities, c 5 s 30.
4  30 Lords Journals 403 (18 April 1763), 561 (10 April 1764), 572 (13 April 1764); Cruise, Dignities, c 5 s 31; 12 Co Rep 112.

# (5) POLITICAL PARTIES

**216. Parties in Parliament.** Members of the two Houses of Parliament sit predominantly in party groupings, although in the House of Lords[1] there are substantial numbers of independent peers. Each party operates a 'whip system'[2] which imposes party discipline and seeks to ensure that the members of a party speak and vote in conformity with the policy of their party. The composition of standing committees[3] of the House of Commons[4] reflects the composition of the House as an oblique reference to the party system[5], and by convention the membership of select committees[6] reflects the party balance in the House and the chairs of select committees are shared between the government party and the opposition[7].

1  As to the House of Lords see para 204 ante; and PARLIAMENT.
2  As to whips see paras 218–219, 546 notes 8–9 post. Some government whips hold sinecure offices in the Treasury or the royal household: see para 354 notes 18–19 post. See also Griffith and Ryle *Parliament: Functions, Practice and Procedures* (1989) pp 113–116. As to the Treasury see paras 512–517 post.
3  As to standing committees see para 410 post; and PARLIAMENT.
4  As to the House of Commons see PARLIAMENT.
5  See HC Standing Orders (1995) (Public Business) no 86(2).

6    As to select committees see para 227 post; and PARLIAMENT.
7    See Griffith and Ryle *Parliament: Functions, Practice and Procedures* (1989) pp 417–420; and paras 217–220, 227 post.

**217. Funding of political parties.** Political parties raise most of their funds privately, and provision of financial help from public sources is limited, and mostly given in kind[1]. All candidates at parliamentary elections are entitled to the use of school premises, or meeting rooms maintained wholly or mainly out of public funds, for the purpose of holding public meetings in furtherance of their candidature[2]. They are also entitled to send, free of postal charge, one electoral communication to each elector or one such communication, unaddressed, to each place in the constituency recognised by Post Office regulations as a delivery point[3]. Opposition parties in Parliament receive financial assistance for their parliamentary work[4].

1    See *Second Report of the Home Affairs Committee: Funding of Political Parties* (HC Paper (1993–1994) no 301); Ewing *The Funding of Political Parties in Britain* (1987); Rawlings *Law and the Electoral Process* (1988) pp 173 et seq.
2    See the Representation of the People Act 1983 s 95 (as amended), s 96 (as substituted and amended); and ELECTIONS vol 15 (Reissue) para 679.
3    See ibid s 91 (as amended); and ELECTIONS vol 15 (Reissue) para 670.
4    As to public finance for opposition parties see para 220 post.

**218. The Opposition.** A number of opposition parties are represented in Parliament, but the opposition party having the greatest numerical strength in the House of Commons[1] is known as 'the Opposition' (or sometimes as 'the official Opposition') and has a leader in each House[2]. 'Her Majesty's opposition' performs essential functions in both Houses of Parliament, criticising the work of the administration in power and continuously offering an alternative administration to the electorate[3]. The opposition is organised on parallel lines to the government, with a leader and a shadow Cabinet, each member of which has the task of observing and criticising the work of a member of the Cabinet or his representative in the other House[4]. The members of the shadow Cabinet sit on the opposition front bench. Like the government, the opposition also has whips in both Houses[5].

The existence of the opposition is recognised by the law in a way analogous to that in which it recognises the Prime Minister[6] and the Cabinet[7], namely, by the indirect method of providing salaries[8].

The institution of a parliamentary opposition originated, and still operates for the most part, as part of a de facto two-party system in which the government has a majority in the House of Commons and its opponents belong largely to one other party. While the opposition in the Commons cannot usually prevent the passage of government business or defeat government motions, it is by convention accorded full right to discuss and criticise the work of the government in debate and by question in each House[9]. In this way the difficulties involved in implementing government policy are exposed and the development of government by a secretive oligarchy is impeded. Moreover, the arrangement of important items of government business is preceded by discussions through the 'usual channels' between the whips of the government and the opposition parties; and informal conversations between the Prime Minister and the Leader of the Opposition are normal before major events of national importance are announced, especially where party differences are not concerned[10].

1    As to the House of Commons see PARLIAMENT.
2    As to the Leader of the Opposition see para 219 post.
3    As to the recognition in parliamentary procedure of the role of the opposition see Erskine May *Parliamentary Practice* (21st Edn, 1989) p 200. See also Griffith and Ryle *Parliament: Functions, Practice and Procedures* (1989) ch 9; and PARLIAMENT.

4    A list of the shadow Cabinet and other opposition front bench speakers is published in *Vacher's Parliamentary Companion* (published quarterly). For the selection of the leader and other officers and party committees see Griffith and Ryle *Parliament: Functions, Practice and Procedures* (1989) pp 105–115.

5    As to whips see paras 219, 546 post.

6    As to the Prime Minister see paras 394–398 post.

7    As to the Cabinet see paras 402–413 post. Note that at least one modern statute has expressly recognised the Cabinet: Data Protection Act 1984 s 27(6) (power to determine whether personal data are exempt from certain provisions of the Act is conferred on a cabinet minister); and see CONFIDENCE AND DATA PROTECTION vol 8(1) (Reissue) para 529 note 5.

8    This recognition was first accorded by the Ministers of the Crown Act 1937 s 5 (repealed), under which a salary was made payable to the Leader of the Opposition. As to the opposition officeholders to whom salaries are now payable see para 219 post.

9    In each session of Parliament there are 20 days, known as 'opposition days' (until 1985 known as 'supply days') when the business chosen by the opposition parties has priority over government business. Of these opposition days, 17 are currently available to the official opposition and three to the second largest opposition party: HC Standing Orders (1995) (Public Business) no 13(2): see Erskine May *Parliamentary Practice* (21st Edn, 1989) pp 200, 261; Griffith and Ryle *Parliament: Functions, Practice and Procedures* (1989) pp 341–343. The allocation of days could alter if the third party were larger or smaller.

10    See also Lord Campion (formerly Clerk of the House of Commons) *Parliament: a Survey* ch 1 at p 30.

**219.   Opposition leaders and whips: salaries and pensions.** Except in the case of a former Prime Minister and First Lord of the Treasury who is in receipt of a specified pension payable by virtue of that office[1], salaries are payable out of the Consolidated Fund of the United Kingdom[2] to the opposition leaders and certain whips at prescribed rates[3]. Opposition members entitled to such salaries are the Leader of the Opposition[4] in the House of Commons and the Leader of the Opposition in the House of Lords, the Chief Opposition Whip[5] in the House of Commons, the Chief Opposition Whip[6] in the House of Lords and not more than two Assistant Opposition Whips in the House of Commons[7]. A person to whom any such salary is payable is entitled to receive only one such salary, but if he is the holder of two or more offices in respect of which a salary is so payable and there is a difference between the salaries payable in respect of those offices, the office in respect of which a salary is payable to him is that in respect of which the highest salary is payable[8].

In addition to their statutory salaries, the Leader of the Opposition and the whips in the House of Commons are entitled to the same parliamentary salary and allowances as ministers[9]. The Leader of the Opposition in the House of Lords and the Chief Opposition Whip in the House of Lords are not eligible for the daily expenses allowances payable in respect of attendance in the House but are entitled, in common with other peers, to reimbursement of their travel expenses between their homes and Westminster for the purpose of attending the House of Lords[10].

The two Leaders of the Opposition and Chief Opposition Whips and the paid Assistant Whips in the House of Commons, participate in a voluntary pension scheme on the same terms as apply to ministers unless they opt out[11].

1    Ie a pension under the Parliamentary and Other Pensions Act 1972 s 26(1): Ministerial and other Salaries Act 1975 s 1(1)(b), Sch 2 Pt II para 3. See also para 426 post. As to the Prime Minister as First Lord of the Treasury see para 395 text and note 5 post.

2    Ministerial and other Salaries Act 1975 ss 1(1)(b), 3(3). As to the Consolidated Fund see para 711 et seq post.

3    Ibid Sch 2 Pt II para 1. Her Majesty may from time to time by Order in Council substitute another figure for that given by Sch 2 as the annual amount of any salary; but no recommendation may be made to Her Majesty to make such an Order in Council unless a draft has been approved by resolution of each House of Parliament: see s 1(4) (as amended). For the current salaries of the Leader of the Opposition (House of Commons); Chief Opposition Whip (House of Commons); Assistant Opposition Whip (House of Commons); Leader of the Opposition (House of Lords); Chief Opposition Whip (House of Lords) see Sch 2 Pt I (amended by the Ministerial and other Salaries Order 1996, SI 1996/1913, art 3, Sch 2).

4    In relation to either House of Parliament, 'Leader of the Opposition' means that member of that House who is for the time being the Leader in that House of the party in opposition to Her Majesty's government having the greatest numerical strength in the House of Commons: Ministerial and other

Salaries Act 1975 s 2(1). If any doubt arises as to which is or was at any material time the party in opposition to Her Majesty's government having the greatest numerical strength in the House of Commons, or as to who is or was at any material time the leader in that House of such a party, the question must be decided for the purposes of the Ministerial and other Salaries Act 1975 by the Speaker of the House of Commons, and his decision, certified in writing under his hand is final and conclusive: s 2(2). If any doubt arises as to who is or was at any time the leader in the House of Lords of the said party, the question must be decided for the purposes of the Act by the Lord Chancellor, and his decision, certified in writing under his hand is final and conclusive: s 2(3).

5    In relation to either House of Parliament, 'Chief Opposition Whip' means the person for the time being nominated as such by the Leader of the Opposition in that House: ibid s 2(1)

6    In relation to the House of Commons, 'Assistant Opposition Whip' means a person for the time being nominated as such, and to be paid as such, by the Leader of the Opposition in the House of Commons: ibid s 2(1).

7    See ibid Sch 2 Pt II para 2.

8    Ibid s 1(5).

9    See the House of Commons Resolutions of 20 December 1971, 828 HC Official Report (5th series), 20 December 1971, col 1248; and para 425 post.

10   See *Companion to the Standing Orders and Guide to the Proceedings of the House of Lords* (1994) p 24–25; *First Report of the Review Body on Top Salaries: Ministers of the Crown and Members of Parliament* (Cmnd 4836) (1971) para 80; and para 425 post.

11   See the Ministerial and Other Pensions and Salaries Act 1991 s 2(2)(c); and para 425 post. As to ministers' salaries see paras 423–426 post.

**220. Public finance for opposition parties.** Opposition parties are eligible to receive public funds to assist in their parliamentary work, known as 'short money'[1]. The amounts paid relate to the votes cast for and seats won by the relevant parties at the previous election. From April 1994 annual upratings linked to the retail price index have taken place. The payments are to be spent exclusively on the parliamentary expenses of each party. Since 1993 a fund of £100,000 has been available for opposition front bench travel, which will also be uprated annually[2].

1    It is so named because it was introduced by Edward Short MP when he was Leader of the House in 1975. See 231 Commons Journals (1974–75) 310.

2    See 249 HC Official Report (6th series), 4 November 1993, col 595.

## (6) POLITICAL BROADCASTING.

**221. Impartiality in broadcasting.** Political broadcasting is regulated partly by the terms of the British Broadcasting Corporation's licence from the government, and partly by statute and the terms of licences between the Independent Television Commission and its licence holders[1]. The ITC must do all that it can to secure that every licensed service complies with the requirement that any news given (in whatever form) in its programmes is presented with due accuracy and impartiality[2], and that due impartiality is preserved on the part of the person providing the service as respects matters of political controversy or relating to current public policy[3]. The BBC is a chartered institution operating under a licence, not bound by statute on this matter, but it seeks to maintain impartiality in the same way[4].

It is an illegal practice for any person to procure the use of transmitting stations outside the United Kingdom with intent to influence voters at an election[5].

By the terms of its charter, and agreement with the Secretary of State for National Heritage, the BBC is required to broadcast an impartial account day by day of the proceedings in Parliament[6].

The ITC must do all that it can to secure that a licensed service must not include (1) any advertisement which is inserted by or on behalf of any body whose objects are wholly or mainly of a political nature[7]; (2) any advertisement which is directed towards any political end[8]; or (3) any advertisement which has any relation to any industrial dispute (other than an advertisement of a public service inserted by, or on behalf of, a government department)[9].

1   As to governmental regulation of broadcasting see para 500 post. As to broadcasting generally see TELECOMMUNICATIONS AND BROADCASTING.
2   Broadcasting Act 1990 s 6(1)(b). The same applies to independent radio services: see s 90(1)(b). As to broadcasting impartiality see TELECOMMUNICATIONS AND BROADCASTING vol 45 para 574.
3   Ibid s 6(1)(c); cf *R v Broadcasting Complaints Commission, ex p Owen* [1985] QB 1153, [1985] 2 All ER 522, DC. See generally Wade and Bradley *Constitutional and Administrative Law* (11th Edn, 1993) pp 171–173, 514–517. The broadcasters have developed a system of 'stopwatch timing' under which the time spent covering the individual parties should be in the same proportions as the agreed division of air time for the party election broadcasts: see *Report of the Hansard Society Commission on Election Campaigns: Agenda for Change* (1991) ch 5.
4   It is not certain to what extent the BBC is under a legally enforceable duty of impartiality: see *Lynch v BBC* [1983] NI 193, (1983) 6 NIJB; *R v Broadcasting Complaints Commission, ex p Owen* [1985] QB 1153, [1985] 2 All ER 522, DC; *Houston v BBC* (1995) Times, 9 May, Ct of Sess. The BBC may not broadcast its own opinions about current affairs or matters of public policy and may not broadcast party political programmes except by agreement with the major parties.
5   See the Representation of the People Act 1983 s 92 (as amended); and ELECTIONS vol 15 (Reissue) para 671; TELECOMMUNICATIONS AND BROADCASTING vol 45 para 570.
6   See the *BBC Charter* (Cmnd 8313) (1981) (amended by a Supplemental Charter (Cmnd 9013) (1983); and *Broadcasting: BBC Charter and Agreement between the Secretary of State for the National Heritage and the BBC* (Cm 3152) (1996) para 3.3, approved by the House of Commons: see 273 HC Official Report (6th series), 15 February 1996, col 1172. As to the Secretary of State for National Heritage see para 499 post.
7   Broadcasting Act 1990 s 8(2)(a)(i).
8   Ibid s 8(2)(a)(ii).
9   Ibid s 8(2)(a)(iii).

**222. Party political broadcasts.** Party political broadcasting is understood to comprise the series of party political broadcasts which occur at intervals between general elections; the parties' broadcasts on the budget; and the special series preceding a general election[1]. These broadcasts are expressly designed to serve the interests of the political parties[2]. The duty of impartiality applies to the allocation of time[3]. In the case of the series between general elections, a limited number of radio and television broadcasting periods is allotted each year, after consultation[4], to the main parties. The British Broadcasting Corporation and Independent Television Commission provide the broadcasting time but the parties themselves decide on its allocation and on the subjects and speakers.

1   As to party election broadcasts see para 223 post; and TELECOMMUNICATIONS AND BROADCASTING vol 45 para 576.
2   See the *Report of the Committee on Broadcasting* (Cmnd 1753) (1960) para 294. As to broadcasts by minority parties see *Evans v BBC and IBA* (1974) Times, 27 February, CA, where it was held that the All-Party Committee on Broadcasting could not lawfully order the broadcasting organisations to vary or cancel a contract made with Plaid Cymru. As to ministerial broadcasts see para 224 post.
3   See *Wilson v Independent Broadcasting Authority* 1979 SC 351; and *Lynch v BBC* [1983] NI 193, (1983) 6 NIJB. See also Rawlings *Law and the Electoral Process* (1988) ch 6.
4   This is not regulated by statute. The allocation was carried out by the unofficial All-party Committee on Party Political Broadcasting, which consists of the major party leaders or officials and representatives of the broadcasters and is chaired by the Prime Minister. However, the actual meetings of this body have become rare, and since 1983 it has been unable to agree on the allocation of time for party political broadcasts, leaving the 'usual channels' and the broadcasters to reach agreement on an 'ad hoc' basis: see *Report of the Hansard Society Commission on Election Campaigns: Agenda for Change* (1991) ch 5; and Rawlings *Law and the Electoral Process* (1988) ch 6.

**223. Party election broadcasts.** During general election campaigns, by agreement between the Independent Television Commission, the British Broadcasting Corporation and the major political parties, time is provided free of charge for party election broadcasts[1]. The agreement covers the number of broadcasts and the amount of time that will be made available. This arrangement is not regulated by statute. The agreed formula for the allocation of time for party election broadcasts is also used to allocate time for coverage of the parties in news and current affairs coverage during the election campaign.

1  See TELECOMMUNICATIONS AND BROADCASTING vol 45 paras 568, 576.

**224. Ministerial broadcasts.** Any minister of the Crown may require announcements to be broadcast[1]. There are two categories of ministerial broadcasts. The first category relates to ministers wishing to explain legislation or administrative policies approved by Parliament, or to seek the co-operation of the public in matters where there is a general consensus of opinion. The British Broadcasting Corporation is obliged by its licence to broadcast such ministerial statements. There is no right of reply by the opposition. The second category relates to more important and normally infrequent occasions when the Prime Minister[2] or one of his senior Cabinet colleagues designated by him wishes to broadcast to the nation in order to provide information or explanation of events of prime national or international importance, or to seek the co-operation of the public in connection with such events. Here the opposition has the right to reply by virtue of the duty of impartiality on the part of the broadcasting bodies[3]. When the opposition exercises this right there will normally also be a broadcast discussion of the issues between a member of the Cabinet and a senior member of the opposition, and other parties with substantial electoral support will be allowed to participate.

1  See the *BBC Charter* (Cmnd 8313) (1981) (amended by a Supplemental Royal Charter dated 13 July 1983 (Cmnd 9013) (1983) cl 13(2)); and *Broadcasting: BBC Charter and Agreement between the Secretary of State for the National Heritage and the BBC* (Cm 3152) (1996), approved by the House of Commons: see 273 HC Official Report (6th series), 15 February 1996, col 1172.
2  As to the Prime Minister see paras 394–398 post.
3  See further paras 221–223 ante.

## (7) PARLIAMENTARY SUPERVISION OF THE EXECUTIVE

**225. Parliamentary scrutiny of government acts and policy.** An important role of the House of Commons[1], and, to a lesser extent of the House of Lords[2], is the scrutiny of the work of ministers and government[3] and the imposition of individual[4] and collective[5] ministerial responsibility. Two aspects of this are the redress of individual grievances[6], and the scrutiny of the wisdom, efficiency and effectiveness of the conduct of government and of individual ministers within it[7].

1  As to the House of Commons see PARLIAMENT.
2  As to the House of Lords see para 204 ante; and PARLIAMENT.
3  See PARLIAMENT.
4  As to individual ministerial responsibility see para 416 post; and PARLIAMENT.
5  As to collective ministerial responsibility see para 417 post.
6  As to the redress of grievances see para 226 post.
7  See further paras 227, 416–417 post.

**226. Parliamentary questions and redress of grievances.** Backbench members of Parliament may ask questions[1] of ministers in order to elicit information and to air concerns. Redress of grievance for members of the public is sought through the asking of parliamentary questions[2]. Ministers are, in principle, expected to answer[3] parliamentary questions, although there are a number of accepted grounds on which questions may not be admitted[4], or answers may be refused[5]. Answers to questions are given either orally or in writing[6].

A member of Parliament who is not satisfied with the answer may seek to raise the matter in debate, in particular in the half-hour debate that takes place on the adjournment at the conclusion of each day's sitting. Alternatively, or additionally, if the complaint is one of maladministration leading to injustice the member may refer the matter to the Parliamentary Commissioner for Administration, who may investigate the matter and report[7]. The Commissioner is responsible to the Select Committee on the Parliamentary Commissioner for Administration, which may pursue a matter if the minister in question does not readily accept the findings of the Commissioner or comply with recommendations for redress to be made to the complainant[8].

In relation to executive agencies in the Civil Service, questions from members of the House of Commons for written answers are usually expected to be addressed to the chief executive of the agency in question rather than to the minister, and it is only if satisfaction is not achieved for the complainant through this route that the minister will deal with the question[9]. Answers of chief executives to questions from members of Parliament are published in a special volume of Hansard since 1993[10].

1    As to notices of questions and the timetable for taking questions see HC Standing Orders (1995) (Public Business) nos 17, 18.

2    See Erskine May *Parliamentary Practice* (21st Edn, 1989) pp 281–297; Griffith and Ryle *Parliament: Functions, Practice and Procedures* (1989) pp 254–262, 352–359, 366–376; and PARLIAMENT.

3    This is an aspect of the conventions that make up individual ministerial responsibility to Parliament: see para 416 post.

4    These include (1) matters which do not relate to the public affairs with which the minister is connected; (2) matters which deal with an action of a minister for which he is not responsible to Parliament; (3) matters which are sub judice; and (4) hypothetical questions: see Erskine May *Parliamentary Practice* (21st Edn, 1989) pp 285–286, 289–291.
     Since 1993 the House of Commons Table Office has abandoned the system of 'blocks' on questions, and questions are now prevented from being tabled if a minister has previously in the same session refused to answer the question: *Second Report from the Public Service Committee: Ministerial Accountability and Responsibility* (HC Paper (1995–96) no 313–I) para 39.

5    Eg on security grounds (see Erskine May *Parliamentary Practice* (21st Edn, 1989) p 292) or because the information is not available or could only be obtained at disproportionate cost. Departments apply a general rule that a cost exceeding a certain sum (£450 in October 1993) justifies refusal to give a written answer. *Questions of Procedure for Ministers* (Cabinet Office, May 1992) suggested that there was a parliamentary convention which determined which questions ministers may answer, but it has been pointed out that these are only ministerial conventions: see the *Second Report from the Public Service Committee: Ministerial Accountability and Responsibility* (HC Paper (1995–96) no 313–I) para 60, which calls for amendment to *Questions of Procedure for Ministers* and a resolution defining the scope of ministers' and civil servants' duties.

6    Erskine May *Parliamentary Practice* (21st Edn, 1989) pp 281–284. As to parliamentary questions generally see the *Report of the Select Committee on Parliamentary Questions* (HC Paper (1971–72) no 39); and the *Third Report from the Select Committee on Procedure: Parliamentary Questions* (HC Paper (1990–91) no 178).

7    As to the Parliamentary Commissioner for Administration see the Parliamentary Commissioner Act 1967; and ADMINISTRATIVE LAW vol 1(1) (Reissue) paras 41–43. See also the *Second Report from the Public Service Committee: Ministerial Accountability and Responsibility* (HC Paper (1995–96) no 313–I) para 65, recommending the amendment of the Parliamentary Commissioner Act 1967 so that members may make a complaint direct to the Commissioner concerning the withholding of information by a government department.

8    See PARLIAMENT. The Select Committee also examines reports from the Health Service Commissioners for England, Scotland and Wales and the Parliamentary Commissioner for Administration for Northern Ireland: HC Standing Orders (1995) (Public Business) no 126(1).

9    See *Government Reply to the Eighth Report from the Treasury and Civil Service Committee: Progress in the Next Steps Initiative* (HC Paper (1989–90) no 481), (Cm 1263); 198 HC Official Report (6th series), 15 November 1991, written answers col 677; 218 HC Official Report (6th series), 9 February 1993, written answers col 609, 612; and Giddings (ed) *Parliamentary Accountability* (1995) ch 7.

10   See the *Third Report of the Select Committee on Procedure: Parliamentary Questions* (HC Paper (1990–91) no 178 para 125); *Seventh Report of the Treasury and Civil Service Committee: Next Steps Initiative* (HC Paper

(1990–91) no 496); *Civil Service Minutes of Evidence of the Treasury and Civil Service Committee: Office of Public Service and Science* (HC Paper (1992–93) no 390-II) p 207. For consideration of the accountability of executive agencies see the *Second Report from the Public Service Committee: Ministerial Accountability and Responsibility* (HC Paper (1995–96) no 313–I) ch V, recommending at para 93 that the government clarify ministers' practice concerning answers by agency chief executives to parliamentary questions, and inform Parliament of the results, and at para 102 that the government review the roles of ministers and agency chief executives and report its conclusions to Parliament in the annual review of 'next steps' agencies.

**227. Select committees of the House of Commons.** Apart from answers to parliamentary questions[1], ministerial statements made to the House[2] and debates in the chamber[3], the principal fora in which the expenditure, administration and policy, and efficiency and effectiveness of ministers and their departments are subjected to scrutiny in the House of Commons are the departmental select committees[4]. These were established in 1979 with the task of examining the expenditure, administration and policy of the principal departments of state[5]. There is a select committee for each government department, and changes in the structure of government departments are normally matched by corresponding changes in the structure of select committees. Membership of the committees in practice reflects the composition of the House, but this is not a requirement of standing orders[6]. The Foreign Affairs Committee, the Home Affairs Committee and the Treasury Committee[7] each has the right to establish a sub-committee[8].

The composition, membership, powers and procedures of select committees are dealt with elsewhere in this work[9].

1   As to parliamentary questions see para 226 ante.
2   See Erskine May *Parliamentary Practice* (21st Edn, 1989) pp 297–298; and PARLIAMENT.
3   See Erskine May *Parliamentary Practice* (21st Edn, 1989) pp 365–384; Griffith and Ryle *Parliament: Functions, Practice and Procedures* (1989) pp 10–13; and PARLIAMENT.
4   See Erskine May *Parliamentary Practice* (21st Edn, 1989) pp 611–661; Drewry (ed) *The New Select Committees* (2nd Edn, 1989); Griffith and Ryle *Parliament: Functions, Practice and Procedures* (1989) ch 11; and PARLIAMENT.
5   See 5 *Stair Memorial Encyclopaedia* paras 428 et seq; and PARLIAMENT.
6   See Erskine May *Parliamentary Practice* (21st Edn, 1989) pp 612–616. Similarly, the allocation of the chairmanship of select committees is a political matter decided by negotiation between the main parties: see Griffith and Ryle *Parliament: Functions, Practice and Procedures* (1989) pp 419–420. The chairmen of the Committee of Public Accounts , the Joint Committee on Statutory Instruments and the Select Committee on European Legislation are by convention members of the Opposition party, and the chairman of the Treasury Committee is by convention a government party backbencher: see Erskine May *Parliamentary Practice* (21st Edn, 1989) pp 551, 660; Griffith and Ryle *Parliament: Functions, Practice and Procedures* (1989) pp 419, 435. Members are appointed to a committee for the remainder of the Parliament (HC Standing Orders (1995) (Public Business) no 130(5)) and thus may not be removed by the whips. See also Erskine May *Parliamentary Practice* (21st Edn, 1989) pp 612, 656.
7   As to the Treasury Committee see para 718 post.
8   See PARLIAMENT.
9   See generally PARLIAMENT. As to select committees and government expenditure see para 718 post.

## (8) PARLIAMENTARY CONTROL OF TAXATION AND PUBLIC EXPENDITURE

**228. Taxation: general principles.** The general principle is that the Crown or its ministers may not impose direct or indirect taxes without parliamentary sanction[1]. It follows that (1) no person can be compelled to make or yield any gift, loan, benevolence or tax without common consent by Act of Parliament[2]; (2) money may not be levied to or for the use of the Crown by pretence of prerogative without grant of Parliament for longer time or in other manner than the same is or may be granted[3]; (3) if money is paid to the Crown on an unlawful demand it is recoverable as of right with interest from the date of the payment[4]; and (4) no exercise of the prerogative which involves the imposition of a charge upon the people can take full effect without parliamentary sanction[5]. There is special provision for the collection of taxes pending the passing of the Finance Act each year[6].

By constitutional usage, no proposal for increased taxation can be initiated except by a minister of the Crown[7], but this rule does not apply to proposals for the alleviation of taxation[8].

1　See PARLIAMENT; and Wade and Bradley *Constitutional and Administrative Law* (11th Edn, 1993) pp 366–367.

2　Petition of Right (1627) s 8. The corresponding provision in Magna Carta (1215) c 12, was to the effect that no scutage or aid other than the three customary feudal aids (as to which see REAL PROPERTY) should be imposed without the consent of the commune concilium. After the Restoration in 1660 these and other feudal revenues ceased with the abolition of the feudal tenures by the Tenures Abolition Act 1660 ss 1, 2 (repealed).

In *R v Hampden, Ship Money Case* (1637) 3 State Tr 826, it was held by seven judges out of twelve that the King could levy ship money. The Long Parliament subsequently passed an Act declaring the writs imposing ship money and the proceedings in *R v Hampden* supra 'contrary to the laws and statutes of the realm, the right of property, the liberty of the subject, and the Petition of Right', and vacated and cancelled the judgment: see the Ship Money Act 1640 (repealed). Parliament's consent to a power to demand payment must be expressed in clear terms: *Congreve v Home Office* [1976] QB 629, [1976] 1 All ER 697, CA (the Home Secretary's discretionary power to revoke a television licence could not lawfully be used to compel the citizen to pay an additional licence fee which was not clearly authorised by statute).

3　Bill of Rights s 1. As to the history and citation of the Bill of Rights see para 35 note 3 ante. There is uncertainty as to the extent to which the imposition of fees and charges for the provision of various services without clear and express legislative authority is a breach of the letter or spirit of s 1: see *A-G v Wilts United Dairies* (1921) 37 TLR 884, CA; on appeal (1922) 91 LJKB 897, HL (minister cannot demand money for a licence for exercising control in a particular way, even though the money goes to a public purpose); *China Navigation Co Ltd v A-G* [1932] 2 KB 197 at 214, CA, per Scrutton LJ (there being no duty on the Crown to provide military protection for British vessels trading in foreign parts, the Crown was entitled to charge for such protection on such terms at it thought fit; no charge is imposed on the subject if he is not bound to accept the service provided: there is no duty to pay money unless the subject requested the service which the Crown was under no duty to afford him); *Yoxford and Darsham Farmers' Association Ltd v Llewellin* [1946] 2 All ER 38, CA (egg marketing compensation fund; no levying of money for the use of the Crown); *R v Richmond upon Thames London Borough Council, ex p McCarthy & Stone Developments Ltd* [1992] 2 AC 48, [1990] 2 All ER 852, CA; revsd sub nom *McCarthy and Stone (Developments) Ltd v Richmond-upon-Thames London Borough Council* [1992] 2 AC 48, [1990] 2 All ER 852, CA; affd [1992] 2 AC 48, [1991] 4 All ER 897, HL (charge levied in respect of pre-planning permission advice by a local planning authority held unlawful in the absence of statutory authority). See also *T and J Brocklebank Ltd v R* [1925] 1 KB 52, CA; *Bristol Channel Steamers Ltd v R* (1924) 131 LT 608; *Marshal Shipping Co v R* (1925) 41 TLR 285 (payments being made as condition of being granted licences); *Congreve v Home Office* [1976] QB 629, [1976] 1 All ER 697, CA. See also para 120 ante; and, on the legality of a levy on foreign exchange transactions, Carey 'A tax by any other name' [1967] British Tax Review p 160. Where fees or charges are imposed without express statutory authority the question would also arise whether this was 'Wednesbury' unreasonable (ie unreasonable in the sense decided by *Associated Provincial Picture Houses Ltd v Wednesbury Corpn* [1948] 1 KB 223, [1947] 2 All ER 680, CA: see generally ADMINISTRATIVE LAW vol 1(1) (Reissue) para 60). Most of the above cases were decided before this principle was expounded in 1948.

4　*Woolwich Equitable Building Society v IRC* [1993]AC 70, sub nom *Woolwich Building Society v IRC (No 2)* [1992] 3 All ER 737, HL. For Law Commission proposals on this subject see *Restitution: Mistakes of Law and Ultra Vires Public Authority Receipts and Payments*, (Law Com no 227) (1994).

5　Thus, a treaty which involves the imposition of a tax needs parliamentary sanction before it can take full effect: see further para 802 post.

6　A resolution of the House of Commons was not sufficient to impose a liability to income tax; an Act of Parliament was required: *Bowles v Bank of England* [1913] 1 Ch 57. Thereafter, to provide for collection of taxes pending the passage of the annual Finance Act, the Provisional Collection of Taxes Act 1913 was passed (now replaced by the Provisional Collection of Taxes Act 1968): see INCOME TAXATION.

7　See Erskine May *Parliamentary Practice* (21st Edn, 1989) p 691.

8　See Erskine May *Parliamentary Practice* (21st Edn, 1989) pp 729–730.

**229. Authorisation and management of taxation.** The care and management of taxes and the machinery for their collection are carried on under permanent Acts[1].

However, rates of income tax, corporation tax and capital gains tax are authorised from year to year by the annual Finance Acts[2]. So important are these taxes requiring annual renewal that Parliament must be summoned annually in order to provide enough revenue (or public income) for current needs[3]. The Comptroller and Auditor General is required to examine whether adequate regulations and procedure exist to secure an effective check on the assessment, collection and proper allocation of revenue and to satisfy himself that they are being duly carried out[4].

1    See eg the Taxes Management Act 1970; the Customs and Excise Management Act 1979; the Income and Corporation Taxes Act 1988; and the Taxation of Chargeable Gains Act 1992: see generally CAPITAL GAINS TAXATION; CUSTOMS AND EXCISE; INCOME TAXATION.
2    See eg most recently the Finance Act 1996 Pt IV (ss 72–182).
3    See Dicey *Law of the Constitution* (10th Edn, 1959) p 446. As to revenue see paras 701–710 post. Income tax is an annual tax: *A-G v Metropolitan Water Board* [1928] 1 KB 833 at 851, CA; *IRC v Sneath* [1932] 2 KB 362, CA; and see INCOME TAXATION vol 23 (Reissue) para 19.
4    As to the Comptroller and Auditor General see paras 724–726 post.

**230. Parliamentary control over public expenditure.** It is a fundamental principle of the constitution of the United Kingdom[1] that Parliament controls the financing of governmental activity[2]. Parliamentary control[3] over expenditure is based upon the principle that all expenditure must rest upon legislative authority[4]. This principle is enforced by making the Consolidated Fund[5] (into which all central government revenue is paid) subject to control by the Comptroller and Auditor General[6], who is an officer of the House of Commons, and therefore independent of the executive government[7]. The Comptroller and Auditor General acts on Treasury request in respect of National Loans Fund lending[8].

1    As to the characteristics of the constitution of the United Kingdom see para 2 et seq ante.
2    It is important to distinguish between parliamentary control of public expenditure, and Treasury control through its Public Expenditure Survey (see para 704 post). See also HM Treasury *Government Accounting* (1989) (amended from time to time and amended most recently (at the date at which this volume states the law) in August 1994); McEldowney 'The Control of Public Expenditure' in Jowell and Oliver (eds) *The Changing Constitution* (3rd Edn, 1994) p 175. As to the Treasury see paras 512–517 post.
3    It is important to distinguish between the control of Parliament, which consists in determining in greater or less detail how the revenue or public income is to be spent, and which therefore ends with the act of voting, and that which is exercised over those who actually expend the grants through the knowledge that accounts will have to be submitted and will be carefully scrutinised: see *Budgetary Reform* (Cm 1867) (1992); McEldowney 'The Control of Public Expenditure' in Jowell and Oliver (eds) *The Changing Constitution* (3rd Edn, 1994) pp 175–207.
4    No payment out of public funds is legal unless it is authorised by statute: *Auckland Harbour Board v R* [1924] AC 318, PC; *R v Secretary of State for Foreign and Commonwealth Affairs, ex p World Development Movement Ltd* [1995] 1 All ER 611, [1995] 1 WLR 386. In 1932 the Committee of Public Accounts (as to which see para 719 post) and the Treasury reached a concordat concerning the requirement to obtain specific legislative authority for expenditure. The Committee of Public Accounts stated that 'where it is desired that continuing functions should be exercised by a government department, particularly where such functions may involve financial liabilities extending beyond a given financial year, it is proper, subject to certain recognised exceptions, that the powers and duties to be exercised should be defined by specific statute.' The Treasury said that 'while they think the Executive government must continue to be allowed a certain measure of discretion in asking Parliament to exercise a power which undoubtedly belongs to it, they agree that practice should normally accord with the view expressed by the Committee [see supra]. The Treasury will, for their part, continue to aim at observance of this principle.' Later in 1932 the Treasury restated their view that 'while it is competent to Parliament, by means of an annual vote embodied in the Appropriation Acts, in effect to extend powers specifically limited by statute, constitutional propriety requires that such extensions should be regularised at the earliest possible date by amending legislation, unless they are of a purely emergency or non-continuing character' (HM Treasury *Government Accounting* 2.2.8, Annex 2.1; see note 2 supra). It is, however, doubtful whether the assumption in the concordat that an annual vote embodied in the Appropriation Acts can extend powers specifically limited by statute is legally valid. The executive government must continue to be allowed a certain measure of discretion in asking Parliament to exercise a power (ie of authorising services by

Appropriation Act alone) which undoubtedly belongs to it: see the Treasury Handbook *Supply and other Financial Procedures of the House of Commons* (1972) para 48.

The Criminal Injuries Compensation Scheme, by which payments were made out of public funds to the victims of crime, ran for some 30 years without specific statutory authority; the legality of the expenditure was never challenged in the courts, and the legality of the scheme was accepted by the courts: see *R v Secretary of State for the Home Department, ex p Fire Brigades Union* [1995] 2 AC 513, [1995] 2 All ER 244, HL. However, as to the statutory Criminal Injuries Compensation Scheme in force under the Criminal Injuries Compensation Act 1995, see para 7 note 21 ante. See also para 701 note 1 post; and PARLIAMENT.

5    As to the Consolidated Fund see para 711 et seq post.
6    See the Exchequer and Audit Departments Act 1866 ss 10–15 (as amended). As to the Comptroller and Auditor General see paras 724–726 post.
7    See the Exchequer and Audit Departments Act 1866 ss 3, 6 (both as amended); National Audit Act 1983 s 1; House of Commons Disqualification Act 1975 s 1(1)(f), Sch 1 Pt III: see paras 713–723 post; and PARLIAMENT.
8    As to the National Loans Fund see paras 727–739 post.

# (9)  INTERNATIONAL PARLIAMENTARY ORGANISATIONS

**231.  Financing of international parliamentary organisations.** The Secretary of State must lay before Parliament each financial year[1] a register of those publicly financed international parliamentary organisations which are in receipt of an annual grant-in-aid to fund both British and international secretariats and which draw their membership from both Houses of Parliament[2]. The register must include the name of the organisation and the amount of money allocated to that organisation in that financial year[3].

1    'Financial year' means the period of 12 months ending with 31 March: Interpretation Act 1978 s 5, Sch 1.
2    International Parliamentary Organisations (Registration) Act 1989 s 1(1). The organisations are the Commonwealth Parliamentary Association and the Inter-Parliamentary Union: s 1(1), Schedule.
3    Ibid s 1(2).

# (10)  PARLIAMENTARY SOVEREIGNTY

**232.  Basic principles.** The Queen in Parliament is said to be sovereign[1]. The courts recognise no limit to Parliament's legislative power[2] save where legislation is incompatible with European Community law[3], and will not seriously entertain any attack on the validity of a public[4] or private Act[5].

1    See Dicey *Law of the Constitution* (10th Edn, 1959) pp 39–85; and Wade and Bradley *Constitutional and Administrative Law* (11th Edn, 1993) pp 65–96. This is now subject to the requirements of European Community law: see paras 23–24 ante; and EUROPEAN COMMUNITIES. This view is to be contrasted with the Scottish view of sovereignty: see paras 52–55 ante.

It must be noted that what follows in this section must be read subject to the overriding principle of the primacy or supremacy of European Community law. See Bradley 'The Sovereignty of Parliament - in Perpetuity' in Jowell and Oliver (eds) *The Changing Constitution* (3rd Edn, 1994) pp 79–107; Wade and Bradley *Constitutional and Administrative Law* (11th Edn, 1993) pp 145–154; Wade, 'Sovereignty and the European Communities' (1972) 88 LQR 1; 5 Stair Memorial Encyclopaedia *Constitutional Law* para 320 et seq; and para 24 ante.

2    It is often said that it would be unconstitutional for the United Kingdom Parliament to do certain things, meaning that the moral, political and other reasons against doing them are so strong that most people would regard it as highly improper if Parliament did these things. But that does not mean that it is beyond the power of Parliament to do such things. If Parliament chose to do any of them, the courts could not hold the Act of Parliament invalid: *Madzimbamuto v Lardner-Burke and George* [1969] 1 AC 645 at 723, [1968] 3 All ER 561 at 573, PC.

'Of the power and jurisdiction of Parliament for making of laws in proceeding by Bill, it is so transcendent and absolute, as it cannot be confined either for causes or persons within any bounds'; 4 Co Inst 36; 'It hath sovereign and uncontrollable authority in the making, confirming, enlarging, restraining, abrogating, repealing, reviving, and expounding of laws concerning matters of all possible denominations, ecclesiastical, or temporal, civil, military, maritime, or criminal: this being the place where that absolute despotic power, which must in all governments reside somewhere, is entrusted by the constitution of these kingdoms'; 1 Bl Com (14th Edn) 160–162.

For examples illustrating the plenitude of Parliament's power see the Continental Shelf Act 1964, Marine etc Broadcasting (Offences) Act 1967; the Representation of the People Act 1983 s 92 (as amended) (extra-territorial legislation); the Act of Settlement; and His Majesty's Declaration of Abdication Act 1936 (alteration of royal succession); Niall MacPherson Indemnity Act 1954 (making an illegal act legal retrospectively); the War Damage Act 1965 (retrospectively depriving claimants of rights to compensation for destruction of their property by the state and thus reversing the decision of the House of Lords in *Burmah Oil Co (Burma Trading) Ltd v Lord Advocate* [1965] AC 75, [1964] 2 All ER 348, HL); the War Crimes Act 1991 (criminal jurisdiction granted retrospectively to courts in the United Kingdom in respect of war crimes committed during the Second World War in Germany by persons who are British citizens or resident in the United Kingdom); the Parliament Acts 1911 and 1949 (which redefined Parliament itself for certain purposes); and the Statute of Westminster 1931 s 3 (which granted full power to Dominion Parliaments to make laws having extra-territorial operation). See also *Mortensen v Peters* (1906) 14 SLT 227 (foreign fisherman convicted of statutory offence committed outside territorial water); *Collco Dealings v IRC* [1962] AC 1, [1961] 1 All ER 762, HL (statute contrary to international law not invalid). As to the citation of the Act of Settlement see para 35 note 3 ante. See also *R v Secretary of State for Social Security, ex p Joint Council for the Welfare of Immigrants* [1996] NLJR 985, CA (regulations withdrawing benefit from certain classes of asylum seeker were unlawful, inter alia, because they offended against basic human rights).

What the statute itself enacts cannot be unlawful, because what the statute says and provides is itself the law, and the highest form of law that is known to this country. It is the law which prevails over every other form of law, and it is not for the court to say that a parliamentary enactment, the highest law in this country, is illegal: *Cheney v Conn (Inspector of Taxes)* [1968] 1 All ER 779 at 782, [1968] 1 WLR 242 at 247 per Ungoed-Thomas J (a taxpayer who had been assessed to tax argued that the provisions of the Finance Act 1964 should not be given legal effect because substantial parts of the receipts from taxes were allocated to the construction of nuclear weapons with the intention of using the weapons, should occasion arise; it was argued that this was a purpose in conflict with a Geneva convention. It was held that if the purposes for which the enactments of the Act of 1964 might be used included an unlawful purpose, the enactments were not thereby vitiated).

3   As to the primacy of European Community law see paras 23–24 ante.

4   This was not always so: see *R v Hampden, Ship Money Case* (1637) 3 State Tr 826. But from the Revolution Settlement at the end of the seventeenth century there have been hardly any attempts to persuade a court that a statute may be invalid. Definitive rulings to the effect that Parliament is sovereign can now be found in *R v Jordan* [1967] Crim LR 483, DC, and *Cheney v Conn (Inspector of Taxes)* [1968] 1 All ER 779, [1968] 1 WLR 242. See also *Ex p Canon Selwyn* (1872) 36 JP Jo 54; and *Hall v Hall* (1944) 88 Sol Jo 383 (county court). See also *Blackburn v A-G* [1971] 2 All ER 1380, [1971] 1 WLR 1037, CA.

5   *British Railways Board v Pickin* [1974] AC 765, [1974] 1 All ER 609, HL. Accordingly, once a bill has received the Royal Assent, a court cannot ask whether members of Parliament were or were not disqualified: *Martin v O'Sullivan (Inspector of Taxes)* [1984] STC 258n, CA. Some doubt has been expressed from time to time whether private Acts of Parliament share the absolute immunity attaching to public Acts; and attempts have been made to attack the validity of private Acts on the ground that they have been obtained improperly by fraud or otherwise. Such attempts have always proved unsuccessful. In *Edinburgh and Dalkeith Rly Co v Wauchope* (1842) 8 Cl & Fin 710 at 723, HL, Lord Campbell declared, obiter, that all that a court of justice can do is look to the Parliament roll, and that, once a bill has passed both Houses and received the Royal Assent, no court of justice can inquire into the mode in which it was introduced into Parliament, nor into what was done previous to its introduction, or what passed in Parliament during its progress in its various stages through both Houses. Moreover, in *Lee v Bude and Torrington Junction Rly Co* (1871) LR 6 CP 576 at 582, Willes J said that if an Act of Parliament has been obtained improperly, it is for the legislature to correct it by repealing it. See also *Waterford, Wexford, Wicklow and Dublin Rly Co v Logan* (1850) 14 QB 672; *Earl of Shrewsbury v Scott* (1859) 6 CBNS 1 at 160; affd at 221, Ex Ch; *Labrador Co v R* [1893] AC 104 at 123, PC; *Hoani Te Heuheu Tukino v Aotea District Maori Land Board* [1941] AC 308 at 322, [1941] 2 All ER 93 at 97, PC. More recently, in *British Railways Board v Pickin* supra, the House of Lords applied these principles in striking out paragraphs of a pleading that called them in question.

The Parliament roll no longer exists. Since 1849 two vellum prints of an Act have been made; one of which is signed by the Clerk of the Parliaments and preserved in the House of Lords Record Office, and the other one is sent to the Public Record Office for preservation: Erskine May *Parliamentary Practice* (21st Edn, 1989) p 535; Wade and Bradley *Constitutional and Administrative Law* (11th Edn, 1993) p 82; and de Smith and Brazier *Constitutional and Administrative Law* (7th Edn, 1994) p 92. As to public records see paras 835–841 post.

**233. Statute and rules of common law or equity.** A statute can alter or abrogate rules of common law or equity[1]. This is very often the case, since most statutes affect the operation of rules of the common law or equity[2].

1 As to statutes generally see STATUTES.
2 See eg the Law of Property Act 1925; the Supply of Goods and Services Act 1982; and the Consumer Protection Act 1987.

**234. Entrenchment of legislation and the doctrine of implied repeal.** If there is repugnancy or incompatibility between one statute and another, the one that is later in date prevails[1]. Thus, any attempt in a statute to protect a statutory provision from express, or even implied, repeal would probably be ineffectual, and it would follow that entrenchment is not possible in the United Kingdom[2].

1 Ie the earlier statute is held to be repealed pro tanto by implication: *Ellen Street Estates Ltd v Minister of Health* [1934] 1 KB 590, CA; and see STATUTES.
2 Acts of Parliament cannot curtail the powers of future Parliaments, since it is a maxim of the common law that 'Acts derogatory to the power of subsequent Parliaments bind not': see 1 Bl Com (14th Edn) 160. Thus, it has been held that Parliament cannot impose limitations on the subject matter of subsequent legislation: *Vauxhall Estates Ltd v Liverpool Corpn* [1932] 1 KB 733, DC; *Ellen Street Estates Ltd v Minister of Health* [1934] 1 KB 590, CA (limiting statute is impliedly repealed: see STATUTES).

This is the orthodox doctrine, which, however, recognises the possibility of Parliament's abdicating and divesting itself of authority either by legally dissolving itself and leaving no means whereby a subsequent Parliament could be legally summoned, or by transferring sovereign authority to another person or body of persons and not preserving its own existence: see Dicey *Law of the Constitution* (10th Edn, 1959) 68 note 1, or by transferring legislative power of limited scope to a supra-national body such as the European Community by Act of Parliament: see para 24 ante. However, even as so qualified, the doctrine is no longer universally accepted by writers on constitutional law; and although any attempt to substitute an alternative doctrine must be highly speculative, some indication must here be given of the factors which might induce, or even compel the courts to change their attitude to statutes and of the arguments or authorities on which they might rely. For many constitutional theorists the question whether parliamentary sovereignty presupposes that Parliament must always remain sovereign and cannot be bound by the legislation of its predecessors, or whether Parliament's sovereignty entitles it to restrict its power to legislate, to impose a special procedure if it is to legislate in areas of particular constitutional importance, or to deprive itself of the power to legislate entirely on any matter, remains open.

Attention has been drawn to various questions which are set out as heads (1)–(6) infra.

(1) Can Parliament, without purporting to restrict its powers, validly make it more difficult to exercise legislative powers by requiring the use of a special 'manner and form' or procedure other than that usually followed by it, for the making of certain changes, usually of special constitutional significance? The new manner and form might, for example, be one requiring a qualified majority, such as two-thirds of those present and voting, of the House of Commons, or the submission of the proposed change to the electorate by way of referendum. Commonwealth authorities (all relating to written constitutions, and in many cases dealing with 'self-entrenched' provisions) suggest that a Parliament is bound to observe the prescribed manner and form when legislating and that, if it does not, the courts will consider either that an improperly constituted assembly is not 'Parliament' or that the purported enactment is not a statute: see *Bribery Comr v Ranasinghe* [1965] AC 172, [1964] 2 All ER 785, PC (Ceylon) (statute not possessing Speaker's certificate showing that it had been passed by required majority declared invalid: it is not inconsistent with the concept of sovereignty that a Parliament should be bound by such 'manner and form' requirements); *Liyanage v R* [1967] 1 AC 259, [1966] 1 All ER 650, PC (Ceylon) (legislation contrary in intention to an entrenched provision declared ultra vires and void); *A-G for New South Wales v Trethowan* (1931) 44 CLR 394, Aust HC; affd [1932] AC 526, PC (purported repeal of entrenched provision without required referendum invalid); *Harris v Donges* [1952] 1 TLR 1245, SA App Div (purported repeal of entrenched provision by Parliament sitting bicamerally, instead of unicamerally as required, declared invalid); for subsequent proceedings see *Minister of the Interior v Harris* 1952 (4) SA 769 (A), SA App Div (South African Parliament not able to declare itself a court in order to overrule *Harris v Donges* supra); and see also *Collins v Minister of the Interior* 1957 (1) SA 552 (A), SA App Div; *R (O'Brien) v Military Governor North Dublin Union Internment Camp* [1924] 1 IR 32, Ir CA (statute passed without necessary declarations

of both Houses declared invalid). It must be noted that in every instance cited the legislature had been established by a pre-existing constitution.

In the United Kingdom, on the other hand, there is no governing instrument which prescribes the law-making powers and the forms which are essential to those powers: see *Bribery Comr v Ranasinghe* [1965] AC 172 at 197, [1964] 2 All ER 785 at 792, PC. Thus, if one is to search for any authority historically and logically prior to the existence of Parliament, one can find it only in the common law. It would then rest with the courts to decide as a matter of common law whether a failure by Parliament to observe a new manner and form prescribed by statute affected the validity of any legislation it purported to enact.

The traditional manner and form of passing legislation, by the Crown with the assent of the two Houses sitting separately, has not always been observed. In fact, the title to the Crown, which is a necessary basis for it, depends ultimately on the revolutionary action of the Convention Parliament of 1689 without the consent of a monarch: see Maitland *Constitutional History of England* (1908) pp 283–285. In *Hall v Hall* (1944) 88 Sol Jo 383 (county court), the plaintiff failed to make good his attack on all legislation subsequent to that event. Moreover, the traditional manner and form was altered by the Parliament Act 1911 so as to dispense with the consent of the House of Lords in certain cases.

It would perhaps be dangerous to draw precise legal inferences from the events that happened in 1911 and 1949 (when the Act of 1911 was amended), for they constituted steps in the progressive exclusion of non-democratic elements from the constitution. However, in *A-G for New South Wales v Trethowan* (1931) 44 CLR 394 at 425, Aust HC, Dixon J raised, obiter, the much more difficult question whether the United Kingdom Parliament could effectually preclude itself by statute from altering specified statutory provisions without previously submitting the alterations to the electorate for its approval. In other words, could Parliament repeal the entrenched provisions without resorting to a referendum, thus restricting, instead of enlarging, popular control of the legislative process. Dixon J left the question unanswered. If put in the form 'can Parliament for certain purposes enlarge its own composition so as to include the electorate as a third House?' it might be difficult to resolve. Some light may be thrown on the question by the fact that by the Northern Ireland Constitution Act 1973 ss 1, 41, Sch 6, Parliament substituted a provision requiring the consent of the majority of the people of Northern Ireland expressed in a poll (see para 68 ante) for the provision in the Ireland Act 1949 s 1(2), affirming that in no event would Northern Ireland or any part of it cease to be part of His Majesty's dominions and of the United Kingdom without the consent of the Parliament of Northern Ireland. The substitution probably makes it easier, rather than more difficult, for Parliament to legislate. But there is force in the suggestion made by de Smith and Brazier *Constitutional and Administrative Law* (7th Edn, 1994) p 99 that if Parliament can make it easier to legislate, as by passing the Parliament Acts 1911 and 1949, or by abolishing the House of Lords, it can also make it harder to legislate. See also Zellick 'Is the Parliament Act Ultra Vires?' (1969) 119 NLJ 716.

(2) Is it a material factor that the requirement of a special manner and form is or is not 'entrenched' by a further requirement that any change in that manner and form may be introduced only by following the same manner and form or some other special manner or form devised for the purpose? In Commonwealth cases, a non-entrenched manner and form requirement in a written constitution has been held to have no particular sanctity and to be impliedly repealed: see *McCawley v R* [1920] AC 691, PC; *Kariapper v Wijesinha* [1968] AC 717, [1967] 3 All ER 485, PC; but cf *Akar v A-G of Sierra Leone* [1970] AC 853, [1969] 3 All ER 384, PC. The New South Wales Parliament was careful to avoid this possibility when it made a change it made in 1929; and in *A-G for New South Wales v Trethowan* [1932] AC 526, PC, the entrenchment was held to be effective. Entrenchment has never been resorted to by the United Kingdom Parliament, and it would probably be as difficult to apply Commonwealth decisions to any attempt at entrenchment as to an attempt to require a special manner and form.

(3) If the Parliament of the United Kingdom were to attempt to impose an entrenching procedure on parliamentary amendment or repeal of legislation, such as a requirement for a two thirds majority in both Houses of Parliament, it would not be possible for the courts to enforce it by holding legislation passed in contravention of the requirements to be void, because the courts have no jurisdiction to inquire into parliamentary procedure. If judicial enforcement of such a procedure were to be possible the law relating to parliamentary privilege and the Bill of Rights s 1 relating to the freedom of the proceedings of Parliament would have to be altered by statute: see *Edinburgh and Dalkeith Rly Co v Wauchope* (1842) 8 Cl and F 710, HL; and *British Railways Board v Pickin* [1974] AC 765, [1974] 1 All ER 609, HL. In Commonwealth countries where the courts have upheld procedural entrenchment the English law relating to parliamentary privilege does not apply or has been overridden by the provisions of the constitutions; and Parliament. As to the history and citation of the Bill of Rights see para 35 note 3 ante.

(4) On the assumption that Parliament could legally require that a statute on a particular topic should be passed according to a special manner and form that made it harder to legislate, could it legally and effectually require a manner and form that made it very difficult or virtually impossible to legislate? The question is not academic, because there have been serious suggestions that human rights and liberties should be irrevocably protected against legislative interference by a Bill of Rights. Moreover, recourse might be had for preference to the model afforded by the former Canadian Bill of Rights (replaced by a Charter of Freedoms in the Constitution Act (Canada) 1982: see infra) which, after recognising and declaring certain human rights and fundamental freedoms to have existed and to continue to exist without discrimination by reason of race etc, enacted that every Canadian law, unless expressly excepted, should be construed and applied so as not to abrogate, abridge or infringe any of the rights and freedoms recognised and declared by the Bill. It must be noted that the Canadian Parliament did not attempt to preclude itself from repealing the Bill or even prescribe a particular manner and form for its repeal. Nevertheless, that fact did not deprive the Bill of a somewhat startling usefulness, as was shown in *R v Drybones* [1970] SCR 282, 9 DLR (3d) 473 (Can SC), where the Bill was held to nullify a provision in a previously existing Act of the Canadian Parliament on the ground that the provision was discriminatory.

Another mechanism for entrenching or protecting from repeal important legislation such as a Bill of Rights would be to include in the statute enacting the Bill of Rights a 'notwithstanding clause' to the effect that provisions in subsequent statutes that were incompatible with the Bill of Rights should not be given effect unless the subsequent Act included an express provision that it was to take effect notwithstanding incompatibility with the Bill of Rights. This device was adopted in the Charter of Freedoms that forms part of the Constitution Act (Canada) 1982 s 33 of which permits derogation from the Charter freedoms only if there is an express declaration in a later Act that it is to operate notwithstanding a provision in the Charter. This clause has been held to be effective in Canada to nullify the effect of later incompatible legislation where no such provision is included in the later Act: see *Re Singh and Minister of Employment and Immigration* (1985) 17 DLR (4th) 422. It may be that the courts in the United Kingdom would regard such a provision as effective to protect a measure against repeal, and as not incompatible with the English doctrine of parliamentary supremacy: see *Macarthys Ltd v Smith* [1979] 3 All ER 325 at 328–329 obiter per Lord Denning MR; and *Garland v British Rail Engineering Ltd* [1983] 2 AC 751, [1982] 2 All ER 402, HL; and Ellis 'Supremacy of Parliament and European Law' (1980) 96 LQR 511–514.

(5) Can Parliament, without abdicating, bind itself irreversibly to accept the validity of certain rights established by an external authority, so as in effect to transfer a portion of its sovereignty to that authority? This is the problem posed by the European Communities Act 1972 s 2(1), (4) (see para 24 ante). The answer appears to be Yes.

(6) The doctrine of parliamentary sovereignty represents nothing more nor less than a series of predictions of how the courts would decide certain issues if properly brought before them. It may be assumed that they would not act unless it became absolutely necessary. Thus in *Blackburn v A-G* [1971] 2 All ER 1380, [1971] 1 WLR 1037, the Court of Appeal refused to decide what it would do if Parliament passed legislation at variance with the EEC Treaty, if and when it should come into force. The court was indeed able to avoid answering the question on the ground that the point at issue concerned only the Crown's prerogative to conclude treaties. Moreover, Stamp LJ said (at 1383 and 1041) that it was no part of the court's function or duty to make declarations in general terms regarding the powers of Parliament. Even if Parliament repealed the European Communities Act 1972, so that a case was no longer hypothetical, a court would probably try to avoid difficult constitutional questions by insisting on proof of a party's locus standi, by deciding on the facts, by applying independent principles of law, or by turning questions of powers into questions of interpretation, to which they would apply their own canons. If avoidance proved impossible, then, in the present climate of judicial opinion, the court would, in all probability, hold that the repeal was valid and effective. It could fortify itself in its refusal to enter into competition with Parliament by reference to the fact that on the one undoubted occasion when a new special manner and form was introduced for a particular kind of legislation, Parliament had, in the Parliament Act 1911 ss 1(2) (as amended), (3), 2(2), (4) (as amended), 3, left it to the Speaker of the House of Commons to decide whether it had been properly used, and had enacted that his certificate should be conclusive for all purposes and should not be questioned in any court of law. On the other hand, in considering whether a purported repeal of the European Communities Act 1972 was valid, a court would not need to inquire into what happened in the legislative process.

## 235. Absence of hierarchy of statutes. There are no degrees of legal validity among statutes; a statute introducing a radical change in the constitution and a statute of a temporary nature made to deal with a passing difficulty are equally valid[1].

1 Thus, the Irish Church Act 1869 (repealed) disestablished the Church of Ireland, although the maintenance of the Established Church in Ireland was made a fundamental term of the union: see the Union with Ireland Act 1800 art 5, as originally enacted. A Parliament can prolong its own life: see the Septennial Act 1715 (repealed), the Parliament and Local Elections Act 1918 (repealed); and the Prolongation of Parliament Acts 1940–1944 (repealed). Parliament may also bind and limit the succession to the Crown: see the Bill of Rights and His Majesty's Declaration of Abdication Act 1936. As to the government of Northern Ireland and the partial repeal of the Government of Ireland Act 1920 and the Ireland Act 1949: see para 68 et seq ante; and PARLIAMENT; STATUTES. As to the history and citation of the Bill of Rights see para 35 note 3 ante.

**236. Political and conventional restraints on the exercise of Parliament's sovereign legislative powers.** Although those who promote and those who draft bills are not under any duty to consider the possible existence of legal restrictions on the power to pass parliamentary legislation, they are bound by restraints of a political or conventional[1] nature and by the need to keep faith with other powers to which the nation is under obligations by treaty or by the rules of international law[2].

1 See *British Coal Corpn v R* [1925] AC 500 at 520, PC: 'The Imperial Parliament could, as a matter of strict law, repeal section 4 of the Statute. But that is theory and has no relation to realities': see also *Manuel v A-G* [1983] Ch 77, [1982] 3 All ER 822, CA; and the Statute of Westminster 1931.

2 How far international law is a part of English law is a matter of some doubt. Some doctrines of international law have been received into common law by judicial decisions, but wherever it has been desired to make provisions in treaties enforceable in the English courts it has been the practice to pass enactments for that purpose.

 A treaty concluded by the government does not alter the laws of the United Kingdom, unless it is incorporated into the laws of the United Kingdom legislation. In particular a treaty cannot give rise to rights enforceable by individuals in United Kingdom courts: *Maclaine Watson & Co Ltd v International Tin Council* [1990] 2 AC 418, [1989] 3 All ER 523, HL. In the European Communities Act 1972 s 2(1), Parliament attributed that effect in advance to some part of what is done from time to time by or under the treaties establishing or regulating the various European Communities: see para 24 ante; EUROPEAN COMMUNITIES; FOREIGN RELATIONS LAW.

**237–300. Presumptions as to Parliament's intention.** The courts apply a number of presumptions when interpreting statutes which seek to protect recognised constitutional principles[1]. However, since 1993 the courts may refer to reports of proceedings in Parliament in order to discover parliamentary intentions in cases of ambiguity or obscurity in a statute or where giving words their literal meaning would lead to absurdity the courts may find that Parliament did not intend these presumptions to apply[2].

In the light of this change, administrative procedures are being put in place for avoiding or correcting any errors or ambiguities arising out of ministerial statements during the passage of legislation. In particular, speeches and speaking notes will generally be reviewed by a department's legal advisers for possible influence on interpretation; the Hansard record of ministers' contributions to debates on legislation will similarly be reviewed to consider whether there is any inaccuracy, and where it seems sensible to do so ministers may more frequently offer to reflect and take further advice on points of interpretation that are raised in debate. If it proves necessary to correct a ministerial statement the aim will be to do this as promptly as possible at an appropriate point during the further consideration of a bill[3].

1 See STATUTES vol 44(1) (Reissue) paras 1369–1498.

2 See *Pepper (Inspector of Taxes) v Hart* [1993] AC 593, [1993] 1 All ER 42, HL.

3 See HL Official Report (5th series), 5 April 1995, written answers col 26.

# 4. THE JUDICIARY

## (1) INTRODUCTION AND FUNCTIONS OF THE JUDICIARY

**301. Introduction.** Of the three main branches of central government, namely, the legislature, the executive and the judiciary, the judiciary comes closest to being separate and independent[1]. For England and Wales this branch comprises most importantly the Supreme Court of Judicature, which consists of the Court of Appeal, the High Court and the Crown Court[2]. The county courts[3] and the magistrates' courts[4] may be seen as a further branch of the judiciary. The Appellate Committees of the House of Lords sit as the supreme court of appeal in the United Kingdom for England and Wales, Scotland and Northern Ireland[5]. In addition there is a network of administrative tribunals[6], many of whose members are part-time appointees, exercising judicial functions, which may also be regarded as part of the judiciary, though the provisions for their appointment, tenure and remuneration differ from those in respect of the Supreme Court and the Lords of Appeal in Ordinary.

It is a feature of the judicial system in England and Wales that there are many part-time judicial office holders, such as deputy High Court judges[7], deputy circuit judges[8] and recorders[9]. These appointees are usually barristers or solicitors in practice. They do not enjoy the high degree of security of tenure applicable to the full-time judiciary[10].

1　As to the doctrine of separation of powers see para 8 ante. In this title it is possible only to treat the major constitutional issues surrounding the judiciary in England and Wales. For full details see COUNTY COURTS; COURTS; MAGISTRATES. As to Scotland see paras 51–56 ante. As to Northern Ireland see paras 67–86 ante. As to non-judicial functions of the judiciary see para 10 ante.

2　See COURTS vol 10 para 843 et seq. For the position in Scotland see para 59 ante; and 5 *Stair Memorial Encyclopaedia* CONSTITUTIONAL LAW para 625 et seq.

3　See generally COUNTY COURTS. The business of the county courts is done by circuit judges, who are also judges of the Crown Court, and district judges and deputy district judges.

4　See generally MAGISTRATES. As to non-judicial functions of magistrates see para 10 ante.

5　No criminal appeals lie to the House of Lords from the High Court of Justiciary in Scotland: Criminal Procedure (Scotland) Act 1975 ss 262, 281; and see 5 *Stair Memorial Encyclopaedia* CONSTITUTIONAL LAW para 644. As to the House of Lords as part of Parliament see further para 204 ante; and PARLIAMENT.

6　See ADMINISTRATIVE LAW vol 1(1) (Reissue) para 13.

7　See COURTS vol 10 para 866.

8　See COURTS vol 10 para 889.

9　See COURTS vol 10 para 890.

10　See COURTS vol 10 paras 866, 889, 890; COUNTY COURTS. See also Brazier *Constitutional Practice* (2nd Edn, 1994) ch 12; Wade and Bradley *Constitutional and Administrative Law* (11th Edn, 1993) ch 18.

**302. Judicial functions.** The principal functions of the judiciary may be described as follows:

(1)　to provide for the orderly resolution of disputes, whether between private individuals or bodies, or involving public bodies or the exercise of public or governmental functions by public or private bodies[1];

(2)　to uphold the principle of legality or the rule of law[2];

(3)　to provide the mechanism through which the coercive powers of the state may be exercised;

(4)　to protect the individual against unlawful state activity[3]; and

(5)　to develop the common law, in which activity they exercise a quasi-legislative function[4].

1   For the bodies and functions subject to judicial review see generally ADMINISTRATIVE LAW vol 1(1)
    (Reissue) para 64.
2   As to the rule of law and the principle of legality see para 6 ante.
3   As to the protection of the rights and freedoms of the individual see paras 101–181 ante.
4   See further para 6 ante. Some judges also exercise a legislative function in the making of rules of procedure
    and practice directions and practice notes: see COURTS vol 10 para 908 et seq.

## (2)  THE INDEPENDENCE OF THE JUDICIARY AND THE SEPARATION OF POWERS

**303. Independence of the judiciary.** The independence of the judiciary is essential to
the rule of law and to the continuance of its own authority and legitimacy. The
independence of the judiciary in England and Wales from political pressures results from
a combination of statute and convention[1]. Thus although the final court of appeal in
England is part of Parliament and although the Lord Chancellor[2] is a member of all three
branches of government and the Law Lords are members of the legislature, a variety of
factors operate to insulate the judiciary as a whole from political pressures[3]. Although
judicial office holders are appointed by the Crown on the advice of the Lord Chancellor[4],
or in the case of Lords of Appeal in Ordinary, the Lord Chief Justice, the Master of the
Rolls, Lords Justices of Appeal, the Vice-Chancellor, and the President of the Family
Division, by the Crown on the advice of the Prime Minister[5], by convention such
appointments are made on merit and not for political reasons[6].

The only practical way of removing judges of the High Court and the Court of
Appeal[7] is upon an address to the Crown by both Houses of Parliament. A similar
provision applies to Lords of Appeal in Ordinary[8]. Other judicial officers enjoy less
security. Circuit judges may be removed by the Lord Chancellor for incapacity or
misbehaviour[9]. Similar provisions apply to district judges[10]. Lay magistrates are appointed
until the age of 70, although they may be removed at the discretion of the Lord
Chancellor at any time[11].

Judicial salaries may be increased by administrative action, but may not be reduced
except by Act of Parliament[12].

Ministers and members of Parliament are prevented by parliamentary rules from
attacking the character of judges[13] or from seeking to influence decisions in the course
of a trial[14].

1   See generally de Smith and Brazier *Constitutional and Administrative Law* (7th Edn, 1994) p 395 et seq.
2   As to the Lord Chancellor see paras 477–497 post.
3   Eg the Law Lords do not generally take part in politically controversial debates (see para 21 text and note
    14 ante); full-time members of the judiciary are disqualified from membership of the House of Commons:
    House of Commons Disqualification Act 1975 s 1(1)(a), Sch 1 Pt I (as amended); and see PARLIAMENT.
    See further 572 HL Official Report (5th series), 5 June 1996, cols 1259–1260, where the shadow Lord
    Chancellor, Lord Irvine of Laing, made a plea for self-restraint by the judges to conserve their reputation
    for political impartiality, and by the ministers when addressing judicial decisions striking down their
    decisions as unlawful.
4   See de Smith and Brazier *Constitutional and Administrative Law* (7th Edn, 1994) p 397.
5   In practice the Prime Minister seeks advice from the Lord Chancellor on appointments: see de Smith
    and Brazier *Constitutional and Administrative Law* (7th Edn, 1994) p 397; Wade and Bradley
    *Constitutional and Administrative Law* (11th Edn, 1994) pp 375–376; Turpin *British Government and the
    Constitution: Text, Cases and Materials* (3rd Edn, 1995) pp 64–65. As to the Prime Minister see paras
    394–398 post.
6   See de Smith and Brazier *Constitutional and Administrative Law* (7th Edn, 1994) p 397 et seq; Wade and
    Bradley *Constitutional and Administrative Law* (11th Edn, 1994) pp 375–376; Turpin *British Government and
    the Constitution: Text cases and Materials* (3rd Edn, 1995) pp 64–65; see also Judicial Appointments 1995
    (Lord Chancellor's Department, 1995) outlining the Lord Chancellor's judicial appointments policies

generally. Separate leaflets issued by the Lord Chancellor's Department deal with senior judicial appointments, circuit judges, district judges and other appointments.

7 Act of Settlement s 3 (repealed in part); and see now the Supreme Court 1981 s 11(3). As to the citation of the Act of Settlement see para 35 note 3 ante. See also de Smith and Brazier *Constitutional and Administrative Law* (7th Edn, 1994) pp 408–409; Wade and Bradley *Constitutional and Administrative Law* (11th Edn, 1994) pp 377–378; Brazier *Constitutional Texts* (1990) ch 11; COURTS vol 10 para 867.

8 See the Appellate Jurisdiction Act 1876 s 6 (as amended); and COURTS vol 10 para 749.

9 Courts Act 1971 s 17(4).

10 See the County Courts Act 1984 s 11(4), (5).

11 See the Justices of the Peace Act 1979 ss 6, 8(2), 10; and MAGISTRATES vol 29 paras 218–221.

12 For Supreme Court judges other than the Lord Chancellor this is provided for by the Supreme Court Act 1981 s 12(3). For Lords of Appeal in Ordinary and certain others, including stipendiary magistrates, the provision is the Administration of Justice Act 1973 s 9(1), (3) (s 9(3) as amended)). For circuit judges the provision is the Courts Act 1971 s 18(2). Note, however, the different provision in respect of district judges, whose salaries are such as the Lord Chancellor, with the concurrence of the Treasury, directs: County Courts Act 1984 s 6(1) (amended by the Courts and Legal Services Act 1990 s 125(3), Sch 18 para 42). As to the remuneration of the Lord Chancellor see para 478 post. As to the Treasury see paras 512–517 post.

13 As to the bringing of charges against High Court judges in the House of Commons, see 866 HC Official Report (5th series), 10 December 1973, cols 42–44. On parliamentary criticism of judges see also Erskine May *Parliamentary Practice* (21st Edn, 1989) pp 344, 377–379. See Wade and Bradley *Constitutional and Administrative Law* (11th Edn, 1994) pp 381–383; Brazier *Constitutional Texts* (1990) ch 11.

14 For the sub judice rule see Erskine May *Parliamentary Practice* (21st Edn, 1989) pp 377–380; Wade and Bradley *Constitutional and Administrative Law* (11th Edn, 1994) pp 382–383.

**304. Immunity of judicial office holders from civil liability.** In order to be sure that judicial officers can discharge their functions impartially and without fear of incurring personal civil liability to anyone aggrieved by their acts, comments or decisions, they are in principle immune at common law from civil actions in respect of acts that would otherwise be tortious providing they are done in a judicial capacity in a court of justice[1]. The Crown is similarly immune[2]. The extent of the immunity of magistrates is less than that of other judicial office holders, as magistrates may be liable for acts outside their jurisdiction where the plaintiff can show bad faith[3].

1 See *Floyd v Barker* (1607) 12 Co Rep 23; *Scott v Stansfield* (1868) LR 3 Ex 220; *Anderson v Gorrie* [1895] 1 QB 668, CA; *Sirros v Moore* [1975] QB 118, [1974] 3 All ER 776, CA; *Re McC (A Minor)* [1985] AC 528, sub nom *McC v Mullan* [1984] 3 All ER 908, HL; and see Olowofoyeku *Suing Judges* (1994). See generally Wade and Bradley *Constitutional and Administrative Law* (11th Edn, 1993) pp 383–386. As to compensation for miscarriages of justice see para 829 post.

2 The Crown Proceedings Act 1947 s 2(5) absolves the Crown from liability for the conduct of any person 'while discharging or purporting to discharge any responsibilities of a judicial nature vested in him'; see further CROWN PROCEEDINGS. Cf the position under a written constitution incorporating a bill of rights (drafted as part of the legislation effecting independence of a former colony from the United Kingdom), where the state may be held liable to compensate a person whose constitutionally protected civil and political rights have been breached by a judge: *Maharaj v A-G of Trinidad and Tobago (No 2)* [1979] AC 385, [1978] 2 All ER 670, PC; and see Olowofoyeku *Suing Judges* (1994). As to the constitutional position of Trinidad and Tobago see COMMONWEALTH vol 6 (Reissue) para 971.

3 Justices of the Peace Act 1979 ss 44, 45 (substituted by the Courts and Legal Services Act 1990 s 108(1)–(4)); and *Sirros v Moore* [1975] QB 118, [1974] 3 All ER 776, CA; *Re McC (A Minor)* [1985] AC 528, sub nom *McC v Mullan* [1984] 3 All ER 908, HL.

## (3) THE RELATIONSHIP BETWEEN THE CROWN AND THE JUDICIARY.

**305. The monarch as the source of justice.** The constitutional status of the judiciary is underpinned by its origins in the royal prerogative and its legal relationship with the Crown, dating from the medieval period when the prerogatives were exercised by the monarch personally. By virtue of the prerogative the monarch is the source and fountain of justice, and all jurisdiction is derived from her[1]. Hence, in legal contemplation, the Sovereign's Majesty is deemed always to be present in court[2] and, by the terms of the coronation oath and by the maxims of the common law, as also by the ancient charters and statutes confirming the liberties of the subject, the monarch is bound to cause law and justice in mercy to be administered in all judgments[3]. This is, however, now a purely impersonal conception, for the monarch cannot personally execute any office relating to the administration of justice[4] nor effect an arrest[5].

1   Bac Abr, Prerogative, D1: see COURTS vol 10 para 704.
2   1 Bl Com (14th Edn) 269.
3   As to the duty to cause law and justice to be executed see head (2) in para 28 ante.
4   2 Co Inst 187; 4 Co Inst 71; *Prohibitions del Roy* (1607) 12 Co Rep 63. James I is said to have endeavoured to revive the ancient practice of sitting in court, but was informed by the judges that he could not deliver an opinion: *Prohibitions del Roy* supra; see 3 Stephen's Commentaries (4th Edn) 357n.
5   YB 1 Hen 7, Mich pl 5; Bac Abr, Prerogative, E1; 1 Bl Com (14th Edn) 269; Bro Abr, Prerogative, 125; Co Litt 3 b.

**306. Writs and legal process.** All writs run with the authority of the Crown[1] and are executed by officers of the Crown; and all judges and magistrates are appointed by and derive their authority, either mediately or immediately, from the Crown[2]. They must, however, exercise their authority in a lawful manner, without deviating from the known and stated forms[3]. The laws are the birthright of the people[4], and the monarch neither has power to change them apart from Parliament[5], nor may she interfere with the due administration of justice[6], and, although her person is above the reach of the law, it is her duty to obey it[7].

1   Formerly all writs ran in the monarch's name, and contained the Royal Command, namely, 'ELIZABETH THE SECOND, by the Grace of God, of the United Kingdom of Great Britain and Northern Ireland and of Our Realms and territories Queen, Head of the Commonwealth, Defender of the Faith', and the issue of the writ was witnessed by the Lord High Chancellor of Great Britain. By virtue of the amendment to RSC Ord 6 r 1, App A by the Rules of the Supreme Court (Writ and Appearance) 1979, SI 1979/1716, the Royal Command and Teste of the Lord Chancellor were omitted from the new form of Writ of Summons. The Queen's association with the legal process was thenceforward to be indicated by a replica of the Royal Arms at the head of the first page of the writ, and its authenticity vouched for by the requirement that every copy of a writ for service on a defendant must be sealed with the seal of the Office of the Supreme Court out of which the writ is issued. 'It should therefore be stressed that the absence of the Royal Command from the Writ will not in any way diminish, detract or derogate from the authority, dignity or effectiveness of the judicial process.' (Supreme Court Practice 1979, 6th Cumulative Supplement para 6/1/10). The omission of the Royal Command 'has made it compatible with international comity to allow service out of the jurisdiction of a copy of the writ itself, instead of such service to be effected under the guise of a "notice of the writ"': Supreme Court Practice 1982 para 6/1/1C.
2   Bac Abr, Prerogative, D1. As to the appointment of judges and magistrates see further paras 301, 303 ante; and COUNTY COURTS; COURTS; MAGISTRATES.
3   Bac Abr, Prerogative, D1; and see ADMINISTRATIVE LAW vol 1(1) (Reissue) para 221.
4   Act of Settlement s 4. See also para 28 ante. As to the citation of the Act of Settlement see para 35 note 3 ante.
5   *Re Grazebrook, ex p Chavasse* (1865) 4 De GJ & Sm 655 at 662. See also paras 28 note 3 ante, 918 post.
6   As to freedom of justice see para 310 post.
7   As to the monarch's duty to obey the law see para 379 note 5 post.

**307. Counties palatine.** The prerogatives relating to the distribution of justice are, in general, inherent in and inseparable from the Crown[1], and although they formerly passed by way of franchise, along with the full jura regalia, to the grantees of the counties palatine of Durham, Chester and Lancaster, the prerogative rights relating to justice within those counties palatine are now in general revested in the Crown[2]. The Courts of Chancery of the County Palatine of Durham and the County Palatine of Lancaster have been merged with the High Court[3], and the jurisdiction of the Chester palatine courts has been abolished[4]. It seems that grants of a like nature would now require the authority of an Act of Parliament[5]. In right of the Duchy of Lancaster the monarch retains the right to appoint high sheriffs throughout the counties of Greater Manchester, Merseyside and Lancashire[6].

1   See Bac Abr, Prerogative, D1; *Christian v Corren* (1716) 1 P Wms 329 at 330.
2   Lancaster was created a county palatine by charter having the authority of Parliament: 4 Co Inst 205, 211: As to the creation and history of the franchise see CROWN LANDS AND PRIVILEGES. Durham and Chester are counties palatine by prescription or custom at least as old as the Conquest (4 Co Inst 211, 216); they were created as a means of defence against the inroads of the Scots and Welsh (see 1 Bl Com (14th Edn) 113–114). As to the county palatine of Durham see CROWN LANDS AND PRIVILEGES. The Earldom and County Palatine of Chester were united to the Crown by Henry III and thence is derived the title of the monarch's eldest son as Earl of Chester: 1 Bl Com (14th Edn) 117. In 1535 certain powers and privileges in relation to counties palatine and liberties were revested in the Crown: Jurisdiction in Liberties Act 1535 ss 1–3 (repealed by the Justices of the Peace Act 1968 s 8(2), Sch 5; and the Courts Act 1971 s 56, Sch 11 Pt II). As to the abolition of the Chester palatine courts see the text and note 4 infra. As to the appointment of officers in Chester on the demise of the Crown see CROWN LANDS AND PRIVILEGES.
3   See the Courts Act 1971 s 41.
4   Law Terms Act 1830 s 14 (repealed). The abolition did not affect the rights of the corporation of Chester: s 15 (repealed).
5   See 4 Co Inst 204; Bac Abr, Courts Palatinate.
6   Local Government Act 1972 s 219(3) (amended by the Statute Law (Repeals) Act 1993).

**308.   Establishment of courts.** As the source and fountain of justice the Crown may issue such commissions to administer the law as are warranted by the common or statute law[1]; but may not, without statutory authority, establish courts to administer any but the common law[2], and may not, it is said, grant the right to hold a court of equity[3]. The Crown may not issue commissions in time of peace to try civilians by martial law[4].

1   Com Dig, Prerogative, D 29. For the power to establish courts outside the United Kingdom see COMMONWEALTH vol 6 (Reissue) paras 990, 1089.
2   Com Dig, Prerogative, D 28; 4 Co Inst 200; *Re Lord Bishop of Natal* (1865) 3 Moo PCCNS 115. As to illegal courts see para 376 post.
3   Bac Abr, Prerogative, F1; Forsyth *Cases and Opinions on Constitutional Law* 172–174. In the counties palatine the right to hold a court of equity passed with the full jura regalia, but such franchise cannot, it seems, be created at the present day: see Bac Abr, Prerogative, F1; and para 307 ante.
4   Petition of Right (1627) ss 7, 8; see para 821 note 1 post. As to martial law see para 821 post.

**309.   The Crown as parens patriae.** As liege lord and protector of the subjects[1], the monarch enjoys the prerogative right of taking care of the persons and estates of minors and mentally disordered persons and of superintending charities, although the exercise of those powers has now been delegated by the monarch or assigned by statute to various authorities.

Jurisdiction in respect of wardships of minors and the care of their estates is expressly assigned to the Family Division of the High Court of Justice[2], whilst local authorities have duties in respect of children in need of care and control[3].

The prerogative of taking care of mentally disordered persons and their estates is no longer exercised, that function being now carried out under statute by the Court of Protection[4]. The prerogative in matters relating to charities is exercised largely by the Lord Chancellor[5], and the administration of charities legislation is the function of the Charity Commissioners[6].

1   As to the monarch as liege lord see para 29 ante.
2   See the Supreme Court Act 1981 s 61, Sch 1 para 3(b) (as amended). As to limitations on the inherent jurisdiction see the Children Act 1989 s 100; and see CHILDREN AND YOUNG PERSONS vol 5(2) (Reissue) para 760 et seq.

3    See the Children Act 1989 s 33; CHILDREN AND YOUNG PERSONS vol 5(2) (Reissue) para 788.
4    See the Mental Health Act 1983 Pt VII (ss 93–113) (as amended); and MENTAL HEALTH vol 30 (Reissue)
     para 1431 et seq.
5    The Chancery Division of the High Court has jurisdiction over trusts, including charitable trusts: see the
     Supreme Court Act 1981 Sch 1 para 1(c). See further CHARITIES vol 5(2) (Reissue) paras 404 et seq, 425.
     As to the Lord Chancellor see paras 477–497 post.
6    See CHARITIES vol 5(2) (Reissue) paras 434–457.

**310. Freedom of justice.** The Crown or its ministers may not interfere with the
ordinary course of justice. Jurors must be duly summoned[1], and excessive bail or fines
may not be required or imposed, nor cruel and unusual punishments inflicted[2].
Moreover, all grants and promises of fines and forfeitures of particular persons before
conviction are illegal and void. The Crown may not bring pressure to bear upon the
judges of the High Court or the Court of Appeal, or upon the Lords of Appeal in
Ordinary, through fear of dismissal, since they hold office during good behaviour,
subject to a power of removal by Her Majesty on an address presented to her by both
Houses of Parliament[3].

1    See the Bill of Rights s 1. As to juries generally see JURIES. As to the history and citation of the Bill of
     Rights see para 35 note 3 ante.
2    Ibid s 1. Under the Convention for the Protection of Human Rights and Fundamental Freedoms
     (1950) (the European Convention of Human Rights) Art 3, no one may be subjected to torture or to
     inhuman or degrading treatment or punishment: see para 124 ante. As to the Convention generally see
     para 122 ante.
3    Supreme Court Act 1981 s 11(3) (re-enacting the Supreme Court of Judicature Act 1875 s 5, which
     itself re-enacted a similar provision (now repealed) in the Act of Settlement s 3): see para 303 ante. As
     to the citation of the Act of Settlement see para 35 note 3 ante. As to the qualifications, appointment,
     tenure and dismissal of judges generally see COURTS. For a recent example of arguably unconstitutional
     pressure brought to bear upon a judge, and the consequent debate in the House of Lords, see 553 HL
     Official Report (5th series), 27 April 1994, col 751 et seq; and see Sir Francis Purchas 'Lord Mackay
     and the judiciary' (1994) 144 NLJ 527; Oliver 'The Lord Chancellor's department and the judges'
     [1994] Public Law 157. For the independence of judicial officers generally see Brazier *Constitutional
     Practice* (2nd Edn, 1994) ch 12.

## (4) THE JUDICIAL COMMITTEE OF THE PRIVY COUNCIL

**311–350. Judicial Committee of the Privy Council.** The ultimate court of appeal,
in all matters where appeal was permissible, was represented originally by the monarch,
as being the source and fountain of justice[1]; and to the Queen in Council, represented
since 1833 by the Judicial Committee of the Privy Council[2], appeals still lie from certain
courts of member states of the Commonwealth[3], from courts of dependent territories[4]
and colonial admiralty courts[5].

The Judicial Committee may hear an appeal to Her Majesty in Council: (1) from the
Courts of Appeal of Jersey and Guernsey and from the Royal Court when sitting in an
appellate capacity[6]; (2) from the Isle of Man[7]; (3) from committees of the General Medical
Council[8] and certain other professional bodies concerned with health[9]; (4) against
schemes of the Church Commissioners under the Pastoral Measure of 1983[10]; and (5)
against a scheme for a cathedral church[11].

The Judicial Committee also has the following rarely used jurisdictions: (a) appeals from
the Arches Court of Canterbury and the Chancery Court of York in faculty causes not
involving matters of doctrine, ritual or ceremonial[12]; (b) appeals from Prize Courts[13]; (c)
disputes under the House of Commons Disqualification Act[14]; (d) appeals from the Court
of Admiralty of the Cinque Ports[15]. The monarch may also refer to the Judicial Committee
any matters whatever, not necessarily being matters arising from a judicial decision[16].

1 Thus the present jurisdiction of the House of Lords may be traced back to the appellate jurisdiction of the King in Council in Parliament. The House of Lords became recognised as the ultimate court of appeal from the King's Bench and Exchequer probably before the time of Henry IV: Rot Parl 1 Hen 4 No 79; cf Rot Parl 50 Edw 3 No 40; and see Baldwin's *The King's Council in the Middle Ages* pp 335–336.

2 See COURTS vol 10 para 767 et seq.

3 These include, by special leave of Her Majesty in Council, usually in criminal cases, but sometimes in a civil case where the appellant has failed to comply with the rules regarding leave by a local court of appeal: Antigua and Barbuda, Bahamas, Barbados, Belize, Grenada, Jamaica, New Zealand, St Christopher and Nevis, St Lucia, St Vincent and the Grenadines, Tuvalu. Appeals also lie from Brunei, where advice is given directly to the Sultan of Brunei: see eg *Royal Brunei Airlines Sdn Bhd v Tan* [1995] 2 AC 378, [1995] 3 All ER 97, PC. See COMMONWEALTH vol 6 (Reissue) para 819. There are also independent republics within the Commonwealth where an appeal lies direct to the Judicial Committee whose orders are then enforceable as Orders of the court of appeal of the territory concerned: Trinidad and Tobago, Singapore (in limited circumstances), The Gambia, Dominica, Kiribati (in limited circumstances), Mauritius.

4 These include Anguilla; Bermuda; British Antarctic Territory; British Indian Ocean Territory; Cayman Islands; Falkland Islands and Dependencies; Gibraltar; Hong Kong (at the date at which this volume states the law); Montserrat; Pitcairn Henderson, Ducie and Oeno (by leave of the Judicial Committee); St Helena and Dependencies; South Georgia and the South Sandwich Islands; the Sovereign Base Areas of Akrotiri and Dhekelia; Turks and Caicos Islands; and the Virgin Islands. See COMMONWEALTH vol 6 (Reissue) para 1041 et seq.

5 See ADMIRALTY vol 1(1) (Reissue) para 539; COMMONWEALTH vol 6 (Reissue) para 1081; COURTS vol 10 para 776.

6 See COMMONWEALTH vol 6 (Reissue) paras 843, 847.

7 See COMMONWEALTH vol 6 (Reissue) para 849.

8 See COURTS vol 10 para 778; and generally MEDICINE.

9 See COURTS vol 10 para 779; and generally MEDICINE.

10 See the Pastoral Measure 1983 s 9, Sch 2; and ECCLESIASTICAL LAW vol 14 para 881.

11 See the Cathedrals Measure 1976 s 3(2), (4); and ECCLESIASTICAL LAW vol 14 para 615.

12 See COURTS vol 10 para 777; ECCLESIASTICAL LAW vol 14 para 1335.

13 See the Naval Prize Act 1864 ss 5, 6; and PRIZE vol 37 para 1386.

14 See the House of Commons Disqualification Act 1975 s 7; and PARLIAMENT.

15 See ADMIRALTY vol 1(1) (Reissue) para 533.

16 Judicial Committee Act 1833 s 4. These are called special references; the Judicial Committee considers them and advises Her Majesty in the same way as on appeals. Matters thus referred have included the legality of telephone tapping where national security was affected (*Interception of Communications* (Cmnd 283) (1957) ('the Birkett Report')); and British policy towards the Falkland Islands (*Falkland Islands review* (Cmnd 8787) (1983) ('the Franks Report'); see further COURTS vol 10 para 781.

# 5. THE EXECUTIVE

## (1) LEGAL STATUS AND POWERS OF THE EXECUTIVE

### (i) The Monarch, the Crown and the Government

**351. The monarch.** In law the monarchy remains legally central to the powers of government. Such powers may be formally vested in the monarch (or the sovereign) or, latterly, the Crown[1]. The monarch's personal functions in the actual administration of the executive are now restricted principally to attaching her signature to various executive documents, the nature and general policy of which have been previously determined by ministers either individually or collectively[2]. In discharging her legal functions the monarch is bound by constitutional conventions which minimise the scope of her discretion[3].

1 See para 353 post.

2 As a matter of convention the monarch ought not to attempt to influence the actions of executive officers without seeking and acting upon the advice of the minister responsible to Parliament. Thus when George

IV wished to influence the Lord Lieutenant of Ireland in exercising the prerogative of mercy, it was pointed out by Sir Robert Peel, then Home Secretary, that the advice of the responsible minister ought first to be asked, and the Crown gave way (see 2 Anson's Law and Custom of the Constitution (4th Edn, 1935) Pt I p 57). The monarch's private correspondence with foreign sovereigns or ministers ought, again as a matter of convention, it is said, to be disclosed to the executive if it touches on political questions, and was habitually so disclosed by Queen Victoria and the Prince Consort (2 Anson's Law and Custom of the Constitution (4th Edn, 1935) Pt I p 56). In paying formal visits of state to the crowned heads of foreign nations the monarch is not necessarily accompanied by any member of the Cabinet, though such visits are jealously regarded by Parliament (see the questions in the House of Commons in 1908 as to the visit to the Tsar of Russia (189 Parliamentary Debates (4th series) 963, 965, 1118, 1262, 1290, 1570, 1571). The monarch's political wishes or intentions ought to be disclosed fully to her ministers, since it is unconstitutional for her to take independent action in foreign politics, and a minister cannot escape responsibility for any independent action which may be taken by the Crown. Thus Lord Somers was impeached for causing the Great Seal to be affixed to the partition treaties concluded by William III in 1698 and 1699 without lawful warrant: *Lord Somers' Case* (1701) 14 State Tr 250 at 253–254. In case of the insistence of the Crown it seems that the constitutional procedure would be for the administration to tender its resignation. On two occasions Lord Hardwicke LC refused to affix the Great Seal to treaties when requested to do so by George II (see 1 Todd's Parliamentary Government p 42; 2 Harris's Life of Hardwicke pp 59, 369). As to the use of the Great Seal see para 909 post.

3    As to constitutional conventions see paras 19–22 ante.

**352. The monarch as head of the executive.** The monarch is the head of the executive, and hence ministers are commonly referred to collectively as 'Her Majesty's government'[1]. The monarch must, as a matter of convention, save in a few very exceptional instances[2], act through or with the co-operation of some other person, usually a servant of the Crown, but the acts which can be performed through or with the co-operation of any particular servant and by any particular mode are limited in number; and in the aggregate such powers do not cover the whole field of government[3].

1    See de Smith and Brazier *Constitutional and Administrative Law* (7th Edn, 1994) p 121.

2    The monarch can open Parliament without the assistance of anyone else. She may also appoint certain of her ministers by merely giving the seals of office into their hands, and dismiss them by merely requiring them to return the seals to her. In exercising these powers, the monarch by convention acts on the advice of the Prime Minister for the time being: see paras 398–399 post. To dissolve Parliament she must act by proclamation under the Great Seal (see para 909 post), which requires the co-operation of the Lord Chancellor, in consequence of an Order in Council, and for this a meeting of the Privy Council needs to be summoned by the Lord President of the Council: see Gordon Walker *The Cabinet* (Revised Edn, 1972) p 84. As to the Privy Council see paras 521–526 post. Apparently the monarch need not ask or accept advice on the question whom she is to call upon to form a new administration; but her choice is almost completely circumscribed by the practice of all parties to elect their leaders, and by the verdict of the House of Commons or of the country at a general election. There may, residually, be a function for the monarch to perform, however, in the event of an inconclusive general election or at any other time when the Prime Minister is, or appears to her to be, unable to command the confidence of the House over a matter of principle if it appears to her that a dissolution would be inappropriate at that time: see paras 21 note 5, 209 ante, 418 post. See also Bogdanor *The Monarchy and the Constitution* (1995) chs 4, 5.

3    Eg powers to do acts which interfere with the liberties of individuals or to raise taxation are excluded. See paras 6–7 ante.

**353. The Crown.** Much of the business of central government is carried on in the name of 'the Crown.' The term 'the Crown' has a number of meanings. Historically it referred to the monarch in whom were united executive, legislative and judicial functions[1]. Thus it may be used to refer to the person of the monarch[2], although this is less commonly used in modern parlance. More frequently 'the Crown' refers to the executive or government. The Crown in this sense is in law a corporation sole or aggregate[3]. However, the term 'the Crown' may also be used to apply to an officer or servant of the Crown[4], or to 'a minister acting in an official capacity'[5]. Some ministers also have separate corporate personality[6].

1   See paras 15–16 ante.
2   See *Re M* [1994] 1 AC 377 at 395, sub nom *M v Home Office* [1993] 3 All ER 537 at 540, HL, per Lord Templeman, and at 407 and 551 per Lord Woolf. See also paras 351–352 ante; and CROWN LANDS AND PRIVILEGES.
3   See *Town Investments Ltd v Department of the Environment* [1978] AC 359, [1977] 1 All ER 813, HL; *Re M* [1994] 1 AC 377 at 424, sub nom *M v Home Office* [1993] 3 All ER 537 at 566, HL. See also 1 Bl Com 292. As to corporations sole and aggregate see CORPORATIONS.
4   *Re M* [1994] 1 AC 377 at 407, sub nom *M v Home Office* [1993] 3 All ER 537 at 551, HL, per Lord Woolf. Prerogative orders may be granted against ministers in their official capacity, but not against the Crown: see *Re M* supra at 416, 424 and 558–559, 566; and see *R v Powell* as reported in (1841) 113 ER 1166.
5   *Re M* [1994] 1 AC 377 at 424, sub nom *M v Home Office* [1993] 3 All ER 537 at 566, HL.
6   See para 363 post.

**354. The government.** The terms 'government' or 'Her Majesty's government' embrace the whole of central government, and they are generally coterminous with 'the Crown'[1]. However, it is convenient to distinguish between the political arm of the executive (that is to say 'the ministry' or, in contemporary parlance, 'the administration') and the permanent professional non-political arm (that is to say the Civil Service[2]).

The term 'minister of the Crown' may be used to denote the holder of an office in Her Majesty's government in the United Kingdom and includes the Treasury[3], the Board of Trade[4] and the Defence Council[5]. It includes, therefore, Secretaries of State, Ministers of State, Parliamentary Under Secretaries of State, and Parliamentary Secretaries[6].

The administration comprises in the first place the Prime Minister[7] and the political heads[8] of public departments. The heads of the major department are of cabinet[9] rank, and according to the present practice, and with certain exceptions[10], are Secretaries of State[11]. Some of these major departments have within them subordinate departments headed by ministers below cabinet rank[12]. Each Secretary of State is supported by at least one Parliamentary Under Secretary of State[13]. The Ministry of Agriculture, Fisheries and Food is the one major department that does not have a Secretary of State at its head[14]. It is now common for a department to have one or more Ministers of State[15], and in some cases they are designated as ministers in charge of subordinate departments[16]. The Treasury has a complicated ministerial staff[17].

Some government whips hold sinecure offices as Lords of the Treasury[18], and other government whips hold sinecure offices in the royal household[19].

Ministers may appoint unpaid Parliamentary Private Secretaries, who are not technically members of the administration, nor are they formally bound by the conventions of collective responsibility[20]. In 1995 the Prime Minister appointed a Deputy Prime Minister with the title First Secretary of State[21].

The Lord Chancellor, who is technically a minister of the Crown[22] with cabinet rank, but is not a Secretary of State, has a department, the direction of which absorbs that part of his time and energy which is not devoted to judicial functions[23]. The Chancellor of the Duchy of Lancaster[24] has minimal departmental duties, and the Lord President of the Council[25] and Lord Privy Seal[26] have none at all; all three can therefore be assigned special tasks to perform, but otherwise serve as ministers without portfolio[27].

1   See para 353 ante.
2   As to the Civil Service generally see paras 549–564 post.
3   As to the Treasury see paras 512–517 post.
4   As to the Board of Trade see para 505 post; and TRADE, INDUSTRY AND INDUSTRIAL RELATIONS vol 47 (Reissue) para 2.
5   As to the Defence Council see paras 443–447 post.
6   See eg the Ministers of the Crown Act 1975 s 8(1).
7   As to the Prime Minister see paras 394–398 post.
8   Ie in contrast to the permanent heads, who are members of the Civil Service.
9   As to the Cabinet see paras 402–413 post.

10  See note 14 infra.

11  As to the office of Secretary of State para 355 et seq post. See also Simcock 'One and many - the Office of Secretary of State' (1992) 70 Public Administration 535.

12  Eg the Overseas Development Administration, a department in the charge of the Minister of State for Foreign and Commonwealth Affairs and Minister for Overseas Development, which is within the Foreign and Commonwealth Office. Other subordinate departments headed by ministers below cabinet rank are the Crown Office for Scotland, the Legal Secretariat of the Law Officers, the Lord Advocate's Department, the Office of Public Service and the Office of the Paymaster General. See further para 427 et seq post.

13  It is now common for a department to have more than one Parliamentary Under Secretary of State: see eg para 465 post. Sometimes they are attached to specific subordinate departments.

14  The designation of the head of the Ministry of Agriculture, Fisheries and Food as 'minister' is a survival from earlier usage. The Ministry of Agriculture, Fisheries and Food also has a Minister of State: see further paras 435–437 post. The Lord Chancellor is a minister of the Crown under the Ministers of the Crown Act 1975 s 8, but is not a Secretary of State: see para 477 post.

15  Eg the Ministry of Defence and the Department of the Environment. See *Questions of Procedure for Ministers* (Cabinet Office, December 1992) (as now revised: see para 416 note 1 post) paras 32–40.

16  Eg in the Department of the Environment there is the Minister for Local Government, Housing and Urban Regeneration, the Minister for the Environment and Countryside, and the Minister for Construction, Planning and Energy Efficiency.

17  See para 515 post.

18  Eg the Parliamentary Secretary to the Treasury, who is the Chief Whip, and the Junior Lords Commissioners of the Treasury.

19  Whips in the House of Commons holding positions in the royal household are the Treasurer of the Household, who is the Deputy Chief Whip, the Comptroller of the Household, the Vice-Chamberlain of the Household. Government whips in the House of Lords are the Captain of the Honourable Corps of the Gentleman at Arms (the Chief Whip) and the Captain of the Queen's Bodyguard of the Yeoman of the Guard (the Deputy Chief Whip) and a number of Lords in Waiting. As to officers of the royal household see para 546 post.

20  As to collective responsibility of ministers see para 417 post.

21  Michael Heseltine was appointed Deputy Prime Minister and First Secretary of State, and charged with giving general assistance to the Prime Minister, with specific responsibility for the competitiveness agenda, the working of government and the presentation of its policies. He took the chair of four cabinet committees and he was given ministerial responsibility for the Cabinet Office, including the Office of Public Service. A previous example of the appointment of a First Secretary of State is the appointment of Mr George Brown in 1967, with responsibility for the Department of Economic Affairs. The designation First Secretary of State was invented for Mr R A Butler by Prime Minister Macmillan in 1962. The only previous example of the formal appointment of a Deputy Prime Minister is the appointment of Mr Clement Attlee from 1942–1945, although William Whitelaw in 1979 and Sir Geoffrey Howe in 1989 were each nominated Deputy Prime Minister: see Brazier *Constitutional Practice* (2nd Edn, 1994) ch 5. See also para 355 text and note 3 post.

22  See the Ministers of the Crown Act 1975 s 8(1).

23  See para 497 post.

24  As to the the Chancellor of the Duchy of Lancaster see CROWN LANDS AND PRIVILEGES. He is at present responsible for the Office of Public Service, which includes the Citizen's Charter Unit and the Efficiency and Effectiveness Group, of which the Efficiency Unit is part: see the List of Ministerial Responsibilities Including Agencies (Cabinet Office, May 1996).

25  See para 526 post. The Lord President of the Council is customarily Leader of the House of Commons. As to the House of Commons see PARLIAMENT.

26  See para 527 post. The Lord Privy Seal is customarily Leader of the House of Lords. As to the House of Lords see para 204 ante; and PARLIAMENT.

27  As a rule, the Paymaster General (as to whom see para 714 post) is a minister without portfolio, available for such special duties as the Prime Minister may assign to him. The Paymaster General is often a Junior Treasury Minister. He heads a subordinate department within the Treasury. Occasionally (as in the Heath administration) there has been a minister specifically designated Minister without Portfolio. It has been the practice from time to time, for instance in the 1992 Conservative administration, for the chairman of the Conservative party to be appointed a minister without portfolio; thus in the list of government at the beginning of the bound HC Official Reports (weekly Hansard) (eg 18–24 July 1996), Dr Brian Mawhinney is listed as Minister without Portfolio. As to of lists of ministers in government see para 399 text and note 5 post.

**355. Office of Secretary of State.** The ordinary method of communication between monarch and subject is through a Secretary[1] of State[2]. There may be held from time to time the office of First Secretary of State[3].

Other than the First Secretary of State, Her Majesty's Principal Secretaries of State are: (1) the Secretary of State for Foreign and Commonwealth Affairs (the Foreign Secretary)[4]; (2) the Secretary of State for the Home Department (the Home Secretary)[5]; (3) the Secretary of State for Trade and Industry[6]; (4) the Secretary of State for Transport[7]; (5) the Secretary of State for Defence[8]; (6) the Secretary of State for National Heritage[9]; (7) the Secretary of State for the Environment[10]; (8) the Secretary of State for Social Security[11]; (9) the Secretary of State for Education and Employment[12]; (10) the Secretary of State for Health[13]; (11) the Secretary of State for Wales[14]; (12) the Secretary of State for Scotland[15]; and (13) the Secretary of State for Northern Ireland[16]. Each of these Secretaries of State heads a department[17].

Although the secretarial duties are divided among the persons presiding over their respective departments of government, the office of Secretary of State is one, and in law each Secretary of State is capable of performing the duties of all or any of the departments[18]. The appointment, which is during pleasure, is made by grant and delivery of the seals of office[19].

The Principal Secretaries of State are members of the Privy Council[20] and are normally members of the Cabinet[21].

1 For the history of the secretariat see Thomas *History of Public Departments* 23–36; 6 Proceedings and Ordinances of the Privy Council (ed Nicolas) (1837) p xcvii; Evans *The Principal Secretary of State (for the period 1558–1680)* (1923); Thomson *The Secretaries of State 1681–1782* (1968); *Harrison v Bush* (1855) 5 E & B 344 at 352; *Entick v Carrington* (1765) 19 State Tr 1029. See also Simcock 'One and many - the Office of Secretary of State' (1992) 70 Public Administration 535. The monarch's Private Secretary (see para 547 post) is not a means of expressing the official will of the Crown.

2 Where there was no indication to the contrary a reference to 'the Secretary of State' was formerly generally taken to import a reference to the Home Secretary: see para 466 post. However, the Interpretation Act 1978 s 5, Sch 1 provides that Secretary of State means one of Her Majesty's Principal Secretaries of State, without further qualification, and in modern enactments 'Secretary of State' may be taken to refer to the Secretary of State exercising functions under the enactment in question. See also note 3 infra. As to the transfer of functions generally see paras 363–365 post.

3 See para 354 text and note 21 ante. It is to be presumed that when this office is held its holder takes precedence over other Secretaries of State.

4 As to the Foreign and Commonwealth Office see paras 459–462 post.

5 As to the Home Office see para 466 et seq post.

6 As to the Department of Trade and Industry see paras 505–508 post.

7 As to the Department of Transport see paras 509–511 post.

8 As to the Ministry of Defence see paras 438–447 post.

9 As to the Department of National Heritage see paras 498–501 post.

10 As to the Department of the Environment see paras 452–458 post.

11 As to the Department of Social Security see paras 502–504 post.

12 As to the Department for Education and Employment see paras 448–451 post.

13 As to the Department of Health see paras 463–465 post.

14 As to the Welsh Office see paras 41–50 ante, 520 post.

15 As to the Scottish Office see paras 51–66 ante, 519 post.

16 As to the Northern Ireland Office see paras 67–86 ante, 518 post.

17 Until recently many of these departments were ministries, headed by ministers. The only surviving ministers are the Minister for the Civil Service (a post held by the Prime Minister) (see paras 395, 427 post), the Minister of Agriculture, Fisheries and Food (see para 435 post), and the Minister of Overseas Development (see para 462 post).

18 33 Parliamentary History 976; *Harrison v Bush* (1855) 5 E & B 344 at 352. In some instances the authority of a Secretary of State derives from the Crown's common law prerogatives which he administers, but in many instances his powers are statutory, in which case the usual practice is for the statute to refer to 'one of Her Majesty's Principal Secretaries of State' or, more frequently, 'the Secretary of State'. Unless the contrary intention appears, 'the Secretary of State' means one of Her Majesty's Principal Secretaries of State for the time being: Interpretation Act 1978 ss 5, 22, 23, Sch 1, Sch 2 para 4(1). See also note 2 supra.

Where powers are conferred jointly upon or divided between two or more ministers a Secretary of State may be described by reference to his functions or by name, eg 'the Secretary of State for Education and Science and the Secretary of State for Wales' (see the Education Act 1973 s 1(3), Sch 1 (as amended)). See also Simcock 'One and many - the Office of Secretary of State' (1992) 70 Public Administration 535.

Where functions are transferred by Order in Council from one minister to another a Secretary of State to whom a transfer is made is frequently described by his full title: see para 363 post.

Powers are occasionally given or transferred to 'a Secretary of State' or 'the Secretary of State', leaving it to be understood from the context or otherwise which Secretary of State is intended; eg the Ministry of Posts and Telecommunications (Dissolution) Order 1974, SI 1974/691, transferred all the functions of the Minister of Posts and Telecommunications to the Secretary of State. In fact, some of those functions were to be exercised by the Home Secretary and others by the Secretary of State for Industry (but all are now exercised by the Secretary of State for Trade and Industry: see the Transfer of Functions (Trade and Industry) Order 1983, SI 1983/1127; and para 505 post). In practice the administration of each Secretary of State is confined to his own department, and the term 'Secretary of State' in any particular statutory context accordingly refers to the Secretary of State whose department normally deals with the subject matter of the provision. Nevertheless, the principle that the office of Secretary of State is one and indivisible remains strictly correct. See Wade and Forsyth *Administrative Law* (7th Edn, 1994) p 55. As to the transfer of functions see paras 363–365 post.

19  33 Parliamentary History 976; *Harrison v Bush* (1855) 5 E & B 344. For the oaths to be taken see the Promissory Oaths Act 1868 s 5, Schedule Pt I (as amended); and para 923 post.

20  As to the Privy Council see paras 521–526 post.

21  At the date at which this volume states the law, as has become the practice, all the Secretaries of State are members of the Cabinet. As to capacity to sit in the House of Commons see the House of Commons Disqualification Act 1975 s 2, Sch 2; and para 400 post. As to the salaries of Secretaries of State see para 423 post. As to the Cabinet see paras 402–413 post.

**356. Actions against a Secretary of State.** An action will lie against a Secretary of State in his personal capacity in respect of unlawful acts, resulting in injury to an individual, done by him personally, or under his direct authority[1].

1   *Wilkes v Lord Halifax* (1769) 19 State Tr 1406; *Cobbett v Grey* (1849) 4 Exch 729; *Sayre v Earl of Rochford* (1776) 20 State Tr 1286. Thus an action will lie for damages for trespass and false imprisonment: *Wilkes v Lord Halifax* supra. In *Dickson v Viscount Combermere* (1863) 3 F & F 527, it was held that an action will not lie against the minister now known as the Secretary of State for Defence for causing the lieutenant-colonel of a regiment to be removed from his office by false charges, unless he has acted dishonestly; and it is probable that such an action would not be maintainable in any case, since the dismissal is the act of the Crown, and he cannot be made liable for advice given by him to the Crown. Indeed a Secretary of State ought not to disclose the advice which he gives to the Crown: *Irwin v Grey* (1863) 1 New Rep 237. The only reported instances of a Secretary of State being held personally liable in tort appear to be *Wilkes v Lord Halifax* supra, and *Sayre v Earl of Rochford* supra; and cf *Cobbett v Grey* supra. For the liability of Crown servants generally see *Re M* [1994] 1 AC 377, sub nom *M v Home Office* [1993] 3 All ER 537, HL; and paras 388–389 post. For the procedure in instituting actions against officers of state see CROWN PROCEEDINGS.

**357. Secretarial seals and orders.** The seals which a Secretary of State controls are the signet, a second secretarial seal and the cachet[1]. The signet is affixed in the Foreign and Commonwealth Office[2] to instruments which authorise the affixing of the Great Seal[3] to powers to treat and to ratifications of treaties, and also to commissions and instructions to colonial governors. The second secretarial seal is affixed to royal warrants and to commissions, and is employed only in the Home Office[4]. The cachet is affixed to envelopes of letters addressed personally by the monarch to the head of a foreign state[5].

Apart from his custody of the seals, a Secretary of State sometimes gives formal expression to the royal pleasure by affixing his signature to documents and orders. Instruments authorising the affixing of the Great Seal to powers to treat and ratifications of treaties are countersigned by a Secretary of State, as are also various royal orders, warrants, commissions and instructions under the sign manual[6].

Proof of any order or regulation issued by or under the authority of a Secretary of State may be given in any legal proceedings in accordance with the Documentary Evidence Act 1868[7].

1 See para 901 post.
2 As to the Foreign and Commonwealth Office see paras 459–462 post.
3 As to the use of the Great Seal see para 909 post.
4 As to the Home Office see para 466 et seq post.
5 As to the use of the seals generally see 2 Anson's Law and Custom of the Constitution (4th Edn, 1935) Pt I p 183. As to the doctrine of the seals with reference to ministerial responsibility see Maitland *Constitutional History of England* (1908) p 393.
6 2 Anson's Law and Custom of the Constitution (4th Edn, 1935) Pt I p 64. Instructions to a colonial governor are exceptional, in as much as they are sealed with the signet, but not countersigned: see 2 Anson's Law and Custom of the Constitution (4th Edn, 1935) Pt I p 64. As to a sign manual warrant as authority for affixing the Great Seal see the Great Seal Act 1884 s 2(1); and para 912 post.
7 See the Documentary Evidence Act 1868 s 2, Schedule (as amended); and EVIDENCE. In some instances this Act has been applied by Order in Council to documents issued by a named Secretary of State: see eg the Transfer of Functions (Education and Employment) Order 1995, SI 1995/2986, art 10(5) (which extends the Documentary Evidence Act 1868 to the Secretary of State for Education and Employment). As to the Secretary of State for Education and Employment see para 448 post.

**358. Miscellaneous powers of Secretaries of State.** The following exceptional powers (inter alia) are vested in a Principal Secretary of State:

(1) the power, by express warrant in writing, to intercept a communication through the post or telecommunications system, in the interests of national security, for the purpose of preventing or detecting serious crime, or safeguarding the economic well-being of the United Kingdom[1];

(2) the power, by order, to signify to a metropolitan magistrate that a requisition (made to the Secretary of State by some person recognised by the Secretary of State as a diplomatic or consular representative of that foreign state) for the surrender of a fugitive criminal of any foreign state, who is in, or suspected of being in, the United Kingdom, has been made, and to require the magistrate to issue a warrant for the apprehension of the fugitive criminal[2];

(3) the power to make, revoke and vary regulations respecting the time, manner and conditions in and under which claims may be made for compensation for damage done by persons who use or threaten unlawful violence[3];

(4) certain powers of proscribing terrorist organisations and excluding persons from Great Britain in order to prevent acts of terrorism[4].

Miscellaneous statutory powers relating to a variety of matters are also conferred upon a Secretary of State[5].

1 See the Interception of Communications Act 1985 s 2; the Post Office Act 1953 s 58(1) proviso (as amended). The warrant must be under the hand of the Secretary of State, except in urgent cases where the Secretary of State has authorised its issue, when it may be signed by a senior official in the department, and endorsed with a statement that the Secretary of State has expressly authorised its issue: see the Interception of Communications Act 1985 s 4. See Feldman *Civil Liberties and Human Rights in England and Wales* (1993) pp 475–491.
2 See the Extradition Act 1989 ss 1, 37(3), Sch 1 paras 4, 13(1), 20; and EXTRADITION. See also the power to deport persons who are not British citizens under the Immigration Act 1971 s 3 (as amended); and see *R v Governor of Brixton Prison, ex p Soblen* [1963] 2 QB 243, [1962] 3 All ER 641, CA; and BRITISH NATIONALITY, IMMIGRATION AND RACE RELATIONS.
3 See the Riot (Damages) Act 1886 s 3(2) (as amended); and *J W Dwyer Ltd v Metropolitan Police District Receiver* [1967] 2 QB 970, [1967] 2 All ER 1051.
4 See the Prevention of Terrorism (Temporary Provisions) Act 1989. See also Bonner *Emergency Powers in Peacetime* (1985); Wade and Bradley *Constitutional and Administrative Law* (11th Edn, 1993) pp 591–595.
5 See the current Official Index of the Statutes in force, Secretary of State.

**359. Secretary of State as designated minister.** For the purposes of the European Communities Act 1972[1] the Secretary of State is a designated minister[2] in relation to certain matters concerning transport, consumer protection, the collection of information on specified subjects and employment[3], and, jointly with the Minister of Agriculture,

Fisheries and Food, in relation to medicinal products and the European Community agricultural policy[4].

1 Ie the European Communities Act 1972 s 2(2), under which, subject to certain restrictions, Her Majesty by Order in Council, and any designated minister or department by regulations, may provide for the implementation of Community obligations (as defined in s 1(2), Sch 1 Pt II), or the exercise of rights under the treaties (as defined in s 1(2) (as amended), 1(3), Sch 1 Pt I). As to the restrictions subject to which the powers are exercisable and the exercise of the powers by statutory instrument see s 2(4), Sch 2. See generally EUROPEAN COMMUNITIES.

2 'Designated minister' means such minister of the Crown as may from time to time be designated by Order in Council in relation to any matter as for any purpose, but subject to such restrictions or conditions, if any, as may be specified by the Order in Council: ibid s 2(2).

3 See the European Communities (Designation) Orders: SI 1972/1811 (as amended); SI 1973/1889; SI 1975/427; SI 1975/1707; SI 1976/897; SI 1976/2141; SI 1977/1718; SI 1981/206; SI 1981/833; SI 1981/1536; SI 1982/847; SI 1982/1675; SI 1983/603; SI 1983/1706; SI 1984/353; SI 1985/749; SI 1985/956; SI 1985/1195; SI 1986/947; SI 1987/448 (as amended); SI 1987/926 (as amended); SI 1988/785; SI 1988/2240; SI 1989/1327; SI 1989/2393; SI 1990/600; SI 1990/1304; SI 1991/187; SI 1991/755; SI 1991/2289 (as amended); SI 1992/707 (as amended); SI 1992/1711; SI 1992/2661; SI 1992/2870 (as amended and partially superseded); SI 1992/3197; SI 1993/595; SI 1993/1571; SI 1993/2661; SI 1994/757; SI 1994/1327; SI 1994/1887; SI 1994/2791 (as amended); SI 1995/262; SI 1995/751 (as amended); SI 1995/2983; SI 1995/3207; SI 1996/266.

4 See the European Communities (Designation) Order 1972, SI 1972/1811, art 2(1)–(4), Schedule; and note 3 supra. See further para 435 post.

**360. Government departments.** Government is generally carried on by or through departments for which ministers are responsible to Parliament[1]. In practice, the term 'government department' is used to refer to offices[2], departments[3], ministries[4] and other bodies[5]. These organisations owe their establishment and organisation partly to the exercise of the royal prerogative power[6] to organise the administration as the Crown sees fit, and partly to statute. Some departments include a number of offices or subordinate departments with ministers at their head[7]. Departments may also contain executive agencies headed by chief executives[8]. Departments exercise powers derived from the common law (generally the royal prerogative) or from statute[9].

Parliament alone can provide departments with the supplies of money necessary for their operations[10]. Their internal arrangements are generally[11] a matter for the royal prerogative or a general de facto power to make administrative dispositions, except in relation to the appointment of accounting officers[12].

The actual creation of an office, department, ministry or other body forming part of central government is often effected by Act of Parliament[13], at other times by Orders in Council[14]. Old-established departments, such as the Treasury[15] and the Home Office, which originally formed parts of the royal household, derive from the exercise of the prerogative, and were established by the independent action of the monarch[16]. When, from the nineteenth century onwards, it became necessary to set up new departments for the internal government of the realm, parliamentary authority was usually obtained for the establishment of a board, such as the Local Government Board[17], or later for the establishment of a ministry such as the Ministry of Labour[18], with a minister at its head. In 1946 provision was made for the transfer of functions between ministers by Order in Council[19].

Departments may be divided into ministerial and non-ministerial departments. The major government departments are ministerial, and civil servants in the departments exercise powers in the name of and on behalf of ministers[20]. However, there are many non-ministerial departments which are Crown bodies, headed by a statutory office-holder or board and staffed by civil servants, and which have their own statutory powers and enjoy varying degrees of independence from the minister who is responsible for them to Parliament[21]. Government departments may be dissolved by Order in Council[22].

Civil proceedings by the Crown may be instituted by an authorised government department in its own name or by the Attorney General, and civil proceedings against the Crown are to be instituted against the appropriate authorised government department, or if none is appropriate, against the Attorney General[23].

1　As to conventions relating to ministerial responsibility to Parliament see paras 416–417 post. As to government departments and ministerial responsibilities see para 427 et seq post.

2　Government offices include the Cabinet Office (see paras 427–434 post), the Home Office (see para 466 et seq post), the Northern Ireland Office (see para 518 post), the Scottish Office (see para 519 post), the Welsh Office (see para 520 post) and the Foreign and Commonwealth Office (see paras 459–462 post).

3　Government departments include the Department of the Environment (see paras 452–458 post), the Department for Education and Employment (see paras 448–451 post), the Department of Health (see paras 463–465 post), the Lord Chancellor's Department (see para 497 post), the Department of National Heritage (see paras 498–501 post), the Department of Social Security (see paras 502–504 post), the Department of Trade and Industry (see paras 505–508 post) and the Department of Transport (see paras 509–511 post).

4　Ministries include the Ministry of Defence (see paras 438–447 post) and the Ministry of Agriculture, Fisheries and Food (see paras 435–437 post).

5　Eg the Board of Trade (see para 505 post; and TRADE, INDUSTRY AND INDUSTRIAL RELATIONS vol 47 (Reissue) para 2), the Board of Inland Revenue (see INCOME TAXATION), Her Majesty's Commissioners of Customs and Excise (see CUSTOMS AND EXCISE), Her Majesty's Stationery Office.

6　Eg the Commissioners of Inland Revenue and the Commissioners of Customs and Excise are appointed by letters patent.

7　Eg the Cabinet Office contains the Office of Public Service (see para 430 post); the Foreign and Commonwealth Office contains the Overseas Development Administration (see para 462 post). See also para 354 ante.

8　See para 551 post.

9　As to the royal prerogative see paras 367–372 post.

10　See para 228 ante.

11　Exceptions include statutory provisions for the constitution of the Commissioners of Inland Revenue and the Commissioners of Customs and Excise, and their relationship with the Treasury: see paras 709–710 post.

12　See para 715 post.

13　Eg the Ministries of Land and Natural Resources, Overseas Development and Technology were created by the Ministers of the Crown Act 1964 ss 1, 2(1)(a) (repealed). They were later dissolved by Order in Council.

14　Eg the Departments of Energy, Industry, Trade, and Prices and Consumer Protection were created by Order in Council (see the Secretary of State (New Departments) Order 1974, SI 1974/692 (partly superseded)). Her Majesty may in connection with any change in departments of the office of Secretary of State or in any change of functions of a Secretary of State make incidental, consequential and supplemental provisions by Order in Council as may be necessary or expedient in connection with the change: see the Ministers of the Crown Act 1975 s 2(1). It seems that statutory authority is required for the creation of departments headed by ministers (as opposed to Secretaries of State): see Brazier *Constitutional Practice* (2nd Edn. 1994) pp 136–137.

15　As to the Treasury see paras 512–517 post.

16　As to the monarch see 351 et seq ante.

17　See the Local Government Board Act 1871 s 2 (as amended).

18　See the New Ministries and Secretaries Act 1916 s 1 (repealed).

19　As to the transfer of functions between ministers see para 363 post. The Ministers of the Crown Act 1975 does not provide for the transfer of functions from non-ministerial departments since their powers are not exercisable by ministers.

20　See *Carltona v Comrs of Works* [1943] 2 All ER 560, CA; and para 365 post.

21　See eg the relationship between Treasury ministers and the Board of Inland Revenue (para 709 post), and the Commissioners for Customs and Excise (para 710 post). See further para 528 post.

22　See the Ministers of the Crown Act 1975 s 1(1)(b); and para 363 post. No such Order in Council which provides for the dissolution of a government department may be made unless, after copies of the draft have been laid before Parliament, each House presents an Address to Her Majesty praying that the order be made: s 5(1).

23　See the Crown Proceedings Act 1947 s 17(2), (3). For the purposes of legal proceedings against the Crown a list of departments is maintained under the Crown Proceedings Act 1947 by the Minister for the Civil Service (as to whom see para 427 post): See CROWN PROCEEDINGS.

**361. Heads of ministerial departments.** The political heads, and Ministers of State and Parliamentary Under Secretaries of ministerial departments, are members of the administration, appointed by the Crown upon the advice of the Prime Minister[1]. Unlike the head of the Civil Service and senior members of a department, they are, therefore, not permanent officers, but owe their official existence to the continuance in power of the political party to which they belong, and retire with every change of administration[2]. They act as the spokespersons in Parliament of the departments which they represent, and determine the general nature of the executive policy which each department is to pursue. Moreover, being members of the administration, they are responsible as a whole for the policy of the principal legislative measures introduced in Parliament which, when they become law, will be the duty of the various departments to administer[3]. The work of administration itself is done by the Civil Service[4], or contracted out to the private sector[5].

1  As to the Prime Minister generally see paras 394–398 post.
2  As to the advantages said to be gained by the combination of a parliamentary head with a permanent staff see Bagehot *The English Constitution* (1963 Edn) ch 8.
3  See para 417 post.
4  As to the Civil Service generally see paras 549–564 post.
5  Eg under the government's market testing and contracting out programmes: see the Deregulation and Contracting Out Act 1994; and *Competing for Quality: Buying Better Public Services* (Cm 1730) (1991); and paras 364, 553 post.

**362. Miscellaneous ministerial powers.** The Ministers of the Crown Act 1975 contains provisions applying to certain ministers and their departments[1].

The minister must take the oath of allegiance, and the official oath[2]. He may appoint such secretaries, officers and servants as he may with the consent of the Minister for the Civil Service[3] determine[4]. The secretaries (other than a Parliamentary Secretary), officers and servants appointed by the minister are paid such salaries or remuneration as the Minister for the Civil Service may determine[5]. The minister's expenses, including any such salaries or remuneration are payable out of money provided by Parliament[6].

The minister is for all purposes a corporation sole[7], and has an official seal which is authenticated by the signature of the minister, a secretary to the ministry or any person authorised by the minister to act in that behalf[8]. The seal must be judicially noticed, and every document purporting to be an instrument made or issued by the minister and sealed with the minister's seal duly authenticated, or purporting to be signed or executed by a secretary to the ministry or any authorised person, must be received in evidence and deemed to be so made or issued without further proof unless the contrary is shown[9]. A certificate signed by the minister that any instrument purporting to be made or issued by him was so made is conclusive evidence of that fact[10].

1  The provisions of the Ministers of the Crown Act 1975 s 6, Sch 1 apply to (1) any minister eligible for a salary under the Ministerial and other Salaries Act 1975 s 1, Sch 1 Pt II head 2 (ie any minister in charge of a public department of Her Majesty's government in the United Kingdom who is not a member of the Cabinet, and whose office is not specified elsewhere in the schedule (see para 423 note 3 post)); and (2) the Secretary of State for Social Services, the Minister for the Civil Service and the Minister of Aviation Supply, and (where appropriate) to their departments, as the corresponding provisions of the Ministers of the Crown Act 1964 Sch 1 (repealed) applied immediately before the passing of the Ministers of the Crown Act 1975: Ministers of the Crown Act 1975 s 6(1), (2).
2  Ibid Sch 1 para 1. The Promissory Oaths Act 1868 has effect as if the name of the minister were included in Schedule Pt I (as amended) to that Act: Ministers of the Crown Act 1975 Sch 1 para 1. As to the oath of allegiance and the official oath see para 923 post.
3  As to the Minister for the Civil Service see paras 395, 427 post.
4  Ministers of the Crown Act 1975 Sch 1 para 2.
5  Ibid Sch 1 para 3.
6  Ibid Sch 1 para 4.

7   As to corporations sole see CORPORATIONS.

8   Ministers of the Crown Act 1975 Sch 1 para 5.

9   Ibid Sch 1 para 6.

10  Ibid Sch 1 para 7. The Documentary Evidence Act 1868 applies to the minister as if his name were included in the first column of the Schedule to that Act, and as if he or a secretary to the ministry or any person authorised by him to act on his behalf were mentioned in the second column of that Schedule, and as if the regulations referred to in that Act included any document issued by the minister: Ministers of the Crown Act 1975 Sch 1 para 8.

### (ii)   The Allocation, Transfer and Exercise of Functions

**363.   Transfer of functions.** Provision may be made by Order in Council[1] for any functions[2] exercised by one minister of the Crown[3] to be transferred to another[4], or to be exercised concurrently with another or to cease to be so exercised[5]. Her Majesty may also by Order in Council provide for the dissolution of the government department in the charge of any minister of the Crown and the transfer to or distribution among such other minister or ministers as may be specified in the order of any functions previously excercisable by the minister in charge of that department[6]. An Order in Council may contain such incidental, consequential and supplemental provisions as may be necessary or expedient to give it full effect[7] and, if it transfers functions in respect of which a minister may sue or be sued by virtue of any enactment, it must provide for the minister to whom the functions are transferred similarly to sue or be sued[8]. Changes in the style or title of ministers of the Crown may also be made by Order in Council[9]. An Order in Council dissolving a government department must be laid before Parliament in draft and requires an affirmative resolution of each House before being made[10]. In any other case an Order in Council is subject to annulment in pursuance of a resolution of either House of Parliament[11]. The powers set out above are not to prejudice any prerogative of the Crown in relation to ministers of the Crown[12]. No statute passed before the powers were conferred[13] is to be construed as limiting them[14].

In connection with any change in the departments of the office of Secretary of State or any change in the functions of a Secretary of State Her Majesty may by Order in Council make such incidental, consequential and supplementary provisions as may be necessary or expedient in connection with the change, including provisions for (1) making the Secretary of State a corporation sole[15]; (2) transferring any property, rights or liabilities to or from a Secretary of State[16]; (3) adapting enactments relating to a Secretary of State or his department[17]; and (4) substituting one Secretary of State or department for another in any instrument, contract or legal proceedings made or commenced before the date when the order takes effect[18]. A certificate issued by a minister of the Crown that any property, vested in any other minister immediately before an order takes effect, has been transferred by virtue of the order to the minister issuing the certificate is conclusive evidence of the transfer[19].

1   Any Order in Council under the Ministers of the Crown Act 1975 may be varied or revoked by a subsequent order made in the like manner and subject to like conditions, so however that the variation or revocation of an order providing for the dissolution of a government department does not affect the dissolution thereof: s 5(3).

2   'Functions' includes powers and duties: ibid s 8(1). As to the transfer of functions by order to an authorised person under the Deregulation and Contracting Out Act 1994 ss 69–79 see para 364 post.

3   'Minister of the Crown' means the holder of an office in Her Majesty's government in the United Kingdom, and includes the Treasury, the Board of Trade and the Defence Council: Ministers of the Crown Act 1975 ss 8(1). Any reference to a minister of the Crown includes a reference to ministers acting jointly: s 5(6). As to the Treasury see paras 512–517 post. As to the Board of Trade see para 505 post; and TRADE, INDUSTRY AND INDUSTRIAL RELATIONS vol 47 (Reissue) para 2. As to the Defence Council see paras 443–447 post.

4    Ibid s 1(1)(a). The Prime Minister is responsible for the overall organisation of the executive and the allocation of functions between ministers in charge of departments. His approval should therefore be sought where changes are proposed that affect this allocation and the responsibilities for the discharge of ministerial functions. This applies where the functions in question are derived from statute or from the exercise of the royal prerogative, or are general administrative responsibilities: see *Questions of Procedure for Ministers* (Cabinet Office, May 1992) (as now revised: see para 416 note 1 post) paras 32–40. As to the royal prerogative see paras 367–372 post.

5    Ministers of the Crown Act 1975 s 1(1)(c). For the purposes of the Ministers of the Crown Act 1975 any functions in respect of which a direction is given in an Order in Council made under s 1(1)(c) are treated as functions transferred; and any reference to the transfer of functions is construed accordingly: s 8(2).

6    Ibid s 1(1)(b).

7    Ibid s 1(2). These may include provisions:
      (1)  for the transfer of property, rights and liabilities held, enjoyed or incurred by any minister of the Crown in connection with any functions transferred or distributed (s 1(2)(a));
      (2)  for the carrying on and completion, by or under the authority of the minister to whom any functions are transferred, of anything commenced by or under the authority of a minister of the Crown before the date when the order takes effect (s 1(2)(b));
      (3)  for such adaptations of the enactments relating to any functions transferred as may be necessary to enable them to be exercised by the minister to whom they are transferred and his officers (s 1(2)(c));
      (4)  for making in the enactments regulating the number of offices in respect of which salaries may be paid or in the House of Commons Disqualification Act 1975 s 2 or Sch 2 (which regulate the number of office-holders who may be elected, and sit and vote, as members of the House of Commons), such modifications as may be expedient by reason of any transfer of functions or dissolution of a department effected by the order (Ministers of the Crown Act 1975 s 1(2)(d)), but not so as to increase the amount of any salary which may be paid, or the aggregate number of persons to whom salaries may be paid, under those enactments or the aggregate number of persons capable of sitting and voting as members of the House of Commons (s 1(3));
      (5)  for the substitution of the minister to whom functions are transferred for any other minister of the Crown in any instrument, contract, or legal proceedings made or commenced before the date when the order takes effect (s 1(2)(e)).
      A certificate issued by a minister that any property vested in any other minister immediately before an order takes effect has been transferred by virtue of the order to the minister issuing the certificate is conclusive evidence of the transfer: s 1(5).

8    Ibid s 1(4).

9    Ibid s 4. The order may contain provisions substituting the new style and title (1) in the enactments (including those mentioned in s 1(2)(d) (see note 7 supra)) relating to the minister; and (2) in any instrument, contract, or legal proceedings made or commenced before the date when the order takes effect: s 4(a), (b).

10   Ibid s 5(1).

11   Ibid s 5(2).

12   Ibid s 5(5).

13   Ie before 6 March 1946: see ibid s 5(4).

14   Ibid s 5(4).

15   Ibid s 2(1)(a). This applies only to changes after 27 June 1974 and to the creation (in that year) of the Departments of Energy, Industry, Trade, and Prices and Consumer Protection: s 2(3).
      Whether a particular Secretary of State is a corporation sole is indicated in the paragraph dealing with his office. As to corporations sole see CORPORATIONS. Where any enactment or any transfer of functions order provides that a named Secretary of State and his successors are to be a corporation sole, anything done by or in relation to any other Secretary of State for the named Secretary of State as a corporation sole has effect as if done by or in relation to the named Secretary of State, and any deed, contract or other instrument to be executed by or on behalf of the named Secretary of State as a corporation sole is valid if under the corporate seal of that Secretary of State authenticated by the signature of any other Secretary of State, or of a secretary to any department of a Secretary of State, or of a person authorised by any Secretary of State to act in that behalf: ibid s 3.

16   Ibid s 2(1)(b); and see note 15 supra.

17   Ibid s 2(1)(c); and see note 15 supra.

18   Ibid s 2(1)(d); and see note 15 supra.

19   Ibid s 2(2), (3); and see note 15 supra.

**364.   Transfer of functions: contracting out.** Any function of a minister[1] or office-holder[2] conferred by or under any enactment[3] and which by virtue of any enactment or rule of law, may be exercised by any officer[4] of his[5] may, by ministerial order, be exercised by such person or the employees[6] of such person (if any) as may be authorised by the minister or office-holder whose function it is[7]. Similarly, a function[8] of a local authority[9] which is conferred by or under any enactment and which may be exercised by an officer of the authority[10] may, if a minister by order so provides, be exercised by, or by the employees of, such person (if any) as may be authorised by the authority whose function it is[11].

Subject to specified exceptions[12], a function is to be excluded from these provisions if (1) its exercise would constitute the exercise of the jurisdiction of any court or tribunal which exercises the judicial power of the state; or (2) its exercise, or a failure to exercise it, would necessarily interfere or otherwise affect the liberty of any individual; or (3) it is a power or right of entry, search or seizure into or of any property; or (4) it is a power or duty to make subordinate legislation[13].

An order under the provisions described above must be made by statutory instrument and may contain provisions (including provisions modifying enactments) which are consequential upon, or supplemental or incidental to, the provisions made by the order and may contain such transitional provisions and savings as appear to the minister by whom the order is made to be appropriate[14]. No order may be made unless a draft of it has been laid before and approved by a resolution of each House of Parliament[15]. Such an order may provide for the function to be exercised either wholly or to a specified extent, either generally or in such cases as may be specified and either unconditionally or subject to the fulfilment of such conditions as may be specified[16].

Anything done or omitted to be done by, or in relation to, the authorised person or an employee of his in, or in connection with, the exercise or purported exercise of the function is to be treated as if it were done by the minister, office-holder, or authority conferring the power as the case may be[17].

Where a person is authorised to exercise any function of a minister, office-holder or local authority and the order or authorisation is revoked at a time when a relevant contract[18] is subsisting the authorised person is entitled to treat the relevant contract as repudiated by the minister, office-holder or local authority (and not as frustrated by reason of the revocation)[19].

In so far as a specified office-holder[20] does not already have power to do so, he may authorise an officer of his to exercise any function of his which is conferred by or under any enactment[21]. Anything done or omitted to be done by an officer so authorised in, or in connection with, the exercise or purported exercise of the function is to be treated as done or omitted to be done by the office-holder in his capacity as such[22].

Provision is made for the disclosure of information, the disclosure of which would otherwise have been restricted by statute or by obligations of confidentiality, where any function of a minister, office-holder or local authority has been contracted out under the above provisions[23].

1 'Minister' has the same meaning in the Deregulation and Contracting Out Act 1994 as 'minister of the Crown' has in the Ministers of the Crown Act 1975 (see para 363 note 3 ante): Deregulation and Contracting Out Act 1994 s 79(1). Any reference to a minister includes references to the Forestry Commissioners and the Intervention Board for Agricultural Produce: s 79(3)(a). However, this is not to be construed as enabling those Commissioners or that Board to make an order under s 69 or 70; and any order under s 69 which relates to a function of the Board is to be made by the ministers (within the meaning of the Agriculture Act 1957): Deregulation and Contracting Out Act 1994 s 79(4).

2 'Office-holder' does not include a minister, an officer of either House of Parliament, the Parliamentary Commissioner for Administration or the Health Service Commissioner for England, for Wales or for Scotland, but subject to that, means: (1) the holder of an office created or continued in existence by a public general Act of Parliament; (2) the holder of an office the remuneration in respect of which is paid out of money provided by Parliament; (3) the registrar of companies for England and Wales and the registrar of companies for Scotland; and (4) the registrar of approved driving instructors: ibid s 79(1).

3 'Enactment' does not include an enactment contained in Northern Ireland legislation but, subject to that, includes an enactment contained in an Act (whenever passed) and an enactment contained in subordinate legislation (whenever made): ibid s 79(1). 'Subordinate legislation' has the same meaning as in the Interpretation Act 1978 (see STATUTES vol 44(1) (Reissue) para 1381): Deregulation and Contracting Out Act 1994 s 79(1).

4 'Officer' in relation to a minister means any person in the Civil Service of the Crown who is serving in his department; and in relation to an office-holder means any member of his staff or any person in the Civil Service of the Crown who has been assigned or appointed to assist him in the exercise of his functions: ibid s 79(1).

5 Ibid s 69(1). The following orders have been made under these provisions: the Contracting Out (Functions in relation to the Registration of Companies) Order 1995, SI 1995/1013; the Contracting Out (Functions of the Official Receiver) Order 1995, SI 1995/1386; the Contracting Out (Highway Functions) Order 1995, SI 1995/1986; the Contracting Out (Administration of Civil Service Pension Schemes) Order 1996, SI 1996/1746. As to the Principal Civil Service Pension Scheme 1974 see para 576 et seq post.

6 'Employee' in relation to a body corporate, includes any director or other officer of that body: Deregulation and Contracting Out Act 1994 s 79(1).

7 Ibid s 69(2). A minister must not make an order in relation to an office-holder without first consulting him: s 69(3).

8 'Function' in relation to a local authority, includes any power to do anything which is calculated to facilitate, or is conducive or incidental to, the exercise of a function: ibid s 79(1).

9 'Local authority' (1) in relation to England, means a county council, district council or London borough council, the Common Council of the City of London, the sub-treasurer of the Inner Temple, the under treasurer of the Middle Temple, the Council of the Isles of Scilly or a parish council; and (2) in relation to Wales, means a county council, county borough council or community council: ibid s 79(1). In relation to any time before 1 April 1996, the above definition has effect as if for the words 'county borough' there were substituted the word 'district': s 79(2). Any reference to a local authority includes references to a joint board and a joint committee: s 79(3)(b). 'Joint board' in relation to England and Wales, means a joint or special planning board constituted for a National Park by order under the Local Government Act 1972 s 184 (as amended), Sch 17 para 1, 3 or 3A (as amended and prospectively repealed), or a joint planning board within the meaning of the Town and Country Planning Act 1990 s 2 (as amended): Deregulation and Contracting Out Act 1994 s 79(1). 'Joint committee' in relation to England and Wales, means a joint committee appointed under the Local Government Act 1972 s 102(1)(b): Deregulation and Contracting Out Act 1994 s 79(1).

10 Ie by virtue of the Local Government Act 1972 s 101 (as amended).

11 Deregulation and Contracting Out Act 1994 s 70(1), (2). A minister must not make an order in relation to a local authority without first consulting such representatives of local government as he considers appropriate: s 70(3). At the date at which this volume states the law, no Order in Council had been made under s 70.

12 Heads (2) and (3) in the text do not exclude any function of the official receiver attached to any court (ibid s 71(2)); and head (3) in the text does not exclude any function of a local authority under, or under regulations made under: the General Rate Act 1967 Pt VI (ss 96–107) (repealed with savings); the Local Government Finance Act 1988 s 22 (repealed with savings), s 62, Sch 4 paras 5–7 (repealed with savings), Sch 9 para 3(2)(b); and the Local Government Finance Act 1992 s 14(3), Sch 4 paras 5–7: Deregulation and Contracting Out Act 1994 s 71(3)(b), (d)– (g).

13 Ibid s 71(1).

14 Ibid s 77(1).

15 Ibid s 77(2).

16 Ibid ss 69(4), 70(4). This also applies to an authorisation given by virtue of an order which may, subject to the provisions of the order, authorise the exercise of a function (see s 69(4)). Such an authorisation must be for a period not exceeding 10 years as is specified in the authorisation, and it may be revoked at any time by the minister or office-holder by whom the authorisation is given, but it must not prevent that minister or office-holder or any other person from exercising the function to which the authorisation relates: ss 69(5), 70(4). In relation to local authorities, any reference to the minister or office-holder by whom the authorisation is given is to be construed as a reference to the local authority by which the authorisation is given: s 70(4).

Where at any time an order is in force under s 70 in relation to any function of a local authority ('authority A'), and arrangements are in force under the Local Government Act 1972 s 101 (as amended) for the exercise of that function by another local authority ('authority B'), it is an implied term of those arrangements that, except with the consent of authority A, authority B must not give any authorisation by virtue of the order in relation to that function: Deregulation and Contracting Out Act 1994 s 70(5).

17 Ibid s 72(1),(2). However, this does not apply for the purposes of so much of any contract made between the authorised person and the minister, office-holder or local authority as relates to the exercise of the function, or for the purposes of any criminal proceedings brought in respect of anything done or omitted to be done by the authorised person (or an employee of his): s 72(3).

18 'Relevant contract' means so much of any contract made between the authorised person and the minister, office-holder or local authority as relates to the exercise of the function: ibid s 73(3).

19 Ibid s 73(1), (2).

20 The specified office-holders are: (1) the registrar of companies for England and Wales and the registrar of companies for Scotland; (2) the official receiver attached to any court; (3) the Comptroller-General of Patents, Designs and Trademarks; (4) the Public Trustee; (5) the traffic commissioner for any traffic area; (6) the registrar of approved driving instructors; and (7) the Registrar General of Births, Deaths and Marriages for Scotland: ibid s 74(4).

21 Ibid s 74(1). Any function of an examiner or other officer of the Patent Office which is conferred by or under any enactment is to be treated as if it were a function of the Comptroller-General of Patents, Designs and Trademarks: see s 79(5), (6). See generally PATENTS AND REGISTERED DESIGNS.

22 Ibid s 74(2). However, this does not apply for the purposes of any criminal proceedings brought in respect of anything done or omitted to be done: s 74(3).

23 See ibid s 75, Sch 15. As to obligations of confidentiality generally see CONFIDENCE AND DATA PROTECTION.

**365. The Carltona principle and delegation of functions.** Where functions entrusted to a minister or to a department are performed by an official employed in the ministry or department, there is generally in law no delegation because the official's act or decision is constitutionally that of the minister[1]. However, some powers may be required to be exercised by the minister personally[2]

Where a statutory power is vested in a particular minister he may not generally delegate its exercise to another minister[3]. However, a minister may contract out of his functions in certain circumstances[4].

An improper assumption of authority by a civil servant which induces a person to do an illegal act cannot be pleaded as justification of that act[5], although, in clear cases, the courts may protect legitimate expectations created by assurances given by a public authority[6].

1 *Carltona Ltd v Comrs of Works* [1943] 2 All ER 560, CA; *Lewisham Metropolitan Borough and Town Clerk v Roberts* [1949] 2 KB 608, [1949] 1 All ER 815, CA. These cases relate to departments with a ministerial head, but since the same rule is applied to local authorities (see *R v Sunderland Corpn* [1911] 2 KB 458 at 462, DC, per Lord Alverstone), it seems clear that the rule could apply to other departments also. But a question may arise whether an official has been properly authorised by the minister to act in a particular situation: see *Woollett v Minister of Agriculture and Fisheries* [1955] 1 QB 103, [1954] 3 All ER 529, CA; *Customs and Excise Comrs v Cure & Deeley Ltd* [1962] 1 QB 340 at 371, [1961] 3 All ER 641 at 660; *R v Skinner* [1968] 2 QB 700 at 706, [1968] 3 All ER 124 at 126, CA; *R v Secretary of State for the Home Department, ex p Oladehinde* [1991] 1 AC 254, [1990] 2 All ER 367, DC; and see *Bushell v Secretary of State for the Environment* [1981] AC 75, [1980] 2 All ER 608, HL. The orthodox position was stated by Sir Robert Armstrong, Head of the Home Civil Service as follows: 'Civil servants are servants of the Crown. For all practical purposes the Crown in this context means and is represented by the government of the day ... the Civil Service as such has no constitutional personality or responsibility separate from the government of the day.': *Duties and Responsibilities of Civil Servants in relation to Ministers: A Note by the Head of the Home Civil Service* 123 HC Official Report (6th series), 2 December 1987, written answers cols 572–575; revised (HC Paper (1993–94) no 27-II). As to the application of this principle to executive agencies see Freedland 'The rule against delegation and the *Carltona* doctrine in an agency context' [1996] Public Law 19; and para 551 post.

2 Eg powers under the Immigration Act 1971 ss 13(5), 14(3) and 15(4) (in respect of exclusion or deportation orders). See also *R v Secretary of State for the Home Department, ex p Oladehinde* [1991] 1 AC 254, [1990] 2 All ER 367, DC.

3 *H Lavender & Son Ltd v Minister of Housing and Local Government* [1970] 3 All ER 871, [1970] 1 WLR 1231.

4 See the Deregulation and Contracting Out Act 1994 Pt II (ss 69–79); and para 364 ante.

5 See *Howell v Falmouth Boat Construction Ltd* [1951] AC 837 at 845, [1951] 2 All ER 278 at 280, HL, per Lord Simonds; see also *A-G for Ceylon v Silva* [1953] AC 461, PC.

6    *R v Liverpool Corpn, ex p Liverpool Taxi Fleet Operators' Association* [1972] 2 QB 299, sub nom *Re Liverpool Taxi Owners' Association* [1972] 2 All ER 589, CA; *Oloniyuh v Secretary of State for the Home Department* [1989] Imm AR 135, CA; *Re Preston* [1985] AC 835, sub nom *Preston v IRC* [1983] 2 All ER 300, HL. See also Wade and Bradley *Constitutional and Administrative Law* (11th Edn, 1993) pp 700–703; Bradley 'Administrative Justice and the Binding Effect of Official Acts' [1981] CLP 1; Wade and Forsyth *Administrative Law* (7th Edn, 1994) pp 418–420.

### (iii)  Sources of Executive Power

**366.  Legal sources of executive power.** The legal sources of governmental power are (1) statutes[1]; (2) the royal prerogative[2]; and (3) common law powers or capacities deriving from the legal personality of the Crown and of ministers[3].

The traditional way in which the executive exercises power is through the promulgation of legislation which is enforceable by the courts. In practice, the state has the monopoly of coercive power[4]. The rule of law or principle of legality[5] has imposed legal restrictions on the exercise of this kind of power, which has been called 'imperium'[6] or 'condign' power[7].

Nowadays other methods of exercising executive power are also significant. These include the use of the resources of government in the form of property and money raised in taxation in order to induce individuals and organisations to behave in accordance with government policy or to enter into negotiated relationships with individuals, organisations and collectivities: this sort of power has been termed 'dominium'[8] or 'property'[9] power. Its use can be observed in the making of grants subject to conditions and guidelines to bodies such as the Further Education Funding Councils for England, Wales and Scotland[10], procurement[11] and the use of contracting[12].

The role of the state has changed since the 1970s from one where the government was predominantly engaged in providing services and unilaterally imposing enforceable obligations to a role in which a wider range of techniques are employed in pursuit of policy, and provision and 'imperium' are increasingly supplemented by 'dominium', enabling, facilitation, regulation and contracting[13].

1    The various statutory powers of government are considered fully in the titles in this work relevant to the areas of law in question. As to statutes generally see STATUTES.
2    As to the royal prerogative see paras 367–372 post.
3    Eg powers or capacities of ownership and contract.
4    See Weber *The Theory of Social and Economic Organisation* (1947) (translated 1964) (Henderson and Parsons (eds)).
5    See para 6 ante.
6    As to the scope and exercise of this power see Daintith 'Regulation by Contract: the New Prerogative' [1979] Current Legal Problems 41; Daintith 'The Techniques of Government' in Jowell and Oliver (eds) *The Changing Constitution* (3rd Edn, 1994).
7    See Galbraith *The Anatomy of Power* (1984).
8    See Daintith 'The Techniques of Government' in Jowell and Oliver (eds) *The Changing Constitution* (3rd Edn, 1994).
9    See Galbraith *The Anatomy of Power* (1984).
10   The Further Education Funding Councils are non-departmental public bodies (as to which see para 951 et seq post) with executive functions. They receive funds from the government and distribute them to universities: see further para 449 post; and EDUCATION.
11   See Turpin *Government Procurement and Contract* (1989); Arrowsmith *Government Procurement Law* (1996). As to the use of the contracting power of government and other public bodies to pursue ulterior policy purposes see Daintith 'Regulation by Contract: the New Prerogative' [1979] Current Legal Problems 41; Ganz 'Comment' [1978] Public Law 333. As to the restrictions on judicial review of government contracting see *R v Lord Chancellor, ex p Hibbit and Saunders (a firm)* (1993) Times, 12 March; Arrowsmith 'Judicial Review and the Contractual Powers of Public Authorities' (1990) 106 LQR 277; Oliver 'Judicial Review and the Shorthandwriters' [1993] Public Law 215. See also para 6 ante.
12   See the Deregulation and Contracting Out Act 1994; and para 364 ante.

13  See Harden *The Contracting State* (1992); Prosser 'Regulation, Markets and Legitimacy'; Daintith 'The
    Techniques of Government'; and Drewry 'Revolution in Whitehall: The Next Steps and Beyond' in
    Jowell and Oliver (eds) *The Changing Constitution* (3rd Edn, 1994); *The Citizen's Charter: Raising the
    Standard* (Cm 1599) (1991); *Competing for Quality: Buying Better Public Services* (Cm 1730) (1991).

## (iv)  The Royal Prerogative

**367.  Meaning of 'royal prerogative'.** Many functions of government are authorised
under the royal prerogative. These include, inter alia, functions in relation to the
organisation of the Civil Service, foreign affairs, defence and mercy[1]. The royal
prerogative may be defined as being that special pre-eminence which the monarch has
over and above all other persons by virtue of the common law[2], but out of its ordinary
course, in right of her regal dignity[3], and includes all the special dignities, liberties,
privileges, powers and royalties allowed by the common law to the Crown of England[4].

1   See paras 801, 809 and 823 et seq post. As to the Civil Service generally see paras 549–564 post.
2   In theory the monarch has supreme sovereignty and pre-eminence, and under the doctrine of perfection,
    can do no wrong: see 1 Bl Com (14th Edn) 241–242, 245–246; *Re M* [1994] 1 AC 377, sub nom *M v
    Home Office* [1993] 3 All ER 537, HL; and generally CROWN LANDS AND PRIVILEGES.
        The person of the monarch is inviolable: see 1 Bl Com (14th Edn) 242; CRIMINAL LAW vol 11(1)
    (Reissue) para 76 et seq (treason); and CROWN LANDS AND PRIVILEGES. The monarch is only bound by
    legislation by express mention or clear implication: see *Thomas v Pritchard* [1903] 1 KB 209, DC; *BBC v
    Johns (Inspector of Taxes)* [1965] Ch 32 at 59–60, [1964] 1 All ER 923 at 929–930, CA, per Willmer LJ;
    and STATUTES vol 44(1) (Reissue) para 1321. The monarch is not bound by custom: Vin Abr,
    Prerogative, T (2); *Anon* (1457) Jenk 83; *Westover v Perkins* (1859) 2 E & E 57; *A-G v Londonderry Bridge
    Comrs* [1903] 1 IR 389 (Crown servants' free passage over ferries). See further CROWN LANDS AND
    PRIVILEGES.
3   1 Bl Com (14th Edn) 239. Literally the term prerogative (*praerogo*) means something demanded before or
    in preference: 1 Bl Com (14th Edn) 239. According to Sir Henry Finch 'by the prerogative that.is law
    almost in every case of the King which is law in no case of the subject': Finch, Discourse on the Law, lib
    ii, 85. The prerogative was described by Dicey as 'both historically and as a matter of actual fact nothing
    else than the residue of discretionary or arbitrary authority which at any given time is legally left in the
    hands of the Crown' (Law of the Constitution (10th Edn) 424). This statement has been cited in a number
    of judgments, eg in *A-G v De Keyser's Royal Hotel Ltd* [1920] AC 508 at 526, HL, per Lord Dunedin, but
    it is not strictly accurate, because the prerogative also includes rights and privileges of various kinds (as to
    these see CROWN LANDS AND PRIVILEGES). The Lord Privy Seal, in a written answer in the House of
    Lords to the question 'what are the categories of powers exercised by ministers exclusively under the royal
    prerogative', said 'the government shares the view of Wade and Bradley, in their work on constitutional
    law, that it is not possible to give a comprehensive catalogue of prerogative powers': 568 HL Official
    Report (5th series), 1 February 1996, written answers, col *118*); Wade and Bradley *Constitutional and
    Administrative Law* (11th Edn, 1993) p 264.
4   Com Dig, Prerogative, A. Powers specially conferred upon the Crown cannot be said to form part of the
    prerogative, although the prerogative has frequently been defined and regulated by statute: see
    *Convocations' Case* (1611) 12 Co Rep 72; and the statute Prerogativa Regis (temp incert), the unrepealed
    portion of which declares the law on certain points as to wreck of the sea, royal fish (c 13) and the
    construction of royal grants (c 17) (as to which see CROWN LANDS AND PRIVILEGES); see also 6 English
    Historical Review 367.
        The use of the term 'the Crown' conveys the correct implication that prerogative powers are, with very
    few exceptions, exercised not by the monarch in person but in her name by her servants. Even where the
    monarch acts in person, she normally acts in accordance with the advice given to her by ministers. See
    paras 351–354 ante; Wade and Bradley *Constitutional and Administrative Law* (11th Edn, 1993) pp 244–245,
    261–264); and de Smith and Brazier *Constitutional and Administrative Law* (7th Edn, 1994) pp 139–142.

**368.  Relations of prerogative to common law and statute.** The prerogative is
thus derived from[1] and limited by the common law, and the monarch can claim no
prerogatives except such as the law allows[2]. In particular no prerogative may be
recognised that is contrary to Magna Carta or any other statute[3], or that interferes with
the liberties of the subject[4].

The courts have jurisdiction, therefore, to inquire into the existence or extent of any alleged prerogative[5], it being a maxim of the common law that the King ought to be under no man, but under God and the law, because the law makes the King[6]. If any prerogative is disputed, the courts must decide the question whether or not it exists in the same way as they decide any other question of law. If a prerogative is clearly established, they must take the same judicial notice of it as they take of any other rule of law[7].

1    Historically it is incorrect to say that the prerogative is 'created' by the common law, because it is the residue of royal authority left over from a time before it was effectually controlled by law; but, since the time of Bracton, who founded the royal authority on law (see note 6 infra), it has been legally correct to use that term.

2    Com Dig, Prerogative, A; *Proclamations' Case* (1611) 12 Co Rep 74 at 75.

3    2 Co Inst 36, 54.

4    1 Bl Com (14th Edn) 245. See also *Ex p Barnsley* (1744) 3 Atk 168 at 171; *Proclamations' Case* (1611) 12 Co Rep 74. The scope of the prerogative in home affairs has been so severely curtailed by statute that it is difficult to see how any act by or authorised by the Crown causing damage to a subject within the realm could be justified as having been lawfully done by virtue of the prerogative. But if that could possibly have occurred in time of peace, it seems that the subject would have a claim to compensation see *Burmah Oil Co (Burma Trading) Ltd v Lord Advocate* [1965] AC 75, [1964] All ER 348, HL, not overruled on this point by the War Damage Act 1965. As to acts done abroad see paras 370, 885 post; and FOREIGN RELATIONS LAW.

5    The instances in the books are numerous. For examples of cases where the courts have determined the extent of prerogative rights see *Darcy v Allen*, known as the *Case of Monopolies* (1602) 11 Co Rep 84b (monopolies); *Case of Monopolies, East India Co v Sandys* (1685) 10 State Tr 371 (exclusive trading licences). For a recent decision see *R v Secretary of State for the Home Department, ex p Northumbria Police Authority* [1989] QB 26, [1988] 1 All ER 556, CA, where the Home Secretary's decision to issue the police with CS gas and plastic baton rounds to deal with serious public disorder was upheld by the Court of Appeal, even though the police authority had refused to approve the supply. It was held that the policy could be justified by virtue of the Crown's prerogative power to act to meet an actual or apprehended breach of the peace. For an article critical of this decision see Bradley 'Police Powers and the Prerogative' [1988] Public Law 298. As to dispensations see para 376 post.

6    Ie *rex non debet esse sub homine, sed sub Deo et lege, quia lex facit regeni*: Bracton, lib 1 C. 8; 12 Co Rep 65; Fleta 2 c 5; Chitty *Law of the Prerogatives of the Crown* 5.

7    'We are indeed bound to take notice of everything that belongs to the Queen's privilege': *Elderton's Case* (1703) 2 Ld Raym 978 at 980 per Holt CJ; 'but if officers of the Crown claim procedural privileges by virtue of the prerogative, they must make out clearly the prerogative': *A-G to Prince of Wales v Crossman* (1866) LR 1 Exch 381 at 386 per curiam. The courts cannot broaden the prerogative: see *BBC v Johns (Inspector of Taxes)* [1965] Ch 32 at 79, [1964] 1 All ER 923 at 941, CA, per Diplock LJ. In a classical summary of the subject Maitland *Constitutional History of England* (1908) pp 418–421 said there is often great uncertainty as to the exact limits of the royal prerogative. Although there is no such doctrine that a prerogative may cease to exist because it is not used, many old prerogative powers, even if not actually abolished by statute, have become clumsy and antiquated and have fallen into disuse. The Crown usually prefers to act under definite statutory powers. See also de Smith and Brazier *Constitutional and Administrative Law* (7th Edn, 1994) pp 144–145. For an article expressing doubts as to a prerogative power see W R Edeson 'The Prerogative of the Crown to Delimit Britain's Maritime Boundary' 89 LQR 364; and Bradley 'Police Powers and the Prerogative' [1988] Public Law 298.

**369. Assignment of prerogatives.** The general rule is that prerogatives cannot be affected[1] or parted with by the Crown[2], except by express statutory authority[3]. However, prerogatives connected with the royal revenues, such as waifs, estrays and the like[4] may be granted out in the form of franchises in certain cases[5]. Some of the prerogatives relating to public government and the right of pardoning offences are usually delegated to the governors[6].

Where, by statute, the Crown is empowered to do what it might previously have done by virtue of its prerogative it can no longer act under the prerogative, and must act under and subject to the conditions imposed by the statute[7]; but the statute may expressly preserve the right to act under the prerogative[8].

Where a prerogative power has been superseded by statute, and the statutory provision is later repealed the prerogative will not revive unless it is a major governmental attribute[9].

1   *Weymouth Corpn v Nugent* (1865) 6 B & S 22.
2   *R v Eduljee Byramjee* (1846) 5 Moo PCC 276. A forfeiture can, however, be waived by the Crown: *Lord Middleton v Power* (1886) 19 LR Ir 1; *R v Secretary of State for Foreign and Commonwealth Affairs, ex p Rees-Mogg* [1994] QB 552 at 570, [1994] 1 All ER 457 at 469, 470, DC (signature of the Treaty on European Union was an exercise and not a transfer of prerogative powers in relation to foreign affairs).
3   Ie just as the kingly dignity is inherent to the royal blood and cannot be transferred to another: see *Oaths before an Ecclesiastical Judge Ex Officio* (1607) 12 Co Rep 26. As to statutes binding the Crown see para 384 post; and CROWN LANDS AND PRIVILEGES. But certain prerogative powers relating to the administration of justice, such as to command a subject by the writ *ne exeat regno* not to leave the realm (see para 815 post), and a number of the prerogative orders such as mandamus, certiorari and prohibition (see ADMINISTRATIVE LAW vol 1(1) (Reissue) paras 109–156), have now come to be exercised by Her Majesty's judges at the instance of aggrieved subjects. Moreover, some prerogatives, such as the power to impress men into the navy, have ceased to be exercised and could hardly be revived: see de Smith and Brazier *Constitutional and Administrative Law* (7th Edn, 1994) pp 141, 143.
4   See CROWN LANDS AND PRIVILEGES. Note that the law of treasure trove, formerly governed by the prerogative, is now embodied in statute: see the Treasure Act 1996.
5   See CROWN LANDS AND PRIVILEGES.
6   As to governors generally see COMMONWEALTH. For the rule that the Crown automatically loses its prerogative power to legislate in a conquered or ceded colony if it grants a representative legislature without reserving the prerogative see COMMONWEALTH vol 6 (Reissue) para 990.
7   *A-G v De Keyser's Royal Hotel Ltd* [1920] AC 508, HL; applied in *Re Azoff-Don Commercial Bank* [1954] Ch 315 at 323–324, [1954] 1 All ER 947 at 950–951 per Wynn Parry J (a case under the Companies Act 1948); see also *Re Mitchell, Hatton v Jones* [1954] Ch 525, [1954] 2 All ER 246 (Crown's right to succeed to property on individual's intestacy depends now on statute); and *Laker Airways Ltd v Department of Trade and Industry* [1977] QB 643, [1977] 2 All ER 182, CA; *Sabally and N'Jie v A-G* [1965] 1 QB 273, [1964] 3 All ER 377, CA. See also para 6 ante; and de Smith and Brazier *Constitutional and Administrative Law* (7th Edn, 1994) p 144.
8   Eg the Trading with the Enemy Act 1939 s 16; see *Bank voor Handel en Scheepvaart NV v Administrator of Hungarian Property* [1954] AC 584, [1954] 1 All ER 969, HL. For other examples see the Crown Proceedings Act 1947 s 11(1); the Royal Assent Act 1967 s 1(2); and the Local Government Act 1972 s 245(10).
9   *New Windsor Corpn v Taylor* [1899] AC 41, HL (where a local customary franchise of tollage was superseded by statutory provisions and the statute was later repealed, it was held that the old franchise was not thereby revived. Cf in *A-G v De Keyser's Royal Hotel Ltd* [1920] AC 508, HL, the court indicated that the prerogative power to requisition for defence purposes in wartime might reasonably be held to lie in suspense while statutory provisions were in force. In *R v Secretary of State for the Home Department, ex p Fire Brigades Union* [1995] 2 AC 513, [1995] 1 All ER 888, CA, an unimplemented statutory scheme under the Criminal Justice Act 1988 ss 108–117, setting up the Criminal Injuries Compensation Scheme, was held to oust the prerogative and therefore render unlawful a later and inconsistent scheme introduced by the Home Secretary under the prerogative (see para 380 note 4 post). See also de Smith and Brazier *Constitutional and Administrative Law* (7th Edn, 1994) p 144; and Colin Munro *Studies in Constitutional Law* (1987) pp 171–172. As to the new statutory Criminal Injuries Compensation Scheme under the Criminal Injuries Compensation Act 1995 see para 7 note 21 ante.

**370. Extent of prerogative.** The prerogative is not confined to the British Islands, but extends to all parts of the Commonwealth of which the Queen is monarch[1] as fully in all respects as to England[2], unless otherwise prescribed by United Kingdom or local enactment.

1   Ie not to those parts that have a republican constitution. However, it extends, as part of the common law, to a protectorate into which the substance of the common law has been introduced: see *Nyali Ltd v A-G* [1956] 1 QB 1, [1955] 1 All ER 646, CA (grant of pontage); affd on a different ground [1957] AC 253, [1956] 2 All ER 689, HL. See *Sabally and N'Jie v A-G* [1965] 1 QB 273 at 293, [1964] 3 All ER 377 at 380–381, CA; and para 6 ante. Clearly the prerogative cannot operate against an alien in an alien land: see *A-G v Nissan* [1970] AC 179 at 229, [1969] 1 All ER 629 at 652, HL, per Lord Pearce. Whether acts done by the armed forces of the Crown who are operating in a foreign territory in time of peace with the consent

of the local sovereign are done by virtue of the prerogative, so as to confer on a British subject a right to compensation for damage done to his property by those forces is doubtful; see further para 885 post.

2    *Re Bateman's Trusts* (1873) LR 15 Eq 355. See also COMMONWEALTH vol 6 (Reissue) para 815.

**371. Classification of prerogatives.** The special privileges enjoyed by the monarch by virtue of the royal prerogative fall naturally under three heads[1]: (1) those concerned with the special qualities of pre-eminence and dignity ascribed to the monarch in her regal capacity; (2) those concerned with the various powers and authorities entrusted to the monarch as the supreme executive officer in the state and exercised in fact by ministers of the Crown; and (3) those concerned with the special privileges enjoyed by the monarch in relation to rights of property, which have been allowed to her for the support of the royal dignity and the increase of the royal revenues[2].

1    By the feudal writers the prerogatives are generally classed as majora and minora regalia, the first relating to the royal pre-eminence and authority, the latter to the royal revenues: see 1 Bl Com (14th Edn) 240–241.
2    See CROWN LANDS AND PRIVILEGES.

**372. Statutory limitations on the prerogative.** The extent of the prerogative being necessarily somewhat vague, it has been necessary at various times to define its limits more accurately by statute[1]. The principal provisions, from a constitutional standpoint, are to be found in four great statutes or charters by which the rights and liberties of the subject are preserved and acts of tyranny by the Crown or its ministers restrained[2]. These statutes must not be regarded as curtailments of existing prerogatives, but as declarations of the fundamental laws of England[3].

1    The prerogative may also, in effect, be in abeyance where statute has enacted provisions which enable what might have been done under the prerogative to be done under the statute: see para 369 ante. In what follows on statutory limitations of the prerogative the Crown may be taken to include the monarch in person, her ministers and officials and all emanations of the Crown.
2    The four great statutes or charters are (1) Magna Carta of Edward I (1297) (see infra); (2) the Petition of Right (1627) (see infra); (3) the Bill of Rights, confirmed by the Crown and Parliament Recognition Act 1689; and (4) the Act of Settlement. As to the history and citation of the Bill of Rights, and as to the citation of the Act of Settlement, see para 35 note 3 ante.
     Magna Carta was first assented to by King John in 1215. It was confirmed, and sometimes extended but more frequently curtailed, more than 30 times between the reigns of Henry III and Henry IV. The confirmation and reissue of 1297, known as the Magna Carta of Edward I (1297) is still in force as to cc 1, 9, 29, 37 (see para 1 note 13 ante), and to that extent still binds the Crown. The same applies to various of the confirming charters, namely the statute 25 Edw 1 (Confirmation of the Charters) (1297), cc 1 (in part), 6; the statute 25 Edw 3 stat 5 (Executors) (1351–2), c 5; the statute 28 Edw 3 (1354), c 3; the statute 7 Hen 4 (Liberties, Charters and Statutes Confirmed) (1405–06), c 1; the statute 4 Hen 5 stat 2 (Confirmation of Charters and Statutes) (1415–16); and the statute 2 Hen 6 (Confirmation of Liberties) (1423), c 1. Constitutionally the most important of these charters is now the Magna Carta of Edward I (1297) (25 Edw 1).
     The Petition of Right (1627) was drawn up by the Commons in 1627, and recited in particular the Magna Carta of Edward I (1297) and the statute 25 Edw I (Statute Concerning Tallage) (1297) (25 Edw I), of which c 1 is still in force. To the petition itself Charles I appended the answer 'Soit droit fait come est desire' (let right be done as is desired).
     As to subsequent amendments and repeals of the Magna Carta of Edward I (1297), the Petition of Right (1627) and the Bill of Rights see para 1 note 13 ante.
3    See 2 Co Inst proëm 3; 1 Bl Com (14th Edn) 128.

## (v) Constitutional Principles governing the Exercise of the Prerogative and Executive Power

**373. General.** Subject to the powers of the Queen in Parliament to legislate expressly[1] to override the principles set out in the following paragraphs, it may be said that a number of constitutional principles have been established by the great statutes or charters[2] and by the courts[3].

1   See paras 202 ante, 374–378 post.
2   As to the four great statutes and charters see para 372 ante.
3   See generally Jowell and Lester 'Beyond *Wednesbury*: Substantive Principles of Administrative Law' [1987] Public Law 368; Sir John Laws 'Is the High Court the Guardian of Fundamental Constitutional Rights?' [1993] Public Law 59; Lord Woolf 'Droit Public – English Style' [1995] Public Law 57; Sir John Laws 'Law and Democracy' [1995] Public Law 72.

## 374. Limitation by Magna Carta.

The Crown or its ministers may not punish, imprison or coerce the subject in an arbitrary manner: no freeman may be taken or imprisoned, or disseised of his freehold, liberties or free customs, or be outlawed or exiled, or in any other wise molested[1]; nor may he be judged[2] or condemned[3], except by the lawful judgment of his peers, or by the law of the land, nor may justice or right be sold, denied or delayed to any man[4].

1   Ie *aut aliquo modo destruatur* (literally 'destroyed'). See *Entick v Carrington* (1765) 19 State Tr 1029.
2   Ie *nec super eum ibimus*.
3   Ie *nec super eum mittimus*.
4   Magna Carta of Edward I (1297), c 29. For subsequent modifications and repeals see para 1 note 13 ante. As to Magna Carta see para 372 note 2 ante. Similar provision was made by the Petition of Right (1627) ss 3, 8 (repealed so far as relevant by the Justices of the Peace Act 1968, Sch 5): see, however, para 375 post.

## 375. Freedom from arrest.

Any power to commit to prison, or to issue warrants of arrest or search warrants, which may have been exercisable at common law by the monarch in person, or by the Privy Council[1], members of the Privy Council or the Secretary of State, whether on their or his own authority or on the special direction of the monarch, has been abolished[2].

1   As to the Privy Council see paras 521–526 post.
2   Justices of the Peace Act 1968 s 1(7) (as originally enacted, replacing the Petition of Right (1627) ss 5, 8). Alien enemies do not enjoy this freedom from arrest and imprisonment: *R v Vine Street Police Station Superintendent, ex p Liebmann* [1916] 1 KB 268; and see WAR. For general powers of arrest see CRIMINAL LAW. As to the office of Secretary of State see para 355 et seq ante.

## 376. Laws may not be suspended.

The Crown may not suspend laws or the execution of laws without the consent of Parliament[1]; nor may it dispense with laws, or the execution of laws[2]; and dispensations by *non obstante* of or to any statute or part of it are void and of no effect except in such cases as are allowed by statute[3].

The Crown or its ministers may not erect courts where persons may be tried in an arbitrary manner, since the issue of commissions to try persons according to the law martial, as is used by armies in time of war[4], and the issue of commissions to erect illegal courts[5], are declared to be against law.

1   Bill of Rights s 1. As to the history and citation of the Bill of Rights see para 35 note 3 ante.
2   Ibid s 1. The words of this provision extend only to the dispensing power 'as it hath been assumed and exercised of late'; this saves the validity of old dispensations (see *Re Case of Eton College* (1815) Special Report by Williams), but the Bill of Rights s 2, rendered invalid all subsequent dispensation with statutes, unless specially allowed by the statutes. See *Vestey v IRC (No 2)* [1980] AC 1148 at 1195, [1979] 3 All ER 976 at 1002–1003, HL (Board of Inland Revenue's claim to the right to dispensed with laws rejected). See also *IRC v National Federation of Self-Employed and Small Business Ltd* [1982] AC 617, [1981] 2 All ER 93, HL.
3   Bill of Rights s 2. This provision does not extend to common law offences, but the King was always held unable to license offences *mala per se*; it was otherwise as to *mala prohibita*: see *Thomas v Sorrell* (1673) Vaugh 330 at 332; *Langdale's Case* (1608) 12 Co Rep 58 at 61; *Anon* (1609) 12 Co Rep 30. An offence

*mala per se* is an act which is intrinsically wrong; one *mala prohibita* is an act which is wrong only because it has been prohibited by law. In ancient days the Crown sometimes purported to give effect to letters patent etc *non obstante* (ie notwithstanding) any statute to the contrary.

4 Petition of Right (1627) s 7. It is still uncertain whether this prohibition applies generally or only to time of peace: see paras 308 ante, 821 note 1, 887 post.

5 Bill of Rights s 1. Particular reference is made by this section to the Court of Commissioners for Ecclesiastical Causes, which James II endeavoured to set up. The section proceeds 'and all other commissions and courts of like nature are illegal and pernicious'. See also the Habeas Corpus Act 1640 ss 2, 3, by which it was enacted that henceforth no court was to be created with similar jurisdiction to that exercised by the Court of Star Chamber, which was thereby abolished, and that neither the Crown nor the Privy Council had or ought to have any jurisdiction by English bill, petition, articles, libel or any other arbitrary way to draw into question, determine or dispose of the lands, goods etc of any subject; heavy penalties and treble damages were also imposed by the Act upon any Lord Chancellor or Keeper of the Great Seal, Lord Treasurer, Keeper of the King's Privy Seal, President of the Council, bishop etc for offences against the Act: ss 4, 5. The Act was repealed as obsolete by the Justices of the Peace Act 1968 s 8(2) (repealed), Sch 5 (repealed). See also 4 Co Inst 200; and para 308 ante. As to the Privy Council see paras 521–526 post.

**377. Impeachment.** The Crown is restrained from shielding its ministers and servants, by means of pardons, from a parliamentary inquiry into illegal acts, for no pardon under the Great Seal[1] is pleadable to an impeachment by the Commons in Parliament[2]. But a pardon may be granted after sentence[3].

1 As to the use of the Great Seal see para 909 post.
2 Act of Settlement s 3. As to the citation of the Act of Settlement see para 35 note 3 ante.
3 See para 823 text and note 5 post.

**378. Taxation.** There is no taxation without the consent of Parliament[1], which must be embodied in statute and expressed in clear terms[2].

1 See the Bill of Rights s 1; and paras 228–229 ante, 701 post. As to the history and citation of the Bill of Rights see para 35 note 3 ante.
2 See *Bowles v Bank of England* [1913] 1 Ch 57; *Congreve v Home Office* [1976] QB 629, [1976] 1 All ER 697, CA. The Provisional Collection of Taxes Act authorises the collection of taxes pending the passage of the annual Finance Act: see paras 228–229 ante.

**379. Judicial review: the extent of the prerogative.** Claims made by the Crown cannot be supported by mere pretence of prerogative, since the courts have power to determine the extent and the legality or otherwise of any alleged prerogative[1]; nor may the extent of the prerogative be enlarged[2] nor illegal acts be rendered justifiable by the plea of the monarch's commands[3] or of state necessity[4]. The Crown is bound to observe the law both by statute and by the terms of the coronation oath, which embodies the contract between the Crown and people upon which the title to the Crown originally depended, and still largely depends[5]. Upon any doubtful point of prerogative the Crown and its ministers must, therefore, bow to the decision of the courts.

At common law the Crown is not entitled by virtue of the royal prerogative to take possession of a subject's property for reasons of state without paying compensation[6]. However, no person is entitled at common law to receive compensation from the Crown in respect of damage to, or destruction of, property within or without the United Kingdom caused by acts lawfully done by, or on the authority of, the Crown during, or in contemplation of the outbreak of, a war in which the monarch was or is engaged[7].

1 See para 368 ante.
2 See *BBC v Johns (Inspector of Taxes)* [1965] Ch 32, [1964] 1 All ER 923, CA; *R v Secretary of State for the Home Department, ex p Northumbria Police Authority* [1989] QB 26, [1988] 1 All ER 556, CA.
3 *R v Earl of Danby* (1685) 11 State Tr 600 at 627, 629, HL.
4 *Entick v Carrington* (1765) 19 State Tr 1029 at 1067; see paras 6 ante, 388 post.

5   See para 28 ante. It is the duty of the Crown and of every branch of the executive to abide by and obey the law. If there is any difficulty in ascertaining it the courts are open to the Crown to sue, and it is the duty of the executive in cases of doubt to ascertain the law, in order to obey it, not to disregard it: *Eastern Trust Co v McKenzie, Mann & Co Ltd* [1915] AC 750 at 759, PC.

6   *A-G v De Keyser's Royal Hotel Ltd* [1920] AC 508, HL; *France Fenwick & Co Ltd v R* [1927] 1 KB 458 at 467; *Bank voor Handel en Scheepvaart NV v Administrator of Hungarian Property* [1954] AC 584 at 638, [1954] 1 All ER 969 at 995, HL, per Lord Keith of Avonholm (his opinion was a dissenting opinion, but this point was not in issue). As regards the construction of legislation conferring powers of compulsory acquisition and the canon that an intention to take property without compensation is not to be imputed to the legislature see COMPULSORY ACQUISITION vol 8(1) (Reissue) para 335.

7   See the War Damage Act 1965 s 1(1), destroying retrospectively the effect of the majority decision in *Burmah Oil Co (Burma Trading) Ltd v Lord Advocate* [1965] AC 75, [1964] 2 All ER 348, HL, that a subject whose property was destroyed or damaged in the exercise of the royal prerogative in relation to war was entitled to compensation, exception being made in the case of battle damage.

**380. Judicial review: the manner of exercise of the prerogative.** Until recently the courts would not enquire into the way in which a prerogative power had been exercised[1]. With the development of judicial review[2], this judicial attitude has changed and the courts have been more willing to review the exercise of discretionary power, whether derived from statute or common law, and hence the courts may be willing to review exercises of the prerogative[3]. The test for reviewability of a prerogative is not the source of the power, but the nature of the function to which it relates and whether it is justiciable[4].

1   See *China Navigation Co Ltd v A-G* [1932] 2 KB 197, CA (manner of disposition of armed forces); *Blackburn v A-G* [1971] 2 All ER 1380, [1971] 1 WLR 1037, CA (entry into a treaty); *Hanratty v Lord Butler of Saffron Walden* (1971) 115 Sol Jo 386 (prerogative of mercy); *Gouriet v Union of Post Office Workers* [1978] AC 435, [1977] 3 All ER 70, HL (Attorney General's consent to the bringing of relator actions).

2   As to judicial review see RSC Ord 53; and generally ADMINISTRATIVE LAW.

3   See *R v Criminal Injuries Compensation Board, ex p Lain* [1967] 2 QB 864, [1967] 2 All ER 182, CA (award by Criminal Injuries Compensation Board, set up under the prerogative, held subject to judicial scrutiny by way of certiorari); *Laker Airways Ltd v Department of Trade and Industry* [1977] QB 643, [1977] 2 All ER 182, CA (withdrawal of designation of airline to operate a transatlantic service); *Council of Civil Service Unions v Minister for the Civil Service* [1985] AC 374, [1984] 3 All ER 935, HL.

4   The most important case in relation to this development has been *Council of Civil Service Unions v Minister for the Civil Service* [1985] AC 374, [1984] 3 All ER 935, HL, in which the Secretary of State for the Foreign and Commonwealth Office decided to exclude trade unions from (Government Communications Headquarters (GCHQ) (as to which see para 473 post), where civil servants were employed. The House of Lords held that such action was in principle reviewable because it concerned the terms of employment of people who, prima facie, had a legitimate expectation that advantages which they had hitherto enjoyed would not be discontinued without their being consulted. The Secretary of State's invocation of the interests of national security, however, served to remove his decision from judicial scrutiny. '...whatever label may be attached to them there have unquestionably survived into the present day a residue of miscellaneous fields of law in which the executive government retains decision-making powers that are not dependent upon any statutory authority but nevertheless have consequences on the private rights or legitimate expectations of other persons which would render the decision subject to judicial review if the power of the decision maker to make them were statutory in origin ... I see no reason why simply because a decision-making power is derived from a common law and not a statutory source it should for that reason only be immune from judicial review' (at 409–410 and at 950 per Lord Diplock). Lord Roskill thought that the right of challenge was not unqualified. 'It must, I think, depend on the subject matter of the prerogative power which is exercised. Many examples were given during the argument of prerogative powers which as at present advised I do not think could properly be made the subject of judicial review. Prerogative powers such as those relating to the making of treaties, the defence of the realm, the prerogative of mercy, the grant of honours, the dissolution of Parliament and the appointment of ministers as well as others are not, I think, susceptible to judicial review because their nature and subject matter are such as not to be amenable to the judicial process' (at 418 and at 956 per Lord Roskill).

    Examples of successful challenges to the exercise of powers conferred by royal prerogative include *R v Secretary of State for the Home Department, ex p Ruddock* [1987] 2 All ER 518, [1987] 1 WLR 1482 (the court acknowledged jurisdiction to examine the issue of a warrant to intercept telephones); *R v Secretary of State for Foreign and Commonwealth Affairs, ex p Everett* [1989] QB 811, [1989] 1 All ER 655, CA (refusal of a passport); *R v Secretary of State for the Home Department, ex p Bentley* [1994] QB 349, [1993] 4 All ER 442, DC (mercy: refusal of a posthumous free pardon); *A-G of Trinidad and Tobago v Phillip* [1995] 1 AC 396, [1995] 1 All ER 93, PC. As to pardons and reprieves see paras 823–830 post. See also *R v Secretary of State for the Home Department, ex p RP and TG* [1994] COD 507, CA (refusal by Criminal Injuries Compensation Board to make an award for an offence of sexual abuse by a parent of a child committed before 1979, when compensation for offences committed 'under the same roof' was not recoverable); *R v Secretary of State for the Home Department, ex p Fire Brigades Union* [1995] 2 AC 513, [1995] 2 All ER 244, HL (refusal of Secretary of State to bring statutory provisions into force). The exercise of the prerogative of mercy under the Constitution of the Bahamas arts 90, 92 in death sentence cases was not amenable to judicial review: *Reckley v Minister of Public Safety and Immigration (No 2)* [1996] 1 AC 527, [1996] 1 All ER 562, PC; following *De Freitas v Benny* [1976] AC 239, [1975] 3 WLR 388, PC.

## (vi)  The Executive's Position in Litigation

**381. Government departments.** Government departments are the agents of the executive, and their acts bind the Crown[1]. Under the Crown Proceedings Act 1947[2], actions for which a remedy is sought against the Crown must normally be instituted against the appropriate authorised government department, or if none is appropriate or there is reasonable doubt as to the identity of the appropriate department, against the Attorney General[3]. In some cases, however, where government officials or departments of state have been invested with the attributes of a corporation, it seems that apart from the Crown Proceedings Act 1947[4] they might be sued in contract in their corporate capacity as principals, though not expressly made liable[5]; but since 1947 this liability has been of little practical importance[6].

Exceptionally, certain government officials or departments, even though not incorporated, have by statute been made capable of suing and being sued[7]. In general, government departments are in the same position as other defendants as regards the period within which proceedings against them must be begun[8].

1  See *A-G v Lindegren* (1819) 6 Price 287. For the special position of the corporations established for nationalised industries see CORPORATIONS.

2  By virtue of the Crown Proceedings Act 1947 the Crown may be liable for the act, eg the tort, of a Crown servant in the course of his official duties, although, it seems, the rule that a superior Crown servant is not personally liable for the acts of his subordinates unless such acts were specifically authorised by the superior is not altered. From the report of *The Truculent* [1952] P 1 at 7, [1951] 2 All ER 968 at 970, it appears that the Admiralty accepted liability for actions by personal representatives of persons killed in a collision involving one of Her Majesty's submarines, and from the same case at [1952] P 1 at 22, [1951] 2 All ER 968 at 981, it appears that a fault existing with the privity of the head of a government department is the fault of the department itself. See CROWN PROCEEDINGS.

3  See the Crown Proceedings Act 1947 s 17(3). The Minister for the Civil Service (as to whom see para 427 post) is required to publish a list of authorised government departments for the purposes of the Act. 'Some of the authorised departments are in fact the description of the official names of individuals or collections of individuals who head the departments': *Re M* [1994] 1 AC 377 at 411, sub nom *M v Home Office* [1993] 3 All ER 537 at 554, HL, per Lord Woolf. See CROWN PROCEEDINGS.

4  See generally CROWN PROCEEDINGS. As to the principle that a corporation may sue see CORPORATIONS.

5  *Re Wood's Estate, ex p Works and Buildings Comrs* (1886) 31 ChD 607 at 621, CA, per Lindley LJ; *Graham v Public Works Comrs* [1901] 2 KB 781 at 788, 790, 791, DC; *Thorn v Public Works Comrs* (1863) 32 Beav 490; *Hawley v Steele* (1877) 6 ChD 521.

6  For a controversy on the point, perhaps academic, whether this liability of government departments has survived the enactment of the Crown Proceedings Act 1947 see Glanville Williams *Crown Proceedings* 6–8; Street *Government Liability* 93–94.

7  A number of such powers were repealed by the Crown Proceedings Act 1947 s 39 (repealed), Sch 2 (repealed), and no such power now exists in the case of any authorised government department within the meaning of s 17 (as amended): see CROWN PROCEEDINGS. By virtue of s 23(3) (as amended), the power continues to exist in the case of inter alios, the Public Trustee (see TRUSTS), the Charity Commissioners (see CHARITIES), and the Registrar of the Land Registry (see LAND REGISTRATION). See also the Administration of Estates Act 1925 s 30(1). As to the construction of such powers see *Minster of Supply v British Thomson-Houston Co Ltd* [1943] KB 478, [1943] 1 All ER 615, CA, overruling

*Rowland v Air Council* (1923) 39 TLR 228 (on appeal on another point (1923) 39 TLR 455, CA); adopted and explained in *The Brabo* [1949] AC 326 at 346, [1949] 1 All ER 294 at 303, HL. The statute which enables the Crown servant to be sued may still permit him to set up privileges or immunities of the Crown, so far as they remain effective since the Crown Proceedings Act 1947.

8    See the Law Reform (Limitation of Actions, &c) Act 1954 s 1 (repealed), which repealed enactments conferring a privileged position on public authorities and persons acting under statutory powers. See also LIMITATION OF ACTIONS.

**382. Civil proceedings against the Crown.** Proceedings by way of petition of right have been abolished in relation to the Crown in respect of any alleged liability in respect of Her Majesty's government in the United Kingdom[1], and are replaced by a right of action in all cases in which a petition of right formerly lay[2]. Certain special proceedings authorised by statute against particular government departments were similarly replaced[3].

The Crown is protected from suit for liability arising otherwise than in respect of Her Majesty's government in the United Kingdom[4]. In general[5], the Crown is subject to liability in tort in respect of Her Majesty's government in the United Kingdom to the same extent as a private individual of full age and capacity for (1) torts committed by the Crown's servants or agents[6]; (2) any breach of the common law duties of an employer to his servants or agents[7]; (3) any breach of the common law duties affecting the ownership, occupation, possession or control of property[8]; and (4) any failure to comply with a statutory duty binding both upon the Crown[9] and upon persons other than the Crown and its officers[10]. In addition the Crown is liable in respect of torts committed by any of its officers in the performance or purported performance of functions conferred upon him in his official capacity as if those functions had been imposed solely by instructions from the Crown[11].

1    See the Crown Proceedings Act 1947 s 40(2). For a refusal to authorise the issue of a writ outside the jurisdiction against a corporation which was held, on evidence, to be the alter ego of the New Brunswick government, and therefore entitled to Crown immunity, see *Mellenger v New Brunswick Development Corpn* [1971] 2 All ER 593, [1971] 1 WLR 604, CA.

2    Crown Proceedings Act 1947 ss 1, 40(2)(b). As to the procedure under that Act see generally CROWN PROCEEDINGS. This provision does not revive a cause of action which, against a defendant other than the Crown, would be statute-barred: *Benson v Home Office* [1949] 1 All ER 48. It appears that in a case falling outside the Crown Proceedings Act 1947 s 40(2)(b), a petition of right still lies (but would have to be in the form used prior to the Petitions of Right Act 1860 (repealed)): see *Franklin v A-G* [1974 QB 185, [1973] 1 All ER 879, where it was held that a petition of right still lay under the Colonial Stock Act 1877 s 20 (as originally enacted). See also *Franklin v R (No 2)* [1974] QB 205 at 212, [1973] 3 All ER 861 at 869, CA; *Barclays Bank Ltd v R* [1974] QB 823, [1974] 1 All ER 305.

3    See the Crown Proceedings Act 1947 s 1. However, mandamus will lie, in a proper case, against a government department: *Padfield v Minister of Agriculture, Fisheries and Food* [1968] AC 997 at 1016, [1968] 1 All ER 694, HL; *R v Customs and Excise Comrs, ex p Cooke v Stevenson* [1970] 1 All ER 1068, [1970] 1 WLR 450, DC. See also *Re M* [1994] 1 AC 377, sub nom *M v Home Office* [1993] 3 All ER 537, HL, in which it was held that there is jurisdiction under the Supreme Court Act 1981 s 31 to make coercive orders, such as injunctions, against ministers of the Crown acting in their official capacity.

4    See the Crown Proceedings Act 1947 ss 2 (as amended), 40(2)(b).

5    For the limitations on proceedings against the Crown see para 383 post.

6    Crown Proceedings Act 1947 s 2(1)(a). 'Agent' includes an independent contractor: s 38(2). However, the Crown is not subject to any greater liabilities in respect of the acts or omissions of an independent contractor than if it were a private person: s 40(2)(d).

7    Ibid s 2(1)(b).

8    Ibid s 2(1)(c).

9    As to what statutes are binding upon the Crown see note 10 infra; and STATUTES.

10   See the Crown Proceedings Act 1947 s 2(2). 'Officer' includes any servant and any minister of the Crown: s 38(2). The Occupiers' Liability Act 1957 binds the Crown, but only to the extent that it is already bound by the Crown Proceedings Act 1947: Occupiers Liability Act 1957 s 6. Duties under ss 2, 3 are treated as statutory duties for the purpose of Crown liability: s 6. The Defective Premises Act 1972 also binds the Crown, but only to the extent that it is bound by the Crown Proceedings Act 1947: Defective Premises Act 1972 s 5. The Highways Act 1980 s 343(1), Sch 23 para 8, which relates

to civil liability for the non-repair of highways and bridges maintainable at the public expense, also binds the Crown: s 58(3).

11 See the Crown Proceedings Act 1947 s 2(2). As to the liability of authorities other than the Crown in analogous circumstances see ADMINISTRATIVE LAW vol 1(1) (Reissue) para 199.

**383. Limitations on proceedings against the Crown.** The provisions of the Crown Proceedings Act 1947 enabling civil proceedings to be taken against the Crown[1] are, however, subject to certain express limitations. Nothing in Part I of that Act[2] extinguishes or abridges any powers or authorities which, if the Act had not been passed, would have been exercisable by virtue of the prerogative of the Crown, or any powers or authorities conferred on the Crown by any statute, and, in particular, nothing in Part I extinguishes or abridges any powers or authorities exercisable by the Crown, whether in time of peace or of war, for the purpose of the defence of the realm or of training or maintaining the efficiency of any of the armed forces of the Crown[3].

No proceedings lie against the Crown for torts committed by servants or agents in respect of an act or omission of a Crown servant or agent unless that act or omission would found an action in tort against him[4], and no proceedings lie under any of these provisions in respect of anything done or omitted by a person in the discharge of judicial responsibilities[5], or in respect of any act, neglect or default of any officer of the Crown, unless appointed directly or indirectly by the Crown and paid wholly out of public funds[6]. Enactments negativing or limiting liability in tort of a government department or officer of the Crown apply in favour of the Crown[7].

The restrictions on proceedings against the Crown in tort in respect of death or personal injury caused to or by a member of the armed forces of the Crown[8] have been suspended[9]. Members of the armed forces, or where appropriate, their dependants, may now sue fellow members for damages for injury or death arising out of their service. Statutory limitations on the liabilities of shipowners are extended with modifications to the Crown in respect of Her Majesty's ships[10], and similar limitations on the liability of owners of docks and canals and of harbour or conservancy authorities are extended to the Crown in its capacity as such an owner or authority[11].

No liability in tort can attach to the Crown in respect of property vesting in the Crown involuntarily by operation of law[12] until the Crown or some person acting on its behalf has taken possession or control or entered into occupation of the property[13].

If any servant or agent of the Crown infringes any plant breeder's rights[14] or makes himself liable to civil proceedings[15] and the infringement or wrong is committed with the authority of the Crown, civil proceedings in respect of the infringement or wrong lie against the Crown[16]. Otherwise no proceedings lie against the Crown in respect of the infringement of plant breeders' rights or of any such injury[17].

Civil proceedings lie against the Crown for an infringement committed by a servant or agent of the Crown, with the authority of the Crown of (1) a patent; (2) a registered trade mark; (3) the right in a registered design; (4) design right; or (5) copyright. Otherwise no proceedings lie against the Crown by virtue of the Crown Proceedings Act 1947 in respect of an infringement of any of those rights[18].

1 See para 382 ante.
2 Ie the Crown Proceedings Act 1947 Pt I (ss 1–12).
3 Ibid s 11(1). A certificate of a Secretary of State to the effect that an act or omission was done under such prerogative powers is conclusive in any proceedings: s 11(2) (amended by the Defence (Transfer of Functions) (No 1) Order 1964, SI 1964/488, art 2, Sch 1, Pt II). It is difficult to see in what way the Crown Proceedings Act 1947 could be thought to extinguish or abridge those powers, and the precise operation of this provision is therefore obscure.
4 Crown Proceedings Act 1947 s 2(1) proviso. As to the operation of continuing limitations on the Crown's liablity in tort see *Mutasa v A-G* [1980] QB 114, [1979] 3 All ER 257 (the Crown has no legal

duty to protect a subject from unlawful arrest and imprisonment). See also *Trawnik v Lennox* [1985] 2 All ER 368, [1985] 1 WLR 544, CA (action against a government department concerning a threatened tort by Crown servants was precluded under s 40(2)(b), and there was no right at common law to sue the Attorney General for a declaration). But cf *Maharaj v A-G of Trinidad and Tobago (No 2)* [1979] AC 385, [1978] 2 All ER 670, PC (where there was a written constitution and a bill of rights which authorised the court to inquire whether the procedure under which the plaintiff had been convicted for contempt contravened the rights to which he was entitled under the constitution).

5　Crown Proceeedings Act 1947 s 2(5).

6　Ibid s 2(6) (amended by the Statute Law (Repeals) Act 1981). It is sufficient for this purpose if the person holds an office certified by the Treasury as being normally so paid; the public funds concerned are the Consolidated Fund of the United Kingdom, money provided by Parliament, and any other fund certified for the purpose: Crown Proceedings Act 1947 s 2(6). As to the Consolidated Fund see para 711 et seq post.

7　Ibid s 2(4).

8　See ibid s 10 (as amended and repealed). As to armed forces see paras 883–890 post; and ROYAL FORCES.

9　This has now been put into suspense by the Crown Proceedings (Armed Forces) Act 1987 s 1 except in relation to anything suffered by a person in consequence of an act or omission before the date on which the Act was passed (ie 15 May 1987). The Crown Proceedings Act s 10 (as amended and repealed) can be revived if it appears to the Secretary of State necessary or expedient to do so, for example, by reason of the imminent national danger or for warlike operations outside the United Kingdom: see the Crown Proceedings (Armed Forces) Act 1987 s 2.

10　See the Merchant Shipping Act 1995 ss 185(3), 186(4), 192(1); and SHIPPING. As to salvage claims against the Crown see the Merchant Shipping Act 1995 s 230(1), (2); and ADMIRALTY vol 1(1) (Reissue) para 327.

11　See ibid ss 191, 192(1); and SHIPPING.

12　Eg bona vacantia, unclaimed wrecks and treasure trove (as to these see further CROWN LANDS AND PRIVILEGES).

13　See the Crown Proceedings Act 1947 s 40(4).

14　As to plant breeders' rights see AGRICULTURE vol 1(2) (Reissue) para 868 et seq.

15　Ie under the Plant Varieties and Seeds Act 1964 s 5 (as amended): see AGRICULTURE vol 1(2) (Reissue) para 882.

16　See ibid s 14(1).

17　See ibid s 14(2). Section 14 has effect as if contained in the Crown Proceedings Act 1947 Pt I: Plant Varieties and Seeds Act 1964 s 14(3). Here again it is difficult to see why the contents of this section are not already covered by the Crown Proceedings Act 1947.

18　Ibid s 3(1) (substituted by the Copyright, Design and Patents Act 1988 s 303(1), Sch 7 para 4(1); and amended by the Trade Marks Act 1994 s 106(2), Sch 5); and see COPYRIGHT; PATENTS; TRADE MARKS.

**384. Statutes.** The Crown is not bound by statute unless the contrary is expressly stated[1], or unless there is a necessary implication to be drawn from the provisions of the Act that the Crown was intended to be bound[2], or there can somehow be gathered from the terms of the relevant Act an intention to that effect[3]. It is by the operation of this rule that Crown property is exempt from local rates, taxation and public health law. The Crown's exemption may be expressly reserved[4]. If repugnant to the body of the Act, a general saving provision will not, it seems, be sufficient to preserve the Crown's rights[5]; but this doctrine has been doubted[6] and the question must, it seems, be governed by the particular circumstances and the extent of the repugnancy.

Though not bound, the Crown may take advantage of statutes[7] unless expressly or impliedly prohibited from doing so[8]. Byelaws made under statutory powers do not bind the Crown, unless expressly or impliedly authorised to do so[9].

The word 'person' in an Act of Parliament is in its ordinary meaning appropriate to include the Crown[10].

1　An example of a provision for the Crown to be bound occurs in the Food Safety Act 1990 s 54(1): 'Subject to the provisions of this section, the provisions of this Act and of regulations and orders made under it shall bind the Crown'. As to statutes generally see STATUTES.

2　*Thomas v Pritchard* [1903] 1 KB 209, DC; *Cooper v Hawkins* [1904] 2 KB 164, DC; and see STATUTES. The test of 'necessary implication' should be viewed strictly, so that in the absence of express words the Crown may be bound by a statute only if the purpose of the statute would be 'wholly frustrated' if the Crown were not bound: *Bombay Province v Bombay Municipal Corpn* [1947] AC 58, PC, per du Parcq LJ at 63; *Madras Electric Supply Corpn Ltd v Boarland (Inspector of Taxes)* [1955] AC 667, [1955] 1 All

ER 753, HL. The exemption belongs also to the Crown in right of the Duchy of Lancaster: *A-G of Duchy of Lancaster v Moresby* [1919] WN 69. In particular, the Crown is not normally bound by a statute imposing a duty or tax: see CROWN LANDS AND PRIVILEGES. From 1937 until 1993 the monarch paid no personal taxes. The Queen, after discussions between the Treasury, the Inland Revenue and the royal household, entered an agreement, with effect from 6 April 1993, which provides that she pay income tax on all her personal income whether from investments or other sources; on that part of the privy purse income which is used for private purposes; she will pay tax on any realised capital gains on her private investments and on the private proportion of assets in the privy purse; and inheritance tax only on bequests or gifts by the monarch other than transfers of assets from one monarch to his or her successor. The arrangements are to be administered by the Inland Revenue. Although these arrangements are voluntary, the Queen and the Prince of Wales intend them to continue indefinitely: see 218 HC Official Report (6th series), 11 February 1993, col 1113. As to the Treasury see paras 512–517 post.

As regards certain statutes, any exemption, immunity or privilege subsisting in favour of the Crown by virtue of this rule of law extends to the service authorities and members of visiting forces and to international headquarters and defence organisations and their members: see the Visiting Forces and International Headquarters (Application of Law) Order 1965, SI 1965/1536, art 12(1); and ROYAL FORCES. For examples of some Acts which bind the Crown see para 382 note 10 ante. The Crown's immunity is being eroded piecemeal by Parliament; its former immunity in respect of National Health Service authorities and premises for the purposes of food legislation and health and safety legislation has been removed: see the National Health Service and Community Care Act 1990 s 60. National Health Service authorities are immune from income and corporation tax: see Income and Corporation Taxes Act 1988 s 519A (as added and amended); and NATIONAL HEALTH. The Road Traffic Regulation Act 1984 s 130 (as amended), the Road Traffic Act 1988 s 183 (as amended) and the Road Traffic Offenders Act 1988 s 92 (as amended) concerning road traffic offences, remove Crown immunity in respect of vehicles and persons in the public service of the Crown. An order for restitution may be made under the Theft Act 1968 s 28 (as amended) in respect of money owed by the Crown: Theft Act 1968 s 28(7) (added by the Criminal Justice Act 1988 s 163). The Parliamentary Corporate Bodies (Crown Immunities etc) Order 1992, SI 1992/1732, puts the Corporate Officer of the House of Lords and the Corporate Officer of the House of Commons in a corresponding position to that of the Crown for the purposes of the application to them of specified legislation: see further PARLIAMENT.

3  See *Lord Advocate v Dumbarton District Council* [1990] 2 AC 580 at 604, [1990] 1 All ER 1 at 18, HL; cf *Bombay Province v Bombay Municipal Corpn* [1947] AC 58, PC; *Madras Electric Supply Corpn Ltd v Boarland (Inspector of Taxes)* [1955] AC 667, [1955] 1 All ER 753, HL.

4  See eg the Crown Proceedings Act 1947 s 40(2)(f); and the Local Government Act 1972 s 271(4).

5  *Yarmouth Corpn v Simmons* (1878) 10 ChD 518 at 528. A saving clause in a statute is generally void if repugnant to the body of the Act: *Alton Woods' Case, A-G v Bushopp* (1600) 1 Co Rep 40b. See also *A-G v Great Eastern Rly Co* (1873) LR 6 HL 367. Quaere whether a general clause saving the Crown's rights refers only to rights of property or in the nature of property: *Yarmouth Corpn v Simmons* supra at 528 per Fry J. See *Lord Advocate v Dumbarton District Council* [1990] 2 AC 580, HL, where the legal basis of Crown immunity was considered. See generally STATUTES vol 44(1) (Reissue) paras 1262, 1401.

6  *Simpson v Scales* (1801) 2 Bos & P 496 at 499, per Rooke J.

7  *Willion v Berkley* (1561) 1 Plowd 223 at 243. See also *Town Investments Ltd v Department of the Environment* [1978] AC 359, [1977] 1 All ER 813, HL; Crown Proceedings Act 1947 s 31(1); and STATUTES. This privilege has, it seems, been applied to visiting forces and to international headquarters and defence organisations: see the Visiting Forces and International Headquarters (Application of Law) Order 1965 art 12(1).

8  *R v Cruise* (1852) 2 I Ch R 65; and see STATUTES.

9  *Gorton Local Board v Prison Comrs* (1887) [1904] 2 KB 165n.

10  *Boarland (Inspector of Taxes) v Madras Electric Supply Corpn* [1953] 2 All ER 467 at 472, [1953] 1 WLR 920 at 928 per Upjohn J; affd [1954] 1 All ER 52, [1954] 1 WLR 87, CA.

**385. Estoppel.** The Crown is not bound by fictions of law[1]. It may possibly take advantage of estoppel by deed[2], though not, it seems, where the estoppel arises through its own letters patent[3].

1  *Anon* (1613) Jenk 286. It has been said that the Crown is not bound by estoppels by deed: see *Coke's Case* (1623) Godb 289 at 299. This applies, it is said, even to estoppels affecting the party through whom the Crown claims: Staundford Prerogativa Regis 64a; *Coke's Case* supra at 291 (release of debt by King's debtor). But all that the authorities seem to show is that if the monarch is deceived in his grant, the grant is void: see the article by F E Farrer in 49 LQR 511; Street *Governmental Liability* 156; and para 864 post.

'I know of no authority for the proposition as applied to estoppel in pais': *A-G to Prince of Wales v Collom* [1916] 2 KB 193 at 204 per Atkin J. Certainly the Crown is bound by equitable estoppel: *A-G to Prince of Wales v Collom* supra; *A-G for Trinidad and Tobago v Bourne* [1895] AC 83, PC; *Plimmer v Wellington Corpn* (1884) 9 App Cas 699, PC. For a statement questioning the principle that estoppel cannot bind the Crown to the detriment of the individual see the remarks of Denning J in *Robertson v Minister of Pensions* [1949] 1 KB 227 at 231; and cf *Western Fish Products Ltd v Penwith District Council* [1981] 2 All ER 204, 77 LGR 185, CA (attempted raising of an estoppel to prevent a statutory body exercising its statutory discretion or performing its statutory duty). See also Fazal 'Reliability of Official Acts and Advice' [1972] Public Law 43. The doctrine of legitimate expectation has mitigated the severity of the rule that estoppel cannot bind the Crown: see generally Wade and Bradley *Constitutional and Administrative Law* (11th Edn, 1993) pp 700–703; de Smith and Brazier *Constitutional and Administrative Law* (7th Edn, 1994) pp 438–440. There is some doubt whether the immunity of the Crown extends to the Duke of Cornwall: *A-G to Prince of Wales v Collom* supra at 204.

2    Co Litt 352a, b.

3    Thus a subject was not estopped, it has been said, if he took a lease of his own land rendering rent by letters patent from the King, because the King was not estopped by his letters patent, and any estoppel ought to be of both parties (see Vin Abr, Estoppel, N 3); but where the King granted land by letters patent to a person who was in fact seised by inheritance, the latter was, it seems, estopped from claiming any other right than by the letters patent, if the right by inheritance was not recited in them (Vin Abr, Estoppel, N 16).

**386.   Receipts.** It is said that the Crown is not bound to offer an acquittance or receipt, but it is said that in discharging a debt the subject ought himself to bring an acquittance and demand it of the monarch[1].

1    Vin Abr, Prerogative, T (2) 13; Bro Abr, Prerogative, pl 101; 2 Co Inst 281.

**387.   Crown contracts for service and for payments.** Since 1968 there have been substantial changes in the structure and organisation of the Civil Service[1]. Nevertheless, it remains the technical position that in the absence of special statutory provisions[2], all contracts of service under the Crown are terminable without notice on the part of the Crown[3]. This is so even if there is an express term to the contrary in the contract[4], for the Crown cannot deprive itself of the power of dismissing a servant at will, and that power cannot be taken away by any contractual arrangement made by an executive officer or department of state[5]. It has even been held that this rule is only part of the wider principle that the Crown cannot by contract fetter its future executive action[6]. If a civil servant is unfairly dismissed, he has recourse to an industrial tribunal for compensation, reinstatement or re-engagement[7].

The Race Relations Act 1976 binds the Crown, but does not invalidate any rules, whenever made, restricting employment in the service of the Crown to persons of particular birth, citizenship, nationality, descent or residence; nor does it render unlawful the publication, display or implementation of any such rules[8]. The Crown is also bound by the Employer's Liability (Defective Equipment) Act 1969[9].

It seems, however, that the Crown can contract unconditionally to make a money payment and can then be sued for non-payment[10].

1    As to the Civil Service generally see paras 549–564 post.

2    Eg the Supreme Court Act 1981 s 11(3).

3    See para 902 post.

4    *Dunn v R* [1896] 1 QB 116, CA. See also *Riordan v War Office* [1959] 3 All ER 552, [1959] 1 WLR 1046; on appeal [1960] 3 All ER 774n, [1961] 1 WLR 210, CA (Army Council Regulations providing for a period of notice did not exclude Crown's right of summary dismissal). See *A-G for Guyana v Nobrega* [1969] 3 All ER 1604, PC (no ruling on claim that the Crown could not unilaterally vary the terms of employment, the court finding that the employment under the original contract had actually been terminated and a new contract substituted for it).

5    *Terrell v Secretary of State for the Colonies* [1953] 2 QB 482 at 499, [1953] 2 All ER 490 at 496 per Lord Goddard CJ.

6   *Rederiaktiebolaget Amphitrite v R* [1921] 3 KB 500; distinguished and criticised by Denning J in
    *Robertson v Minister of Pensions* [1949] 1 KB 227 at 231, [1948] 2 All ER 767 at 770, but his judgment
    was itself criticised in *Howell v Falmouth Boat Construction Ltd* [1951] AC 837 at 845, [1951] 2 All
    ER 278 at 280, HL. Certainly a court will not imply a term in a contract fettering the Crown's future
    executive action: *Board of Trade v Temperley SS Co Ltd* (1926) 26 Ll L Rep 76; affd (1927) 27 Ll L Rep
    230, CA; *Crown Lands Comrs v Page* [1960] 2 QB 274 at 292, 293, [1960] 2 All ER 726 at 735–736,
    CA, per Devlin LJ. See also articles by Mitchell 'Limitations on the Contractual Liabilities of Public
    Authorities' (1950) 13 Mod LR 318, 455. As regards a power of a Crown employee to bind the Crown
    see para 388 post.
7   See the Employment Protection (Consolidation) Act 1978 s 138 (as amended); para 562 post; and
    EMPLOYMENT.
8   See the Race Relations Act 1976 ss 75(1), (5), 75A (as added). There is also exception under European
    Community law, so that freedom of movement of workers does not extend to employment in the public
    service: see EC Treaty art 48(4) (see paras 23–25 ante); and EUROPEAN COMMUNITIES.
9   See the Employers' Liability (Defective Equipment) Act 1969 s 1(4); and EMPLOYMENT.
10  This was the view in *New South Wales v Bardolph* (1934) 52 CLR 455, Aust HC, disapproving the dictum
    of Shee J in *Churchward v R* (1865) LR 1 QB 173 at 209, but approving the contrary dictum of
    Cockburn CJ in that case at 200. Evatt J stated in *New South Wales v Bardolph* supra at 474–475, what in
    his opinion were the requirements for a valid Crown promise to pay money. The decisions in *Commercial
    Cable Co v Government of Newfoundland* [1916] 2 AC 610, PC; *Mackay v A-G for British Columbia* [1922]
    1 AC 457, PC; *A-G v Great Southern and Western Rly Co of Ireland* [1925] AC 754, HL, seem too
    inconclusive to set against the considered opinion of a powerful court in *New South Wales v Bardolph*
    supra; *New South Wales v Bardolph* was cited and followed in *Quintessence Co-ordinators v Governmnent of
    the Republic of Transkei* 1993 (3) SA 184. See also *Australian Woollen Mills Ltd v Commonwealth of Australia*
    [1955] 3 All ER 711, [1956] 1 WLR 11, PC.
        The procedure for obtaining satisfaction of a court order against the Crown for the payment of
    money is governed by the Crown Proceedings Act 1947 s 25(3). See also s 37(1), which, in providing
    that judgment against the Crown is to he satisfied out of money provided by Parliament, is a warning
    that payment must be covered by some sort of appropriation. See also para 230 ante. See further
    CROWN PROCEEDINGS.
        For problems related to alleged overcharging under government contracts see TRADE, INDUSTRY AND
    INDUSTRIAL RELATIONS.

**388. The liability of Crown servants.** At common law servants of the Crown[1]
cannot be made personally liable upon contracts entered into by them in their official
capacity[2], unless the intention to render themselves personally liable appears from the
particular circumstances of the case[3], for they are presumed to contract as agents for the
Crown[4]. Moreover, an action cannot be brought against them in their representative
capacity on a contract[5] or in respect of torts[6], or, it seems, crimes alleged to have been
committed by them. They may, however, be sued and made personally liable for tortious
or criminal acts committed by them in their official capacity[7], without showing malice or
want of probable cause[8], unless that is of the essence of the tort or crime. State necessity[9]
or the orders of the Crown[10] or of a superior officer[11] cannot be pleaded in defence,
except as an act of state in an action by a non-resident alien[12]. In these respects they are
in exactly the same position as any employee of any employer; but Crown servants cannot
be made liable for the wrongful acts of their subordinates, unless the acts can be proved
to have been previously authorised or subsequently ratified by them, so that they are their
own acts[13], for they and their subordinates are not in the position of employer and
employee but are fellow servants of the Crown[14].

If a Crown servant, being in a position which enables him to earn money by use
of his position in the Crown's service, earns money by misuse of that position, the
Crown is entitled to the money thereby earned, even if the acts by which it was earned
were criminal[15].

Where a person holds any office or employment under the Crown on terms which
do not constitute a contract of employment between him and the Crown, those terms
are nevertheless deemed to constitute such a contract for the purposes of: (1) the law
relating to the liability in tort of any person who commits an act which (a) induces

another person to break any contract, interferes with the performance of a contract or induces another person to interfere with its performance, or (b) consists in a threat that a contract will be broken or its performance interfered with, or that any person will be induced to break a contract or to interfere with its performance; and (2) the Trade Union and Labour Relations (Consolidation) Act 1992[16] or any other Act which refers (whether in relation to contracts generally or only in relation to contracts of employment) to any such Act[17].

Judges are exempt from liability for all acts done in the exercise of their jurisdiction[18].

1    As to Crown immunity generally see CROWN PROCEEDINGS. For the purposes of Crown immunity 'Crown servants' should be taken to include all those officers of state and their subordinates who now perform, pursuant to statutory authority, such functions of public government as were formerly the peculiar prerogatives of the Crown (eg the making of war or peace); the immunity extends to these persons only so long as they are acting in the capacity described: *Bank voor Handel en Scheepvaart NV v Administrator of Hungarian Property* [1954] AC 584 at 627, [1954] 1 All ER 969 at 989, HL, per Lord Tucker (a decision on immunity from income tax).

    Crown immunity extends to persons who are the owners or occupiers of property exclusively used for the purposes of government, but the immunity only protects them in respect of liability or disability arising in respect of the ownership or occupation of that property: *Bank voor Handel en Scheepvaart NV v Administrator of Hungarian Property* supra. These are cases of the class called *in consimili casu*. See de Smith and Brazier *Constitutional and Administrative Law* (7th Edn, 1994) pp 193–195.

    As to corporations and Crown status see also CORPORATIONS. As to the position of police officers see *A-G for New South Wales v Perpetual Trustee Co Ltd* [1955] AC 457, [1955] 1 All ER 846, PC; *Fisher v Oldham Corpn* [1930] 2 KB 364; *Lewis v Cattle* [1938] 2 KB 454, [1938] 2 All ER 368, DC; *Coomber (Surveyor of Taxes) v Berkshire Justices* (1883) 9 App Cas 61, HL; and see also *Enever v R* (1906) 3 CLR 969, Aust HC. See also de Smith and Brazier *Constitutional and Administrative Law* (7th Edn, 1994) p 418; and Marshall and Loveday 'The Police: Independence and Accountability' in Jowell and Oliver (eds) *The Changing Constitution* (3rd Edn, 1994).

2    *Macbeath v Haldimand* (1786) 1 Term Rep 172. The principle was followed in *Gidley v Lord Palmerston* (1822) 3 Brod & Bing 275; and in *Palmer v Hutchinson* (1881) 6 App Cas 619, PC. A Secretary of State is like any other government official: see *O'Grady v Cardwell* (1872) 20 WR 342. See also *Felkin v Lord Herbert* (1861) 30 LJCh 798. As to the office of Secretary of State see para 355 et seq ante.

3    *Samuel Bros Ltd v Whetherly* [1907] 1 KB 709 at 715; affd [1908] 1 KB 184, CA (goods ordered on behalf of the commanding officer of a volunteer corps for the use of the corps); *National Bank of Scotland Ltd v Shaw* 1913 SC 133.

4    In *Macbeath v Haldimand* (1786) 1 Term Rep 172, their immunity was put on the ground of public policy; sed quaere. This reasoning was followed in *Dunn v MacDonald* [1897] 1 QB 555, CA, where it was held that the liability of an ordinary agent for breach of warranty of authority does not apply to public servants as agents of the Crown (see at 557 per Chitty LJ); see also *Graham v Stamper* (1692) 2 Vern 147 (goods sold and delivered to the Master of the Buckhounds)). *Dunn v MacDonald* supra, arose out of a contract of service with the Crown; it is uncertain whether, having regard to the peculiarities of such contracts, there was any breach of warranty of authority.

    As agents of the Crown, Crown servants cannot be compelled by any third party to do their duty to the Crown, even if that duty is to pay money to the third party: *Gidley v Lord Palmerston* (1822) 3 Brod & Bing 275; *R v Treasury Lords Comrs* (1872) LR 7 QB 387. A public officer entrusted by the Crown with money for distribution amongst a certain class of persons under the control of the Crown cannot be sued as trustee for the persons interested: *Kinloch v Secretary of State for India* (1882) 7 App Cas 619, HL; *Grenville-Murray v Earl of Clarendon* (1869) LR 9 Eq 11. It seems that it is otherwise where a public officer is entrusted with money issued by government for the use of an individual (*Priddy v Rose* (1817) 3 Mer 86 at 102 per Grant MR; but see *Gidley v Lord Palmerston* supra); or where the relation of trustee and beneficiary exists (*Penn v Lord Baltimore* (1750) 1 Ves Sen 444 at 453 per Lord Hardwicke LC). The use of the term 'trust' in relation to the Crown does not necessarily create a true trust but may create merely a governmental obligation which is not enforceable in the courts. Whether the latter is created in a given case depends on all the circumstances, including whether or not the person named as trustee was described in his personal or in his official capacity: *Tito v Waddell (No 2)* [1977] Ch 106, [1977] 3 All ER 129.

5    *Palmer v Hutchinson* (1881) 6 App Cas 619 at 623, PC. The point is perhaps academic now that actions can be brought in contract against the Crown.

6    *Raleigh v Goschen* [1898] 1 Ch 73; *Hutton v Secretary of State for War* (1926) 43 TLR 106; see the judgment of Atkin LJ in *Mackenzie-Kennedy v Air Council* [1927] 2 KB 517 at 532, CA.

7   See *Re M* [1994] 1 AC 377 at 395, sub nom *M v Home Office* [1993] 3 All ER 537 at 540, HL, per Lord
    Woolf, and at 408, 415 and 552–554, 557–558 per Lord Templeman; *Lonrho plc v Tebbit* [1992] 4 All
    ER 280, CA. In cases of tort the wrong must be brought home to the defendant, eg in an action of
    negligence it must be shown that the defendant himself owed the duty of care: see *Adams v Naylor*
    [1946] AC 543, [1946] 2 All ER 241, HL (decided before the passing of the Crown Proceedings
    Act 1947, and the enacting of the remedies thereby conferred).

8   *Brasyer v Maclean* (1875) LR 6 PC 398; *Raleigh v Goschen* [1898] 1 Ch 73. For the very different position
    of judges and justices of the peace see COURTS; MAGISTRATES. As to offences committed abroad by
    Crown servants see CRIMINAL LAW. As to nomination of individuals for the purposes of criminal
    proceedings relating to government vehicles, under what is now the Road Traffic Offenders Act 1988
    s 94, see *Barnett v French* [1981] 1 WLR 848, 72 Cr App Rep 272, DC; and ROAD TRAFFIC.

9   *Entick v Carrington* (1765) 19 State Tr 1029 at 1067. As to the enforcement of treaties see also para 802
    post. The defence of act of state cannot be set up against a subject (*Walker v Baird* [1892] AC 491, PC),
    or against a resident alien friend (*Johnstone v Pedlar* [1921] 2 AC 262, HL).

10  *R v Earl of Danby* (1685) 11 State Tr 600, HL.

11  *Keighly v Bell* (1866) 4 F & F 763 at 790, 805, NP; *R v Thomas* (1816) 1 Russell on Crime (10th Edn)
    490; and see *Hayling v Okey* (1853) 8 Exch 531, Ex Ch. But for a relaxation of the rule where soldiers
    are concerned see *R v Smith* (1900) 17 Cape of Good Hope Report 561.

12  As to acts of state see FOREIGN RELATIONS LAW.

13  *Raleigh v Goschen* [1898] 1 Ch 73.

14  *Raleigh v Goschen* [1898] 1 Ch 73; *Bainbridge v Postmaster-General* [1906] 1 KB 178, CA; *Lane v Cotton*
    (1701) 1 Ld Raym 646; *Nicholson v Mounsey and Symes* (1812) 15 East 384; *Re M* [1994] 1 AC 377 at 408,
    sub nom *M v Home Office* [1993] 3 All ER 537 at 552, HL. This rule applies only to Crown servants and
    to departments which are considered to be emanations from the Crown, and not eg to local authorities
    or to independent public service corporations: see CORPORATIONS. Where a subordinate illegally does
    an act authorised by a superior official to be done in a legal manner, the superior is not liable: *O'Brien v
    Marquis of Hartington* (1877) IR 11 CL 445. As to the inability of the authority of the Crown to afford a
    defence to an action brought for an illegal act committed by an officer of the Crown see *Feather v R* (1865)
    6 B & S 257 at 296, 122 ER 1191 at 1205; and para 14 ante.

15  *Reading v A-G* [1951] AC 507, [1951] 1 All ER 617, HL (sergeant in the army using his position to enable
    loaded lorries to pass without being inspected).

16  See the Trade Union and Labour Relations (Consolidation) Act 1992 ss 62 (as amended), 65(1)–(5), (as
    amended), 65(7) (as amended), 222, 226(4) (as amended), 273(3) and 276(2).

17  Ibid s 245. The provisions of the Trade Union and Labour Relations (Consolidation) Act 1992 (except
    ss 87(3), 184, 185 and Pt IV ch II (ss 188–198) (as amended)) have effect in relation to Crown
    employment and persons in Crown employment as in relation to other employment and other workers
    or employees: s 273(1), (2). 'Crown employment' means employment under or for the purposes of a
    government department or any officer or body exercising on behalf of the Crown functions conferred by
    an enactment: s 273(3).

18  See para 304 ante.

## 389. Contempt of court.

Coercive orders may not technically be granted against
the Crown, which may not be found to be in contempt of court. Instead, orders may
be granted against a minister or officer of the Crown acting in an official capacity, and
such a minister or officer may be found to be in contempt, either in his official capacity
or personally[1].

1   *Re M* [1994] 1 AC 377, sub nom *M v Home Office* [1993] 3 All ER 537, HL. 'The judges cannot enforce
    the law against the Crown as monarch because the Crown as monarch can do no wrong but judges
    enforce the law against the Crown as executive and against individuals who from time to time represent
    the Crown.... For the purpose of enforcing the law against all persons and institutions, including ministers
    in their official and in their personal capacity, the courts are armed with coercive powers exercisable in
    proceedings for contempt of court': see per Lord Templeman at 395, 540. For the doctrine that the
    monarch can do no wrong see para 14 text and notes 6–7 ante.

## 390. Laches and prescription.

At common law the monarch's right of action was not
barred by negligence or laches, whether on her own part or that of her officers, the
maxim being that time does not run against the monarch[1]. This position has been

modified by statute, and now the Limitation Act 1980 applies in general in actions by or against the Crown[2].

At common law liberties or franchises may be prescribed for or against the Crown[3]. The Crown is bound by those provisions of the Prescription Act 1832 in which it is named[4].

1   Bac Abr, Prerogative, E 6; Com Dig, Prerogative, D 86; Co Litt 90b, 119a; *Willion v Berkley* (1561) 1 Plowd 223 at 243; *Hales v Petit* (1562) Plowd 253 at 261; *Coke's Case* (1623) Godb 289 at 297; *R v Fay* (1878) 4 LR Ir 606, CA; *The Zoe* (1886) 11 PD 72. The maxim is *nullum tempus occurrit regi*: see CROWN LANDS AND PRIVILEGES. As to laches on the part of the Attorney General when suing at the relation of an individual see *A-G v Grand Junction Canal Co* [1909] 2 Ch 505.
2   See the Limitation Act 1980 s 37; and LIMITATION OF ACTIONS.
3   See para 869 post.
4   *Perry v Eames* [1891] 1 Ch 658, approved in *Wheaton v Maple & Co* [1893] 3 Ch 48, CA, where it was held that the Crown, not being named, is not bound by the Prescription Act 1832 s 3, as to ancient lights, though named in and therefore bound by ss 1, 2, relating to rights of common, profits à prendre, ways, use of water or watercourses or other easements.

**391. Choice of forum.** The Crown might in general choose its own forum and sue in what court it pleased, and in this respect the monarch in her private capacity has the former attributes of the Crown[1]. Special modes of redress against the subject by means of informations, inquisitions or inquests of office, extents, scire facias, quo warranto and mandamus were provided by law[2], and still remain in relation to the monarch in her private capacity so far as they are appropriate[3]. The monarch may waive these prerogative remedies and resort to the usual forms of action[4] unless they are inconsistent with the royal dignity[5].

1   4 Co Inst 17; 1 Bl Com (14th Edn) 257; *Willion v Berkley* (1561) 1 Plowd 223; Chitty *Law of the Prerogatives of the Crown* 244–245. The trial of any civil proceedings by or against the Crown in the High Court are to be held at the Royal Courts of Justice (London) unless the court, with the consent of the Crown, otherwise directs: Crown Proceedings Act 1947 s 19(2). However, this does not prejudice the right of the Crown to demand a local venue for the trial of any proceedings in which the Attorney General has waived his right to a trial at bar: s 19(3). This does not bind Her Majesty in her private capacity or affect any proceedings by the Crown otherwise than in right of Her Majesty's government in the United Kingdom: s 40(1), (2)(c). As to the procedure in actions by or against the Crown see COUNTY COURTS; CROWN PROCEEDINGS.
2   Of these remedies Latin and English informations, writs of extent and writs of scire facias were abolished by ibid s 13, Sch 1, except in relation to proceedings by or against Her Majesty in her private capacity and subject to certain other exceptions which include proceedings on the Crown side of the Queen's Bench Division and proceedings by the Crown otherwise than in right of Her Majesty's government in the United Kingdom: ss 23, 40(1), (2)(c). For the meaning of 'civil proceedings' see s 38(2). Informations in the nature of quo warranto (the writ of quo warranto having become obsolete) were abolished by the Administration of Justice (Miscellaneous Provisions) Act 1938 s 9 (repealed). As to injunctions to restrain persons from acting in offices in which they are not entitled to act see s 30. See generally CROWN PROCEEDINGS.
3   See the Crown Proceedings Act 1947 s 40(1).
4   Vin Abr, Prerogative, Q; Bro Abr, Prerogative, pl 130; 1 Roll Abr 373; Chitty *Law of the Prerogatives of the Crown* 245.
5   Eg action of ejectment, which is contrary to the legal fiction that the Crown can never be dispossessed: Bro Abr, Prerogative, pl 89; Staundford, Prerogativa Regis 56b; 1 Bl Com (14th Edn) 257.

**392. Procedure in litigation.** The procedure in the Supreme Court in actions by or against the Crown is regulated by rules of court. This procedure and the government departments which are authorised for the purposes of the Crown Proceedings Act 1947 are considered elsewhere[1].

The Crown is represented in court by the Attorney General or Solicitor General, who appears on behalf of the Crown, since in legal contemplation the 'Sovereign's Majesty is always present in all his courts, though he cannot personally distribute justice'[2].

The common law rule that neither the monarch, nor any person suing to her use, pays or receives costs[3] now survives only in relation to proceedings affecting the monarch in her private capacity[4], and in civil proceedings, including arbitrations, costs are in the discretion of the court[5].

1 See CROWN PROCEEDINGS. As to rules of court see COUNTY COURTS; COURTS; PRACTICE AND PROCEDURE.

   The Crown Proceedings Act 1947 leaves unaltered the substantive law relating to the rights of the Crown in relation to proceedings by the Crown. Thus except as otherwise expressly provided, nothing in the Act affects the law relating to prize, salvage or any criminal proceedings (s 40(2)(a)), or any right of the Crown to control or intervene in proceedings affecting any contract, property or profit s 40(2)(g)). An apparent exception is made by the Merchant Shipping Act 1995 s 230(2), which empowers the Crown to make salvage claims to the same extent as any other salvor. See further ADMIRALTY vol 1(1) (Reissue) para 328.

   As to the preservation of the common law immunity of Her Majesty's ships, aircraft or hovercraft from proceedings in rem, and the substitution for them of proceedings in personam, see the Crown Proceedings Act 1947 s 29(1), (2); Supreme Court Act 1981 s 24(2)(c); RSC Ord 77 r 18; Hovercraft (Application of Enactments) Order 1972, SI 1972/971, art 4, Sch 1 (as amended); and ADMIRALTY vol 1(1) (Reissue) para 400.

2 1 Bl Com (14th Edn) 269.

3 2 Bl Com (14th Edn) 400; *Johnson v R* [1904] AC 817 at 824, PC, per Lord Macnaghten.

4 See the Administration of Justice (Miscellaneous Provisions) Act 1933 s 7 (as amended), s 9.

5 See ibid s 7(1). 'Civil proceedings' includes proceedings by the Crown in the High Court or a county court for the recovery of fines or penalties: see s 7(2); and CROWN PROCEEDINGS. Interest runs on costs awarded to or against the Crown in the High Court unless the court orders otherwise: see the Crown Proceedings Act 1947 s 24(2).

**393. Litigation between subjects affecting the Crown.** If rights of the Crown are or may be called in question in proceedings between persons other than the Crown the Attorney General should be made a party[1]; but where this has not been done, and the Crown's title is clearly proved, the court may give judgment ex officio for the Crown[2]. The Attorney General is a proper party to proceedings which involve a question which directly concerns the Crown, such as the carrying into effect of a treaty of peace[3]. He is also often a proper party to proceedings where the interests of charity in general are in question[4].

An action in which the rights of the Crown in right of the United Kingdom are involved is defectively constituted unless the Crown is represented in that right[5], even though the Crown may be represented in right of some member of the Commonwealth, colony or state[6].

1 *Hovenden v Lord Annesley* (1805) 2 Sch & Lef 607 at 617–618; *A-G v Norstedt* (1816) 3 Price 97; *Esquimalt and Nanaimo Rly Co v Wilson* [1920] AC 358, PC. Unless the Attorney General enters a nolle prosequi, or proceeds with the suit when served, judgment will go in his absence (Bac Abr, Prerogative, E 7); but this may be doubted. For his right to demand a trial at bar see para 535 post; and CROWN PROCEEDINGS.

2 Bac Abr, Prerogative, E 7; Chitty *Law of the Prerogatives of the Crown* 244.

3 It appears that this is also the case if it merely affects a large section of the British public: *Re Chamberlain's Settlement, Chamberlain v Chamberlain* [1921] 2 Ch 533 at 548.

4 See CHARITIES vol 5(2) (Reissue) para 473 et seq.

5 Ie by the Attorney General, or some person authorised by him.

6 Eg New South Wales: *A-G for New South Wales v Williams* [1915] AC 573, PC. On principle the converse rule should apply also, but there is no authority on the point.

# (2) FORMATION, ACCOUNTABILITY AND REMUNERATION OF THE ADMINISTRATION

## (i) The Prime Minister

**394. Appointment of the Prime Minister.** Upon the dismissal or resignation of an administration[1], the monarch[2], following the recognised constitutional practice, summons to her presence the person whom she considers most fitted for the purpose, and requests him to undertake the task of nominating the members of the new administration. Upon acceptance of this commission, and kissing the monarch's hands, the person so chosen becomes known as the Prime Minister, but his retention of that post is in practice dependent, in the first place, upon his ability to form an administration[3].

Nominally the monarch is unfettered in the choice of her ministers, and may summon whom she pleases to fill the office of Prime Minister; nevertheless, owing to the dependence of the executive upon the support of the House of Commons[4], the monarch's choice[5], except in unusual cases, is in practice restricted to the person who seems most likely to have the support of a stable majority in the House of Commons, or, failing such a person, that politician who seems able to form an administration with a reasonable prospect of remaining in office[6]. This will usually be the leader of the party which commands a majority in the House of Commons[7] but if no party commands an overall majority, the party leader who is most likely to be supported by a working majority in that House may be called upon[8]. But, whether this rule is adhered to or not, it is generally conceded that, under the established usage, the ministers of the Crown are entitled to a fair trial in government, at least until it becomes clear that they are unable to obtain that support in the House of Commons which is necessary to enable them to carry on the executive government[9]. And even where it is obvious that the administration does not command the confidence of the House of Commons, it is customary for the latter to extend such support by granting supplies, or otherwise, as may be necessary to enable the executive government of the country to be carried on in a manner becoming to the dignity of the nation until the sense of the electorate can conveniently be taken upon a dissolution, or until a new administration can be formed which commands the requisite majority[10].

No stated rule exists as to the time which may elapse between the dissolution of an existing administration and the appointment of a new one. But the royal summons to the new Prime Minister is invariably made within the space of a few days[11], and any unreasonable delay on the part of the Crown is viewed unfavourably by Parliament[12].

1　As to the dismissal or resignation of an administration see para 418 post. As to the death or resignation of a Prime Minister see para 397 post.

2　As to the monarch see para 351 et seq ante.

3　Lord Granville, for example, failed to form an administration in 1859: see 12 Political History of England p 174.

4　Though nominally the Crown has the free choice of the Prime Minister (see the statement of Sir Robert Peel in 83 Official Report (3rd series), 16 February 1846, col 1004), in practice the choice is limited to the person trusted by the majority of the House of Commons. The necessity for this choice is imposed upon the Crown by Parliament's power in effect to make government impossible by cutting off supplies: see paras 415, 712 post. The House of Commons has, it is said, the right of advising the monarch as to the unfitness of the administration, or in case of urgency, but not so as to render the monarch accountable for the choice of ministers: see the statement of Lord Selkirk in 9 Official Report (1st series), 13 April 1807, col 377; and that of Mr Canning in 23 Official Report (1st series), 21 May 1812, col 267. As to addresses urging the appointment of a strong and efficient administration, or indicating the character of an administration desired by the House, see note 12 infra. As to the House of Commons see PARLIAMENT.

5　The monarch's choice is further circumscribed by the fact that all parties now elect their parliamentary leaders: Mackintosh *The British Cabinet* (3rd Edn, 1977) ch 20. See also para 352 note 2 ante. See also Bogdanor *The Monarchy and the Constitution* (1995) ch 4.

6   Brazier *Constitutional Practice* (2nd Edn, 1994) chs 2, 3; Wade and Bradley *Constitutional and Administrative Law* (11th Edn, 1993) pp 252–255; de Smith and Brazier *Constitutional and Administrative Law* (7th Edn, 1994) pp 174–177.

7   There may be cases where the person to be selected is not obvious, as where there are two or more leading members of the same party, one of whom will not work under the other, eg Lord Palmerston and Lord John Russell in 1859, when Lord Granville was selected, though on his failure to form an administration the post of Prime Minister was eventually filled by Lord Palmerston: see 12 Political History of England p 174. Likewise, in 1923, the choice of Mr Baldwin rather than Lord Curzon was not obvious. This problem is less likely to arise since parties now elect their leaders, but where the leader is elected by the whole party and not only by the parliamentary party it is possible that a leader could be elected that was not acceptable to the majority of the parliamentary party, and who might therefore be unable to command a majority in the House of Commons. See further Brazier *Constitutional Practice* (2nd Edn, 1994) ch 2; Butler *Governing without a Majority: Dilemma for Hung Parliaments in Britain* (2nd Edn, 1986).

8   When, early in 1924, Mr Baldwin was defeated in the House of Commons almost immediately after a general election, the King sent for Mr MacDonald, as the leader of the second largest party in the House, and Mr MacDonald accepted office, on being assured of Liberal support. In 1929 Mr MacDonald again took office with Liberal support, but this time he led the largest party, though it did not possess a parliamentary majority. Although, after the elections of 1910, Mr Asquith became dependent for his majority on the support of the Irish Nationalists and the Labour Party, he did not resign office, so the question of re-appointment did not arise.

     After the general election in February 1974 no party had an overall majority, and the Conservatives, who had had a majority in the outgoing Parliament, were narrowly outnumbered by the Labour Party, although the balance of power was held by the Liberals and other parties. Mr Heath, the former Prime Minister, invited the Liberals to form a coalition which would have enabled him to form a new administration, but they declined and he resigned. The Queen appointed Mr Wilson, the Labour leader, Prime Minister, and he formed an administration, relying on sufficient support from other parties to enable him to command a working majority, until a second general election later in the year gave Labour a narrow (and, in the event, temporary) overall majority. See further de Smith and Brazier *Constitutional and Administrative Law* (7th Edn, 1994) p 101.

     There has sometimes, however, been resort to coalitions where the lines of division are vague, or majorities small (eg the Whigs and Peelites under Lord Aberdeen in 1852). See further Brazier *Constitutional Practice* (2nd Edn, 1994) ch 2; Butler *Governing without a Majority: Dilemma for Hung Parliaments in Britain* (2nd Edn, 1986); Bogdanor *The Monarchy and the Constitution* (1995) chs 4, 6.

9   When Mr Pitt was called to office in 1783 by George III, he had the confidence of the King and of the House of Lords, but not of the majority of the House of Commons. In 1801, when George III replaced Mr Pitt by Mr Addington contrary to the wishes of the majority in the Commons, it was recognised that the King had the sole right of appointment, and that those ministers appointed were entitled at the outset to the constitutional confidence of the House. The same feeling prevailed when Mr Wilson formed his minority administration in March 1974. The usage is supported by the practical consideration that, after the upheaval of an election and particularly when an election has not provided a decisive result, it is in the national interest that there should be a period of political stability so that the necessary processes of government can be carried on.

10   When the administration is in a minority, dissolution or resignation is the recognised procedure, but in the case of dissolution the House of Commons must make itself a party to the transaction by accelerating proceedings, and concurring in temporary measures, so as not to render that course inconvenient (153 Official Report (3rd series), 4 April 1859, cols 1310, 1311). As to parliamentary control of supply see para 712 post.

11   It has been said that changes of administration under ordinary circumstances should be effected within a week (1 Todd's Parliamentary Government p 216); but it seems that no definite time can be laid down, provided the monarch does not delay unnecessarily. Within the present century, the monarch has sent for the new Prime Minister on the same day that the resignation of the old one has been received. In February 1974 the Queen interrupted a Commonwealth tour to return to London for polling day. See Brazier *Constitutional Practice* (2nd Edn, 1994) ch 4.

12   Upon various occasions where delay has occurred, Parliament has taken measures to address the monarch with a request to form a strong and vigorous administration or an indication of the character of the administration desired by the House of Commons.

**395. Status and precedence of the Prime Minister.** Acceptance of the post of Prime Minister entitles the holder to place and precedence next after the Archbishop of York[1]. He enjoys the use of the official residence at 10 Downing Street and of Chequers[2]. By conventional usage the Prime Minister is invariably a member of the House of

Commons[3], and a member of the Privy Council[4]. He usually holds the sinecure office of First Lord of the Treasury[5], and as such receives an annual salary[6]. The Prime Minister is also Minister for the Civil Service[7]. His special duties and privileges, and his relations with the Crown, the Cabinet and Parliament, are defined not by the common law or, in general, by statute law[8] but by recognised usage and practice[9].

1 This rank was conferred upon the then Prime Minister, and all future Prime Ministers, by royal warrant of 2 December 1905: see the London Gazette of that date. The warrant is noticeable as containing an official recognition of the office of Prime Minister. The only earlier official reference appears to be the Treaty of Berlin, in which Lord Beaconsfield described himself as Prime Minister: see 2 Anson's Law and Custom of the Constitution (4th Edn, 1935) Pt I p 139.

   The Prime Minister began to take the position which he at present holds during the Pitt administration, which began in 1783 (2 Todd's Parliamentary Government pp 119–120); but his modern position was not developed until, after the Reform Act (ie the Representation of the People Act 1832 (repealed)), the Cabinet attained its modern position: see para 399 note 4 post. As to the Cabinet see paras 402–413 post. The term 'Prime Minister' in its more modern sense is said to occur first in the writings of Swift: see 2 Anson's Law and Custom of the Constitution (4th Edn, 1935) Pt I p 125.

2 In 1917 the estate of Chequers in Buckinghamshire was conveyed to be administered by certain administrative trustees as a furnished country residence for the Prime Minister: see the Chequers Estate Act 1917 s 1, Schedule; and the Chequers Estate Act 1958 s 1, Schedule. The Chequers Estate Act 1917 appears to be the first statutory recognition of the office of Prime Minister. The Chevening Estate in Kent has been settled upon trust for the use of the Prime Minister or such persons as may be nominated by him: see the Chevening Estate Acts 1959 and 1987. The Prince of Wales accepted such a nomination in 1974: see 873 HC Official Report (5th series), 16 May 1974, written answers col 516.

3 The last member of the House of Lords to be Prime Minister was Lord Salisbury in 1895–1902. The Earl of Home disclaimed his peerage in 1963 to become Sir Alec Douglas-Home shortly after his appointment as Prime Minister. It appears to be established now that the Prime Minister should be a member of the House of Commons: see Wade and Bradley *Constitutional and Administrative Law* (11th Edn, 1993) pp 252–253. The former usage was that he could be a member of either House. As to the House of Commons see PARLIAMENT; and as to the House of Lords see para 204 ante and PARLIAMENT.

4 All members of the Cabinet are invariably members of the Privy Council: see para 404 post. As to the Privy Council see paras 521–526 post.

5 The last Prime Minister who did not hold that office was Lord Salisbury, who was Foreign Secretary. In some instances Prime Ministers in the present century have undertaken departmental duties: eg Mr Baldwin was Chancellor of the Exchequer in 1923; Mr MacDonald was Foreign Secretary in 1924; and Sir Winston Churchill was Minister of Defence in 1951.

   As First Lord of the Treasury, the Prime Minister is a Church Commissioner: Church Commissioners Measure 1947 s 1(2), Sch 1 para 1 (amended by the Synodical Government Measure 1969 s 2(2); and the Church of England (Miscellaneous Provisions) Measure 1992 s 17(1), Sch 3 para 5).

6 This was introduced by the Ministers of the Crown Act 1937 s 4 (repealed). See now the Ministerial and other Salaries Act 1975 s 1(1)(a), Sch 1 Pt I (amended by the Ministerial and other Salaries Order 1996, SI 1996/1913, art 2, Sch 1); see para 423 post. As to the pension of a former Prime Minister and First Lord of the Treasury see para 426 post.

7 As to the Minister for the Civil Service see para 427 post. As to the Civil Service generally see paras 549–564 post.

8 See however note 2 supra.

9 See para 398 et seq post.

## 396. The Prime Minister's Office.
The Prime Minister has an office with a principal private secretary and private secretaries, a diary secretary, a secretary for appointments, a political secretary, parliamentary private secretaries, press secretaries and a parliamentary clerk[1]. He also has a Policy Unit[2], and an Adviser on Efficiency and Effectiveness[3].

1 Civil Service Year Book 1996 col 537. The secretary for appointments deals with recommendations for appointments including those made by the Prime Minister and by the monarch on the advice of the Prime Minister.

2 See the Civil Service Year Book 1996 col 537.

3 The Adviser on Efficiency is a member of the Cabinet Office: Civil Service Year Book 1996 col 71. As to the Cabinet Office see para 427 post.

**397. Death or resignation of the Prime Minister.** The death, resignation or dismissal[1] of the Prime Minister does not necessarily involve the shifting of the government from one political party to another[2]. The other members of the administration do not necessarily retire upon the death or resignation of the Prime Minister, but their offices are in practice invariably placed at the disposal of his successor, who may change or reconstruct the administration as he thinks fit[3].

1 As to dismissal of ministers see para 418 post. See *Adegbenro v Akintola* [1963] AC 614, [1963] 3 All ER 544, PC. See also Kerr *Matters for Judgment* (1987); and Marshall *Constitutional Conventions: the rules and forms of political accountability* (1987) ch II.
2 See 2 Todd's Parliamentary Government p 226.
3 In the past in some cases death, resignation or dismissal of the Prime Minister has been regarded as equivalent to a dissolution of the existing administration: eg the reconstructed ministries on the death of Lord Palmerston in 1865 (see 1 Todd's Parliamentary Government pp 158–159) and in 1908 on the death of Sir Henry Campbell-Bannerman. However, in 1894, when Mr Gladstone retired owing to failing health, the administration was taken over by Lord Rosebery without any general dissolution (see 12 Political History of England p 424). In 1955, Sir Anthony Eden took over Sir Winston Churchill's administration with hardly any change. In 1976 Mr Harold Wilson resigned as Prime Minister and Mr James Callaghan, also Labour, was appointed in his place. And in November 1990 Mrs Margaret Thatcher resigned as Prime Minister and Mr John Major, also Conservative, was appointed in her place. As to appointment of the Prime Minister see para 394 ante; as to the power of the Prime Minister to choose ministers see paras 398–399 post; and as to tenure of office see para 401 post.

**398. The powers of the Prime Minister.** Theoretically the Prime Minister is first among equals in the administration[1], but in practice he possesses considerable power over the composition and operation of the Cabinet[2].

The principal powers exercisable by the Prime Minister derive from the right to advise the monarch on the exercise of prerogative powers relating to the government[3]. These include the appointment and dismissal of ministers[4], and the choice of the date for a general election[5].

Other powers relating to the Cabinet enjoyed by the Prime Minister include de facto control of the cabinet agenda[6] and the right to create new cabinet committees or disband existing ones[7].

Both as head of the government and as Minister for the Civil Service, the Prime Minister has general control over the Cabinet Office[8], whether through the Secretary of the Cabinet[9], the Deputy Prime Minister and First Secretary of State[10], or other bodies and advisers reporting directly to him[11].

The Prime Minister advises the monarch on the making of appointments to the higher judiciary[12] and to the headships of the intelligence and security services[13]. The Prime Minister also advises the monarch on senior home civil service appointments[14] and certain ecclesiastical appointments[15], and makes recommendations for honours[16] and life peerages[17]. Together with the Secretary of State for Foreign and Commonwealth Affairs, the Prime Minister advises the monarch on senior diplomatic appointments[18]; and, with the Secretary of State for Defence, the Prime Minister advises on senior appointments in the armed forces[19].

1 For the appointment of the Prime Minister and the formation of an administration see para 394 ante.
2 See Crossman's Introduction to Bagehot *The English Constitution* (1963 Edn). It has been suggested that the British system, particularly during the 1980s, has moved from cabinet to prime ministerial government, but it has also been said that more recently this move has been to some degree reversed: see generally de Smith and Brazier *Constitutional and Administrative Law* (7th Edn, 1994) pp 178–187; Wade and Bradley *Constitutional and Administrative Law* (11th Edn, 1993) pp 276–280; Brazier *Constitutional*

*Practice* (2nd Edn, 1994) ch 5; Loveland *Constitutional Law: A Critical Introduction* (1996) p 362. As to the Cabinet see paras 402–413 post.

3    The right to advise the monarch is regarded as a constitutional convention: see para 21 ante.

4    See paras 399, 404 post.

5    See paras 21, 209 ante.

6    See para 405 et seq post.

7    As to cabinet committees see para 410 post.

8    As to the Cabinet Office and the Minister for the Civil Service see para 427 post.

9    As to the Secretary of the Cabinet see para 427 text and note 4 post.

10   As to the Deputy Prime Minister and First Secretary of State see para 354 text and note 21 ante; and as to his responsibilities relating to the Cabinet Office and Office of Public Service see para 430 post.

11   See the Civil Service Year Book 1996.

12   See para 901 post.

13   As to the intelligence and security services see paras 471–476 post.

14   As to the Civil Service generally see paras 549–564 post.

15   See ECCLESIASTICAL LAW.

16   See para 832 post.

17   See para 212 ante.

18   See FOREIGN RELATIONS LAW. As to the Secretary of State for Foreign and Commonwealth Affairs see para 459 post.

19   See ROYAL FORCES. As to the Secretary of State for Defence see paras 439–442 post.

### (ii)  Appointment of Ministers

**399.  The Prime Minister's choice of ministers.** In deciding whom to appoint to the administration and in what positions the Prime Minister is limited by convention, by political considerations and by statutory requirements[1]. By convention ministers must normally be members of the House of Commons or the House of Lords[2]. The Chancellor of the Exchequer represents the Treasury in the House of Commons, of which he is necessarily a member[3]. Subject to these requirements the Prime Minister is entitled to choose those of his colleagues who comprise the administration[4] and submit their names for approval to the Crown[5].

1    See Griffith and Ryle *Parliament: Functions, Practice and Procedures* (1989) p 20 et seq. As to statutory limitations see para 400 post. As to the Prime Minister see paras 394–398 ante.

2    A minister may, however, hold office while seeking a seat in Parliament: eg Mr Walker was Foreign Secretary while seeking election in 1964; and Sir Alec Douglas-Home, the Prime Minister, was a member of neither House for a period in 1963 after disclaiming his peerage and before his election to the Commons. As to occasional exceptions in the case of the Law Officers see para 537 post. As to the House of Commons see PARLIAMENT; and as to the House of Lords see para 204 ante and PARLIAMENT.

3    As to the Chancellor of the Exchequer see para 514 post. As to the Treasury see paras 512–517 post.

4    The recognition of this doctrine has been gradual. After the Reform Act (ie the Representation of the People Act 1832 (repealed)), the principle of choice of colleagues by the Prime Minister became recognised with Sir Robert Peel's administration in 1834: 1 Todd's *Parliamentary Government* p 219. Standing Order E of the Parliamentary Labour Party (January 1996) requires that those who have been elected members of the Parliamentary Committee by the Parliamentary Labour Party be appointed members of the Cabinet in the event of a Labour Prime Minister being appointed. As to the Cabinet see paras 402–413 post.

5    Contemporary lists of ministers are published (1) at the beginning of each volume of House of Commons and House of Lords Official Reports (Hansard); (2) annually in the Civil Service Year Book (formerly called the British Imperial Calendar and Civil Service List), together with a list of departmental responsibilities; (3) five times a year in Her Majesty's Ministers and Senior Staff in Public Departments (Cabinet Office); and (4) annually by the Office of Public Service, with a note of ministers', agencies' and non-ministerial departments' responsibilities (see the *List of Ministerial Responsibilities including Agencies* (Cabinet Office, May 1996)). As to the Office of Public Service see para 430 post.

**400.  Numbers in the administration.** Although, in general, the number of ministers who may be appointed is not restricted by law, the creation of any new office involving a charge on public funds requires parliamentary sanction[1] and there is statutory sanction for the payment of salaries to only a certain number of ministerial office-holders[2].

Not more than 95 holders of ministerial offices[3] are entitled to sit and vote in the House of Commons at any one time[4]. For these purposes the following are ministerial offices: (1) Prime Minister and First Lord of the Treasury; (2) Lord President of the Council; (3) Lord Privy Seal; (4) Chancellor of the Duchy of Lancaster; (5) Paymaster General; (6) Secretary of State[5]; (7) Chancellor of the Exchequer; (8) Minister of Agriculture, Fisheries and Food; (9) President of the Board of Trade; (10) Minister of State[6]; (11) Chief Secretary to the Treasury; (12) Minister in charge of a public department of Her Majesty's government in the United Kingdom (if not otherwise excluded); (13) Attorney General; (14) Lord Advocate; (15) Solicitor General; (16) Solicitor General for Scotland; (17) Parliamentary Secretary to the Treasury; (18) Financial Secretary to the Treasury; (19) Parliamentary Secretary[7] in a government department other than the Treasury or not in a department; (20) Junior Lord of the Treasury; (21) Treasurer of Her Majesty's Household; (22) Comptroller of Her Majesty's Household; (23) Vice-Chamberlain of Her Majesty's Household; and (24) Assistant Government Whip[8].

1   Ministerial salaries are voted annually in the estimates: see para 423 post. As to the estimates see para 712 post.
2   As to the number of ministerial salaries payable see para 424 post.
3   Ie offices specified in the House of Commons Disqualification Act 1975 s 2, Sch 2 (which may be modified by Order in Council made under the Ministers of the Crown Act 1975 s 1(2)(d), (3): see para 363 note 7 ante). A copy of the House of Commons Disqualification Act 1975 as from time to time amended by Order in Council must be prepared and certified by the Clerk of the Parliaments and deposited with the rolls of Parliament; and all copies of that Act thereafter to be printed by Her Majesty's printer must be printed in accordance with the copy so certified: s 5(2).
4   Ibid s 2(1). If at any time the number of members of the House of Commons who hold ministerial office exceeds 95 (ie the number entitled to sit and vote in that House under s 2(1)), none except any who were both members of that House and holders of ministerial office before the excess occurred may sit or vote until the number is reduced to 95 by death, resignation or otherwise: s 2(2).
    The purpose of this rule is to limit dominance of the Commons by the executive government. However, ministers also appoint parliamentary private secretaries, who are unpaid, and of whom there are usually some fifty, thus increasing the number of members of Parliament who must support the administration or resign, or be dismissed, to about 150: see Brazier *Constitutional Practice* (2nd Edn, 1994) pp 133–134. However, parliamentary private secretaries are not referred to in *Questions of Procedure for Ministers* (Cabinet Office, May 1992) (as now revised: see para 416 note 1 post) as being bound by collective responsibility. As to collective responsibility see para 417 post.
    As to the House of Commons see PARLIAMENT.
5   'Secretary of State' means one of Her Majesty's principal Secretaries of State: Interpretation Act 1978 s 5, Sch 1. See Simcock 'One and many - the Office of Secretary of State' (1992) 70 Public Administration 535. As to the office of Secretary of State see para 355 et seq ante.
6   'Minister of State' means a member of Her Majesty's government in the United Kingdom who neither has charge of any public department nor holds any other of the offices specified in the House of Commons Disqualification Act 1975 Sch 2 or any office in respect of which a salary is payable out of money provided by Parliament under the Ministerial and other Salaries Act 1975 s 3(1)(b): House of Commons Disqualification Act 1975 s 9(1).
7   'Parliamentary Secretary' includes a person holding ministerial office (however called) as assistant to a member of Her Majesty's government in the United Kingdom, but not having departmental responsibilities: ibid s 9(1).
8   Ibid Sch 2. See PARLIAMENT.

**401. Tenure of office.** All members of the administration hold their offices at the pleasure of the Crown[1], and are dismissable without cause assigned[2]; and, under the recognised usage, the whole administration retires from office collectively with the Cabinet upon a change of administration, when the various offices are placed at the disposal of the new Prime Minister[3].

1   The Crown acts, of course, on the advice of the Prime Minister: see para 352 ante.
2   As to the tenure of office of executive officers generally see para 902 post.

3   2 Todd's Parliamentary Government p 164. It is also customary for all the offices to be placed at the
    disposal of the Prime Minister after an election in which the administration is successful, so that a
    reconstruction of the administration may take place. As to the Prime Minister see paras 394–398 ante and
    as to his choice of ministers see para 399 ante. As to the Cabinet see paras 402–413 post.

## (iii)  The Cabinet

**402.  The Cabinet.** All important questions of policy[1] and the general scope and
character of the legislation to be initiated by the party in power are determined by the
smaller group of senior ministers known as the Cabinet[2], whose functions as a body are
purely consultative and advisory, and whose advice in executive matters the monarch
must, generally, accept[3].

Cabinet and cabinet committee[4] business consists in the main of: (1) questions which
significantly engage the collective responsibility[5] of the administration because they raise
major issues of policy or because they are of critical importance to the public; (2)
questions on which there is an unresolved argument between departments[6].

Details of the executive administration and the ordinary routine work of the executive
are left to the various government offices and departments[7], supervised and controlled, in
the case of such of them as are political departments[8], by individual ministers.

1   This is a convention that is not always observed and there have been occasions when important decisions
    have been taken unilaterally by the Prime Minister or by an inner Cabinet. During the Westland affair in
    1986 Mr Michael Heseltine, the Secretary of State for Defence, resigned because 'the proper
    constitutional practices' as he understood them were not being observed, in that the Prime Minister
    refused to allow cabinet discussion and decision about the appropriate government response to the
    takeover of Westland and imposed a stance of neutrality on cabinet members: see The Observer,
    12 January 1986; and see the *Fourth Report of the Defence Committee: Westland plc: the Government's Decision
    Making* (HC Paper (1985–86) no 519); *The Government's Decision Making: the Government's Response to the
    Third and Fourth Reports from the Defence Committee* (Cmnd 9916) (1986); Marshall 'Cabinet government
    and the Westland Affair' [1986] Public Law 184; Linklater and Leigh *Not Without Honour: The Inside Story
    of the Westland Scandal* (1986); Oliver and Austin 'Political and constitutional aspects of the Westland
    affair' (1987) 40 Parliamentary Affairs 20; and para 416 post. As to the power of deciding what are cabinet
    questions see para 405 post. See also Burch in Young (ed) *Introducing Government* (1993), on the declining
    role of the Cabinet under Mrs Margaret Thatcher. But as to the view that this decline has been reversed
    see para 398 note 2 ante.
2   As to the composition, functions and origin of the Cabinet see paras 403–405 post.
3   As to the monarch see para 351 et seq ante.
4   As to cabinet committees see para 410 post.
5   As to collective responsibility see para 417 post.
6   *Questions of Procedure for Ministers* (Cabinet Office, May 1992) (as now revised: see para 416 note 1 post)
    para 3.
7   As to the departments of state see para 360 et seq ante and para 427 et seq post.
8   Ie the departments whose heads retire from office upon a change of administration. Certain government
    departments do not have political heads, eg the Board of Inland Revenue and the Commissioners of
    Customs and Excise: see INCOME TAXATION, CUSTOMS AND EXCISE. As to non-ministerial departments
    see para 528 post.

**403.  Status of the Cabinet.** The Cabinet does not have its origins in any statute,
though it is recognised by statute law[1], and the rules which regulate its formation and
procedures, and its relations, when formed, with the Crown, Parliament and the
Prime Minister, depend upon the conventional usages which have sprung into
existence since 1688[2], and which have now for the most part become settled
constitutional principles, subject to the modifications rendered necessary by time and
circumstances or by actual changes in existing executive or legislative institutions[3]. A
set of guidelines on procedures and proper conduct has been developed since 1945,

and first published in 1992[4]. In some matters the guidelines reflect the requirements of law[5], but in others they have no legal force[6].

1   See eg the Ministerial and other Salaries Act 1975 s 1(1)(a), Sch 1 Pts I, II (amended by the Ministerial and other Salaries Order 1996, SI 1996/1913, art 2, Sch 1), which provides that, if certain ministers are members of the Cabinet, their salaries are increased: see para 423 post; and the Data Protection Act 1984 s 27(6) (power to determine whether personal data are exempt from certain provisions of the Act is conferred on a cabinet minister).

2   Many of these are set out in *Questions of Procedure for Ministers* (Cabinet Office, May 1992) (as now revised: see para 416 note 1 post). See also para 399 ante and para 404 et seq post.

3   It will be noted that under the common law rule a particular custom must be immemorial (1 Bl Com (14th Edn) 76, 77), legal memory commencing from the beginning of the reign of Richard I in 1189; and that consequently, so long as that rule remains law, the doctrines relating to the Cabinet can never, strictly speaking, become law unless placed upon a statutory basis, the Cabinet being no older than the seventeenth century. It may, however, be said that the decisions arrived at in Parliament as to the constitutionality or otherwise of particular Measures or Acts are as cogent and binding in the conduct of political affairs as are legal decisions in ordinary conduct. It may also be said that the principles to be found embodied in historical precedents have become as firmly settled as the principles of the common law itself, although it is inadvisable to attempt to attach too much binding force to the current rules or conventions in which they are from time to time expressed. Such conventions are altogether more flexible than law. See also paras 7 head (7), 20 ante.

4   Ie *Questions of Procedure for Ministers* (Cabinet Office, May 1992) (as now revised: see para 416 note 1 post). See Hennessy *Whitehall* (1990 Edn) pp 302, 351, 549, 567. As to accountability and conduct of ministers see paras 414–422 post.

5   Eg in relation to secrecy as to cabinet discussions and information (*Questions of Procedure for Ministers* (Cabinet Office, May 1992) (as now revised: see para 416 note 1 post) para 18). See paras 414, 417 post.

6   Eg in relation to preparation of business for the Cabinet and cabinet committees (*Questions of Procedure for Ministers* (Cabinet Office, May 1992) (as now revised: see para 416 note 1 post) paras 6–10). See para 408 post.

**404. Composition of the Cabinet.** The choice of the persons who are to compose the Cabinet rests with the Prime Minister[1]. Although no legal restrictions as to their number or qualifications exist, membership of the Cabinet under modern practice is usually confined to about 20 persons, including the Prime Minister[2]. Persons not holding any office have occasionally been included in the Cabinet[3], and this practice appears to have been recognised by Parliament[4].

Cabinet ministers are invariably members of the Privy Council and must, it seems, be bound by a privy counsellor's oath before they can enter the Cabinet[5].

The names and offices of the ministers comprising the Cabinet are published in official lists, and official communiqués are given to the press containing the names of those who have attended a cabinet meeting, but no legal record is kept of their names[6].

Resignation of office on the part of a cabinet minister is generally understood to involve retirement from the Cabinet unless he is specially summoned to attend[7].

1   As to the powers of the Prime Minister see para 398 ante; and as to the choice of ministers generally see para 399 ante.

2   At one time it might have been said with some degree of confidence that all heads of departments were included in the Cabinet. The growth in the number of departments has meant, however, that it has become necessary to exclude some departmental heads if the Cabinet is not to increase beyond the limited number of people who can take part in manageable discussions. The Ministerial and other Salaries Act 1975 makes express provision for the salaries of ministers in charge of a public department of Her Majesty's government who are not members of the Cabinet: s 1(1)(a), Sch 1 Pt II para 2 (amended by the Ministerial and other Salaries Order 1996, SI 1996/1913, art 2, Sch 1); and see para 423 post.

    More recently there has been some reduction in the number of heads of departments as a result of the transfer of functions previously exercised by two or more departments to a single department headed by a Secretary of State. As to heads of departments see para 361 ante; and as to transfer of functions see paras 363–365 ante.

As to shifts in the balance in the membership of the Cabinet between ministers with seats in the House of Lords and those in the House of Commons see Gordon Walker *The Cabinet* (Revised Edn, 1972) pp 34–35. As to the House of Commons see PARLIAMENT; and as to the House of Lords see para 204 ante and PARLIAMENT.

During the 1914–18 war it was found necessary to establish a War Cabinet, composed of no more than six (for a short period seven) members, of whom only the Chancellor of the Exchequer had departmental duties. This War Cabinet performed all normal functions of the Cabinet, although other ministers attended when business affecting their departments was being considered. For a considerable period General Smuts was a member, although he was a member of neither House of Parliament. Side by side with the War Cabinet were held two sessions of the Imperial War Cabinet, composed of the Prime Ministers of the United Kingdom and the Dominions, together with the Secretaries of State for India and the Colonies. For these developments see in particular the *War Cabinet Report for 1917* (Cd 9005) (1918); and the *War Cabinet Report for 1918* (Cmd 325) (1919).

During the 1939–45 war there was a War Cabinet usually composed of eight or nine ministers. It was attended for periods by General Smuts and by other Commonwealth Prime Ministers visiting London.

3  The practice under Conservative administrations has been to appoint the chair of the Conservative party a minister without portfolio: see para 354 note 27 ante. Most of the members of the War Cabinet from 1916 to 1919 were ministers without portfolio: see note 2 supra.

4  See 6 Official Report (1st series), 3 March 1806, col 327; 142 Official Report (4th series), 9 March 1905, col 864. The Cabinet being in its origin, and still in a sense, a committee of the Privy Council, in theory any privy counsellor may be a member irrespective of any other office he may hold: see 142 Official Report (4th series), 9 March 1905, col 864; 2 Todd's Parliamentary Government p 155. See, however, para 408 note 9 post. As to the Privy Council see paras 521–526 post.

5  Exception was taken in Parliament in 1905 to the inclusion of Lord Cawdor in the list of cabinet ministers attending a council published in the public newspapers before he had been made a privy counsellor. His attendance was excused upon the ground that his presence as First Lord of the Admiralty was required during the discussion: see the statement of Lord Lansdowne in 142 Official Report (4th series), 9 March 1905, col 864.

The duty of secrecy, which applies equally to cabinet ministers and ex-cabinet ministers (see 2 Todd's Parliamentary Government p 195), is said to depend on the fact that they take the privy counsellor's oath, but is more probably a working rule which has been found to be necessary to outspoken discussion in the Cabinet: see Gordon Walker *The Cabinet* (Revised Edn, 1972) pp 26–33, 165–168; Williams *Not in the Public Interest* (1965) ch 2; *Report of the Committee of Privy Counsellors on Ministerial Memoirs* (Cmnd 6386) (1976); see also *A-G v Jonathan Cape Ltd* [1976] QB 752, [1975] 3 All ER 484; and para 417 post. It is for this reason, presumably, that formerly no member was allowed to take any note or record of the proceedings except the Prime Minister (see 88 HC Official Report (5th series), 19 December 1916, col 1343), and that Lord Salisbury used to say that no member should 'Hansardise' his colleagues (Lady Gwendolen Cecil *Life of Robert, Marquis of Salisbury* vol II p 223). The obligation of cabinet secrecy has often been disregarded with impunity: see eg 97 HC Official Report (5th series), 20 August 1917, col 1716 per Mr J G Swift McNeill. For so-called 'unattributable leaks' see Gordon Walker *The Cabinet* (Revised Edn, 1972) p 33 et seq; and para 417 post. The duty of secrecy is regularly waived, with the monarch's consent, in order to enable a retiring minister to explain the reasons for his resignation: see eg the Duke of Devonshire in 1904 (130 Official Report (4th series), 19 February 1904, col 349 et seq). When Mr Michael Heseltine resigned as Secretary of State for Defence during the Westland affair he immediately issued a statement to the press giving his reasons, which were to do with procedures in the Cabinet, without first seeking the consent of the monarch. No criticism was made of this in the press or Parliament: see para 402 note 1 ante.

6  6 Official Report (1st series), 3 March 1806, col 309; 142 Official Report (4th series), 9 March 1905, col 865. After 1800 lists of members of the Cabinet appeared in the Annual Register. As to contemporary lists of ministers see para 399 note 5 ante.

7  For instances when attendance has been invited after resignation see 2 Todd's Parliamentary Government pp 154–155.

## 405. Functions of the Cabinet. In all ordinary matters of administration departmental ministers take full responsibility, subject to the control of the Treasury in matters of expenditure[1]. Questions of policy raising important principles or involving ministerial differences, and questions which are likely to evoke serious debate in Parliament are, in practice, submitted either to the Cabinet or to the Prime Minister[2]; and the Prime Minister may make any subject a matter for discussion by the Cabinet.

The principal functions of the Cabinet may be defined as (1) the final determination of the policy to be submitted to Parliament[3], including decisions as to the contents of the Queen's speech and the legislative timetable; and (2) the determination of the broad economic policy within which the Chancellor of the Exchequer formulates the budget[4].

1    See paras 402, 408–409 post. As to the Treasury see paras 512–517 post.
2    See the *Report of the Committee on the Board of Admiralty* (5 Parliamentary Paper (1861) 168 and (per Sir J S Pakington) 184–186); 2 Todd's Parliamentary Government pp 193–194. 202 ante However, during the Westland affair the Secretary of State for Defence, Mr Michael Heseltine, complained that the Cabinet had not discussed or agreed on policy over the takeover of the helicopter company, Westland, and that policy had been imposed by the Prime Minister, and gave this as one of his reasons for resigning: see para 402 note 1 ante. As to the Prime Minister see paras 394–398 ante.
3    This was the first of three functions identified in the *Report of the Machinery of Government Committee* (Cd 9230) (1918). The other two were the supreme control of the national executive in accordance with the policy prescribed by Parliament, and the continuous co-ordination and delimitation of the activities of the several departments of state; but in modern conditions it is not possible for the Cabinet to perform these functions: see Brazier *Constitutional Practice* (2nd Edn, 1994) ch 6.
4    Under the system of a unified budget whereby one budget statement is made to Parliament in any one year, covering the government's spending plans for the next three years, cabinet ministers have more chance to discuss spending priorities: see *Budgetary Reform* (Cm 1867) (1992) and the *Treasury and Civil Service Committee's Report on the Government's Proposals for Budgetary Reform* (HC Paper (1992–93) no 583); see also para 705 post. For criticism of the system see McEldowney 'The Control of Public Expenditure' in Jowell and Oliver (eds) *The Changing Constitution* (3rd Edn, 1994) pp 175–207. As to the Chancellor of the Exchequer see para 514 post.

**406. Cabinet meetings.** The Cabinet meets regularly, usually once a week when Parliament is in session, but less frequently during the recess. Additional meetings are held when occasion demands, and in times of great emergency the Cabinet is sometimes in almost permanent session[1]. The meetings are held at the Prime Minister's official residence, 10 Downing Street, but if a meeting is called when the House of Commons is actually sitting, the Cabinet usually meets in the Prime Minister's room at the House of Commons[2].

Ministers who are not members of the Cabinet may be invited by the Prime Minister to be present at meetings during the discussion of questions with which they are concerned[3], and non-ministerial experts may, it seems, be summoned to attend for particular purposes[4].

No quorum is necessary before conclusions may be arrived at[5].

1    Eg during the latter part of the 1914–18 war, and during the crisis of August 1931. During the 1939–45 war the War Cabinet normally met once each weekday.
2    2 Todd's Parliamentary Government p 189. As to meetings held elsewhere see Gordon Walker *The Cabinet* (Revised Edn, 1972) pp 99–101. As to the House of Commons see PARLIAMENT. As to the Prime Minister see paras 394–398 ante.
3    A statement will appear on the agenda that a specified minister is invited to attend for a specified item at a specified time: Gordon Walker *The Cabinet* (Revised Edn, 1972) p 109, referring to the practice of the 1964–70 Labour government. As to the agenda see para 408 post.
4    Even before the 1914–18 war, members of the Army Council or a general might be brought in to advise: see 142 Official Report (4th series), 9 March 1905, cols 863–865. During that war the attendance of experts at meetings of the War Cabinet was regular: see *War Cabinet Report for 1917* (Cd 9005) (1918) p 2.
5    See the evidence of the Duke of Newcastle before the Sebastopol Committee (6 Parliamentary Paper (1854–55) Pt 2 p 205).

**407. Proceedings at cabinet meetings.** Except where other ministers are summoned to attend during the discussion of questions with which they are concerned[1] the deliberations of the Cabinet take place in the presence only of members of the Cabinet, of the Chief Whip[2] and of members of the Cabinet Office Secretariat[3].

At meetings of the Cabinet members are on an equal footing, though the views of the Prime Minister are entitled to the greatest weight[4]. Votes are very rare[5].

In case of an irreconcilable difference of opinion, the Prime Minister may require the resignation of any of his colleagues, or, by himself resigning, cause a general dissolution of the administration[6].

1   See para 406 ante.
2   Ie from 1951 onwards: see Gordon Walker *The Cabinet* (Revised Edn, 1972) p 104.
3   As to the Cabinet Office Secretariat see para 428 post.
4   See 155 HC Official Report (5th series), 13 June 1922, col 221. As to the Prime Minister see paras 394–398 ante.
5   'In a Cabinet, at least in the one single Cabinet that I know anything about, there are never votes in the ordinary sense. The Prime Minister, like the clerk of a Quakers' meeting, takes what he considers is the conclusion, and men who disagree have the choice of either acquiescing or resigning from the Cabinet': 256 HC Official Report (5th series), 14 September 1931, col 628 per Mr George Lansbury. But each Prime Minister has his own 'style': see Gordon Walker *The Cabinet* (Revised Edn, 1972) pp 24–25.
6   See the evidence of Sir F T Baring in the *Report of the Committee on the Board of Admiralty* (5 Parliamentary Paper (1861) 168). As to resignation by the Prime Minister see para 397 ante.

**408. Preparation of business.** It is understood that the procedure regarding the summoning of cabinet meetings and the preparation of business is as follows. The Prime Minister instructs the Secretary of the Cabinet regarding the subjects to be placed on the agenda paper, and the Secretary issues to members of the Cabinet a weekly list of questions awaiting consideration[1]. Departments which have memoranda for consideration send them to the Cabinet Office Secretariat[2] in time for them to be circulated two clear days before the cabinet meeting at which they are to be considered, but this rule may be waived with the Prime Minister's sanction in cases of special urgency[3].

Proposals involving expenditure or affecting general financial policy should be discussed with the Treasury before being submitted to the Cabinet or to a cabinet committee[4].

Where proposals affect United Kingdom obligations or interests as a member of the European Community this should be clearly explained[5]. If proposals have manpower implications or may give rise to problems of recruitment, these should be clearly stated after consultation with the Treasury. Any legal implications and matters relating to the impact of the European Convention on Human Rights and Fundamental Freedoms[6] should be cleared or clarified with the Law Officers[7] before circulation. The Cabinet Office will not normally accept a memorandum for circulation to the Cabinet or a cabinet committee unless these steps have been taken[8].

The agenda paper specifies the subjects to be discussed and the memoranda issued in connection with each subject. As a rule it is circulated to every cabinet minister two or three days before the cabinet meeting to which it relates. On the occasion of the first cabinet meeting of a new administration it has been the practice to send, together with the agenda paper, a summons to the meeting in the form of an announcement that a meeting of Her Majesty's servants will be held, at which the minister addressed is desired to attend[9].

All cabinet ministers are expected to attend every meeting and to supply the Prime Minister with their reasons in the event of their being unable to attend[10]. No public announcement is made in advance when a meeting is to be held.

1   *Questions of Procedure for Ministers* (Cabinet Office, May 1992) (as now revised: see para 416 note 1 post) para 6. Memoranda should be circulated in sufficient time to enable ministers to read and digest them and to be properly briefed. As to the Prime Minister see paras 394–398 ante.
2   As to the Cabinet Office and the Secretariat see paras 427–434 post.

3   The objective is that memoranda for the Cabinet and cabinet committees should be circulated at least two full working days and a weekend in advance of the meeting at which they are to be discussed: *Questions of Procedure for Ministers* (Cabinet Office, May 1992) (as now revised: see para 416 note 1 post) para 6. As to cabinet committees see para 410 post.

4   *Questions of Procedure for Ministers* (Cabinet Office, May 1992) (as now revised: see para 416 note 1 post) para 8. See Heath *The Treasury* (1927) pp 57–59. As to the Treasury see paras 512–517 post.

5   As to United Kingdom membership of the European Community see para 23 ante.

6   As to the European Convention on Human Rights and Fundamental Freedoms see para 122–181 ante.

7   As to the Law Officers see para 529 et seq post.

8   *Questions of Procedure for Ministers* (Cabinet Office, May 1992) (as now revised: see para 416 note 1 post) para 8. See 567 HL Official Report (5th series), 29 November 1995, written answers col 45. See also *Cabinet Committee Business: A Guide for Departments* (Cabinet Office, 1995).

9   See the form printed in 2 Marriott's Mechanism of the Modern State p 509. It is noteworthy as disposing of any notion that the modern Cabinet has any formal connection with the Privy Council. As to the Privy Council see paras 521–526 post.

10  See *Questions of Procedure for Ministers* (Cabinet Office, May 1992) (as now revised: see para 416 note 1 post) para 20. Formerly, all the members of the Cabinet were not necessarily summoned to any particular meeting, although when important questions had been fully matured it was usual for a full Cabinet to be convened in order to arrive at a final decision: see 2 Todd's Parliamentary Government p 192.

**409. Records of cabinet meetings.** The cabinet minutes are designed to record clearly and concisely the conclusions which the Cabinet reaches on each subject which comes before it and the grounds on which it reaches them. The minutes record the views of the individual ministers only so far as is necessary to do justice to differences of opinion expressed in the course of discussion. Any suggestions for amendment of cabinet conclusions must reach the Secretary of the Cabinet not later than 24 hours after the circulation of the minutes[1].

Copies of the Cabinet's conclusions are sent to the monarch[2] and to all ministers of cabinet rank. Extracts from them are also sent to ministers summoned to attend the Cabinet for particular items[3].

At this point the responsibility of the Cabinet Office Secretariat[4] in regard to cabinet conclusions ceases[5]. It is the duty of individual ministers to make such communication as they may deem necessary to their respective departments in regard to the conclusions of the Cabinet[6], and to ensure that cabinet decisions are implemented by those departments.

Complete sets of cabinet documents are preserved by the Secretariat for purposes of record. The documents of an administration are treated by the Cabinet Office Secretariat as the special property of that administration, and the rule is strictly observed that the cabinet minutes of one government are not made available for the inspection or use of a subsequent government[7].

1   *Questions of Procedure for Ministers* (Cabinet Office, May 1992) (as now revised: see para 416 note 1 post) para 12. As to the Secretary of the Cabinet see para 427 post.

2   As to the monarch see para 351 et seq ante.

3   See para 406 ante.

4   As to the Cabinet Office and the Secretariat see para 427–434 post.

5   'The Cabinet Secretariat has no executive functions, no administrative functions, displaces no other department and does the work of no other department. Its business is to act as a secretariat, to bring the business of the Cabinet before the Cabinet in proper form, to take such notes of discussions in Cabinet, or cabinet committees, as the Cabinet may require, to record the decisions of the Cabinet, and to see that those decisions are communicated to the departments which have to execute them': Mr Austen Chamberlain in the House of Commons debate on the Cabinet Secretariat (155 HC Official Report (5th series), 13 June 1922, col 223). Strictly speaking, the communication is made to the minister in charge of the department. See also a letter from Sir Maurice Hankey in regard to cabinet minutes: see Mr Lansbury in the House of Commons (261 HC Official Report (5th series), 12 February 1932, cols 1163–1164).

6   *Questions of Procedure for Ministers* (Cabinet Office, May 1992) (as now revised: see para 416 note 1 post) para 13. See 2 Todd's Parliamentary Government pp 195–196. There is no executive department which is supreme over all the others; except that money matters are controlled by the Treasury. As to the Treasury see paras 512–517 post.

7    *Questions of Procedure for Ministers* (Cabinet Office, May 1992) (as now revised: see para 416 note 1 post) paras 14–16. Cabinet minutes are not available for public inspection until the expiration of the period of thirty years beginning with the first day of January in the year next after that in which they were created or such other period, either longer or shorter, as the Lord Chancellor may prescribe: Public Records Act 1958 ss 5(1), 10(1), Sch 1 paras 1, 2 (amended by the Public Records Act 1967 s 1). See also para 840 post.

**410. Cabinet committees.** The Cabinet is assisted by both standing and ad hoc committees[1]. These committees decide some matters on behalf of the Cabinet and prepare others for decision by the Cabinet itself. They also enable those ministers who are not members of the Cabinet to take an active part in discussions and decisions on matters of collective importance.

Standing committees are generally created to deal with those broad topics with which every administration must concern itself, such as defence, economic affairs, home affairs and legislation.

Ad hoc committees are set up to deal with matters the importance of which varies with changing circumstances. The composition and terms of reference of ad hoc committees are settled by the Cabinet.

The Cabinet Office Secretariat[2] provides the secretary, and the procedure and arrangements are closely modelled on those of the Cabinet itself. Particulars of cabinet committees have been published periodically since 1992[3].

1    *Questions of Procedure for Ministers* (Cabinet Office, May 1992) (as now revised: see para 416 note 1 post) para 4 et seq; and for procedures and preparation see *Cabinet Committee Business: A Guide for Departments* (Cabinet Office, December 1995). Cf standing committees of the House of Commons (see para 216 ante and PARLIAMENT); and select committees of the House of Commons (see para 227 ante and PARLIAMENT).

2    As to the Cabinet Office and the Secretariat see paras 427–434 post.

3    The titles, membership and terms of reference of sixteen cabinet committees and ten sub-committees were first published on the instructions of the Prime Minister, Mr John Major, in 1992: *Ministerial Committees of the Cabinet: Membership and Terms of Reference* (Cabinet Office, October 1995). The structure was altered in July 1995, the changes being designed to streamline the current structure and rationalise the arrangement for discussion of policy issues into a smaller number of committees with wide terms of reference (263 HC Official Report (6th series), 18 July 1995, written answers cols *1005–1012* per Mr John Major). For terms of reference, membership and a note of non-members who attend as required or who may be invited to attend all or part of the meetings or who receive papers, see 263 HC Official Report (6th series), 18 July 1995, written answers cols *1005–1012*. Cabinet committees as at October 1995 comprised: (1) committees chaired by the Prime Minister on (a) Economic and Domestic Policy; (b) Defence and Overseas Policy; (c) Nuclear Defence Policy; (d) Northern Ireland; (e) the Intelligence Services; (2) committees chaired by the Deputy Prime Minister and First Secretary of State on (a) Competitiveness; (b) Co-ordination and Presentation of Government Policy; (c) the Environment; (d) Local Government; (3) committees chaired by the Lord President of the Council on (a) Home and Social Affairs; (b) the Queen's Speeches and Future Legislation; (c) Legislation; and (4) the Committee on Public Expenditure chaired by the Chancellor of the Exchequer. The sub-committees included those on Health Strategy, European Questions, Terrorism, Drug Misuse, Women's Issues and London. The list does not include ad hoc committees, and periodic changes are not published. See also *Cabinet Committee Business: A Guide for Departments* (Cabinet Office, 1995). See further Brazier *Constitutional Practice* (2nd Edn, 1994) pp 109–120; and Lee 'Cabinet Procedure' (1986) 64 Public Administration 347.

**411. The monarch and the Cabinet.** Since the reign of George I the monarch has not attended cabinet meetings, being replaced by the Prime Minister[1]. Moreover, the monarch's presence at any meetings of ministers where deliberations or discussions take place is now clearly recognised as being contrary to constitutional practice[2]. The decisions arrived at by ministers must, however, be communicated to the monarch in order to afford her the opportunity of exercising that constitutional criticism with regard to all the departments of state to which she is entitled[3]. The fullest information should also be given to her, both by the Cabinet and by individual ministers, as to the measures proposed to be taken in important matters; and drafts for the monarch's approval and signature, and the papers or dispatches connected with them, should be submitted in time to permit her to become fully acquainted with their nature before coming to a decision[4], the proper course being for all important documents and correspondence to be sent first to the Prime Minister, to be transmitted by him to the monarch, and afterwards circulated among members of the Cabinet. Any measure sanctioned by the Crown should not afterwards be arbitrarily altered or modified[5].

1    Until the reign of George I, the monarch attended cabinet meetings and sometimes gave advice on his own initiative. Queen Anne presided weekly: see 3 Hallam's Constitutional History of England pp 314–315; 2 Todd's Parliamentary Government p 115. For a combination of reasons George I soon ceased to attend, the result being that his place was taken by the leading member of the Cabinet: see Mackintosh *The British Cabinet* (3rd Edn, 1977) pp 50–52. Since the reign of George III the absence of the monarch has been recognised as a constitutional principle (2 Todd's Parliamentary Government p 115; Hearn *The Government of England: its structures and its development* (2nd Edn, 1887) p 208), and only three instances of the presence of the monarch for merely formal purposes have been recorded since the accession of George I (see 2 Todd's Parliamentary Government p 115; 2 Anson's Law and Custom of the Constitution (4th Edn, 1935) Pt I p 53 note 2). As to the monarch see para 351 et seq ante. As to the Prime Minister see paras 394–398 ante.
2    This doctrine was enunciated in Parliament by Lord Granville in 1864 with reference to the attendance of the Queen at a committee of the Privy Council: see 175 Official Report (3rd series), 10 May 1864, col 251.
3    188 Official Report (3rd series), 1867, col 1113 per Mr Disraeli.
4    This is the substance of the detailed instruction sent by Queen Victoria to Lord Palmerston (then Foreign Secretary) through Lord John Russell, then Prime Minister, in 1851: see 119 Official Report (3rd series), 3 February 1852, col 90.
5    See the *Report of Committee on Official Salaries* (15 Parliamentary Paper (1850) evidence no 326).

**412. Access to the monarch.** The Prime Minister acts as the medium of communication between the Cabinet and the Crown[1]. Individual ministers have, however, the right of access to the monarch at all times on matters connected with their own departments; but important communications or correspondence should, it is said, be submitted to the Prime Minister, either beforehand or immediately afterwards[2].

The administration has a constitutional right at all times to tender such advice to the monarch as it thinks fit, and any attempt on the monarch's part to limit the scope or character of that advice, or to exact pledges as to future conduct, either on the formation of an administration or by threats of dismissal, is clearly recognised by the House of Commons as unconstitutional[3].

1    The Prime Minister has a regular weekly audience with the monarch. A copy of the cabinet minutes is sent to the monarch: see para 409 ante. As to the monarch see para 351 et seq ante. As to the Prime Minister see paras 394–398 ante.
2    See 2 Todd's Parliamentary Government p 208.
3    This principle was finally established in 1807, when George III dismissed the Grenville administration for recording in the Council minutes its right at any future time to submit its views upon the Catholic question, which, at the instance of the King, it had pledged itself not to do. The King insisted on the withdrawal of the minute and the substitution of a pledge not to make any proposals in favour of the Catholic claims. Resolutions were formulated in both Houses to the effect that it is contrary to the first duties of the confidential servants of the Crown to restrain themselves by any pledge, express or implied, from offering to the King any advice which circumstances may render necessary for the welfare of the kingdom. No direct vote was taken, although the principle was clearly admitted: see 1 May's Constitutional History (1912 Edn) pp 74–76; 9 Official Report (1st series), 9 April 1907, cols 285, 328–329, 335; 9 Official Report (1st series), 13 April 1907, cols 362, 380; 1 Todd's Parliamentary Government p 91; 2 Todd's Parliamentary Government pp 147–148. As to the House of Commons see PARLIAMENT.

**413. Unanimity of advice.** The advice tendered to the monarch by the Cabinet ought to be unanimous, and it is unconstitutional for the monarch to inquire into the lines of division among members of the government[1]. If the monarch refuses to accept the advice so given, it is recognised that the administration must either revise its decision or resign[2]; but pending the resignation or dismissal of an existing administration and the formation of a new one it is clearly unconstitutional for the monarch to seek formal advice elsewhere[3].

It is not in general constitutional for the monarch to express her political views to any persons except her ministers, though she may listen to the views of others without commenting on them or act as a mediator in heated political quarrels[4].

1   Unanimity of advice and collective responsibility on the part of the Cabinet are correlative: see Lord North *Parliamentary History* (1784) vol 24 p 291; (1783) vol 23 p 678. As to collective responsibility see para 417 post. As to the monarch see para 351 et seq ante.
2   See the statement of Lord Grenville in 1807 (9 Official Report (1st series), 26 March 1807, col 239).
3   As to obtaining informal advice through the monarch's private secretary see CROWN LANDS AND PRIVILEGES.
4   2 Todd's Parliamentary Government pp 202–203, 205; May's Parliamentary Practice (1863 Edn) p 314; Jennings *Cabinet Government* (3rd Edn, 1959) pp 284–296. For a recent exposition of the position see Marshall 'The Queen's Press Relations' [1986] Public Law 505; and de Smith and Brazier *Constitutional and Administrative Law* (7th Edn, 1994) pp 124–125.

## (iv)  Ministerial Conduct and the Accountability of Government

**414. Accountability.** In recognition of the fallibility of government, ministers are accountable in various ways for their own acts and those of their civil servants. Accountability is said to be explanatory and amendatory[1]. Accountability involves ministers having to justify their acts either to Parliament[2], the courts[3] or the electorate[4], and then to make amends if found to have acted unwisely or in breach of the law. Justifications are measured against written or unwritten codes and constitutional understandings, or against legal criteria.

1   Marshall *Constitutional Conventions: the rules and forms of political accountability* (1987) ch IV. See para 416 post.
2   As to accountability to Parliament see para 415 et seq post.
3   As to legal accountability see para 422 post.
4   As to accountability to the public see para 419 et seq post.

**415. Democratic accountability: annual Parliaments.** The necessity for obtaining supplies, which can only be granted by Parliament[1], and without which government could not be carried on, and (at any rate until recent years) the necessity for the continuation of various Acts expiring in each year[2], obliges the Crown to summon Parliament annually, and to observe the conventions and customs of the constitution relating to the conduct of parliamentary and political affairs[3].

1   As to the Crown's inability to impose taxes without parliamentary consent see para 228 ante. As to parliamentary control of supply see para 712 post. A Finance Act is passed annually and occasionally two are passed in one year.
2   The Army Act 1955, the Air Force Act 1955 and the Naval Discipline Act 1957 are examples of Acts which expire annually. By the Armed Forces Act 1991 s 1, these Acts may be continued in force annually by Order in Council until the end of 1996. See further para 887 post. See also the Northern Ireland (Emergency Provisions) Act 1996 s 62, by which that Act is subject to annual renewal.
      The Meeting of Parliament Act 1694 requires that a Parliament be held at least once every three years, but in practice the limitation of Appropriation Acts to one year requires Parliament to meet at least annually; see PARLIAMENT.
3   As to the conventions generally see paras 19–22 ante, and as to the conventions relating to the cabinet system and ministerial responsibility see paras 416–417 post.

**416. Individual ministerial responsibility to Parliament.** Each    minister    is responsible and must answer to Parliament for his or her own acts and policies and for all that is done in his or her department[1]. Theoretically the responsibility of each minister for unlawful conduct may be enforced by impeachment, in bar of which a pardon or the orders of the Crown cannot be pleaded[2]. However, this remedy is now probably obsolete.

In giving an account to Parliament a minister must not knowingly mislead Parliament[3]. He must protect a civil servant who has carried out his explicit order, and must defend a civil servant who acts properly in accordance with the policy laid down by the minister. Except on an important issue of policy or where a claim to individual rights is seriously involved, where an official makes a mistake or causes some delay the minister should acknowledge the mistake and accept the responsibility although he is not personally involved; and he should state that he will take corrective action in the department. Where action has been taken by a civil servant of which the minister disapproves and has no previous knowledge and the conduct of the official is reprehensible, there is no obligation on a minister to endorse what he believes to be wrong or to defend what are clearly shown to be errors of his officers. He remains, however, constitutionally responsible to Parliament for the fact that something has gone wrong, although this does not affect his power to control and discipline his staff[4].

Although in principle ministers are expected to give an account of their departments and answer questions in Parliament, they may refuse to answer questions on a number of grounds, for example that they concern confidential commercial information, or advice received by a minister from a civil servant, or that the information asked for cannot be obtained without undue expense[5]. As far as making amends is concerned there is no legally coercive mechanism to enforce this where no unlawful conduct is involved if the minister does not wish to make amends. A person complaining of injustice in consequence of maladministration may ask a member of Parliament to refer the matter to the Parliamentary Commissioner for Administration[6].

A minister may be called upon in Parliament to make amends or resign if found to be personally at fault, for example if he or she is found to have committed an error of judgment, or to have been negligent in office[7]. If the fault is not that of the minister but of a civil servant it seems there is no duty to resign, though there is still a notional duty to make amends for the fault[8]. In practice ministers do not resign even in the face of parliamentary criticism unless, for instance, they do so voluntarily on the basis that they accept personal responsibility for what has gone wrong[9], or they lose the support of the Prime Minister or the Cabinet[10], or their own backbenchers[11] or they consider that they are too much of an embarrassment to the administration[12].

1    See *Questions of Procedure for Ministers* (Cabinet Office, May 1992) paras 1, 27 (as revised: see infra); Erskine May *Parliamentary Practice* (21st Edn, 1989) pp 281–297; Griffith and Ryle *Parliament: Functions, Practice and Procedures* (1989) pp 254–262, 352–359, 366–376; HC Standing Orders (1995) (Public Business) nos 17, 18. See also para 226 ante. See also Marshall *Constitutional Conventions: the rules and forms of political accountability* (1987) pp 61–67; Wade and Bradley *Constitutional and Administrative Law* (11th Edn, 1993) pp 119–123; Finer 'The Individual Responsibility of Ministers' (1956) 34 Public Administration 377; Turpin 'Ministerial Responsibility' in Jowell and Oliver (eds) *The Changing Constitution* (3rd Edn, 1994) pp 109–151; Brazier 'It is a Constitutional Issue: Fitness for Ministerial Office in the 1990s' [1994] Public Law 431; Woodhouse 'Ministerial responsibility in the 1990s: when do ministers resign?' (1993) 46 Parliamentary Affairs 277. As to standards of conduct see generally para 12 ante.

     *Questions of Procedure for Ministers* has been amended in the light of recommendations in the *First Report of the Committee on Standards in Public Life* (Cm 2850-I) (1995): see *The Government's Response to the First Report of the Committee on Standards in Public Life* (Cm 2931) (1995) Annex A. The revised para 1 provides that all members of the government are expected to behave according to the highest standards of constitutional and personal conduct in the performance of their duties, and sets down seven particular principles, summarised as follows: (1) ministers must uphold the principle of collective responsibility; (2) they are accountable to Parliament for policies, decisions and actions of their departments and agencies; (3) they must not knowingly mislead Parliament and the public and should correct inadvertent errors, and they must be as open as possible, withholding information only when disclosure would not be in the public interest; (4) they must ensure that no conflict arises, or appears to arise, between the public interest and their private interests; (5) they should avoid accepting gifts which might (or might reaonably appear to) compromise their judgment or place them under an improper obligation; (6) ministers in the House of Commons must keep their constituency and ministerial roles separate; (7) ministers must not use public funds for party political purposes, they must uphold the impartiality of the Civil Service, and not ask civil servants to act inconsistently with the Civil Service Code. It is for individual ministers to judge how best to act in order to uphold the highest standards, and noting that ministers can only remain in office for as long as they retain the Prime Minister's confidence. As to the Civil Service Code see para 554 post. For a summary of the government's view of the requirements of ministerial accountability see the memorandum from the Chancellor of the Duchy of Lancaster *Ministerial Accountability and the Provisions of Information by Government to Parliament* (Office of Public Service, 29 March 1996). For a critique of the operation of individual ministerial responsibility see the *Report of the Inquiry into the Export of Defence Equipment and Dual-use Goods to Iraq and related Prosecutions* (HC Paper (1995–96) no 115) vol IV paras K8.1–K8.16 (the 'Scott Report').

For a proposed working definition of 'ministerial responsibility' see the *Second Report of the Public Service Committee: Ministerial Accountability and Responsibility* (HC Paper (1995–96) no 313–I) para 32.

As to government departments see para 427 et seq post and as to the Civil Service generally see paras 549–564 post.

2    As to impeachment see para 377 ante; and COURTS.

3    *Questions of Procedure for Ministers* (Cabinet Office, May 1992) para 1 (as revised: see note 1 supra). For comment on the significance of the word 'knowingly' in this context see *Report of the Inquiry into the Export of Defence Equipment and Dual-use Goods to Iraq and related Prosecutions* (HC Paper (1995–96) no 115) vol IV para K8.5 (the 'Scott Report'); and see Tomkins 'A Right to Mislead Parliament?' (1996) 16 Legal Studies 63.

4    These propositions were formulated in the Crichel Down affair: 530 HC Official Report (5th series), 20 July 1954, cols 1286–1287.

5    Erskine May *Parliamentary Practice* (21st Edn, 1989) pp 285–294, 339–342; *Report of the Select Committee on Parliamentary Questions* (HC Paper (1971–72) no 393); Wade and Bradley *Constitutional and Administrative Law* (11th Edn, 1993) pp 119–123, 217–219; Brazier *Constitutional Practice* (2nd Edn, 1994) pp 140–154. For a discussion of the grounds on which a minister may refuse to answer a question see the *Second Report of the Public Service Committee: Ministerial Accountability and Responsibility* (HC Paper (1995–96) no 313–I) ch III. See also PARLIAMENT.

6    As to the Parliamentary Commissioner for Administration see ADMINISTRATIVE LAW vol 1(1) (Reissue) para 41 et seq. As to the recommended amendment to the Parliamentary Commissioner Act 1967, so that members may make a complaint direct to the Commissioner concerning the withholding of information by a government department, see the *Second Report of the Public Service Committee: Ministerial Accountability and Responsibility* (HC Paper (1995–96) no 313–I) para 65.

7    See text and note 1 supra. It has been said that 'proper and rigorous scrutiny and accountability may be more important to Parliament's ability to correct error than forcing resignations': *Second Report of the Public Service Committee: Ministerial Accountability and Responsibility* (HC Paper (1995–96) no 313–I) para 26.

8    See text and note 1 supra. Mr James Prior, Secretary of State for Northern Ireland stated that he would not resign on the escape of prisoners from the Maze Prison if it were found that the failure was one of administration, not of policy: 47 HC Official Report (6th series), 24 October 1983, cols 23–24; Mr Enoch Powell considered responsibility in the sense of a duty to resign arose where administration of a department was defective: 53 HC Official Report (6th series), 24 October 1983, cols 1060–1061. The minister did not resign. In 1994 the Home Secretary, Mr Michael Howard, endorsed Mr Prior's position, after the escape of prisoners from Whitemoor Prison: see 251 HC Official Report (6th series), 19 December 1994, col 1397; and *Report of the Enquiry into the escape of six prisoners from the Special Security Unit at Whitemoor Prison, Cambridgeshire, on Friday 9th September 1994* (Cm 2741) (1994) (the 'Woodcock Enquiry'). See also the *Report of the Inquiry into the Export of Defence Equipment and Dual-use Goods to Iraq and related Prosecutions* (HC Paper (1995–96) no 115) (the 'Scott Report') ch 8; and the debate on ministerial responsibility in the House of Commons prior to the publication of that report: 271 HC Official Report (6th series), 12 February 1996, cols 674–707.

9    As with the resignation of Lord Carrington as Foreign Secretary (together with his two junior ministers, Mr Humphrey Atkin and Mr Richard Luce) on the Argentine invasion of the Falkland Islands. He accepted that the Foreign Office, under his charge, had made serious errors of judgment and failed to appreciate the significance of intelligence about Argentine intentions in relation to the Falkland Islands: *Report by a Committee of Privy Councillors: The Falkland Islands Review* (Cmnd 8787) (1983); Marshall *Constitutional Conventions: the rules and forms of political accountability* (1987) p 65. Note also the resignation of Sir Nicholas Fairbairn, Solicitor General for Scotland, after a decision not to prosecute in a rape case.

Part of his error had been in speaking to the press about the decision before explaining it to the House of Commons: his letter of resignation is published in The Times, 22 January 1982; and see 16 HC Official Report (6th series), 21 January 1982, col 423. For a list of ministerial resignations, classified, see Butler *British Political Facts 1900–1994* (7th Edn, 1994) pp 68–70.

10 As with the resignation of (1) Mr Norman Lamont as Chancellor of the Exchequer in 1992; (2) Sir Nicholas Fairbairn in 1982 (see note 9 supra); and (3) Mr Nicholas Ridley in 1990. As to those mentioned in heads (2) and (3) see Woodhouse *Ministers and Parliament: Accountability in Theory and Practice* (1994) pp 46–53, 65–71 respectively.

As to the Prime Minister see paras 394–398 ante. As to the Cabinet see paras 402–413 ante.

11 As where Mr Leon Brittan, Secretary of State for Trade and Industry, resigned over what was regarded as his improper authorisation of the disclosure to the press of a letter written by the Solicitor General to Mr Michael Heseltine during the Westland affair: it was mainly because he did not have the support of his own backbenchers that he had to resign, although the Prime Minister took the view that this was not a resigning matter: see the *Fourth Report of the Defence Committee: Westland plc: the Government's Decision Making* (HC Paper (1985–86) no 519); *The Government's Decision Making: the Government's Response to the Third and Fourth Reports from the Defence Committee* (Cmnd 9916) (1986); Woodhouse *Ministers and Parliament: Accountability in Theory and Practice* (1994) pp 106–120. Mrs Edwina Currie resigned after her statements about the extent of salmonella infection in egg production were followed by the collapse of the egg market and brought condemnation from all sides of the House of Commons: her letter of resignation was published in The Independent, 17 December 1989. See Woodhouse *Ministers and Parliament: Accountability in Theory and Practice* (1994) pp 53–65.

12 Mr David Mellor resigned as Secretary of State for National Heritage when his affair with an actress became known and it became known at about the same time that he had accepted free holidays, contrary to the advice in *Questions of Procedure for Ministers* (Cabinet Office, May 1992), from a person with family links with the Palestine Liberation Organisation. He gave as his reason for resigning, ultimately, the embarrassment to his colleagues in government and Parliament caused by press interest in the matters: his letter was published in The Independent, 25 September 1992. He had also lost the support of his own party. See Woodhouse *Ministers and Parliament: Accountability in Theory and Practice* (1994) pp 77–85.

**417. Collective responsibility.** Each administration is collectively responsible to Parliament for its conduct of government[1]. The three elements of this convention are the requirements of unanimity, confidentiality and confidence[2].

In order to preserve the dignity of the nation and the necessary appearance of unanimity which should be displayed by an efficient administration, with regard both to the advice given to the monarch in administrative and executive matters[3], and to legislative measures in Parliament upon all questions which have not been left open, it is recognised as being constitutionally necessary that individual ministers should in general support the decisions arrived at by the Cabinet[4].

Failure to support his colleagues upon vital questions may render a minister liable to dismissal from office[5]; but under the recognised practice, where an individual minister votes against his colleagues on a government question in the House of Commons, it is usual for him to tender his resignation immediately in order to prevent the appearance of disunion in which the administration would otherwise be involved[6]. Where permission has been given to a minister by the Cabinet to vote against the administration upon a particular measure, resignation does not, it seems, necessarily follow[7]; and where in an emergency members of different parties combine to form an administration, the opposition of a minority to important measures may be tolerated if there is agreement on other and still more vital matters, and it is therefore deemed necessary to retain the dissentient members in the Cabinet[8].

Members of the Cabinet owe a duty of confidentiality to the Crown[9] and to one another in respect of what takes place in Cabinet, and publication of cabinet proceedings may be restrained by injunction if the court is satisfied that it is in the public interest to do so[10].

If an administration loses the confidence of the House of Commons, it should resign, or the Prime Minister should seek a dissolution[11].

1  See for instance *Questions of Procedure for Ministers* (Cabinet Office, May 1992) (as now revised: see para 416 note 1 ante) paras 17–19.

2  Marshall *Constitutional Conventions: the rules and forms of political accountability* (1987) pp 55–61. As to collective responsibility generally see Wade and Bradley *Constitutional and Administrative Law* (11th Edn, 1993) pp 112–118; de Smith and Brazier *Constitutional and Administrative Law* (7th Edn, 1994) pp 196–208; Brazier *Constitutional Practice* (2nd Edn, 1994) pp 120–127; Turpin 'Ministerial Responsibility' in Jowell and Oliver (eds) *The Changing Constitution* (3rd Edn, 1994) pp 109–151.

3  See para 413 ante. As to the monarch see para 351 et seq ante.

4  See 126 Official Report (3rd series), 29 April 1853, col 883. An authoritative statement of the classical version of the doctrine is that given by Lord Salisbury in 1878: 'For all that passes in Cabinet every member of it who does not resign is absolutely and irretrievably responsible and has no right afterwards to say that he agreed in one case to a compromise, while in another he was persuaded by his colleagues...It is only on the principle that absolute responsibility is undertaken by every member of the Cabinet, who, after a decision is arrived at, remains a member of it, that the joint responsibility of Ministers to Parliament can be upheld and one of the most essential principles of parliamentary responsibility established': Lady Gwendolen Cecil *Life of Robert, Marquis of Salisbury* vol II pp 219–220. As to the Cabinet see paras 402–413 ante. The doctrine now extends to members of the administration who are not in the Cabinet.

   The conventions of collective responsibility were regarded by the Prime Minister, Mr John Major, as binding on members of the government who hold ministerial office: 263 HC Official Report (6th series), 12 July 1995, written answers col 562. *Questions of Procedure for Ministers* (Cabinet Office, May 1992) (as now revised: see para 416 note 1 ante) in its treatment of collective responsibility in paras 17–19 applies in terms to ministers only. In practice parliamentary private secretaries, though not formally bound by collective responsibility, may find that they are not permitted to speak and vote against the government and that they may be dismissed by the Prime Minister if they do so. See Brazier *Constitutional Practice* (2nd Edn, 1994) pp 140–154. As to the Prime Minister see paras 394–398 ante.

   The unanimity of the administration is the necessary corollary of collective responsibility, and originated contemporaneously. It is now fully recognised that, although individual members may retire without causing the downfall of the administration, on vital questions the government as a whole must stand or fall together.

   The requirement is subject to a number of exceptions. It may be waived by the Prime Minister: so in the campaign leading up to the referendum on the United Kingdom's continued membership of the European Community in 1975 the Prime Minister, Mr Harold Wilson, announced that members of the administration were free to advocate a different view from that of the administration outside Parliament: 889 HC Official Report (5th series), 7 April 1975, written answers col 351; and in 1977 the Prime Minister, Mr James Callaghan, permitted a free vote on the second reading of the European Assembly Elections Bill, which introduced direct elections to the European Assembly. The reasons for this waiver were that the matter divided the Labour party, and at that time the administration was relying on a pact with Liberal members of Parliament for its majority, a term of which related to direct elections to the European Assembly. The Prime Minister said of the requirement of unanimity on that occasion '... I certainly think that the doctrine [of collective responsibility] should apply, except in cases where I announce that it does not': 933 HC Official Report (5th series), 16 June 1977, col 552.

   Other modifications to the rule relate to the frequent toleration by Prime Ministers of leaks to the press by ministers of their disagreement with the government line. In the Westland affair of 1986 the Prime Minister tolerated open disagreements between two members of the Cabinet. The Secretary of State for Defence, Mr Michael Heseltine, objected to the decision imposed by the Prime Minister that ministers should be neutral on the takeover of Westland plc and should not make ministerial statements on the issue without first clearing them with her. An open disagreement on government policy between Mr Heseltine and the Secretary of State for Trade and Industry, Mr Leon Brittan, emerged as a result of which Mr Heseltine resigned voluntarily because he felt that the doctrine of collective responsibility was being imposed without permitting the Cabinet to discuss and agree on policy. Mr Brittan felt obliged to resign because he had undermined a cabinet colleague by authorising the disclosure of confidential information: see Marshall 'Cabinet Government and the Westland Affair' [1986] Public Law 184; *Fourth Report of the Defence Committee: Westland plc: the Government's Decision Making* (HC Paper (1985–86) no 519); *The Government's Decision Making: the Government's Response to the Third and Fourth Reports from the Defence Committee* (Cmnd 9916) (1986); *Seventh Report of the Treasury and Civil Service Committee: Civil Servants and Ministers: Duties and Responsibilities* (HC Paper (1985–86) no 92); *Government Response to the Seventh Report of the Treasury and Civil Service Committee* (Cmnd 9841) (1986). See also Brazier *Constitutional Practice* (2nd Edn, 1994) pp 120–127; and Wass *Government and the Governed* (1984).

   As to the duty to give unanimous advice to the monarch see para 413 ante.

5  Individual ministers must bow to the decision of the majority, or leave to the Crown that full liberty, which the Crown must possess, of no longer continuing the minister in office: see the statement of Lord John Russell in 119 Official Report (3rd series), 3 February 1852, col 90.

6    2 Todd's Parliamentary Government p 329. As to the House of Commons see PARLIAMENT.

7    Thus when Mr Baines voted against the government on the repeal of the navigation laws in 1849 his continued presence in the administration was excused on the ground that he had made that a condition of acceptance of office: see 102 Official Report (3rd series), 14 February 1849, col 681. It seems, particularly in the light of the Prime Minister's increased power in the Cabinet, that the permission of the Prime Minister, not of the Cabinet, will suffice to relieve a minister of the obligations: see note 4 supra and para 398 ante.

8    Thus in January and February 1932, Viscount Snowden, Sir Herbert Samuel, Sir Archibald Sinclair and Sir Donald Maclean, together with other ministers who were not members of the Cabinet, spoke and voted in Parliament against the Tariff Bill introduced by the administration of which they were members, and yet retained their offices. It was, however, understood at the time of their appointment and during the preceding election that they were opposed in principle to protection. The procedure adopted, though it may appear irregular, was obviously more convenient than the unacceptable alternative of two successive reconstructions of the administration; and it serves as a reminder that all the conventions which regulate ministerial responsibility are based on convenience and must therefore give way where a still greater convenience requires it. However, the precedent is not a good one, since the ministers in question resigned soon after. See Wade and Bradley *Constitutional and Administrative Law* (11th Edn, 1993) pp 116–117. For more recent exceptions from the requirement of unanimity see note 4 supra.

9    The duty of confidentiality owed to the Crown derives from the fact that cabinet ministers are by convention members of the Privy Council and as such are required to take the privy counsellors oath: see para 523 post. But see para 404 note 5 ante.

10   *A-G v Jonathan Cape Ltd* [1976] QB 752, [1975] 3 All ER 484 per Lord Widgery CJ. In this case the Attorney General applied to the court for an injunction to restrain the publication of the memoirs of Mr Richard Crossman, who had been a cabinet minister, on the principal ground that publication was a breach of a duty of confidentiality which ought to be prevented by injunction. The court refused the injunction because the diaries related to matters that had taken place some 11 years earlier and it was satisfied that no damage would be caused by disclosure. But the Lord Chief Justice accepted that the expression of individual opinions by cabinet ministers in the course of cabinet discussion are matters of confidence, the publication of which can be restrained by the court when this is clearly necessary in the public interest. Little importance was placed in this decision on the privy counsellor's oath as the origin of the duty of confidentiality. See note 9 supra.

11   Thus when the Labour administration under Mr James Callaghan lost a vote of confidence in 1979 the Prime Minister sought a dissolution, which was granted: Marshall *Constitutional Conventions: the rules and forms of political accountability* (1987) pp 55–56. In 1924 Mr Baldwin resigned after defeat by combined Liberal and Labour votes: Wade and Bradley *Constitutional and Administrative Law* (11th Edn, 1993) p 253. As to loss of the confidence of the House of Commons see further paras 209 note 3 ante, 418 post.

**418. Dismissal of ministers.** The monarch may legally dissolve the administration at any time by dismissal, but the exercise of this power in order to assert the monarch's personal wishes in opposition to the wishes of Parliament, and ultimately of the electorate, is clearly recognised as unconstitutional[1]. However, in cases where the administration still retains the confidence of the House of Commons, but the monarch has reason to believe that the House no longer represents the sense of the electorate, the dismissal of the administration, or the dissolution of Parliament, has been regarded as constitutional; and cases of emergency might conceivably arise where, through the unfitness or incapacity of the administration, the exercise of the power of dismissal would be constitutional, justifiable and proper in order to prevent the adoption of some course of action ruinous to the nation[2].

Under modern usage the exercise of the power of dismissal is unlikely to be required. An adverse vote in the House of Commons on a question of confidence would be followed by resignation of the administration or an appeal to the electorate by dissolution[3].

The continuance of the administration in office is also dependent ultimately upon the goodwill of the electorate, and where on a dissolution the electorate declares itself against the administration by returning a majority opposed to its policy, it is usual for the administration to resign immediately, although in some instances the resignation has been deferred until Parliament has met and a vote of no confidence has been passed[4], or the

Prime Minister has sought to form a coalition government or reach a pact with one or more other parties in the House of Commons[5].

1    Under the modern cabinet system attempts on the part of the Crown to thwart the wishes of Parliament by dismissing the administration have invariably proved unsuccessful, unless upon a dissolution the country has shown itself opposed to the policy of the former Parliament and administration. No attempt has been made in England for over a hundred years. However, in 1975 the Governor General of Australia, Sir John Kerr, dismissed the Prime Minister of Australia, Mr Whitlam, after the refusal by the Upper House of the Australian Parliament, where the opposition was in the majority, to pass Appropriation Bills providing the necessary supply for the government. The Governor General invited the Leader of the Opposition, Mr Fraser, to form an interim administration which would pass the necessary Appropriation Bills and call an election, so that the people could decide. The opposition parties won the election resoundingly, and Mr Fraser formed a coalition government. Since the Governor General represents the monarch this incident may be taken as evidence that the power of the monarch to dismiss an administration survives, although use of that power may give rise to great controversy: see Kerr *Matters for Judgment* (1987); Whitlam *The Truth of the Matter* (1979). As to the monarch see para 351 et seq ante.

2    The Crown, it has been said, is justified in dismissing an administration in whom it feels unable to repose confidence or for want of ability or for unfitness (see 35 Official Report (1st series), 25 March 1801, col 1121 per Mr Pitt; 9 Official Report (1st series), 13 April 1807, col 377 per Lord Selkirk, or where its existence in office is through dissensions or otherwise ruinous to the country (see Mirror of Parliament (1835) pp 28–29 per Lord Brougham). These opinions date from a period when the monarch's personal power was much greater than it is now, and it may well be thought that at the present day the dismissal of ministers who retained the confidence of the House of Commons would at the very least place the monarch in an extremely difficult situation, were the party to which the administration belonged returned with a majority at the next election. See also para 209 ante. As to the House of Commons see PARLIAMENT.

3    See para 417 note 11 ante. No administration supported by a strong and compact majority has resigned or gone to the country as the result of a defeat in the House of Commons, but Mr Chamberlain resigned in 1940 upon a vote which showed that confidence in his administration was waning. When an administration is defeated upon the reduction of a vote in supply, it depends upon the circumstances of the case whether or not it will regard its defeat as a vote of want of confidence. For the circumstances under which governments, though defeated in the House of Commons, even upon an amendment to the Address in reply to the Speech from the Throne, have not resigned office, see Mr Balfour's statement and the debate on the motion for the adjournment of the House: 150 Official Report (4th series), 24 July 1905, col 49 et seq. See also para 209 ante.

4    This principle was marked in 1868 by the resignation of the third Derby and first Disraeli administration upon an adverse verdict at the polls without meeting Parliament: see 12 Political History of England p 220. Of the subsequent ministries only three (namely the first and second Salisbury administrations in 1886 and 1892, and the first Baldwin administration in January 1924), though returned in a minority, awaited a vote of want of confidence before resignation.

5    In February 1974 the administration of Mr Edward Heath lost its majority in the House of Commons. Mr Heath tried to form a coalition with the Liberal party, but failed and resigned as Prime Minister, whereupon Mr Harold Wilson was invited to form a minority administration and did so, relying for a majority on the support of smaller parties in the Commons: see Brazier *Constitutional Practice* (2nd Edn, 1994) ch 3; and para 394 note 8 ante. As to the Prime Minister see paras 394–398 ante.

**419. Accountability to the public: petitions.** In cases where no illegal act has been committed, and consequently no action lies, but where the subject deems himself unduly oppressed by the sentence of a judge or the conduct of an official, the law of the constitution has provided a remedy by petition to the Crown. The exercise of this right cannot be denied, since it is the right of the subject to petition the monarch, and all commitments and prosecutions for so petitioning are illegal[1].

1    Bill of Rights s 1. The necessity for such a provision was proved by the *Seven Bishops' Trial* (1688) 12 State Tr 183. As to statutory provisions against tumultuous petitioning see CRIMINAL LAW. As to petitions for pardon see para 825 post. As to the monarch see para 351 et seq ante. As to the Bill of Rights see para 35 note 3 ante.

**420. Conduct of ministers.** Ministerial behaviour is regulated partly by law[1] and partly by guidelines that have been developed by successive ministries since 1945[2]. The guidelines lay down procedures, and require of ministers that they avoid conflicts between their public duties and private interests[3]. These guidelines include certain legal requirements[4] but they do not themselves have legal force. A minister will be reminded of them by his civil servants, and a minister who disregards them is liable to be censured by the Prime Minister, colleagues, Parliament or the press[5].

The Civil Service Code also contains guidance on the relations between ministers and civil servants[6].

1   As to criminal sanctions for misconduct in public office see para 12 ante.
2   The guidelines are now set out in *Questions of Procedure for Ministers* (Cabinet Office, May 1992), revised in 1995 after the government accepted recommendations in the *First Report of the Committee on Standards in Public Life* (Cm 2850-I) (1995): see the *Government Response to the First Report of the Committee on Standards in Public Life* (Cm 2931) (1995). The 1995 amendments include a statement (1) of the ethical principles and rules contained in *Questions of Procedure for Ministers*; and (2) that it is for individual ministers to judge how best to act in order to uphold the highest standards, and that ministers can only remain in office for as long as they retain the Prime Minister's confidence: see para 416 note 1 ante. As to the Prime Minister see paras 394–398 ante.
3   *Questions of Procedure for Ministers* (Cabinet Office, May 1992) (as revised: see note 1 supra) paras 103–123 advise ministers that they should resign other public appointments on taking up office, resign directorships save those in connection with private family estates, cease to be active in partnerships, dispose of controlling interests in companies which are closely associated with the minister's department or where conflict may arise or appear to arise, transfer investments to a 'blind' trust, avoid speculative investments where accusations of insider dealing may be made, and limit or cease their underwriting membership of Lloyds. On the last point see 247 HC Official Report (6th series), 21 July 1994, written answers cols *551–553*.
4   *Questions of Procedure for Ministers* (Cabinet Office, May 1992) (as revised: see note 1 supra) includes a provision that ministers have a duty to comply with the law, including international law and treaty obligations: see 567 HL Official Report (5th series), 29 November 1995, written answers cols *44–45*. It also specifically provides that ministers are bound by the Companies Securities (Insider Dealing) Act 1985: *Questions of Procedure for Ministers* (Cabinet Office, May 1992) (as so revised) para 115. See generally COMPANIES.
5   Public, press and parliamentary concern about standards of conduct of ministers contributed to the setting up of the Committee on Standards in Public Life under the chairmanship of Lord Nolan, with the following terms of reference: 'To examine current concerns about standards of conduct of all holders of public office, including arrangements relating to financial and commercial activities, and make recommendations as to any changes in present arrangements which might be required to ensure the highest standards of propriety in public life': 558 HL Official Report (5th series), 25 October 1994, col 466; 248 HC Official Report (6th series), 25 October 1994, col 758. See the *First Report of the Committee on Standards in Public Life* (Cm 2850) (1995); and *The Government's Response to the First Report of the Committee on Standards in Public Life* (Cm 2931) (1995); and para 12 ante.
6   As to the Civil Service Code see para 554 post. See also *Duties and Responsibilities of Civil Servants in relation to Ministers: A Note by the Head of the Home Civil Service* 123 HC Official Report (6th series), 2 December 1987, written answers cols *572–575;* revised (HC Paper (1993–94) no 27-II).

**421. Appointments outside government of former ministers.** There are no legal restrictions on the appointments ministers may accept after leaving government, but guidelines provide that ministers may seek advice from the Advisory Committee on Business Appointments[1] about any appointment they wish to take up within two years of leaving office[2].

1   The Advisory Committee on Business Appointments was established to advise on appointments outside government of former civil servants: see para 560 post. It is under the umbrella of the Office of Public Service in the Cabinet Office. As to the Office of Public Service see para 430 post.
2   See *Guidelines on the Acceptance of Appointments outside Government by Former Ministers of the Crown* (Cabinet Office, 1995). These guidelines enable, but do not require, ministers to ask the Advisory Committee on Business Appointments about any appointment they wish to take up within two years of leaving office.

They were drawn up in response to concerns expressed in the *First Report of the Committee on Standards in Public Life* (Cm 2850-I) (1995). They recognise that it is in the public interest that former ministers with experience in government should be able to move into business or into other areas of public life, but that when a former minister takes up a particular appointment there should be no cause for any suspicion of impropriety, for instance that the appointment is a reward for past favours, or that an employing company may gain an unfair advantage from the former minister's access to information while in government. The Advisory Committee on Business Appointments may advise that it sees no objection to the appointment, or it may recommend a delay of up to two years before it is taken up, or that for a similar period the former minister should stand aside from certain activities of the employer. A three month waiting period will normally be expected when the former minister is of cabinet rank unless the committee confirms that the proposed appointment is such that no consideration of improper advantage could apply. Approaches to the committee are considered in strict confidence, and remain confidential if the appointment is not taken up. When a former minister takes up a post which the Advisory Committee on Business Appointments has scrutinised, the committee's advice will be available for publication. The committee produces an annual report, summarising the cases with which it has dealt in the previous year.

**422. Legal accountability.** All ministers and servants of the Crown are accountable to the courts for the legality of their actions, and may be held civilly and criminally liable, in their individual capacities, for tortious or criminal acts[1]. This liability may be enforced either by means of ordinary criminal or civil proceedings or by means of impeachment, a remedy which is probably obsolete[2]. They are also subject to the judicial review jurisdiction of the courts[3].

1    As to the personal liability of Crown servants see para 388 ante.
2    See de Smith and Brazier *Constitutional and Administrative Law* (7th Edn, 1994) p 333. In 1968 the Select Committee on Parliamentary Privilege recommended that the right of impeachment be abolished by statute: *Report of the Select Commitee on Parliamentary Privilege* (HC Paper (1967–68) no 34).

     As to impeachment generally see para 377 ante; and COURTS. Ordinary criminal proceedings might prove illusory, owing to the Crown's power of stopping the trial by the grant of a *nolle prosequi* or a pardon. For relief from civil liability an Act of Parliament is necessary. Such Indemnity Acts are often used also to relieve from criminal liability. For an example of an Act passed to relieve a minister and his subordinate officials from liability for failure to lay a statutory instrument in draft before each House of Parliament, see the Town and Country Planning Regulations (London) (Indemnity) Act 1970 (repealed).
3    As to judicial review see ADMINISTRATIVE LAW.

### (v) Remuneration of Ministers

**423. Fixing of ministerial salaries.** For certain ministerial office-holders, maximum[1] salaries, or the maximum and minimum limits within which the First Lord of the Treasury may determine the salaries to be paid, are laid down by statute[2]. The annual amount, or the maximum or minimum annual amount, of any salary may be altered by Order in Council[3]. The salaries of the Lord Chancellor[4] and the Speaker of the House of Commons[5] are paid out of the Consolidated Fund[6], but other ministerial salaries are payable out of money provided by Parliament[7]; and, since they are voted annually in the estimates[8], they are subject to criticism, variations or disallowance by Parliament.

1    The amount specified in the Ministerial and other Salaries Act 1975 (as amended) as being the amount of any salary payable thereunder out of money provided by Parliament is to be taken to be the maximum amount so payable, and accordingly, the salary so payable in any year in respect of any office may be of a less amount than that so specified: s 4(2).
2    See ibid s 1(1)(a), Sch 1 (as amended: see note 3 infra). As to salaries of the Leaders and Whips of the Opposition see para 219 ante.
3    Ibid s 1(4) (amended by the Ministerial and other Pensions and Salaries Act 1991 s 3). No recommendation may be made to Her Majesty to make such an Order in Council unless a draft has been approved by resolution of each House of Parliament or, if it relates only to the salary to be paid to the Speaker of the House of Commons, by resolution of that House: Ministerial and other Salaries Act 1975 s 1(4) (as so amended).

The salary levels for the following ministers are set out in Sch 1 Pts I–IV (amended by the Ministerial and other Salaries Order 1996, SI 1996/1913, art 2, Sch 1) (but see infra): (1) Prime Minister and First Lord of the Treasury; (2) Chancellor of the Exchequer, Secretary of State, or Minister of Agriculture, Fisheries and Food; (3) for as long as the holder of the office is a member of the Cabinet, any of the offices of Lord President of the Council, Lord Privy Seal, Chancellor of the Duchy of Lancaster, Paymaster General, Chief Secretary to the Treasury, Parliamentary Secretary to the Treasury, or Minister of State; (4) any of the offices listed at (3) supra for as long as the holder of the office is not a member of the Cabinet; (5) minister in charge of a public department of Her Majesty's government in the United Kingdom who is not a member of the Cabinet, and whose office is not specified elsewhere in the Ministerial and other Salaries Act 1975 Sch 1 (as so amended); (6) Financial Secretary to the Treasury; (7) Attorney General; (8) Solicitor General; (9) Captain of the Honourable Corps of Gentlemen at Arms; (10) Parliamentary Secretary other than Parliamentary Secretary to the Treasury; (11) Captain of the Queen's Bodyguard of the Yeomen of the Guard; (12) Treasurer of Her Majesty's Household; (13) Lord in Waiting; (14) Comptroller of Her Majesty's Household, Vice-Chamberlain of Her Majesty's Household, Junior Lord of the Treasury, or Assistant Whip in the House of Commons.

The Ministerial and other Salaries Order 1996 is based on the *Report of the Senior Salaries Review Body on Parliamentary Pay and Allowances* (Cm 3330) (1996).

The salary paid to the holder of any office mentioned in heads (1)–(14) supra must be of the annual amount stated in relation to that office or, as the case may be, of such annual amount not more than the upper figure or less than the lower figure so stated as the First Lord of the Treasury may determine: Ministerial and other Salaries Act 1975 Sch 1 Pt V para 1(1).

A person to whom any salary is payable under s 1(1) is entitled to receive only one such salary, but if he is the holder of two or more offices in respect of which a salary is so payable and there is a difference between the salaries payable in respect of those offices, the office in respect of which a salary is payable to him must be that in respect of which the highest salary is payable: s 1(5).

The date on which the holder of any office listed in head (3) supra becomes or ceases to be a member of the Cabinet must be notified in the London Gazette, and any such notification is conclusive evidence for the purposes of Sch 1 (as so amended): Sch 1 Pt V para 1(2). For an example of such notification see the London Gazette 1 August 1996.

'Junior Lord of the Treasury' means any Lord Commissioner of the Treasury other than the First Lord and the Chancellor of the Exchequer: Ministerial and other Salaries Act 1975 s 4(1). For the meaning of 'Minister of State' see para 400 note 6 ante and for the meaning of 'Parliamentary Secretary' see para 400 note 7 ante.

4   Ibid s 1(2) (amended by the Courts and Legal Services Act 1990 ss 84(d), 125(7), Sch 20; and the Ministerial and other Pensions and Salaries Act 1991 s 3). As to the salary payable to the Lord Chancellor see para 478 post.

5   Ministerial and other Salaries Act 1975 s 1(3) (amended by the Ministerial and other Salaries Order 1996 art 5). The Speaker of the House of Commons is to be paid an annual salary, and on a dissolution of Parliament the Speaker of the House of Commons at the time of the dissolution is deemed for this purpose to remain Speaker until a Speaker is chosen by the new Parliament: Ministerial and other Salaries Act 1975 s 1(3) (as so amended).

6   As to the Consolidated Fund see para 711 et seq post.

7   Ministerial and other Salaries Act 1975 s 3(1). The salaries payable in respect of the offices of (1) Treasurer of Her Majesty's Household; (2) Comptroller of Her Majesty's Household; (3) Vice-Chamberlain of Her Majesty's Household; (4) Captain of the Honourable Corps of Gentlemen at Arms; (5) Captain of the Queen's Bodyguard of the Yeomen of the Guard; and (6) Lord in Waiting, are to be paid out of money so provided as part of the expenses of the Treasury: s 3(1). The sums payable out of money provided by Parliament in respect of the salary of the Chancellor of the Duchy of Lancaster must be reduced by the amount of the salary payable to him otherwise than out of moneys so provided in respect of his office: s 3(2).

8   As to the estimates see para 712 post.

## 424. Number of ministerial salaries payable.
In the case of certain offices a salary may be paid[1] to more than one holder of the office at the same time, although restrictions are placed on the number of salaries which may be paid at the same time[2].

Thus the number of Secretaries of State[3] to whom salaries may be paid is subject to the limitation that not more than 21 cabinet level salaries[4] may be paid at the same time[5].

The number of Ministers of State[6] to whom salaries may be paid is subject to the limitation that not more than 50 cabinet level and ministerial salaries[7] may be paid at the same time[8].

The number of Parliamentary Secretaries[9], other than Parliamentary Secretary to the Treasury, to whom salaries may be paid is subject to the limitation that not more than 83 cabinet level, ministerial and parliamentary secretary level salaries[10] may be paid at the same time[11].

The number of salaries paid at the same time to Junior Lords of the Treasury[12] may not exceed five[13]; to Assistant Whips in the House of Commons, seven[14]; and to Lords in Waiting, five[15].

1   Ie under the Ministerial and other Salaries Act 1975 s 1(1)(a), Sch 1 (amended by the Ministerial and other Salaries Order 1996, SI 1996/1913, art 2, Sch 1): see para 423 ante.
2   Ministerial and other Salaries Act 1975 Sch 1 Pt V para 2. Under the power to transfer functions (see para 363 ante) Her Majesty may, by Order in Council, make provisions which modify the enactments regulating the number of offices in respect of which salaries may be paid: Ministers of the Crown Act 1975 s 1(1), (2)(d).
3   For the meaning of 'Secretary of State' see para 400 note 5 ante.
4   Ie salaries paid in accordance with the Ministerial and other Salaries Act 1975 Sch 1 Pt I (as amended: see note 1 supra). See para 423 ante.
5   Ibid Sch 1 Pt V para 2(a). Thus the intention is that the Cabinet should consist of not more than 22 members, including the Lord Chancellor. The inconvenient limitation to nine, formerly imposed on the number of Secretaries of State by the Ministerial Salaries Consolidation Act 1965 s 2(1) (repealed), has been abolished. The size of the Cabinet can, of course, be increased provided the additional members are paid non-cabinet salaries: see the Ministerial and other Salaries Act 1975 Sch 1 Pt II (as amended: see note 1 supra); and para 423 ante.
6   For the meaning of 'Minister of State' see para 400 note 6 ante.
7   Ie salaries paid in accordance with the Ministerial and other Salaries Act 1975 Sch 1 Pts I and II (as amended: see note 1 supra). See para 423 ante.
8   Ibid Sch 1 Pt V para 2(b).
9   For the meaning of 'Parliamentary Secretary' see para 400 note 7 ante.
10  Ie salaries paid in accordance with the Ministerial and other Salaries Act 1975 Sch 1 Pts I and II (as amended: see note 1 supra) taken together with salaries to any Parliamentary Secretary in accordance with Sch 1 Pt IV (as amended: see note 1 supra). See para 423 ante.
11  Ibid Sch 1 Pt V para 2(c).
12  For the meaning of 'Junior Lord of the Treasury' see para 423 note 3 ante.
13  Ministerial and other Salaries Act 1975 Sch 1 Pt V para 2(d).
14  Ibid Sch 1 Pt V para 2(e).
15  Ibid Sch 1 Pt V para 2(f).

**425. Ministers' parliamentary salaries and allowances.** In   addition   to   their statutory salaries[1], ministers who are members of the House of Commons receive a parliamentary salary[2]. They are also entitled to certain parliamentary allowances: these comprise the secretarial and travelling allowances payable to all members[3], a supplementary London allowance[4] and, for those with constituencies outside the London area, an allowance in respect of constituency duties which involve their spending nights away from their only or main residence.

Certain ministers and other office-holders may be entitled to a grant if, before the age of 65, they cease to hold a relevant office[5] and do not again become a holder of a relevant office within three weeks[6]. The amount to which such a person is entitled is salary-related, being an amount equal to one-quarter of the annual amount of the salary which was being paid to that person in respect of that office immediately before he ceased to hold office[7].

Ministers in the House of Lords, though not eligible for the daily expenses allowance payable in respect of attendance in the House, are entitled, in common with other peers, to reimbursement of their travel expenses between their homes and Westminster for the purpose of attending the House of Lords[8].

Free residences are enjoyed by the Prime Minister and First Lord of the Treasury, the Lord Chancellor, the Home Secretary, the Secretary of State for Foreign and

Commonwealth Affairs, the Chancellor of the Exchequer, the Chancellor of the Duchy of Lancaster and the Parliamentary Secretary to the Treasury[9].

Certain ministers and office-holders in the House of Lords[10] are entitled to an allowance, based on the rate of overnight expenses recoverable by other members of the House[11]. This allowance will not be regarded as part of the salary in respect of the relevant office for pension purposes or for the purposes of payment of salary-related grants[12].

1   See paras 423–423 ante.
2   See 828 HC Official Report (5th series), 20 December 1971, col 1248. See also Judge 'The Politics of MPs' Pay' (1984) 37 Parliamentary Affairs 59.
3   See 828 HC Official Report (5th series), 20 December 1971, cols 1248–1249; and PARLIAMENT.
4   This is not payable to a minister who holds a paid office in respect of which an official residence is provided from public funds: 828 HC Official Report (5th series), 20 December 1971, col 1249.
5   'Relevant office' means (1) any office, other than that of Prime Minister and First Lord of the Treasury, in respect of which a salary is payable in accordance with the Ministerial and other Salaries Act 1975 s 1, Sch 1 (amended by the Ministerial and other Salaries Order 1996, SI 1996/1913, art 2, Sch 1) (see para 423 ante); (2) any position in respect of which a salary is payable in accordance with the Ministerial and other Salaries Act 1975 s 1, Sch 2 (amended by the Ministerial and other Salaries Order 1996 art 3, Sch 2) (see para 219 ante); (3) the office of Chairman of Ways and Means and any office of Deputy Chairman of Ways and Means in respect of which a salary is payable out of money provided by Parliament; and (4) the office of Chairman of Committees of the House of Lords and any office of Deputy Chairman of Committees of the House of Lords in respect of which a salary is payable out of such money: Ministerial and other Pensions and Salaries Act 1991 s 4(6).
6   Ibid s 4(1). Such a payment is to be made out of money provided by Parliament or charged on and paid out of the Consolidated Fund according as the salary payable in respect of that office is payable out of such money or charged on and paid out of that fund: s 8(1). There must be charged on and paid out of the Consolidated Fund or, as the case may be, paid out of money provided by Parliament any increase attributable to this Act in the sums charged on and payable out of that fund or payable out of such money under any other Act: s 8(3). As to the Consolidated Fund see para 711 et seq post.
    Payment may not be made until the end of the three week period mentioned in s 4(1): s 4(4). No payment may be made under these provisions where a person has ceased to hold a relevant office on his death: s 4(5).
7   Ibid s 4(2). The amount is reduced if the person was a member of the House of Commons immediately before he ceased to hold the office: s 4(3). Where a person ceases to hold a relevant office while Parliament is dissolved, the amount is reduced if he was a member of the House of Commons immediately before the dissolution: s 4(7).
8   See the *First Report of the Review Body on Top Salaries: Ministers of the Crown and Members of Parliament* (Cmnd 4836) (1971) para 80.
9   *First Report of the Review Body on Top Salaries: Ministers of the Crown and Members of Parliament* (Cmnd 4836) (1971) para 79 App I.
10  Ie (1) any member of the House of Lords who holds an office in respect of which a salary is payable in accordance with the Ministerial and other Salaries Act 1975 Sch 1 (as amended: see note 5 supra) (see para 423 ante); (2) any member of the House of Lords who holds a position in respect of which a salary is payable in accordance with the Ministerial and other Salaries Act 1975 Sch 2 (as amended: see note 5 supra) (see para 219 ante); and (3) the Chairman of Committees and Principal Deputy Chairman of Committees of the House of Lords: Ministerial and other Pensions and Salaries Act 1991 s 5(1).
11  Ibid s 5; and the Lords Office-holders Allowance Order 1991, SI 1991/772. The allowance payable to a person within note 10 heads (1) or (3) supra is to be paid out of money provided by Parliament and the allowance payable to a person within note 10 head (2) supra is to be charged on and paid out of the Consolidated Fund: Ministerial and other Pensions and Salaries Act 1991 s 8(2). There must be charged on and paid out of the Consolidated Fund or, as the case may be, paid out of money provided by Parliament any increase attributable to this Act in the sums charged on and payable out of that fund or payable out of such money under any other Act: s 8(3).
12  Ibid s 5(4). As to salary-related grants see text and notes 5–7 supra.

## 426. Pensions for former Prime Minister or Speaker of the House of Commons.

In respect of a person who ceases to hold the office of Prime Minister and First Lord of the Treasury or the office of Speaker of the House of Commons after 28 February 1991[1], the annual amount of pension payable will be equal to one-half of the annual salary payable in respect of that office at the time when that person ceases to hold it[2]. The pensions of Prime Ministers who ceased to hold office after 28 February 1991 will be deemed to begin on the day following the last day of service in respect of which the pension is payable[3].

For a person who ceased to hold the office of Prime Minister before 28 February 1991, the annual amount of pension payable at that date[4] is increased by the sum required to bring it up to what it would be by virtue of these provisions if he had ceased to hold office immediately after 28 February 1991[5]. For the purposes of the Pensions (Increase) Act 1971, the pension of such a person is now deemed to have begun on 28 February 1991 so that pension increase will be payable on the whole of the amount as increased by the Ministerial and other Pensions and Salaries Act 1991[6] as if it were a pension which began on that date[7].

These pensions are charged on and payable out of the Consolidated Fund[8]; but no such pension is payable to any person so long as he is in receipt of any salary payable out of the Consolidated Fund or the revenue of the Duchy of Lancaster, or any salary payable out of money provided by Parliament, other than a salary or allowance payable out of money so provided in respect of his membership of the House of Commons[9].

The Prime Minister and First Lord of the Treasury and the Speaker of the House of Commons may elect to contribute to the Parliamentary Contributory Pension Fund[10] out of his remuneration as a member of the House while holding that office[11], but any pension may not be calculated by reference to service as a member of the House of Commons before 28 February 1991[12].

On the death of a person who holds or has held office as Prime Minister and First Lord of the Treasury or Speaker of the House of Commons provision is made for the benefit of surviving spouses and children[13].

1 Ministerial and other Pensions and Salaries Act 1991 s 1(4). As to the pension payable to a person who has ceased to hold the office of Lord Chancellor see para 479 post. As to the Prime Minister see paras 394–398 ante. As to the Speaker of the House of Commons see PARLIAMENT.
2 Parliamentary and other Pensions Act 1972 s 26(3), (4) (substituted by the Ministerial and other Pensions and Salaries Act 1991 s 1(1)).
3 Pensions (Increase) Act 1971 s 8(2) (applied by the Pensions Increase (Past Prime Ministers) Regulations 1991, SI 1991/787, reg 3).
4 Ie under the Parliamentary and other Pensions Act 1972 s 26(3) (as originally enacted) or the Ministerial Salaries Consolidation Act 1965 s 3 (repealed).
5 Ministerial and other Pensions and Salaries Act 1991 s 1(5).
6 See the text and notes 4 and 5 supra.
7 Pensions Increase (Past Prime Ministers) Regulations 1991 regs 3, 4.
8 Parliamentary and other Pensions Act 1972 s 26(5). As to the Consolidated Fund see para 711 et seq post.
9 Ibid s 26(2).
10 As to the Parliamentary Contributory Pension Fund see PARLIAMENT.
11 Parliamentary and other Pensions Act 1987 s 2(3) (amended by the Ministerial and other Pensions and Salaries Act 1991 s 2(1)). An election to contribute to the fund must be in accordance with regulations: Parliamentary and other Pensions Act 1987 s 2(3) (as so amended); and see the Parliamentary Pensions (Amendment) Regulations 1992, SI 1992/599 (amended by the Parliamentary Pensions (Consolidation and Amendment) Regulations 1993, SI 1993/3253); the Parliamentary Pensions (Additional Voluntary Contributions Scheme) Regulations 1993, SI 1993/3252 (as modified by the Insurance Companies (Third Insurance Directives) Regulations 1994, SI 1994/1696); and the Parliamentary Pensions (Consolidation and Amendment) Regulations 1993. Certain enactments and subordinate legislation have effect as if contained in regulations made under the Parliamentary and other Pensions Act 1987 s 2: see s 2, Sch 2.
12 Ministerial and other Pensions and Salaries Act 1991 s 2(2).
13 Parliamentary and other Pensions Act 1972 s 27; Parliamentary Pensions (Consolidation and Amendment) Regulations 1993 regs K1, K2, K3; Pensions for Dependants of the Prime Minister or Speaker (Designated Provisions) Regulations 1995, SI 1995/1443, reg 2.

## (3) CENTRAL GOVERNMENT: DEPARTMENTS AND MEMBERS OF THE GOVERNMENT, LEGAL ADVISERS AND THE ROYAL HOUSEHOLD

### (i) The Cabinet Office

**427. The Cabinet Office.** The Cabinet Office[1] is comprised of the Cabinet Office Secretariat[2] and the Office of Public Service[3]. At its head is the Secretary of the Cabinet[4], who reports to the Prime Minister as Minister for the Civil Service[5].

The Minister for the Civil Service is for all purposes a corporation sole[6]. He has an official seal which is authenticated by his signature or that of a secretary to the department, or that of any person authorised by the minister to act in that behalf[7]. The seal must be officially and judicially noticed[8]. Every document purporting to be an instrument made or issued by the minister and to be sealed with his corporate seal duly authenticated, or to be signed or executed by a secretary to the department or any duly authorised person, is to be received in evidence and deemed to be so made or issued without further proof unless the contrary is shown[9]. A certificate signed by the minister that an instrument purporting to be made or issued by him was so made or issued is conclusive evidence of the fact[10]. Proof of any instrument of the minister may be given, in accordance with the Documentary Evidence Act 1868[11].

The Minister for the Civil Service is assisted by the First Secretary of State and Deputy Prime Minister, and a minister without portfolio[12].

The ministerial office of the Chancellor of the Duchy of Lancaster[13] is situated in the Cabinet Office and the costs are currently borne upon the Cabinet Office vote[14].

1 The Cabinet Office has developed from the War Cabinet Secretariat established to service the War Cabinet in December 1916: see generally Mosley *The Story of the Cabinet Office* (1969). The Prime Minister answers parliamentary questions relating to the Cabinet Office: see eg 872 HC Official Report (5th series), 9 April 1974, cols 151–153. The Parliamentary Commissioner for Administration cannot investigate the conduct of the Cabinet Office: see the Parliamentary Commissioner Act 1967 s 4(1), Sch 2 note 6 (substituted by the Parliamentary and Health Service Commissioners Act 1987 s 1(1), (2), Sch 1; amended by the Transfer of Functions (Science) Order 1992, SI 1992/1296, art 6(1), Schedule para 3(d)). As to the Parliamentary Commissioner for Administration see ADMINISTRATIVE LAW vol 1(1) (Reissue) para 41 et seq.

    See also the Civil Service Year Book 1996 col 67 et seq; and *Cabinet Committee Business: A Guide for Departments* (Cabinet Office, December 1995).
2 As to the Cabinet Office Secretariat see para 428 post.
3 As to the Office of Public Service see para 430 post.
4 This post, which was at various times combined with that of Secretary of the Committee of Imperial Defence, or of Clerk to the Privy Council, or of Permanent Secretary to the Treasury, became independent in 1962. As to the Cabinet see paras 402–413 ante.
5 See the Civil Service Year Book 1996 col 67. As to the Prime Minister see paras 394–398 ante. As to the transfer of functions to the Minister for the Civil Service see the Ministers of the Crown Act 1975 ss 1, 2; Minister for the Civil Service Order 1968, SI 1968/1656; Minister for the Civil Service Order 1971, SI 1971/2099; Transfer of Functions (Minister for the Civil Service and Treasury) Order 1981, SI 1981/1670; Transfer of Functions (Minister for the Civil Service and Treasury) Order 1987, SI 1987/2039; Transfer of Functions (Minister for the Civil Service and Treasury) Order 1991, SI 1991/188; Transfer of Functions (Science) Order 1992, SI 1992/1296; Transfer of Functions (Treasury and Minister for the Civil Service) Order 1992, SI 1992/1737; Transfer of Functions (Treasury and Minister for the Civil Service) Order 1995, SI 1995/269. As to the transfer of functions generally see para 363 ante. As to the Civil Service generally see paras 549–564 post.
6 Ministers of the Crown Act 1975 s 6(2), Sch 1 para 5. As to corporations sole see CORPORATIONS.
7 Ibid Sch 1 para 5. As to secretarial seals see para 357 ante.
8 Ibid Sch 1 para 6.
9 Ibid Sch 1 para 6.
10 Ibid Sch 1 para 7.

11  Ibid Sch 1 para 8; and as to the Documentary Evidence Act 1868 see generally EVIDENCE.

12  See the Civil Service Year Book 1996 1996 cols 67–68.

13  The Chancellor of the Duchy of Lancaster has few duties associated with the duchy. Incumbents of this office are therefore always allocated other duties (see eg para 430 post), as is the practice with ministers without portfolio. As to the duchy see CROWN LANDS AND PRIVILEGES.

14  See the *Supply Estimates 1995–96 for the year ending 31 March 1996* (HC Paper (1994–95) no 271–XVIII). As to votes as heads of expenditure and as to estimates see para 712 post.

## 428. The Cabinet Office Secretariat.

Among the principal duties of the Cabinet Office Secretariat are (1) to record the proceedings of the Cabinet and its committees; (2) to transmit decisions made by these bodies to the departments responsible for giving effect to them or otherwise interested; (3) to prepare agenda papers, to arrange for the attendance of ministers and other persons concerned, and to procure and circulate documents required for discussion; and (4) to attend to correspondence connected with the work of the Cabinet[1]. The stated aim of the Cabinet Office Secretariat is to provide an effective, efficient and impartial service to the Cabinet and its committees. It has no executive powers beyond servicing the Cabinet and committees and co-ordinating departmental contributions to the government's work[2].

The Secretary of the Cabinet is also the Head of the Home Civil Service[3]. He is assisted by senior civil servants within the Economic and Domestic Affairs and Legislation Secretariat; the Defence and Overseas Affairs Secretariat; the Joint Intelligence Organisation; the European Secretariat; the Telecommunications Secretariat; the Establishment Officers Group; and the Ceremonial Branch[4].

1  War Cabinet Report for 1917 (Cd 9005). There has hardly been any change since that date.

   Until 1916 deliberations of the Cabinet took place only in the presence of members of the Cabinet, except where other persons were summoned to assist with special knowledge or advice (see para 406 ante). No official record of the proceedings was kept, though the decisions arrived at might be embodied in the form of written minutes to be communicated to the monarch by the Prime Minister; and indeed it was customary for the Prime Minister to write a letter to the monarch after every cabinet meeting, setting out what had been decided. No agenda was prepared, and members might be called upon to make decisions suddenly, and without sufficient information about the point at issue, though it was usual to circulate written memoranda, dispatches and other documents which were intended for perusal by members of the Cabinet, in cabinet dispatch boxes, of which each member had a master key.

   With the growth of government business early in the present century the defects of the system became apparent, and during the 1914–18 war it broke down entirely. In 1902 a Committee of Imperial Defence, with a permanent secretariat, had been set up, and during the earlier stages of the 1914–18 war this secretariat was used first for the War Council, then for the Dardannelles Committee, then for the War Committee, and finally for the War Cabinet. During 1917, 1918 and 1919 it increased very greatly in size, and it met with serious criticism. The Cabinet Secretariat, as it had now become, was successfully defended in a debate in the House of Commons in June 1922, but at the end of the year the new Conservative government found it necessary to reduce it considerably. It was, however, retained, and each succeeding government has found its services indispensable.

   For the history of the War Cabinet Secretariat see the *War Cabinet Report for 1917* (Cd 9005) (1918); *War Cabinet Report for 1918* (Cmd 325) (1919); and articles by Clement Jones in the Empire Review for December 1923 and January 1924. For the later developments see The Times, 23 December 1931 per Sir John Simon. See also the Eleventh Haldane Memorial Lecture delivered by Lord Hankey on 22nd May 1942; and Mosley *The Story of the Cabinet Office* (1969).

   As to the Cabinet see paras 402–413 ante. As to functions of the Cabinet Office Secretariat see para 407 et seq ante. See also *Cabinet Committee Business: A Guide for Departments* (Cabinet Office, December 1995).

2  See the Cabinet Office, Privy Council Office and Parliament Annual Report: *The Government's Expenditure Plans 1995–96 to 1997–98* (Cm 2820) (1995).

3  See the Civil Service Year Book 1996 col 67. As to the Civil Service generally see paras 549–564 post.

4  See the Civil Service Year Book 1996 col 67 et seq; and see also Dynes and Walker *The Times Guide to the New British State: The Government Machine in the 1990s* (1995) pp 32–33. The Establishment Officers Group consists of a Personnel division; an Infrastructure division; a Finance division; and Internal Audit unit; and a Historical and Records section: Civil Service Year Book 1996 cols 78–79.

**429. Parliamentary Counsel Office.** Parliamentary Counsel are included within the Cabinet Office group[1]. They are responsible for drafting government bills, amendments to them and any motions, including financial resolutions, to be tabled in connection with them[2]. Parliamentary Counsel also advise government departments on all aspects of parliamentary procedure when bills are introduced[3]. The office is headed by the First Parliamentary Counsel[4].

1  See the Civil Service Year Book 1996 col 529; and the Cabinet Office, Privy Council Office and Parliament Annual Report: *The Government's Expenditure Plans 1995–96 to 1997–98* (Cm 2820) (1995).
2  See the Civil Service Year Book 1996 col 529. Parliamentary Counsel are not, however, responsible for drafting bills relating only to Scotland, which are dealt with by the Lord Advocate's Department: see the Civil Service Year Book 1996 col 881; and paras 63 ante, 530 post.
3  See the Civil Service Year Book 1996 col 529.
4  See the Civil Service Year Book 1996 col 529.

**430. The Office of Public Service.** The Office of Public Service was set up within the Cabinet Office[1] in 1992 in order to take over most of the functions of the Civil Service Department[2], together with the science functions of what was the Department of Education and Science[3]. The Permanent Secretary of the Office of Public Service reports both to the Secretary of the Cabinet and through the Chancellor of the Duchy of Lancaster to the Deputy Prime Minister and First Secretary of State, and ultimately to the Prime Minister as Minister for the Civil Service[4]. The Office of Public Service is responsible[5] for the competitiveness agenda[6]; the progress and development of deregulation[7]; raising the standard of public services, including the privatised utilities, through the Citizen's Charter programme[8]; and improving the effectiveness and efficiency of central government and science and technology policy and the science budget[9]. Its Civil Service responsibilities include the market testing programme and efficiency scrutinies; the 'next steps' initiative[10]; the effective and efficient use of information systems in government[11]; recruitment, training and development; senior and public appointments and interchange; equal opportunities; duties and standards of conduct and the promotion of greater openness in government.

The Office of Public Service has four executive agencies[12]: (1) the Civil Service College; (2) the Civil Service Occupational Health and Safety Agency; (3) Recruitment and Assessment Services; and (4) the Chessington Computer Centre.

1   As to the Cabinet Office see para 427 ante.
2   As to the Civil Service generally see paras 549–564 post.
3   As to the transfer of functions to the Minister for the Civil Service see para 427 ante. As to the transfer of functios generally see para 363 ante.
4   See the Civil Service Year Book 1996. As to the Minister for the Civil Service see para 427 ante, 550 post.
5   See the Civil Service Year Book 1996 col 68.
6   As to the Competitiveness Division see para 434 post.
7   As to the Deregulation Unit see para 433 post.
8   As to the Citizen's Charter Unit see para 431 post.
9   As to the Efficiency Unit see para 432 post.
10  As to the 'next steps' initiative see para 551 post.
11  Ie through CCTA: The Government Centre for Information Systems. See the Civil Service Year Book 1996 col 76.
12  There are other government agencies, eg Her Majesty's Stationery Office and the Central Office of Information, which are also departments in their own right. As to non-ministerial departments generally see para 528 post. As to executive agencies see further para 551 post.

**431. Citizen's Charter Unit.** The Citizen's Charter Unit of the Office of Public Service was set up in order to implement, develop and co-ordinate the programme of action arising from the Citizen's Charter proposals[1]. These proposals cover all public services, including government departments, 'next steps' agencies[2], nationalised industries, local authorities, the National Health Service, courts, police, emergency services, and the key utilities in the private sector. The aim is that over a period of ten years standards which can be expected from public services will be provided. There will be publication of actual performance against those standards; information on how public services are run; public consultation; helpful and courteous service from public servants; an effective complaints procedure; and value for money[3].

1   *The Citizen's Charter: Raising the Standard* (Cm 1599) (1991).
2   As to the 'next steps' initiative see para 551 post.
3   The Charter programme is to be pursued in a number of ways, with the approach varying from service to service in different parts of the United Kingdom. The initiatives and ideas of the Charter programme are to raise standards in the way most appropriate to each service. See *The Citizen's Charter: Raising the Standard* (Cm 1599) (1991). By 1994 there were 38 Charters covering the main public services; and 98 organisations had received a Charter Mark award by October 1994, making 227 awards in total over a period of three years. See *The Citizen's Charter Second Report* (Cm 2540) (1994).

**432. Efficiency Unit.** The Efficiency Unit is also part of the Office of Public Service[1]. Its aim is to improve the value for money of the resources used by government departments and to maintain the impetus in opening central government work to competition[2]. The unit is establishing efficiency plans and scrutinies, but the most significant of the unit's reforms is the 'next steps' initiative[3].

1   In 1979 Sir Derek Rayner was appointed by the Prime Minister to advise on ways of improving efficiency in Whitehall, which led to the setting up of the Efficiency Unit. The Efficiency Unit became part of the Office of Public Service in 1992.
2   See the Civil Service Year Book 1996 col 71.
3   See the Report of the Efficiency Unit to the Prime Minister *Improving Management in Government: The Next Steps* (Efficiency Unit of the Cabinet Office, 1988); and para 551 post. See also the Cabinet Office, Privy Council Office and Parliament Annual Report: *The Government's Expenditure Plans 1995–96 to 1997–98* (Cm 2820) (1995).

**433. Deregulation Unit.** The Deregulation Unit of the Office of Public Service has been established in order to administer the deregulation initiative, the aim of which is to reduce administrative and regulatory burdens and hence to contribute to competitiveness[1]. The stated aims of the deregulation initiative are: (1) to secure specific deregulatory changes; (2) to minimise the burden of new domestic and European Community regulation; and (3) to improve guidance, advice and enforcement[2]. The Deregulation Unit co-ordinates the use by departments of the streamlined procedures for deregulating primary legislation[3].

1   See *Competitiveness: Forging Ahead* (Cm 2867) (1995).
2   See the Civil Service Year Book 1996 col 70.
3   Ie under the Deregulation and Contracting Out Act 1994: see para 364 ante.

**434. Competitiveness Division.** The aim of the Competitiveness Division of the Office of Public Service is to ensure that government policies have the maximum practical benefit on the competitiveness of the United Kingdom[1].

1   See the Civil Service Year Book 1996 col 69.

### (ii) The Ministry of Agriculture, Fisheries and Food

**435. The Minister of Agriculture, Fisheries and Food.** The Minister of Agriculture, Fisheries and Food is the successor to the Board of Agriculture and Fisheries[1]. He is a corporation sole for the purposes of acquiring and holding land or other property[2]. He takes the oath of allegiance and official oath[3]. He may appoint two or more secretaries, including assistant secretaries, and such officers and servants as with the sanction of the Minister for the Civil Service he may determine[4]. He is currently assisted by a Minister of State and two Parliamentary Secretaries[5].

The Minister of Agriculture, Fisheries and Food has an official seal which is officially and judicially noticed, and is authenticated by his signature or by the signature of the secretary or an assistant secretary[6] or of a person authorised by the minister[7]. Documents which purport to have been issued by the minister and to be sealed with his seal, duly authenticated, are received in evidence and deemed to be so issued without further proof unless the contrary is shown[8]. A certificate signed by the minister that an instrument purporting to be made or issued by him was so made or issued is conclusive evidence of the fact[9]. Proof of orders or regulations of the minister may be given, in accordance with the Documentary Evidence Act 1868[10], in all legal proceedings[11].

The ministry is an authorised government department for the purpose of suing and being sued[12], and is subject to investigation by the Parliamentary Commissioner for Administration[13].

For the purposes of the European Communities Act 1972[14] the minister is a designated minister[15] in relation to medicinal products and the common agricultural policy of the European Economic Community[16].

The expenses of the Ministry of Agriculture, Fisheries and Food are provided by Parliament[17].

1 See the Ministry of Agriculture and Fisheries Act 1919 s 1, which empowered the Crown to appoint a Minister of Agriculture and Fisheries (s 1(1)) and provided that the Board of Agriculture and Fisheries should be deemed to be the predecessor of the first person to be so appointed (s 1(3)). The board was established as the Board of Agriculture by the Board of Agriculture Act 1889 s 1 (repealed), and renamed the Board of Agriculture and Fisheries by the Board of Agriculture and Fisheries Act 1903 s 1(1). The minister's style and title was changed to that of Minister of Agriculture, Fisheries and Food when the functions of the Minister of Food were largely transferred to him by the Transfer of Functions (Ministry of Food) Order 1955, SI 1955/554, art 3(1). As to the transfer of functions generally see para 363 ante. As to the minister's salary see para 423 ante.

2 Ministry of Agriculture and Fisheries Act 1919 s 1(2); Transfer of Functions (Ministry of Food) Order 1955 art 3(3). As to corporations sole see CORPORATIONS.

3 Board of Agriculture Act 1889 s 8(2); Board of Agriculture and Fisheries Act 1903 s 1(1); Ministry of Agriculture and Fisheries Act 1919 s 1(1); Transfer of Functions (Ministry of Food) Order 1955 art 3(3).

4 Board of Agriculture Act 1889 s 5(1); Board of Agriculture and Fisheries Act 1903 s 2(2); Board of Agriculture and Fisheries Act 1909 s 1(1); Ministry of Agriculture and Fisheries Act 1919 s 1(1); Ministers of the Crown Act 1937 s 11, Sch 4 (repealed); Transfer of Functions (Ministry of Food) Order 1955 art 3(3); Ministers of the Crown (Parliamentary Secretaries) Act 1960 s 4(1), Sch 1; Minister for the Civil Service Order 1968, SI 1968/1656, art 2(1). As to the power to appoint inspectors of fisheries see the Ministry of Agriculture and Fisheries Act 1919 s 1(1); Transfer of Functions (Ministry of Food) Order 1955 art 3(3). As to paying out of money provided by Parliament the salaries of the minister's secretaries (other than the Parliamentary Secretary), officers and servants, see the Board of Agriculture Act 1889 s 5(2), (3); Board of Agriculture and Fisheries Act 1903 s 1(1), (9); Ministry of Agriculture and Fisheries Act 1919 s 1(1); Ministers of the Crown Act 1937 s 11, Sch 4 (repealed); Transfer of Functions (Ministry of Food) Order 1955 art 3(3); Ministers of the Crown (Parliamentary Secretaries) Act 1960 s 4(1), Sch 1.
As to the Minister for the Civil Service see para 427 ante.

5 See the Civil Service Year Book 1996 col 37.

6 As to the appointment of secretaries see the text and note 4 supra.

7 Board of Agriculture Act 1889 s 6(2). As to secretarial seals see para 357 ante.

8 Ibid s 7(1).

9 Ibid s 7(2).

10 Ie in accordance with the Documentary Evidence Act 1868 s 2; and the Documentary Evidence Act 1882 s 2: see EVIDENCE.

11 Documentary Evidence Act 1895 s 1.

12 See the list published under the Crown Proceedings Act 1947 s 17(1) (as amended); and CROWN PROCEEDINGS.

13 Parliamentary Commissioner Act 1967 s 4(1), Sch 2 (substituted by the Parliamentary and Health Service Commissioners Act 1987 s 1(1), (2), Sch 1). As to the Parliamentary Commissioner for Administration see ADMINISTRATIVE LAW vol 1(1) (Reissue) para 41 et seq.

14 Ie the European Communities Act 1972 s 2(2): see para 359 ante.

15 For the meaning of 'designated minister' see para 359 note 2 ante.

16 European Communities (Designation) Order 1972, SI 1972/1811 (as amended); and the European Communities (Designation) Order 1976, SI 1976/897. For other areas in which he is the designated minister see the following European Communities (Designation) Orders: SI 1973/1889; SI 1975/427; SI 1976/2141; SI 1981/833; SI 1982/847; SI 1982/1675; SI 1988/785; SI 1988/2240; SI 1989/1327; SI 1989/2393; SI 1990/1304; SI 1991/755; SI 1992/2661; SI 1994/757; SI 1995/751.

17 See the *Supply Estimates 1995–96 for the year ending 31 March 1996* (HC Paper (1994–95) no 271–III).

**436. Functions.** The Minister of Agriculture, Fisheries and Food is responsible for the supervision and implementation of government policy relating to agriculture, horticulture and the fishing industry in England[1]. He is responsible for policies relating to safety and quality of food in the United Kingdom, including composition, labelling, additives, contaminants and new production processes[2]. He has responsibilities in connection with the administration of the common agricultural and fisheries policies of the European Community[3], being jointly responsible for the Intervention Board[4]; and also has responsibilities for various national support schemes[5] including emergency and strategic food reserves[6]. He is responsible for the administration of policies for the control and eradication of animal, fish and plant diseases[7], and the improvement and drainage of agricultural land[8]. The minister has responsibility for the protection and the enhancement of the countryside and the marine environment, for flood defence and for other rural issues[9]. The Ministry of Agriculture, Fisheries and Food is the licensing authority for veterinary medicines and the registration authority for pesticides; provides scientific and technical services and advice to farmers and growers; and commissions research[10]. The Forestry Commission exercises its functions in England subject to the direction of the minister[11].

1 Some functions in relation to agriculture and the fishing industry in Wales are the joint responsibility of the minister and the Secretary of State for Wales. In some instances statutes are administered by the minister jointly with the Secretary of State for Wales or, in the case of functions exercisable as regards Great Britain, by the minister acting jointly with the Secretary of State for Scotland or with the Secretary of State for Scotland and the Secretary of State for Wales. See the Transfer of Functions (Wales) Order 1969 (SI 1969/388); the Transfer of Functions (Wales) (No 1) Order 1978, SI 1978/272 (partially revoked by the Food Act 1984 s 134, Sch 11 (repealed)), which divides certain functions relating in particular to agriculture, fisheries, water resources, water supply and land drainage between the minister and the Secretary of State for Wales; and see also the Transfer of Functions (Radioactive Substances) (Wales) Order 1990, SI 1990/2598. See generally AGRICULTURE, FISHERIES, FOOD. As to the transfer of functions to the minister see para 435 ante. As to the transfer of functions generally see para 363 ante.

2 See the Food Safety Act 1990 s 4(1); and FOOD. See also the Civil Service Year Book 1996 col 37.

3 See para 435 text and notes 14–16 ante.

4 The Intervention Board for Agricultural Produce is a separate government department subject to the direction and control of the Minister of Agriculture, Fisheries and Food and the Secretaries of State respectively concerned with agriculture in Wales, Scotland and Northern Ireland acting jointly: see the European Communities Act 1972 s 6(1), (8); the Agriculture Act 1957 s 11; and note 1 supra. It is an executive agency, and is the government body within the United Kingdom for receiving and accounting for funding provided in accordance with the Common Agricultural Policy: see the Civil Service Year Book 1996 col 462. Its aims and objectives are set out in the Ministry of Agriculture, Fisheries and Food and the Intervention Board Annual Report: *The Government's Expenditure Plans 1995–96 to 1997–98:* (Cm 2803) (1995). As to the Common Agricultural Policy of the European Community see AGRICULTURE vol 1(2) (Reissue) para 1001 et seq; and as to the Intervention Board see AGRICULTURE vol 1(2) (Reissue) para 1007. As to non-ministerial departments generally see para 528 post. As to executive agencies see para 551 post.

5 See eg AGRICULTURE vol 1(2) (Reissue) para 565 et seq.

6 See the *Supply Estimates 1995–96 for the year ending 31 March 1996* (HC Paper (1994–95) no 271–III).

7   As to animal diseases see ANIMALS vol 2 para 482 et seq and AGRICULTURE vol 1(2) (Reissue) para 1028
    et seq; as to plant diseases see AGRICULTURE vol 1(2) (Reissue) para 1037; and as to the diseases of fish
    see FISHERIES vol 18 para 689 et seq.
8   See AGRICULTURE vol 1(2) (Reissue) para 501 et seq.
9   See the Civil Service Year Book 1996 col 37.
10  See the Civil Service Year Book 1996 col 37.
11  See the Forestry Act 1967 ss 1(4), 49(1). In the case of Wales, directions are given by the Secretary of
    State for Wales: ss 1(4), 49(1), (2). Directions are usually given by the minister and the Secretary of State
    jointly: s 1(5). As to the Forestry Commission see FORESTRY.

**437. Organisation.** The Minister of Agriculture, Fisheries and Food and the Minister
of State are assisted by a Permanent Secretary[1]. The groups reporting direct to the
Permanent Secretary are the Agriculture Commodities, Trade and Food Production
Directorate; the Food Safety Directorate; the Countryside, Marine Environment and
Fisheries Directorate; the Chief Scientist's Group; the Legal Department; the Finance
group; the Establishment Department; and the Information Division[2]. There is also a
Regional Services Division (which also advises on information technology matters)[3].

The Agricultural Commodities, Trade and Food Production Directorate comprises
two European Community Divisions; the Livestock Group; Arable Crops and
Horticulture; and Food, Drink and Marketing Policy[4].

The Food Safety Directorate is comprised of the Food Safety and Science Group; the
Veterinary Field and Investigation Service; the Chief Veterinary Officer's Group;
Agricultural Inputs; and Animal Health[5].

The Countryside, Marine Environment and Fisheries Directorate consists of
Fisheries; Land Use, Conservation and Countryside; Environment Policy; and
Economics and Statistics[6].

The minister has several executive agencies to which he has delegated responsibility,
namely: the Agricultural Development and Advisory Service, with regional consultancy,
research and statutory centres through England and Wales[7]; the Central Science
Laboratory[8]; the Central Veterinary Laboratory[9]; the Pesticides Safety Directorate[10]; the
Veterinary Medicines Directorate[11]; and the Meat Hygiene Service[12].

1   For a full description of the organisation of the Ministry of Agriculture, Fisheries and Food see the Civil
    Service Year Book 1996 cols 37–65. As to the Civil Service generally see paras 549–564 post.
2   See the Civil Service Year Book 1996 cols 37–57.
3   See the Civil Service Year Book 1996 cols 57–60.
4   See the Civil Service Year Book 1996 cols 42–45.
5   See the Civil Service Year Book 1996 cols 45–52.
6   See the Civil Service Year Book 1996 cols 53–57.
7   See the Civil Service Year Book 1996 cols 60–63.
8   See the Civil Service Year Book 1996 cols 63–64.
9   See the Civil Service Year Book 1996 col 64.
10  See the Civil Service Year Book 1996 col 64.
11  See the Civil Service Year Book 1996 col 65.
12  The Meat Hygiene Service was established on 1 April 1995, and is the most recent executive agency: see
    the Ministry of Agriculture Fisheries and Food and the Intervention Board Annual Report: *The
    Government's Expenditure Plans 1995–96 to 1997–98* (Cm 2803) (1995). As to executive agencies see para
    551 post.

## (iii)   The Ministry of Defence

**438. General.** In 1964 arrangements were made under the royal prerogative for a
Principal Secretary of State to be charged with general responsibility for defence; for
the establishment of a Defence Council having powers of command and administration
over Her Majesty's armed forces, and of an Admiralty Board, an Army Board and an

Air Force Board to be charged (under the Defence Council) with the administration of matters relating to the naval, military and air forces respectively[1]; and the appropriate statutory functions were transferred[2] to the Secretary of State for Defence[3] and the Defence Council[4].

The Ministry of Defence is an authorised government department for the purpose of suing and being sued[5], and is subject to investigation by the Parliamentary Commissioner for Administration[6]. The expenses of the Ministry of Defence are provided by Parliament[7].

The Ministry of Defence is headed by the Secretary of State for Defence, assisted by the Minister of State for the Armed Forces, the Minister of State for Defence Procurement and a Parliamentary Under Secretary of State[8]. They are assisted by two principal advisers, the Chief of the Defence Staff and the Permanent Under Secretary of State[9].

1    See the Defence (Transfer of Functions) Act 1964 s 1(1); and Letters Patent dated 16 March 1964 (revoked). The government's decision of principle that there should be 'one unified Ministry of Defence and that it should be comprised of the essential core of the Admiralty, the War Office and the Air Ministry' was announced by the Minister of Defence on 4 March 1963: see 673 HC Official Report (5th series), 4 March 1963, col 39. The proposed new arrangements, providing for a unified Ministry of Defence and for a Secretary of State for Defence who would have complete control both of defence policy and of the machinery for the administration of the three services, were set out in the White Paper *Central Organisation for Defence* (Cmnd 2097) (1963). The publication of the white paper was followed by a House of Commons debate (682 HC Official Report (5th series), 31 July 1963, col 465), in which the Minister of Defence specified (see cols 468–472) the following guiding principles on which the reorganisation was to be based: (1) there should be a single unified Ministry of Defence, under a single Secretary of State with clear lines of authority and responsibility; (2) machinery must exist to enable decentralisation, particularly that of day-to-day administration, to be effective; (3) the relationship with the Ministry of Aviation should be carefully defined, and must ensure much closer co-operation between the two departments; (4) the organisation must be flexible, and adaptable to change; (5) a proper balance must be struck between the military, civil and scientific components; and (6) the individual loyalties and traditions of 'the fighting men' must be preserved. See also ROYAL FORCES vol 41 para 2.

2    Ie by the Defence (Transfer of Functions) Act 1964 s 1(1); and the Defence (Transfer of Functions) (Appointed Day) Order 1964, SI 1964/487. Under the Defence (Transfer of Functions) Act 1964 s 3(1), consequential and transitional provisions may be made to adapt enactments or legislative instruments by Order in Council to the new arrangements and to repeal such as are no longer required (see the Defence (Transfer of Functions) (No 1) Order 1964, SI 1964/488 (amended by SI 1972/1922 (revoked) and SI 1972/1955 (revoked)); the Defence (Transfer of Functions (No 2) Order 1964, SI 1964/489 (amended by SI 1972/316 and SI 1972/419); and the Defence (Transfer of Functions) Order 1965, SI 1965/1126). Subject to any such provision made by Order in Council, the new authorities are substituted in enactments or legislative instruments for the previously existing service authorities: Defence (Transfer of Functions) Act 1964 s 3(2). The effect of anything done previously under the old arrangements is preserved: s 3(3), (4). Nothing in the Act is to prejudice any power exercisable by virtue of the prerogative of the Crown: s 4(3). As to the prerogative in relation to the royal forces see para 886 post; and generally ROYAL FORCES. As to the transfer of functions generally see para 363 ante.

3    As to the functions of the Secretary of State for Defence see para 441 post.

4    As to the Defence Council see paras 443–447 post.

5    See the list published under the Crown Proceedings Act 1947 s 17(1) (as amended); and CROWN PROCEEDINGS.

6    Parliamentary Commissioner Act 1967 s 4(1), Sch 2 (substituted by the Parliamentary and Health Service Commissioners Act 1987 s 1(1), (2), Sch 1). As to the Parliamentary Commissioner for Administration see ADMINISTRATIVE LAW vol 1(1) (Reissue) para 41 et seq. For these purposes the Ministry of Defence includes the Defence Council and the Admiralty, Army and Air Force Boards: Parliamentary Commissioner Act 1967 Sch 2 note 1 (as so substituted).

7    See the *Supply Estimates 1995–96 for the year ending 31 March 1996* (HC Paper (1994–95) no 271–I).

8    See the Civil Service Year Book 1996 col 136. The structure of the Ministry of Defence is explained in a Table in the Ministry of Defence Annual Report: *The Government's Expenditure Plans 1995–96 to 1997–98* (Cm 2801) (1995) Annex A; and the responsibilities of each minister are set out in the Ministry of Defence Annual Report: *The Government's Expenditure Plans 1995–96 to 1997–98* (Cm 2801) (1995) Annex B.

9    See the Civil Service Year Book 1996 col 137.

**439. Secretary of State for Defence: incorporation and authentication of documents.** The Secretary of State for Defence is a corporation sole, with a corporate seal, for all purposes relating to the acquisition, holding, management or disposal of property[1].

The Secretary of State's corporate seal is to be authenticated by the signature of a Secretary of State or of an Under Secretary of State in the Ministry of Defence or of any person authorised by a Secretary of State to act in that behalf[2]. The seal is to be officially and judicially noticed[3]. Every document purporting to be an instrument made or issued by the Secretary of State and to be sealed with his corporate seal duly authenticated, or to be signed by an Under Secretary of State in the Ministry of Defence or any duly authorised person, is to be received in evidence and deemed to be so made or issued without further proof unless the contrary is shown[4].

1　Defence (Transfer of Functions) Act 1964 s 2(1) (amended by the Ministers of the Crown Act 1974 s 4(3), Sch 3 (repealed)). As to acts done for him by another Secretary of State see para 363 ante. As to corporations sole see CORPORATIONS. As to secretarial seals see para 357 ante.
2　Defence (Transfer of Functions) Act 1964 s 2(5).
3　Ibid s 2(5)(a).
4　Ibid s 2(5)(b). See also the Documentary Evidence Act 1868 s 2, Schedule; the Documentary Evidence Act 1882 s 2; the Defence (Transfer of Functions) (No 1) Order 1964, SI 1964/488, art 2(1), (3), Sch 1 Pt I (amended by SI 1972/1922 (revoked) and SI 1972/1955 (revoked)); and EVIDENCE.

**440. Secretary of State for Defence: land and other property.** The Secretary of State for Defence has succeeded to all property, rights and liabilities in the United Kingdom or elsewhere of the Minister of Defence, or of the Admiralty, or of the Secretary of State for War or for Air, or of the Army or Air Council, including property, rights and liabilities held or incurred by any of them jointly with any other person[1].

1　Defence (Transfer of Functions) Act 1964 s 2(2); and the Defence (Transfer of Functions) (Appointed Day) Order 1964, SI 1964/487. For the powers exercisable under the Defence Acts 1842–1873 (as amended), the Lands Clauses Consolidation Acts Amendment Act 1860 (as amended) and the Military Lands Act 1892 (as amended), and also the exemption from personal liability under the Defence Act 1842 (as amended) enjoyed by the Secretary of State for Defence as successor to the Secretary of State for War, see ROYAL FORCES.
　　See also the Secretaries of State (Government Oil Pipe-line and Petroleum Licences) Order 1989, SI 1989/150, which transferred to the Secretary of State for Defence all the property, rights and liabilities comprising or related to the government oil pipe-line and storage system, which were vested in any other minister of the Crown.

**441. Secretary of State for Defence: functions.** The Secretary of State for Defence is charged with general responsibility for defence[1]. The functions conferred by any enactment[2] on the former Minister of Defence[3], the Secretary of State for War[4], the Secretary of State for Air[5] and, with certain exceptions[6], the Admiralty[7] have been transferred to him[8]. Certain functions of the former Minister of Aviation Supply[9] and of the United Kingdom Atomic Energy Authority[10] have also been transferred to him; and he also exercises functions under the Firearms Act 1968[11]. The Meteorological Office and the Hydrographic Office are now executive agencies of the Ministry of Defence[12].

1　Ie under the royal prerogative: see para 438 ante. As to the functions of the Secretary of State for Defence generally see ROYAL FORCES vol 41 para 2. As to the transfer of functions to the Secretary of State see para 438 ante. As to the transfer of functions generally see para 363 ante.
2　This extends also to any legislative instrument having effect under any enactment: see the Defence (Transfer of Functions) Act 1964 s 1(7).
3　The Minister of Defence was charged with the formulation and general application of a unified policy relating to the armed forces of the Crown as a whole and their requirements: see the Ministry of Defence Act 1946 s 1 (repealed). The minister's functions were defined in greater detail in the White Paper *Central Organisation for Defence* (Cmd 6923) (1946); see also *Statement relating to Defence* (Cmd 7042) (1947).

4    The Secretary of State for War was responsible, both to the Crown and to Parliament, for all the business
     of the Army Council. He could specially reserve to himself any business which he pleased, but the
     responsibility for all other business was assigned in accordance with rules laid down by Order in Council
     dated 21 May 1947. The internal organisation of the War Office dated substantially from 1904, when the
     system of dual control of military administration, by the Secretary of State for War and the Commander
     in Chief, gave place to a distribution of administrative duties among the Secretary of State for War and
     the other members of a newly established Army Council. For the complicated history of the War Office
     see 2 Anson's Law and Custom of the Constitution (4th Edn, 1935) Pt II pp 222–240; Hampden Gordon
     *The War Office* (1935).

5    The Secretary of State for Air was President of the Air Council, which was organised on similar lines to
     the Army Council. He could specially reserve to himself any business which he pleased, but the
     responsibility for all other business was assigned in accordance with rules laid down by Order in Council:
     see the Air Force (Constitution) Act 1917 s 8 (repealed).

6    Ie those transferred to the Defence Council: see the Defence (Transfer of Functions) Act 1964 s 1(3) (as
     amended); and para 444 post. Although the functions conferred on the Admiralty by any enactment
     contained in the Naval Discipline Act 1957 were in general transferred to the Defence Council, any
     power to make or delegate the making of orders, regulations or rules which was conferred on the
     Admiralty by ss 50, 58, 64, 79, 81, 82, 110 (relating to the practice and procedure etc of disciplinary courts
     and courts-martial, to the execution of their sentences, and to related matters) were transferred to the
     Secretary of State: see the Defence (Transfer of Functions) Act 1964 s 1(3)(b), (4).

7    The Board of Admiralty was responsible for the affairs of the Royal Navy and the Royal Marines. From
     1708 onwards, except for a short period in 1827, the Board of Admiralty consisted of the commissioners
     for the time being for executing the office of Lord High Admiral of the United Kingdom, with the
     addition of a Permanent Secretary and of a Parliamentary and Financial Secretary. Its constitution was
     regulated from time to time by Orders in Council and letters patent under the royal prerogative: see the
     Order in Council dated 25 March 1951. As to the history of the Admiralty see 2 Anson's Law and Custom
     of the Constitution (4th Edn, 1935) Pt I p 201.

8    Defence (Transfer of Functions) Act 1964 s 1(2). See further ROYAL FORCES.

9    See the Ministry of Aviation Supply (Dissolution) Order 1971, SI 1971/719, art 2(2); and para 442 post.

10   See the Atomic Energy Authority (Weapons Group) Act 1973 s 1; and para 442 post.

11   Functions of the Defence Council under the Firearms Act 1968 ss 5, 12(2) were transferred to the
     Secretary of State by the Transfer of Functions (Prohibited Weapons) Order 1968, SI 1968/1200.

12   See the Civil Service Year Book 1996 col 200; and *Next Steps Review 1995* (Cm 3164) (1995) pp 122,
     124. As to executive agencies see para 551 post.

**442. Procurement of supplies.** The Secretary of State for Defence relies largely on
his inherent powers under the prerogative in exercising his procurement functions[1].
However, on the dissolution of the Ministry of Aviation Supply in 1971 the minister's
functions relating to supply activities under the Ministry of Supply Act 1939[2] were
transferred to the Secretary of State[3].

The 1939 Act was consolidated in the Supply Powers Act 1975[4], which empowers
the Secretary of State to acquire, produce or process articles for the public service[5] or
articles to be exchanged for such articles; to sell, exchange or otherwise dispose of any
such articles or any government surplus materials[6]; to store and transport any such
articles and materials; and to do all such things, including the erection of buildings and
the execution of works, as appear to him necessary or expedient for the exercise of
these powers[7].

The Secretary of State has power to make grants or loans to facilitate the
augmentation of, or the improvement of storage for, stocks of articles required for the
public service[8]; and to require periodical and other returns as to such stocks and
facilities available for production and storage from persons producing, dealing in or
having control of such articles[9].

No information with respect to an individual business which has been obtained
under the provisions of the Supply Powers Act 1975 may be disclosed without the
consent of the person carrying on the business[10]. This does not, however, prevent the
disclosure of information to a government department or any person authorised by a
government department requiring that information for the purpose of the discharge of

the functions of that department, or for the purposes of any prosecution for an offence under these provisions[11]. Disclosure of information in contravention of these provisions constitutes an offence[12].

Certain enactments principally relating to land were applied to the Minister of Supply[13] and are now applied to the Secretary of State in connection with his supply powers[14]. The property, rights and liabilities of the Minister of Aviation Supply were transferred to the Secretary of State for Defence, except any property outside the United Kingdom which was not capable of transfer by Order in Council, and the rights and liabilities in relation to any such property; and the person from time to time holding office as Secretary of State for Defence is to be the Minister of Aviation Supply so long as any property, rights or liabilities remain vested in that minister[15]. The official seal of the Minister of Aviation Supply is to be authenticated by the signature of the minister or any person authorised by him to act in that behalf[16].

The transfer from the Minister of Aviation Supply did not include certain of the minister's powers in relation to land[17], but anything done by or in relation to the minister under those powers has effect as if done by or in relation to the Secretary of State for Defence under his corresponding powers[18].

The functions of the Minister of Aircraft Production which had originally been transferred from the Secretary of State for Air, and which were transferred in 1946 by Order in Council to the Minister of Supply[19], subsequently became otiose and this order has been repealed[20].

The Secretary of State for Defence is now to carry on any activities which were formerly[21] those of the Weapons Group of the United Kingdom Atomic Energy Authority and which involve the doing of work on explosive nuclear devices[22]. Land and premises which belonged to the authority and were held by the Weapons Group and, with exceptions, property, rights, liabilities and obligations which belonged to or were incumbent upon the authority and appertained to the Weapons Group, have been transferred to the Secretary of State for Defence[23].

1   These functions are mainly exercised in the Ministry of Defence within the Procurement Executive which was set up on 2 August 1971 following the White Paper *Government Organisation for Defence Procurement and Civil Aerospace* (Cmnd 4641) (1971). As to procurement see generally ROYAL FORCES. As to the Secretary of State's powers to establish trading funds see the Government Trading Funds Act 1973 s 1 (substituted by the Government Trading Act 1990 s 1(1)); and para 743 post.

2   Ie the Ministry of Supply Act 1939 s 2 (repealed: see note 4 infra). The functions which had been conferred by the Ministry of Supply Act 1939 on the Minister of Supply (whose title was subsequently changed to that of Minister of Aviation: Minister of Aviation Order 1959, SI 1959/1768, art 3(1) (revoked)) were transferred in 1967 to the Minister of Technology (see the Ministry of Aviation (Dissolution) Order 1967, SI 1967/155, art 2(1)). In 1970, when the functions of the Minister of Technology were for the most part transferred to the Secretary of State for Trade and Industry, the Minister was restyled the Minister of Aviation Supply in conformity with the nature of the functions remaining vested in him: Secretary of State for Trade and Industry Order 1970, SI 1970/1537, art 2(2).

3   Ministry of Aviation Supply (Dissolution) Order 1971, SI 1971/719, art 2(2). As to the transfer of functions generally see para 363 ante.

4   The Ministry of Supply Act 1939 is repealed by the Supply Powers Act 1975 s 8(1), Sch 2 Pt I. The Supply Powers Act 1975 consolidates the outstanding provisions of the 1939 Act.

5   'Articles required for the public service' means: (1) articles required for the purpose of the discharge of its functions by any government department (including a Northern Ireland department), by the United Kingdom Atomic Energy Authority, the Civil Aviation Authority, or any Research Council within the meaning of the Science and Technology Act 1965 s 1; (2) articles required for the defence of any part of the Commonwealth, including any territory under Her Majesty's protection or in which Her Majesty has jurisdiction, or for the maintenance or restoration of peace and security in any part of the world or for any measures arising out of a breach or apprehended breach of peace in any part of the world; (3) articles required by any international organisation of which the United Kingdom is a member or (where the relevant international agreement so provides) by any other member of such an organisation; (4) articles which in the opinion of the Secretary of State would be essential for the needs of the community in the

event of war; (5) articles for supply to a person carrying on an undertaking which includes the production of articles of that or any other description where that person requests the Secretary of State to supply those articles and the Secretary of State is satisfied that the supply will serve the interests of the community; (6) anything which in the opinion of the Secretary of State is or is likely to be necessary for or in connection with the production of any such articles as are mentioned in heads (1)–(5) supra; 'works required for the public service' is to be construed accordingly; and 'articles' includes substances: Supply Powers Act 1975 s 7.

By virtue of the Visiting Forces and International Headquarters (Application of Law) Order 1965, SI 1965/1536, 'articles required for the public service' includes articles required for the service of any visiting force or of any headquarters (for the meaning of which see art 3 (as amended)): art 4(1).

6   'Government surplus materials' means surplus articles of any government department (including a Northern Ireland department), and surplus articles of the government of any country outside the United Kingdom to be disposed of by Her Majesty's government in the United Kingdom in pursuance of an agreement between those governments: Supply Powers Act 1975 s 7.

7   Supply Powers Act 1975 s 1(1). As to inspections in connection with the production of any articles see s 1(2).

8   Payments are to be made in accordance with arrangements approved by the Treasury: ibid s 3. As to offences connected with obtaining payments under s 3, and as to penalties, see s 6.

9   Ibid s 4.

10  Ibid s 5(1).

11  Ie an offence under ibid s 6: s 5(2). Cf the more detailed provisions of the Statistics of Trade Act 1947 s 9 (as amended).

12  Supply Powers Act 1975 s 6(1).

13  See the Ministry of Supply (Transfer of Powers) (No 1) Order 1939, SR & O 1939/877 (revoked).

14  Ie through the effect of the transfer of functions orders mentioned in note 2 supra.

15  Ministry of Aviation Supply (Dissolution) Order 1971 art 2(2).

16  Ministers of the Crown Act 1975 s 6(2), Sch 1; and the Ministry of Aviation Supply (Dissolution) Order 1971 art 3(1).

17  Neither any Order in Council made under the Ministry of Supply Act 1939 s 2(2), (3) (now consolidated in the Supply Powers Act 1975 s 2: see note 4 supra), nor the Emergency Laws (Miscellaneous Provisions) Act 1953 s 1, Sch 1 para 8, were to have effect in relation to the Secretary of State: see the Ministry of Aviation Supply (Dissolution) Order 1971, art 3(2), Schedule para 1(2). Neither were references to the Minister in the Ministry of Supply Act 1939 s 2(2), (3) (now consolidated: see supra) or the Industrial Expansion Act 1968 s 13, Sch 3 para 1 (repealed) to include the Secretary of State for Defence: Ministry of Aviation Supply (Dissolution) Order 1971 Schedule para 1(1) (revoked). As to the exercise of the power to apply statutes to the Minister of Supply, see the Ministry of Supply (Transfer of Powers) (No 1) Order 1939 arts 5, 6, Schs 1, 2 (revoked).

18  Ministry of Aviation Supply (Dissolution) Order 1971 Schedule, para 1(2). As to the corresponding powers of the Secretary of State for Defence see the Defence (Transfer of Functions) Act 1964 s 2(3), (4); and para 440 ante.

19  See the Ministry of Aircraft Production (Dissolution) Order 1946, SR & O 1946/374 (revoked).

20  See the Industrial Expansion Act 1968 s 18, Sch 4 (repealed).

21  Ie before 1 April 1973: see the Atomic Energy Authority (Weapons Group) Act 1973 (Appointed Day) Order 1973, SI 1973/463.

22  Atomic Energy Authority (Weapons Group) Act 1973 s 1(1). As to functions of the Secretary of State in connection with nuclear devices see also the Atomic Weapons Establishments Act 1991. As to atomic energy and radioactive substances see FUEL AND ENERGY vol 19(2) (Reissue) para 1101 et seq.

23  See the Atomic Energy (Weapons Group) Act 1973 s 1(2), (3).

**443. The Defence Council: constitution.** The Defence Council consists of the Secretary of State for Defence as chairman, the Minister of State for the Armed Forces, the Minister of State for Defence Procurement, the Parliamentary Under Secretary of State for Defence, the Chief of the Defence Staff, the Permanent Under Secretary of State of the Ministry of Defence, the Chief of the Naval Staff and First Sea Lord, the Chief of the General Staff, the Chief of the Air Staff, the Vice-Chief of the Defence Staff, the Chief of Defence Procurement for the Ministry of Defence, the Chief Scientific Adviser of the Ministry of Defence and the Second Permanent Under Secretary of State of the Ministry of Defence[1].

The Permanent Under Secretary of State is secretary of the Defence Council, but the council may appoint other persons to act as secretary or secretaries in addition to the Permanent Under Secretary[2].

The powers and duties of the Defence Council may be exercised and performed by any two members, and any document may be signed on its behalf by any two members or by the secretary or person acting as secretary[3].

1  Letters Patent dated 4 May 1993; see the London Gazette, 7 May 1993.
2  Letters Patent dated 4 May 1993.
3  Letters Patent dated 4 May 1993. A certificate purporting to be given under the hand of the secretary (or person acting as secretary) to the Defence Council that any person was at a time specified in the certificate a member of the Defence Council, the Admiralty Board, the Army Board or the Air Force Board is to be evidence of the fact certified: Defence (Transfer of Functions) Act 1964 s 1(6).

**444. The Defence Council: functions.** Certain functions have been transferred to the Defence Council. These are the functions exercised under the royal prerogative as to command and administration of the royal forces and appointments in those forces[1], together with the functions conferred by any enactment[2] on the Army Council or on the Air Council, and the functions conferred on the Admiralty: (1) by any enactment by which similar functions are conferred on the Army Council or on the Air Council; or (2) by any enactment contained in the Naval Discipline Act 1957 except for those transferred to the Secretary of State[3] or by the provisions as to Royal Marines in the Army Act 1955[4].

Subject to any directions of the Defence Council, the council's functions under any enactment[5] may be discharged by the Admiralty Board, the Army Board or the Air Force Board; and for the purposes of any enactment, anything done by or in relation to any of those boards in or in connection with the discharge of any such functions of the Defence Council is to be of the same effect as if done by or in relation to the Defence Council[6].

1  Letters Patent dated 4 May 1993.
2  For the purposes of the Defence (Transfer of Functions) Act 1964 s 1 (as amended), 'enactment' includes any legislative instrument having effect under an enactment, or any Order in Council transferring to the Defence Council functions conferred by such an instrument on the Admiralty and which would apart from the order be transferred to the Secretary of State: s 1(7).
3  Ie those transferred by ibid s 1(4): see para 441 note 6 ante.
4  Ie the Army Act 1955 s 210, Sch 7 (as amended): Defence (Transfer of Functions) Act 1964 s 1(3) (amended by the Statute Law (Repeals) Act 1989 s 1(1), Sch 1 Pt XI).
5  The Defence Council's functions under the Naval Discipline Act 1957 ss 70–72 (as amended) are excluded: Armed Forces Act 1971 s 51. See also note 6 infra. These functions may be discharged by the Admiralty Board or by any officer empowered in that behalf by that board: see the Naval Discipline Act 1957 s 70(4) (added by the Armed Forces Act 1971 s 51). As to the meaning of 'enactment' see note 2 supra.
6  Defence (Transfer of Functions) Act 1964 s 1(5). Section 1(5) applies to functions conferred by enactments passed after the Act, except in so far as its application is expressly or impliedly excluded: s 1(5). Section 1(5) is repealed so far as it relates to the functions of the Defence Council under the Naval Discipline Act 1957 ss 70–72 (as amended): Armed Forces Act 1971 s 51; and see note 5 supra.

**445. The Admiralty Board of the Defence Council.** The Admiralty Board is concerned with the administration of matters relating to the naval forces[1]. It is composed of the Secretary of State for Defence as chairman, the Minister of State for the Armed Forces, the Minister of State for Defence Procurement, the Parliamentary Under Secretary of State for Defence, the Chief of the Naval Staff and First Sea Lord, the Second Permanent Under Secretary of State of the Ministry of Defence, the Second Sea Lord and Commander in Chief Naval Home Command, the Commander in Chief Fleet, the Controller of the Navy, the Chief of Fleet Support and the Assistant Chief of the Naval Staff[2].

1   Defence (Transfer of Functions) Act 1964 s 1(1)(b).
2   The power to establish the board is conferred by Letters Patent dated 4 May 1993, but the precise composition of the board is not prescribed.

**446. The Army Board of the Defence Council.** The Army Board is concerned with the administration of matters relating to the military forces[1]. It is composed of the Secretary of State for Defence as chairman, the Minister of State for the Armed Forces, the Minister of State for Defence Procurement, the Parliamentary Under Secretary of State for Defence, the Chief of the General Staff, the Second Permanent Secretary of State of the Ministry of Defence, the Adjutant General, the Quartermaster General, the Master General of the Ordnance, the Commander in Chief Land Command, and the Assistant Chief of the Defence Staff[2].

1   Defence (Transfer of Functions) Act 1964 s 1(1)(b).
2   The power to establish the board is conferred by Letters Patent dated 4 May 1993, but the precise composition of the board is not prescribed.

**447. The Air Force Board of the Defence Council.** The Air Force Board is concerned with the administration of matters relating to the air forces[1]. It is composed of the Secretary of State for Defence as chairman, the Minister of State for the Armed Forces, the Parliamentary Under Secretary of State for Defence Procurement, the Parliamentary Under Secretary of State for Defence, the Chief of the Air Staff, the Second Permanent Under Secretary of State for Defence, the Air Member for Personnel/Air Officer Commanding in Chief Personnel and Training Command, the Air Member for Logistic/Air Officer Commanding in Chief Logistic Command, the Controller Aircraft and the Air Officer Commanding in Chief Strike Command[2].

1   Defence (Transfer of Functions) Act 1964 s 1(1)(b).
2   The power to establish the board is conferred by Letters Patent dated 4 May 1993, but the precise composition of the board is not prescribed.

## (iv) The Department for Education and Employment

**448. The Secretary of State for Education and Employment.** The Ministry of Education was created in 1944, in succession to the Board of Education[1]. In 1964, following the appointment of a Principal Secretary of State by the style and title of Secretary of State for Education and Science, the functions of the Minister of Education and the Minister of Science were brought together[2]; but since 1992 the scientific functions have once again been separated[3], leaving the Department for Education with overall responsibility for education in England and Wales[4]. In 1995, the Secretary of State for Education took over most of the functions of the Secretary of State for Employment[5].

The Secretary of State for Education and Employment is a corporation sole[6]. He has an official seal which is authenticated by his signature or that of a secretary to the Department for Education and Employment or of any person authorised by the Secretary of State[7]. The seal is officially and judicially noticed; and a document purporting to be an instrument made or issued by the Secretary of State and either sealed with his seal duly authenticated or signed or executed by a secretary to the Department for Education and Employment or by a duly authorised person, is to be deemed to be so made or issued without further proof unless the contrary is shown[8]. A certificate signed by the Secretary of State that an instrument purporting to be made or issued by him was so made or issued is conclusive evidence of the fact certified[9]. Proof of any document of the Secretary of State may be given in accordance with the Documentary Evidence Act 1868[10].

The Department for Education and Employment is subject to investigation by the Parliamentary Commissioner for Administration[11], and is an authorised government department for the purpose of suing and being sued[12]. The expenses of the department are provided by Parliament[13].

1   A Minister of Education was appointed in 1944: Education Act 1944 s 1(1) (as originally enacted); Education (Date of Appointment of Minister) Order 1944, SR & O 1944/937. The minister succeeded to the office of the President of the Board of Education (which had been created under the Board of Education Act 1899 (repealed)): Education Act 1944 s 2(1).

2   Secretary of State for Education and Science Order 1964, SI 1964/490, arts 1(1), 2(1), (4), 3(2)(b). The order substituted the Secretary of State for Education and Science for the Minister of Education and the Minister of Science respectively where membership or chairmanship of any body or any trusteeship was held by virtue of his office (arts 1(1), 2(2)), and dissolved the Ministry of Education and the Office of the Minister for Science (art 2(1)). Functions of the Lord President of the Council transferred to the Secretary of State for Education and Science (arts 1(1), 2(3)) were exercisable under statutes since repealed.

3   See the Transfer of Functions (Science) Order 1992, SI 1992/1296.

4   See EDUCATION vol 15 (Reissue). The Secretary of State for Wales exercises many of the education functions of the Secretary of State for Education (formerly the Secretary of State for Education and Science, and now the Secretary of State for Education and Employment) in relation to Wales by virtue of the Transfer of Functions (Wales) Order 1970, SI 1970/1536, (as amended) and the Transfer of Functions (Wales) (No 2) Order 1978, SI 1978/274. As to the office of Secretary of State see para 355 et seq ante. As to the transfer of functions generally see para 363 ante.

5   See the Transfer of Functions (Education and Employment) Order 1995, SI 1995/2986. The functions of the Department of Employment have been divided between four departments, with the largest share going to the Department for Education, the other three being the Department of Trade and Industry (see paras 505–508 post), the Department of the Environment (see paras 452–458 post); and the Central Statistical Office (now the Office for National Statistics: see para 516 post). The Secretary of State for Employment and Productivity succeeded to the Minister of Labour (Secretary of State for Employment and Productivity Order 1968, SI 1968/729, art 2), and his title was changed to the Secretary of State for Employment in 1970 (Secretary of State for Trade and Industry Order 1970, SI 1970/1537, art 3(1)). As to education functions see para 449 post; and as to employment functions see para 450 post.

6   Transfer of Functions (Education and Employment) Order 1995 art 10(1). As to corporations sole see CORPORATIONS.

7   Ibid art 10(2). As to secretarial seals see para 357 ante.

8   Ibid art 10(3).

9   Ibid art 10(4).

10  Ibid art 10(5); and see EVIDENCE.

11  Parliamentary Commissioner Act 1967 s 4(1), Sch 2 (substituted by the Parliamentary and Health Service Commissioners Act 1987 s 1(1), (2), Sch 1; amended by the Transfer of Functions (Science) Order 1992; and the Transfer of Functions (Education and Employment) Order 1995 art 11(1), Schedule para 5). As to the Parliamentary Commissioner for Administration see ADMINISTRATIVE LAW vol 1(1) (Reissue) para 41 et seq.

12  See the list published under the Crown Proceedings Act 1947 s 17(1) (as amended); and CROWN PROCEEDINGS.

13  See the *Supply Estimates 1995–96 for the year ending 31 March 1996* (HC Paper (1994–95) no 271–X).

**449. Educational functions.** The Secretary of State is required to promote the education of the people of England and Wales[1]. There have been significant changes in the national education system since 1979, with the powers of local education authorities reduced in favour of greater autonomy for the schools themselves and with the introduction of grant maintained schools[2]. The Secretary of State's control over the development of the national education system has increased through his function of approving schemes for local management of schools[3] and through his duty to establish a National Curriculum[4]. He makes funds available to the Further Education Funding Councils for Education for England and for Wales[5].

1   Education Act 1993 s 1. The Secretary of State concerned, in relation to England, is the Secretary of State for Education and Employment or, in relation to Wales, the Secretary of State for Wales: see para 448 note 4 ante. The Secretary of State must exercise his powers in respect of those bodies in receipt of public funds

which, for the purpose of promoting primary, secondary and further education in England and Wales, (1) carry responsibility for securing that the required provision for primary, secondary or further education is made in schools, or institutions within the further education sector, in or in any area of England or Wales; or (2) conduct schools or institutions within the further education sector in England and Wales: s 2(1). He must, in the case of his powers to regulate the provision made in schools and institutions within the further education sector, exercise his powers with a view, among other things, to improving standards, encouraging diversity and increasing opportunities for choice: s 2(2). For the special position of Wales see the Education Act 1993 ss 4, 86–91, 252–253; and EDUCATION vol 15 (Reissue) para 4.

2    See also the right of the parent to express a preference for a school, which circumscribes the power of local education authorities to place children in schools: Education Act 1980 s 6 (as amended). As to the acquisition of grant maintained status see EDUCATION vol 15 (Reissue) para 11 et seq. As to the powers and duties of local education authorities see EDUCATION vol 15 (Reissue) para 22 et seq.

3    See EDUCATION vol 15 (Reissue) para 4 et seq.

4    See the Education Reform Act 1988 s 4 (as amended); and EDUCATION vol 15 (Reissue) para 106 et seq.

5    The Further Education Funding Councils for England and for Wales were established under the Further and Higher Education Act 1992 s 1. The Secretary of State may make grants to each of the councils of such amounts and subject to such terms and conditions as he may determine: s 7.

## 450. Employment functions.

The Secretary of State is now responsible for the training and employment services formerly operated by the Manpower Services Commission[1].

In connection with the provision and encouragement of work-related training, the National Council for Vocational Qualifications[2] was set up to establish a system of vocational qualifications related to standards of competence required by business and industry[3]. Through the Operations Directorate[4], the Department for Education and Employment is responsible for the Training and Enterprise Councils[5].

The Secretary of State is also assisted by the Employment Service Agency[6]. It is an executive agency and has the functions of assisting unemployed people to find work and of paying benefits to those entitled to them while they seek work[7]. The Employment Service Agency is establishing a network of job centres to provide access to government training and employment programmes and services for unemployed people[8].

The department also has a central role in the formulation and co-ordination of policy on the labour market[9].

1    The Manpower Services Commission was set up under the Employment and Training Act 1973 s 1 (repealed). It was to make such arrangements as it considered appropriate for the purpose of assisting persons to select, train for, obtain and retain employment suitable for their ages and capacities: s 2(1) (as originally enacted). The Manpower Services Commission was renamed the Training Commission: Employment Act 1988 s 24(1) (repealed). The Training Commission was then dissolved (Employment Act 1989 s 22) and its functions were transferred to the Secretary of State (Training Commission (Incidental and Transitional Provisions) Order 1988, SI 1988/1905). See *Employment for the 1990s* (Cm 540) (1988). See also EMPLOYMENT vol 16 (Reissue) para 435.

2    The National Council for Vocational Qualifications (NCVQ) was set up following the publication of a White Paper (*Working together: Education and training* (Cmnd 9823) (1986)). See the Department of Employment Annual Report: *The Government's Expenditure Plans 1995–96 to 1997–98* (Cm 2805) (1995).

3    Qualifications which satisfy the required criteria are called National Vocational Qualifications (NVQs).

4    As to the Operations Directorate see para 451 post; and the Civil Service Year Book 1996 col 210.

5    The Training and Enterprise Councils are private sector companies which manage local training and enterprise activities in England under a performance-based contract: see the Civil Service Year Book 1995 col 197. They are gradually replacing the Industrial Training Boards. As to the Industrial Training Boards see EMPLOYMENT vol 16 (Reissue) para 443 et seq.

6    The Employment Service Agency is the successor to the Employment Service Agency of the Manpower Services Commission: see note 1 supra. See also the Department of Employment Annual Report: *The Government's Expenditure Plans 1995–96 to 1997–98* (Cm 2805) (1995).

7    See the Civil Service Year Book 1996 col 210. As to executive agencies see para 551 post.

8    See the Civil Service Year Book 1996 col 210.

9    The Strategy, International and Analytical Services Directorate is responsible for promoting a competitive and efficient labour market; and the Employment and Lifetime Learning Directorate advises on, and carries out, government policy on training and the labour market, and is also responsible for employer training and equal opportunities: Civil Service Year Book 1996 cols 209–210. See also para 451 post.

**451. Organisation.** The Department for Education and Employment is headed by the Secretary of State for Education and Employment, who is assisted by two Ministers of State, three Parliamentary Under Secretaries of State and two Joint Permanent Secretaries[1].

The department is divided into seven directorates[2]: (1) Personnel and Support Services; (2) Finance; (3) Strategy, International and Analytical Services, whose brief extends to EC and international issues and the European Social Fund; (4) Schools, which deals with the organisation and funding of schools, with curricular issues, and with the Pupils, Parents and Youth Service; (5) Further and Higher Education and Youth Training, which deals with curricular issues, qualifications, careers education and guidance, education business links, further and higher education and student support; (6) Employment and Lifetime Learning, which deals with active labour market policy, training for the unemployed, employer training, equal opportunities, and education and training technology; and (7) Operations, which deals with Training and Enterprise Councils, Careers Service, and Industry Training Organisations[3]. There are also three executive agencies: the Employment Service Agency[4], the Teachers' Pensions Agency[5] and the Teacher Training Agency[6].

The Office for Standards in Education (OFSTED) is a non-ministerial government department, headed by Her Majesty's Chief Inspector of Schools in England[7].

1   See the Civil Service Year Book 1996 col 208.
2   See the Civil Service Year Book 1996 cols 209–210. As to the Civil Service generally see paras 549–564 post.
3   As to training and employment functions see para 450 ante.
4   See the Civil Service Year Book 1996 col 210; and para 450 ante. As to executive agencies see para 551 post.
5   See the Civil Service Year Book 1996 col 215.
6   See the Civil Service Year Book 1996 col 215.
7   See the Civil Service Year Book 1996 col 565. As to the Office of Her Majesty's Chief Inspector of Schools in Wales see the Civil Service Year Book 1996 col 938. As to non-ministerial departments generally see para 528 post.

## (v) The Department of the Environment

**452. Constitution and organisation of the department.** The Department of the Environment was set up to perform the functions of the dissolved Ministries of Housing and Local Government, of Transport and of Public Buildings and Works[1]. At its head is the Secretary of State for the Environment, who is assisted by the Minister for Local Government, Housing and Urban Regeneration, the Minister for the Environment and Countryside, the Minister for Construction, Planning and Energy Efficiency and two Parliamentary Under Secretaries of State[2]. There is also a Permanent Secretary[3].

The Department of the Environment is organised, under the Permanent Secretary, into groups[4]: (1) Organisation and Establishments and Administration Resources Group[5]; (2) Central Management and Analysis Unit[6]; (3) Directorate of Communication[7]; (4) Local Government and Planning[8]; (5) Cities and Countryside Group[9]; (6) Property Holdings and Central Support Services Group[10]; (7) Housing and Construction Group[11]; (8) Environment Protection Group[12]; (9) Chief Scientist Group[13]; and (10) Legal Group[14].

The department is responsible for the following executive agencies: (a) Building Research Establishment; (b) The Buying Agency; (c) Planning Inspectorate; (d) Security Facilities Executive; and (e) The Queen Elizabeth II Conference Centre[15]. The Health and Safety Commission[16] comes under the aegis of the Department of the Environment[17]; and there is now also an Environment Agency[18].

The Department of the Environment is an authorised government department for the purpose of suing and being sued[19], and is subject to investigation by the Parliamentary Commissioner for Administration[20]. The expenses of the department are provided by Parliament[21].

1	The Ministry of Housing and Local Government, the Ministry of Transport and the Ministry of Public Buildings and Works were dissolved, and all their functions were transferred to the Secretary of State, by the Secretary of State for the Environment Order 1970, SI 1970/1681 (as amended). Functions and property of the Secretary of State for the Environment with respect to historic buildings, the national heritage and functions relating to the Sports Council were transferred to the Secretary of State for National Heritage by the Transfer of Functions (National Heritage) Order 1992, SI 1992/1311: see para 498 post. Energy efficiency functions of the former Secretary of State for Energy were transferred to the Secretary of State for the Environment by the Transfer of Functions (Energy) Order 1992, SI 1992/1314. Functions and property in connection with Inner City Task Forces were transferred to the Secretary of State for the Environment from the Secretary of State for Trade and Industry by the Transfer of Functions (Inner City Task Forces) Order 1992, SI 1992/1316. As to the Secretary of State for Trade and Industry see para 506 post. As to the office of Secretary of State see para 355 et seq ante. As to the transfer of functions generally see para 363 ante. As to the transfer of property, rights and liabilities held by the Secretary of State to corporate bodies established under the Parliamentary Corporate Bodies Act 1992 see PARLIAMENT. As to the functions of the department see paras 454–458 post.

2	See the Civil Service Year Book 1996 col 220.

3	See the Civil Service Year Book 1996 col 221.

4	See the Civil Service Year Book 1996; and the Department of the Environment Annual Report: *The Government's Expenditure Plans 1995–96 to 1997–98* (Cm 2807) (1995). As to the Civil Service generally see paras 549–564 post.

5	See the Civil Service Year Book 1996 col 221 et seq.

6	See the Civil Service Year Book 1996 col 227.

7	See the Civil Service Year Book 1996 col 227 et seq.

8	See the Civil Service Year Book 1996 col 228 et seq; and paras 454–455 post.

9	See the Civil Service Year Book 1996 col 237 et seq; and paras 455, 458 post.

10	As from April 1996, departments are to take responsibility as principals for the property they occupy, and a new central agency is to be reconstituted from Property Holdings, called Property Advisers to the Civil Estate.

	At December 1995, the prime responsibility of Property Holdings was stated to be to manage the government's Office Estate so as to provide accomodation for departments efficiently and effectively: see the Department of the Environment Annual Report: *The Government's Expenditure Plans 1995–96 to 1997–98* (Cm 2807) (1995); and the Civil Service Year Book 1996 col 245 et seq.

11	See the Civil Service Year Book 1996 col 252 et seq; and para 456 post.

12	See the Civil Service Year Book 1996 col 260 et seq; and para 458 post.

13	See the Civil Service Year Book 1996 col 273.

14	See the Civil Service Year Book 1996 col 273 et seq.

15	See the Civil Service Year Book 1996 col 276 et seq; and the *Next Steps Review 1995* (Cm 3164) (1995) p 140. As to executive agencies see para 551 post.

16	As to non-ministerial departments generally see para 528 post.

17	See the Civil Service Year Book 1996 col 389.

18	As to the Environment Agency see para 458 post.

19	See the list published under the Crown Proceedings Act 1947 s 17(1) (as amended); and CROWN PROCEEDINGS.

20	Parliamentary Commissioner Act 1967 s 4(1), Sch 2 (substituted by the Parliamentary and Health Service Commissioners Act 1987 s 1(1), (2), Sch 1). As to the Parliamentary Commissioner for Administration see ADMINISTRATIVE LAW vol 1(1) (Reissue) para 41 et seq.

21	See the *Supply Estimates 1995–96 for the year ending 31 March 1996* (HC Paper (1994–95) no 271–VII).

**453. The Secretary of State for the Environment.** The Secretary of State for the Environment is a corporation sole[1].

The corporate seal of the Secretary of State for the Environment is authenticated by the signature of a Secretary of State, a secretary to the Department of the Environment or a person authorised by a Secretary of State to act in that behalf[2]. The seal is officially and judicially noticed[3]. A document purporting to be an instrument made or issued by the Secretary of State for the Environment and to be sealed with his seal duly authenticated or to be signed or executed by a secretary to the Department of the Environment or a person authorised by a Secretary of State to act in that behalf is to be received in evidence and be deemed to be so made or issued without further proof unless the contrary is shown[3]. A certificate signed by the Secretary of State for the Environment that any instrument purporting to be made or issued by him or by the Minister of Housing and Local Government, the Minister of Transport or the Minister of Public Building and Works was so made or issued is conclusive evidence of that fact[4].

No stamp duty is chargeable on any instrument by which a conveyance, transfer or lease is made or agreed to be made to or with the Secretary of State for the Environment[5].

1   Secretary of State for the Environment Order 1970, SI 1970/1681, art 3(2) (amended by the Ministers of the Crown Act 1974 s 4(3), Sch 3 (repealed)). As to corporations sole see CORPORATIONS.
2   Secretary of State for the Environment Order 1970 art 3(3). As to secretarial seals see para 357 ante.
3   Ibid art 3(4).
4   Ibid art 3(5).
5   Finance Act 1987 s 55.

**454. Local government.** As successor to the Minister of Housing and Local Government[1], the Secretary of State for the Environment has responsibility for the structure and functioning of local government[2]. The Secretary of State determines the amount of government grants to local authorities in the form of rate support grants[3] and may limit, or 'cap', the level of council tax[4] levied by a local authority in any one year[5]. The Department of the Environment is responsible for non-domestic rating and for compulsory competitive tendering in the provision of local government services[6]. The Secretary of State is empowered to give directions in cases where it appears to him that a local authority has not complied with the competitive tendering legislation[7].

1   See para 452 text and note 1 ante.
2   Much has been written on the relationship between central and local government, tracing the increasing control of central government over local authorities: eg de Smith and Brazier *Constitutional and Administrative Law* (7th Edn, 1994) pp 451–453; Griffith *Central Departments and Local Authorities* (1966) ch 1; Elliott *Central-Local Government Relations* (1982); Loughlin *Local Government in the Modern State* (1986); Loughlin 'The Restructuring of Central-Local Government Relations' in Jowell and Oliver (eds) *The Changing Constitution* (3rd Edn, 1994) p 261–293. See also LOCAL GOVERNMENT vol 28 para 1380 et seq.
3   As to rate support grants see LOCAL GOVERNMENT vol 28 para 1262 et seq. The proportion of local government expenditure being met by grants from central government has increased from around 10% in 1890 to nearly 50% in 1980: see Bennett *Central Grants to Local Governments: The Political and Economic Impact of the Rate Support Grant in England* (1982) p 44.
4   Ie the local tax introduced under the Local Government Finance Act 1992 to replace the community charge, or 'poll tax', which itself was introduced under the Local Government Finance Act 1988 to replace the old system of domestic rates. As to the council tax see RATING.
5   See the Local Government Finance Act 1992 Pt I Ch V (ss 53–64) (as amended); and RATING. As to the capping of local authority budgets, and the amount of the reductions, see the Department of the Environment Annual Report: *The Government's Expenditure Plans 1995–96 to 1997–98* (Cm 2807) (1995).
6   As to compulsory competitive tendering see the Local Government Act 1988 (as amended); and LOCAL GOVERNMENT.
7   Ibid s 14 (amended by the Local Government Act 1992 s 11, Sch 1 para 14).

**455. Planning.** As successor to the Ministry of Housing and Local Government[1], the Department of the Environment inherited responsibilities with regard to town planning, town development and land use[2]. Under the consolidating planning legislation of 1990, the central authority for the purposes of the Town and Country Planning Acts[3] is, in England, the Secretary of State for the Environment and, in Wales, the Secretary of State for Wales[4]. The Secretary of State has the power to give financial assistance for urban regeneration[5] and to establish, by statutory instrument, Urban Development Corporations to secure the regeneration of the area in which they operate[6]. The department approves development plans[7] prepared by local planning authorities[8], and makes regulations with regard to their form and content and the procedure surrounding their preparation. It issues departmental circulars and Planning Policy Guidance Notes, which are the main source of policy guidance on planning matters[9]. The Secretary of State has quasi–judicial functions in relation to planning appeals[10].

1   See para 452 text and note 1 ante.
2   See the Secretary of State for the Environment Order 1970, SI 1970/1681 (as amended); and para 452 ante. As to planning generally see TOWN AND COUNTRY PLANNING.
3   Ie the Town and Country Planning Act 1990; the Planning (Listed Buildings and Conservation Areas) Act 1990; the Planning (Hazardous Substances) Act 1990; and the Planning (Consequential Provisions) Act 1990. See TOWN AND COUNTRY PLANNING vol 46 (Reissue) para 2.
4   See TOWN AND COUNTRY PLANNING vol 46 (Reissue) para 10. Certain functions and property of the Secretary of State for the Environment with respect to historic buildings and the national heritage were transferred to the Secretary of State for National Heritage by the Transfer of Functions (National Heritage) Order 1992, SI 1992/1311: see para 452 note 1 ante and para 498 post. As to the transfer of functions generally see para 363 ante.
5   Ie under the Housing and Planning Act 1986 s 27(1) (substituted by the Leasehold Reform, Housing and Urban Development Act 1993 s 174). See TOWN AND COUNTRY PLANNING vol 46 (Reissue) para 1348 et seq.
6   Ie under the Local Government, Planning and Land Act 1980 s 135 (amended by the Leasehold Reform, Housing and Urban Development Act 1993 s 179). As to Urban Development Corporations see TOWN AND COUNTRY PLANNING vol 46 (Reissue) para 1271 et seq. For a full description of the various measures taken to assist in urban regeneration see the Department of the Environment Annual Report: *The Government's Expenditure Plans 1995–96 to 1997–98* (Cm 2807) (1995).
7   As to development plans see TOWN AND COUNTRY PLANNING vol 46 (Reissue) para 39 et seq.
8   Ie under the Town and Country Planning Act 1990 Pt II Ch 1 (ss 10–28) (as amended). As to local planning authorities see TOWN AND COUNTRY PLANNING vol 46 (Reissue) para 11.
9   As to departmental circulars and Planning Policy Guidance Notes see TOWN AND COUNTRY PLANNING vol 46 (Reissue) para 6.
10  See the Town and Country Planning Act 1990 ss 78–79 (as amended). See TOWN AND COUNTRY PLANNING vol 46 (Reissue) para 846 et seq.

**456. Housing.** As successor to the Ministry of Housing and Local Government[1], the Department of the Environment inherited responsibilities and functions in relation to housing[2], rent control and building regulation[3]. Through the Housing and Construction Group[4], the department is responsible for housing finance, including the 'right to buy' scheme. The department sponsors the Housing Corporation[5] and Housing Action Trusts[6], and determines housing investment programme allocations for local authorities[7].

1   See para 452 text and note 1 ante.
2   'Housing' includes public and private sector housing. As to housing generally see HOUSING.
3   See the Secretary of State for the Environment Order 1970, SI 1970/1681 (as amended); and HOUSING vol 22 para 414 et seq.
4   See the Civil Service Year Book 1996 col 252 et seq.
5   As to the Housing Corporation see HOUSING vol 22 paras 429–444. The Housing Corporation is a non-departmental public body which oversees the activities of the housing association sector. As to housing associations see HOUSING vol 22 para 445 et seq. See also the Civil Service Year Book 1996 col 260. As to non-departmental public bodies generally see para 951 et seq post.
6   Housing Action Trusts are non-departmental public bodies dedicated to the regeneration and the improvement of housing: see the Housing Act 1988 Pt III (ss 60–92); and HOUSING vol 22 para 523A.
7   See the Department of the Environment Annual Report: *The Government's Expenditure Plans 1995–96 to 1997–98* (Cm 2807) (1995) para 1.1.40 et seq. See also the Civil Service Year Book 1996 col 259.

**457. Countryside.** As successor to the Ministry of Housing and Local Government[1], the Department of the Environment has responsibility for safeguarding the English countryside and coastline together with their wildlife, and has a particular duty to protect endangered or rare species and their habitat[2]. In carrying out those responsibilities, it works through non-departmental bodies[3] now known as the Countryside Commission[4] and English Nature[5]; and government agencies, such as the Rural Development Commission[6]. The department also gives financial assistance to National Park authorities[7] and the Broads Authority[8].

1 See para 452 text and note 1 ante.
2 As to the powers of protection under the National Parks and Access to the Countryside Act 1949 (as amended) and the Wildlife and Countryside Act 1981 (as amended) see OPEN SPACES AND HISTORIC BUILDINGS vol 34 para 462 et seq.
3 As to non-departmental public bodies generally see para 951 et seq post.
4 As to the Countryside Commission see OPEN SPACES AND HISTORIC BUILDINGS vol 34 paras 422, 443 et seq; and the Civil Service Year Book 1996 col 752.
5 English Nature is the name of the Nature Conservancy Council for England, which works with the Countryside Council for Wales through the Joint Nature Conservation Committee: Environmental Protection Act 1990 ss 128(1), (4), 131(1). See OPEN SPACES AND HISTORIC BUILDINGS vol 34 para 423 et seq.
6 See the Department of the Environment Annual Report: *The Government's Expenditure Plans 1995–96 to 1997–98* (Cm 2807) (1995). As to the Rural Development Commission see the Civil Service Year Book 1996 col 791.
7 National Park authorities are established under the Environment Act 1995 s 63, either replacing existing authorities or in connection with the designation of any area as a new National Park. As to National Parks generally see OPEN SPACES AND HISTORIC BUILDINGS.
8 The Broads Authority is established by the Norfolk and Sufolk Broads Act 1988 s 1, Sch 1. In relation to land in the Broads, the Broads Authority is a local planning authority: Town and Country Planning Act 1990 s 5 (amended by the Planning and Compensation Act 1991 s 32, Sch 7 paras 8, 9).

**458. Environment.** The Department of the Environment is responsible, through the Environment Protection Group[1], for environmental protection. The newly established Environment Agency[2] takes on the pollution control functions of the National Rivers Authority and the London Waste Regulation Authority[3]. The agency's pollution control powers are exercisable for the purpose of preventing or minimising, or remedying or mitigating the effects of, pollution of the environment[4]. The agency must also, to such extent as it considers desirable, generally promote (1) the conservation and enhancement of inland and coastal waters and associated land; (2) the conservation of flora and fauna which are dependent on an aquatic environment; and (3) the use of such waters and land for recreational purposes[5]. The protection of sites of special interest is also carried out through the agency[6].

The department is responsible for regulating air quality[7], noise levels[8], waste, litter, recycling and radioactive waste[9]. The Water Directorate of the Environment Protection Group includes the Drinking Water Inspectorate[10].

1 See the Civil Service Year Book 1996 col 260 et seq.
2 The Environment Agency is established by the Environment Act 1995 s 1, Sch 1. The Agency came into being on 1 April 1996, which was the specified transfer date for transfer of functions: see the Environment Agency (Transfer Date) Order 1996, SI 1996/234. As to the transfer of functions see note 3 infra. See generally PUBLIC HEALTH.
3 The functions, property, rights and liabilities of the National Rivers Authority, the waste regulation authorities and the disposal authorities, and the pollution control and health and safety functions of various inspectors and of the Secretary of State, are transferred to the Environment Agency: Environment Act 1995 ss 2(1), (2), 3. The National Rivers Authority and the London Waste Regulation Authority are abolished: s 2(3). As to the transfer of functions generally see paras 363–365 ante.
4 Ibid s 5(1). Pollution control powers include regulation of industrial pollution under the Environmental Protection Act 1990 (as amended) and the storage, use and disposal of radioactive substances in accordance with the Radioactive Substances Act 1993: see the Environment Act 1995 s 5(5).
5 Ibid s 6(1).

6   See ibid s 8.
7   Ie under the Clean Air Act 1993. See PUBLIC HEALTH vol 38 para 213 et seq.
8   Ie under the Environmental Protection Act 1990 (amended by the Noise and Statutory Nuisance Act 1993). As to noise nuisances see PUBLIC HEALTH vol 38 para 424 et seq.
9   See the Department of the Environment Annual Report: *The Government's Expenditure Plans 1995–96 to 1997–98* (Cm 2807) (1995); and the Civil Service Year Book 1996 col 265 et seq.
10  See the *Supply Estimates 1995–96 for the year ending 31 March 1996* (HC Paper (1994–95) no 271–VII); and see the Civil Service Year Book 1996 col 268 et seq.

## (vi)  The Foreign and Commonwealth Office

**459.  The Secretary of State for Foreign and Commonwealth Affairs.** The Secretary of State for Foreign and Commonwealth Affairs is responsible for the work of the Foreign and Commonwealth Office and the Diplomatic Service[1].

The Secretary of State is assisted by four Ministers of State, one of whom is primarily Minister for Overseas Development[2]. The Permanent Under Secretary of the Foreign and Commonwealth Office is at the same time Head of the Diplomatic Service, and advises the Secretary of State on all aspects of foreign policy[3]. Answering to the Permanent Under Secretary there is (1) a Political Director, responsible for Western Europe and International Organisations; (2) an Economic Director, responsible for International Organisations, Economic Advisers and European Union; (3) a Chief Clerk, responsible for Public Departments, Protocol, Personnel and Security, Resources, General Services, the Government Hospitality Fund and Overseas Estates; (4) a Legal Adviser responsible for Legal Advisers; and (5) Deputy Under Secretaries responsible for (a) the Americas, Northern Asia and Pacific, South and East Asia, Africa and Overseas Trade; (b) International Security, Aid Policy and the Permanent Under Secretary's Department; and (c) the Middle East and North Africa, and Central and Eastern Europe. There are also policy planning staff within the Foreign and Commonwealth Office[4].

The Secretary of State is empowered to make regulations for the Diplomatic Service, including the division of the service into branches and grades, conditions of employment, salaries and retirement provisions[5].

The Secretary of State for Foreign and Commonwealth Affairs is now a corporation sole, with a corporate seal[6]. The corporate seal is authenticated by the signature of a Secretary of State or of an Under Secretary of State in the Foreign and Commonwealth Office, or by a person authorised by a Secretary of State to act for the purpose[7]. The seal is to be officially and judicially noticed[8]. Every document purporting to be an instrument made or issued by the Secretary of State for Foreign and Commonwealth Affairs and to be sealed with that seal duly authenticated, or to be signed or executed by an Under Secretary of State in the Foreign and Commonwealth Office or by an authorised person, is to be received in evidence and deemed to be so made or issued without further proof unless the contrary is shown[9]. A certificate signed by the Secretary of State for Foreign and Commonwealth Affairs that any instrument purporting to be made or issued by him was so made or issued is conclusive evidence of the fact[10].

The Foreign and Commonwealth Office is subject to investigation by the Parliamentary Commissioner for Administration[11]. Its expenses are provided by Parliament[12].

1   The Foreign Office Order in Council 1943 amalgamated the former Foreign Office and Diplomatic Service, the Commercial Diplomatic Service and the Consular Service into the Foreign Service. The Diplomatic Service Order in Council dated 20 November 1964 merged the Foreign Service, the Commonwealth Service and the Trade Commission to form the Diplomatic Service.

    The Secretary of State for Foreign and Commonwealth Affairs Order 1968, SI 1968/1657, transferred all functions of the Secretary of State for Foreign Affairs and the Secretary of State for Commonwealth Affairs to the Secretary of State for Foreign and Commonwealth Affairs. The Secretary of State for Commonwealth Affairs was known as the Secretary of State for Commonwealth Relations until the

Commonwealth Relations Office and the Colonial Office were combined into the Commonwealth Office: see the Secretary of State for Commonwealth Affairs Order 1966, SI 1966/950 (spent). The Commonwealth Relations Office was formerly called the Dominions Office. As to the transfer of functions generally see para 363 ante. As to the office of Secretary of State see para 355 et seq ante.

2　See the Civil Service Year Book 1996 col 295. As to the Overseas Development Administration see para 462 post.

3　See the Civil Service Year Book 1996 col 295.

4　As to the structure and functions of the Foreign and Commonwealth Office see the Civil Service Year Book 1996 col 295 et seq; and the Foreign and Commonwealth Office Annual Report, including Overseas Development Administration: *The Government's Expenditure Plans 1995–96 to 1997–98* (Cm 2802) (1995). As to the Civil Service generally see paras 549–564 post.

5　Diplomatic Service Order in Council 1991 (as amended). The regulations regarding such matters as salaries, allowances and pensions require the concurrence of the Office of Public Service: Diplomatic Service Order in Council 1991 art 5. As to the Office of Public Service see para 430 ante.

6　See the Secretary of State for Foreign and Commonwealth Affairs Order 1983, SI 1983/146, art 2(1). The Secretary of State for Foreign and Commonwealth Affairs Order 1983 was made consequent on the conferring on the Secretary of State for Foreign and Commonwealth Affairs of certain functions in relation to immoveable property abroad. As to corporations sole see CORPORATIONS. As to secretarial seals see para 357 ante.

7　Ibid art 2(2).

8　Ibid art 2(3).

9　Ibid art 2(3).

10　Ibid art 2(4).

11　Parliamentary Commissioner Act 1967 s 4(1), Sch 2 (substituted by the Parliamentary and Health Service Commissioners Act 1987 s 1(1), (2), Sch 1). The Commissioner has special jurisdiction in respect of consular actions abroad: Parliamentary Commissioner Act 1967 s 6(5) (added by the Parliamentary Commissioner (Consular Complaints) Act 1981 s 1). As to the Parliamentary Commissioner for Administration see ADMINISTRATIVE LAW vol 1(1) (Reissue) para 41 et seq.

12　See the *Supply Estimates 1995–96 for the year ending 31 March 1996* (HC Paper (1994–95) no 271–II).

**460. Functions.** The Secretary of State for Foreign and Commonwealth Affairs[1] is primarily responsible to the Crown and to Parliament for formulating and conducting the foreign policy[2] of the country. He conducts the correspondence with Commonwealth and foreign governments and is responsible for the appointment of United Kingdom representatives to Commonwealth and foreign countries (subject, as the case may be, to royal or prime ministerial approval in the case of Ambassadors or High Commissioners). He has formal duties in connection with the making of treaties[3] and with the reception of the representatives of foreign states and in presenting them to the monarch. It used to be the case that the Secretary of State or the Permanent Under Secretary of State was usually present when matters of state were discussed between the monarch and a foreign minister, or a foreign monarch, or his representative; but it is now often the practice for one of the Ministers of State to be in attendance, depending upon the circumstances of the meeting. The Foreign and Commonwealth Office is responsible for the arrangements for state or official visits abroad[4].

The Secretary of State has the responsibility for ensuring the good government of the dependent territories[5] and for their relations with foreign states.

The Secretary of State accounts for the greater part of the grant in aid voted by Parliament to the BBC World Service[6], to the British Council[7] and to international organisations[8]. He also has functions in connection with United Kingdom membership of the European Community[9].

1　As to the transfer of functions to the Secretary of State for Foreign and Commonwealth Affairs see para 459 ante.

2　The stated aims of the United Kingdom's foreign policy are (1) to enhance the security and prosperity of the United Kingdom and the dependent territories; and (2) to promote and protect British interests and influence overseas, including the welfare of British nationals: Foreign and Commonwealth Office Annual

Report, including Overseas Development Administration: *The Government's Expenditure Plans 1995–96 to 1997–98* (Cm 2802) (1995).

3  As to the treaty-making power see paras 801–802 post.

4  See the Civil Service Year Book 1996 col 310.

5  As to the dependent territories see COMMONWEALTH.

6  The World Service is a constituent part of the BBC, but has complete editorial and managerial independence: see the Foreign and Commonwealth Office Annual Report, including Overseas Development Administration: *The Government's Expenditure Plans 1995–96 to 1997–98* (Cm 2802) (1995). See also the Civil Service Year Book 1996 col 302.

7  See the Foreign and Commonwealth Office Annual Report, including Overseas Development Administration: *The Government's Expenditure Plans 1995–96 to 1997–98* (Cm 2802) (1995). See also the Civil Service Year Book 1996 col 298.

8  See the Foreign and Commonwealth Office Annual Report, including Overseas Development Administration: *The Government's Expenditure Plans 1995–96 to 1997–98* (Cm 2802) (1995).

9  See *Political Co-operation by the Member States of the European Communities* (Cmnd 5432) (1973).

**461. Crown Agents.** The Crown Agents were established as a statutory body[1] on 1 January 1980[2]. They are empowered to act in the capacity of agents for any scheduled authority[3] and to carry on certain prescribed activities anywhere in the world in their own right[4]. They may also perform functions anywhere in the world ancillary to those activities[5]. Further, the agents may in certain circumstances be required to act for a particular scheduled authority[6].

Where the agents undertake any activity in their agency capacity involving the making of payments by them on the principal's behalf, they must ensure that they hold a sufficient sum from the principal to cover payment or must obtain an irrevocable letter of credit from him enabling them to recover the sum involved[7]. The agents have power to invest sums received by them from a principal for disbursement or investment[8]. On being so required by the minister, the agents must review their affairs and their subsidiaries' and report to him[9], and similarly they are obliged to furnish him with such information as he may from time to time require[10]. Every year they must prepare an annual report on the performance of their functions and on their policies, programmes and plans[11].

Only a member of the Crown Agents may be appointed as a director of a subsidiary of the agents unless the minister approves it or different arrangements expressly apply[12]. The agents must ensure that their subsidiaries do not exceed the agents' authority, but this does not apply to involvement in activities for which a subsidiary has received ministerial approval if the agents themselves could have obtained that approval[13]. No wholly-owned subsidiary may issue shares, stock or debentures to anyone except the agents, another wholly-owned subsidiary or their nominees; nor may it transfer any interest it holds in another wholly-owned subsidiary to anyone but them[14].

The Crown Agents must be financially self-supporting and be able to achieve a rate of return and to allocate such funds as the minister prescribes to reserve[15]. Moneys held by them other than as agents must be held or invested in accordance with regulations[16]. Any excess in the agents' revenue may be required to be paid over to the minister[17]. The agents have certain temporary and long-term borrowing powers[18] which are subject to limitations[19], and grants and loans may be made to them by the minister[20]. Any sums borrowed by the agents may be guaranteed by the Treasury as the Treasury sees fit[21]. The agents must keep proper accounts and records, and must, if directed by the minister, prepare a statement of accounts of their own and all their subsidiaries' dealings[22]. The minister has a general power to give the agents directions in any financial matter relating to functions performed in their own right[23]. The agents must ensure that they and their subsidiaries are appropriately insured against insurable financial risks arising out of all their activities[24].

As from a day to be appointed, the property, rights and liabilities of the Crown Agents are to be vested in a successor company nominated by the Secretary of State[25]. The commencing capital debt of the Crown Agents[26] must be repaid[27]. The successor company must issue securities[28] to the Secretary of State as he may from time to time direct with the approval of the Treasury[29]. The government may, with the consent of the Treasury, acquire securities of the successor company, or rights to subscribe for such securities[30]. The Secretary of State may not dispose of securities or rights without the consent of the Treasury[31]. The Crown Agents continue in existence after the appointed day for the purpose of performing certain residual functions[32]. Once the Secretary of State is satisfied that the residual functions are substantially discharged he may, after consulting the Crown Agents and the successor company, by order dissolve the Crown Agents from a day specified in the order[33].

1   The body consists of between six and ten full-time or part-time members appointed by the Minister of Overseas Development, who also appoints a chairman and deputy chairman: Crown Agents Act 1979 s 1(3)–(4). As to the appointment and tenure of members see s 1(6), Sch 1 paras 1–6; as to the remuneration of members see Sch 1 paras 7–9. Members are disqualified for membership of the House of Commons: House of Commons Disqualification Act 1975 s 2, Sch 2 (amended by the Crown Agents Act 1979 Sch 1 para 9). As to proceedings of the Crown Agents see the Crown Agents Act 1979 Sch 1 paras 10–12; as to staff see Sch 1 paras 13–15; as to delegation of functions see Sch 1 para 16; and as to instruments and contracts see Sch 1 paras 17–18.
    The full title of the Crown Agents is the Crown Agents for Oversea Governments and Administrations: see s 1(1), (2).
2   Ibid s 1(1), (2). Crown Agents Act 1979 (Appointed Day) Order 1979, SI 1979/1672. All property, rights, liabilities and obligations of the previous body vested in the new body except those reserved to the Crown Agents Holding and Realisation Board: see the Crown Agents Act 1979 ss 2, 25, 26, 27, 28, Sch 2, Sch 5; and text and note 25 infra.
3   As to the scheduled authorities, which are in the nature of governments, government departments, international organisations and bodies, public authorities, and charitable organisations, see ibid s 3, Sch 3. As to the activities which they may carry out in the capacity of agent see s 4, Sch 4.
4   See ibid ss 3, 5; and the Crown Agents (Additional Powers) Order 1990, SI 1990/2303.
5   See the Crown Agents Act 1979 s 6(1). As to limitations on this power see s 6(2)–(4).
6   See ibid s 7.
7   Ibid s 8(1), (2).
8   See ibid s 8(3)–(7) (s 8(5) amended by the Finance Act 1987 s 72(7), Sch 16 Pt XI); the Banking Act 1987 s 108(1), Sch 6 para 8; and by virtue of the Banking Co-ordination (Second Council Directive) Regulations 1992, SI 1992/3218, Sch 10 para 10.
9   See the Crown Agents Act 1979 s 9.
10  See ibid s 10.
11  See ibid s 11.
12  See ibid s 12(1)(a).
13  See ibid s 12(1)(b), (c).
14  See ibid s 12(2).
15  See ibid ss 13, 14. As to the commencing capital debt in respect of property and rights transferred to the agents see s 17 (amended by the Crown Agents (Amendment) Act 1986 s 1).
16  See the Crown Agents Act 1979 s 15. Such regulations are not statutory instruments, and are not recorded in this work.
17  See ibid s 16(1), (3), (4). If not required by the minister, the excess may be used by the agents as they see fit: s 16(2).
18  See ibid s 18.
19  Ibid s 19. Total debts must not exceed £50 million, which figure may be increased to £80 million by order: see s 19(1). At the date at which this volume states the law, no such order had been made.
20  See ibid s 20 (amended by the Finance Act 1982 s 153(4)).
21  See the Crown Agents Act 1979 s 21.
22  See ibid s 22 (amended by the Companies Act 1989 s 23; and the Companies Act 1989 (Eligibility for Appointment as Company Auditor) (Consequential Amendments) Regulations 1991, SI 1991/1997).
23  See the Crown Agents Act 1979 s 23.
24  See ibid s 24.

25  Crown Agents Act 1995 s 1(1), (3). The Secretary of State may nominate any registered company which at the appointed day is wholly owned by the Crown: see s 1(2). The order appointing a day or nominating a company may be varied or revoked by subsequent order before the property rights and liabilities become vested by virtue of these provisions: s 1(4). For transitional provisions dealing with agreements, transactions etc operating before the appointed day see s 1(5), Sch 1 paras 1, 2. As to the effect on contracts of employment and pensions see Sch 1 paras 3, 4. The words 'Crown Agents' may form part of the name of the successor company, a holding company of the successor company, or a subsidiary of the successor company: see s 6. As to the effect of the transfer on statutory accounts see s 5; as to the effect on the liability for corporation tax see s 7.

As to the constitution and functions of the Crown Agents Holding and Realisation Board after the appointed day see the Crown Agents Act 1979 s 25, Sch 5 (both as amended by the Crown Agents Act 1995 s 11).

On the appointed day substantial parts of the Crown Agents Act 1979 will be repealed, namely ss 1(7), 2–24, 27(2), (3) (part), 28, 30(3)(a) (part), 31(1) (part), (2), (3), Sch 1 para 7 (part), 8, 9, 11, 13–15, Schs 2–4, Sch 5 paras 8 (part), 23 (part), Sch 6 Pt II: Crown Agents Act 1995 s 13(2), Sch 2 Pt I.

At the date at which this volume states the law, no order had been made appointing a day for the purposes of these provisions.

26  Ie the commencing capital debt under the Crown Agents Act 1979 s 17: see note 15 supra.

27  Crown Agents Act 1995 s 2(1). The Secretary of State may, with Treasury approval, direct the time and manner of repayment: s 2(1), (4). If he so directs, with Treasury approval, before the appointed day, the Crown Agents may be deemed to have assumed a debt to the Secretary of State, the terms of which are such as may be determined from time to time by the Secretary of State with Treasury approval: s 2(2), (4). Sums received by the Secretary of State under s 2(1) must be paid into the National Loans Fund, and sums received by way of repayment of capital or interest on a debt under s 2(2) must be paid into the Consolidated Fund: s 2(3). As to the National Loans Fund see para 727 et seq post; and as to the Consolidated Fund see para 711 et seq post.

28  Securities must be issued at such time or times and on such terms, and any shares issued must be of such nominal value, as the Secretary of State may, with the approval of the Treasury, direct: s 3(3), (4), (5).

29  Ibid s 3(1), (5). He must not give such a direction, however, after the company has ceased to be wholly owned by the Crown: s 3(2). Any dividends or other payments received under this provision must be paid into the Consolidated Fund: s 3(6).

30  Ibid s 4(1).

31  Ibid s 4(2). Any dividends or other payments received in right of or on the disposal of such securities must be paid into the Consolidated Fund: s 4(4).

32  Ibid s 8(1). Those functions relate to the effective vesting of property in the successor company under foreign law (s 9), and the preparation of final reports and accounts (s 10). During the transitional period the minimum number of members of Crown Agents is reduced to two, and no remuneration is payable: s 8(2). Any expenses incurred by Crown Agents during that period must be met by the successor company: s 8(3).

33  Ibid s 8(4). On the dissolution of Crown Agents, the Crown Agents Act 1979 ss 1 (remainder), 30(3)(a) (part), and Sch 1 (remainder) are repealed: Crown Agents Act 1995 s 13(2), Sch 2 Pt II.

## 462. Overseas Development Administration.

The Ministry of Overseas Development[1] has been dissolved and the functions of the Minister of Overseas Development[2] have been transferred to the Secretary of State for Foreign and Commonwealth Affairs[3].

There is a Minister of State responsible for the overseas aid programme[4], assisted by the Permanent Secretary and a Deputy Secretary[5]. The Overseas Development Administration is divided into (1) the Finance Division; (2) the Personnel and Organisation Division; (3) the Africa Division; (4) the Asia and Pacific Division; (5) the International Division; (6) the Eastern European and Western Hemisphere Division; (7) the Latin America, Caribbean and Atlantic Department; (8) the Education Division; (9) the Engineering Division; (10) the Health and Population Division; (11) the Natural Resources Division; and (12) the Economic and Social Division[6]. The Overseas Development Administration is also responsible for the Natural Resources Institute, an executive agency which assists developing countries to improve the productivity and sustainable management of their natural resources through the application of science and technology[7].

In addition to providing bilateral assistance, the Overseas Development Administration works in conjunction with other countries through international institutions, particularly the European Union, the United Nations and the World Bank[8].

The expenses of the Overseas Development Administration are provided by Parliament[9].

1    The Ministry of Overseas Development was first created in 1964. Provisions concerning the minister and his department were contained in the Ministers of the Crown Act 1964 (repealed). Functions were transferred to the minister by the Minister of Overseas Development (No 1) Order 1964, SI 1964/1849; the Minister of Overseas Development (No 2) Order 1964, SI 1964/2050; the Transfer of Functions (Overseas Pensions) Order 1965, SI 1965/1528; the Transfer of Functions (Miscellaneous) Order 1967, SI 1967/486; and the Transfer of Functions (Secretary of State and Minister of Overseas Development) Order 1967, SI 1967/973.

2    The Minister of Overseas Development was concerned with the formulation and execution of policies to help the economic development of less developed countries, and administered the British programme of development aid.

3    The functions of the minister were transferred to the Secretary of State in 1970 by the Transfer of Functions (Overseas Aid) Order 1970, SI 1970/1682. The overseas aid functions were exercised by the Secretary of State for Foreign and Commonwealth Affairs, assisted by a Minister for Overseas Development, until the Ministry of Overseas Development was again given departmental status: Ministers of the Crown Act 1974 s 3(3)–(5), Sch 1 (repealed); and the Minister of Overseas Development Order 1974, SI 1974/1264. In 1979 the ministry was again dissolved and its functions transferred to the Secretary of State, or in the case of functions relating to certain specified bodies to the Secretary of State for Foreign and Commonwealth Affairs: Ministry of Overseas Development (Dissolution) Order 1979, SI 1979/1451. As to the office of Secretary of State see para 355 et seq ante. As to the transfer of functions generally see para 363 ante. As to the Secretary of State for Foreign and Commonwealth Affairs see para 459 ante.

4    The purpose of the aid programme is to promote the development or maintain the economy of any country or territory outside the United Kingdom, or the welfare of its people: Overseas Development and Co-operation Act 1980 s 1(1).

5    See the Civil Service Year Book 1996 col 520.

6    As to the organisation of the Overseas Development Administration see the Civil Service Year Book 1996 col 520 et seq; and the Foreign and Commonwealth Office Annual Report, including Overseas Development Administration: *The Government's Expenditure Plans 1995–96 to 1997–98* (Cm 2802) (1995). As to the Civil Service generally see paras 549–564 post.

7    See the Civil Service Year Book 1996 col 527 et seq; and the Foreign and Commonwealth Office Annual Report, including Overseas Development Administration: *The Government's Expenditure Plans 1995–96 to 1997–98* (Cm 2802) (1995). The Administration is currently considering options for the future ownership of the Natural Resources Institute. As to executive agencies see para 551 post.

8    See the Civil Service Year Book 1996 col 520.

9    See the *Supply Estimates 1995–96 for the year ending 31 March 1996* (HC Paper (1994–95) no 271–II).

## (vii)  The Department of Health

**463.  Functions of the department.** The Department of Health was established in 1988, when the Department of Health and Social Security[1] was divided into two departments, each with its own Secretary of State[2]. The Department of Health is responsible for promoting and protecting the health of the nation, providing a National Health Service in England[3] and social care[4].

It is the duty of the Secretary of State[5] to continue the promotion in England and Wales of a comprehensive health service designed to secure improvement in the physical and mental health of the people of those countries, and in the prevention, diagnosis and treatment of illness[6]. The Secretary of State discharges his responsibility for the provision of local health services through the National Health Service Executive[7], which itself is responsible for the central management and guidance of National Health Service trusts[8], health authorities and certain special health authorities[9]. Where he finds the provision of general medical, dental, opthalmic or pharmaceutical services inadequate in any particular area or district, the Secretary of State may authorise the health authority to make such arrangements as he may approve, or may himself make the necessary arrangements[10].

The department is an authorised department for the purpose of suing and being sued[11], and is subject to investigation by the Parliamentary Commissioner for Administration[12]. Complaints about the Health Service are investigated by the National Health Service Commissioners[13]. The expenses of the department are provided by Parliament[14].

1   The functions of the Minister of Health and the Minister of Social Security were transferred in 1968 to the Secretary of State for Social Services, who was responsible for the Department of Health and Social Security: see the Secretary of State for Social Services Order 1968, SI 1968/1699.
2   See the Transfer of Functions (Health and Social Security Order) 1988, SI 1988/1843. As to the transfer of functions generally see para 363 ante. As to the office of Secretary of State see para 355 et seq ante.
3   The central authority for the administration of the law relating to the National Health Service in Wales is the Secretary of State for Wales: see the Transfer of Functions (Wales) Order 1969, SI 1969/388, art 2(1). See generally NATIONAL HEALTH AND SOCIAL SECURITY vol 33 para 143 et seq.
4   See the Civil Service Year Book 1996 col 355.
5   Ie the Secretary of State for Health in England or the Secretary of State for Wales in Wales: see note 3 supra.
6   See the National Health Service Act 1977 s 1(1).
7   As to the National Health Service Executive see the Civil Service Year Book 1996 col 368 et seq; and para 465 post.
8   The Secretary of State may by order establish National Health Service Trusts (1) to assume responsibility for the ownership and management of hospitals or other establishments or facilities which were previously managed or provided by health authorities or special health authorities; or (2) to provide and manage hospitals or other establishments or facilities: National Health Service and Community Care Act 1990 s 5(1) (amended by the Health Authorities Act 1995 s 2(1), Sch 1 Pt II paras 65, 69). See also the Department of Health Annual Report: *The Government's Expenditure Plans 1995–96 to 1997–98* (Cm 2812) (1995); and NATIONAL HEALTH AND SOCIAL SECURITY.
9   As to health authorities and special health authorities see NATIONAL HEALTH AND SOCIAL SECURITY.
10  See the National Health Service Act 1977 s 56 (amended by the Health Authorities Act 1995 Sch 1 Pt I paras 1, 37); and NATIONAL HEALTH AND SOCIAL SECURITY vol 33 paras 86, 95, 101.
11  See the list published under the Crown Proceedings Act 1947 s 17(1) (as amended); and CROWN PROCEEDINGS.
12  Parliamentary Commissioner Act 1967 s 4(1), Sch 2 (substituted by the Parliamentary and Health Service Commissioners Act 1987 s 1(1), (2), Sch 1; amended by the Transfer of Functions (Health and Social Security) Order 1988, SI 1988/1843).
13  Previously complaints about the National Health Service were excluded from the jurisdiction of the Parliamentary Commissioner for Administration, but the National Health Service Act 1977 introduced a scheme of Health Service Commissioners to investigate complaints: see now the Health Service Commissioners Act 1993 (as amended). As to the Health Service Commissioners see NATIONAL HEALTH AND SOCIAL SECURITY vol 33 para 182 et seq.
14  See the *Supply Estimates 1995–96 for the year ending 31 March 1996* (HC Paper (1994–95) no 271–XII).

**464. The Secretary of State for Health.** The Secretary of State for Health is a corporation sole, with a corporate seal[1]. The corporate seal of the Secretary of State for Health is authenticated by the signature of a Secretary of State, or of a secretary to the Department of Health, or of a person authorised by a Secretary of State to act in that behalf[2]. The seal is officially and judicially noticed[3]. Every document purporting to be an instrument made or issued by the Secretary of State for Health and to be sealed with his seal duly authenticated, or to be signed or executed by a secretary to the Department of Health or an authorised person, is to be received in evidence and deemed to be so made or issued without further proof unless the contrary is shown[4]. A certificate signed by the Secretary of State for Health that any instrument purporting to be made or issued by him was so made or issued is conclusive evidence of that fact[5].

1   Transfer of Functions (Health and Social Security) Order 1988, SI 1988/1843 art 4(1). As to the transfer of functions to the Secretary of State for Health see para 463 ante. As to corporations sole see CORPORATIONS. As to secretarial seals see para 357 ante.
2   Ibid art 4(2).

3    Ibid art 4(3).
4    Ibid art 4(3).
5    Ibid art 4(4).

**465. Organisation.** The Secretary of State for Health is assisted by a Minister of State, three Parliamentary Under Secretaries, the Permanent Secretary, the Chief Medical Officer and the Chief Executive of the National Health Service Executive[1]. The Department of Health includes: (1) the Departmental Resources and Services Group; (2) the Social Care Group[2]; (3) the Public Health Group[3]; and (4) the National Health Service Executive[4]. There is a National Health Service Policy Board, of which the Secretary of State is the chairman[5].

There are four executive agencies accountable to the Secretary of State for Health: (a) the Medicines Control Agency; (b) the Medical Devices Agency; (c) NHS Estates; and (d) the NHS Pensions Agency[6].

1    See the Civil Service Year Book 1996 col 355 et seq. As to the National Health Service see NATIONAL HEALTH AND SOCIAL SECURITY.
2    The Social Care Group covers the whole range of social care functions, including care for the elderly and the mentally ill, disability services and children's services.
3    The Public Health Group deals with wider public health functions including health aspects of environment and food. See the White Paper *The Health of the Nation* (Cm 1986) (1992).
4    As to the structure and organisation of the Department of Health see the Civil Service Year Book 1996 col 356 et seq. As to the Civil Service generally see paras 549–564 post.
5    See the Civil Service Year Book 1996 col 356.
6    See the Civil Service Year Book 1996 col 385 et seq. As to executive agencies see para 551 post.

## (viii)  The Home Office

### A.  THE HOME OFFICE GENERALLY

**466. The Home Secretary.** Apart from the matters which are especially assigned to his department, the Secretary of State for the Home Department (the 'Home Secretary'), performs all the functions[1] which fell to the King's Secretary before the present departmental organisation of the executive came into existence. The Home Secretary presides over the Home Office[2].

The Home Office is now concerned almost exclusively with England and Wales, but relations between the United Kingdom government and the Channel Islands and the Isle of Man[3] fall within its scope[4].

The Home Office is an authorised government department for the purpose of suing and being sued[5], and is subject to investigation by the Parliamentary Commissioner for Administration[6]. Its expenses are provided by Parliament[7].

1    As to the functions of the Home Secretary see paras 467–469 post.
2    It has been said that the Home Secretary is first in precedence among the Secretaries of State: 2 Anson's Law and Custom of the Constitution (4th Edn, 1935) Pt II p 19. It seems that this is no longer the case, and that 'Secretary of State' no longer necessarily imports a reference to the Home Secretary. The Interpretation Act 1978 s 5, Sch 1 provides that in any Act, unless the contrary intention appears, 'Secretary of State' means one of Her Majesty's Principal Secretaries of State; and in modern enactments 'Secretary of State' may be taken to refer to the Secretary of State exercising functions under the enactment in question. The term 'First Secretary of State' is not, however, obsolete: Mr Michael Heseltine is currently known as Deputy Prime Minister and First Secretary of State. As to the office of Secretary of State generally see para 355 et seq ante. As to the transfer of functions generally see para 363 ante.
3    As to the constitutional status of the Channel Islands and the Isle of Man see COMMONWEALTH vol 6 (Reissue) para 838 et seq.
4    See Newsam *The Home Office* (1954); and the Civil Service Year Book 1996 col 406. As to Scotland see paras 51–66 ante, 519 post.

5    See the list published under the Crown Proceedings Act 1947 s 17(1) (as amended); and CROWN
     PROCEEDINGS.
6    Parliamentary Commissioner Act 1967 s 4(1), Sch 2 (substituted by the Parliamentary and Health Service
     Commissioners Act 1987 s 1(1), (2), Sch 1): see PARLIAMENT. As to the Parliamentary Commissioner for
     Administration see ADMINISTRATIVE LAW vol 1(1) (Reissue) para 41 et seq.
7    See the *Supply Estimates 1995–96 for the year ending 31 March 1996* (HC Paper (1994–95) no 271–VIII).

**467. Communications between Crown and subject.** The Home Secretary is the
proper and usual medium of communication between Crown and subject, and signifies
the Crown's pleasure both to individuals and to departments. He notifies to certain great
local officials matters of state intelligence, such as declarations of war, treaties of peace,
and royal births and deaths[1]. Addresses and petitions to the monarch in person, as opposed
to the Queen in Council, are received and transmitted by him[2]. Thus, petitions for the
exercise of the prerogative of mercy are addressed to him[3].

In the majority of cases in which formal expression is to be given to the monarch's
will, it is the Home Secretary's duty to cause the necessary document to be prepared, and
to countersign it[4].

1    See 2 Anson's Law and Custom of the Constitution (4th Edn, 1935) Pt II pp 19–20.
2    2 Anson's Law and Custom of the Constitution (4th Edn, 1935) Pt II p 20.
3    See para 825 post. See also Troup *The Home Office* (1925) ch V; and Newsam *The Home Office* (1954) ch XI.
4    Two classes of royal warrants are submitted to the monarch from the Home Office: (1) warrants of various
     kinds which are prepared at the Home Office for Her Majesty's signature, and are countersigned and
     sealed by the Home Secretary; and (2) warrants which are prepared at the Crown Office, on instructions
     from the Secretary of State, for the passing of letters patent under the Great Seal. The second class of
     warrants, which constitute the authority of the Lord Chancellor for the sealing of letters patent, are
     countersigned by the Secretary of State, but are not sealed by him. As to letters patent under the Great
     Seal see para 920 post. As to public documents generally see paras 906–922 post. The only seal which is
     in use in the Home Office is the second secretarial seal. As to secretarial seals see para 357 ante.

**468. General functions.** The Home Secretary is primarily concerned with matters of
administration affecting the internal well-being of the country, so far as those matters have
not been especially vested in other departments[1], and he exercises powers of
administration, supervision and control.

These matters include functions connected with civil defence[2], the fire services[3],
coroners[4], licensing and inspection under the legislation relating to controlled drugs[5],
animal welfare including the licensing of experiments on animals[6], explosives[7], charities[8]
and elections[9]. The Home Office also deals with cremations, burials and exhumations;
firearms; poisons; liquor licensing; theatre and cinema licensing; and scrutiny of local
authority bye-laws[10].

The Home Secretary is responsible for immigration policy, nationality matters
including the acquisition of citizenship by registration and naturalisation, the enforcement
of immigration laws and applications for asylum[11]. He is also responsible for the
extradition of criminal offenders[12]. He is responsible for the co-ordination of policy
concerning ethnic minorities and legislation against racial discrimination[13].

He has functions relating to betting, gaming and lotteries and appoints members of
the Gaming Board for Great Britain[14].

The Home Secretary is also a Church Commissioner[15].

1    See the Civil Service Year Book 1996 col 406.
2    See the Civil Defence Act 1948 ss 1, 9(2). See also the *Supply Estimates 1995–96 for the year ending
     31 March 1996* (HC Paper (1994–95) no 271–VIII); and WAR vol 49 para 164.
3    See the Fire Services Act 1947 (as amended). See also the *Supply Estimates 1995–96 for the year ending
     31 March 1996* (HC Paper (1994–95) no 271–VIII); and FIRE SERVICES vol 18 para 472.
4    See CORONERS.

5   See the Misuse of Drugs Act 1971 (as amended); and MEDICINES vol 30 (Reissue) para 1001.

6   See the Animals (Scientific Procedures) Act 1986 (as amended); and ANIMALS vol 2 (Reissue) para 429 et seq.

7   See the Explosives Act 1875 (as amended); the Explosives Act 1923; the Fireworks Act 1951 (as amended); the Health and Safety at Work etc Act 1974 (as amended); and EXPLOSIVES.

8   The Charity Commission is a separate department, but accountable directly to the Home Secretary: see the Home Office and Charity Commission Annual Report: *The Government's Expenditure Plans 1995–96 to 1997–98* (Cm 2808) (1995). See also CHARITIES. As to non-ministerial departments generally see para 528 post.

9   Eg see the Representation of the People Act 1983 (as amended); and the Parliamentary Constituencies Act 1986 (as amended); and ELECTIONS.

10  See the Civil Service Year Book 1996 col 406. Certain functions of the Secretary of State relating to legal aid and costs in criminal cases have been transferred to the Lord Chancellor: see the Transfer of Functions (Legal Aid in Criminal Proceedings and Costs in Criminal Cases) Order 1980, SI 1980/705. As to the Lord Chancellor see paras 477–497 post. Property, rights and liabilities in connection with any wireless telegraphy functions have been transferred from the Home Secretary to the Secretary of State for Trade and Industry: see the Transfer of Functions (Trade and Industry) Order 1983, SI 1983/1127. As to the Secretary of State for Trade and Industry see para 506 post. Property, rights and liabilities in connection with broadcasting functions or functions relating to safety of sports grounds have been transferred from the Home Secretary to the Secretary of State for National Heritage: see the Transfer of Functions (National heritage) Order 1992, SI 1992/1311. As to the Secretary of State for National Heritage see para 499 post. As to the office of Secretary of State see para 355 et seq ante. As to the transfer of functions generally see para 363 ante.

11  See BRITISH NATIONALITY, IMMIGRATION AND RACE RELATIONS.

12  See the Extradition Act 1989; and EXTRADITION. The Home Secretary may also have the power to issue the prerogative writ *ne exeat regno*, to keep a subject within the realm in time of war: see para 815 post.

13  See the Race Relations Act 1976 (as amended); and BRITISH NATIONALITY, IMMIGRATION AND RACE RELATIONS.

14  Eg see the Gaming Act 1968 (as amended); the Lotteries and Amusements Act 1976 (as amended); and BETTING, GAMING AND LOTTERIES.

15  See the Church Commissioners Measure 1947 s 1(2), Sch 1 para 1 (amended by the Synodical Government Measure 1969 s 2(2)); and the Church of England (Miscellaneous Provisions) Measure 1992 s 17(1), Sch 3 para 5); and ECCLESIASTICAL LAW.

**469. Functions relating to public order.** The maintenance of public order falls within the department of the Home Secretary[1]. As the minister responsible for law and order, the Home Secretary has a general responsibility for the system of criminal justice[2]. He may recommend the exercise of the prerogative of mercy[3]; and he is responsible for considering claims for compensation for wrongful conviction[4]. The department's concerns also include sentencing policy and practice; criminal procedure in magistrates' courts and the higher courts; appeals; juries; evidence; obscene publications; victims of crime; criminal injuries compensation[5]; the law on the rehabilitation of offenders; and policy on the repatriation of prisoners[6].

The general supervision of the police is entrusted to the Home Secretary, who is responsible for the provision of an effective and efficient police service[7]. His objectives are as follows: (1) to maintain and, if possible, increase the number of detections for violent crimes; (2) to increase the number of detections for burglaries of people's homes; (3) to target and prevent crimes which are a particular local problem, including drug-related criminality, in partnership with the public and local agencies; (4) to provide high visibility policing so as to reassure the public; and (5) to respond promptly to emergency calls from the public[8]. The Home Secretary is the police authority for the metropolitan police district[9].

The Home Office is responsible for the general supervision of prisons[10]. The Prison Service became an executive agency on 1 April 1993[11]. The Home Secretary has power to provide young offender institutions[12], and he has powers in relation to the detention of persistent young offenders in secure training centres[13]. He has important functions in relation to probation and after-care[14], the regulation of community service work[15], the approval of bail hostels and probation hostels[16]; and he may make rules regulating the monitoring arrangements to be made for persons subject to curfew orders[17]. He also has functions in relation to the Parole Board[18]; and he advises the Crown on the appointment of Her Majesty's Chief Inspector of Prisons[19].

1   *Harrison v Bush* (1855) 5 E & B 344 at 353.
2   Responsibility for magistrates' courts has been transferred from the Home Secretary to the Lord Chancellor's department by the Transfer of Functions (Magistrates' Courts and Family Law) Order 1992, SI 1992/709. As to the Lord Chancellor's department see para 497 post. As to the transfer of functions generally see para 363 ante.
3   As to pardons and reprieves see paras 823–830 post.
4   Ie compensation under the Criminal Justice Act 1988 s 133 (as amended). There may be ex gratia payment if the criteria for eligibility under that Act are not met: see HC Official Report (6th series), 15 April 1991, written answers cols 6–7.
5   As to the Criminal Injuries Compensation scheme see CRIMINAL LAW vol 11(2) (Reissue) para 1499 et seq; and *R v Secretary of State for the Home Department, ex p Fire Brigades Union* [1995] 2 AC 513, [1995] 1 All ER 888, CA.
6   See the Civil Service Year Book 1996 cols 407–408.
7   Police Act 1964 s 38 (amended by the Police and Magistrates' Courts Act 1994 s 20); Police and Magistrates' Courts Act 1994 s 4. The principle underpinning the Act is that policing should remain a local service and that responsibility for it should lie with local police authorities, subject to standards set by the Home Secretary: see the Home Office and Charity Commission Annual Report: *The Government's Expenditure Plans 1995–96 to 1997–98* (Cm 2808) (1995). As to the organisation, administration and powers of the police and the Home Secretary's powers and duties in relation to the police force see POLICE.
8   Police (Secretary of State's Objectives) Order 1994, SI 1994/2678, art 2.
9   Police Act 1964 s 62 (substituted by the Police and Magistrates' Courts Act 1994 s 44, Sch 5 Pt I para 15).
10  See the Prison Act 1952 (as amended); and PRISONS vol 37 para 1105.
11  See *Next Steps Review 1995* (Cm 3164) (1995) p 106; and the Civil Service Year Book 1996 col 424 et seq.
12  Prison Act 1952 s 43(1)(aa) (added by the Criminal Justice Act 1988 s 170(1), Sch 15 para 11; amended by the Criminal Justice and Public Order Act 1994 s 18(3)).
13  See the Criminal Justice and Public Order Act 1994 Pt I (ss 1–24).
14  See the Probation Service Act 1993 (as amended); and MAGISTRATES.
15  See the Probation Service Act 1993 s 26.
16  See the Probation Service Act 1993 s 27.
17  Criminal Justice Act 1991 s 15 (amended by the Probation Service Act 1993 s 32(2), (3), Sch 3 para 10, Sch 4); and see CRIMINAL LAW vol 11(2) (Reissue) para 1218.
18  See the Criminal Justice Act 1991 s 32, Sch 5 (respectively amended and substituted by the Criminal Justice and Public Order Act 1994 ss 149, 168(2), Sch 10 para 70).
19  983 HC Official Report (5th Series), 30 April 1980, col 1395. See also PRISONS vol 37 para 1110.

**470. Organisation.** The Home Secretary is assisted by three Ministers of State, two Parliamentary Under Secretaries of State, and a Permanent Under Secretary of State[1].

The Home Office includes: (1) the Legal Adviser's Branch; (2) the Criminal Policy Department; (3) the Research and Statistics Department; (4) the Criminal Justice and Constitutional Department; (5) Her Majesty's Inspectorate of Probation; (6) the Fire and Emergency Planning Department; (7) Her Majesty's Fire Service Inspectorate; (8) the Police Department; (9) Her Majesty's Inspectorate of Constabulary; (10) the Equal Opportunities and General Department; (11) the Immigration and Nationality Department; (12) Her Majesty's Inspectorate of Prisons for England and Wales; (13) the Personnel and Office Services Department; and (14) the Finance Department[2]. There is also a Central Information and Systems Division and a Communications Directorate[3].

The Home Office has four executive agencies: (a) the Forensic Science Service; (b) Her Majesty's Prison Service; (c) the United Kingdom Passport Agency; and (d) the Fire Service College[4].

1   See the Civil Service Year Book 1996 cols 406–407.
2   See the Civil Service Year Book 1996 col 407 et seq; and the Home Office and Charity Commission Annual Report: *The Government's Expenditure Plans 1995–96 to 1997–98* (Cm 2808) (1995).
3   See the Civil Service Year Book 1996 cols 419, 421.
4   See the Civil Service Year Book 1996 col 422 et seq. As to executive agencies see para 551 post.

## B.   THE SECURITY AND INTELLIGENCE SERVICES

**471. Security Service.** The Security Service is now on a statutory basis under the authority of the Secretary of State[1]. Its functions are the protection of national security, in particular from threats of espionage, terrorism and sabotage, from the activities of agents of foreign powers and from actions intended to overthrow or undermine parliamentary democracy by political, industrial or violent means[2]. It is also concerned with safeguarding the economic well-being of the United Kingdom against threats posed by actions or intentions of persons outside the British Islands[3].

The operations of the Service are under the control of a Director-General who is appointed by the Secretary of State[4]. The Director-General prepares an annual report on the work of the Service to the Prime Minister[5] and the Secretary of State and may at any time report to either of them on any matter relating to its work[6]. The Director-General is responsible for the efficiency of the Service and it is his duty to ensure that there are arrangements[7] for securing that no information is obtained by the Service except so far as necessary for the proper discharge of its functions, or disclosed by it except so far as necessary for that purpose or for the purpose of preventing or detecting any serious crime or for the purpose of any criminal proceedings[8]. However, the disclosure of information is regarded as necessary for the proper discharge of the functions of the Security Service if it consists of the disclosure of records subject to and in accordance with the Public Records Act 1958[9] or the disclosure of information, subject to and in accordance with arrangements approved by the Secretary of State, to the Comptroller and Auditor General for the purposes of his functions[10].

The Director-General is also under a duty to ensure that the Service does not take any action to further the interests of any political party[11].

1   Security Service Act 1989 s 1(1). Any expenses of the Secretary of State under the Security Service Act 1989 are defrayed out of money provided by Parliament: s 6. As to the indivisibility of the office of Secretary of State see para 355 ante. The functions of the Secretary of State under this Act are exercised variously by the Home, Defence and Foreign Secretaries.
       In 1909, in response to rising fears about German espionage, the War Office set up, without any statutory authority, a service called MO5 which later became known as MI5. It was combined with the Metropolitan Police counter-subversion division in 1935, and was renamed the Security Service, although its domestic branch is still widely known as MI5: see Wade and Bradley *Constitutional and Administrative Law* (11th Edn, 1993) p 560; and also *Lord Denning's Report* (Cmnd 2152) (1963) on the Profumo Scandal.
2   Security Service Act 1989 s 1(2).
3   Ibid s 1(3). As from a day to be appointed it will also be the function of the Security Service to act in support of the activities of police forces and other law enforcement agencies in the prevention and detection of serious crime: s 1(4) (prospectively added by the Security Service Act 1996 s 1(1)).
4   Security Service Act 1989 s 2(1).
5   As to the Prime Minister see paras 394–398 ante.
6   Security Service Act 1989 s 2(4).
7   These arrangements must be such as to ensure that information in the possession of the Service is not disclosed for use in determining whether a person should be employed, or continue to be employed, by any person, or in any office or capacity, except in accordance with provisions approved by the Secretary of State: ibid s 2(3).
8   Ibid s 2(2)(a) (amended by the Intelligence Services Act 1994 s 11(2), Sch 4 para 1).
9   As to public records see paras 835–841 post.

10   Security Service Act 1989 s 2(3A) (added by the Intelligence Services Act 1994 Sch 4 para 1). As to the
     Comptroller and Auditor General see paras 724–726 post.
11   Security Service Act 1989 s 2(2)(b). As from a day to be appointed the Director-General will also be under
     a duty to ensure that there are arrangements, agreed with a person designated by the Secretary of State,
     for co-ordinating the activities of the Service in pursuance of s 1(4) (as prospectively added: see note 3
     supra) with the activities of police forces and other law enforcement agencies: s 2(2)(c) (prospectively
     added by the Security Service Act 1996 s 1(2)). Also as from a day to be appointed the Secretary of State
     must designate for the purposes of the Security Service Act 1989 s 2(2)(c) (as prospectively added: see
     supra) a person who is or has been a chief officer of police of a police force in England and Wales, the
     chief officer of a police force in Scotland or the chief constable of the Royal Ulster Constabulary: s 2(3B)
     (prospectively added by the Security Service Act 1996 s 1(3)).

**472. Secret Intelligence Service.** The Secret Intelligence Service ('the Intelligence
Service') is now on a statutory basis under the authority of the Secretary of State[1]. Its
functions are the obtaining and provision of information relating to the actions or
intentions of persons outside the British Islands[2] and the performance of other tasks
relating to the actions or intentions of such persons[3]. These functions are exercisable only
in the interests of national security (with particular reference to the defence and foreign
policies of Her Majesty's government in the United Kingdom), in the interests of the
economic well-being of the United Kingdom, or in support of the prevention or
detection of serious crime[4].

The operations of the Intelligence Service continue to be under the control of Chief
of the Intelligence Service who is appointed by the Secretary of State[5]. He is responsible
for the efficiency of the Service and it is his duty to ensure that there are arrangements
for securing that no information is obtained by the Intelligence Service except so far as
necessary for the property discharge of its functions and that no information is disclosed
by it except so far as necessary for that purpose, in the interests of national security, for
the purpose of the prevention or detection of serious crime or for the purpose of any
criminal proceedings[6]. However, the disclosure of information is regarded as necessary for
the proper discharge of the functions of the Intelligence Service if it consists of the
disclosure of records subject to and in accordance with the Public Records Act 1958[7], or
the disclosure of information, subject to and in accordance with arrangements approved
by the Secretary of State, to the Comptroller and Auditor General[8] for the purposes of
his functions[9].

It is also the duty of the Chief of the Intelligence Service to ensure that the Service
does not take any action to further the interests of any United Kingdom political party[10].

The Chief of the Intelligence Service prepares an annual report on the Service to the
Prime Minister[11] and the Secretary of State, and may at any time report to either of them
on any matter relating to its work[12].

1   See the Intelligence Services Act 1994 s 1(1). The Secret Intelligence Service is otherwise known as MI6:
    see Wade and Bradley *Constitutional and Administrative Law* (11th Edn, 1993) p 560; de Smith and Brazier
    *Constitutional and Administrative Law* (7th Edn, 1994) p 519–521. As to the indivisibility of the office of
    Secretary of State see para 355 ante. The functions of the Secretary of State under this Act are exercised
    variously by the Home, Defence and Foreign Secretaries.
2   Intelligence Services Act 1994 s 1(1)(a).
3   Ibid s 1(1)(b).
4   Ibid s 1(2).
5   Ibid s 2(1).
6   Ibid s 2(2)(a).
7   As to public records see paras 835–841 post.
8   As to the Comptroller and Auditor General see paras 724–726 post.
9   Intelligence Services Act 1994 s 2(3).
10  Ibid s 2(2)(b).
11  As to the Prime Minister see paras 394–398 ante.
12  Security Service Act 1989 s 2(4).

**473. The Government Communications Headquarters.** The    Government
Communications Headquarters (GCHQ)[1] is now on a statutory basis under the
authority of the Secretary of State[2]. Its functions are (1) the monitoring or interference
with electromagnetic, acoustic and other emissions and any equipment producing such
emissions, the obtaining and provision of information derived from or related to such
emissions or equipment and from encrypted material; and (2) the provision of advice
and assistance about languages (including terminology used for technical matters), and
cryptography and other matters relating to the protection of information and other
material, to the armed forces of the Crown, to Her Majesty's government in the United
Kingdom or to a Northern Ireland Department or to any other organisation which is
determined for the purposes of this provision in such manner as may be specified by
the Prime Minister[3]. The functions relating to the monitoring of emissions[4] are
exercisable only in the interests of national security, with particular reference to the
defence and foreign policies of Her Majesty's government in the United Kingdom[5], in
the interests of the economic well-being of the United Kingdom in relation to the
actions or intentions of persons outside the British Islands[6], or in support of the
prevention or detection of serious crime[7].

The operations of GCHQ continue to be under the control of a Director appointed
by the Secretary of State[8]. The Director is responsible for the efficiency of GCHQ and it
is his duty to ensure that there are arrangements for securing that no information is
obtained by GCHQ except so far as necessary for the proper discharge of its functions and
that no information is disclosed by it except so far as necessary for that purpose or for the
purpose of any criminal proceedings[9]. However, the disclosure of information is regarded
as necessary for the proper discharge of the functions of GCHQ if it consists of the
disclosure of records subject to and in accordance with the Public Records Act 1958[10],
or the disclosure of information, subject to and in accordance with arrangements
approved by the Secretary of State, to the Comptroller and Auditor General[11] for the
purposes of his functions[12]. It is also the duty of the Director to ensure that GCHQ does
not take any action to further the interests of any United Kingdom political party[13].

The Director prepares an annual report on the work of the GCHQ to the Prime
Minister and the Secretary of State and may at any time report to either of them on any
matter relating to its work[14].

1   In the Intelligence Services Act 1994, 'GCHQ' refers to the Government Communications Headquarters
    and to any unit or part of a unit of the armed forces of the Crown which is for the time being required
    by the Secretary of State to assist the Government Communications Headquarters in carrying out its
    functions: s 3(3).
2   Ibid s 4(1). As to the indivisibility of the office of Secretary of State see para 355 ante. The functions of the
    Secretary of State under this Act are exercised variously by the Home, Defence and Foreign Secretaries.
3   Ibid s 3(1). See also the Interception of Communications Act 1985; and Wade and Bradley *Constitutional
    and Administrative Law* (11th Edn, 1993) pp 574–577. As to the Prime Minister see paras 394–398 ante.
4   See the Intelligence Services Act 1994 s 3(1)(a); and the text to note 3 supra.
5   Ibid s 3(2)(a).
6   Ibid s 3(2)(b).
7   Ibid s 3(2)(c).
8   Ibid s 4(1).
9   Ibid s 4(2)(a).
10  As to public records see paras 835–841 post.
11  As to the Comptroller and Auditor General see paras 724–726 post.
12  Intelligence Services Act 1994 s 4(3).
13  Ibid s 4(2)(b).
14  Ibid s 4(4).

**474. Authorisation of certain actions.** No entry on or interference with property or with wireless telegraphy[1] is unlawful if it is authorised by a warrant issued by the Secretary of State[2].

The Secretary of State may, on an application made by the Security Service[3], the Intelligence Service or GCHQ[4], issue a warrant authorising the taking of such action as is specified in the warrant in respect of any property or wireless telegraphy so specified, provided he is satisfied that certain grounds have been met[5].

A warrant authorising the taking of action in support of the prevention or detection of serious crime may not relate to property in the British Islands[6]. The Security Service may make an application for a warrant to be issued authorising that Service, or a person acting on its behalf, to take action as is specified in the warrant on behalf of the Intelligence Service or GCHQ even if such action would not otherwise be within its functions[7]. However, the Security Service may not make an application for a warrant except where the action proposed to be authorised by the warrant is action in respect of which the Intelligence Service or GCHQ could make such an application, and is to be taken otherwise than in support of the prevention or detection of serious crime[8].

The Secretary of State may also authorise a person to do any act outside the British Islands for which he would otherwise be liable under the criminal or civil law of any part of the United Kingdom[9]. The Secretary of State must not give such an authorisation unless he is satisfied that certain grounds have been met[10]. The authorisation may be general or may relate to a particular act, person or operation and may be subject to specified conditions[11].

An authorisation or warrant may not be given except under the hand of the Secretary of State or, in an urgent case where the Secretary of State has expressly authorised it to be given and a statement of that fact is endorsed on it, under the hand of a senior official of his department[12]. Both warrants and authorisations last for six months if issued by the Secretary of State, unless renewed for a further six months by the Secretary of State who must cancel an authorisation or warrant if he is satisfied that any act authorised by it is no longer necessary[13].

1  'Wireless telegraphy' has the same meanings as in the Wireless Telegraphy Act 1949 and, in relation to wireless telegraphy, 'interfere' has the same meaning as in that Act: Intelligence Services Act 1994 s 11(1)(e).

2  Ibid s 5(1).

3  See para 471 ante.

4  As to the Intelligence Service see para 472 ante; and as to GCHQ see para 473 ante.

5  Intelligence Services Act 1994 s 5(2). The grounds are as follows:

   (1)  that he thinks it necessary for the action to be taken on the ground that it is likely to be of substantial value in assisting, as the case may be (a) the Security Service in carrying out any of its functions under the Security Service Act 1989; (b) the Intelligence Service in carrying out any of its functions under Intelligence Services Act 1994 s 1; or (c) GCHQ in carrying out any function which falls within s 3(1)(a): s 5(2)(a);

   (2)  that he is satisfied that what the action seeks to achieve cannot reasonably be achieved by other means: s 5(2)(b); and

   (3)  that he is satisfied that satisfactory arrangements are in force under the Security Service Act 1989 s 2(2)(a) (see para 471 ante), the Intelligence Services Act 1994 s 2(2)(a) (see para 472 ante) or s 4(2)(a) (see para 473 ante) with respect to the disclosure of information obtained by virtue of s 5 and that any information obtained under the warrant will be subject to those arrangements: s 5(2)(c).

6  Ibid s 5(3). As from a day to be appointed s 5(3) is substituted as follows. A warrant issued on the application of the Intelligence Service or GCHQ for the purpose of the exercise of their functions under s 1(2)(c) or 3(2)(c) may not relate to property in the British Islands: s 5(3) (prospectively substituted by the Security Service Act 1996 s 2). A warrant issued on the application of the Security Service for the purposes of the exercise of their function under the Security Service Act 1989 s 1(4) may not relate to property in the British Islands unless it authorises the taking of action in relation to conduct within the Intelligence Services Act 1994 s 5(3B) (as prospectively substituted): s 5(3A) (prospectively substituted by

the Security Service Act 1996 s 2). Conduct is within the Intelligence Services Act 1994 s 5(3B) (as prospectively substituted) if it constitutes (or if it took place in the United Kingdom, would constitute) one or more offences, and either (1) it involves the use of violence, results in substantial financial gain or is conduct by a large number of persons in pursuit of a common purpose; or (2) the offence or one of the offences is an offence for which a person who has attained the age of 21 and has no previous convictions could reasonably be expected to be sentenced to imprisonment for a term of three years or more: s 5(3B) (prospectively substituted by the Security Service Act 1996 s 2).

7   Intelligence Services Act 1994 s 5(4).
8   Ibid s 5(5).
9   Ibid s 7(1), (2).
10  The Secretary of State must not give an authorisation under ibid s 7 unless he is satisfied:
   (1)  that any acts which may be done in reliance on the authorisation or, as the case may be, the operation in the course of which the acts may be done will be necessary for the proper discharge of a function of the Intelligence Service: s 7(3)(a);
   (2)  that there are satisfactory arrangements in forced to secure (a) that nothing will be done in reliance on the authorisation beyond what is necessary for the proper discharge of a function of the Intelligence Service; and (b) that, in so far as any acts may be done in reliance on the authorisation, their nature and likely consequences will be reasonable, having regard to the purposes for which they are carried out: s 7(3)(b); and
   (3)  that there are satisfactory arrangements in force under s 2(2)(a) with respect to the disclosure of information obtained by virtue of s 7 and that any information obtained by virtue of anything done in reliance on the authorisation will be subject to those arrangements: s 7(2)(c).
11  Ibid s 7(4).
12  Ibid ss 6(1), 7(5). 'Senior official', in the Intelligence Services Act 1994, in relation to a department is a reference to an officer of or above Grade 3 or, as the case may require, Diplomatic Service Senior Grade: s 11(1)(d).
13  See ibid ss 6(2)–(4), 7(6)–(8). Sections 5, 6 have effect in relation to the Security Service so that a warrant issued under the Security Service Act 1989 s 3 (repealed) is treated as a warrant under the Intelligence Services Act 1994 s 5: see s 5(5), (6).

## 475. The Intelligence and Security Committee.

The Prime Minister[1], after consultation with the Leader of the Opposition[2], appoints the members (one of whom is the Chairman) of the Intelligence and Security Committee ('the Committee')[3]. The Committee examines the expenditure, administration and policy of the Security Service, the Intelligence Service and GCHQ[4].

The Committee consists of nine members who are drawn both from members of the House of Commons[5] and from members of the House of Lords[6]; none of whom is a minister of the Crown[7]. A member of the Intelligence and Security Committee holds office for the duration of the Parliament in which he is appointed[8]. Past service is not a bar to appointment as a member[9]. A member may resign at any time by notice to the Prime Minister[10], but must vacate office if he ceases to be a member of the House of Commons, or of the House of Lords, or he becomes a minister of the Crown or if he is required to do so by the Prime Minister on the appointment[11] of another person as a member in his place[12].

The Committee may determine its own procedure[13]. However, it is laid down that the requisite number for a quorum is three[14] and that in the event of an equality of voting among the Committee members, the Chairman has a casting vote[15]. The Chairman may appoint another member to act as Chairman at any Committee meeting in his absence but in this case the appointed person does not have a casting vote[16].

If the Director-General of the Security Service, the Chief of the Intelligence Service or the Director of GCHQ is asked by the Committee to disclose any information, he must either arrange for it to be made available to the Committee subject to and in accordance with arrangements approved by the Secretary of State; or inform the Committee that it cannot be disclosed either because it is sensitive information[17] which, in his opinion, should not be made available; or because the Secretary of State has determined that it should not be disclosed[18]. The fact that any particular information is sensitive information does not prevent its disclosure if the Director-General, the Chief of the Intelligence Service or the Director of GCHQ considers it safe to disclose it[19]. Information which has not been disclosed to the Committee on the ground that it is sensitive must be disclosed to it if the Secretary of State considers it desirable in the public interest[20]. The Secretary of State must not make a determination restricting disclosure with respect to any information on the grounds of national security alone and, he must not make such a determination unless the information appears to him to be of such a nature that, if he were requested to produce it before a departmental select committee of the House of Commons, he would think it proper not to do so[21]. The disclosure of information to the Committee is regarded for the purposes of the Security Service Act 1989 and the Intelligence Services Act 1994, as necessary for the proper discharge of the functions of the Security Service, the Intelligence Service, or as the case may require, GCHQ[22].

The Committee makes an annual report on the discharge of its functions to the Prime Minister and may at any time report to him on any matter relating to the discharge of those functions[23]. The Prime Minister must lay before each House of Parliament a copy of each annual report made by the Committee together with a statement as to whether any matter has been excluded from that copy[24]. If it appears to the Prime Minister, after consultation with the Committee, that the publication of any matter in a report would be prejudicial to the continued discharge of the functions of either of the Services or GCHQ, the Prime Minister may exclude that matter from the copy of the report as laid before each House of Parliament[25].

1   As to the Prime Minister see paras 394–398 ante.
2   Ie the Leader of the Opposition within the meaning of the Ministerial and other Salaries Act 1975. As to the Leader of the Opposition see paras 218–219 ante.
3   See the Intelligence Services Act 1994 s 10(1), (3).
4   Ibid s 10(1). As to GCHQ see para 473 ante.
5   As to the House of Commons see PARLIAMENT.
6   As to the House of Lords see para 204 ante; and PARLIAMENT.
7   Intelligence Services Act 1994 s 10(2). 'Minister of the Crown' has the same meaning as in the Ministers of the Crown Act 1975: s 11(1)(c).
8   Intelligence Services Act 1994 s 10(4), Sch 3 para 1(1).
9   Ibid Sch 3 para 1(4).
10  Ibid Sch 3 para 1(3).
11  Ie under ibid s 10(3): see Sch 3 para 1(2).
12  Ibid Sch 3 para 1(2).
13  Ibid Sch 3 para 2(1).
14  Ibid Sch 3 para 2(4).
15  Ibid Sch 3 para 2(2).
16  Ibid Sch 3 para 2(3).
17  For these purposes, 'sensitive information' is:
    (1)  information which might lead to the identification of, or provide details of, sources of information, other assistance or operational methods available to the Security Service, Intelligence Service or GCHQ: ibid Sch 3 para 4(a);
    (2)  information about particular operations which have been, are being or are proposed to be undertaken in pursuance of any of the functions of those bodies: Sch 3 para 4(b);
    (3)  information provided by, or by an agency of, the government of a territory outside the United Kingdom where that government does not consent to the disclosure of the information: Sch 3 para 4(c).
18  Ibid Sch 3 para 3(1).
19  Ibid Sch 3 para 3(2).
20  Ibid Sch 3 para 3(3).
21  Ibid Sch 3 para 3(4).
22  Ibid Sch 3 para 3(5).
23  Ibid s 10(5). The Committee made its first interim report in May 1995: see the *Interim Report of the Intelligence and Security Committee* (Cm 2873) (1995). In that report, the committee identified a number of

major issues upon which it will report in the future (para 10). The topic for its first major inquiry is: 'how the Agencies have adapted in general to the new situations post-Cold War and, in particular, how tasks and the priorities attached to them have altered, and whether the resources now provided are appropriate to those tasks and used in a cost effective way' (para 11). The first Chairman of the Intelligence and Security Committee is the Rt Hon Tom King, CH, MP.

24  Intelligence Services Act 1994 s 10(6).

25  Ibid s 10(7).

**476. Commissioners and tribunals.** The Prime Minister[1] appoints a Commissioner who, among his powers, may review the issue of warrants to the Security Service[2] and another Commissioner who may review the issue of warrants and the authorisation of acts outside the British Islands to the Intelligence Service and GCHQ[3] except in so far as those powers relate to the Security Service[4]. The persons appointed as Commissioners are those who hold or have held high judicial office[5], and they hold office as Commissioners in accordance with the terms of their appointment, being paid such allowances as the Treasury may determine[6]. The Secretary of State may, after consultation with the Commissioners and with the approval of the Treasury as to numbers, provide the Commissioners with such staff as the Secretary of State thinks necessary for the discharge of the Commissioners' functions[7].

It is the duty of every member of the Security Service, the Intelligence Service and GCHQ and every official of the department of the Secretary of State to disclose to the Commissioners such documents or information as they may require for the purpose of enabling them to discharge their functions[8]. Both Commissioners must report annually on the discharge of their functions to the Prime Minister, and a copy of each report must be laid before each House of Parliament but may exclude any material considered by the Prime Minister after consultation with the Commissioner, to be prejudicial to the functions of the Security Service, Intelligence Service or GCHQ; a statement as to whether any such matter has been excluded must also be laid before Parliament[9].

There is one tribunal which is established for the purpose of investigating complaints about the Security Service and another to investigate complaints about the Intelligence Service and GCHQ[10]. Both tribunals consist of not less than three or more than five members, appointed by Her Majesty by royal warrant[11], each of whom must be (1) a person who has a 10 year general qualification; (2) an advocate or solicitor of Scotland of at least 10 years' standing; or (3) a member of the Bar of Northern Ireland or a solicitor of the Supreme Court of Northern Ireland of at least 10 years' standing[12]. A member must vacate office at the end of a period of five years from the day of appointment but he is eligible for reappointment[13]. He may be relieved of office by Her Majesty at his own request or removed by Her Majesty on an address presented to her by both Houses of Parliament[14]. A member of the tribunal may be appointed President or a Vice-President by royal warrant[15].

The Secretary of State may, after consultation with the tribunal and with Treasury approval as to numbers, provide the tribunal with such staff as he thinks necessary for the proper discharge of its functions[16]. The Secretary of State pays the tribunal members such remuneration and allowances as he may determine with Treasury approval, and he also defrays such of the tribunal's expenses as he may with Treasury approval[17].

Subject to certain requirements[18], the tribunal may determine its own procedure[19]. The functions of the tribunal in relation to any complaint are capable of being carried out in any place in the United Kingdom, by any two or more members of the tribunal designated for the purpose by the President; and different members of the tribunal may carry out functions in relation to different complaints at the same time[20]. It is the duty of every member of the Security Service, Intelligence Service or GCHQ to disclose or give to the relevant tribunal such documents or information as it may require for the purpose of enabling it to carry out its functions[21]. The tribunal may authorise any member of staff to obtain any document or information on the tribunal's behalf[22]. The tribunal must carry out its functions in such away as to secure that no document or information disclosed or given to the tribunal by any person is disclosed without his consent to any complainant, to any person (other than the Commissioner) holding office under the Crown or to any other person; and accordingly, the tribunal must not, except in certain circumstances[23] give any reasons for a determination notified by them to a complainant[24].

The Commissioners must assist the tribunals in the discharge of their duties[25]. A decision of a Commissioner or a tribunal, including a decision as to the jurisdiction of each, is not subject to appeal or liable to be questioned by any court[26].

Any person[27] may complain to the relevant tribunal if he is aggrieved by anything which he believes the Security Service, Intelligence Service or GCHQ has done in relation to him or to any property[28] of his; and, unless the tribunal considers that the complaint is frivolous or vexatious, it must investigate it in accordance with statutory provisions[29].

If the complaint is to the Security Service tribunal, that tribunal must then investigate whether the complainant has been the subject of inquiries by the Security Service[30], and if it finds that he has but that those inquiries had ceased at the time when the complaint was made, it must determine whether, at the time when the inquiries were instituted, the Security Service had reasonable grounds for deciding to institute inquiries about the complainant in the discharge of its functions[31]. If the Security Service tribunal finds such inquiries were continuing at the time when the complaint was made, it must determine whether, at that time, the Security Service had reasonable grounds for deciding to continue them[32]. Where it appears to the tribunal that the inquiries were made about the complainant on the ground of his membership of a category of persons regarded by the Security Service as requiring investigation in the discharge of its functions, it must regard the Security Service as having reasonable grounds for deciding to institute or continue such inquiries about the complainant if the tribunal considers that the Security Service had reasonable grounds for believing him to be a member of that category[33]. If in such a case the tribunal considers that the Security Service may not be justified in regarding all members of a particular category as requiring investigation it must refer that matter to the Commissioner[34]. If the complainant alleges that the Security Service disclosed information for use in determining whether he should be employed, or continue to be employed, by any person or in any office or capacity specified by him, the tribunal must investigate whether the Security Service has disclosed information for that purpose, and if it finds that they have done so, it must determine whether the Security Service had reasonable grounds for believing the information to be true[35]. If the complainant alleges that anything has been done by the Security Service in relation to any of his property, the tribunal must refer the complaint to the Commissioner who must investigate whether a warrant has been issued[36] in respect of that property and if he finds that such a warrant has been issued he must, applying the principles applied by a court on an application for judicial review, determine whether the Secretary of State was acting properly in issuing or renewing the warrant[37]. The Commissioner must then inform the Security Service tribunal of his conclusions on any complaint referred to him[38].

If and so far as the complainant alleges that anything has been done by the Intelligence Services or GCHQ in relation to any property of the complainant, the Intelligence Services tribunal must refer the complaint to the Commissioner[39]. If in the course of the investigation of the complaint by that tribunal, it considers that it is necessary to establish whether an authorisation was given[40] to the doing of any act, it must refer so much of the complaint as relates to the doing of that act to the Commissioner[41]. Where any such reference is made to the Commissioner, he must investigate as the case may require, whether a warrant was issued[42] in relation to the property concerned; or whether an authorisation was given[43] to the doing of the act in question[44]. If the Commissioner finds that a warrant was issued or an authorisation was given, he must, applying the principles applied by a court on an application for judicial review, determine whether the Secretary of State was acting properly in issuing or renewing the warrant or, as the case may be, in giving or renewing the authorisation[45]. Subject to these provisions, the tribunal must investigate whether the Intelligence Service or, as the case may be, GCHQ has obtained or provided information or performed any other tasks in relation to the actions or intentions of the complainant; and if so, whether, applying the principles applied by a court on an application for judicial review, the Intelligence Service or GCHQ had reasonable grounds for doing what it did[46].

If in any case investigated by the Security Service tribunal or the Intelligence Services tribunal, the tribunal's conclusions on the matters which it is required to investigate are such that no determination is made by it in favour of the complainant; but it appears to the relevant tribunal from the allegations made by the complainant that it is appropriate for there to be an investigation into whether the Security Service, the Intelligence Service or GCHQ has in any other respect acted unreasonably in relation to the complainant or his property, it must refer the matter to the Commissioner[47]. The Commissioner may report any such matter referred to him to the Secretary of State who may take such action[48] in the light of the report as he thinks fit[49].

1   As to the Prime Minister see paras 394–398 ante.
2   Ie by the Secretary of State under the Intelligence Services Act 1994 ss 5, 6: Security Service Act 1989 s 4(3) (amended by the Intelligence Services Act 1994 s 11(2), Sch 4 para 2). As to the Security Service see para 471 ante.
3   Ie by the Secretary of State under ibid ss 5–7: see s 8(3). As to the Intelligence Service see para 472 ante; and as to GCHQ see para 473 ante.
4   Ibid s 8(3). In the Intelligence Services Act 1994 'the Commissioner' means the Commissioner appointed under s 8: s 11(1)(b).
5   Ie within the meaning of the Appellate Jurisdiction Act 1876: see Security Service Act 1989 s 4(1); Intelligence Services Act 1994 s 8(1).
6   Security Service Act 1989 s 4(2); Intelligence Services Act 1994 8(2). As to the Treasury see paras 512–517 ante.
7   Security Service Act 1989 s 4(8); Intelligence Services Act 1994 s 8(8).
8   Security Service Act 1989 s 4(4); Intelligence Services Act 1994 s 8(4).
9   Security Service Act 1989 s 4(5), (6), (7); Intelligence Services Act 1994 s 8(5), (6), (7).
10   Security Service Act 1989 s 5(1); Intelligence Services Act 1994 s 9(1).
11   See the Security Service Act 1989 s 5(2), Sch 2 para 1(2); Intelligence Services Act 1994 s 9(3), Sch 2 para 1(2).
12   Security Service Act 1989 Sch 2 para 1(1) (amended by the Courts and Legal Services Act 1990 s 71(2), Sch 10 para 74)); Intelligence Services Act 1994 Sch 2 para 1(1). For the meaning of a 'general qualification' see the Courts and Legal Services Act 1990 s 71.
13   Security Service Act 1989 Sch 2 para 1(3); Intelligence Services Act 1994 Sch 2 para 1(3).
14   Security Service Act 1989 Sch 2 para 1(4), (5); Intelligence Services Act 1994 Sch 2 para 1(4), (5).
15   Security Service Act 1989 Sch 2 para 2(1); Intelligence Services Act 1994 Sch 2 para 2(1). A person ceases to be President or Vice-President if he ceases to be a member of the tribunal: Security Service Act 1989 Sch 2 para 2(3); Intelligence Services Act 1994 Sch 2 para 2(3). If at any time the President is temporarily unable to carry out the functions of the President, the Vice-President must carry them out: Security Service Act 1989 Sch 2 para 2(2); Intelligence Services Act 1994 Sch 2 para 2(2).
16   Security Service Act 1989 Sch 2 para 6(1); Intelligence Services Act 1994 Sch 2 para 6(1).
17   Security Service Act 1989 Sch 2 para 5(1), (2); Intelligence Services Act 1994 Sch 2 para 5(1), (2).
18   Ie subject to the Security Service Act 1989 Sch 2 para 4(2); Intelligence Services Act 1994 Sch 2 para 4(2): see text and note 32 infra).
19   Security Service Act 1989 Sch 2 para 4(3); Intelligence Services Act 1994 Sch 2 para 4(3).
20   Security Service Act 1989 Sch 2 para 3; Intelligence Services Act 1994 Sch 2 para 3.
21   Security Service Act 1989 Sch 2 para 4(1); Intelligence Services Act 1994 Sch 2 para 4(1).

22 Security Service Act 1989 Sch 2 para 6(2); Intelligence Services Act 1994 Sch 2 para 6(2).

23 Ie except in reports under Security Service Act 1989 Sch 1 para 5(1)(b) (see text and note 31 infra); Intelligence Services Act 1994 Sch 1 para 6(1)(b) (see text and note 46 infra): see the Security Service Act 1989 Sch 2 para 4(2); Intelligence Services Act 1994 Sch 2 para 4(2).

24 Security Service Act 1989 Sch 2 para 4(2); Intelligence Services Act 1994 Sch 2 para 4(2).

25 Security Service Act 1989 s 5(3); Intelligence Services Act 1994 s 9(2).

26 Security Service Act 1989 s 5(4); Intelligence Services Act 1994 s 9(4). As to ouster clauses such as these see *Anisminic v Foreign Compensation Commission* [1969] 2 AC 147, [1969] 1 All ER 208, HL; *R v Cornwall County Council, ex p Huntington* [1994] 1 All ER 694, CA; and COURTS vol 10 para 720.

27 The persons who may complain to the tribunal include any organisation and any association or combination of persons: Security Service Act 1989 s 5(1), Sch 1 para 8(1); Intelligence Services Act 1994 s 9(3), Sch 1 para 9.

28 References to a complainant's property include references to any place where the complainant resides or works: Security Service Act 1989 Sch 1 para 8(2); Intelligence Services Act 1994 Sch 1 para 11(b). Reference in the Intelligence Services Act 1994 Sch 1 to a complainant's property also includes a reference to any wireless telegraphy transmission originated or received or intended to be received by him: Sch 1 para 11(a).

29 Security Service Act 1989 Sch 1 para 1; Intelligence Services Act 1994 Sch 1 para 1. No complaint may be entertained if and so far as it relates to anything done before the date on which the relevant Schedule came into force: Security Service Act 1989 Sch 1 para 9(1); Intelligence Services Act 1994 Sch 1 para 10(1). The Security Service Act 1989 came into force on 18 December 1989: Security Service Act 1989 (Commencement) Order 1989, SI 1989/2093. The Intelligence Services Act 1994 came into force on 15 December 1994: Intelligence Services Act 1994 (Commencement) Order 1994, SI 1994/2734.

30 Security Service Act 1989 Sch 1 para 2(1). Where any inquiries about a person were instituted before the date on which Sch 1 came into force (ie 18 December 1989: see note 29 supra) and no decision had been taken before that date to discontinue them, Sch 1 para 2 has effect as if the inquiries had been instituted on that date: Sch 1 para 9(2).

31 Ibid Sch 1 para 2(2). Where the Security Service tribunal determines under Sch 1 para 2 or 3 that the Security Service did not have reasonable grounds for the decision or belief, it must (1) give notice to the complainant that it has made a determination in his favour; and (2) make a report of its findings to the Secretary of State and the Commissioner: Sch 1 para 5(1). Where the tribunal gives a complainant notice of such a determination, the tribunal may (a) if the determination is made under Sch 1 para 2, order inquiries by the Security Service about the complainant to be ended and any records relating to such inquiries to be destroyed (Sch 1 para 6(1)(a)); (b) if the determination is made under Sch 1 para 2 or 3, direct the Secretary of State to pay to the complainant such sum by way of compensation as may be specified by the tribunal (Sch 1 para 6(1)(b)).

Where no such determination is made by the tribunal or the Commissioner the tribunal must give notice to the complainant that no determination in his favour has been made on his complaint: Sch 1 para 5(3).

32 Ibid Sch 1 para 2(3). See also Sch 1 para 5(1); and note 3 supra.

33 Ibid Sch 1 para 2(4).

34 Ibid Sch 1 para 7(1).

35 Ibid Sch 1 para 3. See also Sch 1 paras 5(1), 6(1)(b); and text and note 31 supra.

36 Ie under ibid s 3 or the Intelligence Services Act 1994 s 5: see Security Service Act 1989 Sch 1 para 4(1) (as amended).

37 Ibid Sch 1 para 4(1) (amended by the Intelligence Services Act 1994 s 11(2), Sch 4 para 3). The Security Service tribunal must give notice to the complainant of any determination in his favour by the Commissioner under the Security Service Act 1989 Sch 1 para 4: Sch 1 para 5(2). Where the tribunal gives the complainant notice of such a determination it may (1) quash any warrant in respect of any property of the complainant which the Commissioner has found to have been improperly issued or renewed and which he considers should be quashed (Sch 1 para 6(2)(a)); (2) if the Commissioner considers that a sum should be paid to the complainant by way of compensation, direct the Secretary of State to pay to the complainant such sum as the Commissioner may specify (Sch 1 para 6(2)(b)).

Where no such determination is made by the tribunal or the Commissioner the tribunal must give notice to the complainant that no determination in his favour has been made on his complaint: Sch 1 para 5(3).

38 Ibid Sch 1 para 4(2).

39 Intelligence Services Act 1994 Sch 1 para 2.

40 Ie under ibid s 7: see Sch 1 para 4. The Commissioner must inform the tribunal of his conclusion on any reference made to him under Sch 1 para 2 or 4: Sch 1 para 5(3).

41 Ibid Sch 1 para 4. See also Sch 1 para 5(3); and note 40 supra.

42 Ie under ibid s 5 (see para 474 ante): see Sch 1 para 5(1)(a).

43 Ie under ibid s 7 (see para 474 ante): see Sch 1 para 5(1)(b).

44 Ibid Sch 1 para 5(1). The Intelligence Services tribunal must give notice to the complainant of any determination in his favour by the Commissioner: Sch 1 para 6(2). Where the Intelligence Services tribunal gives a complainant notice of such a determination, the tribunal may do either or both of the following: (1) quash any warrant or authorisation which the Commissioner found to have been improperly issued, renewed or given and which he considers should be quashed (Sch 1 para 8(2)(a)); (2) direct the Secretary of State to pay to the complainant such sum by way of compensation as may be specified by the Commissioner (Sch 1 para 8(2)(b)).

45 Ibid Sch 1 para 5(2). See also Sch 1 para 6(2); and text and note 37 supra.

46 Ibid Sch 1 para 3. Where the Intelligence Services tribunal determines under Sch 1 para 3 that the Intelligence Service or, as the case may be, GCHQ did not have reasonable grounds for doing what it did, it must (1) give notice to the complainant that it has made a determination in his favour; and (2) make a report of its findings to the Secretary of State and the Commissioner: Sch 1 para 6(1). Where the Intelligence Services tribunal gives notice of such a determination, the tribunal may do either or both of the following: (a) direct that the obtaining and provision of information in relation to the complainant or, as the case may be, the conduct of other activities in relation to him or to any property of his must cease and that any records relating to such information so obtained or provided or such other activities must be destroyed (Sch 1 para 8(1)(a)); (b) direct the Secretary of State to pay to the complainant such sum by way of compensation as may be specified by the Intelligence Services tribunal (Sch 1 para 8(1)(b)).

Where no such determination is made by the Intelligence Services tribunal or the Commissioner, the tribunal must give notice to the complainant that no determination in his favour has been made on his complaint: Sch 1 para 6(3).

47 Security Service Act 1989 Sch 1 para 7(2); Intelligence Services Act 1994 Sch 1 para 7(1).

48 Such action in relation to the Security Service includes any action which the Security Service tribunal has power to take or direct under the Security Service Act 1989 Sch 1 para 6 (see notes 3 and 8 supra): Sch 1 para 7(3). Such action in relation to the Intelligence Services includes any action which the Intelligence Services tribunal has power to take or direct under the Intelligence Services Act 1994 Sch 1 para 8(1), (2); Sch 1 para 8(3).

49 Security Service Act 1989 Sch 1 para 7(3); Intelligence Services Act 1994 Sch 1 para 7(2), 8(3).

## (ix) The Lord Chancellor and the Lord Chancellor's Department

**477. Appointment of Lord Chancellor.** 'The Lord Chancellor' means[1] the Lord High Chancellor of Great Britain for the time being[2]. The Lord Chancellor is appointed by the monarch on the recommendation of the Prime Minister, and the appointment is made by the monarch delivering the Great Seal of the United Kingdom into his custody[3] and addressing him by the title of his office[4].

There are no statutory qualifications for the office[5]; but it has long been the practice to appoint a member or former member of the Bar, often but by no means always from among the Bench or someone who has been Attorney General or Solicitor General[6]. It is provided by statute that the office may be held by a Roman Catholic[7].

On appointment, the Lord Chancellor takes the oath of allegiance, the official oath and the judicial oaths[8].

1 Interpretation Act 1978 ss 5, 23(1), Sch 1, Sch 2 para 4(1), (4). This applies, except when used with reference to Ireland only, when it means the Lord Chancellor of Ireland for the time being (Sch 2 para 4(4)). However, the office of Lord Chancellor of Ireland has been abolished: see the Irish Free State (Consequential Provisions) Act 1922 s 2, Sch 2 Pt II. References in enactments to the Lord Chancellor of Ireland are to be construed as references to the Lord Chief Justice of Northern Ireland: General Adaptation of Enactments (Northern Ireland) Order 1921, SR & O 1921/1804, art 5.

2 Interpretation Act 1978 Sch 1, Sch 2 Pt II. Cf the definitions in the Great Seal Act 1884 s 4 (see para 912 note 2 post), and in the Great Seal (Offices) Act 1874 s 3 (see para 921 note 2 post).

3 See 3 Bl Com (14th Edn) 47; Office of the Lord Chancellor (attributed without warrant to Ellesmere) (1651 Edn) 15. As to the use of the Great Seal of the United Kingdom see para 909 post.

4 1 Campbell's Lives of the Lord Chancellors (1845 Edn) 21. The appointment was occasionally formerly made by patent or writ of privy seal, or by suspending the Great Seal around the neck: 1 Campbell's Lives of the Lord Chancellors (1845 Edn) 21.

5 The Supreme Court Act 1981 s 10(3) (as amended), which specifies the qualifications of judges of the Supreme Court, makes no reference to the Lord Chancellor.

6    Lord Chancellors who were previously judges include Viscount Sankey (1929–35), Lord Maugham
     (1938–39) and Lord Simonds (1951–54); those who were previously Law Officers include Viscount
     Hailsham (1928–29, 1935–38), Viscount Caldecote (1939–40), Lord Simon (1940–45), Lord Jowitt
     (1945–51), Lord Kilmuir (1954–62), Lord Dilhorne (1962–64), Lord Elwyn-Jones (1974–79), Lord
     Havers (1987) and Lord Mackay of Clashfern (1987-date). Lord Chancellors who had been neither judges
     nor law officers include Lord Haldane (1912–15, 1924), Lord Gardiner (1964–70) and Lord Hailsham of
     St Marylebone (1970–74) and (1979–87). See Heuston *Lives of the Lord Chancellors* 1885–1940 (1987). As
     to the Law Officers see para 529 et seq post. As to the judiciary see paras 301–311 ante.

7    Lord Chancellor (Tenure of Office and Discharge of Ecclesiastical Functions) Act 1974 s 1. If the office
     is held by a Roman Catholic, Her Majesty in Council may provide for his visitational or ecclesiastical
     functions, and any patronage to livings normally in the Lord Chancellor's gift, to be performed by the
     Prime Minister or any other minister: s 2.
         As to the possibility of a Jewish Lord Chancellor, the Religious Disabilities Act 1846 s 2, by which Her
     Majesty's subjects professing the Jewish religion were to be subject to the same laws as Protestant subjects
     in respect to their schools, places for religious worship, educational and charitable purposes, and the
     property held therewith, and not further or otherwise, has been repealed: Statute Law (Repeals) Act
     1989. The Jews Relief Act 1858 s 3, which provided that the Act should not be construed as enabling a
     person professing the Jewish religion to become Lord Chancellor, was repealed by the Promissory Oaths
     Act 1871, as was 21 & 22 Vict c 48 (Oaths of Allegiance &c and Relief of Jews)(1858). In the light of
     these repeals, particularly the repeal of the Religious Disabilities Act 1846, it is unclear whether a person
     professing the Jewish religion would be appointed Lord Chancellor without clarifying legislation.

8    See para 923 post.

**478. Salary.** The Lord Chancellor receives an annual salary[1] of such sum as, together
with the amount payable to him as Speaker of the House of Lords[2], amounts to £2,500
a year more than the salary for the time being payable to the Lord Chief Justice[3]. This
figure may be altered by Order in Council[4]. The Lord Chancellor is also provided with
an official residence at the public expense[5].

1    The salary is charged on and paid out of the Consolidated Fund: Ministerial and other Salaries Act 1975
     s 1(2). As to the Consolidated Fund see para 14.A1381 post.
2    The Lord Chancellor's salary as Speaker of the House of Lords is £2,500: see 327 HL Official Report
     (5th series), 1 February 1972, col 685.
3    Ministerial and other Salaries Act 1975 s 1(2) (amended by the Courts and Legal Services Act 1990
     ss 84(d), 125(7), Sch 20; the Ministerial and other Pensions and Salaries Act 1991 s 3(1); and the
     Ministerial and other Salaries Order 1996, SI 1996/1913, art 4). The salary is set at this high figure in
     order to provide 'headroom for proper payment of the judges': see 327 HL Official Report (5th series),
     1 February 1972, col 685. As to the salary of the Lord Chief Justice see the Supreme Court Act 1981 s 12
     (as amended); and COURTS.
4    Ministerial and other Salaries Act 1975 s 1(4) (amended by the Ministerial and other Pensions and Salaries
     Act 1991 s 3(1)). No recommendation may be made to Her Majesty to make an Order in Council unless
     a draft of the Order has been approved by resolutions of each House of Parliament: Ministerial and other
     Salaries Act 1975 s 1(4).
5    See the *First Report of the Review Body on Top Salaries: Ministers of the Crown and Members of Parliament*
     (Cmnd 4836) (1971) para 79 App I.

**479. Pension.** Her Majesty may by letters patent under the Great Seal[1] grant the
Lord Chancellor an annuity, payable out of the Consolidated Fund[2], to commence on
his ceasing to hold office and to be payable for life except in so far as its duration or
amount is limited by the letters patent to periods when he does not hold any office of
profit under the Crown or to take account of the salary or profits of any such other
office[3]. The maximum rate at which the annuity was payable was originally £5,000 a
year[4]. The annual amount of pension payable to a person resigning the office of Lord
Chancellor after 27 February 1991 is equal to the aggregate of one half of the annual
salary payable in respect of his tenure of that office, and one half of the salary payable
to that person as speaker of the House of Lords at the time when he ceases to hold
those offices[5].

The Lord Chancellor may on resignation receive a lump sum equal to twice the annual amount of pension[6].

The office of Lord Chancellor is included among those for which the widows', widowers' and children's pension schemes for holders of judicial offices is established[7].

1    As to the use of the Great Seal see para 909 post. As to letters patent under the Great Seal see para 920 post.
2    As to the Consolidated Fund see para 711 et seq post.
3    See the Lord Chancellor's Pension Act 1832 s 3 (amended by the Statute Law Revision Act 1980; the Statute Law (Repeals) Act 1981; and the Parliamentary and other Pensions Act 1972 s 28). The annuity may not exceed an amount calculated in accordance with the Parliamentary and other Pensions Act 1972 s 28(1) (see text and note 5 infra): Lord Chancellor's Pension Act 1832 s 3 (as so amended).

    A former Lord Chancellor who is entitled to a pension under s 3 and a pension in respect of judicial office he has held may not receive more than one pension: see the Judicial Pensions Act 1981 s 4.
4    See the Lord Chancellor's Pension Act 1832 s 3 (as originally enacted).
5    Parliamentary and other Pensions Act 1972 s 28(1) (substituted in relation to persons ceasing to hold office after 27 February 1991 by the Ministerial and other Pensions and Salaries Act 1991 s 1(2), (4)).
6    See the Judicial Pensions Act 1981 ss 16(1), 17(1), 26.
7    See ibid ss 18–29 (as amended); and see also eg the Superannuation (Children's Pensions) (Earnings Limit) Order 1994, SI 1994/350. As to the pensions for holders of judicial offices see generally COURTS.

**480. Tenure of office.** The Lord Chancellor holds office during pleasure[1], and, as a member of the ministry and the Cabinet[2] under the established usage, retires from or accepts office with the party to which he belongs[3]. The office is in practice determined by the voluntary surrender of the Great Seal[4] into the hands of the monarch upon retirement from office or resignation, or by the monarch's demanding it in person or sending a messenger for it under the sign manual upon dismissal[5].

1    The Lord Chancellor is expressly excepted from the provisions of the Supreme Court Act 1981, as to tenure of office during good behaviour applicable to the judges of the High Court and of the Court of Appeal: s 11(1), (3). As to the judiciary see paras 301–311 ante.
2    As to the Lord Chancellor's membership of the ministry see para 205 note 1 ante. As to his membership of the Cabinet see para 482 post. As to the Cabinet see paras 402–413 ante.
3    As to the retirement of the ministry as a whole see para 401 ante.
4    As to the use of the Great Seal see para 909 post.
5    1 Campbell's Lives of the Lord Chancellors (1845 Edn) 22.

**481. Precedence and place in Parliament.** The Lord Chancellor has precedence next after the Archbishop of Canterbury[1]. If of the degree of baron of Parliament or above he is to sit and be placed, together with certain other officers[2], on the left side of the Parliament chamber on the higher part of the form of the same side above all dukes, except the monarch's sons, brothers, uncles, nephews[3], or the monarch's brothers' or sisters' sons[4]. If below the degree of baron, the Lord Chancellor, together with those other officers, is to sit and be placed at the uppermost parts of the sacks in the middle of the Parliament chamber, either there to sit upon one form, or upon the uppermost sack, the one of them above the other in the prescribed order[5].

When presiding in the House of Lords[6] the Lord Chancellor occupies the Woolsack[7], and votes without leaving it[8]. He must always speak uncovered, and when he addresses the House otherwise than as president he is to go to his own place as a peer[9]. By virtue of his office (but only if he is a baron or above of Parliament) he in fact goes to the left of the chamber, above all dukes not being of the blood royal[10].

1    See Burke's Peerage, Table of Precedence.
2    Ie the Lord Treasurer, Lord President of the Council and Lord Privy Seal, if of the degree of baron or above.
3    This word in the Act would appear to be an error for 'grandsons' or some other word, in view of the provisions immediately following.
4    House of Lords Predecence Act 1539 s 4; see PEERAGES AND DIGNITIES vol 35 (Reissue) para 937.

5   Ibid s 8 (amended by the Statute Law Revision Act 1888).
6   See para 483 post. As to the House of Lords see para 204 ante; and PARLIAMENT.
7   See HL Standing Orders (1994) (Public Business) no 15. Technically the Woolsack is not within the House: Erskine May *Parliamentary Practice* (21st Edn, 1989) p 174.
8   See HL Standing Orders (1994) (Public Business) no 52. Since 1991 provision has been made whereby the Lord Chancellor may 'in exceptional circumstances' vote by passing through a lobby: see the *Companion to the Standing Orders and Guide to the Proceedings of the House of Lords* (1994) p 99.
9   HL Standing Orders (1994) (Public Business) no 16. The Lord Chancellor must not adjourn the House, or do anything else as the 'mouth' of the House without the prior consent of the Lords, and any matter on which there is a difference of opinion among the Lords must be put to the question: HL Standing Orders (1994) (Public Business) no 16.
10  House of Lords Precedence Act 1539 s 4. See also the text to note 4 supra.

**482. Offices held by Lord Chancellor.** The Lord Chancellor is usually a member of the Cabinet, not, it is said, as of right, but because his duties as holder of the Great Seal make him a necessary party to the innermost councils of the Crown[1]. Retirement from the office of Lord Chancellor is generally understood to involve retirement from the Cabinet[2]. For the same reason he is also a member of the Privy Council[3]. The Lord Chancellor is a Church Commissioner[4].

1   2 Anson's Law and Custom of the Constitution (4th Edn, 1935) Pt I p 169. The Lord Chancellor was not a member of the War Cabinets from 1916–19 and 1940–45, or of the Churchill 'Caretaker' Cabinet 1945. As to the Cabinet see paras 402–413 ante.
2   See para 404 ante. As to the use of the Great Seal see para 909 post.
3   1 Campbell's Lives of the Lord Chancellors (1845 Edn) p 15, commenting on a statement in Selden, Office of Lord Chancellor, s 3, to the effect that he is a privy counsellor by virtue of his office.
4   Church Commissioners Measure 1947 s 1(2), Sch 1 para 1 (amended by the Synodical Government Measure 1969 s 2(2)); and the Church of England (Miscellaneous Provisions) Measure 1992 s 17(1), Sch 3 para 5); and see ECCLESIASTICAL LAW.

**483. Speaker of the House of Lords.** The Lord Chancellor is ex officio Speaker of the House of Lords[1] in its legislative capacity and, except when the House is in Committee[2], always presides there when present without any commission or express authority[3].

The Lord Chancellor is invested with no more authority than an ordinary member, so that the rules for preserving order are enforced not by him but by the House itself[4]. The House itself therefore determines questions of precedence in addressing it, although it is customary to give precedence to the Lord Chancellor when he rises[5].

If during any adjournment the Lord Chancellor is satisfied that the public interest requires it, he may give notice for the meeting of the House on an earlier day than that to which it stands adjourned[6].

The Lord Chancellor puts forward the names of House of Lords members to serve on the Joint Committee on Consolidation Bills[7]. He appoints the Clerks at the Table subject to the approval of the House[8].

1   If not a peer the Lord Chancellor now invariably receives a peerage on appointment. However, it is not legally necessary that he should be a peer and he may act as Speaker before his patent of creation has been made out: see the instances cited at Erskine May *Parliamentary Practice* (21st Edn, 1989) p 174. As to the House of Lords see para 204 ante; and PARLIAMENT.
2   When the House is in Committee the Lord Chancellor leaves the Woolsack and the Lord Chairman of Committees presides: HL Standing Orders (1994) (Public Business) no 59.
3   HL Standing Orders (1994) (Public Business) no 15. It is the duty of the Lord Chancellor ordinarily to attend the House of Lords as Speaker; if he is absent his place on the Woolsack may be taken either by a Deputy Speaker authorised under the Great Seal by the Queen or by a Deputy Chairman appointed by the House; if neither a Deputy Speaker nor a Deputy Chairman is present the Lords may choose their own Speaker during the vacation: HL Standing Orders (1994) (Public Business) no 15. As to the Lord Chancellor's functions when the House is acting judicially see para 492 post.

4   HL Standing Orders (1994) (Public Business) no 17. See also para 481 note 9 ante. He may, however, call to order members who converse in the space behind the Woolsack while the House is sitting: see HL Standing Orders (1994) (Public Business) no 19.

5   Erskine May *Parliamentary Practice* (21st Edn, 1989) p 434.

6   HL Standing Orders (1994) (Public Business) no 14(1).

7   See HL Standing Orders (1994) (Public Business) no 49.

8   *Companion to the Standing Orders and Guide to the Proceedings of the House of Lords* (1994) p 20.

**484. The Lord Chancellor and the monarch.** In a number of instances the Lord Chancellor is the formal medium of communication between the monarch and Parliament. If the monarch is not present to open a new Parliament in person it is the Lord Chancellor's duty to inform the House of the fact and of the appointment of a commission under the Great Seal to perform that duty and, after the Commons have been summoned, to make a similar announcement to the members of both Houses[1]. After the letters patent appointing the commissioners have been read, he directs the Commons to retire to elect a Speaker, and on the following day he signifies the monarch's approval of the election[2]. On the prorogation of Parliament the Queen's speech is read by the Lord Chancellor[3]. When a new session of Parliament is opened by the Queen in person, the Lord Chancellor presents her speech to her for reading to both Houses, and when the Queen is not present in person it is he who reads her speech[4]. When a joint address is to be presented to the monarch by both Houses, the Lord Chancellor reads the address and presents it to Her Majesty[5]. The list of bills which are ready for the royal assent are submitted to the Queen by the Lord Chancellor[6].

1   Erskine May *Parliamentary Practice* (21st Edn, 1989) p 225. As to the opening of Parliament when the monarch is not present see PARLIAMENT.

2   Erskine May *Parliamentary Practice* (21st Edn, 1989) p 227.

3   Erskine May *Parliamentary Practice* (21st Edn, 1989) pp 223, 236.

4   Erskine May *Parliamentary Practice* (21st Edn, 1989) p 233.

5   Erskine May *Parliamentary Practice* (21st Edn, 1989) pp 567–568.

6   Erskine May *Parliamentary Practice* (21st Edn, 1989) p 527.

**485. Judicial appointments.** As head of the judicial administration the Lord Chancellor recommends persons to Her Majesty for appointment as judges of the High Court[1], circuit judges[2] and recorders[3]. As a temporary measure to facilitate the disposal of business in the High Court or the Crown Court he may appoint deputy judges of the High Court[4] and deputy circuit judges and assistant recorders[5]. He may authorise the continuance in office of certain judges beyond normal retirement age until 75 years of age[6]; and may extend the term for which a recorder is appointed[7].

With the concurrence of at least one other senior judge[8] he may declare the office of a judge of the Supreme Court vacant if he is satisfied by medical evidence that the judge is disabled by permanent infirmity from performing his duties and is for the time being incapable of resigning[9]. He may remove a circuit judge on the grounds of incapacity or misbehaviour[10] and a recorder on those grounds or for failure to comply with the terms of his appointment as to the frequency and duration of the occasions on which he is to be available to undertake the duties of a recorder[11].

Stipendiary magistrates in commission areas outside the Inner London area and the City of London are appointed by Her Majesty on the recommendation of the Lord Chancellor and may be removed from office only on his recommendation[12]. He designates one of the metropolitan stipendiary magistrates to be the chief metropolitan stipendiary magistrate[13]. In order to avoid delays in the administration of justice he may appoint acting metropolitan stipendiary magistrates[14] and he may remove metropolitan stipendiary magistrates for inability or misbehaviour[15]. Except for commission areas where the function is that of the Chancellor of the Duchy of Lancaster[16], justices of the peace other than stipendiary magistrates are appointed on behalf of Her Majesty by the Lord Chancellor and are removed in the same manner[17].

With the approval of the Treasury[18], the Lord Chancellor determines the salaries to be paid to Lords of Appeal in Ordinary[19], judges of the Supreme Court[20], judges of the Court of Session[21], judges of the Supreme Court of Northern Ireland[22], metropolitan stipendiary magistrates[23], stipendiary magistrates in commission areas outside the Inner London area and the City of London[24] and circuit judges[25], and the remuneration and allowances to be paid to recorders[26].

1   This does not apply to the Lord Chief Justice of England, the President of the Family Division or the House of Lords, the responsibility for whose appointment rests with the Prime Minister: see para 303 ante. As to the judiciary see paras 301–311 ante. As to the appointment and number of judges generally see COUNTY COURTS; COURTS.

2   Courts Act 1971 s 16(1). With the concurrence of the Minister for the Civil Service he fixes from time to time the maximum number of circuit judges: s 16(2). As to the Minister for the Civil Service see paras 427 ante, 550 post.

3   Ibid s 21(1), (2) (s 21(2) amended by the Courts and Legal Services Act 1990 s 71(2), Sch 10 para 32(1)).

4   Supreme Court Act 1981 s 9(4).

5   Courts Act 1971 s 24(1) (s 24 substituted by the Supreme Court Act 1981 s 146).

6   See the Judicial Pensions and Retirement Act 1993 ss 1, 26(4)–(6), 30(1), Sch 1.

7   Courts Act 1971 ss 21, (4)(5), 24(1A) (s 21(5) amended by the Judicial Pensions and Retirement Act 1993 s 26(10), Sch 6 para 9(1); s 24 as substituted: see note 5 supra; s 24(1A) added by the Judicial Pensions and Retirement Act 1993 Sch 6 para 9(2)).

8   If the judge under consideration is any of the Lord Chief Justice, the Master of the Rolls, the President of the Family Division or the Vice-Chancellor, the Lord Chancellor must act with the concurrence of at least two others of them; if the judge under consideration is a Lord Justice of Appeal, the Lord Chancellor must have the concurrence of the Master of the Rolls; if the judge is a puisne judge of any division of the High Court, the Lord Chancellor must have the concurrence of the senior judge of the division in question, namely, the President of the Family division, the Vice-Chancellor, or the Lord Chief Justice (as President of the Queen's Bench Division: Supreme Court Act 1981 ss 11(9), 151(1).

9   Ibid s 11(9).

10   Courts Act 1971 s 17(4).

11   Ibid s 21(6).

12   Justices of the Peace Act 1979 s 13(3). As to commission areas see ss 1, 2 (both as amended); and MAGISTRATES vol 29 para 207.

13   Ibid s 31(3).

14   Ibid s 15(1).

15   Ibid s 31(4)(c).

16   See ibid s 68(1). As to the Duchy of Lancaster see CROWN LANDS AND PRIVILEGES.

17   Ibid s 6 (amended by the Administration of Justice Act 1982 s 65). As to the Lord Chancellor's functions generally in relation to justices of the peace see MAGISTRATES.

18   As to the Treasury see paras 512–517 ante.

19   See the Administration of Justice Act 1973 ss 9(1)(a); and the Transfer of Functions (Minister for the Civil Service and Treasury) Order 1981, SI 1981/1670. At the request of the government, judicial salaries may be examined by the Review Body on Top Salaries. See eg the *Thirty-third Report of the Review Body on Top Salaries* (Cm 2015) (1992).

20   Supreme Court Act 1981 s 12(1). This refers to judges of the Supreme Court other than the Lord Chancellor.

21   Administration of Justice Act 1973 s 9(1)(c). In this instance the consent required is that of the Secretary of State for Scotland: s 9(1).

22   Ibid s 9(1)(d).

23   Ibid s 9(1)(e).

24   Ie stipendiary magistrates appointed under the Justices of the Peace Act 1979 s 13 (see text and note 12 supra): Administration of Justice Act 1973 s 9(1)(f) (amended by the Justices of the Peace Act 1979 s 71, Sch 2 para 23).

25   Courts Act 1971 s 18(1). This does not however apply to the office holders who became circuit judges when that Act came into force: see s 18(1), Sch 2 Pt II.

26   Ibid s 21(7).

**486. Functions relating to judicial administration.** The Lord Chancellor may request a former Lord Chancellor[1], a Lord of Appeal in Ordinary who is an ex officio judge of the Court of Appeal[2], a judge of the High Court or a former judge of the Court of Appeal or of the High Court[3] to sit as a judge of the Court of Appeal. He may request a judge of the Court of Appeal to sit as a judge of the High Court or the Crown Court[4]. He may request a circuit judge or a recorder to sit as a judge of the High Court[5]. When he considers it desirable he may require a judge of the Court of Appeal, a judge of the High Court or a recorder who consents to do so to sit as judge for a county court district[6].

The Lord Chancellor directs to what division puisne judges of the High Court are to be attached and, with their consent, may direct their transfer[7] from one division to another[8].

He assigns circuit judges to county court districts[9], and he determines which of the circuit judges, deputy circuit judges or recorders are to discharge the functions of official referees[10].

Among his functions relating to the nomination of members of the judiciary to particular offices or duties are those of nominating puisne judges of the High Court to be judges of the Patents Court[11], the Admiralty Court[12], or the Commercial Court[13] and judges of the High Court to hear appeals from Pensions Appeal Tribunals[14]. He also nominates members of the Restrictive Practices Court[15], selects one of the judges of that court to be the court's president[16], and recommends to Her Majesty persons for appointment by her as non-judicial members of that court[17].

1 Supreme Court Act 1981 s 2(2)(b). As to the judiciary see paras 301–311 ante.
2 Ibid s 2(2)(c).
3 Ibid s 9(1), Table.
4 Ibid s 9(1), Table.
5 Ibid s 9(1), Table (amended by the Administration of Justice Act 1982 s 58).
6 County Courts Act 1984 s 5(3).
7 Transfer from any division requires the concurrence of the senior judge of that division (see para 485 note 8 ante): Supreme Court Act 1981 s 5(2).
8 Ibid s 5(2).
9 County Courts Act 1984 s 5(1).
10 Supreme Court Act 1981 s 68(1) (amended by the Administration of Justice Act 1982 s 59).
11 Supreme Court Act 1981 s 6(2). As to the Patents Court see PATENTS vol 35 (Reissue) para 714 et seq.
12 Ibid s 6(2). As to the Admiralty Court see ADMIRALTY vol 1(1) (Reissue) para 301 et seq.
13 Ibid s 6(2). As to the Commercial Court see PRACTICE AND PROCEDURE vol 37 para 591 et seq.
14 Pensions Appeal Tribunals Act 1943 s 6(2).
15 Restrictive Practices Court Act 1976 s 2(1)(a). He also recommends any increase in the number of members of that court: s 4(1)(a). As to the Restrictive Practices Court see TRADE, INDUSTRY AND INDUSTRIAL RELATIONS vol 47 (Reissue) para 252 et seq.
16 Ibid s 2(1).
17 Ibid s 3(1). He has power to remove appointed members: see s 3(2) (as amended).

**487. Functions relating to the business of the courts.** The Lord Chancellor has powers to give directions with regard to the business of the courts. These include the power by order to direct:

(1)    that any business vested in the High Court but not assigned to any division, is to be assigned to a specified division or divisions[1];

(2)    that any business assigned to any division is to be assigned to any other division[2]; and

(3)    that any proceedings are to cease to be assigned to a special judge of the High Court[3].

He also has power to give directions: (a) waiving the requirements that justices of the peace are included in the Crown Court when the court is hearing appeals or proceedings on committal for sentence[4]; and (b) granting solicitors the right of audience in the Crown Court[5].

In addition various matters are determined in accordance with directions given by or on behalf of the Lord Chancellor, including (i) the places at which, and the days and times when, the Crown Court sits[6]; (ii) subject to rules of court, the places at which, and the days and times when, the High Court sits outside the Royal Courts of Justice[7]; and (iii) the distribution of official referees' business[8]. Certain other matters require his concurrence, including directions given by or on behalf of the Lord Chief Justice as to the allocation of Crown Court cases respectively to a judge of the High Court and to a circuit judge or recorder and the distribution of Crown Court business generally[9]; and as to the allocation of cases to a Crown Court comprising justices of the peace[10]. The Lord Chancellor may now direct by order that there are to be district probate registries of the High Court at such places and for such districts as he specifies[11].

The Lord Chancellor also has powers in relation to the jurisdiction of county courts. Thus, he may by order exclude any county court from exercising bankruptcy jurisdiction[12] and the county courts in which proceedings may be brought by the Commission for Racial Equality are appointed to have jurisdiction by orders made by him[13].

The Lord Chancellor is responsible for the summoning of jurors for service to the Crown Court, the High Court and county courts[14].

1    Supreme Court Act 1981 s 61(3)(a), (4).
2    Ibid s 61(3)(b). Jurisdiction may be exercised concurrently: s 61(4). An order requires the concurrence of the senior judges (see para 485 note 8 ante) of both the divisions concerned: s 61(5).
3    Ibid s 63(2).
4    See ibid s 74(4), (5). As to those requirements see s 74(1), (2).
5    See ibid s 83 (substituted by the Courts and Legal Services Act 1990 s 67).
6    Supreme Court Act 1981 s 78(3).
7    Ibid s 71(2).
8    Ibid s 68(6) (amended by the Administration of Justice Act 1982 s 59).
9    Supreme Court Act 1981 s 75(1).
10   Ibid s 75(2).
11   Ibid s 104.
12   See the Insolvency Act 1986 s 374; and BANKRUPTCY vol 3(2) (Reissue) para 7.
13   See the Race Relations Act 1976 s 67(1); and BRITISH NATIONALITY, IMMIGRATION AND RACE RELATIONS vol 4(2) (Reissue) para 200.
14   Juries Act 1974 s 2(1). See generally JURIES vol 26 para 611.

**488. Appointment and removal of court officers.** With the concurrence of the Treasury as to numbers and salaries, the Lord Chancellor appoints the masters of the Supreme Court[1] and, with Treasury concurrence as to salaries, district judges and deputy district judges[2]. He also appoints the conveyancing counsel of the Supreme Court[3], district registrars, joint district registrars and deputy district registrars[4], district probate registrars, part-time and provisional district probate registrars[5] and deputies for Supreme Court officers[6]. With Treasury approval, the Lord Chancellor may permit certain of these persons to remain in office beyond the normal retirement age where he considers it desirable in the public interest[7].

He may constitute, on a permanent or temporary basis, one or more advisory committees to advise him on such questions relating to the Supreme Court and the county courts as he may from time to time refer to them[8].

With the concurrence of the Treasury as to numbers and salaries the Lord Chancellor may appoint such officers and other staff for the Supreme Court[9] and county courts as appear to him necessary for setting up a unified administrative court service, for discharging any statutory functions in those courts conferred on officers so appointed, and generally for carrying out the administrative work of those courts[10]. He may enter into contracts with other persons for the provision of officers and staff for such purposes[11], not including functions of making judicial decision, or exercising judicial discretion or a power of arrest[12].

1    See the Supreme Court Act 1981 s 89(1), Sch 2 Pt II (Sch 2 substituted by the Courts and Legal Services Act 1990 s 71(2), Sch 10 para 49); the Mental Health Act 1983 s 93(2); and the Transfer of Functions (Minister for the Civil Service and Treasury) Order 1981, SI 1981/1670. The offices in question include Queen's Bench and Chancery masters, the Master of the Crown Office, the Master of the Court of Protection, registrars of the Family Division, taxing masters, bankruptcy registrars and taxing masters, the registrar, assistant registrars and deputy assistant registrars of criminal appeals and the Admiralty Registrar. As to the judiciary see paras 301–311 ante. As to the Treasury see paras 512–517 ante.

2    See the County Courts Act 1984 ss 6, 8 (both amended by the Courts and Legal Services Act 1990 s 125(3), Sch 18 para 42; s 8 further amended by the Judicial Pensions and Retirement Act 1993 ss 26(10), 31(4), Sch 6 para 17(1), Sch 9).

3    See the Supreme Court Act 1981 s 131 (amended by the Courts and Legal Services Act 1990 Sch 10 para 48). Business is distributed among them in such order and manner as the Lord Chancellor thinks fit.

4    See the Supreme Court Act 1981 ss 100, 102 (both as amended).

5    Ibid Sch 2 Pt III (Sch 2 as substituted: see note 1 supra).

6    Ibid s 91 (as amended).

7    See ibid s 92 (as amended); and see further COURTS.

8    Courts Act 1971 s 30.

9    This includes district probate registries: ibid s 27(1) (s 27 substituted by the Deregulation and Contracting Out Act 1994 s 76, Sch 16 para 2).

10   Courts Act 1971 s 27(1) (as substituted: see note 9 supra). The Principal Civil Service Pension Scheme 1974 (as to which see paras 576–613 post) applies, with necessary adaptations, to such officers and staff as it applies to other civil servants: Courts Act 1971 s 27(2) (as so substituted).

11   See ibid s 27(3), (5), (8) (as substituted: see note 9 supra). The power is exercisable by order made by statutory instrument: see s 27(7) (as so substituted). Before making such an order the Lord Chancellor must consult with the senior judges (ie the Lord Chief Justice, the Master of the Rolls, the President of the Family Division and the Vice-Chancellor): s 27(6), (9) (as so substituted).

12   Ibid s 27(4) (as substituted: see note 9 supra).

**489. Other functions relating to the administration of justice.** The Lord Chancellor is a member of the committee by which the Rules of the Supreme Court are made and appoints the judges (other than the senior judges) and the practising lawyers from among whom its other members are selected[1]. He is a member of the Crown Court Rule Committee[2] and appoints a number of its members[3]. He appoints the County Court Rule Committee and has power to allow, disallow or alter rules made by it[5]. Non-contentious probate rules made by the President of the Family Division require his concurrence[6]. He makes rules relating to insolvency after consulting the Insolvency Rules Committee[7].

He has functions with respect to the fees to be taken in court proceedings. With the advice and consent of the judges and the concurrence of the Treasury he fixes the fees to be taken in the High Court and the Court of Appeal[8], and with the concurrence of the Treasury those to be taken in county courts[9] and the Crown Court[10]. He has power to make rules with the concurrence of the Treasury with respect to funds in court[11].

1    See the Supreme Court Act 1981 s 85(1), (3) (s 85(1) as amended). As to the judiciary see paras 301–311 ante.

2    See ibid s 86(1) (as amended).

3    Ibid s 86(3), (4) (s 86(4) as amended).

4    County Courts Act 1984 s 75(7)–(10) (as amended).

5    Ibid s 75(9). He also directs when the rules are to come into operation: s 75(10).

6    Supreme Court Act 1981 s 127(1).

7    Insolvency Act 1986 ss 411–413 (as amended).

8    Supreme Court Act 1981 s 130(1), (2)(a). See also the Insolvency Act 1986 ss 414–415 (fees in bankruptcy proceedings); and the Companies Act 1985 s 663(4) (fees in winding up proceedings). As to the Treasury see paras 512–517 post.

9    County Courts Act 1984 s 128(1).

10   Supreme Court Act 1981 s 130(1), (2)(b), which also provides that the concurrence of the Lord Chief Justice is required.

11   Administration of Justice Act 1982 s 38(7).

**490. Other powers with respect to appointments.** Among the appointments made by the Lord Chancellor are those of the Chief Land Registrar[1], the Public Trustee[2], the General Commissioners of Income Tax[3], the members of the Law Commission[4], the chairman of the Foreign Compensation Commission[5], and the members[6] of the Council on Tribunals[7].

In numerous instances appointments to statutory tribunals are made by the Lord Chancellor, among them being the following: the president and members of the Immigration Appeal Tribunal[8], the members of the Pensions Appeal Tribunals[9], the president and members of the Lands Tribunal[10], the chairmen and panels of members of the Agricultural Land Tribunals[11], the chairmen of Independent Schools Tribunals[12], the chairmen and members[13] of Mental Health Review Tribunals[14], and the President of the Industrial Tribunals and the legal panels of members of such tribunals[15]. He appoints the panels of persons from among whom the chairmen of certain statutory tribunals are selected by the minister who makes the appointments[16]. In the case of certain statutory tribunals or panels constituted for the purposes of any such tribunals a minister who has power to terminate a person's membership may exercise the power only with the consent of the Lord Chancellor[17].

1   Land Registration Act 1925 s 126(1).
2   Public Trustee Act 1906 s 8(1) (substituted by the Public Trustee and Administration of Funds Act 1986 s 1(3), Schedule para 1).
3   Taxes Management Act 1970 s 2(2) (amended by the Finance Act 1988 s 134(1)).
4   Law Commissions Act 1965 s 1(1) (amended by the Administration of Justice Act 1982 s 64).
5   Foreign Compensation Act 1950 s 1(1).
6   Ie the members other than the Parliamentary Commissioner for Administration, who is a member by virtue of his office: Tribunals and Inquiries Act 1992 s 2(3).
7   Ibid s 2(1). The Lord Chancellor exercises this function in conjunction with the Lord Advocate. As to the Lord Advocate see para 63 ante.
8   Immigration Act 1971 s 12, Sch 5 Pt II paras 6, 7 (s 12 amended by the Transfer of Functions (Immigration Appeals) Order 1987, SI 1987/465, art 3(1), (2); Sch 5 Pt II para 7 amended by the Courts and Legal Services Act 1990 s 71(2), Sch 10 para 34). The Lord Chancellor also appoints the chief adjudicator: Immigration Act 1971 Sch 5 Pt I para 1 (amended by the Transfer of Functions (Immigration Appeals) Order 1987 art 3(3)).
9   Pensions Appeal Tribunals Act 1943 s 6(1), Schedule para 2 (substituted by the Judicial Pensions and Retirement Act 1993 s 26(1), Sch 6 para 39).
10  Lands Tribunal Act 1949 s 2.
11  Agriculture Act 1947 s 73(2), Sch 9 paras 13–15 (Sch 9 paras 13–15 substituted by the Agriculture Act 1958 s 8(1), Sch 1 Pt I para 5; subsequently amended by the Courts and Legal Services Act 1990 Sch 10 para 6(1), (2); and by the Judicial Pensions and Retirement Act 1993 Sch 6 para 46).
12  Education Act 1944 s 72(1), Sch 6 paras 1(a), 4.
13  Members, other than those who are legally qualified, are appointed by the Lord Chancellor after consultation with the Secretary of State for Health: Mental Health Act 1983 s 65(2), Sch 2 para 1(b), (c).
14  Ibid Sch 2 paras 1(a), 3.
15  Industrial Tribunals (Constitution and Rules of Procedure) Regulations 1993, SI 1993/2687, regs 3, 5.
16  See the Tribunals and Inquiries Act 1992 s 6(1).
17  See ibid s 7 (amended by the Pensions Act 1995 ss 122, 151, 177, Sch 3 para 21(a), Sch 5 para 16(1), (2), Sch 7 Pt III; and the Tribunals and Inquiries (Friendly Societies) Order 1993, SI 1993/3258).

**491. Judicial duties in the Supreme Court.** The Lord Chancellor is president of the Supreme Court[1], one of the judges of the Court of Appeal[2] and a member of the High Court of Justice[3]. He is also president of the Chancery Division of the High Court[4]. A former Lord Chancellor remains an ex officio member of the Court of Appeal[5], but may not be required to sit and act as a judge of that court unless, upon the request of the Lord Chancellor, he consents to do so[6]. While so sitting and acting, the former Lord Chancellor ranks after the Lord Chief Justice and the Master of the Rolls, with Lords of

Appeal in Ordinary according to the priority of dates upon which they respectively became Lord Chancellor or Lords of Appeal in Ordinary[7].

As a judge the Lord Chancellor has no jurisdiction in Scotland, but only certain statutory powers which are not of a judicial nature[8].

1 Supreme Court Act 1981 s 1(2). As to the judiciary see paras 301–311 ante.
2 Ibid s 2(1)(a).
3 Ibid s 4(1)(a). As such he has in general equal power, authority and jurisdiction in any division of the court: s 4(3).
   He has no jurisdiction as a judge of the High Court to hear an application for a writ of habeas corpus: Administration of Justice Act 1960 s 14(2). Nor has he any jurisdiction to hear an application for bail: see *Re Kray, Re Kray, Re Smith* [1965] Ch 736, [1965] 1 All ER 710, Lord Gardiner LC. As to his original powers, in common with the judges of the courts of common law, with regard to the issue of writs of habeas corpus and of prohibition, see 1 Campbell's Lives of the Lord Chancellors (1845 Edn) 12; 2 Anson's Law and Custom of the Constitution (4th Edn, 1935) Pt I p 166; *Crowley's Case* (1818) 2 Swan 1, LC.
4 Supreme Court Act 1981 s 5(1)(a).
5 Ibid s 2(2)(b).
6 Ibid s 2(2).
7 Ibid s 13(1)(b). As to whether the Court of Appeal is bound by the decision of a Lord Chancellor sitting alone in the old Court of Appeal in Chancery before the transfer of its jurisdiction and powers to the Court of Appeal by the Supreme Court of Judicature Act 1873 s 18 see *Re Lloyd, Lloyd v Lloyd* [1903] 1 Ch 385 at 392, CA.
8 See *Stuart v Marquis of Bute* (1861) 9 HL Cas 440 at 454–455.

**492. Judicial duties in the House of Lords and Privy Council.** As Speaker of the House of Lords[1] the Lord Chancellor presides over the House when sitting as the highest court of appeal[2]. If present, he also takes the chair in any Appellate or Appeal Committee[3]. If a peer, a former Lord Chancellor is qualified to form one of the quorum of Lords of Appeal necessary when the House of Lords hears appeals[4].

The Lord Chancellor is also a member of the Judicial Committee of the Privy Council[5].

1 See para 483 ante. As to the House of Lords see para 204 ante; and PARLIAMENT. As to the judiciary see paras 301–311 ante.
2 In cases of impeachment of a commoner, but not of a peer, the Lord Chancellor presided: see further Erskine May *Parliamentary Practice* (21st Edn, 1989) pp 67–68. Special provision is made for deputy speakers when the House is sitting judicially, by a Commission of 22 May 1969: see Erskine May *Parliamentary Practice* (21st Edn, 1989) p 174.
3 HL Standing Orders (1994) (Public Business) no 83(4), which further provides that, in the Lord Chancellor's absence the chair is taken by the senior Lord of Appeal in Ordinary present.
4 Appellate Jurisdiction Act 1876 ss 5(3), 25 (s 25 amended by the Statute Law Revision Act 1894; the Administration of Justice Act 1965 s 34, Sch 2; and the Justices of the Peace Act 1979 s 8(2), Sch 5 Pt I).
5 See the Judicial Committee Act 1833 s 1 (amended by the Statute Law Revision Act 1874; and the Statute Law Revision (No 2) Act 1888); the Appellate Jurisdiction Act 1887 s 3; and the Appellate Jurisdiction Act 1876 s 25 (as amended: see note 4 supra). As to the Judicial Committee of the Privy Council see para 311 ante; and COURTS vol 10 para 767 et seq.

**493. Effect of the Judicature Acts.** Except as expressly therein directed, the Supreme Court of Judicature Act 1873 did not affect the office or position of the Lord Chancellor, and his officers remained attached to him as if the Act had not been passed; all duties which any officer of the Court of Chancery might, when the Act came into force on 1 November 1875, be required to perform in aid of any of the Lord Chancellor's duties, may be required to be performed by such officer when transferred to the Supreme Court, and by his successors[1].

Any duty, authority or power imposed or conferred by any statute, law or custom on the Lord Chancellor immediately before 1 January 1982 and not incident to the administration of justice in any court of law continues to be performed and exercised by him in the same manner as formerly[2].

1   Supreme Court of Judicature Act 1873 s 94 (repealed and not re-enacted by the Supreme Court of Judicature (Consolidation) Act 1925 s 226(1), Sch 6 (repealed, but not so as to alter the law). The 1925 Act was consolidated, with amendments, in the Supreme Court Act 1981.

2   See ibid s 44(1), (2), which came into force on 1 January 1982: s 153(2).

**494. Judicial duties of Commissioners of the Great Seal.** When the Great Seal is in commission, the Lords Commissioners are to represent the Lord Chancellor for the purposes of the Supreme Court Act 1981 and the County Courts Act 1984[1]. The senior Lord Commissioner for the time being may, however, exercise the powers vested in the Lord Chancellor by those Acts in relation to the appointment of officers[2] and the senior Lord Commissioner may also exercise the powers vested in the Lord Chancellor by the Supreme Court Act 1981 in relation to any act for which the concurrence or presence of the Lord Chancellor is required by that Act[3].

1   Supreme Court Act 1981 s 129; County Courts Act 1984 s 146. Cf the Great Seal Act 1688 s 1 (Lords Commissioners of the Great Seal declared to have the same powers as the Lord Chancellor: see para 912 note 2 post). As to the use of the Great Seal see para 909 post.

2   Supreme Court Act 1981 s 129(a); County Courts Act 1984 s 146.

3   Supreme Court Act 1981 s 129(b).

**495. Custody of the Great Seal.** The Lord Chancellor is the custodian of the Great Seal[1]. Unless the Great Seal is in commission[2], it remains in the custody of the Lord Chancellor[3]. The Great Seal is kept in the Office of the Clerk of the Crown in Chancery[4].

When a worn-out seal is replaced or when a new seal is introduced on a change of the royal arms or style, the old seal becomes the property of the Lord Chancellor. In theory the old seal is first broken, the monarch destroying its virtue by breaking or 'damasking' it by giving it a gentle blow with a hammer[5]. The seal formerly in use also becomes the Lord Chancellor's property when a new seal is introduced following a demise of the Crown[6].

1   As to the monarch's appointment of the Lord Chancellor by delivery of the Great Seal see para 477 ante. As to the use of the Great Seal see para 909 post.

2   As to Lords Commissioners of the Great Seal see the Great Seal Act 1688 s 1; the Great Seal Act 1884 s 4; and para 912 note 2 post.

3   As to the Lord Chancellor's functions in relation to the Great Seal see the Great Seal Act 1884; and para 912 et seq post.

4   As to the Clerk of the Crown in Chancery see the Great Seal (Offices) Act 1874; the Crown Office Act 1890; and para 921 post. As to the Office of the Clerk of the Crown in Chancery see the Civil Service Year Book 1996 col 478.

5   1 Campbell's Lives of the Lord Chancellors (1845 Edn) 25.

6   On a demise of the Crown the Great Seal continues to be used until the successor to the Crown gives order to the contrary: Succession to the Crown Act 1707 s 9 (amended by the Statute Law Revision Act 1888).

**496. Other duties.** Those duties of the Lord Chancellor which derived from the fact that he represented the Crown before the development of the various departments of government or which arose through the Crown acting in its capacity of parens patriae or from his role as 'keeper of the King's conscience' have now for the most part been delegated or assigned by statute to various authorities[1].

However, he still exercises the visitatorial jurisdiction of the Crown over certain charitable corporations[2]. He exercises the patronage of the monarch's livings of the value of £20 or under[3]; in this he acts by custom independently of the Crown[4]. He appoints the Lord Chancellor's Visitors under the Mental Health Act 1983[5] and is one of the persons by whom the statutory jurisdiction for the management of the property and affairs of mental patients is exercisable[6].

A number of modern statutes have extended the scope of the Lord Chancellor's duties which are administrative in nature. Thus the Court Service is now an executive agency for which he is accountable[7]; he has functions of a supervisory nature with respect to the legal advice and assistance and legal aid system[8]; functions in relation to Agricultural Land Tribunals which formerly belonged to the Minister of Agriculture, Fisheries and Food[9] are now exercisable by the Lord Chancellor[10]; the direction of the Public Record Office has been transferred to him and he is in general responsible for public records[11]; and he has general responsibility for the work of the Law Commissions and, thus, for law reform in England and Wales[12].

1   See para 309 ante.
2   See CHARITIES vol 5(2) (Reissue) para 419.
3   These values are those in the Queen's books and not the actual values.
4   2 Anson's Law and Custom of the Constitution (4th Edn, 1935) Pt I p 167.
5   See the Mental Health Act 1983 s 102(2); and MENTAL HEALTH vol 30 (Reissue) para 1506.
6   See ibid ss 93(1), 94(1) (as amended); and MENTAL HEALTH vol 30 (Reissue) para 1434.
7   The Court Service became an executive agency in April 1995. Its role is to provide administrative support to the Court of Appeal, the High Court, the Crown Court, county courts and those tribunals for which the Lord Chancellor has responsibility: see the Lord Chancellor's and Law Officers' Departments Annual Report: *The Government's Expenditure Plans 1995–96 to 1997–98* (Cm 2809) (1995) p 12 et seq; and the Civil Service Year Book 1996 cols 485–486. As to executive agencies see para 551 post.
8   See generally LEGAL AID vol 27(2) (Reissue) paras 1852–1859, 1999, 2040, 2062.
9   Ie those conferred on the Minister by the Agriculture Act 1947 s 73 (as amended): see AGRICULTURE vol 1(2) (Reissue) para 971 et seq.
10  Agriculture Act 1958 ss 5, 9(1); see AGRICULTURE vol 1 (Reissue) para 971.
11  See the Public Records Act 1958 s 1(1); and para 837 post.
12  See the Law Commission Act 1965 ss 3(1)–(4), 6(2) (s 6(2) amended by the Transfer of Functions (Secretary of State and Lord Advocate) Order 1972, SI 1972/2002). See further para 957 post. The Lord Chancellor is also president of the Statute Law Committee.

**497.  The Lord Chancellor's Department.** The Lord Chancellor's Department, in which the Lord Chancellor is assisted by a Permanent Secretary, who is also the Clerk of the Crown in Chancery, comprises the Principal Establishments and Finance Office, the Judicial Appointments Group, the Legal Group and the Policy Group[1].

The Principal Establishments and Finance Office comprises the Planning and Communications division, the Personnel Management division, the Finance division, the Accommodation and Magistrates' Courts Building division, and the Internal Assurance division[2].

The Judicial Appointments Group consists of the Circuit Bench division, the District Bench and Tribunals division, the Magistrates' (Appointments) division, the Magistrates' Training division, the Judicial Studies Board and the Policy and Conditions of Service division[3].

The Legal Group, which is professionally accountable direct to the Permanent Secretary but otherwise forms part of the Policy Group, consists of the Legal Advice and Litigation division, the Rules of Court and Regulations division, the International division, the Property and Public Law division and the Statutory Publications Office[4].

The Policy Group consists of the Legal Aid division, the Legal Aid Reform Team, the Family Policy division, the Policy Group Secretariat, the Agency Monitoring Unit, the Legal Services Development division, the Criminal Policy division, the Magistrates' Courts divisions and the Woolf Inquiry team[5].

The Court Service is an executive agency of the Lord Chancellor's Department[6]. Its role is to provide administrative support to the Court of Appeal, the High Court, the Crown Court, county courts and those tribunals for which the Lord Chancellor has responsibility[7]. The Lord Chancellor appoints Her Majesty's Chief Inspector of the

Magistrate's Court Service and such number of inspectors as he considers appropriate to inspect and report to the Lord Chancellor on the organisation and administration of magistrates' courts[8].

The Public Trust Office is also an executive agency of the Lord Chancellor's Department[9]. It exercises functions of the Public Trustee, and administrative functions of the Court of Protection[10].

The Lord Chancellor's Office is subject to investigation by the Parliamentary Commissioner for Administration[11]. The expenses of the office are provided by Parliament[12].

1  For the organisation and staff of the Lord Chancellor's Department see the Civil Service Year Book 1996 col 478 et seq.
2  See the Civil Service Year Book 1996 cols 483–484.
3  See the Civil Service Year Book 1996 cols 479–480.
4  See the Civil Service Year Book 1996 cols 482–483.
5  See the Civil Service Year Book 1996 cols 480–482.
6  See para 496 note 7 ante. As to executive agencies see para 551 post.
7  See the Lord Chancellor's and Law Officers' Departments Annual Report: *The Government's Expenditure Plans 1995–96 to 1997–98* (Cm 2809) (1995) paras 13, 54.
8  Police and Magistrates' Courts Act 1994 s 86; and see MAGISTRATES.
9  See the Civil Service Year Book 1996 cols 489–490; and the Lord Chancellor's and Law Officers' Departments Annual Report: *The Government's Expenditure Plans 1995–96 to 1997–98* (Cm 2809) (1995).
10  See the Civil Service Year Book 1996 cols 489–490; and see generally TRUSTS vol 48 (Reissue) paras 655–681.
11  Parliamentary Commissioner Act 1967 s 4(1), Sch 2 (substituted by the Parliamentary and Health Service Commissioners Act 1987 s 1(1), (2), Sch 1). As to the Parliamentary Commissioner for Administration see ADMINISTRATIVE LAW vol 1(1) (Reissue) para 41 et seq.
12  *Supply Estimates 1995–96 for the year ending 31 March 1996* (HC Paper (1994–95) no 271–IX).

## (x)  The Department of National Heritage

**498. Constitution of the department.** The Department of National Heritage was set up in 1992 taking functions from the Lord President of the Council, the Department for Education and Science, the Department of the Environment, the Department of Trade and Industry, the Department of Employment and the Home Office[1]. At its head is the Secretary of State for National Heritage, assisted by two Parliamentary Under Secretaries and the Permanent Secretary[2].

The department is an authorised government department for the purpose of suing and being sued[3], and is subject to investigation by the Parliamentary Commissioner for Administration[4]. The expenses of the department are provided by Parliament[5].

1  Transfer of Functions (National Heritage) Order 1992, SI 1992/1311. That Order transferred (1) functions and property relating to museums, libraries, the arts etc from the Lord President of the Council; (2) functions and property relating to historical records etc relating to transport from the former Secretary of State for Education and Science; (3) functions and property relating to historic buildings, the national heritage and the Sports Council from the Secretary of State for the Environment; (4) property relating to the film industry from the Secretary of State for Trade and Industry; (5) property relating to tourism from the Secretary of State for Employment; and (6) property relating to broadcasting and safety of sports grounds from the Secretary of State for the Home Department.

As to the transfer of such functions prior to the establishment of the Department of National Heritage see particularly the Transfer of Functions (Arts and Libraries) Order 1979, SI 1979/907; the Transfer of Functions (Arts, Libraries and National Heritage) Order 1981, SI 1981/207; the Transfer of Functions (Arts, Libraries and National Heritage) Order 1983, SI 1983/879; the Transfer of Functions (Arts, Libraries and National Heritage) Order 1984, SI 1984/1814; and the Transfer of Functions (Arts, Libraries and National Heritage) Order 1986, SI 1986/600. As to the transfer of functions generally see para 363 ante.
2  See the Civil Service Year Book 1996 col 497.

3   See the list published under the Crown Proceedings Act 1947 s 17(1) (as amended); and CROWN
    PROCEEDINGS.
4   Parliamentary Commissioner Act 1967 s 4(1), Sch 2 (substituted by the Parliamentary and Health Service
    Commissioners Act 1987 s 1(1), (2), Sch 1; amended by the Transfer of Functions (National Heritage)
    Order 1992). As to the Parliamentary Commissioner for Administration see ADMINISTRATIVE LAW vol
    1(1) (Reissue) para 41 et seq.
5   See the *Supply Estimates 1995–96 for the year ending 31 March 1996* (HC Paper (1994–95) no 271–XI).

**499. Secretary of State for National Heritage.** The Secretary of State for National
Heritage is a corporation sole[1].

The corporate seal of the Secretary of State for National Heritage is authenticated by
the signature of a Secretary of State, a secretary to the Department of National Heritage,
or a person authorised by a Secretary of State to act in that behalf[2]. The seal is officially
and judicially noticed[3]. A document purporting to be an instrument made or issued by
the Secretary of State for National Heritage and to be sealed with his seal duly
authenticated, or to be signed or executed by a secretary to the Department of National
Heritage or a person authorised by the Secretary of State to act in that behalf is to be
received in evidence and be deemed to be so made or issued without further proof unless
the contrary is shown[4]. A certificate signed by the Secretary of State for National Heritage
that any instrument purporting to be made or issued by him was so made or issued is
conclusive evidence of that fact[5].

1   Transfer of Functions (National Heritage) Order 1992, SI 1992/1311, art 2(1). As to corporations sole
    see CORPORATIONS.
2   Ibid art 2(2). As to secretarial seals see para 357 ante.
3   Ibid art 2(3).
4   Ibid art 2(3).
5   Ibid art 2(4).

**500. Functions of the department.** The Department of National Heritage exercises
regulatory and supervisory functions[1] designed to create conditions which will:

(1)   preserve ancient sites, monuments and historic buildings and increase their
      accessibility for study and enjoyment, both now and in the future[2];

(2)   maintain, increase and make available the national collection of books, works
      of art, scientific objects and other records and artefacts of the past and of the
      present[3];

(3)   encourage the living arts, including the performing arts, the visual and plastic arts,
      broadcasting, film and literature, to flourish[4];

(4)   increase variety and choice in broadcasting and competition in the provision of
      services, while maintaining programme standards and quality[5];

(5)   increase the opportunities for sport and recreation both for champions and for the
      general public[6];

(6)   encourage inward and domestic tourism[7].

The department is responsible for the National Lottery[8]. The net proceeds of the
National Lottery are paid to the Secretary of State[9] who pays any sums received into the
National Lottery Distribution Fund[10], for payment into the Consolidated Fund for
meeting expenditure relating to the lottery[11], and for expenditure on the arts, sport, the
national heritage, charitable expenditure and projects to mark the year 2000 and the
beginning of the third millenium[12].

1   See the Department of National Heritage Annual Report: *The Government's Expenditure Plans 1995–96
    to 1997–98* (Cm 2811) (1995) p 1. As to the transfer of functions to the department see para 498 ante.
2   The Secretary of State exercises powers derived inter alia from the Crown Lands Act 1851 (see CROWN
    LANDS AND PRIVILEGES); the Ancient Monuments and Archaeological Areas Act 1979 (see OPEN SPACES

AND HISTORIC BUILDINGS); and the Planning (Listed Buildings and Conservation Areas) Act 1990 (see TOWN AND COUNTRY PLANNING). The Secretary of State sponsors English Heritage (formerly known as the Historic Buildings and Monuments Commission: see the Civil Service Year Book 1996 col 756), which acts as his statutory adviser and exercises numerous regulatory and executive functions in relation to the built heritage: see the National Heritage Act 1983 ss 33 (as amended), 34; the Civil Service Year Book 1996 col 756; and OPEN SPACES AND HISTORIC BUILDINGS.

3    The Secretary of State has statutory responsibility for the British Library (British Library Act 1972) and for the Public Lending Right (Public Lending Right Act 1979) and he is responsible for the Royal Commission on Historical Manuscripts (first appointed by Royal Warrant of 2 April 1869: see LIBRARIES AND SCIENTIFIC AND CULTURAL INSTITUTIONS vol 28 para 408). He has a general statutory obligation under the Public Libraries and Museums Act 1964 to ensure that local library authorities in England provide a comprehensive and efficient public library service. The Secretary of State is responsible for grants to the Museums and Galleries Commission (in existence since 1930: Treasury Minute, 28 November 1930; and see LIBRARIES AND SCIENTIFIC AND CULTURAL INSTITUTIONS vol 28 para 417) and has various powers with regard to national museums and art galleries: see eg the National Heritage Acts 1980 and 1983; and the Museums and Galleries Act 1992. See generally LIBRARIES AND SCIENTIFIC AND CULTURAL INSTITUTIONS.

4    The Secretary of State provides funds in order to achieve this objective largely through the Arts Council of England incorporated by Royal Charter dated 1 April 1994: see the Civil Service Year Book 1996 col 741; and LIBRARIES AND SCIENTIFIC AND CULTURAL INSTITUTIONS.

5    As to broadcasting generally see TELECOMMUNICATIONS AND BROADCASTING. The Secretary of State has published a White Paper on the future of the British Broadcasting Corporation, whose Charter expires in December 1996: see *The Future of the BBC: Serving the Nation, Competing World-Wide* (Cm 2621) (1994). The Secretary of State has also published proposals on a new legislative framework: see *Media Ownership* (Cm 2872) (1995). The Secretary of State appoints the chairman and deputy chairman of the Independent Television Commission, the Broadcasting Complaints Commission and the Broadcasting Standards Council: Broadcasting Act 1990 ss 1(2), 142(3), 151(2).

6    The Secretary of State has functioned mainly through the work of the Sports Council incorporated by Royal Charter dated 4 February 1972. As to the reorganisation of the Sports Council into the Sports Council for England and the United Kingdom Sports Council see the Civil Service Year Book 1996 cols 794–795. The Secretary of State appoints the chairman and other members of the Football Licensing Authority: Football Spectators Act 1989 s 8(3).

7    The Department of National Heritage sponsors the tourism industry, in particular through the Tourist Boards (established by the Development of Tourism Act 1969 s 1 (as amended)). The Secretary of State appoints the chairman and members of the British Tourist Authority: s 1(2); Transfer of Functions (National Heritage) Order 1992, SI 1992/1311. See also TRADE, INDUSTRY AND INDUSTRIAL RELATIONS vol 47 (Reissue) para 813 et seq.

8    See the National Lottery etc Act 1993. The Secretary of State appoints the Director General of the National Lottery: s 3. See generally BETTING, GAMING AND LOTTERIES.

9    Ibid s 5(6).

10   Ibid s 21(2).

11   See ibid s 31.

12   Ibid s 22. See also the Department of National Heritage Annual Report: *The Government's Expenditure Plans 1995–96 to 1997–98* (Cm 2811) (1995) p 8.

## 501. Organisation.

The Department of National Heritage is organised into five groups, an information division and two executive agencies[1]. The groups are as follows: (1) the Arts, Sports and Lottery Group[2]; (2) the Libraries, Galleries and Museums Group[3]; (3) the Broadcasting and Media Group[4]; (4) the Heritage and Tourism Group[5]; and (5) the Resources and Services Group[6].

The Historic Royal Palaces Agency was established in 1989 and is responsible for managing the Historic Royal Palaces open to the public[7]. The Royal Parks Agency, established in 1993, is responsible for managing and policing the nine royal parks and some other open spaces in London[8].

Additionally the department works with 44 non-departmental public bodies and five public corporations[9].

1    See the Civil Service Year Book 1996 col 496 et seq; and the Department of National Heritage Annual Report: *The Government's Expenditure Plans 1995–96 to 1997–98* (Cm 2811) (1995). As to the Civil

Service generally see paras 549–564 post. As to executive agencies see para 551 post.

2 The Arts, Sports and Lottery Group consists of divisions concerned with (1) arts; (2) sport and recreation; (3) the National Lottery; and (4) the Government Art Collection: Civil Service Year Book 1996 cols 498–500.

3 The Libraries, Galleries and Museums Group consists of four divisions concerned with (1) libraries; (2) the British Library project; (3) museums and galleries; and (4) cultural property: Civil Service Year Book 1996 cols 500–502.

4 The Broadcasting and Media Group consists of four divisions concerned with (1) broadcasting policy; (2) broadcasting legislation; (3) broadcasting and audiovisual sponsorship; and (4) the media: Civil Service Year Book 1996 cols 502–504.

5 The Heritage and Tourism Group consists of three divisions concerned with (1) heritage; (2) the royal estates; and (3) tourism: Civil Service Year Book 1996 cols 504–507.

6 The Resources and Services Group consists of four divisions concerned with (1) finance; (2) strategy and systems; (3) personnel; and (4) pay and delegations: Civil Service Year Book 1996 cols 507–509.

7 See the Civil Service Year Book 1996 cols 509–510; and *Next Steps Review 1995* (Cm 3164) (1995) p 6. The palaces are: The Tower of London; Hampton Court Palace with its gardens and park; Kensington Palace State Apartments with the Royal Ceremonial Dress Collection and Orangery; the Banqueting House, Whitehall; and Kew Palace with Queen Charlotte's Cottage. The agency is sponsored by the Royal Estates Division of the Heritage and Tourism Group (see note 5 supra): Civil Service Year Book 1996 col 506.

8 See the Civil Service Year Book 1996 cols 510–511; and *Next Steps Review 1995* (Cm 3164) (1995) p 10. The parks are: Hyde Park; Kensington Gardens; St James' Park and the Green Park; Regent's Park and Primrose Hill; Greenwich Park; Richmond Park and Bushy Park. See the Civil Service Year Book col 511; the Crown Lands Act 1851 s 22 (as amended); and CROWN LANDS AND PRIVILEGES. The agency is sponsored by the Royal Estates Division of the Heritage and Tourism Group (see note 5 supra): Civil Service Year Book 1996 col 506.

9 See the Civil Service Year Book 1996 col 496. The five public corporations are the British Broadcasting Corporation; the Independent Television Commission; Channel Four Television Corporation; S4C; and the Radio Authority.

## (xi) The Department of Social Security

**502. Functions of the department.** The Department of Social Security was created in 1988, when the Department of Health and Social Security was divided into two departments, each with its own Secretary of State[1]. The Department of Social Security is responsible for the development and delivery of the social security programme, and for the operation of the National Insurance fund.

The department is an authorised department for the purpose of suing and being sued[2], and is subject to investigation by the Parliamentary Commissioner for Administration[3]. The expenses of the department are provided by Parliament[4].

1 Transfer of Functions (Health and Social Security) Order 1988, SI 1988/1843.
  As to the transfer of relevant functions prior to the creation of the two new departments see (in chronological order): the Transfer of Functions (Ministry of Pensions) Order 1953, SI 1953/1198; the Ministry of Social Security Act 1966 ss 1, 2 (repealed); and the Secretary of State for Social Services Order 1968, SI 1968/1699 (as amended). As to the transfer of functions generally see para 363 ante. As to the Department of Health see paras 463–465 ante. As to the office of Secretary of State see para 355 et seq ante.

2 See the list published under the Crown Proceedings Act 1947 s 17(1) (as amended); and CROWN PROCEEDINGS.

3 Parliamentary Commissioner Act 1967 s 4(1), Sch 2 (substituted by the Parliamentary and Health Service Commissioners Act 1987 s 1(1), (2), Sch 1; amended by the Transfer of Functions (Health and Social Security) Order 1988). As to the Parliamentary Commissioner for Administration see ADMINISTRATIVE LAW vol 1(1) (Reissue) para 41 et seq.

4 See the *Supply Estimates 1995–96 for the year ending 31 March 1996* (HC Paper (1994–95) no 271–XIII).

**503. The Secretary of State for Social Security.** The Secretary of State for Social Security is a corporation sole[1]. The corporate seal of the Secretary of State for Social Security is authenticated by the signature of a Secretary of State, or of a secretary to that department, or of a person authorised by a Secretary of State to act in that behalf[2]. The seal is officially and judicially noticed[3]. Every document purporting to be an instrument made or issued by the Secretary of State for Social Security and to be sealed with his seal duly authenticated, or to be signed or executed by a secretary to the Department of Social Security, is to be received in evidence and to be deemed to be so made or issued without further proof unless the contrary is shown[4]. A certificate signed by the Secretary of State for Social Security shall be conclusive evidence of that fact[5].

1 Transfer of Functions (Health and Social Security) Order 1988, SI 1988/1843 art 4(1). As to corporations sole see CORPORATIONS.
2 Ibid art 4(2). As to secretarial seals see para 357 ante.
3 Ibid art 4(3).
4 Ibid art 4(3).
5 Ibid art 4(4).

**504. Organisation.** The Department of Social Security has the greatest expenditure in the government[1]. The Secretary of State is assisted by two Ministers of State (one in the House of Commons and one in the House of Lords) and three Parliamentary Under Secretaries. The departmental headquarters is small, and consists of the Social Security Policy Group, the Resource Management and Planning Group and the Solicitors Office[2]. The greater part of the department is devolved into the five executive agencies described below[3]:

(1) the Benefits Agency (or Social Security Benefits Agency), which administers and delivers benefits[4]; within that division, and under the Director of Medical Services and Chief Medical Adviser to the Department of Social Security, is the Medical Services section, which provides a specialist medical examination service of claimants of health related benefits[5];

(2) the Contributions Agency (or Social Security Contributions Agency), which ensures compliance with national insurance law and maintains national insurance records[6];

(3) the Child Support Agency (or Social Security Child Support Agency), which was set up to implement the child support system of child maintenance[7];

(4) the War Pensions Agency (or Social Security War Pensions Agency), which administers payment of war disablement and war widows pensions, and provides appropriate support[8];

(5) the Information Technology Services Agency (or Social Security Information Technology Services Agency), which provides information technology to the department and its agencies[9].

1 The Department of Social Security accounted for 28% of planned public expenditure in 1995–96, approximately £85,000 million. Expenditure on benefits accounts for 95% of the social security programme, while the costs of administering the benefits and collecting national insurance contributions accounts for the remaining 5%: Department of Social Security Annual Report: *The Government's Expenditure Plans 1995–96 to 1997–98* (Cm 2813) (1995) pp 4, 9. This compares with £597 million in 1949–50.
2 The Social Security Policy Group consists of five divisions each concerned with a group of social security and national insurance benefits, together with an information division which is concerned with liaison with the media, public enquiries and national publicity: Civil Service Year Book 1996 cols 550–554.
   The Resource Management and Planning Group consists of the private office, the Corporate Strategy and Personnel division, the Analytical Services division, and the Planning and Finance division: Civil Service Year Book 1996 cols 547–550.
   The Solicitors Office consists of two divisions of solicitors concerned with advice and legal services on social security matters, legal proceedings, and staffing matters: Civil Service Year Book 1996 cols 554–556.
3 The Resettlement Agency, which operated hostels for single homeless people, ceased to operate on 1 April 1996, and its residual functions reverted to the Social Security Policy Group: see the Civil Service Year Book 1996 cols 552–553, 564. As to executive agencies see para 551 post.

4   See the Civil Service Year Book 1996 cols 557–561; and the Department of Social Security Annual
    Report: *The Government's Expenditure Plans 1995–96 to 1997–98* (Cm 2813) (1995) p 75.
5   See the Civil Service Year Book 1996 cols 559–561; and *Next Steps Review 1995* (Cm 3164) (1995) p 154.
6   See the Civil Service Year Book 1996 cols 562–563; and *Next Steps Review 1995* (Cm 3164) (1995) p 80.
    As to contributions and benefits see generally NATIONAL HEALTH AND SOCIAL SECURITY.
7   See the Civil Service Year Book 1996 cols 561–562; and *Next Steps Review 1995* (Cm 3164) (1995)
    p 164. As to child support see CHILDREN vol 5(2) (Reissue) paras 862–924.
8   See the Civil Service Year Book 1996 col 564; and *Next Steps Review 1995* (Cm 3164) (1995) p 158.
9   See the Civil Service Year Book 1996 cols 563–564; and *Next Steps Review 1995* (Cm 3164) (1995) p 272.

## (xii)  The Department of Trade and Industry

**505. The Department of Trade and Industry.** The Department of Trade and
Industry was formed in 1983 by an amalgamation of the Department of Trade and the
Department of Industry[1].

The Department of Trade and Industry is headed by the Secretary of State for Trade
and Industry, who is also the President of the Board of Trade[2]. He is assisted by Ministers
of State or Parliamentary Under Secretaries of State[3].

The Department of Trade and Industry, and the Board of Trade, are subject to
investigation by the Parliamentary Commissioner for Administration[4]. The expenses of
the department are provided by Parliament[5].

1   Transfer of Functions (Trade and Industry) Order 1983, SI 1983/1127. The civil aviation and shipping
    functions of the Secretary of State for Trade were transferred to the Secretary of State for Transport:
    art 2(3). As to the Secretary of State for Transport see para 509 post.
        There had previously been a Department of Trade and Industry established by the Secretary of State
    for Trade and Industry Order 1970, SI 1970/1537; its functions were distributed between other
    departments by the Secretary of State (New Departments) Order 1974, SI 1974/692: see TRADE,
    INDUSTRY AND INDUSTRIAL RELATIONS vol 47 (Reissue) para 2. By the Transfer of Functions
    (Financial Services) Order 1992, SI 1992/1315, a number of functions previously exercised by the
    Secretary of State in the area of financial services were transferred to the Treasury so as to be exercisable
    by the Treasury alone, by the Secretary of State and the Treasury acting jointly or by the Secretary of
    State and the Treasury acting concurrently. As to the Treasury see paras 512–517 post. The present
    department is an amalgamation of the former Departments of Trade, Industry, Energy, Prices and
    Consumer Protection, effected by the Secretary of State for Trade Order 1979, SI 1979/578; the
    Transfer of Functions (Trade and Industry) Order 1983; and the Transfer of Functions (Energy) Order
    1992, SI 1992/1314. Functions of the Home Secretary relating to wireless telegraphy were also
    transferred to the Secretary of State for Trade and Industry by the Transfer of Functions (Trade and
    Industry) Order 1983. It has also assumed functions relating to small businesses which were previously
    entrusted to the Secretary of State for Employment: Transfer of Functions (Small Businesses) Order
    1992, SI 1992/1297; functions relating to employment also previously exercised by the Secretary of
    State for Employment: Transfer of Functions (Education and Employment) Order 1995, SI 1995/2986
    (see para 507 post); and functions relating to science previously exercised by the Minister for the Civil
    Service and the Chancellor of the Duchy of Lancaster: Transfer of Functions (Science) Order 1995,
    SI 1995/2985. As to the Secretary of State for Education and Employment see para 448 ante. As to the
    Minister for the Civil Service see paras 427 ante, 550 post.
        As to the transfer of relevant functions prior to the re-establishment of the Department of Trade and
    Industry in 1983, or prior to the transfer of functions from other departments to the Department of Trade
    and Industry in 1992, see 5 Halsbury's Statutory Instruments *Constitutional Law* (1994 Reissue) 101–104.
    As to the transfer of functions generally see para 363 ante. As to the functions of the Department of Trade
    and  Industry see para 507 post.
2   The Board of Trade was (and still is) a committee of the Privy Council set up by Order in Council dated
    23 August 1786 and charged with the general responsibility for advising on 'trade and foreign plantations':
    see the definition in the Harbours and Passing Tolls etc Act 1861 s 65. Its meetings became steadily less
    frequent and its functions came to be exercised by or on behalf of the President of the Board of Trade,
    an unpaid post now held by the Secretary of State for Trade and Industry. In 1992, on becoming the
    Secretary of State for Trade and Industry, Mr Michael Heseltine resumed the use of the title President of
    the Board of Trade: see Department of Trade and Industry Press Notice P/92/241. At the date at which
    this volume states the law, the Secretary of State for Trade and Industry, Mr Ian Lang, continues to use

the title: see the Civil Service Year Book 1996 col 568. As to the execution of documents and the proof of orders and regulations of the board see the Harbours and Passing Tolls etc Act 1861 s 67; the Documentary Evidence Act 1868 s 2, Schedule; and EVIDENCE. For a history of the Board of Trade see Foreman *Shoes and Ships and Sealing Wax*. The functions of the Board of Trade are exercisable concurrently by the Secretary of State for Trade and Industry and the functions of the President, other than his functions in the board and any power to act for the board, are likewise so exercisable concurrently: see the Secretary of State for Trade and Industry Order 1970, SI 1970/1537, art 2(1); see also TRADE, INDUSTRY AND INDUSTRIAL RELATIONS vol 47 (Reissue) para 2.

3    At the date at which this volume states the law, the Secretary of State for Trade and Industry is assisted by a Minister of State (departmental spokesman in the House of Lords); the Minister for Industry and Energy; the Minister for Trade; the Parliamentary Under Secretary of State for Trade and Industry (Minister for Company Affairs); the Parliamentary Under Secretary of State for Science and Technology (Minister for Science and Technology); the Parliamentary Under Secretary of State for Competition and Consumer Affairs (Minister for Competition and Consumer Affairs); and the Parliamentary Under Secretary of State for Small Business, Industry and Energy (Minister for Small Business): see the Civil Service Year Book 1996 cols 568–569.

4    Parliamentary Commissioner Act 1967 s 4(1), Sch 2 (substituted by the Parliamentary and Health Service Commissioners Act 1987 s 1(1), (2), Sch 1); Transfer of Functions (Trade and Industry) Order 1983 art 5(1); and see PARLIAMENT. As to the Parliamentary Commissioner for Administration see ADMINISTRATIVE LAW vol 1(1) (Reissue) para 41 et seq.

5    See the *Supply Estimates 1995–96 for the year ending 31 March 1996* (HC Paper (1994–95) no 271–IV).

**506. The Secretary of State for Trade and Industry.** The Secretary of State is a corporation sole and has a corporate seal[1]. His corporate seal is authenticated by the signature of a Secretary of State, or of a secretary to the Department of Trade and Industry, or of a person authorised by a Secretary of State to act in that behalf[2]. The corporate seal must be officially and judicially noticed[3], and every document purporting to be an instrument made or issued by the Secretary of State for Trade and Industry, and to be sealed with the seal authenticated as above, or to be signed or executed by a secretary to the Department of Trade and Industry or a person authorised as above, must be received in evidence and be deemed to be so made or issued without further proof unless the contrary is shown[4]. A certificate signed by the Secretary of State for Trade and Industry that any instrument purporting to be made or issued by him was so made or issued is conclusive evidence of that fact[5].

1    Secretary of State for Trade and Industry Order 1970, SI 1970/1537, art 4(1). As to the establishment of the Department of Trade and Industry by that order, and its re-establishment by the Transfer of Functions (Trade and Industry) Order 1983, SI 1983/1127, see para 505 note 1 ante. As to corporations sole see CORPORATIONS. As to secretarial seals see para 357 ante.

2    Secretary of State for Trade and Industry Order 1970 art 4(2). As to secretarial seals see para 357 ante.

3    Ibid art 4(3).

4    Ibid art 4(3).

5    Ibid art 4(4).

**507. Functions.** The Department of Trade and Industry is responsible for general trade policy, nationally, within the European Community and overseas. There are divisions within the department dealing with, inter alia, competitiveness and new initiatives for encouraging improved performance of United Kingdom suppliers[1]; support for small businesses, including their setting up and development; international trade policy dealing with the General Agreement on Tariffs and Trade, and the Organisation for Economic Co-operation and Development; tariff issues and duty relief schemes; international investment policy; general commodity policy; import licensing policy and administration; policy and co-ordination on Single Market issues; bilateral market access with individual countries; anti-dumping; export control; United Nations sanctions; and nuclear non-proliferation[2]. The department is responsible for the British Overseas Trade Board, which advises businesses on export promotion[3].

The Department of Trade and Industry is also responsible for standardisation, including co-operation with the British Standards Institute, European standardisation policy and national measurement systems. The Vehicles, Metals and Minerals division deals with issues relating to the industrial minerals industry; sponsorship of steel and associated industries; the Multilateral Steel Agreement; motor vehicle trade and sponsorship of the vehicle component sector and of car and commercial vehicle manufacturing; sponsorship of shipbuilding, ship repair and marine equipment. The Aerospace division covers relations with the various sectors of the aerospace industry. The department is a partner in the British National Space Centre which co-ordinates United Kingdom civil space activities. There are also divisions for electronics and engineering and textiles and retailing[4].

The department includes the Office of Science and Technology which provides a central focus for the development of government policy on science, engineering and technology. It is responsible for the science budget and the work of the Research Councils[5].

The department has statutory responsibilities in the area of telecommunications and radio communications, including the appointment of the Director General of Telecommunications and the granting of licences[6]. The department has functions on the supply side of broadcasting by way of sponsorship of telecommunications and radiocommunications equipment, innovation support, and initiatives to support export activity[7].

The department has certain supervisory powers over the Post Office[8]. The Secretary of State has statutory powers to give such general directions as to the exercise of its powers as he considers to be in the national interest[9].

Government responsibility in relation to matters of fuel and energy is vested in the department[10]. The Secretary of State may make orders regulating or prohibiting the use or supply of petroleum, gas or electricity[11].

The Department of Trade and Industry is the successor to the functions of the Department of Prices and Consumer Affairs[12]. It is responsible for policy on mergers, monopolies, restrictive trade practices, anti-competitive practices and international (including European Community) aspects of competition policy; for corporate and individual insolvency; for policy on intellectual property and the administration of the patents, designs and trade marks legislation; and for weights and measures legislation[13]. As such, the department is accountable for the Monopolies and Mergers Commission[14], for the Insolvency Service[15], for the Patent Office[16], and for the National Weights and Measures Laboratory[17].

The Secretary of State has powers to authorise and supervise insurance companies under the Insurance Companies Act 1982 and policy responsibility for legislation in that field[18]. He also has responsibility for the development and administration of company law, under which he has powers to investigate the affairs and conduct of companies under the Companies Acts 1985 and 1989[19].

The department also has responsibility for functions of the former Department of Employment in relation to industrial relations, pay, redundancy payments, work permits, the conciliation service and Industrial Tribunals[20].

1 Government White Paper *Competitiveness: Helping Business to Win* (Cm 2563) (1994). The Department of Trade and Industry continues to have responsibilities in these areas, although the primary responsibility for competitiveness and deregulation has been assumed by the First Secretary of State, with Cabinet Office support: see paras 430, 433–434 ante.

2 See the Civil Service Year Book 1996 col 570 et seq. See also the Department of Trade and Industry Annual Report: *The Government's Expenditure Plans 1995–96 to 1997–98* (Cm 2804) (1995).

3 Department of Trade and Industry Annual Report: *The Government's Expenditure Plans 1995–96 to 1997–98* (Cm 2804) (1995) p 32.

4	See the Civil Service Year Book 1996 col 581 et seq; Department of Trade and Industry Annual Report: *The Government's Expenditure Plans 1995–96 to 1997–98* (Cm 2804) (1995) pp 22–23, 25.

5	See the Civil Service Year Book 1996 col 617 et seq.

6	Ie under the Telecommunications Act 1984 and the Wireless Telegraphy Acts 1949 to 1967: see TELECOMMUNICATIONS AND BROADCASTING.

7	See the Civil Service Year Book 1996 cols 573–594. The principal regulatory functions are now the responsibility of the Department of National Heritage: see para 500 ante; and TELECOMMUNICATIONS AND BROADCASTING.

8	See the Civil Service Year Book 1996 col 595; and generally POST OFFICE.

9	See the Post Office Act 1969 s 11 (amended by the British Telecommunications Act 1981 ss 62, 89, Sch 6 Pt II); and POST OFFICE.

10	See the Civil Service Year Book 1996 cols 596–600. As to the transfer of functions relating to fuel and energy prior to 1992 see FUEL AND ENERGY vol 19(1) (Reissue) para 501. Functions are also allocated to the Department of the Environment and the Treasury. All the former functions of the Secretary of State for Energy were transferred by the Transfer of Functions (Energy) Order 1992, SI 1992/1314, to the Secretary of State for Trade and Industry, except for energy efficiency functions which were transferred to the Secretary of State for the Environment. See also the Department of Trade and Industry Annual Report: *The Government's Expenditure Plans 1995–96 to 1997–98* (Cm 2804) (1995) pp 62–69. As to the Department of the Environment see paras 452–458 ante. As to the Treasury see paras 512–517 post.

11	See the Energy Act 1976 s 1; and see FUEL AND ENERGY vol 19(1) (Reissue) para 502.

12	Secretary of State for Trade Order 1979, SI 1979/578; Transfer of Functions (Trade and Industry) Order 1983, SI 1983/1127.

13	See the Civil Service Year Book 1996 cols 604–609.

14	See generally TRADE, INDUSTRY AND INDUSTRIAL RELATIONS vol 47 (Reissue) paras 111–149.

15	See generally BANKRUPTCY AND INSOLVENCY.

16	See generally PATENTS AND REGISTERED DESIGNS vol 35 (Reissue) para 662 et seq.

17	See generally WEIGHTS AND MEASURES.

18	See INSURANCE vol 25 (Reissue) para 846 et seq.

19	See generally COMPANIES.

20	See the Transfer of Functions (Education and Employment) Order 1995, SI 1995/2986.

**508. Organisation.** The Department of Trade and Industry is organised into eight units (sometimes known as commands), each headed by a Deputy Secretary (or equivalent) reporting to the Permanent Secretary, as described below[1].

(1)	Trade Policy and Export Promotion, which is further divided into the International Trade Policy division, the European Community and Trade Relations division, the Export Control and Non-proliferation division; also in this unit, under the control of the Director-General of Export Promotion and Head of the Joint Export Promotion Directorate, are the Joint Export Promotion Directorate, the Projects Export Promotion division, the Oil and Gas Projects and Supplies Office, the Exports to Asia, Africa and Australasia division, and the Exports to Europe and the Americas division[2].

(2)	Industry, which is further divided into the Technology and Innovation Policy division, the Chemicals and Biotechnology division, the Vehicles, Metals and Minerals division, the Aerospace division, the British National Space Centre, the Electronics and Engineering division, the Textiles and Retailing division, the Telecommunications division, and the Posts[3]. There is also within this command one executive agency, the Radiocommunications Agency, responsible for international regulatory and policy issues concerning radio communications and for the management of the civil radio spectrum in the United Kingdom[4].

(3)	Energy, which is further divided into the Atomic Energy division, the Environment and Energy Technologies division, the Coal division, the Electricity division, the Nuclear Fuels division, the Oil and Gas division, the Energy Policy and Analysis Unit and the Nuclear Power Privatisation Team[5].

(4)	Regional and Small Firms, which is further divided into the Regional Development division, Invest in Britain Bureau, the Small Firms and Business

Link division, the Management and Technology Services division and the government offices for the regions[6].

(5) Corporate and Consumer Affairs, which includes the Laboratories, the Companies division, the Industrial Relations division, the Insurance division, the Competition Policy division and the Consumer Affairs division[7]. The command has seven executive agencies under its supervision, namely: Companies House[8], the National Weights and Measures Laboratory[9], the Laboratory of the Government Chemist[10], the Insolvency Service[11] and the Patent Office[12].

(6) The Solicitor's Office, which includes the Investigation Division (responsible for investigations under the Companies Acts, the Financial Services Act 1986 and Insurance Companies Act 1986 and for subsequent criminal and some civil proceedings), and the legal advisory divisions[13].

(7) Establishment and Finance, which includes the Economics and Statistics division, the Personnel division, the Finance and Resource Management division, the Services Management division, Internal Audit, and the Information division[14]. The command is responsible for one executive agency, the Accounts Services Agency[15].

The Department of Trade and Industry also includes the Office of Science and Technology[16].

1 See the Civil Service Year Book 1996 col 568 et seq; and the Department of Trade and Industry Annual Report: *The Government's Expenditure Plans 1995–96 to 1997–98* (Cm 2804) (1995) p 11.
2 See the Civil Service Year Book 1996 cols 570–581.
3 See the Civil Service Year Book 1996 cols 581–595.
4 See the Civil Service Year Book 1996 col 625; Department of Trade and Industry Annual Report: *The Government's Expenditure Plans 1995–96 to 1997–98* (Cm 2804) (1995); and see also *Next Steps Review 1995* (Cm 3164) (1995) p 146. As to executive agencies see para 551 post.
5 See the Civil Service Year Book 1996 cols 595–600.
6 See the Civil Service Year Book 1996 cols 600–604.
7 See the Civil Service Year Book 1996 cols 600, 604–609.
8 See the Civil Service Year Book 1996 cols 620–621; *Next Steps Review 1995* (Cm 3164) (1995) p 326.
9 See the Civil Service Year Book 1996 col 623; *Next Steps Review 1995* (Cm 3164) (1995) p 338.
10 See the Civil Service Year Book 1996 cols 622–623; *Next Steps Review 1995* (Cm 3164) (1995) p 308.
11 See the Civil Service Year Book 1996 cols 621–622; *Next Steps Review 1995* (Cm 3164) (1995) p 328.
12 See the Civil Service Year Book 1996 cols 623–625; *Next Steps Review 1995* (Cm 3164) (1995) p 340.
13 See the Civil Service Year Book 1996 cols 609–614.
14 See the Civil Service Year Book 1996 cols 614–617.
15 *Next Steps Agencies in Government Review 1994* (Cm 2750) (1994) p 1.
16 See para 507 text and note 5 ante.

## (xiii) The Department of Transport

**509. The Secretary of State for Transport.** The Secretary of State for Transport[1] is assisted by one Minister of State and two Parliamentary Under Secretaries. He is a corporation sole and has a corporate seal[2]. The corporate seal of the Secretary of State for Transport is authenticated by the signature of a Secretary of State, a secretary to the Department of Transport or a person authorised by a Secretary of State to act in that behalf[3]. The seal is officially and judicially noticed[4]. A document purporting to be an instrument made or issued by the Secretary of State for Transport and to be sealed with his seal duly authenticated or to be signed or executed by a secretary to the Department of Transport or a person authorised by a Secretary of State to act in that behalf is to be received in evidence and be deemed to be so made or issued without further proof unless the contrary is shown[5]. A certificate signed by the Secretary of State for Transport that any instrument purporting to be made or issued by him was so made or issued is conclusive evidence of that fact[6].

No stamp duty is chargeable on any instrument made by, to or with the Secretary of State for Transport[7].

The department is an authorised government department for the purposes of suing and being sued[8], and is subject to investigation by the Parliamentary Commissioner for Administration[9]. The expenses of the department are provided by Parliament[10].

1    A separate Department of Transport was created in 1976, and the transport functions of the Secretary of State for the Environment were transferred to the Secretary of State for Transport by the Secretary of State for Transport Order 1976, SI 1976/1775. That arrangement continued until 1979, when a Ministry of Transport was again formed, and, by the Minister of Transport Order 1979, SI 1979/571, all functions which had been conferred on the Secretary of State for Transport were transferred to the Minister. In 1981, by the Transfer of Functions (Transport) Order, SI 1981/238, there were transferred to the Secretary of State for Transport all functions of the Minister for Transport which, immediately before the coming into operation of the Minister of Transport Order 1979, were, by virtue of the Secretary of State for Transport Order 1976, exercisable by that Secretary of State, and the functions under the Development of Rural Wales Act 1976 s 5(1), Sch 3, the Local Government, Planning and Land Act 1980 ss 84(5), 85(1) (both repealed), and the Highways Act 1980 ss 258, 300(2), Sch 1, paras 7, 8, 14, 15, 18, 19, 21, so far as exercisable jointly by the Minister of Transport and the Secretary of State. All other functions of the Minister of Transport were transferred to the Secretary of State. In 1983, by the Transfer of Functions (Trade and Industry) Order 1983, SI 1983/1127, shipping and aviation functions were transferred from the Department of Trade and Industry to the Department of Transport. As to the Department of Trade and Industry see paras 505–508 ante.
        As to the transfer of relevant functions prior to 1976 see 5 Halsbury's Statutory Instruments vol 5 (1994 Reissue) *Constitutional Law* pp 104–105. As to the transfer of functions generally see para 363 ante.
2    Secretary of State for Transport Order 1976 art 4(1). As to corporations sole see CORPORATIONS. As to secretarial seals see para 357 ante.
3    Ibid art 4(2).
4    Ibid art 4(3).
5    Ibid art 4(3).
6    Ibid art 4(4).
7    Ibid art 4(5); Minister of Transport Order 1979, SI 1979/571, art 3(2).
8    See the list published under the Crown Proceedings Act 1947 s 17(1) (as amended); and CROWN PROCEEDINGS.
9    Parliamentary Commissioner Act 1967 s 4(1), Sch 2 (substituted by the Parliamentary and Health Service Commissioners Act 1987 s 1(1), (2), Sch 1); Secretary of State for Transport Order 1976, SI 1976/1775. As to the Parliamentary Commissioner for Administration see ADMINISTRATIVE LAW vol 1(1) (Reissue) para 41 et seq.
10    See the *Supply Estimates 1995–96 for the year ending 31 March 1996* (HC Paper (1994–95) no 271–VI).

**510.  Functions.** Government responsibility for transport by road, rail, sea and air in the United Kingdom is divided between the Secretaries of State for Transport, Scotland, Wales and Northern Ireland[1].

The Secretary of State is the highway authority for the trunk road network which includes most motorways[2]. He is also responsible for driver testing and licensing throughout the United Kingdom[3]; operator licensing for road haulage and passenger carrying operators in Great Britain[4]; regulating the road haulage industry in Great Britain[5]; vehicle testing and type approval in Great Britain[6]; the construction and use of vehicles[7]; the form and content of highway markings and traffic signs and signals in Great Britain[8]; and collecting vehicle excise duty and vehicle registration duty throughout the United Kingdom[9].

In relation to national railways, the Secretary of State acts as sponsor for the railway in Great Britain and sets its overall policy framework and objectives[10]. The Railways Act 1993 provides for the securing by the Secretary of State, as soon as is reasonably practicable, that the function of providing railway services in Great Britain is performed by private sector operators[11]. The Secretary of State acts as sponsor for London Regional

Transport, and sets its policy framework and financial regime[12]. The Secretary of State is also responsible for orders made under the Transport and Works Act 1992 authorising the construction and operation of railways, tramways and other systems of guided transport[13].

In relation to local transport, the Secretary of State is responsible for general policy on local buses, taxis, trams and trolley buses and for the administration of the fuel duty rebate scheme for local buses[14].

In relation to civil aviation, the Secretary of State is charged with the general duty of organising, carrying out and encouraging measures for the development of civil aviation, for the designing, development and production of civil aircraft, for the promotion of safety and efficiency in their use, and for research into air navigation[15]. He has the power to establish and maintain aerodromes for civil aviation and to acquire land for such purpose[16].

In relation to shipping, the Secretary of State, together with the Marine Safety Agency[17] and the Coastguard Agency[18], regulates shipping in United Kingdom waters to maintain and improve marine safety[19]; takes or co-ordinates measures to prevent and minimise the effects of marine pollution[20]; provides up to date information for inclusion in charts and other assistance with navigation[21]; and co-ordinates search and rescue, inquiries and investigations in the event of accidents at sea[22].

1   The Secretary of State is responsible for promoting the efficiency of the transport market and its contribution to the economy; conserving the environment; promoting transport safety and the mobility of disabled people; furthering United Kingdom transport interests overseas, and planning for civil emergencies: Department of Transport Annual Report: *The Government's Expenditure Plans 1995–96 to 1997–98* (Cm 2806) (1995) para 1.1. As to the increase of passenger and freight travel in the period 1952–1992 see Dynes and Walker *The Times Guide to the New British State: The Government Machine in the 1990s* (1995) p 60. As to the Secretary of State for Wales see para 45 ante. As to the Secretary of State for Scotland see para 64 ante. As to the Secretary of State for Northern Ireland see para 83 ante. As to the office of Secretary of State see para 355 et seq ante.

2   As to the Secretary of State's duties as highway authority under the Highways Act 1980 see HIGHWAYS vol 21 (Reissue) para 46. The responsibility for managing, maintaining and improving the national motorway and trunk road network in England is now exercised by the Highways Agency, an agency of the Department of Transport, those functions having been contracted out by virtue of the Contracting Out (Highway Functions) Order 1995, SI 1995/1986; see also *Trunk Roads in England 1994 Review* (HM Stationery Office, 1994).

3   As to the Secretary of State's duties of testing and licensing see generally ROAD TRAFFIC vol 40 para 148 et seq. The responsibilities have been devolved to the Driver and Vehicle Licensing Agency: see para 511 post.

4   Licensing authorities act under the general direction of the Secretary of State: Public Passenger Vehicles Act 1981 s 4(4)(a) (substituted by the Transport Act 1985 s 3(2)); and the Goods Vehicles (Licensing of Operators) Act 1995 s 1(2). See ROAD TRAFFIC vol 40 para 731 et seq.

5   Ibid s 57(1), (2); and see ROAD TRAFFIC vol 40 para 737 (regulations by the Secretary of State concerning carriage of goods by road).

6   See ROAD TRAFFIC vol 40 para 219 et seq. The Vehicle Certification Agency is responsible for administering the European Community and domestic schemes for type approval, whereby new models of vehicles and components, and the production lines making them, are certified as meeting acceptable standards. The Vehicle Inspectorate carries out annual roadworthiness tests on heavy goods vehicles and public service vehicles and supervises the 'MOT' testing of cars, light goods vehicles and motor cycles. As to the Vehicle Certification Agency and the Vehicle Inspectorate see para 511 post.

7   See eg the Motor Vehicles (Construction and Use) Regulations 1986, SI 1978/1078 (as amended): and ROAD TRAFFIC vol 40 para 87 et seq.

8   See the Traffic Signs Regulations and General Directions 1994, SI 1994/1519; and ROAD TRAFFIC vol 40 para 353 et seq.

9   See the Vehicle Excise and Registration Act 1994 ss 6, 22; the Road Vehicles (Registration and Licensing) Regulations 1971, SI 1971/450 (as amended); CUSTOMS AND EXCISE; and ROAD TRAFFIC.

10  Department of Transport Annual Report: *The Government's Expenditure Plans 1995–96 to 1997–98* (Cm 2806) (1995) p 21.

11  Railways Act 1993 s 113. The Secretary of State appoints the Rail Regulator, supported by the Office of the Rail Regulator, and the Director of Passenger Rail Franchising, supported by the Office of Passenger

Rail Franchising, in order to assist in the process of privatisation and in the control and regulation of the industry: see the Railways Act 1993 s 1; Department of Transport Annual Report: *The Government's Expenditure Plans 1995–96 to 1997–98* (Cm 2806) (1995) p 23; and RAILWAYS, INLAND WATERWAYS AND PIPE-LINES.

12 See the London Regional Transport Act 1984 s 2 (as amended). As to the Secretary of State's powers and responsibilities in relation to London Regional Transport see LONDON GOVERNMENT.

13 See the Transport and Works Act 1992 s 1.

14 See the Department of Transport Annual Report: *The Government's Expenditure Plans 1995–96 to 1997–98* (Cm 2806) (1995).

15 Civil Aviation Act 1982 s 1(1): see AVIATION vol 2 (Reissue) para 1032. The day to day responsibility for the regulation of civil aviation rests with the Civil Aviation Authority: see ss 2–4 (as amended); and see also the Department of Transport Annual Report: *The Government's Expenditure Plans 1995–96 to 1997–98* (Cm 2806) (1995) p 54; and AVIATION vol 2 (Reissue) paras 1044–1062.

16 Civil Aviation Act 1982 ss 25, 41; and see AVIATION vol 2 (Reissue) para 1033.

17 See para 511 post.

18 See para 511 post.

19 See the Merchant Shipping Act 1995 ss 85, 86; and generally SHIPPING.

20 See ibid ss 128, 129, 293; and SHIPPING.

21 See ibid s 90; and SHIPPING.

22 See the Merchant Shipping Act 1995 Pt XI (ss 267–273) (accident investigations and inquiries); and generally SHIPPING.

**511. Organisation.** The Department of Transport consists of a number of groups, as described below.

(1) Railways, which includes divisions dealing with, inter alia, finance, corporate affairs and safety; international railways; the Channel Tunnel rail link; and railway economics[1].

(2) Roads, Local Transport and Transport Policy, which includes divisions dealing with highways; buses and London Transport; taxis and London projects; local transport policy; traffic policy; driver information and traffic management; road and vehicle safety; and freight and road haulage[2].

(3) Aviation, Shipping and International Directorate, containing divisions dealing with shipping policy; investigation of marine accidents; ports; civil aviation; international aviation; and the investigation of air accidents[3].

(4) Central Services, consisting of the Directorate of Personnel Management; the Central Services Directorate; the Chief Scientist's Unit; the Executive Agencies Directorate; the Mobility Unit; and the Transport Security division[4].

The department also has legal and information divisions[5].

The department has eight executive agencies[6]: the Coastguard Agency[7]; the Driving Standards Agency[8]; the Driver and Vehicle Licensing Agency[9]; the Highways Agency[10]; the Marine Safety Agency[11]; the Transport Research Laboratory[12]; the Vehicle Certification Agency[13]; the Vehicle Inspectorate[14].

1 See the Civil Service Year Book 1996 cols 632–634; and see the Department of Transport Annual Report: *The Government's Expenditure Plans 1995–96 to 1997–98* (Cm 2806) (1995) p 7.

2 See the Civil Service Year Book 1996 cols 635–640.

3 See the Civil Service Year Book 1996 cols 640–645.

4 See the Civil Service Year Book 1996 cols 645–653.

5 See the Civil Service Year Book 1996 cols 632 et seq.

6 As to executive agencies see para 551 post.

7 See the Civil Service Year Book 1996 cols 653–655; Department of Transport Annual Report: *The Government's Expenditure Plans 1995–96 to 1997–98* (Cm 2806) (1995) p 11; and *Next Steps Review 1995* (Cm 3164) (1995) p 14.

8 See the Civil Service Year Book 1996 col 656; the Department of Transport Annual Report: *The Government's Expenditure Plans 1995–96 to 1997–98* (Cm 2806) (1995) p 12; and *Next Steps Review 1995* (Cm 3164) (1995) p 40.

9   See the Civil Service Year Book 1996 col 657; the Department of Transport Annual Report: *The Government's Expenditure Plans 1995–96 to 1997–98* (Cm 2806) (1995) p 12; and *Next Steps Review 1995* (Cm 3164) (1995) p 30.

10  See the Civil Service Year Book 1996 cols 658–665; the Department of Transport Annual Report: *The Government's Expenditure Plans 1995–96 to 1997–98* (Cm 2806) (1995) p 12; and *Next Steps Review 1995* (Cm 3164) (1995) p 44.

11  See the Civil Service Year Book 1996 cols 665–666; the Department of Transport Annual Report: *The Government's Expenditure Plans 1995–96 to 1997–98* (Cm 2806) (1995) p 12; and *Next Steps Review 1995* (Cm 3164) (1995) p 332.

12  See the Civil Service Year Book 1996 col 667; the Department of Transport Annual Report: *The Government's Expenditure Plans 1995–96 to 1997–98* (Cm 2806) (1995) p 13; and *Next Steps Review 1995* (Cm 3164) (1995) p 314.

13  See the Civil Service Year Book 1996 col 667; the Department of Transport Annual Report: *The Government's Expenditure Plans 1995–96 to 1997–98* (Cm 2806) (1995) p 13; and *Next Steps Review 1995* (Cm 3164) (1995) p 346.

14  See the Civil Service Year Book 1996 cols 667–668; the Department of Transport Annual Report: *The Government's Expenditure Plans 1995–96 to 1997–98* (Cm 2806) (1995) p 13; and *Next Steps Review 1995* (Cm 3164) (1995) p 348.

### (xiv)  The Treasury

**512. The Treasury.** 'The Treasury' means the Commissioners of Her Majesty's Treasury[1]. In 1816 the offices of Lord High Treasurer of Great Britain and of Lord High Treasurer of Ireland were united in one office, the Lord High Treasurer of the United Kingdom of Great Britain and Ireland[2], the holder of which has the same powers over the revenue in Scotland[3] as in England. The functions of the Lord High Treasurer became expressly exercisable by the Treasury commissioners[4].

Executive agencies closely linked with the Treasury include the Paymaster General's Office[5] and the Exchequer Office, Scotland. The Board of Customs and Excise and the Board of Inland Revenue are also closely associated with the Treasury, and together they are known as the revenue departments[6]. The Treasury also has close contacts with the Bank of England[7].

The Treasury is an authorised government department for the purpose of suing and being sued[8]. The Treasury, including the subordinate departments and the office of any minister whose expenses are defrayed out of money provided by Parliament for the service of the Treasury[9], are subject to investigation by the Parliamentary Commissioner for Administration[10].

1   Interpretation Act 1978 ss 5, 22, Sch 1, Sch 2 para 4(1). As to the commissioners see para 513 post. See generally Barnett *Inside the Treasury* (1982); Roseveare *The Treasury: the evolution of a British institution* (1969); Young *But Chancellor: an Enquiry into the Treasury* (1984); Pliatsky *Getting and Spending: public expenditure, employment and inflation* (1984 Edn); Kynaston *Chancellor of the Exchequer* (1980).

2   See the Consolidated Fund Act 1816 s 2 (as amended).

3   See the Crown Lands (Scotland) Act 1835 s 1, whereby the rights of the Crown in Scotland as *ultimus haeres* are vested in the Treasury.

4   Consolidated Fund Act 1816 s 3 (as amended). The last Lord High Treasurer resigned in 1714. The office has been in commission ever since, and there is no reference in the Interpretation Act 1978 to the Lord High Treasurer in the definition of Treasury: see text and note 1 supra.

5   As a rule the Paymaster General is a minister without portfolio available for such special duties as the Prime Minister may assign. As to the functions of the Paymaster General's Office see para 714 post. As to executive agencies see para 551 post.

6   See paras 708–710 post.

7   As to the Bank of England see generally BANKING vol 3 (Reissue) paras 1–8.

8   See the list published under the Crown Proceedings Act 1947 s 17(1) (as amended); and CROWN PROCEEDINGS.

9   See the *Supply Estimates 1995–96 for the year ending 31 March 1996* (HC Paper (1994–95) no 271–XVII).

10  Parliamentary Commissioner Act 1967 s 4(1), Sch 2 (substituted by the Parliamentary and Health Service Commissioners Act 1987 s 1(1), (2), Sch 1). For this purpose the Treasury does not include the Cabinet Office: Parliamentary Commissioner Act 1967 Sch 1 note 6. As to the Parliamentary Commissioner for Administration see ADMINISTRATIVE LAW vol 1(1) (Reissue) para 41 et seq.

**513. Treasury commissioners.** The office of Lord High Treasurer is executed by commissioners[1], the power to appoint commissioners by letters patent under the Great Seal being expressly recognised by statute[2]. The commissioners are not disqualified for membership of the House of Commons[3].

The commissioners constituting the Treasury Board are the First Lord of the Treasury[4], the Chancellor of the Exchequer, and a varying number of Junior Lords[5] appointed by the Crown upon the nomination of the First Lord. In practice the board does not meet. The Chancellor of the Exchequer is the only member of the board whose duties are of a financial nature; the others have purely political duties[6].

1   See para 512 text and notes 1–4 ante. Any instrument or act required by statute or otherwise to be done by or under the hands of the commissioners or any three or more of them is binding if done by or under the hands of any two or more of them: Treasury Instruments (Signature) Act 1849 s 1 (amended by the Statute Law Revision Act 1891). Any requisition or request for a credit under the Exchequer and Audit Departments Act 1866 ss 13, 15 (both as amended), or the National Loans Act 1968 s 1(3), may be signed by any two of the following persons, namely, the Secretaries of the Treasury and such officers as the Treasury may from time to time appoint to that duty: Finance Act 1975 s 56. See further para 711 post.

2   Consolidated Fund Act 1816 s 2 (as amended). As to letters patent under the Great Seal see para 920 post.

3   Ie they are not disqualified by the House of Commons Disqualification Act 1975: see s 2, Sch 2 (as amended); and PARLIAMENT.

4   This office is generally held by the Prime Minister: see para 395 ante.

5   Not more than five Junior Lords may be paid salaries out of money provided by Parliament: see the Ministerial and other Salaries Act 1972 s 1(1)(a), Sch 1 Pt V para 2(d); and para 424 ante.

6   The Junior Lords are government whips: see para 354 ante.

**514. The Chancellor of the Exchequer.** The Chancellor of the Exchequer is not only a Treasury commissioner; he is appointed, by separate patents, and by the delivery of the Exchequer seals, Chancellor of the Exchequer and Under Treasurer[1]. He is assisted by the Chief Secretary, the Financial Secretary, the Paymaster General, the Economic Secretary and the Permanent Secretary to the Treasury, who in turn is assisted by seven directors[2].

As a political officer, the Chancellor of the Exchequer represents the Treasury in the House of Commons, of which he is necessarily a member. He is responsible for the direction of economic and financial policy and the control of public expenditure. By his budget proposals he formulates the demands to be made upon Parliament for the annual sums required to carry on the government of the country and adjusts the relationship between revenue and expenditure[3].

The Chancellor of the Exchequer is also the minister responsible for Her Majesty's Customs and Excise and the Board of Inland Revenue and for several smaller departments. He is a Commissioner for the Reduction of the National Debt[4], a Church Commissioner[5] and the Master of the Mint[6], and takes part in the annual nomination of sheriffs[7].

1   2 Anson's Law and Custom of the Constitution (2nd Edn, 1935) Pt I p 191. As to his salary see para 423 ante. As to the Treasury commissioners see para 513 ante.

2   See the Civil Service Year Book 1996 col 672; and see para 517 post.

3   As to the effect of United Kingdom membership of the European Community on the Chancellor of the Exchequer's functions in this connection see the European Monetary Union requirements as contained in the EC Treaty art 3A (added by the Treaty on European Union signed at Maastricht on 7 February 1992 (the 'Maastricht Treaty') (Cm 1934). As to European economic and monetary union see Wyatt and Dashwood *European Community Law* (3rd Edn) pp 661–669. As to the presentation of the budget see para 705 post.

4   National Debt Reduction Act 1786 s 14 (amended by the Statute Law Revision Act 1871; and the Statute Law Revision Act 1888).

5    See the Church Commissioners Measure 1947 s 1(2), Sch 1 para 1 (amended by the Synodical Government Measure 1969 s 2(2); and the Church of England (Miscellaneous Provisions) Measure 1992 s 17(1), Sch 3 para 5); and ECCLESIASTICAL LAW.

6    See the Coinage Act 1971 s 4(1). The Royal Mint is responsible for the production of coins, medals, seals, dies and commemorative medallions: see the Civil Service Year Book 1996 col 543. See further MONEY.

7    See the Sheriffs Act 1887 s 6(1) (amended by the Statute Law Revision Act 1908); and SHERIFFS.

**515. Treasury ministers.** The Treasury has four ministers in addition to the Chancellor of the Exchequer, namely the Chief Secretary, the Financial Secretary and an Economic Secretary, who rank as Secretaries to the Treasury Board[1], and the Paymaster General. They advise the Chancellor as appropriate on policy[2].

The Paymaster General has particular responsibility under the Chancellor of the Exchequer for customs and excise duties and taxes, the European Community budget, the environment, charities and the Office of the Paymaster General[3].

The Chief Secretary has particular responsibility under the Chancellor of the Exchequer for the control of public expenditure (including local authority and nationalised industry finance), all supply estimates being presented to the House of Commons in his name; value for money in the public services (including 'next steps' services[4]), procurement policy, competitive tendering and market testing[5].

The Financial Secretary has particular responsibility under the Chancellor of the Exchequer for parliamentary financial procedure, including the approval of financial resolutions etc[6]; he also has responsibility for other parliamentary financial business (public accounts committee, Comptroller and Auditor General, exchequer and audit acts); general oversight of the Inland Revenue; privatisation; Civil Service pay and personnel management; competition and deregulation policy[7].

The Economic Secretary has particular responsibility for monetary policy; and for banks, building societies and other financial institutions. He is also responsible for the Royal Mint, the Government Actuary's Department, the Government Centre for Information Systems, the Valuation Office, and international financial issues and institutions (other than those relating to the European Community)[8].

1    Additionally there is a Parliamentary Secretary to the Treasury, who is the government Chief Whip in the House of Commons; he has responsibilities in respect of parliamentary business and as political adviser to the Cabinet (see the *First Report of the Review Body on Top Salaries: Ministers of the Crown and Members of Parliament* (Cmnd 4836) (1971) para 104 App I), and has no connection with the work of the Treasury. As to his salary see para 423 ante. When he is not a member of the Cabinet it is the practice to invite him to all cabinet meetings. As to the Cabinet see paras 402–413 ante.

2    As to ministerial responsibilities see the current edition for the time being of Dod's Parliamentary Companion.

3    As to the Paymaster General see further para 714 post. See also the Chancellor of the Exchequer's smaller departments and net payments to European Community institutions Annual Report: *The Government's expenditure plans 1995–96 to 1997–98* (Cm 2817) (1995) p 79.

4    As to 'next steps' agencies in government see *Next Steps Review 1995* (Cm 3164) (1995); and generally para 551 post.

5    A Chief Secretary was first appointed in 1961: see Bridges *The Treasury* p 162, referring to a statement made by the Prime Minister on 9 October 1961. The Chief Secretary has been a member of the Cabinet since 1977. For his responsibilities see the Chancellor of the Exchequer's smaller departments and net payments to European Community institutions Annual Report: *The Government's expenditure plans 1995–96 to 1997–98* (Cm 2817) (1995) p 79; and Dod's Parliamentary Companion. As to supply procedure see para 712 post.

6    The officials of the House of Commons will not place a financial resolution on the agenda of the House unless it has the initials of the Financial Secretary: see Bridges *The Treasury* p 35.

7    See the Chancellor of the Exchequer's smaller departments and net payments to European Community institutions Annual Report: *The Government's expenditure plans 1995–96 to 1997–98* (Cm 2817) (1995) p 79; and Dod's Parliamentary Companion.

8    See the Chancellor of the Exchequer's smaller departments and net payments to European Community institutions Annual Report: *The Government's expenditure plans 1995–96 to 1997–98* (Cm 2817) (1995) p 79; and Dod's Parliamentary Companion.

**516. Functions.** The principal functions[1] of the Treasury are (1) to manage the national economy as a whole; (2) subject to Parliament, to impose and regulate taxation and the collection of the revenue, for which purpose it has the assistance of the Board of Inland Revenue and Her Majesty's Customs and Excise[2]; (3) to control public expenditure, chiefly through the preparation each year of public expenditure forecasts and the preparation or supervision of supply estimates for the House of Commons[3]; (4) to arrange for the provision of the funds required from day to day to meet the necessities of the public service, for which purpose it is entrusted with extensive borrowing powers; (5) to prescribe the manner in which public accounts are kept[4]; and (6) to initiate and carry out measures affecting the national debt[5], banking[6], building societies[7] and certain other financial services[8].

The Chancellor of the Exchequer has responsibility for the Office of National Statistics, formed from the merger of the Central Statistical Office and the Office of Population Censuses and Surveys[9].

A number of functions formerly exercised by the Treasury have been transferred to other departments, and functions formerly exercised by other departments have been transferred to the Treasury[10].

1   See also paras 514–515 ante.
2   See generally paras 707–710 post.
3   See para 704 post. As to supply procedure see para 712 post.
4   As to public accounts generally see paras 715–723 post.
5   See generally MONEY.
6   See generally BANKING.
7   See eg BUILDING SOCIETIES.
8   See generally the Financial Services Act 1986; the Transfer of Functions (Financial Services) Order 1992, SI 1992/1315; and MONEY.
9   See the Transfer of Functions (Registration and Statistics) Order 1996, SI 1996/273.
10  See the transfer of functions orders listed at 5 Halsbury's Statutory Instruments *Constitutional Law* (1994 Reissue) 106.

**517. Organisation.** The work of the Treasury is carried out by seven directorates, as described below.

(1)   Macro-economic Policy and Prospects, which includes units concerned with economic prospects; fiscal and macro-economic policy; economic briefing and analysis; inflation and monetary policy; debt and reserves management; and economist group management[1].

(2)   International Finance, which includes units concerned with European Union finances, future strategy and co-ordination; developing countries, debt and export finance; international financial institutions and the former Soviet Union; trade policy and developments, world economic issues and regional/country analysis[2].

(3)   Budget and Public Finances, which includes units concerned with general expenditure policy and statistics; exchequer funds and accounts; public sector finances; tax and the budget (including tax economics and administration); strategic management; public sector pay policy; departmental pay systems; public service pensions; and overseas allowances[3].

(4)   Spending, which is concerned with aid, diplomacy and intelligence; defence; agriculture; social security; health; heritage and central departments; education; employment and training; home and legal; local government; housing, urban and government property; Scotland, Wales, Northern Ireland, environment and planning; and central operational research and economics[4].

(5) Financial Management, Reporting and Audit (including the Treasury Officer of Accounts), which is concerned with central accountancy; government accountancy services management; audit policy and advice; resource accounting and budgeting; finance and purchasing; and Treasury internal audit[5].

(6) Finance Regulation and Industry (including credit institutions), which is concerned with financial services; securities and markets policy; general financial issues; securities and investment services; industry issues; private finance; transport issues; privatisation; competition, regulation and energy markets; and procurement policy and practice[6].

(7) Personnel and Support, including personnel policy and management; information systems; accommodation and security; and outplacement services[7].

1  See the Civil Service Year Book 1996 cols 677–678.
2  See the Civil Service Year Book 1996 cols 676–677.
3  See the Civil Service Year Book 1996 cols 674–676.
4  See the Civil Service Year Book 1996 cols 681–683.
5  See the Civil Service Year Book 1996 cols 683–685.
6  See the Civil Service Year Book 1996 cols 678–681.
7  See the Civil Service Year Book 1996 cols 673–674.

## (xv)  The Northern Ireland Office

**518. The Secretary of State for Northern Ireland.** The powers of the Governor of Northern Ireland under the Government of Ireland Act 1920 were transferred in 1972 on a temporary basis to the Secretary of State and a Secretary of State for Northern Ireland was appointed to assume responsibility for Northern Ireland affairs. The Secretary of State is a member of the Cabinet and heads a department known as the Northern Ireland Office[1].

1  See paras 67–86 ante.

## (xvi)  The Scottish Office

**519. The Secretary of State for Scotland.** Scottish affairs, that is to say matters of relevance only to Scotland and the Scottish aspects of matters relevant to the United Kingdom, fall within the field of responsibility of the Scottish Office, which is presided over by the Secretary of State for Scotland[1].

1  See paras 51–66 ante.

## (xvii)  The Welsh Office

**520. The Secretary of State for Wales.** Welsh affairs, that is to say matters of relevance only to Wales and the Welsh aspects of matters relevant to the United Kingdom, fall within the field of responsibility of the Welsh Office, which is presided over by the Secretary of State for Wales[1].

1  See paras 41–50 ante.

## (4) THE PRIVY COUNCIL

**521. Meaning of 'Privy Council'.** Since 1708 there has been one Privy Council for Great Britain[1], which superseded the previous Privy Councils for England and Scotland respectively. Unless the contrary intention appears, the use of the term 'Privy Council' in statutes, except when used with reference to Ireland only, means the Lords and others for the time being of Her Majesty's Most Honourable Privy Council[2]. On the Union with Ireland in 1801 the Privy Council for Ireland remained separate from the Privy Council for Great Britain[3], and on the establishment of a separate government for Northern Ireland, a Privy Council for Northern Ireland was established, which, as respects Northern Ireland, entirely succeeded to and took the place of the Privy Council for Ireland[4].

1  Union with Scotland (Amendment) Act 1707 s 1. The Privy Council for Great Britain is to have the same powers and authorities as the Privy Council for England lawfully had and exercised at the time of the Union, and none other: s 1. As to the Judicial Committee of the Privy Council see para 311 ante; and COURTS vol 10 para 767 et seq.
2  See the statement of Lord Grenville in 1807 (9 Parliamentary Debates (1st series) 239).
3  Union with Ireland Act 1800 art 8 s 3 (repealed by the Statute Law (Repeals) Act 1993). His Majesty was empowered to continue the Privy Council of Ireland to be his Privy Council for that part of the United Kingdom called Ireland: art 8 s 3 (repealed).
4  Irish Free State (Consequential Provisions) Act 1922 s 1(1), Sch 1 para 2(1)–(3) (partially repealed by the Northern Ireland Constitution Act 1973 s 41(1)(a), Sch 6, Pt I). No new appointment to the Privy Council for Northern Ireland has been possible since 1973: s 32(3).

**522. Membership of the Privy Council.** The Privy Council is composed of an unlimited number of persons, appointed solely at the pleasure of the Crown on advice from the Prime Minister[1] without formal grant or letters patent and no previous qualification is, in general, legally necessary. With the exception of citizens of the Republic of Ireland, only British citizens are qualified to be privy counsellors[2]. Appointment is for life though a privy counsellor may be removed on advice or at his or her request[3].

The members of the Privy Council[4] are invariably chosen by the Crown from amongst noblemen of high rank, persons who have held or hold high political, judicial or ecclesiastical office, distinguished politicians from other parts of the Commonwealth, persons eminent in science or letters or very senior civil servants. The near relatives of the monarch[5], the archbishops[6], the Prime Minister, the Lord Chancellor[7], the Speaker of the House of Commons[8], the Bishop of London[9], cabinet ministers[10], great officers of State and of Household, the Queen's Private Secretary[11], the Lords of Appeal in Ordinary[12], the Lord Chief Justice[13], the Master of the Rolls[14], the President of the Family Division of the High Court of Justice[15], and the Lords Justices of Appeal[16], are from the nature of their position or offices generally understood to have a claim to appointment[17]. In recent years the leaders of opposition[18] parties have also been appointed so that they can be given classified information 'on privy counsellor terms'[19] should the need arise.

1  As to the Prime Minister see paras 394–398 ante.
2  See the Act of Settlement s 3 (as amended); Status of Aliens Act 1914 s 28, Sch 3 (repealed); British Nationality Act 1948 s 31, Sch 4 Pt I (repealed); Ireland Act 1949 s 3(1)(b). Naturalised British subjects are eligible for appointment: *R v Speyer* [1916] 2 KB 858, CA. As to the citation of the Act of Settlement see para 35 note 3 ante.
3  Mr John Profumo and Mr John Stonehouse were removed from the Privy Council at their own request in 1963 and 1976 respectively: see de Smith and Brazier *Constitutional and Administrative Law* (7th Edn, 1994) p 165n. See further para 524 text and note 7 post.
4  At the date at which this volume states the law, the membership of the Council amounts to some 400 persons. A list of privy counsellors is published annually in Whitaker's Almanack.

5   It seems that near relatives of the monarch are not necessarily required to take the privy counsellor's oath (2 Todd's Parliamentary Government p 55 note (h), citing Haydn *Book of Dignities* pp 120, 129, 137, 145), but are introduced into the Privy Council.

6   It is said that the Archbishops of Canterbury and York claim membership by prescriptive right: see 2 Todd's Parliamentary Government p 161.

7   As to the Lord Chancellor see paras 477–497 ante.

8   As to the Speaker of the House of Commons see PARLIAMENT.

9   As to the Bishop of London see ECCLESIASTICAL LAW.

10  As to the Cabinet see paras 402–413 ante.

11  As to the Queen's Private Secretary see para 547 post.

12  As to the Lords in Appeal in Ordinary see COURTS.

13  As to the Lord Chief Justice see COURTS.

14  As to the Master of the Rolls see COURTS; SOLICITORS.

15  As to the President of the Family Division see COURTS.

16  As to the Lords Justices of Appeal see COURTS.

17  See 2 Todd's Parliamentary Government p 54.

18  As to the Opposition see para 218 ante.

19  See paras 523–524 post.

**523. The privy counsellor's oath.** Privy counsellors are required to take the privy counsellor's oath[1] or an affirmation in lieu of that oath[2]. The substance of the oath is: (1) to be a true and faithful servant of the Crown; (2) not to countenance any word or deed against the monarch, but to withstand the same to the utmost of his power, and to reveal it to the monarch or the Privy Council; (3) to declare his true and faithful opinion upon all matters before the Privy Council; (4) to keep secret all matters revealed or treated of in the Privy Council[3]; (5) not to reveal matters so treated of touching any of his colleagues without the consent of the monarch or the Privy Council; (6) to bear faith and allegiance to the Crown, and to defend its jurisdiction and powers against all foreign princes, persons, prelates, states or potentates; and (7) generally to act in all things as true and faithful servants of the Crown[4].

1   For the form of privy counsellor's oath see the Report of the Oaths Committee 1867 (Parliamentary Paper 1867 vol 31, 84) where a form of declaration recommended in place of the oath is given. As to oaths of office generally see paras 923–927 post. See also the *Report of the Committee of Privy Counsellors on Ministerial Memoirs* (Cmnd 6386) (1976); and Hennessy *Whitehall* (1990 Edn) p 349.

2   See the Oaths Act 1978 ss 5(1)–(4), 6; and EVIDENCE.

3   This obligation to keep revealed matters secret is thought to be the origin of the requirement of confidentiality in the Cabinet, whose members are also privy counsellors (although the decision in *A-G v Jonathan Cape Ltd* [1976] QB 752, [1975] 3 All ER 484, relied not on this reasoning but on the principle of public interest based on the doctrine of collective cabinet responsiblity: see para 417 notes 9–10 ante). The duty of confidentiality also explains the appointment to the Privy Council of leaders of opposition parties and others to whom it may be necessary in the public interest to communicate confidential information. Len Murray, general secretary of the Trades Union Congress, was appointed to the Privy Council so that he could be consulted on the 'social contract' policy of the Labour Government: see Hennessy *Whitehall* (1990 Edn) pp 350–351. As to duties of confidentiality generally see CONFIDENCE AND DATA PROTECTION.

4   See note 1 supra.

**524. Precedence of privy counsellors.** Privy counsellors are called to office by the monarch's invitation, and after taking the oath of allegiance[1] and the privy counsellor's oath[2], or an affirmation in lieu of either of those oaths[3], their names are inscribed in the Privy Council book.

Privy counsellors enjoy no special salary or emoluments, but are entitled to the style of 'Right Honourable' and to precedence, following Knights of the Garter and of the Thistle, next after the eldest sons of barons[4].

The office of privy counsellor is not affected by the demise of the Crown[5], and members of the House of Commons do not vacate their seats upon appointment[6]. Privy counsellors are dismissable at the pleasure of the monarch simply by the striking of their names off the Privy Council book[7].

1   For the form of oath of allegiance see the Promissory Oaths Act 1868 ss 2, 10. The oath of allegiance in this form is taken in lieu of the oath of allegiance, supremacy and abjuration taken by privy counsellors before the passing of the Promissory Oaths Act 1868: s 14(2) (amended by the Statute Law (Repeals) Act 1977). As to oaths of office see paras 923–927 post.

2   As to the privy councillor's oath see para 523 ante.

3   See the Oaths Act 1978 ss 5(1)–(4), 6; para 523 text and note 2 ante; and EVIDENCE.

4   This precedence was conferred by letters patent of 9, 10 and 14 Jac 1.

5   See the Demise of the Crown Act 1901 s 1(1); and CROWN LANDS AND PRIVILEGES.

6   See 174 Parliamentary Debates (3rd series) col 1197, where it is stated that it is customary for a new writ to be issued on the vacation of a seat by acceptance of an office of profit, before admission to the Privy Council.

7   Counsellors were frequently so dismissed in earlier periods of history. Thus, the Duke of Devonshire's name was struck off by George III in 1762, and Fox was struck off in 1798 on Mr Pitt's advice for a seditious speech, although he was later reinstated upon the advice of Lord Grenville: 2 Todd's Parliamentary Government p 53 note (b), citing Haydn *Book of Dignities*. Sir Edgar Speyer was removed from the Privy Council following the 1914–18 war due to his pro-German sympathies: see de Smith and Brazier *Constitutional and Administrative Law* (7th Edn, 1994) p 165n.

**525. Privy Council meetings.** Meetings of the Privy Council ('the Queen in Council'), or of committees of the Privy Council, are summoned[1] by the Clerk of the Council in Ordinary[2]. The monarch presides in person at Privy Council meetings, the Lord President of the Council, who is appointed simply by declaration of the Queen in Council, taking up his position on her right[3]. The monarch is not present at meetings of committees of the Privy Council[4]. Once a minister has accepted a summons to a meeting of the Privy Council this should take precedence over all other engagements[5].

Although orders issued by the Privy Council are still expressed to be made by the Crown with the advice of the Privy Council, the Privy Council itself has ceased to exercise its former deliberative and consultative functions, except through the medium of its committees[6], and meets principally to confer formal approval upon documents, the purport and tenor of which have been previously considered and decided upon by the Cabinet, committees of the Privy Council, or the various ministers and government departments. In the exercise of the manifold powers entrusted to it by statute the Privy Council acts largely as a secondary legislative chamber complementary to Parliament[7].

Other transactions which take place at meetings of the Privy Council are the administration of official oaths, appointments to offices under the Crown by delivery of the various seals, and the 'pricking' of high sheriffs for the current year[8].

All formal acts of the Privy Council are expressed either in the form of Orders in Council, which are authenticated by the signature of the Clerk of the Council, or by proclamations which are signed by the monarch[9].

1   In the case of an ordinary Privy Council the summons runs: 'Let the Messenger acquaint the Lords and others of Her Majesty's Most Honourable Privy Council that a Council is appointed to meet at the Court at Buckingham Palace, on ... day the ... day of this instant, at ... of the clock'. In the case of a committee meeting, the summons is directed to the Lords of the Council, informing them that a committee of their lordships is appointed to meet at the Council Chamber, Whitehall. The quorum for Privy Council meetings is three, but four members are usually summoned. It rests with the Privy Council Office to decide who shall be summoned: *Appendix to the Second Report of the Royal Commission on the Civil Service* (Cd 6535) (1912), evidence of Sir Almeric W FitzRoy, Clerk of the Privy Council, qq 12936, 12955.

2   A deputy may be appointed in the absence of the Clerk of the Council in Ordinary subject to provisions to be made by Order in Council, and the acts of the deputy are to be valid in all respects as the acts of the Clerk in Ordinary himself: Clerk of the Council Act 1859 s 1. The oaths to be taken by the Clerk of the Council and the Keeper of the Council Chamber, for which declarations are recommended to be substituted, are given in the Report of the Oaths Committee 1867 (Parliamentary

Paper, 1867 vol 31, 85). Declarations may be made in place of an oath under the Promissory Oaths Act 1868: see s 12(4); and para 926 post.

3 This is the present practice: cf 2 Anson's Law and Custom of the Constitution (4th Edn, 1935) Pt I p 162. Formerly, it seems, the Chancellor sat on the right, and the President on the left: see 2 Todd's Parliamentary Government pp 58–59. The Lord President of the Council is also Leader of the House of Commons: see the periodically published lists of government; and para 399 text and note 5 ante.

4 As to the form of summons see note 1 supra. The presence of the monarch at committees of the Privy Council where deliberations or consultations take place is now fully recognised as unconstitutional: see the statement of the Earl of Granville in 1864 (175 Parliamentary Debates (3rd series) 251).

5 *Questions of Procedure for Ministers* (Cabinet Office, May 1992) (as now revised: see para 416 note 1 ante) para 2.

6 The Privy Council was originally the Crown's chief advisory council. After the Revolution of 1688 the Cabinet took the place of the Privy Council as chief advisory body, and certain provisions of the Act of Settlement restoring the old deliberative functions to the Privy Council were repealed before the Act came into operation by the Security of the Succession, etc Act 1705 ss 27, 28 (repealed). As to the citation of the Act of Settlement see para 35 note 3 ante.

7 The variety and scope of the matters to which the orders and proclamations relate, and which obtain the force of law without previous parliamentary criticism, are worthy of comment, extending as they do from the regulation of colonial institutions to the formulation of rules relating to the details of domestic administration. Orders in Council are especially used when it is desired to cover the operations of several departments, such as to effect transfers of functions between departments: see para 363 ante. For the documents by which the powers of the Privy Council are exercised see the current Index to Government Orders. See also para 907 post.

8 As to pricking the sheriffs see SHERIFFS vol 42 para 1104.

9 Orders in Council may be, but are not necessarily, statutory instruments. For an example of an Order in Council which is not a statutory instrument see the Civil Service Order in Council 1995 (as amended); and para 549 note 12 ante. Proclamations are published in the London, Edinburgh and Belfast Gazettes as appropriate.

## 526. Privy Council office and committees.

The preparation of business for the Privy Council and its committees is the function of the Privy Council Office, for which the Lord President of the Council is responsible[1]. The Clerk of the Privy Council, who is the permanent head, and the Deputy Clerk of the Council, are appointed by the monarch on his recommendation[2].

To a great extent, the work of the office is of a formal character, such as the preparation of orders for submission to the Queen in Council, but even where, as is usually the case, the orders come from the various departments concerned ready drafted, the labour of printing, reading, editing and issuing them in a final and accurate form devolves upon the officers of the Privy Council[3]. There is also a considerable amount of necessary work in which the Privy Council has the initiative and control[4]. Most of this work in practice is done in the Privy Council Office, at the discretion of the Lord President, and to this extent the office is a real administrative department, which exercises prerogative and statutory powers; but in theory the business of the office is the work of committees of the Privy Council, for which the Lord President acts[5]. Some of the work is, however, actually done by committees, although they do not always meet, but discharge their functions by circulation of papers[6]. Except where they are empowered to act without reference to the Queen in Council, the advice given by committees of the Council is eventually embodied in formal Orders in Council.

Committees of the Privy Council may be appointed at any time by the Crown, on the advice of the Lord President[7], to advise upon particular questions, and in addition to the Judicial Committee[8] by which the Privy Council's appellate jurisdiction is exercised, there are certain standing committees to advise on matters connected with the universities of Oxford and Cambridge[9], Scottish universities[9], constitutional questions affecting the Channel Islands and the Isle of Man, the baronetage[10] and honours[11]. Other functions substantially performed by the Privy Council Office under the prerogative or statutory powers include the granting of charters to charitable, mercantile, learned, scientific, educational or professional bodies whose statutes or byelaws also have to be approved by the Privy Council; the consideration of university statutes[12]; and various statutory functions relating to professions[13].

The Board of Trade was originally established as a committee of the Privy Council[14].

The legal jurisdiction of the Privy Council, which mainly consists in appeals from various courts abroad[15], ecclesiastical appeals[16], and appeals from disciplinary committees for the medical and other professions[17], is exercised by the Judicial Committee of the Privy Council[18].

1  *Appendix to the Second Report of the Royal Commission on the Civil Service* (Cd 6535) (1912), evidence of Sir A W FitzRoy, p 389 at 398: 'The Council Office is the Privy Council in motion'. As to the Lord President's salary see para 423 ante. The Lord President of the Council is ex officio a Church Commissioner: Church Commissioners Measure 1947 s 1(2), Sch 1 para 1 (amended by the Synodical Government Measure 1969 s 2(2); and the Church of England (Miscellaneous Provisions) Measure 1992 s 17(1), Sch 3 para 5); and ECCLESIASTICAL LAW.

2  *Appendix to the Second Report of the Royal Commission on the Civil Service* (Cd 6535) (1912), evidence of Sir A W FitzRoy, q 12988.

3  *Appendix to the Second Report of the Royal Commission on the Civil Service* (Cd 6535) (1912) p 399.

4  *Appendix to the Second Report of the Royal Commission on the Civil Service* (Cd 6535) (1912) q 12820.

5  *Appendix to the Second Report of the Royal Commission on the Civil Service* (Cd 6535) (1912) p 400.

6  *Appendix to the Second Report of the Royal Commission on the Civil Service* (Cd 6535) (1912) qq 12931, 12932.

7  *Appendix to the Second Report of the Royal Commission on the Civil Service* (Cd 6535) (1912) q 12952. Any privy counsellor who is learned in any particular subject may be called upon to give advice to the Privy Council: q 12978.

8  As to the Judicial Committee of the Privy Council see para 311 ante; and COURTS vol 10 para 767 et seq.

9  The standing committees on the universities are established in consequence of the Universities of Oxford and Cambridge Act 1877 s 44 (repealed) (see EDUCATION), and the Universities (Scotland) Act 1889 s 9.

10  *Appendix to the Second Report of the Royal Commission on the Civil Service* (Cd 6535) (1912), evidence of Sir A W FitzRoy, p 400.

11  The Political Honours Scrutiny Committee consists of three privy counsellors who are not members of the government. They report initially to the Prime Minister on the suitability of persons to be recommended for the award of titles and dignities at CBE level and above for political or any other services: see the *Report of the Royal Commission on Honours* (Cmd 1789) (1922). See also the Honours (Prevention of Abuses) Act 1925. Although the name of the committee was unaltered, its function was expanded by the Prime Minister to include examination of recommendations based on non-political services: see 974 HC Official Report (5th series), 26 November 1979, col 880. The Queen must be informed of the committee's view if the Prime Minister proceeds despite the committee's recommendation: see de Smith and Brazier *Constitutional and Administrative Law* (7th Edn, 1994) p 168; and para 832 post.

12  Under the Education Reform Act 1988 s 205 (as amended), the Privy Council was given the task of considering modifications to university statutes submitted to them by the University Commissioners, including the removal of tenure of staff.

13  See eg the Pharmacy Act 1954 ss 3, 11, 15, 16, 22, Sch 1; Medical Act 1983 ss 1, 6–9, 11, 28, 31, 32, 40, 43, 50–53, Sch 1 Pts I, II, III, Sch 4 (as amended); Dentists Act 1984 ss 1, 9, 11, 12, 16, 19, 51, Sch 1 (as amended), Sch 3 (as amended); Opticians Act 1989 ss 1, 8, 12, 13, 16 (as amended), 22 (as amended), 27 (as amended), 31, 33–35, Sch 1; Professions Supplementary to Medicine Act 1960 ss 1–5, 8, 9, 10–12, Sch 1 (as amended), Sch 2 (as amended); Veterinary Surgeons Act 1966 ss 1 (as amended), 3–5, 17, 21–23, 25, Sch 1, Sch 2 Pt I; the Osteopaths Act 1993 ss 1, 11, 14–16, 18, 34–36, 40, Schedule; the Chiropractors Act 1994 ss 1, 10, 14–16, 18, 34–36, 41, Schedule; and MEDICINE.

14  Civil List and Secret Service Money Act 1782 s 15 (repealed). As to the Board of Trade see para 505 ante; and TRADE, INDUSTRY AND INDUSTRIAL RELATIONS vol 47 (Reissue) para 2.

15  See COMMONWEALTH vol 6 (Reissue) para 819, and paragraphs in that title relating to particular countries.

16  See the Pastoral Measure 1983 s 9(2); and ECCLESIASTICAL LAW.

17  See note 13 supra; and MEDICINE.

18  See note 8 supra.

## (5) THE LORD PRIVY SEAL

**527. Status of Lord Privy Seal.** Since the passing of the Great Seal Act 1884, which renders the use of the Privy Seal in all cases unnecessary[1], the office of Lord Privy Seal is a purely honorary one. It usually confers cabinet rank upon its holder, and is utilised for the purpose of enabling a minister to be a member of that body without holding an office to which definite duties are attached or to perform special functions which do not fall within the scope of a department[2]. The salary attaching to the office, which in earlier times was usually unpaid, varies according to whether or not the holder is a member of the Cabinet[3].

1 See the Great Seal Act 1884 s 3 (repealed).
2 The present Lord Privy Seal is Leader of the House of Lords: see the Civil Service Year Book 1996 col 493. In the recent past a holder of the office was responsible for the Civil Service Department under the Prime Minister (ie the Minister for the Civil Service). As to the Civil Service generally see paras 549–564 post. An earlier Lord Privy Seal was Leader of the House of Commons. As to the House of Commons see PARLIAMENT. For the history of the office see 2 Anson's Law and Custom of the Constitution (4th Edn, 1935) Pt I p 171. As to ministers without portfolio see para 354 text and note 27 ante.
3 As to ministerial salaries see para 423 ante.

## (6) NON-MINISTERIAL DEPARTMENTS

**528. Other offices forming part of the Crown.** Apart from the great departments of state, of which the principal political officer is a Secretary of State or a minister, there are many 'non-ministerial departments' and executive agencies, which are staffed by servants of the Crown[1]. Many of these have special relationships with a major ministerial department[2]. Offices forming part of the Crown may come into existence for a temporary purpose[3].

1 Non-ministerial departments are headed by office-holders, boards or commissioners, and often have specific statutory responsibilities. Non-ministerial departments include the Charity Commission, the Crown Estate, Her Majesty's Customs and Excise, the Office of Electricity Regulation, the Export Credits Guarantee Department, the Office of Fair Trading, the Forestry Commission, the Registry of Friendly Societies, the Office of Gas Supply, the Government Actuary's Department, the Health and Safety Commission, Her Majesty's Stationery Office, the Central Office of Information, the Board of Inland Revenue, the Intervention Board, Her Majesty's Land Registry, the Law Commission, the National Investment and Loans Office, the Office of the National Lottery, the Department for National Savings, Ordnance Survey, the Serious Fraud Office, the Office for Standards in Education, the Office of Telecommunications, and the Office of Water Services: see the Civil Service Year Book 1996.
   The Central Statistical Office and the Office of Population Censuses and Surveys have been merged to form a new department, the Office for National Statistics: see the Civil Service Year Book 1996 cols 91, 531; and para 516 ante.
   As to government departments generally see para 360 ante. As to the Civil Service generally see paras 549–564 post. As to the extent of Crown immunity for servants of the Crown see para 388 ante. As to non-departmental public bodies, whose staff are generally not Crown servants, see para 951 et seq post.
2 Eg the relationship between Treasury ministers and the Board of Inland Revenue (see para 709 post); and Treasury ministers and the Commissioners for Customs and Excise (see para 710 post). As to the Treasury ministers see para 515 ante.
3 Eg the Custodian of Enemy Property and Administrators of Enemy Property for particular ex-enemy countries: see the Trading with the Enemy Act 1939 s 7; Distribution of German Enemy Property Act 1949 s 1(3); and WAR.

# (7) LEGAL REPRESENTATIVES AND ADVISERS OF THE CROWN

**529. The Attorney General and the Solicitor General.** The Queen cannot appear in her own courts to support her interests[1] in person, but is represented by her attorney[2], who bears the title of Her Majesty's Attorney General[3].

The Attorney General is primarily an officer of the Crown, and is in that sense an officer of the public[4]. Although he performs to some extent judicial functions[5] both at common law and by statute, he does not constitute a court in the ordinary sense, so that prohibition will not lie against him[6].

In his absence or incapacity, the duties devolve upon the Solicitor General[7]. When the office of Attorney General is vacant or the Attorney General is unable to act through absence or illness or he authorises the Solicitor General to act in a particular case, any functions authorised or required by an enactment to be discharged by the Attorney General may in general be discharged by the Solicitor General[8]. The Solicitor General also represents the Crown where distinct interests require to be separately represented[9].

The offices of Attorney General and Solicitor General are conferred by patent, and are held during pleasure. Neither the Attorney General nor the Solicitor General may engage in private practice[10].

The Attorney General and the Solicitor General are assisted by the Legal Secretariat to the Law Officers, itself headed by a Legal Secretary[11].

In general, the Attorney General and the Solicitor General are consulted before the government is committed to critical decisions involving legal considerations[12].

1 In *R v Gregory* (1672) 2 Lev 82, a declaration *quod dominus rex venit coram domino rege* was allowed after some demur, but characterised by Hale CJ as 'well enough, but unmannerly'.

2 *R v Austen* (1821) 9 Price 142n: 'the King sues by his attorney' or 'the Attorney sues for the King' are only different forms of expressing the same thing. It is the monarch who, by his attorney, gives the court to understand and be informed of the matter which is being brought to its notice: *Wilkes v R* (1770) Wilm 322 at 327, HL; see also *A-G to Prince of Wales v St Aubyn* (1811) Wight 167. See further *A-G v Ellis* (1959) Times, 21 January (injunction to restrain publication of information relating to royal family, in breach of undertaking).

3 Cf note 7 infra. As to the functions of the Attorney General see Edwards *The Law Officers of the Crown* (1964).

4 *A-G v Brown* (1818) 1 Swan 265 at 294; *R v Wilkes* (1770) 4 Burr 2527 at 2570 (on appeal 4 Burr 2576, HL). He may also represent the public: see eg AVIATION vol 2 (Reissue) para 1521.

5 *R v Comptroller-General of Patents, ex p Tomlinson* [1899] 1 QB 909, CA.

6 *Re Van Gelder's Patent* (1888) 6 RPC 22 at 27, CA.

7 The Solicitor General has always been the general deputy of the Attorney General, and subordinate to him: *Wilkes v R* (1770) Wilm 322 at 329–330, HL; 6 Holdsworth's History of English Law pp 462–463, 469–470. He has never had any special connection with the Court of Chancery: 6 Holdsworth's History of English Law (7th Edn) pp 469–470.

8 Law Officers Act 1944 s 1(1). This applies in the case of any enactment passed before 13 July 1944 which makes no provision for enabling the Solicitor General to act in place of the Attorney General or which enables him to act only in certain circumstances (see eg the Explosive Substances Act 1883 s 9(1)), and to any enactment passed since that date which does not provide to the contrary: Law Officers Act 1944 s 1(1)(i), (ii). When the office of Attorney General is vacant, documents, notices, proceedings etc required to be served on or taken against the Attorney General may be served on or taken against the Solicitor General, except in so far as any enactment passed since 13 July 1944 provides to the contrary: s 1(2).

As to the effect of a change of Attorney General during proceedings see *Hamilton v A-G* (1880) 7 LR Ir 223; affd (1881) 9 LR Ir 271, CA.

9 *A-G v Galway Corpn* (1828) 1 Mol 95 at 101n; *A-G v Dean and Canons of Windsor* (1860) 8 HL Cas 369; and see other instances cited in Robertson *Civil Proceedings by and against the Crown* p 15. See also *Ellis v Duke of Bedford* [1899] 1 Ch 494 at 504, 518, CA; *A-G v Duke of Richmond (No 2)* [1907] 2 KB 940.

10 As to their salaries see para 423 text and note 3 ante. Any fees payable to them are carried to the Consolidated Fund: Law Officers Fees Act 1872 s 1. As to the political position of the Attorney General and the Solicitor General see para 537 post.

11 See the Civil Service Year Book 1996 cols 474–475. Proposals that the Legal Secretariat be merged with the Treasury Solicitor's Department to form a single Law Officers' Department, presided over by the

Attorney General, with the Treasury Solicitor as Permanent Secretary and head of a centrally managed Government Legal Service, have not been implemented. As to the proposals for reform see the *Review of Government Legal Services (the Andrew Report)* (Cabinet Office, 1989) ch V.

12　See *Questions of Procedure for Ministers* (Cabinet Office, May 1992) (as now revised: see para 416 note 1 ante) paras 22–26, which set out the circumstances in which the Law Officers should normally be consulted by ministers or their officials. By convention, written opinions of the Law Officers, unlike other ministerial papers, are generally made available to succeeding administrations, but should not be disclosed outside government without their authority: *Questions of Procedure for Ministers* (Cabinet Office, May 1992) (as so revised) para 24. As to ministerial records see para 409 text and note 7 ante; and as to the duty of confidentiality see para 417 ante.

**530. Other law officers.** The Crown is represented in Scotland by separate law officers under the titles of the Lord Advocate and the Solicitor General for Scotland[1]. The Attorney General has precedence of the Lord Advocate, even on the hearing of a Scottish appeal in the House of Lords[2].

There is no longer a separate Attorney General for Northern Ireland[3]; the Attorney General by virtue of his office is Attorney General for Northern Ireland[4], and the Solicitor General acts for him when necessary as in England[5].

There are separate law officers for the Duchy of Lancaster[6], the County Palatine of Durham[7] and the Duchy of Cornwall[8].

1　As to the law officers of the Crown in Scotland see para 63 ante. See also the Civil Service Year Book 1996 col 881.
2　*A-G v Lord Advocate* (1834) 2 Cl & Fin 481 at 485, HL.
3　As to the office of Attorney General for Northern Ireland see the Government of Ireland Act 1920 s 8(3), (4) (repealed); the Supreme Court of Judicature (Northern Ireland) Order 1921, SR & O 1921/1802, art 2(2); the Office of Attorney General Act (Northern Ireland) 1923 (NI); and the Northern Ireland (Temporary Provisions) Act 1972 s 1 (expired). See also para 75 ante.
4　Northern Ireland Constitution Act 1973 s 10(1).
5　See ibid s 10(2), (3).
6　See para 538 post; and the Civil Service Year Book 1996 col 18.
7　See para 539 post.
8　The Attorney General of the Duchy of Cornwall is the legal agent of the Prince of Wales: see the Civil Service Year Book 1996 col 17; and CROWN LANDS AND PRIVILEGES.

**531. The Attorney General in the courts.** The Attorney General is the head of the Bar[1], and has precedence over all Queen's Counsel[2]. However, generally speaking he has no greater legal rights than other members of the Bar, in so far that he or any person appointed to act for him must conform to the rules of the court in which the proceeding in which he is engaged takes place, the courts exercising over him the same authority that they exercise over every other suitor or his advocate[3]. He would not be permitted to prosecute any proceeding which was merely vexatious, or which had no legal object[4]; and where the representatives of the Crown claim to be on a different footing from the subject as regards procedure they must clearly establish their claim[5].

In the eyes of the court the Attorney General's opinion is entitled to no more authority than that of any other member of the Bar[6]. No general right of reply on the part of the Attorney General is recognised by the courts[7]. Admissions by the Attorney General bind the Crown as to matters of fact, but not as to matters of law[8]. It appears that the court has no power to compel the Attorney General to be examined as a witness[9].

The Attorney General represents the Crown in the courts in all matters in which rights of a public character come into question[10]. He must be plaintiff in any civil proceedings by the Crown unless an authorised government department sues in its own name and may be defendant in any civil proceedings against the Crown unless an authorised government department is clearly the appropriate defendant[11]. He is a necessary party to the assertion of public rights even where the moving party is a private individual[12]; although it is otherwise where a public body has a private right of action peculiar to itself as, for example, for maintaining the quality of a commodity supplied to the public[13]; and again where a private person can show that he has suffered special damage to a private right over and above any injury suffered by the general public[14]. He is generally a necessary party to charity proceedings, in order to represent the beneficial interest, or the objects, of the charity[15]. The Attorney General has a right of intervention at the invitation or with the permission of the court in a private suit whenever it may affect the prerogatives of the Crown, including its relations with foreign states, or raises any question of public policy on which the executive may have a view which it may desire to bring to the notice of the court[16]. The Attorney General can be sued, as representing the Crown, for a declaration of right[17]. On an application for a declaration of adoption or legitimacy, the court may at any stage of the proceedings, of its own motion or on the application of any party to the proceedings, direct that all necessary papers in the matter be sent to the Attorney General; and the Attorney General, whether or not he is sent papers in relation to an application for such a declaration, may intervene in the proceedings in such manner as he thinks necessary or expedient, and argue before the court any question in relation to the application which the court considers it necessary to have fully argued[18].

1    *R v Comptroller-General of Patents, ex p Tomlinson* [1899] 1 QB 909, CA.

2    See BARRISTERS vol 3(1) (Reissue) para 434.

3    Eg the Attorney General has no right to usurp the functions of the judge in directing the jury as to the law.

4    *R v Prosser* (1848) 11 Beav 306; see also *R v Home* (1778) 20 State Tr 651 at 740, HL; *R v Hunt* (1820) 1 State Tr NS 171 at 315; *Tobin v R* (1863) 32 LJCP 216 at 224.

5    *A-G to Prince of Wales v Crossman* (1866) LR 1 Exch 381 at 386; and see *Nireaha Tamaki v Baker* [1901] AC 561 at 576, PC.

6    *R v Hunt* (1820) 1 State Tr NS 171.

7    This is clearly so in the House of Lords: *Lord Advocate v Lord Dunglas* (1842) 9 Cl & Fin 173, HL; see also *O'Connell v R* (1844) 11 Cl & Fin 155 at 185, HL. In the Queen's Bench Division, there is doubt. In *R v Treasury Lords Comrs, ex p Lord Brougham* (1851) 16 QB 357, the Attorney General was heard in reply on his suggestion that the reply should be by consent, but on condition that it should be considered neither an exercise of the right on the part of the Crown, nor an acknowledgment on his part as Attorney General that such a right did not exist; see also *R v Archbishop of Canterbury* (1848) 11 QB 483 at 560n. For the practice in revenue cases see *Marquis of Chandos v IRC* (1851) 6 Exch 464 at 478; and Robertson *Civil Proceedings by and against the Crown* pp 12–13. In the Admiralty Court a reply was allowed in *The Parlement Belge* (1879) 4 PD 129 at 144; on appeal (1880) 5 PD 197, CA. As to the Chancery Division, it was said in *Hilton v Lord Granville* (1847) 2 New Pract Cas 262 that as a matter of prerogative the Attorney General has a general right of reply on behalf of the Crown when a motion is made in which the Crown is directly interested. In criminal cases the Attorney General's right of reply in trials on indictment was abolished by the Criminal Procedure (Right of Reply) Act 1964 s 1(1)(a). A right of reply has been exercised in opposing proceedings for prerogative remedies: *R v Commanding Officer 39th Battalion Royal Fusiliers, ex p Kutchinsky* (2 March 1918, unreported). See generally CROWN PROCEEDINGS.

8    *A-G v Bagg* (1658) Hard 125 at 129; *Wall v Pennington* (1660) Hard 170.

9    *R v Home* (1778) 20 State Tr 651 at 740, HL.

10    See eg CHARITIES vol 5(2) (Reissue) paras 473–480.

11    Crown Proceedings Act 1947 s 17(2), (3), (4); and see CROWN PROCEEDINGS.

12    *A-G v Shrewsbury (Kingsland) Bridge Co* (1882) 21 ChD 752; *A-G v Ashbourne Recreation Ground* [1903] 1 Ch 101; *A-G v Wimbledon House Estate Co Ltd* [1904] 2 Ch 34; *Boyce v Paddington Borough Council* [1903] 2 Ch 556, CA (revsd on other grounds sub nom *Paddington Corpn v A-G* [1906] AC 1, HL); *A-G v Bastow* [1957] 1 QB 514, [1957] 1 All ER 497; *A-G v Smith* [1958] 2 QB 173, [1958] 2 All ER 557. It has been said that the jurisdiction of the Attorney General to decide in what cases it is proper for him to sue on behalf of relators is absolute; and, certainly, his jurisdiction has not yet been successfully reviewed in the courts: see *LCC v A-G* [1902] AC 165, HL; *Gouriet v Union of Post Office Workers* [1978] AC 435, [1977] 3 All ER 70, HL. As to the review by the courts of prerogative powers see paras 379–380 ante. As to relator actions generally see PRACTICE AND PROCEDURE. *Gouriet v Union of Post Office Workers* supra concerned the highly unusual procedure of using civil proceedings to enforce the criminal law, and it has been said that only the Attorney General should be permitted to follow that

procedure: see Wade and Forsyth *Administrative Law* (7th Edn, 1994) pp 606–607, 700–702. See also *Ashby v Ebdon* [1985] Ch 394, [1984] 3 All ER 869. See the different approach adopted by the House of Lords on standing to bring judicial review proceedings of governmental powers: *IRC v National Federation of Self-Employed and Small Businesses Ltd* [1982] AC 617, [1981] 2 All ER 93, HL.

13   *LCC v South Metropolitan Gas Co* [1904] 1 Ch 76, CA, where in an action by plaintiffs against the company (incorporated under private Acts) for a declaration affirming their rights to test the quality of gas supplied to the public on Sundays, and for an injunction restraining the defendants from interfering, it was held that the Attorney General was not a necessary party.

14   See *Ex p Island Records Ltd* [1978] Ch 122, [1978] 3 All ER 824, CA.

15   *Ware v Cumberlege* (1855) 20 Beav 503; *Hauxwell v Barton-upon-Humber UDC* [1974] Ch 432, [1973] 2 All ER 1022; see CHARITIES vol 5(2) (Reissue) para 473.

16   *Adams v Adams (A-G intervening)* [1971] P 188, [1970] 3 All ER 572.

17   See *Dyson v A-G* [1911] 1 KB 410, CA; *Dyson v A-G* [1912] 1 Ch 158, CA. As to declarations in proceedings against the Crown see the Crown Proceedings Act 1947 s 21; and CROWN PROCEEDINGS.

18   Family Law Act 1986 s 59(1), (2). See CHILDREN AND YOUNG PERSONS vol 5(2) (Reissue) para 722.

**532. Law officers and Parliament.** The Attorney General and Solicitor General are summoned, together with the judges, to attend the House of Lords at the beginning of every Parliament[1].

When a peerage claim is made by petition to the Crown, the petition is referred to the Attorney General. If he is satisfied that a prima facie case has been established, he generally advises the Crown to refer it to the House of Lords, which refers it to the Committee of Privileges for report. The Attorney General attends the hearing before the committee both as assistant, by virtue of his writ of attendance, and as protector of the interests of the Crown as fountain of honour[2].

The Attorney General acts as prosecutor for both Houses of Parliament. In the case of offences directly concerning the House of Commons, the House directs the Attorney General to prosecute; in the case of offences not directly concerning the House, the House addresses to the Crown a request that the Attorney General be directed to prosecute[3].

1   They are summoned as members of the ancient concilium regis (4 Co Inst 4), their places being among those persons who are under the degree of a baron of Parliament: House of Lords Precedence Act 1539 s 8. Although they are summoned to Parliament, their opinion is not taken by the House of Lords sitting as the highest appellate tribunal. For the history of their summons, effect and practice see 206 HL Official Report (5th series), 19 November 1957, cols 377–382. As to the House of Lords see para 204 ante; and generally PARLIAMENT.

2   *Barony of Saye and Sele Case* (1848) 1 HL Cas 507 at 511n. It is said that the Attorney General is entitled to sit within the bar: *Barony of Saye and Sele Case* supra. See generally COURTS; PEERAGES AND DIGNITIES.

3   See Erskine May *Parliamentary Practice* (21st Edn, 1989) p 111 and journals there referred to. As to the House of Commons see generally PARLIAMENT.

**533. Nolle prosequi.** The Crown, being always present in court, cannot be nonsuited[1], but the Attorney General has power to enter a nolle prosequi on any indictment[2], and can do so without calling upon the prosecutor to show cause why that should not be done[3]. The right to enter a nolle prosequi in civil proceedings no longer exists[4].

1   Bro Abr, Nonsuit, 68; and see para 305 ante.

2   Until the abolition of criminal informations (see the Criminal Law Act 1967 s 6(6)), the Attorney General could also enter a nolle prosequi on any information. For an early instance of the entering of a nolle prosequi see 4 Co Inst 20. For a more recent instance see (1951) 101 L Jo 225. See generally Edwards *The Law Officers of the Crown* (1964) p 226 et seq.

3   *R v Allen* (1862) 1 B & S 850. A nolle prosequi can only be entered by or on the authority of the Attorney General, not by a private prosecutor (*R v Dunn* (1843) 1 Car & Kir 730). See, however, *R v Rowlands* (1851) 17 QB 671. It can be entered after, as well as before, verdict: *R v Leatham* (1861) 7 Jur NS 674. See also CRIMINAL LAW.

4   Ie in consequence of the Crown Proceedings Act 1947. See the former RSC Ord LXVIII r 1(c) (revoked). For a statement of the former right see *R v Evans* (1819) 6 Price 480 at 481.

**534. Criminal matters.** In connection with the administration of the criminal law, the Attorney General and Solicitor General were formerly included in the commission of the peace for every county[1], but this is no longer the case[2]. The Attorney General may be instructed to prosecute in important cases, and his consent may be required before certain criminal proceedings may be undertaken[3].

1 See the Order in Council dated 22 February 1878, Schedule, r 1 (amended by SI 1969/1070) (revoked).
2 See the Crown Office (Forms and Proclamations Rules) Order 1992, SI 1992/1730, r 2, Schedule Pt II Forms A to D (amended by SI 1996/276).
3 See eg the Prevention of Terrorism (Temporary Provisions) Act 1989 s 19. See also CRIMINAL LAW vol 11(1) (Reissue) para 639.

**535. Trial at bar.** The Attorney General is entitled to demand a trial at bar[1] as of right in civil actions[2] where the Crown is interested[3], but the practice seems now to have fallen into disuse. There is no longer that right in criminal cases, and all proceedings on indictment must be brought before the Crown Court[4].

1 Trial at bar is a trial by jury before two or more judges.
2 The Attorney General's right to claim a trial at bar is expressly preserved by the Crown Proceedings Act 1947: see ss 19(3), 40(2)(g). His application for a trial at bar cannot be refused, the court relying on his discretion: *A-G v Walsh* (1832) Hayes & Jo 65. The rule for a trial at bar when granted on the Attorney General's application is absolute in the first instance (*Paddock v Forrester* (1840) 1 Man & G 583), but it is open to the other party to show subsequently that the Attorney General has been misinformed, and that the Crown is not interested, whereupon the rule will be set aside (*Dixon v Farrer* (1886) 18 QBD 43, CA). The court had power to make the order at the instance of a private prosecutor, even though the Attorney General declined to interfere: *Anderson v Gorrie* (1894) 10 TLR 383, CA. The right to trial at bar was not taken away by the Judicature Acts, the trial being thereafter by a divisional court: *Anderson v Gorrie* supra; *Dixon v Farrer* supra.
3 The Crown's interest need not be such as to affect its property directly, or the property of the Crown as head of the state: *Lord Bellamont's Case* (1700) 2 Salk 625; *Dixon v Farrer* (1886) 18 QBD 43, CA. The Attorney General is entitled to a trial at bar where the interests of the Crown as Duke of Lancaster come into question: *Brown v Lord Granville* (1835) 1 Har & W 270.
4 See the Supreme Court Act 1981 s 46(1).

**536. The Attorney General's administrative functions.** The Attorney General's certificate or fiat is necessary in many cases before proceedings in which the Crown may be interested can be initiated[1], and many statutes provide that prosecutions for offences under them cannot be instituted without the consent or certificate of the Attorney General or Solicitor General[2], or that proceedings require consultation with or some action by the Attorney General[3]. The Attorney General's decision is conclusive[4], so that no mandamus will lie to compel him to grant a fiat except in the event of his refusing to hear an application[5]. However, the fiat cannot be arbitrarily withheld[6].

1 See PRACTICE AND PROCEDURE. An example is a relator action: see Wade and Forsyth *Administrative Law* (7th Ed, 1994) pp 601–610.
2 See eg the Prevention of Corruption Act 1906 s 2(1); and the Solicitors Act 1974 s 42(2). For a full list see the current Index to the Statutes in Force under the heading 'Attorney General'.
3 See eg the Charities Act 1993 s 33(7) (information sent to Attorney General with a view to proceedings by him): see CHARITIES vol 5(2) (Reissue) para 468.
4 *R v Comptroller-General of Patents, ex p Tomlinson* [1899] 1 QB 909, CA; *Ex p Newton* (1855) 4 E & B 869.
5 *Ex p Newton* (1855) 4 E & B 869; *Ex p Costello* (1868) IR 2 CL 380; *Ex p Blackburn* [1956] 3 All ER 334, [1956] 1 WLR 1193, CA (affd 40 Cr App Rep 131, HL).
6 See CROWN PROCEEDINGS.

**537. Political position.** The Attorney General and Solicitor General, and the Lord Advocate and Solicitor General for Scotland, are members of the administration[1], and are the Crown's principal advisers on points of law[2]. They are usually members of the House of Commons, but not included in the Cabinet; however, there have been exceptional cases of an Attorney General in the Cabinet, and law officers have at different times been out of Parliament[3]. The Lord Advocate alone is necessarily, under the present practice, a member of the Privy Council[4]. The Attorney General is by virtue of that office also the Attorney General for Northern Ireland[5].

1   In performing his non-political functions, such as entering a nolle prosequi to stop a trial of an indictable offence, or giving leave to institute certain classes of criminal proceedings, the Attorney General by convention exercises an independent discretion, not dictated by his colleagues in the government, though he may consult them in a case with political implications: see de Smith and Brazier *Constitutional and Administrative Law* (7th Edn, 1994) p 413.

2   For that purpose the Attorney General and Solicitor General are assisted by the Legal Secretariat to the Law Officers, composed of a small number of civil servants: see the Civil Service Year Book 1996 cols 474–475.

3   Eg Sir Douglas Hogg, Attorney General, was a member of the Cabinet from 1924–29; Sir William Jowitt, Attorney General, was without a seat in 1931, and Sir Henry Slesser, Solicitor General, was without a seat in 1924. The Solicitor General for Scotland is not invariably a member of the House of Commons; eg neither W I Stewart QC (appointed in 1972) nor John McCluskey QC (appointed in 1974) were members. See also 1 Lowell's Government of England p 133 note 3. As to the House of Commons see PARLIAMENT. As to the Cabinet see paras 402–413 ante.

4   As to the Privy Council see paras 521–526 ante.

5   See para 530 ante.

## 538. The Attorney General of the Duchy of Lancaster.

The Attorney General of the Duchy of Lancaster is appointed by patent under the seal of the Duchy of Lancaster[1] to represent the interests of the Crown in respect of the Duchy[2]. He is disqualified for membership of the House of Commons[3].

1   *A-G of Duchy of Lancaster v Duke of Devonshire* (1884) 14 QBD 195. As to the counties palatine see para 307 ante. As to the Duchy of Lancaster see CROWN LANDS AND PRIVILEGES.

2   The Court of Chancery of the County Palatine of Lancaster was merged with the High Court by the Courts Act 1971 s 41. A Court of Duchy Chamber still exists, at least in theory.

3   House of Commons Disqualification Act 1975 s 1, Sch 1 Pt III. As to the House of Commons see PARLIAMENT.

## 539. County Palatine of Durham.

Within the County Palatine of Durham the interests of the Crown are represented by the Attorney General or Solicitor General of the County Palatine of Durham[1]. It is apprehended that similar principles are applicable to the law officers of the County Palatine of Durham as in the case of the Attorney General of the Duchy of Lancaster[2].

1   The Court of Chancery of the County Palatine of Durham and Sadberge was merged with the High Court by the Courts Act 1971 s 41. As to the counties palatine see para 307 ante. See also CROWN LANDS AND PRIVILEGES.

2   See para 538 ante.

## 540. Solicitors to public departments.

All persons appointed to act as solicitors on behalf of the Crown under the directions of the Treasury, Inland Revenue, or Commissioners of Customs and Excise, or of any commissioners or other persons having the management of any other branch of the revenue[1], and the Solicitor of the Ministry of Agriculture, Fisheries and Food[2], may act and practise as solicitors in any place within the United Kingdom without complying with the conditions to which solicitors are ordinarily subject as to admission, certificates or otherwise[3]. In addition to these persons, the solicitors to the Post Office, the Admiralty and the War Office were exempted from the provisions of the Solicitors Act 1843[4]. Solicitors to public departments, including the department of the Church Commissioners[5], and the clerks or officers appointed to act for the solicitors of those public departments, were generally exempted from the provisions of the Attorneys and Solicitors Act 1874[6]. The person appointed to act as solicitor to the Duchy of Cornwall is entitled to practise as the solicitor for the affairs of the duchy without conforming to the regulations imposed upon solicitors by the Solicitors Acts[7].

1   Revenue Solicitors' Act 1828 s 1. See also the Attorneys and Solicitors Act 1874 s 12, and the Solicitors Act 1860 s 33 (both repealed; but see note 3 infra). Pleadings served by a person purporting to have been appointed solicitor on behalf of the Crown under the direction of the Inland Revenue Commissioners cannot be treated as a nullity because they do not contain an allegation to the effect that revenue matters are in question: *West v Taunton* (1830) 6 Bing 404.

2   Small Holding Colonies Act 1916 s 9 (amended by the Statute Law (Repeals) Act 1973); Ministry of Agriculture and Fisheries Act 1919 s 1(1); Transfer of Functions (Ministry of Food) Order 1955, SI 1955/554, art 3(1). As to the Ministry of Agriculture, Fisheries and Food see paras 435–437 ante.

3   The Solicitors Act 1974 provides that nothing in that Act is to prejudice or affect any rights or privileges of the solicitor to the Treasury, any other public department, the Church Commissioners or the Duchy of Cornwall, or require any such officer or any clerk or officer appointed to act for him to be admitted or enrolled or to hold a practising certificate in any case where it would not have been necessary for him to be admitted or enrolled or to hold that certificate if the Act had not been passed: s 88(1).

4   Solicitors Act 1843 s 47 (repealed). See note 3 supra.

5   See the Church Commissioners Measure 1947 s 15(2); and ECCLESIASTICAL LAW.

6   Attorneys and Solicitors Act 1874 s 12 (repealed); see note 3 supra. The section exempted clerks or officers from the penalties imposed upon persons who were not duly qualified, but did not expressly confer the right to act and practise as a solicitor in any court. Even though he is not a barrister or solicitor, any officer or other person authorised by the Commissioners of Customs and Excise may conduct proceedings relating to customs or excise before a magistrates' court or examining justices and any person admitted as a solicitor and employed by the commissioners may act as a solicitor in such proceedings in England, Wales or Northern Ireland, even though he does not hold a practising certificate: Customs and Excise Management Act 1979 s 155. As to clerks or officers of the Commissioners of Inland Revenue see also the Inland Revenue Regulation Act 1890 s 27 (amended by the Finance Act 1896 s 38); and see generally SOLICITORS.

7   Stannaries Act 1855 s 31. See note 3 supra.

**541. The Treasury Solicitor.** The Treasury Solicitor is a corporation sole, his official style being that of Solicitor for the affairs of Her Majesty's Treasury[1]. He has perpetual succession by that name, with a capacity to acquire and hold in that name land, government securities, shares in any public company, securities for money and real and personal property of every description[2]. He has capacity to sue and be sued, to execute deeds, make leases, to enter into engagements binding on himself and his successors in office, and to do all other acts necessary or expedient to be done in the execution of the duties of his office[3]. He has an official seal, and any document purporting to be sealed with that seal is receivable in evidence of the particulars stated in it[4].

The Treasury Solicitor acts for the Crown in matters falling within his department, including probate matters in which the Crown has an interest[5]. He may also, by direction of the Crown, act in cases where a person in a public capacity is a party to proceedings in which the Crown has an interest[6]. He acts as solicitor for and is the proper person to serve in respect of legal proceedings against those authorised government departments who do not have their own departmental solicitors[7]. He is also the Queen's Proctor[8].

The Treasury Solicitor's Department, the expenses of which are provided by Parliament[9], has Advisory and Litigation Divisions, a Bona Vacantia Division, a Resources and Services Division and a Lawyers' Management Unit[10]. The department also provides legal services to the Treasury, the National Heritage Department, the Office of Public Service, the Department for Education and Employment, the Ministry of Defence, and the Department of Transport[11]. The Treasury Solicitor's Department has an executive agency, Government Property Lawyers[12], which provides conveyancing and lands advisory services to departments and public bodies.

1 Treasury Solicitor Act 1876 s 1. As to the Treasury see paras 512–517 ante. As to corporations sole see CORPORATIONS.
2 Ibid s 1.
3 Ibid s 1.
4 Ibid s 1.
5 For the Treasury Solicitor's duties in connection with the administration of the property of intestates to which the Crown has become entitled see ibid ss 2, 4, 7 (amended by the Administration of Estates Act 1925 s 30(4)); Treasury Solicitor (Crown's Nominee) Rules 1931, SR & O 1931/1097 (amended by SI 1968/1521). The statutory provisions requiring administrators to produce sureties do not apply where administration is granted to the Treasury Solicitor: Supreme Court Act 1981 s 120(5). For the provisions applicable where administration of a deceased's estate is granted to a nominee of the Crown, whether the Treasury Solicitor or a person nominated by the Treasury Solicitor, see the Administration of Estates Act 1925 s 30; and EXECUTORS. As to the Treasury Solicitor's duties in connection with the property and rights of dissolved companies to which the Crown has become entitled as bona vacantia (ie under the Companies Act 1985 s 654) see the Companies Act 1985 ss 656–657; and COMPANIES. For cases where the Treasury Solicitor was constituted a trustee of forfeited property see *Re ex-Tsar of Bulgaria* (1919) 35 TLR 714; and *Re ex-Tsar of Bulgaria* (1919) 36 TLR 9; both cases revsd on appeal, but not on a point affecting those functions, sub nom *Re Ferdinand, ex-Tsar of Bulgaria* [1921] 1 Ch 107, CA.
6 *Brownsea Haven Properties Ltd v Poole Corpn* [1958] Ch 574 at 581, [1958] 1 All ER 205, CA. The Treasury Solicitor is by virtue of his appointment a qualified solicitor, and, therefore, a litigant for whom he acts as solicitor by direction of the Crown is entitled to recover costs: *R v Archbishop of Canterbury* [1903] 1 KB 289 at 292, CA; but see *Re Eastwood, Lloyds Bank Ltd v Eastwood* [1975] Ch 112, [1973] 3 All ER 1079 (profit costs not allowed on taxation).
The Treasury Solicitor is a trust corporation for the purposes of the Law of Property Act 1925, the Settled Land Act 1925, the Trustee Act 1925, the Administration of Estates Act 1925, and the Supreme Court Act 1981: see the Law of Property (Amendment) Act 1926 s 3(1) (amended by the Supreme Court Act 1981 s 152(1), Sch 5). For his duties in relation to Crown proceedings see the Crown Proceedings Act 1947 ss 17, 18; and CROWN PROCEEDINGS.
7 See ibid s 17; and CROWN PROCEEDINGS.
8 As to the Queen's Proctor see para 545 post.
9 See the *Supply Estimates 1995–96 for the year ending 31 March 1996* (HC Paper (1994–95) no 271–IX).
10 See the Civil Service Year Book 1996 col 686 et seq.
11 See the Civil Service Year Book 1996 col 686 et seq.
12 Formerly the Treasury Solicitor's Conveyancing Division, and now relocated to Taunton under the recommendations of the *Review of Government Legal Services (the Andrew Report)* (Cabinet Office, 1989). See further the *Next Steps Review 1995* (Cm 3164) (1995) p 256. See also the Civil Service Year Book 1996 col 691. Proposals that the Legal Secretariat be merged with the Treasury Solicitor's Department have not been implemented: see para 529 note 11 ante. As to executive agencies see para 551 post.

**542. The Duchy Solicitor.** The Duchy Solicitor is a corporation sole, his official style being that of Solicitor for the affairs of the Duchy of Lancaster[1]. He stands in the same relation to the affairs of the duchy as the Treasury Solicitor to the other affairs of the Crown, and for the execution of his duties has much the same powers[2].

1 Duchy of Lancaster Act 1920 s 3(1). As to the counties palatine see para 307 ante. As to the Duchy of Lancaster see CROWN LANDS AND PRIVILEGES. As to corporations sole see CORPORATIONS.
2 Ibid s 3 (amended by the Administration of Estates Act 1925 s 30(4)); and the Statute Law (Repeals) Act 1981 s 1(1), Sch 1 Pt I); see also the Administration of Estates Act 1925 s 55(1)(xxv); and para 541 ante. The statutory provisions requiring administrators of deceased persons' estates to produce sureties do not apply where administration is granted to the Duchy Solicitor: Supreme Court Act 1981 s 120(5); and see EXECUTORS. The Duchy Solicitor is a trust corporation for the purposes of the Law of Property Act 1925, the Settled Land Act 1925, the Trustee Act 1925, the Administration of Estates Act 1925, and the Supreme Court Act 1981: see the Law of Property (Amendment) Act 1926 s 3 (amended by the Supreme Court Act 1981 s 152(1), Sch 5). The Intestates Estates Act 1884 s 8 applies the Act to the Duchy of Lancaster in the case of deaths occurring before 1 January 1926. See also *Re Best's Goods* [1901] P 333; and EXECUTORS.

**543. Assistant solicitors.** An assistant solicitor for the affairs of Her Majesty's Treasury, on behalf of the Treasury Solicitor, may take any oath, make any declaration, verify any account, execute any deed or do any act or thing which the Treasury Solicitor, in the exercise of his duties as Treasury Solicitor, is required or authorised under Act of Parliament or otherwise to take, make, verify, execute or do[1].

The assistant solicitor for the affairs of the Duchy of Lancaster may act in exactly the same way on behalf of the Duchy Solicitor[2].

1   Treasury Solicitor Act 1876 s 3.
2   Duchy of Lancaster Act 1920 s 3(4).

**544. The Crown Prosecution Service.** The Crown Prosecution Service[1] is headed by the Director of Public Prosecutions[2], who acts under the superintendence of the Attorney General[3]. It is the duty of the Director of Public Prosecutions (1) to take over the conduct of all criminal proceedings, other than specified proceedings[4], instituted on behalf of a police force[5]; (2) to institute and have the conduct of criminal proceedings in any case where it appears to him that the importance or difficulty of the case makes it appropriate that proceedings should be instituted by him or it is otherwise appropriate for proceedings to be instituted by him[6]; (3) to take over the conduct of all binding over proceedings instituted on behalf of a police force[7]; (4) to take over the conduct of all proceedings concerning forfeiture of obscene articles[8]; (5) to give, to such extent as he considers appropriate, advice to police forces on all matters relating to criminal offences[9]; (6) to appear for the prosecution, when directed by the court to do so, on appeals under certain provisions[10]; (7) to discharge such other functions as the Attorney General may from time to time assign[11].

The Director of Public Prosecutions is appointed by the Attorney General[12], and must have a ten year general qualification[13]. The Director of Public Prosecutions may designate as a Crown Prosecutor[14] any member of the Crown Prosecution Service who has a general qualification[15]; he must divide England and Wales into areas, which may be varied from time to time[16], and for each area he must designate a Chief Crown Prosecutor responsible for supervising the operation of the Crown Prosecution Service in that area[17].

The Director of Public Prosecutions issues a Code for Crown Prosecutors[18] giving guidance on general principles to be applied (a) in determining whether proceedings for an offence should be instituted or discontinued, or what charges should be preferred[19]; and (b) in considering, in any case, representations to be made about the mode of trial suitable for that case[20].

1   The Crown Prosecution Service was set up in 1986 under the Prosecution of Offences Act 1985 Pt I (ss 1–15). See generally CRIMINAL LAW vol 11(1) (Reissue) para 645 et seq; and see also the Lord Chancellor's and Law Officers' Departments Annual Report: *The Government's Expenditure Plans 1995–96 to 1997–98* (Cm 2809) (1995).
2   See the Civil Service Year Book 1996 col 109; and CRIMINAL LAW vol 11(1) (Reissue) para 637. The office of Director of Public Prosecutions was created by the Prosecution of Offences Act 1879. In 1884 the director's duties were transferred to the Treasury Solicitor (Prosecution of Offences Act 1884 s 2 (repealed)), but in 1908 the office was reconstituted and separated from that of the Treasury Solicitor (Prosecution of Offences Act 1908 s 1(1)). For a general discussion of the office of Director of Public Prosecutions see Edward *The Law Officers of the Crown* (1964) p 367.
3   Prosecution of Offences Act 1985 s 3(1). As to the submitting of an annual report to the Attorney General which is laid before Parliament see s 9; and CRIMINAL LAW vol 11(1) (Reissue) para 641. As to the Attorney General see para 529 et seq ante.
4   Ie proceedings which fall within any category for the time being specified by order made by the Attorney General for the purposes of ibid s 3: s 3(3). See further CRIMINAL LAW vol 11(1) (Reissue) para 646.
5   Ibid s 3(2)(a).
6   Ibid s 3(2)(b).
7   Ibid s 3(2)(c).
8   Ie all proceedings begun by summons issued under the Obscene Publications Act 1959 s 3: Prosecution of Offences Act 1985 s 3(2)(d).
9   Ibid s 3(2)(e).

10  Ibid s 3(2)(f). As to the relevant provisions see CRIMINAL LAW vol 11(1) (Reissue) para 646.
11  Ibid s 3(2)(g).
12  Ibid s 2(1).
13  Ie a ten year general qualification within the meaning of the Courts and Legal Services Act 1990 s 71: Prosecution of Offences Act 1985 s 2(2) (substituted by the Courts and Legal Services Act 1990 s 71(2), Sch 10 para 60). A person has a general qualification if he has a right of audience in relation to any class of proceedings in any part of the Supreme Court, or all proceedings in county courts or magistrates' courts: Courts and Legal Services Act 1990 s 71(3)(c).
14  As to Crown Prosecutors generally see CRIMINAL LAW vol 11(1) (Reissue) para 647.
15  Prosecution of Offences Act 1985 s 1(3).
16  Ibid s 1(5).
17  Ibid s 1(1)(b), (4).
18  The Director of Public Prosecutions may from time to time make alterations in the code: ibid s 10(2). The provisions of the code, and any alteration, must be set out in the his report to the Attorney General (see note 3 supra): s 10(3).
19  Ibid s 10(1)(a).
20  Ibid s 10(1)(b).

**545.  The Queen's Proctor.** The Queen's Proctor represents the Crown in maritime[1] and matrimonial causes. Under the present practice the office is always held by the Treasury Solicitor[2].

In every case of a petition for divorce, nullity proceedings or a petition for presumption of death and dissolution of marriage the court may, if it thinks fit, direct all necessary papers in the matter to be sent to the Queen's Proctor, who is required, under the Attorney General's directions, to instruct counsel to argue before the court any question in relation to the matter which the court considers it necessary or expedient to have fully argued[3]. The Queen's Proctor is entitled to charge the costs of these proceedings as part of the expenses of his office[4].

Where the Queen's Proctor is invited to assist the court by attending to argue a question of law as amicus curiae, he does not become a party to the suit and accordingly he has no right of appeal[5].

At any time during the progress of the proceedings or before the decree is made absolute, any person not a party to the suit[6], or the trial judge[7], may give information to the Queen's Proctor on any matter material to the due decision of the case, and the Queen's Proctor may then take such steps as the Attorney General considers necessary or expedient[8].

If during the progress of a suit the court decides to send information to the Queen's Proctor, the court can either pronounce a decree nisi or adjourn the proceedings, if it considers that the information available at that stage is not sufficient for a decree to be pronounced[9].

Under the directions of the Attorney General and by leave of the court, the Queen's Proctor has power to intervene in a cause[10] before the decree nisi has been pronounced, in which case the court gives directions that the Queen's Proctor be represented at the hearing and as to the part to be taken by him in the proceedings[11]. After the pronouncement of a decree nisi but before the decree is made absolute the Queen's Proctor may also, under the Attorney General's directions, show cause why the decree should not be made absolute by reason of material facts not having been brought before the court[12].

In any case in which the Queen's Proctor intervenes or shows cause against the decree nisi the court may make such order as to costs as may be just[13].

1  This includes prize, as to which see ADMIRALTY vol 1(1) (Reissue) para 351; and PRIZE.
2  As to the Treasury Solicitor see para 541 ante.
3  Matrimonial Causes Act 1973 ss 8(1)(a), 15, 19(4); and see DIVORCE vol 13 para 1001 et seq.
4  Ibid ss 8(3)(a), 15, 19(4).

5 *Day v Day* [1957] P 202, [1957] 1 All ER 848.
6 *Squires v Squires* [1959] 2 All ER 85, [1959] 1 WLR 483.
7 *Middlebrook v Middlebrook* [1965] P 262, [1965] 1 All ER 404.
8 Matrimonial Causes Act 1973 ss 8(1)(b), 15, 19(4): see DIVORCE vol 13 para 1003 et seq.
9 *Middlebrook v Middlebrook* [1965] P 262, [1965] 1 All ER 404. On a petition for divorce it is the court's duty to inquire, so far as it reasonably can, into any facts alleged by the petitioner and the respondent: see the Matrimonial Causes Act 1973 s 1(3); and DIVORCE.
10 Under the directions of the Attorney General he may have the proceedings watched: *Hudson v Hudson* (1875) 1 PD 65.
11 *Sloggett v Sloggett* [1928] P 148. Before this decision it was thought that he could not be given leave to intervene unless collusion were suspected, but this case made it clear that intervention was not confined to this class of case.
12 Matrimonial Causes Act 1973 ss 9(1), 15, 19(4); see DIVORCE.
13 Ibid ss 8(2), 15, 19(4).

## (8) THE OFFICERS OF THE HOUSEHOLD

**546. The royal household.** The various offices connected with the royal household, which were originally of an hereditary nature, and descendible in certain families, have long ceased to be such[1]; and, except with regard to the forms and ceremonies observed at the coronation of the monarch, when the privileges of some of the ancient hereditary officers are still exercisable subject to allowance by the Court of Claims[2], the duties and functions connected with it are now performed by persons appointed for that purpose by the monarch, and selected in part, as to the principal offices, from among the members of the party in power, either in the Lords or Commons[3].

Moreover, until the beginning of the twentieth century it was generally recognised as the constitutional practice[4] that the principal officers of the household should be included in the political arrangements made on a change of administration, and retire from office with the party to which they owed their appointment[5], the offices, when filled, to which this rule applied being, it was said[6], those of the Lord Steward, the Lord Chamberlain, the Vice-Chamberlain, the Master of the Horse, the Treasurer of the Household, the Comptroller of the Household, the Captain of the Corps of Gentlemen at Arms, the Captain of the Corps of Yeomen of the Guard, the Chief Equerry or Groom in Waiting, and the Lords in Waiting[7]. In 1924 it was decided[8] that the only officers to go out with a change of government should be the Treasurer, the Comptroller, and the Vice-Chamberlain of the Household, who are government whips, and Lords in Waiting[9].

1 The officers of the household originally formed the first circle round the monarch, and in them is to be found the first elements of a ministry of state: see 1 Stubbs's Constitutional History of England p 343. The principal officers in the Norman household appear to have been the treasurer, chamberlain, steward, butler, constable and marshal, and these eventually became hereditary (eg see 1 Stubb's Constitutional History of England pp 344–345, 353–354), whilst as to certain of them duplicate offices were created for state or ministerial purposes (eg the treasurer: see 1 Stubbs's Constitutional History of England p 355). Certain of the latter now only appear at the coronation ceremonies: see CROWN LANDS AND PRIVILEGES.

However, some of the offices connected with, although not today part of, the actual royal household still exist and descend by inheritance, eg the Lord Great Chamberlain and the Earl Marshal, both of whom are numbered among the great officers of state. The principal instance of the separation of offices for state and domestic purposes is the Lord Chamberlain and the Lord Great Chamberlain.
2 See CROWN LANDS AND PRIVILEGES.
3 The principal officers are for the most part peers or members of the House of Commons: 2 Todds' Parliamentary Government p 723. As to the House of Commons see PARLIAMENT. As to the House of Lords see para 204 ante; and PARLIAMENT.
4 This usage appears to have become recognised from the reign of George III: see 1 Todd's Parliamentary Government pp 188–189.
5 As to offices connected with the coronation see CROWN LANDS AND PRIVILEGES.
6 2 Todd's Parliamentary Government pp 163–164.

7　The list also included the offices of the Clerk Marshal and the Master of the Buckhounds, now defunct.

8　The reference is to a 'gentleman's agreement' made in 1924 by which it was decided that the monarch should nominate to all the household posts except three of the Lords in Waiting and the Treasurer, Comptroller and Vice-Chamberlain of the Household, the latter three being ex-officio government whips in the House of Commons and therefore political; that the names of the other three Lords in Waiting and of the three great officers of state (the Lord Chamberlain, the Lord Steward and the Master of the Horse), although selected by the monarch, should continue to be submitted by the Prime Minister; and that these non-political members of the household should undertake not to speak or vote against the government and not to engage in political activities: see Nicolson *King George V* (1952) pp 390–391.

9　The remaining offices were to be in the monarch's personal gift. In recent years the Captain of the Corps of Gentlemen at Arms and the Captain of the Corps of Yeomen of the Guard have acted with the Lords in Waiting as government whips in the House of Lords and have thus become political appointments changing with the government.

## 547. The monarch's Private Secretary.

The Private Secretary to the monarch is appointed by the monarch personally[1] and paid by her out of money granted to her under the Civil List[2]. It is the Private Secretary's function to keep the monarch informed on all current topics and on all basic issues in order to enable her to exercise her right to be consulted by ministers and to encourage and warn them[3]; and for this purpose the Private Secretary makes himself acquainted with relevant periodical and other literature. Whilst he is not a constitutional adviser to the monarch, who is under no duty to follow such advice as he may give, he is at liberty to obtain information from any source, including members of parties who are not included in the government of the day. In so doing he must preserve the same political impartiality as the monarch herself is expected to exercise. His activity as an impartial go-between has been and may be of critical importance in a constitutional crisis[4].

1　The Private Secretary is also Private Secretary of the Queen of Australia, of Canada, of New Zealand and of each other member of the Commonwealth remaining within Her Majesty's Dominions. He is made a member of the Privy Council, at the monarch's request. As to the Privy Council see paras 521–526 ante. The Prime Minister of the United Kingdom plays no part in the choice of appointment of a Private Secretary.

2　See CROWN LANDS AND PRIVILEGES.

3　See Bagehot *The English Constitution* (1963 Edn) p 111.

4　As to the monarch's Private Secretary see generally Jennings *Cabinet Government* (3rd Edn, 1959) pp 59, 343; Wheeler Bennett *King George VI: His Life and Reign* (1958) pp 817–823; Emden *Behind the Throne*; and see also para 355 note 1 ante. General Grey was gazetted as the Queen's Private Secretary in 1867 (see Emden *Behind the Throne* p 148). This appears to have been the first express recognition of the office. Sir Herbert Taylor had in effect been Private Secretary for a few years from 1805, and later held a similar position under William IV; and the task was subsequently performed continuously by Prince Albert or other officers of the household. William III had used Lord Sunderland in very much the same capacity.

## 548. The Mistress of the Robes.

In the case of a queen regnant, the practice generally accepted as constitutional appears to be that, in addition to the regular offices of the household[1], the Mistress of the Robes and the Ladies of the Bedchamber should be included in the political arrangements made on a change of administration, where those offices are held by ladies connected with outgoing ministers, but not where, as at the present day, they are held by ladies without any political connection[2]. However, this rule does not appear always to have been strictly enforced[3].

1　As to the royal household see para 546 ante.

2　Difficulties arose as to the change of household officers by the Prince Regent on the attempted formation of a ministry by Lord Moira in 1812, although the constitutional principle appears to have been recognised both by the Prince Regent and in Parliament, where it was stated that a change in the particular circumstances was not deemed advisable: see 23 Official Report (1st series) col 453. The bedchamber question in 1839 led to Sir Robert Peel's abandonment of the task of forming a ministry, the Queen having declined to comply with his request for a change of the ladies of the household: see

47 Official Report (3rd series) cols 983, 985, 987. A minute drawn up by the Melbourne ministry expressed the view that it was reasonable for the efficiency and stability of the administration, and for giving those marks of the constitutional support of the Crown which were required to enable it to act usefully to the public service, that the great officers of the court and situations in the royal household held by members of Parliament should be included in the political arrangements made on a change of administration, but that a similar principle should not be applied to the offices held by ladies of Her Majesty's household: 47 Official Report (3rd series) col 1001. Two years later, when Sir Robert Peel was again called to office, the principle affirmed by him appears to have been accepted as constitutional by Queen Victoria.

3  See 2 Anson's Law and Custom of the Constitution (4th Edn, 1935) Pt I p 137, citing Gladstone *Gleanings of Past Years* p 40.

# (9) THE CIVIL SERVICE

## (i) In general

**549. The Civil Service generally.** The Civil Service[1] comprises the Home Civil Service and the Diplomatic Service. In general, the staff of all government departments, other than the Foreign and Commonwealth Office, are members of the Home Civil Service. The Foreign and Commonwealth Office[2] is staffed partly by members of the Diplomatic Service (who also serve in British diplomatic missions abroad) and partly by members of the Home Civil Service.

Civil servants are 'servants of the Crown, other than holders of judicial or political offices, who are employed in a civil capacity and whose remuneration is paid wholly and directly out of moneys voted by Parliament'[3]. This excludes ministers of the Crown, the staff of the two Houses of Parliament[4], members of the armed forces, the police, local government, nationalised industries and the National Health Service[5]. The two principal roles of the Civil Service are support for ministers on policy matters and the management and provision of public services[6].

The Minister for the Civil Service[7] has power to make regulations or give instructions for controlling the conduct of the Home Civil Service and providing for the classification, remuneration and other conditions of service of persons serving in it[8]. The Secretary of State for Foreign and Commonwealth Affairs has similar power in respect of the Diplomatic Service, subject to the concurrence of the Minister for the Civil Service regarding such matters as salaries, allowances and pensions[9]. The Civil Service is generally under the control of the Treasury, with the Office of Public Service[10]. For the most part[11] the regulations which govern the Civil Service have no statutory basis, and are made under the prerogative[12].

1  As to the Civil Service generally see Armstrong 'The Role and Character of the Civil Service' (56 Proceedings of the British Academy 209, 221); Parris *Constitutional Bureaucracy* (1969); Hennessy *Whitehall* (1990 Edn); *Report of the Committee on the Civil Service* (Cmnd 3638) (1968) (the 'Fulton Report').

2  As to the Foreign and Commonwealth Office see paras 459–462 ante.

3  *Report of the Committee on the Civil Service* (Cmnd 3638) (1968) App A; see also the Crown Proceedings Act 1947 s 2(6) (as amended); and CROWN PROCEEDINGS.

4  The staff of the two Houses of Parliament hold office on terms virtually identical with those applying to the Civil Service, but the staff of the House of Commons are employed by the House of Commons Commission and are not therefore servants of the Crown: House of Commons (Administration) Act 1978 ss 2, 5(2); Erskine May *Parliamentary Practice* (21st Edn, 1989) p 192; the Clerk of the Parliaments in the House of Lords is appointed by the Crown by letters patent, and he employs most other staff of the House of Lords, who are therefore not civil servants: see the Clerk of Parliaments Act 1824 ss 2, 5 (both as amended).

5   The size of the Civil Service was 732,000 in 1979, 565,000 in January 1993, and 524,000 in January 1995, with the likelihood of further significant reduction in the four years following: see *The Civil Service: Taking Forward Continuity and Change* (Cm 2748) (1995) para 3.17.

6   *The Civil Service: Continuity and Change* (Cm 2627) (1994) para 1.3. The Civil Service Code states that 'The constitutional and practical role of the Civil Service is, with integrity, honesty, impartiality and objectivity, to assist the duly constituted government, of whatever political complexion, in formulating policies of the government, carrying out decisions of the government and in administering public services for which the government is responsible': para 1. As to the code see para 554 note 1 post.

7   As to the Minister for the Civil Service see paras 427 ante, 550 post.

8   See the Civil Service Order in Council 1995 art 10 (amended by the Civil Service (Amendment) Order in Council 1995). As to Orders in Council see further note 12 infra.

9   Diplomatic Service Order 1991 art 5; Minister for the Civil Service Order 1968, SI 1968/1656, art 2. See also para 459 ante.

10  Except for the period 1968–1981, when the general control of the service was transferred to a newly created Civil Service Department, thereby implementing the recommendations of the *Report of the Committee on the Civil Service* (Cmnd 3638) (1968) (the 'Fulton Report'): see the Minister for the Civil Service Order 1968, SI 1968/1656; and the Minister for the Civil Service Order 1971, SI 1971/2099. In 1981, the Civil Service Department was abolished, and its functions divided between the Treasury and a newly created Management and Personnel Office within the Cabinet: Treasury and Civil Service Committee *Reports 1980–81* (Cmnd 8170) (1981); Transfer of Functions (Minister for Civil Service and Treasury) Order 1981, SI 1981/1670. The Treasury regained control over manpower, pay, allowances and pensions. The Management and Personnel Office was concerned with organisation, overall efficiency, recruitment, training and personnel management: see *Efficiency in the Civil Service* (Cmnd 8293) (1981). The Management and Personnel Office was itself abolished in 1987 (Transfer of Functions (Minister for Civil Service and Treasury) Order 1987, SI 1987/2039), with the Treasury effectively reassuming the control it exercised before 1968. The Prime Minister remains the Minister for the Civil Service: see para 427 ante. See also para 550 post. As to the Treasury see paras 512–517 ante.

11  For an exception see the Deregulation and Contracting Out Act 1994; and para 553 post.

12  Eg the Civil Service Order in Council 1982, and the Civil Service Order in Council 1991 (both as amended). As at 8 July 1996, the operative Order in Council is the Civil Service Order in Council 1995 (amended by the Civil Service (Amendment) Order in Council 1995; and the Civil Service (Amendment) Order in Council 1996). See *Council of Civil Service Unions v Minister for the Civil Service* [1985] AC 374, [1984] 3 All ER 935, HL, particularly at 409, 950 per Lord Diplock. For the status of the regulations see also Wade and Bradley *Constitutional and Administrative Law* (11 Edn, 1993) pp 296–297.

   Civil Service Orders in Council are not listed as statutory instruments, but copies are obtainable from the Privy Council Office. The 1995 Order (as amended) is set out as Annex A to the Introduction to the Civil Service Management Code (1996). As to the Civil Service Management Code (1996) see para 554 note 1 post.

   The government retains an open mind about legislation in some limited areas, particularly with regard to rules concerning the terms and conditions of employment of civil servants and the Civil Service Code: see *The Civil Service: Taking Forward Continuity and Change* (Cm 2748) (1995) para 2.16.

**550. The structure and organisation of the Civil Service.** Responsibility for the Civil Service is now divided between the Treasury and the Office of Public Service, which is part of the Cabinet Office[1]. The Cabinet Secretary is the Head of the Home Civil Service and advises the Prime Minister in his capacities as head of government and Minister for the Civil Service[2].

In 1853 the Northcote-Trevelyan Report[3] recommended changes which led in due course to the creation of a modern, cohesive, unified and politically impartial Civil Service, with competitive entry and freedom from political interference. Following the Fulton Report in 1968[4], which recommended that 'all civil servants should be organised in a single grading structure', considerable progress towards common pay and grading arrangements was made, giving rise to the Senior Open Structure (Grades 1, 1A, 2 and 3), Grade 4, Grades 5–7, professional, technical and scientific grades, executive and support grades, clerical and secretarial grades and industrial staff[5].

However, the Civil Service continues to undergo radical change, inspired by a desire to achieve efficiency and cost effectiveness, and an improved service to the public[6]. The emphasis has moved away from organisational uniformity, towards a federal structure of more autonomous units[7], with a small central core of civil servants involved in policy making and servicing ministers[8]. There has now been established the Senior Civil Service, broader then the Senior Open Structure, in which apart from Permanent Secretary there are no central grades[9]. Individual departments and agencies have power to decide which posts are included in the Senior Civil Service[10]. Below the Senior Civil Service departments and agencies have power to make their own grading and pay structures[11].

The Civil Service Commissioners are appointed by Her Majesty in Council, and hold office during pleasure. They have functions relating to recruitment and selection practices[12], approval of appointments in the Senior Civil Service[13] and the hearing and determination of appeals under the Civil Service Code[14]. Their functions may be exercised by the First Civil Service Commissioner or such other of them as he authorises, or by any officer of the Commissioners authorised by them[15]. The Commissioners may from time to time authorise other persons to perform specified functions[16]. They are subject to investigation by the Parliamentary Commissioner for Administration[17], but actions taken in respect of appointments and certain other matters may not be investigated[18].

1   See the Transfer of Functions (Minister for the Civil Service and Treasury) Order 1991, SI 1991/188; the Transfer of Functions (Treasury and Minister for the Civil Service) Order 1995, SI 1995/269. As to the Treasury see paras 512–517 ante; and as to the Office of Public Service see para 430 ante. As to the Minister for the Civil Service see para 427 ante. See also the *Fifth Report of the Treasury and Civil Service Committee: The Role of the Civil Service* (HC Paper (1993–94) no 27) paras 228–243, especially at para 231. See also note 2 infra.

2   See the *Fifth Report of the Treasury and Civil Service Committee: The Role of the Civil Service* (HC Paper (1993–94) no 27) para 243. The Minister for the Civil Service has power to make regulations and give instructions concerning the number and grading of posts in the Civil Service, the classification of posts and employees, pay and conditions (such as retirement, redundancy reinstatement and re-employment of persons, and redeployment of staff): Civil Service Order in Council 1995 art 10(a). As to the Civil Service Order in Council 1995 see para 549 note 12 ante.

3   The text of the 1853 report is reproduced at Appendix B of the Fulton Report (as to which see note 4 infra).

4   See the *Report of the Committee on the Civil Service* (Cmnd 3638) (1968) (the 'Fulton Report') paras 67, 198.

5   See the former Civil Service Management Code (1994). The current such code is the Civil Service Management Code (1996) (see para 554 note 1 post).

6   See the remarks of Sir Robin Butler, Head of the Home Civil Service and Cabinet Secretary, in giving evidence before the Treasury and Civil Service Committee: '[the Civil Service] has had to change because the world outside is changing…Parliament and the public expect it to change…Parliament and the public want to see a Civil Service that improves the service which it gives to the public, that is the aim of all of this. If one looks outside, one sees delegation going on, so that decisions are made near the point of delivery of services, so that there is the greatest possible competition for the provision of those services, so that it is done efficiently and the taxpayer's money is used to best effect' (*Fifth Report of the Treasury and Civil Service Committee: The Role of the Civil Service* (HC Paper (1993–94) no 27-II), Q 1351.

7   See para 551 post.

8   Policy work is estimated to engage about 10% of the current Civil Service: *The Civil Service: Continuity and Change* (Cm 2627) (1994) para 2.5.

9   See the Civil Service Management Code (1996) para 6.1.

10  See ibid para 5.1.1.

11  Ibid para 7.1.1. For a rationale see *The Civil Service: Continuity and Change* (Cm 2627) (1994) para 3.23 et seq. Fears have been expressed that the introduction of performance-related pay could undermine the ethos of the Civil Service and undermine political impartiality: *First Report of the Committee on Standards in Public Life* (Cm 2850) (1995) para 3.48.

12  See the Civil Service Order in Council 1995 art 4; and para 556 post.

13  See ibid art 5, Schs 1, 2 (art 5 amended, and Sch 1 substituted, by the Civil Service (Amendment) Order in Council 1996).

14  Civil Service Order in Council 1995 art 4(5) (added by the Civil Service (Amendment) Order in Council 1995). As to the Civil Service Code see para 554 note 1 post.

15  Civil Service Order in Council 1995 art 9(1).

16  See ibid art 9(2).

17  Parliamentary Commissioner Act 1967 s 4(1), Sch 2 (substituted by the Parliamentary and Health Services
    Commissioners Act 1987 s 1(1), and s 1(2), Sch 1 respectively).

18  Parliamentary Commissioner Act 1967 s 5(3), Sch 3 para 10 (amended by the Parliamentary and Health
    Services Commissioners Act 1987 s 1(3)(c); and the Parliamentary Commissioner Order 1983,
    SI 1983/1707).

**551. Executive agencies in the Civil Service.** Many of the structural reforms
produced by the Fulton Report[1] have been abandoned, but recommendations for
'accountable management' and the call for an inquiry into the possibility of hiving off
functions[2] to executive boards or agencies have been resurrected in a new guise in the
context of the 'next steps' initiative[3] resulting in a Civil Service with a federal structure
of more or less autonomous units[4] known as executive or 'next steps' agencies[5]. Staff in
the 'next steps' agencies remain civil servants[6] and within the diversity of functions are
said to be unified by the five fundamental values, namely: impartiality, integrity,
objectivity, selection and promotion on merit, and accountability through ministers to
Parliament[7]. Each agency operates within a framework document and business plan. Key
performance targets are set annually by the appropriate minister and are announced to
Parliament. Each agency has a chief executive, directly accountable to the minister. The
majority of chief executives are appointed through open competition[8]. Pay and grading
are gradually being devolved to the agencies themselves[9]. The delegation to departments
and agencies of employment matters has been facilitated by the Civil Service
(Management Functions) Act 1992[10]. The privatisation of government functions is kept
under review at the time of the review of each agency, now every five years[11].

1   Ie the *Report of the Committee on the Civil Service* (Cmnd 3638) (1968) (the 'Fulton Report').

2   See *The Reorganisation of Central Government* (Cmnd 4506) (1970) para 14 envisaging 'a sustained effort to
    ensure that…executive blocks of work will be delegated to accountable units of management, thus
    lessening the load on departmental top management'. The first such units were: the Civil Aviation
    Authority (1971); the Procurement Executive (1971); the Property Services Agency (1972); the
    Manpower Services Commission (1974); the Royal Ordnance Factories (1974); and the Royal Mint
    (1975): see Giddings (ed) *Parliamentary Accountability: A Study of Parliament and Executive Agencies* (1995)
    ch 1. The Efficiency Unit (see para 432 ante) undertook a series of small scale efficiency scrutinies in
    government departments, most notably the Department of the Environment's Management Information
    System for Ministers (MINIS), in 1980. In 1982, the government launched the Financial Management
    Initiative, whose aims were, in summary, that each department should define its objectives and set up
    systems to measure performance in relation to those objectives and should develop a well defined
    responsibility for making the best use of their resources, including a scrutiny of output and value for
    money: see *Efficiency and Effectiveness in the Civil Service: Government observation on the Third Report of the
    Treasury and Civil Service Select Committee* (Cmnd 8616) (1982) para 13. As to the accountability to
    Parliament of executive agencies see para 226 ante.

3   The terms of reference of the enquiry led by Sir Robin Ibbs leading to the publication of the report of
    the Efficiency Unit to the Prime Minister *Improving Management in Government: The Next Steps* (Efficiency
    Unit of the Cabinet Office, 1988) were: 'to assess the progress achieved in managing the Civil Service;
    to identify what measures had been successful in changing attitudes and practices; to identify institutional,
    administrative, political and managerial obstacles to better management and efficiency that still remain;
    and to report to the Prime Minister on what further measures should be taken'. The next steps initiative
    has generally been carried out without a full parliamentary debate since the need for legislation has, with
    the exception of trading funds under the Government Trading Act 1990 (see paras 743–751 post), been
    considered and rejected, and the reforms have been achieved by administrative means. The government
    has, however, undertaken to consider a Civil Service Act in the context of contracts of employment for
    civil servants and the Civil Service Code introduced in 1995 (see para 554 note 1 post): see *The Civil
    Service: Taking Forward Continuity and Change* (Cm 2748) (1995) para 2.16. Nevertheless, the development
    of the 'next steps' programme has been subject to a good deal of parliamentary scrutiny: see the *Eighth
    Report of the Treasury and Civil Service Committee: Civil Service Management Reform: The Next Steps*
    (HC Paper (1987–88) no 494); the *Fifth Report of the Treasury and Civil Service Committee: Developments in
    the Next Steps Programme* (HC Paper (1988–89) no 348); the *Seventh Report of the Treasury and Civil Service
    Committee: The Next Steps Initiative* (HC Paper (1990–91) no 496); the *Sixth Report of the Treasury and Civil*

*Service Committee: The Role of the Civil Service: Interim Report* (HC Paper (1992–93) no 390); and the *Fifth Report of the Treasury and Civil Service Committee: The Role of the Civil Service* (HC Paper (1993–94) no 27).

4    See the report of the Efficiency Unit to the Prime Minister *Improving Management in Government: The Next Steps* (Efficiency Unit of the Cabinet Office, 1988) para 12: '...the advantages which a unified Civil Service are intended to bring are seen as outweighed by the practical disadvantages, particularly beyond Whitehall itself. [The Efficiency Unit was told that] the advantages of an all-embracing pay structure are breaking down, that the uniformity of grading frequently inhibits effective management and that the concept of a career in the Civil Service has little relevance for most civil servants whose horizons are bounded by their local office or, at most, by their department'. See also at para 44: 'The aim should be to establish a quite different way of conducting the business of government. The central Civil Service should consist of a relatively small core engaged in the function of servicing ministers and managing departments, who will be the 'sponsors' of particular policies and services. Responding to these departments will be a range of agencies employing their own staff, who may or may not have the status of Crown servants, and concentrating on the delivery of their particular service, with clearly defined responsibilities between the Secretary of State and the Permanent Secretary on the one hand and the Chairmen or Chief Executives of the agencies on the other. Both departments and their agencies should have a more open and simplified structure'.

5    See the report of the Efficiency Unit to the Prime Minister *Improving Management in Government: The Next Steps* (Efficiency Unit of the Cabinet Office, 1988) para 21: 'once the policy objectives within the framework are set, the management of the agency should then have as much independence as possible in deciding how those objectives are met. A crucial element in the relationship would be a formal understanding with ministers about the handling of sensitive issues and the lines of accountability in a crisis. The presumption must be that, provided management is operating within the strategic direction set by ministers, it must be left as free as possible to manage within that framework'. By December 1995, there were 109 agencies, and in addition 23 executive units of HM Customs and Excise and 27 executive offices of the Inland Revenue which work on 'next steps' lines, employing 69% of the Civil Service (over 360,000 staff). These are listed in *Next Steps Review 1995* (Cm 3164) (1995); and the Civil Service Year Book 1996 pp lxxix–xc.

6    *Next Steps Review 1995* (Cm 3164) (1995). See also *The Civil Service: Taking Forward Continuity and Change* (Cm 2748) (1995) para 2.1.

7    See *The Civil Service: Continuity and Change* (Cm 2627) (1994) paras 1.3, 2.7, restating the evidence of Sir Robin Butler, Secretary to the Cabinet and Head of the Home Civil Service, to the Treasury and Civil Service Committee. The statement of these values was adopted in the *Fifth Report of the Treasury and Civil Service Committee: The Role of the Civil Service* (HC Paper (1993–94) no 27) para 72; and see *The Civil Service: Taking Forward Continuity and Change* (Cm 2748) (1995) para 2.2. The Public Service Committee recommended that framework documents should specify more precisely the respective roles of ministers and agency chief executives, and that the government should invite select committees to comment on framework documents and agency corporate plans before thay are published and when they are reviewed: *Second Report of the Public Service Committee: Ministerial Accountability and Responsibility* (HC Paper (1995–96) no 313–I) paras 122–123

8    See *Career Management and Succession Planning Study* (Efficiency Unit, 1993) (the 'Oughton Report'); and *Next Steps Review 1995* (Cm 3164) (1995). As to the role of the Civil Service Commissioners see para 550 ante. See also the government's response to the recommendations made in *The Civil Service: Taking Forward Continuity and Change* (Cm 2748) (1995) at pp 39–40; and the Office of Public Service and Science Memorandum to the Treasury and Civil Service Committee (HC Paper 1994–95) no 27). The Office of Public Service and Science is now the Office of Public Service: see para 430 ante.

9    By 1 April 1995, 29 agencies and the two revenue departments, over 60% of the Home Civil Service, had delegated responsibility for their own pay and pay-related conditions of service. On 1 April 1996, responsibility for pay and grading of staff below senior levels was delegated to all departments and agencies: see *Next Steps Review 1995* (Cm 3164) (1995) p 12; and *The Civil Service: Taking Forward Continuity and Change* (Cm 2748) (1995) para 3.15.

10   See para 552 post.

11   In order to ensure that the widest range of views are taken into account when an agency is reviewed, these reviews are publicly announced, to enable those with an interest in the agency and its work to contribute to the discussion of its future organisation and status. Each review is announced in Parliament and the responsible department issues a press notice: *Next Steps Review 1995* (Cm 3164) (1995) pp III–X.

By November 1995 a number of agencies had been privatised including 'Forward', the Civil Service catering organisation ('because there does not seem to be any good reason for the Treasury to be in the sandwich-making business'), the Driver Vehicles and Operators Information Technology Agency and the National Engineering Laboratory. Warren Spring Laboratory merged with AEA Technology in 1994 to create a new National Environmental Technology Centre within the Atomic Energy Authority. The government has announced its intention to transfer to the private sector the Crown

Agents (see para 461 ante), the Electrical Equipment Certification Service, the Transport Research Laboratory and the Laboratory of the Government Chemist: see the *Fifth Report of the Treasury and Civil Service Committee: The Role of the Civil Service* (HC Paper (1993–94) no 27) para 177; and *The Civil Service: Taking Forward Continuity and Change* (Cm 2748) (1995) para 3.8. The privatisation of public functions remains controversial: 'It would be ironic if the single most successful Civil Service reform programme of recent decades came to be regarded by the government which initiated it simply as a transitional phase. We believe that the value of Agency status as an instrument for improving efficiency and quality of service in the Civil Service would be considerably reduced if Agency status came to be seen principally as a staging post to the private sector': *Fifth Report of the Treasury and Civil Service Committee: The Role of the Civil Service* (HC Paper (1993–94) no 27) para 179. See also *The Civil Service: Taking Forward Continuity and Change* (Cm 2748) (1995) at p 32. See also the possible effects of the Deregulation and Contracting Out Act 1994 Pt II (ss 69–79), considered by Freedland 'Privatising Carltona: Part II of the Deregulation Act 1994' [1995] Public Law 21.

**552. Management functions.** A minister of the Crown[1] in whom is vested a function delegated by Her Majesty with respect to the management of Her Majesty's Home Civil Service which has been the subject of a transfer of functions order[2], may, to such extent and subject to such conditions[3] as he thinks fit, delegate the function to any other servant of the Crown[4]. Without prejudice to any rule of law with respect to carrying out of functions under the authority of a person in charge of a government department, where a function is so delegated otherwise than to such a person, the person to whom the function is delegated may, subject to the terms of the delegation, authorise a servant of the Crown for whom he is responsible to carry out the function on his behalf[5].

The minister whose sanction is required for the exercise of any statutory power which (1) relates to the appointment or management of members of Her Majesty's Home Civil Service, and (2) requires for its exercise the sanction of a minister of the Crown (whether by way of approval, consent, agreement or otherwise) may, to such extent and subject to such conditions as he thinks fit[6], authorise its exercise without his sanction[7]. Where by virtue of any statutory provision the sanction required for the exercise of such a power itself requires the sanction (whether by way of approval, consent, agreement or otherwise) of a minister of the Crown, the power is exercisable subject to the approval of that minister[8].

1   'Minister of the Crown' has the same meaning as in the Ministers of the Crown Act 1975 s 8(1) (see para 363 ante): Civil Service (Management Functions) Act 1992 s 3(2).
2   'Transfer of functions order' means an Order in Council under the Ministers of the Crown (Transfer of Functions) Act 1946 s 1 (repealed) or the Ministers of the Crown Act 1975 s 1 (see para 363 ante): Civil Service (Management Functions) Act 1992 s 1(5).
3   Without prejudice to this provision, such conditions may include a condition prohibiting, to such extent as may be specified in the condition, the carrying out of the function under the authority of the person to whom it is delegated: ibid s 1(3).
4   Ibid s 1(1), (2). See paras 363–365 ante.
5   Ibid s 1(4).
6   Without prejudice to this provision, such conditions may include a condition prohibiting, to such extent as may be specified in the condition, the exercise of the power concerned under the authority of the person by whom it is exercisable: ibid s 2(3).
7   Ibid s 2(1), (2).
8   Ibid s 2(4).

**553. Market testing in the Civil Service.** Under a programme known as the Competing for Quality programme[1], government departments are to conduct market testing in order to establish, for certain activities, where it is possible for them to be performed either by public servants or by the private sector, which alternative presents the better value for money[2]. Where the activity is transferred to the private sector, the accountability of ministers to Parliament remains unchanged[3]. Part II of the Deregulation and Contracting Out Act 1994[4] empowers ministers to make orders to facilitate the contracting out of functions exercised by government[5].

1 See the White Paper *Competing for Quality: Buying Better Public Services* (Cm 1730) (1991), launched as part of the Citizen's Charter initiative. As to the Citizen's Charter see para 431 ante.
2 It has been argued that the programme does not take sufficient account of the intangible benefits of the Civil Service ethos: 'the programme would undermine public service values, including impartiality, integrity and confidentiality, and the wider commitment to public service rather than private gain': see the *Fifth Report of the Treasury and Civil Service Committee: The Role of the Civil Service* (HC Paper (1994–95) no 27) paras 180–195. In the period up to 30 September 1993, the government set itself the target of market testing activities valued at £1,449 million and involving over 44,000 civil servants. The exercise fell considerably short of target, although by the end of September 1993 it had led to savings of approximately £100 million: *Fifth Report of the Treasury and Civil Service Committee: The Role of the Civil Service* paras 187–188. The programme for 1993–1994 consisted of activities valued at £830 million, and involving 35,000 staff: *Fifth Report of the Treasury and Civil Service Committee: The Role of the Civil Service* (HC Paper (1994–95) no 27) para 189. See also *The Civil Service: Taking Forward Continuity and Change* (Cm 2748) (1995) at pp 32–33.
3 *Fifth Report of the Treasury and Civil Service Committee: The Role of the Civil Service* (HC Paper (1994–95) no 27) para 194; and *The Government's Guide to Market Testing* (Efficiency Unit, 1993) para 9.21.
4 Ie the Deregulation and Contracting Out Act 1994 Pt II (ss 69–79).
5 See paras 363–365 ante. The government has announced an intention to contract out the administration of the Civil Service pension scheme; the collection of business statistics; food safety enforcement and the Rent Registration Service in Scotland: *The Civil Service: Taking Forward Continuity and Change* (Cm 2748) (1995) para 3.11. As to Civil Service pensions see paras 565–619 post.

**554. Ethical standards.** The framework for maintaining standards in the Civil Service is laid down in a series of documents governing the conduct of civil servants[1]. Duties include the duty to serve the government in accordance with the principles set out in the Civil Service Code[2], recognising the accountability of civil servants to ministers or office holders; the duty of all public officers to discharge public functions reasonably and according to the law; and the duty to comply with the law, including international law and treaty obligations[3], and to uphold the administration of justice, and ethical standards governing particular professions[4]. The Civil Service Code applies to all civil servants, summarising the framework within which they work. It must be seen in the context of the duties and responsibilities of ministers[5].

The code states the duty of civil servants to conduct themselves with integrity, impartiality and honesty, to give honest and impartial advice to ministers, without fear or favour, and to make all information relevant to a decision available to ministers. Civil servants should not deceive or knowingly mislead ministers, Parliament or the public[6]. They should endeavour to deal with affairs of the public sympathetically, efficiently, promptly and without bias and maladministration, and to ensure the proper, effective and efficient use of public money[8].

Civil servants should not misuse their official position or information acquired in the course of their official duties[9], and they should not without authority disclose official information which has been communicated in confidence within government, or received in confidence from others[10]. They should conduct themselves so as to deserve and retain the confidence of ministers[11].

Where a civil servant considers that he or she is being asked to act in a manner which is illegal, improper, unethical or in breach of constitutional convention or a professional code, or which may involve possible maladministration or is otherwise inconsistent with the standards of conduct prescribed in the Civil Service Code, the civil servant should report the matter in accordance with procedures laid down in departmental guidance or rules of conduct. A civil servant should also report to the appropriate authorities evidence of criminal or unlawful activity by others and may also report in accordance with departmental procedures if he becomes aware of other breaches of the code or is required to act in a way which, for him, raises a fundamental issue of conscience[12].

Where a civil servant is not satisfied with the response to such a report he may report the matter in writing to the Civil Service Commissioners[13]. If thereafter a civil servant remains dissatisfied he should either carry out instructions or resign from the Civil Service. Former civil servants should continue to observe their duties of confidentiality after they have left Crown employment[14].

1   For a full list see the *Sixth Report of the Treasury and Civil Service Committee: The Role of the Civil Service: Interim Report* (HC Paper (1992–93) no 390-II) pp 36–37. The key documents are listed below.

   (1)   *The Duties and Responsibilities of Civil Servants in relation to Ministers: A Note by the Head of the Home Civil Service*: see 123 HC Official Report (6th series), 2 December 1987, written answers cols *572–575* (the 'Armstrong memorandum').

   (2)   The Civil Service Management Code (1996), issued under the Civil Service Order in Council 1995 art 10(b) (amended by the Civil Service (Amendment) Order in Council 1995: see para 549 note 12 ante); particularly important is para 4.1 Annex A, which sets out the Civil Service Code, the text of which was previously published in 566 HL Official Report (5th series), 30 October 1995, written answers, cols *146–148*. As to the Civil Service Order in Council 1995 (as amended) see para 549 note 12 ante.

   (3)   *Questions of Procedure for Ministers* (Cabinet Office, May 1992) (as now revised: see paras 416 note 1, 420 ante).

   (4)   *Departmental Evidence and Response to Select Committees* (Cabinet Office, December 1994) (formerly the 'Osmotherly rules'), which set out the rules for civil servants appearing before select committees of the House of Commons, laying down that officials who give evidence to select committees do so on behalf of their ministers and under their directions (para 38).

   There are procedures relating to advice on the use of public money from Accounting Officers (*The Responsibilities of an Accounting Officer* paras 13–14). See eg the *Seventeenth Report of the Committee of Public Accounts, Pergau Hydro-Electric Project* (HC Paper (1993–94) no 155) paras 46, 47, 52; and the *Treasury Minute of the Seventeenth to Twenty-first Reports from the Committee of Public Accounts 1993–94* (Cm 2602) para 13. There are also internal resolution procedures: 'These procedures generally have no formal status. They are not described in the documents we have discussed above. They are confidential and usually take place orally. They do not depend on any special provision in any of these documents, other than the duty of civil servants to give impartial and objective advice. They depend essentially upon what might be termed the Civil Service's powers of moral suasion': *Fifth Report of the Treasury and Civil Service Committee: The Role of the Civil Service* (HC Paper (1994–95) no 27) para 96.

   In 1995 the government formulated four policies intended to help preserve standards of conduct in the light of greater delegation and more movement in and out of the Civil Service. These were (a) the establishment of a new Senior Civil Service; (b) a new handbook for agency chief executives; (c) a new Civil Service Code (see head (2) supra); (d) an independent line of appeal for civil servants to the Civil Service Commissioners: *The Civil Service: Taking Forward Continuity and Change* (Cm 2748) (1995). In the *First Report of the Committee on Standards in Public Life* (Cm 2850) (1995) the Committee on Standards in Public Life (the 'Nolan Committee') welcomed these proposals (see paras 3.48–3.72), and made a number of recommendations:

   (i)    the performance pay arrangements for the Senior Civil Service should be structured so as not to undermine political impartiality (para 3.48);

   (ii)   the Civil Service Code (see head (2) supra) should cover circumstances in which a civil servant, while not personally involved, is aware of wrongdoing or maladministration taking place (see text and note 12 infra) (para 3.51);

   (iii)  the operation of the appeals system should be disseminated as openly as possible, and the Civil Service Commissioners should report all successful appeals to Parliament (para 3.52);

   (iv)   departments and agencies should nominate one or more officials entrusted with the duty of investigating staff concerns raised confidentially (para 3.53);

   (v)    the Cabinet Office should continue to survey and disseminate best practice on maintaining standards of conduct to ensure that basic principles of conduct are being properly observed (para 3.59);

   (vi)   there should be regular surveys in departments and agencies of the knowledge and understanding staff have of ethical standards which apply to them, and where such surveys indicate problem areas, guidance should be reinforced and disseminated appropriately, particularly by way of additional training (para 3.61).

   The Committee also elaborated seven principals of public life, which apply to all who serve the public: see para 12 ante.

2   As to the Civil Service Code see note 1 head (2) supra.

3   In response to a written question in the House of Lords, the government has revised *Questions of Procedure for Ministers* (Cabinet Office, May 1992), so as to include the duty to comply with the law, including international law and treaty obligations: see 567 HL Official Report (5th series), 29 November 1995, written answers cols *44–45*. See also para 416 note 1 ante.

4   Civil Service Code para 4.

5   See the Civil Service Code para 3. The responsibilities are set out in *Questions of Procedure for Ministers* (Cabinet Office, May 1992) (as now revised: see para 416 note 1 ante), and include the duty not to ask civil servants to act inconsistently with the Civil Service Code; the duty to consider advice given by the Civil Service as well as others; and the duty to comply with the law including international law and treaty obligations: see the Civil Service Code para 3.

6   See the Civil Service Code paras 1, 5.

7   See the Civil Service Code para 6.

8   See the Civil Service Code para 7.

9   See the Civil Service Code para 8.

10  See the Civil Service Code para 10.

11  See the Civil Service Code para 9.

12  See the Civil Service Code para 11. This is restated in the Civil Service Management Code (1996) para 12.1.5.

13  See the Civil Service Code para 12.

14  See the Civil Service Code para 13.


**555. Accountability.** One of the essential characteristics of the Civil Service is the principle that civil servants are accountable to their ministers, and ministers alone are accountable to Parliament[1]. A minister is accountable to Parliament for everything that goes on within his department, in the sense that Parliament can call the minister to account for it[2]. This remains the case when a large part of public functions are exercised by 'next step' executive agencies[3]: the government is clear that the line of accountability through ministers to Parliament remains unbroken and that they are accountable to Parliament for the policy, administration and resources of their departments, including operational action, successes and mishaps, whatever the extent of delegation and whether they were personally involved or not[4].

The practice in relation to questions from members of the House of Commons about the actions of executive agencies is as follows: where letters to ministers from members or written parliamentary questions concern operational matters to do with executive agency activity, they are referred in the first instance to the agency chief executive, whose answers are published in the Official Report. Ministers continue to answer written questions which raise policy issues and all oral questions, and in cases where the response from the chief executive does not satisfy the questioner. Where a member of Parliament seeks to raise an issue by correspondence the policy now is to encourage that correspondence to be addressed directly to the chief executive rather than to the minister[5].

1   See paras 21, 416 ante. The government's view is that officials who give evidence to select committees do so on behalf of, and under the direction of, their ministers: *Departmental Evidence and Response to Select Committees* (Cabinet Office, December 1994) para 38. This position is not always accepted by the House of Commons: see the *Report of the Procedure Committee* (HC Paper (1989–90) no 19) para 153 ('It is important to note that the *Memorandum of Guidance* [the precursor to *Departmental Evidence*] has no parliamentary status whatever'). For a discussion of the accountability of civil servants to their ministers, and the rights of select committees to receive evidence from civil servants, see the *Second Report of the Public Service Committee: Ministerial Accountability and Responsibility* (HC Paper (1995–96) no 313–I) ch IV. In relation to executive agencies see ch V, and as to the accountability of witnesses see ch VI.

    Civil servants are servants of the Crown. Constitutionally, the Crown acts on the advice of ministers and civil servants owe their loyalty to the duly constituted government: Civil Service Code para 2. The Civil Service Code is set out as Annex A to para 4.1 of the Civil Service Management Code (1996) (see para 554 note 1 ante), the text having been previously published in 566 HL Official Report (5th series), 30 October 1995, written answers, cols *146–148*. See also Giddings (ed) *Parliamentary*

*Accountability: A Study of Parliament and Executive Agencies* (1995); the *Report of the Committee on the Civil Service* (Cmnd 3638) (1968) (the 'Fulton Report') para 23 ('accountability to Parliament and the public is not a constitutional platitude; it is an integral part of the daily life of many civil servants'); *The Duties and Responsibilities of Civil Servants in relation to Ministers: A Note by the Head of the Home Civil Service* 123 HC Official Report (6th series), 2 December 1987, written answers cols 572–575 (the 'Armstrong memorandum') (see para 554 note 1 ante). Exceptions arise where civil servants are accounting officers: see paras 715, 751 post.

2     A distinction has been drawn between accountability, in the sense of ministerial accountability for all that a department does, and responsibility, in the sense of the personal involvement and responsibility of ministers for all the actions of their departments and agencies, given the realities of delegation and dispersed responsibility for much business: see the Cabinet Office *Memorandum on Ministerial Accountability and Responsibility* set out in the *Fifth Report of the Treasury and Civil Service Committee: The Role of the Civil Service* (HC Paper (1994–95) no 27-II) p 188. The distinction was much criticised by the Treasury and Civil Service Committee (see HC Paper (1994–95) no 27 paras 118–140), but this criticism was largely rejected in *The Civil Service: Taking Forward Continuity and Change* (Cm 2748) (1995) pp 27–28. See also *Departmental Evidence and Response to Select Committees* (Cabinet Office, December 1994) para 39. The distinction has also been examined by the Public Service Committee, which concluded that it is not possible to distinguish between accountability and responsibility. 'Ministers have an obligation to Parliament which consists in insuring that government explains its actions. Ministers also have an obligation to respond to criticism made in Parliament in a way that seems likely to satisfy it – which may include, if necessary, resignation.': *Second Report of the Public Service Committee: Ministerial Accountability and Responsibility* (HC Paper (1995–96) no 313–I) para 21.

3     As to 'next steps' agencies see para 551 ante.

4     See *The Civil Service: Taking Forward Continuity and Change* (Cm 2748) (1995) pp 28, 31.

The difficulties raised by this position were demonstrated in the government and parliamentary responses to the findings of Sir John Learmont's *Review of Prison Service Security in England and Wales and the Escape from Parkhurst Prison on Tuesday 3 January 1995* (Cm 3020) (1995). The Home Secretary claimed that he had been entitled to interfere in the management of the Prison Service, and agreed that he had done so, but maintained that he was not responsible, in the sense of being to blame, for the defects that had been found in it. He accepted however that he was 'accountable' in the sense that he had to take remedial action, and dismissed the Director of the Prison Service. The Director of the Prison Service complained that the Home Secretary had interfered inadvisedly, and denied that he himself was to blame for the escapes. He refused to resign and so was dismissed by the Home Secretary: see 264 HC Official Report (6th series), 16 October 1995, cols 30–43; 264 HC Official Report (6th series), 19 October 1995, cols 502–550. The Public Service Committee accepted that ministers were accountable to Parliament, but recommended, inter alia, (1) a resolution stressing the duty of ministers and civil servants to co-operate with Parliament when it discharges its functions of holding the executive to account; and (2) a review of the roles of ministers and agency chief executives and a report of the conclusions to Parliament: *Second Report of the Public Service Committee: Ministerial Accountability and Responsibility* (HC Paper (1995–96) no 313–I) paras 60, 82, 83, 102.

5     See the *Fifth Report of the Treasury and Civil Service Committee: The Role of the Civil Service* (HC Paper (1993–94) no 27) para 170; and see *The Civil Service: Taking Forward Continuity and Change* (Cm 2748) (1995) p 31. See also Giddings (ed) *Parliamentary Accountability: A Study of Parliament and Executive Agencies* (1995). As to answering parliamentary questions relating to these agencies see para 226 text and notes 9–10 ante. The accountability of agency chief executives and the responsibilities of ministers and chief executives have been considered by the Public Service Committee, which recommended that there be a presumption that ministers will agree to requests by select committees for agency chief executives to give evidence, and that agency chief executives should give evidence on matters which are delegated to them in the framework document: *Second Report of the Public Service Committee: Ministerial Accountability and Responsibility* (HC Paper (1995–96) no 313–I) paras 113–114.

## 556. Admission and recruitment to the Civil Service. Generally, departments and agencies are responsible for their own recruitment practices and procedures within the framework set down by the Civil Service Order in Council 1995[1], and the Recruitment Code issued under it by the Civil Service Commissioners[2]. The responsibility for appointment to the Civil Service has moved from the Treasury to the Minister for the Civil Service[3].

The minister may make regulations, inter alia, relating to the recruitment of persons to situations in the Civil Service, and prescribing the qualifications for appointment, including qualifications relating to age, knowledge, ability, professional attainment, aptitude and potential[4].

Generally, all appointments to the Senior Civil Service[5] have to be approved in writing by the Civil Service Commissioners[6]. Appointments in the Civil Service must generally be on merit on the basis of fair and open competition[7], and the appointee must satisfy such qualifications as may be prescribed[8]. Responsibility for ensuring that recruitment is so conducted rests with the Permanent Secretary or chief executive of each department or agency[9].

In general, no person who is neither a Commonwealth citizen[10], nor a British protected person[11] nor a citizen of the Republic of Ireland[12] may be appointed to any office or place in the Civil Service[13]. There are exceptions to this rule[14] and applicants with dual nationality will be eligible provided that one of the nationalities meets the requirements[15].

Appointment to the post of Permanent Secretary is by the Prime Minister acting on the advice of the Head of the Home Civil Service; other senior appointments must be approved by the Prime Minister upon the advice of the Head of the Home Civil Service, who in turn is advised by the Senior Appointments Selection Committee[16]. A person taking up a first appointment in the Senior Civil Service must now sign a written contract of employment[17].

1   Ie the Civil Service Order in Council 1995 (as amended): see para 549 note 12 ante.
2   The Civil Service Commissioners' Recruitment Code is made under the Civil Service Order in Council 1995 art 4(2); the text of the code is set out in the Civil Service Management Code (1996) para 1.1 Annex A. The former Civil Service Commission was abolished in 1991 and its functions taken over by two executive agencies, the Civil Service College, and the Recruitment and Assessment Agency. For the purposes of the Civil Service Order in Council 1995, the Commissioners are the persons for the time being appointed by Her Majesty in Council to be Her Majesty's Civil Service Commissioners: art 1. As to the Civil Service Management Code (1996) see para 554 note 1 ante.
3   Transfer of Functions (Treasury and Minister for the Civil Service) Order 1995, SI 1995/269, art 2. As to the Minister for the Civil Service see paras 427, 550 ante.
4   See the Civil Service Order in Council 1995 art 10(c), (d). See also para 549 note 8 ante. The formal requirements for recruitment are set out in the Civil Service Management Code (1996) paras 1.1.1–1.1.14; and the Civil Service Commissioners' Recruitment Code (as to which see note 2 supra). Particular provision is made with regard to age, health, character and nationality: Civil Service Management Code (1996) paras 1.1.6–1.1.11, 1.1 Annex B. As to the recruitment of disabled persons see the Civil Service Order in Council 1995 art 7; and the Civil Service Commissioners' Recruitment Code paras 2.31–2.33. The provision for equal opportunity in the management code is comprehensive and includes monitoring by the Cabinet Office, and the appointment by departments and agencies of equal opportunity officers to have overall responsibility for the implementation of equal opportunity policy, monitoring and reviewing progress: see the Civil Service Management Code (1996) Section 2 (paras 2.1.1–2.1.9).
5   As to the Senior Civil Service see para 550 text and notes 9–10 ante.
6   Civil Service Order in Council 1995 art 5(1). The exceptions are for appointments of less than 12 months or for certain appointments specified in art 3 (see note 7 infra): art 5(1). Approval may be conditional or unconditional: see art 5(1), (2), Sch 2.
7   Civil Service Order in Council 1995 art 2(1)(a). As to the Civil Service Order in Council 1995 (as amended) see para 549 note 12 ante. It is the function of the Civil Service Commissioners to maintain the principle: art 4(1). The Commissioners must audit recruitment policies and practices within the Civil Service to establish whether the Civil Service Commissioners' Recruitment Code is being observed, and may require appointing authorities to publish summary information relating to recruitment and to exceptions to the code: Civil Service Order in Council 1995 art 4(3), (4); Civil Service Commissioners' Recruitment Code Section 3 (paras 3.1–3.3). As to exceptions see infra. The Commissioners must publish an annual report: see the Civil Service Order in Council 1995 art 8 (substituted by the Civil Service (Amendment) Order in Council 1995).
    The principles of selection on merit and fair and open competition are set out in the Civil Service Commissioners' Recruitment Code (as to which see note 2 supra). There are limited exceptions to the principles set out in that code and in the Civil Service Order in Council 1995, in relation to: (1) an appointment made directly by the Crown; (2) the appointment of an adviser to a minister, where the appointment does not last beyond the administration; (3) short term appointments, and extensions and

conversions into permanency; (4) secondments; (5) the reappointment of former civil servants; (6) transfers of staff into the Civil Service; (7) the appointment of surplus acceptable candidates to posts where departments have found a consistent shortfall of suitable candidates; (8) disabled candidates; and (9) exceptionally, appointment at the discretion of the Civil Service Commissioners where (a) the person is of proven distinction and the appointment is justified for exceptional reasons relating to the needs of the service; or (b) where after fair and open competition the appointment is made not in order of merit: Civil Service Order in Council 1995 arts 3, 6; Civil Service Commissioners' Recruitment Code Section 2 (paras 2.1–2.35).

8   Civil Service Order in Council 1995 art 2(1)(b).

9   Civil Service Commissioners' Recruitment Code para 1.8.

10  For these purposes a Commonwealth citizen is any person who has the status of a Commonwealth citizen under the British Nationality Act 1981, including British citizens, British subjects with the right of abode in the United Kingdom, British dependent territories citizens, British overseas citizens, and British nationals (overseas): Civil Service Management Code (1996) para 1.1 Annex B. See also BRITISH NATIONALITY, IMMIGRATION AND RACE RELATIONS.

11  A British protected person is a member of any class of person declared to be a British protected person by Order in Council under the British Nationality Act 1981 or by virtue of the Solomon Islands Act 1978: Civil Service Management Code (1996) para 1.1 Annex B.

12  British Nationality Act 1981 s 51(4).

13  Aliens Restriction (Amendment) Act 1919 s 6. The Race Relations Act 1976 preserves the validity of nationality rules governing eligibility for employment in the service of the Crown and certain prescribed public bodies: see s 75(5).

14  See the European Communities (Employment in the Civil Service) Order 1991, SI 1991/1221 (enabling nationals of other European Community member states and certain family members to be employed in non-reserved Civil Service posts); the European Economic Area Act 1993 (enabling nationals of member states of the European Free Trade Area (EFTA), except Switzerland and Liechtenstein, to be employed in the Civil Service, together with certain family members, in non-reserved posts); and the Aliens Employment Act 1955 s 1 (permitting the employment of aliens in exceptional circumstances, in cases where no suitably qualified British subject is available, or where the alien possesses exceptional qualifications and experience, by way of certificate made by the Minister for the Civil Service; and requiring a list of such certificates to be laid before both Houses of Parliament). The total number of aliens thus employed in 1995 is 12. See generally the Civil Service Management Code (1996) para 1.1.8–1.1.11, Annex B.

15  Ibid para 1.1 Annex B.

16  Ibid para 5.2.1. As to the Head of the Home Civil Service see para 550 ante.

17  Ibid para 5.3.2.

**557. Tenure of office.** In theory civil servants hold office during the pleasure of the Crown[1], and are therefore dismissable at any time without cause assigned[2]. In practice, however, permanent officials are invariably treated as holding office during good behaviour[3], and are not removed except in cases of misconduct[4], inefficiency or ill health, although there is in addition provision for compulsory premature retirement in the public interest on structural grounds[5], grounds of limited efficiency[6] and redundancy[7].

Formerly the courts would not entertain an action for wrongful dismissal, even though the civil servant could prove the existence of a contract in which the Crown purported to restrict its right to dismiss him[8]. Latterly, however, legally binding collective agreements can be concluded between the Crown as employer and representatives of its staff[9], which would give those representatives standing to sue for breaches of any conditions of service covered by those agreements[10]. Moreover, a civil servant has a right to bring an action for unfair dismissal or to sue on his conditions of service[11]. The result is to make his situation virtually the same as that of the employee of any ordinary employer; in neither case can the employee insist on continuing to be employed, but in both he can recover damages for unfair dismissal[12].

1  See, however, the Civil Service Management Code (1996) para 5.3.2, under which persons appointed to the Senior Civil Service must now sign a written contract. The government favours contracts in which employment is for an indefinite term, but with specified periods of notice. The government is considering legislation in connection with the terms and conditions of employment of civil servants:

*The Civil Service: Taking Forward Continuity and Change* (Cm 2748) (1995) para 4.9. As to the Senior Civil Service see para 550 text and notes 9–10 ante. As to the Civil Service Management Code (1996) see para 554 note 1 ante.

2　See para 902 post. In other respects the Crown may enter into contracts with civil servants in respect of matters connected with their employment (at any rate, in regard to their pay): *Sutton v A-G* (1923) 39 TLR 294, HL. But see Freedland 'Privatising *Carltona*: Part II of the Deregulation Act 1994' [1995] Public Law 21; and Fredman and Morris *The State as Employer* (1989). See also CROWN PROCEEDINGS.

3　See para 903 post.

4　As to what constitutes misbehaviour in office see para 903 post.

5　See the Civil Service Management Code (1996) para 11.6.4.

6　See ibid para 11.6.5.

7　See ibid paras 11.6.1–11.6.2.

8　*Re Hales' Petition of Right* (1918) 34 TLR 341 (affd sub nom *Hales v R* 34 TLR 589, CA); *Denning v Secretary of State for India in Council* (1920) 37 TLR 138; *Rodwell v Thomas* [1944] KB 596, [1944] 1 All ER 700; and see para 902 post.

9　Under the Trade Union and Labour Relations (Consolidation) Act 1992 ss 62(7), 273–276 (as amended), the terms under which Crown employees are employed are deemed to constitute a contract of employment for certain purposes; see further EMPLOYMENT.

10　See ibid s 179.

11　See the Employment Protection (Consolidation) Act 1978 s 138 (as amended). See also *R v Civil Service Appeal Board, ex p Bruce* [1988] 3 All ER 686, DC; *McLaren v Home Office* [1990] ICR 824, [1990] IRLR 338, CA; *R v Lord Chancellor's Department, ex p Nangle* [1992] 1 All ER 897, DC.

12　As to orders for reinstatement following unfair dismissal see the Employment Protection (Consolidation) Act 1978 ss 68, 69 (both as amended); and EMPLOYMENT vol 16 (Reissue) paras 364–366.

**558. Pay.** The remuneration of civil servants in the Senior Civil Service[1] is determined according to procedures set down in the Civil Service Management Code (1996), within a framework laid down by the Cabinet Office[2].

Departments and agencies have authority to determine conditions relating to remuneration of their own staff outside the Senior Civil Service[3]. The arrangements developed must, inter alia, accord with government policy and observe spending controls, and must be performance-related[4].

A civil servant may probably sue for arrears of his pay[5]. In general he is entitled to a pension according to rules made by the Minister for the Civil Service[6].

1　As to the Senior Civil Service see para 550 text and notes 9–10 ante.

2　Civil Service Management Code (1996) paras 7.1.10–7.1.18. Departments and agencies have discretion as to the allocation of staff to prescribed pay bands, and the detailed operation of their pay schemes: paras 7.1.12–7.1.13. As to the Civil Service Management Code (1996) see para 554 note 1 ante. As to the Cabinet Office see paras 427–434 ante.

3　See the Civil Service Management Code (1996) paras 7.1.1–7.1.8.

4　Ibid paras 7.1.1–7.1.2.

5　The contrary was stated, probably obiter, by Lord Blackburn in the Scottish case of *Mulvenna v The Admiralty* 1926 SC 842, followed by Pilcher J in *Lucas v Lucas and High Comr for India* [1943] P 68, [1943] 2 All ER 110, and by the Judicial Committee of the Privy Council in *High Comr for India v Lall* (1948) LR 75 IA 225, PC. But Sir Douglas Logan's adverse criticism in 61 LQR 260 of the decision in *Lucas v Lucas and High Comr for India* supra was cited with approval by Lord Diplock in *Kodeeswaran v A-G of Ceylon* [1970] AC 1111 at 1123, PC; Lord Blackburn's reasoning in *Mulvenna v The Admiralty* supra was disapproved and the decisions in *Lucas v Lucas and High Comr for India* supra and *High Comr for India v Lall* supra virtually overruled, the latter as having been made per incuriam.

6　See generally paras 565–619 post. As to the Minister for the Civil Service see paras 427, 550 ante.

**559. Discipline in the Home Civil Service.** The Minister for the Civil Service is empowered to make regulations or give instructions for controlling the conduct of Her Majesty's Home Civil Service, including the making and amendment of a civil service code[1]. In the exercise of this power he has issued instructions which are contained in the Civil Service Management Code[2] and the Civil Service Code[3]. The minister is responsible for this central framework governing the conduct of civil servants, but departments and agencies are responsible for defining the standards of conduct they require of their staff and for ensuring that these fully reflect the central framework[4].

1    Civil Service Order in Council 1995 art 10(b) (amended by the Civil Service (Amendment) Order in Council 1995). As to the Civil Service Order in Council 1995 (as amended) see para 549 note 12 ante. As to the Minister for the Civil Service see paras 427, 550 ante.
2    The Civil Service Management Code, first issued in 1993 and reissued in 1996, replaced the Civil Service Pay and Conditions Code, which in turn replaced the Estacode. Estacode was not published, and was issued only to officers whose duties required it. The Civil Service Management Code (1996) is widely available and may be bought from Her Majesty's Stationery Office. For the provisions of the code relating to discipline see paras 4.5.1–4.5.15.
3    As to the Civil Service Code see para 554 note 1 ante.
4    Civil Service Management Code (1996) para 4.1.2. See para 560 post.

**560. Conduct of civil servants.** Civil servants are subject to a general code of conduct, the central framework of which derives from the need for them to be, and to be seen to be, honest and impartial in the exercise of their duties. They must not allow their judgment or integrity to be compromised in fact or by reasonable implication[1]. The particular principles set out apply.

(1)    Civil servants must not misuse information which they acquire in the course of their official duties or disclose information which is held in confidence within government, nor without authority disclose official information which has been communicated in confidence within government, or received in confidence from others. They must not seek to frustrate the policies, decisions or actions of government either by declining to take, or abstaining from, action which flows from ministerial decisions or by unauthorised, improper or premature disclosure outside the government of any information to which they have had access as civil servants[2].

(2)    Civil servants must not take part in any political or public activity which compromises, or might be seen to compromise, their impartial service to the government of the day or any future government[3].

(3)    Civil servants must not misuse their official position or information acquired in the course of their official duties to further their private interests or those of others. Conflicts of interest may arise from financial interests and more broadly from official dealings with, or decisions in respect of, individuals who share a civil servant's private interests (for example, freemasonry, membership of societies, clubs and other organisations, and family). Where a conflict of interest arises, civil servants must declare their interest to senior management so that senior management can determine how best to proceed[4].

(4)    Civil servants must not receive gifts, hospitality or benefits of any kind from a third party which might be seen to compromise their personal judgment or integrity[5].

Rules restrict the making of government contracts with, and purchases from, and sales to, government departments and agencies by civil servants who have outside business interests. Departments and agencies must require their staff to report relevant business interests[6].

Full-time civil servants are generally not allowed to undertake outside occupations which would require their attendance during normal official hours, which would impair their usefulness as public servants or which might conflict with the interests of their departments or be inconsistent with their position as public servants[7].

The Business Appointments Rules have been drawn up to provide independent scrutiny of business appointments which independent civil servants propose to take up in the first two years after they leave the Civil Service[8]. Certain senior civil servants, and senior members of the diplomatic and armed services, and other civil servants who have been engaged in particular kinds of work, must obtain government approval before accepting, within two years of leaving Crown employment, offers of any form of full-time, part-time or fee-paid employment in the United Kingdom or overseas in a public or private company or in the service of a foreign government or its agencies[9].

It is an offence for a person who is or has been a Crown servant to disclose certain categories of information without authority[10].

1   See the Civil Service Management Code (1996) para 4.1.3. As to the Civil Service Management Code (1996) see para 554 note 1 ante. Departments and agencies must use these principles as their defining framework, ensure that their own rules fully reflect those standards and incorporate any additional rules necessary to reflect local needs and circumstances.

2   See ibid para 4.1.3a. See generally *A-G v Observer Ltd, A-G v Times Newspapers Ltd* [1990] 1 AC 109, sub nom *A-G v Guardian Newspapers Ltd (No 2)* [1988] 3 All ER 545, HL: the duty of confidentiality owed by a civil servant to the Crown might be displaced by the public interest in the disclosure of iniquity, but only if the civil servant has exhausted all methods short of publication to deal with the iniquity but the Crown would not be entitled to an injunction against disclosure unless it could show a detriment to the public interest if the material were published; its remedy for unlawful disclosure might be an account for profits. Disciplinary proceedings might be taken under the contract of employment. See generally CONFIDENCE AND DATA PROTECTION vol 8(1) (Reissue) para 434. Where the information disclosed is no longer secret and confidential, the Crown cannot claim publication profits unless there has been a specific contractual undertaking: see *A-G v Blake (Jonathan Cape Ltd, third party)* [1996] EMLR 382.

3   See the Civil Service Management Code (1996) para 4.1.3b. For the arrangements whereby civil servants are allowed to hold non-executive directorships of private sector companies see 568 HL Official Report (5th series), 1 February 1996, col 119.

4   See the Civil Service Management Code (1996) para 4.1.3c.

5   See ibid para 4.1.3c.

6   See generally ibid paras 4.3.1–4.3.10 (standards of propriety), and Annex 4.3A (rules on acceptance of outside appointments by Crown servants), Annex 4.3B (guidance for departments and agencies on the rules in Annex 4.3A).

7   See ibid para 4.3.4.

8   Ibid Annex 4.3A. The aim of the rules is (1) to avoid any suspicion that the advice and decisions of a civil servant might be influenced by the hope or expectation of future employment with a particular firm or organisation; or (2) to avoid the risk that a particular firm might gain an improper advantage over its competitors by employing someone who has had access to technical or other information which those competitors might regard as their own trade secrets or to information relating to proposed developments in government policy which may affect that firm or its competitors: Annex 4.3A para 3. See also 273 HC Official Report (6th series), 4 March 1996, col 5.

9   Ibid Annex 4.3A paras 6–12. Offers of employment must be reported, even if the civil servant in question is not considering taking it up: paras 13–14.

10  See the Official Secrets Act 1989 ss 2–6 (as amended); and CRIMINAL LAW vol 11(1) paras 245–252. See Wade and Bradley *Constitutional and Administrative Law* (11th Edn, 1993) pp 571–573; the *Report of the Departmental Committee on Section 2 of the Official Secrets Act 1911* (Cmnd 5104) (1972) (the 'Franks Report').

**561. Activities involving the use of official information or experience.** Under the Copyright, Designs and Patents Act 1988, copyright in any works made by civil servants in the course of their employment is Crown copyright[1]. Civil servants must obtain prior permission from their head of department or agency chief executive before entering into any arrangement regarding the publication of any articles or material produced as part of their official duties[2].

Civil servants must not take part in any activities or make any public statement which might involve disclosure of official information or draw upon experience gained in their official capacity without the prior approval of their department or agency. They must clear in advance material for publication, broadcasts or other public discussion which draws on official information or experience[3].

It is accepted that the fullest possible exposition should be afforded to Parliament and to the public of the reasons for government policies and decisions when those policies and decisions have been formulated and are announced, and that a better public understanding should be created about the way in which the processes of government work and about the factual or technical background to government policies and decisions. Since House of Commons Select Committees were reorganised along departmental lines in 1979, civil servants have increasingly been called upon to give evidence to such committees, often in public. But civil servants should not disclose (1) in order to preserve the collective responsibility of ministers, the advice given to ministers by their departments, nor information about departmental exchanges on policy issues, nor the level at which decisions were taken or the manner in which a minister has consulted his colleagues, nor information about cabinet committees or their decisions; (2) advice given by a law officer, except when expressly authorised by that law officer; (3) the private affairs of individuals or institutions on which any information has been supplied in confidence[4].

Civil servants should also avoid giving written evidence about or discussing the following: (a) questions in the field of political controversy[5]; (b) sensitive information of a commercial or economic nature[6]; (c) matters the disclosure of which might impair the effectiveness of the conduct of international relations[7]; (d) specific cases where the minister has or may have a quasi-judicial or appellate function, such as in relation to planning applications and appeals, or where the matter is being considered by the courts or Parliamentary Commissioner[8].

The Code of Practice on Access to Government Information[9] sets out the information which is and is not available to the public upon request. Disputes about the provision of government information are subject to review by the Parliamentary Commissioner for Administration[10], to whom a complaint is made through a member of Parliament, about a decision under the Code of Practice[11].

1    See the Copyright, Designs and Patents Act 1988 s 163. See also *A-G v Blake (Jonathan Cape Ltd, third party)* [1996] EMLR 382, cited in para 560 note 2 ante; and COPYRIGHT.

2    Civil Service Management Code (1996) para 4.2.9. The matter will then need to be referred on to Her Majesty's Stationery Office to consider the copyright implications: para 4.2.9.

3    Civil Service Code of Management (1996) para 4.2.4. See also *The Duties and Responsibilities of Civil Servants in relation to Ministers: A Note by the Head of the Home Civil Service* 123 HC Official Report (6th series), 2 December 1987, written answers cols *572–575* (the 'Armstrong memorandum'); and see paras 555, 560 ante.

4    This list is taken from *Departmental Evidence and Response to Select Committees* (Cabinet Office, December 1994) paras 66–73, 79 (see para 554 note 1 ante). The restrictions in these rules have been criticised: see eg the *Second Report of the Select Committee on Trade and Industry* (HC Paper (1985–86) no 305-I) paras 10, 13; and Lord Crowther Hunt in a Memorandum to the former Expenditure Committee (*Eleventh Report of the Expenditure Committee* (HC Paper (1976–77) no 353-III) App 48 para 70). See also *The Civil Service: Continuity and Change* (Cm 2627) (1994) para 2.32. See also *Departmental Evidence and Response to Select Committees* (Cabinet Office, December 1994) para 62.

5    Civil Service Management Code (1996) para 4.4.15.

6    See *Departmental Evidence and Response to Select Committees* (Cabinet Office, December 1994) para 78.

7    See *Departmental Evidence and Response to Select Committees* (Cabinet Office, December 1994) para 77.

8    See *Departmental Evidence and Response to Select Committees* (Cabinet Office, December 1994) paras 74–76.

9    The Code of Practice came into force on 4 April 1994, following a White Paper on *Open Government* (Cm 2290) (1993); see the *Annual Report of the Parliamentary Commissioner for Administration for 1994* (HC Paper (1994–95) no 307) ch 2; the *Second Report of the Parliamentary Commissioner for Administration* (HC Paper (1994–95) no 91); Birkinshaw 'I only ask for information – the White Paper on Open Government' [1993] Public Law 557.

10   As to the Parliamentary Commissioner for Administration (the Parliamentary Ombudsman) see para 226 ante; and ADMINISTRATIVE LAW vol 1(1) (Reissue) para 41 et seq.

11   *The Civil Service: Continuity and Change* (Cm 2627) (1994) para 2.31. The government has proposed legislation on statutory right of access to personal records and to health and safety information held by the public sector: para 2.31.

**562. Civil Service appeals.** Civil servants have a right of appeal against management decisions that affect them adversely[1]. Departments and agencies must put in place appropriate appeal arrangements and inform staff of their rights of appeal[2]. A civil servant also has the right of appeal to the Civil Service Appeal Board in cases of: (1) refusal to allow participation in political activities; (2) forfeiture of superannuation; (3) dismissal and early retirement; and (4) non-payment of compensation to civil servants dismissed on inefficiency grounds[3].

The Civil Service Appeal Board is an independent appeals body comprising three people sitting together: the appointed chairman or deputy chairman and two other members, one from the Official Side panel and one from the Trade Union Side panel. The proceedings are informal, and vary with the category of appeal brought before it[4].

In cases coming within head (1) above, the board recommends to the department or agency that permission to undertake a particular activity should or should not be granted, or that conditions should be applied to the granting of permission. If the head of department or agency does not accept a recommendation of the board that permission be granted, the department or agency must submit the case for final decision to the minister[5].

In cases coming within head (2) above, the board's judgement will be accepted by the Cabinet Office[6].

In cases coming within head (3) above, if the board decides that the dismissal was unfair, it may recommend reinstatement, or specify what compensation is to be paid, or recommend other appropriate action[7]. In limited efficiency dismissal cases, the Department must accept the recommendations of the Board with regard to payment under the provisions of the Principal Civil Service Pension Scheme[8].

In cases coming within head (4) above, the head of department or agency will normally be expected to accept the recommendations of the board[9].

1 Civil Service Management Code (1996) para 12.1.1. As to appeals where a civil servant has a crisis of conscience see para 7.7.5; the Civil Service Code para 11; and para 554 text and note 12 ante. As to the Civil Service Code and the Civil Service Management Code (1996) see para 554 note 1 ante.
2 Civil Service Management Code (1996) paras 12.1.2–12.1.3.
3 Ibid para 12.1.13.
4 See ibid para 12.1.12.
5 See ibid paras 12.1.14–12.1.22.
6 See ibid paras 12.1.23–12.1.25. As to the Cabinet Office see paras 427–434 ante.
7 See ibid paras 12.1.26–12.1.32, 12.1.34.
8 See ibid para 12.1.33.
9 See ibid paras 12.1.35–12.1.39.

**563. Security in the Civil Service.** Security procedures have been in place since 1948[1]. The current policy[2] is that in the interests of national security and of safeguarding parliamentary democracy, no one should be employed in connection with work the nature of which is vital to the security of the state who: (1) is, or has been, involved in, or associated with (a) espionage, (b) terrorism, (c) sabotage, or (d) actions intended to overthrow or undermine parliamentary democracy by political, industrial or violent means; or (2) is, or has recently been, a member of any organisation which has advocated such activities; or (3) is, or has recently been, associated with any such organisation, or any of its members, in such a way as to raise reasonable doubts about his reliability; or (4) is susceptible to pressure from any such organisation or from a foreign intelligence service or a hostile power; or (5) suffers from defects of character which may expose him to blackmail or other influence by any such organisation or by a foreign intelligence service or which may otherwise indicate unreliability.

The two main procedures were formerly positive vetting and the purge[3]. Now different levels of vetting are in operation, depending upon the sensitivity of the information with which the individual concerned comes into contact. Positive vetting (S)[4] is the level of clearance required before regular access to secret information can be authorised, this being a full record check, and if necessary further inquiries; positive vetting (TS)[5] is required before regular and constant access to top secret information can be authorised, and also at the discretion of the Foreign and Commonwealth Office in posts abroad, or, at the discretion of the Home Office, the Northern Ireland Office and the Scottish Office in certain circumstances, or, at departmental discretion before employment in a departmental security post, or, at the discretion of the security and intelligence agencies to members of their ancillary staff. In addition to the record checks, there are checks on creditworthiness and interviews with colleagues, family and friends; extended positive vetting[6] is the most rigorous level of clearance now applied to members of the security and intelligence agencies, and consists of the same sort of enquiries as positive vetting (TS) but in greater depth[7].

Additionally, security checks known as reliability checks may be carried out in various circumstances, primarily to ensure that the character of the individual concerned is such that he can be trusted in circumstances where he may gain access to information of importance to national security[8].

Where the investigations uncover character defects, such as financial instability, untruthfulness or irregular sexual or marital relations, an appeal against any adverse finding lies to the permanent head of the individual's department. In all other cases, the appeal against an adverse finding is to a panel of three advisers, two of whom are normally civil servants, with a judge of the High Court as chairman[9].

The reasonableness of a decision to withdraw positive vetting clearance is not reviewable by the courts[10].

Similar rules and procedures apply to the Diplomatic Service and indeed to government contractors and their employees engaged on work classified as involving national security[11].

In January 1964 a Standing Security Commission was appointed with the duty, when so requested by the Prime Minister[12], of investigating and reporting upon the circumstances in which a breach of security is known[13] to have occurred in the public service and upon any related failure of departmental security arrangements or neglect of duty; and in the light of any such investigation to advise whether any change in security arrangements is necessary or desirable[14]. The chairman is a High Court judge and there is a panel of six members of whom two are selected to sit with the chairman on the occasion of each investigation[15].

1   The security procedure is entirely administrative and governed by regulations and departmental memoranda: Treasury Memorandum, 5 May 1948; Treasury Memorandum, 1 March 1957. See *Report of the Commission on Security Procedures in the Public Service* (Cmnd 1681) (1962) (the 'Radcliffe Report'); the *Statement on the Recommendations of the Security Commission* (Cmnd 8540) (1982); and (in relation to the Ministry of Defence and government contractors) the *First Report of the Select Committee on Defence, Session 1982–83: Positive Vetting Procedures in Her Majesty's Services and the Ministry of Defence* (HC Paper (1982–83) no 242). See also Hollingsworth and Norton-Taylor *Black list: the Inside Story of Political Vetting* (1989); Fredman and Morris *The State as Employer* (1989); Jackson 'Individual Rights and National Security' (1957) 20 MLR 364; Leigh and Lustgarten 'Employment, Justice and Detente: the Reform of Vetting' [1991] 54 MLR 613; Austin in Jowell and Oliver (eds) *The Changing Constitution* (3rd Edn, 1994).

2   See 177 HC Official Report (6th series), 24 July 1990, written answers cols *159–161*. These are a revision of the 1985 procedures (see 76 HC Official Report (6th series), 3 April 1985, written answers col *621*).

3   *Security Procedures in the Public Service* (Cmnd 1681) (1962).

4   This may be abbreviated to PV (S).

5   This may be abbreviated to PV (TS).

6   This may be abbreviated to EPV.

7   177 HC Official Report (6th series), 24 July 1990, written answers col *160*.

8   177 HC Official Report (6th series), 24 July 1990, written answers col *161*.

9   The procedure of the hearing before the three advisers has been criticised for not complying with the rules of natural justice. Details of the charges are not made available if this would involve the disclosure of sources. There is no right to know of the evidence nor to lead witnesses in defence, nor is there a right to cross examine witnesses testifying against the appellant. The employee is not entitled to representation, although a friend is allowed to be present during his opening statement, and for as long as the three advisers consider appropriate. See *R v Secretary of State for the Home Department, ex p Hosenball* [1977] 3 All ER 452, [1977] 1 WLR 766, CA; Fredman and Morris *The State as Employer* (1989) p 233; de Smith and Brazier *Constitutional and Administrative Law* (7th Edn, 1994) pp 220–221; Wade and Bradley *Constitutional and Administrative Law* (11th Edn, 1993) p 565.

10  *R v Director of Government Communications Headquarters, ex p Hodges* (1988) Times, 26 July, DC.

11  See 177 HC Official Report (6th series), 24 July 1990, written answers cols *159–161*.

12  Before putting a request to the commission the Prime Minister consults with the Leader of the Opposition. As to the Prime Minister see paras 394–398 ante. As to the Leader of the Opposition see paras 218–219 ante.

13  The procedure was later altered so that a reference could be made to the commission as soon as the government was satisfied or had good reason to think that a breach of security had occurred: see 716 HC Official Report (5th Series), 22 July 1965, cols 1845–1846.

14  687 HC Official Report (5th series), 21 January 1964, col 1271. The commission may if necessary act as a tribunal of inquiry under the Tribunals of Inquiry (Evidence) Act 1921 (see EVIDENCE): 687 HC Official Report (5th series), 21 January 1964, cols 1272–1273. See also the commission's recommendations as to security procedure (*Report of the Standing Security Commission* (Cmnd 2722) (1965) para 125); and the announcement that the government had accepted all the recommendations in whole or in part (723 HC Official Report (5th series), 25 January 1966, written answers, col *23*). See further the *Report of a Board of Inquiry appointed by the Prime Minister* (Cmnd 1773) (1965); [1964] Public Law 184; [1965] Public Law 352; [1966] Public Law 177.

15  As originally appointed the commission consisted of a High Court judge and two members: see 687 HC Official Report (5th series), 21 January 1964, col 1272. The number of members was increased in 1965: see 716 HC Official Report (5th series), 22 July 1965, col 1846. See Leigh and Lustgarten 'Employment, Justice and Detente: the Reform of Vetting' (1991) 54 MLR 613.

**564. Political activities of civil servants.** Any person who for the time being is employed in the Civil Service of the Crown[1], whether in an established capacity or not, and whether for the whole or part of his time, is disqualified for membership of the House of Commons[2] and of the European Parliament[3]. Moreover, unless he belongs to one of the excepted classes, no person for the time being so employed may issue an address to electors or in any other manner publicly announce himself or allow himself to be publicly announced as a candidate or prospective candidate for election to Parliament for any constituency[4].

Political activities that may be subject to restriction are defined as follows:

(1)   at national level: (a) holding, in a party political organisation, office which impinges wholly or mainly on party politics in the field of Parliament or the European Parliament; (b) speaking in public on matters of national political controversy; (c) expressing views on such matters in letters to the press, or in books, articles or leaflets; (d) being announced publicly as a candidate for Parliament or the European Parliament; and (e) canvassing on behalf of a candidate for Parliament or the European Parliament or on behalf of a political party[5]; and

(2)   at local level: (a) candidature for, or co-option to, local authorities; (b) holding office in a party political organisation, impinging wholly or mainly on party politics in the local field; (c) speaking in public on matters in letters to the press, or in books, articles or leaflets; and (d) canvassing on behalf of candidates for election to local authorities or a local political organisation[6].

Civil servants are divided, for the purposes of political activity into those who are 'politically free' and those who are 'politically restricted'. The politically free category are those in industrial and non-office grades, and they may take part in all political activity[7]. The politically restricted category are members of the Senior Civil Service[8] and immediately below, and other specified staff[9]. They must not take part in national political activities, and must seek permission to take part in local political activities[10].

All civil servants must resign from the Civil Service upon formal adoption as a parliamentary candidate or prospective candidate[11]. Civil servants in the politically restricted category who are candidates for election must complete their last day of service before their adoption papers are completed[12]. Civil servants in the politically free category who are not successfully elected must be reinstated by their department or agency if they apply within a week of declaration day. If they are elected, they must still be subsequently reinstated if they cease to be a member after an absence from the Civil Service of not more than five years and they have at least ten years service before the election, and they apply for reinstatement within three months of ceasing to be a member[13]. Departments and agencies have the discretion to reinstate politically restricted civil servants following resignation to stand for election to Parliament or to the European Parliament. Discretion to reinstate should normally be exercised only where it is possible to post staff to non-sensitive areas[14].

Politically free category civil servants must nevertheless seek permission to take part in national or local political activities, unless they are in a grade or area that has already been given permission under a specific mandate from the department or agency[15].

Civil servants must not take part in any political activity when on duty, or in uniform, or on official premises[16].

All civil servants who do not belong to the politically free group must take particular care to express political comment with moderation, particularly about matters for which their own ministers are responsible; to avoid comment altogether about matters of controversy affecting the responsibility of their own ministers; and to avoid personal attacks. They must generally retain at all times a proper reticence in matters of political controversy so that their impartiality is beyond question[17].

Individual civil servants do not need permission to take part in trade union activity, though they have no right to do so[18]. Elected trade union representatives may comment on government policy when representing the legitimate interests of their members, but must make clear when they do so that they are expressing views as representatives of the union and not as civil servants[19].

1 'Civil service of the Crown' includes the Civil Service of Northern Ireland, Her Majesty's Diplomatic Service and Her Majesty's Overseas Civil Service: House of Commons Disqualification Act 1975 s 1(3).
2 Ibid s 1(1)(b). A person is not disqualified by reason of his being a member of the Royal Observer Corps unless he is employed as such for the whole of his time: s 3(3).
3 Servants of the Crown, Parliamentary, European Assembly and Northern Ireland Assembly (Candidature) Order 1987; Civil Service Management Code (1996) para 4.4.19.
4 Servants of the Crown, Parliamentary, European Assembly and Northern Ireland Assembly (Candidature) Order 1987; Civil Service Management Code (1996) para 4.4.21.
5 Ibid para 4.4.1a; see also Fredman and Morris *The State as Employer* (1989) pp 217–218.
6 Civil Service Management Code (1996) para 4.4.1b.
7 Ibid para 4.4.2.
8 As to the Senior Civil Service see para 550 text and notes 9–10 ante.
9 Civil Service Management Code (1996) para 4.4.9
10 Ibid para 4.4.9
11 Ibid paras 4.4.19–4.4.21.
12 Ibid para 4.4.21.
13 Ibid para 4.4.6
14 See ibid paras 4.4.7–4.4.8.
15 Ibid para 4.4.10.
16 Ibid para 4.4.11.
17 Ibid paras 4.4.13–4.4.15.
18 Ibid para 4.4.16. See *Council of Civil Service Unions v Minister for the Civil Service* [1985] AC 374, [1984] 3 All ER 935, HL (Civil Service unions have a legitimate expectation derived from past practice that they

will be consulted before civil servants' terms and conditions of service, including the freedom to belong to trade unions, are altered, unless considerations of national security indicate otherwise; Minister for the Civil Service was entitled to give an instruction withdrawing trade union membership entitlements from certain civil servants on national security grounds).

19   Civil Service Management Code (1996) para 4.4.16.

## (ii)   Civil Service Superannuation

### A.   IN GENERAL

**565. Civil Service superannuation generally.** The grant of superannuation benefits in respect of service in the Civil Service of the state is regulated by the Principal Civil Service Pension Scheme 1974[1], except in relation to those civil servants who, with the approval of the Minister for the Civil Service[2], are subject to other superannuation schemes[3]. These are schemes operated under the Federated Superannuation System for Universities[4], the Federated Superannuation Scheme for Nurses and Hospital Officers[5], and any other scheme approved by the minister[6].

Pensions of governors overseas have been briefly considered elsewhere[7].

1   As to the Principal Civil Service Pension Scheme 1974 see paras 576–613 post. The Principal Civil Service Pension Scheme 1974 was laid before Parliament on 19 November 1974 under the Superannuation Act 1972 s 2(11). Provision is made by Parliament (see the Superannuation Act 1972 s 26(1)) in the *Supply Estimates 1995–96 for the year ending 31 March 1996* (HC Paper (1994–95) no 271–XVIII). Separate estimates are laid before Parliament for half pay or military, naval or air force pensions.

2   As to the Minister for the Civil Service see paras 427, 550 ante.

3   See the Superannuation Act 1965 s 89 (repealed with savings: see the Superannuation Act 1972 s 29(2), Sch 7 para 2(1)); Minister for the Civil Service Order 1968, SI 1968/1656, art 2(1)(c). Provisions regarding injury warrants remain applicable to those civil servants: see the Superannuation Act 1972 Sch 7 para 2(2). Regulations may assimilate the superannuation benefits payable to civil servants with those applicable to civil servants generally: see the Superannuation Act 1965 s 89(3) (repealed with savings) and authorise a similar increase of their pensions see the Pensions (Increase) Act 1971 s 13(2), (5) (s 13(2) amended by the Superannuation Act 1972 s 29(1), Sch 6 para 88).

4   See also the Pensions Increase (Federated Superannuation System for Universities) Regulations 1972, SI 1972/877 (amended by SI 1974/737; SI 1975/1383; SI 1977/286; SI 1977/863; and SI 1980/1869); and see the Federated Superannuation System for Universities (Temporary Service) Regulations 1949, SI 1949/1890 (amended by SI 1949/2116; and modified by SI 1963/1219); Federated Superannuation System for Universities (War Service) Regulations 1949, SI 1949/1891; Federated Superannuation System for Universities (Reckoning of Certain Previous Service) Regulations 1963, SI 1963/1219. Superannuation of teachers is considered in EDUCATION vol 15 (Reissue) para 89 et seq.

5   See the Pensions Increase (Federated Superannuation Scheme for Nurses and Hospital Officers) (Civil Service) Regulations 1972, SI 1972/395 (amended by SI 1973/1068; and SI 1984/1751).

6   Superannuation Act 1965 s 89(4) (repealed with savings). The full list is set out in the Pensions Manual vol 1: *Introduction to the PCSPS* Appendix 1.2 and is as follows: Teachers' Superannuation Scheme; Scottish Teachers' Superannuation Scheme; National Health Service Superannuation Scheme; Hovercraft Superannuation Scheme; Merchant Navy Officers' Pension Fund; United Kingdom Atomic Energy Authority Principal Non-Industrial Superannuation Scheme; United Kingdom Atomic Energy Authority Industrial Superannuation Scheme; Local Government Pension Scheme; Firemen's Pension Scheme; Police Pension Scheme.

7   See COMMONWEALTH vol 6 (Reissue) para 996.

**566. Entitlement to benefits.** Formerly all benefits were discretionary[1], although there was a well-founded expectation that they would be paid. Now, however, the Minister for the Civil Service[2] is empowered, in making a scheme, to specify benefits as mandatory or discretionary according to choice[3]; and the Principal Civil Service Pension Scheme 1974 has provided that, with a few exceptions[4], benefits are to be[5] or will be paid[6]. Thus by implication, there is a right to payment, subject, of course, to the provision of money by Parliament[7].

1   See the Superannuation Act 1965 s 79 (repealed). The earliest Superannuation Act was in 1834.
2   As to the Minister for the Civil Service see paras 427, 550 ante. As to the contracting out of his functions
    see para 567 note 2 post.
3   See the Superannuation Act 1972 s 1(1)(a).
4   See eg the Principal Civil Service Pension Scheme 1974 r 3.8 (discretionary death benefits to nominated
    persons); and para 591 post.
5   See eg ibid r 3.1 (ordinary retirement); and para 588 post.
6   See eg ibid r 3.4 (retirement on medical grounds); and para 590 post.
7   See paras 565 note 1 ante, 567 text and note 9 post.

## B.  SUPERANNUATION ACT 1972

**567. Power to make, maintain and administer schemes.** The Minister for the
Civil Service[1] may make, maintain and administer schemes[2] (whether contributory or not)
making provision for pensions, allowances or gratuities which are to be paid, or may be
paid[3], by him to such persons as he may determine who are employed in the Civil Service
of the state[4] or in certain other employments[5] or are holders of certain offices[6]. Although
the schemes are non-statutory, a copy of a principal Civil Service pension scheme or a
scheme amending or revoking it[7] must be laid before Parliament before it comes into
operation[8]. Moreover, the periodic control of the House of Commons is preserved by the
rule that all money needed to operate the schemes must be provided by Parliament[9].

The Principal Civil Service Pension Scheme 1974 now sets out the pension and
related provisions for the civil service[10].

1   As to the Minister for the Civil Service see paras 427, 550 ante.
2   Superannuation Act 1972 s 1(1)(a). The minister may, to such extent and subject to such conditions as
    he thinks fit, delegate to any other minister or officer of the Crown any functions exercisable by him by
    virtue of s 1 or any scheme made under it: s 1(2). The object of the Act was to remove the necessity for
    successive applications to Parliament for legislation by giving the minister full power to act as the need
    arises, after consultation with the Civil Service unions. The responsibility for Civil Service pensions has
    been transferred from the Treasury to the Minister for the Civil Service: Transfer of Functions (Treasury
    and Minister for the Civil Service) Order 1995, SI 1995/269, art 3, Schedule. The function of
    administering schemes under the Superannuation Act 1972 s 1(1) or (2) may be exercised by (or
    by employees of) such person as may be authorised in that behalf by the minister or office-holder
    whose function it is: Contracting Out (Administration of Civil Service Pension Schemes) Order 1996,
    SI 1996/1746, arts 2, 3. As to the Treasury see paras 512–517 ante.
3   Ie subject to the fulfilment of such requirements and conditions as may be prescribed by the scheme:
    Superannuation Act 1972 s 1(1)(a). Where a money purchase scheme under s 1 includes provision
    enabling a member to elect for the benefits which are to be provided to or in respect of him from any
    authorised provider whom he may specify, then the scheme may make provision for the making of such
    an election to have the effect, in such cases as the scheme may specify, of discharging any liability to the
    Treasury to pay those benefits to or in respect of that member, although it may not be so framed as to
    have the effect that benefits under it may only be provided in a manner which discharges Treasury
    liability: Superannuation Act 1972 s 1(2A) (added by the Pensions (Miscellaneous Provisions) Act 1990
    s 8(1)). 'Money purchase scheme' has the meaning given by the Pension Schemes Act 1993 s 181(1); and
    'authorised provider' in relation to any benefit, means a person authorised under the Financial Services
    Act 1986 Pt I Ch III (ss 7–14) (as amended) to provide that benefit: Superannuation Act 1972 s 1(9)
    (added by the Pensions (Miscellaneous Provisions) Act 1990 s 8(2); amended by the Pension Schemes
    Act 1993 s 190, Sch 8 para 6). 'Authorised provider' includes any European institution acting in the
    course of home-regulated investment business carried on by it in the United Kingdom: see the Banking
    Co-ordination (Second Council Directive) Regulations 1992, SI 1992/3218, reg 82(1), Sch 10 para 5.
4   Superannuation Act 1972 s 1(1)(a), (4)(a).
5   Ibid s 1(1)(a), (4)(b). The employments are listed in Sch 1 (as extensively amended). The minister may,
    by order, either remove any employment or office from those listed (s 1(5)(c)) or, provided the
    remuneration of persons serving in it is paid out of money provided by Parliament or the Consolidated
    Fund (as to which see para 711 et seq post) (s 1(6)), add any employment or office to those listed (s 1(5)(a),
    (b)). The minister may also by order provide that schemes include persons in employment remunerated
    out of a fund established by or under an Act of Parliament: s 1(7). As to payments to the minister of
    benefits out of the fund in such scheme see s 2(5). An order, which must be made by statutory instrument

subject to annulment by resolution of either House of Parliament (s 1(8)(d)), may be retroactive (s 1(8)(a)), may include transitional or other supplementary provisions (s 1(8)(b)) and may vary or revoke previous orders (s 1(8)(c)). Orders made under s 1(5) are: the Superannuation (Crown Solicitor for Northern Ireland) Order 1974, SI 1974/1085; the Superannuation (Listed Employments and Offices) Order 1975, SI 1975/599; the Superannuation (Lyon King of Arms and Lyon Clerk) Order 1979, SI 1979/1540; the Superannuation (National Audit Office) Order 1983, SI 1983/1942; the Superannuation (Lay Observers) Order 1985, SI 1985/1855; the Superannuation (Museums and Galleries Commission) Order 1986, SI 1986/2119; the Superannuation (Valuation and Community Charge Tribunals) Order 1989, SI 1989/1674; the Superannuation (National Museums and Galleries on Merseyside) Order 1990, SI 1990/757; and the Superannuation (Admission to the Principal Civil Service Pension Scheme) Order 1995, SI 1995/1293. At the date at which this volume states the law no order had been made under the Superannuation Act 1972 s 1(7). The list has been frequently and extensively amended by statute: see 33 Halsbury's Statutes (4th Edn) (1993 Reissue) p 481.

6    Superannuation Act 1972 s 1(1)(a), (4)(c), Sch 1 (as amended: see further note 5 supra).

7    Different schemes may be made in relation to different classes of persons and 'the Principal Civil Service Pensions Scheme' means the principal scheme relating to persons in employment in the Home Civil Service or the Diplomatic Service: ibid s 2(10).

8    Ibid s 2(11).

9    Ibid s 26(1)(a); and see para 565 note 1 ante.

10   As to the Principal Civil Service Pension Scheme 1974 see paras 576–613 post.


**568. Power to amend or revoke schemes.** A scheme[1] may amend or revoke any previous scheme[2]. The Minister for the Civil Service[3] may by order repeal or amend any provision in a statute or statutory instrument where it appears to him to be inconsistent with a scheme or to have become unnecessary or to require modification for the purposes of a scheme[4]. The order may have retroactive effect, may revoke any previous order, and must be made by statutory instrument subject to annulment in pursuance of a resolution of either House of Parliament[5].

1    Ie a scheme under the Superannuation Act 1972 s 1(1): see para 567 ante.

2    Ibid s 2(9).

3    As to the Minister for the Civil Service see paras 427, 550 ante. As to the power of that minister to delegate for the purposes of the Superannuation Act 1972, and as to the contracting out of functions under that Act, see para 567 note 2 ante.

4    Ibid s 6(1). At the date at which this volume states the law, there have been 24 scheme amendments, all approved by Parliament. For the complete list see the Pensions Manual vol 1: *Introduction to the PCSPS* para 2.1 Annex A.

5    Superannuation Act 1972 s 6(2).


**569. Consultation with interested parties.** Before making a scheme[1] the minister[2] must consult either with persons appearing to him to represent persons likely to be affected by the scheme or with the persons likely to be affected[3]. Moreover, although a scheme may have retroactive effect[4], no provision in it which would have the effect of reducing the amount of any pension, allowance or gratuity directly referable to rights accrued before the coming into force of the scheme, whether by virtue of service rendered, or contributions paid or any other things done, may be made unless the persons consulted agree to it[5].

1    Ie a scheme under the Superannuation Act 1972 s 1(1): see para 567 ante.

2    Ie the Minister for the Civil Service or, if he so directs in relation to a particular scheme, the minister of the Crown specified in the direction: ibid s 1(3). As to the Minister for the Civil Service see paras 427, 550 ante. As to the power of that minister to delegate for the purposes of the Superannuation Act 1972, and as to the contracting out of functions under that Act, see para 567 note 2 ante.

3    Ibid s 1(3). As to what amounts to consultation see the cases cited in ADMINISTRATIVE LAW vol 1(1) (Reissue) para 82.

4    See ibid s 2(4).

5    See ibid s 2(3) (substituted by the Pensions (Miscellaneous Provisions) Act 1990 s 9).

**570. Ministerial determinations.** A scheme[1] may provide for the Minister of the Civil Service[2] to determine questions arising under it and for his decision to be final[3]. However, before he determines any such questions, the minister may, and if directed by the High Court must, refer any questions of law arising out of such questions for determination by the High Court on a case stated[4]. An appeal from the determination of the High Court lies to the Court of Appeal only with leave of either court[5].

1 Ie a scheme under the Superannuation Act 1972 s 1(1): see para 567 ante.
2 As to the Minister for the Civil Service see paras 427, 550 ante. As to the power of that minister to delegate for the purposes of the Superannuation Act 1972, and as to the contracting out of functions under that Act, see para 567 note 2 ante.
3 Ibid s 2(6). As to the review of 'final' decisions see ADMINISTRATIVE LAW vol 1(1) (Reissue) para 73.
4 See ibid s 2(7).
5 See ibid s 2(8).

**571. Incapacitation or death as a result of injury or disease.** Where a scheme[1] makes provision with respect to benefits payable to or in respect of a person[2] who is incapacitated or dies as a result of an injury sustained or disease contracted in circumstances prescribed by the scheme, it may make the like provision in relation to a person who is employed[3] in a civil capacity for the purposes of, or holds office in, Her Majesty's government in the United Kingdom and who is incapacitated or dies as a result of an injury or disease so sustained or contracted[4].

If, when providing for benefits in the case of incapacity or death due to injury or disease, a scheme requires the Minister for the Civil Service[5] to take into account any damages[6] recovered or recoverable by or on behalf of the recipient, but he makes payments without taking such damages into account, he has the right[7] in certain circumstances[8] to recover all or part of the payments[9] from the recipient[10].

1 Ie a scheme under the Superannuation Act 1972 s 1(1): see para 567 ante.
2 Ie a person to whom ibid s 1 applies: see para 567 ante.
3 Ie whether temporarily or permanently, and whether for reward or not: ibid s 2(1).
4 Ibid s 2(1).
5 As to the Minister for the Civil Service see paras 427, 550 ante. As to the power of that minister to delegate for the purposes of the Superannuation Act 1972, and as to the contracting out of functions under that Act, see para 567 note 2 ante.
6 Ie damages in respect of that injury, disease or death: ibid s 3(2).
7 Ie if and when he is satisfied that there are any damages to be so taken into account: ibid s 3(2).
8 Proceedings may not be brought after the death of the recipient (ibid s 3(4)(a)) or after the expiration of two years from the date when the amount of the damages was finally determined or the determination first came to the minister's knowledge, whichever date is the later (s 3(4)(b)). A certificate issued by the minister stating the date when the determination first came to his knowledge is admissible in any proceedings as sufficient evidence of that date: s 3(5).
9 Where the amount of the payments is less than the net amount of the damages, the amount of the payments is recoverable: ibid s 3(2)(a). Where the amount of the payments is not less than the net amount of the damages, the amount recoverable is the net amount of the damages: s 3(2)(b). So far as any amount recoverable represents a payment from which income tax had been deducted before payment, the proper allowance must be made in respect of the deduction: s 3(3). 'The net amount of the damages' means the amount of the damages after deduction of any tax payable in the United Kingdom or elsewhere to which the damages are subject: s 3(3).
10 Ibid s 3(1), (2). This is without prejudice to any right of the minister under the scheme to take damages into account by withholding or reducing any further sums otherwise payable to the recipient: s 3(6). The provision applies also in relation to payments made before 25 March 1972 in accordance with a warrant under the Superannuation Act 1965 s 18 (repealed): Superannuation Act 1972 s 29(2), Sch 7 para 2(2): Superannuation Act 1972 (Commencement No 1) Order 1972, SI 1972/325.

**572. Compensation for loss of office etc.** A scheme[1] may make provision for the payment by the Minister for the Civil Service[2] of pensions, allowances or gratuities by way of compensation to or in respect of persons[3] who suffer loss of office or employment, or loss or diminution of emoluments[4] in such circumstances, or by reason of the happening of such event, as may be prescribed by the scheme[5].

1   Ie a scheme under the Superannuation Act 1972 s 1(1): see para 567 ante.

2   As to the Minister for the Civil Service see paras 427, 550 ante. As to the power of that minister to delegate for the purposes of the Superannuation Act 1972, and as to the contracting out of functions under that Act, see para 567 note 2 ante.

3   Ie persons to whom the Superannnuation Act 1972 s 1 (as amended) applies: see para 567 ante.

4   As to the meaning of 'emoluments' see *R v Postmaster General* (1878) 3 QBD 428, CA; *Shelford v Mosey* [1917] 1 KB 154 at 159, DC, per Lord Reading CJ; *R v Lyon, ex p Harrison* [1921] 1 KB 203, DC; *Hartland v Diggines* [1926] AC 289, HL; *Kiddie v Port of London Authority* (1929) 93 JP 203; *Stoke Newington Borough Council v Richards* [1930] 1 KB 222, DC; *Re Wickham and Paddington Corpn's Arbitration* [1946] 2 All ER 68.

5   Superannuation Act 1972 s 2(2).

**573. Transfers to or from other employment.** The Minister for the Civil Service[1] may pay or receive transfer values[2], make payments by way of a return of contributions, with or without interest[3], and make such payments as he thinks fit towards provision of superannuation benefits outside a scheme[4].

1   As to the Minister for the Civil Service see paras 427, 550 ante. As to the power of that minister to delegate for the purposes of the Superannuation Act 1972, and as to the contracting out of functions under that Act, see para 567 note 2 ante.

2   Ibid s 1(1)(b) (in relation to persons leaving the Civil Service for other employment or entering it from other employment).

3   Ibid s 1(1)(c).

4   See ibid s 1(1)(d).

**574. Distribution without probate.** Where on the death of a person there is due to him or his personal representatives from a government department[1] a sum not exceeding £5000[2] in respect of salary, wages or other emoluments or of superannuation benefits[3], the whole or any part of the sum may be paid by the appropriate authority[4] to the personal representatives, without need for probate or other proof of their title, or to any person[5] appearing to the authority to be beneficially entitled to the deceased's personal or movable estate[6].

1   'Government department' includes a body or institution listed in the Superannuation Act 1972 s 1, Sch 1 (as amended) (see para 567 ante): s 4(3).

2   The Treasury may make an order under the Administration of Estates (Small Payments) Act 1965 s 6(1), substituting a higher amount: see the Superannuation Act 1972 s 4(2). The amount was increased to £5000 under the Administration of Estates (Small Payments) (Increase of Limit) Order 1984, SI 1984/539. As to the Treasury see paras 512–517 ante.

3   Ie superannuation benefits payable by virtue of a scheme under the Superannuation Act 1972 s 1 (as amended) (see para 567 ante): s 4(1).

4   'Appropriate authority' means the minister in charge of the government department, the body, or the trustees or other authority responsible for the institution, as the case may be, from whom the sum is due: ibid s 4(4).

5   Payment may also be made among a number of persons: see ibid s 4(1).

6   See ibid s 4(1). When payment has been made the person paid, and not the authority, is liable to account for the amount paid: s 4(1). This rule also applies in relation to a person to whom a payment was made under the Superannuation Act 1965 s 93 (repealed): Superannuation Act 1972 s 29(2), Sch 7 para 2(3).

**575. Assignment.** Any assignment of or charge on, and any agreement to assign or charge, any benefit payable under a scheme[1] is void[2], but without prejudice to the power of a court[3] to order a bankrupt's pension to be paid to the trustee in bankruptcy[4].

1   Ie a scheme under the Superannuation Act 1972 s 1(1): see para 567 ante.
2   Ibid s 5(1).
3   Ie under the Insolvency Act 1986 s 310 (as amended): see BANKRUPTCY AND INSOLVENCY vol 3(2) (Reissue) paras 437–439.
4   Superannuation Act 1972 s 5(2) (amended by the Insolvency Act 1985 s 235(1), Sch 8 para 19(b); and the Insolvency Act 1986 s 439(2), Sch 14).

## C. PRINCIPAL CIVIL SERVICE PENSION SCHEME 1974

### (A) Introduction

**576. The scheme.** The Principal Civil Service Pension Scheme 1974 came into operation on 19 November 1974[1]. It revoked and replaced the provisions deemed[2] to be the Principal Civil Service Pensions Scheme by the Superannuation Act 1972[3].

1   Principal Civil Service Pension Scheme 1974 r 1.1 (as originally made). The scheme was laid before Parliament on 19 November 1974 under the Superannuation Act 1972 s 2(11). It has been amended by Principal Civil Service Pension Scheme (Amendment) Schemes, laid before Parliament on: 22 April 1975; 28 July 1977; 31 July 1978; 27 March 1980; 4 November 1980; 31 July 1984; 26 March 1987; 30 June 1987; 30 September 1987; 30 March 1988; 26 May 1988; 27 July 1988; 26 May 1989; 6 July 1989; 1 December 1989; 20 December 1989; 28 January 1991; 12 February 1992; 14 December 1994; 9 January 1995; 31 January 1995; 19 July 1995; 18 January 1996. Except where otherwise stated, references to the Principal Civil Service Pension Scheme 1974 are to the scheme as amended and issued as Issue 2 in February 1996.
2   See the Superannuation Act 1972 s 2(12), Sch 2, which lists the provisions (all now repealed) deemed to constitute a pension scheme replaced by the Principal Civil Service Pension Scheme 1974.
3   Principal Civil Service Pension Scheme 1974 r 1. 2 (as originally made).

**577. Application of the scheme.** The Principal Civil Service Pension Scheme 1974 applies to the following persons whose service ends on or after 1 June 1972[1], namely all persons serving full time or part time in the Civil Service[2] except (1) casual staff; (2) staff engaged (including former civil servants re-employed) on a fee-paid or sessional basis; (3) staff whose terms of appointment state them to be outside the Civil Service superannuation arrangements; (4) unestablished staff engaged locally overseas; (5) staff who are covered for their service in the Civil Service by another occupational pension scheme; and (6) part-time staff who (a) before 1 October 1982 worked less than 18 hours per week; or (b) on or after 1 October 1982 and on or before 31 December 1994 worked less than 15 hours per week[3].

1   Principal Civil Service Pension Scheme 1974 r 1.1, which applies except where otherwise stated. Rules 9.1–9.16 contain transitional provisions which apply to staff whose service ended on or after 29 February 1972 and before 1 June 1972: r 1.2. As to references to the Principal Civil Service Pension Scheme 1974 see para 576 note 1 ante.
    The Occupational Pension Schemes (Disclosure of Information) Regulations 1986, SI 1986/1046 (as amended), provide inter alia for the disclosure of information about occupational pension schemes to the members of the schemes and to others. Those regulations are revoked and replaced as from 6 April 1997 by the Occupational Pension Schemes (Disclosure of Information) Regulations 1996, SI 1996/1655. The Occupational Pension Schemes (Managers) Regulations 1986, SI 1986/1718 (as amended) make provision as to who is to be treated as the manager of a public service pension scheme and as such responsible for disclosure: in the case of a government scheme, the government department responsible for its administration is treated as the manager of the scheme, and in any other case, it is the board, council, commission, person or body responsible for its administration.

2    'Civil Service' means the Civil Service of the state or any of the employments or offices listed in the
Superannuation Act 1972 s 1, Sch 1, as subsequently amended by any order under s 1(5) (see para 567
note 5 ante): Principal Civil Service Pension Scheme 1974 r 1.3. As to the application of the scheme to
court officers and staff see para 488 note 10 ante.

3    Ibid r 1.4(i)–(vi). Part-time staff are excluded from the scheme only in relation to the periods described
in heads (a) and (b) in the text: r 1.4. The exclusion under head (b) in the text does not apply where
service qualifies under r 2.7 or r 2.7a (see para 580 post): r 1.4(vi)(b).

*(B)   Reckonable Service*

**578.   Reckonable service and qualifying service.** In the Principal Civil Service
Pension Scheme 1974, 'reckonable service' means service in the Civil Service[1] or
elsewhere which reckons towards a pension under the scheme, and 'qualifying service'
(which is usually, but not necessarily, the same as reckonable service) means service which
counts towards the qualifying period for benefits[2]. In all cases reckonable and qualifying
service are counted in years and fractions of a year, each day counting as one 365th part
of a year[3]. Subject to exceptions, reckonable service is governed by general principles[4].

1    For the meaning of 'Civil Service' see para 577 note 2 ante.
2    Principal Civil Service Pension Scheme 1974 r 1.5. Except where otherwise stated, reckonable service is
also qualifying service, and service which is not reckonable service is not qualifying service: r 2.2. As to
references to the Principal Civil Service Pension Scheme 1974 see para 576 note 1 ante.
3    Ibid r 1.5.
4    So far as the reckoning of service before 1 June 1972 is concerned, the provisions of ibid rr 2.1–2.31 are
subject to any direction made before that date by the Treasury or the minister under the Superannuation
Act 1965 or any enactment repealed by that Act: Principal Civil Service Pension Scheme 1974 r 2.1.
Apart from certain exceptions (see rr 1.6a–1.7 (determination of pensionable pay), r 1.17(ii) (effect of
additional voluntary contributions), rr 4.15(ii), 4.16(ii) (death in service)) reckonable service cannot
exceed 40 years by the retiring age or 45 years in total: r 2.3. As to the different kinds of service which
are treated as reckonable or qualifying service see para 579 et seq post.
        In certain circumstances reckonable service may be enhanced, eg in relation to the resignation of a civil
servant whose resignation was desirable for management reasons, or where a person moves from a higher
to a lower substantive grade: see rr 3.10d, 3.24a(ii).
        In the Principal Civil Service Pension Scheme 1974 'minister' means the Minister for the Civil
Service: r 1.13g. As to the Minister for the Civil Service see paras 427, 550 ante. As to the Treasury see
paras 512–517 ante. As to the power of that minister to delegate for the purposes of the Superannuation
Act 1972, and as to the contracting out of functions under that Act, see para 567 note 2 ante.

**579.   Full-time service.** Continuous full-time service in the Civil Service[1] on or after
14 July 1949 reckons in full for pension[2]. Continuous full-time service before that date
reckons in full if given in an established or permanent unestablished capacity[3].
Continuous full-time service before that date reckons at half its actual length if given in
an unestablished capacity[4].

1    For the meaning of 'Civil Service' see para 577 note 2 ante.
2    See the Principal Civil Service Pension Scheme 1974 r 2.4. As to references to the Principal Civil Service
Pension Scheme 1974 see para 576 note 1 ante.
3    See ibid r 2.5.
4    See ibid r 2.6. Where unestablished service is followed by established service full reckoning may begin
before the date of establishment: r 2.6(ii), Appendix 2. Unestablished service given before 14 July 1949
while under 18 does not reckon at all: r 2.6(i). As to the position where service began before
27 June 1935 see r 2.6(iii).

**580.   Part-time service.** Part-timers for the purposes of the Principal Civil Service
Pension Scheme 1974 are those who work less than the full-time conditioned hours for
the grade and those whose conditions of service require them to work full-time for some,

but not all weeks. With effect from 1 January 1995 part-timers are eligible to be members of the scheme without restriction on the number of hours worked[1].

Between 1 October 1982 and 31 December 1994 part-timers were eligible to be members when the average conditioned hours were more than 15 hours per week. Before 1 October 1982, the minimum limit was 18 hours per week conditioned hours for the grade[2].

Where a person employed on a casual appointment is appointed to a post as a civil servant a proportion of his service under the casual appointment may count as qualifying and reckonable service[3].

1    See the Principal Civil Service Pension Scheme 1974 rr 1.4(vi), 1.10(iv). As to references to the Principal Civil Service Pension Scheme 1974 see para 576 note 1 ante.

2    See ibid rr 2.7–2.7b. Part-time service given under 18 years of age before 1 June 1972 does not, however, qualify at all: r 2.7(c). A person is not entitled to a pension at all until he has performed the necessary qualifying service. Thus any shorter period of service will not be reckonable. But, conversely, there are situations in which a person who has completed the qualifying period cannot reckon it for pension. As to reckonable and qualifying service see para 578 ante.

3    See ibid r 2.32, which applies to persons employed on casual appointments or as civil servants on or after 20 July 1995 with casual service on or after 1 April 1993.

**581. Broken service.** Where there is a break between reckonable service and earlier service in the Civil Service[1], then in certain circumstances that earlier service may count as reckonable and qualifying[2].

1    For the meaning of 'Civil Service' see para 577 note 2 ante.

2    See the Principal Civil Service Pension Scheme 1974 rr 2.9, 3.25–3.37a, Appendix 7; and para 595 post. As to reckonable and qualifying service see para 578 ante. As to references to the Principal Civil Service Pension Scheme 1974 see para 576 note 1 ante.

**582. Leave.** Annual leave and maternity leave on full pay, and special leave, injury leave and sick absence on full or half pay count as reckonable service, but in general unpaid leave and leave at pension rate neither qualify nor reckon[1].

1    See the Principal Civil Service Pension Scheme 1974 r 2.10. For exceptions to these rules see r 2.10 (i)-(vi). As to reckonable and qualifying service see para 578 ante. As to references to the Principal Civil Service Pension Scheme 1974 see para 576 note 1 ante.

**583. War service and national service.** No period of service in the armed forces may reckon if it also reckons for the purpose of naval, military or air force non-effective pay[1]. Subject to this exception, any service in the armed forces during which a civil servant was eligible to receive balance of civil pay may reckon as if it were a continuation of his service in the Civil Service[2].

A civil servant whose service in the Civil Service was interrupted by war service may reckon his war service and any subsequent unestablished service in the Civil Service before reinstatement in his former post as if it were service in his former post[3].

An established or unestablished civil servant who was called up for compulsory national service on or after 1 July 1947 may reckon his national service as if he had stayed in the Civil Service[4].

1    See the Principal Civil Service Pension Scheme 1974 r 2.11. As to references to the Principal Civil Service Pension Scheme 1974 see para 576 note 1 ante.

2    Ibid r 2.12. For the meaning of 'Civil Service' see para 577 note 2 ante.

3    Ibid r 2.13. This is subject to certain conditions (as to which see r 2.13). There are special provisions in favour of civil servants who were prevented by call-up from taking up their established appointments or who entered the Civil Service between 3 September 1939 and 30 June 1950 or through a reconstruction

competition after 30 June 1950 and had performed service in the armed forces, the merchant navy or mercantile marine or one of the women's services between those dates: see rr 2.14, 2.15.

4	See ibid r 2.16. There are provisions in favour of a person who was prevented by that service from taking up his established post: see r 2.16. Similar provisions apply to civil servants recalled for certain service in the reserve and auxiliary forces: see rr 2.17, 2.17a.

**584. Other service outside the Civil Service.** Previous service outside the Civil Service[1] counts as reckonable or qualifying service[2] in accordance with rules varying with the nature of the previous service[3].

1	For the meaning of 'Civil Service' see para 577 note 2 ante.
2	As to reckonable and qualifying service see para 578 ante.
3	See the Principal Civil Service Pension Scheme 1974 rr 2.18–2.22.
	Rule 2.18 relates to civil servants who were transferred from other services under block transfers. These services and the rules relating to the transfers are listed in Appendix 3: Supreme Court Officers (Pensions) Act 1954 s 2(7) (secretaries or clerks to High Court judges etc); Superannuation Act 1965 s 37 (repealed) (Imperial War Graves Commission); s 92 (repealed); Government of India (India Office Pensions) Order 1936, SR & O 1936/1034; Unemployment Assistance Board (Superannuation) Rules 1935, SR & O 1935/592; National Insurance and Civil Service (Superannuation) Rules 1948, SI 1948/2434 (approved societies); Superannuation (Transfer of Silicosis Medical Officers) Rules 1949, SI 1949/168 (revoked); Superannuation (Reckoning of Certain Previous Service) Rules 1949, SI 1949/1803 (local government, Safety in Mines Research Board, and War Agricultural Executive Committee); Commonwealth Telegraphs (Cable and Wireless Ltd Pension) Regulations 1955, SI 1955/1893 (amended by SI 1971/61); Commonwealth Telegraphs (Cable and Wireless Ltd Pension) Regulations 1962, SI 1962/196 (amended by SI 1968/1979); Superannuation (Roehampton Hospital and Civil Service) Transfer Rules 1957, SI 1957/1723; Superannuation (Wartime Social Survey and Civil Service) Transfer Rules 1957, SI 1957/1989; Superannuation (Polish Education Committee and Civil Service) Transfer Rules 1959, SI 1959/191; Superannuation (British Council and Civil Service) Transfer Rules 1959, SI 1959/1922; Superannuation (Imperial Institute and Civil Service) Transfer Rules 1959, SI 1959/1923; Superannuation (National Assistance Board) Transfer Rules 1959, SI 1959/1985 (amended by SI 1961/1376; and SI 1965/2130); Superannuation (Imperial Forestry Institute and Civil Service) Transfer Rules 1961, SI 1961/1775; Superannuation (Low Temperature Research Station and Civil Service) Transfer Rules 1961, SI 1961/1776; Superannuation (Pest Infestation Laboratory and Civil Service) Transfer Rules 1961, SI 1961/1777; Superannuation (Transfer of Hostels Staff) Rules 1962, SI 1962/158; Superannuation (Transfer of Agricultural Staff) Rules 1963, SI 1963/1220; Superannuation (Institutes for the Blind and Civil Service) Transfer Rules 1964, SI 1964/719; Superannuation (Anti-Locust Research Centre and Civil Service) Transfer Rules 1964, SI 1964/1720; Superannuation (National Buildings Record) Transfer Rules 1965, SI 1965/1040; Superannuation (City of London Collectors of Taxes and Civil Service) Transfer Rules 1965, SI 1965/1558; Superannuation (Tropical Research Units and Civil Service) Transfer Rules 1966, SI 1966/776; Superannuation (Pool of Soil Scientists and Civil Service) Transfer Rules 1969, SI 1969/402; Superannuation (Hovercraft Development Ltd and Civil Service) Transfer Rules 1970, SI 1970/1331; Superannuation (General Medical Council and Civil Service) Transfer Rules 1970, SI 1970/1357 (revoked); Superannuation (Pest Infestation Laboratory and Civil Service) Transfer Rules 1971, SI 1971/1726.
	The Principal Civil Service Pension Scheme 1974 r 2.19 relates to individual civil servants who transferred before 1 June 1972 from other employments covered by the following instruments listed in Appendix 4: Local Government and Civil Service (Superannuation) Rules 1936, SR & O 1936/651 (amended by SR & O 1940/1976, SR & O 1947/2809); Superannuation (Transfers between the Civil Service and Public Boards) Rules 1950, SI 1950/1539 (revoked) (previously amended by SI 1952/1330; SI 1954/263; SI 1955/127; SI 1955/1427; SI 1958/2092; SI 1959/2015; SI 1960/1466; SI 1961/377; SI 1963/1760; SI 1964/1719; SI 1964/1800; SI 1966/454; SI 1966/705; SI 1967/89; SI 1967/1111; SI 1968/471; SI 1969/1382; SI 1970/744; SI 1970/1563; SI 1971/752; and the Principal Civil Service Pension Scheme (Transfer Scheme) 1972); Superannuation (Transfers from the Civil Service to the Fire Services) Rules 1952, SI 1952/917 (revoked); Superannuation (the Civil Service and the Federated Superannuation System for Universities) Transfer Rules 1953, SI 1953/337 (revoked) (previously amended by SI 1966/453; and the Principal Civil Service Pension Scheme (Transfer Scheme) 1972); Superannuation (Civil Service and Imperial Institute) Transfer Rules 1954, SI 1954/981 (revoked); Superannuation (Civil Service and Jersey Civil Service) Transfer Rules 1956, SI 1956/976 (revoked) (previously amended by SI 1966/450); Superannuation (Civil Service and Northern Ireland Health Service) Transfer Rules

1957, SI 1957/1222 (revoked) (previously amended by SI 1966/451); Superannuation (Civil Service and Isle of Man Authorities) Transfer Rules 1957, SI 1957/2229 (revoked) (previously amended by SI 1966/449); Superannuation (Civil Service and Northern Ireland Local Government) Transfer Rules 1960, SI 1960/819 (revoked) (previously amended by SI 1966/452; and SI 1968/779); National Health Service (Superannuation) Regulations 1961, SI 1961/1441; Superannuation (Civil Service and Agricultural Research Organisations) Transfer Rules 1965, SI 1965/1827 (revoked) (previously amended by SI 1966/447); Superannuation (Civil Servants and Members of the House of Commons) Transfer Rules 1966, SI 1966/769 (revoked) (previously amended by SI 1967/614); Superannuation (Transfers between the Civil Service and the Police) Rules 1966, SI 1966/1586 (revoked); Superannuation (Civil Service and Local Government) Interchange Rules 1968, SI 1968/72; Superannuation (Civil Service and Public Transport Services) Transfer Rules 1968, SI 1968/841 (revoked) (previously amended by the Principal Civil Service Pension Scheme (Transfer Scheme) 1972); Superannuation (Territorial and Auxiliary Forces Associations and Civil Service) Transfer Rules 1968, SI 1968/34 (revoked); Superannuation (Teaching and Civil Service) Interchange Rules 1970, SI 1970/260; and Superannuation (Civil Service and Northern Ireland Teaching Service) Transfer Rules 1971, SI 1971/2013.

The Principal Civil Service Pension Scheme 1972 rr 2.19a, 2.19b make provision in relation to staff previously employed by Territorial and Auxiliary Forces Associations.

Rule 2.20, relates to civil servants who join on or after 1 June 1972 under the transfer provisions of rr 6.2–6.28 (as to which see para 611 post).

Rule 2.21 provides that a civil servant with previous service in a public office (as defined by the Superannuation Act 1965 s 39 (as amended); the Superannuation (Designation of Public Offices) Order 1965, SI 1965/1357; and the Superannuation (Designation of Public Offices) Order 1967, SI 1967/666) may count that service as reckonable or qualifying. The rules for doing so are set out in the Superannuation (Public Offices) Rules 1967, SI 1967/364 (amended by SI 1968/2071; SI 1972/1762; and SI 1982/1207), made under the Superannuation Act 1965 ss 38, 42(1) (repealed).

**585. Added years.** A number of civil servants who entered the Civil Service[1] before 1 June 1972 were awarded added years of reckonable service under the Superannuation Act 1965[2]. For those entering the Civil Service on or after that date the minister[3] has discretion to grant added years if there are special circumstances to justify this[4]. Subject to certain limits a civil servant may increase his reckonable and qualifying service by buying added years at full cost to himself[5].

1　For the meaning of 'Civil Service' see para 577 note 2 ante.
2　See the Superannuation Act 1965 s 24 (repealed), and the Principal Civil Service Pension Scheme 1974 r 2.23. As to references to the Principal Civil Service Pension Scheme 1974 see para 576 note 1 ante.
3　Ie the Minister for the Civil Service: see para 578 note 4 ante.
4　Principal Civil Service Pension Scheme 1974 r 2.24. Additionally, added years may be granted to a civil servant over 60 who remains in a post at the same or a higher grade, where staff recruitment or retention problems in his department justify the grant of added years: see r 2.4a.
5　Ibid r 2.25. As to the rules for buying added years see rr 7.1–7.26. As to reckonable and qualifying service see para 578 ante.

**586. Service overseas.** Service in certain places overseas reckons at one and a half times the length at which it would otherwise have reckoned[1].

1　See the Principal Civil Service Pension Scheme 1972 r 2.29, Appendix 6. This provision does not apply for the purposes of qualifying (as opposed to reckonable) service, and it is subject to exceptions: r 2.30. The retiring age is also reduced: see r 2.31. As to reckonable and qualifying service see para 578 ante. As to references to the Principal Civil Service Pension Scheme 1974 see para 576 note 1 ante.

**587. Opting out.** Membership of the Principal Civil Service Pension Scheme is not a condition of Civil Service[1] employment. Members may opt out of the scheme in favour of alternative pension arrangements[2]. The scheme applies to a person joining the Civil Service unless he exercises an option that it is not so to apply[3]. A person who has opted out may elect that the scheme is to reapply to him, provided that he is under 55 and satisfies tests with regard to his state of health[4].

1    For the meaning of 'Civil Service' see para 577 note 2 ante.
2    Principal Civil Service Pension Scheme 1974 rr 1.4a(i), (iii), 1.4b(ii), 1.4c(ii). The scheme then ceases to
     apply to such a person: r 1.4a(ii). As to references to the Principal Civil Service Pension Scheme 1974 see
     para 576 note 1 ante.
3    See ibid r 1.4c(i), (ii).
4    See ibid r 1.4d.

## *(C)  Retirement and Death Benefits*

**588. Ordinary retirement.** Subject to the other provisions of the Principal Civil
Service Pension Scheme 1974, a civil servant who retires on or after reaching the retiring
age must be paid (1) an annual pension of one-eightieth of his pensionable pay multiplied
by the length of his reckonable service; and (2) a lump sum of three-eightieths of his
pensionable pay multiplied by the length of his reckonable service[1]. A civil servant may
surrender the lump sum for the commutation value as an increase in pension payments[2].

1    See the Principal Civil Service Pension Scheme 1974 r 3.1. As to reckonable service see para 578 ante.
     Pensionable pay is determined under rr 1.6a–1.7. As to references to the Principal Civil Service Pension
     Scheme 1974 see para 576 note 1 ante. If a civil servant serving beyond retiring age completes 45 years'
     reckonable service an additional lump sum may be paid in respect of further service (see r 3.2), but there
     is no absolute right to receive this payment (r 8.1). Further provision is made as to the calculation of
     benefits in relation to designated appointments (ie appointments where the civil servant is paid more than
     the pay band maximum, or where he is promoted by two or more grades: see rr 3.1b–3.1d. As to the
     calculation of widows', widowers' and dependants' pension benefits and contributions see r 4.66.
2    See ibid r 3.1a.

**589. Premature retirement: the Civil Service Compensation Scheme.**
Benefits are payable under the Civil Service Compensation Scheme[1] to: (1) a civil servant
who is compulsorily retired early on grounds of structure, limited efficiency or
redundancy[2]; (2) a civil servant who is compulsorily retired early under the flexible
category[3]; and (3) a civil servant aged 50 or over with at least five years' qualifying service
who is retired under the approved category[4].

   Particular provision is made in relation to (a) civil servants who are retired within
three years of their retiring age[5]; (b) service overseas[6]; (c) resettlement leave[7]; (d) part-
time service[8]; (e) widows' and dependants' benefits[9]; (f) allocation of part of benefits[10]; (g)
repackaging of benefits[11]; (h) transfers[12]; (i) re-employment of persons to whom former
rules applied[13]; (j) interim arrangements[14]; (k) fixed term appointments[15]; and (l)
compensation in lieu of notice for Crown servants[16].

1    The Civil Service Compensation Scheme was laid before Parliament on 9 January 1995 under the
     Superannuation Act 1972 s 1 (see para 567 ante); it has been amended by Civil Service Compensation
     Scheme (Amendment) Schemes on 19 July 1995, 18 January 1996 and 1 April 1996. The scheme replaces
     the Principal Civil Service Pension Scheme 1974 section 10 (the former rules) with effect from 1 January
     1995. The former rules are set out as Appendices 1 and 2 to the Civil Service Compensation Scheme. As
     to the Principal Civil Service Pension Scheme 1974 see para 576 note 1 ante.
2    Civil Service Compensation Scheme r 2.1. The benefits are determined in accordance with rr 2.2–2.9.
3    See ibid rr 3.1–3.4.
4    See ibid rr 4.1–4.2.1.
5    See ibid r 5.1.
6    See ibid r 5.2.
7    See ibid r 5.3.
8    See ibid rr 5.4–5.5.
9    See ibid r 5.6.
10   See ibid r 5.7.
11   See ibid rr 5.8–5.14.
12   See ibid r 5.15.
13   See ibid rr 6.1–6.7. As to the former rules see note 1 supra.

14  See ibid rr 7.1–7.11.
15  See ibid rr 8.1–8.4.
16  See ibid rr 9.1.1–9.2.2.

**590. Retirement on medical grounds.** A civil servant (other than a person on a period appointment) who is retired on medical grounds and who would qualify for a pension on ordinary retirement[1], or who is eligible for a preserved pension[2] with five or more years' qualifying service will be paid an ill health pension and lump sum[3].

1  As to the benefits payable on ordinary retirement see para 588 ante.
2  Ie a preserved pension under the Principal Civil Service Pension Scheme 1974 r 3.11, r 3.17 or r 3.24a: see paras 581 ante, 592 post. As to references to the Principal Civil Service Pension Scheme 1974 see para 576 note 1 ante.
3  See ibid rr 3.4–3.4b. These will be calculated in the way described in r 3.1 (see para 588 ante), but with his reckonable service enhanced as described in r 3.4. Provision is also made for retirement on medical grounds after at least two but less than five years' qualifying service: (see r 3.5, but note that such payments (ill health payments) are discretionary: r 8.1). A civil servant retired on medical grounds may be treated as having resigned if: (1) he has not satisfied the health standard as specified from time to time by the minister; or (2) he has made a false declaration as to his health or suppressed a material fact when applying to join (or rejoin) the scheme: rr 3.6, 3.7. For the meaning of 'minister' see para 578 note 4 ante.

**591. Death benefits.** If a civil servant dies in service a death benefit may be paid to one person nominated by him to receive it, or, in the absence of a valid nomination, to his personal representatives[1]. The death benefit will be the greater of (1) two years' pensionable pay; and (2) the lump sum that would have been paid if he had been retired on medical grounds at the date of his death[2].

1  Principal Civil Service Pension Scheme 1974 r 3.8. There is no absolute right to receive this benefit: r 8.1. A nomination is invalid if: (1) the person nominated was the nominator's husband or wife at the time of the nomination, but the marriage has come to an end; (2) the minister considers that payment is not reasonably practicable or would be subject to the common law rule of forfeiture; (3) the person nominated has died; or (4) the nomination was not in correct form: r 3.8(ii). A nomination may be revoked by subsequent notice in writing in correct form: r 3.8(iii). There are special provisions for part-time service in the last three years of reckonable service (r 3.8(vi)), for the position where a civil servant had been transferred from standard to non-standard pay terms (r 3.8a) and for death after retirement (rr 3.9, 8.1).
    As to references to the Principal Civil Service Pension Scheme 1974 see para 576 note 1 ante. For the meaning of 'minister' in the scheme see para 578 note 4 ante.
2  Ibid r 3.8(v). Where death occurred before 1 July 1987, the position is the same as is set out in the text except that for 'two years' pensionable service' there should be read 'his pensionable service': see r 3.8(iv).

**592. Resignation.** A civil servant who resigns may be eligible for payment of a transfer value to his new employer[1]. A civil servant who:

(1)  resigns with two or more years' qualifying service; or

(2)  is a woman civil servant who leaves the Civil Service[2] after the end of the tax year before she reaches 60; or

(3)  was formerly entitled to rights under a personal pension scheme in respect of which a transfer payment has been made into the Principal Civil Service Pension Scheme,

and who does not opt for the payment of a transfer value, will be awarded a preserved pension and lump sum[3]. These will be brought into payment when he reaches the retiring age[4].

1  See the Principal Civil Service Pension Scheme 1974 r 3.10. This is subject to the conditions set out in Section 6 (transfers): see para 611 post. As to references to the Principal Civil Service Pension Scheme 1974 see para 576 note 1 ante. Alternatively, a civil servant may opt to receive immediate payment of the pension and lump sum after actuarial reduction: see para 593 post.

Short-service payments may be paid to civil servants who resigned before 6 April 1988 with at least two but less than five years' qualifying service: see rr 3.17, 3.18, 8.1.

2 For the meaning of 'Civil Service' see para 577 note 2 ante.

3 Principal Civil Service Pension Scheme 1974 r 3.11.

4 Ibid r 3.11. They will be calculated in the way described in r 3.1 (see para 588 ante). There are special provisions for prison officers (rr 3.12, 3.13), for immediate or early payment to persons who fall ill before reaching the age of 60 (r 3.14) or on compassionate grounds (see r 3.15), and for a death benefit to persons who die before a preserved pension and lump sum come into payment (rr 3.16, 8.1).

**593. Actuarially reduced pensions.** Where a civil servant aged 50 or over resigns and is eligible for a preserved pension and lump sum[1] he may opt for immediate payment of the preserved pension and lump sum after actuarial reduction[2], instead of the full amounts which would be paid at retiring age[3]. The minister[4] must be satisfied that the pension so reduced does not amount to less than the guaranteed minimum pension payable under statute[5]. A civil servant may at any time before they would otherwise be brought into payment, opt for payment of the preserved pension and lump sum after actuarial reduction[6].

1 See para 592 ante.

2 The actuarial reduction is calculated by reference to factors provided by the scheme actuary: Principal Civil Service Pension Scheme 1974 r 3.10a. As to the position where a civil servant has a reduced retiring age under r 2.31 (see para 586 ante) see r 3.10b. As to references to the Principal Civil Service Pension Scheme 1974 see para 576 note 1 ante.

3 See ibid r 3.10a(i). This may also apply where a person moves from a higher to a lower substantive grade: see r 3.10(a)(ii).

4 For the meaning of 'minister' in the scheme see para 578 note 4 ante.

5 Principal Civil Service Pension Scheme 1974 r 3.10a. The statute in question is the Social Security Pensions Act 1975 s 35(1).

6 See the Principal Civil Service Pension Scheme 1974 r 3.10c.

**594. Modification on account of national insurance benefits.** A pension will be reduced to take account of flat-rate national insurance pensions[1] or graduated national insurance pensions[2].

1 See the Principal Civil Service Pension Scheme 1974 rr 3.19–3.21. These rules apply similarly to superannuation allowances deemed to have been granted under the scheme by the Superannuation Act 1972 s 29(2), Sch 7 para 1(1) (savings consequent on repeals of former legislation): Principal Civil Service Pension Scheme 1974 r 3.23a. As to references to the Principal Civil Service Pension Scheme 1974 see para 576 note 1 ante.

2 See ibid rr 3.22, 3.23.

**595. Re-employment and employment on a lower grade.** Detailed provision is made by the Principal Civil Service Pension Scheme 1974 governing the pension to be awarded where a civil servant is re-employed in the Civil Service[1] according to whether he is re-employed in a grade the same as, or lower than, or higher than, his grade on retirement, and according to whether he is re-employed on full-time or part-time work[2].

Provision is also made for the case where a civil servant moves from a higher to a lower substantive grade before the retiring age[3], or has been transferred from standard pay terms to non-standard pay terms for a fixed period before the retiring age[4].

1 For the meaning of 'Civil Service' see para 577 note 2 ante.

2 See the Principal Civil Service Pension Scheme 1974 rr 3.25–3.37a. As to references to the Principal Civil Service Pension Scheme 1974 see para 576 note 1 ante. For the application of the provisions relating to widows' (or widowers') pension, dependants' pension, or invalidity pension see r 4.62.

3 See ibid rr 3.24–3.24f.

4 See ibid r 3.24g.

**596. Special cases and gratuities.** Special provisions apply to: (1) persons who left the Civil Service before 1 June 1972 on approved employment terms or with an award on retirement on or after the age of 50 years[1]; (2) gratuities for unestablished service before 31 May 1972 given by a civil servant who later (but before 1 June 1982) resigned or retired[2]; (3) marriage gratuities for women civil servants resigning on or after 1 June 1972, but before 1 June 1982[3].

1   See the Principal Civil Service Pension Scheme 1974 r 3.45. Such persons remain subject to the Superannuation Act 1965 ss 7, 40, 46 (repealed). Provision is also made for certain civil servants who were established before 27 June 1935: see Principal Civil Service Pension Scheme 1974 rr 3.46–3.48.
2   See ibid rr 3.38–3.41, 8.1.
3   See ibid rr 3.42–3.44, 8.1.

### (D) Injury Benefits

**597. Qualifying conditions.** Injury benefits[1] may be paid to a civil servant[2] who: (1) is injured in the course of official duty[3]; or (2) suffers an injury as a result of an attack or similar act which is directly attributable to his employment or office[4]; or (3) contracts a disease to which he is exposed by the nature of his duty[5]; or (4) having been recruited in the United Kingdom, suffers an injury while in an area outside the United Kingdom which is directly attributable to the existence in that area of a state of war, revolution or serious disturbance or as a direct result of deliberate acts of the local population or of sporadic political disturbances[6]; or (5) having been recruited in the United Kingdom, suffers an aggravation of a disease from which he is already suffering, as a result of his duty outside the United Kingdom[7].

1   Such benefits are not payable if the injury or disease is wholly or mainly due to the person's own serious or culpable misconduct or negligence: Principal Civil Service Pension Scheme 1974 r 11.3. As to references to the Principal Civil Service Pension Scheme 1974 see para 576 note 1 ante.
2   Ie persons serving in full-time or part-time employment in the Civil Service who are injured or contract a disease on or after 29 February 1972, if the Injury Warrants 1952–71 applied to them, or on or after 1 June 1972 if those warrants did not apply: ibid r 11.1. Persons who satisfied the conditions of those warrants and whose service had not ended before 29 February 1972 are also included: r 11.2. It should be noted that this is wider than membership of the scheme itself. For the meaning of 'Civil Service' see para 11.1324 note 2 ante.
3   Ibid r 11.3(i), which further provides that the injury is directly attributable to the nature of the duty or arises from an activity reasonably incidental to the duty. An injury suffered during a journey between the person's place of residence and official premises is not included, unless it is a duty journey: r 11.4(i), (ii). Neither is an injury if it is not related to the person's official duty and is suffered during his main meal break, even if it is on official premises: r 11.4(iii).
4   See ibid r 11.3(ii).
5   Ibid r 11.3(iii).
6   Ibid r 11.3(iv).
7   Ibid r 11.3(v).

**598. Eligibility for benefit.** A person satisfying the qualifying conditions[1] whose earning capacity is impaired because of injury or disease may be paid an annual allowance[2], a lump sum[3], or both, according to his circumstances[4].

1   See para 597 ante. As to injury suffered during temporary service outside the United Kingdom see the Principal Civil Service Pension Scheme 1974 r 11.11. As to references to the Principal Civil Service Pension Scheme 1974 see para 576 note 1 ante.
2   The amount of annual allowance is calculated in accordance with a scale of guaranteed minimum income rates appropriate to the circumstances of the case: see ibid r 11.7. The appropriate guaranteed minimum income takes into account any occupational pension or any specified national insurance benefits payable: rr 11.7, 11.8. As to review of allowances see r.11.10.

3　The lump sum is calculated according to the impairment of earning capacity and the amount of pensionable pay: see ibid r 11.9.

4　See ibid r 11.6. Where damages are or will be recovered in respect of any injury or disease for which injury benefits may be paid, the allowance or lump sums may be withheld or reduced: see r.11.19. If the civil servant is an apprentice or, because of his youth is paid less than a corresponding adult worker, the injury benefit will be calculated as if he had been paid adult rates: see r 11.20.

**599. Injury benefits payable to widows, widowers and dependants.** An annual allowance and a lump sum[1] may be paid to the widow or widower[2] and dependants[3] of a civil servant who satisfies the qualifying conditions for benefit[4] and who dies as a direct result of his injury or disease[5].

1　Such benefits are paid in accordance with the Principal Civil Service Pension Scheme 1974 rr 11.13–11.18. As to references to the Principal Civil Service Pension Scheme 1974 see para 576 note 1 ante.

2　Any reference in those provisions to 'eligible widow' includes a reference to 'eligible widower': see rr 4.21a, 11.12, 11.16. For the meaning of 'eligible widow' see ibid r 4.4; and para 602 note 7 post.

3　Dependants include each eligible child (see ibid rr 4.26–4.28; and para 606 post), a wholly or mainly dependant parent, and any incapacitated children, brothers or sisters who were wholly or mainly dependant on the civil servant at the time of his death: rr 11.12(b)–(d), 11.14, 11.15.

4　See para 597 ante.

5　See the Principal Civil Service Pension Scheme 1974 rr 11.12, 11.13.

**600. Persons employed for government purposes and ministers.** An annual allowance and a lump sum may be paid to a person (or his spouse or dependants) who, although not a civil servant, is employed in a civil capacity for government purposes and whose earning capacity is impaired, or who dies, because of injury or disease occurring after 31 May 1972[1].

Benefit is also payable to a person holding government office whose earning capacity is impaired because of injury or disease occurring on or after 29 February 1972[2].

1　Principal Civil Service Pension Scheme 1974 rr 11.21–11.23, and see rr.11.3, 11.4 sub-para 1 ante. Such employment may be temporary or permanent, or for reward or not: r 11.21. As to references to the Principal Civil Service Pension Scheme 1974 see para 576 note 1 ante.

2　See ibid rr 11.24–11.27.

*(E) Widows', Widowers' and Dependants' Benefits*

**601. Widows' pensions application.** The provisions of the Principal Civil Service Pension Scheme 1974 relating to widows' pensions apply to all male pensionable civil servants in service on or after 1 June 1972[1].

1　Principal Civil Service Pension Scheme 1974 r 4.1. As to references to the Principal Civil Service Pension Scheme 1974 see para 576 note 1 ante.

**602. Widows' pensions: contributions and benefits.** While in service a civil servant must pay periodical contributions of 1t of salary or wages until the end of pensionable service[1].

If a civil servant

(1)　dies in service with two or more years' qualifying service[2]; or

(2)　dies in service on or after reaching retiring age[3]; or

(3)　dies after retiring with a pension[4]; or

(4)　dies in service and was formerly entitled to rights under a personal pension scheme in respect of which a transfer payment has been made to the Principal Civil Service Pension Scheme[5],

then a widow's pension[6] will be paid if he leaves an eligible widow[7].

There is provision for a guaranteed minimum pension if the civil servant's employment becomes contracted out, unless (a) the pension rights have been transferred out of the scheme; or (b) the widow forfeits the pension for misconduct; or (c) the pension ceases because she remarries or lives with another man as his wife[8].

1   See the Principal Civil Service Pension Scheme 1974 r 4.9, which makes further provision as to the assessment of contributions. As to references to the Principal Civil Service Pension Scheme 1974 see para 576 note 1 ante. A civil servant may opt to pay additional periodical contributions: rr 4.12–4.14. As to contributions due in respect of purchased added years (see para 585 ante), married and unmarried civil servants, and as to the collection of such contributions, see rr 4.15–4.19, 4.59–4.60.
2   Ibid r 4.3(ii). As to qualifying service see para 578 ante.
3   Ibid r 4.3(iii).
4   Ie a pension under ibid r 3.1 (see para 588 ante), or an ill health pension under r 3.4 (see para 590 ante), or a preserved pension under r 3.11 or 3.24a(ii) (see para 592 ante): r 4.3(iv).
5   Ibid r 4.3(v).
6   As to the annual amount of a widow's pension see ibid rr 4.6–4.7a, 4.68.
7   Ibid r 4.3. 'Eligible widow' means a woman to whom the civil servant was married at the time of his death, and who was not cohabiting with another man; if he retired before 6 April 1978 she must have been married to him at some time while he was a civil servant: r 4.4. The pension is payable for life unless she remarries or cohabits with any man, in which case it may cease to be payable or may be reduced: see r 4.5.
    There are special provisions where: (1) a civil servant dies leaving an eligible widow but there is no entitlement to a widow's pension (r 4.8(i), (ii)); or (2) there is no eligible widow but dependants are left in the care of some other person (rr 4.8(iii), (iv), 4.68); (3) there has been part-time service in the last three years of reckonable service or where the civil servant dies during a period of re-employment (r 4.8a); or (4) where the civil servant was transferred to non-standard pay terms for a fixed period (r 4.67).
8   See ibid r 4.19a. As to the transfer of pension rights out of the scheme see para 611 post. As to forfeiture for misconduct see para 613 post. As to the effect of remarriage or cohabitation on a widow's pension see note 7 supra.

**603. Widowers' pensions application.** The provisions of the Principal Civil Service Pension Scheme 1974 relating to widowers' pensions apply to all female pensionable civil servants in service on or after 1 July 1987, including those who had before that date been paying contributions under voluntary arrangements[1].

1   See the Principal Civil Service Pension Scheme 1974 r 4.20a(i). It also applies to female civil servants who died on or before 30 June 1987 and opted to pay voluntary contributions, and others who had so opted but had no service after that date: see r 4.20a(ii). As to references to the Principal Civil Service Pension Scheme 1974 see para 576 note 1 ante.

**604. Widowers' pensions: contributions and benefits.** While in service a civil servant must pay periodical contributions of 1.5 per cent of salary or wages until the end of pensionable service[1].
    If a civil servant
(1)   dies in service with two or more years' qualifying service[2]; or
(2)   dies in service on or after reaching retiring age[3]; or
(3)   dies after retiring with a pension[4]; or
(4)   dies in service and was formerly entitled to rights under a personal pension scheme in respect of which a transfer payment has been made to the Principal Civil Service Pension Scheme[5],
then a widower's pension[6] will be paid if she leaves an eligible widower[7].
    There is provision for a guaranteed minimum pension if the civil servant's employment becomes contracted out, unless (a) the pension rights have been transferred out of the scheme; or (b) the widower forfeits the pension for misconduct; or (c) the pension ceases because he remarries or lives with another woman as her husband[8].

1  See the Principal Civil Service Pension Scheme 1974 r 4.22, which makes further provision as to the assessment of contributions. As to references to the Principal Civil Service Pension Scheme 1974 see para 576 note 1 ante. A civil servant may opt to pay additional periodical contributions: r 4.22aa. As to contributions due in respect of purchased added years (see para 585 ante), married and unmarried civil servants, and as to the collection of such contributions, see rr 4.22c–4.23d, 4.59–4.60.

2  Ibid r 4.21(ii). As to qualifying service see para 578 ante.

3  Ibid r 4.21(iii).

4  Ie a pension under ibid r 3.1 (see para 588 ante), or an ill health pension under r 3.4 (see para 590 ante), a preserved pension under r 3.11 or 3.24a(ii) (see para 592 ante), or an actuarially reduced pension under r 3.10a (see para 593 ante): r 4.21(iv).

5  Ibid r 4.21(v).

6  As to the annual amount of a widower's pension see ibid rr 4.21c–4.21e, 4.68.

7  Ibid r 4.21. 'Eligible widower' means a man to whom the civil servant was married at the time of her death, and who was not cohabiting with another woman; if she retired on or before 5 April 1988 he must have been married to her at some time while she was a civil servant: r 4.21a. The pension is payable for life unless he remarries or cohabits with any woman, in which case it may cease to be payable or may be reduced: see r 4.21b.

   There are special provisions where: (1) a civil servant dies leaving an eligible widower but there is no entitlement to a widowers' pension (r 4.21f(i), (ii)); or (2) there is no eligible widower but dependants are left in the care of some other person (rr 4.21f(iii), (iv), 4.68); (3) there has been part-time service in the last three years of reckonable service or where the civil servant dies during a period of re-employment (r 4.21g); or (4) where the civil servant was transferred to non-standard pay terms for a fixed period (r 4.67).

8  See ibid r 4.21i. As to the transfer of pension rights out of the scheme see para 611 post. As to forfeiture for misconduct see para 613 post. As to the effect of remarriage or cohabitation on a widower's pension see note 7 supra.

**605. Children's pensions: application.** The provisions for non-contributory children's pensions apply to all pensionable civil servants in service on or after 1 June 1972[1].

1  See the Principal Civil Service Pension Scheme 1974 rr 4.24, 4.34. As to references to the Principal Civil Service Pension Scheme 1974 see para 576 note 1 ante.

**606. Children's pensions: contributions and benefits.** Children's pensions under the Principal Civil Service Pension Scheme are non-contributory[1]. If a civil servant:

(1)   dies in service[2]; or

(2)   dies after retiring with a pension[3]; or

(3)   dies after resigning or opting out of the scheme with a preserved pension[4],

a children's pension will be paid if he leaves one or more eligible children[5]. The amount of the pension is generally one-quarter or one-third of the civil servant's pension, depending on whether the child is in the care of his widow or in the care of some other person[6].

The pension is normally payable to the civil servant's widow or widower if they are in her (or his care), or to the children's guardian if they are in the care of some other person[7]. An eligible child may receive a children's pension in respect of not more than two civil servants to whom the scheme applies[8].

1  See the Principal Civil Service Pension Scheme 1974 r 4.34. As to references to the Principal Civil Service Pension Scheme 1974 see para 576 note 1 ante.

2  Ibid r 4.25(i)(b). This applies to death occurring after 1 April 1980; prior to that date there was a requirement of at least 5 years' qualifying service: see r 4.25(i)(a).

3  Ie a pension under ibid r 3.1 (see para 588 ante), or an ill health pension under r 3.4 (see para 590 ante), or an actuarially reduced pension under r 3.10a (see para 593 ante): r 4.25(ii)(a)–(c). This applies to death occurring after 1 April 1980; prior to that date there was a requirement of at least 5 years' qualifying service: r 4.25(ii).

4    Ie after leaving or opting out with a preserved pension under ibid r 3.11 (see para 592 ante) or r 3.24a(ii) (see para 595 ante): r 4.25(ii)(d), (e). This applies to death occurring after 1 April 1980; prior to that date there was a requirement of at least 5 years' qualifying service: r 4.25(ii).

5    Ibid r 4.25. As to the position where the civil servant was transferred to non-standard pay terms for a fixed period see r 4.67. In general 'eligible child' means:

    (1)   a child of the civil servant or his spouse (including such a child born after the death of the civil servant);

    (2)   a child of a dead brother, sister or child of the civil servant; or

    (3)   a brother or sister of the civil servant,

who is (a) under 17 years of age, or (b) receiving full-time education, or (c) undergoing full-time training of at least two years' duration for any trade, profession or vocation during which he receives not more than a specified maximum allowable remuneration: r 4.26(a)–(c), (i)–(iii). 'Child' includes legally adopted children, step children and illegitimate children, and 'brother' and 'sister' include half brothers and half sisters: r 4.26. If (b) or (c) supra applies, the education must have continued uninterrupted from age 17, unless the minister decides (or at his direction, the scheme administrator decides) to overlook breaks in education: r 4.26

    However (in relation to death occurring on or after 1 July 1987), 'eligible child' generally excludes (i) any child (other than a posthumous child) not dependent on the civil servant at the time of his death; (ii) where the person dies after ceasing to be a civil servant, any child who would not have been eligible at the date of the when pensionable service ended if the civil servant had died on that date: r 4.27. As to the minister's discretion to treat children as eligible see r 4.28. For the meaning of 'minister' in the scheme see para 578 note 4 ante.

6    See ibid rr 4.30, 4.68. As to the maximum amounts payable see r 4.31.

7    See ibid rr 4.24, 4.32. If the children are in the care of more than one person, the pension will be paid in the appropriate persons: r 4.32. In all cases the pension is to be applied for the benefit of the children: r 4.32.

8    See ibid r 4.33b.

## 607. Invalidity pensions: application.

A pensionable civil servant may nominate for an invalidity pension a person who (1) is such that he would count as an eligible child[1] if the civil servant were to die; (2) is permanently incapacitated[2]; and (3) is wholly or mainly dependent on the civil servant[3]. A nomination ceases to be valid if the nominator revokes it, if the nominee ceases to be permanently incapacitated or wholly or mainly dependent on the civil servant[4], if the nominee dies or if the nominee marries the civil servant[5]. There may be only one valid nomination at any time[6].

1    Ie an eligible child under the Principal Civil Service Pension Scheme 1974 rr 4.24–4.34: see para 606 ante. As to references to the Principal Civil Service Pension Scheme 1974 see para 576 note 1 ante.

2    'Permanently incapacitated' means that because of a specific mental or physical disability which is likely to be permanent, the child in question is unlikely to be able to earn his own living: ibid r 4.36.

3    See ibid r 4.35. The civil servant's periodical contributions in relation to widow's (or widower's) pension, adult dependant's pension and the purchase of added years, must not exceed a stated amount: see r 4.35. A valid nomination for a 'life pension' under the provisions operating before the Principal Civil Service Pension Scheme 1974 may be deemed to be a nomination for an invalidity pension: r 4.36.

4    Ie if he enters a hospital or institution maintained by the state, and ceases to be maintained by the civil servant: ibid r 4.38.

5    See ibid r 4.38.

6    See ibid r 4.39.

## 608. Invalidity pensions: contributions and benefits.

While in service a civil servant will pay periodical contributions of 2 per cent of salary or wages from 1 June 1973 or, if later, from the date of his nomination[1]. If he:

    (1)   dies in service[2]; or

    (2)   dies after retiring with a pension[3]; or

    (3)   dies after resigning or opting out of the scheme with a preserved pension[4],

and if his nomination is still valid, an invalidity pension will be payable to the person chosen by the minister[5] to receive it[6]. The pension is payable from the day after the death of the civil servant or, if later, when the nominee reaches 17. It ceases (a) when the nominee marries or lives with another person as spouse, unless it is restored on compassionate grounds, or (b) on the nominee's death[7].

1  See the Principal Civil Service Pension Scheme 1974 r 4.44. For further details and for variations see rr 4.45–4.53, 4.59–4.60. As to references to the Principal Civil Service Pension Scheme 1974 see para 576 note 1 ante.

2  Ibid r 4.41(i)(b). This applies to death occurring after 1 April 1980; prior to that date there was a requirement of at least 5 years' qualifying service: see r 4.41(i)(a).

3  Ie a retirement pension under ibid r 3.1 (see para 588 ante), an ill health pension under r 3.4 (see para 590 ante), or an actuarially reduced pension under r 3.10a (see para 593 ante): r 4.41(ii)(a)–(c).

4  Ie after leaving or opting out with a preserved pension under ibid r 3.11 (see para 592 ante) or r 3.24a(ii) (see para 595 ante): r 4.41(ii)(d), (e). This applies to death occurring after 1 April 1980; prior to that date there was a requirement of at least 5 years' qualifying service: r 4.41(ii).

5  For the meaning of 'minister' in the scheme see para 578 note 4 ante.

6  Principal Civil Service Pension Scheme 1974 r 4.41. If the person chosen is not the nominee, the pension must be applied for his benefit: r 4.41. As to the time payment begins and ceases see r 4.42. As to the annual amount of the pension see rr 4.43, 4.50. As to the position where the civil servant was transferred to non-standard pay terms for a fixed period see r 4.67.

7  Ibid r 4.42.

**609. Pensions for adult dependants.** Where a civil servant had a valid nomination for a life pension in force under the provisions of the Superannuation Act 1965 for an adult dependant, those provisions continue to apply[1].

1  Principal Civil Service Pension Scheme 1974 r 4.54. These pensions are being phased out as obsolete, and replaced by the new scheme for invalidity pensions under rr 4.35–4.53: see paras 607–608 ante. As to references to the Principal Civil Service Pension Scheme 1974 see para 576 note 1 ante.

*(F)  Allocations and Transfers*

**610. Allocations.** A person who is granted a pension under the Principal Civil Service Pension Scheme[1] or an annual compensation payment under the Civil Service Compensation Scheme[2] may at the time the pension or payment comes into payment or at any time thereafter, allocate part of that pension or payment either in favour of the person who is his spouse at the time of the allocation, or in favour of a person who is his dependant at the time of the allocation, provided that while serving in the Civil Service[3] he was normally employed in the United Kingdom or was a member of a grade in the service normally recruited there[4].

1  Ie a pension (other than an ill health pension) under the Principal Civil Service Pension Scheme 1974 rr 3.1–3.48: see para 588 et seq ante. As to references to the Principal Civil Service Pension Scheme 1974 see para 576 note 1 ante.

2  See para 589 ante.

3  For the meaning of 'Civil Service' see para 577 note 2 ante.

4  Principal Civil Service Pension Scheme 1974 r 5.1. See further rr 5.2–5.11.

**611. Transfers.** The Principal Civil Service Pension Scheme 1974 contains detailed provision for the payment and receipt of transfer values in respect of persons leaving or entering the Civil Service[1] on or after 1 June 1972[2].

1  For the meaning of 'Civil Service' see para 577 note 2 ante.

2  See the Principal Civil Service Pension Scheme 1974 rr 6.1 (introduction), 6.2–6.21 (outgoing transfers generally), 6.22–6.28 (incoming transfers), 6.29–6.32 (mixed transfer values), 6.33–6.34 (old cases, etc), 6.35–6.39 (miscellaneous provisions). As to references to the Principal Civil Service Pension Scheme 1974 see para 576 note 1 ante.

## (G) *Discretionary Benefits*

**612. Entitlement to benefits: minister's discretion.** The following benefits under the Principal Civil Service Pension Scheme will be paid at the discretion of the minister[1], and nothing in the scheme extends or may be construed to extend to give any person an absolute right to them[2], namely: (1) payments for service after completion of 45 years' reckonable service or five years' reckonable service during re-employment after retiring age[3]; (2) ill health payments[4]; (3) death benefits in respect of civil servants who die in service[5] or after retirement[6] or before a preserved pension and lump sum comes into payment[7]; (4) injury benefits[8].

1  For the meaning of 'minister' see para 578 note 4 ante.
2  See the Principal Civil Service Pension Scheme 1974 r 8.1. As to references to the Principal Civil Service Pension Scheme 1974 see para 576 note 1 ante. Rule 8.1(ii), (v) refers to certain benefits no longer payable, namely: short service payments (rr 3.3, 3.17); unestablished and marriage gratuities (rr 3.38, 3.42).
3  Ie payments under ibid r 3.2 (see para 588 ante) or r 3.32a: r 8.1(i). For the meaning of 'reckonable service' see para 578 ante.
4  See ibid rr 3.5, 8.1(iii), and para 590 ante.
5  See ibid rr 3.8, 8.1(iv); and para 591 ante.
6  See ibid rr 3.9, 8.1(iv); and para 591 ante.
7  See ibid rr 3.16, 8.1(iv); and para 592 ante.
8  See ibid rr 8.1(vi), 11.1–11.27; and paras 597–600 ante.

## (H) *Forfeiture*

**613. Forfeiture for misconduct.** The minister[1] has power to withhold benefits payable under the Principal Civil Service Pension Scheme 1974 where a civil servant or former civil servant is convicted of:

(1)  one or more offences under the Official Secrets Acts 1911–89 for which the person concerned has been sentenced to a term of imprisonment of at least ten years, or has been sentenced on the same occasion to two or more consecutive terms amounting in aggregate to at least ten years[2]; or

(2)  an offence in connection with any employment to which the scheme applies, certified by a minister of the Crown either to have been gravely injurious to the state or to be liable to lead to a loss of confidence in the public service[3].

Before benefits may be forfeited, the person concerned will be entitled to appeal against the forfeiture to an independent board nominated by the minister; and where an appeal is made, the minister will accept the board's judgment on whether or not the appellant's pension benefits should be forfeited[4].

1  For the meaning of 'minister' see para 578 note 4 ante.
2  Principal Civil Service Pension Scheme 1974 r 8.2(i). As to references to the Principal Civil Service Pension Scheme 1974 see para 576 note 1 ante. As to the Official Secrets Acts 1911–89 see CRIMINAL LAW vol 11(1) (Reissue) para 243 et seq.
3  Principal Civil Service Pension Scheme 1974 r 8.2(ii).
4  Ibid r 8.2.

### D.  INCREASE OF PENSIONS

**614. Official pensions.** Official pensions[1] comprise certain specified state pensions, certain specified pensions payable out of local funds[2] and certain other specified pensions[3]. State pensions include ministerial and parliamentary pensions[4], European Parliament pensions[5], Civil Service pensions[6], judicial pensions[7], police and firemen's pensions[8], teachers' pensions[9], national health service pensions[10], diplomatic, colonial and overseas service pensions[11], and certain other pensions[12].

The Treasury[13] may by regulations[14] provide that other pensions are to be dealt with as if they were official pensions[15], and the minister, with consent the Lord Chancellor or the Secretary of State, may by regulations direct that the provisions of the Pensions (Increase) Act 1971 are to apply to any official pension subject to modifications, adaptations and exceptions[16].

1   In the Pensions (Increase) Act 1971 'pension' includes:
    (1)   any allowance or other benefit payable, whether in respect of the pensioner's own services or those of any other person, by virtue of any superannuation scheme, statutory or otherwise, including a scheme providing injury or death benefits;
    (2)   any compensation payable in respect of retirement in pursuance of an enactment, or in respect of loss, abolition or relinquishment of office occasioned by reorganisation or transfer of functions of local authorities, or in respect of diminution of emoluments; and
    (3)   compensation payable in pursuance of the provisions of a scheme under the Superannuation Act 1972 ss 1, 2 (as amended) (ie the Civil Service Compensation Scheme: see para 589 ante),
    but it does not include money purchase benefits: Pensions (Increase) Act 1971 s 8(1) (amended by the Superannuation Act 1972 s 29(1), Sch 6 para 86; and the Pensions (Miscellaneous Provisions) Act 1990 s 1(5)). 'Money purchase benefit' has the same meaning as in the Social Security Act 1986 s 84(1): Pensions (Increase) Act 1971 s 17(1) (definition added by the Pensions (Miscellaneous Provisions) Act 1990 s 7(3)).
    A pension does not include a return of contributions: see the Pensions (Increase) Act 1971 s 9(1) (amended by the Pensions (Miscellaneous Provisions) Act 1990 s 7(2)). As to the application of the Pensions (Increase) Act 1971 to gratuities and lump sums see s 9 (as amended).
2   Except as otherwise provided by the Pensions (Increase) Act 1971, it is the duty of a pension authority to increase, in accordance with the Act, a pension payable out of local funds: s 5(1) (amended by the Superannuation Act 1972 s 29(1), Sch 6 para 85). As to the pensions payable out of local funds see the Pensions (Increase) Act 1971 ss 4, 5, 15 (all as amended), Sch 2 Pt II (as amended). 'Pension authority' means the authority by which the pension is payable (although in the case of a pension payable in respect of the Raw Cotton Commission the pension authority is the Treasury); but the Treasury or, with the approval of the Treasury, the Secretary of State may by regulations provide for a pension authority's functions to be performed for it by some other authority: s 7(1), Sch 2 Pt III para 66. As to the apportionment of certain costs of increases between authorities see s 7(2), Sch 3. As to the transfer of functions under the Pensions (Increase) Act 1971 from the Minister for the Civil Service to the Treasury see note 13 infra. As to the Treasury see paras 512–517 ante.
3   See ibid s 5(1), Sch 2.
4   Ibid Sch 2 Pt I paras 1–3A (paras 1–3 amended by the Parliamentary and Other Pensions Act 1972 s 31(2), and the Statute Law (Repeals) Act 1986; para 3A added by the Parliamentary and Other Pensions Act 1972 s 31(1); substituted by the Parliamentary and Other Pensions Act 1987 s 6(1), Sch 3 para 3).
5   Pensions (Increase) Act 1971 Sch 2 para 3B (added by the European Parliament (Pay and Pensions) Act 1979 s 4(7); amended by virtue of the European Communities (Amendment) Act 1986 s 3).
6   Pensions (Increase) Act 1971 Sch 2 Pt I para 4 (amended by the Superannuation Act 1972 s 29(1), Sch 6 para 89(a)).
7   Pensions (Increase) Act 1971 Sch 2 Pt I paras 4A, 7, 10, 11, 13 (para 4A added by the Judicial Pensions and Retirement Act 1993 s 22(1); para 13 amended by the Administration of Justice Act 1973 s 5, Sch 1 Pt IV para 11(2)).
8   Pensions (Increase) Act 1971 Sch 2 Pt I paras 14–16A (para 15 amended by the Police Pensions Act 1976 s 13(1), Sch 2 para 8; and the Police and Magistrates' Courts Act 1994 s 44, Sch 5 Pt II para 17; paras 15A, 16A added by the Superannuation Act 1972 Sch 6 para 89(b), (c)).
9   Pensions (Increase) Act 1971 Sch 2 Pt I paras 17–20A (para 20 amended, and para 20A added, by the Superannuation Act 1972 Sch 6 para 89(b), (d), (e)).
10  Pensions (Increase) Act 1971 Sch 2 Pt I paras 22–23A (paras 22, 23 amended, and para 23A added, by the Superannuation Act 1972 Sch 6 para 89(g)–(i), Sch 8; para 22 further amended by the National Health Service Reorganisation Act 1973 s 57, Sch 4 para 133). Reference is also made to pensions granted on the passing of the National Insurance Act 1946: see the Pensions (Increase) Act 1971 Sch 2 Pt I paras 24, 25 (amended by the Superannuation Act 1972 Sch 6 para 89(j)).
11  Pensions (Increase) Act 1971 Sch 2 Pt I paras 27–29 (para 27A added by the Overseas Pensions Act 1973 s 4(3)).
12  Pensions (Increase) Act 1971 s 5(1), Sch 2 Pt I paras 30–38 (para 37 amended by the Reserve Forces Act 1980 s 157, Sch 9 para 11).

13  Functions under the Pensions (Increase) Act 1971 originally exercisable by the Minister for the Civil Service are now exercisable by the Treasury, by virtue of the Transfer of Functions (Minister for the Civil Service and Treasury) Order 1981, SI 1981/1670. As to the Minister for the Civil Service see paras 427, 550 ante. As to the transfer of functions generally see para 363 ante.

14  Regulations under the Pensions (Increase) Act 1971 s 5 may provide for increases to take effect from a date before that on which the regulations were made: s 5(4).

15  Ibid s 5(2). See the Pensions Increase (Compensation to Court Officers) Regulations 1973, SI 1973/382; Pensions Increase (Compensation to Clerks to General Commissioners) Regulations 1973, SI 1973/1954; Pensions Increase (Local Authorities' etc Pensions) Regulations 1974/1740 (amended by SI 1983/1315; SI 1986/391; and SI 1989/417); Pensions Increase (Northern Ireland Reserved Services) Regulations 1976, SI 1976/146; Pensions Increase (Specification of Pensions) Regulations 1977, SI 1977/1652; Pensions Increase (Welsh Development Agency) Regulations 1978, SI 1978/211; Pensions Increase (Parliamentary Commissioner) Regulations 1979, SI 1979/622; Pensions Increase (Civil Service Supplementary (Earnings Cap) Pension Scheme 1994) Regulations 1995, SI 1995/1683.

16  Pensions (Increase) Act 1971 s 5(3) (amended by the Social Security Pensions Act 1975 s 65(1), Sch 4 para 18; the Minister of Overseas Development Order 1974, SI 1974/1264, art 5(3); and the Ministry of Overseas Development (Dissolution) Order 1979, SI 1979/1451, art 3(3), Sch 3), and see note 13 supra). See the Increase of Pensions (Police and Fire Services) Regulations 1971, SI 1971/1330 (amended by SI 1973/432; and SI 1973/965); Increase of Pensions (Teachers' Family Benefits) Regulations 1971, SI 1971/1614; Pensions Increase (Injury Warrant Pensions) Regulations 1971, SI 1971/1616; Pensions Increase (Judicial Pensions) Regulations 1972, SI 1972/71 (amended by SI 1973/495; SI 1974/984; SI 1974/2029; SI 1978/1808; SI 1991/786; SI 1992/736); Pensions Increase (Speakers' Pensions) Regulations 1972, SI 1972/1653 (amended by SI 1979/762; and SI 1991/788); Pensions Increase (Parliamentary Pensions) Regulations 1973, SI 1973/1838 (amended by SI 1976/348); Pensions Increase (Parliamentary Pensions) Regulations 1972, SI 1972/1655; Pensions (Increase) Act 1971 (Modification) (Teachers) Regulations 1972, SI 1972/1676; Increase of Pensions (Teachers' Family Benefits) Regulations 1972, SI 1972/1905; Increase of Pensions (Governors) Regulations 1976, SI 1976/889; Pensions Increase (Past Prime Ministers) Regulations 1991, SI 1991/787. See also the Pensions Increase (Police Compensation) Regulations 1974, SI 1974/1333; Pensions Increase (Civil Service Early Retirement Pension Scheme 1992) Regulations 1993, SI 1993/806.

**615. Increases of official pensions beginning before specified dates.** Except as otherwise provided[1], if any qualifying condition[2] is satisfied or the pension is a widow's pension[3], an official pension[4] may be increased by the pension authority[5] in respect of any period beginning on or after 1 December 1978[6].

Except as otherwise provided, a pension beginning[7] before the year 1969 may be increased by the amount necessary to bring the rate up to the 1969 standard[8] and by a further specified percentage of the rate as so increased[9]. A pension beginning on or before 1 April 1969 but not earlier than that year may be increased by the same specified percentage of the basic rate[10]; and pensions beginning at later dates may be increased by progressively decreasing rates[11].

Provision was made for the increase of basic rate of certain official pensions specified by regulations[12] which began after 1 January 1973 and before 7 November 1974 (or some later date prescribed as the date on which a principal pay increase for the period ending before 7 November 1974 was to take effect), which were affected by specified counter-inflationary legislation[13].

1  As to the power to direct that the provisions of the Pensions (Increase) Act 1971 are to apply to an official pension subject to modifications etc see s 5(3) (as amended); and para 614 ante.

2  For the qualifying conditions see para 617 post.

3  'Widow's pension' means a pension payable in respect of the services of the pensioner's deceased husband: Pensions (Increase) Act 1971 s 17(1) (substituted by the Pensions (Increase) Act 1974 s 3(3)).

4  For the meaning of 'official pension' see para 614 ante.

5  For the meaning of 'pension authority' see para 614 note 2 ante.

6  Pensions (Increase) Act 1971 s 1(1) (s 1 substituted by the Pensions (Increase) Act 1974 s 3(3)(a); and by virtue of the Pensions Increase (Annual Review) Order 1978, SI 1978/1211).

7  As to when a pension is deemed to begin see the Pensions (Increase) Act 1971 s 8(2) (amended by the Pensions (Miscellaneous Provisions) Act 1990 s 1(5)).

8 The rate is arrived at by applying to the basic rate of pension the multiplier given in the Pensions (Increase) Act 1971 s 1, Sch 1, for the year in which the pension began: s 1(1)(a) (as substituted: see note 6 supra). For the meaning of 'basic rate' see note 10 infra.

9 Ibid s 1(1)(a) (as substituted: see note 6 supra). This increase takes the place of those authorised by the Pensions (Increase) Acts 1920 to 1969 (repealed with savings), but in certain cases the increase is to be of the larger amount specified by reference to increases that might have been made under these Acts: see the Pensions (Increase) Act 1971 ss 1(2), 6 (s 1(2) as substituted: see note 6 supra; s 6 amended by the Pensions (Increase) Act 1974 s 3(3), (4)); Pensions (Preservation of Increases) Order 1971, SI 1971/1316.

10 Pensions (Increase) Act 1971 s 1(1)(b) (as substituted: see note 6 supra). 'Basic rate' means the annual rate of a pension apart from any increase under or by reference to the Pensions (Increase) Act 1971 or any enactment repealed by that Act or any corresponding increase made otherwise than under or by reference to that Act or any enactment repealed by that Act but including any increase in that annual rate in consequence of the Pensions (Increase) Act 1974 (see text and notes 12–13 infra): Pensions (Increase) Act 1971 s 17(1) (amended by the Pensions (Increase) Act 1974 s 1(3)).

11 See the Pensions (Increase) Act 1971 s 1(1)(c)–(u) (as substituted: see note 6 supra).

12 Ie the Pensions Increase (Civil Service Pensions) Regulations 1974, SI 1974/715; the Pensions Increase (Teachers) Regulations 1974, SI 1974/813; Pensions Increase (Trustee Savings Banks Pensions) Regulations 1974, SI 1974/914; the Pensions Increase (National Health Service Pensions) Regulations 1974, SI 1974/975; the Pensions Increase (Judicial Pensions) Regulations 1974, SI 1974/985; the Pensions Increase (Modification) (Police and Fire Services) Regulations 1974, SI 1974/1531; the Pensions Increase (Police and Fire Services) Regulations 1974, SI 1974/1532; the Pensions Increase (Metropolitan Civil Staffs) Regulations 1974, SI 1974/1702; the Pensions Increase (Coroners) Regulations 1974, SI 1974/1729; the Pensions Increase (Local Authorities' etc Prescribed Pensions) Regulations 1974, SI 1974/1778; and certain instruments relating to service in Northern Ireland.

13 See the Pensions (Increase) Act 1974 ss 1, 2, 4 (as amended), Schedule. That Act authorised increases in the specified pensions, which had been effected by the deferment of increase of emoluments under the Counter-Inflation (Temporary Provisions) Act 1972 (repealed) and the Counter-Inflation Act 1973 (repealed in all relevant respects).

**616. Annual reviews and increases of official pensions.** The Treasury[1] must, by order laid before Parliament, provide for the increase in rates of official pensions[2]. The increase is the percentage, or fraction of the percentage, by which the Secretary of State for Social Security has directed by virtue of his powers to increase the level of benefit having regard to movements in prices[3]. The annual rate of an official pension may, if a qualifying condition[4] is satisfied or the pension is a derivative[5] or substituted pension[6] or relevant injury pension[7], be increased as provided in the order as to the annual rate and in respect of any lump sum payable at the relevant time[8].

1 As to the transfer of functions to the Treasury see para 614 note 13 ante. As to the Treasury generally see paras 512–517 ante.

2 See the Social Security Pensions Act 1975 s 59 (as amended). 'Official pension' has the same meaning as in the Pensions (Increase) Act 1971 (see para 614 ante): Social Security Pensions Act 1975 s 59(7) (amended by the Pensions (Miscellaneous Provisions) Act 1990 s 21(4), Sch 3 para 20).

3 Social Security Pensions Act 1975 s 59(1) (amended by the Social Security (Consequential Provisions) Act 1990 s 4, Sch 2 para 34; and the Pensions (Miscellaneous Provisions) Act 1990 s 1(7)); Social Security Administration Act 1992 ss 150(1)(c), 151(1) (amended by the Pensions Act 1995 s 130(2)). See the Social Security Benefits Up-rating Order 1995, SI 1995/559.

4 As to the qualifying conditions see para 617 post.

5 'Derivative pension' means one which is not payable in respect of the pensioner's own services: Pensions (Increase) Act 1971 s 17; applied by virtue of the Social Security Pensions Act 1975 s 59(7) (as amended: see note 2 supra).

6 'Substituted pension' means a pension granted in consideration of the surrender of the whole or part of another pension: Pensions (Increase) Act 1971 s 17 (as applied: see note 5 supra).

7 'Relevant injury pension' means a pension paid to a person in respect of

(1) his absence from work by reason only of an injury sustained, or disease contracted, by him in the course of his employment by virtue of which his entitlement to the pension arises; or

(2) his having accepted less favourable terms and conditions of employment by reason of ill-health suffered by him in consequence of such an injury or disease,

but it does not include a pension the rate of which is periodically recalculated by reference to the rate of salary the pensioner could reasonably be expected to have received had he not sustained the injury or contracted the disease in question: ibid s 17(1) (definition substituted by the Pensions (Miscellaneous Provisions) Act 1990 s 1(6)).

8 See the Social Security Pensions Act 1975 s 59(1) (as amended); and eg the Pensions Increase (Review) Order 1996, SI 1996/800.

**617. Qualifying conditions.** A pension, other than a derivative[1] or substituted[2] pension or a relevant injury pension[3], may not be increased unless one of the qualifying conditions is satisfied[4]. For a pension payable in respect of the pensioner's own services the qualifying conditions are that the pensioner (1) has attained the age of 55 years[5]; or (2) has retired on account of physical or mental infirmity[6] from the office or employment in respect of which or on retirement from which the pension is payable[7]; or (3) has at least one dependant[8]; or (4) the pension authority[9] is satisfied that the pensioner is disabled by physical or mental infirmity[10].

1 For the meaning of 'derivative pension' see para 616 note 5 ante.
2 For the meaning of 'substituted pension' see para 616 note 6 ante.
3 For the meaning of 'relevant injury pension' see para 616 note 7 ante.
4 Pensions (Increase) Act 1971 s 3(1) (amended by the Pensions (Increase) Act 1974 s 3(3)(a); and the Pensions (Miscellaneous Provisions) Act 1990 s 1(1)).
5 Pensions (Increase) Act 1971 s 3(2)(a) (amended by the Pensions Increase (Reduction of Qualifying Age) Order 1972, SI 1972/1299), made under the Pensions (Increase) Act 1971 s 3(8) (amended by the Pensions (Miscellaneous Provisions) Act 1990 s 3(c)).
6 A pensioner is to be deemed to be disabled by physical or mental infirmity if he is permanently incapacitated by such infirmity from engaging in any regular full-time employment: Pensions (Increase) Act 1971 s 3(5).
7 Ibid s 3(2)(b).
8 Ibid s 3(2)(c) (amended by the Pensions (Miscellaneous Provisions) Act 1990 s 1(2)(b); and the Pensions Act 1995 ss 171(1), (2), 177, Sch 7 Pt IV).
   This condition was withdrawn as from 1 January 1993 to the extent of the following provisions: (1) the Pensions (Increase) Act 1971 s 3(2)(c) will continue to apply to an existing pension until it falls to be increased on or after 1 January 1993 in consequence of any other provision of s 3(2); (2) where a pension commences on or after 1 January 1993 and the person has not yet reached the age of 55, s 3(2)(c) will continue to have effect in relation to so much of the pension as is referable to service rendered before 1 January 1993 until it falls to be increased under any other provision of s 3(2): s 3(9)–(11) (added by the Pensions (Miscellaneous Provisions) Act 1990 s 1(4); s 3(10), (11) amended by the Pensions Act 1995 s 171(3)–(5)).
   'Dependant' means, in relation to a pensioner, a person who the pension authority is satisfied is wholly or mainly supported by the pensioner and who either has not attained the age of 17 years or is receiving full-time instruction at an educational establishment or undergoing training for a trade, profession or vocation in such circumstances that he is required to devote the whole of his time to that training for a period of not less than two years: Pensions (Increase) Act 1971 s 3(6) (amended by the Pensions (Miscellaneous Provisions) Act 1990 s 1(3)(b)).
   In certain circumstances where the pension was payable to a woman at 31 August 1971, her dependants may include (a) her (or her deceased husband's) father, mother, brother, sister, child, uncle or aunt; (b) the child of any such person; (c) her step-father or step-mother; or (d) a person undergoing training in any trade, vocation or profession: see the Pensions (Increase) Act 1971 s 3(7) (amended by the Children Act 1975 s 108(1)(b), Sch 4 Pt I).
9 For the meaning of 'pension authority' see para 614 note 2 ante.
10 Pensions (Increase) Act 1971 s 3(2) (amended by the Pensions (Miscellaneous Provisions) Act 1990 s 1(2)).

**618. Re-employment.** Where a person has been in receipt of an official pension[1] in respect of any service and in consequence of any further service the pension falls to be recalculated as to its basic rate[2] and is to be treated as beginning at a later date, the rate of the pension as recalculated and with any increase under Part I of the Pensions (Increase) Act 1971[3] may be further increased up to the rate, if higher, at which it would have been payable with any such increase if the further service had not been rendered and, in the case of specified pensions[4], the length of the previous service had been increased by the length of the further service[5].

1   For the meaning of 'official pension' see para 614 ante.
2   For the meaning of 'basic rate' see para 615 note 10 ante.
3   Ie the Pensions (Increase) Act 1971 Pt I (ss 1–9) (as amended).
4   Ie the pensions specified in ibid s 4(4) (amended by the Superannuation Act 1972 s 29(1), Sch 6 para 84).
5   Pensions (Increase) Act 1971 s 4(1). An official pension may be similarly increased where a person has terminated his service in circumstances such that, without rendering further reckonable service, he is or may become eligible for a pension, but has not been in receipt of the pension before being re-employed: s 4(2) (amended by the Pensions (Miscellaneous Provisions) Act 1990 s 2(2). 'Reckonable service', in relation to a person and his official pension, means service which falls to be taken into account in calculating the basic rate of the pension: Pensions (Increase) Act 1971 s 4(2A) (added by the Pensions (Miscellaneous Provisions) Act 1990 s 2(3)). As to the effect of re-employment on the calculation of increase in a derivative pension see the Pensions (Increase) Act 1971 s 4(3) (amended by the Pensions (Miscellaneous Provisions) Act 1990 s 2(4)).

**619-700. Pensions under approved schemes.** The Treasury[1] may make regulations[2] conferring on persons who

(1)   are or have been employed in the civil service of the state, were recruited and are or were employed in a territory outside the United Kingdom, and are or were subject to a superannuation scheme approved by the Treasury[3]; or

(2)   are or have been employed in the civil service of the state or in any specified capacity[4] and are or were subject to specified superannuation schemes[5],

such benefits, enjoyable after the termination of the employment, as appear to the Treasury to be appropriate having regard to the benefits provided by Part I of the Pensions (Increase) Act 1971[6] for persons whose superannuation benefits are regulated by the Principal Civil Service Pension Scheme 1974[7] and, in the case of civil servants falling within head (1) above, having regard also to the circumstances of the territory in question[8].

1   As to the Treasury see paras 512–517 ante.
2   With Treasury approval, regulations may also be made by the Secretary of State: Pensions (Increase) Act 1971 s 13(4) (amended by the Minister of Overseas Development Order 1974, SI 1974/1264; and the Ministry of Overseas Development (Dissolution) Order 1979, SI 1979/1451). As to the transfer of functions to the Treasury see para 614 note 13 ante. As to the transfer of functions generally see para 363 ante.
3   Pensions (Increase) Act 1971 s 13(1)(a)–(c).
4   Ie any capacity listed in ibid s 13, Sch 6 (amended by the Police and Magistrates' Courts Act 1994 s 93, Sch 9 Pt I; and the Local Government Superannuation Regulations 1974, SI 1974/520, reg M1(1), Sch 18 Pt I para 7).
5   Pensions (Increase) Act 1971 s 13(2)(a), (b). The schemes so specified are schemes operated under the Federated Superannuation System for Universities, the Federated Superannuation Scheme for Nurses and Hospital Officers or any other scheme approved by the Treasury: s 13(2)(b). As to the Treasury's power to make regulations with respect to persons employed by a local authority and subject to the foregoing schemes see the Pensions (Increase) Act 1971 s 13(3) (amended by the Pensions (Increase) Act 1974 s 3(4)(a)). See also the Pensions Increase (Approved Schemes) (Local Government) Regulations 1972, SI 1972/931 (amended by SI 1975/503); Pensions Increase (Wheat Commission) Regulations 1972, SI 1972/387; Pensions Increase (Federated Superannuation Scheme for Nurses and Hospital Officers) (Civil Service) Regulations 1972, SI 1972/395 (amended by SI 1973/1068; and SI 1984/1751); Pensions Increase (Federated Superannuation System for Universities) Regulations 1972, SI 1972/877 (amended by SI 1974/737; SI 1975/1383; SI 1977/286: SI 1977/863; SI 1980/1869); Pensions Increase (Approved Schemes) (National Health Service) Regulations 1976, SI 1976/1451 (amended by SI 1989/711; and SI 1991/2419); Pensions Increase (Federated Superannuation Scheme for Nurses and Hospital Officers) (Metropolitan Civil Staffs) Regulations 1972, SI 1972/1241; Pensions Increase (Power Jets) Regulations 1973, SI 1973/942.
6   Ie the Pensions (Increase) Act 1971 Pt I (ss 1–9) (as amended); see para 614 et seq ante.
7   As to the Principal Civil Service Pension Scheme 1974 see paras 576–613 ante.
8   Pensions (Increase) Act 1971 s 13(1), (2) (both amended by the Superannuation Act 1972 s 29(1), Sch 6 para 88). As to the powers of the Secretary of State, with the approval of the Treasury, to increase or supplement other overseas pensions, see the Pensions (Increase) Act 1971 ss 10, 11 (as amended), 11A (as added), 12, Schs 4 (as amended), 5; and cf COMMONWEALTH vol 6 (Reissue) para 1016.

# 6. REVENUE AND PUBLIC FINANCE

## (1) BASIC PRINCIPLES

**701. Revenue vests in the Crown.** In traditional constitutional theory, public revenue[1] is vested in the Crown[2]. In its origin the revenue at the disposal of the Crown was derived from the land, prerogative rights and privileges of the monarch[3], supplemented by aids granted by the Commons[4].

1  The term 'revenue' is commonly used to refer to income from taxation. However, it may also be used to refer to money at the disposal of the Crown (ie the government). The chief sources of revenue are: Crown property surrendered to the nation (see CROWN LANDS AND PRIVILEGES); taxation; income from government-held land, shares and other property; money realised from the sale or disposal of property, fees and charges, and other profits or fiscal prerogatives of the Crown. The term used to cover this wider sense of revenue in HM Treasury *Government Accounting* is 'public income': HM Treasury *Government Accounting* (August 1994) 1.1.1. See para 230 note 2 ante.
   Details of the national revenue and expenditure are published annually among the House of Commons papers. The main papers are the following (1) the financial statement of past and estimated future revenue and expenditure, and of proposed changes in taxation, which is laid before the House of Commons by the Chancellor of the Exchequer when opening his budget (See *Budgetary Reform* (Cm 1867) (1992); and paras 228 ante, 705 post); (2) statutory accounts of payments into and out of the Consolidated Fund (as to which see para 711 et seq post) and payments into and out of the National Loans Fund (as to which see paras 727–739 post), and statutory statements containing additional information regarding the transactions, assets and liabilities of the Consolidated Fund and of the National Loans Fund: see the National Loans Act 1968 s 21 (1)-(3); (3) the 'appropriation accounts' of the sums granted by Parliament for civil and defence services: see the Exchequer and Audit Departments Act 1866 s 22 (as amended), Sch A (as substituted and amended).
   House of Commons papers contain reports of the Comptroller and Auditor General (as to whom see paras 724–726 post) not only in respect of civil and defence services accounts, but also in respect of certain revenue and store accounts (see further PARLIAMENT). See also the Exchequer and Audit Departments Act 1921 s 5 (as amended).
2  However, this is a simplification of the current position, as many revenues do not vest in the Crown. Examples include council tax, which is payable to local authorities (see generally RATING), and charges made by non-departmental public bodies which do not form part of the Crown. As to non-departmental public bodies see para 951 et seq post.
3  See CROWN LANDS AND PRIVILEGES.
4  As to the House of Commons see PARLIAMENT.

**702. Crown land and prerogative revenue.** Revenue[1] from Crown land and from prerogative rights is now customarily placed at the disposal of Parliament by the monarch on his or her accession[2], and such rights as are preserved to the Crown in respect of it are exercised upon constitutional advice and have no appreciable effect upon the public revenue[3].

1  For the meaning of 'revenue' see para 701 note 1 ante.
2  See the Civil List Act 1952, preamble para 1; and CROWN LANDS AND PRIVILEGES.
3  See ibid s 13(2); the Civil List Act 1972 s 8(3); and see *The Odessa, The Woolston* [1916] 1 AC 145, PC. See also the Remission of Penalties Act 1859; and CROWN LANDS AND PRIVILEGES.

**703. Parliamentary control over public expenditure.** Parliamentary control is exercised in respect of (1) the raising of revenue[1]; (2) its expenditure[2]; and (3) the audit of public accounts[3].

1  For the meaning of 'revenue' see para 701 note 1 ante. As to the sources of revenue in particular see para 707 post.
2  As to parliamentary control of expenditure see para 230 ante.
3  As to the audit of public accounts see paras 716–723 post.

**704. Treasury control over public expenditure.** The department through which the executive exercises central control in all matters affecting the revenue[1] is the Treasury[2]. The Treasury requires that its sanction be obtained for all departmental expenditure, and any expenditure by a department outside its delegated authority is considered by the Treasury to be irregular (that is to say illegal) if it does not have Treasury approval[3]. The control exercised by the Treasury rests not only upon specific enactments[4], but also upon the constitutional practice according to which the Chancellor of the Exchequer[5], its ministerial head, presents all proposals for raising money to the House of Commons[6] in his budget speech[7]. The government reviews its public expenditure annually. A committee consisting of Treasury civil servants and financial officers called the Public Expenditure Survey Committee prepares a report for the Chancellor of the Exchequer[8]. The Public Expenditure Survey is based on each department's projected costs and sets out a review of the spending plans for the next two years and makes proposals for the following year; and after further ministerial discussions the results of the survey are published in the autumn statement which is issued in November[9].

The Treasury issues a loose-leaf guide for the use of accounting officers[10] and departments setting out conventions and practices relating to accounting[11] and it also produces a Treasury handbook giving guidance about House of Commons procedures[12].

Control of borrowing upon the public credit is exercised through the Treasury[13].

1    For the meaning of 'revenue' see para 701 note 1 ante.

2    As to the Treasury see paras 512–517 ante. See also the Treasury handbook entitled Treasury Handbook *Supply and other Financial Procedures of the House of Commons* (1972); HM Treasury *Government Accounting* (see para 230 note 2 ante); Epitome of the Reports from the Committee of Public Accounts vol I (1857–1937), vol II (1938–69) and subsequent reports with Treasury minutes all published by the Treasury. See also McEldowney *Public Law* (1994) pp 303–313; McEldowney 'The Control of Public Expenditure' in Jowell and Oliver (eds) *The Changing Constitution* (3rd Edn, 1994).

3    HM Treasury *Government Accounting* 2.4.1, 2.4.11, 45.6.5.

4    See eg the Exchequer and Audit Departments Act 1866 ss 10 (as amended), 11, 13–15 (as amended), 18–20, 22 (as amended), 23 (as amended), 31, 34 (as amended), 41, 43, 44; the Consolidated Fund Act 1816 s 2 (as amended); the Inland Revenue Regulation Act 1890 s 1; the Crown Estate Act 1961 s 2(3)–(6); and the National Loans Act 1968 s 21(1)–(3).

5    As to the Chancellor of the Exchequer see para 514 ante.

6    As to the House of Commons see PARLIAMENT.

7    As to the budget see para 705 post.

8    See de Smith and Brazier *Constitutional and Administrative Law* (7th Edn, 1994) pp 307–308; and Wade and Bradley *Constitutional and Administrative Law* (11th Edn, 1993) pp 364–365.

9    For the timetable of the financial year see para 705 note 6 post.

10   As to accounting officers see para 715 post.

11   See HM Treasury *Government Accounting* (see para 230 note 2 ante).

12   Ie the Treasury Handbook *Supply and other Financial Procedures of the House of Commons* (1972). See also *Supply Estimates 1995–96 Summary and Guide* (Cm 2775) (1995).

13   See further para 727 et seq post.

**705. The budget.** Until December 1993[1], the Chancellor of the Exchequer[2] traditionally presented his budget[3] to the House of Commons[4] in early April, following, in recent years, an autumn statement in November. Since 1993, under the unified budget system[5], one statement is made to Parliament in late November or early December, concerning the administration's tax plans for the coming year and its spending plans for the next three years[6].

Once the Chancellor has made his budget statement, immediate changes in taxation and duty rates are authorised by formal resolutions passed by the House of Commons, and at the conclusion of the subsequent debate on the budget the House agrees to a series of resolutions, including those which give renewed authority for the collection of the annual taxes. These resolutions are later embodied in the annual Finance Act[7].

1   See *Budgetary Reform* (Cm 1867) (1992); and Treasury and Civil Service Committee: *The Government's Proposals for Budgetary Reform* (HC Paper (1992–93) no 583).
2   As to the Chancellor of the Exchequer see para 514 ante.
3   For a fuller account of the budget procedure see PARLIAMENT.
4   As to the House of Commons see PARLIAMENT.
5   See *Budgetary Reform* (Cm 1867) (1992).
6   See *Budgetary Reform* (Cm 1867) (1992); HM Treasury press releases 10 March 1992 and 31 March 1992.
      The Chancellor of the Exchequer's budget statement to Parliament is accompanied by (1) the detailed material previously contained in the autumn statement and the financial statement and budget report; (2) a summary of the main budget tax and spending changes; (3) an analysis of departmental spending plans for the next three years; (4) a description of the main tax and National Insurance contribution measures and their revenue consequences; (5) a statement of the government's medium term financial strategy; (6) the short term economic forecast and the public sector borrowing requirement; (7) detailed material on the likely out-turn for the public finances in the current year, and the revenue (or public income) forecasts for the year ahead; and (8) information on the cost of tax reliefs.
      There is a revised timetable which fits within the existing financial year running from April to March. In November/December the autumn budget statement is presented to Parliament. The Winter supplementary estimates for the current year and the votes on account are presented in December and given statutory effect by the first Consolidated Fund Act and must be voted on by 6 February (see para 712 post). In January the Finance Bill is introduced into the House of Commons and in February/March further details of the new public expenditure plans are published in departmental reports and a statistical supplement to the budget. The main supply estimates for the forthcoming financial year, further Spring supplementary estimates for the current year and excess votes for the previous year are presented to Parliament before the beginning of the next financial year and these must be voted on by 18 March (see para 712 post). The financial year begins in April. Royal Assent must be given to the Finance Act by 5 May: see the Provisional Collection of Taxes Act 1968 s 1(3)(a) (amended by the Finance Act 1993 s 205(4)). In June a second short term economic forecast is published and there may be debates and votes on the total of government spending for the year. A Consolidated Fund (Appropriation) Bill which appropriates the year's expenditure to specific services is passed in July and given Royal Assent as the Appropriation Act. It covers the balance of the main estimates for the then current financial year and must be voted on by 5 August (see para 712 post). See further *Budgetary Reform* (Cm 1867) (1992).
7   As to the constitutional principles involved in levying taxes see paras 228–229 ante.

**706. Charges upon the public revenues.** It is a constitutional principle that any charge upon the public revenues[1], whether payable out of the Consolidated Fund, the National Loans Fund or other sources, must be authorised by resolution of the House of Commons[2], and that no motion for such a resolution must be introduced in the Commons except upon the recommendation of the Crown[3] expressed through a member of the government. The observance of this principle is enforced by House of Commons Standing Orders[4]. The effect of these orders is that private members, including the opposition, are unable to propose increased charges on public funds or to secure the passage of legislation involving expenditure out of public funds without a financial resolution. Where the main object of a bill is to create a charge on public funds, it may be introduced only by a minister of the Crown[5].

The Crown, being the executive power, is charged with the management of all the revenue of the state, and with all payments for the public service. The Crown, therefore, acting with the advice of its responsible ministers, makes known to the House of Commons the financial requirements of the government; the Commons in return grant supplies, and the ways and means to meet them through taxes, and the appropriation of other sources of the public income. The participation of the House of Lords[6] is confined to assenting to such financial requirements of the government as require statutory authorisation. The withholding of their assent is effective only for a month. Effectively, therefore, the functions of Parliament are exercised by the House of Commons in matters of financial control[7]. Thus the Crown demands money, the

Commons grant it, and the House of Lords assent to the grant. However the Commons do not vote money unless it is required by the Crown; nor do they impose or augment taxes, unless such taxation is necessary for the public service as declared by the Crown through its constitutional advisers[8].

It is a principle of the highest constitutional importance that no public charge can be incurred except on the initiative of the Crown[9].

1    A charge 'upon the public revenue' or 'upon public funds' means an obligation to make a payment out of the Consolidated Fund or the National Loans Fund: HM Treasury *Government Accounting* 3.2.1. (see para 230 note 2 ante). As to the Consolidated Fund see para 711 et seq post. As to the National Loans Fund see paras 727–739 post.
2    HC Standing Orders (1995) (Public Business) no 47. As to the House of Commons see PARLIAMENT.
3    See HC Standing Orders (1995) (Public Business) no 46. This principle therefore applies to all provisions in a bill or amendments to a bill.
4    See the standing orders cited in notes 2–3 supra.
5    See HC Standing Orders (1995) (Public Business) no 48.
6    As to the House of Lords see PARLIAMENT.
7    HM Treasury *Government Accounting* 1.1.1.
8    HM Treasury *Government Accounting* 1.1.2; and also 1.1.4–1.1.6.
9    Erskine May *Parliamentary Practice* (21st Edn, 1989) p 691: and also pp 684–694; and McEldowney 'The Control of Public Expenditure' in Jowell and Oliver (eds) *The Changing Constitution* (3rd Edn, 1994).

## (2)  SOURCES AND COLLECTION OF REVENUE

**707.  Principal sources of revenue.** The revenue[1] dependent upon annual legislative authority[2] is that produced by income tax and corporation tax[3].

The principal other sources of revenue are constituted by value added tax[4], insurance premium tax[5], excise duties[6] (which include tobacco, oil, beer, spirits, wine, motor vehicle duties, general and pool betting duties[7]), air passenger duty[8], gaming licence duty[9], bingo duty[10] and gaming machine licence duty[11], petroleum revenue tax[12], broadcast receiving licence duties[13], capital gains tax[14], inheritance tax[15] and stamp duty[16].

The hereditary revenues of the Crown are surrendered to the nation by each succeeding monarch for the term of his or her life in return for the Civil List. These surrendered hereditary revenues are the net surplus revenue produced by Crown land[17], miscellaneous receipts derived from small branches of the hereditary revenues of the Crown surrendered to the nation, and other casual revenues[18]. Receipts in the form of fees and charges imposed by government departments for the provision of services[19] are treated by the Treasury as casual revenues unless otherwise provided for by statute[20]. Receipts from the privatisation of industries and services also form part of the public revenue[21].

All such revenues are paid into the Consolidated Fund unless there is a statutory provision to different effect, and are thus subject to parliamentary control[22].

Customs duty is now a European Community tax collected by the British government and paid over to the European Community[23].

1    For meaning of 'revenue' see para 701 note 1 ante.
2    See eg the annual Finance Act; and PARLIAMENT.
3    The Income and Corporation Taxes Act 1988 imposes the charge to income tax and corporation tax. The Taxes Management Act 1970 enacts the machinery for the management, assessment and collection of both taxes. See INCOME TAXATION.
4    See the Value Added Tax Act 1994; and VALUE ADDED TAX.
5    See the Finance Act 1994 Pt III ss 48–52; and INSURANCE.
6    The management of excise duties is provided for under the Customs and Excise Management Act 1979; see CUSTOMS AND EXCISE.

7   See the Betting and Gaming Duties Act 1981 ss 1–8 (ss 1, 6, 7 as amended), Sch 1 (as amended). The Betting and Gaming Duties Act 1981 is to be construed as one with the Customs and Excise Management Act 1979: Betting and Gaming Duties Act 1981 s 35(1), (2); see BETTING vol 4(1) (Reissue) para 106 et seq; and CUSTOMS AND EXCISE.

8   See the Finance Act 1994 ss 28–44 (ss 30, 39 as amended), Sch 6 (as amended); and AVIATION.

9   See the Betting and Gaming Duties Act 1981 ss 13–16 (ss 14, 15 as amended), Sch 2 (as amended); and CLUBS vol 6 (Reissue) para 388 et seq.

10   See ibid ss 17–20 (as amended), Sch 3 (as amended); and CLUBS vol 6 (Reissue) para 397 et seq.

11   See ibid ss 21–26 (as amended), Sch 4 (as amended); and BETTING vol 4(1) (Reissue) para 195 et seq.

12   See the Petroleum Revenue Tax Act 1980; and FUEL AND ENERGY vol 19(2) (Reissue) para 1801 et seq.

13   See the Wireless Telegraphy Act 1949 s 2 (as amended); and TELECOMMUNICATIONS AND BROADCASTING vol 45 para 526.

14   See the Taxation of Chargeable Gains Act 1992; and CAPITAL GAINS TAXATION.

15   See the Inheritance Tax Act 1984 (formerly known as the Capital Transfer Tax Act 1984); and INHERITANCE TAXATION. Inheritance tax is collected and managed by the Commissioners of Inland Revenue: see para 709 post.

16   See STAMP DUTIES. Stamp duties are under the care and management of the Commissioners of Inland Revenue: see the Stamp Duties Management Act 1891 ss 1, 27; and see para 709 post.

17   See the Civil List Act 1952 s 1; and CROWN LANDS AND PRIVILEGES.

18   See ibid s 1; and CROWN LANDS AND PRIVILEGES. The Civil List Act 1831 s 2 provided for the surrender of all casual revenues of the Crown. The Civil List Act 1837 provided for the surrender of the casual revenues of the Crown which had been surrendered by the 1831 Act. On that basis it is the practice of the Treasury (as to which see paras 512–517 ante) to treat all non-statutory revenue, including fees and charges not otherwise provided for by statute, as casual 'hereditary revenue' and thus payable into the Consolidated Fund (as to which see para 711 et seq post) and subject to parliamentary control: HM Treasury *Government Accounting* 22.2.12 (see para 230 note 2 ante). As to the power to remit payment of hereditary revenues into the Exchequer see CROWN LANDS AND PRIVILEGES. As to fines and forfeitures imposed or forfeited before the courts see para 828 post; and CRIMINAL LAW; MAGISTRATES. Property accruing to the monarch and received by the Treasury Solicitor under administration or forfeiture is paid into the Crown's Nominee Account: see the Treasury Solicitor Act 1876 s 4; and EXECUTORS.

19   Eg fees paid for the issue of passports and driving licences: see *The Fees and Charges Guide* (HM Treasury, 1992). As to whether such fees and charges are to be regarded as covered by the provisions of the Bill of Rights s 1 see para 228 ante. As to the history and citation of the Bill of Rights see para 35 note 3 ante.

20   Eg fees charged by trading funds such as Companies House and the Land Registry, which are governed by trading fund provisions: see note 18 supra; and para 743 et seq post.

21   As to the presentation of privatisation receipts to Parliament see para 726 text and note 13 post.

22   As to the Consolidated Fund see para 711 et seq post.

23   Customs duties were progressively abolished between the United Kingdom and the other member states of the European Community so that by 1 July 1977 there were no customs duties: see the European Communities Act 1972 s 5 (as amended); EC Treaty art 95; and CUSTOMS AND EXCISE.

**708. Authorities principally responsible for collecting revenue.** The bulk of the revenue[1] is collected by the Commissioners of Inland Revenue[2] and the Commissioners of Customs and Excise[3]; and most of the remainder is collected by the Post Office[4], local authorities[5], the Secretary of State for Transport[6] and the Crown Estate Commissioners[7].

1   For the meaning of 'revenue' see para 701 note 1 ante.

2   As to the Commissioners of Inland Revenue see para 709; and INCOME TAXATION.

3   As to the Commissioners of Customs and Excise see para 710 post; and CUSTOMS AND EXCISE.

4   See generally POST OFFICE.

5   As to the management and collection of revenue by local authorities see CUSTOMS AND EXCISE.

6   See eg the Vehicle Excise and Registration Act 1994 s 6; and CUSTOMS AND EXCISE.

7   See CROWN LANDS AND PRIVILEGES.

**709. The Commissioners of Inland Revenue.** The Commissioners of Inland Revenue (frequently referred to collectively as the Board of Inland Revenue[1]) are appointed by letters patent under the Great Seal[2], and hold office during Her Majesty's pleasure[3]. Two of their number form a quorum, except where anything is by statute or otherwise expressly directed or authorised to be done by one commissioner[4]. On the death, resignation or retirement of a member of the board and the admission of a new member, fresh letters patent are sealed.

In the performance of their duty, it is an important constitutional principle that the commissioners are free from day to day control by ministers in how they carry out their functions in collecting tax in individual cases, although they are legally subject to the authority, direction and control of Treasury ministers[5]. Income tax, corporation tax, capital gains tax[6], inheritance tax[7], petroleum revenue tax[8] and stamp duties[9] are under the commissioners' care and management.

The commissioners have the important function of advising Treasury ministers, principally the Chancellor of the Exchequer[10], on questions of tax policy in regard to the taxes under their care, including proposals for new or amending legislation, in particular to stop avoidance of tax, and for alterations in the law deemed advisable in view of adverse decisions of the courts. Advice to ministers upon particular provisions in a bill dealing with specific changes in the tax legislation is given by revenue[11] civil servants[12]. The commissioners are responsible to the Chancellor of the Exchequer.

The commissioners' annual report for the year ended 31 March is presented to Parliament by the Financial Secretary to the Treasury, and published as a command paper. Extra-statutory concessions were formerly notified in an appendix to these reports, but are now published separately[13].

The commissioners appoint inspectors of taxes and collectors, who act under their directions[14].

1  See eg the Taxes Management Act 1970 s 1(1).
2  As to use of the Great Seal see para 909 post.
3  See the Inland Revenue Regulation Act 1890 s 1(1). The commissioners are required to make a declaration of secrecy before taking office: see the Taxes Management Act 1970 ss 6 (as amended), 119(2), Sch 1 (as amended), Sch 4 para 1. As to offices held during pleasure see para 902 post.
4  See the Inland Revenue Regulation Act 1890 s 2.
5  See ibid s 1(2). The relationship is a delicate one. The trend has been for ministers to expect to be told more about the running of the department and even about individual cases than was the case some 20 years ago, but the fundamental principle remains that the collection of tax is the responsibility of the Board and ministers are informed after the event, if at all. As to the Treasury see paras 512–517 ante.
6  See the Taxes Management Act 1970 s 1(1); and INCOME TAXATION.
7  See the Inheritance Tax Act 1983 s 215; and INHERITANCE TAXATION.
8  See the Oil Taxation Act 1975 s 1(5), Sch 2 para 1(1); and PETROLEUM REVENUE TAX.
9  See the Stamp Duties Management Act 1891 ss 1, 27; and STAMP DUTIES.
10  As to the Chancellor of the Exchequer see para 514 ante.
11  For the meaning of 'revenue' see para 701 note 1 ante.
12  As to the Civil Service generally see paras 549–564 ante.
13  As to extra-statutory concessions see para 7 note 15 ante. Extra-statutory concessions are published in Inland Revenue Press Releases and compiled in booklet IR 1. See further INCOME TAXATION.
14  See the Taxes Management Act 1970 s 1(2); and the Inland Revenue Regulation Act 1890 s 4. Inspectors and collectors of taxes exercise their functions in relation to income tax, corporation tax, capital gains tax and petroleum revenue tax by virtue of the office they hold and not under authority derived from the Board. This position contrasts with their functions relating to inheritance tax, and to the position of officers appointed by the Commissioners of Customs and Excise: in those cases authority is derived from the Board and the Commissioners of Customs and Excise respectively.

**710. The Commissioners of Customs and Excise.** The Commissioners of Customs and Excise are appointed by letters patent under the Great Seal[1] and hold their appointments at Her Majesty's pleasure[2]. Subject to the general control of Treasury ministers, they are charged with the duty of collecting, accounting for and otherwise managing the revenues of customs and excise[3]. They are also responsible for the collection and management of value added tax[4] and gaming and betting duties[5].

1  As to use of the Great Seal see para 909 post.
2  See the Customs and Excise Management Act 1979 s 6(1) (as amended). As to offices held during pleasure see para 902 post.
3  Ibid s 6(2). Thus, the commissioners are not subject to the detailed control of the Treasury and are responsible for the day to day management of these revenues. As with the Commissioners of Inland Revenue (see para 709 ante), it is an important constitutional principle that the commissioners are free from day to day control by ministers in how they carry out their functions in collecting tax in individual cases, although they are legally subject to the authority, direction and control of Treasury. As to the Treasury see paras 512–517 ante. The collection and management of excise duties were transferred from the Commissioners of Inland Revenue to the Commissioners of Customs (who were renamed the Commissioners of Customs and Excise) by the Excise Transfer Order 1909, SR & O 1909/197, made under the Finance Act 1908 s 4 (repealed). That order was revoked by the Customs and Excise Act 1952 s 320(5), but substantially re-enacted by that Act. See further CUSTOMS AND EXCISE. Officers appointed by the commissioners exercise functions under authority derived from the Board.
4  See the Value Added Tax Act 1994 s 58, Sch 11 para 1(1); and VALUE ADDED TAX.
5  See the Betting and Gaming Duties Act 1981; and BETTING, GAMING AND LOTTERIES.

## (3)  THE CONSOLIDATED FUND AND ISSUES OF PUBLIC MONEY

### (i)  The Consolidated Fund

**711. The Consolidated Fund.** All central government revenue[1] derived from taxation or other sources[2] is, save where otherwise provided for[3], paid into an account with the Bank of England called the 'Account of Her Majesty's Exchequer'[4]. The money so credited forms one fund known as the 'Consolidated Fund'[5], from which issues may be made only on legislative authority[6], and it is this requirement that secures parliamentary control over government expenditure. It is for this reason that requirements that revenue be paid into the Consolidated Fund are of constitutional importance[7].

Receipts from privatisation are normally paid into the Consolidated Fund as excess appropriations in aid on departmental votes after the expenses of the sale have been deducted[8]. The transactions of the Consolidated Fund come under review in the annual accounts of the Fund which are examined and certified by Comptroller and Auditor General and presented to Parliament[9].

1  This principle does not apply to revenue of other public bodies, such as local authorities. For the meaning of 'revenue' see para 701 note 1 ante.
2  As to sources of revenue see para 707 ante.
3  Ie except (1) where statute provides otherwise (eg the Exchequer and Audit Departments Act 1866 s 10 (as amended), which enables the commissioners to make deductions before surrendering tax revenues to the exchequer); (2) money directed by statute or by the Treasury (as to which see paras 512–517 ante) to be applied as an appropriation in aid of money provided by Parliament for a particular service (see the Public Accounts and Charges Act 1891 s 2), or to be paid into a specific fund (eg the National Insurance Fund). See HM Treasury *Government Accounting* 3.3 (see para 230 note 2 ante). As to appropriations in aid see PARLIAMENT.
    As to the use of private sector banks instead of the Paymaster General and the Bank of England see booklet DAO (GEN) 4/94, March 1994; and HM Treasury *Government Accounting* 28. As to the Paymaster General see para 714 post.
4  See the Exchequer and Audit Departments Act 1866 s 10 (as amended); and HM Treasury *Government Accounting* 3.2.5. This is the central account of the government. It is strictly a cash account. Revenue or public income from whatever source and all government receipts are paid into it: see the Exchequer Extra Receipts Act 1868 s 1; the Treasury Solicitor Act 1876 s 4(2); the Treasury Bills Act 1877 s 5 (as amended); the Coinage Act 1971 ss 4(7) (restricted by the Government Trading Funds Act 1973 s 7(2)). As to the terms 'Exchequer' and 'Consolidated Fund' see note 6 infra. As to payment to the Exchequer of money borrowed upon the public credit see paras 728–729 post. As to payment of hereditary revenues

to the Exchequer see the Civil List Act 1952 s 1; and CROWN LANDS AND PRIVILEGES. The exception mentioned in note 1 supra applies in respect of revenues, from whatever source, so paid.

5 See the Consolidated Fund Act 1816 s 1 (as amended); and HM Treasury *Government Accounting* 3. The Consolidated Fund was established originally for the United Kingdom of Great Britain and Ireland: see the Consolidated Fund Act 1816 s 1 (as amended). Separate funds were constituted for Southern Ireland (now the Republic of Ireland) and Northern Ireland by the Government of Ireland Act 1920 s 20 (as originally enacted); that Act ceased to apply to the territory that is now the Republic of Ireland in consequence of the Irish Free State (Consequential Provisions) Act 1922 s 1 (as originally enacted).

The use of the terms 'Exchequer' and 'Consolidated Fund', and the relation between them, are matters of historical development. From about the twelfth century the Exchequer was, among other things, the King's purse into which all royal revenue and out of which all royal expenditure were paid. At first there was one account of the Exchequer, but with the growth of its revenue and expenditure in the course of centuries the practice grew of keeping a separate account for a particular source of revenue and for the expenditure to which that revenue was appropriated. Those separate accounts became so numerous and complicated to check that in 1787 it was decided to abolish them and to put all public revenue into, and to charge all public expenditure on, one 'Consolidated Fund'. See further PARLIAMENT.

6 See the Exchequer and Audit Departments Act 1866 s 11. The Treasury may only draw upon the account if the Comptroller and Auditor General (see paras 724–726 post) has certified that the drawing is in accordance with Parliament's authority: see ss 11, 13 (as amended). It is a prevalent literary and financial practice to treat 'Exchequer' and 'Consolidated Fund' as virtually synonymous and interchangeable terms, but since the passing of the National Loans Act 1968, the statutory convention has been to enact that money be paid into the Consolidated Fund (instead of enacting that it be paid into the Exchequer): National Loans Act 1968 s 1(8).

7 As to parliamentary control of expenditure see para 230 ante.

8 See HM Treasury *Government Accounting* 22.2.9. Other receipts may be surrendered as Consolidated Fund extra receipts: see HM Treasury *Government Accounting* 22.2.10.

9 See HM Treasury *Government Accounting* 3.2.19; and paras 724–726 post.

## (ii) Issues of Public Money

**712. Supply procedure.** Supply is the granting by Parliament of money to the Crown. This is voted annually[1]. Funds voted by Parliament under the Consolidated Fund Acts and the Appropriation Acts[2] are only available for expenditure during the financial years specified in the Acts. Any money which has been voted by Parliament for a particular year, but which is not needed to meet expenditure chargeable to that year is surrendered to the Consolidated Fund and cannot be carried forward into the next financial year[3].

The government lays before the House of Commons in March each year, before the beginning of the new financial year, its main supply estimates containing a request for funds for the forthcoming financial year, based on the new spending plans for the year ahead announced in the budget[4]. Part I of each estimate forms the basis of a single supply resolution, covering all the estimates[5], which is normally voted on by members of Parliament in the House of Commons before the end of July. A Consolidated Fund (Appropriation) Bill is then brought in and passed before Parliament rises for the Summer recess. The resulting Appropriation Act authorises departments to spend up to the amounts requested in the main supply estimates, any revised estimates and any Summer supplementary estimates[6]. The Appropriation Act gives parliamentary authority for the total sums requested to be issued from the Consolidated Fund, and also limits the way in which this money can be spent by prescribing how the overall sum is to be appropriated to particular estimates in order to finance specified services. It also appropriates to individual votes[7] sums provided under Consolidated Fund Acts passed since the previous Appropriation Act. Parliament does not normally approve the main estimates until the end of July or early August, so funds for early months of the financial year are provided by a system of votes on account. These are normally presented to Parliament in the previous November, along with the Winter supplementary estimates for the then current year. Once these resolutions have been approved by the House of Commons, they are embodied in legislation authorising issue of moneys from the Consolidated Fund[8], known as the Consolidated Fund Acts.

1     Three days (other than Fridays) before 5 August in each session are allotted for the consideration of supply estimates (known as 'estimates days'): see HC Standing Orders (1995) (Public Business) no 52. The time available on estimates days is allocated on the advice of the Liaison Committee (as to which see HC Standing Orders (1995) (Public Business) no 131; and PARLIAMENT).

       The primary purpose of the supply estimates is to provide the means by which the government seeks from Parliament sufficient funds and fresh parliamentary authority for the greater part of its own expenditure each year. When voted, the funds are drawn from the Consolidated Fund (as to which see para 711 et seq post). This expenditure is all within the 'control total' (ie the aggregate of the elements of public expenditure which the government plans and controls to achieve its wider objective for general public expenditure). This covers central government's own expenditure, local authority expenditure and the external financing requirements of nationalised industries and other public corporations. The main exceptions are cyclical social security and grants to certain central government bodies whose own expenditure is counted in the control total. The main elements of the control total not funded through supply estimates are (1) central government expenditure which is funded directly from other sources, such as the National Insurance Fund (see NATIONAL HEALTH); (2) certain salaries and other payments which are made, by statute, direct from the Consolidated Fund; (3) credit approvals issued by central government to local authorities; (4) market and overseas borrowing of nationalised industries and other public corporations; and (5) local authority self-financed expenditure: see *Supply Estimates 1995–96, Summary and Guide* (Cm 2775) (1995) para 2.2. For the format of and information given in estimates see HM Treasury *Government Accounting* 11 (see para 230 note 2 ante). As to the changes in the form of the supply estimates for 1996–1997 and subsequent years see the *Third Report of the Treasury and Civil Service Committee: The Form of the Estimates* (HC Paper (1993–94) no 192); *Third Special Report: The Form of the Estimates: the Government's Response to the Third Report of the Committee in Session 1993–94* (HC Paper (1993–94) no 441); and the *Fourth Report of the Treasury and Civil Service Committee: Simplified Estimates and Resource Accounting* (HC Paper (1994–95) no 212).

       Three estimates days each session are, however, taken in government time: (a) the first must be taken before 6 February (by which date the House must vote on the account for the coming financial year and the Winter supplementary estimates for the current year); (b) the second must be taken before 18 March (by which date the House must vote on the Spring supplementary estimates); and (c) the third must be taken before 5 August (by which date the House must vote on the main estimates and the Summer supplementary estimates): see HC Standing Orders (1995) (Public Business) no 53. As to supplementary estimates see note 6 infra.

       Detailed parliamentary scrutiny of government estimates on the floor of the House has long been abandoned. There is, however, growing attention to expenditure plans, and consequently to supply estimates, by select committees (as to which see paras 227 ante, 718 post; and PARLIAMENT). See the *Eighth Report of the Committee of Public Accounts* (HC Paper (1986–87) no 98); Likierman *Public Expenditure* (1988); McEldowney *Public Law* (1994) pp 313–316; and Elliott 'The control of public expenditure' in Jowell and Oliver (eds) *The Changing Constitution* (2nd Edn, 1989) p 165.

       The Committee of Public Accounts reported that 'Parliament's consideration of the annual estimates - the key constitutional control - remains largely a formality'. However, the estimates are still important as they provide the framework for the appropriation accounts which are audited by the National Audit Office (as to which see para 720 post) and examined by the Committee of Public Accounts (as to which see para 719 post).

2     The parliamentary scrutiny of Consolidated Fund Bills and Appropriation Bills is purely formal since the 'Jopling reforms' to HC Standing Orders (1995) (Public Business). When a motion has been made for the second reading of a Consolidated Fund or Appropriation Bill, the question must be put forthwith, no order must be made for the committal of the bill and the question for the third reading must be put forthwith; and may be decided at any hour, though opposed: see HC Standing Orders (1995) (Public Business) no 54; and PARLIAMENT. There is therefore no scope for parliamentary debate or amendment.

3     This is the concept of 'annuality': see HM Treasury *Government Accounting* 11.2.21 (see para 230 note 2 ante).

4     As to the budget see para 705 ante.

5     This is known as the 'roll-up'.

6     A 'supplementary estimate' may be presented by the Treasury for parliamentary approval if, later in the year, a department's needs turn out to be greater than estimated or new services are introduced. The supplementary estimates for Summer, Winter and Spring may be passed under accelerated procedure at certain times: see HC Standing Orders (1995) (Public Business) nos 52, 53. Should money have been spent in excess of that voted, retrospective authority (after investigation by the Committee of Public

Accounts) is given by March of the following year: see Erskine May *Parliamentary Practice* (21st Edn, 1989) p 702. As to the Treasury see paras 512–517 ante.

Supplementary estimates may be used to redistribute the amount of money between subheads of the same vote as well as to increase it: HM Treasury *Government Accounting* 11.4.30. See also PARLIAMENT.

7 Since the Exchequer and Audit Departments Act 1866 the supply estimates have been divided into classes, usually one class per major department. Each class is divided into heads of expenditure, known as 'votes'. Thus, each department will have a number of votes. There were between two and 22 votes per class in 1995–96. The number of votes is to be reduced from 1996–97: see *Supply Estimates: Summary and Guide* (Cm 2775) (1995–96); McEldowney *Public Law* (1994) pp 313–317; and PARLIAMENT.

8 See *Supply Estimates: Summary and Guide* (Cm 2775) (1995–96) ch 5; and para 711 et seq ante.

**713. Authorisation for issue of public money.** Issues of money from the Consolidated Fund[1] are authorised by statute either for Consolidated Fund services or for supply services[2]. The expenditure of the former is charged on and payable out of the Consolidated Fund[3], and may continue from year to year, so long as the relevant statutory provisions remain in force, without further legislative authority. The major payment of this kind out of the Consolidated Fund is to the National Loans Fund towards service of the national debt[4]. Other payments include those to the European Community, and certain payments to Northern Ireland[5]. Payments from the Consolidated Fund also include the Civil List[6], and expenditure on salaries of persons who are intended to be independent of the government of the day and whose conduct should in consequence not be open to discussion in the ordinary course[7].

Expenditure on supply services is met out of money provided by Parliament, and may not commence, or continue from year to year, unless authority has previously been provided by Parliament[8]. Supply services may arise for discussion each year, and the Treasury ministers must be prepared to defend the expenditure to the House of Commons[9]. Hence the estimated expenditure, to cover which Parliament is asked to vote supplies, must first have been submitted to and approved by the Treasury[10]. Estimates must be prepared and presented, and in part voted, before the commencement of the financial year for which they provide[11].

The House of Commons approves the estimates. During that process it becomes necessary for the government to obtain authority for drawing money from the Consolidated Fund. This is arranged before the end of March[12] by passing a Consolidated Fund Act authorising payment from the Consolidated Fund in respect of the supply for the opening period of the ensuing financial year and towards making good the supply voted for the expiring financial year[13]. Other Consolidated Fund Acts are passed from time to time during the financial year. Generally in late July or early August, just before the Summer adjournment, an Appropriation Act[14] is passed, authorising a further payment from the Consolidated Fund and appropriating the total amounts granted since the previous Appropriation Act, retrospectively from the date of the passing of the first of the Acts mentioned in a schedule to it. The foregoing Acts authorise the Bank of England to advance to the Treasury, on 'ways and means advances', any sum required to meet temporary requirements within the total amount specified in them[15].

The payments authorised for Consolidated Fund and supply services need a further authorisation from the Comptroller and Auditor General[16], who must satisfy himself, in the case of supply services, that the amount requisitioned is within the total sum voted by Parliament for the year of account[17].

1 As to the Consolidated Fund see para 711 et seq ante.
2 As to supply procedure see para 712 ante.
3 See the Public Revenue and Consolidated Fund Charges Act 1854 s 1 (as amended).
4 As to payments for the service of the national debt see para 732 post; and MONEY.
5 See Erskine May *Parliamentary Practice* (21st Edn, 1989) p 691.
6 See CROWN LANDS AND PRIVILEGES.

7　Such as the Speaker of the House of Commons, members of the judiciary, the Comptroller and Auditor General (see paras 724–726 post), the Parliamentary Commissioner for Administration, the Leader of the Opposition and the Opposition whips.

8　See generally PARLIAMENT.

9　As to the Treasury see paras 512–517 ante. As to the House of Commons see PARLIAMENT.

10　As to Treasury control of expenditure see para 704 ante; and Erskine May *Parliamentary Practice* (21st Edn, 1989) ch 27.

11　As to supply procedure see para 712 ante.

12　The financial year ends on 31 March: Interpretation Act 1978 s 5, Sch 1, Sch 2 para 4(1) (amended by the Family Law Reform Act 1987 s 33(1), (4), Sch 2 para 74, Sch 4). For the timetable of the financial year see para 705 note 6 ante.

13　This payment from the Consolidated Fund for the expiring financial year is to make good any supplementary sums required. The February or Spring supplementary estimates are voted in supply in time to be incorporated in the March Consolidated Fund Act. The Summer supplementary estimates are disposed of together with the main estimates for the current financial year which have to be authorised before 5 August. The November or Winter supplementary estimates and the vote on account for the following financial year must be disposed of in supply not later than 6 February: see para 712 ante.

14　As to the annual Appropriation Act see para 712 text and note 2 ante. The financial year itself normally overlaps two sessions; the expenditure of a particular year needs to be authorised by more than one Appropriation Act, and every Appropriation Act contains provisions for the finance of years other than the year to which it mainly relates: see Erskine May *Parliamentary Practice* (21st Edn, 1989) pp 707–709.

15　See Erskine May *Parliamentary Practice* (21st Edn, 1989) ch 29.

16　As to the Comptroller and Auditor General see paras 724–726 post.

17　See the Exchequer and Audit Departments Act 1866 ss 13, 15 (both as amended); and PARLIAMENT.

**714. The Paymaster General.** The Paymaster General is the ministerial head of an office[1] subordinate to the Treasury and through which the Treasury controls the issue of money to each government department[2]. He is appointed by warrant under the sign manual[3] (countersigned by the Treasury) and he holds office during the pleasure of the Crown[4], and retires upon a change of government. Official duties as Paymaster General are nominal[5], the duties of that office being entrusted to a permanent Assistant Paymaster General[6]. The office of Paymaster General does not disqualify the holder from sitting and voting in the House of Commons[7].

Having been authorised by the Comptroller and Auditor General[8] to grant a credit for supply services within the total amount granted by the current Consolidated Fund Acts[9], the Treasury instructs the Bank of England to transfer money from the Exchequer account (ie the Consolidated Fund[10]) to the Paymaster General's supply account, from which transfers are made by him as necessary to a drawing account. Departmental drafts for payment to the public are made on this drawing account. The Paymaster General also maintains various other accounts on behalf of government departments. The Pay Office records show the amount of each vote[11] granted by Parliament for every department, and as money is issued from the drawing account the appropriate vote account is debited up to the limit of the total sums granted.

The Treasury may make rules and regulations and issue such orders from time to time in all matters relating to the office of Paymaster General, for the safety, economy and advantage of the public service as they see fit[12]. These rules, regulations and orders are to be observed by the Comptroller and Auditor General and the Bank of England[13].

1　The office is styled 'The Office of Her Majesty's Paymaster General'; and consists of a paymaster general with such number of officers, clerks and assistants, and with such salaries as are fixed and regulated from time to time by the Treasury: Paymaster General Act 1835 s 3 (amended by the Statute Law Revision (No 2) Act 1888; the Statute Law Revision Act 1890; and the Statute Law (Repeals) Act 1981). As to the Treasury see paras 512–517 ante.

2　As to the Treasury's control of matters affecting the revenue or public income see para 704 ante. As to the Paymaster General's salary see para 423 ante.

3　As to the sign manual see para 908 ante.

4    Paymaster General Act 1835 s 4 (amended by the Statute Law Revision (No 2) Act 1888; the Statute Law
     Revision Act 1890; and the Statute Law (Repeals) Act 1981). See paras 901–902 post.

5    The person holding the office of Paymaster General is usually a minister without portfolio: see para 512
     note 5 ante.

6    The duties and salary of the Assistant Paymaster General are prescribed by Treasury Minute.

7    Ie it is not an office mentioned in the House of Commons Disqualification Act 1975 s 2, Sch 2 (as
     amended): see further PARLIAMENT.

8    As to the Comptroller and Auditor General see paras 724–726 post.

9    As to such authorisation and payment see para 713 text and notes 12–15 ante.

10   As to the Consolidated Fund see para 711 et seq ante.

11   As to votes see para 712 note 7 ante.

12   Paymaster General Act 1848 s 1 (amended by the Statute Law Revision Act 1891). A return setting out
     all the rules, regulations and orders that have been prescribed and issued by the Treasury must be laid
     before Parliament within six weeks from the date of issue if Parliament is then sitting; and if not sitting,
     within six weeks from the day of the next ensuing meeting of Parliament: Paymaster General Act 1848
     s 5 (amended by the Statute Law Revision Act 1891).

13   Paymaster General Act 1848 s 1 (as amended: see note 12 supra).

### (iii)  Public Accounts

**715.  Accounting officers.** In each government department a particular officer in that
department (usually the Permanent Secretary), called the accounting officer[1], appointed
by the Treasury[2], is made personally responsible to Parliament for the regularity (that is
to say the legality) of any expenditure from each vote[3], and for rendering, in due course,
the 'appropriation account'[4], that is the final account of the year's expenditure and
receipts which, after audit by the Comptroller and Auditor General[5], who is an officer of
the House of Commons, is laid before Parliament[6]. The accounting officer is a member
of the department's staff and not of the Treasury's staff.

In addition the chief executive of each executive agency is appointed 'agency
accounting officer' by the Treasury if it has its own vote or is a trading fund[7]. If an
executive agency does not have its own vote the departmental accounting officer
designates the chief executive as agency accounting officer[8].

The senior full time official in each non-departmental public body[9] which is in receipt of
grant or grant in aid from a government department, and in some other non-departmental
public bodies, has responsibilities similar to those of an accounting officer, and is sometimes
formally designated as such by the appropriate departmental accounting officer.

It is the accounting officer's duty to satisfy himself that the proposed expenditure is
within the ambit of the vote[10], and that any Treasury authority which may be necessary
has been obtained. The accounting officer has the responsibility to advise the minister on
all matters of financial propriety and regularity[11]. If a minister overrules an accounting
officer's advice against expenditure the accounting officer minutes his advice and the fact
that the minister overruled it and reports the matter to the Comptroller and Auditor
General[12]. He is free to point out to a minister that the department may receive criticism
from the Committee of Public Accounts[13].

The personal responsibility of the accounting officer is a fundamental feature of the
financial system. He is liable to be called to appear before the Committee of Public
Accounts to answer questions on the use of the funds for which he is responsible, and he
is directly accountable to the House of Commons[14] for his acts and is, it seems, liable to
personal surcharge[15].

Although vouching for propriety and regularity is an important part of his
responsibilities, equally if not more important is his responsibility for securing economy
in the administration of the expenditure under his control. It is for this reason that it is
the general rule to appoint as accounting officer the senior officer responsible to his

minister for the activities covered by the vote. His duties and responsibilities are made clear to him in his formal letter of appointment[16].

Internal audits are carried out in departments by units responsible to the accounting officer, under guidance issued by the Treasury[17].

1   See the Exchequer and Audit Departments Act 1866 s 22 (as amended); and HM Treasury *Government Accounting* 6 (see para 230 note 2 ante). See also McEldowney *Public Law* (1994) pp 304–306.

2   As to the Treasury see paras 512–517 ante.

3   As to votes see para 712 note 7 ante.

4   Exchequer and Audit Departments Act 1866 s 22 (as amended); and see para 701 note 1 ante.

5   As to the Comptroller and Auditor General see paras 724–726 post.

6   As to the audit of public accounts see para 716 post.

7   See the Government Trading Funds Act 1973 s 4(6) (as amended); and paras 743–751 post. For the responsibilities of an accounting officer see HM Treasury *Government Accounting* 6.1, 17.1.9.

8   See HM Treasury *Government Accounting* 6.1.

9   Non-departmental public bodies do not normally form part of the Crown and thus they do not have their own votes and are not strictly covered by the accounting officer provisions. The Committee on Standards in Public Life recommended that the responsibilities of accounting officers in those bodies be emphasised and audit procedures be reviewed: *First Report of the Committee on Standards in Public Life* (Cm 2850) (1995). The government's response is set out in *Spending Public Money: Governance and Audit Issues* (Cabinet Office/Treasury, March 1996). The government will ensure that the Comptroller and Auditor General has inspection reports over all executive non-departmental public bodies which he does not audit: see 273 HC Official Report (6th series) 7 March 1996, written answers cols *301–306*. As to non-departmental public bodies generally see para 951 et seq post.

10   Except in the case of trading funds, since they are not within the supply system: see paras 743–751 post.

11   See HM Treasury *Government Accounting* 6.1.1–6.1.12.

12   See HM Treasury *Government Accounting* 6.1.5 (memorandum entitled *Responsibilities of an Accounting Officer*). See eg the Overseas Development Agency accounting officer's reservation minute issued in relation to the Pergau Dam in Malaysia: *Third Report of the Committee of Foreign Affairs: Public Expenditure: Pergau Hydro-electric Project, Malaysia, the Aid and Trade Provision and Related Matters* (HC Paper (1993–94) no 271); and see White, Harden and Donnelly 'Audit, accounting officers and accountability: the Pergau Dam affair' [1994] Public Law 526.

13   HM Treasury *Government Accounting* 6.1.5 (memorandum entitled *Responsibilities of an Accounting Officer* paras 13–15). As to the Committee of Public Accounts see para 719 post.

14   As to the House of Commons see PARLIAMENT.

15   This inference may be drawn from the Exchequer and Audit Departments Act 1866 s 43 which provides for relief from surcharge.

16   See Treasury memorandum published as Appendix A to the *First, Second, Third and Fourth Reports from the Committee of Public Accounts together with the Proceedings of the Committee, Minutes of Evidence, Appendices and Index* (HC Papers (1950–51) nos 100-I, 183-I, 184-I, 241-I); and HM Treasury *Government Accounting* 6.1.5.

17   See *Government Internal Audit Manual* (2nd Edn, 1988) published by the Treasury.

**716. Audit of public accounts.** The accounts[1] of all government departments and most public bodies (excluding local authorities) relating to the raising of money through taxation and spending of public funds are transmitted annually to the Comptroller and Auditor General[2], who is an officer of the House of Commons, for examination, certification and report, and then laid, together with any report, before the House of Commons or both Houses of Parliament[3] so that it may be ascertained whether the relevant directions have been carried out[4].

The Comptroller and Auditor General must examine the accounts of any person or body specified by an order made by the Treasury[5] by statutory instrument; and no such order may be made unless a draft of it has been laid before and approved by a resolution of the House of Commons[6]. He must examine any such accounts with as little delay as possible, and when the examination is completed he must sign a certificate to the account recording the result of his examination, and a copy of the account is sent to the person or body in question[7].

The accounts of the receipt of revenue by the Commissioners of Customs and Excise and the Commissioners of Inland Revenue and the accounts of every receiver of money which is by law payable into the Exchequer, is examined by the Comptroller and Auditor General on behalf of the House of Commons in order to ascertain that adequate regulations and procedure have been framed to secure an effective check on the assessment, collection and proper allocation of revenue, and he must satisfy himself that any such regulations and procedure are being duly carried out[8]. He must make such examination as he thinks fit with respect to the correctness of the sums brought to account in respect of the revenue, and he must present a report on the results of the examination[9].

The Comptroller and Auditor General also examines stock and store accounts[10] on behalf of the House of Commons in order to ascertain that adequate regulations have been made for control and stocktaking, and that the regulations are duly enforced and that any requirements of the Treasury have been complied with; he then reports to the House of Commons with the result of the examination[11].

Each financial year, statements of account are prepared, showing the income and expenditure of any operations of the department for which the Treasury considers it desirable that such statements should be prepared, together with such balance sheets and statements of profit and loss and particulars of costs as the Treasury may require[12]. These accounts are transmitted to the Comptroller and Auditor General and presented to Parliament before specified dates[13]. He then examines the accounts on behalf of the House of Commons and certifies and reports on them to the Commons[14].

In some cases where the Secretary of State has the power to appoint the auditor of a non-departmental public body he may choose to appoint the Comptroller and Auditor General[15]. The Comptroller and Auditor General may charge a fee for auditing the accounts of a person or body[16]. However, he must not without the consent of a minister of the Crown charge a fee for auditing the accounts of a person or body whose functions are discharged on behalf of the Crown[17]. Any fee received by the Comptroller and Auditor General must be paid by him into the Consolidated Fund[18].

In the case of appropriation accounts, every such account must be examined by the Comptroller and Auditor General on behalf of the House of Commons[19]. In the examination of such accounts he must satisfy himself that the money expended has been applied to the purpose or purposes for which the grants made by Parliament were intended to provide and that the expenditure conforms to the authority which governs it[20].

The Comptroller and Auditor General, after satisfying himself that the vouchers have been examined and certified as correct by the accounting department, may, in his discretion and having regard to the character of the departmental examination, in any particular case admit the sums so certified without further evidence of payment in support of the charges to which they relate[21].

If, in examining an appropriation account, it appears to the Comptroller and Auditor General that the account includes any material expenditure requiring the authority of the Treasury which has been incurred without such authority he must report that fact to the Treasury, and any such unauthorised expenditure must, unless sanctioned by the Treasury, be regarded as not being properly chargeable to a parliamentary grant, and must be reported to the House of Commons[22]. He must also report to the House of Commons any important change in the extent or character of any examination made by him[23].

In order that such examination may as far as possible proceed pari passu with the transactions of the several accounting departments, the Comptroller and Auditor General has free access, at all convenient times, to the books of account[24] and other documents relating to the accounts of such departments, and may require the several departments concerned to furnish him from time to time, or at regular periods, with accounts of the transactions of such departments respectively up to such times or periods[25].

These accounts and reports are referred to and considered by a select committee known as the Committee of Public Accounts which is set up every session by the House of Commons for this purpose[26].

1   As to the furnishing of accounts see para 723 post.
2   As to the Comptroller and Auditor General see paras 724–726 post.
3   Eg certificates under the Exchequer and Audit Departments Act 1921 s 5 (as amended) are given to the House of Commons alone. Certificates under the Government Trading Funds Act 1973 s 4(6) (as amended) are given to 'Parliament'. As to the House of Commons see PARLIAMENT.
4   See the Exchequer and Audit Departments Act 1866 s 5 (as amended), s 22 (as amended), s 25, Sch A (as substituted); the Exchequer and Audit Departments Act 1921 s 1 (as amended) (examination of appropriation accounts), s 2 (as amended) (examination of accounts of receipts of revenue), s 3 (as amended) (examination of other cash accounts), s 4 (examination of stock and store accounts) and s 5 (as amended) (preparation and examination of trading etc accounts); the National Loans Act 1968 s 21 (as amended); and the Government Trading Funds Act 1973 s 4(6) (as amended). The Exchequer and Audit Departments Act 1921 ss 3, 5 (both as amended) do not apply to Post Office accounts: see the Post Office Act 1961 ss 12(2), 28(1), Schedule. Nor does the Exchequer and Audit Departments Act 1921 s 5 (as amended) apply to a service financed, during any financial year, by means of a trading fund established under the Government Trading Funds Act 1973: see s 4(7) (as amended). See also HM Treasury *Government Accounting* 7.1.8–7.1.10 (see para 230 note 2 ante). Not all accounts furnished to the Comptroller and Auditor General are certified and not all have to be reported on; it depends on the precise wording of the statute or agreement under which the audit is carried out. The Treasury may require any accounts, whether or not relating to the receipt or expenditure of public funds, to be transmitted to the Comptroller and Auditor General for examination. As to the examination by the Comptroller and Auditor General of the Exchange Equalisation Account see MONEY.
5   As to the Treasury see paras 512–517 post.
6   Exchequer and Audit Departments Act 1921 s 3(1) (substituted by the National Audit Act 1983 s 12): see also the Comptroller and Auditor General (Examination of Accounts) Order 1984, SI 1984/1078.
7   Exchequer and Audit Departments Act 1921 s 3(2) (amended by the National Audit Act 1983 s 12).
8   Exchequer and Audit Departments Act 1921 s 2(1) (amended by the Post Office Act 1961 s 28(1), Schedule).
9   Exchequer and Audit Departments Act 1921 s 2(2).
10  Stock and store accounts must be kept in all cases where, in the opinion of the Treasury, the receipts, expenditure, sale, transfer or delivery of any securities, stamps, provisions or stores the property of the Crown in any government department is of sufficient amount or character to require the keeping of such accounts: see ibid s 4(1).
11  Ibid s 4(1).
12  Ibid s 5(1) (amended by the Government Trading Act 1990 s 3(1)).
13  Exchequer and Audit Departments Act 1921 s 5(2). See the Exchequer and Audit Departments Act 1866 Sch A (substituted by the Exchequer and Audit Departments Act 1921 s 6, Sch 1).
14  Exchequer and Audit Departments Act 1921 s 5(3) (amended by the Government Trading Act 1990 s 3(1)).
15  See HM Treasury *Government Accounting* 7.1.11. As to non-departmental public bodies see para 951 et seq post. In such cases the Comptroller and Auditor General will not have audit rights, but he may have inspection rights. If the non-departmental public body is a company the Comptroller and Auditor General will not be qualified to act as auditor under the Companies Acts: see further COMPANIES.
16  National Audit Act 1983 s 5(1).
17  Ibid s 5(2). However, this provision is not to be construed as authorising the charging of a fee for the audit by agreement of the accounts of any other person or body unless the agreement so provides: s 5(2).
18  Ibid s 5(3). As to the Consolidated Fund see para 711 et seq ante.
19  See the Exchequer and Audit Departments Act 1921 s 1(1).
20  Ibid s 1(1).
21  Ibid s 1(2) (amended by the National Audit Act 1983 s 14, Sch 5).
22  Exchequer and Audit Departments Act 1921 s 1(3) (amended by the National Audit Act 1983 s 11). This statement is known as a 'regularity opinion'. As a matter of practice and not statutory requirement, from 1995–96 the Comptroller and Auditor General will give regularity opinions on all accounts he audits. As to value for money audit and examination see para 717 post.
23  Exchequer and Audit Departments Act 1921 s 1(4).
24  A plan of account books and accounts, adapted to the requirements of each service, must be designed under the superintendence of the Treasury; and the Treasury may prescribe the manner in which each department of the public service keeps its accounts: Exchequer and Audit Departments Act 1866 s 23 (amended by the Exchequer and Audit Departments Act 1921 s 9(1)).

25  Exchequer and Audit Departments Act 1866 s 28 (amended by the Exchequer and Audit Departments Act 1921 s 9(2)). The department charged with the duty of preparing the appropriation account must, if required to do so by the Comptroller and Auditor General, transmit to him a balance sheet and verify the balances appearing upon the appropriation account, provided always that he may, if he thinks fit, require the department to transmit to him in lieu of such balance sheet a certified statement showing the actual disposition of the balances appearing upon the appropriation account on the last day of the period of such account: see the Exchequer and Audit Departments Act 1866 s 25. The appropriation account must also be accompanied by a statement explaining the disposal of balances and the cause of any excess expenditure: see s 26.

26  As to the Committee of Public Accounts see para 719 post; and PARLIAMENT.

**717. Economy, efficiency and effectiveness of examinations.** The Comptroller and Auditor General[1] may carry out examinations (known as 'value for money audit') into the economy, efficiency and effectiveness[2] with which any department, authority[3] or other body has used its resources in discharging its functions[4]. This does not, however, entitle the Comptroller and Auditor General to question the merits of the policy[5] objectives of any department, authority or body in respect of which an examination is carried out[6].

The departments, authorities and other bodies to which this provision applies are:

(1)  any department in respect of which appropriation accounts are required to be prepared[7];

(2)  any National Health Service body required to keep accounts[8];

(3)  any other authority or body whose accounts are required to be examined and certified by, or are open to the inspection of, the Comptroller and Auditor General by virtue of any enactment[9];

(4)  any authority or body[10] whose accounts are required to be examined and certified by, or are open to the inspection of, the Comptroller and Auditor General by virtue of any agreement[11] made between that authority or body and a minister of the Crown[12].

Value for money auditing extends to privatisation of industries to consider whether good value has been received for assets sold[13]. However, the Comptroller and Auditor General is not empowered to examine nationalised industries or local government[14].

Where the Comptroller and Auditor General's functions in relation to an authority or body falling within head (3) or (4) above are by the enactment or agreement in question restricted to particular activities of the authority or body, any examination must be correspondingly restricted[15].

If the Comptroller and Auditor General has reasonable cause to believe that any authority or body (with specified exceptions[16]) appointed, or whose members are required to be appointed, by or on behalf of the Crown, has in any of its financial years received more than half its income[17] from public funds[18] he may carry out an examination into the economy, efficiency and effectiveness with which it has in that year used its resources in discharging its functions[19]. However, this does not entitle the Comptroller and Auditor General to question the merits of the policy objectives of any authority or body in respect of which an examination is carried out[20]. In determining whether the income of an authority or body is such as to bring it within this provision the Comptroller and Auditor General must consult that authority or body and the Treasury[21].

The Comptroller and Auditor General has a right of access at all reasonable times to all such documents as he may reasonably require for carrying out any examination[22] and is entitled to require from any person holding or accountable for any such document such information and explanation as are reasonably necessary for that purpose[23].

The Comptroller and Auditor General may report to the House of Commons the results of any examination carried out by him under these provisions[24].

1   As to the Comptroller and Auditor General see paras 724–726 post.
2   The National Audit Office has itself defined economy, efficiency and effectiveness as follows: 'Economy is concerned with minimising the cost of resources with regard to appropriate quality (in short, spending less). Efficiency is concerned with the relationship between output of goods, services or other results and the resources used to produce them (in short, spending well). Effectiveness is concerned with the relationship between intended results and the actual results of projects, programmes or other activities (in short, spending wisely)': see *A Framework for Value for Money Audits (Treasury Minute on the First Four Reports from the Committee of Public Accounts)* (Cmnd 9755) (1985–86) paras 21–23; *Treasury Minute on the First, Third to Sixth and Eighth to Seventeenth Reports from the Committee of Public Accounts Session 1980–81* (Cmnd 8413) (1981) para 87. As to efficiency and effectiveness see also *Report of the Treasury and Civil Service Committee: Efficiency and Effectiveness in the Civil Service* (HC Paper (1981–82) no 236); HM Treasury *Government Accounting* 7.1.12, 7.1.14, 7.1.24–7.1.28 (see para 230 note 2 ante); and McEldowney *Public Law* (1994) pp 326–333.
3   'Authority' includes any person holding a public office: National Audit Act 1983 s 6(7).
4   Ibid s 6(1).
5   'Policy' in relation to any such authority, includes any policy of the government so far as relating to the functions of that department: ibid s 6(7).
6   Ibid s 6(2).
7   Ie under the Exchequer and Audit Departments Act 1866: National Audit Act 1983 s 6(3)(a).
8   Ie under the National Health Service Act 1977 s 98 or the National Health Service (Scotland) Act 1978: National Audit Act 1983 s 6(3)(b).
9   Ibid s 6(3)(c).
10  Ie any authority or body which does not fall within ibid s 7: see text and notes 17–21 infra.
11  References to an agreement made by a minister include references to conditions imposed by him in pursuance of any statutory power in that behalf, whether in connection with the provision of financial assistance or otherwise: ibid s 6(7).
12  Ibid s 6(3)(d). No examination may be carried out by the Comptroller and Auditor General in respect of such an authority or body unless the carrying out of such an examination is included expressly or by implication in the functions exercisable by him under the agreement in question; but where (1) the agreement was made by a minister before 1 January 1984 and is not such as to allow any such examination; or (2) a minister makes an agreement after 1 January 1984 for the exercise by the Comptroller and Auditor General in respect of any authority or body of any such functions, the minister must, subject to s 6(6) (see infra), use his best endeavours to secure from the authority or body in question such rights as will enable examinations to be carried out in respect of that authority or body: s 6(5). 'Minister' or 'minister of the Crown' includes any department falling within head (1) in the text: s 6(7). Section 6(5) does not oblige a minister to seek to obtain any rights except at the request of the Comptroller and Auditor General, and the obligations of a minister under s 6(5) do not apply to any organisation which is the subject of an Order in Council under the International Organisations Act 1968 s 1 (as amended) or s 4 (as amended): National Audit Act 1983 s 6(6).
13  See McEldowney *Public Law* (1994) pp 324–325; McEldowney 'The National Audit Office and Privatisation' (1991) 54 Modern Law Review 933–955; Beauchamp 'The National Audit Office: Its Role in Privatisation' (1990) Public Money and Management pp 55–58; *Treasury Minute on the First Four Reports from the Committee of Public Accounts* (Cmnd 9755) (1985–86); Graham and Prosser 'Privatising Public Enterprises: Constitutions, the State and Regulation in Comparative Perspective' (1991); Graham and Prosser 'Privatising Nationalised Industries: Constitutional Issues and New Legal Techniques' (1987) 50 Modern Law Review pp 16–51.
14  Local authorities are subject to audit by the Audit Commission (see LOCAL GOVERNMENT). The remaining nationalised industries have their own procedures for audit issued by the Nationalised Industries Chairman's Group Financial Panel.
15  National Audit Act 1983 s 6(4).
16  The following authorities or bodies are specifically excepted: British Airways Board; British Coal Corporation; British Railways Board; British Shipbuilders; British Steel Corporation; British Waterways Board; Central Electricity Generating Board; Electricity Council and Area Boards within the meaning of the Electricity Act 1947; North of Scotland Hydro-electric Board; South of Scotland Electricity Board; Civil Aviation Authority; London Regional Transport; Post Office; Scottish Transport Group; British Broadcasting Corporation; Sianel Pedwar Cymru: ibid s 7(4), Sch 4 (amended by the Telecommunications Act 1984 s 109(6), Sch 7 Pt III; London Regional Transport Act 1984 s 24; Oil and Pipelines Act 1985 s 7(4), Sch 4 Pt II; Airports Act 1986 s 83(5), Sch 6 Pt I; Gas Act 1986 s 67(4), Sch 9 Pt III; Coal Industry At 1987 s 1(2), Sch 1 para 44; Coal Industry Act 1987 s 10(3), Sch 3 Pt II; Water Act 1989 s 190(3), Sch 27 Pt I; Broadcasting Act 1990 s 203(1), Sch 20 para 36; National Bus Company (Dissolution) Order 1991, SI 1991/510, art 5(4), Schedule). As from a day to be appointed the British Steel Corporation entry is repealed: British Steel Act 1988 s 16(3), Sch 2 Pt II. As from a day to be appointed the Central Electricity

Generating Board, the Electricity Council and Area Boards within the meaning of the Electricity Act 1947, the North of Scotland Hydro-electric Board and the South of Scotland Electricity Board entries are repealed: Electricity Act 1989 s 112(4), Sch 18. As from a day to be appointed the British Coal Corporation entry is repealed: Coal Industry Act 1994 s 67(1), (8), Sch 9 para 29, Sch 11 Pt IV.

17 'Income' includes capital receipts: National Audit Act 1983 s 7(6).
18 Money is received from public funds if it is paid (1) by a minister of the Crown out of moneys provided by Parliament or out of the National Loans Fund; or (2) by an authority or body which itself falls within ibid s 7(1) (see the text to note 19 infra), including an authority or body falling within that subsection, but in either case, any money paid as consideration for the acquisition of property or the supply of goods or services or as remuneration, expenses, pensions, allowances or similar benefits for or in respect of a person as the holder of an office must be disregarded: s 7(5). As to the National Loans Fund see paras 727–739 post.
19 Ibid s 7(1), (4).
20 Ibid s 7(2).
21 Ibid s 7(3). As to the Treasury see paras 512–517 post.
22 Ie any examination under ibid s 6 or s 7: see text and notes 1–21 supra.
23 Ibid s 8(1). This applies only to documents in the custody or under the control of the department, authority or body to which the examination relates: s 8(2).
24 Ibid s 9.

**718. Select committees and government expenditure.** Certain departmentally-related select committees are empowered to examine the expenditure, administration and policy of their respective government departments[1]. They examine the use or proposed use of public money by scrutinising the relevant estimates[2] or the annual reports of their departments. The annual reports contain the department's expenditure plans for the following three years, and present in more detailed form the results of the government's annual Public Expenditure Survey as they apply to each department[3]. Many select committees take formal evidence from their department's accounting officers or principal finance officers, or both[4].

The Treasury Committee, together with the Committee of Public Accounts[5] is also responsible for considering changes to the form of the estimates and other financial information presented to the House of Commons[6], including changes proposed by the Treasury[7]. No such changes are introduced until these committees have been consulted, and in certain cases (such as changes in the form of the appropriation accounts or changes in the rules relating to virement[8]) the specific approval of the Committee of Public Accounts is required before the Treasury can proceed[9].

1 See HC Standing Orders (1995) (Public Business) no 130. As to select committees see para 227 ante; and PARLIAMENT.
2 As to supply estimates see para 712 ante.
3 As to the Public Expenditure Survey see para 704 ante.
4 The select committees may appoint specialist advisers to supply information: see HC Standing Orders (1995) (Public Business) no 130(4). As to accounting officers see para 715 ante.
5 As to the Committee of Public Accounts see para 719 post.
6 As to the House of Commons see PARLIAMENT.
7 Erskine May *Parliamentary Practice* (21st Edn, 1989) p 696. As to the Treasury see paras 512–517 post. In addition, both the Treasury Committee and, in particular, the Select Committee on Procedure, consider possible changes in the financial procedures of the House, either in response to government proposals, or as part of the regular process of bringing procedure into line with the contemporary requirements of the House and its members.
8 As to 'virement' (the use of savings under one subhead to meet expenditure under another) see further HM Treasury *Government Accounting* 11.7 (see para 230 note 2 ante); and Erskine May *Parliamentary Practice* (21st Edn, 1989) p 698.
9 See Erskine May *Parliamentary Practice* (21st Edn, 1989) p 696.

**719. The Committee of Public Accounts.** The Committee of Public Accounts[1] acts on behalf of Parliament to examine and report on accounts and public expenditure[2].

Its primary task is to ensure that funds voted by Parliament have been used for their prescribed purpose and the basis of its deliberations are the investigations carried out by the Comptroller and Auditor General. It is also empowered to carry out examinations into the economy, efficiency and effectiveness with which any department, authority or other body, audited by the Comptroller and Auditor General, has used its resources in discharging its functions. The committee may also consider other material submitted to it from the National Audit Office[3] which has not been presented to the House of Commons[4]. The reports made to the House by the Committee of Public Accounts are debated annually, and its rulings and related Treasury minutes are published[5]. The Committee has full power to call for such further explanations as it may require and may in its reports recommend, retrospectively when necessary, that any expenditure which has been incurred in excess of or without parliamentary authority should be sanctioned by additional grants, provision for which is commonly made in the next following Appropriation Act[6]. It may also recommend that expenditure be disallowed and that an accounting officer be personally surcharged for such unauthorised expenditure[7].

1   If at any time after the passing of the National Audit Act 1983 the name of the Committee of Public Accounts is changed or the functions discharged by that Committee or functions substantially corresponding thereto, are discharged by a different Committee of the House of Commons, references in the National Audit Act 1983 to the Committee of Public Accounts must be construed as a reference to that Committee by its new name or, as the case may be, to the Committee for the time being discharging those functions: s 13(1). Any questions arising under this provision must be determined by the Speaker of the House of Commons: s 13(2).

2   See HC Standing Orders (1995) (Public Business) no 122; Erskine May *Parliamentary Practice* (21st Edn, 1989) pp 660–1; Drewry *The New Select Committees* (2nd Edn, 1989); Griffith and Ryle *Parliament: Functions, Practice and Procedures* (1989) pp 441–444; and PARLIAMENT. The committee seeks to be non-partisan in its activities, particularly where they concern questions of financial regularity and efficiency. Many of the reports of the Comptroller and Auditor General (see paras 724–726 post) considered by the Committee of Public Accounts in modern times, however, concern 'value for money' audits (as to which see para 717 ante; and HM Treasury *Government Accounting* 7.1.24–7.1.28 (see para 230 note 2 ante)), where questions of the financial efficacy of government policies are inevitably engaged. Although the committee's criticisms and recommendations must by their nature be retrospective, they always receive careful attention by the government: see de Smith and Brazier *Constitutional and Administrative Law* (7th Edn, 1994) 309–310; Wade and Bradley *Constitutional and Administrative Law* (11th Edn, 1993) pp 362–363; Griffith and Ryle *Parliament: Functions, Practice and Procedures* (1989) pp 441–444.

3   As to the National Audit Office see para 720 post.

4   See Erskine May *Parliamentary Practice* (21st Edn, 1989) p 661.

5   See eg *Sale of Rover Group plc to British Aerospace plc* (HC Paper (1991–92) no 51): recommendation that the Treasury draw up further guidance on the best practices to be adopted in future privatisations. See also Treasury Minutes: Cm 2618 (1994), on the Report of the Committee of Public Accounts on English Estates (a non departmental body sponsored by the Department of the Environment) and property disposal; Cm 2175 (1993) on the Nineteenth Report of the Committee on Public Accounts *The Vehicle Inspectorate: Progress and the First Executive Agency* (HC Paper (1992–93) no 118); Treasury Minute Cm 2732 (1994), on the Fortieth Report of the Committee of Public Accounts 1993–94, on Property Services in the English Occupied Royal Household. As to the Treasury see paras 512–517 post.

6   See generally PARLIAMENT.

7   As to accounting officers see para 715 post.

## 720. The National Audit Office.

The National Audit Office consists of the Comptroller and Auditor General[1] (who is the head of the office) and the staff appointed by him[2]. He may appoint such staff as he considers necessary for assisting him in the discharge of his functions[3]. The staff are appointed at such remuneration and on such other terms and conditions as the Comptroller and Auditor General may determine[4]. Neither the Comptroller and Auditor General nor any member of the National Audit

Office staff are to be regarded as holding office under Her Majesty or as discharging any functions on behalf of the Crown[5].

The National Audit Office's expenses are defrayed out of money provided by Parliament[6].

1  As to the Comptroller and Auditor General see paras 724–726 ante.
2  National Audit Act 1983 s 3(1). The National Audit Office replaces the Exchequer and Audit Department which was set up under the Exchequer and Audit Departments Act 1866.
3  National Audit Act 1983 s 3(2).
4  Ibid s 3(3). Employment as a member of the staff of the National Audit Office is included among the kinds of employment to which a superannuation scheme under the Superannuation Act 1972 s 1 (as amended) can apply; and in exercising his powers under the National Audit Act 1983 s 3(3) the Comptroller and Auditor General must have regard to the desirability of keeping the remuneration and other terms and conditions of employment of the staff of that office broadly in line with those applying to persons employed in the Civil Service of the state: s 3(4). As to the Civil Service generally see paras 549–564 ante. As to Civil Service pay see para 558 ante. As to Civil service pensions see paras 565–619 ante.
      On the establishment of the National Audit Office the Comptroller and Auditor General was placed under a duty to make, by a date determined by the Public Accounts Commission (as to which see para 721 post), an offer of employment (irrevocable for three months) as a member of the staff of the National Audit Office to each person employed in the Civil Service of the state in the Exchequer and Audit Department immediately before 1 January 1984 (the date on which the Act came into force): see ss 3(7), 15, Sch 2 para 2(1), (2). The terms of the offer to any person were to be not less favourable than the terms on which he was employed on the date of the offer: Sch 2 para 2(1). Such a person's of employment in the Civil Service counts as a period of employment as a member of the staff of that office and the change of employment does not break the continuity of the period of employment: Sch 2 para 2(3). The agreed redundancy procedures applicable to persons employed in the Civil Service did not apply to such a person; and if he ceased to be employed on becoming a member of the National Audit Office staff in consequence of these provisions, or having unreasonably refused such an offer made to him, he is not treated as having retired on redundancy: Sch 2 para 2(4).
5  Ibid s 3(5) (amended by the Official Secrets Act 1989 s 16(4), Sch 2).
6  National Audit Act 1983 s 4(1). This, however, does not affect the Exchequer and Audit Departments Act 1957 s 1(4) or the Superannuation Act 1972 s 13 (as substituted) (under which the salary etc of the Comptroller and Auditor General are charged on and issued out of the Consolidated Fund); and any sums payable to him in consequence of any liability for breach of duty (whether arising under a contract or otherwise) incurred by him or a member of the staff of the National Audit Office in performing his functions in respect of any audit or examination are charged on and issued out of that fund: National Audit Act 1983 s 4(6).

**721. The Public Accounts Commission.** The Public Accounts Commission ('the Commission') was established by the National Audit Act 1983[1]. The Comptroller and Auditor General[2] prepares an estimate of the expenses of the National Audit Office[3] and the Commission examines the estimate and lays it before the House of Commons[4] with such modifications, if any, as the Commission thinks fit[5]. In doing so, the Commission must have regard to any advice given by the Committee of Public Accounts[6] and the Treasury[7]. The Commission must appoint a person to be responsible as accounting officer for preparing appropriation accounts for the National Audit Office[8], and he discharges such other duties as the Commission may determine[9].

The Commission consists of the member of the House of Commons who is for the time being the Chairman of the Committee of Public Accounts, the Leader of the House of Commons and seven other members of the House of Commons appointed by the House, none of whom is a minister of the Crown[10], and the Commission elects a chairman from among its members[11]. It may appoint one of the Commissioners to act as chairman at any meeting of the Commission in the absence of the elected chairman[12] and it may determine its own procedure[13]. The Commission must from time to time present to the House of Commons a report on the exercise of its functions[14].

A member of the Commission, other than the ex officio member[15], must vacate his office if he ceases to be a member of the House of Commons or if another person is nominated or appointed in his place[16]. Subject to this, a member of the Commission, other than the ex officio member, must hold office for the duration of the Parliament in which he is nominated or appointed and for the specified further period[17], and he may resign at any time by notice to the Commission[18]. Past service is no bar to nomination or appointment as a member of the Commission[19].

On a dissolution of Parliament the person who is then the Chairman of the Committee of Public Accounts must continue in office as a member of the Commission until a new Chairman of that Committee is appointed[20]. On a dissolution of Parliament the members of the Commission, other than the ex officio member, must continue in office until members are nominated or appointed in their place[21]. However, this is subject to the provision that where, at any time after Parliament has been dissolved, it appears that a member of the Commission, other than the ex officio member, has not been validly nominated as a candidate at the ensuing general election or, although so nominated, has not been elected a member of Parliament at that election, the member must resign from the Commission forthwith[22].

The validity of any proceedings of the Commission is not affected by any vacancy among the members of the Commission or by any defect in the appointment or nomination of any Commissioner[23].

1 See the National Audit Act 1983 s 2(1).
2 As to the Comptroller and Auditor General see paras 724–726 post.
3 As to the National Audit Office see para 720 ante.
4 As to the House of Commons see PARLIAMENT.
5 National Audit Act 1983 s 4(2).
6 As to the Committee of Public Accounts see para 719 ante.
7 National Audit Act 1983 s 4(3). As to the Treasury see paras 512–517 post.
8 Ie accounts of the appropriation of the supply granted for that office by the Appropriation Act of each year: see ibid s 4(4).
9 Ibid s 4(4).
10 Ibid s 2(2).
11 Ibid s 2(4), Sch 1 para 3.
12 Ibid Sch 1 para 4(3).
13 Ibid Sch 1 para 4(2).
14 Ibid s 2(3). See eg the *Seventh Report of the Public Accounts Commission* (HC Paper (1993–94) no 567). Such reports are normally published biennially.
15 'The ex officio member' means the Chairman of the Committee of Public Accounts: National Audit Act 1983 Sch 1 para 1(5).
16 Ibid Sch 1 para 1(1).
17 Ibid Sch 1 para 1(2). As to the further specified period see the text to notes 20–21 infra.
18 Ibid Sch 1 para 1(3).
19 Ibid Sch 1 para 1(4).
20 Ibid Sch 1 para 2(1).
21 Ibid Sch 1 para 2(2).
22 Ibid Sch 1 para 2(3). However, nothing in Sch 1 para 2(2) or (3) must be taken as preventing any such member from resigning otherwise than in pursuance of Sch 1 para 2(3): see Sch 1 para 2(3).
23 Ibid Sch 1 para 4(1).

**722. Auditor of the National Audit Office.** The Public Accounts Commission[1] appoints an auditor for the National Audit Office[2] who is a member of one or more of a specific list of bodies or has such other qualifications as may be approved by the Commission; and a firm must not be appointed unless each of its members is a member of one or more of those bodies[3]. The bodies referred to are: (1) the Institute of Chartered Accountants in England and Wales[4]; (2) the Institute of Chartered Accountants of Scotland[5]; (3) the Association of Certified Accountants[6]; (4) the Chartered Institute of Public Finance and Accountancy[7]; (5) the Institute of Chartered Accountants in Ireland[8]; and (6) any other body of accountants established in the United Kingdom and for the time being approved by the Commission[9]. The auditor must be appointed at such remuneration and on such other terms and conditions as the Commission may determine; and the remuneration of the auditor must be defrayed as part of the expenses of the National Audit Office[10]. The auditor has the power to carry out economy, efficiency and effectiveness examinations of the use of resources by the National Audit Office[11], and he has a right of access at all reasonable times to all such documents as appear to him necessary for the purposes of the audit and he is entitled to require from any person holding or accountable for any such documents such information and explanation as he thinks necessary for those purposes[12]. On completion of his examination the auditor must certify the appropriation account[13] and submit it, together with his report on it, to the Commission for presentation to the House of Commons[14].

1   As to the Public Accounts Commission see para 721 ante.
2   National Audit Act 1983 s 4(5). As to the National Audit Office see para 720 ante.
3   Ibid s 4(5), Sch 3 para 1(1)
4   Ibid Sch 3 para 1(2)(a).
5   Ibid Sch 3 para 1(2)(b).
6   Ibid Sch 3 para 1(2)(c).
7   Ibid Sch 3 para 1(2)(d).
8   Ibid Sch 3 para 1(2)(e).
9   Ibid Sch 3 para 1(2)(f).
10  Ibid Sch 3 para 1(3).
11  Ibid Sch 3 para 2. As to economy, efficiency and effectiveness examinations see para 717 ante.
12  Ibid Sch 3 para 3.
13  The Exchequer and Audit Departments Act 1921 s 1(1), (2), (4) (examination of appropriation accounts) (see para 716 text and notes 20–21, 23 ante) applies, with necessary modifications, to the examination by the auditor of the appropriation accounts of the National Audit Office as they apply to the examination by the Comptroller and Auditor General of the appropriation accounts of a public department: National Audit Act 1983 Sch 3 para 4(1).
14  Ibid Sch 3 para 4(2).

**723. Daily and annual accounts.** Daily accounts of receipts and issues from the Consolidated Fund[1] and the National Loans Fund[2] are required to be furnished to the Comptroller and Auditor General[3]. Annual accounts of payments into and out of those two funds must also be furnished to him by the Treasury for him to examine, certify and report on and lay copies, together with his report, before each House of Parliament[4]. Annual accounts of services financed by votes (called 'appropriation accounts') must also be submitted to the Comptroller and Auditor General[5].

1   As to the Consolidated Fund see para 711 et seq ante.
2   As to the National Loans Fund see paras 727–739 post.
3   See the Exchequer and Audit Departments Act 1866 ss 10, 13, 15 (all as amended); National Loans Act 1968 s 1(2): see paras 716 ante, 727 post. As to the Comptroller and Auditor General see paras 724–726 post.
4   Ibid s 21(1), (2). They must be sent not later than the end of November following the end of the financial year to which they relate: s 21(2). The Treasury must also prepare statements containing additional information regarding the transactions, assets and liabilities of the two funds, and lay copies of the statements before each House of Parliament not later than 31 December next following the end of that financial year: s 21(3). As to the Treasury see paras 512–517 ante.
5   See the Exchequer and Audit Departments Act 1866 ss 22 (as amended), 23 (as amended), 25, 26, Sch A (as amended); and PARLIAMENT.

### (iv)  The Comptroller and Auditor General

**724. The office of Comptroller and Auditor General.** The  Comptroller  and Auditor General, by virtue of his office, is an officer of the House of Commons[1] and the head of the National Audit Office[2] and is appointed by the Crown by letters patent under the Great Seal[3]. The power of appointment of the Crown is exercisable on an address presented by the House of Commons, and no motion may be made for such an address except by the Prime Minister[4] acting with the agreement of the Chairman of the Committee of Public Accounts[5]. The person holding the office of Comptroller and Auditor General is by that name a corporation sole[6].

The Comptroller and Auditor General holds his office during good behaviour, subject to removal by the Crown on an address by both Houses of Parliament, and he may not hold any other office under the Crown, nor may he be a peer of the realm[7]. As an officer of the House of Commons[8] he is disqualified for membership of the House[9].

The staff of the Comptroller and Auditor General are no longer civil servants, but are appointed by and answerable to him[10], and the estimates of expenditure of the National Audit Office are prepared and laid before the House of Commons not by the Treasury[11], but the Public Accounts Commission[12]. Subject to any duty imposed on him by statute, the Comptroller and Auditor General has complete discretion in the discharge of his functions, and, in particular, in determining whether to carry out any examination under the National Audit Act 1983[13] and as to the manner in which any such examination is carried out, but in determining whether to carry out any such examination, he must take into account any proposals made by the Committee of Public Accounts[14].

1   National Audit Act 1983 s 1(2). See further Erskine May *Parliamentary Practice* (21st Edn, 1989) p 198; and PARLIAMENT.
2   As to the National Audit Office see para 720 ante.
3   On the death, resignation or other vacancy in the office of the Comptroller and Auditor General, the Crown may, by letters patent nominate and appoint a successor who has the same powers, authorities and duties and who is paid the same salary, annuity or pension out of the Consolidated Fund: Exchequer and Audit Departments Act 1866 s 6 (amended by the Statute Law Revision Act 1893; and the Statute Law (Repeals) Act 1975). As to the Consolidated Fund see para 711 et seq ante. As to use of the Great Seal see para 909 post.
4  ʹ As to the Prime Minister see paras 394–398 ante.
5   National Audit Act 1983 s 1(1).
6   Ibid s 3(7), Sch 2 para 1.
7   Exchequer and Audits Departments Act 1866 s 3 (amended by the Statute Law Revision Act 1893; the Statute Law (Repeals) Act 1975; and the House of Commons Disqualification Act 1957 s 14(1), Sch 4 Pt I). As to offices held during good behaviour see para 903 post.
8   National Audit Act 1983 s 1(2), (4).
9   See the House of Commons Disqualification Act 1975 s 1, Sch 1 Pt III.
10  See the National Audit Act 1983 s 3(2); and para 720 ante.
11  As to the Treasury see paras 512–517 ante.
12  As to the Public Accounts Commission see para 721 ante.
13  See the National Audit Act 1983 ss 6–9; and para 717 ante. For a discussion of the office and effectiveness of Comptroller and Auditor General see Wade and Bradley *Constitutional and Administrative Law* (11th Edn, 1993) pp 361–363; de Smith and Brazier *Constitutional and Administrative Law* (7th Edn, 1994) pp 310–312.
14  National Audit Act 1983 s 1(3).

**725. Comptroller and Auditor General's salary and pension.** The Comptroller and Auditor General's salary and any pension or other benefit granted is charged on and issued out of the Consolidated Fund[1]. He is paid the same salary as if he were employed in the Civil Service of the state in such appointment as the House of Commons[2] may by resolution from time to time determine; and such a resolution may take effect from the date on which it is passed or from such other date as may be specified in the resolution[3]. The salary payable to the Comptroller and Auditor General is abated by the amount of any pension payable to him in respect of any public office in the United Kingdom or elsewhere to which he had previously been appointed or elected[4].

The Comptroller and Auditor General holding office on or after 31 March 1995[5] is entitled, if he was a member of a judicial pension scheme[6] immediately before he first holds that office, to elect[7] between (1) the scheme of pensions and other benefits under that judicial pension scheme (his 'former scheme')[8]; (2) (if different from his former scheme) the scheme of pensions and other benefits constituted by the Judicial Pensions and Retirement Act 1993[9] (the '1993 scheme')[10]; and the scheme of pensions and other benefits applicable to the Civil Service of the state (the 'Civil Service scheme')[11]; and, if he is not entitled to make such an election, or if he is so entitled but fails to make such an election, he must be treated as if he had been so entitled and had elected for the Civil Service scheme[12]. If a Comptroller and Auditor General who held the office before 31 March 1995 has made an election under the former enactments[13] for the old judicial scheme[14], he is entitled to make an election between the old judicial scheme[15] and the 1993 scheme[16]; and if he fails to make an election he must be taken to have elected for the old judicial scheme[17]. If a Comptroller and Auditor General who held office before 31 March 1995 has made an election under the former enactments for the civil service scheme, or has failed to make an election under those enactments (so that he is taken to have elected for the Civil Service scheme) he is treated as if he had been entitled to make an election under these provisions and he had elected for the civil service scheme[18].

Where he elects for the 1993 scheme[19] he is entitled, when he ceases to hold office as Comptroller and Auditor General, to a pension under Part I of the Judicial Pensions and Retirement Act 1993 at the appropriate annual rate if he has held that office for at least five years and either he has attained the age of 65 or he is disabled by permanent infirmity for the performance of his office; and subject to certain provisions[20] the provisions which provide for benefits in respect of earnings in excess of pension-capped salary, appeals and transfer of accrued rights[21] apply in relation to him and his service in the office of Comptroller and Auditor General as they apply in relation to a person to whom Part I of the Judicial Pensions and Retirement Act 1993 applies[22].

The Minister for the Civil Service may make regulations for purposes supplementary to these provisions[23]. Any statutory instrument so made is subject to annulment in pursuance of a resolution of the House of Commons[24]. Any such regulations may, without prejudice to certain provisions relating to employment in more than one public office[25], make special provision with respect to the pensions and other benefits payable to or in respect of a person to whom his former scheme, the 1993 scheme, the civil service scheme or the old judicial scheme, applies, or has applied, in respect of any service other than service as Comptroller and Auditor General[26]. Such special provision includes (a) provision for aggregating (i) other service falling within his former scheme, the 1993 scheme or the old judicial scheme with service as Comptroller and Auditor General; or (ii) service as Comptroller and Auditor General with such other service, for the purpose of determining qualification for, or entitlement to, or the amount of benefit under the scheme in question; and (b) provision for increasing the amount of the benefit payable under any of the schemes mentioned in head (i) above, in the case of a person to whom that scheme applied in respect of an office held by him before appointment as Comptroller and Auditor General, up to the amount that would have been payable under that scheme if he had retired from that office on the ground of permanent infirmity immediately before his appointment[27].

1   Exchequer and Audit Departments Act 1957 s 1(4); Superannuation Act 1972 s 13(14) (s 13 substituted by the Judicial Pensions and Retirement Act 1993 s 25, Sch 4 Pt I). As to the Consolidated Fund see para 711 et seq ante.

2   As to the House of Commons see PARLIAMENT.

3   Exchequer and Audit Departments Act 1957 s 1(1) (substituted by the Parliamentary and Other Pensions and Salaries Act 1976 s 6(1)). In relation to any time before the first resolution takes effect, the salary payable to the holder of the office of Comptroller and Auditor General is the same salary as if he were employed in the Civil Service of the state as a permanent secretary: Exchequer and Audit Departments

Act 1957 s 1(2) (substituted by the Parliamentary and Other Pensions and Salaries Act 1976 s 6(1)). As to Civil Service remuneration see para 558 ante.

4   Exchequer and Audit Departments Act 1957 s 1(3) (substituted by the Parliamentary and Other Pensions and Salaries Act 1976 s 6(3)). His salary may still be increased by resolution of the House of Commons. In computing the salary of a former holder of the office of Comptroller and Auditor General for the purposes of the Superannuation Act 1972 s 13 (as substituted) any abatement of that salary, any temporary abatement of that salary in the national interest and any voluntary surrender of that salary in whole or in part must be disregarded: Exchequer and Audit Departments Act 1957 s 1(3A) (added by the Parliamentary and Other Pensions and Salaries Act 1976 s 6(3)).

5   Ie the day on which the Judicial Pensions and Retirement Act 1993 Sch 4 Pt I came into force: see the Superannuation Act 1972 s 13(1), (15) (as substituted: see note 1 supra).

6   'Judicial pension scheme' means any public service pension scheme as defined in (1) the Pension Schemes Act 1993 s 1 (Superannuation Act 1972 s 13(15)(a) (as substituted (see note 1 supra); s 13(15)(a) amended by the Pension Schemes Act 1993 s 190, Sch 8 para 8)); or (2) the Pension Schemes (Northern Ireland) Act 1993 s 1 (Superannuation Act 1972 s 13(15)(b) (as substituted (see note 1 supra); s 13(15)(b) amended by the Pension Schemes (Northern Ireland) Act 1993 s 184, Sch 7 para 13)).

7   Any power to make an election is exercisable within such time and in such manner as may be prescribed in the regulations: Superannuation Act 1972 s 13(9) (as substituted: see note 1 supra).

8   See ibid s 13(1)(a) (as substituted). Where a person elects under these provisions for his former scheme, that scheme applies, subject to regulations, as if his service as Comptroller and Auditor General were service which was subject, in his case, to that scheme: s 13(4) (as substituted: see note 1 supra).

9   Ie the Judicial Pensions and Retirement Act 1993 Pt I (ss 1–18) (as amended): Superannuation Act 1972 s 13(1), (15) (as substituted: see note 1 supra).

10   See ibid s 13(1)(b) (as substituted).

11   Ie a Civil Service scheme under ibid s 1: see s 13(1)(c) (as substituted). Where a person elects for the Civil Service scheme, the Principal Civil Service Pension Scheme within the meaning of s 2 (as amended) and for the time being in force applies, subject to regulations as if his service as Comptroller and Auditor General were service in employment in the Civil Service of the state: s 13(7) (as so substituted). As to the Principal Civil Service Pension Scheme 1974 see paras 576–613 ante.

12   Superannuation Act 1972 s 13(1) (as substituted: see note 1 supra).

13   'Former enactments' means ibid s 13 as it had effect from time to time before 31 March 1995: s 13(15) (as substituted: see note 1 supra).

14   'Old judicial scheme' means the statutory scheme of pensions and other benefits applicable under or by virtue of the Judicial Pensions Act 1981 to the judicial offices listed in the Judicial Pensions Act 1981 s 1: Superannuation Act 1972 s 13(15) (as substituted: see note 1 supra).

15   See ibid s 13(2)(a) (as substituted).

16   See ibid s 13(2)(b) (as substituted).

17   Ibid s 13(2) (as substituted: see note 1 supra). Where a person elects for the old judicial scheme, that scheme and the former enactments continue, subject to regulations, to have effect in relation to him and his service in the office of Comptroller and Auditor General: s 13(8) (as so substituted).

18   Ibid s 13(3) (as substituted: see note 1 supra).

19   Ie under ibid s 13(1)(b) or 13(2)(b): see s 13(5) (as substituted).

20   Ie the provisions of ibid s 13(6)–(15) (as substituted) and the regulations made under that section: see s 13(5) (as substituted).

21   Ie the Judicial Pensions and Retirement Act 1993 Pt I (other than ss 1(1)–(4), 2), ss 19, 20, 23 and Sch 2 (as amended): see the Superannuation Act 1972 s 13(5) (as substituted).

22   Ibid s 13(5) (as substituted: see note 1 supra). As to the persons to whom the Judicial Pensions and Retirement Act 1993 Pt I applies see the Judicial Pensions and Retirement Act 1993 s 1.

Subject to the regulations, a person who elects for the 1993 scheme is treated:

(1)   as if the office of Comptroller and Auditor General were a qualifying judicial office (within the meaning of the Judicial Pensions and Retirement Act 1993) by virtue of inclusion among the offices specified in Sch 1 Pt I;

(2)   as if his election were an election as mentioned in s 1(1)(d) so that s 12, which provides for the transfer of accrued rights into the scheme, applies;

(3)   as if his pension by virtue of the Superannuation Act 1972 s 13 (as substituted) were a pension under the Judicial Pensions and Retirement Act 1993 s 2 (and, accordingly, a judicial pension, within the meaning of that Act); and

(4)   for the purpose of determining, in the event of his death, the rate of any surviving spouse's or children's pension payable under ss 5–8 in respect of his service as Comptroller and Auditor General, as if references in those sections to the annual rate of the deceased's judicial pension were references (a) where a pension had commenced to be paid to him by virtue of the Superannuation Act 1972 s 13(5) (as substituted), to the appropriate annual rate of that pension; or (b) where no

such pension had commenced to be paid to him, to the rate that would have been the appropriate annual rate of the pension payable to him by virtue of s 13(5)(b) (as substituted), had he not died, but been disabled by permanent infirmity for the performance of the duties of his office on and after the date of death;

and, in the application of the Judicial Pensions and Retirement Act 1993 to the Comptroller and Auditor General (whether by virtue of the Superannuation Act 1972 s 13(1)(a) or (b) or 13(2)(b) (as substituted) the references to the appropriate minister in the Judicial Pensions and Retirement Act 1993 ss 13 (as amended) (election for personal pension), 19 (benefits in respect of earnings in excess of pension-capped salary), 20 (appeals), Sch 2 (as amended) (transfer of accrued rights) are taken as references to the Minister for the Civil Service and the power conferred by Sch 2 para 2 to make regulations is exercisable by the Minister for the Civil Service: Superannuation Act 1972 s 13(6) (as substituted: see note 1 supra). (Note that by the Transfer of Functions (Treasury and Minister for the Civil Service) Order 1995, SI 1995/269, arts 3, 5(2), Schedule para 7, references to the Treasury in the Superannuation Act 1972 s 13 (as substituted) have been replaced with references to the Minister for the Civil Service). As to the Treasury see paras 512–517 post. As to the Minister for the Civil Service see para 427 ante.

For regulations made under s 13(5) or (6) (as so substituted) see the Judicial Pensions (Appeals) Regulations 1995, SI 1995/635; the Judicial Pensions (Transfer of Accrued Benefits) Regulations 1995, SI 1995/637; and the Judicial Pensions (Additional Benefits for Disregarded Earnings Regulations 1995, SI 1995/640.

23   Superannuation Act 1972 s 13(10) (as substituted: see note 1 supra).
24   Ibid s 13(13) (as substituted: see note 1 supra).
25   Ie the Superannuation Act 1965 s 38 (as amended) or s 39A (as added and amended).
26   Superannuation Act 1972 s 13(11) (as substituted: see note 1 supra).
27   Ibid s 13(12) (as substituted: see note 1 supra).

## 726. Functions of the Comptroller and Auditor General. The duties of the Comptroller and Auditor General[1] are twofold.

As Comptroller he ensures that all revenue is paid into the Consolidated Fund[2], and he authorises, on Treasury[3] request, National Loans Fund[4] lending. His authority to the Bank of England is required before the Treasury may draw money from the funds. He must see that the limits of expenditure authorised by Parliament are not exceeded[5]. Anything which under any Act is required to be done by the Comptroller and Auditor General may be done by a principal officer of his department authorised for that purpose by the Comptroller and Auditor General[6]. An authority given[7] to certify and report on accounts for the House of Commons[8] or each House of Parliament extends only to accounts in respect of which the Speaker of the House of Commons has certified to that House or, as the case may be, the Speaker has certified to that House and the Lord Chancellor to the House of Lords[9], that the Comptroller and Auditor General is unable to do so himself, and ceases on a vacancy arising in the office of Comptroller and Auditor General[10].

As Auditor General he carries out statutory[11] and non-statutory[12] certification audits to confirm the proper presentation of receipts and payments in accounts, that sums voted by Parliament have been spent on the intended purposes and the propriety and probity of departmental operations. This includes appropriation accounts of departments. Receipts for privatisation and expenses are presented to Parliament in the form of a standard government appropriation account relevant to the government department responsible for the sale. The Comptroller and Auditor General provides an audit certificate which states his opinion as to whether the account properly presents the expenditure and receipts of the vote or it presents a true and fair view where accounts are prepared on an income and expenditure basis[13]. He may seek an explanation from the department if he is dissatisfied with the accounts and may qualify his certificate with his reservations[14]. If Treasury authority has not been given where it was required the matter is reported to the Treasury[15].

As Auditor General he is also empowered to carry out examinations into the economy, efficiency and effectiveness with which a government department or other body has used its resources[16]. A similar power is conferred on the Comptroller and Auditor General in relation to specified authorities or bodies which he has reasonable cause to believe have in any of their financial years received more than half their incomes from public funds[17].

1    As to the office of Comptroller and Auditor General see para 724 ante.
2    As to the Consolidated Fund see para 711 et seq ante.
3    As to the Treasury see paras 512–517 post.
4    As to the National Loans Fund see paras 727–739 post.
5    See HM Treasury *Government Accounting* 7.1.16 (see para 230 note 2 ante).
6    Exchequer and Audit Departments Act 1957 s 2(2). The reference to the department of the Comptroller
     and Auditor General is to be construed as a reference to the National Audit Office: National Audit Office
     Act 1983 s 3(6).
7    Ie under the Exchequer and Audit Departments Act 1957 s 2(3).
8    As to the House of Commons see PARLIAMENT.
9    As to the House of Lords see para 204 ante; and PARLIAMENT.
10   Exchequer and Audit Departments Act 1957 s 2(3).
11   See HM Treasury *Government Accounting* 7.1.8–7.1.11.
12   At the request of the Treasury and by agreement between the appropriate minister and the bodies
     concerned, the Comptroller and Auditor General audits the accounts of a number of other bodies. These
     include some non-departmental public bodies, such as the Arts Council and the British Council which
     receive most of their funds by way of government grants. The Comptroller and Auditor General also
     audits some international bodies to which the United Kingdom contributes funds, eg the UN Food and
     Agriculture Organisation, the International Labour Organisation, the International Maritime
     Organisation and the World Maritime University. This is done not on behalf of Parliament, but at the
     invitation of and for the purposes laid down by the governing boards of the bodies concerned: see HM
     Treasury *Government Accounting* 7.1.12–7.1.13. The Comptroller and Auditor General also audits a
     number of Commonwealth organisations by agreement.
13   See HM Treasury *Government Accounting* 7.1.15.
14   See HM Treasury *Government Accounting* 7.1.17.
15   See HM Treasury *Government Accounting* 7.1.18; and the Exchequer and Audit Departments Act
     1921 s 1(3).
16   See the National Audit Act 1983 ss 6, 7; and para 717 ante.
17   See ibid s 7(1), (2), (3); and para 717 ante.

# (4) THE NATIONAL LOANS FUND

**727. Origin and character of the National Loans Fund.** The National Loans
Fund was established on 1 April 1968[1] as a separate vehicle for all central government
borrowing operations and most of the domestic lending transactions previously met from
the Consolidated Fund[2]. It is an account at the Bank of England for which the Treasury[3]
is responsible and the method of its operation is similar to that which applies to the
Consolidated Fund[4]. Money paid into the National Loans Fund is to form one general
fund to meet all outgoings from the fund, and daily statements of all money paid into and
out of the fund, in such form as the Treasury may direct, must be sent by the Bank of
England to the Comptroller and Auditor General[5]. The Comptroller and Auditor
General is to grant, from time to time at the request of the Treasury, credits[6] on the
National Loans Fund for sums payable out of the fund[7] and, subject to the provision for
the daily balancing of the fund[8], all payments out of the fund must be made by the
Treasury in accordance with the credits so granted[9].

1    See the National Loans Act 1968 s 1(1).
2    As to the Consolidated Fund see para 711 et seq ante.
3    As to the Treasury see paras 512–517 ante.
4    See the National Loans Act 1968 s 1(1). However, no provision in any Act requiring money to be paid into
     the Exchequer is to be construed as requiring or authorising money to be paid into the National Loans Fund:
     s 1(7).
5    Ibid s 1(2). As to the Comptroller and Auditor General see paras 724–726 ante.
6    Such credits may be signed by any two of the Secretaries of the Treasury and such officers as the Treasury
     may from time to time appoint to that duty: Finance Act 1975 s 56.
7    Ie under the National Loans Act 1968 or any other Act: see the National Loans Act 1968 s 1(3).
8    Ie subject to ibid s 18 (as to which see para 740 post).
9    Ibid s 1(3).

**728. The national debt: authority for borrowing.** Since 1968, when all the then existing powers of government borrowing were repealed, any money which the Treasury[1] considers it expedient to raise for the purpose of promoting sound monetary conditions in the United Kingdom and any money required for providing the sums required to meet any excess of payments out of the National Loans Fund over receipts into the National Loans Fund; and for providing any necessary working balance in it, may be raised in such a manner and on such terms and conditions as the Treasury thinks fit; and the money so raised is to be paid into the National Loans Fund[2]. The terms, as to interest or otherwise, on which any balance for the time being in the National Loans Fund is to be held are to be such as may be agreed between the Treasury and the Bank of England[3].

1   As to the Treasury see paras 512–517 ante.
2   National Loans Act 1968 s 12(1) (amended by the Finance Act 1982 s 152(1)).
3   National Loans Act 1968 s 12(1A) (added by the Finance Act 1982 s 152(2)).

**729. Methods of raising money.** In order to raise money the Treasury[1] may create and issue such securities, at such rates of interest and subject to such conditions as to repayment, redemption and other matters (including provision for a sinking fund) as it thinks fit[2]. This power to raise money extends to raising money either within or outside the United Kingdom and either in sterling or in any other currency or medium of exchange, whether national or international[3].

The principal of and interest on any money borrowed and of any money due under the securities issued, together with any sums required to be set aside for the purpose of any sinking fund, any other sums to be paid by the Treasury in accordance with the terms on which it borrows, and any expenses incurred in connection with the raising of money or the issue, repayment or redemption of securities, are to be charged on and paid out of the National Loans Fund with recourse to the Consolidated Fund[4].

The power to raise money extends to the issue of Treasury bills[5]. The Bank of England may lend any sums which the Treasury has power to borrow[6].

1   As to the Treasury see paras 512–517 ante.
2   National Loans Act 1968 s 12(2). As to the power to exchange securities see para 731 post. With a view to facilitating the raising of money by means of the issue of securities under s 12, the National Debt Commissioners may acquire securities issued under s 12 and transfer such securities: Finance Act 1993 s 211. As to the national debt see MONEY.
3   National Loans Act 1968 s 12(3).
4   Ibid s 12(4). See also the National Debt Act 1972 s 8(1).
5   Ie under the Treasury Bills Act 1877: National Loans Act 1968 s 12(5)(b); and as to Treasury bills see para 730 post. As to the National Savings Bank see the National Savings Bank Act 1971; it is not covered by the normal provisions for the raising of money. As to national savings instruments generally see MONEY.
6   National Loans Act 1968 s 12(7) (amended by the Statute Law (Repeals) Act 1973).

**730. Treasury bills.** A Treasury bill is a bill for the payment out of the National Loans Fund with recourse to the Consolidated Fund to a named recipient or bearer, at a date not later than 12 months from the date of issue, of the principal sum named in the bill[1]. Treasury bills are issued by the Bank of England on the authority of a Treasury warrant[2]. Interest is payable at such rate and in such manner as the Treasury may direct[3].

1   See the Treasury Bills Act 1877 ss 4, 5 (as amended). Regulations as to the preparation, issue and cancellation of Treasury bills and prevention of fraud in relation to them may be made by the Treasury from time to time: see s 9 (as amended). For the prescribed form of Treasury bills see the Treasury Bills Regulations 1968, SI 1968/414 (amended by SI 1988/1603; and SI 1991/1667). As to the Treasury see paras 512–517 ante.
2   Treasury Bills Act 1877 s 8(1) (amended by the Statute Law (Repeals) Act 1977; and the Finance (No 2) Act 1992 ss 79, 82, Sch 18).
3   Treasury Bills Act 1877 s 4.

**731. Exchange of securities.** The Treasury[1] may enter into arrangements or agreements for varying the terms on which Her Majesty's government in the United Kingdom has borrowed money or issued securities (whether before or after the passing of the National Loans Act 1968), and may create and issue securities for that purpose[2]. For the purpose of carrying out any arrangement for the exchange (whether on or before maturity and whether with or without any further payment) of securities the Treasury may in particular create and issue new securities[3]. The Treasury may by statutory instrument[4] make rules with respect to the surrender, issue or exchange of securities for those purposes[5].

Rules made with respect to the exchange of securities may include provision for requiring holders of the securities which are to be redeemed desiring to receive repayment in cash in respect of their holdings, to apply in that behalf in accordance with the rules[6], and for securing that, if no such application is made within such period as may be provided in the rules, the holder is deemed to have accepted the offer[7]. The Treasury may cancel any securities surrendered to it and may undertake to make payments[8], upon such terms and conditions as it thinks fit, to the holders or otherwise as part of the arrangement or agreement[9].

Any money required by the Treasury for the purpose of carrying out any such arrangement is to be charged on and paid out of the National Loans Fund with recourse to the Consolidated Fund[10]; and any money received by the Treasury is to be paid into the National Loans Fund[11].

1    As to the Treasury see paras 512–517 ante.
2    National Loans Act 1968 s 14(1).
3    Ie under ibid s 12 (as amended) (see para 729 ante): s 14(2).
4    The rules must be made by statutory instrument subject to annulment in pursuance of a resolution of the House of Commons: ibid s 14(11).
5    See ibid s 14(3); and the Exchange of Securities Rules 1962, SI 1962/868; the Exchange of Securities (No 2) Rules 1962, SI 1962/906; the Exchange of Securities (No 3) Rules 1962, SI 1962/1219; the Exchange of Securities (No 4) Rules 1962, SI 1962/2140; the Exchange of Securities (No 5) Rules 1962, SI 1962/2167; the Exchange of Securities (No 6) Rules 1962, SI 1962/2486; the Exchange of Securities (Consolidation) Rules 1962, SI 1962/1562; the Exchange of Securities Rules 1963, SI 1963/490; the Exchange of Securities (General) Rules 1963, SI 1963/935 (amended by SI 1965/1289, SI 1969/1325); and the Exchange of Securities (General) Rules 1979, SI 1979/1678 (amended by SI 1985/1147).
6    National Loans Act 1968 s 14(4)(a).
7    Ibid s 14(4)(b). The rules may specify the persons who may apply in cases where (1) any holder of securities which may be exchanged has died, or is outside the United Kingdom, or is of unsound mind, or is an infant, pupil or minor, or is otherwise under a disability; or (2) a stop notice is in force with respect to a holding: s 14(5).
8    A warrant by the Bank of England or the Bank of Ireland for making any such payment is deemed to be a cheque within the meaning of the Bills of Exchange Act 1882 and is exempt from stamp duty: National Loans Act 1968 s 14(7).
9    Ibid s 14(6).
10   Ibid s 14(8).
11   Ibid s 14(9).

**732. Payments for service of national debt.** The Treasury[1] must from time to time pay out of the Consolidated Fund[2] into the National Loans Fund sums equal to the excess of the amounts required to meet charges on the National Loans Fund for the service of national debt[3] over the amounts paid into the National Loans Fund which represent interest on loans by the government or which, in the Treasury's opinion, ought to be treated in the same way as interest on loans by the government[4]. Payments must be effected without the granting of credits by the Comptroller and Auditor General[5].

1   As to the Treasury see paras 512–517 ante.
2   As to the Consolidated Fund see para 711 et seq ante.
3   'Charges on the National Loans Fund for the service of national debt' means all payments to be made out of the National Loans Fund which represent (1) interest on debt charged on the National Loans Fund; (2) expenses incurred in connection with the raising of money or the issue, repayment or redemption of securities; (3) money required for the purpose of carrying out any arrangement under the National Loans Act 1968 s 14; or (4) sums payable under s 16(7): s 15(3). See further MONEY.
4   Ibid s 15(1).
5   Ibid s 15(2). This is so, notwithstanding the provisions of Exchequer and Audit Departments Act 1866 s 13 (as amended) (see para 713 text and notes 6–7 ante): National Loans Act 1968 s 15(2). As to the Comptroller and Auditor General see paras 724–726 ante.

**733. Treasury control of bank and government stock accounts.** The Treasury[1] exercises control with regard to the banks at which departments may open accounts, the consolidation of accounts, the opening of accounts of government stocks or annuities, and the sale and transfer of those stocks[2].

1   As to the Treasury see paras 512–517 ante.
2   See the Exchequer and Audit Departments Act 1866 ss 18–20; para 704 ante; and MONEY. As to the charge of government annuities on the National Loans Fund see para 738 post. See HM Treasury *Government Accounting* 28 (see para 230 note 2 ante) and leaflet DAO (GEN) 4/94, March 1994 for guidance on when departments can use the services of private sector banks instead of the Paymaster General's Office and the Bank of England. As to the Paymaster General see para 714 ante.

**734. Payment for management services.** Payment is to be made to the Banks of England and Ireland for the management of government securities[1] of such sums as may be agreed upon with the Treasury[2]. With certain exceptions, the sums payable are to be met out of the National Loans Fund with recourse to the Consolidated Fund[3].

1   'Government securities' means securities of Her Majesty's government in the United Kingdom and securities issued under the Irish Land Act 1903, the Irish Land Act 1909 and the Northern Ireland Land Act 1925: National Loans Act 1968 s 16(7). Such sums required to be paid in respect of the management of securities issued under the Northern Ireland Land Act 1925 are now to be met out of the National Loans Fund with recourse to the Consolidated Fund: Finance Act 1981 s 137(3). See further MONEY.
2   See the National Loans Act 1968 s 16(7) (as amended). As to the Treasury see paras 512–517 ante.
3   Ibid s 16(9). As to the Consolidated Fund see para 711 et seq ante.

**735. Government lending: transfer to National Loans Fund.** Most enactments[1] which authorise advances or loans out of the Consolidated Fund[2], or create commencing capital debts or other obligations to that fund, or authorise payments out of that fund which are to be repaid out of votes[3], have been amended so as to substitute in them references to the National Loans Fund for references to the Consolidated Fund. Accordingly, most such government loans, including those made to finance the public corporations, are made not out of the Consolidated Fund but out of the National Loans Fund[4].

1   Ie the enactments listed in the National Loans Act 1968 s 2, Sch 1 (both as amended).
2   As to the Consolidated Fund see para 711 et seq ante.
3   Ie after consideration of supply estimates; see para 712 ante; and PARLIAMENT.
4   As to the suspension of certain payments into the National Loans Fund in respect of new towns see the Finance Act 1983 s 45; and TOWN AND COUNTRY PLANNING vol 46 (Reissue) para 1171.

**736. Local loans.** The Treasury[1] may issue out of the National Loans Fund such sums as are required by the Public Works Loan Commissioners to make loans as authorised by the National Loans Act 1968, or any future Act[2]. Interest on such loans is to be paid at such rates as the Treasury may from time to time determine[3]. For any loan or class of loans, the Treasury may determine or approve either a fixed rate of interest or a variable rate of interest[4].

On each occasion when it determines or approves a fixed rate of interest for a loan or class of loans, the Treasury must satisfy itself that the rate would be at least sufficient to prevent a loss if (1) the loan, or any loan of that class, (a) were made forthwith, and (b) were met out of money borrowed by the Treasury at the lowest rate at which the Treasury is for the time being able to borrow money, of whatever amount, for a comparable period and on other comparable terms; and (2) the interest on the money so borrowed, together with the Treasury's expenses of borrowing, were set off against the interest received on the loan[5]. On each occasion when it determines or approves a variable rate of interest for a loan or class of loans, the Treasury must satisfy itself that the rate would be at least sufficient to prevent a loss if (i) the loan, or any loan of that class, (A) were made forthwith, (B) were to be repaid at the end of its first interest period and (C) were met out of money borrowed by the Treasury at the lowest rate at which the Treasury is for the time being able to borrow money, of whatever amount for a comparable period; and (ii) the interest on the money so borrowed were set off against the interest received on the loan[6].

If, in the case of a loan of any class, an undertaking[7] was given to the person to whom the loan was to be made that the rate of interest which would apply to that loan would be that which, at the time specified in or determined in accordance with the undertaking, was or would be in force for loans of that class, and before the loan was made, the determination or approval of that rate of interest was withdrawn[8] or otherwise ceased to be effective, the applicable rate of interest is that which was in force for loans of that class at the time specified in or determined in accordance with the undertaking[9].

All sums paid or applicable in or towards the discharge of the principal or interest of any loans made by the Public Works Loan Commissioners, whether before or after the coming into force of the National Loans Act 1968, must be paid by the commissioners into the National Loans Fund[10].

The aggregate of any commitments of the Public Works Loan Commissioners outstanding in respect of undertakings entered into by them to grant loans and any amount outstanding in respect of the principal of any local loans must not exceed £55,000 million or such other lower or higher sum not exceeding £70,000 million, as the Treasury may from time to time specify by order made by statutory instrument[11], a draft of which must be laid before and approved by a resolution of the House of Commons[12].

1 As to the Treasury see paras 512–517 ante.
2 National Loans Act 1968 s 3(1). See also LOCAL GOVERNMENT. As to the Public Works Loan Commissioners see MONEY.
3 Ie in accordance with ibid s 5 (as substituted and amended): s 3(2).
4 Ibid s 5(2) (s 5 substituted by the Finance Act 1982 s 153(1)). A fixed rate of interest is a specified rate or a formula rate which is to be applied, throughout the period of the loan or any loan of that class, with the value which it has when the loan is made: National Loans Act 1968 s 5(2)(a) (as so substituted). A variable rate of interest is a formula rate which is to be applied, for each of the successive periods of the loan or any loan of that class which are of a length specified in the determination or approval (referred to as interest periods), with the value which it has at the beginning of that period: s 5(2)(b) (as so substituted). 'Formula rate' means a rate which is so expressed (whether by means of a formula or otherwise) that it will or may have different values at different times: s 5(2) (as so substituted).

   Different fixed rates of interest may be determined or approved in respect of loans which are to be made for the same length of time; and different variable rates of interest may be determined or approved for loans which are to have interest periods of the same length: s 5(7) (as so substituted).
5 Ibid s 5(3) (as substituted: see note 4 supra).
6 Ibid s 5(4) (as substituted: see note 4 supra). If at any time the Treasury is satisfied that a rate of interest determined or approved in the case of a class of loans would not meet the requirements of s 5(3) or (4)

(as so substituted) if it were determined or approved at that time, that determination or approval must be withdrawn at the earliest convenient time, and from that or such later time as may be convenient another rate determined or approved in accordance with s 5(3) or (4) (as so substituted) must come into force for further loans of that class: s 5(5) (as so substituted; subsequently amended by the Finance Act 1983 s 44).

The Treasury may in determining or approving a rate of interest take into account any consideration justifying a rate higher than that required by the National Loans Act 1968 s 5(3) or (4) (as so substituted): s 5(6) (as so substituted).

7   'Undertaking' means an undertaking given by the person by whom the loan in question was to be made and, where that person is not the Treasury, given by that person with the consent of the Treasury: ibid s 5(5B) (added by the Finance Act 1983 s 44).

8   Ie by virtue of the National Loans Act 1968 s 5(5) (as substituted and amended).

9   Ibid s 5(5A) (added by the Finance Act 1983 s 44).

10   National Loans Act 1968 s 3(3). Where security for a loan is enforced in any manner, the net receipts only must be so paid into the National Loans Fund: s 3(3). Subject to any statutory limit (see text and note 11 infra) the commissioners' power of making loans includes power to enter into undertakings to make loans: s 3(5) (amended by the Finance Act 1984 s 128(6), Sch 23 Pt XIV).

11   National Loans Act 1968 s 4(1) (s 4 substituted by Finance Act 1984 s 125(1); and amended by the Finance Act 1990 s 130).

12   National Loans Act 1968 s 4(2) (as substituted: see note 11 supra).

**737. The Exchange Equalisation Account.** Such sums as the Treasury[1] may determine may be issued to the Exchange Equalisation Account[2] out of the National Loans Fund at such times and in such manner as the Treasury may direct[3]; and such sums as are for the time being outstanding constitute a liability of that account to that fund[4]. If at any time the Treasury is of opinion that the assets in sterling of that account are for the time being in excess of what is required for the purposes of the account[5] it may direct that the excess be paid into the National Loans Fund[6].

1   As to the Treasury see paras 512–517 ante.

2   As to the Exchange Equalisation Account generally see MONEY.

3   Exchange Equalisation Account Act 1979 s 2(1).

4   Ibid s 2(2).

5   See ibid s 1.

6   Ibid s 2(3).

**738. Government annuities.** All immediate life annuities[1] and immediate savings bank annuities must be charged on and issued out of the National Loans Fund at such times as the Treasury may direct[2], with recourse to the Consolidated Fund[3].

1   Ie annuities mentioned in the Government Annuities Act 1929 s 8(1) (as amended). Generally speaking, no new annuities or insurances can be granted under that Act: see the Finance Act 1962 s 33 (as amended); and MONEY.

2   Government Annuities Act 1929 s 8(1) (amended by the Finance Act 1962 s 34(6), (7), Sch 11 Pt VI; the Statute Law Revision Act 1963; and the National Loans Act 1968 s 8(2)).

3   National Loans Act 1968 s 8(1). As to the Consolidated Fund see para 711 et seq ante.

**739. Profits of the Issue Department of the Bank of England.** The profits of the Issue Department of the Bank of England must be paid into the National Loans Fund[1]. The assets held in that department must be valued at market prices, at such times and in such manner as may be agreed between the Treasury[2] and the Bank of England, but at least once in each financial year[3]. If, as the result of this valuation, the value of the assets then held in the department falls short of the total amount of the Bank of England notes then outstanding, the Treasury must assume a liability to the department of an amount equal to the difference[4], to be charged on the National Loans Fund with recourse to the Consolidated Fund[5]. The liability will be subject to such conditions as to repayment and other matters as may be agreed between the Bank of England and the Treasury, but is not to bear interest[6].

1   National Loans Act 1968 s 9(1).
2   As to the Treasury see paras 512–517 ante.
3   National Loans Act 1968 s 9(2).
4   Ibid s 9(3).
5   Ibid s 9(4)(c).
6   Ibid s 9(4)(b).

# (5) RELATIONSHIP BETWEEN THE CONSOLIDATED FUND AND THE NATIONAL LOANS FUND

**740. Daily balancing of the Consolidated Fund.** On any day on which payments into the Consolidated Fund exceed payments out of that fund, the Treasury[1] must pay out of the Consolidated Fund into the National Loans Fund sums equal to that excess[2]. On any day on which payments out of the Consolidated Fund exceed payments into that fund the Treasury must pay out of the National Loans Fund into the Consolidated Fund sums equal to that excess[3]. All such payments may be effected without the granting of credits by the Comptroller and Auditor General[4].

1   As to the Treasury see paras 512–517 ante.
2   National Loans Act 1968 s 18(2). As to the Consolidated Fund see para 711 et seq ante. As to the National Loans Fund see paras 727–739 ante.
3   Ibid s 18(3).
4   Ibid s 18(5). This is so, notwithstanding the Exchequer and Audit Departments Act 1866 s 13 (as amended) (see para 713 text and notes 6–7 ante), or the National Loans Act 1968 s 1(3) (see para 727 text and note 9 ante): s 18(5). As to the Comptroller and Auditor General see paras 724–726.

**741. Liabilities and assets of the National Loans Fund.** The excess for the time being of the liabilities of the National Loans Fund over its assets is treated as a liability of the Consolidated Fund to the National Loans Fund[1]. The liability to pay interest on that excess is deemed to be satisfied by any payment[2] made from the Consolidated Fund to the National Loans Fund for the service of the national debt[3].

1   National Loans Act 1968 s 19(1). As to the National Loans Fund see paras 727–739 ante. As to the Consolidated Fund see para 711 et seq ante. The liabilities of the National Loans Fund consist of the nominal amount of the debt outstanding and charged to that fund, as determined by the Treasury, and the assets of the fund are the aggregate of any balance in that fund and the amount of principal, as determined, of advances, loans and other payments outstanding and due to that fund: s 19(4) (amended by the Finance Act 1982 s 152(3)). As to the Treasury see paras 512–517 ante.
2   Ie under the National Loans Act 1968 s 15 (see para 732 ante).
3   Ibid s 19(2). See further MONEY.

# (6) THE CONTINGENCIES FUND

**742. Contingencies Fund.** The Contingencies Fund is a reserve fund[1] intended to meet payments for urgent services in anticipation of parliamentary approval for those services[2]. The Treasury[3] may authorise total advances outstanding from the fund not exceeding 2 per cent of the previous year's total estimates provision[4]. Money withdrawn from the fund must be repaid. Legislation giving authority for the expenditure must be introduced at the earliest possible time[5].

1   See the Contingencies Fund Act 1974; HM Treasury *Government Accounting* 11.6 (see para 230 note 2 ante); the *Sixth Report of the Treasury and Civil Service Select Committee: Budgetary Reform* (HC Paper (1981–82) no 137), Appendix 20, pp 167–194; McEldowney *Public Law* (1994) pp 316–317; McEldowney 'The Contingencies Fund and the Parliamentary Scrutiny of Public Finance' [1988] Public Law pp 232–245; and MONEY.

2 For general guidance on the use of the Contingencies Fund, including the circumstances in which it may be used to finance new services see HM Treasury *Government Accounting* 6, 11. The criterion is not convenience, but urgency in the public interest. If the amount of money involved, or the potentially contentious nature of the proposal is such as to create special difficulty in justifying anticipation of specific parliamentary approval, it may be necessary to consider the alternative of immediate presentation of a supplementary estimate, outside the normal timetable, to be followed by a special Consolidated Fund Bill: HM Treasury *Government Accounting* 11.6.4.

3 As to the Treasury see paras 512–517 post.

4 Contingencies Fund Act 1974 s 1(1). See also McEldowney *Public Law* (1994) pp 316–317; McEldowney 'The Contingencies Fund and Parliamentary Scrutiny of Pubic Finance' [1988] Public Law pp 232–245.

5 The fund should not be drawn upon for any purpose for which the statutory authority of Parliament is required until legislation seeking that authority has been given its second reading. The issue is whether the government of the day is prepared to take the responsibility of assuming that legislation being considered by Parliament will pass into law: HM Treasury *Government Accounting* 11.6.6–11.6.7.

## (7) GOVERNMENT TRADING FUNDS

**743. Establishment of trading funds.** A trading fund is a method of financing and accounting for the activities of a government department, executive agency or part of a department, outside the usual system of supply estimates and appropriation accounts[1].

If it appears to any minister of the Crown[2] (1) that any operations of a government department for which he is responsible are suitable to be financed by means of a trading fund[3] and, in particular, to be so managed that the revenue[4] of the fund would consist principally of receipts in respect of goods or services provided in the course of the operations in question, and (2) that the financing of the operations in question by means of a trading fund would be in the interests of the improved efficiency and effectiveness of the management of those operations, he may by order[5] establish a trading fund for the operations in question as from a day appointed by the order[6]. Expenditure and income are met from or paid into the trading fund, which thus operates outside the supply system[7].

Where a minister proposes to make an order in respect of any operations which are not already financed by means of trading fund and he considers that the operations in question consist substantially in the provision of goods or services[8] in the United Kingdom otherwise than to government departments, and that an opportunity to make representations to him should be given, he must take appropriate steps to give such an opportunity to such persons as appear to him to be appropriate[9].

An order establishing a trading fund must designate as the authorised lender[10] either the National Loans Fund or the responsible minister[11].

1 As to supply procedure and appropriation accounts see para 712 ante. A trading fund has standing authority under the Government Trading Funds Act 1973 (as amended) to use its receipts to meet its outgoings. Its receipts are paid into the fund and payments are made out of the fund without the need for further parliamentary authority through annual supply estimates. Moneys in the hands of a trading fund at the end of the financial year do not have to be surrendered to the Consolidated Fund: see HM Treasury *Government Accounting* 17.1.4 (see para 230 note 2 ante).

The Government Trading Act 1990 makes substitutions in and amendments to the Government Trading Funds Act 1973 which is set out in full as a schedule to the 1990 Act: see the Government Trading Act 1990 s 2(5), Sch 1.

2 'Minister of the Crown' means the holder of an office in Her Majesty's government, including the Treasury: Government Trading Funds Act 1973 s 1(7) (s 1 substituted by the Government Trading Act 1990 s 1(1)). References in the Government Trading Funds Act 1973 to a minister of the Crown include ministers acting jointly, but an order may not designate more than one minister as the authorised lender: s 1(9) (as so substituted). As to the Treasury see paras 512–517 ante.

An order establishing a trading fund for operations carried on by a person appointed in pursuance of any enactment may provide (1) for the fund to be under the control and management of that person instead of the responsible minister; and accordingly (2) for the Government Trading Funds Act 1973 to have effect as if certain references to the responsible minister were references to that person: see s 1(6) (as substituted). 'The responsible minister', in relation to any operations of a department of the government, means the minister of the Crown responsible for that department: s 1(7) (as so substituted).

3    Ie a fund established under ibid: s 1(1)(a) (as substituted: see note 2 supra).

4    For the meaning of 'revenue' see para 701 note 1 ante.

5    The power to make an order is exercisable only with Treasury concurrence: Government Trading Funds Act 1973 s 1(2) (as substituted: see note 2 supra).

The power to make an order under s 1 (as so substituted) is exercisable by statutory instrument and includes the power to vary or revoke such an order, but no such order may alter the authorised lender in relation to any fund: s 6(1) (substituted by the Government Trading Act 1990 s 2(3)). No order establishing a trading fund or extending or restricting the funded operations may be made unless a draft of a statutory instrument containing it has been laid before the House of Commons and approved by a resolution of that House: Government Trading Funds Act 1973 s 6(2) (amended by the Government Trading Act 1990 s 2(3)). If such a statutory instrument is made without a draft having been approved by a resolution of the House of Commons it is subject to annulment in pursuance of a resolution of that House: Government Trading Funds Act 1973 s 6(3) (amended by the Government Trading Act 1990 s 2(3)(c)). 'Funded operations', in relation to a trading fund, means the operations for which the fund is established: Government Trading Funds Act 1973 s 1(7) (as substituted: see note 2 supra)

Orders made under the Government Trading Funds Act 1973 in force on the day before the Government Trading Act 1990 was passed continue to have effect with the necessary modifications as if made under the 1973 Act s 1 (as substituted): Government Trading Act 1990 s 5(2). The Government Trading Act 1990 received royal assent on 26 July 1990. See HMSO Trading Fund Order 1980, SI 1980/456 (amended by SI 1994/1192; and SI 1994/2470); Vehicle Inspectorate Trading Fund Order 1991, SI 1991/773 (amended by SI 1992/471); Property Services Agency Supplies Trading Fund Order 1976 Revocation Order 1991, SI 1991/856; Central Office of Information Trading Fund Order 1991, SI 1991/857 (amended by SI 1992/43); Buying Agency Trading Fund Order 1991, SI 1991/875 (amended by SI 1992/123; SI 1995/1665; and SI 1996/1080); Companies House Trading Fund Order 1991, SI 1991/1795; Patent Office Trading Fund Order 1991, SI 1991/1796; Fire Service College Trading Fund Order 1992, SI 1992/640; Defence Research Agency Trading Fund Order 1993, SI 1993/380; Defence Evaluation and Research Agency Trading Fund Order 1995, SI 1995/650; Land Registry Trading Fund Order 1993, SI 1993/938; Land Registry Trading Fund (Additional Assets) Order 1996, SI 1996/750; Medicines Control Agency Trading Fund Order 1993, SI 1993/751; Chessington Computer Centre Trading Fund Order 1993, SI 1993/948; Hydrographic Office Trading Fund Order 1996, SI 1996/773; Meteorological Office Trading Fund Order 1996, SI 1996/774.

6    Government Trading Funds Act 1973 s 1(1) (as substituted: see note 2 supra).

7    HM Treasury *Government Accounting* 1.1.9 and 17.

8    References to the provision of services include the provision of any authority required for carrying on any activity or exercising any right, and the performance of any other functions in connection with the regulation of any activity or right: Government Trading Funds Act 1973 s 1(8) (as substituted: see note 2 supra).

9    Ibid s 1(3) (as substituted: see note 2 supra). Where a minister has taken such steps to give an opportunity for representations to be made about a proposed order, he must, before laying a draft instrument containing the order giving effect to the proposal, lay a report before Parliament about the representations received and his conclusions: s 6(4) (substituted by the Government Trading Act 1990 s 2(3)(d)).

10   Ie the source of issues to the fund by way of loan: Government Trading Funds Act 1973 s 1(4) (as substituted: see note 2 supra). Issues to the fund by way of loan by the responsible minister must be made out of money provided by Parliament, and the right to repayment of such issues rank as an asset of the Consolidated Fund: s 1(5) (as so substituted). As to the Consolidated Fund see para 711 et seq ante.

11   Ibid s 1(4) (as substituted: see note 2 supra).

**744. Assets and liabilities of funds.** Where any minister of the Crown[1] proposes to make an order establishing a trading fund[2] for any operations or to lay an order extending the funded operations[3] he must with Treasury[4] concurrence determine what Crown assets and liabilities[5] are properly attributable to the operations for which the fund is to be established or, as the case may be, the additional operations, and are suitable to be appropriated to the fund[6]. Where an order establishing a trading fund provides for any assets and liabilities to be appropriated as assets and liabilities of the fund, the amount by which the values of those assets exceed the amounts of those liabilities, less any amount treated by virtue of the order as public dividend capital[7], or any amount treated by virtue of the order as reserves or (where the order provides for both public dividend capital and reserves) the aggregate of those amounts, is originating debt[8] of the fund[9]. The responsible minister may from time to time, in the case of any such fund, with Treasury concurrence determine what additional Crown assets and liabilities are properly attributable to the funded operations and suitable to be appropriated to the fund, and provide by order for the assets and liabilities in question to be appropriated as assets and liabilities of the fund[10]. He may also from time to time with Treasury concurrence by order provide for any assets and liabilities of a fund to cease to be assets and liabilities of the fund[11].

1    For the meaning of 'minister of the Crown' see para 743 note 2 ante.
2    As to the nature and establishment of trading funds see para 743 ante.
3    For the meaning of 'funded operations' see para 743 note 5 ante.
4    As to the Treasury see paras 512–517 ante.
5    'Liabilities', in relation to a trading fund, does not include liabilities in respect of any amount issued to the fund under the Government Trading Funds Act 1973 s 2B (as added): s 1(7) (s 1 substituted by the Government Trading Act 1990 s 1(1)); and see para 746 post.
6    Government Trading Funds Act 1973 s 2(1)(a) (s 2 substituted by the Government Trading Act 1990 s 1(1)). The order must provide for the assets and liabilities so determined to be appropriated as assets and liabilities of the fund: Government Trading Funds Act 1973 s 2(1)(b) (as so substituted; subsequently amended by the Finance Act 1991 ss 119, 123, Sch 19 Pt VIII). The values or amounts of assets and liabilities must be determined by the responsible minister in accordance with Treasury directions: Government Trading Funds Act 1973 s 2(2A) (s 2 as so substituted: s 2(2A) added by the Finance Act 1991 s 119, Sch 19 Pt VIII). An order providing for any assets and liabilities to be appropriated as, or to cease to be, assets and liabilities of a trading fund may describe them in general terms: Government Trading Funds Act 1973 s 2(7) (as so substituted). For the meaning of 'responsible minister' see para 743 note 2 ante.
7    As to public dividend capital see para 745 post.
8    'Originating debt', in relation to a trading fund, means any amount remaining after any repayment or reduction of the amount which, by virtue of the Government Trading Funds Act 1973 s 2(3), (4) (both as substituted), is the originating debt of the fund: s 1(7) (as substituted: see note 5 supra).
9    Ibid s 2(3) (as substituted: see note 6 supra; subsequently amended by the Finance Act 1993 s 210, Sch 22 para 2). The originating debt is to be treated as having been issued to the fund under the Government Trading Funds Act 1973 s 2B (as added) on the day appointed by the order: s 2(3) (as so substituted and amended). See also s 2(4) (as substituted and amended) which contains similar provisions to s 2(3) (as substituted and amended) in relation to a trading fund established by a previous order, providing that the amounts are to be added to the originating debt of the fund.
10   Ibid s 2(2) (as substituted: see note 6 supra; subsequently amended by the Finance Act 1991 Sch 19 Pt VIII). The values or amounts of assets and liabilities must be determined by the responsible minister in accordance with Treasury directions: Government Trading Funds Act 1973 s 2(2A) (s 2 as so substituted: s 2(2A) added by the Finance Act 1991 s 119).
11   Government Trading Funds Act 1973 s 2(5) (as substituted: see note 6 supra). However, this power is not exercisable where s 4A (as added) applies: s 2(5) (as so substituted); and see para 749 post. In the case of any originating debt or public dividend capital which he determines with Treasury concurrence to be properly attributable to the assets and liabilities in question, the responsible minister may repay, out of money provided by Parliament, the whole or part of the debt or make a repayment into the Consolidated Fund in reduction or extinguishment of the capital, and by order made with Treasury concurrence provide for the reduction or extinguishment of any capital remaining thereafter: s 2(6) (as so substituted).

**745. Public dividend capital.** An order providing for any assets and liabilities[1] to be appropriated as assets and liabilities of a trading fund[2] may provide for any amount by which the values of the assets exceed the amounts of the liabilities to be treated as public dividend capital[3] of the fund[4]. If the responsible minister[5] considers it appropriate to do so, he may with Treasury[6] concurrence issue out of money provided by Parliament an amount to the fund as public dividend capital[7].

For any financial year in which a trading fund has public dividend capital, there must be paid out of the fund into the Consolidated Fund such sums (if any) by way of return on that capital and its reserves as the responsible minister may determine, with Treasury concurrence, having regard to any balance in the fund at the end of that year and the amount of the balance which appears to the responsible minister and the Treasury to be in the nature of distributable profit[8].

1 As to the meaning of 'liabilities' see para 744 note 5 ante.
2 As to the nature and establishment of trading funds see para 743 ante.
3 Public dividend capital ranks as asset of the Consolidated Fund: Government Trading Funds Act 1973 s 2A(4) (s 2A added by the Government Trading Act 1990 s 1(1)). As to the Consolidated Fund see para 711 et seq ante.
4 Government Trading Funds Act 1973 s 2A(1) (as added: see note 3 supra).
5 For the meaning of 'responsible minister' see para 743 note 2 ante.
6 As to the Treasury see paras 512–517 ante.
7 Government Trading Funds Act 1973 s 2A(2A) (s 2A as added: see note 3 supra; s 2A(2A) added by the Finance Act 1993 s 210, Sch 22 para 3). The Government Trading Funds Act 1973 s 2A(2A) (as added) has effect instead of s 2A(2) (as added) after the day on which the Finance Act 1993 was passed: s 2A(2A) (as so added). Where any sum is issued to a trading fund under s 2B (as added) (see para 746 post), the responsible minister may with Treasury concurrence pay out of the fund into the Consolidated Fund a corresponding sum in reduction or extinguishment of any public dividend capital: s 2A(3) (as so added).
8 Ibid s 2A(5) (as added: see note 3 supra).

**746. Borrowing by funds.** No amount may be paid into a trading fund[1] by way of loan except in accordance with the following provisions[2]. The authorised lender[3] may issue by way of loan to a trading fund sums required for the funded operations[4]. Sums issued under these provisions must be repaid out of the fund on such terms, and interest on them must be paid at such variable or fixed rates and at such times as the Treasury[5] may determine[6]. In the case of any trading fund where the authorised lender is a minister of the Crown[7], repayment of any amount outstanding in respect of the principal of any sum issued under these provisions[8] may, with Treasury concurrence, be made to the minister instead of into the Consolidated Fund[9] and applied by him as money provided by Parliament[10].

An order establishing a trading fund which is made after 27 July 1993[11] must provide that the maximum specified in the order must not be exceeded by the aggregate of: (1) the total outstanding at any given time in respect of amounts issued to the fund under the above provisions (other than as originating debt)[12]; and (2) the total at that time constituting public dividend capital issued to the fund[13].

The sum of the maxima in force in respect of all trading funds at any time must not exceed £2,000 million[14].

1 As to the nature and establishment of trading funds see para 743 ante.
2 Government Trading Funds Act 1973 s 2B(1) (s 2B added by the Government Trading Act 1990 s 1(1)).
3 As to the meaning of 'authorised lender' see para 743 text and note 10 ante.
4 Government Trading Funds Act 1973 s 2B(2) (as added: see note 2 supra). For the meaning of 'funded operations' see para 743 note 5 ante.
5 As to the Treasury see paras 512–517 ante.
6 Government Trading Funds Act 1973 s 2B(3) (as added: see note 2 supra). A rate of interest for any amount so issued by the responsible minister must be determined as if the National Loans Act 1968 s 5 (as substituted) (see para 736 ante) had effect in respect of it and s 5(5A), 5(5B) (both as added) apply accordingly: Government Trading Funds Act 1973 s 2B(4) (as so added). For the meaning of 'responsible minister' see para 743 note 2 ante.
7 For the meaning of 'minister of the Crown' see para 743 note 2 ante.
8 Ie other than repayment before the due date: Government Trading Funds Act 1973 s 2B(5) (as added: see note 2 supra).
9 As to the Consolidated Fund see para 711 et seq ante.
10 Government Trading Funds Act 1973 s 2B(5) (as added: see note 2 supra).
11 Ie the day on which the Finance Act 1993 was passed.
12 Government Trading Funds Act 1973 s 2C(1)(a) (s 2C added by the Finance Act 1993 s 210, Sch 22 para 4). For the meaning of 'originating debt' see para 744 note 8 ante.
13 Government Trading Funds Act 1973 Act s 2C(1)(b) (as added: see note 12 supra). As to public dividend capital see para 745 ante. As to provisions relating to orders made on or before 27 July 1993 see s 2C(2) (as added).
14 Ibid s 2C(3) (as added: see note 12 supra). The Treasury may by order made by statutory instrument increase or further increase this limit by any amount, not exceeding £1,000 million, specified in the order

but not so as to make the limit exceed £4,000 million: s 2C(4) (as so added). No such order may be made unless a draft of a statutory instrument containing it has been laid before the House of Commons and approved by a resolution of that House: s 2C(5) (as added: see note 12 supra).

**747. Initial reserves.** An order[1] providing for any assets and liabilities[2] to be appropriated as assets and liabilities of a trading fund[3] may provide for any part of the amount by which the values of the assets exceed the amounts of the liabilities to be treated as reserves[4] in the accounts of the fund, and may provide for the maintenance of such reserves[5].

1    Ie an order made after 27 July 1993 (the day on which the Finance Act 1993 was passed): see Government Trading Funds Act 1973 s 2AA(4) (s 2AA added by the Finance Act 1993 s 210, Sch 22 para 2).
2    As to the meaning of 'liabilities' see para 744 note 5 ante.
3    As to the nature and establishment of trading funds see para 743 ante.
4    'Reserves' means reserves whether general, capital or otherwise; and an order may provide for different kinds of reserves: Government Trading Funds Act 1973 s 2AA(2) (as added: see note 1 supra).
5    Ibid s 2AA(1) (as added: see note 1 supra). However, this does not prejudice the operation of s 4(2) (see para 750 post) in relation to a trading fund; and s 4(2) does not prejudice the operation of s 2AA(1) (as added) in relation to a trading fund: s 2AA(3) (as added: see note 1 supra).

**748. Payments into and out of trading funds.** There must be paid into a trading fund[1] all receipts in respect of the funded operations[2] and there must be paid out of the fund all expenditure incurred by the responsible minister[3] in respect of those operations, except expenditure in respect of liabilities[4] not appropriated to the fund[5]. Provision is now made for a case where operations cease to be funded[6].

Payment must be made into the Consolidated Fund[7] of such sums as may be appropriate as representing accruing liabilities of the Treasury[8] in respect of pensions (including increases of pensions), gratuities and other similar benefits for persons who have been employed in the funded operations and in respect of the administrative expenses attributable to those liabilities and their discharge[9]. Where the Treasury is the responsible minister for the fund, it is for the Treasury to determine the sums payable, the amount of any payment and the time at which it is to be made; and in other cases it is for the responsible minister to determine the sums payable in agreement with the Treasury, subject to any Treasury directions as to the amount or time of the payment[10].

The enactments relating to public receipts, expenditure and accounting are to have effect subject to the foregoing provisions, except as may be directed by the Treasury from time to time[11].

1    As to the nature and establishment of trading funds see para 743 ante.
2    For the meaning of 'funded operations' see para 743 note 5 ante.
3    For the meaning of 'responsible minister' see para 743 note 2 ante.
4    As to the meaning of 'liabilities' see para 744 note 5 ante.
5    Government Trading Funds Act 1973 s 3(1) (substituted by the Government Trading Act 1990 s 2(1)(a)).
6    As to operations ceasing to be funded see para 749 post. Nothing in the Government Trading Funds Act 1973 affects the powers conferred in relation to fees and charges by the Finance (No 2) Act 1987 s 102: Government Trading Funds Act 1973 Act s 3(4) (added by the Government Trading Act 1990 s 2(1)(c)).
7    As to the Consolidated Fund see para 711 et seq ante.
8    As to the Treasury see paras 512–517 ante.
9    Government Trading Funds Act 1973 s 3(2) (amended by the Transfer of Functions (Minister for the Civil Service and Treasury) Order 1981, SI 1981/1670; and the Government Trading Act 1990 s 2(1)(b)).
10   Government Trading Funds Act 1973 s 3(2)(a), (b) (amended by the Transfer of Functions (Minister for the Civil Service and Treasury) Order 1981).
11   Government Trading Funds Act 1973 s 3(3). If any question arises whether any particular sums are required by those provisions to be paid into, or out of, the trading fund, that question must be determined by the Treasury: 3(3).

**749. Operations ceasing to be funded.** Provision is made for a case where any operations for which a trading fund[1] is established are to cease to be funded operations[2]. These provisions apply whether the operations ceasing to be funded represent the whole or part of the funded operations or are to cease altogether or to be funded operations of another fund or, while continuing to be operations of a government department, be financed by other means[3].

Where the operations ceasing to be funded are to cease altogether, if the values of the assets[4] of the fund exceed the amounts of its liabilities[5], the amount or excess in question must be applied first towards the repayment of the debt[6] and then paid into the Consolidated Fund[7] in reduction or extinguishment of any public dividend capital[8]. If in any other case it appears to the responsible minister that any amount standing in the reserves[9] of the fund is surplus to any foreseeable requirements of the funded operations, or the revenues of the fund for the last financial year exceed the total sums properly chargeable to revenue account for that year, the amount or excess must be applied in the same way[10]. The responsible minister may repay any debt remaining after the application of the above provisions or make a payment into the Consolidated Fund in reduction or extinguishment of any public dividend capital so remaining[11]. Where the operations ceasing to be funded represent only part of the funded operations, the responsible minister may by order with Treasury concurrence reduce or extinguish any originating debt, or public dividend capital, remaining after the application of the preceding provisions[12].

1   As to the nature and establishment of trading funds see para 743 ante.
2   For the meaning of 'funded operations' see para 743 note 2 ante.
3   Government Trading Funds Act 1973 s 4A(1) (s 4A added by the Government Trading Act 1990 s 1(2)). Where operations ceasing to be funded represent only part of the funded operations, the responsible minister must by order provide for such assets and liabilities of the fund as he may with Treasury concurrence determine to be properly attributable to the operations ceasing to be funded, to cease to be assets and liabilities of the fund: Government Trading Funds Act 1973 s 4A(2) (as so added). For the meaning of 'responsible minister' see para 743 note 2 ante. As to the Treasury see paras 512–517 ante.
4   Where the operations ceasing to be funded represent only part of the funded operations, references to assets and liabilities are to the assets and liabilities of the fund by virtue of an order under ibid s 4A(2) (as added: see note 3 supra).
5   See note 4 supra.
6   References to debt, originating debt or public dividend capital are to so much of any debt, originating debt or public dividend capital as the responsible minister may with the concurrence of the Treasury determine to be attributable to the operations ceasing to be funded: Government Trading Funds Act 1973 s 4A(3) (as added: see note 3 supra). 'Debt' means any amount outstanding in respect of the principal of or interest on sums issued under s 2B (as added) (see para 746 ante): s 4A(3) (as so added). 'Originating debt' includes any amount outstanding in respect of interest on such debt: s 4A(3) (as so added). As to public dividend capital see para 745 ante.
7   As to the Consolidated Fund see para 711 et seq ante.
8   Government Trading Funds Act 1973 s 4A(4), (6) (as added: see note 3 supra). Where the operations ceasing to be funded represent the whole of the funded operations, if any balance remains after the surplus amount or excess in question has been duly applied, the responsible minister must pay the balance into the Consolidated Fund: s 4A(6) (as so added).
9   For the meaning of 'reserves' see para 747 note 4 ante.
10  Government Trading Funds Act 1973 s 4A(5) (as added: see note 3 supra).
11  Ibid s 4A(7) (as added: see note 3 supra).
12  Ibid s 4A(8) (as added: see note 3 supra).

**750. Management of trading funds.** A trading fund[1] is to be under the control and management of the responsible minister[2], who is under a duty (1) to manage the funded operations[3] so that the revenue of the fund consists principally of receipts in respect of goods or services provided in the course of the funded operations and is not less than sufficient, taking one year with another, to meet outgoings which are properly chargeable to revenue account; and (2) to achieve such further financial advantages as the Treasury[4] may from time to time, by minute laid before the House of Commons, indicate as having been determined by the responsible minister, with Treasury concurrence, to be desirable of achievement[5].

With Treasury concurrence, the responsible minister may establish and maintain general, capital and other reserves[6] in the accounts of the trading fund[7]. If at any time it appears to the responsible minister that any amount standing in the reserves of the trading fund is surplus to any foreseeable requirements of the funded operations, he may with Treasury concurrence pay that amount out of the fund and into the Consolidated Fund[8]. If, in the case of a trading fund not having public dividend capital[9], the revenues of the fund for a financial year exceed the total sums properly chargeable to revenue account for that year, the responsible minister may with Treasury concurrence, apply the excess for such purposes of the funded operations as he may determine, or pay the whole or part of the excess into the Consolidated Fund[10]. Any money in the fund which appears to the responsible minister not to be immediately required for the funded operations may be invested by him in such government securities[11] as the Treasury may approve, including Treasury bills and ways and means advances[12].

1   As to the nature and establishment of trading funds see para 743 ante.
2   For the meaning of 'responsible minister' see para 743 note 2 ante.
3   For the meaning of 'funded operations' see para 743 note 5 ante.
4   As to the Treasury see paras 512–517 ante.
5   Government Trading Funds Act 1973 s 4(1) (amended by the Government Trading Act 1990 ss 2(2)(a), 5(4), Sch 2 Pt II).
6   For the meaning of 'reserves' see para 747 note 4 ante.
7   Government Trading Funds Act 1973 s 4(2).
8   Ibid s 4(3) (amended by the Government Trading Act 1990 s 2(2)(b)). As to the Consolidated Fund see para 711 et seq ante.
9   As to public dividend capital see para 745 ante.
10  Government Trading Funds Act 1973 s 4(4) (substituted by the Government Trading Act 1990 s 2(2)(c)).
11  Ie securities of the government of the United Kingdom or of the government of Northern Ireland: see Government Trading Funds Act 1973 s 4(5).
12  Ibid s 4(5).

**751–800. Accounting.** The Treasury[1] must appoint an accounting officer[2] for the trading fund[3], with responsibility for keeping the fund's accounts and proper records in relation to it, and preparing and signing a statement of the accounts[4] for each financial year[5]. The accounting officer must send to the responsible minister[6] in respect of each financial year the annual statement of accounts and a report in such form and containing such information as to the performance of the funded operations as the Treasury may require[7]. The responsible minister must publish any such report, together with the annual statement of accounts (unless the Treasury otherwise directs), in such manner as the Treasury may require[8].

1   As to the Treasury see paras 512–517 ante.
2   As to accounting officers generally see para 715 ante.
3   As to the nature and establishment of trading funds see para 743 ante.
4   The annual statement of accounts must comply with any directions given by the Treasury as to the information to be contained in it, the manner in which such information is to be presented or the methods and principles according to which the statement is to be prepared, and contain such additional information as the Treasury may require to be provided for the information of Parliament: Government Trading Funds Act 1973 s 4(6)(a) (amended by the Government Trading Act 1990 s 2(2)(d)). The statement in respect of each financial year must, on or before 30 November next following the end of that year, be transmitted to the Comptroller and Auditor General (see paras 724–726 ante), who must examine and certify the statement and lay copies of it, together with a report on it, before Parliament: Government Trading Funds Act 1973 s 4(6)(b).

5    See ibid s 4(6) (as amended). As respects any financial year during the whole of which any operations of a government department are funded operations of a trading fund, the Exchequer and Audit Departments Act 1921 s 5 does not apply to those operations, but otherwise the Government Trading Funds Act 1973 s 4(6) (as amended) is without prejudice to the Exchequer and Audit Departments Act 1866: Government Trading Funds Act 1973 s 4(7) (amended by the Government Trading Act 1990 s 2(2)(f)). For the meaning of 'funded operations' see para 743 note 5 ante.

6    For the meaning of 'responsible minister' see para 743 note 2 ante.

7    Government Trading Funds Act 1973 s 4(6A) (added by the Government Trading Act 1990 s 2(2)(e)).

8    Government Trading Funds Act 1973 s 4(6A) (as added: see note 7 supra). Where any enactment other than the Government Trading Funds Act 1973 requires a report to be prepared for any period as to the funded operations and sent to any person, and/or laid before Parliament, an order may provide for that requirement to be treated as satisfied by preparing the report for the financial year and sending it to that person, or laying it before Parliament, or both or, as the case may be, so sending it or laying it by the time or times specified in the order: s 4(6B) (added by the Government Trading Act 1990 s 2(2)(e)).


# 7.  MISCELLANEOUS FUNCTIONS OF THE CROWN

## (1)  THE MAKING OF TREATIES

**801. Conduct of foreign affairs and power to make treaties.** The Crown is the representative of the nation in the conduct of foreign affairs, and what is done in such matters by the royal authority is the act of the whole nation, and binding, in general, upon the nation without further sanction[1].

The Crown, therefore, enjoys the sole right of appointing ambassadors, diplomatic agents, consuls and other officers, through whom relations with foreign nations are conducted, and of receiving those of foreign states; of making treaties; declaring peace and war; and generally of conducting all foreign affairs[2]. Such matters are entrusted in general to the absolute discretion of the Crown, acting through the recognised constitutional channels upon the advice of the Cabinet or the Secretary of State for Foreign and Commonwealth Affairs, unfettered technically by any direct supervision, parliamentary or otherwise[3].

The treaty-making power is vested in the Crown[4], and is carried out by agents appointed by the Crown and acting on its behalf[5]. Formal authority is required to sign or ratify a treaty on behalf of the Crown, or to express some other form of consent to be bound by a treaty. Under both international and British constitutional practice this is done in the form of full powers[6]. In concluding a treaty, the Crown always acts in its sovereign character, and never as agent or trustee for any of its subjects unless it expressly declares itself to be so acting[7]. The courts will not impugn the treaty-making power of the Crown[8] unless it has been regulated by statute, as in certain matters in the field of European Community law[9]. When Parliament wishes to fetter the Crown's treaty-making power in relation to Community law, it does so in express terms[10].

1    1 Bl Com (14th Edn) 252. Anything done in such matters without the royal authority is merely the act of private persons: 1 Bl Com (14th Edn) 252.

2    1 Bl Com (14th Edn) 252–253, 257. As to ambassadors and diplomatic agents generally see FOREIGN RELATIONS LAW. As to declarations of war and treaties of peace see paras 809–810 post.

3    An indirect means of control is, however, supplied by the customary or conventional law of the constitution relating to the Cabinet system and the doctrine of ministerial responsibility. Moreover, it is recognised as a constitutional maxim or convention that declarations of peace and war, and the conduct of foreign relations, must be in conformity with the wishes of Parliament, and in certain cases treaties require special parliamentary sanction (see para 802 post). As to the Cabinet and the Secretary of State for Foreign and Commonwealth Affairs, see paras 402–413, 459 ante. The relations of ministers of the Crown with foreign powers should be conducted through the proper official and diplomatic channels, and, it seems, be fully disclosed to and open to the criticism and supervision of the Cabinet and of the

government as a whole. Deviation from this course on the part of ministers with regard to matters of state exposes their motives to the danger of misinterpretation and is not tolerated by the House of Commons. The danger incurred by a minister who conducts a secret correspondence with foreign powers or agents is clearly shown by the impeachment of the Earl of Danby (see *R v Earl of Danby* (1685) 11 State Tr 600 at 621–622, HL), where the first article of the impeachment charged him with having 'traitorously encroached to himself regal power by treating in matters of peace and war with foreign ministers and ambassadors, and giving instructions to His Majesty's ambassadors abroad without communicating the same to the Secretaries of State and the rest of His Majesty's Council'.

4  1 Bl Com (14th Edn) 256. It is part of the monarch's prerogative to make treaties, leagues and alliances with foreign states and princes: 1 Bl Com (14th Edn) 256. As to the necessity for confirmation by the legislature in certain cases see para 802 post. For the meaning of 'treaty' see FOREIGN RELATIONS LAW vol 18 para 1769.

5  For a treaty concluded between heads of State, the instrument conferring the power is passed under the Great Seal on the authority of a sign manual warrant countersigned by the Secretary of State for Foreign and Commonwealth Affairs: see 2 Anson's Law and Custom of the Constitution (4th Edn, 1935) Pt I p 65. As to use of the Great Seal see para 909 post. As to the sign manual see para 908 post. Now, however, it is the practice, according to the Foreign and Commonwealth Office, for the considerable majority of treaties to be concluded as between governments. In such cases, the full powers are signed by the Secretary of State for Commonwealth and Foreign Affairs. Some United Kingdom representatives abroad hold (*ad personam*, but in virtue of their office) general full powers covering treaties concluded with, or under the auspices of, the international organisations to which they are accredited. Conversely, the mere negotiation of the terms of a treaty does not require formal authority, and may be undertaken in many different ways by government representatives at different levels. Where, however, the negotiation takes place at an international conference, delegates would normally require, under the rules regulating the particular conference in question, written credentials.

6  See FOREIGN RELATIONS LAW vol 18 paras 1771–1772.

7  *Rustomjee v R* (1876) 2 QBD 69 at 73, CA, per Lord Coleridge CJ. Therefore, no subject can by legal proceedings compel the Crown to distribute money received on his behalf under the terms of a treaty with a foreign state, though there may be a moral duty to do so. See also *Civilian War Claimants Association Ltd v R* [1932] AC 14, HL. The same reasoning was applied to rights acquired by the German government in *German Property Administrator v Knoop* [1933] Ch 439. As to Crown agents see para 461 ante.

8  *Blackburn v A-G* [1971] 2 All ER 1380 at 1383, [1971] 1 WLR 1037 at 1040, CA; *McWhirter v A-G* [1972] CMLR 882, CA.

9  No treaty which provides for an increase in the powers of the European Parliament is to be ratified by the United Kingdom unless it has been approved by an Act of Parliament: European Parliamentary Elections Act 1978 s 6(1). See also *R v Secretary of State for Foreign and Commonwealth Affairs, ex p Rees-Mogg* [1994] QB 552, [1994] 1 All ER 457, DC.

10  See *R v Secretary of State for Foreign and Commonwealth Affairs, ex p Rees-Mogg* [1994] QB 552 at 567, [1994] 1 All ER 457 at 467, DC, per Lloyd LJ.

**802. Parliamentary sanction to treaties.** Treaties concluded by the Crown are binding upon the state without express parliamentary sanction, but the previous consent of, or subsequent action by, the legislature may be necessary in certain cases to ensure that rights and obligations arising under the treaty can be enforced[1]. A treaty to which Her Majesty's government is a party does not alter the laws of the United Kingdom[2]. Where treaties require internal legislative action for their implementation, this may be done either by Act of Parliament[3], or by delegated legislation[4]. The method by which Parliament gives effect to obligations appears not to affect the manner in which courts resolve problems of interpretation that arise from, for example, discrepancies between the statutory words and the words of the treaty[5]. Treaties may expressly require the parties to them to enact legislation to achieve the treaty's objectives[6]. In other cases, the parties are given a wide margin of discretion over the way they choose to do this, as long as the ultimate objective is achieved[7]. There are important areas in which the conclusion of treaties within specified limits is authorised by Parliament in advance, and the terms of the treaty become directly applicable through scheduling to an order[8].

According to the practice known as the Ponsonby Rule[9], it is 'the intention of His Majesty's Government to lay on the table of both Houses of Parliament every treaty, when signed, for a period of 21 days[10], after which the treaty will be ratified and published and circulated in the Treaty Series. In the case of important treaties, the Government will, of course, take an opportunity of submitting them to the House for discussion within this period ...His Majesty's Government desire that Parliament should...exercise supervision over agreements, commitments and understandings by which the nation may be bound in certain circumstances and which may involve international obligations...although no signed and sealed document may exist...During our term of office we shall inform the House of all agreements, commitments and undertakings which may in any way bind the nation to specific action in certain circumstances'[11]. In certain cases of urgency ministers have decided to depart from the letter of the Ponsonby Rule and in these cases they have sought the express consent of Parliament to ratification, usually by means of a ministerial statement made in debate or in answer to a parliamentary question or (usually if Parliament is not sitting) by consulting the leaders of the opposition parties[12]. However, the Ponsonby rule is still current practice for treaties which have been signed, subject to ratification[13]. After signature, the Ponsonby Rule applies when the consent of the United Kingdom to be bound by the treaty is subject to a further formal act, such as ratification.

If a treaty is not within the Ponsonby Rule, but needs legislation before it can be brought into force in the United Kingdom, it is the practice to lay a text before Parliament before the legislation (whether primary or subordinate) is debated[14].

In the case of the treaties relating to the European Community the European Communities Act 1972 specifically provides that all such rights, powers, liabilities, obligations and restrictions from time to time created or arising by or under the treaties, and all such remedies and procedures from time to time provided for by or under the treaties, as in accordance with the treaties were without further enactment to be given legal effect or used in the United Kingdom should be recognised and available in United Kingdom law and be enforced, allowed and followed accordingly[15]. Her Majesty may by Order in Council declare that a treaty is to be regarded as a Community treaty[16].

1   As to treaties involving interference with private rights see *The Parlement Belge* (1879) 4 PD 129 (revsd on other grounds [1880] 5 PD 197), where the question was whether the Crown had power by treaty to render Belgian packet boats immune from actions brought by a British subject: Sir R Phillimore held that the making of such a treaty was 'a user of treaty-making power of the Crown without precedent, and in principle contrary to the laws of the constitution'. See also *Walker v Baird* [1892] AC 491, PC; and *Republic of Italy v Hambros Bank and Gregory (Custodian of Enemy Property)* [1950] Ch 314, [1950] 1 All ER 430, where it was held that a treaty did not of itself alter the law, but needed legislation for its implementation. Cf *McWhirter v A-G* [1972] CMLR 882, CA (the courts will not take cognisance of a treaty until it has been embodied in an Act of Parliament). See also *A-G for Canada v A-G for Ontario* [1937] AC 326, HL; *Cheney v Conn (Inspector of Taxes)* [1968] 1 All ER 779, [1968] 1 WLR 242; *J H Rayner (Mincing Lane) v Department of Trade and Industry* [1989] Ch 72, sub nom *Maclaine Watson & Co Ltd v Department of Trade and Industry* [1988] 3 All ER 257; affd [1990] 2 AC 418, [1989] 3 All ER 523, HL.

In England there is no codified list of subjects upon which the Crown has power to bind the subject by treaty without parliamentary sanction; but where any reasonable doubt arises, it is usual either to obtain statutory authority beforehand, or to stipulate in the treaty that the consent of the legislature shall be obtained (2 Anson's Law and Custom of the Constitution (4th Edn, 1935) Pt II pp 137–142 dealing with the cession of territory). Now that treaties regularly require ratification to become binding, the authority of Parliament need only be obtained for ratification. Thus, for example, certain peace treaties made after the 1939–45 war had to be ratified before they came into force; and since they affected the private rights of British subjects, the Treaties of Peace (Italy, Roumania, Bulgaria, Hungary and Finland) Act 1947 and the Japanese Treaty of Peace Act 1951 were passed, giving the Crown powers of subordinate legislation enabling it to carry the treaties into effect. As to ratification see FOREIGN RELATIONS LAW vol 18 para 1776.

Since the treaty-making power is exercised upon the advice of ministers responsible to the House of Commons, the consent of that House can normally be expected as a matter of course. That is not necessarily true of the House of Lords, which, for example, declined to ratify the Declaration of London in 1909. See also the Treaties (Parliamentary Approval) Bill 1996 (HL Bill 27), a private member's bill introduced by Lord Lester of Herne Hill, which proposes a requirement that all treaties concluded by the United Kingdom which are subject to ratification are approved by Parliament before they are ratified and after publication of an explanatory memorandum on the significance of the treaty: see 569 HL Official Report (5th series), 28 February 1996, col 1530 et seq. As to the House of Commons see PARLIAMENT. As to the House of Lords see para 204 ante; and PARLIAMENT.

2    *J H Rayner (Mincing Lane) Ltd v Department of Trade and Industry* [1990] 2 AC 418 at 476, sub nom *Maclaine Watson & Co Ltd v Department of Trade and Industry* [1989] 3 All ER 523 at 526, HL. 'There is a well established rule that the making of a treaty is an executive act, while the performance of its obligations, if they entail alteration of the existing domestic law, requires legislative action': *A-G for Canada v A-G for Ontario* [1937] AC 326 at 347, HL, per Lord Atkin. '... the stipulations of a treaty duly ratified do not ... by virtue of the treaty alone have the force of law': *A-G for Canada v A-G for Ontario* supra at 347 per Lord Atkin. 'Except to the extent that a treaty becomes incorporated into the laws of the United Kingdom by statute, the courts have no power to enforce treaty rights and obligations at the behest of a sovereign government or at the behest of a private individual': *J H Rayner (Mincing Lane) Ltd v Department of Trade and Industry* supra at 476, 526 per Lord Templeman.

3    Such primary legislation will therefore receive the detailed attention of Parliament; see further STATUTES. See eg the Carriage of Goods by Sea Act 1971; and Higgins 'The United Kingdom' in Jacobs and Roberts (eds) *The Effect of Treaties in Domestic Law* (1987) ch 7. This is normally effected by passing a short Act to which the convention is scheduled; see eg the Carriage by Air Act 1961 embodying the Warsaw Convention of 1929 (amended at the Hague in 1955); the Recognition of Trusts Act 1987, giving effect to the 1984 Hague Convention on the law applicable to trusts and their recognition; the Civil Jurisdiction and Judgments Act 1982, giving effect to the 1968 Brussels Convention on jurisdiction and the enforcement of judgments in civil and commercial matters between the members states of the European Community. As to the attempts to incorporate the Convention for the Protection of Human Rights and Fundamental Freedoms (1950) see para 103 ante.

4    See eg the International Organisations Act 1968, which enables privileges and immunities to be granted to certain international organisations: see FOREIGN RELATIONS LAW vol 18 paras 1597–1598. As to subordinate legislation generally see STATUTES vol 44(1) (Reissue) paras 1499–1526.

5    See *Salomon v Customs and Excise Comrs* [1967] 2 QB 116, [1966] 3 All ER 871, CA. 'It is a principle of construction of United Kingdom statutes, now too well established to call for citation of authority, that the words of a statute passed after the treaty has been signed and dealing with the subject matter of the international obligation of the United Kingdom, are to be construed, if they are reasonably capable of bearing such a meaning, as intended to carry out the obligation and not to be inconsistent with it': *Garland v British Rail Engineering Ltd* [1983] 2 AC 751 at 771, [1982] 2 WLR 918 at 934–935, HL, per Lord Diplock. See also para 104 ante.

6    See the Conventions on international crimes, eg the Convention on the Prevention and Punishment of the Crime of Genocide 1948, which the United Kingdom has ratified (see the Genocide Act 1969), and more recent conventions on aviation, security, hi-jacking and the protection of diplomats.

7    See eg the Convention for the Protection of Human Rights and Fundamental Freedoms (1950) Art 1; *Ireland v United Kingdom* A 25 (1978), 2 EHRR 25, ECtHR; and para 122 ante.

8    See eg under the Extradition Act 1989 s 4 (as amended); the Income and Corporation Taxes Act 1988 s 788; the Social Security Administration Act 1992 s 179 (as prospectively amended).

9    The Ponsonby Rule was derived from an undertaking given to Parliament by the Under Secretary of State for Foreign Affairs, Arthur Ponsonby; see 171 HC Official Report (5th series) 1924 cols 2001–2004.

10   The period of 21 days is taken to refer to sitting days of the House of Commons, although they need not be within the same Parliament or session of Parliament.

11   See the *Report of the Select Committee on the European Communities, Political Union: Law-Making Powers and Procedures* (HL Paper (1990–91) no 80) App 4 at p 56. See also Higgins 'The United Kingdom' in Jacobs and Roberts (eds) *The Effect of Treaties in Domestic Law* (1987) ch 7; and Erskine May *Parliamentary Practice* (21st Edn, 1989) p 215. Approximately one in four treaties entered into by the United Kingdom is subject to the Ponsonby Rule.

12   *Report of the Select Committee on the European Communities, Political Union: Law-Making Powers and Procedures* (HL Paper (1990–91) no 80) App 4 at p 57.

13   566 HL Official Report (5th series), 1 November 1995, written answers col 159. On 6 May 1981, it was announced that bilateral double taxation agreements would no longer fall under the Ponsonby Rule. Their texts would no longer be tabled in the Command Papers series but would continue to be published in the Treaty Series of Command Papers after entry into force: 4 HC Official Report (6th series) 6 May 1981, written answers, col 82.

     It is interesting to note that there was no Parliamentary approval or even debate when the Attlee government ratified the Convention for the Protection of Human Rights and Fundamental Freedoms (1950) ('the European Convention on Human Rights'), nor when the Wilson government accepted the right of individual petition under Art 25 of the Convention in January 1966, nor indeed when the second Wilson government ratified the International Convention on Civil and Political Rights in 1976: see Lester 'Fundamental Rights: The United Kingdom Isolated?' [1984] Public Law 46; and Lester 'Taking Human Rights Seriously' (1994–95) 5 Kings College Law Journal pp 2–3. As to the question of the status of these conventions which create rights and obligations in the absence of the necessary legislation see paras 103–104 ante. It should be noted that proposals for cabinet or ministerial committees should cover the impact of the European Convention on Human Rights: *Questions of Procedure for Ministers* (Cabinet Office, May 1992) (as now revised: see para 416 note 1 ante). See also *Minister for Immigration and Ethnic Affairs v Teoh* (1995) 128 ALR 353, Aust HC, which held that ratification by Australia of the Convention on the Rights of the Child created a legitimate expectation, in the absence of statutory or executive indications to the contrary, that administrative decision-makers would act in accordance with the Convention. See also Saunders 'Articles of Faith or Lucky Breaks? The Constitutional Law of International Agreements in Australia' (1995) 17 Sydney Law Review 148.

14  See the *Report of the Select Committee on the European Communities, Political Union: Law-Making Powers and Procedures* (HL Paper (1990–91) no 80) App 4 at p 57.

15  European Communities Act 1972 s 2(1): see EUROPEAN COMMUNITIES. The Act also empowered Her Majesty by Order in Council and designated ministers and departments by regulations to make provision for implementing Community obligations, enabling treaty rights to be enjoyed, and generally dealing with matters arising out of or relating to any such obligations or rights (see s 2(2)), made provision for meeting the expenses of membership of the Communities (see s 2(3), (4)), for the interpretation of the treaties in accordance with Community law and for proof of the treaties and evidence of Community instruments (see s 3 (as amended)), and made necessary consequential amendments to United Kingdom law (see Pt II (ss 4–12 (as amended)); Companies Act 1985). See the *Report of the Select Committee on the European Communities, Political Union: Law-Making Powers and Procedures* (HL Paper (1990–91) no 80); and Forman 'The European Communities Act 1972: The Government's Position on the Meaning and Effect of its Constitutional Provisions' (1973) 10 CML Rev 39.

16  See the European Communities Act 1972 s 1(3). However, a treaty of major significance which affects the structure or financing of the Communities is added to the list of Community Treaties in s 2 by primary legislation. No treaty which provides for an increase in the powers of the European Parliament may be ratified by the United Kingdom unless it has been approved by an Act of Parliament: European Parliamentary Elections Act 1978 s 6. See in particular the European Communities (Amendment) Act 1986 which made the necessary domestic law changes following the Single European Act, and the European Communities (Amendment) Act 1993 following upon the Treaty on European Union 1992 ('the Maastricht Treaty) (on which see Rawlings 'Legal Politics: The United Kingdom and Ratification of the Treaty on European Union (Part One)' [1994] Public Law 254. As to Community Treaties see para 24 note 2 ante.

## (2) FOREIGN COMPENSATION COMMISSION.

**803. Compensation payable by foreign governments, international organisations etc.** Her Majesty may, by Order in Council[1], make provision for various administrative and financial matters in contemplation of Her Majesty's government in the United Kingdom receiving or, where the government has received, compensation paid by another country (or its government) by an international organisation or by an international tribunal[2]. Provision may be made for:

(1)  the prescribing of categories of person who may apply to the Foreign Compensation Commission for the purpose of establishing claims to participate in the compensation[3];

(2)  the imposition of conditions that must be fulfilled before such applications can be considered[4];

(3)  the prescribing of matters that must be established to the satisfaction of the commission by persons making such applications[5];

(4)  the registration by the commission of such claims and the making of reports by the commission in respect of such claims[6];

(5)  the investigation and determination by the commission of such claims[7];

(6)  the surrender to the commission of documents of title relating to property in respect of which claims are established, and the abandonment or extinction of rights in respect of which claims are established[8];

(7) the distribution by the commission of any sums paid to them by the government of the United Kingdom out of compensation[9]; and

(8) any supplementary or incidental matters for which provision appears to Her Majesty to be necessary or expedient[10].

1 Any Order in Council made under the Foreign Compensation Act 1950 may be revoked or varied by a further Order in Council: s 8(1). All Orders in Council made under the Act are subject to annulment by resolution of either House of Parliament: s 8(2).

2 Ibid 3(1) (substituted by the Foreign Compensation (Amendment) Act 1993 s 1). An 'international organisation' means an organisation of which two or more countries (or their governments) are members, and includes any committee or other subordinate body of such an organisation: Foreign Compensation Act 1950 s 3(3) (as so substituted). An 'international tribunal' means any tribunal, court or other body or person that in pursuance of (1) an agreement between two or more countries (or their governments) and one or more international organisation; or (2) a decision or resolution of an international organisation or a conference attended by representatives of two or more countries (or their governments), performs, or is appointed (whether permanently or temporarily) to perform, any function of a judicial or quasi-judicial nature: s 3(3) (as so substituted).

The Foreign Compensation Act 1950 dealt specifically with agreements between Her Majesty's government and the governments of Yugoslavia and Czechoslovakia, and to that extent is spent. The Foreign Compensation Act 1962 was passed inter alia to enable the Secretary of State to make payments to the commission out of money provided by Parliament, to be treated as though it represented payments from a foreign government: this was done in order to supplement the Egyptian Compensation Fund out of such money. The Foreign Compensation Act 1969 empowered the commission to receive and distribute assets in the United Kingdom which became available for the settlement of claims under the Anglo-Soviet agreement of 5 January 1968.

As to Orders made in the exercise of the Foreign Compensation Act 1950 s 3 (as originally enacted) see the Foreign Compensation (Hungary) (Registration) Order 1954, SI 1954/219 (amended by SI 1954/1371); the Foreign Compensation (Roumania) (Registration) Order 1954, SI 1954/221 (amended by SI 1959/1295); the Foreign Compensation (Czechoslovakia) (Registration) Order 1960, SI 1960/849 (amended by SI 1961/585; and SI 1964/698); the Foreign Compensation (Roumania) Order 1961, SI 1961/1832 (amended by SI 1964/494; and SI 1966/444); the Foreign Compensation (Hungary) Order 1963, SI 1963/1148 (amended by SI 1967/813); the Foreign Compensation (Egypt) Order 1971, SI 1971/2104; the Foreign Compensation (German Democratic Republic) (Registration) Order 1975, SI 1975/410; the Foreign Compensation (Romania) Order 1976, SI 1976/1154; the Foreign Compensation (People's Republic of China) (Registration) Order 1980, SI 1980/1720; the Foreign Compensation (Czechoslovakia) Order 1982, SI 1982/1073; the Foreign Compensation (Union of Soviet Socialist Republics) (Registration and Determination of Claims) Order 1986, SI 1986/2222 (amended by SI 1987/663); the Foreign Compensation (Union of Soviet Socialist Republics) (Distribution) Order 1987, SI 1987/663; the Foreign Compensation (People's Republic of China) Order 1987, SI 1987/2201.

3 Foreign Compensation Act 1950 s 3(2)(a) (as substituted: see note 2 supra).
4 Ibid s 3(2)(b) (as substituted: see note 2 supra).
5 Ibid s 3(2)(c) (as substituted: see note 2 supra).
6 Ibid s 3(2)(d) (as substituted: see note 2 supra).
7 Ibid s 3(2)(e) (as substituted: see note 2 supra).
8 Ibid s 3(2)(f) (as substituted: see note 2 supra).
9 Ibid s 3(2)(g) (as substituted: see note 2 supra).
10 Ibid s 3(2)(h) (as substituted: see note 2 supra).

**804. Constitution of the Foreign Compensation Commission.** The Foreign Compensation Commission is a body corporate consisting of a paid chairman[1] appointed by the Lord Chancellor[2] and such number of other paid members so appointed as the Secretary of State may with the approval of the Minister for the Civil Service determine[3]. Subject to specific provision for the chairman[4], every member of the commission must hold and vacate his office in accordance with the terms of his appointment, and a member of the commission who ceases to hold office is eligible for re-appointment[5]. The commission has power to hold land and may act notwithstanding a vacancy among its members[6]. The commission pays to its members such remuneration (whether by way of salary or fees) and allowances as the commission may with the approval of the Minister for the Civil Service determine[7]. It also, as regards any persons who are or have been members of the commission, pays to or in respect of them such pensions or other benefits in connection with their retirement or death, or such sums towards the provision of pensions or other such benefits, as may be so determined[8]. Members of the commission are disqualified for membership of the House of Commons[9].

1 The chairman of the commission must vacate his office on the day on which he attains the age of 70 years; but this is subject to the Judicial Pensions and Retirement Act 1993 s 26(4)–(6) (power to authorise continuance in office up to the age of 75 years): Foreign Compensation Act 1950 s 1(3A) (added by the Judicial Pensions and Retirement Act 1993 ss 26(10), (11), 27, Sch 6 para 25, Sch 7).
2 As to the Lord Chancellor see paras 477–497 ante.
3 Foreign Compensation Act 1950 s 1(1). See also the Minister for the Civil Service Order 1968, SI 1968/1656. As to the Minister for the Civil Service see para 427 ante.
4 See the Foreign Compensation Act 1950 s 1(3A) (as added); and note 1 supra.
5 Ibid s 1(3) (amended by the Judicial Pensions and Retirement Act 1993 Sch 6 para 25, Sch 7).
6 Foreign Compensation Act 1950 s 1(2) (amended by the Statute Law (Repeals) Act 1974).
7 Foreign Compensation Act 1950 s 1(5). See also the Minister for the Civil Service Order 1968; and the Minister for the Civil Service Order 1971, SI 1971/2099.
8 Foreign Compensation Act 1962 s 3(1). This provision does not have effect in relation to a chairman or former chairman of the commission who is person to whom the Judicial Pensions and Retirement Act 1993 Pt I (ss 1–18) (as amended) applies, except to the extent provided by or under that Act: Foreign Compensation Act 1962 s 3(1A) (added by the Judicial Pensions and Retirement Act 1993 s 31(3), Sch 8 para 4).
9 House of Commons Disqualification Act 1975 s 1, Sch 1 Pt II. As to the House of Commons see PARLIAMENT.

**805. Procedure.** The Foreign Compensation Commission makes rules, which are subject to the Lord Chancellor's approval[1], regulating its procedure for determining applications under the Foreign Compensation Act 1950; and such rules may prescribe time limits within which such applications must be made and may confer powers on the commission for enforcing the attendance of witnesses and their examination on oath, affirmation or otherwise, and for compelling the production of documents and the furnishing of information, and for the taking of evidence abroad[2]. Such rules may provide that the application must, if the commission so directs or the applicant so desires, be the subject of an oral hearing and that the applicant is entitled to appear in person or to be represented[3]. Her Majesty may by Order in Council prescribe the number of members who may determine applications on behalf of the commission, and the Order may prescribe different numbers in relation to different classes of applications[4].

1 The power of the Lord Chancellor to approve rules made under the Foreign Compensation Act 1950 s 4 (as amended) is exercisable by statutory instrument, which is subject to annulment by resolution of either House of Parliament: Foreign Compensation Act 1950 s 8(3). As to the Lord Chancellor see paras 477–497 ante.
2 Ibid s 4(2). If any person (1) on being summoned, in accordance with rules made under s 4 (as amended), as a witness before the commission, fails to attend; or (2) being in attendance as a witness refuses to take an oath or make an affirmation required in accordance with such rules to be taken or made, or to answer any question to which the commission may legally require an answer; or (3) being required in accordance with such rules to produce any document or furnish any information, fails without reasonable excuse to comply with that requirement; or (4) does any other thing which would, if the commission had been a court of law having power to commit for contempt of court, have been contempt of court; the chairman of the commission may certify the offence of that person under his hand to the High Court, and the court may inquire into the alleged offence and may punish or take steps for the punishment of that person in like manner as if he had been guilty of contempt of court: s 5(1). A witness before the commission is entitled to the same immunities and privileges as if he were a witness before the High Court: s 5(2).
  As to the commission's main rules see the Foreign Compensation Commission Rules 1956, SI 1956/962 (amended by rules approved by SI 1964/638; SI 1968/164; and modified by rules approved by SI 1958/1995; SI 1991/2684). The rules provide for a procedure very similar to that of a court of justice and in addition to the matters specified in the Foreign Compensation Act 1950 s 4(2),

provide for a public oral hearing at the option of either the applicant or the commission. It has, however, been the commission's practice to make rules regulating the procedure for each category of claims to be determined; see the Foreign Compensation Commission (Egypt) Rules Approval Instrument 1972, SI 1972/219 (modified by SI 1991/2684); the Foreign Compensation Commission (Romania) Rules Approval Instrument 1976, SI 1976/1646 (modified by SI 1991/2684); the Foreign Compensation Commission (Czechoslovakia) Rules Approval Instrument 1982, SI 1982/1110 (amended by rules approved by SI 1985/697; and modified by SI 1991/2684); the Foreign Compensation Commission (Union of Soviet Socialist Republics) Rules Approval Instrument 1987, SI 1987/143 (modified by SI 1991/2684); and the Foreign Compensation Commission (People's Republic of China) Rules Approval Instrument 1988, SI 1988/153 (modified by SI 1991/2684).

3    Foreign Compensation Act 1950 s 4(3) (amended by the Statute Law (Repeals) Act 1989).

4    Foreign Compensation Act 1950 s 4(1).

**806. Determinations of the Foreign Compensation Commission.** The Foreign Compensation Commission has power to determine any question as to the construction or interpretation of any provision of an Order in Council[1] with respect to claims falling to be determined by it[2]; but if required to do so by (1) a claimant; or (2) any person appointed by the commission to represent the interests of any fund out of which the claim would, if allowed, be met, who is aggrieved by any such determination[3] of the commission or by any determination on any question of law relating to its jurisdiction, the commission must state and sign a case for the decision of the Court of Appeal[4]. Such a person may, with a view to requiring the commission to state and sign a case, request the commission to furnish a written statement of the reasons for any determination, but the commission is not obliged to state the reasons for any determination unless it is given on a claim in which a question as to the construction or interpretation of an Order in Council or as to the jurisdiction of the commission arises[5]. If the Court of Appeal decides a question on a case stated and signed by the commission on a provisional determination in any proceedings, there is no right to require the commission to state and sign a case on a final determination of that question in those proceedings[6]. Except where the commission may be required to state and sign a case and except in so far as proceedings may be brought by any person questioning a determination of the commission on the ground that it is contrary to natural justice, no determination of the commission on any claim may be called in question in any court of law[7].

1    Ie an Order in Council under the Foreign Compensation Act 1950 s 3 (as substituted): see para 803 ante.

2    Foreign Compensation Act 1969 s 3(1).

3    'Determination' includes a determination which under rules under the Foreign Compensation Act 1950 s 4(2) (see para 805 text and note 2 ante) is a provisional determination, and anything which purports to be a determination: Foreign Compensation Act 1969 s 3(3).

4    Ibid s 3(2), (6). The Foreign Compensation Act 1969 s 3 (as amended), while confirming the commission's power to determine questions of construction of Orders in Council, provides for appeals against determinations in certain circumstances. The right of appeal was exercised in *Kesten v Cooper, Benyami v Cooper* (1970) 114 Sol Jo 704, CA. Notwithstanding anything in the Appellate Jurisdiction Act 1876 s 3 (right of appeal to the House of Lords from decisions of the Court of Appeal), no appeal lies to the House of Lords from a decision of the Court of Appeal on an appeal under the Foreign Compensation Act 1969 s 3 (as amended): s 3(8). As to the House of Lords see PARLIAMENT.

5    Ibid s 3(5). Any such request must be in writing, and may be disregarded unless (1) it is received by the commission within the period of four weeks beginning with the date on which the commission sends notice of the determination in question or such other period as may be provided for by or under rules under the Foreign Compensation Act 1950 s 4(2) (see para 805 text and note 2 ante); or (2) it is received by the commission within the period of eight weeks beginning with that date or the period of four weeks beginning with the date on which the commission sends a statement of reasons for the determination in question, whichever expires last, or within such other period as may be provided for by or under rules of court: Foreign Compensation Act 1969 s 3(7).

6    Ibid s 3(4).

7    Ibid s 3(9), (10).

**807. Administrative and financial provisions.** Her Majesty may make provision by Order in Council with respect to the following administrative and financial matters:

   (1)   the quorum and proceedings of the Foreign Compensation Commission[1];

   (2)   the appointment of officers and servants of the commission and the payment of remuneration and allowances to them[2];

   (3)   the management and investment of any moneys in the hands of the commission[3];

   (4)   any other matters for which Her Majesty considers it necessary or expedient to provide for the purposes of enabling the commission to exercise its functions[4];

   (5)   the disposal of any sums in the hands of the commission which it is not practicable to distribute[5];

   (6)   the winding up of the commission[6].

It may also be provided by Order in Council that the commission's expenses attributable to the distribution of any particular fund are met out of that fund[7]; subject to the exercise of this power the commission's expenses are defrayed out of moneys provided by Parliament[8].

The commission is required to prepare accounts for each financial year[9] and, as soon as possible after the end of each financial year it must submit its accounts for that year to the Secretary of State who must transmit the accounts to the Comptroller and Auditor General who must examine and certify them and lay copies together with his report on them before Parliament[10]. The commission must also prepare an annual report on the exercise of its functions during each financial year and submit it to the Secretary of State who lays copies before Parliament[11].

1   Foreign Compensation Act 1950 s 7(1)(a).
2   Ibid s 7(1)(b). This extends to the making, in relation to persons who are or have been such officers or servants, of provision with respect to pensions or other benefits in connection with their retirement or death: Foreign Compensation Act 1962 s 3(2).
3   Foreign Compensation Act 1950 s 7(1)(c).
4   Ibid s 7(1)(d).
5   Ibid s 7(1)(e).
6   Ibid s 7(1)(f). See also the Foreign Compensation (Staff) (Superannuation Benefits) Order 1977, SI 1977/2148.
7   Foreign Compensation Act 1950 s 7(2) proviso. This applies in relation to payments made by virtue of the Foreign Compensation Act 1962 s 3 (as amended) as it applies in relation to other expenses of the commission: Foreign Compensation Act 1962 s 3(3). Orders in Council are made annually under this power and each Order in Council supersedes that of the previous year; see the Foreign Compensation (Financial Provisions) Orders 1974, SI 1974/249; SI 1975/409; SI 1976/220; SI 1977/239; SI 1978/180; SI 1979/109; SI 1980/186; SI 1981/240; SI 1984/128; SI 1985/168; 1986/219; 1987/164, 1028; SI 1988/244; SI 1989/481; SI 1990/589; SI 1991/190; SI 1992/228; SI 1993/224. The latest Order in Council was SI 1993/2806 but it, like the others, is now spent.
8   Foreign Compensation Act 1950 s 7(2); Foreign Compensation Act 1962 s 3(3).
9   'Financial year' means the period of twelve months ending with 31 March: Foreign Compensation Act 1950 s 6(3) (amended by the Statute Law (Repeals) Act 1989).
10   Foreign Compensation Act 1950 s 6(1). As to the Comptroller and Auditor General see paras 724–726 ante.
11   Ibid s 6(2).

## (3) THE UNITED NATIONS

**808. Measures under United Nations charter.** The Crown has statutory power to make by Order in Council such provision as appears to it necessary or expedient in order to apply effectively any measures which it is called upon to take under Article 41 of the Charter of the United Nations[1] by the Security Council of the United Nations[2].

1   For the Charter of the United Nations see TS 67; Cmd 7015 (1946). Article 41 of the charter relates to measures not involving the use of armed force. As to the United Nations generally see FOREIGN

RELATIONS LAW vol 940 para 1811–1815.

2    United Nations Act 1946 s 1(1). Orders in Council, which must be laid before Parliament (s 1(4) (amended by the Statute Law Revision Act 1963)), may be varied or revoked by subsequent orders (s 1(3)). Orders may be so made as to extend to any part of Her Majesty's dominions (other than dominions within the meaning of the Statute of Westminster 1931) and, to the extent that Her Majesty has jurisdiction therein, to any other territory in which she has from time to time jurisdiction (other than territories which are being administered by the government of such a dominion as aforesaid): United Nations Act 1946 s 1(2) (amended by the Burma Independence Act 1947 s 5, Sch 2 Pt I; the Zimbabwe Act 1979 s 6(3), Sch 3; and the Statute Law (Repeals) Act 1995). The terms of this limitation are now obsolete and it must be assumed that no attempt would now be made to extend an order to any independent member of the Commonwealth.

The following Orders in Council have been made under the United Nations Act 1946 s 1 (as amended), imposing sanctions on Angola, Haiti, Iraq and Kuwait, Liberia, Libya, Rwanda, Serbia and Montenegro, Somalia, South Africa and the former Yugoslavia:

   (1)   As to Angola see the Angola (United Nations Sanctions) Order 1993, SI 1993/2355; Angola (United Nations Sanctions) (Dependent Territories) Order 1993, SI 1993/2356; Angola (United Nations Sanctions) (Channel Islands) Order 1993, SI 1993/2357; Angola (United Nations Sanctions) (Isle of Man) Order 1993, SI 1993/2358.

   (2)   As to Haiti see the Haiti (United Nations Sanctions) Order 1994, SI 1994/1323; Haiti (United Nations Sanctions) (Dependent Territories) Order 1994, SI 1994/1324; Haiti (United Nations Sanctions) (Channel Islands) Order 1994, SI 1994/1325; Haiti (United Nations Sanctions) (Isle of Man) Order 1994, SI 1994/1326.

   (3)   As to Iraq and Kuwait see the Iraq and Kuwait (United Nations Sanctions) Order 1990, SI 1990/1651 (amended by SI 1990/1768; and SI 1990/2144); Iraq and Kuwait (Dependent Territories) Order 1990, SI 1990/1652 (amended by SI 1990/1770); Iraq and Kuwait (United Nations Sanctions) (Bermuda) Order 1990, SI 1990/1769; Iraq and Kuwait (United Nations Sanctions) (Channel Islands) Order 1990, SI 1990/1771; Iraq and Kuwait (United Nations Sanctions) (No 2) Order 1990, SI 1990/1987; Iraq and Kuwait (United Nations Sanctions) (Dependent Territories) (No 2) Order 1990, SI 1990/1988; Iraq (United Nations) (Sequestration of Assets) Order 1993, SI 1993/1244; Iraq (United Nations) (Sequestration of Assets) (Dependent Territories) Order 1993, SI 1993/1245; Iraq (United Nations) (Sequestration of Assets) (Isle of Man) Order 1993, SI 1993/1575; Iraq (United Nations) (Sequestration of Assets) (Guernsey) Order 1993, SI 1993/1798; Iraq (United Nations) (Sequestration of Assets) (Jersey) Order 1993, SI 1993/1799.

   (4)   As to Liberia see the United Nations Arms Embargoes (Liberia, Somalia and the Former Yugoslavia) Order 1993, SI 1993/1787 (amended by SI 1994/1637). See also the United Nations Arms Embargoes (Dependent Territories) Order 1995, SI 1995/1032.

   (5)   As to Libya see the Libya (United Nations Prohibition of Flights) Order 1992, SI 1992/973; Libya (United Nations Prohibition of Flights) (Dependent Territories) Order 1992, SI 1992/974; Libya (United Nations Sanctions) Order 1993, SI 1993/2807; Libya (United Nations Sanctions) (Dependent Territories) Order 1993, SI 1993/2808; Libya (United Nations Sanctions) (Channel Islands) Order 1993, SI 1993/2811; Libya (United Nations Sanctions) (Isle of Man) Order 1993, SI 1993/2812.

   (6)   As to Rwanda see the United Nations Arms Embargoes (Liberia, Somalia and the Former Yugoslavia) Order 1993, SI 1993/1787 (amended by SI 1994/1637). See also the United Nations Arms Embargoes (Dependent Territories) Order 1995.

   (7)   As to Serbia and Montenegro see the Serbia and Montenegro (United Nations Sanctions) Order 1992, SI 1992/1302; Serbia and Montenegro (United Nations Sanctions) (Dependent Territories) Order 1992, SI 1992/1303; Serbia and Montenegro (United Nations Prohibition of Flights) Order 1992, SI 1992/1304; Serbia and Montenegro (United Nations Prohibition of Flights) (Dependent Territories) Order 1992, SI 1992/1305; Serbia and Montenegro (United Nations Sanctions) (Channel Islands) Order 1992, SI 1992/1308; Serbia and Montenegro (United Nations Sanctions) Order 1993, SI 1993/1188 (amended by SI 1994/2673); Serbia and Montenegro (United Nations Sanctions) (Dependent Territories) Order 1993, SI 1993/1195 (amended by SI 1994/2674); Serbia and Montenegro (United Nations Sanctions) (Channel Islands) Order 1993, SI 1993/1253; Serbia and Montenegro (United Nations Sanctions) (Isle of Man) Order 1993, SI 1993/1254.

   (8)   As to Somalia see the United Nations Arms Embargoes (Liberia, Somalia and the Former Yugoslavia) Order 1993, SI 1993/1787 (amended by SI 1994/1637). See also the United Nations Arms Embargoes (Dependent Territories) Order 1995.

   (9)   As to South Africa see the South Africa (United Nations Arms Embargo) (Prohibited Transactions) Revocations Order 1994, SI 1994/1636.

(10) As to the former Yugoslavia see the United Nations Arms Embargoes (Liberia, Somalia and the Former Yugoslavia) Order 1993, SI 1993/1787 (amended by SI 1994/1637). See also the United Nations Arms Embargoes (Dependent Territories) Order 1995.

See further *R v Searle; R v KCS Products Ltd; R v Borjanovic* (1995) 16 Cr App Rep (S) 944, CA.

## (4)  THE MAKING OF WAR AND PEACE

**809. State of war.** When war with a foreign state has been commenced either by a formal declaration or by actual hostilities, the effect is to prohibit all commerce and intercourse between British subjects resident in British territory and the subjects of that state, or with persons residing there[1].

1    Trading with the enemy is an offence at common law. It is also a statutory offence under the Trading with the Enemy Act 1939; Emergency Laws (Miscellaneous Provisions) Act 1953. See generally WAR.

**810. Treaty of peace.** War can be commenced or terminated only by the authority of the Crown[1]. Termination of war is usually[2] effected by a treaty of peace[3] and announced to the nation by proclamation or Order in Council[4]. Proclamations and Orders in Council of this nature were made after the 1939–45 war[5], as also after the 1914–18 war. It may be found necessary for the interpretation of documents referring to the duration of the war in various terms to fix one date, irrespective of the state with which peace was concluded[6].

1    1 Bl Com (14th Edn) 257–258.
2    An example of the termination of war by means of an agreement not amounting to a peace treaty is afforded by the agreement with Thailand of 1 January 1946: see Cmd 8140; see also Cmd 9090.
3    As to parliamentary sanction to peace treaties in certain cases see para 802 ante. As to the greater latitude usually allowed to the exercise of the prerogative in wartime see para 811 post.
4    It is usual on such occasions to publish notices as to the signing and ratification of the treaty of peace in the London Gazette, and after ratification the fact that peace is established is usually announced by proclamation.
5    After the 1939–45 war treaties were signed on 10 February 1947 with Italy and Roumania (Cmd 7486), Bulgaria and Hungary (Cmd 7485), and Finland (Cmd 7484), and the state of war with those countries ended on 15 September 1947 (London Gazette, 16 September 1947). The Treaties of Peace (Italy, Roumania, Bulgaria, Hungary and Finland) Act 1947, gave power to make Orders in Council for carrying these into effect. The following orders were made: the Treaty of Peace (Bulgaria) Order 1948, SI 1948/114; the Treaty of Peace (Finland) Order 1948, SI 1948/115; the Treaty of Peace (Hungary) Order 1948, SI 1948/116; (see also *Bank voor Handel en Scheepvaart NV v Administrator of Hungarian Property* [1954] AC 584, [1954] 1 All ER 969, HL); the Treaty of Peace (Italy) Order 1948, SI 1948/117; the Treaty of Peace (Roumania) Order 1948 SI 1948/118. The state of war with Austria was declared to have ended on 16 September 1947 (see London Gazette, 16 September 1947). A treaty for the re-establishment of an independent and democratic Austria was signed on 15 May 1955, and the Austrian State Treaty Act 1955 gave power to make Orders in Council to carry the treaty into effect. The state of war with Germany was declared to have ended on 9 July 1951 (see London Gazette, 9 July 1951); see also *Re Grotrian, Cox v Grotrian* [1955] Ch 501, [1955] 1 All ER 788, where, for the purpose of construing a condition in a will relating to peace being declared, it was held that a declaration of the termination of war also brought about a state of peace. Conventions were signed on 26 May 1952 comprising (1) the Convention on Relations between the Three Powers and the Federal Republic of Germany; (2) the Convention on the Rights and Obligations of Foreign Forces and their Members in the Republic; (3) the Finance Convention; and (4) the Convention on the Settlement of Matters arising out of the War and the Occupation; these conventions were amended by the Protocol on the Termination of the Occupation Regime in the Federal Republic of Germany signed on 3 October 1954 (Cmd 9368).
     A Treaty of Peace with Japan and a Protocol to it were signed in San Francisco on 8 September 1951 (Cmd 8392), and the Japanese Treaty of Peace Act 1951 gave power to make Orders in Council to carry the treaty and protocol into effect. The order made under this power is the Japanese Treaty of Peace Order 1952, SI 1952/862 (amended by the Industrial Expansion Act 1968 s 18(2), Sch 4 (repealed)).
6    After the 1914–18 war the Termination of the Present War (Definition) Act 1918 gave power to declare by Order in Council the date of the termination of the war. This was exercised by Order in Council

dated 12 August 1921, SR & O 1921/1276, which declared it to be 31 August 1921. For cases in which questions arose concerning the termination of the war or conclusion of peace see *Kotzias v Tyser* [1920] 2 KB 69; *Lloyd v Bowring* (1920) 36 TLR 397; *Rattray v Holden* (1920) 36 TLR 798; *Re Rawson, Rigby v Rawson* (1920) 124 LT 498; *Ruffy-Arnell and Baumann Aviation Co Ltd v R* [1922] 1 KB 599; *Re Gunn, Gunn v Public Trustee* [1922] WN 337. No such general Act has been passed to determine the date of termination of the Second World War, but the duration of temporary Acts is generally limited by some such expression as 'until such date as His Majesty may by Order in Council declare to be the date on which the emergency that was the occasion of the passing of this Act came to an end': see eg the Execution of Trusts (Emergency Provisions) Act 1939 s 7 (repealed) and the Execution of Trusts (Emergency Provisions) Act (End of Emergency) Order 1948, SI 1948/1165 (now lapsed), declaring 31 May 1948 to be the date. A separate Order in Council concerning the particular Act is required for each Act: *Willcock v Muckle* [1951] 2 KB 844, [1951] 2 All ER 367, DC. See also *R v Phillips; R v Grecian; R v Blackledge; R v Mason* [1996] 1 Cr App Rep 326, CA (concerning the Export of Goods (Control) Order 1987, SI 1987/2070 (revoked), and the Export of Goods (Control) Order 1989, SI 1989/2376 (revoked), made under the Import, Export and Customs Powers (Defence) Act 1939 s 1(1), where it was held that in the absence of an Order in Council, the legislation was still in force).

**811. Royal prerogative in time of war.** In time of war and in matters relating to war the Crown enjoys generally a somewhat wider latitude in the exercise of the prerogative than in time of peace, for in such matters more stringent measures than are ordinarily allowed by the common or statute law are frequently rendered necessary for the public safety or for the restoration of peace and good order. Thus it is possible that the exercise of martial law is to some extent permissible in time of war, and various prerogatives relating to the relations between British subjects and those of foreign countries are allowed to the Crown in time of war[1].

Presumptions in favour of the liberty or property of the subject, which are usually of great effect in interpreting statutes in time of peace, become relatively weak in time of war when the safety of the realm is in danger[2].

1   As to martial law see para 821 post.
2   The counter-maxim *salus populi suprema lex* ('the safety of the people is the paramount law') is applied as a corrective. See eg *R v Halliday* [1917] AC 260 at 270, HL; *Ronnfeldt v Phillips* (1918) 35 TLR 46, CA; *Hudson's Bay Co v Maclay* (1920) 36 TLR 469 at 475; *Liversidge v Anderson* [1942] AC 206, [1941] 3 All ER 338, HL. See also WAR. As to review of the exercise of prerogative powers see paras 379–380 ante.

**812. Defence regulations.** In time of war the Crown may enter on the land of a subject, for example to erect fortifications[1] or to dig for saltpetre[2], but in both the 1914–18 and 1939–45 wars special powers were conferred by statute and regulations to take necessary action with regard to the requisition of property, the entry on land and many other national needs, and the wide scope of those powers rendered unnecessary recourse to the royal prerogative[3]. In carrying out duties under legislation passed to meet the needs of the nation in war or emergency, a person is not necessarily to be regarded as acting in implementation of the Crown's prerogative in relation to the making of war or peace[4].

1   *Warren v Smith, Magdalen College Case* (1615) 1 Roll Rep 151 at 152.
2   See King's Prerogative in Saltpetre (1606) 12 Co Rep 12.
3   See the Defence of the Realm (Consolidation) Act 1914 (repealed), and the Emergency Powers (Defence) Act 1940 s 1 (repealed), which gave power to make Defence Regulations requiring persons 'to place themselves, their services and their property' at the disposal of the Crown.
4   *Bank voor Handel en Scheepvaart NV v Slatford* [1953] 1 QB 248 at 289, [1952] 2 All ER 956 at 967, CA, per Sir Raymond Evershed MR; on appeal without affecting that dictum sub nom *Bank voor Handel en Scheepvaart NV v Administrator of Hungarian Property* [1954] AC 584, [1954] 1 All ER 969, HL.

**813. Requisitioning of British ships.** The Crown has a prerogative right in a national emergency to requisition British ships in territorial waters[1].

1   *The Sarpen* [1916] P 306 at 311, CA; *The Broadmayne* [1916] P 64 at 67–68, CA. The Crown exercised this power by proclamation of 3 August 1914. For an argument in favour of the view that the prerogative extends to British ships both on the high seas and in a foreign port see Holdsworth 'The Power of the Crown to requisition British Ships in a National Emergency' (1919) 35 LQR 12. The emergency need not amount to an 'instant and urgent necessity': *Crown of Leon (Owners) v Admiralty Comrs* [1821] 1 KB 595 at 604, DC.
    As to the Crown's right of angary (the right to appropriate the property of a neutral) see FOREIGN RELATIONS LAW vol 18 para 1903.

**814. Booty and prize.** Enemy property captured by a land force belongs to the Crown as booty of war, and enemy vessels, together in certain circumstances with neutral vessels, seized by Her Majesty's ships constitute prize and also belong to the Crown[1]. The Crown formerly had the power at common law and by statute to allot a portion of booty or of prize to the officers and men engaged in the capture[2]. The prerogative right to grant prize money to officers and crew has now been abolished[3].

1   *Banda and Kirwee Booty* (1866) LR 1 A & E 109; *The Adjutant* [1919] P 41; and see generally PRIZE.
2   *The Elsebe* (1804) 5 Ch Rob 173 at 181. Army Prize Money Act 1832 s 2 (repealed); Naval Prize Act 1864 s 55(1) (amended by the Prize Act 1939 s 1(2), Schedule Pt I).
3   Prize Act 1948 s 9(1).

**815. War: leaving the country.** There is authority for the use of proclamations in wartime to restrain any persons or classes of persons from leaving the country[1]. The common law writ of ne exeat regno might possibly also still be used as a state writ to prevent departure from the country in time of war[2]. The Crown may lay embargoes on shipping in wartime[3].

In anticipation of the outbreak of war in 1939 the Crown's prerogative powers were augmented by wide powers to make defence regulations by Order in Council[4], and those powers were used to control the departure of shipping and British subjects from the country.

1   'The established law is that the King may prohibit any of his subjects from leaving the realm': 1 Bl Com (14th Edn) 270. As to prohibiting persons from leaving the realm by proclamation see 3 Co Inst 179; Fitz Nat Brev 85; Vin Abr, Prerogative, Ia.
2   Ne exeat regno was originally a state writ granted by the Chancellor on the application of a Secretary of State either with or without cause shown: see Bacon's Law Tracts, Ordinance No 89: 1 Bl Com (14th Edn) 266; 4 Mod Rep 177 note (b). As to the present use of the writ see EQUITY vol 16 (Reissue) para 734. See also the powers of the Secretary of State under the Prevention of Terrorism (Temporary Provisions) Act 1989 to issue exclusion orders; and para 116 ante.
3   1 Bl Com (14th Edn) 263. Embargoes in time of peace are illegal: see Hale *de Portibus Maris* c 9; and PORTS AND HARBOURS.
4   Emergency Powers (Defence) Act 1939 s 1(1) (repealed). See also WAR.

**816. Recalling subjects.** The Crown enjoys the right of recalling subjects from abroad by letters under the Great Seal served by the Queen's messenger[1], disobedience to which formerly rendered the person's property in the realm liable to seizure under a commission issued by the Exchequer until the recall was complied with[2]. This prerogative, so far as it is not obsolete, applies, it seems, either in time of war or in time of peace.

1   3 Co Inst 180; 1 Hawk PC 22. The privy seal is also mentioned, but its use has now been abolished. As to use of the Great Seal see para 909 post.
2   3 Co Inst 180. This passage was cited at first instance in *HRH Prince Ernest Augustus of Hanover v A-G* [1955] Ch 440 at 447, [1955] 1 All ER 746 at 749; revsd [1956] Ch 188, [1955] 3 All ER 647, CA; affd sub nom *A-G v HRH Prince Ernest August of Hanover* [1957] AC 436, [1957] 1 All ER 49, HL.

**817. Alien enemies; blockades.** No subject of an enemy's country may enter the realm during war, and if he does so, or if he embarks upon the high seas in a vessel of his own country whilst a state of war prevails, both his person and his goods are liable to seizure[1].

1  1 Bl Com (14th Edn) 259. By the Declaration of Paris 1856 a neutral flag protects hostile goods so long as they are not contraband of war: see 10 Hertslet's Commercial Treaties p 547. For the control of aliens generally in peace or in war see BRITISH NATIONALITY, IMMIGRATION AND RACE RELATIONS vol 4(2) (Reissue) para 66; FOREIGN RELATIONS LAW vol 18 para 1723 et seq; and WAR.

**818. Explosives; arms; land.** The Crown possesses certain statutory powers, applicable in time of war or peace, relating to the control of the importation and exportation of explosives, arms and ammunition, and the control of stores of explosives[1]. There are also statutory powers for the compulsory acquisition of land and the stopping up of footpaths, which may be exercised by the Secretary of State for Defence for the service of his department or the defence of the realm[2].

1  See CUSTOMS AND EXCISE; EXPLOSIVES; and TRADE, INDUSTRY AND INDUSTRIAL RELATIONS (as regards exports and imports generally).
2  See HIGHWAYS vol 21 (Reissue) paras 172–176.

**819. Compulsory service.** The Crown may also demand, and is entitled to, the personal services of every man capable of bearing arms in case of sudden invasion or dangerous rebellion, but except on such occasions it has no power, unless such a power is conferred by statute, to compel enlistment[1].

1  *Broadfoot's Case* (1743) Fost 154 at 157–159, 175. During the 1914–18 war and since, this power was not resorted to by the Crown, which preferred to obtain the passing of Acts of Parliament imposing compulsory service: see ROYAL FORCES; WAR.

## (5) EXECUTIVE POWERS IN EMERGENCIES

**820. Power to deal with emergencies.** The Crown has the same power as a private individual of taking all measures which are absolutely and immediately necessary for the purpose of dealing with an invasion or other emergency[1]. The Crown further has prerogative power to take action to maintain the peace[2]. It has also been suggested that the Crown has by its prerogative a right to take steps to deal with an apprehended emergency, even to the extent of interfering with the rights of the subject[3], although this is almost certainly incorrect[4]; but, although this proposition cannot, probably, be maintained in its generality, the Crown has certain discretionary powers in time of war or emergency, for example the power of requisitioning ships[5]. However, no person is entitled at common law to receive from the Crown compensation in respect of damage to or destruction of property caused by acts lawfully done by or on the authority of the Crown during, or in contemplation of, the outbreak of a war in which the monarch was or is engaged[6].

1  *R v Hampden, Ship Money Case* (1637) 3 State Tr 826 at 975, 1011–1013 (Holborne's argument). Emergency legislation arising out of the 1939–45 war is considered in WAR. See also the *Report of the Inquiry into the Export of Defence Equipment and Dual-Use Goods to Iraq and Related Prosecutions* (HC Paper (1995–96) no 115) (the 'Scott Report') paras C1.20–C1.27. The Convention for the Protection of Human Rights and Fundamental Freedoms (1950) Art 15 permits a member state to take measures derogating from its obligations under the Convention 'in time of war or other public emergency threatening the life of the nation'; see para 168 ante. As to the Convention generally see para 122 ante.

2   *Harrison v Bush* (1855) 5 E & B 344 at 353. The power to take action to maintain the peace includes the power to supply equipment to a chief constable where the equipment is necessary to deal with either an actual or an apprehended threat to the peace: *R v Secretary of State for the Home Department, ex p Northumbria Police Authority* [1989] QB 26, [1987] 2 All ER 282, DC.

3   *Re Petition of Right* [1915] 3 KB 649 at 659, CA, per Lord Cozens-Hardy MR. See also note 4 infra.

4   The decision cited in note 3 supra, was adversely criticised by the House of Lords on appeal and the case was afterwards settled, the Crown consenting to pay compensation to the suppliants: see *Re X's Petition of Right* (1916) 32 TLR 699, HL. The opinion of Lord Cozens-Hardy MR is moreover in conflict with the arguments of Hampden's counsel in *R v Hampden, Ship Money Case* (1637) 3 State Tr 826, and in agreement with those put forward by the judges for the decision, which was afterwards reversed by the Ship Money Act 1640 (repealed). It is doubtful whether it is reconcilable with the decision in *A-G v De Keyser's Royal Hotel Ltd* [1920] AC 508, HL.

    During the 1939–45 war power was taken under Emergency Powers (Defence) Acts to set up special civilian courts for the trial of offenders in areas within the United Kingdom where by reason of actual or apprehended enemy action the military situation might be such that criminal justice could not be administered by the ordinary courts. These powers were never in fact exercised, and expired on 23 February 1946.

5   *The Broadmayne* [1916] P 64, CA. See also para 813 ante. The law gives no right of action for injury sustained in raising bulwarks for defence against the King's enemies: *Governor and Co of British Cast Plate Manufacturers v Meredith* (1792) 4 Term Rep 794 at 797 per Buller J; but, by statute, compensation is payable on the exercise of requisitioning and other powers conferred by emergency legislation: see COMPULSORY ACQUISITION vol 8(1) (Reissue) para 3.

6   The contrary was held by a majority in *Burmah Oil Co (Burma Trading) Ltd v Lord Advocate* [1965] AC 75, [1964] 2 All ER 348, HL, exception being made of damage or destruction in actual battle. The decision was deprived of effect and the law settled in the sense expressed above by the War Damage Act 1965 s 1(1).

**821. Martial law.** The Crown may not issue commissions in time of peace to try civilians by martial law[1]; but when there exists a state of actual war, or of insurrection, riot or rebellion amounting to war[2], the Crown and its officers may use the amount of force necessary in the circumstances to restore order[3]. This use of force is sometimes termed 'martial law'[4]. Once a state of actual war exists[5] the civil courts have no authority to call in question the actions of the military authorities[6], but it is for the civil courts to decide, if their jurisdiction is invoked, whether a state of war exists which justifies the application of martial law[7]. The powers, such as they are, of the military authorities cease and those of the civil courts are resumed ipso facto with the termination of the state of war[8]; and, in the absence of an Act of Indemnity, the civil courts may inquire into the legality of anything done during the state of war[9]. Even if there is an Act of Indemnity couched in the usual terms, malicious acts will not be protected[10]. Whether this power of using extraordinary measures is really a prerogative of the Crown or whether it is merely an example of the common law right and duty of all, ruler and subject alike, to use the amount of force necessary to suppress disorder[11], is not quite free from doubt[12]. It is, however, clear that so-called military courts set up under martial law are not really courts at all[13], and so an order of prohibition will not issue to restrain them[14]. Probably the correct view to take of martial law itself is that it is no law at all[15]. No state of martial law was declared in the United Kingdom during the two world wars[16].

1   Petition of Right (1627) ss 7, 8; *Ex p Marais* [1902] AC 109 at 115, PC, per the Earl of Halsbury LC ('the framers of the Petition of Right knew well what they meant when they made a condition of peace the ground of the illegality of unconstitutional procedure'). The words of the Petition of Right are obscure, and can be made to bear a wider interpretation. However, the issue of commissions of martial law has long been discontinued, and the term 'martial law' is now generally applied to that state of affairs which exists in time of war, when the Crown by proclamation, or by notice issued by the military authorities, warns the public that certain offences will be tried and punished by a military court. There are no English examples; for the terms of the notice issued in other countries see *Ex p Marais* supra at 113 (South Africa); *R v Allen* [1921] 2 IR 241 at 261 (Ireland). When, shortly before

the 1939–45 war, the Emergency Powers (Defence) Act 1939 (repealed) was passed, the making of provision for trial by courts-martial of persons not subject to the Naval Discipline Act or to military or air force law was expressly excepted from the powers to make defence regulations: Emergency Powers (Defence) Act 1939 s 1(5) (repealed).

2   See note 7 infra.

3   *R v Hampden, Ship Money Case* (1637) 3 State Tr 826 at 976 (Holborne's argument), and at 1162 per Croke J; *R v Nelson and Brand* (1867) Cockburn's Charge 59 at 85; Forsyth *Cases and Opinions on Constitutional Law* pp 198–199.

4   Forsyth *Cases and Opinions on Constitutional Law* pp 198–199, 556–557.

5   See note 7 infra.

6   *Ex p Marais* [1902] AC 109 at 115, PC; *Elphinstone v Bedreechund* (1830) 1 Knapp 316, PC; *A-G for Cape of Good Hope v Van Reenen, A-G for Cape of Good Hope v Smit* [1904] AC 114, PC; *R v Allen* [1921] 2 IR 241; *R (Garde) v Strickland* [1921] 2 IR 317; *R (Ronayne and Mulcahy) v Strickland* [1921] 2 IR 333; *Higgins v Willis* [1921] 2 IR 386. These Irish cases were complicated by the existence of special legislation giving the military authorities extraordinary powers to put down the insurrection, and the argument was put forward that there was no need in the circumstances for the 'exercise of martial law', and so the court should intervene. This argument was rejected in these cases, but in *Egan v Macready* [1921] 1 IR 265 it was accepted, and the prisoner released. In a later case, to which the special legislation did not apply, the same judge followed *Ex p Marais* supra; see *R (Childers) v Adjutant-General of the Provisional Forces* [1923] 1 IR 5. See also *Johnstone v O'Sullivan* [1923] 2 IR 13, CA.

7   *R (Garde) v Strickland* [1921] 2 IR 317 at 329. For the old view as to when a state of war will be deemed to exist see Opinions of Coke and Rolle, cited in 2 Rushworth's Historical Collections, Pt II, Appendix 79, 81 ('The time of peace is when the Courts of Westminster are open'). 'If the Chancery and Courts of Westminster be shut up… it is time of war, but if the courts be open it is otherwise; yet if war be in any part of the kingdom that the sheriff cannot execute the king's writ, then is tempus belli' (1 Hale PC 344; Hale, History of the Common Law 42–43; Co Litt 249a, b). The criterion was modified in *Ex p Marais* [1902] AC 109 at 114, PC, where it was said that the fact that for some purposes the civil tribunals have been permitted by the military authorities to pursue their ordinary course is not conclusive that war is not raging. It is, however, doubtful whether there is any question of permission from the military authorities, for in *R (Garde) v Strickland* supra at 331, Molony CJ protested that he sat in virtue of the King's commission and not by any permission of the military authorities. Of course, the fact that the courts need military protection in order to function is evidence of a state of war: see *R (Childers) v Adjutant-General of the Provisional Forces* [1923] 1 IR 5.

8   See *Wolfe Tone's Case* (1798) 27 State Tr 613 at 625; *Higgins v Willis* [1921] 2 IR 386; *R (O'Brien) v Military Governor of North Dublin Union Military Internment Camp* [1924] 1 IR 32, Ir CA.

9   *Higgins v Willis* [1921] 2 IR 386.

10   *Wright v Fitzgerald* (1799) 27 State Tr 759 at 765; Indemnity Act 1920 s 1(1) (repealed).

11   As to this see *R v Pinney* (1832) 3 B & Ad 947; and Lord Justice Bowen's Report on the Featherstone Riots 1893–94 (Cd 7234).

12   See the remarks of Blackburn J in *R v Eyre* (1868) Finlason's Report at 74. In favour of the view that the power to proclaim martial law in proper circumstances exists as a prerogative of the Crown there may be cited the clauses of certain statutes authorising the exercise of martial law in Ireland, which save the right of the Crown 'for the public safety to resort to the exercise of martial law against open enemies and traitors: see 27 Geo 3 c 15 (1787) (Irish); Suppression of Rebellion in Ireland Act 1803 (repealed); Suppression of Disturbances and Associations in Ireland Act 1833 s 40 (repealed).

In favour of the opposing view there may be cited *R v Nelson and Brand* (1867) Cockburn's Charge 59 at 74; *Grant v Gould* (1792) 2 Hy Bl 69 at 98; *R v Eyre* supra at 73–74 per Blackburn J; Forsyth *Cases and Opinions on Constitutional Law* 198–199, 553, 556–557.

There does not seem to be much practical difference in the consequences of holding one view or the other; on either view the powers of the Crown and its officials are limited both as to their extent and their duration by the necessity of the case. This at least was the opinion of the King's Bench Division in Ireland in *R (Ronayne and Mulcahy) v Strickland* [1921] 2 IR 333; and the Court of Appeal in *Johnstone v O'Sullivan* [1923] 2 IR 13, CA, considered that any government has an inherent power to organise a force to suppress rebellion. In *Egan v Macready* [1921] 1 IR 265, O'Connor MR held that the exercise of martial law was a part of the royal prerogative, and as such was regulated by the Restoration of Order in Ireland Act 1920 (repealed), and accordingly he held that the civil courts retained jurisdiction to interfere with the military authorities and compel them to act in accordance with the Act (see *A-G v De Keyser's Royal Hotel Ltd* [1920] AC 508, HL), disagreeing in this with the decision of the King's Bench Division in *R v Allen* [1921] 2 IR 241.

It is customary for Parliament to pass Acts of Indemnity after the occasion is over, perhaps because the existence of the prerogative is doubtful, and certainly because it is necessary to protect persons who have acted in good faith in a time of war or insurrection (for examples of such Acts see the

Indemnity and Special Tribunals Act 1900 (No 6 of 1900) (Cape of Good Hope); the General Indemnity Act 1902 (No 4 of 1902) (Cape of Good Hope); and the Indemnity Act 1920 (repealed)). Such Acts usually substitute a right to compensation from the public funds (s 2). They are not generally so drawn as to protect persons who have acted in bad faith and without due regard to humanity (see text and note 10 supra).

13   *Tilonko v A-G of Natal* [1907] AC 93 at 94, PC, per Lord Halsbury; *Re Clifford and O'Sullivan* [1921] 2 AC 570, HL.

14   *Re Clifford and O'Sullivan* [1921] 2 AC 570, HL.

15   *Tilonko v A-G of Natal* [1907] AC 93 at 94, PC, per Lord Halsbury: 'It is by this time a very familiar observation that what is called 'martial law' is no law at all. The notion that 'martial law' exists by reason of the proclamation... is an entire delusion. The right to administer force against force in actual war does not depend upon the proclamation of martial law at all. It depends upon the question whether there is war or not'. See also the opinion of Sir John Campbell, Attorney General, and Sir R M Rolfe, Solicitor General, with regard to the Canadian disturbances in 1838: Forsyth *Cases and Opinions on Constitutional Law* 198.

16   The Emergency Powers (Defence) (No 2) Act 1940, gave authority for special war zone courts to exercise criminal jurisdiction if, on account of military action, criminal justice had to be more speedily administered than in the ordinary courts; see Wade and Bradley *Constitutional and Administrative Law* (11th Edn, 1993) pp 584–587.
     Where Her Majesty's forces are in armed occupation of hostile territory, it is competent to her commanders to declare that martial law shall prevail in that territory, and to lay down rules which they deem essential for the preservation of her forces and military stores. In such a case, the jurisdiction of courts-martial extends over all persons resorting to that territory (not being in the military or naval service of an independent sovereign): see Stephens, Gifford and Smith, *Manual of Naval Law* (4th Edn) pp 127–128. It is this species of martial law that the Duke of Wellington had in mind when he described it as the will of the general in command of the army. But martial law in this sense is quite outside the range of municipal law: 'Martial law must be distinguished according as it is a foreign or international fact or as it is a domestic or municipal fact' (Mr Cushing (Attorney General of the United States of America) in 8 Opinions of Attorneys-General 369). After the occupation of Germany in 1944 a system of courts was set up by the allied forces and exercised jurisdiction under ordinances promulgated by the allies as occupying forces; it came to an end in 1955.

## 822. Proclamation of emergency.

**822. Proclamation of emergency.** If it appears to Her Majesty that events of a specified nature have occurred or are about to occur, Her Majesty may by proclamation declare that a state of emergency exists[1]. These events are those of such a nature as to be calculated, by interfering with the supply and distribution of food, water, fuel or light, or with the means of locomotion, to deprive the community, or any substantial portion of the community, of the essentials of life. No proclamation is to be in force for more than one month, without prejudice to the issue of another proclamation at or before the end of that period[2].

Where a proclamation of emergency has been made, the occasion of it must forthwith be communicated to Parliament[3]. If Parliament is at the time separated by such adjournment or prorogation as will not expire within five days, a proclamation must be issued for the meeting of Parliament within five days, and Parliament must meet and sit accordingly[4].

Where a proclamation of emergency has been made, and so long as it remains in force, the Crown has power by Order in Council to make regulations for securing the essentials of life to the community[5]. Such regulations must be laid before Parliament as soon as may be after they are made, and are not to continue in force after the expiration of seven days from the time when they are so laid unless a resolution is passed by both Houses providing for their continuance[6]. The regulations may be added to, altered or revoked by resolution of both Houses or by regulations made in like manner and subject to the like provisions as the original regulations[7]. The expiry or revocation of any regulations so made is not to be deemed to have affected their previous operation, or the validity of any action taken under them, or any penalty or punishment incurred in respect of any contravention or failure to comply with them, or any proceeding or remedy in respect of any such punishment or penalty[8].

Emergency regulations may confer or impose on a Secretary of State or other government department, or any other persons in the service of the Crown or acting on behalf of the Crown, such powers and duties as the Crown may deem necessary (1) for the preservation of the peace; (2) for securing and regulating the supply and distribution of food, water, fuel, light and other necessities; (3) for maintaining the means of transit or locomotion; and (4) for any other purposes essential to the public safety and the life of the community[9]. The regulations may make such provisions incidental to these powers as may appear to the Crown to be required for making the exercise of them effective[10], but they may not impose any form of compulsory military service or industrial conscription, or make it an offence to take part in a strike, or peacefully to persuade others to do so[11].

Emergency regulations may also provide for the trial, by courts of summary jurisdiction, of persons guilty of offences against them; but the maximum penalty is to be imprisonment for three months or a fine not exceeding level five on the standard scale[12] or both, or not exceeding a lesser amount together with the forfeiture of any goods or money in respect of which the offence has been committed[13]. The existing procedure in criminal cases is not to be altered, nor is there to be any fine or imprisonment without trial[14].

1   Emergency Powers Act 1920 s 1(1) (amended by the Emergency Powers Act 1964 s 1). Such proclamations are known as proclamations of emergency: Emergency Powers Act 1920 s 1(1) (as so amended).
2   Ibid s 1(1) (as amended: see note 1 supra).
3   Ibid s 1(2).
4   Ibid s 1(2). Parliament must sit on the day appointed by the proclamation, and must continue to sit and act in like manner as if it had stood adjourned or prorogued to the same day: s 1(2).
5   Ibid s 2(1).
6   Ibid s 2(2).
7   Ibid s 2(4) (amended by the Statute Law Revision Act 1963; and the Statute Law (Repeals) Act 1986).
8   Emergency Powers Act 1920 s 2(5).
9   Ibid s 2(1).
10   Ibid s 2(1).
11   Ibid s 2(1) proviso.
12   'Standard scale' means the standard scale of maximum fines for summary offences as set out in the Criminal Justice Act 1982 s 37(2) (as substituted): Interpretation Act 1978 s 5, Sch 1 (amended by the Criminal Justice Act 1988 s 170(1), Sch 15 para 58(a)). See CRIMINAL LAW vol 11(2) (Reissue) para 808; and MAGISTRATES. At the date at which this volume states the law, the standard scale is as follows: level 1, £200; level 2, £500; level 3, £1,000; level 4, £2,500; level 5, £5,000: Criminal Justice Act 1982 s 37(2) (substituted by the Criminal Justice Act 1991 s 17(1)). As to the determination of the amount of the fine actually imposed, as distinct from the level on the standard scale which it may not exceed, see the Criminal Justice Act 1991 s 18 (substituted by the Criminal Justice Act 1993 s 65); and MAGISTRATES.
13   Emergency Powers Act 1920 s 2(3) (amended by the Criminal Justice Act 1982 s 41; and the Statute Law (Repeals) Act 1993). See also the Criminal Justice Act 1948 s 1(2).
14   Emergency Powers Act 1920 s 2(3) proviso.

## (6) PARDONS AND REPRIEVES

**823. Pardons.** The Crown enjoys the exclusive right of granting pardons[1], a privilege which cannot be claimed by any other person either by grant or prescription[2]. It is usually delegated to colonial governors and to Governors General[3], although in so doing the monarch does not entirely divest herself of the prerogative[4].

In general, pardon may be granted either before or after conviction[5]; but no pardon is pleadable in bar of an impeachment by the Commons[6], and the penalty of imprisonment for life imposed by statute for committing to prison out of the realm cannot be remitted[7]. A pardon may be granted posthumously[8].

The right of pardon is, moreover, confined to offences of a public nature where the Crown is prosecutor and has some vested interest either in fact or by implication[9]; and where any right or benefit is vested in a subject by statute or otherwise, the Crown, by a pardon, cannot affect it or take it away[10]. The prerogative to grant pardons extends to ecclesiastical disciplinary offences[11].

1  According to figures supplied by the Home Office, 22 free pardons were granted in 1993 (19 in 1992; 29 in 1991; 28 in 1990). Of these, 21 were on grounds affecting the original conviction and one on account of technical irregularities in the conviction or sentence; none were granted as a reward for assistance to the authorities and none on medical or compassionate grounds. In 1993, there were 34 remissions of sentence (67 in 1992; 49 in 1991 and 100 in 1990). Of these, seven were granted as a reward for assistance to the authorities; two on medical grounds and 25 classified as 'other cases'. The Crown's right to grant a free pardon is not affected by the Rehabilitation of Offenders Act 1974 s 4(1) (which deals with the effect of rehabilitation for the purposes of the law): s 7(1)(a).
2  See 3 Co Inst 233.
3  See COMMONWEALTH vol 6 (Reissue) para 1000 note 1. As to governors generally see COMMONWEALTH vol 6 (Reissue) para 994 et seq.
4  See the Speaker's ruling of 10 March 1947 (434 HC Official Report (5th series), 10 March 1947, col 959), and his further statement on 1 May 1947 (436 HC Official Report (5th series), 1 May 1947, col 2185).
5  3 Co Inst 233; and see *R v Boyes* (1861) 1 B & S 311. If granted before conviction it must be specially pleaded: *R v Boyes* supra.
6  Act of Settlement s 3. This provision does not negative the Crown's right of pardoning after impeachment. Thus three of the lords impeached and attainted in 1715 were subsequently pardoned. The principle of excluding a pardon as a bar to an impeachment by the Commons was first affirmed in the case of the Earl of Danby by a resolution of the House of Commons: see Commons Journals, 5 May 1679. As to the citation of the Act of Settlement see para 35 note 3 ante.
7  Habeas Corpus Act 1679 s 11; Criminal Law Act 1967 s 13(2), Sch 4 Pt III para 1.
8  See *R v Secretary of State for the Home Department, ex p Bentley* [1994] QB 349, [1993] 4 All ER 442, DC, where the Divisional Court invited the Home Secretary to reconsider his decision to refuse a posthumous pardon.
9  3 Co Inst 235–240.
10 *Biggin's Case* (1599) 5 Co Rep 50a, b; *Hall's Case* (1604) 5 Co Rep 51a. So the Crown may not pardon the commission of a public nuisance before conviction whilst it continues (Bac Abr, Pardon, B); nor release a recognisance to keep the peace, nor discharge an action already begun so as to deprive a common informer of the penalty (3 Co Inst 238), the maxim of law applicable in all such cases being *non potest rex gratiam facere cum injuria et damno aliorum* ('the King cannot confer a favour on one man to the injury and damage of others'): see 3 Co Inst 236; *Thomas v Sorrell* (1673) Vaugh 330 at 343). As to the Crown's power to remit penalties in certain cases, even though payable to a private person, see para 828 note 2 post.
11 See the Ecclesiastical Jurisdiction Measure 1963 s 83(2)(a), which provides that nothing in that Act affects any royal prerogative.

## 824. Nature of pardon.

**824. Nature of pardon.** The pardon is part of the prerogative of mercy. The prerogative is not an arbitrary monarchical right of grace and favour[1], but a constitutional safeguard against mistakes[2]. The prerogative of mercy is capable of being exercised in many different circumstances and over a wide range[3]. The prerogative is a flexible power and its exercise can and should be adapted to meet the circumstances of the particular case[4].

Formerly pardons were in all cases required to pass under the Great Seal[5], but a pardon in respect of any offence, if granted by warrant under the royal sign manual[6], countersigned by the Secretary of State, has now the same effect as a pardon under the Great Seal[7].

1  *Burt v Governor General of New Zealand* [1992] 3 NZLR 672 at 681.
2  *R v Secretary of State for the Home Department, ex p Bentley* [1994] QB 349 at 365, [1993] 4 All ER 442 at 455, DC, per Watkins LJ.

3    *R v Secretary of State for the Home Department, ex p Bentley* [1994] QB 349 at 363, [1993] 4 All ER 442 at 453, DC, per Watkins LJ.

4    *R v Secretary of State for the Home Department, ex p Bentley* [1994] QB 349 at 365, [1993] 4 All ER 442 at 454, DC, per Watkins LJ.

5    *Bullock v Dodds* (1819) 2 B & Ald 258 at 277; *Gough v Davies* (1856) 2 K & J 623; 4 Bl Com (14th Edn) 400. As to use of the Great Seal see para 909 post.

6    As to the sign manual see para 908 post.

7    Criminal Law Act 1967 s 9.

**825. Grant of pardon.** A pardon is usually granted on the advice of the Home Secretary[1], to whose notice the matter is brought either on a recommendation to mercy by the judge when passing sentence[2], or on petition by the criminal himself or friends on his behalf[3]. The exercise of the prerogative of mercy in a case where a death sentence is under consideration cannot be the subject of discussion in Parliament until the sentence has been carried out[4]. The courts may not inquire into the merits of the exercise of the prerogative, but there may be cases in which its exercise is reviewable[5]. While a power to pardon can expunge past offences, it cannot be used to dispense with criminal responsibility for an offence which has not yet been committed, and waive responsibility for future offences[6].

Where a person has been convicted on indictment and found not guilty by reason of insanity, or been found by a jury to be under disability and to have done the act or made the omission charged against him, the Secretary of State[7] may, if he thinks fit, at any time either refer the whole case to the Court of Appeal, the case being then treated for all purposes as an appeal to the court by that person, or, if the Secretary of State desires the court's assistance on any point arising in the case, refer that point to the court for its opinion on it, in which event the court must consider the point so referred, and furnish the Secretary of State with its opinion accordingly[8].

1    As to the manner in which petitions are dealt with by the Home Office see the *Report of the Committee of Inquiry into the case of Adolf Beck* (Cd 2315) (1904). The uncontrolled responsibility of the Home Secretary in the matter of reprieves goes back at least as far as 1830: see Mackintosh *The British Cabinet* (2nd Edn) p 328 note 4. See also Sir Edward Troup *The Home Office (Whitehall Series)* ch V.

2    *R v Oxford County Inhabitants* (1811) 13 East 411 at 416 note (b).

3    This right to petition cannot be denied, having been expressly confirmed by the Bill of Rights s 1: see para 419 ante. As to the history and citation of the Bill of Rights see para 35 note 3 ante.

4    See the Speaker's ruling of 10 March 1947 (434 HC Official Report (5th series), 10 March 1947, col 959); and his statement of 1 May 1947 (436 HC Official Report (5th series), 1 May 1947, col 2179) ('A minister is responsible to the King, and not to the House, for the advice he proposes to tender to His Majesty, though he is responsible to the House for the advice once it has been tendered'). Cf the discussion on a disallowed motion relating to the prerogative of mercy in the House on 27 January 1953 (510 HC Official Report (5th series), 27 January 1953, cols 845–864). Although sentence of death may still be pronounced in a few cases of crime, of which high treason is one, the abolition of capital punishment for murder by the Murder (Abolition of Death Penalty) Act 1965 (made permanent by resolution of both Houses of Parliament on 31 December 1969) obviates the need to exercise the prerogative of mercy to negative a death sentence.

5    Eg where the Home Secretary has taken into account irrelevant or discriminatory considerations. It is for the courts to decide on a case by case basis whether the matter in question is reviewable or not. In 1992 the Home Secretary, Mr Kenneth Clarke, refused to recommend a posthumous pardon for Derek Bentley. His refusal was the subject of an application for judicial review brought by the late Mr Bentley's sister. Watkins LJ held that the Home Secretary had not given sufficient consideration to the availability of a conditional pardon, suitable to the circumstances of this case. No order was made but the court invited the Home Secretary to consider afresh that possibility: *R v Secretary of State for the Home Department, ex p Bentley* [1994] QB 349, [1993] 4 All ER 442, DC. See also *Burt v Governor General of New Zealand* [1992] 3 NZLR 672. The exercise of the prerogative of mercy under the Constitution of the Bahamas arts 90 and 92 in death sentence cases was not amenable to judicial review: *Reckley v Minister of Public Safety and Immigration (No 2)* [1996] 1 AC 527, [1996] 1 All ER 562, PC; following *De Freitas v Benny* [1976] AC 239, [1975] 3 WLR 388, PC.

6    *A-G of Trinidad and Tobago v Phillip* [1995] 1 AC 396, [1995] 1 All ER 93, PC.

7   Ie normally the Home Secretary. As to the performance of the duties of a Secretary of State by one or
    any of them see para 355 text and note 18 ante.

8   Criminal Appeal Act 1968 s 17(1) (amended by the Criminal Procedure (Insanity and Unfitness to
    Plead) Act 1991 ss 7, 8(2), Sch 3 para 4). Note that this provision is to be repealed, as from a day to
    be appointed, by the Criminal Appeal Act 1995 ss 3, 29(2), Sch 3. As the reference of a whole case
    is treated as an appeal, further appeal, if a point of general public importance is involved, will lie to
    the House of Lords: see the Criminal Appeal Act 1968 s 33. As to the House of Lords see para 204
    ante; and PARLIAMENT.

## 826. Effect of pardon.

Pardons may be free[1], conditional[2] or in the form of a
remission or partial remission of sentence[3]. The effect of a free pardon is to clear the
person from all consequences of the offence for which it is granted[4], and from all
statutory or other disqualifications following upon conviction[5], but not to remove
the conviction[6].

1   As to the policy of successive Home Secretaries in granting free pardons see *R v Secretary of State for the
    Home Department, ex p Bentley* [1994] QB 349, [1993] 4 All ER 442, DC.

2   A conditional pardon substitutes for one punishment another, lesser sentence. As to the policy of
    successive Home Secretaries in granting conditional pardons see *R v Secretary of State for the Home
    Department, ex p Bentley* [1994] QB 349, [1993] 4 All ER 442, DC; and *A-G of Trinidad and Tobago v
    Phillip* [1995] 1 AC 396, [1995] 1 All ER 93, PC (considering the validity of pardons subject to lawful
    conditions, such as the prompt laying down of arms in the case of insurrection).

3   See *R v Secretary of State for the Home Department, ex p Bentley* [1994] QB 349, [1993] 4 All ER 442, DC.

4   Bac Abr, Pardon, H; *Hay v Tower Division of London Justices* (1890) 24 QBD 561 at 565; 2 Hale
    PC 278. The effect is confined to the offence for which it was granted: see *R v Harrod* (1846)
    2 Car & Kir 294. 'The effect of a free pardon is such as, in the words of the pardon itself, to remove
    from the subject of the pardon 'all pains penalties and punishments whatsoever that from the said
    conviction may ensue', but not to eliminate the conviction itself ... . Constitutionally, the Crown no
    longer has a prerogative of justice, but only a prerogative of mercy. It cannot therefore ... remove a
    conviction, but only pardon its effects. The Court of Appeal, Criminal Division, is the only body
    which has statutory power to quash a conviction': *R v Foster* [1985] QB 115 at 130, [1984] 2 All
    ER 679 at 687, CA, per Watkins LJ. See also *A-G of Trinidad and Tobago v Phillip* [1995] 1 AC 396,
    [1995] 1 All ER 93, PC, where, following an insurrection in which the Prime Minister and other
    ministers were held hostage, the acting President granted a pardon in the form of a general amnesty
    to the rebels. The rebels were subsequently arrested and charged with treason, murder and other
    offences, but were granted a writ of habeas corpus and ordered to be released from detention on the
    grounds that the pardon was valid. The pardon was held by the Privy Council to be invalid because
    it related to offences which had not yet been committed.

5   *Hay v Tower Division of London Justices* (1890) 24 QBD 561; *Bennet v Easedale* (1626) Cro Car 55. In the
    days when a conviction disqualified a man from being a witness, a pardon removed the disqualification:
    *Fine's Case* (1623) Godb 288; *R v Gully* (1773) 1 Leach 98 at 99; 2 Hawk PC (1824 Edn) 547. The
    disqualification was removed in all cases by the Evidence Act 1843 (repealed). As to the equitable claim
    of an accomplice who turns King's evidence to the mercy of the Crown see *R v Rudd* (1775) 1 Leach
    115 at 121, 125. Quaere whether, since the decision in *R v Secretary of State for the Home Department, ex p
    Bentley* [1994] QB 349, [1993] 4 All ER 442, DC, it is still the case that a pardon makes a person, as it
    were, a new man, so as to enable him to maintain an action against any person afterwards defaming him
    in respect of the offence for which he was convicted: see *Cuddington v Wilkins* (1615) Hob 67 at 81;
    2 Hawk PC (1824 Edn) 547; and cf *Leyman v Latimer* (1878) 3 ExD 352.

6   See *R v Foster* [1985] QB 115, [1984] 2 All ER 679, CA.

## 827. Proclamations promising pardon.

A proclamation promising pardon does
not have the legal effect of a pardon, but following such a proclamation the court will
defer execution of sentence and so allow time for the prisoner to apply for a pardon[1].

1   *R v Garside and Mosley* (1834) 2 Ad & El 266. As to the cases in which a person has an equitable claim to
    pardon see *R v Rudd* (1775) 1 Leach 115; 2 Hawk PC, c 37. See also See also *A-G of Trinidad and Tobago
    v Phillip* [1995] 1 AC 396, [1995] 1 All ER 93, PC, cited in para 826 note 4 ante.

**828. Reprieves.** The Crown may exercise the prerogative right of granting a reprieve, which is effected by announcing its pleasure in any way to the court[1], and may remit penalties in certain cases[2].

1   2 Hale PC 412. Reprieves may also be granted by the judge on his own initiative: 2 Hale PC 412. The Crown's right to grant a reprieve is not affected by the Rehabilitation of Offenders Act 1974 s 4(1) (which deals with the effect of rehabilitation for the purposes of the law): s 7(1)(a).
2   Her Majesty may remit in whole or in part any sum of money imposed under any Act as a penalty or forfeiture on a convicted offender, even though the money is payable in whole or in part to some party other than the Crown. Imprisonment for non-payment of any sum of money so imposed may also be remitted, even though the money may be payable in whole or in part to some party other than the Crown: Remission of Penalties Act 1859 s 1 (amended by the Statute Law Revision Act 1892; and the Northern Ireland (Modification of Enactments No 1) Order 1973, SI 1973/2163, art 14(2), Sch 6). As to the circumstances under which the Remission of Penalties Act 1859 applies see *Todd v Robinson* (1884) 12 QBD 530; *Bradlaugh v Clarke* (1883) 8 App Cas 354 at 374, HL. As to the effect of the remission of a penalty or forfeiture see *Gough v Davies* (1856) 2 K & J 623. See also CRIMINAL LAW.

**829. Compensation for miscarriages of justice.** There is statutory provision for the payment of compensation in cases of miscarriages of justice[1]; and there is still a residuary prerogative power to make ex gratia payments to those who have spent a period in custody following a wrongful conviction or charge[2].

1   See the Criminal Justice Act 1988 s 133 (as amended); and CRIMINAL LAW vol 11(2) (Reissue) paras 1521–1522.
2   See CRIMINAL LAW vol 11(2) (Reissue) paras 1523–1524.

**830. Criminal Cases Review Commission.** The Criminal Appeal Act 1995 contains provisions creating a body corporate to be known as the Criminal Cases Review Commission. The commission is to refer summary convictions to the Crown Court, and convictions on indictment to the Court of Appeal, if it considers that there is a real possibility that the conviction, verdict or finding would not be upheld were the reference to be made because of an argument or evidence not raised in the proceedings which led to it, or if there are other exceptional circumstances which the commission considers justify the making of a reference[1].

1   See the Criminal Appeal Act 1995 Pt II (ss 8–25) (in force as from a day to be appointed under s 32): and CRIMINAL LAW.

## (7) THE GRANTING OF HONOURS

**831. Titles of honour.** By convention the monarch's powers in relation to honours are exercised on the advice of the Prime Minister. The monarch enjoys the sole right of conferring all titles of honour, dignities and precedence[1], and no subject can acquire a new title or dignity except by grant from the Crown, unless it be conferred by Act of Parliament[2], or acquired by marriage (in the case of a female)[3], or obtained by prescription, which, however, presupposes a lost grant[4].

Titles of honour are conferred either by express grant in the form of letters patent, or by writ of summons in the case of peerages, or by direct corporeal investiture, as in the case of knights[5].

1   4 Co Inst 361, 363; 1 Bl Com (14th Edn) 271. The King is the fountain of all honour and dignity: *Prince's Case* (1606) 8 Co Rep 1a at 18b. The Crown's right of granting precedence was declared by the House of Lords Precedence Act 1539 s 1. As to honours conferred upon British subjects by foreign

states see PEERAGES AND DIGNITIES.

2    Com Dig, Dignity, C 5. The House of Lords cannot by itself confer a new title, although it enjoys the right of adjudicating on disputed peerage claims if the Crown refers the question to it: see *R v Knollys* (1694) 1 Ld Raym 10. As to the House of Lords see para 204 ante; and PARLIAMENT.

3    Co Litt 16b.

4    Co Litt 16a.

5    1 Bl Com (14th Edn) 272. See also PEERAGES AND DIGNITIES.

**832. Conferring of honours.** Subject to certain restrictions[1], the monarch can create any new title or dignity which did not exist before[2], and can confer any title or precedence upon such of her subjects as she pleases[3].

It is usual, however, where titles are conferred as a reward for parliamentary or other public services, for the Crown to be guided by the advice of the Prime Minister[4]; and although no stated rule exists as to the times at which honours are conferred, such occasions as the birthday of the monarch, New Year's Day, or a change of administration, are usually marked by the bestowal of honours.

It is the regular practice for each incoming Prime Minister to appoint three Privy Counsellors to act as a Political Honours Scrutiny Committee, for the purpose of considering the character and antecedents of persons on whom it is proposed to confer honours, and to report to the Prime Minister[5].

1    As to restrictions on the right to create peers see para 212 ante.

2    *Anon* (1611) 12 Co Rep 81; 1 Bl Com (14th Edn) 271.

3    4 Co Inst 361. By the free distribution of peerages the Crown might ensure the passing of any measure by the House of Lords, as was done by Queen Anne in 1712 with regard to the Treaty of Utrecht. In 1719 a bill restraining the creation of peers within certain limits was passed by the House of Lords but rejected by the Commons. No statutory restraint has since been attempted (see Pike *Constitutional History of the House of Lords* (1894) p 363). As to the House of Commons see PARLIAMENT. As to the House of Lords see para 204 ante; and PARLIAMENT.

4    Her Majesty reserves to herself an absolute discretion in conferring the Order of Merit, the Order of the Garter, the Order of the Thistle and the Royal Victorian Order.

5    See the Report of the *Royal Commission on Honours* (Cmd 1789) (1922) paras 24–28; and see eg 57 HL Official Report (5th series), 26 June 1924, col 1068. See further para 526 note 11 ante.

**833. Prevention of abuses.** It is an offence to obtain or attempt to obtain any gift, money or valuable consideration as an inducement or reward for procuring or endeavouring to procure the grant of a dignity or title of honour; and it is also an offence to make or offer such a gift[1].

1    See the Honours (Prevention of Abuses) Act 1925 s 1(1), (2); Criminal Law Act 1967 s 1(1). As to the penalties for these offences see the Honours (Prevention of Abuses) Act 1925 s 1(3) (as amended); and CRIMINAL LAW vol 11(1) (Reissue) para 285.

**834. Arms, awards and decorations.** The Crown has a prerogative right to grant arms[1], awards[2], decorations and medals[3].

1    For an example of a royal licence to adopt a changed surname and arms see the London Gazette, 19 November 1971.

2    As to the royal warrant creating the Queen's Award to Industry in recognition of outstanding achievements in industry in increasing exports or in technological innovation see the London Gazette, 22 March 1964, and the London Gazette, 13 April 1971.

3    For an example of the award of the Queen's Police Medal for Distinguished Service see the London Gazette, 19 March 1996.

## (8) PUBLIC RECORDS

**835. Definition of public records.** The term 'public records' in the Public Records Act 1958 includes not only written records but records conveying information by any other means whatsoever[1]. Subject to certain provisions[2], administrative and departmental records belonging to Her Majesty, whether in the United Kingdom or elsewhere, in right of Her Majesty's government in the United Kingdom and, in particular (1) records of, or held in, any department of the government; or (2) records of any office, commission or other body or establishment whatsoever under the government, are public records[3]. However, this does not apply to:

(a)　records of any government department or body which is wholly or mainly concerned with Scottish affairs, or which carries on its activities wholly or mainly in Scotland[4];

(b)　registers, or certified copies of entries in registers, being registers or certified copies kept or deposited in the General Register Office under or in pursuance of any enactment, whether past or future, which provides for the registration of births, deaths, marriages or adoptions[5];

(c)　records of the Duchy of Lancaster[6];

(d)　records of the office of the Public Trustee relating to individual trusts[7].

The administrative and departmental records of the bodies and establishments set out in the Act[8] are public records, whether or not they are records belonging to Her Majesty[9].

Records[10] of specified courts and tribunals (but not those courts or tribunals whose jurisdiction extends only to Scotland or Northern Ireland[11]) are also public records for the purposes of the Act[12], and so are records of the Chancery of England[13].

Public records include (i) all records within the meaning of the Public Record Office Act 1838 or to which that Act was applied which, at the commencement of the Public Records Act 1958[14], were in the custody of the Master of the Rolls in pursuance of that Act[15]; (ii) all records which at the commencement of the Public Records Act 1958 were in the Public Record Office and under the charge and superintendence of the Master of the Rolls[16]; and (iii) all records forming part of the same series as any series of documents falling under heads (i) or (ii) above[17].

Her Majesty may by Order in Council direct that any description of records not falling within the foregoing provisions are to be treated as public records, but no recommendation may be made to make such an order unless a draft of it has been laid before Parliament and approved by resolution of each House of Parliament[18]. A question whether any records or description of records are public records must be referred to and determined by the Lord Chancellor[19].

1　Public Records Act 1958 s 10(1).
2　Ie the provisions of ibid s 10(1), Sch 1 para 2.
3　Ibid Sch 1 paras 1, 2(1).
4　Ibid Sch 1 para 2(2)(a).
5　Ibid Sch 1 para 2(2)(b).
6　Ibid Sch 1 para 2(2)(c). This is subject to the provisions of Sch 1 para 4: see text and notes 10–12 infra.
7　Ibid Sch 1 para 2(2)(d).
8　The bodies and establishments under government departments are: (1) Agricultural Wages Board; (2) Agricultural Wages Committees; (3) National Farm Survey; (4) Official seed testing station for England and Wales; (5) Meteorological Office; (6) National Health Service Authorities (including National Health Service Trusts) other than local health authorities; (7) Family Practitioner Committees; (8) Health Service hospitals within the meaning of the National Health Service Act 1977 (except (a) records of endowments passing to Boards of Governors under the National Health Service Act 1946 s 7; (b) records relating to funds held by hospital boards and committees under ss 59, 60; (c) records of private patients admitted under s 5; (d) records of property passing to regional, area or district health authorities

or special health authorities under the National Health Service Reorganisation Act 1973 ss 23–26 or the National Health Service Act 1977 s 92; (e) records of property held by a regional, area or district health authority or special health authority under the National Health Service Reorganisation Act 1973 s 21 or s 22, or the National Health Service Act 1977 s 90 or s 91); (f) records of trust property passing to a health authority or special health authority by virtue of the Health Authorities Act 1995 or under the National Health Service Act 1977 s 92 or held by a health authority under s 90 or s 91 of that Act); (9) Welsh Board of Health; (9) Office of the Metropolitan Police Commissioner; (10) Office of the Receiver for the Metropolitan Police District; (11) National Dock Labour Board; (12) National Institute of Houseworkers Limited; (13) Wages Boards and Wages Councils; (14) National Insurance Advisory Committee; (15) Industrial Injuries Advisory Council; (16) Attendance Allowance Board; (17) National Insurance and Industrial Injuries Joint Authorities; (18) Workmen's Compensation Supplementation Board; (19) Pneumoconiosis and Byssinosis Benefit Board; (20) Occupational Pensions Board; (21) Air Transport Advisory Council; (22) Airworthiness Requirements Board; (23) Civil Aviation Authority; (24) Legal Aid Board: Public Records Act 1958 Sch 1 para 3 Table Pt I (amended by the Defence (Transfer of Functions) Act 1964 ss 1, 3(2); the National Heritage Act 1983 s 40, Sch 6; the Secretary of State for Social Services Order 1968, SI 1968/1699, art 5(4); the National Health Service Reorganisation Act 1973 ss 57, 58, Sch 4 para 82; the National Health Service Act 1977 s 129, Sch 15 para 22; the Health Services Act 1980 ss 1, 2, Sch 1 Pt I para 12; the Health Authorities Act 1995 s 2(1), Sch 1 para 90; the Family Practitioner Committees (Consequential Modifications) Order 1985, SI 1985/39; the National Health Service and Community Care Act 1990 s 66(1), Sch 9 para 6; the Secretary of State for Employment and Productivity Order 1968, SI 1968/729; the National Insurance (Old Persons' and Widows' Pensions and Attendance Allowances) Act 1970 s 9, Sch 2 Pt 1 para 2; the Social Security Act 1973 s 100, Sch 27 para 19(a), (b); the Social Security Pensions Act 1975 s 65(3), Sch 5; the Transfer of Functions (Trade and Industry) Order 1983, SI 1983/1127; the Civil Aviation Act 1982 s 109, Sch 15 para 3; and the Legal Aid Act 1988 s 45(1), (3), Sch 5 para 1). As from a day to be appointed the entries 'Authorised Conveyancing Practitioners Board' and 'Conveyancing Ombudsman' are inserted at the appropriate places by the Courts and Legal Services Act 1990 s 125(3), Sch 18 para 1(1). As from a day to be appointed the entry 'Occupational Pensions Board' is repealed by the Pensions Act 1995 ss 151, 177, Sch 5 para 1, Sch 7 Pt III.

Other establishments and organisations are: Anglo-Egyptian Resettlement Board; Armouries; Board of Trustees of the National Museums and Galleries on Merseyside; British Coal Corporation; British Museum (including the Natural History Museum); British Telecommunications; Catering Wages Commission; Coal Authority; Coal Industry Social Welfare Organisation; Commission on Industrial Relations; Countryside Council for England and Wales; Crown Agents for Oversea Governments and Administrations (before and after their reconstitution as a body corporate) except when acting for governments or authorities outside Her Majesty's Dominions; Crown Agents Holding and Realisation Board; Curriculum and Assessment Authority for Wales; Data Protection Registrar; Development Commission; Environment Agency; Funding Agency for Schools; Further and Higher Education Funding Councils for England and Wales; Historic Buildings and Monuments Commission for England; Imperial War Museum; Irish Sailors' and Soldiers' Land Trust; Legal Services Ombudsman; London Museum; Lord Chancellor's Advisory Committee on Legal Education and Conduct; Millenium Commission; Monopolies Commission; National Audit Office; National Gallery; National Maritime Museum; National Parks Commission; National Portrait Gallery; National Savings Committee; Nature Conservancy Council for England; Office of the Director General of Fair Trading; Pensions Ombudsman; Post Office; Remploy Limited; Royal Botanic Gardens, Kew; Royal Greenwich Observatory; Schools Curriculum and Assessment Authority; Schools Funding Council for Wales; Science Museum; Tate Gallery; Teacher Training Agency; Traffic Director for London; Trustee Savings Banks Inspection Committee; United Kingdom Atomic Energy Authority; University Grants Committee; Victoria and Albert Museum; Wallace Collection; War Works Commission; any body established for the purpose of determining the boundaries of constituencies of the Parliament of the United Kingdom, or of local authorities in England or Wales: Public Records Act 1958 Sch 1 para 3 Table Pt II (amended by the Post Office Act 1969 s 75(1); the Employment and Training Act 1973 s 14(1), Sch 3 para 5 (repealed); the Fair Trading Act 1973 s 139, Sch 12; the Employment Protection Act 1975 s 125(1), (3), Sch 16 Pt IV para 6, Sch 18; the Crown Agents Act 1979 s 32, Sch 6 Pt I; the British Telecommunications Act 1981 s 56(1); the National Audit Act 1983 s 3(7), Sch 2 para 4; the National Heritage Act 1983 s 40, Sch 5 para 3; the Data Protection Act 1984 s 3(6), Sch 2 Pt III para 14; the Coal Industry Act 1987 ss 1(2), 10(3), Sch 1 para 6, Sch 3 Pt II; the Courts and Legal Services Act 1990 s 125(3), Sch 18 para 1(1); the Environmental Protection Act 1990 s 128, Sch 6 para 17; the Local Government Reorganisation (Miscellaneous Provisions) Order 1990, SI 1990/1765, art 3(2); the Road Traffic Act 1991 s 52(2), Sch 5 para 10; the Further and Higher Education Act 1992 s 93(1), Sch 8 Pt II para 68; the Education Act 1993 ss 253(2), 307(1), Sch 15 para 1, Sch 19 para 34; the National Lottery etc Act 1993 s 40(2), Sch 6 para 13; the Coal Industry Act 1994 s 67(1), Sch 9 para 6; the Education Act

1994 s 24, Sch 2 para 1; the Environment Act 1995 s 120(1), Sch 22 para 4; the Pensions Act 1995 s 173, Sch 6 para 1). As from a day to be appointed the entry 'Criminal Cases Review Commission' is inserted by the Criminal Appeal Act 1995 s 29(1), Sch 2 para 3. As from a day to be appointed the entries 'Occupational Pensions Regulatory Authority' and 'Pensions Compensation Board' are inserted by the Pensions Act 1995 Sch 5 para 1.

See also the Crown Estate Act 1961 s 9, Sch 2 Pt II para 5(3). All records of the Palatine Court are deemed to be records of the Supreme Court; and all records of the local court are deemed to be records of county courts and may be dealt with accordingly under the Public Records Act 1958: Courts Act 1971 ss 41(2), 42(4), Sch 5 Pt I para 5, Pt II para 14.

Any description of government department, court, tribunal or other body or establishment by reference to which a class of public records is framed extends to a government department, court, tribunal or other body or establishment, as the case may be, which has ceased to exist whether before or after the commencement of the Public Records Act 1958: Sch 1 para 8.

9 Ibid Sch 1 para 3(1). This does not apply to records in any museum or gallery mentioned in note 8 supra which form part of its permanent collections (that is to say records which the museum or gallery has acquired otherwise than by transfer from or arrangements with a government department): Sch 1 para 3(2).

10 'Records' for the purposes of ibid Sch 1 para 4 (as amended), includes records of any proceedings in the court or tribunal in question and includes rolls, writs, books, decrees, bills, warrants and accounts of, or in the custody of, the court or tribunal in question: Sch 1 para 4(3).

11 Ibid Sch 1 para 4(2).

12 The following descriptions are public records for the purposes of the Public Records Act 1958:

    (1) records of, or held in any department of the Supreme Court (including any court held under a commission of assize) (Sch 1 para 4(1)(a));

    (2) records of county courts and of any other superior or inferior court of record established since the passing of the County Courts Act 1846 (Public Records Act 1958 Sch 1 para 4(1)(b));

    (3) records of courts of quarter sessions (Sch 1 para 4(1)(d));

    (4) records of magistrates' courts (Sch 1 para 4(1)(e));

    (5) records of coroners' courts (Sch 1 para 4(1)(f));

    (6) records of courts-martial held whether within or outside the United Kingdom by any of Her Majesty's forces raised in the United Kingdom (Sch 1 para 4(1)(g));

    (7) records of naval courts held whether within or outside the United Kingdom under the enactments relating to merchant shipping (Sch 1 para 4(1)(h));

    (8) records of any court exercising jurisdiction held by Her Majesty within a country outside Her dominions (Sch 1 para 4(1)(i));

    (9) records of any tribunal (by whatever name called) (a) which has jurisdiction connected with any functions of a department; or (b) which has jurisdiction in proceedings to which such a government department is a party or to hear appeals from decisions of such a government department (Sch 1 para 4(1)(j));

    (10) records of the Lands Tribunal or of any Rent Tribunal or Local Valuation Court (Sch 1 para 4(1)(k));

    (11) records of the Industrial Court, of the Industrial Disputes Tribunal and of the National Arbitration Tribunal (which was replaced by the Industrial Disputes Tribunal) (Sch 1 para 4(1)(l));

    (12) records of umpires and deputy umpires appointed under the National Service Act 1948 or the Reinstatement in Civil Employment Act 1944 (Public Records Act 1958 Sch 1 para 4(1)(m));

    (13) records of ecclesiastical courts when exercising the testamentary and matrimonial jurisdiction removed from them by the Court of Probate Act 1857 and the Matrimonial Causes Act 1857 respectively (Public Records Act 1958 Sch 1 para 4(1)(n));

    (14) records of the Data Protection Tribunal (Sch 1 para 4(1)(nn) (added by the Data Protection Act 1984 s 3(6), Sch 2 Pt III para 14));

    (15) records of such other courts or tribunals (by whatever name called) as the Lord Chancellor may by order contained in a statutory instrument specify (Public Records Act 1958 Sch 1 para 4(1)(o)).

Note that the courts of assize were abolished by the Courts Act 1971 s 1(2) (repealed) and the courts of quarter sessions were abolished by the Courts Act 1971 s 3 (repealed). The Supreme Court consists of the Court of Appeal and the High Court together with the Crown Court: Supreme Court Act 1981 s 1.

13 Public Records Act 1958 Sch 1 para 5.

14 Ie 1 January 1959: see ibid s 13(3).

15 Ibid Sch 1 para 6(a).

16 Ibid Sch 1 para 6(b).

17 Ibid Sch 1 para 6(c).

18 Ibid Sch 1 para 7(1). See the Public Records (British Railways Board) Order 1984, SI 1984/546; and the Public Records (Commission for the New Towns) Order 1984, SI 1984/547.

19   Public Records Act 1958 Sch 1 para 7(2). The Lord Chancellor must include his decisions on such questions in his annual report to Parliament and must from time to time compile and publish lists of the departments, bodies, establishments, courts and tribunals comprised in Sch 1 paras 2, 3 (as amended) and 4 (as amended) and lists describing more particularly the categories of records which are, or are not, public records as defined in Sch 1: Sch 1 para 7(2).

**836. Legal validity of public records.** The legal validity of any record is not affected by its removal under the provisions of the Public Records Act 1958, or of the Public Record Office Acts 1838 to 1898, or by any provisions in those Acts with respect to its legal custody[1].

A copy of or extract from a public record[2] in the Public Record Office purporting to be examined and certified as true and authentic by the proper officer[3] and to be sealed or stamped with the seal of the Public Record Office is admissible as evidence in any proceedings without any further or other proof if the original record would have been admissible as evidence in those proceedings[4].

1   Public Records Act 1958 s 9(1).
2   For the meaning of 'public record' see para 835 ante.
3   Reference to the 'proper officer' is a reference to the Keeper of Public Records or any other officer of the Public Record Office authorised in that behalf by the Keeper of Public Records and, in the case of copies and extracts made before the commencement of the Public Records Act 1958, the deputy keeper of the records or any assistant record keeper appointed under the Public Record Office Act 1838: Public Records Act 1958 s 9(2).
4   Ibid s 9(2). As to evidence generally see CRIMINAL LAW vol 11(2) (Reissue) paras 1055–1186; EVIDENCE.

**837. General responsibility for public records.** The Lord Chancellor[1] is generally responsible for the execution of the Public Records Act 1958 and must supervise the care and preservation of public records[2]. He is advised by an Advisory Council on Public Records on matters concerning public records in general and, in particular, on those aspects of the work of the Public Record Office which affect members of the public who make use of the facilities provided by it[3]. The Lord Chancellor must lay before Parliament an annual report on the work of the Public Record Office and this must include any report made to him by the Advisory Council on Public Records[4].

However, the Master of the Rolls remains responsible for the records of the Chancery of England[5].

1   As to the Lord Chancellor see paras 477–497 ante.
2   Public Records Act 1958 s 1(1). As to his responsibility for court records see para 841 post. For the meaning of 'public records' see para 835 ante.
3   Ibid s 1(2). The Master of the Rolls is chairman of the council and the other members are appointed by the Lord Chancellor on such terms as he may specify: s 1(2).
4   Ibid s 1(3).
5   Ibid s 7(1). These records are in his custody and he may determine the place of deposit (s 7(1)), but as long as they are deposited in the Public Record Office they are in the custody of the Keeper of Public Records and subject to the Lord Chancellor's directions (s 7(2)). However, subject to this, the Master of the Rolls does not have charge and superintendence over, or custody of, any public records, and any public records which were in the custody of the Master of the Rolls at the commencement of the Public Records Act 1958 (other than records of the Chancery of England) are thereafter in the custody of the Keeper of Public Records or such other officer as the Lord Chancellor may from time to time appoint: s 7(3). The Master of the Rolls may delegate his functions to a judge of the Supreme Court: see the Courts and Legal Services Act 1990 s 73.

**838. The Public Record Office and other places of deposit.** The Lord Chancellor[1] may appoint a Keeper of Public Records to take charge, under his direction, of the Public Record Office and the records in it[2]. The Keeper of Public Records has the custody of public records in the Public Record Office[3], and must take all practicable steps for their preservation[4].

He may do everything necessary or expedient for maintaining the utility of the Public Record Office[5].

The Public Record Office is subject to investigation by the Parliamentary Commissioner for Administration[6].

If the Lord Chancellor considers that a place other than the Public Record Office affords suitable facilities for safe keeping and preservation of records and public inspection, he may, with the agreement of the authority who will be responsible for records deposited in that place, appoint it as a place of deposit for any class of records selected[7] for permanent preservation[8]. Public records in such a place of deposit are in the custody of such officer as the Lord Chancellor may appoint[9].

1   As to the Lord Chancellor see paras 477–497 ante.

2   Public Records Act 1958 s 2(1), (2). With Treasury concurrence, the Lord Chancellor may also appoint other persons to serve there at such remuneration as the Treasury may from time to time direct: s 2(1), (2). See the Civil Service Yearbook 1996 col 540. For the meaning of 'public records' see para 835 ante. As to the Treasury see paras 512–517 ante.

3   Public Records Act 1958 ss 4(5), 7(2).

4   Ibid s 2(3).

5   Ibid s 2(4). He may in particular:
    (1)   compile and make available indexes and guides to, and calendars and texts of, the records in the Public Record Office (s 2(4)(a));
    (2)   prepare publications concerning the activities of and facilities provided by the Public Record Office (s 2(4)(b));
    (3)   regulate the conditions under which members of the public may inspect public and other records or use the other facilities at the Public Record Office (s 2(4)(c));
    (4)   provide for the making and authentication of copies of, and extracts from, records required as evidence in legal proceedings or for other purposes (s 2(4)(d));
    (5)   accept responsibility for the safe keeping of records other than public records (s 2(4)(e));
    (6)   make arrangements for the separate housing of films and other records which have to be kept under special conditions (s 2(4)(f));
    (7)   lend records, in a case where the Lord Chancellor gives his approval, for display at commemorative exhibitions or for other special purposes (s 2(4)(g));
    (8)   acquire records and accept gifts and loans (s 2(4)(h)).

6   See the Parliamentary Commissioner Act 1967 s 4(1) (as substituted), Sch 2 (as substituted); and PARLIAMENT.

7   Ie under the Public Records Act 1958 s 3: see para 839 post.

8   Ibid s 4(1). In choosing a place of deposit for public records of (1) the Crown Court or magistrates' courts; or (2) courts of coroners of counties or boroughs, the Lord Chancellor must have regard to any arrangements made by the person for the time being responsible for the records with respect to the place where those records are to be kept and, where he does not follow any such arrangements, he must, so far as practicable, proceed on the principle that the records of any such court ought to be kept in the area of the administrative county or county borough comprising the area for which the court acts or where it sits, except in a case where the authorities or persons appearing to the Lord Chancellor to be mainly concerned consent to the choice of a place of deposit elsewhere: s 4(2); Courts Act 1971 s 56(1), Sch 8 para 2 Table item 4.

    Before appointing a place of deposit as respects public records of a class for which the Lord Chancellor is not himself responsible, he must consult with the minister or other person, if any, who appears to him to be primarily concerned and, where the records of the Crown Court the records of which are subject to the directions of a custos rotulorum, the Lord Chancellor must consult him: Public Records Act 1958 s 4(4); Courts Act 1971 s 3 (repealed). The custos rotulorum (keeper of the county records) was appointed for a county under the Custos Rotulorum Act 1545 s 1 (repealed).

    The Lord Chancellor may at any time direct that public records be transferred from the Public Record Office to another place of deposit or from such a place of deposit to the Public Record Office or another place of deposit (Public Records Act 1958 s 4(3)) and public records in the Public Record Office or other place of deposit must be temporarily returned at the request of the person by whom or department or office from which they were transferred (s 4(6)).

9   Ibid s 4(5).

**839. Selection and preservation of public records.** Every person responsible for public records[1] of any description which are not in the Public Record Office or a place of deposit appointed[2] by the Lord Chancellor[3] must make arrangements[4] for the selection of those which ought to be preserved permanently and for their safe-keeping[5]. Public records prior to 1660 must be selected for permanent preservation[6]. The Keeper of Public Records is responsible for co-ordinating and supervising all action taken[7]. Public records selected for permanent preservation must normally be transferred not later than 30 years after creation either to the Public Record Office or to another appointed[8] place of deposit directed by the Lord Chancellor[9]. He may, if it appears to him in the interests of the proper administration of the Public Record Office, direct that the transfer of any class of records be suspended until arrangements for their reception have been completed[10].

The records of the Chancery of England, certain records of ecclesiastical courts and certain public records in the custody of the University of Oxford are excluded from these provisions[11].

All original wills and other documents which are under the control of the High Court in the Principal Registry or in any district probate registry must be deposited and preserved in such places as the Lord Chancellor may direct; and any wills or other documents so deposited must, subject to the control of the High Court and to probate rules, be open to inspection[12].

Where private documents have remained in the custody of a court in England and Wales for more than 50 years without being claimed, the Keeper of Public Records may, with the approval of the Master of the Rolls, require their transfer to the Public Record Office, whereupon they become public records[13].

Public records which have been rejected as not required for permanent preservation must be destroyed or, in the case of records for which some person other than the Lord Chancellor is responsible, with the approval of the Lord Chancellor, otherwise disposed of[14], as may public records in the Public Record Office or other appointed[15] place of deposit which are duplicated by other public records selected for permanent preservation, or which for some other special reason should not be permanently preserved[16].

1    For the meaning of 'public records' see para 835 ante. As to court records see para 841 post.
2    Ie under the Public Records Act 1958 s 4(1): see para 838 ante.
3    As to the Lord Chancellor see paras 477–497 ante.
4    Any question as to the person whose duty it is to make arrangements under the Public Records Act 1958 s 3 with respect to any class of public records must be referred to the Lord Chancellor for his decision: s 3(7).
5    Ibid s 3(1).
6    Ibid s 3(3).
7    Ibid s 3(2). See also the Public Record Office Corporate Plan (1995–96 to 1997–98) (PRO 1994), where the Public Record Office's stated fundamental aim is 'to assist and promote the study of the past through the public records in order to inform the present and the future'.
8    See note 2 supra.
9    Public Records Act 1958 s 3(4). Provided that any records may be retained after the said period if, in the opinion of the person responsible for them, they are required for administrative purposes or ought to be retained for any other special reason and, where that person is not the Lord Chancellor, the Lord Chancellor has been informed of the facts and given his approval: s 3(4) proviso.
     The provisions of s 3 do not make it unlawful for the person responsible for any public record to transmit it to the Keeper of the Records of Scotland or to the Public Record Office of Northern Ireland: s 3(8).
10   Ibid s 3(5).
11   See ibid ss 7(2), 8(5) (as amended), (6).
12   Supreme Court Act 1981 s 124.
13   Public Records Act 1958 s 8(4).
14   Ibid s 3(6).
15   See note 2 supra.
16   Public Records Act 1958 s 6.

**840. Access to public records.** Public records[1] in the Public Record Office, other than those to which the public had access before transfer there, are not available for public inspection until the expiration of 30 years beginning with 1 January in the next year after that in which they were created[2]. Special provisions relating to the imposition of conditions and the extension of the period apply to records containing information obtained from the public under such conditions that opening to public inspection after the period would or might constitute a breach of good faith on the part of the government or the person who obtained the information[3].

Subject to the above provisions, to certain enactments restricting disclosure of information obtained from the public except for certain limited purposes[4] and to any other Act or instrument containing a similar restriction, the Keeper of Public Records must arrange for reasonable facilities for public inspection and the obtaining of copies of public records in the Public Record Office[5].

In the case of public records in other places of deposit[6] the Lord Chancellor must require arrangements to be made for public inspection comparable to those made as above and subject to corresponding restrictions[7].

1 For the meaning of 'public records' see para 835 ante.
2 Public Records Act 1958 s 5(1) (amended by the Public Records Act 1967 s 1). The Lord Chancellor may prescribe some other period either longer or shorter as respects any particular class of public records: Public Records Act 1958 s 5(1). As to cabinet records see 608 HC Official Report (5th series), 2 July 1959, cols 62–63. The Keeper of Public Records may permit a person to inspect any records if he has obtained special authority given by an officer of a government department or other body who is accepted by the Lord Chancellor as qualified to give that authority: s 5(4). Former ministers may not evade the 30 year rule by publishing their own accounts of Cabinet meetings: see 881 HC Official Report (5th series), 15 November 1974, written answers cols *271–274*. As to the Lord Chancellor see paras 477–497 ante.
3 See the Public Records Act 1958 s 5(2).
4 See ibid s 5(3), Sch 2 (as amended).
5 Ibid s 5(3). With the concurrence of the Treasury, the Lord Chancellor may by regulations prescribe the fees for the inspection of records under the charge of the Keeper of Public Records, authenticated copies or extracts from such records and for other services afforded by officers of the Public Record Office and authorise the remission of fees in prescribed cases: s 2(5). The fees so received are paid into the Exchequer: s 2(6). See the Public Record Office (Fees) Regulations 1994, SI 1994/2353. As to the Treasury see paras 512–517 ante. As to payments into the Exchequer and the Consolidated Fund see para 711 text and notes 4–5 ante.
6 See the Public Records Act 1958 s 4; and para 838 ante.
7 Ibid s 5(5).

**841. Responsibility for court records.** The Lord Chancellor[1] is responsible for the public records[2] of every court of record or magistrates' court which are not in the Public Record Office or an appointed[3] place of deposit and may determine the officer to have the custody of any such records[4].

1 As to the Lord Chancellor see paras 477–497 ante.
2 For the meaning of 'public records' see para 835 ante.
3 Ie under the Public Records Act 1958 s 4: see para 838 ante.
4 Ibid s 8(1).

# (9) RIGHTS OF THE CROWN IN RELATION TO PROPERTY

**842. Priority of Crown rights.** Where the Crown's right and that of a subject meet at one and the same time, that of the Crown is in general preferred, the rule being *detur digniori*[1].

Thus the Crown cannot have a joint property with any person in one entire chattel, or one which is not capable of division, and where the title of the Crown and a subject concur, the Crown takes the whole[2]. So if an indivisible chattel or a debt are assigned to the Crown and a subject, or where two persons have a joint property in such a chattel or debt and one person assigns his share to the Crown, or where a bond is made to the Crown and a subject, the Crown takes the whole[3], for the Crown cannot be a partner with a subject; nor can the Crown become a joint owner of a chattel real by grant or contract, but takes the whole[4]. Where, however, a share of real property becomes vested in the monarch by descent, or, it seems, otherwise, she may become at law a joint tenant, though she takes beneficially only an undivided share in proceeds of sale[5]; and the monarch and a subject may in equity be tenants in common[6].

1    Ie 'let it be given to the worthier': see Co Litt 30b; *Quick's Case* (1611) 9 Co Rep 129a at 129b; *Wardens and Commonalty of Sadlers' Case* (1588) 4 Co Rep 54b at 55a; *A-G v Andrew* (1655) Hard 23; Bac Abr, Prerogative, E, 4. For a discussion of the nature of the Crown's priority see *Re Irish Employers Mutual Insurance Association Ltd* [1955] IR 176 at 202 et seq.
2    Co Litt 30; 1 Bl Com (14th Edn) 409; *Willion v Berkley* (1561) 1 Plowd 223 at 243.
3    1 Bl Com (14th Edn) 409; *Willion v Berkley* (1561) 1 Plowd 223 at 243. See also *Mines' Case* (1567) 1 Plowd 310 at 323, Ex Ch; *Miles v Williams* (1714) 10 Mod Rep 243 at 245; *R v Fairclough* (1597) Cro Eliz 265. Quaere whether the principle applies in the case of a gift by a subject: *R v Fairclough* supra.
4    1 Bl Com (14th Edn) 409.
5    This, it is apprehended, is the effect of the Law of Property Act 1925 ss 34, 208, on the older authorities, ie Co Litt 180b, 186a, 190a; Bac Abr, Joint Tenants, B; 2 Bl Com (14th Edn) 184; *Willion v Berkley* (1561) 1 Plowd 223 at 247; Chitty *Law of the Prerogatives of the Crown* pp 210, 248. Under a gift to the monarch and a subject and their heirs, the monarch and subject take beneficially as tenants in common and not as joint tenants: Chitty *Law of the Prerogatives of the Crown* pp 210–211.
6    Bro Abr, Prerogative, 105.

**843. Personal property.** Personal property of the Crown is not subject to the law relating to wreck, estrays or waifs[1], or distress for rent[2]. No custom which goes to the person or goods binds the Crown[3], and it is, therefore, exempt from all customary rates and tolls[4].

1    Vin Abr, Prerogative, T, 2; *Willion v Berkley* (1561) 1 Plowd 223 at 243.
2    See CROWN LANDS AND PRIVILEGES.
3    Com Dig, Toll, G, 1.
4    Vin Abr, Prerogative, T, 2; *Anon* (1457) Jenk 83.

**844. Trusts.** It seems that the monarch may be a trustee[1], but in law could not be seised to a use[2], or be compelled to execute the use[3], and in effect land so vested in the monarch was discharged from the use[4].

1    Chitty *Law of the Prerogatives of the Crown* p 378. As to trusts generally see TRUSTS.
2    *Willion v Berkley* (1561) 1 Plowd 223 at 238; Bac Abr, Prerogative, E, 1; 1 Cru Dig, Use, cap III, s 8. On this ground the monarch could not convey by the old forms of bargain and sale, covenant to stand seised, or lease and release: Chitty *Law of the Prerogatives of the Crown* p 378. But the monarch could apparently be a beneficiary, if both the conveyance and the declaration of use were by matter of record: Bacon, Law Tracts, Reading on the Statute of Uses, 349 (7 Collected Works (Spedding) 438).
3    1 Cru Dig, Use, cap III, s 8; Bac Abr, Prerogative, E, 1.
4    Bac Abr, Prerogative, E, 1. The Statute of Uses (1535) was repealed by the Law of Property Act 1925 s 207, Sch 7 (now repealed), which substituted trusts for use (see s 1(9)).

**845. Appointment as executor.** The monarch may be appointed executor, but as she cannot be presumed to have leisure to perform the duties, she may nominate such persons to do so as she thinks fit, against whom actions may be brought. She may also appoint others to take accounts of such executors[1].

1    4 Co Inst 335; Bac Abr, Prerogative, E, 1; Chitty *Law of the Prerogatives of the Crown* p 379. As to executors generally see EXECUTORS AND ADMINISTRATORS.

**846. Rents.** The Crown may, in general, reserve rents to a stranger, though a subject may not do so[1]; but a reservation of rent to an officer for the time being, who is removable at will, is bad[2].

The Crown may also, it seems, reserve rents out of incorporeal hereditaments, such as commons or fairs[3].

1   Co Litt 143b; 2 Roll Abr 447; *Saffron Walden Case* (1583) Moore KB 159 at 162.
2   *Borough's Case* (1695) 1 Ld Raym 36.
3   Bac Abr, Prerogative, E, 3; Co Litt 47a, n (1).

**847. Distress.** The Crown could at common law distrain without attornment[1]; and may distrain for a rent service, fee farm rent, rentcharge, or rentseck, whether acquired by grant or forfeiture, upon the land out of which the rent is reserved, or upon all other land of the tenant, even though held of other lords, provided the land is in the tenant's actual possession; if it is underlet for years or at will, the undertenant's goods are not liable[2] unless the land was underlet after the rent accrued due to the Crown[3]. The Crown may, perhaps, distrain on the highway[4]. The prerogatives relating to distress do not pass to the Crown's grantee[5].

A tenant may, it seems, replevy[6] on a distress for rent by the Crown[7], but not on a distress for fee farm rent[8] or other duty to the Crown[9].

1   Co Litt 309b; and see DISTRESS.
2   2 Co Inst 132, 184; 4 Co Inst 119; Bro Abr, Prerogative, 68, 77; Vin Abr, Prerogative, F; Bac Abr, Prerogative, E, 3; Chitty *Law of the Prerogatives of the Crown* p 209. The Crown can, it seems, distrain even though the land is under a sequestration out of Chancery, though this is doubtful: *A-G v Coventry Corpn* (1715) 1 P Wms 306 at 307.
3   1 Roll Abr 670.
4   2 Co Inst 131. As to distress for lawful tolls see HIGHWAYS vol 21 (Reissue) para 141.
5   Bro Abr, Prerogative, 68; Vin Abr, Prerogative, F.
6   As to replevin see DISTRESS vol 13 paras 373–381.
7   Bro Abr, Replevin, 51; Bac Abr, Replevin, C.
8   *R v Oliver* (1717) Bunb 14. As to a seizure in order to condemnation see *Cawthorne v Campbell* (1790) Anst 205n at 212.
9   See Bro Abr, Replevin, 51; Bac Abr, Replevin, C. As to distress generally see DISTRESS.

**848. Crown leases.** Where Crown leases are made with a clause of re-entry on non-payment of rent, no demand for payment is required, but on non-payment the Crown may re-enter[1]. This right does not, however, extend to the Crown's grantee[2]; nor to land in the Duchy of Lancaster[3]; nor, it seems, where there is an express provision requiring demand in a lease made either originally by the Crown, or by some other person of whom the Crown has acquired the reversion[4].

1   Co Litt 201b; Bro Abr, Prerogative, pl 101; *Boroughe's Case* (1596), 4 Co Rep 72b at 73a.
2   Co Litt 201b; *Boroughe's Case* (1596) 4 Co Rep 72b; *Buskin v Edmunds* (1595) Moore KB 598; *Kidwelly v Brand* (1550) Plowd 69 at 70; *Anon* (1553) Dyer 87b.
3   *Bonnye's Case* (1584) Moore KB 149 at 154; *Saffron Walden Case* (1583) Moore KB 159 at 161.
4   *Knight's Case* (1588) Moore KB 199 at 210.

# (10) ROYAL GRANT

## (i) In general

**849. Crown grants.** At common law grants by the Crown are generally void unless made under the Great Seal[1]. Thus grants of freehold interests in land, honours, franchises and liberties, offices in fee or for life, and, it is said, chattels real, may not be granted by the Crown at common law except by matter of record[2], namely by charter or letters patent under the Great Seal and enrolled either on the patent rolls or the close rolls[3]. It seems, however, that certain leases could be validly granted under the Exchequer seal[4].

Grants of lands in the duchy and county palatine of Lancaster were required to be passed under the seals of the duchy and county palatine respectively[5].

Personalty, such as goods or choses in action, did not require the authority of the Great Seal, but could legally be passed under the Privy Seal[6].

Grants of property vested in the King in his body natural required, in general, the same formalities as grants of property vested in him in his body politic[7].

1    2 Bl Com (14th Edn) 346; and see the authorities cited in note 2 infra. As to use of the Great Seal see para 909 post.
2    *Lane's Case* (1586) 2 Co Rep 16b; Vin Abr, Prerogative, C, b; Com Dig, Patent, C, 2; 2 Bl Com (14th Edn) 346; Vin Abr, Prerogative, F, b.
3    2 Bl Com (14th Edn) 346. Instruments enrolled on the patent rolls are addressed to subjects at large, whilst close roll patents are directed to particular persons for particular purposes and sealed on the outside: 2 Bl Com (14th Edn) 346. As to the patent rolls see also Scargill-Bird, Guide to Public Records (R S) 34, 35; and as to the close rolls see The Close Rolls (Rec Com), Introduction. For forms of letters patent to be used on creation of certain peerages and dignities see the Crown Office (Forms and Proclamations Rules) Order 1992, SI 1992/1730 (as amended).
4    *Lane's Case* (1586) 2 Co Rep 16b; *Predyman v Wodry* (1606) Cro Jac 109; Com Dig, Patent, C, 3.
5    Co Inst 209; Com Dig, Patent, C, 4; *Duchy of Lancaster Case* (1561) 1 Plowd 212 at 218. A presentation to a church, the advowson of which belonged to the duchy, might, it seems, pass under the Great Seal, though a grant of the next avoidance required the duchy seal: see Vin Abr, Prerogative, D, b.
6    Vin Abr, Prerogative, F, b; Com Dig, Patent, C, 5. There seems to be some doubt how far writing was necessary: see Bro Abr, Prerogative, pl 61. It seems that choses in action could always be assigned by the Crown by express words, though at common law they could not be assigned by a subject so as to pass the right to the grantee to sue in his own name: see *Ford and Sheldon's Case* (1606) 12 Co Rep 1, Ex Ch; Bro Abr, Prerogative, 40; Co Litt 232b, n (1); Vin Abr, Prerogative, M, b. This doctrine appears to have applied only to a debt or liquidated demand, and not to a right of action for damages: see Vin Abr, Prerogative, M, b; Bro Abr, Choses in Action, pl 11. In cases where writing is required such grants would now, it seems, pass under the sign manual (as to which see para 908 post).
7    *Duchy of Lancaster Case* (1561) 1 Plowd 212.

## 850. Common law grants to the monarch.

At common law grants to the monarch of a freehold interest or term of years, or a surrender, had to be made by matter of record, as by deed enrolled[1], and grants to her in her body natural required the same formalities as grants to her in her body politic[2]; but she might take goods and choses in action without matter of record[3].

1    *Duchy of Lancaster Case* (1561) 1 Plowd 212 at 213, 213a; Bro Abr, Prerogative, pl 41, 56, 57, 93; Vin Abr, Prerogative, Z, c.
2    *Duchy of Lancaster Case* (1561) 1 Plowd 212.
3    Vin Abr, Prerogative, Z, c; Bro Abr, Prerogative, pl 36, 40, 50; Bac Abr, Choses in Action, pl 4. Choses in action could always be assigned by or to the Crown: see the authorities cited in para 849 note 6 ante.

## 851. Countersigning grants.

It is said that grants or warrants[1] which can be made under the sign manual[2] ought to be countersigned by one of the principal Secretaries of State, or by the Lords of the Treasury, except where an Act of Parliament directs that the monarch may do a certain thing under the sign manual, in which case it seems that they need not be so countersigned[3].

1    This does not include a royal warrant to a tradesman, which is not something in the nature of an exercise of the royal prerogative; it is nothing more than an intimation by a proper authority representing the Crown that a particular tradesman is a person who has had dealings with the monarch

in a particular branch of business: *Re Imperial Tobacco Co (of Great Britain and Ireland) Ltd's Trade Marks* [1915] 2 Ch 27 at 44, CA, per Lord Cozens-Hardy MR.

2   As to the sign manual see para 908 post.

3   Com Dig Patent, C, 7. As to the office of Secretary of State see para 355 et seq ante. As to the Lords of the Treasury see paras 512–513 ante.

**852. Departmental grants.** It seems that some grants might pass through certain offices, such as the Admiralty or Treasury[1], under the sign manual[2] without the authority of the signet, the Great Seal[3] or the Privy Seal[4].

1   As to the Treasury see paras 512–517 ante.

2   As to the sign manual see para 908 post.

3   As to use of the Great Seal see para 909 post.

4   2 Bl Com (14th Edn) 347. The necessity for use of the signet was abolished by 14 & 15 Vict c 82 (Great Seal) (1851) (repealed); the necessity for use of the Privy Seal was abolished by the Great Seal Act 1884 s 3 (repealed).

**853. Statutory provisions.** The common law rules relating to Crown grants have been largely superseded by statute[1].

Where a grant is directed by statute to be made in a particular manner, it is doubtful whether it can be legally effected in any other manner[2]; but in the absence of statutory provisions it seems that the common law rules still apply.

1   As to the disposal of Crown land, and the Crown private estates see CROWN LANDS AND PRIVILEGES.

2   *Earl of Southampton's Case* (1541) Dyer 50a. See also *A-G v De Keyser's Royal Hotel Ltd* [1920] AC 508 at 540, HL.

**854. Fees and duties.** Although stamp duty is no longer payable on a grant by letters patent under the Great Seal[1], certain fees may be payable as appointed by the Lord Chancellor[2].

1   See the Finance Act 1938 s 51 (repealed). As to stamp duty see para 857 post; and STAMP DUTIES. As to use of the Great Seal see para 909 post.

2   See the Great Seal (Offices) Act 1874 s 9 (as amended); and para 922 post. As to the Lord Chancellor see paras 477–497 ante.

**855. Re-entry.** When a right of re-entry upon land or other hereditaments has accrued to the Crown, the right may be exercised or enforced without inquisition being taken or office found or any actual re-entry being made on the premises[1].

1   Queen's Remembrancer Act 1859 s 25 (the words 'or her successors' in this section were repealed by the Statute Law Revision Act 1892). This provision was considered in *A-G v Parsons* [1955] Ch 664 at 678, 682, [1955] 2 All ER 466 at 473, 476, CA; but on appeal [1956] AC 421, [1956] 1 All ER 65, HL, the decision was reversed and the question did not arise.

**856. Proof of Crown grant.** A grant from the Crown is proved by production of the original under the Great Seal[1] or the royal sign manual[2], or by exemplifications or examined copies or, under the Evidence Act 1851[3] by certified copies[4]. If the original cannot be produced and the vendor's solicitor informs the purchaser where the grant can be found, it seems that the purchaser is not entitled to a copy but must have it examined at the office where it is kept[5].

1   As to use of the Great Seal see para 909 post.

2   2 Bl Com (14th Edn) 346. As to the sign manual see para 908 post.

3   See the Evidence Act 1851 s 14.

4    1 Williams *The Law of Vendor and Purchaser* (4th Edn, 1936) pp 119, 186; Taylor *Law of Evidence* (12th Edn, 1931) s 1527.

5    Sugden *Vendor and Purchaser* (14th Edn, 1862) p 431; 1 Dart *Vendor and Purchaser* (8th Edn) p 315. As to grants from the Crown generally see para 849 ante.

**857. Stamp duty.** Except where express provision to the contrary is made by statute an instrument relating to property belonging to the Crown or to the monarch's private property is charged with the same stamp duty as an instrument of the same kind relating to property belonging to a subject[1].

1    See the Stamp Act 1891 s 119; and STAMP DUTIES vol 44(1) (Reissue) paras 1001, 1094.

### (ii) Construction of Grants

**858. Effect of grants.** Because the monarch is a corporation sole[1], grants which she makes bind her successors even though those successors are not expressly named[2]. Similarly a grant to the monarch simply is sufficient to pass a fee simple estate[3].

1    As to corporations sole see CORPORATIONS vol 9 paras 1206–1207.
2    Bac Abr, Prerogative, E, 2; Co Litt 9; *Duchy of Lancaster Case* (1561) 1 Plowd 212.
3    Bac Abr, Prerogative, E, 3. Where either after 31 December 1925 or before 1 January 1926 any property or any interest in it is or has been vested in a corporation sole (including the Crown), the same, unless and until otherwise disposed of by the corporation, passes and devolves to and vests in and is deemed always to have passed and devolved to or vested in the successors from time to time of that corporation: Law of Property Act 1925 s 180(1).

**859. Operation of grants.** Grants under the Great Seal[1] require no delivery and take effect from the date expressed in the grant; but they are effectual even if undated, since the sealing and enrolment are sufficient[2].

1    As to use of the Great Seal see para 909 post.
2    Vin Abr, Prerogative, G, b, 3.

**860. Construction of grants.** Contrary to the ordinary rule applicable to grants by a subject[1], grants by the Crown are usually construed most favourably for the Crown[2]. Thus a Crown grant of a manor with all land accepted or reputed as parcel of it will only pass such land as has belonged to the manor immemorially and of truth and right[3], and under the grant of a manor or land with the appurtenances the right to advowsons does not pass[4].

A grant of 'franchises' will not generally pass the right to treasure trove[5], nor will a grant of 'land' pass the right to mines[6], unless they are expressly mentioned. Flotsam, jetsam, and lagan or ligan[7] will not pass under a grant of 'wreck'[8]; and a grant of land 'and the mines therein contained' will not be sufficient to pass the right to royal mines of gold and silver[9], the rule in such cases being that general words will not pass prerogative rights by implication[10], or unless expressly mentioned[11]; and where under a general term both things royal and things base may be included, only the latter will pass[12].

Rights which do not form part of the prerogative will sometimes pass even though they are not expressly mentioned. Thus under a grant to burgesses of a town with all its appurtenances, the Crown being the owner of the soil and the right to toll-traverse, the right to toll-traverse has been held to pass[13]; and under a grant of a rectory, all churches and vicarages belonging to it being expressly excepted, the right to a perpetual curacy passed as not forming part of the exception[14]. No definite rule can, however, be laid down in such cases, each being governed by its own merits[15].

Where a grant by the Crown cannot take effect without some further act or grant on the part of the Crown, that further act or grant will not be implied and the grant is void[16].

1   Ie that grants are to be taken most strongly against the grantor: 2 Bl Com (14th Edn) 346. See generally DEEDS.

2   2 Bl Com (14th Edn) 346; *A-G v Ewelme Hospital* (1853) 17 Beav 366; *Knight's Case* (1588) 5 Co Rep 54b; Vin Abr, Prerogative, O, c; Com Dig, Grant, G, 12; Bac Abr, Prerogative, E, 4; *Hudson's Bay Co v A-G for Canada* [1929] AC 285 at 294, PC.

3   2 Roll Abr 186. But see *Gennings v Lake* (1629) Cro Car 168, where a grant of messuages and all land to the said messuages belonging or with them devised was held to pass land enjoyed with the manor for a convenient time.

4   Statute Prerogativa Regis (temp incert c 17) (amended by the Crown Estate Act 1961 s 9(4) (repealed), Sch 3 Pt I (repealed)). The Statute Prerogativa Regis does not extend to lay advowsons such as the nomination of the master of an almshouse: see *A-G v Ewelme Hospital* (1853) 17 Beav 366.

5   *A-G v Trustees of British Museum* [1903] 2 Ch 598. As to treasure trove see CORONERS; and CROWN LANDS AND PRIVILEGES. Note that the law of treasure trove, formerly governed by the prerogative, is now embodied in statute: see the Treasure Act 1996.

6   *Woolley v A-G of Victoria* (1877) 2 App Cas 163, PC; *Hudson's Bay Co v A-G for Canada* [1929] AC 285, PC.

7   As to the meaning of these terms see CROWN LANDS AND PRIVILEGES.

8   *Sir Henry Constable's Case* (1601) 5 Co Rep 106a.

9   *Mines' Case* (1567) 1 Plowd 310 at 336, Ex Ch. A grant of all coal mines 'within the commons, waste grounds, or marshes' within a lordship, with a proviso that the grant should be construed strictly against the Crown and most strictly and beneficially for the grantee, was held to pass coal lying under the foreshore of an estuary and forming part of the manor: *A-G v Hanmer* (1858) 27 LJCh 837.

10  See the *Royal Fishery of the Banne's Case* [1610] Dav 55 at 57.

11  *A-G v Trustees of British Museum* [1903] 2 Ch 598 at 612; Vin Abr, Prerogative, C, c; Com Dig, Grant, G, 7. As to rights embraced by words of reference to a previous grant see *A-G v Marquis of Downshire* (1816) 5 Price 269; *Dyke v Walford* (1848) 5 Moo PCC 434 at 487. See also the *Royal Fishery of the Banne's Case* [1610] Dav 55, where a grant by the Crown of land and fishing rights except for three-quarters of the fishing rights in the River Banne ('exceptis tribus partibus piscationis fluminis de Banne') was held not to pass the right of the Crown to the remaining quarter of the several fishery in the tidal portion of the river.

12  *Basket v Cambridge University* (1758) 1 Wm Bl 105 at 118.

13  *Brett v Beales* (1829) Mood & M 416 at 426. As to tolls generally see HIGHWAYS; MARKETS AND FAIRS.

14  *Arthington v Bishop of Chester* (1790) 1 Hy Bl 418.

15  As to the right to take tolls under the grant of a fair see *Earl of Egremont v Saul* (1837) 6 Ad & El 924; *Stamford Corpn v Pawlett* (1830) 1 Cr & J 57. As to what passes under a grant of titles see *Holdsworth v Fairfax* (1834) 3 Cl & Fin 115, HL; *A-G v Lord Eardley* (1820) 8 Price 39; *Governors of Lucton Free School v Scarlett* (1828) 2 Y & J 330; affd sub nom *Scarlet v Governors of Lucton Free School* (1836) 10 Bli NS 592, HL. A specific portion of Crown land cannot be claimed under general words in a grant: see *Parmeter v A-G* (1813) 10 Price 412, HL.

16  Thus land granted to an alien, at a time when aliens could not hold land, would not have enured to make him a denizen: *Knight's Case* (1588) 5 Co Rep 54b; see Bro Abr, Patents, pl 62; and see Vin Abr, Prerogative, G, c; *Basket v Cambridge University* (1758) 1 Wm Bl 105 at 118; *Englefield's Case* (1591) 7 Co Rep 11b; 2 Bl Com (14th Edn) 347. For the meaning of 'denizen' see para 31 note 1 ante.

**861. Rules of construction.** The general rule of construction[1] is capable of important relaxations in favour of the subject. Thus if the intention is obvious, a fair and liberal interpretation must be given to the grant to enable it to take effect[2], and the operative part, if plainly expressed, may take effect notwithstanding qualifications in the recitals[3].

The grant will also be construed in favour of the subject where it is expressed to be made, not at the solicitation of the latter, but, as is frequently the case, 'by special favour, out of certain knowledge, and mere motion of the King'[4].

If the grant is for valuable consideration it must be construed strictly in favour of the grantee, for the honour of the monarch[5]; and where two constructions are possible, one valid and the other void, that which is valid ought to be preferred[6], for the honour of the monarch ought to be more regarded than the monarch's profit[7]. Where, however, two interpretations may be given to the grant, both of which are good, that which is more favourable to the Crown is in many cases preferred[8].

1   As to the general rule of construction of grants see para 860 ante.
2   2 Co Inst 496–497.
3   *Legat's Case* (1612) 10 Co Rep 108b.
4   Ie *ex speciali gratia, certa scientia, et mero motu regis*: *Alton Woods' Case, A-G v Bushopp* (1600) 1 Co Rep 40b; *Legat's Case* (1612) 10 Co Rep 108b, Com Dig, Grant, G, 12; Vin Abr, Prerogative, E, c (3); 2 Bl Com (14th Edn) 347.
5   2 Co Inst 496–497; *Molyn's Case* (1598) 6 Co Rep 5b; *Whistler's Case* (1613) 10 Co Rep 63a at 65a.
6   *Bewley's Case* (1611) 9 Co Rep 130b; *Molyn's Case* (1598) 6 Co Rep 5b; *Churchwardens of St Saviour's, Southwark, Case* (1613) 10 Co Rep 66b at 67b.
7   Com Dig, Grant, G, 12; *Earl of Rutland's Case* (1608) 8 Co Rep 55a.
8   *Earl of Rutland's Case* (1608) 8 Co Rep 55a; *Alton Woods' Case, A-G v Bushopp* (1600) 1 Co Rep 40b at 45a, 53a. Licences and passports to alien enemies to trade or reside in British territory during wartime, which were occasionally granted in the early years of the nineteenth century, were construed liberally for the grantee: *Flindt v Scott* (1814) 5 Taunt 674, Ex Ch; *Vaughan v Lemcke* (1825) 7 Dow & Ry KB 236. See also WAR.

**862. User.** Evidence of user may be adduced to explain the meaning of a grant, and in such cases a more liberal interpretation will frequently be given to it[1]. Thus evidence of acts of ownership will be admitted to show that the foreshore passed under the grant of an adjacent manor[2], or under a grant of land[3], even though not expressly mentioned.

1   See *Sutton Harbour Improvement Co v Plymouth Guardians* (1890) 63 LT 772, where usage extending over the last 150 years was admitted to explain the meaning of a charter of 1440.
2   *A-G v Jones* (1862) 2 H & C 347; *Calmady v Rowe* (1844) 6 CB 861; *Le Strange v Rowe* (1866) 4 F & F 1048; *Re Walton-cum-Trimley Manor, ex p Tomline* (1873) 28 LT 12; *Healy v Thorne* (1870) IR 4 CL 495; *Re Belfast Dock Act 1854, ex p Earl of Ranfurly* (1867) IR 1 Eq 128; *Lord Advocate v Young* (1887) 12 App Cas 544, HL; *Hamilton v A-G* (1880) 5 LR Ir 555; *Daly v Murray* (1885) 17 LR Ir 185, CA.
3   *Hastings Corpn v Ivall* (1874) LR 19 Eq 558; *Brew v Haren* (1877) IR 11 CL 198, Ex Ch; affirming (1874) IR 9 CL 29.

**863. Uncertainty.** Where there is found to be uncertainty as to what is granted, the grant will in general be void not only as against the grantee but also against the monarch, because a presumption of deceit is raised[1]. Thus a grant of a parcel of land without describing what parcel[2], or of debts accrued within a certain period without specifying what debts[3], is void for uncertainty.

The common law rule, that that which is capable of being made certain is to be treated as certain[4], obtains with regard to such grants[5]; and a grant with such privileges as a named person enjoyed[6], and a grant of a manor to hold as fully and completely[7] as it came into the hands of the monarch by attainder of a named person or under such conditions as are contained in certain letters patent[8], have been held not void for uncertainty.

1   Vin Abr, Prerogative, F, c; Bac Abr, Prerogative, F, 2.
2   *Stockdale's Case* (1611) 12 Co Rep 86; *Parmeter v A-G* (1813) 10 Price 412, HL.
3   *Stockdale's Case* (1611) 12 Co Rep 86.
4   Ie *id certum est quod certum reddi potest*.
5   Com Dig, Grant, G, 5; Vin Abr, Prerogative, R, c.
6   *Lord Darcy's Case* (1596) Cro Eliz 512 at 513.
7   Ie *adeo plene et integre*.
8   *Whistler's Case* (1613) 10 Co Rep 63a.

**864. Deceit.** In general, grants will be void for deceit (that is to say, it will be presumed that the Crown is deceived in the grant) upon three grounds: (1) where the Crown grants a greater or different estate than it is entitled to; (2) where the same estate or part of it has already been granted to another, and the prior grant is not recited; (3) where the Crown has been deceived in the consideration expressed in the grant[1].

Thus where property was granted by the Crown for an estate in fee in possession, and it turned out that the same property had already been granted under a lease for years which had several years to run and which was not recited in the grant, the grant in fee was held to be void, it being inconsistent with the monarch's honour to grant two interests in possession at the same time[2]. This principle would, it seems, apply only to cases where the prior grant is of record (for example, enrolled), and where, therefore, the subject cannot be deceived[3]; and the second grant will not be void if the prior grant is recited, for then there is no uncertainty and the Crown is not deceived[4]; and, generally when a reversion is granted by the Crown, it is usually necessary that the previous term or estate still in being, and which is of record, should be recited[5].

The Crown's title need not, however, be recited[6], and if the facts are recited and a wrong conclusion of law or fact is drawn from them, this will not avoid the grant[7]. Therefore a recital that the Crown is entitled by escheat, whereas it is really entitled by inheritance, or a misdescription of the grantee[8], will not avoid the grant.

1   *Gledstanes v Earl of Sandwich* (1842) 4 Man & G 995. See also, as to false consideration, 2 Roll Abr 189, pl 15, 25; *Barwick's Case* (1597) 5 Co Rep 93b; 2 Bl Com (14th Edn) 347; *Penn v Lord Baltimore* (1750) 1 Ves Sen 444 at 451. As to the grant of a greater or different estate see Com Dig, Grant, G, 8; 2 Bl Com (14th Edn) 348.
2   *Alcock v Cooke* (1829) 5 Bing 340 at 349; see also *Alton Woods' Case, A-G v Bushopp* (1600) 1 Co Rep 40b; *Earl of Rutland's Case* (1608) 8 Co Rep 55a at 57a; *Wing v Harris* (1591) Cro Eliz 231 at 232.
3   *Alcock v Cooke* (1829) 5 Bing 340 at 349 per Best CJ; *Alton Woods' Case, A-G v Bushopp* (1600) 1 Co Rep 40b at 45a.
4   *Earl of Rutland's Case* (1608) 8 Co Rep 55a at 56b; *Alcock v Cooke* (1829) 5 Bing 340 at 349 per Best CJ. As to what constitutes a sufficient recital of a prior grant see *Bozoun's Case* (1584) 4 Co Rep 34b at 35b; Vin Abr, Prerogative, R, b.
5   Vin Abr, Prerogative, Q, b; Com Dig, Grant, G, 10.
6   *Alton Woods' Case, A-G v Bushopp* (1600) 1 Co Rep 40b at 45b, 51a; *Englefield's Case* (1591) Moore KB 303 at 318, 320.
7   *Duke of Chandos's Case* (1606) 6 Co Rep 55a.
8   Eg that he is a knight when he is not: see *R v Bishop of Chester* (1696) 1 Ld Raym 292 at 304.

**865.   Mistake.** A grant will be void where the Crown is prejudiced by a mistake in a material point, either in its tenure or profit[1]; or where a recital which sounds for the Crown's benefit turns out to be false[2]; for example that the grant is made in consideration of the surrender of a lease when the lease is in fact void[3]; or if land is granted on a false suggestion that the land is of less value than it really is[4]; or where the grant is to take effect on the determination of a former grant which is in fact determined[5]. In such cases the grant will be void even though derivative titles depend upon it[6].

1   Bac Abr, Prerogative, F, 2.
2   See 2 Roll Abr 188; *Cholmley's Case* (1597) 2 Co Rep 50a at 54; *Earl of Devonshire's Case* (1607) 11 Co Rep 89a at 90; *Anon* (1576) 3 Dyer 352a.
3   *Barwick's Case* (1597) 5 Co Rep 93b at 94a.
4   2 Roll Abr 188, pl 15; *Penn v Lord Baltimore* (1750) 1 Ves Sen 444 at 451.
5   *Holt v Roper* (1559) 3 Leon 5 at 6; *Auditor Curle's Case* (1610) 11 Co Rep 2b at 4b; 2 Roll Abr 188.
6   *Cumming v Forrester* (1820) 2 Jac & W 334 at 342.

**866.   Avoidance of grants of offices with fees.** Where a patent of the receivership of a court was granted for the grantee's life with a fee, and the court was afterwards dissolved by statute[1], the whole patent was void[2]. Where, however, an office of stewardship of a manor, a parkership or the like was granted, with a fee for exercising the office, the fee remained, it was said, even if the monarch or the lord aliened the manor, disparked the park, or discharged the office; where the fee arises from the profits of the office, the monarch or other grantor cannot generally destroy the grant of the fee by determining the office[3].

1　1 Mar sess 2, c 10 (Dissolution of Courts) (1553) (repealed).
2　*Anon* (1561) Jenk 225, Ex Ch. That is because the grantee concurs in the Act of Parliament (*Anon* supra).
3　*Anon* (1561) Jenk 225, Ex Ch.

## (iii)　Presumption of Grants

**867. Presumed grant.** In disputes relating to land or incorporeal hereditaments between subject and subject a grant from the Crown will in some cases be presumed in order to support a possessory title, even where the acts of user or enjoyment relied upon would not necessarily be sufficient to displace the title of the Crown itself[1]. Thus possession over a period of 350 years, although commencing within the time of legal memory, has been held sufficient to support the presumption of a grant from the Crown, though such a grant would not have been effectual without matter of record and no such record in fact existed[2]; and the grant of an advowson, although expressly excepted from a former grant, was presumed good after continued possession for 133 years, as evidenced by title deeds and three presentations[3]. Other examples of the same principle are to be found[4].

1　*Wyse v Leahy* (1875) IR 9 CL 384. As to possession of the foreshore see *Hastings Corpn v Ivall* (1874) LR 19 Eq 558. See also *Goodtitled Parker v Baldwin* (1809) 11 East 488. See also *Wheaton v Maple & Co* [1893] 3 Ch 48 at 51, 56, CA, per Kekewich J, that in a proper case a lost grant may be presumed against the Crown, as established by *Goodman v Saltash Corpn* (1882) 7 App Cas 633, HL. In *Hunwick v Essex Rivers Catchment Board* [1952] 1 All ER 765 at 767, Croom-Johnson J doubted whether the Crown could dedicate as a highway a pathway on top of a sea wall used for a long period by the public.
2　*Kingston-upon-Hull Corpn v Horner* (1774) 1 Cowp 102.
3　*Gibson v Clark* (1819) 1 Jac & W 159.
4　As to the presumption of a supplementary and confirmatory grant of undefined shares in land see *Des Barres v Shey* (1873) 29 LT 592 at 595, PC. As to user by exercise of sporting rights etc see *Harper v Charlesworth* (1825) 6 Dow & Ry KB 572. As to what constitutes sufficient user of the foreshore see *Le Strange v Rowe* (1866) 4 F & F 1048. As to evidence of user and presumption of grants in the case of several fisheries in tidal waters see *Harris v Earl of Chesterfield* [1911] AC 623, HL; *Tighe v Sinnott* [1897] 1 IR 140; *Smith v Andrews* [1891] 2 Ch 678; *Little v Wingfield* (1859) 11 ICLR 63, Ex Ch; affg (1858) 8 ICLR 279; *O'Neill v Allen* (1859) 9 ICLR 132. As to the presumption of a grant of the soil in the case of a several fishery see *Hanbury v Jenkins* [1901] 2 Ch 401; and FISHERIES. As to the acquisition of an ancient ferry see *General Estates Co v Beaver* [1914] 3 KB 918 at 925, CA (vill to vill); *Hammerton v Earl of Dysart* [1916] 1 AC 57 at 79, HL (point to point); and HIGHWAYS vol 21 (Reissue) para 879 et seq.

**868. No presumption against statutory restraint.** Where the Crown is expressly restrained by statute from making the grant, no such grant can be presumed even after continued acts of ownership and enjoyment[1]. Thus no grant of a several fishery in tidal rivers and arms of the sea subsequent to Magna Carta can be presumed, the Crown having been restrained by that statute from making fresh grants affecting the public right of fishing[2].

1　*Goodtitled Parker v Baldwin* (1809) 11 East 488.
2　See *Malcolmson v O'Dea* (1863) 10 HL Cas 593 at 618; *Lord Fitzhardinge v Purcell* [1908] 2 Ch 139 at 167; and FISHERIES. There is, however, some doubt whether this was the effect of the Magna Carta of Edward I (1297), c 16 (repealed): see *Neill v Duke of Devonshire* (1882) 8 App Cas 135 at 177, HL. See also CROWN LANDS AND PRIVILEGES.

**869. Adverse possession and prescription.** In actions to recover land 30 years' possession by a subject affords, in general, a valid statutory title as against the Crown[1], and in such cases a grant will be presumed[2]. Where no statutory protection is afforded as against the Crown, user or enjoyment extending over a definite period must in some cases be alleged, otherwise a valid grant cannot be presumed[3].

In the case of franchises or liberties, 20 years' uninterrupted enjoyment affords valid evidence of title upon which a grant may be presumed at common law[4]. In this and in all other cases of prescriptive title as against the Crown not provided for by statute[5], though immemorial enjoyment need not necessarily, it seems, be alleged[6], it is apprehended that no grant would be presumed if acts of ownership by the Crown within the period of legal memory were proved[7].

1   See the Limitation Act 1980 ss 15(1), 15(7), Sch 2 para 10. For the meaning of 'land' see s 38. The period for the foreshore is 60 years: Sch 2 para 11(1). See also CROWN PROCEEDINGS; LIMITATION OF ACTIONS.
2   As to the application of this principle to foreshore see *A-G v Portsmouth Corpn* (1877) 25 WR 559.
3   Ie in cases where the Crown has been prohibited by statute from making grants (eg Magna Carta: see para 868 ante), by which the Crown is restrained from making grants in derogation of public rights. As to free fisheries in tidal or navigable waters see para 868 ante.
4   See the authorities cited in note 5 infra.
5   As to presumption of various grants see *Merttens v Hill* [1901] 1 Ch 842 (manor); *Kingston-upon-Hull Corpn v Horner* (1774) 1 Cowp 102; *Foreman v Free Fisheries and Dredgers of Whitstable* (1869) LR 4 HL 266 (tolls on shipping); *Turner v Walsh* (1881) 6 App Cas 636, PC (highway: user for 21 years); *Campbell v Wilson* (1803) 3 East 294 (right of way); *Gibson v Clark* (1819) 1 Jac & W 159 (advowson); *Roe d Johnson v Ireland* (1809) 11 East 280 (enfranchisement of copyhold); *Simpson v Gutteridge* (1816) 1 Madd 609 (extinction of fee farm rents). See generally *Read v Brookman* (1789) 3 Term Rep 151 at 158, 159; *Lord Pickering v Lord Stamford* (1793) 2 Ves 272 (bill for an account of personal estate under a bequest in 1754 claimed to be void under the Statute of Mortmain); *Wheaton v Maple & Co* [1893] 3 Ch 48, CA; *Brune v Thompson* (1843) 4 QB 543 (jury directed not to presume grant – which should be of record, and not produced – on evidence of usage).
6   Eg a claim to a port or harbour: see *Jenkins v Harvey* (1835) 1 Gale 23 at 27, per Parke B. For a case where a claim to fix moorings on the foreshore by immemorial user was upheld see *A-G v Wright* [1897] 2 QB 318, CA.
7   Ie since, in the absence of statutory provisions, no time runs against the Crown, and no laches is attributable to it: see para 390 ante. The time of legal memory has long been fixed to commence from the beginning of the reign of Richard I: see 2 Co Inst 238, 239; 2 Bl Com (14th Edn) 31.

### (iv)  Grants which may or may not be made

**870.  Derogatory grants.** The monarch is restrained from making grants in derogation of the common law or statute. Thus she cannot suspend or dispense with laws or the execution of laws[1]; or grant a right to hold a court of equity[2]; or, perhaps, create a mode of descent unknown to the common law[3]; nor can she grant the right to commit a public nuisance[4].

1   Bill of Rights s 1. See also para 376 ante. As to the history and citation of the Bill of Rights see para 35 note 3 ante.
2   As to restrictions on the Crown's right to establish courts see para 308 ante.
3   Vin Abr, Prerogative, M, b, pl 23; 2 Roll Abr 164. As to the limitation of a title in a manner unknown to the common law see *Devon Peerage Case* (1831) 2 Dow & Cl 200, HL; *Cope v Earl De la Warr* (1873) 8 Ch App 982; *Wiltes' Peerage Claim* (1869) LR 4 HL 126; and see para 212 ante; and PEERAGES AND DIGNITIES.
4   See *A-G v Burridge, Portsmouth Harbour Case* (1822) 10 Price 350. As to public nuisances see NUISANCE.

**871.  Exceptions.** In some instances grants by the Crown are valid which would have been invalid at common law if made by a subject. Thus a grant by the Crown to the inhabitants of a parish may be good, even though it would not have been effectual at common law if made by a subject[1]; and a grant in fee by the Crown may contain a condition against alienation[2]. A grant by the Crown of unascertained shares in land was held not to be void for uncertainty after continued possession, a confirmatory grant being presumed in such a case[3].

1   *Willingale v Maitland* (1866) LR 3 Eq 103 at 109, where the grant of a profit à prendre to the inhabitants of a parish was held good as a grant to the parish qua corporation; the grant in this case being the right to

take lopwood was in derogation of the Crown's forestal rights: otherwise, it seems, it might have been bad. See also *Chilton v London Corpn* (1878) 7 ChD 735 at 741–743; and COMMONS vol 6 (Reissue) para 516.

2   *Fowler v Fowler* (1865) 16 I Ch R 507. As to whether the Crown is bound by the rule against perpetuities see *Cooper v Stuart* (1889) 14 App Cas 286 at 290, PC; and PERPETUITIES. The Perpetuities and Accumulations Act 1964 binds the Crown: s 15(7).

3   *Des Barres v Shey* (1873) 29 LT 592 at 595, PC.

**872. Taxes and tolls.** The Crown cannot by grant impose new taxes or enlarge old ones[1]. However, in certain cases where the grant is for the public utility and there is a quid pro quo to the public, a grant of the right to take a toll is valid[2]. Thus grants of pontage and murage are valid[3]; markets, fairs, ferries and harbours may be granted with the right to take tolls or dues[4]; and tolls on the highway may be claimed by grant or prescription, though they may not, it is said, be granted at the present day[5].

All such tolls and dues must, in general, have a reasonable commencement and be fair and moderate in their amount; otherwise the franchise will be void[6].

1   2 Co Inst 58, 60, 62–63; Bill of Rights s 1. As to the history and citation of the Bill of Rights see para 35 note 3 ante.
2   Vin Abr, Prerogative, M, b, pl 18. That consideration to the public is essential in the case of markets and fairs is shown by the writ of ad quod damnum, which is issued by the Crown before the grant of a market or fair: see Bac Abr, Fairs, A; and MARKETS AND FAIRS.
3   As to grants of pontage and murage see para 880 post.
4   As to tolls in markets and fairs see MARKETS AND FAIRS; as to ferries see HIGHWAYS; as to harbour dues see PORTS AND HARBOURS.
5   Bac Abr, Prerogative, F, 1. Toll-thorough can, it seems, only be claimed where consideration is shown by keeping the highway in repair, or the like, whereas toll-traverse may be claimed without showing consideration, though such is presumed by the law: see *Lord Pelham v Pickersgill* (1787) 1 Term Rep 660 at 667, per Ashurst J; *Hill v Smith* (1812) 4 Taunt 520 at 531; and see HIGHWAYS vol 21 (Reissue) para 141.
6   2 Bl Com (14th Edn) 37; *Heddy v Wheelhouse* (1597) Cro Eliz 558 at 559 per Popham J, and at 591. See also the authorities cited in note 5 supra.

**873. Exemption from taxes or tolls.** The monarch may not grant exemptions from taxes or charges imposed by Act of Parliament[1], but may grant exemptions from tolls in markets due to herself or in respect of markets subsequently to be granted, though not in respect of tolls due in an old fair or market belonging to a subject[2]. Similar principles would, it seems, be applicable in the case of other tolls[3].

The Crown may also grant exemptions from serving in certain public offices, such as sheriffs[4].

1   See Vin Abr, Prerogative, K, c; 2 Roll Abr 199; Bill of Rights s 1. As to the history and citation of the Bill of Rights see para 35 note 3 ante.
2   Com Dig, Prerogative, D, 33; 2 Co Inst 221; Bac Abr, Fairs, D, 2.
3   See Vin Abr, Prerogative, K, c; 2 Roll Abr 198; Com Dig, Prerogative, D, 33.
4   As to the theoretical power to compel and exempt from service as a sheriff or parish constable see para 27 note 1 ante.

**874. Reversionary interests.** In general, the Crown may grant reversionary interests. Thus it may grant a reversionary interest in land, or an office may be granted in reversion if it be such that the monarch cannot exercise it personally[1]; but a corody or a right of presentation cannot, it is said, be given in reversion, since the Crown has the right only when the corody or church becomes void[2].

1   See *Earl of Rutland's Case* (1608) 8 Co Rep 55a at 55b.
2   *Earl of Rutland's Case* (1608) 8 Co Rep 55a at 55b. As to the Crown's rights of presentation generally see ECCLESIASTICAL LAW. The Crown's right to corodies, namely to send one of its chaplains to be maintained by the bishop, or to have a pension allowed him until the bishop promotes him to a benefice (1 Bl Com (14th Edn) 280) has fallen into disuse.

**875. Monopolies.** Grants of monopolies by the Crown are bad at common law[1], except in the case of patents for new inventions[2]. Grants of patents for inventions, together with the registration of designs, are regulated by statute[3], and in certain cases national corporations have been granted by statute monopolies as respects their undertakings[4].

1　*Case of Monopolies* (1602) 11 Co Rep 84b (grant for the exclusive making and importing of playing cards held to be a monopoly, and therefore void).

2　*Case of Monopolies* (1602) 11 Co Rep 84b. This right of the Crown was recognised by the judges in that case.

3　As to patents and designs generally, and the special position of the Crown, see PATENTS; TRADE MARKS.

4　As to national corporations see CORPORATIONS.

**876. Freedom of trade.** All British subjects have equal rights of trading within the dominions and dependencies of the Crown, unless prohibited or restricted (for example, by the need to obtain a licence) by Act of Parliament. The Crown may not, therefore, by charter or otherwise, grant exclusive trading licences to any person or corporation[1]. Licences may be granted to alien enemies to trade and bring actions in time of war[2].

1　Commons Journals, 19 January 1694. The Statute of Monopolies (1623) s 9, expressly excepted the right of corporations, and of any companies or societies of merchants, from the operation of the Act, and it was held in the case of *Case of Monopolies, East India Co v Sandys* (1685) 10 State Tr 371 (known as 'the Great Case of Monopolies'), that a grant to the East India Company of the sole right of trading to the East Indies was good. On a petition of the merchants for creating a new East India Company in 1694 the House of Commons resolved 'that all subjects of England have equal rights to trade to the East Indies unless prohibited by Act of Parliament': Commons Journals, 19 January 1694; see also 5 Parliamentary History 828. Trade in India was not, however, thrown open to the public until 1813: see the East India Company Act 1813 ss 2, 3 (repealed); and see TRADE, INDUSTRY AND INDUSTRIAL RELATIONS.

2　As to licences to trade in time of war see WAR. A licence is conclusive, and neither its validity nor the policy inducing it can be questioned in a court: see *Bugsier Reederei-und-Bergungs Akt v SS Brighton (Owners)* [1951] 2 TLR 409.

**877. Anticipatory grants.** Where land escheats to Her Majesty in right of the Crown or of the Duchy of Lancaster, or to the Duke of Cornwall or Her Majesty in right of the Duchy of Cornwall, then, without prejudice to the rights of other persons, the land vests accordingly and may be dealt with, and any proceedings may be taken in relation to it, without the title by escheat being found of record by inquisition or otherwise[1]; but the Crown may not grant land 'when it shall escheat'[2].

The Crown may, in general, grant a mere possibility or an interest depending on a contingency[3].

1　Crown Estate Act 1961 s 8(3). Although escheat is abolished as regards the estates of persons deceased on or after 1 January 1926 (Administration of Estates Act 1925 s 45(1)(d)), this provision will apply where the legal estate in land vests in the Crown on the dissolution of a company or in cases where the Treasury Solicitor has disclaimed a bankrupt's property.

2　See *A-G v Farmen* (1676) T Raym 241.

3　Vin Abr, Prerogative, C, 2; Bac Abr, Prerogative, F, 3.

**878. Annuities.** A Crown grant of an annuity will be void at common law unless charged upon possessions of the Crown[1].

1　*Anon* (1695) 1 Salk 58: and see CHOSES IN ACTION vol 6 (Reissue) para 75.

### (v)  Grants of Franchises

**879. Franchises.** Whilst certain franchises remain in the hands of the Crown they form part of the royal prerogative, and do not exist as franchises until they have been granted out as such to the subject[1]. These include royal mines, wrecks, waifs and estrays, royal fish and swans[2]. These may be validly granted as franchises, notwithstanding the general rule which prevents the Crown from parting with its prerogatives[3]. But under a general grant of 'franchises' such rights, being part of the jura regalia or 'flowers of the Crown', will not pass, since they have no existence as franchises until they have been expressly granted[4].

Other franchises may be granted not out of but by virtue of the prerogative; but until so granted they have no legal existence[5]. Instances are markets and fairs[6], ferries[7], pontage and murage[8], corporations[9], counties palatine, counties corporate[10] and the cinque ports. Such franchises may become vested in the Crown after their creation by grant from a subject, forfeiture, escheat, intestacy or other means, and would then probably pass under a grant of franchises generally.

All franchises may be claimed either by grant, or by long and immemorial usage and prescription, which presupposes a former grant; and in the latter case 20 years' uninterrupted enjoyment is, in general, presumptive evidence in favour of a claimant[11].

A franchise vested in a subject merges and becomes absolutely extinct if it reverts to the Crown[12].

1   *Groenvelt's Case* (1697) 1 Ld Raym 213 at 214; Vin Abr, Prerogative, M, b, pl 20; *A-G v Trustees of British Museum* [1903] 2 Ch 598 at 612.
2   As to these prerogatives see CROWN LANDS AND PRIVILEGES. Note that the law of treasure trove, formerly governed by the prerogative, is now embodied in statute: see the Treasure Act 1996.
3   By the Civil List Act 1952 s 1, the hereditary revenues are surrendered to the nation during the Queen's reign, but the rights and powers exercisable with regard to them are preserved: see s 13(2). The foregoing franchises might therefore still be granted, it seems, for valuable consideration.
4   *A-G v Trustees of British Museum* [1903] 2 Ch 598.
5   See Bac Abr, Prerogative, F.
6   Markets and fairs, with the tolls belonging, can only be set up by grant or prescription: 2 Co Inst 220; 1 Bl Com (14th Edn) 273; *Merchant Adventurers' Co v Rebow* (1687) 3 Mod Rep 126 at 127; Bac Abr, Fairs, A, 1. As to markets and fairs generally see MARKETS AND FAIRS.
7   As to the Crown's right to grant a ferry with toll see Bac Abr, Prerogative, F, 1; 2 Roll Abr 171; Com Dig, Prerogative, D, 48; Vin Abr, Prerogative, M, b. As to ferries generally see HIGHWAYS vol 21 (Reissue) paras 876–895.
8   As to the grant of pontage and murage see para 880 post.
9   As to the creation of corporations see para 881 post.
10   As to the grant of franchises of counties corporate see para 882 post.
11   *Bealey v Shaw* (1805) 6 East 208 at 215; *Weld v Hornby* (1806) 7 East 195 at 199; *Goodtitled Parker v Baldwin* (1809) 11 East 488 at 491. As to prescriptive rights of fishing in tidal waters see para 867 note 4 ante.
12   *Abbot of Strata Mercella's Case* (1591) 9 Co Rep 24a; *Duke of Northumberland v Houghton* (1870) LR 5 Exch 127 at 131 per Martin B.

**880. Pontage and murage.** Pontage and murage are the rights granted to persons who erected new bridges, or walls for purposes of defence or the like, to take a toll for the keeping and repairing of the bridge or wall respectively, and may be claimed by prescription[1], but only so long, it is said, as the bridge or wall remains useful[2]. Under the prerogative the Crown may grant pontage in a protectorate[3].

1   Bac Abr, Prerogative, F, 1; Com Dig, Prerogative, D, 48; 2 Roll Abr 171.
2   Bac Abr, Prerogative, F, 1; Vin Abr, Prerogative, M, b, pl 19.
3   See *Nyali Ltd v A-G* [1956] 1 QB 1, [1955] 1 All ER 646, CA; affd on a different ground [1957] AC 253, [1956] 2 All ER 689, HL.

**881. Corporations.** At common law the Crown enjoys the exclusive right of creating corporations by charter[1], except such corporations as exist by custom and with the implied consent of the Crown, for example the monarch, and ecclesiastical persons such as bishops, parsons, vicars and churchwardens, who are at common law corporations by virtue of their office[2]. A corporation may exist by prescriptive right, which presupposes a former grant, as in the case of the City of London[3], and the Crown may grant the right to create a corporation, for he who acts through another acts himself[4].

1   See CORPORATIONS.
2   1 Bl Com (14th Edn) 471, 472.
3   1 Bl Com (14th Edn) 472; 2 Co Inst 330.
4   Ie *qui facit per alium facit per se*: 1 Bl Com (14th Edn) 473.

**882. Municipal franchises.** At common law the Crown may grant to a town the right or franchise of choosing its own sheriff[1], or of having its own justices to the exclusion of the county justices[2]. The Crown also frequently exercised the right of granting to a city or town the franchise of being a 'county corporate', or county in itself apart from the general body of the county, with its own sheriffs and officers exclusive of the county officers[3].

All these powers of the Crown were superseded as from 1 April 1974[4]; but on a petition from the council of a district, the Crown may by charter confer on that district the status of a borough[5]. Any privileges or rights belonging immediately before 1 April 1974 to the citizens or burgesses of an existing city or borough belong on and after that date to the inhabitants of the area of the existing city or borough[6]; and where the Crown confers on a district the status of a borough (for which charter trustees are not constituted), the charter may provide that any such privileges or rights shall belong to the inhabitants of the whole or any part of the district[7].

1   Vin Abr, Prerogative, M, b, 18, 21: see SHERIFFS.
2   See *Blankley v Winstanley* (1789) 3 Term Rep 279. The jurisdiction of borough justices is concurrent with the county jurisdiction unless the contrary appears: *R v Sainsbury* (1791) 4 Term Rep 451. As to commissions of the peace see the Local Government Act 1972 s 217 (repealed); and the Justices of the Peace Act 1979 ss 1–5 (as amended), 71, Sch 1 para 3.
3   1 Bl Com (14th Edn) 119; see LOCAL GOVERNMENT.
4   See the Local Government Act 1972 s 1.
5   See ibid s 245(1). The Act also preserves the prerogative to grant the status of city or royal borough: see s 245(10); and LOCAL GOVERNMENT vol 28 para 1083.
6   Ibid s 246(1).
7   Ibid s 246(2)(b) (amended by the Charter Trustees Act 1985 s 1(2)).

# (11)  ARMED FORCES

## (i)  Basic Principles

**883. Standing army.** The government, or in traditional terms the Crown or its ministers, is prevented from exercising despotic power by means of military force because it is not permitted to raise or keep a standing army within the kingdom in time of peace without the consent of Parliament[1]. Soldiers and mariners may not be billeted upon private persons[2], unless under statutory authority[3].

1   Bill of Rights s 1. See generally Wade and Bradley *Constitutional and Administrative Law* (11th Edn, 1993) ch 16. As to the history and citation of the Bill of Rights see para 35 note 3 ante.
2   Petition of Right (1627) ss 6, 8.
3   As to the billeting of soldiers and airmen see ROYAL FORCES; and as to the requisition of property in times of war or emergency see WAR.

**884. Statutory control.** Although the supreme command and governance of the royal forces are vested in the Crown at common law and by statute[1], most matters relating to them are today primarily regulated by statute, for example the raising or embodying of the regular, reserve, territorial and auxiliary forces and their subjection, when raised or embodied, to special codes of military or naval discipline; the general mode of enlistment and term of service of soldiers, sailors and airmen, with many other matters relating to the pay, pensions, decorations, effects, billeting, privileges and exemptions, and civil duties and liabilities of soldiers, sailors and airmen; and the requisitioning of vehicles[2]. The general administration of the Acts relating to these matters is controlled by the Ministry of Defence[3].

1  As to supreme command of the royal forces see para 886 post.
2  As to these see ROYAL FORCES.
3  As to the Ministry of Defence see paras 438–447 ante.

**885. The service ministries.** Apart from these statutory provisions, many wide and important powers relating to the royal forces are still retained by the Crown, whose discretionary authority is exercised on the advice of the Secretary of State for Defence[1], and through the recognised executive channels of the Ministry of Defence[2] and the Defence Council[3], the Admiralty Board[4], the Army Board[5] and the Air Force Board[6]. The powers left to the control of the Crown and its servants embrace such matters as the selection and appointment of the officers to whom the supreme command is delegated and the apportionment of their duties; the grouping and disposal of the various ships, battalions, and squadrons, and other naval, military or air force units at home and abroad, in time of peace or war; and generally all matters relating to the organisation, disposition, personnel, armament and maintenance of the naval, military and air forces[7]. Whether all acts done in the exercise of such powers and not authorised by statute are necessarily done by virtue of the royal prerogative is doubtful[8].

1  As to the Secretary of State for Defence see paras 439–441 ante.
2  As to the Ministry of Defence see paras 438–447 ante.
3  As to the Defence Council see paras 443–444 ante.
4  As to the Admiralty Board of the Defence Council see para 445 ante.
5  As to the Army Board of the Defence Council see para 446 ante.
6  As to the Air Force Board of the Defence Council see para 447 ante.
7  See generally ROYAL FORCES. As to the extent to which these powers may be subject to judicial review see *China Navigation Co Ltd v A-G* [1932] 2 KB 197, CA; *Chandler v DPP* [1964] AC 763, [1962] 3 All ER 142, HL. As to judicial review and the manner of exercise of the prerogative see para 380 ante; and ADMINISTRATIVE LAW.
8  The matter was raised in *Nissan v A-G* [1968] 1 QB 286, [1967] 2 All ER 200; on appeal [1968] 1 QB 286 at 327, [1967] 2 All ER 1238, CA; affd sub nom *A-G v Nissan*, cited infra, but not in such a form as to require a definite answer, the particular issue to be decided being whether the acts in question were acts of state (see FOREIGN RELATIONS LAW). In the Court of Appeal Lord Denning MR was clearly of opinion that when Her Majesty sends her troops overseas to duty in a foreign land, without the authority of Parliament, but with the accord of the foreign sovereign, it is done by virtue of the royal prerogative, since there is no other warrant for it ([1968] 1 QB 286 at 340, [1967] 2 All ER 1238 at 1244, CA). In the House of Lords Lord Pearce (*A-G v Nissan* [1970] AC 179 at 229, [1969] 1 All ER 629 at 652, HL) substantially agreed with that view on the ground that the prerogative is the power which directs the movement of forces abroad and is the warrant for their presence abroad; accordingly when monarch and subject meet through the operation of the prerogative in an army overseas, there seems no inherent reason why the prerogative should not be valid. The other Law Lords either did not mention the point or preferred not to commit themselves. It is submitted that the opinions expressed by Lord Denning MR and Lord Pearce are correct. See also Gilmour 'British Forces Abroad and the Responsibility for their Actions' [1970] Public Law 121–152.

## (ii)　The Command of the Forces

**886. The supreme command.** The supreme government and command of all forces by sea, land and air, and of all defence establishments is vested in the Crown by prerogative right at common law and by statute[1].

The monarch has, however, long since ceased to exercise the supreme command in person[2], and is expressly empowered to make regulations as to the persons, being members of Her Majesty's forces[3], in whom command over those forces or any part or member of them is to be vested, and as to the circumstances in which that command is to be exercised[4].

The formulation and general application of a unified policy relating to the armed forces as a whole and their requirements is the duty of the Secretary of State for Defence[5], who is a member of the Cabinet[6].

1　Com Dig, Prerogative, C 3; 13 Car 2 stat 1 c 6 (Militia) (1661). Under the Regulation of the Forces Act 1871 s 6 (repealed), all powers etc over volunteers formerly vested in lieutenants of counties reverted to and became exercisable by Her Majesty through her Secretary of State or any officers to whom such powers etc might be delegated with the advice of the Secretary of State. All officers in the volunteers hold their commissions from the Her Majesty, and such commissions are to be prepared, authenticated and issued as those of Her Majesty's land forces: Reserve Forces Act 1980 s 117(1) (repealed as from a day to be appointed by the Reserve Forces Act 1996 s 131(2), Sch 11). This recital was applied to the former Territorial and Army Volunteer Reserve: see Order in Council dated 19 March 1908 SR & O 1908/256 (having effect as if made under the Reserve Forces Act 1980 s 152(1) (as prospectively repealed: see supra). The Territorial and Army Volunteer Reserve is now known as the Territorial Army: see the Reserve Forces Act 1982 s 1 (prospectively repealed by the Reserve Forces Act 1996 Sch 11). As to the office of Secretary of State see para 355 et seq ante.
2　The King gave up the personal command of the army in 1793, when the first Commander-in-Chief was created: see 10 Hunt and Poole's Political History of England p 362; 1 Clode's Military Forces of the Crown p 240.
3　'Member of Her Majesty's Forces' includes any person in command of an aircraft: Army Act 1955 s 177(2).
4　Ibid s 177(1); Air Force Act 1955 s 177(1). These provisions were enacted to remove doubts as to the powers previously vested in officers and others. They are not to be deemed to affect any power otherwise vested in Her Majesty: Army Act 1955 s 177(3); Air Force Act 1955 s 177(3).
5　As to the Secretary of State for Defence see paras 439–441 ante.
6　As to the Cabinet see paras 402–413 ante.

## (iii)　Maintenance and Discipline of the Royal Forces

**887. Legislative authority for maintaining the armed forces and discipline in them.** The Crown is expressly prohibited from raising or keeping a standing army within the kingdom in time of peace unless with the consent of Parliament[1]. Moreover, the issue of commissions of martial law by the Crown, and the subjection of any person in time of peace to any other than the established laws of the realm as enacted by Parliament, is contrary to the constitution[2]. The necessary authority for the maintenance of the military forces to be employed for the safety of the United Kingdom and the defence of the possessions of the Crown and for keeping discipline in them is supplied annually by statute or Order in Council[3].

The raising and maintenance of the Royal Air Force are authorised by a permanent Act[4], but as the Air Force Act 1955, by which discipline is enforced, expires annually, annual legislation by statute or Order in Council is needed for its continuance, in the same way as for the army[5].

The regular naval forces are maintained by the Crown without any direct statutory authority, none being required by the law of the constitution[6]. Their discipline is provided for by the Naval Discipline Act 1957, which, although by tradition and in principle permanent, is now made to expire every five years unless continued in force year by year by Order in Council according to the same rules as those applicable to the army and the air force[7].

The Royal Marines are a separate corps of the regular forces[8]. An officer, warrant officer, non-commissioned officer or marine of the Royal Marines, the Royal Marines Reserve or the Royal Fleet Reserve continues to be subject to military law notwithstanding that he may, for the time being, be subject to the Naval Discipline Act 1957[9].

1    Bill of Rights s 1. As to the prohibition of quasi-military organisations enacted in the Public Order Act 1936 s 2 see CRIMINAL LAW. As to compulsory national service, which generally came to an end in 1962, see ROYAL FORCES. As to the history and citation of the Bill of Rights see para 35 note 3 ante.

2    See Magna Carta of Edward I (1297), c 29; Petition of Right (1627) ss 7, 8; and see the Bill of Rights. As to the legal position of the armed forces generally see ROYAL FORCES.

     Military justice was administered originally in the Court of the Constable and Earl Marshal. Both these offices were hereditary, and on the former being extinguished by the attainder of the Duke of Buckingham in the reign of Henry VIII the jurisdiction of the court should have reverted to the Crown, but the court seems to have continued to exist, until in 1703 it was said that without the Constable the court was not properly constituted: *Chambers v Jennings* (1702) 7 Mod Rep 125, an opinion regarded as obiter and disapproved by Lord Goddard in *Manchester Corpn v Manchester Palace of Varieties Ltd* [1955] P 133 at 149, [1955] 1 All ER 387 at 393, High Court of Chivalry. Serious doubt has been cast upon the connection between martial law and the court: see Squibb, High Court of Chivalry 8–9. The office of Earl Marshal is still hereditary in the family of the Duke of Norfolk. See Adye, Courts-martial 3. The term 'military law' is now applied to the legal code under the Army Act 1955, whilst the term 'martial law' is applied to proclamations of martial law by the Crown: see para 821 ante.

3    After the revolution of 1688 the standing army was placed on a legal footing by means of annual Mutiny Acts: see 1 Clode's Military Forces of the Crown pp 363–364. From 1881 onwards the annual Army Act took the place of the Mutiny Act. An important change was made in 1955, when the Army Act 1955 was enacted to remain in force for one year, with power conferred to continue it annually up to a maximum of five years by Order in Council to be approved in draft by resolution of each House of Parliament. These provisions have been contained in subsequent Armed Forces Acts continuing the Army Act 1955 for further periods of five years and conferring power to extend it annually by Order in Council: see eg the Armed Forces Act 1991 s 1 (repealed as from 1 September 1996 by the Armed Forces Act 1996 ss 35(2), 36(4), Sch 7 Pt III); and the Army, Air Force and Naval Discipline (Continuation) Order 1995, SI 1995/1964, which provides for the continuation in force of the Army Act 1955, the Air Force Act 1955 and the Naval Discipline Act 1957; and see the Armed Forces Act 1996 s 1(1) (continuing those Acts until 31 August 1997), (2) (providing for their further continuance by Order in Council), and (3) (limiting their ultimate continuance to the end of the year 2001).

4    See the Air Force (Constitution) Act 1917 s 1.

5    The Air Force Act 1955 contained provisions for its annual continuation by Order in Council up to a maximum of five years, in the same way as the Army Act 1955. See now the Armed Forces Act 1991 s 1 (repealed: see note 3 supra); the Army, Air Force and Naval Discipline (Continuation) Order 1995; the Armed Forces Act 1996 s 1; and note 3 supra.

6    The maintenance of the naval forces does not appear to have been regarded by Parliament as a menace to the liberties of the subject, hence the absence of enactments compelling parliamentary sanction. An indirect control has, however, always been exercised by Parliament in the granting of supplies necessary to meet the expenses of the annual estimates for the navy. As to entry and service in the Royal Navy see the Royal Navy Terms of Service (Ratings) Regulations 1982, SI 1982/834 (as amended); and ROYAL FORCES.

7    See the Armed Forces Act 1991 s 1 (repealed: see note 3 supra); the Army, Air Force and Naval Discipline (Continuation) Order 1995; the Armed Forces Act 1996 s 1; and note 3 supra.

8    Army Act 1955 s 210(1).

9    Ibid s 210(3) (amended by the Navy, Army and Air Force Reserves Act 1959 s 2, Schedule; the Armed Forces Act 1971 s 75, Sch 3 para 4(1); and the Armed Forces Act 1981 s 28(1), Sch 4 para 1(1)). See further ROYAL FORCES.

**888. Territorial forces and naval, army and air reserves.** In addition to the regular forces, Her Majesty is empowered to maintain the Territorial Army[1], the Royal Auxiliary Air Force, the Royal Naval Reserve, the Army Reserve and the Air Force

Reserve[2]. These forces consist of such number of officers and men or women as may from time to time be provided by Parliament[3].

The Home Guard has also been established as part of the armed forces of the Crown, being a force consisting of such persons as may voluntarily undertake to serve in the Home Guard without pay and be accepted for service[4].

1   The Territorial Army was formerly known as the Territorial and Army Volunteer Reserve: Reserve Forces Act 1982 s 1 (repealed as from a day to be appointed by the Reserve Forces Act 1996 s 131(2), Sch 11).
2   As to all these forces see generally ROYAL FORCES.
3   See eg the Reserve Forces Act 1980 s 5(2) (repealed and replaced as from a day to be appointed by the Reserve Forces Act 1996 ss 3(1), 132(4), Sch 11).
4   The Home Guard is believed to be in abeyance, although it appears that it has not formally been disbanded. As to the Home Guard see ROYAL FORCES vol 41 para 311 et seq.

**889. Women's services.** The Crown's power, vested whether by statute or prerogative, to raise and maintain land and air forces includes power to raise and maintain forces consisting of or including women[1], which are known as the Women's Royal Army Corps and the Women's Royal Air Force.

Members of the Women's Royal Naval Service have never been declared to be members of the armed forces of the Crown, though in fact on enrolment they contract to observe a code of discipline similar to that for the Royal Navy[2].

1   Army and Air Force (Women's Service) Act 1948 s 1: see ROYAL FORCES vol 41 paras 17, 313.
    By virtue of the Sex Discrimination Act 1975 (Application to Armed Forces etc) Regulations 1994, SI 1994/3276, the legislation on sex discrimination and equal pay apply to the armed forces. This is in order to comply with obligations under EC Council Directive 76/207 (OJ L39 14.2.76 p 40). For criticism of the inadequacy of the regulations see 561 HL Official Report (5th series), 16 February 1995, col 852.
2   See further ROYAL FORCES.

**890–900. Courts-martial appeals.** Appeal lies from a decision of a court-martial to the Courts-Martial Appeal Court[1]. The monarch's prerogative of mercy is not, however, affected by the establishment of this court, nor is her prerogative power to quash a conviction by a court-martial affected by it[2].

1   See the Courts-Martial (Appeals) Act 1968 s 8 (as amended). As to the Courts-Martial Appeal Court see COURTS vol 10 paras 953–956; ROYAL FORCES vol 41 para 520 et seq.
2   See ibid s 54. This is subject to a procedural qualification as to the time for the exercise of the prerogative power to quash a conviction: see s 54(1). As to the prerogative of mercy see para 823 ante.

# 8. FORMALITIES, DOCUMENTS AND OATHS

## (1) APPOINTMENT TO AND TENURE OF OFFICES

**901. Appointment.** The manner in which judicial officers, members of the administration and executive officers generally are appointed by the Crown varies according to the different offices; but the more important posts are conferred directly by the Crown either (1) by delivery of seals of office, as in the case of the Lord Chancellor, the Lord Privy Seal and the Principal Secretaries of State[1]; (2) by letters patent under the Great Seal[2], as in the case of the Treasury Commissioners[3] and Lords of Appeal in Ordinary, Lords Justice of Appeal and High Court Judges[4]; (3) by warrant under the royal sign manual[5], as in the case of the Paymaster General, circuit judges and recorders and stipendiary magistrates[6]; (4) by commission under the sign manual and signet, as in the case of overseas governors[7]; or (5) by declaration of the monarch herself in Council, as in the case of the Lord President of the Council.

Appointments of the Attorney General and the Solicitor General take effect from the approval by the monarch of the Prime Minister's recommendation and are confirmed by letters patent[8]. District judges are appointed by the Lord Chancellor by way of an instrument of appointment[9].

The Civil Service Commissioners for testing the qualifications of candidates for permanent appointments in the Home Civil Service and the Diplomatic Service are appointed by Order in Council made under the prerogative[10]. Her Majesty may, by Order in Council, from time to time as the occasion may require, regulate the grant of commissions in the navy, army and air force[11] and direct that commissions prepared under the authority of the sign manual may be issued without the sign manual but be signed by the Secretary of State for Defence or by the Secretary of State and a member or members of the Defence Council[12].

Some ministerial offices, notably those of Lord Chancellor[13] and Secretary of State[14] derive from the prerogative[15]. Other ministerial offices are now established under statutory provisions. Secretaries of State[16] and certain ministers in charge of a public department of government who are not members of the Cabinet are corporations sole[17]. Both prerogative and statutory appointees exercise such statutory functions as are conferred on the minister from time to time. Functions may be transferred by Order in Council from one minister to another[18]. The style and title of ministers may be altered[19], and departments may be dissolved by Order in Council[20]. Statutory authority is required if a new ministerial office is to have corporate personality, except that of Secretary of State[21].

1   The secretarial seals are the signet, the second secretarial seal, and the cachet. The office of the signet has now been abolished (see the Great Seal Act 1851 s 2 (repealed)), and each department now uses its own signet. An example of its use is in the commissions of appointment of and instructions to overseas governors. See also para 357 ante.
2   As to use of the Great Seal see para 909 post.
3   See the Consolidated Fund Act 1816 s 2 (as amended).
4   As to letters patent and documents under the Great Seal see para 920 post.
5   As to the sign manual see para 908 post.
6   See the Paymaster General Act 1835 s 4 (as amended) (and para 714 ante); the Courts Act 1971 ss 16, 21 (both as amended); and the Justices of the Peace Act 1979 s 13 (as amended). Appointments, once made, are announced in the London Gazette.
7   There are usually three documents: (1) Order in Council or letters patent constituting the office of governor; (2) instructions under the sign manual and signet; and (3) the commission under the sign manual and signet appointing the governor to act pursuant to (1) and (2): see COMMONWEALTH vol 6 (Reissue) para 995.
8   As to the law officers of the Crown see para 529 et seq ante.
9   See the County Courts Act 1984 s 6 (as amended).
10  See eg the Civil Service Order in Council 1995. As to the commissioners see para 550 ante.
11  See eg the Officers' Commissions (Army) Order 1967, dated 23 March 1967, under which first commissions in the regular, reserve and auxiliary military forces are issued under the sign manual in the form set out in the schedule to the order and are to be countersigned by two members of the Defence Council or of the Army Board. See also ROYAL FORCES.
12  See the Officers' Commissions Act 1862 s 1 (as amended).
13  As to the appointment of the Lord Chancellor see para 477 ante.
14  'Secretary of State' means one of Her Majesty's Principal Secretaries of State: Interpretation Act s 5 1978, Sch 1. As to the office of Secretary of State see para 355 et seq ante.
15  As to the royal prerogative see paras 367–380 ante.
16  See the Ministers of the Crown Act 1975 ss 2(1)(a), 3; and para 363 ante.

17  See ibid s 6(1), Sch 1 para 5; Ministerial and other Salaries Act 1975 s 1(1)(b), Sch 1 Pt II (as amended); and para 363 ante. As to corporations sole see CORPORATIONS.

18  See the Ministers of the Crown Act 1975 s 1(1)(a); and para 363 ante.

19  See ibid s 4; and para 363 ante.

20  See ibid s 1(1)(b); and para 363 ante.

21  See de Smith and Brazier *Constitutional and Administrative Law* (7th Edn, 1994) pp 195–196.

**902. Tenure of office.** Except where it is otherwise provided by statute[1], all public officers and servants of the Crown hold their appointments at the pleasure of the Crown[2], and all, in general, are subject to dismissal at any time without cause assigned[3]. The courts will not entertain an action for wrongful dismissal[4], even though the officer can prove the existence of a contract in which the Crown purports to restrict its right to dismiss him[5]. These rules once made the position of civil servants legally precarious, though in practice dismissal would take place only as the result of well-established disciplinary processes. Now, however, although the Crown still retains the right to dismiss at pleasure, the legal position of the civil servant has been greatly changed[6].

Where an office held during good behaviour is conferred by letters patent, procedure by writ of scire facias on the Crown side of the Queen's Bench Division of the High Court or impeachment may, it seems, be necessary in order to vacate the office[7]. There are, however, several offices which are held neither during pleasure nor during good behaviour[8]. Some offices are specially protected by the terms of their appointment[9].

1  See *Gould v Stuart* [1896] AC 575, PC; and para 903 post.

2  *Dunn v R* [1896] 1 QB 116 at 119, CA, per Lord Herschell LC. See also *A-G for Guyana v Nobrega* [1969] 3 All ER 1604, PC; and para 387 ante.

3  As to officers in the army and navy see *Re Tufnell* (1876) 3 ChD 164. See also *Grant v Secretary of State for India* (1877) 2 CPD 445; *Dickson v Viscount Combermere* (1863) 3 F & F 527; and CROWN PROCEEDINGS. As to civil servants in the colonial service see *Shenton v Smith* [1895] AC 229, PC; *Re Governor General and Executive Council of New South Wales, ex p Robertson* (1858) 11 Moo PCC 288.

4  See the cases cited in note 3 supra; and generally EMPLOYMENT.

5  *Re Hales's Petition of Right* (1918) 34 TLR 341; affd sub nom *Hales v R* (1918) 34 TLR 589, CA; *Denning v Secretary of State for India in Council* (1920) 37 TLR 138; *Rodwell v Thomas* [1944] KB 596, [1944] 1 All ER 700. It is submitted that, in so far as it is in conflict with the statement in the text, the opinion expressed in *Reilly v R* [1934] AC 176, PC, is wrong.

6  As to the tenure of office of civil servants see para 557 ante.

7  See *Re Governor-General and Executive Council of New South Wales, ex p Robertson* (1858) 11 Moo PCC 288. The methods of determining an office held during good behaviour (which would, it seems, be applicable) were stated in the case of Sir Jonah Barrington to be (1) scire facias; (2) criminal information; (3) impeachment; and (4) the exercise of the inquisitorial and judicial jurisdiction of the House of Lords (see 62 Lords Journals 6026, 4 June 1830). Criminal informations were abolished by the Criminal Law Act 1967 s 6(6). Proceedings by scire facias in relation to title to an office, being proceedings whereby a Crown grant, charter or franchise could be rescinded, are obsolescent; but scire facias upon the Crown side of the Queen's Bench Division of the High Court, which is the remedy here in question, was not abolished by the Crown Proceedings Act 1947 s 23 (as amended), Sch 1, owing to the saving in s 38(2), whereby proceedings on the Crown side are excluded from being civil proceedings within the Act. Proceedings by impeachment are probably obsolete.

8  Eg a full-time immigration adjudicator holds and vacates his office in accordance with the terms of his appointment and, on ceasing to hold office, is eligible for re-appointment: Immigration Act 1971 s 12(b) (substituted by the Transfer of Functions (Immigration Appeals) Order 1987, SI 1987/465, art 3(2), Sch 5 para 2(1)). However, this is subject to the provision that an adjudicator must vacate his office on the day on which he attains the age of 70, subject to the Judicial Pensions and Retirement Act 1993 s 26(4)–(6) (power to authorise continuance in office up to the age of 75): Immigration Act 1971 Sch 5 para 2(3) (added by the Judicial Pensions and Retirement Act 1993 s 26(1), Sch 6 para 38).

9  Eg the Crown Estate Commissioners (see the Crown Estate Act 1961 s 1(7), Sch 1 para 1(5); and CROWN LANDS AND PRIVILEGES).

**903. Offices expressed to be held during good behaviour.** Judges of the High Court and of the Court of Appeal, with the exception of the Lord Chancellor[1], the Lords of Appeal in Ordinary[2], the Comptroller and Auditor General[3], and the Parliamentary Commissioner for Administration[4] hold their offices during good behaviour, subject to a power of removal upon an address to the Crown by both Houses of Parliament[5]. Such offices may, it is said, be determined for want of good behaviour without an address to the Crown, either by writ of scire facias[6] or impeachment, or by the exercise of the inquisitorial and judicial jurisdiction vested in the House of Lords[7]. The grant of an office during good behaviour creates an office for life or until retirement age[8] determinable upon breach of the condition[9]. High Court judges, Lords Justices of Appeal and Heads of Division holding office during good behaviour who become incapacitated may have their offices declared to have been vacated by the Lord Chancellor[10].

'Behaviour' means behaviour in matters concerning the office[11], except in the case of conviction upon an indictment for any infamous offence of such a nature as to render the person unfit to exercise the office, which amounts legally to misbehaviour although not committed in connection with the office[12]. 'Misbehaviour' as to the office itself means improper exercise of the functions appertaining to the office, or non-attendance, or neglect of or refusal to perform the duties of the office[13].

1　See the Supreme Court Act 1981 s 11(3). Colonial judges hold office during pleasure: see *Terrell v Secretary of State for the Colonies* [1953] 2 QB 482, [1953] 2 All ER 490. As to the tenure of judicial office holders see para 303 ante; and ADMINISTRATIVE LAW vol 1(1) (Reissue) para 10; COURTS. As to the Lord Chancellor see paras 477–497 ante.

2　See the Appellate Jurisdiction Act 1876 s 6 (as amended); and COURTS vol 10 para 749.

3　See the Exchequer and Audit Departments Act 1866 s 3 (as amended). As to the Comptroller and Auditor General see paras 724–726 ante.

4　See the Parliamentary Commissioner Act 1967 s 1(2) (as amended). A person appointed to the Commissioner may be relieved of office by Her Majesty at his own request, or may be removed from office by Her Majesty in consequence of addresses from both Houses of Parliament, and must in any case vacate office on completing the year of service in which he attains the age of 65 years: s 1(3).

5　See also paras 8, 303 ante.

6　See further para 902 note 7 ante.

7　*Barrington's Case* (1830) 62 Lords Journals 599 at 602; and see para 902 note 7 ante. As to the House of Lords see para 204 ante; and PARLIAMENT.

8　As to the retirement ages for judicial officers see the Judicial Pensions and Retirement Act 1993 s 26; and ADMINISTRATIVE LAW vol 1(1) (Reissue) para 10; COURTS.

9　Co Litt 42a.

10　See the Supreme Court Act 1981 s 11(8), (9); and COURTS.

11　4 Co Inst 117.

12　See *R v Richardson* (1758) 1 Burr 517 at 539 (removal from office).

13　*Earl of Shrewsbury's Case* (1610) 9 Co Rep 42a at 50a.

**904. Women in office.** A person must not be disqualified by sex or marriage from the exercise of any public function, from being appointed to or holding any civil or judicial office or post, or from entering or assuming or carrying on any civil profession or vocation, or for admission to any incorporated society (whether incorporated by Royal Charter or otherwise)[1].

If the terms of a contract under which a woman is employed at an establishment in Great Britain do not include (directly or by reference to a collective agreement or otherwise) an equality clause they are deemed to include one[2]. An equality clause has the effect of ensuring that where a woman and a man are employed on like work in the same employment the woman's contract does not include any term which is less favourable[3]. This applies to (1) service for the purposes of a minister of the Crown or government department other than service of a person holding a statutory office; or (2) service on behalf of the Crown for purposes of a person holding a statutory office or purposes of a statutory body, as it applies to employment by a private person[4]. It also applies in relation to service as a relevant member of the House of Commons staff as in relation to service for the purposes of a minister of the Crown or government department[5].

1   Sex Disqualification (Removal) Act 1919 s 1 (amended by the Courts Act 1971 ss 35(7), 56, Sch 11 Pt I; the Criminal Justice Act 1972 s 64(2), Sch 6 Pt I; and the Statute Law (Repeals) Act 1989). See also the Sex Discrimination Act 1975 ss 6, 8 (both as amended).
2   See the Equal Pay Act 1970 s 1(1) (as substituted); and EMPLOYMENT vol 16 para 767.
3   See ibid s 1(2); and EMPLOYMENT vol 16 (Reissue) para 215.
4   See ibid s 1(8) (as substituted).
5   See ibid s 1(10A) (as added). As to the House of Commons see PARLIAMENT.

**905. Removal from office.** Where an office is held during good behaviour subject to a power of removal by the Crown on an address from both Houses of Parliament, proceedings may, it seems, be initiated by a petition to either House of Parliament, praying for an address to the Crown[1], or by articles of charge presented to the House of Commons[2] by a member[3] (though such a proceeding has been so long out of use that it is doubtful whether it is still available[4]); or proceedings may be originated in either House by a resolution for an address to the Crown to appoint a committee of inquiry into the conduct of the person designated[5], although preferably they should be commenced in the House of Commons[6].

The charges upon which the proceedings are grounded must, however, be distinctly and specifically alleged, and must be such as would, if proved, be sufficient to warrant an address to the Crown for dismissal[7]. If the facts alleged are sufficient, the House may proceed to refer the matter for inquiry either to a select committee or to a committee of the whole House[8], but in either case opportunity should, it seems, be given to the officer whose conduct is impugned to make his defence on a public inquiry at the Bar either of the Lords or Commons[9]. If an address to the Crown is agreed upon, it is communicated to the other House, and if not rejected there, is ultimately conveyed to the Crown, which replies in accordance with the terms of the address[10].

1   See *Fox's Case* (1805) 45 Lords Journals 181, 203 at 204.
2   As to the House of Commons see PARLIAMENT.
3   See *M'Cleland's Case* (1819) 74 Commons Journals 493 (27 June 1819); 40 Parliamentary Debates 850–854.
4   See 866 HC Official Report (5th series), 10 December 1973, col 42.
5   *Barrington's Case* (1830) 85 Commons Journals 196 (18 March 1830).
6   In *Fox's Case* (1805) 45 Lords Journals 181, 203, the proceedings were commenced by petition from the House of Lords, but were subsequently abandoned on a resolution to the effect that no criminal complaint can be preferred originally in the Lords, that the House of Commons is the grand inquest of the High Court of Parliament, and that House alone can bring complaints before the Lords for high crimes and misdemeanours (see 7 Parliamentary Debates (1st series), 757–758). A protest against this course was, however, recorded by Lords Abercorn, Eldon, and others (see at 788), and the resolution would not now, it is apprehended, be acted upon.
7   Thus in *M'Cleland's Case* (1819) 74 Commons Journal 493 (27 June 1819) a motion to refer the matter for inquiry was rejected on the ground that no such corrupt conduct had been imputed as would justify inquiry (see 74 Commons Journal 493; 40 Parliamentary Debates 850–854). In *Lord Abinger's Case* (1843) 66 Parliamentary Debates (3rd series) 1037, the complaint was the use of objectionable expressions in charges to the jury; but the motion to refer for inquiry was negatived because the charges were not specific (see 66 Parliamentary Debates (3rd series) 1102, 1129–1130).
8   For reference to a select committee see *Chief Baron O'Grady's Case* (1821) 76 Commons Journals 499; 78 Commons Journals 321. In *Barrington's Case* (1830) 85 Commons Journals 196 (18 March 1830), a select committee was appointed to inquire into the report of the commission of inquiry in Ireland, and Sir Jonah was permitted to attend. The report of the select committee was ultimately considered in a committee of the whole House (see 85 Commons Journals 653 (18 March 1830), and Sir Jonah petitioned for a trial at the bar, but this was refused (see Mirror of Parliament (1830) 1702, 1863, 1897). As to select committees see para 227 ante; and PARLIAMENT.

9   In *Barrington's Case* (1830) 85 Commons Journals 196 (18 March 1830), evidence on oath having been taken and fully considered previously, the House refused a trial at the bar of the House, although it was questioned whether an address ought to be voted without a full public inquiry (see Mirror of Parliament (1830) 1702, 1863, 1897). On the subsequent proceedings in the House of Lords a petition for trial at the bar of the House was granted (see 62 Lords Journals 599 at 602 (4 June 1830)).

10   *Barrington's Case* (1830) 85 Commons Journals 196 (18 March 1830). For the terms of the reply see 62 Lords Journals 915, and 85 Commons Journals 653 (22 July 1830). This appears to be the only case in which the proceedings were carried to a final conclusion.

# (2) PUBLIC DOCUMENTS

**906. Public documents.** The monarch's wishes or commands in executive matters are made known to the nation, or to the individuals particularly concerned, by means of various documents, of which the most formal are (1) Orders in Council[1]; (2) warrants, commissions or orders under the sign manual[2]; or (3) proclamations, writs, letters patent, letters close, charters, grants, and other documents under the Great Seal[3].

Apart from the prerogative power of the monarch executive authority is often expressly conferred on the Crown and its ministers by statute, and by virtue of the statutes conferring the powers is exercised by means of various written instruments, of which the most important are (a) Orders in Council; and (b) orders, schemes, warrants, regulations or rules[4].

1   As to Orders in Council see para 907 post.

2   As to the sign manual see para 908 post.

3   As to use of the Great Seal see para 909 post. An Order in Council or a royal warrant issued under prerogative powers may place a duty on a minister to carry out its provisions, but this duty is owed only to the Crown and a subject cannot enforce the performance by legal proceedings: *Griffin v Lord Advocate* 1950 SC 448; *R v Secretary of State for War* [1891] 2 QB 326, CA. In *Griffin v Lord Advocate* supra, it was left undecided how far these principles apply in relation to an Order in Council made under statutory powers.

4   This statement of types of instruments is not intended to be exhaustive; eg regulations may empower a minister to give directions to particular persons. As to what instruments are statutory instruments and subject to the provisions of the Statutory Instruments Act 1946 see STATUTES.

**907. Orders in Council.** Orders in Council are the general medium by which the manifold statutory powers conferred upon the Crown are exercised[1], although they may also be employed in expressing the wishes of the Crown with regard to matters falling within its discretionary authority by virtue of the prerogative[2]. They are formulated by the various ministers or departments concerned with the particular matter to which the orders relate, and their general policy is determined by the Cabinet[3]; they are expressed to be made by the monarch by and with the advice of the Privy Council at meetings of the Privy Council, which are held at such times as the exigencies of public business require, and are signed by the Clerk of the Council[4]. Orders in Council may, but need not, be statutory instruments[5].

1   For the various matters to which such orders relate see the current Index to Government Orders.

2   Eg legislation for Crown colonies, regulations with regard to trade and commerce in time of war etc. For the relation of such prerogative Orders in Council to international law, as administered by prize courts see FOREIGN RELATIONS LAW; WAR. As to the enforcement of Orders in Council see para 906 note 3 ante.

3   As to the Cabinet see paras 402–413 ante.

4   As to the Privy Council generally see paras 521–526 ante.

5   See further para 525 note 9 ante. As to statutory instruments generally see STATUTES.

**908. Sign manual.** Orders, warrants and commissions under the sign manual are used under the powers conferred by the common or statute law, and relate to a variety of matters, such as the appointment of executive officers[1], circuit judges and recorders[2], and the authorisation of the performance of executive acts[3].

In some cases the sign manual, warrant or order requires the addition of one of the secretarial seals[4]. Where such confirmation is not necessary, sign manual documents are usually required to be countersigned by a Secretary of State or other responsible minister or ministers[5].

1 Eg governors of overseas territories; first commissions in land forces: see para 901 ante.

2 For examples of appointments of circuit judges and recorders under the royal sign manual see eg the London Gazette, 20 .. lay 1996.

3 Eg warrants for affixing the Great Seal to executive documents, countersigned by the necessary minister (see para 912 post); pardons, countersigned by the Secretary of State (Criminal Law Act 1967 s 9: see para 824 ante); orders for the issue of public money by the Treasury, counter-signed by two or more of the Treasury Commissioners (see the Exchequer and Audit Departments Act 1866 s 14; Treasury Instruments (Signature) Act 1849 s 1 (as amended)). As to the Treasury Commissioners see para 513 ante. As to the Treasury generally see paras 512–517 ante.

4 As to secretarial seals and authority for sealing see paras 357 ante, 912 post. As to grants by the Admiralty and Treasury see para 852 ante.

5 See note 2 supra. As to the office of Secretary of State see para 355 et seq ante.

**909. Use of Great Seal of the United Kingdom.** Since the date of the Union with Scotland on 1 May 1707 it is expressly provided that the Great Seal of the United Kingdom is to be used for sealing writs to elect and summon the Parliament of Great Britain, and for sealing all treaties with foreign princes and states, and all public acts, instruments and orders of state which concern the whole of the United Kingdom, which includes Great Britain and Northern Ireland[1], and in all other matters relating to England as the Great Seal of England was used prior to that date[2].

1 As to the Union of Great Britain and Ireland into one kingdom see the Union with Ireland Act 1800 art 1. For the construction of references to the United Kingdom in enactments passed before the establishment of the Irish Free State (now the Republic of Ireland) see the Irish Free State (Consequential Adaptation of Enactments) Order 1923, SR & O 1923/405, art 2. In every public document issued after the passing of the Royal and Parliamentary Titles Act 1927 the expression 'United Kingdom' means, unless the context otherwise requires, Great Britain and Northern Ireland: Royal and Parliamentary Titles Act 1927 s 2(2) (amended by the Interpretation Act 1978 s 25(1), Sch 3). As to Irish seals see para 911 post.

2 Union with Scotland Act 1706 art 24. As to the Union between England and Scotland see paras 51, 53 ante.

**910. Scottish seals.** As from the date of the Union with Scotland on 1 May 1707 the privy seal, signet, casset (casket) signet of the Justiciary Court, quarter seal, and seals of courts then used in Scotland were directed to be continued, but were to be altered and adapted to the state of the Union as the monarch should think fit[1]. The seals and the keepers of them are subject to regulations made by Parliament[1].

As from that date a seal is directed always to be kept in Scotland and made use of in all things relating to private rights or grants which usually passed the Great Seal of Scotland prior to the Union, and which only concern offices, grants, commissions and private rights within that kingdom[2].

1 Union with Scotland Act 1706 art 24. As to the Union between England and Scotland see paras 51, 53 ante.

2 Ibid art 24. Until such seal should be appointed by the monarch, the Great Seal of Scotland then existing was directed to be used for such purposes: art 24.

**911. Irish seals.** Following the establishment of the Irish Free State, provision was made for a Great Seal of Northern Ireland[1] which was to be kept in the custody of the governor and to be used for all matters in Northern Ireland for which the Great Seal of Ireland was formerly used[2]. Upon the abolition of the office of governor[3] the custody of the seal passed to the Secretary of State[4].

1   As to Northern Ireland see paras 67–86 ante.
2   See the Irish Free State (Consequential Provisions) Act 1922 (Session 2) s 1 (as amended), Sch 1 para 2(4).
3   Ie by the Northern Ireland Constitution Act 1973 s 32(1).
4   Ibid s 40(1), Sch 5 para 4.

**912. Authority for sealing.** A warrant under the sign manual[1], countersigned by the Lord Chancellor[2], or by one of the principal Secretaries of State[3], or by the Lord High Treasurer or two of the Treasury Commissioners[4], is a necessary and sufficient authority for passing any instrument[5] under the Great Seal of the United Kingdom[6], according to the tenor of the warrant[7].

Any instrument which might on 28 July 1884 be passed under the Great Seal by the fiat or under the authority or directions of the Lord Chancellor, or otherwise without passing through any other office, may continue to be so passed[8].

1   As to the mode of signing in the case of illness or absence of the monarch see CROWN LANDS AND PRIVILEGES. The documents sent to the monarch from the Crown Office are (1) the warrant for attaching the Great Seal; (2) the instrument itself; and (3) the docket, or short note of the contents of the instrument: see 2 Anson's Law and Custom of the Constitution (4th Edn, 1935) Pt I p 63. This docket is different from that which is required in the case of letters patent.
2   'Lord Chancellor' means the Lord High Chancellor of Great Britain and, if there is a Lord Keeper or Lords Commissioners of the Great Seal of the United Kingdom, the Great Seal Act 1884 is to apply as if such Lord Keeper or Lords Commissioners were substituted for the Lord Chancellor, and a warrant may be countersigned by any two of such Lords Commissioners: Great Seal Act 1884 s 4. By the Lord Keeper Act 1562 (repealed) the Lord Keeper of the Great Seal was declared to have the same authority as the Lord Chancellor. The office is now obsolete. By the Great Seal Act 1688 Lords Commissioners of the Great Seal are declared to have the same powers as the Lord Chancellor or Lord Keeper of the Great Seal: Great Seal Act 1688 s 1. As to the Lord Chancellor see paras 477–497 ante.
3   As to the office of Secretary of State see para 355 et seq ante.
4   As to the Lord High Treasurer and the Treasury Commissioners see paras 512–513 ante.
5   'Instrument' includes any letters patent, letters close, writ, commission and grant, and any document required to be passed under the Great Seal of the United Kingdom: Great Seal Act 1884 s 4.
6   The Great Seals of Scotland and Northern Ireland are authorised to be used in certain circumstances: see paras 910–911 ante. As to the seal of the Duchy of Lancaster see CROWN LANDS AND PRIVILEGES.
7   Great Seal Act 1884 s 2(1). The passage of documents under the Great Seal formerly required more complicated processes and authorities. These included inter alia the affixing of the Privy Seal, which was abolished by s 3 (repealed).
8   Ibid s 2(1) proviso. In the following cases the royal sign manual is not required: (1) the fiat of the Lord Chancellor is sufficient for commissions of the peace, writs of summons to peers to attend the House of Lords on succeeding to the title, and for the old writs of dedimus giving power to administer oaths, supersedeas staying the exercise of a jurisdiction, and mittimus authorising the removal of records from one court to another (which writs were issued under the Great Seal: see para 919 post); (2) the warrant of the Speaker of the House of Commons is sufficient for writs for by-elections; (3) Orders in Council are used in the case of writs for the summons of a new Parliament, for charters incorporating towns (see however para 882 ante), and for warrants from the Foreign and Commonwealth Office (formerly the Colonial Office) (see 2 Anson's Law and Custom of the Constitution (4th Edn, 1935) Pt I pp 68–69). Letters patent signifying the royal assent to bills are signed by the monarch before sealing (see the Royal Assent Act 1967 s 1(1); Crown Office (Forms and Proclamations Rules) Order 1992, SI 1992/1730 (as amended)); and it seems, the same practice is observed as to commissions to open Parliament (see 2 Anson's Law and Custom of the Constitution (4th Edn, 1935) Pt I p 68).

**913. Preparation of documents.** The Lord Chancellor[1] may from time to time make rules relating to the preparation of warrants and instruments[2], and the manner in which instruments are to be passed under the Great Seal[3]; but every warrant must be prepared by the Clerk of the Crown in Chancery[4]. A committee of the Privy Council[5] may by order make, and when made from time to time revoke, add to or alter, rules[6] prescribing the mode in which documents[7] are to be prepared, whether to be printed or written or partly printed and partly written and whether to be printed or written on paper, parchment or any other fitting material[8]. The form in which documents are to be worded may be prescribed by rules made by Order in Council[9].

1 For the meaning of 'Lord Chancellor' in these provisions see para 912 note 2 ante. As to Lord Chancellor see paras 477–497 ante.

2 For the meaning of 'instrument' see para 912 note 5 ante.

3 Great Seal Act 1884 s 2(2). Such rules may be revoked or varied by the Lord Chancellor: s 2(2). All earlier rules so made are now consolidated in the Crown Office (Preparation and Authentication of Documents Rules) Order 1988, SI 1988/1162.

4 Great Seal Act 1884 s 2(2).

5 The committee consists of the Lord Chancellor, the Lord Privy Seal and a principal Secretary of State acting in case of difference according to the opinion of any two of them: see the Crown Office Act 1877 s 4. As to the Privy Council see paras 521–526 ante.

6 The rules, which may be revoked, added to or altered, must be laid before both Houses of Parliament: ibid s 5 (amended by the Statute Law (Repeals) Act 1986 s 1(1), Sch 1 Pt XII). As to the laying of documents before Parliament see further STATUTES.

7 'Document' means any writ, commission, letters patent, letters close, or document of such a character, or belonging to such a class, as would at the date of passing of the Crown Office Act 1877 be required to be or usually would be authenticated by being passed under the Great Seal: s 7.

8 Ibid s 5(3).

9 Ibid s 3(1). Rules are to be laid before Parliament as mentioned in note 6 supra: see s 3 (as amended). All previous subordinate legislation is now replaced by the Crown Office (Forms and Proclamations Rules) Order 1992, SI 1992/1730 (as amended), which allows appropriate modifications to be made to the prescribed wording of writs of summons and dissolution, commissions of the peace, letters patent and royal assents under the Great Seal necessitated by the circumstances to be provided for in the document; and amends the prescribed forms of words to be used in the commissions signifying the royal assent in cases where an Act has been passed in accordance with the provisions of the Parliament Acts 1911 and 1949.

**914. Wafer Great Seal.** Impressions of the Great Seal made, as directed by a committee of the Privy Council[1], on embossed paper, wax, wafer or any other material when attached to or embossed on documents[2], confer the same validity in all respects as if the document itself had been authenticated by or passed under the Great Seal[3]. The committee may by order make, and when made from time to time revoke, add to or alter, rules[4] prescribing the documents to which a wafer Great Seal is to be attached[5]; but it is not necessary to the validity of a document to prove that attachment or embossing of a wafer Great Seal was authorised and no evidence to the contrary may be received[6].

1 As to the composition of the committee of the Privy Council see para 913 note 5 ante. As to the Privy Council see paras 521–526 ante.

2 For the meaning of 'document' see para 913 note 7 ante.

3 Crown Office Act 1877 s 4. Provision is also made for the use of wafer Privy Seals; see s 4. The need for the use of the Privy Seal was, however, abolished by the Great Seal Act 1884 s 3 (repealed).

4 As to the power to revoke, vary, add to or alter rules, the laying of rules before Parliament, and the validity of rules see the Crown Office Act 1877 s 5 (as amended); and para 913 note 6 ante.

5 Ibid s 5(2). Earlier rules are now consolidated in the Crown Office (Preparation and Authentication of Documents Rules) Order 1988, SI 1988/1162, which makes no reference to letters patent for inventions. Letters patent for inventions were listed in the Rules dated 22 February 1878 r 1. A patent sealed with the seal of the Patent Office has, however, the same effect as if sealed with the Great Seal: see the Patents Act 1949 ss 19(1), 21(1).

6 Crown Office Act 1877 s 5(3) proviso (a). Engrossing may in all cases be dispensed with, and, so far as seems to the committee convenient, printing must be adopted: s 5(3) proviso (b).

**915. Misuse of Great Seal.** Making or preparing a warrant for passing an instrument[1] under the Great Seal, or procuring an instrument to be passed under that seal, otherwise than as provided by the Crown Office Act 1877 or the Great Seal Act 1884[2] is an offence[3].

1    For the meaning of 'instrument' see para 912 note 5 ante.
2    As to authority for sealing see para 912 et seq ante.
3    Great Seal Act 1884 s 2(3). See also the Criminal Law Act 1967 s 1(1), abolishing the classification of offences as felonies or misdemeanours; and CRIMINAL LAW vol 11(1) (Reissue) para 42.

**916. Royal proclamations.** In general, proclamations may legally be made and issued only by the authority of the Crown, and must be passed under the Great Seal[1], and no private person may make and issue a proclamation, unless the practice is warranted by custom[2], or unless he is expressly authorised to do so[3]. Breach of this provision is punishable by fine and imprisonment[4].

Rules[5] may be made by Order in Council making regulations as to the manner of publication of royal proclamations and as to the towns to which copies of such proclamations are to be sent and, generally, as to the best mode of making such proclamations known to the public[6]. Any royal proclamation is valid in law as respects England, Scotland and Northern Ireland if it is published in the London Gazette, the Edinburgh Gazette and the Belfast Gazette respectively[7]. Copies of proclamations may be sent to High Sheriffs, Sheriffs, Lord Mayors and Mayors in England and Wales[8].

When legally made and issued a royal proclamation is to be judicially noticed, and is of the same validity as an Act of Parliament[9]. Any breach of its provisions is punishable by fine and imprisonment[10].

1    *Keyley v Manning* (1630) Cro Car 180.
2    An instance of such a custom is the proclamation issued by members of the Privy Council and others announcing the accession of a new monarch, as to which see CROWN LANDS AND PRIVILEGES. As to the Privy Council see paras 521–526 ante.
3    *Proclamations' Case* (1611) 12 Co Rep 74 at 76; *Knightly's Case* (1530) Bro Abr, Proclamations, pl 10 (where Sir Edmund Knightly, acting as executor, made and issued a proclamation that the creditors of the deceased were to come in and prove by a certain day; he was fined and imprisoned because he did it publicly and without authority).
4    *Knightly's Case* (1530) Bro Abr, Proclamations, Pl 10.
5    The rules, which may be revoked, added to or altered, must be laid before both Houses of Parliament: see the Crown Office Act 1877 s 3 (as amended). As to laying of documents before Parliament see further STATUTES.
6    Ibid s 3(2). See also the Crown Office (Forms and Proclamations Rules) Order 1992, SI 1992/1730 (as amended).
7    Crown Office Act 1877 s 3 proviso (3); Government of Ireland (Miscellaneous Adaptations) (Northern Ireland) Order 1923, SR & O 1923/803, art 3. On important occasions, such as a declaration of peace, the issue of the royal proclamation is sometimes accompanied by various forms and ceremonies.
8    See the Crown Office (Forms and Proclamations Rules) Order 1992 r 3.
9    Such proclamations are acts of subordinate legislation, as to which see para 7 note 11 ante; and STATUTES.
10   *Proclamations' Case* (1611) 12 Co Rep 74 at 75.

**917. Use of proclamations.** Proclamations may legally be used to call attention to the provisions of existing laws[1], or to make or alter regulations over which the Crown has a discretionary authority, either at common law or by statute[2]. Thus, the Crown may by proclamation summon or dissolve Parliament[3], declare war or peace[4], and promulgate blockades and lay embargoes on shipping in time of war[5].

The fact that martial law is in force would, it seems, be notified by means of proclamations if such a course were rendered necessary by a state of war[6] and there is authority for their use to restrain persons from leaving the realm in time of war, in order to prevent their rendering assistance to the enemy[7]; but these and other similar prerogatives in time of war, being created for the public safety, are strictly limited by necessity[8].

Proclamations may also legally be used when the Crown is authorised by statute to put in force statutory provisions which would otherwise remain dormant[9].

1  Eg in the case of war between two states friendly to the United Kingdom, to the provisions of the Foreign Enlistment Act 1870, as to which see CRIMINAL LAW. See eg the Proclamation of Neutrality dated 11 February 1904, SR & O 1904/201, issued in connection with the Russo-Japanese War.
2  1 Bl Com (14th Edn) 269–270; Bac Abr, Prerogative, D, 8; *Proclamations' Case* (1611) 12 Co Rep 74.
3  See PARLIAMENT.
4  As to declarations of war and treaties of peace see paras 809–810 ante; and FOREIGN RELATIONS LAW.
5  See further para 817 ante.
6  As to martial law generally see para 821 ante.
7  See 1 Bl Com (14th Edn) 270; Fitz Nat Brev 85; 3 Co Inst 179.
8  See the speech of Lord Erskine in 1808 (10 Parliamentary Debates 961).
9  Eg the Criminal Law and Procedure (Ireland) Act 1887 (repealed). As to prohibiting the importation or exportation of explosives, arms, ammunition etc see para 818 ante. As to proclamations declaring that a state of emergency exists see para 822 ante.

**918. Restrictions on proclamations.** Under the general rule which restrains the Crown from legislating apart from Parliament, it is well settled that the monarch's proclamation, unless authorised in that behalf by statute, cannot enact any new law, or make provisions contrary to old ones[1]. The monarch's proclamation may not restrict the liberties of the subject in matters upon which the law is silent[2]. Thus it has been held that the King could not by proclamation prohibit the erection of new buildings in and about London, or the making of starch from wheat, for that would be to alter the law of the land[3]. Where, in order to prevent famine, and Parliament not being assembled, an embargo was laid on all ships laden with wheat and flour in time of peace, contrary to express statutory provisions, it was found necessary to indemnify by statute the advisers of the Crown, and all persons acting under the proclamation[4].

1  *Re Grazebrook, ex p Chavasse* (1865) 4 De GJ & Sm 655 at 662; *Grieve v Edinburgh and District Water Trustees* 1918 SC 700. It was provided by 31 Hen 8 c 8 (Proclamation by the Crown) (1539) that certain proclamations issued with the advice of the council were to have the force of statutes, but this provision was repealed by 1 Edw 6 c 12 (Treason and Felony) (1547) s 5 (repealed). Proclamations were, however, frequently issued and enforced by the Star Chamber until 1640, when that court was abolished (see para 376 ante).
2  *Proclamations' Case* (1611) 12 Co Rep 74 at 75.
3  *Proclamations' Case* (1611) 12 Co Rep 74 at 75. This opinion was given by the two Chief Justices and two Barons of the Exchequer after conference with the Privy Council. See also the same case as reported in 2 State Tr 726: 'The King cannot create any offence which was not an offence before, for then he may alter the law of the land in his proclamation in some high point... The law of England is divided into three parts: the common law, statute law, and custom; but the King's proclamation is none of these... The King has no prerogative but that which the law of the land allows him'. As to the right of the Crown to legislate in British settlements having no representative government see COMMONWEALTH vol 6 (Reissue) para 989.
4  See 7 Geo 3 c 7 (Indemnity) (1766) (repealed). This was the last occasion upon which the Crown attempted to legislate by proclamation. The Crown's action was later defended by Lord Camden on the ground of necessity (see 19 Parliamentary History p 1248), but it constituted an exercise of the suspending power forbidden by the Bill of Rights: see para 376 ante. As to the history and citation of the Bill of Rights see para 35 note 3 ante.

**919. Writs under the Great Seal.** Writs under the Great Seal are in the form of a command to do or abstain from doing a certain thing, and are used for a variety of purposes, such as for summoning a person to the House of Lords[1], and thus conferring a new peerage, or confirming an already existing one[2], for summoning a new Parliament[3] or for by-elections[4]. Writs of dedimus, supersedeas and mittimus were also issued under the Great Seal[5]. Writs of summons in actions are not so issued, but are under the seal of the officer of the office out of which they are issued[6].

Writs under the Great Seal directed to particular persons for particular purposes are sometimes closed up and sealed on the outside, and are then known as writs close, or letters close, and are recorded in the close rolls[7].

1 As to the House of Lords see para 204 ante; and PARLIAMENT.
2 See 1 Bl Com (14th Edn) 400; and PEERAGES AND DIGNITIES.
3 See para 912 note 8 ante. As to the persons to whom the writs are directed see PARLIAMENT.
4 See para 912 note 8 ante; and PARLIAMENT.
5 As to use of the Great Seal see para 909 ante. These were the old writs of *dedimus potestatem* giving power to administer oaths, *supersedeas* staying the exercise of a jurisdiction, and *mittimus* authorising the removal of records from one court to another.
6 RSC Ord 6 r 7(3); and see PRACTICE AND PROCEDURE. Writs of habeas corpus are issued out of the Crown Office except where they affect minors, in which case they are issued out of the Principal Registry of the Family Division: see Ord 57 r 5(1); Ord 54 r 11. Writs of subpoena in aid of an inferior court or tribunal issue out of the Crown Office but otherwise are issued out of either the Central Office or the appropriate district registry: see Ord 38 rr 14, 19. Certain writs may now be issued out of Chancery chambers: Ord 57 r 5(1). See also para 306 ante.
7 Ie literae clausae, as distinguished from letters patent, which are recorded on the patent rolls: see 2 Bl Com (14th Edn) 346; and para 849 note 3 ante.

**920. Letters patent and other documents under the Great Seal.** Letters patent are used for ratifying treaties with foreign powers[1], for conferring titles or dignities[2], for creating and conferring offices[3] and for conferring authority to perform particular functions[4]. Grants are used for creating or passing franchises[5] and other rights of property. Charters are used for creating corporations[6]. All these documents are issued under the Great Seal, and documents authorising the making and ratification of treaties are passed under the Great Seal under the authority of a sign manual warrant[7],

Where the Crown acts on the advice of the Privy Council, as in grants of charters to towns or other bodies, it is said to be necessary that an Order in Council should be made before the issue of the warrant. An Order in Council may itself be sufficient following upon a royal proclamation, as in the case of the issue of writs for a new Parliament[8].

1 2 Anson's Law and Custom of the Constitution (4th Edn, 1935) Pt I p 66. As to treaty-making powers generally see para 801 ante.
2 See 1 Bl Com (14th Edn) 400; and PEERAGES AND DIGNITIES. For the form of letters patent for the creation of peers see the Crown Office (Forms and Proclamations Rules) Order 1992, SI 1992/1730 (as amended).
3 Eg the creation of the office of governor of a dependent territory (see para 901 note 7 ante); and the appointment of judges (see COURTS).
4 Eg royal assent to bills by commission: see the Crown Office (Forms and Proclamations Rules) Order 1992 (as amended).
5 As to franchises see para 879 ante.
6 See CORPORATIONS.
7 As to the sufficiency of a sign manual warrant see para 912 ante; and as to the necessity for passing the treaties themselves under the Great Seal see para 801 ante.
8 See 2 Anson's Law and Custom of the Constitution (4th Edn, 1935) Pt I p 69.

**921. Clerk of the Crown in Chancery.** The duties and powers of the Clerk of the Petty Bag, other than those relating to solicitors and to the administration of justice[1], were transferred in 1874 to the Clerk of the Crown in Chancery, and are now performed by and vested in the clerk or his officers in such manner as the Lord Chancellor[2] may from time to time direct[3]. The duties and powers so transferred include all those relating to any writs or letters patent passed under the Great Seal[4]. All the duties and powers of the Clerk of the Patents were also transferred to the Clerk of the Crown in Chancery or his officers in such manner as the Lord Chancellor may from time to time direct[5].

It continues to be lawful for Her Majesty from time to time under the royal sign manual[6] to appoint a fit person to fill the office of Clerk of the Crown in Chancery, and the Clerk of the Crown in Chancery continues to perform the duties of the office of Keeper or Clerk of the Hanaper[7]. The statutory and other duties of the Secretary of Presentations were transferred to the Clerk of the Crown in Chancery, or to such of the Lord Chancellor's officers as he may direct, in 1890[8].

The salary of the Clerk of the Crown in Chancery is such as the Treasury[9] may assign to him, and the salaries of the Clerk of the Crown in Chancery and of his officers, and the expenses of his office, are paid out of money provided by Parliament[10].

The Clerk of the Crown in Chancery and his deputy are officers both of the House of Lords and the House of Commons[11].

1   As to the nature of these duties see the Great Seal (Offices) Act 1874 s 5 (as amended).
2   'Lord Chancellor' means the Lord High Chancellor of Great Britain or the commissioners for executing the office of such Lord High Chancellor: ibid s 3. See also para 912 note 2 ante. As to the Lord Chancellor see paras 477–497 ante.
3   Ibid s 5 (amended by the Statute Law Revision (No 2) Act 1893). If any doubt arises as to whether any duty or power of the Clerk of the Petty Bag is or is not transferred to the Clerk of the Crown in Chancery such doubt is to be determined by the Lord Chancellor, whose decision is final: Great Seal (Offices) Act 1874 s 5 (as so amended).
4   See ibid s 5 (as amended). As to the use of wafer seals in lieu of the Great Seal see the Crown Office Act 1877 ss 4, 5 (as amended); and para 914 ante. As to the preparation and wording of documents to be passed under the Great Seal see ss 3(1), 5(3); and para 913 text and notes 8–9 ante.
5   Great Seal (Offices) Act 1874 s 6 (amended by the Statute Law Revision Act 1883; and the Statute Law Revision (No 2) Act 1893). Nothing in the Great Seal (Offices) Act 1874 applies to the Clerk of the Commissioners of Patents so far as related to letters patent under the Patent Law Amendment Act 1852 and the Acts amending it: Great Seal (Offices) Act 1874 s 6 (as so amended).
6   As to the royal sign manual see para 908 ante.
7   Great Seal (Offices) Act 1874 s 8 (amended by the Statute Law (Repeals) Act 1973). Writs relating to the business of the subject were originally kept 'in hanaperio' (in a hamper).
8   Crown Office Act 1890 s 1(2). The Lord Chancellor may make regulations respecting the passing and preparation of instruments prepared or issued by the Clerk of the Crown in Chancery under the transferred powers: see s 1(3). This power does not appear to have been exercised.
9   As to the Treasury see paras 512–517 ante.
10  Great Seal (Offices) Act 1874 s 8 (amended by the Statute Law Revision (No 2) Act 1893).
11  See Erskine May *Parliamentary Practice* (21st Edn, 1989) pp 191–192. As to his role as an officer of the House of Lords see PARLIAMENT. His role as an officer of the House of Commons is confined to elections; see further ELECTIONS. As to the House of Commons see PARLIAMENT.

**922. Fees.** The Lord Chancellor[1], with the concurrence of the Treasury[2], may from time to time by order appoint the fees to be taken in the office of or by the Clerk of the Crown in Chancery[3], or by any of his officers, or by any person performing the duties of messenger or pursuivant of the Great Seal[4] or gentleman of the chamber attending the Great Seal or purse-bearer to the Lord Chancellor or chaff wax sealer or deputy sealer, and may from time to time by order increase, reduce, add to or abolish such fees for the time being taken in such office or by such officer[5]. No fees other than those so appointed are to be taken in the office of the Clerk of the Crown in Chancery[6]. By virtue of orders made under this power, fees in cash[7] must be paid in the office of the Clerk of the Crown in Chancery upon the making and sealing of various grants, writs, commissions and other executive documents[8].

1   For the meaning of 'Lord Chancellor' in this context see para 921 note 2 ante.
2   As to the Treasury see paras 512–517 ante.
3   As to the Clerk of the Crown in Chancery see para 921 ante.

4    All duties and powers required to be performed by or vested in the messenger or pursuivant of the Great
     Seal are performed by and vested in such officer as the Lord Chancellor may from time to time direct:
     Great Seal (Offices) Act 1874 s 4 (amended by the Statute Law Revision Act 1883; the Parliament
     (Elections and Meetings) Act 1943; and the Statute Law (Repeals) Act 1995). As to use of the Great Seal
     of the United Kingdom see para 909 ante.
5    Great Seals (Offices) Act 1847 s 9 (amended by the Statute Law Revision Act 1883; and the Statute Law
     (Repeals) Act 1995).
6    Great Seal (Offices) Act 1874 s 9 (as amended: see note 5 supra).
7    See the Treasury Order dated 30 June 1891, made under the Public Office Fees Act 1879, prescribing
     the mode of collecting fees in the Crown Office in Chancery.
8    See the Order dated 20 June 1871 appointing fees to be taken in the office of the Clerk of the Crown in
     Chancery; the Orders dated 18 July 1871 appointing fees to be taken in the Great Seal Patent Office and
     in the office of the Lord Chancellor's Secretary of Presentations; the Order dated 8 August 1881 as to fees
     in respect of warrants for letters patent. See also the Crown Office Fees (Election Papers) Order 1922,
     SR & O 1922/1393; the Crown Office Fees (Judicial Appointments) Order 1936, SR & O 1936/610;
     the Crown Office Fees (Honours and Dignities) Order 1937, SR & O 1937/497; and the Crown Office
     Fees Order 1994, SI 1994/600.

## (3) OATHS OF OFFICE AND JUDICIAL OATHS

**923. Oaths to be taken.** As soon as may be after their acceptance of office the
following executive officers and members of the judiciary must take the oath of allegiance
and official or judicial oath, in the form and manner prescribed[1]: First Lord of the
Treasury[2], Chancellor of the Exchequer[3], Lord Chancellor[4] (as an executive officer), Lord
President of the Council[5], Lord Privy Seal[6], Secretaries of State[7], President of the Board
of Trade[8], Lord Steward[9], Lord Chamberlain[10], Earl Marshal[11], Master of the Horse[12],
Chancellor of the Duchy of Lancaster[13], Paymaster General[14], Minister of Agriculture,
Fisheries and Food[15], any Minister of State who is eligible for a salary under the
Ministerial Salaries Act 1975[16], Lord Chancellor of Great Britain (as a member of the
judiciary)[17], Recorder of London[18], Justices of the Peace for counties and boroughs[19],
district judges (including a district judge of the principal registry of the Family Division)[20],
Master of the Queen's Bench Division[21], Master of the Chancery Division[22], Registrar in
Bankruptcy of the High Court[23], Taxing Master of the Supreme Court[24], Admiralty
Registrar[25], Lord Chief Justice[26], Master of the Rolls[27], President of the Family
Division[28], Vice Chancellor[29], Lord Justice of Appeal[30], puisne judge of the High Court[31],
circuit judges[32], recorders[33] and the Master of the Court of Protection[34].

Any person who objects to being sworn may be permitted to make his solemn
affirmation instead of taking an oath, and this applies in relation to a person to whom it
is not reasonably practicable without inconvenience or delay to administer an oath in the
manner appropriate to his religious beliefs as it applies in relation to a person objecting to
be sworn[35].

If any officer specified declines or neglects, when an oath required to be taken by him
is duly tendered, to take such oath, he must, if he has already entered on his office, vacate
it and if he has not entered office he must be disqualified from entering it; but no person
may be compelled, in respect of the same appointment to the same office, to take such
oath more than once[36].

1    For the prescribed forms of oath see the Promissory Oaths Act 1868 ss 2–4. Where in any oath under the
     1868 Act the name of the present monarch is expressed, the name of the monarch of the United Kingdom
     for the time being is to be substituted: s 10. As to the mode of taking the oaths see para 924 post.
2    Ibid s 5, Schedule Pt I (amended by the Statute Law Revision Act 1953; the Defence (Transfer of
     Functions) (No 1) Order 1964, SI 1964/488, art 2, Sch 1 Pt II; the Post Office Act 1969 s 141, Sch 11
     Pt II; the Secretary of State for the Environment Order 1970, SI 1970/1681, art 5(3), Sch 4; and the
     Statute Law (Repeals) Act 1977). The office of First Lord of the Treasury is held by the Prime Minister:
     see para 395 ante.

3	Promissory Oaths Act 1868 Schedule Pt I (as amended: see note 2 supra). As to the Chancellor of the Exchequer see para 514 ante.

4	Ibid Schedule Pt I (as amended: see note 2 supra). As to the Lord Chancellor see paras 477–497 ante.

5	Ibid Schedule Pt I (as amended: see note 2 supra). As to the Lord President of the Council see paras 525–526 ante.

6	Ibid Schedule Pt I (as amended: see note 2 supra). As to the Lord Privy Seal see para 527 ante.

7	Ibid Schedule Pt I (as amended: see note 2 supra). As to the office of Secretary of State see para 355 et seq ante.

8	Ibid Schedule Pt I (as amended: see note 2 supra). As to the President of the Board of Trade see para 505 text and note 2 ante.

9	Ibid Schedule Pt I (as amended: see note 2 supra). As to the Lord Steward see para 546 ante.

10	Ibid Schedule Pt I (as amended: see note 2 supra). As to the Lord Chamberlain see para 546 ante.

11	Ibid Schedule Pt I (as amended: see note 2 supra). As to the Earl Marshal see para 546 ante.

12	Ibid Schedule Pt I (as amended: see note 2 supra). As to the Master of the Horse see para 546 ante.

13	Ibid Schedule Pt I (as amended: see note 2 supra). As to the Chancellor of the Duchy of Lancaster see para 354 note 24 ante; and CROWN LANDS AND PRIVILEGES.

14	Ibid Schedule Pt I (as amended: see note 2 supra). As to the Paymaster General see para 714 ante.

15	See the Board of Agriculture Act 1889 s 8(2); the Ministry of Agriculture and Fisheries Act 1919 s 1(1); and the Transfer of Functions (Ministry of Food) Order 1955, SI 1955/554, art 3(1). As to the Minister of Agriculture, Fisheries and Food see para 435 ante.

16	Ie under the Ministerial and other Salaries Act 1975 s 1(1), Sch 1 Pt II head 2: Ministers of the Crown Act 1975 s 6(1): see para 362 note 1 ante.

17	Promissory Oaths Act 1868 s 6 (amended by the Statute Law Revision Act 1875), Schedule Pt II (amended by the Statute Law Revision Act 1893; the Statute Law (Repeals) Act 1977; and the Supreme Court Act 1981 s 152(4), Sch 7).

18	Promissory Oaths Act 1868 Schedule Pt II (as amended: see note 17 supra). As to the Recorder of London see LONDON GOVERNMENT.

19	Ibid Schedule Pt II (as amended: see note 17 supra); and see generally MAGISTRATES.

20	Courts and Legal Services Act 1990 s 76(1)(a), (2); and see generally COURTS.

21	Ibid s 76(1)(b), (2); and see generally COURTS.

22	Ibid s 76(1)(c), (2); and see generally COURTS.

23	Ibid s 76(1)(d), (2); and see generally COURTS.

24	Ibid s 76(1)(e), (2); and see generally PRACTICE AND PROCEDURE.

25	Ibid s 76(1)(f), (2); and see generally ADMIRALTY.

26	Supreme Court Act 1981 s 10(1), (4); and see generally COURTS.

27	Ibid s 10(1), (4); and see generally COURTS.

28	Ibid s 10(1), (4); and see generally COURTS.

29	Ibid s 10(1), (4); and see generally COURTS.

30	Ibid s 10(4); and see generally COURTS.

31	Ibid s 10(4); and see generally COURTS.

32	Courts Act 1971 s 22(1), (3); and see generally COURTS.

33	Ibid s 22(1), (3); and see generally COURTS.

34	Mental Health Act 1983 s 93(3); and see generally MENTAL HEALTH.

35	Oaths Act 1978 s 5(1), (2). A person who may be permitted under s 5(2) to make his solemn affirmation may also be required to do so: s 5(3). A solemn affirmation is of the same force and effect as an oath: s 5(4). See further EVIDENCE.

36	Promissory Oaths Act 1868 s 7 (amended by the Statute Law (Repeals) Act 1981).

**924. How oaths are taken.** Members of the Cabinet take the oath of allegiance and the official oath in the presence of the Queen in Council[1]. The oaths are taken by the Chancellor of the Duchy of Lancaster in the presence of Her Majesty alone[2], and by other executive officers[3] in the presence of the Lord Chancellor or the Lord President of the Council or a Secretary of State[4].

The oath of allegiance and the judicial oath are taken by the Lord Chief Justice[5], Master of the Rolls[6], President of the Family Division[7], Vice-Chancellor[8], Lord Justice of Appeal[9], puisne judges of the High Court[10], circuit judges[11] and the Master of the Court of Protection[12] in the presence of the Lord Chancellor. Recorders take the oaths before a judge of the Court of Appeal or of the High Court or a circuit judge[13]. District judges (including a district judge of the principal registry of the Family Division), Master of the Queen's Bench Division, Master of the Chancery Division, Registrar in Bankruptcy of the High Court, Taxing Master of the Supreme Court and the Admiralty Registrar take the oath of allegiance and judicial oath before a judge of the High Court or a circuit judge[14]. The oaths of allegiance and judicial oath are to be taken by justices of the peace before such persons as Her Majesty may from time to time appoint, or before the Lord Chancellor, or in open court before a judge of the High Court or in open court at the general sessions of the peace for the county or place in which the justice is to act[15].

1   Promissory Oaths Order 1939, SR & O 1939/916, art 1.
2   Order in Council dated 9 August 1872; Promissory Oaths Order 1939 art 2.
3   As to these officers see para 923 ante.
4   Promissory Oaths Order 1939 art 1.
5   See the Supreme Court Act 1981 s 10(1), (4); and para 923 ante.
6   See ibid s 10(1), (4); and para 923 ante.
7   See ibid s 10(1), (4); and para 923 ante.
8   See ibid s 10(1), (4); and para 923 ante.
9   See ibid s 10(4); and para 923 ante.
10   See ibid s 10(4); and para 923 ante.
11   See the Courts Act 1971 s 22(2); and para 923 ante.
12   See the Mental Health Act 1983 s 93(3); and para 923 ante.
13   See the Courts Act 1971 s 22(2); and para 923 ante.
14   See the Courts and Legal Services Act 1990 s 76(1); and para 923 ante.
15   Promissory Oaths Act 1871 s 2. See also the Supreme Court Act 1981 s 19. 'General sessions' means a meeting of all the justices of the peace. See further MAGISTRATES vol 29 para 214.

**925. Special oaths.** Other cases in which special oaths are required to be taken by persons before entering upon offices or dignities are the oaths of homage by archbishops and bishops[1], the oaths required to be taken by peers, baronets or knights upon their creation[2], by members of Parliament on taking their seats[3], by members of the clergy[4], by members of the Privy Council[5], and by persons in the army and auxiliary forces[6]. There are many other instances[7].

1   See the Promissory Oaths Act 1868 s 14(3); and ECCLESIASTICAL LAW vol 14 para 469.
2   See PEERAGES AND DIGNITIES. The oath of allegiance in the form provided by the Promissory Oaths Act 1868 s 2, is to be substituted for the oaths of allegiance, supremacy and abjuration or any of them required to be taken in such cases: s 14(5).
3   Ie under the Parliamentary Oaths Act 1866. The form of oath prescribed by that Act has been replaced by the oath of allegiance under the Promissory Oaths Act 1868: see ss 8 (as amended), 14(1); and PARLIAMENT.
4   Ie under the Clerical Subscription Act 1865. The form of oath prescribed by that Act has been replaced by the oath of allegiance under the Promissory Oaths Act 1868: see ss 8 (as amended), 14(1); and ECCLESIASTICAL LAW.
5   See ibid s 14(2) (as amended); and para 524 ante. As to the Privy Council see paras 521–526 ante.
6   See ibid s 14(6) (as amended); and ROYAL FORCES.
7   Nothing in the Promissory Oaths Act 1868 affects the oaths mentioned in the text and notes 1–6 supra or any of the following: (1) the oath of canonical obedience to the bishop or archbishop taken by bishops on consecration (see s 14(4)); (2) the oath taken by aliens on being naturalised (see s 14(7) (as amended)); (3) any power of substituting a declaration for an oath vested in the Treasury by the Statutory Declarations Act 1835 (see the Promissory Oaths Act 1868 s 14(9) (as amended)); (4) any oath required or authorised by Act of Parliament to be taken or made for the purpose of attesting any fact or verifying any account or document (see s 14(10)); (5) any oath required to be taken by any juror, witness or other person as a preliminary to or in the course of any proceedings (see s 14(12)).
    The various oaths required to be taken by public officers in 1867 are set out fully in the report of the Oaths Committee 1867 (Parliamentary Papers 1867 vol 31), by which declarations in place of the oaths were recommended. As to the substitution of declarations in lieu of oaths see para 926 post. Affirmations in lieu of oaths may be made in certain circumstances: see para 923 note 35 ante. All oaths indirectly disqualifying Roman Catholics from certain offices were abolished by certain nineteenth century statutes. Roman Catholics are no longer disqualified for the office of Lord Chancellor: see para 477 text and note 7 ante.

**926. Declaration in lieu of oath.** Except in the case of those offices in respect of which statutory provision has been made for the taking of oaths[1] or it is provided that the taking of oaths is to continue[2], a declaration has been substituted for an oath wherever an oath was formerly required to be taken on or as a condition of accepting any employment or office[3]. Where a declaration has been substituted for an oath, any person, guild, body corporate, or society which formerly had the power to alter such oath, or to substitute another oath in its place, may exercise a like power with regard to such declaration[4]. The making of the declaration has the same effect in all respects as the taking of the oath[5], and failure to make the declaration entails the same penalties and disabilities as failure to take the oath[6].

The Treasury[7] has power to substitute a statutory declaration where under statutes relating to specified departments or under departmental regulations an oath, solemn affirmation or affidavit is required to be taken or made for any purpose[8]. Where a statutory declaration has been so substituted an oath may not be administered[9]. Whenever any declaration is so made, the fees that would have been due and payable on the taking or making any legal oath, solemn affirmation or affidavit are due and payable on making and subscribing such declaration[10].

1  As to those offices see para 923 ante.

2  See the Promissory Oaths Act 1868 s 14(1)–(6) (as amended); and para 925 ante.

3  Ibid s 12(4). For example, a declaration of fidelity may be substituted in the case of anyone accepting employment or office in Her Majesty's honourable band of Gentlemen at Arms or body guard of Yeomen of the Guard or in any other department of Her Majesty's household, with the addition (in cases where it seems appropriate to Her Majesty by Order in Council to make such addition) of a declaration of secrecy to be observed by the declarant with respect to matters coming within his cognisance by reason of his employment or office: s 12(1). Where an oath was formerly required on accepting office in or under a municipal corporation or on or as a condition of admission to membership of or participation in the privileges of any municipal corporation, there may be substituted a declaration that the declarant will faithfully perform the duties of his office or that he will faithfully demean himself as a member of, or a participator in the privileges of, the corporation as appropriate: s 12(2). A declaration to the like effect of an oath may be substituted where an oath was required to be taken on admission to membership or fellowship or participation in the privileges of any guild, body corporate, society or company, provided that if any two or more of the members with the concurrence of the majority of the members present and voting at a meeting specially summoned for the purpose, object to any statement contained in such declaration on the grounds of its relating to duties which by reason of change of circumstances have become obsolete, they may appeal to one of Her Majesty's Principal Secretaries of State to omit such statement, and the decision of the Secretary of State is final: s 12(3).

4  Ibid s 15.

5  Ibid s 12(5). See also the Promissory Oaths Act 1871 s 1(2), which provides that where a person is prevented or relieved by the Promissory Oaths Act 1868 from taking an oath as required by the conditions of an appointment he is, on performing any other conditions, to be entitled to the office in the same way as if the conditions relating to the oaths had been performed.

6  Promissory Oaths Act 1868 s 13.

7  As to the Treasury see paras 512–517 ante.

8  Statutory Declarations Act 1835 s 2 (amended by the Statute Law Revision (No 2) Act 1888; the Statute Law Revision Act 1890; the Crown Estates Act 1961 ss 9(4), 10(2), Sch 3 Pt II; and the Post Office Act 1969 s 137, Sch 8 Pt I). This power is not affected by anything in the Promissory Oaths Act 1868: see s 14(9); and para 925 note 7 ante. When the Treasury has substituted in writing under their hands and seals a declaration in lieu of an oath, solemn affirmation or affidavit, they must, as soon as conveniently may be, cause a copy of the instrument substituting the declaration to be inserted and published in the London Gazette; and from and after the expiration of 21 days following the day of the date of the gazette in which it has been published, the provisions of the Statutory Declarations Act 1835 extend and apply to each and every case specified in the instrument in the same manner as if it were specified and named in the Act: s 3 (amended by the Statute Law Revision (No 2) Act 1888; and the Statute Law Revision Act 1890).

As to the exercise of this power see Treasury Warrants dated 7 December 1835, 27 June 1836 and 11 July 1836.

The Universities of Oxford and Cambridge and various other bodies may make statutes, byelaws or orders authorising and directing the substitution of a declaration in lieu of an oath, solemn affirmation or affidavit; provided that such statutes, byelaws or orders are duly made and passed according to the charter, laws or regulations of the particular university or body so authorised: Statutory Declarations Act 1835 s 8 (amended by the Statute Law Revision (No 2) Act 1888).

As to the offence of knowingly and wilfully making a false statement in a declaration see the Perjury Act 1911 s 5; Criminal Justice Act 1948 s 1(2); Criminal Law Act 1967 s 1(1); and CRIMINAL LAW.

9    Statutory Declarations Act 1835 s 4 (amended by the Statute Law Revision (No 2) Act 1888; and the Statute Law Revision Act 1890). See generally EVIDENCE.

10   Statutory Declarations Act 1835 s 19 (amended by the Statute Law Revision (No 2) Act 1888).

**927–950.  Effect of oath.** A person is bound by an oath administered in such form and with such ceremonies as he may accept without objection or declare to be binding[1]. If he has made a false statement in taking the oath he may be convicted of an offence[2].

1    See the Oaths Act 1978 s 4(1); Perjury Act 1911 s 15(1); and PRACTICE AND PROCEDURE vol 37 para 454.

2    See ibid s 2(1); Criminal Justice Act 1948 s 1(1), (2); Criminal Law Act 1967 s 1(1); and CRIMINAL LAW.

# 9.  NON-DEPARTMENTAL PUBLIC BODIES AND INFORMATION GATHERING INSTITUTIONS

## (1)  NON-DEPARTMENTAL PUBLIC BODIES

**951.  General.** There is a growing number of non-departmental public bodies[1] in the United Kingdom which are independent of ministerial control and therefore independent of full ministerial responsibility to Parliament. Non-departmental public bodies are said to have a role in the processes of government in the United Kingdom but are not government departments or part of a government department[2]. Thus, non-departmental public bodies are distinguishable from executive agencies which are within departments[3]. Non-departmental public bodies are also known as 'quangos' (quasi-autonomous non-governmental organisations)[4]. However, this term is also applied to National Health Service bodies, which are not generally regarded as non-departmental public bodies[5].

Non-departmental public bodies may be classified in various ways, but the government classifies them as (1) executive bodies[6]; (2) advisory bodies[7]; (3) tribunals[8]; and (4) other bodies, including boards of visitors[9]. Executive bodies carry out a wide range of operational and regulatory functions, various scientific and cultural and some commercial or semi-commercial activities[10]. Advisory bodies are usually composed of a group of experts in a particular sphere advising the government on one issue and tribunals have a judicial or quasi-judicial function[11].

1    There are more than 1,200 non-departmental public bodies listed in *Public Bodies* (Office of Public Service, 1995). See also the *Non-Departmental Public Bodies: A Guide for Departments* (Office of Public Service, 1979).

2    See the *Report on Non-departmental Public Bodies* (Cmnd 7797) (1980); and *Public Bodies* (Office of Public Service, 1995).

3    As to executive agencies in the Civil Service see para 551 ante.

4    As to the acronym 'quango', coined by Anthony Barker, see the entry in the *Oxford English Dictionary*; and Weir and Hall (eds) *Ego Trip: Extra-Governmental Organisations in the United Kingdom and their Accountability (The Democratic Audit of the United Kingdom)* (1994) p 6. See particularly Barker *Quangos in Britain* (1982).

5   See further the *First Report of the Committee on Standards in Public Life* (Cm 2850-I) (1995) ch 4. As to the National Health Service see NATIONAL HEALTH.

6   *Public Bodies* (Office of Public Service, 1995) identifies 320 executive non-departmental government bodies. The classification of non-departmental public bodies is derived from the *Report on Non-Departmental Public Bodies* (Cmnd 7797) (1980) (the 'Pliatzky Report').

The Democratic Audit of the United Kingdom, drawing on (1) answers to parliamentary questions in 1993, (2) *Public Bodies* (Office of Public Service and Science, 1993), and (3) the Civil Service Year Book 1993, identified a large number of executive bodies which were not recognised by the government as quangos or public bodies at all, and gave to them and to recognised non-departmental public bodies the name 'extra-governmental organisations'. These executive bodies numbered 5,521 in all, and included over 4,500 bodies operating at local level under appointed or self-appointed committees, including training and enterprise councils, which are private companies, and voluntary and charitable bodies such as registered housing associations, further education and sixth form college corporations and grant maintained schools. All such bodies perform public functions for the government and deliver public services. They are almost wholly funded by government and act under the direction of government ministers and their departments and major executive bodies under government control like the Housing Corporation or the Funding Agency for Schools. They were estimated to spend £46.6 billion in 1992–93: Weir and Hall (eds) *Ego Trip: Extra-Governmental Organisations in the United Kingdom and their Accountability (The Democratic Audit of the United Kingdom)* (1994). See also Davis and Stewart *The Growth of Government by Appointment* (1994).

7   In 1995 there were 699 advisory bodies: see *Public Bodies* (Office of Public Service, 1995).

8   There are over 70 tribunals classified as non-departmental public bodies: see *Public Bodies* (Office of Public Service, 1995).

9   There are over 130 boards of visitors: see *Public Bodies* (Office of Public Service, 1995).

10   See the *First Report of the Committee on Standards in Public Life* (Cm 2850-I) (1995) p 66 para 4.

11   See the *First Report of the Committee on Standards in Public Life* (Cm 2850-I) (1995) p 66 para 4.

## 952. Legal status of non-departmental public bodies.

There is no fixed legal status for non-departmental public bodies. They may be incorporated by royal charter[1] or by statute[2]. Some have the status of private companies[3]. Others were originally private bodies taken into public ownership but retaining their original corporate personality[4]. Generally non-departmental public bodies do not form part of the Crown[5].

1   Eg the Arts Council of Great Britain and the British Broadcasting Corporation.

2   Eg the Audit Commission (created under the National Audit Act 1983), and the Higher Education Funding Councils for England, Wales, Scotland and Northern Ireland (created under the Further and Higher Education Act 1992).

3   Eg the Securities and Investments Board to which the Secretary of State has power to transfer regulatory functions under the Financial Services Act 1986.

4   Eg the Bank of England, which was first established as a private bank in 1694 and was taken into public ownership under the Bank of England Act 1946.

5   Enabling statutes generally provide expressly that a non-departmental public body is not to be regarded as a servant or agent of the Crown or as enjoying any status, immunity or privilege of the Crown: see eg the Gas Act 1986 s 2(5), Sch 2 para 1 (in relation to the Gas Consumers' Council). For the position of the BBC see *BBC v Johns (Inspector of Taxes)* [1965] Ch 32, [1964] 1 All ER 923, CA. As to the position of a national health service hospital board see *Pfizer Corpn v Ministry of Health* [1965] AC 512, [1965] 1 All ER 450, HL (board held to be acting on behalf of the Ministry of Health and entitled, therefore, to benefit from the special rights of the Crown under patent law for importing drugs).

## 953. Relations between non-departmental public bodies and government departments.

The members of non-departmental public bodies are normally appointed by ministers in the departments from which they receive their funds. These departments are commonly referred to as 'sponsoring departments'[1]. Each government department is responsible for making appointments to the executive non-departmental public bodies under its aegis[2]. The Office of Public Service[3] maintains a list of potential candidates for membership. In 1995 the office of Commissioner for Public Appointments was established by Order in Council[4] with the role of advising, regulating and monitoring the appointment of individuals as members of boards of executive non-departmental public bodies in accordance with the overriding principle of appointment on merit, but with the minister retaining the ultimate responsibility for approving appointments[5].

The relationship between the non-departmental public body and its sponsoring department is necessarily one at 'arm's length' either because the work is of an executive character which does not require ministers to take responsibility for its day-to-day management; or because the work is more effectively carried out by a single-purpose organisation rather than by a government department with a wide range of functions; or in order to involve people from outside government in the direction of the organisation; or as a self-denying ordinance on the part of government and Parliament, in order to place the performance of a particular function outside the party political arena[6]. The staff employed in non-departmental public bodies are not generally civil servants[7].

Sponsoring departments make payments to non-departmental public bodies by way of either grants[8] or grants in aid[9]. The sponsoring department approves the expenditure of non-departmental public bodies that receive their money by way of outright grant voted by Parliament. The accounting officer of the sponsoring department is responsible for the vote and, where the grant or grant in aid is large, the body's senior full-time official is formally designated as accounting officer by the departmental accounting officer and is responsible for the efficient and proper application of the money[10].

Ministers are not generally entitled to give directions as to the day-to-day activities of non-departmental public bodies[11] nor are they responsible to Parliament for such activities. However, ministers may be entitled by statute to give directions of a general character to the body in question[12]. Ministers are responsible to Parliament for the appointments they make, and for giving or failing to give such directions and for the bodies' underlying efficiency and effectiveness. Ministers are therefore in a position to remove members (according to the terms of their appointment[13]) if dissatisfied with their performance, and to adjust their budgets taking their performance into account.

1   See *Public Bodies* (Office of Public Service, 1995).

2   In September 1994 the various types of non-departmental public bodies had the following numbers of members: (1) executive bodies - 3,850 members; (2) advisory bodies - 10,065 members; (3) tribunals - 21,975 members; and (4) boards of visitors - 1,782 members: *Public Bodies* (Office of Public Service and Science, 1994).

3   As to the Office of Public Service (formerly known as the Office of Public Service and Science) see para 430 ante. The Public Appointments Unit in the Office of Public Service produces a *Guide to Public Appointments Procedures*.

4   Public Appointments Order in Council 1995. The office was established in response to recommendations in the *First Report of the Committee on Standards in Public Life* (Cm 2850-I) (1995); see 267 HC Official Report (6th series), 23 November 1995, written answers col *234*. The Commissioner for Public Appointments produced a draft code of practice for public appointments, and guidance for consideration by the Public Service Committee which endorsed it: see the *First Report of the Public Service Committee: the Code of Practice for Public Appointments* (HC Paper (1995–96) no 168) para 22. *The Commissioner for Public Appointments' Guidance on Appointments of Non-departmental Public Bodies and National Health Service Bodies* (Office of the Commissioner for Public Appointments, April 1996) incorporates the code of practice for public appointments endorsed by the Public Service Committee. The Public Appointments Unit of the Cabinet Office issued *Supplementary Guidance on Public Appointments* (Cabinet Office, May 1996), which was intended to be complementary to the *Commissioner for Public Appointments' Guidance on Appointments of Non-departmental Public Bodies and National Health Service Bodies* (see supra).

5   267 HC Official Report (6th series), 23 November 1995, written answers col *234*. See also *First Report of the Committee on Standards in Public Life* (Cm 2850-I) (1995) ch 4; and *The Government's Response to the First Report of the Committee on Standards in Public Life* (Cm 2931) (1995).

6   *Report on Non-Departmental Public Bodies* (Cmnd 7797) (1980) (the 'Pliatzky Report') (which contains guidance to government departments on the creation and supervision of non-departmental public bodies by departments.

7   However, the Health and Safety Executive, the Health and Safety Commission and the Advisory, Conciliation and Arbitration Service are non-departmental public bodies, and are Crown bodies staffed

    by civil servants. All other non-departmental public bodies are non-Crown and their employees are not civil servants. As to the Civil Service generally see paras 549–564 ante.

8   See HM Treasury *Government Accounting* 13.2 (see para 230 note 2 ante).

9   See HM Treasury *Government Accounting* 13.3.

10  See HM Treasury *Government Accounting* 6.1.4, 6.1.7–6.1.12; and as to accounting officers see para 715 ante.

11  However, there are exceptions. The Treasury may issue formal directions to the Bank of England, although this power has not been exercised: see the Bank of England Act 1946 s 4 (as amended); and BANKING. As to the Treasury see paras 512–517 ante.

12  The British Broadcasting Corporation is in a special position. It operates under a licence that is renewable periodically after negotiation with the minister in the Department of National Heritage (formerly with the Home Office) and sets out in detail the aims, objectives and duties of the corporation for the period of the licence.

13  As to terms of public appointments and removal from office see paras 901–905 ante.

## 954. Relations between non-departmental public bodies and Parliament.

The Comptroller and Auditor General[1] audits the accounts of several non-departmental public bodies[2] and their members may be summoned to appear before the Public Accounts Committee and other select committees[3].

1   As to the Comptroller and Auditor General see paras 724–726 ante.

2   Eg the British Council and the National Museum of Wales: see HM Treasury *Government Accounting* 7.1.11, 7.1.12, 7.1.14 (see para 230 note 2 ante). For a summary of the bodies that are subject to full audit by the Comptroller and Auditor General and those where he has been appointed as external auditor but nevertheless has full access to the body's books and records see *Public Bodies* (Office of Public Service, 1995).

3   *Report on Non-departmental Public Bodies* (Cmnd 7797) (1980) (the 'Pliatzky Report') para 71. Select committees are entitled to examine the expenditure, administration and policy of 'associated public bodies' of the principal government departments: see HC Standing Orders (1995) (Public Business) no 130(1). The term 'associated public bodies' is not defined but the Chancellor of the Duchy of Lancaster, introducing the new standing orders providing for departmental select committees in 1979, indicated that 'the test in every case will be whether there is a significant degree of ministerial responsibility for the body concerned': 969 HC Official Report (5th series), 25 June 1979, col 44 et seq. The rules of accountability and external audit arrangements for executive non-departmental public bodies are found in *Spending Public Money: Governance and Audit Issues* (Cm 3179) (1996). See also 273 HC Official Report (6th series), 7 March 1996, written answers col *301*.

## 955. Parliamentary Commissioner for Administration's jurisdiction over non-departmental public bodies.

Some non-departmental public bodies are subject to the jurisdiction of the Parliamentary Commissioner for Administration[1]. He is entitled to investigate complaints of maladministration made in respect of bodies listed in the schedule to the Parliamentary Commissioner Act 1967[2]. These may only include bodies or authorities whose functions are exercised on behalf of the Crown[3] and bodies established under an Act of Parliament or Order in Council or by a minister, that fulfil certain criteria as to the source of their income and the power of appointment[4].

1   As to the Parliamentary Commissioner for Administration see ADMINISTRATIVE LAW vol 1(1) (Reissue) para 41 et seq.

2   See the Parliamentary Commissioner Act 1967 s 4, Sch 2 (substituted by the Parliamentary and Health Service Commissioners Act 1987 s 1(1), (2), Sch 1); and ADMINISTRATIVE LAW vol 1(1) (Reissue) para 41.

3   See, however, para 952 note 5 ante.

4   See the Parliamentary Commissioner Act 1967 Sch 2. For a body's inclusion in Sch 2 at least half of the body's income must be derived from revenues voted directly by Parliament: see *Non-Departmental Public Bodies: A Guide for Departments* (Office of Public Service, 1979) para 3.5.1.

## (2) INFORMATION-GATHERING INSTITUTIONS

**956. In general.** For the proper exercise of their powers, legislative and administrative authorities require to be furnished with information. It will often be wise for authorities to consult interested or expert parties before exercising powers or introducing legislation, in order to secure that the proposal is workable or to determine whether it will be regarded as legitimate and so win the co-operation that may be necessary to the effectiveness of the measure in question. An exceptional form of consultation is a referendum, of which very few have been held in the United Kingdom[1]. They have been regarded as consultative only and not binding on government. A referendum is thus a method of consulting public opinion and informing government and Parliament before legislation is introduced, and of legitimating that legislation.

To obtain information, members of Parliament ask questions of ministers[2] and the Houses of Parliament make use of select committees[3]. Government departments commonly issue Green Papers inviting responses before a White Paper is produced containing the considered proposals of the department for legislation. Administrative authorities, such as departments of state or local authorities, rely to a great extent on their own officers, such as health and safety inspectors[4], environmental health officers[5], weights and measures inspectors[6], or inspectors of constabulary[7] or schools[8].

Many government departments and public corporations have associated with them permanent consultative or advisory committees or councils[9]. Other permanent commissions[10] or councils[11] have an independent existence. While some of them can act on their own initiative[12], others investigate only such questions as are submitted to them by other authorities[13].

Royal commissions[14], inquiries[15] and departmental or inter-departmental committees[16] are specially set up from time to time to investigate specific topics. These inquiries may not only engage in fact finding, but also provide a forum for soliciting public or expert opinion. The conduct of certain kinds of inquiries set up for particular purposes is governed by permanent arrangements[17]. Public local inquiries into planning and land use issues are usually conducted by inspectors in the service of the appropriate departments[18].

Neither parliamentary nor subordinate legislation is ordinarily embarked on without consultation with non-governmental bodies[19]. In some cases such consultation is necessary[20].

1    Examples include the poll held in Northern Ireland in 1973 to determine whether it should remain part of the United Kingdom (see the Northern Ireland (Border Poll) Act 1972; and para 68 text and note 4 ante); the referendum in 1975 on whether the United Kingdom should remain a member of the Common Market (see the Referendum Act 1975 (repealed); and EUROPEAN COMMUNITIES vol 51 para 1.24); the referendum in Scotland under the Scotland Act 1978 on the proposal for establishing a Scottish Parliament (see para 66 ante); and the referendum in Wales under the Wales Act 1978 on proposals for establishing a Welsh Assembly (see para 44 ante). In both the Scotland Act 1978 and the Wales Act 1978 there was a requirement that it should not take effect unless not less than 40% of the total electorate voted in favour.
2    As to parliamentary questions see para 226 ante.
3    Inquiries by select committees have formed the basis of legislation by receiving evidence and recommending changes: see the *Fifth Report of the Home Affairs Committee: the Law relating to Public Order* (HC Paper (1979–80) no 756); and the *First Report of the Home Affairs Committee: Representation of the People Acts* (HC Paper (1982–83) no 32). As to select committees see further para 227 ante; and PARLIAMENT.
4    See HEALTH AND SAFETY AT WORK vol 20 (Reissue) para 471 et seq.
5    See PUBLIC HEALTH vol 38 para 70.
6    See WEIGHTS AND MEASURES vol 50 para 49.
7    See POLICE vol 36 para 258.

8   See EDUCATION vol 15 (Reissue) para 154.

9   Eg the Post Office Users' National Council was set up under the Post Office Act 1969 ss 14–15 (as amended): see POST OFFICE vol 36 paras 633–641. See also Wade and Bradley *Constitutional and Administrative Law* (11th Edn, 1993) pp 320–321.

10  Eg the Law Commission (as to which see para 957 post).

11  Eg the Council on Tribunals (as to which see para 958 post; and ADMINISTRATIVE LAW vol 1(1) (Reissue) para 48 et seq).

12  Eg the Law Commission and the Council on Tribunals. The Council on Tribunals acts in part on its own initiative and in part when matters are referred to it: see further para 958 post.

13  Eg the Law Reform Committee and the Criminal Law Revision Committee: see Wade and Bradley *Constitutional and Administrative Law* (11th Edn, 1993) pp 399–400.

14  Eg the *Redcliffe-Maud Commission on Local Government* (Cmnd 4040) (1969); *Royal Commission on Criminal Justice* (Cm 2263) (1993).

15  Eg the *Report of the Inquiry into the Export of Defence Equipment and Dual-Use Goods to Iraq and Related Prosecutions* (HC Paper (1995–96) no 115) (the 'Scott Report').

16  Eg the 'Franks Committee': see the *Report of the Committee on Administrative Tribunals and Enquiries* (Cmnd 218) (1957); the *Report of the Committee of Inquiry into Human Fertilization and Embryology* (Cmnd 9314) (1984); the *Review of Press Self-Regulation* (Cm 2135) (1993).

17  Eg tribunals of inquiry by the Tribunals of Inquiry (Evidence) Act 1921 (see paras 959–961 post); public local inquiries by the Tribunals and Inquiries Act 1992 (see para 958 post).

18  Eg planning inquiries are held by the Department of the Environment: see generally TOWN AND COUNTRY PLANNING.

19  Eg the County Councils Association, the District Councils Association, the Confederation of British Industry and the Trades Union Congress.

20  This is particularly the case with delegated legislation, for example the Social Security Administration Act 1992 ss 170 (as amended), 172–174 which require the Social Security Advisory Committee to be consulted on proposed regulations. Under the Tribunals and Inquiries Act 1992 ss 8 (as amended), 9, the Council on Tribunals must be consulted about procedural rules for tribunals and statutory inquiries.

**957. The Law Commissions.** The body of commissioners known as the Law Commission was set up to promote the reform of English law[1]. It consists of a chairman and four other commissioners appointed by the Lord Chancellor[2] except during any temporary vacancy[3]. There is also a Scottish Law Commission[4].

The commissioners of the Law Commission and the Scottish Law Commission, other than a commissioner who holds a high judicial office[5], receive such salaries or remuneration as may be determined with the approval of the Treasury[6] by the Lord Chancellor (or the Lord Advocate as the case may be)[7]. A commissioner is also entitled to such pension, allowance or gratuity on his retirement or death, or such contributions or other payments towards provision for such payments as may be determined[8]. As soon as such a determination has been made, the Lord Chancellor (or Lord Advocate as the case may be) lays before each House of Parliament, a statement of the amount of the pension, allowance or gratuity or contributions or other payments towards them in pursuance of the determination[9].

The Lord Chancellor may appoint such officers and servants of the Law Commission and the Lord Advocate may appoint such officers of the Scottish Law Commission, as he may determine with the approval of the Treasury as to number and conditions of service[10]. The Treasury may make regulations[11] providing for the counting of service as an officer or servant or either of the commissions as pensionable service in any other capacity under the Crown or vice versa[12]. The commissions' expenses so incurred, including the remuneration of officers and servants appointed, are payable out of moneys provided by Parliament[13].

Each commission must keep the law under review with a view to its systematic development and reform, including in particular its codification, the elimination of anomalies, the repeal of obsolete and unnecessary enactments, the reduction of the number of separate enactments and generally its simplification and modernisation[14]. In the exercise of their functions the commissioners must act in consultation with each other[15].

Approved programmes and proposals for reform must be laid before Parliament[16], as must the annual reports which the commissions are required to make[17]. The commissions have published a large number of reports and working papers, some of which have led to legislation[18].

1    See the Law Commissions Act 1965 s 1(1) (as amended), (5).
2    As to the Lord Chancellor see paras 477–497 ante.
3    Law Commissions Act 1965 s 1(1) (amended by the Administration of Justice Act 1982 s 64). The persons appointed must appear to the Lord Chancellor to be suitably qualified by the holding of judicial office or by experience as a person having a general qualification within the meaning of the Courts and Legal Services Act 1990 s 71 or as a teacher of law in a university: Law Commissions Act 1965 s 1(2) (amended by the Courts and Legal Services Act 1990 s 71(2), Sch 10 para 25). A 'general qualification' means a right of audience in relation to all proceedings in the Supreme Court or all proceedings in county courts or magistrates' courts: s 71(3)(c). A person appointed to be a commissioner must be appointed for a term not exceeding five years and subject to such conditions as may be determined by the Lord Chancellor at the time of his appointment: Law Commissions Act 1965 s 1(3). However, a commissioner may at any time resign his office and a person ceasing to be a commissioner is eligible for reappointment: s 1(3). A person holding judicial office may be appointed as a commissioner without relinquishing that office, but, unless otherwise provided by the terms of his appointment, he is not required to perform his duties as holder of that office while he remains a member of the commission: s 1(4).
4    See ibid s 2; and paras 63 text and note 9, 65 ante.
5    'High judicial office' has the same meaning as in the Appellate Jurisdiction Act 1876 (as amended): Law Commissions Act 1965 s 6(2).
6    As to the Treasury see paras 512–517 ante.
7    Law Commissions Act 1965 s 4(1) (amended by the Transfer of Functions (Secretary of State and Lord Advocate) Order 1972, SI 1972/2002, arts 2(1)(e), 3(3)(c)). Such salaries or remuneration are payable out of moneys provided by Parliament: Law Commissions Act 1965 s 4(4).
8    Ibid s 4(2). Such sums are payable out of moneys provided by Parliament: s 4(4).
9    Ibid s 4(3) (amended by the Transfer of Functions (Secretary of State and Lord Advocate) Order 1972 arts 2(1)(e), 3(3)(c)).
10   Law Commissions Act 1965 s 5(1) (amended by the Transfer of Functions (Secretary of State and Lord Advocate) Order 1972 arts 2(1)(e), 3(3)(c)).
11   This power to make regulations is exercisable by statutory instrument which is subject to annulment in pursuance of a resolution of either House of Parliament: Law Commissions Act 1965 s 5(3).
12   Ibid s 5(2).
13   Ibid s 5(4).
14   Ibid s 3(1). For this purpose it is the duty of each commission to:
     (1)  receive and consider any proposals for the reform of the law which may be made or referred to them (s 3(1)(a));
     (2)  prepare and submit to the minister from time to time programmes for the examination of different branches of the law with a view to reform, including recommendations to the agency (whether the commission or another body) by which any such examination should be carried out (s 3(1)(b));
     (3)  undertake, pursuant to any such recommendations approved by the minister, the examination of particular branches of the law and the formulation, by means of draft bills or otherwise, of proposals for reform therein (s 3(1)(c));
     (4)  prepare from time to time at the request of the minister comprehensive programmes of consolidation and statute law revision, and to undertake the preparation of draft bills pursuant to any such programme approved by the minister (s 3(1)(d));
     (5)  provide advice and information to government departments and other authorities or bodies concerned at the instance of the government with proposals for the reform or amendment of any branch of the law (s 3(1)(e));
     (6)  obtain any such information as to the legal systems of other countries as appears to the commissioners likely to facilitate the performance of their functions (s 3(1)(f)).
     'Minister' means the Lord Chancellor in relation to the Law Commission and the Lord Advocate in relation to the Scottish Law Commission: s 6(2) (amended by the Transfer of Functions (Secretary of State and Lord Advocate) Order 1972 art 3(3)(b)).
15   Law Commissions Act 1965 s 3(4).
16   See ibid s 3(2).

17  Ibid s 3(3).
18  See eg the Animals Act 1971 (which implemented, with modifications, the recommendations in the *Law Commission's Report on Civil Liability for Animals* (Law Com no 13)); the Wild Creatures and Forest Laws Act 1971 (which implemented a report on statute law revision *Statute Law Revision Second Report* (August 1970) (Law Com no 28); the Public Order Act 1986 (which implemented *Criminal Law: Offences Relating to Public Order* (October 1983) (Law Com no 123)); the Family Law Reform Act 1987 (which implemented *Family Law: Illegitimacy* (December 1982) (Law Com no 118)); the Children Act 1989 (which implemented *Family Law: Review of Child Law, Guardianship and Custody* (July 1988) (Law Com no 172)). The Law Commission, in the *Twenty-eighth Annual Report, 1993* (Law Com no 223), expressed concern over the delay in the implementation of its law reform reports, pointing out that only four had been implemented since 1990. See also Sir Thomas Bingham 'The European Convention on Human Rights: Time to Incorporate' (1993) 109 LQR 390.

**958.   Council on Tribunals.** The Council on Tribunals[1] is required to keep under review the constitution and working of specified[2] tribunals and to make reports on them[3]. In addition, the council is required to consider and report on such particular matters as may be referred to it under the Tribunals and Inquiries Act 1992 with respect to tribunals other than courts of law, whether or not within the category of specified tribunals, or any such tribunal[4]. It is also required to consider and report on such matters as may be so referred to it, or as it may determine to be of special importance, with respect to administrative procedures involving, or which may involve, the holding by or on behalf of a minister of a statutory inquiry, or any such procedure[5].

1   As to the Council on Tribunals generally see ADMINISTRATIVE LAW vol 1(1) (Reissue) para 48 et seq.
2   For the tribunals specified for this purpose see the Tribunal and Inquiries Act 1992 s 1(1), Sch 1; and ADMINISTRATIVE LAW vol 1(1) (Reissue) para 49.
3   See ibid s 1. As to the persons to whom the council reports see ADMINISTRATIVE LAW vol 1 (Reissue) para 48.
4   See ibid s 1.
5   See ibid s 1.

**959.   Tribunals of inquiry.** One of the means by which Parliament can investigate a situation prior to taking action upon it is the setting up of a tribunal of inquiry. The essential function of such a tribunal is to report to Parliament; if action needs to be taken it is for Parliament, not the tribunal, to make the necessary provision[1].

Where it has been resolved by both Houses of Parliament that it is expedient that a tribunal be established for inquiring into a definite matter described in the resolution as of urgent public importance, and a tribunal is so appointed either by the Crown or a Secretary of State, the instrument by which the tribunal is appointed, or any supplemental instrument, may provide for the application to the tribunal of the Tribunals of Inquiry (Evidence) Act 1921[2].

1   The history of judicial inquiries is set out in the *Report of the Royal Commission on Tribunals of Inquiry* (Cmnd 3121) (1966) paras 6–21. The circumstances in which an inquiry is appropriate are rumoured instances of lapses in accepted standards of public administration and other matters causing public concern which cannot be dealt with by ordinary civil or criminal processes but which require investigation to allay public anxiety: para 22. As to tribunals of inquiry generally see ADMINISTRATIVE LAW vol 1(1) (Reissue) para 13 et seq. See further Wade and Bradley *Constitutional and Administrative Law* (11th Edn, 1993) pp 659–661.
    For examples of powers to apply the provisions of the Tribunals of Inquiry (Evidence) Act 1921 see the Agricultural Marketing Reorganisation Commissions (see AGRICULTURE vol 1(2) (Reissue) para 703). For examples of tribunals of inquiry not set up under the Tribunals of Inquiry (Evidence) Act 1921 see the inquiry into the Profumo scandal (*Lord Denning's Report* (Cmnd 2152) (1963)); the *Inquiry into the Supervision of the BCCI* (HC Paper (1992–93) no 198); and the *Report of the Inquiry into the Export of Defence Equipment and Dual-Use Goods to Iraq and Related Prosecutions* (HC Paper (1995–96) no 115) (the 'Scott Report'). The *Report of the Committee of Inquiry into Complaints about Ashworth Hospital* (Cm 2028-I) (1992) recommended a comprehensive review of public inquiries.

2    See the Tribunals of Inquiry (Evidence) Act 1921 s 1(1). For the consequences of the application of the Act see paras 960–961 post. As to the procedure before the tribunal see the *Report of the Royal Commission on Tribunals of Inquiry* (Cmnd 3121) (1966) paras 16–19; and 40 Court Forms (2nd Edn) (1996 Issue) 148–151. These tribunals are comparatively rare. For examples see the *Report of the Tribunal Appointed to inquire into the Disaster at Aberfan on 21 October 1966* (HL Paper (1966–67) no 316), (HC Paper (1966–67) no 553); the *Report of the Tribunal appointed to inquire into certain issues in relation to the circumstances leading up to the cessation of trading by the Vehicle and General Insurance Company Limited* (HL Paper (1971–72) no 80), (HC Paper (1971–72) no 133); and the *Inquiry into Disorders in Northern Ireland ('Bloody Sunday')* (Cmd 566) (NI) (April 1972).

## 960. Evidence before tribunals of inquiry.

Where it is provided that the Tribunals of Inquiry (Evidence) Act 1921 applies[1], a tribunal has all the powers, rights and privileges in respect of certain matters which are vested in the High Court, or in Scotland the Court of Session, or a judge of either of those courts, on the occasion of an action[2]. The matters specified are (1) enforcing the attendance of witnesses and examining them on oath, affirmation or otherwise[3]; (2) compelling the production of documents[4]; and (3) subject to rules of court, issuing a commission or request to examine witnesses abroad[5]. A summons signed by one or more of the tribunal's members may be substituted for, and is equivalent to, any formal process capable of being issued in any action for enforcing the attendance of witnesses and compelling the production of documents[6]. A witness before any such tribunal is entitled to the same immunities and privileges as if he were a witness in civil proceedings before the High Court or the Court of Session[7].

In specified circumstances the tribunal's chairman may certify an offence by a person under his hand to the High Court, or in Scotland the Court of Session. The court may then inquire into the alleged offence and, after hearing any witnesses who may be produced against or on behalf of the person charged with the offence and after hearing any statement in defence, may punish or take steps for the punishment of that person as if he had been guilty of contempt of the court[8]. The specified circumstances are if any person (a) on being duly summoned as a witness before a tribunal makes default in attending[9]; or (b) being in attendance as a witness refuses to take an oath or to produce any document in his power or control legally required by the tribunal, or to answer any relevant question to which the tribunal may legally require an answer[10]; or (c) does any other thing which would, if the tribunal had been a court of law having power to commit for contempt, have been contempt of that court[11].

1 .  As to the application of the Tribunals of Inquiry (Evidence) Act 1921 see para 959 ante.

2    See ibid s 1(1) (amended by the Statute Law (Repeals) Act 1995).

3    Tribunals of Inquiry (Evidence) Act 1921 s 1(1)(a). As to the attendance and examination of witnesses generally see EVIDENCE.

4    Ibid s 1(1)(b). As to the discovery of documents generally see DISCOVERY.

5    Ibid s 1(1)(c). As to the taking of evidence from witnesses out of the jurisdiction see EVIDENCE.

6    See ibid s 1(1) (as amended: see note 2 supra).

7    Ibid s 1(3) (amended by the Civil Evidence Act 1968 s 17(1)(a)). As to the immunity and privileges of witnesses generally see EVIDENCE.

8    Tribunals of Inquiry (Evidence) Act 1921 s 1(2).

9    Ibid s 1(2)(a).

10   Ibid s 1(2)(b). See *A-G v Clough* [1963] 1 QB 773, [1963] 1 All ER 420; *A-G v Mulholland* [1963] 2 QB 477, [1963] 1 All ER 767, CA. A person may be excused by his status as a witness from answering a particular question: see the text and note 7 supra.

11   Tribunals of Inquiry (Evidence) Act 1921 s 1(2)(c). The provisions of the Contempt of Court Act 1981 (except s 9(3)) are expressly applied to tribunals to which the 1921 Act applies: see the Contempt of Court Act 1981 s 20(1). As to contempt of court generally see CONTEMPT. For a general consideration of the application of the law of contempt to these tribunals see the *Report of the Interdepartmental Committee on the Law of Contempt as it Affects Tribunals of Inquiry* (Cmnd 4078) (1969).

**961. Powers of tribunals of inquiry.** A tribunal to which the Tribunals of Inquiry (Evidence) Act 1921 applies[1] may not refuse to allow the public, or any portion of the public, to be present at any of its proceedings unless in its opinion it is in the public interest expedient to do so for reasons connected with the subject matter of the inquiry or the nature of the evidence to be given[2].

A tribunal is empowered to authorise the representation before it of any person appearing to it to be interested[3] by counsel or solicitor or otherwise, or it may refuse to allow that representation[4].

1   As to the application of the Tribunals of Inquiry (Evidence) Act 1921 see para 959 ante.
2   Ibid s 2(a).
3   As to the meaning of 'interested' see the *Report of the Tribunal Appointed to Inquire into the Disaster at Aberfan on 21 October 1966* (HC Paper (1966–67) no 553) para 6; *Report of the Tribunal Appointed to Inquire into the Vassall Case and Related Matters* (Cmnd 2009) (1963) para 7.
4   Tribunals of Inquiry (Evidence) Act 1921 s 2(b).

# INDEX

## Constitutional Law and Human Rights

COMMISSIONERS OF CUSTOMS AND EXCISE
  appointment and tenure of office, 710
  control over, 710n[3]
  responsibilities, 710
COMMISSIONERS OF INLAND REVENUE
  advisory functions, 709
  annual report, 709
  appointment and tenure of office, 709
  control over, 709n[5]
  taxes and duties, responsibility for, 709
COMMITTEE
  Cabinet, 410
  Privy Council, of, 526
  Public Accounts, of, 719
  Select, 227, 718
COMMON AGRICULTURAL POLICY
  designated minister, 435
COMMON LAW
  Crown grants, 849, 850
  descent of Crown, 34
  royal prerogative, and, 368
  rules of, and statute, 233
COMMONWEALTH
  written constitution, countries having, 1n[12]
COMPENSATION
  loss of office etc (civil servants), 572
  miscarriage of justice, for, 829
COMPLAINT
  European Commission of Human Rights, to, 172
COMPTROLLER AND AUDITOR GENERAL
  appointment and tenure of office, 724
  appropriation accounts submitted to, 723
  audit of public accounts, 716
  certification audits, 726
  death, resignation or other vacancy, 724n[3]
  discretion of, 724
  fees, powers to charge, 716
  Foreign Compensation Commission, audit of accounts, 807

**References are to paragraph numbers; superior figures refer to notes**

References are to paragraph numbers; superior figures refer to notes

**References are to paragraph numbers; superior figures refer to notes**

**References are to paragraph numbers; superior figures refer to notes**

**References are to paragraph numbers; superior figures refer to notes**

**References are to paragraph numbers; superior figures refer to notes**

EXECUTIVE—*continued*
　transfer of functions—*continued*
　　minister's certificate as to, 363
　　Order in Council, by, 363
　　power to transfer, 363
EXECUTIVE AGENCY
　'Next Steps' initiative, 551
　non-departmental public body distinguished,
　　951
　parliamentary questions, as to, 226
　pay and conditions, determination of, 558
　privatisation, 551n[11]
EXECUTOR
　Crown appointed as, 845
EXPLOSIVES
　control over, 818
EXTRADITION
　criminal charge, exclusion as, 136
　detention pending, 133
FAIR
　grant or prescription, by, 879n[6]
FAMILY LIFE
　family: meaning, 151
　Human Rights Convention, 151
　right to respect for, 113, 151
FERRY
　Crown's right to grant, 879n[7]
FOOTPATH
　stopping up in time of war, 818
FORCED LABOUR
　*meaning*, 126n[1]
　Human Rights Convention, 126
FOREIGN AND COMMONWEALTH
　　OFFICE
　expenses, 459
　history of, 459n[1]
　Ministers of State, 459
　organisation, 459
　Overseas Development Administration, 462
　Parliamentary Commissioner, investigation by,
　　459
　Secretary of State. *See* SECRETARY OF STATE
　　(FOREIGN AND COMMONWEALTH
　　AFFAIRS)
FOREIGN COMPENSATION COM-
　　MISSION
　accounts and audit, 807
　administrative provisions, 807
　annual report, 807
　appointment and tenure of office, 804
　case stated by, 806
　chairman, 490, 804n[1]
　compensation payable, 803
　constitution, 804
　countries subject of Orders, 803n[2]
　determination of questions, 806
　financial provisions, 807
　legislation, 803n[2]
　Orders in Council, 803n[1]
　procedure, 805
　remuneration etc, 804

FOREIGN COMPENSATION COM-
　　MISSION—*continued*
　request for statement of reasons, 806n[5]
　rules of procedure, 805n[2]
FRANCHISE (LIBERTY)
　corporation, creation of, 881
　ferry, 879n[7]
　grant of, 879
　markets and fairs, 879n[6]
　municipal, 882
　nature of, 879
　pontage and murage, 880
　royal prerogative, 879
FREE MOVEMENT (WORKERS)
　European Economic Area, 23
　European Union, 116n[3]
FREEDOM OF EXPRESSION
　Human Rights Convention, 158, 159
FREEDOM OF SPEECH
　English law, 107
　Human Rights Convention, 158, 159
FURTHER EDUCATION FUNDING
　　COUNCIL
　function, 366n[10]
　functions of Secretary of State, 449n[5]
　non-departmental public body, 366n[10]
GENERAL COMMISSIONERS
　Lord Chancellor, appointment by, 490
GOVERNMENT
　*meaning*, 16, 354
　bodies exercising governmental functions, 13
　borrowing, National Loans Fund. *See*
　　NATIONAL LOANS FUND
　Cabinet. *See* CABINET
　Crown. *See* CROWN
　defeat in Parliament leading to dissolution, 209n[2]
　department. *See* GOVERNMENT DEPARTMENT
　executive, the, 16
　executive functions, 9
　extra-governmental organisations, 951n[6]
　Government Communications Headquarters.
　　*See* GOVERNMENT COMMUNICATIONS
　　HEADQUARTERS
　Head of State, 14
　Her Majesty's government: meaning, 16
　information-gathering institutions, 956
　judiciary. *See* JUDICIARY
　legal basis of, 5
　legal status, 354
　legality, principle of, 6
　Parliament, necessity for, 203
　powers—
　　Crown as source of, 15
　　specific legal sources, 7
　　strict separation, absence of, 8
　privatisation of functions, 551n[11]
　right to participate in, 118
　three main branches of, 301
　trading fund. *See* GOVERNMENT TRADING
　　FUND
　unitary character, 4

**References are to paragraph numbers; superior figures refer to notes**

**References are to paragraph numbers; superior figures refer to notes**

**References are to paragraph numbers; superior figures refer to notes**

POLITICAL PARTY—*continued*
  Parliament, in, 216
  public finance for opposition parties, 220
  whip system, 216
PONTAGE
  nature and grant of, 880
PRESCRIPTION (LEGAL)
  corporation existing by, 881
  Crown grant, 869
  Crown's position, 390
PRIME MINISTER
  access to monarch, 412n[1]
  allocation of functions to departments, 363n[4]
  appointment, 394
  Cabinet, powers as to, 398
  Chequers and Chevening, 395n[2]
  Commissioners and tribunals as to Security and Intelligence Services, appointment, 476
  considerations for selection of, 394
  death of, 397
  delay in appointment, 394n[11,12]
  Deputy, 354n[21]
  head of administration, 354
  Intelligence and Security Committee, appointment, 475
  Lord Chancellor's appointment, 477
  member of House of Commons, 395n[3]
  ministers, choice of, 399
  office and staff, 396
  official residences, 395
  pension entitlement, 426
  powers, 398
  precedence, 395
  remuneration, 423, 425, 426
  resignation, effect of, 397
  status, 395
PRINCE OF WALES
  creation of, 50
PRIVACY
  English law, 110
  Human Rights Convention. *See under* EUROPEAN CONVENTION ON HUMAN RIGHTS
PRIVATE BILL
  Scotland, applying to, special procedure, 58
PRIVATISATION
  government functions, 551n[11]
  receipts paid into Consolidated Fund, 711
  value for money audit, 717
PRIVILEGE
  freedom of expression, and, 107
PRIVY COUNCIL
  *meaning*, 521
  Cabinet members of, 404
  committees, 526
  functions, 525
  Judicial Committee. *See* JUDICIAL COMMITTEE OF PRIVY COUNCIL
  legal jurisdiction, 526
  meetings, 525
  membership. *See* PRIVY COUNSELLOR

PRIVY COUNCIL—*continued*
  Northern Ireland, 521n[4]
  Political Honours Scrutiny Committee, 526n[11]
  Privy Council Office, 526
  summons to meeting, 525n[1]
PRIVY COUNSELLOR
  appointment, 522
  monarch's Private Secretary, 547n[1]
  number of, 522
  oath, 523
  precedence, 524
  qualifications, 522
  removal, 522
  style, 524
PRIZE
  war, in time of, 814
PROCLAMATION
  accession, of, 40
  authority for, 916
  custom, authorisation by, 916n[2]
  judicial notice of, 916
  restrictions on, 918
  rules as to, 916n[5]
  sealing, 916
  use of, 917
PROPERTY
  Crown rights. *See under* CROWN
  right to—
    English law, 120
    Human Rights Convention, 165
PUBLIC ACCOUNTS
  accounting officer, 715
  audit, 716
  Committee of Public Accounts, 719
  economy, efficiency and effectiveness examinations, 717
  money received from public funds: meaning, 717n[18]
  National Audit Office. *See* NATIONAL AUDIT OFFICE
  non-departmental public bodies, 715n[9]
  parliamentary control, 703
  Public Accounts Commission, 721
  select committees, 718
  Treasury Committee, 718
  unauthorised expenditure, 716
  value for money audit, 717
  virement, 718
PUBLIC AUTHORITY
  bodies exercising public or governmental functions, 13
PUBLIC BODY
  non-departmental. *See* NON-DEPARTMENTAL PUBLIC BODY
  value for money audit, exclusions, 717n[16]
PUBLIC DOCUMENT
  authority for sealing, 912
  Clerk of the Crown in Chancery, 921
  Great Seal. *See* GREAT SEAL
  Order in Council, 907
  proclamation. *See* PROCLAMATION

**References are to paragraph numbers; superior figures refer to notes**

PUBLIC DOCUMENT—*continued*
 rules for preparation of, 913n[9]
 sign manual, 908
 statutory instruments, 906
 types of, 906
PUBLIC EXPENDITURE. *See also* PUBLIC
  MONEY
 accounts. *See* PUBLIC ACCOUNTS
 Chancellor of the Exchequer, control by, 704
 Contingencies Fund, 742
 control total, 712n[1]
 heads of, 712n[7]
 parliamentary control over, 230, 703
 Public Expenditure Survey, 704
 supplementary estimates, 712
 supply estimates, 705, 712, 713, 718
 supply procedure, 712
 Treasury control, 704
PUBLIC INTEREST IMMUNITY
 Scotland, 55
PUBLIC LENDING RIGHT
 Secretary of State responsible for, 500n[5]
PUBLIC MONEY. *See also* PUBLIC EXPENDI-
  TURE
 authorisation of issue, 713
 Contingencies Fund, 742
 estimates days, 712n[1]
 Pay Office records, 714
 Paymaster General, 714
 supply procedure, 712
PUBLIC OFFICE
 affirmation instead of oath, 923
 appointment to, 901
 corruption, 12n[5]
 good behaviour, held during, 903
 Nolan Committee, 12n[5]
 oath. *See* OATH (office, of)
 principles of public life, 12
 removal from, 905
 secretarial seals, 357, 901n[1]
 sex discrimination, 904
 tenure, 902
PUBLIC ORDER
 free assembly, and, 109
 Home Secretary's functions, 469
PUBLIC RECORD OFFICE
 Lord Chancellor's functions, 496
PUBLIC RECORDS
 *meaning*, 835
 access to, 840
 Advisory Council, 837
 authentication, 836
 Chancery records, 837n[5]
 court records, responsibility for, 841
 departmental bodies and establishments, records
  of, 835n[8]
 indexes and guides, 838n[5]
 inspection and copies, 840
 Keeper, 838
 legal validity, 836
 places of deposit, 838

PUBLIC RECORDS—*continued*
 proper officer: meaning, 836n[3]
 Public Record Office, 838
 Public Records Act 1958 purposes, for, 835n[12]
 publication, 839
 responsibility for, 837
 selection, 839
 thirty year rule, 840n[2]
PUBLIC TRUSTEE
 Lord Chancellor, appointed by, 490
PUBLIC WORKS LOAN COMMISSIONERS
 interest rate, 736
 sums issued out of National Loans Fund, 736
QUEEN'S PROCTOR
 functions, 545
 matrimonial causes functions, 545
 Treasury Solicitor as, 545
RACIAL DISCRIMINATION
 Human Rights Convention, 164
RAPE
 inhuman treatment, as, 124n[2]
 wife, of, retrospectivity and Human Rights
  Convention, 148n[14]
RECEIPT
 Crown, by, 386
RECORDS
 court records, responsibility for, 841
 public. *See* PUBLIC RECORDS
RECRUITMENT
 Civil Service, 556
REGULATIONS
 emergency regulations, 822
 power to make—
  Paymaster General, as to, 714n[12]
  pension of Comptroller and Auditor General,
   as to, 725
RELIGION
 freedom of—
  English law, 108n[3]
  Human Rights Convention, 156, 157
REMUNERATION
 civil servants, 558
 Comptroller and Auditor General, 725
 Foreign Compensation Commission, 804
 Law Commission members, 957
 minister of the Crown. *See under* MINISTER OF
  THE CROWN
 Opposition. *See under* OPPOSITION
RENT
 Crown rights, 846
REPRIEVE
 prerogative right, 828
REPUBLICAN COUNTRY
 royal prerogative, 370n[1]
RESIGNATION
 Prime Minister, of, 397
REVENUE. *See also* TAX
 *meaning*, 701n[1]
 Account of Her Majesty's Exchequer, 711
 budget, 705
 casual revenues, 707

References are to paragraph numbers; superior figures refer to notes

**References are to paragraph numbers; superior figures refer to notes**

**References are to paragraph numbers; superior figures refer to notes**

TITLE OF HONOUR
abuse, prevention of, 833
conferring of, 832
form of grant, 831
granting of, 831
TOLL
Crown grant, 872, 873
TORTURE
*meaning*, 124n[1]
Human Rights Convention, 124
TOURISM
Department of National Heritage, functions, 500n[10]
TOWN
municipal franchises, 882
TRADE
Crown grant of licence for, 876
TRADE AND INDUSTRY
Department of. *See* DEPARTMENT OF TRADE AND INDUSTRY
Secretary of State. *See* SECRETARY OF STATE (TRADE AND INDUSTRY)
TRADE UNION
Civil Service, 564n[18, 19]
TRAINING AGENCY
functions, 450n[2]
TRAINING COMMISSION
establishment and dissolution, 450n[1]
TRANSLATION
criminal proceedings, in, defendant's right to, 147
TRANSPORT
Department of. *See* DEPARTMENT OF TRANS-PORT
Secretary of State. *See* SECRETARY OF STATE (TRANSPORT)
TREASURY
*meaning*, 216n[2], 512
authorised department, 512
bank and government stock accounts, control of, 733
borrowing, control of, 704
Chancellor of the Exchequer, 514
Chief Secretary, 515
Civil Service, control of, 549
commissioners, 513
Consolidated Fund, drawings on, 711n[6]
Contingencies Fund, 742
directorates, 517
Economic Secretary, 515
Exchange Equalisation Account, 737
exchange of securities, 731
executive agencies, 512
expenses of, 512
Financial Secretary, 515
functions, 516
local loans, 736
Lord High Treasurer, 512
ministers, 515
organisation, 514, 517

TREASURY—*continued*
Parliamentary Commissioner, investigation by, 512
Paymaster General, 714
public expenditure, control over, 704
revenue departments, 512
secretaries to the Treasury Board, 515
statutory declaration in lieu of oath, powers, 926n[8]
trading funds. *See* GOVERNMENT TRADING FUND
transfer of functions, 516n[8-10]
Treasury bills, 730
Treasury Committee, 718
TREASURY SOLICITOR
administration of deceased's estates, 541n[5]
assistant solicitor, 543
authentication of documents, 541
department's functions and expenses, 541
Government Property Lawyers, 541n[12]
Queen's Proctor, 541, 545
status and functions, 541
trust corporation, as, 541n[6]
TREATY
Crown's treaty-making power, 801
European Communities, 24n[2], 802n[15, 16]
incorporation into UK legislation, 236n[2]
letters patent, ratification by, 920
parliamentary sanction, 802
peace, of, 810
Ponsonby Rule, 802
signing of, 801n[5]
TRIAL
bar, at Attorney General's right to demand, 535
fair, right to. *See under* CONVENTION FOR THE PROTECTION OF HUMAN RIGHTS AND FUNDAMENTAL FREEDOMS
TRIBUNAL
Government Communications Headquarters, as to, 476
independence and impartiality under Human Rights Convention, 140
inquiry, of. *See* TRIBUNAL OF INQUIRY
Lord Chancellor, appointments made by, 490
non-departmental public bodies, 951n[8]
Northern Ireland, in, 84
Scotland, 62
Security and Intelligence Services, 476
TRIBUNAL OF INQUIRY
contempt, 960n[11]
evidence, 960
function, 959
hearing in public, 961
history of, 959n[1]
legal representation, 961
powers, 961
witnesses, compelling attendance of, 960
TRUST
Crown rights, 844
UNFAIR DISMISSAL
civil servants, 387

# Words and Phrases

**References are to paragraph numbers; superior figures refer to notes**